World Mythology

DISCARDED

World Mythology

AN ANTHOLOGY OF THE GREAT MYTHS AND EPICS

THIRD EDITION

Donna Rosenberg

NTC Publishing Group
a division of NTC/CONTEMPORARY PUBLISHING GROUP
Lincolnwood, Illinois USA

Photo Credits:
Page 1, 3 (detail and all such subsequent details): Foto Marburg/Art Resource, NY; **79, 82 (detail and all such subsequent details):** Christie's Images; **289, 291 (detail and all such subsequent details):** Wolfgang Kaehler/Corbis; **367, 369 (detail and all such subsequent details):** Erich Lessing/Art Resource, NY; **457, 459 (detail and all such subsequent details):** Werner Forman/Art Resource, NY; **507, 509 (detail and all such subsequent details):** Christie's Images; **567, 570 (detail and all such subsequent details):** Giraudon/Art Resource, NY.

Sponsoring Editor: Marisa L. L'Heureux
Product Manager: Judy Rudnick
Art Director: Ophelia Chambliss
Production Coordinator: Denise Duffy-Fieldman
Cover illustration: Tony Stone Images

ISBN: 0-8442-5965-9 (hardbound)
ISBN: 0-8442-5966-7 (softbound)

Published by NTC/Contemporary Publishing Group, Inc.,
4255 West Touhy Avenue, Lincolnwood (Chicago), Illinois 60646-1975 U.S.A.
© 1999 NTC/Contemporary Publishing Group, Inc.

0 QB 0 9 8 7 6 5 4 3 2

Library of Congress Cataloging-in-Publication Data

Rosenberg, Donna.
  World mythology : an anthology of the great myths and epics /
Donna Rosenberg. -- 3rd ed.
    p.   cm.
  Includes bibliographical references and index.
  ISBN 0-8442-5965-9. -- ISBN 0-8442-5966-7 (pbk.)
  1. Mythology.   I. Title.
BL311.R63 1998
291.1'3--dc21   98-45342
                                              CIP

To Dick, my favorite hero.

The coward believes he will live forever
    If he holds back in the battle.
But in old age he shall have no peace
    Though spears have spared his limbs.

Cattle die, kindred die,
    Every man is mortal:
But I know one thing that never dies,
    The glory of the great deed.

The Elder Edda, "Words of the High One"
(Translated by Paul B. Taylor and W. H. Auden)

Of possessions cattle and fat sheep are things to be had for the lifting, and tripods can be won, and the tawny high heads of horses, but a man's life cannot come back again, it cannot lifted nor captured again by force, once it has crossed the teeth's barrier. For my mother Thetis the goddess of the silver feet tells me I carry two sorts of destiny toward the days of my death. Either, if I stay here and fight beside the city of the Trojans, my return home is gone, but my glory shall be everlasting; but if I return home to the beloved land of my fathers, the excellence of my glory is gone, but there will be a long life left for me, and my end in death will not come to me quickly. And this would be my counsel to others also, to sail back home again . . .

The Iliad, Book IX
(Translated by Richard Lattimore)

Contents

Preface

World Mythology presents the major myths from around the world in a manner that preserves their appeal as fine literature. My retelling of each myth is based on scholarly English translations of the original material. I have retained the principal plot, characterization, style, and cultural values of the original, although a one-volume edition has made it necessary to shorten the longer epics. My goal, with these shortened epics, has been to try to tell them so well that readers will wish to go on to enjoy them in a fine, unabridged translation.

The myths are arranged geographically into seven major cultural groups: the Middle East; Greece and Rome; the Far East and the Pacific Islands; the British Isles; Northern Europe; Africa; and the Americas. In order to facilitate cross-cultural comparisons and contrasts, I have included creation, fertility, and hero myths from each culture. An introduction to each myth includes historical background, literary analysis, and an evaluation of the myth's appeal. Each myth is followed by interpretative questions. Notes at the end of *World Mythology* provide additional information about each myth, regarding my sources, selected supplementary sources, and, often, a wealth of additional information that will enhance critical study and further reading pleasure.

World Mythology reflects the fact that we live in an exciting and challenging time. We live in an exciting time because the world is becoming smaller. We are becoming more familiar with its diverse cultures and more aware of the many ways that they have enriched each other through the centuries. This is reflected, in this new edition, in revised introductions and additional notes to our most cherished epics, introductions and notes that now reveal the cultural complexity of these works—the ways in which, even when they were written, they reflected different cultures, both old and contemporary.

We live in a challenging time because we recognize an ever-increasing need to view all members of the human family as related, and we need the knowledge and the experience that will help us to understand and respect each culture's unique contributions to our own life experience. The study of world mythology helps to give us this knowledge and this experience.

World Mythology introduces you to stories that are among the greatest in the history of the world. It is interesting that the people who created these stories lived in all parts of the world. However, "interest" is not enough to unite all human beings into one great human family, because "interesting" is a word that describes the mind's reaction to something outside of itself. These myths—the greatest of stories—appeal to the human heart, and so they arouse feelings within each reader. These myths involve emotion: anticipation, excitement, hope, love, dread, despair, sorrow, and empathy. The great myths belong to the listener as well as to the bard who recites them. They belong to the reader as well as to the poet who has written them. Readers feel these stories—they quicken their pulse, and they bring tears to their eyes. Readers think about these stories—tonight they invade their dreams, and tomorrow they open a new world of experience, for they have become part of their readers' lives.

Those who study world mythology find that their world has become both smaller and larger. Their world has become smaller because they realize that they share the humanity of the people to whom these myths belong, no matter where and when they have lived. Their world becomes larger because they respect and appreciate cultures that they never knew existed. It is in this way that readers come to know that human beings are remarkably alike through time and across space.

Myths reflect human nature, with its needs and desires, hopes and fears. Myths reveal the human condition. Creation myths satisfy the need to have roots. Fertility myths respond to the need for economic stability in an unpredictable world. Hero myths provide models for human behavior. Myths reveal cultural responses to the ever-important questions: Who am I? How should I lead my life? Thus, they reveal the different ways in which human beings respond to the issues that unite them.

The study of comparative mythology leads readers to learn more about themselves as well as more about others. By seeing the ways in which the characters in the great myths respond to the issues that confront them, readers gain insight into themselves and become able to evaluate the nature of their own lives. Like the heroes of every culture, all people today confront choices that force them to reconcile their personal wishes with their responsibility to others. Like these heroic figures, all people today must confront tasks in the course of their daily lives that appear to be insurmountable. They, too, must be courageous and determined if they are to achieve their goals. The study of the hero teaches that great character is as important as great deeds.

The study of world mythology leads readers to broaden their knowledge, understanding, and appreciation of interrelationships. They learn that, from the time of the earliest cities, through travel, trade, and talk, people have learned from each other. Their technology has traveled, and their great stories—the myths and legends in their oral and written traditions—have traveled. In this way, for centuries, one culture has continued to enrich another.

The world's myths continue to inspire many creative and intellectual pursuits. They enrich the appreciation of literature, art, and music and can lead to greater interest in history, religion, psychology, anthropology, and archaeology.

Introduction

Myths symbolize human experience and embody the spiritual values of a culture. Every society preserves its myths, because the beliefs and worldview found within them are crucial to the survival of that culture. Myths usually originate in an ancient, oral tradition. Some explain origins, natural phenomena, and death; others describe the nature and function of divinities; while still others provide models of virtuous behavior by relating the adventures of heroes or the misfortunes of arrogant humans. Myths often include elements from legend and folklore. They depict humans as an integral part of a larger universe, and they impart a feeling of awe for all that is mysterious and marvelous in life.

Although most of the myths in *World Mythology* were created by people who lived in societies that were much less complex than our own, they address fundamental questions that each thinking person continues to ask: Who am I? What is the nature of the universe in which I live? How do I relate to that universe? How much control do I have over my own life? What must I do in order to survive? How can I lead a satisfying life? How can I balance my own desires with my responsibilities to my family and my community? How can I reconcile myself to the inevitability of death? Therefore, myths are an important way to understand ourselves. Because they provide a variety of answers to these questions, they present us with new possibilities, and by considering these possibilities, we gain insight into our own attitudes and values.

Myths are also an important way to understand our connection to other people at a time when the welfare of each culture depends on the attitudes and actions of other cultures. The answers to these questions have produced a body of myths from diverse cultures that closely resemble each other in subject, although the treatment of each issue naturally varies from one society to another. Despite the unique perspective of each culture, their shared concerns tie human beings to one another across the globe and throughout history.

Moreover, their shared concerns performed this function in ancient times as well as in our own day. What has largely gone unnoticed is the mobility of oral, and even written, literature in ancient times and the cultural influence that one ancient culture had on another. The great epics cry out to be told, and so they traveled the seaways with merchants, sailors, visitors, warriors, immigrants, scholars, and professional entertainers who were part historian and part storyteller. Particularly if they lived in a colony, in an empire, or near major trade routes, professionally trained bards knew and performed the literature of other cultures, as well as their own. This process not only preserved the greatest myths—the epics of any culture—but it made it possible for the most skilled of bards and poets to enhance their own renditions, both oral and written, of their own culture's epics by creatively adapting the appealing aspects of the epics from other cultures, such as particular relationships between pairs of characters, important themes, and artistic style.

All too often, centuries later, a culture has considered its myths, with pride, to be totally homegrown. Yet the warriors as well as the historians of ancient Greece and Rome were interested in the ethnology of foreign peoples, and they recorded what they learned, either firsthand or from other sources. Their surviving histories and essays reveal that the world's greatest epics reflect the cultural influence of peoples who preceded them by hundreds and even thousands of years. Moreover, archaeologists in the twentieth century have unearthed thousands of clay tablets and opened many tombs that help us understand ancient cross-cultural connections. Revised introductions in this book to *The Iliad* and *Beowulf* reflect what scholars, both old and new, have learned about the cultures that influenced the authors of these epics and their orally transmitted material.

In part because human beings are all part of one family, and in part because of cross-cultural contacts, the following themes are common in world mythology: The first parents are often the gods of sky and earth. The creator-god usually fashions the first human beings from parts of the earth—perhaps clay, trees, rocks, or plants. The gods destroy at least one world of mortals by causing a great flood. In the world, as in nature, birth, maturity, and death are often followed by rebirth. Heroes are children of gods who have an unusual birth, possess extraordinary strength, kill monsters with the help of special weapons, embark on an arduous journey, descend into the Underworld as part of their tasks, and have an unusual death.

An inherent part of many myths is the belief in one or more divine powers who create life and control the direction of the universe. Throughout the world, these divinities, whether in human or in animal form, are anthropomorphic in that they think, act, and speak like human beings. They differ primarily in their attitude toward mortals. Some gods, like those of Greece, Egypt, India, and North America, appreciate the merits of human beings, are sympathetic to them, and try to help them. Other gods, like those of Sumer, Babylonia, and northern Europe (the Norse gods), tend to be indifferent to the fate of human beings. Still others, like Sedna, from the Inuit people of North America, are unpredictable, and their people must take constant care so as not to offend them.

Where an oral myth has been told to, and written down by, an outsider, the authenticity of the myth can be clouded by the teller's distortions or the outsider's biases. The myths from the Middle East, Greece and Rome, and, to some extent, China and Japan have retained their authenticity because they were written down by people within the culture for their own use. In other cultures, like those of

India and China, the myths of earlier peoples were transcribed by people who intentionally imposed their own values on them, and it is sometimes possible to discern the original form of the myth.

However, in most cultures, like those of the Americas, Africa, and Ireland, the myths were part of an oral tradition that, of necessity, was communicated by the historian, through an interpreter, to a missionary or an anthropologist. Therefore, the authenticity of these myths depends on the motivation and the objectivity of three different parties. In some cultures, the historian was not permitted to reveal sacred material to an outsider (even the uninitiated in his own society). In other cultures, consciously or unconsciously, the outsiders were uncomfortable with pagan beliefs and values, and they intentionally or inadvertently changed what they heard so that it conformed with their own attitudes and values.

THE PURPOSE OF MYTHS

Myths were originally created as entertaining stories with a serious purpose. Their broad appeal has enabled them to survive for hundreds and sometimes thousands of years. A myth's serious purpose is either to explain the nature of the universe (creation and fertility myths) or to instruct members of the community in the attitudes and behavior necessary to function successfully in that particular culture (hero myths and epics). The Hittite myth of Telepinu, the Ainu epic *Kotan Utunnai,* the Micmac myth "Caught by a Hairstring," and the Yekuhana myth of Wanadi permit the reader to enter the world of a different culture and to see that world in a way that conveys the mystery of the universe and the fragility of human life.

A particular culture may be interested in the creation of the entire universe, beginning with divine beings who separate earth and sky. Many cultures start with the beginning of the universe—a chaotic, formless mass that a god separates, as do Bumba in the Boshongo and Bakuba myth from Africa and P'an Ku in the myth from China. In other cultures, like the Babylonian, the Greek, the Maori from New Zealand, the Toltec/Aztec from Mexico, and the Maya from Guatemala, the universe begins with a group of two or more gods, who multiply so that each can have his or her particular role in the universal scheme. In still other cultures, a creator-god, like Wanadi in the Yekuhana myth from Venezuela or Viracocha in the Tiahuanaco/Aymara myth from Peru, brings life to earth in the form of plants, animals, and human beings.

In contrast, some cultures are interested in myths that explain the origin of their own people and enhance their nationalistic spirit. For example, the Navajo people depict their journey upward through four worlds into a fifth world. Similarly, the Irish Celts are concerned with the settling of Ireland, and the Yoruba people explain the creation of Ife, their sacred city-state.

The myths of other cultures explain the continued existence of evil in the universe. Myths like *Wanadi* from the Yekuhana people of Venezuela, *Esfandyar* from Persia, "Quetzalcoatl" from Toltec/Aztec people of Mexico, and "The Woman Who Fell from the Sky" from the Iroquois/Huron people of the United States and Canada depict a universe in which a good divinity and an evil divinity wage constant war on earth for the human soul.

According to many myths, human beings are not perfect creatures even though a god created them. In many cultures, the creator-god must fashion and destroy, usually through a flood, a succession of races. This theme is found world-wide, from the Hindu myths of India to the myths of the Maya of Central America and the Yoruba myths of Africa. One of the most elaborate flood myths comes from Sumer and Babylonia.

All cultures explain how human beings acquired particular foods and the agricultural tools that permitted them to become civilized. Some myths, like the Hittite myth of Telepinu, the Japanese myth of Amaterasu, and the African myth from Dahomey, involve gods who have been insulted and must be appeased for fertility to be restored. The Telepinu myth includes powerful metaphorical incantations designed to enlist the god's aid. The Greek myth of Demeter and Persephone is a masterpiece of psychological complexity.

The myths of other cultures involve a divine figure who teaches agricultural skills to human beings. Viracocha introduces the Aymara/Tiahuanaco people to a more complex and civilized way of life, just as Wanadi does for the Yekuhana people and Quetzalcoatl does for the Toltec people. Other myths, like the Chinese myth of Chi Li, show a heroic figure rescuing humanity by killing a monster that has destroyed the fertility of the land. Similarly, in the Hawaiian myth, Maui tames the sun so that his people will have more light in which to pursue the activities that are necessary for their survival. The myths of many people involve trickster twins, such as Lodge-Boy and Thrown-Away from the Crow people in the United States, who kill monsters and so make the world safe for their people.

The heroic myths and epics of a society teach its members the appropriate attitudes, behavior, and values of that culture. These myths are of particular interest and value to us. Not only are they exciting adventure stories, but in these myths we see ourselves, drawn larger and grander than we are, yet with our human weaknesses as well as our strengths.

Heroes are the models of human behavior for their society. They earn lasting fame—the only kind of immortality possible for human beings—by performing great deeds that help their community, and they inspire others to emulate them. Heroes are forced by circumstance to make critical choices where they must balance one set of values against competing values. They achieve heroic stature in part from their accomplishments and in part because they emerge from their trials as more sensitive and thoughtful human beings.

Yet heroes are not the same throughout the world. Achilles, Gilgamesh, Heracles, Jason, the young Beowulf, Sigurd the Volsung, the hero of *Kotan Utunnai,* and Bakaridjan Kone, for example, come from cultures where individuals may earn fame in a variety of ways. This permits them to express their individuality. In contrast, Rama must always remember and follow dharma, the particular form of proper and righteous behavior that the Hindu culture expects of a person in his or her political, economic, and social position. Esfandyar must remain true to the principles of his religion, Zoroastrianism. Aeneas must always act in a way that is compatible with his god-given destiny. Arthur must keep the knights of the Round Table in harmony with one another and with him for the good of Britain, and in his old age, Beowulf, as the war-king of the Geats, must protect his people by fighting a dragon that is destroying his country.

In spite of their extraordinary abilities, no hero is perfect. Yet their human weaknesses are often as instructive as their heroic qualities. Their imperfections allow ordinary people to identify with them and to like them, for everyone has similar psychological needs and conflicts.

Many of the greatest heroes cannot accept mortality. Gilgamesh so fears death that he undertakes a long and perilous journey in search of the secret of immortality. Ultimately, he learns to be satisfied with the immortality that comes from enduring accomplishments. Achilles much choose between death with honor and a long, undistinguished life. When he feels deprived of honor on the battlefield, he chooses life, and only the unforeseen ramifications of that choice cause him to change his mind. Hector and Beowulf are forced to choose heroic deaths because they cannot live with the stain of cowardice.

Unlike most heroes, Heracles knows that he will become immortal after he has accomplished his labors. His primary concern is to avoid the labors because he refuses to be controlled by a cowardly king. In contrast, the immortality of lasting fame is so important to Gassire that he will do anything to achieve it, even if it destroys his people. Bakaridjan Kone must confront his loss of fame and decide what he is willing to do in order to regain it. Jason is so impressed with his fame that he feels entitled to act as he wishes, with no serious thought about the consequences.

The hero myths examine the relationship between the individual's desires and his or her responsibilities to society. Often the choice is crucial but uncomplicated: whether or not to risk death to save the community. The hero who chooses to risk death acquires honor and lasting fame; the hero who chooses safety is denied both. Esfandyar, Heracles, Beowulf, and Chi Li make the world a safer place by killing many monsters. The hero of *Kotan Utunnai* helps his people by fighting valiantly against the enemy.

In the major epics, the issue is the same, but the circumstances are infinitely more complex. When a leader places his or her own desires before the needs of the community, both the community and the individual suffer. Agamemnon and Achilles quarrel over a slave girl because public honor is the key to self-esteem. Similarly, Lancelot and Guinevere place their love above their loyalty to King Arthur, thereby destroying the Round Table and putting Britain into the hands of power-hungry local rulers. Aeneas places the needs of his community above his personal desires but loses his own humanity. Similarly, Rama places the needs of his community above his love for Sita, causing great personal tragedy for both of them. On the other hand, Gassire earns fame by placing his personal desires before the needs of his community, and Jason loses fame for the same reason. Bakaridjan Kone's community supports his heroism even though it is at the expense of an innocent community.

Heroes define themselves by how they relate to external circumstances. They acquire lasting fame by performing deeds of valor, but they acquire even greater heroic stature by winning an inner battle against their desires. Hector fights a greater battle because he first must overcome his fear of Achilles. Both he and Beowulf fight against a superior foe, knowing that they will die in the process yet choosing to die with honor rather than to live without self-esteem and public approval. In contrast, Quetzalcoatl is outmatched when Tezcatlipoca preys upon his vanity, and Jason is destroyed when his vanity leads him to dishonor Medea, his wife and benefactor.

We should not be intimidated by the external characteristics of the hero: an immortal parent, unusual birth, aristocratic social position, and divine sponsorship. We could say that Heracles can perform great tasks because his father is Zeus. We do this in our own lives whenever we attribute someone's success primarily to luck instead of to individual courage, perseverance, and ability. However, this attitude is not personally helpful. Although these heroes lived long ago in cultures very different from our own, they can still serve as models for us. We too must often risk our self-esteem and our reputation by making difficult choices and by attempting tasks where we fear failure. We too want to live in such as way that we are remembered for our good deeds.

THE MATRIARCHAL SOCIETY

A knowledge of the basic difference between Mother Earth–centered matriarchal religions and the Father Sky–centered patriarchal religions is crucial to an understanding of the symbolic content of many myths. The political, economic, social, and religious foundation of the matriarchal society was the agricultural year. The importance of agriculture fostered a cyclical view of life, emphasizing the progression of all living matter from birth to maturity to death to rebirth. Even in lands where the climate remained relatively stable from one season to the next, people could see the connection between the development of their own lives and the development of life among plants and animals.

In the matriarchal society, the Great Goddess or Mother Goddess personified Mother Earth and was the supreme deity. She functioned in three related forms. As Goddess of the Underworld, she controlled the three-stage cycle of life: the period of birth and childhood; the fertile period of maturity and reproduction; and the sterile period of old age, with its decline and death.

As Goddess of the Earth, she controlled the three-stage cycle of the seasons: spring—the period of birth or rebirth, and budding growth; summer—the fertile period of blossoming and harvest; and winter—the sterile period of decay, barrenness, and death or dormancy.

As Goddess of the Sky, she was the great Moon Goddess, who appeared in her three-stage cycle of phases: as the new and waxing moon—the period of birth or rebirth, and growth; as the full moon—the period of maturity; and as the waning moon—the period of decline and death or dormancy.

Consequently, the Great Goddess was the source of all human life and the source of all food. To survive, societies needed to produce children and to produce food. They knew how dependent they were upon the blessings of the Great Goddess, and they worshipped her properly so they would receive those blessings.

The queen embodied the spirit the Great Goddess, and she wielded great political, economic, social, and religious power. Other women were considered daughters of the Great Goddess. Thus, all women in the matriarchal society were highly valued, and many of them held important positions. Women were the heads of their families, and inheritance passed from a mother to her daughters, with the youngest daughter being most important because, presumably, she would be the last to die and thus would continue the family line the longest. Children were reared by their mother and her brother, while the father lived in the home of his mother and helped rear his sister's children. The children's primary moral obligations were to their mother and their siblings.

When the male's role in procreation became understood and valued, the queen took a husband, called the sacred king, for one year. At first, he was her brother or her son, but later he was a youth who symbolized her son. Many youths competed for the great honor of being sacred king. They had to win many contests involving physical strength and the skillful use of the bow. Heracles' tasks against the Nemean lion, the Cretan bull, the Erymanthian boar, and Artemis's deer represent typical contests. Odysseus's participation in an archery contest where the winner will marry Penelope is an echo of this tradition.

Each spring, when the seeds of the new crops were sown, the past year's sacred king would be sacrificed as part of a major religious ceremony. The priestesses of the Mother Goddess would eat his flesh in order to acquire his powers of fertility, and the fields and farm animals would be sprinkled with his blood so they too would become fertile. Then, in a religious ceremony, the queen would take a new sacred king for the coming year.

The sacred king gradually gained more power. He increased the length of his reign to eight years by choosing a substitute, or surrogate, sacred king to die in his place. At the end of each year, the real king would retire from public view into a burial chamber or cave for one to three days, while the surrogate sacred king reigned in his place. The priestesses of the Great Goddess would sacrifice the surrogate king in a sacred ceremony and use his flesh and blood to ensure the fertility of the community. Then the real king would resume his duties for the coming year.

When Gilgamesh rejects Ishtar's marriage proposal, he related the ways that she has destroyed previous mates. Ishtar retaliates by causing the death of Enkidu, who functions as Gilgamesh's surrogate. Demeter in Greek culture and Amaterasu in Japanese culture are examples of the Great Goddess. Moreover, vestiges of the pre-Hellenic matriarchal culture remain in the Greek myths of Jason, Medea, Heracles, Achilles, and Paris.

By 2400 B.C., aggressive tribes worshipping a supreme male god who was a father-figure or a successful warrior had begun to invade many matriarchal communities. They brought with them a new social and political order in which males dominated. Kings gained enough power to change the old social system to one in which kings ruled by heredity and animals were sacrificed to win the favor of the gods.

Some cultures depict a world view in which one generation of gods replaces another, the newer gods being more civilized and capable than the earlier ones. For example, Zeus conquers Cronus in Greek mythology, and Marduk conquers Tiamat in Babylonian mythology. The battle between one family of gods and another often reflects the political and religious conflict between the indigenous people, who were farmers and worshipped the Great Goddess or the Mother Goddess, and a warlike invading people, who worshipped male sky gods. Zeus's conquest of Cronus and the Titans reflects the political conquest of one people by another, and his liaisons with many Mother Goddesses in addition to Hera, his wife, represent a compromise in which the invader's religion was united with each local religion. Similar changes are reflected in Babylonian mythology, where a religion in which Marduk is the principal god incorporates the older gods.

ACADEMIC PERSPECTIVES ON MYTHS

Because myths are symbols of human experience, they can be analyzed in a variety of ways, depending upon the perspective of the scholar. Years ago, many scholars viewed myths as symbols of the external environment. Those who crated myths were thought to have observed nature and interpreted the behavior of human beings in a parallel manner. For example, heroes were considered symbols of the sun. They wielded swords that symbolized the sun's rays against monsters that symbolized clouds and night, the enemies of the sun. Each hero story was thus a symbol of the conflict between day and night and, by extension, between good and evil.

In the twentieth century, the symbolic interpretation of myths moved from the external environment to the internal environment of the unconscious mind. Sigmund Freud and his followers view myths as the expression of the individual's unconscious wishes, fears, and drives. For example, Otto Rank explains the characteristics of the traditional hero in terms of infantile hostility, childhood fantasies, and rebellion against one's father.

Carl Jung and his followers, among them Carl Kerenyi, Erich Neumann, and, more broadly, Joseph Campbell, view myths as the expression of a universal, collective unconscious. In their theory, innate psychological characteristics, common to all human beings, determine how people throughout the world and throughout history experience and respond to the process of living. The contents of the collective unconscious are divided into archetypes—such as the mother, the child, the hero, the trickster, and the giant—but these are simply image frameworks. A particular individual's life experiences determine in what particular shape and form the archetypal images will be expressed. Thus, the fact that myths from around the world contain many similar themes reflects the existence of a common collective unconscious. The fact that they differ in their treatment of these themes reflects the influence of each culture's particular physical, social, economic, and political environment on the archetypes.

Scholars in this century have interpreted myths in other ways as well. Mircea Eliade, a historian of religions, views myths as the essence of religion, conceived from a genuine religious experience. It is the sacred experience that gives myths their structure and their utility. The ancient world contained a multitude of coexisting religious ideas and forms: different types of monotheism and polytheism (both female-dominated and male-dominated), nature worship, and ancestor worship. Consequently, numerous similarities and connections exist from one culture to another. This is evident from the study of various aspects of the religious experience, such as the nature of divinities, creation myths, sacrifices, rituals, death, and paradise.

The anthropologist Paul Radin views myths from an economic perspective. The individual's actual struggle for survival in the face of economic uncertainty, caused by an insufficient food supply and poor technology, creates fears that life will be unhappy and short. Religious leaders manipulate these fears for their own material benefit, often in concert with the political leaders of the community.

The anthropologist Claude Lévi-Strauss views myths as abstract constructions rather than narrative tales or symbols of experience. The structure of all human minds is identical and is revealed by the similar ways people solve their problems. Myths are identical products from identical minds, so myths from around the world possess a common structure. They reveal the conflict between opposing forces—such as life and death or nature and culture. To discover the meaning of a particular myth, one must focus on its underlying structure rather than its narrative content or any symbolic meaning. This structure invariably reveals tensions in social relations or economic problems. The analysis of myths proves that human beings, no matter how primitive their technology, are not mentally inferior. Their myths demonstrate that they possess the intellectual capacity to understand the world in which they live.

Part of the fascination of mythology involves viewing it from a variety of perspectives simultaneously. Each discipline offers a valuable contribution, increasing our appreciation of the whole.

World Mythology

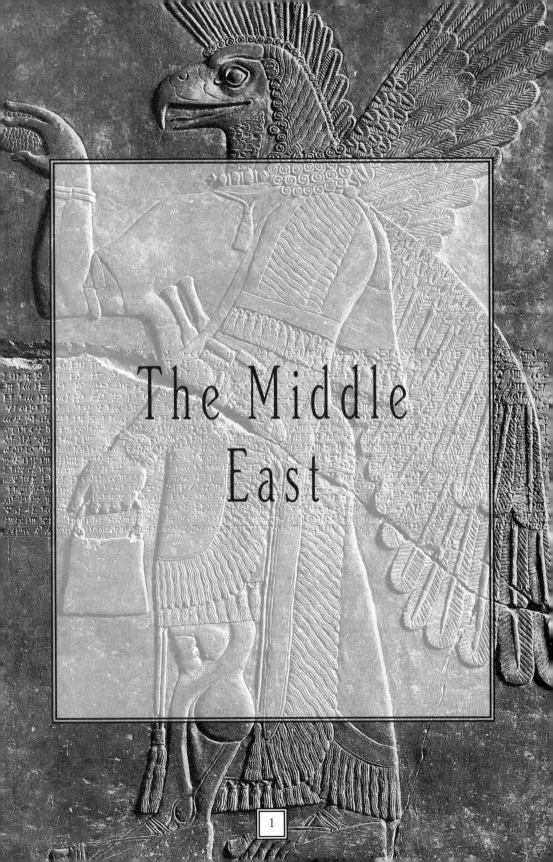

The Middle East

The myths from the Middle East, which date from 2500 B.C., are the oldest recorded literature in the world. Yet they reveal a universe of gods and heroes who react to the human condition as we know it today. The gods of Sumer, Babylonia, and Egypt have human personalities and human needs, and they enjoy helping a favorite mortal.

In ancient Middle Eastern cultures, the ability to perform magic tricks was considered proof of the ability to govern the world. In the *Enuma elish,* the Babylonian creation epic, a male divinity, Marduk, pits his great magical powers against the original female divinity, Tiamat. Because he possesses stronger magic, Marduk wins and becomes the new ruler of the universe.

Egyptian myths reflect Egypt's isolated culture and therefore are quite different from the myths of Egypt's neighbors, Sumer and Babylonia. The ancient Egyptian view of the universe included predictable, helpful divinities who combated an evil that could never be permanently conquered. The Egyptians also believed in resurrection for deserving human beings. The myth of Osiris, Isis, and Horus was so important that the Egyptians pictorially depicted it on the walls of their temples.

The Hittite myth about Telepinu addresses fertility. Possibly because the first part of the tablet is missing, the reason for the anger that Telepinu feels is not explained; the myth simply describes how the god must be appeased in order for life on earth to continue and flourish.

The Sumerian/Babylonian epic *Gilgamesh* presents what may be the first tragic hero. Gilgamesh wants what many other human beings wish to possess—the immortality of everlasting life. He takes a perilous journey in the hope of achieving his wish, but he learns that human beings are not destined to acquire this type of immortality. Despite his disappointment, Gilgamesh learns much from his journey. He learns to value the ordinary pleasures in life, and he decides to perform deeds that will bring him lasting fame—the only form of immortality that is available to human beings. This epic also reveals how the gods of Sumer and Babylonia, unlike the Egyptian gods, are unpredictable. Many of them are most memorable for their quick tempers and impulsive behavior.

The Persian legend about Esfandyar brings ancient Persia's two greatest heroes into conflict with one another. Rostam is one of the world's greatest traditional heroes. He has devoted his life to making his society a better place in which to live, and he has no ambition beyond heroism. In contrast, Esfandyar wants, above all, to become king of Persia, and his religious principles lead him to obey a command that is unjust, unnecessary, and ultimately self-destructive.

HISTORICAL BACKGROUND

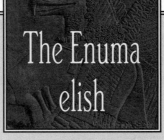
The Enuma elish

The Babylonian creation myth is the epic known as *The Enuma elish* from its opening words, which mean "when on high." It was recorded in cuneiform (wedge-shaped) script upon seven clay tablets that were found by British archaeologists in the 1840s in their excavations at Nineveh, in what is now Iraq. These tablets were part of the library of King Ashurbanipal, who ruled from 668 to 627 B.C.

German excavations at Ashur (not far from Nineveh), begun in 1902, uncovered another version of *The Enuma elish*. This version is identical to the one at Nineveh except for the substitution of the name of the Assyrian national god (Ashur) for the Babylonian national god (Marduk). Therefore, this epic appears to have been important to the Assyrians as well as to the Babylonians.

Although these cuneiform tablets date back only to about 1000 B.C., their content and style indicate that the story recorded on them may have existed as early as 1900 B.C. In the introduction to his famous legal code, Hammurabi, who ruled the Babylonians from 1728 to 1686 B.C., refers both to *The Enuma elish* and to Marduk: "At the time when Anu, king of the gods, and Enlil, lord of heaven and earth and the god who determines the destiny of the land, first made Marduk supreme among the gods, then assigned to Marduk Enlil's role as king over all human beings, and finally made Babylon supreme among the nations of the world, at that time Anu and Enlil chose me, Hammurabi, the religious and god-fearing prince, to enrich the lives of the people by caus-ing justice to shine upon the land like the sun, thereby destroying all that is evil."

Each year in Babylon, *The Enuma elish* was solemnly recited and drama-tized as part of the ten-day New Year festival, which marked the beginning of the autumn season. The holiday was a serious one that emphasized the reestablishment of order in the universe, the renewal of life, and the determination of all human destinies for the coming year.

Scholars believe that the Babylonians pantomimed the battle depicted in *The Enuma elish* between the forces of chaos and the forces of order. Chaos would reign in the streets of Babylon until Marduk was freed. Then he would lead a procession, symbolizing the forces of the gods, against Tiamat and her demon forces. After Marduk had defeated Tiamat and her rebellious forces in a mock battle and had established order in the universe, the Babylonians would carry his image in a triumphant parade through the streets. In this magical way, the people hoped to influence the gods who controlled human destinies and persuade them to usher in a year of fertility, abundance, and good fortune.

The people of Babylon may also have considered this myth to have magical power over the Tigris and Euphrates Rivers. These rivers overflowed their banks each spring and often ravaged the countryside with severe flooding. Residents used the magic of incantation and dramatization to try to protect their community against the devastation of these terrible spring floods.

The myth honoring Marduk glorifies both the patron god of Babylonia—who had created the universe and brought order out of chaos—and the city of Babylon, for the gods built the temple of Marduk in Babylon to be their earthly home. The myth thus combines both religious and secular political aspects. Just as the destinies of human beings were determined in the course of the New Year holiday, so, too, the political fate of Babylonia was being decided.

Thus, *The Enuma elish* epic is more than a creation myth. The Babylonians took the traditional Sumerian creation myth and reshaped it to serve new national, religious, and political purposes. The explanation of the creation of the universe became the story of the rise to supreme power of the storm god Marduk and the glorification of his earthly city of Babylon.

BABYLONIAN RELIGION

The three greatest Sumerian divinities—Anu, god of the sky, Enlil, god of the air, and Ea, god of the earth—still existed among the Babylonian divinities. Then Marduk, who possessed both a great birthright as Ea's son and extraordinary abilities of his own, was born. Once Marduk entered the assembly of the gods, they gave him Enlil's role in the universe, so that Enlil was a god in name only, without function or power. Marduk became the supreme god, given the honor of creating the universe and of keeping it functioning. Further, Marduk was responsible for the creation of human beings, whose purpose it was to serve the gods. All gods and all mortals obeyed Marduk's will.

Marduk achieved power by means of a religious revolution, and his victory established a new order and a new way of looking at the universe. The Sumerian gods had been the substance of the universe, not merely representing but actually being the land, the water, and the heavens. When Marduk gave them new roles, he created the universe as the Babylonians recognized it. He organized the elements that already existed (the gods) to bring order out of chaos.

It is also significant that Marduk built the new order upon the ruins of an order that was even older than that explained in Sumerian mythology. The earliest people of Babylonia were farmers. They worshipped the Great Goddess or Mother Goddess to ensure the fertility of their fields and themselves and, therefore, to ensure the survival of their community. Therefore, when Marduk is victorious over Tiamat, his victory represents that of a new male-dominated patriarchal religion over a female-dominated matriarchal religion, in which Tiamat was the Great Goddess or Mother Goddess.

Tiamat originally presided over a universe that was far from the chaos that Marduk is called upon to organize. As the Great Goddess, she functioned in three related forms. As Goddess of the Underworld, she controlled the three-stage cycle of life: first, the period of birth and childhood; then the fertile period of maturity and reproduction; and last, the sterile period of old age, with its decline and death. As Goddess of the Earth, she controlled the three-stage cycle of the seasons: first, spring (the period of birth or rebirth and budding growth); then, summer (the fertile period of blossoming and harvest); and last, winter (the sterile period of decay, barrenness, and death or dormancy). As Goddess of the Sky, she was the great Moon Goddess, who appeared in her three-stage cycle of phases: first, as the new and waxing moon (the period of birth or rebirth and growth); then, as the full moon (the period of maturity); and last, as the waning moon (the period of decline and death or dormancy).

However, the Babylonians transform Tiamat's earlier role in the *Enuma elish*. Tiamat, who originally was the Great Goddess or Mother Goddess and who had given birth to all of the original gods, now became their enemy. She who originally was good and protected the lives of her children now became evil and attempted to destroy those children. She who originally had given birth to the best of the gods now gave birth to monsters and demons. She who originally was more powerful than her husband and her sons now was easily defeated by a new god who was immune to her potent magic.

Under Marduk, order emerged out of chaos, life emerged from dead matter, and nature was renewed each year. Nevertheless, the universe and the gods within it were not predictable or reliable. Even the powerful king Marduk was always dependent upon the goodwill and the help of the gods for success. Life after death promised no rewards for earthly achievements—just darkness, dust, deprivation, and eternal boredom. Therefore, the Babylonians believed that human beings had to make the most of their earthly lives, in a world that lacked security and hope.

e⌒ɔ

PRINCIPAL GODS*

TIAMAT: *Babylonia:* Great Goddess or Mother Goddess; Mother Earth, who nourishes all life; wife of Apsu; mother of Anshar, Kishar, and Mummu; ruler of salt waters. *Sumer:* counterpart of Nintu

APSU: *Babylonia:* husband of Tiamat; father of Anshar, Kishar, and Mummu; ruler of all the gods and sweet waters. *Sumer:* counterpart of Anu

MUMMU: *Babylonia:* son of Tiamat and Apsu; god of mist

ANSHAR: *Babylonia:* son of Tiamat and Apsu; brother and husband of Kishar

KISHAR: *Babylonia:* daughter of Tiamat and Apsu; sister and wife of Anshar

ANU (An): *Babylonia:* god of the sky; son of Anshar and Kishar. *Sumer:* god of the sky; husband of Nintu; father and ruler of all the gods

NINTU (Ki): *Sumer:* a Great Goddess or Mother Goddess like Tiamat; wife of Anu; mother of all the gods; created the first human beings out of clay

ENLIL: *Babylonia:* god of the air between earth and sky. *Sumer:* son of Anu and Nintu; god of air and agriculture; became ruler of the gods along with Anu

ISHTAR (Inanna): *Sumer:* first, daughter of Anu, later of Sin; a Great Goddess or Mother Goddess; goddess of love and war

EA: *Babylonia:* son of Anu; husband of Damkina; father of Marduk; ruler of all the gods and sweet water after Apsu; god of wisdom, arts, and crafts. *Sumer:* son of Nintu; ruler of the earth; god of wisdom, arts, and crafts

DAMKINA: *Babylonia:* wife of Ea; mother of Marduk

MARDUK: *Babylonia:* son of Ea and Damkina; wisest and most accomplished god; becomes ruler of all the gods. *Sumer:* counterpart of Anu and Enlil

KINGU: *Babylonia:* commands Tiamat's forces against Marduk

SIN: god of the moon; father of Shamash

SHAMASH: son of Sin; god of the sun; protects the poor, the wronged, and the traveler

*For the most part, the Babylonians adopted the earlier Sumerian gods. Important distinctions between the Babylonian and Sumerian gods are noted.

THE ENUMA ELISH

In the beginning, only water and the mist that hovered above it existed. Father Apsu personified and ruled the sweet waters, Mother Tiamat personified and ruled the salt waters, and both waters flowed together as one. Mummu, their son, existed in the mist that covered them. Neither the heavens high above nor the firm earth below existed yet. Neither marshland nor pastureland had as yet appeared upon the waters. As yet, no huts of matted reeds had been fashioned.

Then the gods Anshar and Kishar were formed within the sweet waters of Apsu and the salt waters of Tiamat, and they emerged from the waters. In time, Anshar and Kishar became the parents of Anu, who became god of the heavens. Anu, in turn, became the father of Ea. Ea surpassed both his father and his grandfather, for he was wiser, more understanding, and stronger than they, and he was skilled in the use of magic. He became god of the earth, and he had no rival among the great gods.

The young gods joined together and had merry times. They were so rowdy that they disturbed Tiamat as they surged back and forth, and their exuberance caused her to resent their presence. As time passed, the Mother Goddess came to hate their behavior, but she did not know how to deal with them. She asked Apsu to talk to them, but when he tried, they ignored him.

Apsu, Tiamat, and Mummu sat down together to discuss the problem. Apsu announced, "I cannot abide the way the gods are behaving! Their clamor continues incessantly both day and night, so that I can never get any sleep. I desperately need peace and quiet! Since they will not listen to my pleas, I will have to stop their raucous activities the only way I can, by destroying them!"

Her husband's words angered Tiamat. She replied, "I understand exactly how you feel, Apsu. You know that I have complained about the same problem. However, your solution is evil! Will we destroy the children that we ourselves created? Their manners are rude, and their activities are annoying, but we must try to be understanding."

Mummu, however, supported Apsu. "I advise you to ignore Tiamat's opinion in this matter," he counseled. "Proceed with your plan and destroy the gods, for they show no respect for your authority. They are unruly both day and night, and their behavior gives you no peace." Apsu's face glowed with pleasure when he heard Mummu's opinion, for he enjoyed the evil plan that he had in mind.

The gods quickly learned of Apsu and Mummu's plot against them. When they first heard the news, they cried. Then they sat in silence, unable to think of a way to avoid their fate.

But Ea, who was the wisest, the most clever, and the most accomplished of the gods, soon thought of a way to spoil the scheme of Apsu and Mummu. First he created a magic circle to protect the gods and placed them safely within it. Then he recited a sacred spell upon the deep waters of Apsu, causing Apsu to fall into a sound sleep and Mummu to remain powerless.

Ea then placed Apsu in chains, removed his crown and halo, and placed them on his own head. When he had taken the symbols of kingship, he killed Apsu. He then bound Mummu, leading him about wherever he wished by a rope drawn through Mummu's nose.

Once he had conquered his enemies, Ea made his home upon Apsu and the sweet waters that had belonged to him. There, deep within the waters, he rested peacefully with his wife, Damkina. His splendid house became the house of destinies; his sacred room became the room of fates.

In time Ea and Damkina became the parents of Marduk, the wisest and most able of all of the gods. Even though he was born fully grown, goddesses fed Marduk from the day of his birth and made him awesome to behold. From the beginning, Marduk appeared to be a natural leader, and as soon as Ea saw his son, his paternal heart filled with gladness. Ea made Marduk a double god so that he would surpass all the other gods in form and in strength. Four sparkling eyes shone forth from Marduk's face, enabling him to see everything, and four large ears extended outward, enabling him to hear everything. Whenever Marduk moved his lips, fire blazed forth from his mouth.

"Our son is the sun of the heavens!" Ea exclaimed. Indeed, Marduk wore the halos of ten gods upon his head, so that the brightness of his rays was awesome to behold. He inspired terror as well as majesty in all who beheld him.

Meanwhile, Anu created the winds of the north, south, east, and west, and these tempests violently disturbed Tiamat's waters. When some of the gods suffered in the dreadful windstorms and could find no rest, they designed evil within their hearts.

Led by Kingu, they said to their mother, "When Ea and the gods who helped him killed Apsu, our father, you allowed them to do it. Now Anu has created this terrible fourfold wind, which disturbs your body and keeps us awake, and you have allowed him to do it. Our eyes are weary from lack of sleep! Apparently you do not love us, for you do nothing! Think about your husband and Mummu, whom those gods defeated. You have been left all alone! Why not rouse yourself and avenge Apsu and Mummu by attacking the gods? We will support you!"

Tiamat was very pleased to hear these words of encouragement. "You have given me good advice," she replied. "I will create monsters to help us, and then we will fight against those gods!"

The rebellious gods now felt free to express their anger. They met both day and night in order to plan their revolt.

Meanwhile, Tiamat created monster serpents as her invincible weapons. She filled their bodies with venom instead of blood and gave them sharp teeth and long fangs. She fashioned terrifying dragons and crowned them with halos like the gods, so that anyone who looked upon them would perish from fright. Once the serpents stood upright, no one would be able to stand against them. She created eleven monsters in all: the viper, the dragon, the sphinx, the great lion, the mad dog, the scorpion-man, three mighty storm demons, the dragonfly, and the centaur.

Then Tiamat chose Kingu to be commander-in-chief of her monsters and the rebellious gods. "I have cast my spell upon you, Kingu," she told him. "I have given you the power to counsel all the gods in the assembly. You now rule supreme and are my only companion. Your command will be everlasting, and your word will endure!" With these words, Tiamat fastened the Tablet of Destinies upon Kingu's chest.

In this way, Tiamat prepared to fight against her children in order to avenge the death of Apsu. Knowing nothing of fear, the monsters gathered around her and marched at her side. They were angry and ready for battle. Tiamat exclaimed, "May your great poison conquer our enemies!"

As soon as Ea heard that Tiamat and Kingu were leading a revolt against the gods, he went to Anshar, his grandfather, and informed him of their preparations for battle. Anshar was very concerned. "Ea, you have killed Apsu, and now you must kill Kingu, who marches at the head of Tiamat's forces!"

Ea tried his best to please his grandfather. But as soon as he saw Tiamat and her forces, his heart filled with terror, and he could not summon the courage to face them. Ashamed of his cowardice, he retreated and returned to Anshar. "Tiamat, Kingu, and Tiamat's monster serpents will never respond to my magic!" he exclaimed. "They are much more powerful than I am!"

Then Anshar turned to Anu and said, "You are both courageous and strong! Take a stand against Tiamat. Surely you can resist Kingu's attack!"

Anu obeyed his father's command and took the road to Tiamat. However, when he saw her terrifying forces, he did not have the courage to face her. Like Ea, he returned to Anshar in shame. "I am not strong enough to carry out your wishes," he confessed.

Anshar, Anu, and Ea sat in silence. "No god," they thought, "can face Tiamat and her forces in battle and survive!"

Finally Anshar joyfully exclaimed, "Marduk, the hero, will avenge us! He is very strong, and he is great in battle! Ea, bring your son before us!"

When Marduk stood before them, he announced, "Do not be concerned. I will go and carry out your heart's desire! After all, it is not as if a male has come against you. Tiamat, for all her weapons, is only a woman! So, Father of the Gods, rejoice and be happy. Soon you will be able to tread upon Tiamat's neck!"

"My son," Anshar replied, "you are the wisest of the gods. Calm Tiamat with your sacred spell. Take your storm chariot and go quickly. Kingu and Tiamat's monster serpents will not be able to drive you away. Defeat them!"

Marduk rejoiced to hear the words of Anshar. He replied, "Anshar, if I am to avenge you, conquer Tiamat, and save the lives of the gods, then call all of the gods to assembly and proclaim my supreme destiny! Let my word determine the fates! Let whatever I create remain fixed. Let my command be everlasting, and let my word endure!"

Anshar called his adviser to his side and said, "Tell all the gods about Tiamat's revolt against us, and explain how Marduk will surely succeed where Ea and Anu have failed. Tell them to assemble here. After we have feasted upon good bread and wine, we will decree the destinies for Marduk, our avenger."

So it came to pass that the gods met in assembly and glorified Marduk. First they built a princely throne for him, from which he presided. Then they said, "You, Marduk, are the most important of the great gods. Your rule is unrivaled. It has the authority of Anu, god of the sky. From this day forth, when we gather in assembly your word will be supreme. Your decrees will be everlasting. No one among the gods will disobey your word. We grant you kingship over the entire universe. It will be within your power to raise or to bring low, to create or to destroy."

Then the gods brought forth a garment, placed it before Marduk, and said, "To prove your power, make this garment vanish and reappear. Now, reveal the extent of your power!"

Marduk then commanded the garment: "Vanish!" And it disappeared. He commanded: "Appear!" And it reappeared in one piece. When the gods saw the power of his words, they joyfully announced, "Marduk is king!" Then they gave him his throne, his sceptre, and his ceremonial robes. Finally they gave him unequaled weapons to use against his enemies.

"Your weapons will not fail; you will indeed destroy your enemies," they said to him. "Spare the life of the one who trusts you, but pour out the life of the god who is evil. Go now and cut off the life of Tiamat. May the winds carry her blood to secret places. May you return successful, having accomplished your purpose."

Marduk then constructed a great bow for himself, attached an arrow to it, and hung it at his side. In his right hand he grasped his mace. In his left hand he held a plant that destroyed poison. At his side he carried a net he had created to enclose Tiamat when he captured her. In front he set lightning. He filled his body with a blazing flame. Then he placed the winds of the four directions about him so that Tiamat could not escape.

Marduk then brought forth the evil wind, the whirlwind, the hurricane, the fourfold wind, the sevenfold wind, the cyclone, and the matchless wind and sent all seven winds to stir up the inside of Tiamat, goddess of the salt waters. He harnessed his team of four beasts—the Destroyer, the Relentless, the Trampler, and the Flier—to his invincible storm chariot, which inspired with terror anyone who gazed upon it. Marduk mounted his chariot, and Smiter, who was fearsome in battle, took up position at his right, while Combat, who could repel the most ardent fighters, took up position at his left. Both monsters possessed sharp teeth and tongues that dripped venom.

Finally, Marduk encased himself in a terrifying coat of armor and placed his fearsome halos upon his head. He smeared red paste upon his lips as a magical protection against the forces of evil. Last of all, he called forth the flooding rainstorm, his mighty weapon. Then he set forth to meet the raging Tiamat.

The sight of Marduk sent terror into Kingu's heart and distracted his mind. Kingu's forces could not face Marduk's brilliance and turned away in fright.

Marduk then raised his mighty weapon, the flooding rainstorm, against the enraged Tiamat and said, "Why have you begun such an evil conflict? You are attacking your own children! Do you not love them? Sons are fighting against their fathers, and you have no cause to hate them! You have conferred upon Kingu a rank to which he is not rightfully entitled. Although you are armed with weapons and surrounded by your forces, I ask you to stand against me in single combat!"

At these words, Tiamat lost her senses. Her legs shook and she cried aloud, using all of her magic. Then Tiamat and Marduk fought in single combat. Marduk spread out his net to enfold her. When Tiamat opened her mouth to consume him, Marduk drove the evil wind into her mouth in order to keep it open. The other winds entered Tiamat's body, broadly extending it. Marduk then shot her with his bow. The arrow tore into her stomach and ripped through her body, splitting her heart and killing her.

Marduk then threw down Tiamat's body and stood upon it. Once she was dead the gods who had marched at her side retreated in terror, desperately attempting to save their own lives. But Marduk's forces encircled them and permitted no escape. Marduk took the rebellious gods prisoner, smashed their weapons, and confined them in his net. Then he imprisoned them in cells.

Marduk bound with chains the band of eleven demons who had marched on Tiamat's right, then trampled their bodies. He imprisoned Kingu, took from him the Tablet of Destinies—which was not rightfully his—sealed the Tablet, and fastened it upon his own breast.

Once Marduk had subdued all his enemies, he returned to Tiamat, stamped on her legs, and crushed her skull with his mace. When he had severed her arteries, the north wind bore her blood to the secret places. Marduk then divided Tiamat's body into two parts like a shellfish. Half of Tiamat he set up as the sky; the other half he formed into the earth. From Tiamat's saliva, he created the clouds and filled them with water, but he himself took charge of the winds, the rain, and the cold. He put Tiamat's head into position to form the mountains of the earth, and he caused the Tigris and the Euphrates rivers to flow from her eyes.

Marduk then directed Anu to rule the heavens, Ea to rule the earth, and Enlil to rule the air between heaven and earth. He divided the year into months and days. He caused the moon, Sin, to shine at night in various phases as a way of marking the days of the month. He created the sun, giving the days to Shamash as he had given the nights to Sin.

When he had created order in the universe, Marduk handed over the shrines he created to Ea. The Tablet of Destinies he gave to Anu. He restored the bound gods who had helped Tiamat to their fathers. Finally, he turned Tiamat's eleven monsters into statues to remind the gods of the futility of revolt.

When he returned to Anu, Enlil, and Ea, Marduk announced, "I have hardened the ground in order to build a luxurious house and temple where you will spend the night whenever you descend from heaven and meet in assembly. I will call my temple Babylon, which means 'the houses of the great gods.' Skilled craftsmen will build it."

The gods asked Marduk, "Who will have authority in the temple you have built? Who will have your power on the earth that you have created? Establish Babylon as our home forever! Let someone bring us our daily ration, and we will continue to perform the tasks that we have always performed. Let Ea, who is skillful in all crafts, prepare the plans for Babylon, and we will be the workers."

Marduk's heart filled with joy to hear their response. "I will collect blood and create bones," he said to Ea, "and from them, I will create a savage and call him 'man.' His job will be to serve the gods so that they may rest at ease."

Ea, the wise, replied, "Call the gods to assembly. Tell them to give us the god who led Tiamat to rebel. Let that god perish so that human beings can be formed out of his blood."

When Marduk had assembled the gods, he said, "Declare under oath who among you devised the revolt and led Tiamat to rebel. Deliver him to me to take the responsibility, the blame, and the punishment upon himself. The rest of you will then be able to live in peace."

The gods who had rebelled revealed that the instigator of their revolt had been Kingu. Then they bound him and presented him to Marduk and Ea.

Ea killed Kingu, severed his blood vessels, and fashioned the first human beings out of Kingu's blood. Then Ea explained to them that the purpose of their lives was to serve the gods.

The gods had now been freed for a life of ease. But first, in order to honor Marduk and thank him for saving them, they worked for two years to construct Babylon, their earthly home. When the temple was completed, the gods gathered within its walls and celebrated. Then they praised Marduk's future.

"May Marduk rule unsurpassed among the gods," they declared. "May he shepherd the human race that he created. May he establish for them the rites of religious worship: the food to be offered, the incense to be smelled, and the sacred spells to be recited. May all human beings remember to praise and honor Marduk to the end of days. May they serve and support their gods and tend their sanctuaries without fail. May they improve their lands, build their shrines, and remember the Mother Goddess."

The gods concluded their celebration by proclaiming the fifty names and qualities that Marduk possessed, for they wished to honor their supreme god's glorious ways and deeds. Finally they said, "Let the shepherd and the herdsman rejoice in Marduk so that their lands may be fertile and they may prosper. The command of Marduk is unalterable; whatever he says, no god will change. Vast is his mind, and broad is his sympathy. Yet when Marduk is angry, no god can withstand his wrath. Let Marduk's command be supreme, both in the heavens above and upon the earth below, for Marduk has destroyed Tiamat and has achieved everlasting kingship."

❧ QUESTIONS FOR
Response, Discussion, and Analysis

1. In ancient times, one sign of being fit to rule was the ability to perform miracles or magic. What can Marduk do? What other leaders could perform extraordinary feats?

2. Marduk conquers Tiamat in a war. How is he superior to her as a divinity? How does the war between the gods reflect human life?

3. Why did the gods want to create human beings? How did this affect the lives of Babylonians?

HISTORICAL BACKGROUND

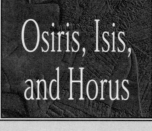

Osiris, Isis, and Horus

Civilization developed in Egypt between 4000 and 3000 B.C. The years between 3500 and 2500 B.C. were a Golden Age in which Egypt flowered politically, economically, and artistically. In about 3000 B.C., Upper Egypt and Lower Egypt united, becoming the first great nation of the Western world. About that time, the Egyptians invented *hieroglyphics,* a kind of picture-writing, which permitted them to record their thoughts and thus to establish a written heritage. By 2500 B.C., Re, the sun god, was the principal god, and the belief in Osiris, god of life, death, and resurrection, was widespread and of major importance. The great pyramids also had been constructed by that period, and the *Pyramid Texts* recorded important religious ideas.

In the years between 3500 and 2500 B.C., the political, economic, and religious climate in Egypt was very different from that in Mesopotamia, the other great ancient civilization of the West. Separated from the rest of the ancient world by large expanses of desert and by the Mediterranean Sea, the Egyptians lived in cultural isolation for many hundreds of years.

Until about 1700 B.C., civilization in Egypt proceeded without serious disruptions or significant outside influence. Egypt was more politically stable than Mesopotamia, so the people could concentrate on improving the quality of their lives. The Egyptians also kept to themselves economically. While the cuneiform (wedge-shaped) script of the Mesopotamians was adopted by many of the communities with which they traded, Egypt's economic isolation meant that its system of writing was not adopted by other peoples.

The differences between the physical environments in which the Mesopotamian and Egyptian civilizations developed led to profound differences in religion. In Egypt, for example, the Nile River flooded and receded with a predictable regularity. In Mesopotamia, however, the Tigris and Euphrates Rivers would flood fiercely and unpredictably, widely changing their courses from one year to the next and destroying everything in their paths. While the Egyptians feared that the Nile would dry up permanently and wither their culture, they had less cause for concern than those in Mesopotamia, who suffered the floods of the Tigris and Euphrates Rivers. Thus, the Egyptians envisioned kindly gods who were inevitably more gentle than those of the Mesopotamians.

EGYPTIAN RELIGION

Religious ideas influenced Egyptian politics, science, art, and literature. Like most ancient peoples, the earliest Egyptians prayed to their gods for children, success in farming and hunting, and success in war. However, from earliest times, the Egyptians also believed in the divine aspect of human beings and in the idea that when a human being died he or she left life on earth and began life in another world. In addition, the ancient Egyptians believed that their king—the pharaoh—was god and man combined. He was both king and priest, both a human being and the son of the sun god.

The great pyramid tombs of the kings and queens of Egypt testify to the Egyptian belief in the afterlife. The tombs, surviving to this day, contained not only mummified corpses but everything the ruler would need in the next life. For example, the tomb of King Tutankhamen—a tomb that was fortunate enough to escape grave robbers—revealed an incredible wealth of material: sculptures, wall paintings, and writings describing daily life; furniture; household utensils; wigs; jewelry; games; and musical instruments. Many of the golden and jeweled burial objects reveal a beauty and intricate design unequaled among the civilizations of the ancient world—and unsurpassed even today.

The Nile River was the lifeblood of the ancient Egyptians. Its waters created lush, fertile farmlands. Vegetation flourished along its banks, supporting the lives of animals and human beings.

In contrast, the desert was the great environmental enemy of the ancient Egyptians. It represented death, for human beings could not survive in such a hot, dry wasteland. It sheltered wild, poisonous animals and many evil spirits and appeared to lie in wait. Every summer, the intense heat and desert winds would cause the Nile to become slow and narrow. Although their river's flood cycle was predictable, the fear of death from famine haunted the earliest Egyptians. The nearby desert reminded these people that their existence was fragile. So the annual flooding of the Nile brought great relief and celebration. Water brought the rebirth of the land and provided sustenance and survival to human beings.

From earliest times, Osiris was the god of grain and of the Nile; like the Nile, he nourished all life. In his own and neighboring lands, he taught people what grains to cultivate, how to irrigate the land, and how to prevent unwanted flooding. Just as the Nile flooded, dried up, and flooded again, so Osiris lived, died, and was reborn. His death represented the death of vegetation when the Nile dried up. His regeneration represented the rebirth of vegetation when the Nile flooded in the spring.

Osiris was both god and man. The son of a god, Osiris was king of Egypt and the earth, and he caused both to be fertile and to prosper. After Osiris's death, his father, Re, who was the great god of the sun, made Osiris king of the gods and king of the Other World. Osiris's resurrection gave the ancient Egyptians the hope that they could share his destiny. Just as the gods had helped Osiris return to life, so they would help human beings who had led good lives gain life after death.

The worship of Osiris was particularly significant because it turned the ancient Egyptian people away from cannibalism. Once the Egyptians came to believe that the human being was part divine, they viewed living humans with more respect and the human corpse as sacred. Once they came to believe that the key to their immortality was to have lived a good life on earth, their relationships with one another improved immeasurably.

Osiris was a particularly appealing god because he had also been a man. Because he had suffered and died, he could emphathize with the suffering and death of each human being. Because he was a god, he could help people in both this world and the next. Osiris began as the example of a man who, with the help of the gods, regained life after death. In time, he became the god who caused the deceased person to achieve resurrection.

Horus, Osiris's son, became Osiris's counterpart on the earth once Osiris became Lord of the Other World. In effect, Horus was a form of the resurrected Osiris. He inherited his father's kingdom and restored the order, justice, and prosperity that had existed under his father's reign. Horus was called the avenger of Osiris because he had performed the tasks involved in resurrecting his father's body. As Osiris's son, Horus acted as an intermediary between Egyptians who were destined to die and Osiris, who could grant them immortality.

The spirit of the newly dead person would appear before Horus and tell the god all of the good deeds that he or she had performed in life, to show why that individual deserved resurrection. Osiris would then take the person's heart (symbolizing conscience) and place it on one side of a great balance scale; a feather (symbolizing law) would be placed on the opposite side. A jury would watch the balance of the scale, and the god Thoth—lord and maker of law—would record the result.

A person who had led a good life would have a heart lighter than the feather and would be granted new life in Osiris's kingdom, where he or she would live just as on earth. If the heart weighed more than the feather, however, the jackal that was sitting near the scale would eat the person's heart and mummy, and he or she would remain dead. Thus, Osiris was also the god of truth and judge of the dead. He conducted this trial, which rewarded the virtuous and punished evildoers.

Isis, Osiris's sister and wife, was the greatest goddess in Egypt. She was called the Great Goddess, the Mother Goddess, the lady of green crops, and the lady of abundance. She represented both the devoted and loyal wife and the loving and nurturing mother. As an earth goddess, Isis created every living thing and nourished and protected all that she had created. Like Osiris, Isis was a human being as well as a goddess. Her persistent search for the body of Osiris and her trials while she reared Horus in the papyrus swamps endeared her to the Egyptian people. After Isis was reunited with Osiris, she remained in the Other World with him, giving life and food to the dead.

Set, Osiris's brother and enemy, represented the evil in the universe: natural catastrophes—such as earthquakes and storms—darkness, destruction, and death. He was the god of the desert through which he wandered. Naturally, Set plotted against Osiris, Isis, and Horus because they represented the forces of good. Good triumphed over evil in that Set could not destroy Osiris and Horus, no matter how clever his attempts. Yet the gods did not destroy Set either. Evil would continue to exist in the world.

Between 2500 and 1500 B.C., Osiris gradually became as important as Re, the god of the sun. By 1850 B.C., the great religious festival of Osiris was held annually at Abydos, in Upper Egypt, where Isis had found Osiris's head. The focus of the Abydos festival was the dramatic presentation of the story of Osiris: his death and dismemberment (which was a common ancient burial custom), the finding of the pieces of his corpse, and his return to life. There Horus had resurrected Osiris's body, and there the door to the Other World was located. Therefore, the dead person was judged at Abydos and was either permitted to enter the Other World or condemned to eternal death. Wealthy Egyptians chose to be buried at Abydos.

APPEAL AND VALUE

It is clear from the earliest existing writings of the Egyptians that the story of Osiris, Isis, and Horus was very well known. Numerous references to parts of the story exist in ancient Egyptian sources, the *Pyramid Texts* and *The Book of the Dead*. However, either the ancient Egyptian writers saw no need to retell such a popular tale, or the narratives that once existed have long since disappeared. The only existing narrative of the entire story is that of the Greek Plutarch, who wrote *De Iside et Osiride* in about A.D. 70. Considering that the story may well have been four thousand years old by that time, it is amazing that Plutarch's Egyptian sources were so accurate.

The fact that this myth continued to live in a form so close to the original for many thousands of years testifies to the timelessness of the values it contains. A wife's devotion to her husband has appealed to countless generations of human beings in cultures around the world. Equally appealing and enduring is the nurturance that a mother gives her child. As in ancient Egypt and in Plutarch's day, these values are steadfast.

Moreover, throughout time, human beings have had to confront the forces of evil in the universe. Like Osiris's brother Set, evil can be conquered temporarily, but it cannot be destroyed permanently. History and our own experiences confirm this to be true. In every age, people have feared their mortality and wanted to avoid death. The myth of Osiris gave Egyptians hope for life after death.

OSIRIS, ISIS, AND HORUS

Nut, goddess of the sky, was very beautiful and kind. She was married to Re, god of the sun and creator of all. But she also made love to her brother, Geb, god of the earth, and Thoth, lord of divine words. When Re discovered that Nut had secretly slept with Geb, his heart filled with rage and he cursed his wife. "You will not give birth to the child that is within you in any month of any year!" he exclaimed.

Nut's kind heart filled with sorrow at the thought that she would not become a mother. Tearfully she approached Thoth and said, "Re has cursed me so that I cannot give birth in any month of any year! Is there anything you can do to help me? Surely, one of the children within me is yours!"

Thoth replied, "Do not spoil your beauty with your tears. Instead, let good cheer chase your grief from your heart. Trust me to find a way to help you. I promise that before the next year begins, you will be called Mother of the Gods!"

Thoth's eyes sparkled as he left Nut and went off to find Moon. "Since you love to play games," he said to Moon, "I will agree to play as many games as you like if you will help me. Every time I win, I want you to give me a small part of your illumination. You will never miss the light, but it will be very useful to me. Do you agree?"

"I do not mind at all," Moon replied, "as long as you take very little light each time."

So it came to pass that Thoth and Moon played many games in the course of the next months. As they had agreed, whenever Thoth won a game he took from Moon a small part of her illumination. He then put this fragment of light aside and saved it.

Finally, Thoth had collected so many fragments of light that, when he put them together, they created five complete days. Thoth then added the five days he had won from Moon to the normal solar year of 360 days.

In this way, Thoth avoided the curse that Re had placed upon Nut. When the solar year came to an end, Nut gave birth to five children, one on each of the extra five days that Thoth had created. As Thoth had predicted, from that time on Nut was known as Mother of the Gods.

Re was the father of both Osiris, who was born on the first of these five days, and Horus the Elder, who was born on the second day. At Osiris's birth a voice called out from the heavens, "The good and great King Osiris, lord of all the earth, has been born!"

Geb was the father of both Set, who chose to be born on the third day, and Nephthys, who was born on the fifth day. Set showed his aggressive spirit from the moment of birth. While Nut's four other children were born at the proper time, Set chose the time and manner of his own birth. He cut an opening in his mother's side and forced his way into the world. In time, he married his sister Nephthys.

Thoth was the father of the Great Goddess Isis, lady of green crops, who was born on the fourth day. Thoth was the most intelligent of the gods. He was called lord of divine words because he possessed the magical power to compel whomever he chose to listen to and obey the words he uttered. Thoth taught his daughter something of this power. Isis and Osiris loved one another from the time they shared their mother's womb. In time, they became husband and wife.

Osiris became king of Upper and Lower Egypt and earned lasting fame for himself and his subjects. When he began his rule, his people were nomads. They lived a simple life, wandering from place to place and gathering the fruits of the earth. Osiris united these tribes and taught them to be a highly civilized people. First he made his subjects more industrious. He taught them the arts of farming so they could acquire more and better foods from the earth. Then Osiris gave his subjects a body of laws so they could live and work together in peace. Finally, he taught his subjects to revere and worship the gods. Osiris was the ideal king, and his rule created a Golden Age in Egypt.

When Osiris had improved the lives of his own people in these ways, he traveled to other parts of the world to convince the inhabitants to accept his ideas. He persuaded his listeners by entertaining them, setting his ideas to music and singing hymns and songs.

While Osiris was away from Egypt on these ventures, Set searched for an opportunity to take over the country. He was unable to succeed, for Isis and her father sensed his ambition and watched him carefully.

After Osiris returned, Set became even more determined to rule Egypt. One night, while Osiris was asleep, Set secretly measured the king's body. He then commanded his craftspeople to construct a wooden box that could contain Osiris. He ordered the best artists in the land to decorate it so beautifully that it would be a work of art. Finally, he convinced seventy-two of Osiris's subjects to join him in planning a revolt.

Soon thereafter, Set entertained the conspirators and Osiris at an elaborate feast. At the end of the meal, he had his servants bring the beautiful wooden box into the dining hall. As he had anticipated, the box was admired by all of his guests.

Pretending to jest, Set announced, "Whoever among you would like to own this beautiful box should climb into it. I promise to give it as a gift to the person whose body is a proper fit. However, your body must fit exactly when you lie down. If you are so tall that your head or your legs overhang the box, or if you are so short that your body leaves a space at the head or foot of the box, then you will not qualify for the gift."

As Set had planned, his dinner companions eagerly gathered around the beautiful box, each awaiting his turn to try it. One after another, each guest climbed inside the box and attempted to lie down as Set had directed. But no one fit exactly. Finally Osiris took his turn, climbing into the box and lying down. The fit was exact.

Osiris had hardly settled himself inside the box when the conspirators quickly nailed the box lid in place, imprisoning the unsuspecting king. To make certain that Osiris would suffocate, the conspirators next poured melted lead over the box. Then they carried the box to the Nile River and dumped it into the water. The current carried the box to the mouth of the Nile, where it became lodged in the papyrus swamps in the eastern part of the delta.

The people who lived near the city of Chemmis were the first to hear about the murder of Osiris, and they spread word of Set's terrible deed. When Isis heard about Osiris's death, her heart overflowed with grief. She immediately cut off one of her locks as a sign of mourning and put on the clothing worn by a woman mourning the death of a loved one. Then she set off in search of the box.

As the Great Goddess wandered tirelessly from place to place throughout Egypt, her mournful cries interrupted farmers laboring in their fields, craftspeople working in their shops, and even those who slept soundly at night. Isis walked from town to town, questioning everyone she met. Finally, she found a group of children who had watched the box drift into the papyrus swamps at the mouth of the Nile, and they told her the direction it had gone.

Isis eventually learned that the box finally had become lodged among the branches of a tamarisk bush in the papyrus swamps near Byblos. This bush had grown into a very large tree, and the box had been completely enclosed within the tree's trunk.

The king of the country, Melcarthus, was unaware of the box. When he heard of this large tree, he had his servants chop it down and bring it to his palace. Trees of great size were rare in his country, and he had a specific use for its huge trunk. He placed it in the center of his dining hall to help support the roof of his palace. The use of this tree trunk as a column was talked of far and wide.

In time, Isis heard about the fate of the large tamarisk tree. She traveled to the town near King Melcarthus's palace and seated herself beside the fountain where women came to draw water for their households. The goddess sat there in silence until Queen Astarte's handmaidens arrived for water. Then she spoke with them in a very kind, friendly fashion. She braided their hair for them and perfumed them with the aroma of her own body.

The handmaidens returned to their queen with the exciting news of the strange woman they had met by the fountain. Queen Astarte immediately announced to her servants, "I want to meet this marvelous stranger who can transfer her own perfume to the hair and skin of other people! Go to the town fountain quickly, before she leaves. Find her, and bring her to the palace at once!"

So it came to pass that Isis entered King Melcarthus's palace and met the queen. Queen Astarte was so delighted with Isis that, before long, she asked the Mother Goddess to become the nurse of one of her sons. In time, Isis told the queen her story and asked for permission to cut open the pillar that supported the roof of the palace. With the queen's permission, she did so and removed the box without harming the ceiling.

Once Isis was alone, she fell upon the box with loud cries of mourning. Then she took leave of the royal family and returned to Egypt, taking the sealed box with her.

Upon reaching a remote place in the desert, Isis stopped and opened the box. The sight of her beloved husband, lying still and lifeless, was more than her heart could bear. The Great Goddess placed her face against the face of Osiris, embraced his body, and wept with grief. Then she placed the wings of a bird upon her arms and hovered over Osiris, flapping her wings in order to create air for him to breathe.

Finally, using knowledge that her father, Thoth, had taught her, she skillfully uttered the magical words of power in a way that she knew would bring temporary life to Osiris. Osiris returned to life! With delight, Isis embraced her great love and enjoyed him for as long as she could. Then, when Osiris once again lay lifeless and still, Isis replaced his body in the box. She carefully hid the box in a remote, isolated place where it would be safe from harm.

In time, Isis gave birth to Osiris's son, whom she named Horus. As the Mother Goddess gazed upon her newborn child, her heart overflowed with joy. She hoped that one day Horus would avenge his father's death and would inherit his kingdom.

Shortly thereafter Thoth, lord of divine words, visited his daughter. "Listen to my counsel, Isis, and obey me," he said. "Those who follow the advice of another live and prosper. You must now escape from the eye of Set, and I will help you. If you will hide your child from Set until he is grown, he will become doubly strong. Then he surely will avenge the death of his father and will sit upon his father's throne.

"However," Thoth continued, "until that time comes, Horus will never be far from danger. Therefore, I will teach you the words of power that will protect Horus from death on earth, in the world above, and in the Other World."

Isis followed her father's advice. That evening, she left the house with Horus and seven scorpion-helpers. The Mother Goddess said to them, "My child and I are all alone in the world. Because of the death of my husband, my sorrow surpasses the grief of anyone in Egypt. So turn your faces to the ground and take me to a hidden place where I may rear my child in safety and in peace."

With three of the scorpions leading the way, Isis brought Horus to an island in the papyrus swamps of the Nile delta. There she secretly nursed and reared her child. Isis would often hide Horus among the papyrus plants while she went into a nearby city to acquire food for herself and her child.

"Have no fear, dear Horus, my glorious son," she would croon. "Your grandfather and I will keep every evil thing from you, for you are the father of all that is yet to be created. You will be in no danger, either on land or in the water. The sting of the most poisonous snake will not kill you, nor will the strongest lion be able to crush you. For you are the son of Osiris and Isis, and in time you will become lord of all the earth as your father was before you!"

Yet one day when Isis returned from the city, she found Horus lying lifeless and still with the mark of a scorpion bite upon him. She immediately recognized the treachery of Set. Isis leaned over the body of her baby son and carefully began to chant the magical words that Thoth had taught her. As she intoned the words, the color gradually returned to Horus's face, and his limbs began to stir. By the time Isis finished, Horus was smiling up at his mother. The infant had been restored to life. He grew up to be a healthy young man, skilled in the arts of medicine that his mother taught him.

It came to pass that Set was hunting in the desert by moonlight one night when he accidentally came upon the box that Isis had hidden. He recognized it instantly and opened it at once. As he gazed upon the corpse of his rival, Set's heart filled with implacable hatred and rage. In a mad fury, the evil god tore the corpse of Osiris into fourteen pieces. Then Set traveled throughout the kingdom of Egypt, scattering the pieces of Osiris wherever his whim led him.

Not long thereafter, Isis heard about Set's latest attack upon Osiris. Her sister Nephthys, although married to Set, was always loyal to Isis. Therefore, Nephthys accompanied Isis and Horus on the search for Osiris. They sailed up and down the Nile in a papyrus boat, and wandered throughout the country until they had located the various fragments of Osiris's body. Wherever they found a piece, Isis collected it and buried in its place a small figurine of Osiris. Isis then placed a tomb over each figurine. She hoped that this would mislead Set and give the time that she and Nephthys needed to find and heal Osiris.

When Isis found Osiris's head at Abydos, she possessed all fourteen pieces of his body. With Nephthys to help her, Isis set to work at once. First, they arranged Osiris's head, torso, limbs, heart, and organs as they would be in life. Next, the goddesses connected the various parts with wax. Then, they prepared a long piece of linen cloth by smearing sweet-smelling ointments upon it and sprinkling it with spices that would preserve Osiris's body from decay. Finally, they wrapped Osiris's body in the treated linen cloth and buried it.

Once Osiris was properly buried, Horus prepared to do his part to return his father to life. He led Isis and Nephthys to the world of the dead, where they found Osiris. Then the two goddesses pronounced the magical words of power that would bring Osiris new life. Gradually, the dead god came back to life; he began to breathe, his eyelids fluttered, and he moved his limbs.

Horus then removed his eternal eye, placed it in his father's mouth, and directed him to swallow it. Osiris immediately became much stronger and regained the ability to see, speak, and walk. With the help of Re, Horus set up a ladder so tall that it reached from the Other World up to the world of the gods above the earth. Osiris slowly climbed up to join the gods, with Isis leading the way and Nephthys behind him. The gods welcomed Osiris warmly, for they were delighted to have him living among them once again.

Once Osiris had rejoined the gods, Re made him their king and king of the Other World. Horus then became king of Upper and Lower Egypt in his father's place.

Now that Horus had taken his place among the gods, Osiris decided that the time had come to deal with Set. He tested Horus's readiness to avenge his father's murder.

"What is the most glorious deed a man can perform?" Osiris asked his son.

Horus replied, "To take revenge upon one who has injured his father or mother."

"What animal is most useful to a warrior?" his father asked.

"A horse," said Horus.

"Why not a lion?" his father asked in surprise.

Horus replied, "A lion is more powerful, but a horse is much quicker. Therefore, a horse can help a warrior capture a fleeing enemy better than a lion can."

Osiris was pleased to hear his son's responses, for they showed that he was mature enough to fight Set. Osiris then taught Horus how to use weapons of war and encouraged his son to take vengeance upon Set.

Horus and Set did fight each other, first in the form of two men and then in the form of two bears. The battle was so fierce that it lasted for three days and three nights. Osiris, Isis, and Thoth watched its progress. Joy flooded their hearts when Horus finally won and took Set prisoner.

But once Horus had conquered Set, Isis suddenly felt great pity for him. In her sympathy for her fallen enemy, Isis used her father's magical power with words. "Drop your weapons, Horus!" she cried.

Horus found himself powerless to resist. In spite of his own intentions, his weapons fell to the ground. Set was free!

Horus's heart filled with sudden rage and hatred toward his mother. "How can you do this to me, Mother?" he cried. "How can you let her do it, Grandfather?

Father, did you train me to win, only to see me lose in my moment of victory? Set has been our enemy for so long! He is evil, and his ways are cruel beyond imagining!"

No one replied to Horus's accusations. He watched, helpless, as Set ran away. In a fury, Horus then tore after Isis like a panther chasing its prey. When he caught her, he fought as fiercely as he had fought with Set. Finally, Horus cut off her head.

Thoth immediately used his magical words of power to change his daughter's head into the head of a cow, and he quickly attached it to her body. Horus then knew that Set would have to remain free, at least for the time being. He would conquer him, but in some other way.

Set was still determined to become king of Upper and Lower Egypt. He next tried to acquire the throne by accusing Horus of being an illegitimate child of Isis and, therefore, not the legal heir to the kingdom. However, when the gods met in assembly to discuss the matter, Thoth convinced them that Horus was indeed the legitimate child of Isis and Osiris. The lord of divine words brought forth a great balance scale and weighed the testimony of Set on one scale and Osiris's defense on the other. When the balance registered in favor of Osiris, he, Isis, and Horus were recognized as speakers of truth, while Set was unmasked as a liar. As a result, Osiris became judge of the dead in the Hall of Judgment, weighing their testimony on the great balance scale just as Thoth had weighed his.

But Set did not give up. Twice more he challenged Horus, and twice more he lost in combat. At last he accepted Horus's right to rule the kingdom of Osiris.

So it came to pass that the assembly of gods formally acclaimed Horus to be lord of all the earth as his father had been before him. Horus once again established order and justice, and with his reign prosperity returned.

Since he had been born from the seed of his dead father, Horus was chosen to be the intermediary between the living and the dead. Men and women would pray to him while they were still alive, asking him to notice their good lives and plead with Osiris for their resurrection after death.

Once Horus had inherited his father's kingdom, Isis remained with Osiris in the Other World and always accompanied him. She was satisfied and happy. Her husband had returned to life and love. Her son had avenged his father. The gods had proclaimed the truth of their words against Set's accusations. The kingdom of Upper and Lower Egypt was in good hands, and all was well.

❧ QUESTIONS FOR
Response, Discussion, and Analysis

1. This myth celebrates the idea of the cyclical nature of life: birth, maturity, death, and rebirth. What role does Isis perform in this cycle? Osiris? Horus?

2. What is the function of the villain Set? Why does Horus not kill him? Why does Isis free him? Would the myth have been more appealing if Horus had killed him? Explain.

This Hittite nature myth fits the pattern of the god who disappears, causing the earth to become barren. It contains the ritual for restoring the presence of the god and, with his presence, fertility.

Like other myths of its pattern, the Telepinu myth could account for the changing seasons in nature because it emphasizes the cycle of birth, death, and rebirth. If this is the myth's purpose, then it is not necessary to know the specific cause of Telepinu's anger, for presumably Telepinu will disappear whenever he becomes very angry, and something will anger him each year before the arrival of the winter season. (The first third of the Telepinu tablet was broken off and has never been found. Possibly that is why the story never reveals the cause of Telepinu's anger. However, at a later point in the story, Telepinu is given the opportunity to explain his behavior and chooses not to do so.)

Some scholars think this myth was retold and the rituals reenacted whenever the Hittites wanted to expel the forces of evil from their communities. In many cultures, such "housecleaning" rituals were performed before the beginning of the new year or the spring planting season.

TELEPINU

One day Telepinu, the god who made living things fertile, became furious and shouted, "I am so angry! No one should come near me!" He was so upset that he tried to put his right shoe upon his left foot and his left shoe upon his right foot. This made him even angrier.

Finally he fixed his shoes and stalked off. He took with him the ripening grain, the fertile winds, and the abundant growth in fields, meadows, and grassy plains. He went into the country and wandered into a secluded meadow that was sheltered among a grove of trees. There exhaustion overcame him, and he fell asleep.

Telepinu's rage upset the entire world of nature. Mist swirled over the countryside, fogging the windows of houses. Smoke invaded people's homes. In their fireplaces, the logs smoldered and would not burn. Cattle, sheep, and people no longer conceived. The lambs and the calves were neglected by their mothers. Even those already pregnant with new life could not give birth.

Corn, wheat, and barley no longer grew in the fields. All vegetation withered and died. Without moisture, the mountains and hills dried up. The trees also shriveled and could bring forth no fresh growth. The pastures became parched, and the springs evaporated. Famine arose in the land; both human beings and gods feared that they would all die of starvation.

The great sun god prepared a meal and invited the thousand gods. They ate, but could not satisfy their hunger; they drank, but could not quench their thirst.

Tarhun, the storm god, looked among the many gods and became anxious about his son. "Telepinu is not here," he announced. "He has become angry and has taken with him every growing thing!"

The great gods and the lesser gods began to search for Telepinu. They wandered over hill and dale. They crossed lakes and streams. But they could not find him.

The sun god then sent forth the swift eagle, saying, "Go look for Telepinu. Search every high mountain! Search the deep valleys! Search the blue waves of the sea!"

The eagle searched far and wide but could not find Telepinu. Finally it returned to the sun god and said, "I have looked everywhere for Telepinu. I have soared over the high mountains, I have dipped into the deep valleys, and I have skimmed over the blue waves of the sea. I found no trace of the noble god Telepinu!"

The storm god became worried and angry. He went to his father and said, "Who has offended my son so that the seeds have dried up and everything has withered?"

His father replied, "No one has offended him but you. You are the one who is responsible!"

Tarhun responded, "You are wrong! I am not responsible!"

His father then said, "I will look into the matter. If I find that you are guilty, I will kill you! Now, go look for Telepinu!"

Tarhun then approached Nintu, the Mother Goddess, and said, "Telepinu has become so angry that the seeds have died and everything has dried up. My father tells me that it is my fault. He intends to look into the matter, and he will kill me. What has happened? What will we do? If Telepinu is not found soon, we will all die of hunger!"

Nintu replied, "Calm yourself and do not be afraid. If it is your fault, I will correct it. If it is not your fault, I will also correct it. Meanwhile, go and search for Telepinu! Your winds can travel far and wide."

So Tarhun began to search for Telepinu. He went to his son's city and knocked at the gate of his house, but no one responded and the gate remained closed. Then he lost his temper and broke into Telepinu's house, but he still could not find his son. So he gave up and returned to Nintu. "I cannot find him at home," he said. "Where else should I search?"

Nintu replied, "Calm yourself. I will bring him to you. Bring me the bee. I will instruct it, and it will search for Telepinu." Tarhun did as Nintu requested and soon returned with the bee.

Nintu said to it, "Little bee, go and search for Telepinu! When you find him, sting his hands and his feet. Sting him until he springs to his feet! Then take some of your wax, and wipe his eyes and feet. Purify him and bring him before me!"

As Tarhun watched Nintu with the little bee, he said, "The great gods and the lesser gods have searched for Telepinu without finding him. How do you expect a bee to do any better than we did? Its wings are very small and weak, and it is a very small and weak creature. How can it succeed where the gods have failed?" Nintu replied, "Despite your doubts, Tarhun, the bee will find Telepinu. Just wait patiently, and you will see!"

The bee left the city and searched everywhere for Telepinu. It searched the streaming rivers and the murmuring springs. It searched the rounded hills and the rugged mountains. It searched the barren plains and the leafless woodlands. The length of its journey was a great strain, and as the little bee flew it began to consume the honey and the wax within its body.

Finally, the bee found Telepinu as he lay asleep in a meadow amid a grove of trees. It stung his hands and his feet and finally aroused Telepinu from his deep sleep. Once he stood up, the bee took some of its wax and wiped Telepinu's eyes and his feet. After it had purified him, it asked him what he was doing sleeping in the meadow.

Telepinu replied furiously, "I simply became very angry and walked away. How dare you awaken me from my sleep! How dare you force me to talk to you when I am so angry!"

Telepinu grew still more enraged. He stalked about, causing further damage. He dammed whatever springs still bubbled. He made the flowing rivers overflow their banks, creating devastating floods. Water now flooded houses and destroyed cities. In this way, Telepinu caused the death of sheep, cattle, and human beings.

The gods became very frightened and asked, "Why has Telepinu become so angry? What will we do? What will we do?"

The great sun god then declared, "Let the goddess of healing and magic calm Telepinu's anger with her sacred chants! And fetch a male human being. Let him use his magic to purify Telepinu!"

The goddess of healing and magic chanted: "Oh, Telepinu, here lies sweet and soothing essence of cedar. Let what has been deprived be restored! Here is sap to purify you. Let it strengthen your heart and your soul! Here lies an ear of corn. Let it attract your heart and your soul! Here lies sesame. Let your heart and your soul be comforted by it! Here lie figs. Just as figs are sweet, even so let your heart and your soul become sweet! Just as the olive holds oil within it and the grape holds wine within it, so may you, in your heart and soul, have good feelings toward the king and treat him kindly!"

Telepinu came to her in a stormy rage. Lightning flashed and thunder rumbled upon the dark earth as he arrived.

Then the goddess of healing and magic chanted: "When Telepinu was angry, his heart and his soul burned like brushwood. So let his rage, anger, wrath, and fury burn themselves out! Just as malt is barren and cannot be used for seed or for bread, so let his rage, anger, wrath, and fury become barren! When Telepinu was angry, his heart and his soul were a burning fire. As this fire was quenched, let his rage, anger, wrath, and fury be quenched too!"

She concluded, "Oh, Telepinu, give up your rage, your anger, your wrath, and your fury! Just as water in a pipe cannot flow upward, may your rage, anger, wrath, and fury not return!"

When the gods gathered in assembly under the tree, the male human being said, "Oh, Telepinu, when you left the tree on a summer day, the crops became diseased. Oh Telepinu, stop your rage, anger, wrath, and fury! Oh, tree, you wear white clothing in the spring, but in autumn your clothing is blood red. When the ox goes beneath you, you rub off its hair. When the sheep goes beneath you, you rub off its wool. Now rub off Telepinu's rage, anger, wrath, and fury. When the storm god arrives and is fearfully angry, the priest halts his progress. When a pot of porridge starts to boil over, the stirring of a spoon halts its progress. May my words halt Telepinu's rage, anger, wrath, and fury!

"Let Telepinu's rage, anger, wrath, and fury depart!" the man prayed. "Let them leave the house, the window, the courtyard, the gate, the gateway, and the road of the king. Let them stay far removed from the thriving field, the garden, and the orchard."

He continued, "Let them go the way the sun god travels each night, into the Netherworld. The doorkeeper has unlocked the seven bolts and opened the seven doors of the Underworld. Bronze containers with metal lids and handles stand deep within the dark earth. Whatever enters them does not leave them because it perishes there. Let these containers receive Telepinu's rage, anger, wrath, and fury, and let them never return!

"I have purified Telepinu!" the man concluded. "I have removed the evil from his body. I have removed his rage, his anger, his wrath, and his fury!"

And so it came to pass. Telepinu returned to his house and cared again for his land. The mist left the windows, the smoke left the house, and the fire burned on the hearth. Telepinu let the sheep enter the fold and the cattle enter the pen. The mother cared for her child, the ewe cared for her lamb, and the cow cared for her calf. Telepinu cared for the king and the queen, giving them both long life and strength.

A pole was set up before Telepinu, and from it the fleece of a sheep was suspended. It signified abundance: plentiful grain and wine, fat cattle and sheep, and successive generations of children. It signified fruitful breezes and fertility for every living thing.

❧ QUESTIONS FOR
Response, Discussion, and Analysis

1. How does Telepinu behave? What kind of person would he be? Would you like him? Why or why not?

2. Why is it necessary for a mortal to pacify Telepinu?

3. What purpose do the prayerlike chants at the end of the myth serve? Why does the myth say the same thing in so many ways?

HISTORICAL BACKGROUND

The epic of *Gilgamesh* was written on clay tablets in cuneiform (wedge-shaped) script at least 1300 years before Homer wrote *The Iliad* and *The Odyssey*. However, the first of these tablets was not discovered until excavations at Nineveh, begun in 1845, uncovered the library of Ashurbanipal, the last great king of Assyria (668–627 B.C.). Among the 25,000 tablets was the Assyrian version of *Gilgamesh*.

The epic gained international importance in 1862, when an expert in cuneiform published an outline of *Gilgamesh* along with his translation of part of the Assyrian version of the flood. The similarity between the flood story in the *Gilgamesh* epic and the description of the flood in the Bible led archaeologists to intensify their search for more cuneiform tablets.

Today scholars have available tablets containing portions of the *Gilgamesh* epic from many of the ancient countries in the Middle East, dating from 2100 to 627 B.C.—including some recently found in the library of Ebla, the latest ancient kingdom to be discovered. Scholars believe that stories of the adventures of Gilgamesh that existed in the oral tradition of Sumer were first written down in approximately 2100 B.C.

Between 1600 and 1000 B.C., the epic had been inscribed in Akkadian (Babylonian), Hittite, and Hurrian translations, some following the Sumerian versions and some branching off into wider variations, but all keeping the Sumerian names of characters and gods. A priest by the name of Sin-leqi-unninni, who probably lived during this time, is given credit for creating the late Akkadian version of the epic. Scholars think that he took the available Sumerian tales and imposed a uniform focus upon them, so that a series of separate adventures became the dramatic story of Gilgamesh's search for immortality. Sin-leqi-unninni integrated the Sumerian flood story into the epic and also created the friendship between Gilgamesh and Enkidu.

Gilgamesh apparently was a real king of Uruk, in southern Mesopotamia, sometime between 2700 and 2500 B.C. At that period Sumer had city-states, irrigation, laws, and various forms of literature. The writings of the time reveal that the people valued justice, freedom, and compassion. The strong walls of Uruk are attributed to Gilgamesh, and he may well have ventured into the wilderness in order to bring timber to his region, for wood was a valuable building material that this region lacked.

The Sumerian view of the gods as unpredictable and therefore frightening reflects the unpredictable and disturbing nature of the world in which they lived. For example, the Tigris and the Euphrates Rivers often radically changed their paths from season to season, a phenomenon that must have wreaked havoc on the farms and cities in the area. The flood in Gilgamesh is probably the specific, catastrophic flood that scholars think occurred in southern Mesopotamia in approximately 2900 B.C. It became a popular subject in the literature of the time.

Traces of an earlier, matriarchal religion remain in *Gilgamesh* as well as in *The Enuma elish*, the Babylonian creation epic. For example, the Temple of Anu and Ishtar belongs to Ishtar alone. The priestess from the temple who is chosen to civilize Enkidu is highly esteemed in her society. Her role in the temple closely connects her with the Great Goddess or Mother Goddess and sanctifies her sexual relationships.

In addition, *Gilgamesh* depicts Ishtar as a Great Goddess. When she wants Gilgamesh to marry her, he refuses because he knows that marriage to the Great Goddess will bring him certain death. He further insults Ishtar by listing the ways she has killed many of her previous mates. Ishtar becomes furious with Gilgamesh and retaliates by contriving to cause his death. However, his friend Enkidu dies instead, unwittingly serving as a substitute sacred king.

THE EARLIEST HERO

Gilgamesh is an unusual hero in that his major quest has an intellectual purpose: the acquisition of knowledge. In addition to possessing courage, he must have great determination, patience, and fortitude in order to reach his destination. After enduring physical hazards, he must wage a battle against despair when he learns that he cannot become immortal. He must find experiences that make life worthwhile, and he must find ways of perpetuating his name. Later heroes start by accepting what Gilgamesh questions; they are born into societies that have already determined the acceptable ways in which a person can achieve fame and an immortal name.

APPEAL AND VALUE

Gilgamesh is the earliest major recorded work of literature, and Gilgamesh is the first human hero in literature. The epic has universal appeal among Western cultures because it reaffirms the similarities in human nature and human values across time and space. The epic reveals the importance of friendship and love, pride and honor, adventure and accomplishment, and also the fear of death and the wish for immortality. It speaks as clearly to us as it spoke to those who lived when it was written, almost four thousand years ago.

Gilgamesh learns that the only type of immortality that he or any other mortal can achieve is lasting fame through performing great deeds and constructing enduring monuments. He also learns that life is precious and should be enjoyed to the fullest. His discovery during his long and arduous journey is a lesson that we too must learn in the course of our own lives.

Like Gilgamesh, we must fight the despair of failure and death, and we must choose what we will value in life and have the freedom to make these choices.

PRINCIPAL CHARACTERS*

GILGAMESH: king of Uruk who searches for immortality
LUGALBANDA: heroic father of Gilgamesh; earlier king of Uruk
NINSUN: goddess mother of Gilgamesh; priestess of Shamash
ENKIDU: best friend of Gilgamesh
HUMBABA: giant who guards the Cedar Forest of Lebanon
SIDURI: alewife whom Gilgamesh meets on his journey
UTANAPISHTIM: king of Shurippak; survivor of the Sumerian flood
URSHANABI: Utanapishtim's boatman

*For a list of the Sumerian gods, see page 5.

GILGAMESH

Chapter 1

Gilgamesh angers his people with his arrogance and selfishness. The gods create Enkidu to teach him humility.

Notice the strong walls of our city of Uruk! These walls were built by Gilgamesh on a foundation created in ancient times by the seven wise men, who brought great knowledge to our land. The top of our outer wall shines with the brightness of copper, but it is made of burnt brick. Now study the inner walls of our city. Examine the fine brickwork. These walls, too, surpass all others! No human being, not even a king, will ever be able to construct more impressive walls than Gilgamesh built around our city of Uruk! Now approach the majestic Temple of Anu and Ishtar. No mortal, not even a king, will ever be able to build a structure as beautiful as the one Gilgamesh created! Climb up and walk upon the walls of Uruk. Examine the fine brickwork. Admire the majestic Temple of Anu and Ishtar. Gaze upon one man's supreme achievement!

Who was the Gilgamesh who built these walls of lasting fame? Who was the Gilgamesh who built this most majestic temple? Gilgamesh was the renowned king of the city of Uruk. To his people, Gilgamesh was a tyrant who became a great hero.

Gilgamesh left his city to learn how to avoid death, and he returned having learned how to live. In the course of his travels, he saw everything throughout the land. Because he thought about what he had seen, he came to know everything that makes a person wise.

When Gilgamesh returned, he inscribed his travels and his thoughts upon stone tablets and placed these tablets on the strong walls of Uruk. He described the time before and during the great flood. He described his long, tiring journey in search of everlasting life. And he revealed the hidden mysteries of life and death that he had discovered. He wanted his knowledge to help his people improve their lives.

Read what Gilgamesh inscribed in stone upon the strong walls of the city of Uruk so that you, too, may gain wisdom.

Gilgamesh was two-thirds god and one-third man. His mother was the wise goddess Ninsun. His father was the noble Lugalbanda, a mortal who had also been king of Uruk.

Gilgamesh was such a godlike person that his people knew the gods had favored him. Nintu, the great Mother Goddess who had fashioned the first human beings out of clay, had also created Gilgamesh. Radiant Shamash, god of the sun, had given him great beauty. Adad, god of storms, had given him great courage. Ea, god of wisdom, had given him the capacity to learn from his experiences and to become the wisest of men. Yet, despite his goddess mother and all of his divine gifts, Gilgamesh was not a god, but a man. Therefore, he was doomed to share the common fate of all human beings, which is death.

When Gilgamesh was a young king, he was as willful and fearsome as a wild bull. He was the supreme wrestler and warrior. He knew no fear. He had no respect for tradition. He used the sacred drum as he wished. He did whatever he wished even when it hurt others. The fact that his behavior disturbed his companions did not restrain him.

Finally the nobles in Uruk became very distressed by Gilgamesh's behavior. They complained to one another, "Gilgamesh is incredibly arrogant, both day and night. Is this the way our king should act? It is true that the shepherd of our strong-walled city should be bold, but a king should also be majestic and wise! Gilgamesh interferes in the lives of his subjects beyond his right as king. Even in the households of his nobles and warriors, he intrudes between husband and wife, between mother and daughter, and between father and son."

The heavenly gods heard the complaints of the nobles of Uruk and met in assembly to discuss Gilgamesh's behavior. Anu, father of the gods, called the Mother Goddess before the assembly and said, "You created the hero Gilgamesh, mighty and wild bull of a man that he is! Now create an equally strong and courageous man, Enkidu, to be just like Gilgamesh. Make the spirit in Enkidu's heart like that of the warrior god, Ninurta, so that it will match the untamed spirit in Gilgamesh's heart.

"Then send Enkidu into Uruk, and let these two giants among men fight with one another. Enkidu will teach Gilgamesh his proper place in the world. Gilgamesh must be forced to recognize that, godlike though he is, he is not a god. Once he learns that he has limitations like all human beings, then the people in the strong-walled city of Uruk will be able to live in peace."

When she heard these words, Nintu conceived in her mind the image of a second heroic man, whom she created in the form of the god Anu. She washed her hands and pinched off a hunk of clay. Very carefully she drew the design she had envisioned upon it and threw the clay upon the broad, grassy plain a three-day journey from Uruk. Thus she created the hero Enkidu.

Enkidu came to life as a fully grown man. In some ways he looked as much like an animal as like a man, for his entire body was covered with shaggy hair. Long hair sprouted abundantly upon his head like rich fields of wheat. Like the god of cattle, he clothed himself in animal skins. Enkidu lived like a wild creature, away from the company of human beings and among the animals of the plain. He was aware of neither people nor land. Like his companions, the gazelles, he fed upon the grass of the plain. Along with the wild beasts at the watering place, he pushed for his turn to drink.

One day a hunter, who lived by trapping the wild animals, discovered Enkidu drinking at the watering place with the wild beasts. Amazed by the sight of such a strange human being, the hunter returned to the watering place on each of the following three days. Each time, he stared in fascination when he saw Enkidu among the wild animals. Each time, the sight of the mighty savage so frightened the hunter that he took his hounds and returned to his home, where he sat in silence, terrified of the wild man.

Finally the hunter said to his father, "For the past three days, I have seen a wild man at the watering place who appears to have come out of the hills. He is so strong that surely he is the mightiest in the land. In fact, the spirit of Anu, father of the heavenly gods, must live within his body! From what I have been able to observe of his habits, he seems to wander over the hills. He feeds with the gazelles on the grass of the plain, and he drinks at the watering place with the wild beasts who gather there.

"I am too afraid to approach him," the hunter confessed, "and yet he is robbing me of my livelihood. He fills in with dirt the pits I dig, and he tears up the traps I set. He releases the beasts and the smaller creatures of the plain whenever my devices catch them, and I can no longer capture any game!"

His father replied, "My son, the heroic King Gilgamesh lives in the strong-walled city of Uruk, which is only three days' journey from here. No one is mightier than he is! Even this wild man of whom you speak cannot possibly equal his strength! Gilgamesh is so strong that the spirit of Anu must live within his body!

"Therefore, you must go to the strong-walled city of Uruk and tell Gilgamesh about this mighty wild man. Bring back a priestess from the temple and let her educate this savage man in the ways of human beings. Let her meet him at the watering place. He will be attracted by her beauty. Once he embraces her, the beasts on the plain will regard him as a stranger and will associate with him no longer. He will be forced to become a human being."

The hunter took his father's advice and followed the road to the strong-walled city of Uruk. As soon as the king heard the hunter's tale, he sent a priestess from the temple to teach the wild man how to act like a human being.

After a journey of three days, the hunter and the priestess reached the home of the hunter. They spent the entire day sitting by the watering place, but Enkidu never appeared among the wild beasts. Early on the second day, the hunter and his companion returned to the watering place. They watched as the wild beasts and the creeping creatures came there to drink. Finally Enkidu, the mighty savage who was accustomed to feeding upon the grass of the plain with the gazelles and drinking at the watering place with the wild beasts, arrived.

"There he is!" the hunter exclaimed. "That is the savage man I have brought you to see! As soon as he sees you, he will approach you. Do not be afraid, for I am certain he will not hurt you. Let him get to know you, and teach him what it is to be a human being."

Enkidu was fascinated by the woman, and he spent six days and seven nights with her. He forgot the grassy plain where he had been born, the hills where he had roamed, and the wild animals that had been his companions. Later, when he was ready to rejoin the wild beasts of the plain, they sensed that Enkidu was now a human being. Even the gazelles drew away from him in fright.

Enkidu was so surprised by their change in behavior that, at first, he stood completely still. When he tried to rejoin them, he found that he could no longer run with the speed of a gazelle. He was no longer the wild man that he had been. However, he had gained something in return for the speed that he had lost, for he now possessed greater understanding and wisdom. He returned to the woman, sat down at her feet, and looked into her face attentively.

Chapter 2

Enkidu and Gilgamesh fight and become friends.

The priestess said, "Enkidu, when I look upon you now, I can see that you have become wise like one of the heavenly gods. Why do you still want to roam over the grassy plains with the wild beasts? Leave this wild country to the shepherds and the hunters, and come with me. Let me take you into the strong-walled city of Uruk, to the marketplace and to the sacred Temple of Anu and Ishtar. In Uruk you will meet the mighty King Gilgamesh. He has performed great heroic deeds, and he rules the people of the city like a wild bull. You will love him as you love yourself."

Enkidu's heart longed for a friend, so he said, "I will do as you suggest. Take me to Uruk, where the mighty king Gilgamesh rules the people like a wild bull. I will boldly address him and challenge him to a wrestling match. 'I am the strongest one!' I will shout. 'I was born on the grassy plain, and my strength is mighty!'"

"Come then, Enkidu," the woman replied. "You must give up your wild ways and prepare to live like a man among other men. You must learn to eat the food other men eat, to wear the kind of clothes other men wear, and to sleep upon a bed instead of on the ground."

Placing her cape upon his shoulders, the woman took Enkidu's hand and, as a mother leads her child, led him into the nearby shepherd's hut. A number of shepherds immediately gathered around and offered him some of their bread and beer. But when Enkidu saw that the shepherds expected him to eat and drink as they did, he could only stare in embarrassment and gag at the unfamiliar refreshments. He could not bring himself to taste such food, for he had lived by sucking the milk from wild animals, and the strange smell and appearance of the bread and beer repelled him.

When Enkidu refused to eat the bread and drink the beer, the priestess said, "You must learn to eat this bread, for it sustains human life, and you must learn to drink the strong drink, for that is the custom in this land."

Enkidu accepted her advice, and when he had eaten and drunk he was happy. He then cut his hair, oiled his body, and put on the customary clothing of a man. He became truly human, and he looked like a young noble. "Before we leave for Uruk," he said, "I will use my weapon to kill the wolves and the lions so the shepherds can rest at night."

Once Enkidu had done what he could to make the life of the shepherds easier, he and the priestess began their three-day journey. "You will like the city of Uruk," she said to him. "The people dress in festive clothing as if each day is a holiday. The young men are strong and athletic, and the young women are perfumed and attractive.

"I will point out Gilgamesh to you," she continued, "although you should recognize him. Like you, he enjoys life. He glows with manhood, and his whole appearance reveals his strength. He is stronger by far than you are, for he leads an active life both day and night. If he ever rests, no one is aware of it!

"Enkidu, you must curb your arrogance," the priestess warned. "Do not be too bold with Gilgamesh! Shamash, god of the sun, loves him. Anu and Enlil, who rule the heavenly gods, and Ea, god of wisdom, have made him very wise. Even before we arrive from the country, Gilgamesh will be expecting you, for he will have seen you in his dreams."

Meanwhile, Gilgamesh approached his mother, the wise and beloved goddess Ninsun, and told her his dreams so that she could explain them to him. "Mother," he began, "I dreamed last night that I walked among the nobles on a beautiful evening. As the stars in the heavens sparkled above me, one star, in form like Anu himself, fell out of the sky. This star-being landed right at my feet and blocked my path.

"When I tried to lift it," Gilgamesh continued, "it was much too heavy for me. When I tried to push it away, I could not move it. There the star-being stood, unconquerable, right in the middle of our strong-walled city! The people of Uruk rushed from their homes and gathered around it, while my companions, the nobles, kissed its feet. Much to my surprise, I loved this star-being! I placed my carrying strap upon my forehead, and with the help of my companions, I was able to lift it upon my back and bring it to you. However, when I placed it at your feet, you made it fight with me!"

Ninsun replied, "This star of heaven, in form like Anu himself, which suddenly descended upon you, which you could not lift and could not push away, which you loved, and which you placed at my feet and I made fight with you—this is, in fact, a man just like you, named Enkidu. He was born on the grassy plains, and the wild creatures have raised him. When Enkidu arrives in Uruk, you will meet him and embrace him, and the nobles will kiss his feet. Then you will bring him to me.

"Your heart will be joyful," Gilgamesh's mother continued, "for Enkidu will become your dearest companion. He is the strongest man in the land, with the strength of heavenly Anu. He is the kind of friend who will save his friend in time of need. The fact that you loved him in your dream means that he will always be your dearest friend. This is the meaning of your dream."

Then Gilgamesh said, "Mother, when I lay down again, I had another dream. This time, a strangely shaped axe lay upon the street within our strong-walled city, and all of the people of Uruk stood gathered around it. I loved it as soon as I saw it, so I picked it up and brought it to you. But when I placed it at your feet, you made it fight with me."

His wise mother replied, "Your second dream means the same as your first dream. The axe is the heroic Enkidu, who possesses the strength of heavenly Anu. When he arrives in Uruk, he will become your companion and your dearest friend."

Then Gilgamesh said, "It surely seems that, by Enlil's command, a dear friend and counselor has come to me, and I will be a dear friend and counselor to him in return."

When Enkidu and the priestess were not far from the city, a strange man approached and looked as if he wished to speak with them.

"Please bring that man to me," Enkidu said to the woman. "I would like to know his name and why he has come."

The stranger said to Enkidu, "Our king, Gilgamesh, lives without any self-restraint. He thinks that he has the right to do whatever he chooses, without considering the rights of others and the traditions of our land. The assembly of the heavenly gods decreed at his birth that, as the king of Uruk, Gilgamesh would have the right to sleep with a bride on the first night of her marriage. Yet Gilgamesh has abused and extended this privilege. Therefore, the people of our city fear and resent him!"

When Enkidu heard this, his face became pale with anger. He said to himself, "When I meet this king who rules the people of Uruk like a wild bull, I will teach him to know his proper place and to respect the rights and wishes of other people!"

Soon Enkidu entered the strong-walled city of Uruk, with the priestess following close behind him. As he stood in the marketplace, the people of Uruk immediately gathered around the heroic-looking stranger and blocked his path.

"Why this man looks just like our king!" they exclaimed. "Look how similar his build is! He is not as tall, but his bones look stronger. The milk of the wild creatures has given him prodigious strength. Surely he is the mightiest man in our land! Now the clamor of weapons in contests of arms will echo throughout Uruk!"

The nobles rejoiced. "A godlike hero has appeared in our city as a match for our own great king! Godlike Gilgamesh has met his equal!" they proclaimed.

That night, when Gilgamesh was walking toward the Temple of Anu and Ishtar, the two great men met in the marketplace of the land. As the king approached the temple, Enkidu placed himself in the middle of the gateway, gathered his strength, and stuck out his foot to prevent Gilgamesh from passing through the gate. Amazed and angered, Gilgamesh wrestled with the presumptuous stranger. For a long while, the two giants fought one another like two bulls. They shattered the gateposts and made the wall shake.

Finally, Gilgamesh bent his knee to the ground and turned away from Enkidu. His fury suddenly left him, for he realized that this presumptuous stranger must be the Enkidu of his dreams. His dreams had revealed the truth, for Gilgamesh knew that he had indeed met his match in Enkidu.

When he saw that Gilgamesh had turned away, Enkidu said with the greatest respect, "Hail to you, Gilgamesh, whom Enlil has made king of the people! Your mother, the goddess Ninsun, has given birth to a great son! You tower over those you rule!"

The two men then embraced each other and became the dearest of friends.

Chapter 3

Gilgamesh and Enkidu prepare to travel to the Cedar Forest and to meet the evil giant Humbaba.

One day Enkidu's eyes filled with tears, for his heart was sad. Gilgamesh, hearing his friend sigh bitterly, said to him, "Enkidu, my friend, why do your eyes fill with tears, and why do you sigh with such bitterness?"

Enkidu replied, "I am crying for my lost strength. When I lived among the animals upon the grassy plain, I was swift and strong. Here in the strong-walled city of Uruk, my arms hang useless by my sides. Inactivity has turned me into a weakling!"

"I know how to heal the grief in your heart," Gilgamesh replied. "The fierce giant Humbaba lives at the base of the Cedar Mountain, home of the heavenly gods in the Cedar Forest of Lebanon in the land of the living. Come with me to slay him, and then we will have banished all evil from the land."

"You cannot mean what you are saying," Enkidu replied. "You can speak with great courage because you have never seen Humbaba. Although I have never seen him either, I learned from the wild creatures about the Cedar Forest and the evil giant who guards it.

"The forest extends over an area of 30,000 square miles," Enkidu explained. "Its span is so large that a person can enter it and never find his way out again. And as for Humbaba, the very thought of fighting that monstrous giant fills my heart with horror! Enlil, ruler of the heavenly gods, has appointed him watchman. He preserves the Cedar Forest by terrifying anyone who dares to enter it. His face is as fearsome as a lion's. His dreadful roar resounds throughout the forest like a river that is swollen with flood. His teeth are those of a dragon, and flames issue forth from his mouth. With each breath he consumes every reed and tree in his path. Nothing that burns can escape being devoured by that monster! Why would you choose to pit yourself against a being who is more powerful than you are?"

"I know that it is my fate to die, sooner or later," Gilgamesh explained. "Before my life comes to an end, I would like to make a name for myself. So I intend to climb the Cedar Mountain! When those in time to come remember the great names of the past, I would like my name to be among them. I will bring the names of the heavenly gods with us, so that they too will be remembered."

"We cannot enter the Cedar Forest," Enkidu repeated. "Humbaba watches over the forest without ever resting. He can hear the wild cows when they are two hundred miles away."

Gilgamesh responded, "My friend, who can reach heaven? Only the gods live forever with radiant Shamash. The days of human beings are numbered, and whatever they achieve is like the wind! Why do you fear death when, like all human beings, it is your fate to die? What has become of your heroic strength? Is it not better to do your best to gain fame than to wait patiently and quietly for the day of your death? Fame and glory will give life to your name even after your death.

"If you are still afraid to fight Humbaba," Gilgamesh continued, "then let me walk ahead of you while you encourage me to be brave. Even if I fail, I will have made a lasting name for myself. People will say of me, 'Gilgamesh died fighting the fierce giant Humbaba!'"

"I will not walk behind you, my friend," Enkidu replied. "While you are traveling toward the land of the living, I will remain in the strong-walled city of Uruk. I will inform your mother of your great glory. Let the wise goddess Ninsun proclaim your fame to all the people! I will inform your mother of your impending death. Let the wise goddess Ninsun weep bitter tears as she grieves for her lost son!

"As for me, I do not choose to die," Enkidu continued. "I do not wish to be destroyed by fire. I am not ready to have my shroud cut. I am not ready to make that journey upon the Euphrates River."

Gilgamesh said, "Your fear fills my heart with sadness. With my own hands I will kill Humbaba, cut down the cedars, and bring their fragrant wood to strong-walled Uruk. In this way, I will make a lasting name for myself. I will order the blacksmith to forge new weapons for us: axes to chop and blades to shape the wood, and mighty swords to use against Humbaba. I wish to see this giant whose name fills our land with terror. I will overcome him in the Cedar Forest! Then all peoples will know how strong the king of Uruk is!"

Enkidu replied, "Oh, Gilgamesh, if your heart is set upon such an adventure and you are determined to enter the land of the living, then I will reluctantly accompany you. However, you must tell radiant Shamash. He is in charge of the Cedar Forest, and surely you will need his help."

So Gilgamesh chose two young goats, one white and one brown, and offered them to Shamash with a prayer. "Oh, heavenly Shamash, I wish to enter the Cedar Forest of Lebanon in the land of the living, and I wish that you would help me."

"I know that your strength is great, Gilgamesh," radiant Shamash replied. "You are, indeed, a great warrior. But why are you attempting such an adventure? Why does the land of the living interest you?"

Gilgamesh tearfully answered, "Oh, radiant Shamash, please listen to my words. We human beings are not as blessed as the heavenly gods, for we cannot live forever. Every day in my city of Uruk, people die! When I look over the strong walls of my city, I see the Euphrates River bearing their dead bodies.

"Sooner or later even I, though a king, will have to face that fate. Even I will have to make that last journey. Death makes the human heart heavy with grief. No matter how tall he is, a mortal cannot reach heaven. No matter how wide he is, a mortal cannot stretch over the earth.

"Yet before my life comes to an end," Gilgamesh concluded, "I would like to make a name for myself. I would like to enter the land of the living and climb the Cedar Mountain. When future generations remember the great names of the past, I would like my name to be among them. I will bring the names of the heavenly gods with me, so that your names too will be remembered."

Shamash heard Gilgamesh's words and accepted his tears as a sacred offering. The radiant god felt pity for Gilgamesh's human fate and was merciful to him. "I will be your ally against Humbaba," he told Gilgamesh. "I will confine in mountain caves the snake that poisons with its tongue, the dragon that scorches with its fire, the raging flood that destroys the land, and the quick flashes of lightning that cannot be conquered. They will not be able to cause trouble for you during the course of your adventure."

When Gilgamesh heard the words of Shamash, his heart filled with joy. He called the elders of Uruk to assembly and informed them of his plan. They were not convinced by his enthusiasm.

"Your youthful spirit fills your heart, Gilgamesh," they said to their king, "but it has blinded your eyes to what you are doing. Listen to our advice. We hear that the Cedar Forest extends over an area of thirty thousand square miles. Who among human beings is brave enough to enter it? We hear that Humbaba is a creature to be feared. Who among human beings can face his weapons? The monster roars like a river swollen with flood, and his fiery breath brings death.

"Why do you want to face such an enemy?" they asked. "You could not choose a more unequal contest! However, if we cannot convince you to change your mind, then go with our blessing. May your god, Shamash, protect you and bring you safely back to strong-walled Uruk!"

Gilgamesh knelt before radiant Shamash. Raising his hands in prayer, he said, "Heavenly Shamash, I am on my way. Guard my soul. Protect me and bring me safely back to Uruk. I am taking a road I have never traveled. I want to walk with joy in my heart."

Gilgamesh then set about recruiting some of his countrymen. "He who is responsible for a household, stay home!" he commanded. "He who is responsible for his mother, remain with her! However, if you are a single man and you would like to join me on this greatest of heroic adventures, I invite fifty of you to come along with me into the land of the living, where Humbaba guards the Cedar Forest. There we will slay the monster and banish all evil from the land!"

The men of Uruk obeyed Gilgamesh. Those who were supporters of their families stayed behind, while fifty youths prepared to accompany Gilgamesh upon the great adventure.

Gilgamesh ordered the metalsmiths to cast the enormous bronze axe that he would call his "might of heroism," along with axes and swords for all his companions. Then he ordered servants to cut wood from the apple, the box, and the willow trees to be fashioned into other weapons and tools. When all of the adventurers had been properly equipped, Gilgamesh's servants brought their king his weapons. They gave him his bow, a quiver full of arrows, and an assortment of cutting and shaping tools, and they placed his axe, the "might of heroism," and his sword upon his belt.

When the group was ready to leave, the people cried, "May you return safely to our city!"

Then the elders gave Gilgamesh their final advice: "Do not put too much faith in your own strength, Gilgamesh. Allow Enkidu to travel the road in front of you, for he knows the way to the Cedar Forest and he is experienced in battle. Let Enkidu precede you through the forest and over the mountain passes. Let his eyes see clearly that he may protect himself and you, for the person who treads first protects the friends and companions who follow behind him.

"At night," they advised, "before you rest, you must dig a well so that the water in your waterskin will always be fresh. Remember to offer cool water to radiant Shamash, and never forget to honor your father, Lugalbanda. Then, after you kill Humbaba, you must remember to wash your feet as the gods require.

"May your god go with you, Gilgamesh," the elders concluded. "May Shamash heed your prayers. May he open before your feet the obstructed path, the closed road, and the formidable mountain. May the night bring you nothing to fear. May your father stay with you and protect you. May you live to attain your wish."

Then the assembled elders addressed Enkidu, saying, "We, the assembly, entrust our king to you. Protect your friend and companion, and return him to us safely."

Once they had received the blessing of the assembly of elder nobles, Gilgamesh said to Enkidu, "Let us go before my mother, priestess of Shamash.

The great queen Ninsun, who possesses broad knowledge and great wisdom, will surely send us forth with her blessing."

Hand in hand, the two friends entered Ninsun's chamber. Gilgamesh said, "Mother, I have determined to make a great journey that will take me upon a strange road to the Cedar Forest and the home of Humbaba. There I face a battle whose outcome is uncertain, for I will attempt to kill Humbaba in order to remove all evil from the land. Each day that passes from the day of my departure until the day of my return, pray to Shamash on my behalf, for he too hates evil."

Ninsun put on her ceremonial robe, placed an ornament upon her breast, and crowned her head with a diadem. She climbed the stairs to the top of the temple-palace, where she stood upon the roof and offered incense to radiant Shamash.

Raising her arms to the god of the sun, Ninsun cried, "Why have you given me a son like Gilgamesh? Why have you given him such a restless heart? Why would you have him make such a journey upon a strange road? Why must he face Humbaba in the Cedar Forest?"

She prayed, "Oh, Shamash, I ask you to protect my son each day that passes from his departure until his return. And when at the end of each day you go to your rest, commend my son to the watchers of the night! Protect him in the Cedar Forest as he slays the fierce Humbaba, for he will remove all evil from the land, and you also hate evil."

Ninsun then smothered the incense and called to Enkidu, "You are not my own child as Gilgamesh is, mighty Enkidu, but I am now formally adopting you. Go with my blessing, and return safely to Uruk."

Chapter 4

Gilgamesh and Enkidu reach the Cedar Forest and kill Humbaba.

Enkidu then said to Gilgamesh, "Let us be on our way. Follow me, and have no fear in your heart. I know the road that Humbaba travels and the place where he lives."

In only three days, Gilgamesh, Enkidu, and the young men walked a distance that would usually take six weeks. After sixty miles, they stopped to eat. When they had traveled another ninety miles, they prepared to spend the night. Then, before radiant Shamash they dug a well. They walked one hundred fifty miles each day and crossed seven mountains. Finally they arrived at the gateway to the Cedar Forest, which was guarded by Humbaba's watchman, whom they killed.

There Gilgamesh fell into a deep sleep. Enkidu prodded the king's body, but he did not awaken. He spoke to Gilgamesh, but he did not reply. "Oh, Gilgamesh," Enkidu cried, "how long will you lie here asleep? The young men of Uruk who have accompanied us are waiting for you at the base of the Cedar Mountain!"

At last Gilgamesh heard Enkidu's words and rose quickly to his feet. He stood upon the earth like a great bull, put his mouth to the ground, and bit the dust. Then he stood erect and clothed himself with words of heroism as if he were putting on his robe. "By the lives of my father, Lugalbanda, and my mother, Ninsun, who gave birth to me," Gilgamesh swore, "I will not return to the strong-walled city of Uruk until I have entered the Cedar Forest in the land of the living and have fought with Humbaba, whether he is a man or a god! By the lives of my father, Lugalbanda, and my mother, Ninsun, who gave birth to me, may I achieve such glory that all who look upon me will view my deeds with wonder!

"Let us call the young men and hurry, Enkidu," Gilgamesh continued. "We want to find Humbaba before he travels beyond our reach."

Enkidu replied, "Oh, let us not walk deep into the Cedar Forest! When I opened this gate, my hands became weak. I no longer have the strength to protect either you or myself!"

"Do not be afraid, Enkidu," Gilgamesh assured his friend. "You know how to fight, and you are experienced in battle. If you will just touch my robe, you will not be afraid of death, and your hands and your arms will regain their former strength.

"Now, come!" Gilgamesh commanded. "Let us go forward and face this adventure together. Be of good courage! When we come face to face with Humbaba, if we are afraid, we will conquer our fear. Even if we feel terror, we will conquer our terror. The man who walks in front protects himself and his companion. Even if he dies in the process, he has made a lasting name for himself. The man who is a coward is not at peace with himself and leaves nothing behind to give him a good name."

They found themselves at the green mountain. Without further conversation, they stood still and looked around them. When they looked at the entrance to the Cedar Forest, they noticed the tremendous height of the cedar trees. They saw that the path that Humbaba was accustomed to walking was straight and clear. They looked upon the Cedar Mountain, which was the home of the heavenly gods. The face of the mountain was covered with a luxurious blanket of stately, shade-bearing cedar trees.

That night, Gilgamesh awakened Enkidu at midnight and said, "I had a strange dream, Enkidu. A mountain crumbled and fell upon me. Then a fine-looking man appeared. He pulled me out from under the mountain, gave me water to drink, and then helped me to stand upon my feet."

Enkidu replied, "Your dream is good, Gilgamesh. Humbaba is the mountain that fell upon you. We will seize him, kill him, and toss his body upon the plain." The next day, when they had walked sixty miles in the Cedar Forest, they stopped to eat. After another ninety miles, they prepared to spend the night. Then they dug a well before Shamash. Gilgamesh approached the mountain with an offering of a fine meal and said, "Mountain, bring me a dream."

Gilgamesh fell asleep with his head upon his knees. Once again he found himself wide awake in the middle of the night. "Enkidu, my friend," he said, "I have had an awesome dream! It is so disturbing that surely it is not favorable! I dreamed that I seized a wild bull of the plains. When I grabbed it, the bull stirred up so much dirt that the dust made the sky dark. Then the bull seized me and sapped my strength so that I was forced to retreat before it. But once I was at its mercy, the bull gave me food to eat and water from its waterskin to drink!"

Enkidu replied, "The wild bull of your dream, my friend, is really heavenly Shamash. When we need his help, he will hold our hands. It is he who let you drink from his waterskin. He watches over you, and he will bring you honor. In your dream, radiant Shamash is encouraging us to accomplish one thing that will be remembered after we have died. Certainly the deed must be to slay the monstrous giant Humbaba!"

Gilgamesh then said to Enkidu, "When we approach Humbaba, what should we do about his servants?"

Enkidu answered, "My friend, first capture the mother bird, for without their mother, where can the chicks go? Therefore, let us first kill Humbaba. We can find and kill his servants later, for like chicks, they will run around frantically in the grass."

Gilgamesh listened to the advice of his friend. In order to attract Humbaba's attention, he lifted his axe and cut down one of the cedars.

Although they were more than two miles away from Humbaba's cedar house, the giant heard the noise and became furious. He left his house and fastened his eye, the eye of death, upon the two friends. He shook his head warningly and roared, "Who has come here? Who is damaging the precious trees that grow upon my mountains? Who has cut down one of my cedars?"

At the sound of Humbaba's roar, Gilgamesh suddenly trembled with fear. Enkidu saw the terror in his heart and said, "My friend, remember the words you spoke to the people of Uruk! Remember why we have made this journey! Now let courage enter your heart, and prepare to kill this monstrous giant!"

Gilgamesh gathered his courage and called out to Humbaba, "I, Gilgamesh, king of Uruk, have felled your cedar! By the lives of my father, Lugalbanda, and my mother, Ninsun, who gave birth to me, I have come to the Cedar Forest in the land of the living in order to fight you to the death and banish all evil from the land!"

Then Shamash from high in heaven spoke to Gilgamesh and Enkidu. "Approach Humbaba, and have no fear. Just do not let him enter his house." Shamash then hurled mighty winds upon Humbaba. Eight winds—the great wind, the north wind, the south wind, the whirlwind, the storm wind, the chill wind, the tempestuous wind, and the hot wind—arose against the fierce giant and beat against him from all sides so that he was unable to move in any direction.

Meanwhile, Gilgamesh, Enkidu, and the young men began to fell the cedars, trim their crowns, bundle them, and lay them at the foot of the mountain. When Gilgamesh had felled the seventh cedar, he found himself face to face with Humbaba.

Gilgamesh pushed the monstrous giant against the wall of his house and gently slapped his face as if he were pressing a kiss on him.

Humbaba's teeth shook with fear as he pleaded, "Heavenly Shamash, help me! I know neither my mother, who gave birth to me, nor my father, who reared me. In this land of the living, it is you who have been my mother and my father!"

"Gilgamesh!" Humbaba then entreated. "I swear by the life in heaven, the life upon the earth, and the dead in the nether world that I will subject myself to you and become your servant. I will let you cut down my trees and even build houses with them."

As he listened to Humbaba's pleas, Gilgamesh felt pity for the giant. To Enkidu, the king said, "Should I not let the trapped bird flee the cage? Should I not let the captured man return to his mother?"

Enkidu said to Gilgamesh, "Do not listen to Humbaba's pleas! Do not let him talk you into freeing him, for he is a clever and dangerous enemy. He must not remain alive! The evil demon Death will devour even the greatest of human beings if he does not use good judgment. I assure you that if you let the trapped bird flee the cage, if you let the captured man return to his mother, then you most certainly will not return to Uruk and the mother who gave birth to you!"

"Enkidu," complained Humbaba, "you are only a servant and yet you have spoken evil words about me!"

However, Gilgamesh listened to Enkidu's wise advice. He took his axe, the "might of heroism," and his sword from his belt. Then he struck Humbaba upon the neck. Enkidu also struck the monstrous giant upon the neck. With the third blow Humbaba fell to the ground, and Enkidu sliced off his head. For six miles round about, the cedars echoed the sound of Humbaba's body hitting the earth. Gilgamesh and Enkidu stood amazed that they had actually killed the giant of the Cedar Forest of Lebanon.

Gilgamesh then continued into the forest, where he cut down Humbaba's cedar trees. The young men of strong-walled Uruk cut and tied them in preparation for their return to the city.

Chapter 5

Gilgamesh refuses to marry Ishtar, the goddess of love and fertility. She retaliates by sending the ferocious Bull of Heaven into Uruk. Gilgamesh and Enkidu kill the bull. Enkidu insults Ishtar and then becomes ill and dies.

When Gilgamesh returned to strong-walled Uruk, he cleaned and polished his weapons. He unbraided his dirty hair, washed it, and threw it back loosely over his shoulders. He then changed into clean clothes. Finally, he wrapped his royal, fringed cape about his shoulders, fastened it with a sash at his waist, and placed his crown upon his head.

When the goddess Ishtar saw Gilgamesh dressed in his royal clothing, she admired his great beauty and said to him, "Come marry me, Gilgamesh! You will be my husband, and I will be your wife."

She added, "I will harness for you a jeweled and golden chariot, with golden wheels and brass horns. Storm demons will be your mighty steeds and will pull your chariot. The fragrance of cedar will greet you when you enter our house. Kings, princes, and nobles all will bow before you, kiss your feet, and bring you the fruits of the plains and the hills as tribute. Even the mountains and the plains will pay tribute to you. Your goats will give birth to triplets, your sheep to twins. Your colts will have the strength of burden-bearing mules. The horses that pull your chariot will be famous racers. The ox that pulls your plow will have no equal."

"And why should I marry you?" Gilgamesh asked. "You have harmed everyone you have ever loved! Listen, for I am happy to list your lovers for you. You loved Tammuz when you were young, but you left him and caused him to weep year after year. You struck the spotted shepherd-bird that you loved and broke his wing. Now, year after year, he stays in the orchards and cries, 'My wing! My wing!' Then you loved a stallion that was famous in war. First you whipped and spurred him into galloping twenty-one miles, and then you made him drink muddy water, causing him to die! His mother still weeps for him.

"Then," Gilgamesh continued, "you loved the herdsman who placed piles of ash-cakes at your feet, and every day he killed the finest of his goats for your pleasure. You rewarded his love by striking him and turning him into a wolf! His own shepherd boys drove him away from the flocks, and his hounds bit into his legs. Then you loved your father's gardener of the palm trees. Every day he brought you baskets of ripe dates for your table. You turned him into a mole and buried him in the earth, where he cannot move either up or down! If I let you love me, you would only treat me as poorly as you have treated all of your other lovers!"

Gilgamesh added, "You are like a pan of white-hot coals that go out in the cold. You are like a back door that fails to keep out the blasts of a tempest. You are like a palace that crushes the king within it. You are like a headdress that does not cover the head. You are like an elephant that shakes off its carpet. You are like pitch that blackens the one who carries it. You are like a waterskin that soaks the person who carries it. You are like a limestone rock that falls from the stone wall. You are like a shoe that pinches the foot of the one who wears it."

Ishtar became enraged as she listened to his words. She went up to heaven and tearfully complained to her father, Anu. "Father," she began, "Gilgamesh has hurled great insults upon me! He has recounted to my face all of my wicked deeds!"

Anu replied, "I believe that you started the quarrel and caused Gilgamesh to tell you of your shameful deeds."

Undaunted by his criticism, Ishtar pleaded, "Father, please give me the Bull of Heaven and let me use it to kill Gilgamesh. If you refuse, I will break the bolts and smash the gates of the Underworld, letting them stand open. I will cause the dead to rise to the world above, where they will eat among the living and outnumber them."

Anu replied, "If I give you the Bull of Heaven, there will be seven years of famine in the land of Uruk. Have you gathered and stored enough grain to feed the people through those lean years? Have you grown enough grass for all the animals?"

Ishtar said, "Yes, Father, I have stored grain for the people, and I have provided the beasts with grass to last seven lean years."

Then Anu gave Ishtar the Bull of Heaven, and the goddess led the bull into the strong-walled city of Uruk. When the bull snorted, pits opened in the earth and two hundred young men of Uruk fell into them and died. With its next snort, more pits opened in the earth and two hundred more young men of Uruk fell into them and died. With its third snort, the bull sprang upon Enkidu.

Enkidu leaped up and seized the Bull of Heaven by its horns. The bull foamed at the mouth and blew its foam into Enkidu's face. Then it struck him with the tassled end of its tail. Enkidu held fast, and Gilgamesh came to his aid. As the two heroes fought with the bull, Enkidu chased it and hung onto the thick part of its tail. Gilgamesh finally killed it by thrusting his sword between its neck and its horns. Then the two friends tore its heart from its body and dedicated it to Shamash.

Ishtar then climbed upon the strong walls of Uruk and shouted, "Woe to Gilgamesh, for he has insulted me by killing the Bull of Heaven!"

Upon hearing these words, Enkidu tore off the right thigh of the Bull of Heaven and threw it in the face of the goddess. "If I could capture you as I captured this bull," he shouted to Ishtar, "I would treat you as I have treated it!"

Ishtar then gathered the temple women and mourned over the right thigh of the Bull of Heaven. Meanwhile, Gilgamesh gathered the armorers, the craftspeople, and the artisans and told them to take the parts of the bull they could use. Gilgamesh himself kept the valuable horns and hung them in his bedroom. He then made an offering of oil to honor his dead father, Lugalbanda.

Next, the two friends washed their hands in the Euphrates River and rode together through the market street of Uruk. The people gathered to gaze upon them, and singers sang praises. Gilgamesh asked, "Who is the best of the heroes? Who is the most noble among men?"

The people replied, "Gilgamesh is the best of the heroes! Gilgamesh is the most noble among men!"

That evening Gilgamesh held a joyous celebration in the palace to mark the victory over the Bull of Heaven. During the night Enkidu had a dream. He awakened Gilgamesh and said, "My friend, listen to my dream. The great gods, Anu and Enlil, wise Ea, and radiant Shamash met together. Anu said to Enlil, 'Because Gilgamesh and Enkidu have killed Humbaba and the Bull of Heaven, the one who removed the cedars from the mountain must die!' Enlil replied, 'Gilgamesh will not die, but Enkidu should die.'"

Enkidu's dream made him ill with fear. With the coming of day, he raised his head and wept before radiant Shamash. With tears streaming down his face also, Gilgamesh said, "Oh, dear Brother! Why would the gods spare me and punish you? Will I sit down at the door of the spirits of the dead and never be able to see you, my dear brother, again?"

Enkidu cursed the events in his life that had brought him to the point of death. Raising his eyes, he said, "Oh, you gate to the Cedar Forest that hurt my hands! How I admired your size and your beautiful, fragrant cedar! Your wood is unsurpassed in all the land! Surely a master craftsman built you. But if I had known, oh gate, that your beauty would bring about my death, I would have set upon you with my axe and destroyed you!

"And Shamash," Enkidu continued, "I ask you to destroy the power and wealth of the hunter. May his life displease you. May the beasts escape from the traps he sets. May his heart be sad."

Enkidu then said, "I curse you, young woman of the temple, most of all and for all time to come! May you never have a house that pleases you. May you eternally be forced to live in the dust of the crossroad. May the desert be your bed. May you be unwelcome where other women gather. May the shadow of a wall give you your only comfort. May thorns and brambles tear your feet. May the refuse of the road, the dirty and the thirsty, strike your cheek. May the drunkard soil with his vomit any place you enjoy."

When radiant Shamash heard these words, he called down from heaven. "Enkidu, why do you curse the young woman of the temple? She gave you food worthy of the gods and drink worthy of royalty. She clothed you with fine garments and led you to your best friend, Gilgamesh."

The god continued, "And has Gilgamesh not treated you like a king? He has given you a royal bed on which to sleep. He has seated you in comfort at his left hand. He has honored you and has encouraged the princes of the earth to kiss your feet. When you die, he will make the people of Uruk weep over you. Sorrow in their hearts will then overcome any thought of joy. He will make his people serve you even after your death. When you depart, Gilgamesh will let his hair grow long and will wander over the grassy plains clad in a lion skin."

When Enkidu heard the words of Shamash, his heart became calm. "I who have cursed you will now bless you, woman of the temple," he said. "May kings, princes, and nobles love you. May you receive jewels and gold. May anyone who does not respect you be punished. May poverty find his storehouse and his home. May the priest let you enter the presence of the gods."

Still feeling sick, Enkidu lay down all alone. The next morning he said to Gilgamesh, "My friend, last night I had another dream. The heavens groaned, and the earth replied. While I was standing alone between heaven and earth, a young man with a very dark face and with claws like the talons of an eagle leaped upon me and overpowered me. Then he transformed my arms into the wings of a bird. He led me along the road of no return into the House of Darkness and Dust, which no one can leave once he has entered it."

Enkidu continued, "Those who live there dwell in eternal darkness, and there is no way to return to the land of the living. Their food consists of clay and dust. They are clothed with wings, like birds. I saw many people there who had been royalty during their lives on earth. All of the rulers I saw had removed their crowns, for they are of no use in the House of Darkness and Dust."

By the end of the day following Enkidu's unfavorable dream, he was ill. For the next twelve days he remained in bed, and his suffering increased. Finally he called Gilgamesh to his side and said, "The goddess Ishtar has cursed me! I will not die honorably like one who falls in battle."

Gilgamesh cried, "May the bear, the hyena, the panther, the tiger, the deer, the leopard, the lion, the oxen, the ibex, and all the wild creatures of the plain weep for you. May your tracks in the Cedar Forest weep for you unceasingly, both night and day. May the Ula River, along whose banks we used to walk, weep for you. May the pure Euphrates, where we used to draw water for our waterskins, weep for you."

Gilgamesh continued, "May the nobles of strong-walled Uruk weep for you. May the warriors of Uruk weep for you. May those in Uruk who praised your name weep for you. May those who provided grain for you to eat weep for you. May those who put salve on your back weep for you. May those who put beer in your mouth weep for you. May the young woman of the temple who put fragrant oil upon you weep for you."

Gilgamesh's heart overflowed with grief and loneliness when Enkidu died. The king said, "Oh, elders of strong-walled Uruk, listen to me! I weep for my friend Enkidu. I moan bitterly like a wailing woman. An evil demon has robbed me of my dearest friend. He was like the bow in my hand, like the dagger in my belt, like the axe and the sword at my side, like the shield that protects me, like my ceremonial robe, and like my glorious royal decorations.

"Oh, Enkidu," Gilgamesh said to the body of his dead friend. "You chased the wild creatures of the hills and the panther of the grassy plains! Together we conquered all things! We climbed the mountains. We seized and killed the Bull of Heaven. We overthrew Humbaba, who lived in the Cedar Forest. What kind of sleep has come upon you, Enkidu, that you cannot hear me? You do not lift your head. When I touch your heart, it does not beat!"

Gilgamesh covered his friend in rich clothing and veiled him as a bride is veiled. First he roared over Enkidu's death like a lion. Then he cried over him like a lioness deprived of her cubs. Back and forth before Enkidu's body he paced, tearing out his hair and flinging off his clothing as if it were unclean.

With the first glow of dawn, Gilgamesh issued a summons throughout the land for coppersmiths, goldsmiths, jewelers, and engravers. "Create a statue of my friend Enkidu," he commanded. "Choose jewels for his breast and fashion his body from the purest gold."

Then Gilgamesh said to his friend, "Oh, Enkidu, I gave you a couch of honor on which to lie. I seated you on a seat of ease at my left, so that the princes of the earth would kiss your feet. I will make the people of strong-walled Uruk weep over your death. These once joyful people will now lament and be sad, and they will perform services for you. And once you are gone, I will let my hair grow long and roam over the grassy plains clad in a lion skin."

Chapter 6

Gilgamesh goes to Utanapishtim, the survivor of the great flood, to learn how a human being can gain immortality. He travels through a long, dark tunnel, receives advice from the alewife Siduri, and finally is taken by boat to Utanapishtim.

Gilgamesh wandered the grassy plain, bitterly weeping over the death of his dearest friend. "When I die," he said to himself, "my fate will be just like Enkidu's! Grief tears at my heart, and fear of death gnaws at my stomach. I must travel as quickly as my feet will take me to the home of Utanapishtim (*uta:* he found + *napishtim:* life), who is called the Faraway. He is a human being just as I am. Yet he has found everlasting life and has joined the assembly of the heavenly gods. Surely he can teach me how to live for days without end!"

Gilgamesh traveled alone across the grassy plain and the scorching desert. One night, upon a mountain pass, he was confronted by two lions. The sight of them flooded his heart with terror. Raising his head to the moon, Gilgamesh prayed, "Oh, Sin, god of the light that brightens the night sky, protect me!"

Then Gilgamesh courageously drew the dagger from his belt and raised the axe in his hand. Approaching the beasts as straight as the flight of an arrow, he killed them, skinned them, and chopped them into pieces. He wrapped his body in their warm skins, for his own clothing had already become torn and tattered. He ate some of their flesh, for the food he had carried with him no longer could sustain him.

After many weeks of travel over land and sea, Gilgamesh came to Mount Mashu, whose twin peaks reach to the roof of heaven and guard Shamash as the sun rises and sets each day. There he found scorpion-men guarding the gate to the mountain. The halos around their heads dazzled the mountain itself, and their glance could kill any human being their eyes fixed upon. The sight of these guards caused Gilgamesh's heart to flood with terror. However, he forced himself to gather his courage and continue forward.

When they saw Gilgamesh approaching, one of the scorpion-men called to his wife, "This man who has come before us has flesh like the heavenly gods! He must be one of them!"

The scorpion-woman replied, "No, only two-thirds of him is god; one-third is human. The man who stands before you is Gilgamesh, king of strong-walled Uruk."

The scorpion-man then addressed Gilgamesh. "Child of the gods, why have you made such a difficult journey to this distant place? Tell me why you have wandered so far over land and sea."

Gilgamesh replied, "I have come to find Utanapishtim, the Faraway. I know that he has found everlasting life and has joined the assembly of the heavenly gods. I wish to talk with him about life and death."

The scorpion-man said, "Gilgamesh, no human being has ever found Utanapishtim! It is beyond the courage of any human being to make the journey! In order to reach the Faraway, you must first travel through a tunnel deep within the mountains. The tunnel extends for thirty-six miles in darkness black as pitch. From one rising of the sun to the next, no light penetrates that darkness."

Gilgamesh took the words of the scorpion-man into his mind and into his heart, but he was not dissuaded from making the journey. "I intend to take that path," he said. "Neither pain, nor sorrow, nor tears, nor extreme cold, nor scalding heat will stop me! Open the gate of the mountain so that I can continue my journey!"

The scorpion-man replied, "I will open the gate of Mount Mashu to you, Gilgamesh. Go in safety, and may your feet bring you a safe return as well!"

Gilgamesh entered the tunnel of Mount Mashu. He kept the words of the scorpion-man alive in his mind and in his heart so that knowledge of what lay before him would lessen his fear of the darkness.

Gilgamesh traveled from east to west as the sun travels each day. When he had walked three miles, so thick was the darkness that he could see nothing ahead of him and nothing behind him, for there was no light. When he had walked nine miles, so thick was the darkness that he could see nothing ahead of him and nothing behind him, for there was no light. When he had walked eighteen miles, so thick was the darkness that he could see nothing ahead of him and nothing behind him, for there was no light.

When he had walked twenty-four miles, he was weary and impatient, and he cried out in protest. So thick was the darkness that he could see nothing ahead of him and nothing behind him, and still there was no light.

When Gilgamesh had walked twenty-seven miles, so thick was the darkness that he could see nothing ahead of him and nothing behind him, for still there was no light. But he could now feel a wind blowing into his face, so he quickened his steps. When he had walked thirty-three miles, he saw the rose color of dawn in the sky in front of him, and by the time he had walked thirty-six miles, the sky ahead of him was bright from the light of the sun.

Upon leaving the tunnel, Gilgamesh came upon an orchard of jewel-bearing trees. The jeweled fruits and foliage dazzled his eyes as they sparkled in the sun-light. A light wind helped show off their beauty by leading them in a graceful dance among their branches. Gilgamesh gazed in fascination at the glorious garden. For a short while, he forgot his grief and his pain, his fatigue and his fear. He was certain that he had entered the garden of the heavenly gods.

While Gilgamesh gazed in wonder at the orchard, radiant Shamash looked down from the sky and saw a human being clothed in animal skins. When he realized that the figure he saw was that of Gilgamesh, he became concerned. Shamash approached Gilgamesh and said, "Where are you going? You will not find the life for which you are searching."

Gilgamesh replied, "After wandering over the grassy plain and the scorching desert, must I lay my head in the heart of the earth, where there are no stars and no sun, and sleep the endless sleep? I want my eyes to feast upon the sun! I want its light and its warmth to fill my heart with joy! Light drives away the darkness!"

Shamash then left Gilgamesh to his journey, and in a short time, Gilgamesh reached the sea. There he saw the alewife Siduri living in a cottage by the shore of the deep sea.

Siduri was sitting in her yard, gazing into the distance, when she noticed the haggard-looking, shaggy-haired stranger clothed in animal skins. When she saw that he intended to talk with her, Siduri's heart flooded with fear. She said to herself, "This man looks like a murderer! I wonder where he is going!" Obeying the counsel of her heart, she got up, locked the door of her house, and barred her gate with the crossbar.

Gilgamesh, watching her, picked up his pointed staff and placed his hand on the gate. Then he said, "Alewife, what do you see that has made you bolt your door and bar your gate? Tell me, or else I will shatter your gate and smash your door!

"I am Gilgamesh, king of strong-walled Uruk," he continued. "I have overthrown and killed Humbaba, who guarded the Cedar Forest in the land of the living. I have seized and slaughtered the Bull of Heaven, and I have slain the lions who guarded the mountain passes."

Siduri said, "If you are indeed the hero you say you are, then why are your cheeks so pale and your face so gaunt? Why do you look like a stranger who has traveled here from afar with the ravages of heat and cold seared upon your face? Why does grief tear at your heart and fear gnaw at your stomach? And why do you roam over the grassy plain and the scorching desert searching for the home of the wind?"

Gilgamesh replied, "Oh, Alewife, I have crossed the mountains from the east, as the sun rises, and I have roamed like a hunter over the grassy plain and the scorching desert. I have had to kill the bear, the hyena, the lion, the panther, the tiger, the stag, and the ibex. I have eaten the flesh of wild beasts and crawling creatures, and when my clothing hung about me in tatters, I had to wrap my body in their skins.

"Why should I not look as I look and wander as I wander?" Gilgamesh continued. "Enkidu, my friend, whom I dearly loved and who endured all kinds of hardships with me and helped me conquer all things, has met the fate of all human beings. Ever since Enkidu died, I have felt that he took my life with him on his journey to the House of Darkness and Dust!"

Gilgamesh concluded, "Because Enkidu has died, I fear my own death! How then can I be silent? How then can I be still? My friend, whom I dearly loved, has returned to clay! In time, must I also lay my head in the heart of the earth, where there are no stars and no sun, and sleep the endless sleep? Oh, Alewife, now that I have seen your face, do not make me see my death, which I dread!"

Siduri replied, "Gilgamesh, where are you roaming? The life that you are seeking you will not find. When the heavenly gods created human beings, they kept everlasting life for themselves and gave us death.

"So, Gilgamesh, accept your fate," Siduri advised. "Each day, wash your head, bathe your body, and wear clothes that are sparkling fresh. Fill your stomach with delicious food. Play, sing, dance, and be happy both day and night. Delight in the pleasures that your wife brings you, and cherish the little child who holds your hand. Make every day of your life a feast of rejoicing! This is the task that the gods have set before all human beings. This is the life you should seek, for this is the best life a mortal can hope to achieve."

"You may have given me good advice, Alewife," Gilgamesh replied. "Nevertheless, tell me, which is the way to Utanapishtim, the Faraway? Living on the shore of the sea as you do, you must be able to tell me the signs that mark the way. If necessary, I will cross the deep sea. Otherwise, I will continue to roam like a hunter over the grassy plain and the scorching desert."

Siduri replied, "Gilgamesh, there is no way to cross this deep sea! Since the beginning of time, no one who has come here has been able to travel over these waters."

Then Siduri added, "I have thought of one possibility. Perhaps Urshanabi, the boatman of Utanapishtim, would be willing to help you. He possesses sacred stone figures, which he keeps in the forest. If he will permit you to accompany him, I advise you to cross the deep sea with him. If not, you must withdraw and return to your strong-walled city of Uruk."

When Gilgamesh heard these words, anger flooded his heart. He drew the dagger from his belt and raised the axe in his hand. He entered the forest and sought to threaten the boatman who possessed the sacred stone figures. He found the sacred images, but not the boatman. He approached the images as straight as the flight of an arrow and in his rage he shattered them.

Urshanabi, who was close by, saw the gleam of Gilgamesh's dagger and heard the sound of the destruction. He ran to Gilgamesh and asked, "Who are you, and what are you doing here? Why do you look like a traveler from afar, with the ravages of heat and cold seared upon your face?"

Gilgamesh replied, "You must be Urshanabi! Gilgamesh is my name, and I am king of the strong-walled city of Uruk. I have crossed the mountains from the east, as the sun rises, and have come a long way. My friend, whom I dearly loved, has returned to clay. I am afraid that, in time, I also must lay my head in the heart of the earth and sleep the endless sleep.

"Urshanabi, show me the road to Utanapishtim, the Faraway!" Gilgamesh pleaded. "If necessary, I will cross the deep sea. Otherwise, I will continue to roam like a hunter over the grassy plain and the scorching desert. Oh, Urshanabi, take me to Utanapishtim!"

Urshanabi replied, "Your angry hands have hindered the sea journey. In your rage, you have destroyed the sacred stone images that enable me to cross the deep sea without touching the Waters of Death. Go into the forest, cut 120 poles, each 100 feet long, and bring them to me."

Gilgamesh took the dagger from his belt, raised the axe in his hand, and went into the forest. After he had returned to Urshanabi with the poles, the two men climbed into the boat, cast off into the waves of the deep sea, and drifted away. In three days they covered the distance it would have taken another craft a month and a half to cover. Then they found themselves at the Waters of Death.

Urshanabi said to Gilgamesh, "Take one of the poles and push us forward, but be careful not to let your hand touch the Waters of Death!"

Gilgamesh could use each pole only once if he wished to keep his hand completely dry, so it was not very long before he had used up all 120 poles. Then he pulled up his tunic and held it aloft as a sail.

While they were sailing upon the Waters of Death, Utanapishtim spied them far in the distance. "Why have the sacred stone images of the boat been broken?" he asked himself. "Why is someone riding in the boat who is not her master?"

When the boat landed, Utanapishtim, the Faraway, looked upon Gilgamesh and said, "Who are you, and why have you come here? And tell me, why are your cheeks so pale and your face so gaunt? Why do you look like a traveler from afar, with the ravages of heat and cold seared upon your face? Why does grief tear at your heart and fear gnaw at your stomach? And why do you roam over the grassy plain and the scorching desert searching for the home of the wind?"

Gilgamesh replied, "My name is Gilgamesh, and I am king of the strong-walled city of Uruk. I have crossed the mountains from the east, as the sun rises, and have come a long way. Why should my cheeks not be pale and my face drawn? Why should I not look like a traveler from afar, with the ravages of heat and cold seared upon my face? Why should my heart not be torn with grief and my stomach gnawed by fear? And why should I not roam over the grassy plain and the scorching desert searching for the home of the wind?

"Enkidu, my dear friend, who chased the wild creatures of the hills and the panthers of the plain, who scaled the mountains with me, who endured all kinds of hardships with me and helped me conquer all things, who helped me seize and slaughter the Bull of Heaven and overthrow and kill Humbaba in the Cedar Forest, Enkidu, whom I dearly loved, has met the fate of all human beings."

Gilgamesh continued, "I wept over Enkidu's body for seven days and seven nights. I hoped that my sorrow and my pleas would arouse him from his endless sleep. The burden of my friend's death weighs heavily upon my heart. Ever since Enkidu died, I have felt that he took my life with him on his journey to the House of Darkness and Dust.

"Because Enkidu has died, I fear my own death! How then can I be silent? How then can I be still? My friend, whom I dearly loved, has returned to clay! In time, must I also lay my head in the heart of the earth, where there are no stars and no sun, and sleep the endless sleep?

"My eyes have seen little of sweet sleep, and my joints have felt much pain," Gilgamesh concluded. "I have roamed like a hunter over all lands, including the grassy plain and the scorching desert. I have crossed high mountains and choppy seas to come face to face with you, Utanapishtim. I wish to talk with you about life and death. I know that you have found everlasting life and have joined the assembly of the gods. I too wish to live on earth forever. Teach me what you know, so I can live as you do!"

Utanapishtim, the Faraway, replied, "Oh, Gilgamesh, do we build a house that will last forever? Do we seal arguments forever? Do brothers divide property into equal shares forever? Does hatred persist forever? Does the river rise and flood its banks forever? Should no one experience death? Since ancient times, nothing has been permanent. The shepherd and the noble have an identical fate—death."

Utanapishtim concluded, "When the heavenly gods gather in assembly, they decree the fate of each human being. The gods determine both life and death for every human being, but they do not reveal the day of anyone's death."

Chapter 7

Utanapishtim tells Gilgamesh about the great flood: how it came about, what it was like, and how he survived.

Gilgamesh said to the Faraway, "I know that you can live for days without end, Utanapishtim, but your features look the same as my own. Nothing about you looks strange; you resemble me in every way. I had expected that you would wish to do battle, but here you are, lying lazily upon your back. You appear to feel as I do, no longer interested in contests with the sword or with the bow. Tell me, how did you acquire everlasting life? How did you join the assembly of the heavenly gods?"

Utanapishtim replied, "Gilgamesh, I will reveal to you a secret of the gods." And so he began his tale.

You are familiar with the city of Shuruppak, on the banks of the Euphrates River. When both the city itself and the gods within it were already old, the gods decided to bring forth a great flood. Enlil, ruler of all the gods, called them together in assembly.

"The people who live upon the broad earth have become numerous beyond count, and they are too noisy," he complained. "The earth bellows like a herd of wild oxen. The clamor of human beings disturbs my sleep. Therefore, I want Adad to cause heavy rains to pour down upon the earth, both day and night. I want a great flood to come like a thief upon the earth, steal the food of these people, and destroy their lives."

Ishtar supported Enlil in his wish to destroy all of humanity, and then all the other gods agreed with his plan. However, Ea did not agree in his heart. He had helped human beings to survive upon the earth by creating rich pastures and farmland. He had taught them how to plow the land and how to grow grain. Because he loved them, he devised a clever scheme.

When Ea heard Enlil's plan, he appeared to me in a dream and said, "Stand by the wall of your reed hut, and I will speak with you there. Accept my words and listen carefully to my instructions. I will reveal a task for you."

I found myself wide awake, with Ea's message clearly etched in my mind. So I went down to the reed hut and stood with my ear to the wall as the god had commanded. "Utanapishtim, king of Shuruppak," a voice said. "Listen to my words, and consider them carefully! The heavenly gods have decreed that a great rainstorm will cause a mighty flood. This flood will engulf the cult-centers and destroy all human beings. Both the kings and the people whom they rule will come to a disastrous end. By the command of Enlil, the assembly of the gods has made this decision.

"Therefore," Ea continued, "I want you to abandon your worldly possessions in order to preserve your life. You must dismantle your house and construct a giant ship, an ark that you should call Preserver of Life.

"Make sure the ship's dimensions are equal in length and width," Ea counseled. "Build it of solid timber so the rays of Shamash will not shine into it. Take care to seal the structure well. Take aboard your wife, your family, your relatives, and the craftspeople of your city. Bring your grain and all of your possessions and goods. Take the seed of all living things, both the beasts of the field and the birds of the heavens, aboard the ship. Later, I will tell you when to board the ship and seal the door."

I replied, "Ea, my lord, I will do as you have ordered. However, I have never built a ship. Draw a design of this ark on the ground for me, so that I can follow your plan. And when the people of Shuruppak ask me what I am doing, how will I respond?"

Ea then replied to me, his servant, "I am drawing the design of the ship upon the ground for you as you have asked. As for the people of Shuruppak, tell them, 'I have learned that Enlil hates me so that I can no longer live in your city, nor can I place my feet anywhere in that god's territory. Therefore, I will go down to the deep and live with my lord Ea. However, Enlil intends to shower you with abundance. After a stormy evening, you will find the most unusual birds and fish, and your land will be filled with rich harvests.'"

With the first glow of dawn, I began to construct my giant ship. The people of Shuruppak gathered about me with great interest. The little children carried the sealing materials, while the others brought wood and everything else I would need. By the end of the fifth day of hard labor, I had constructed the framework for my ship. The floor space measured an entire acre. The length, width, and height each measured 200 feet.

I divided the height of the ark so that the interior had seven floors, and I divided each level into nine sections. I hammered water plugs into it and stored supplies. I made the craft watertight. Every day I killed cattle and sheep for the people and feasted the workers with red wine, white wine, and oil as though they were water from the Euphrates. We celebrated each day as if it were a great holiday!

Finally, on the seventh day I completed my preparations and moved the ship into the water. When two-thirds of the ship had entered the water, I loaded into it whatever remained that I intended to take with me. This included what silver and gold I possessed and what living things I had. I put aboard my family and relatives. I put aboard all of the craftspeople. I put aboard animals of the field, both wild and tame.

Ea had given me a time by which I had to be ready to depart. He had said to me, "When Adad causes the heavens to darken with terrible storm clouds, board the ship and seal the entrance."

So I watched the heavens carefully. When they looked awesome with the gloom of an impending storm, I boarded the ship and sealed the entrance with clay. Long before the storm began to rage upon us, we cast off our ship's cables and prepared to let the sea carry us wherever it would.

The people of the land watched, bewildered and quiet, as Adad turned all that had been light into darkness. The powerful south wind blew at his side, uniting the hurricane, the tornado, and the thunderstorm. It blew for a full day, increasing speed as it traveled, and shattered the land like a clay pot.

In order to observe the catastrophe the heavenly gods lifted up their torches so that the land might blaze with light. But the storm wind raged furiously over the land like a battle. It brought forth a flood that buried the mountains and shrouded the people. No person could see another, and the gods looking down from heaven could not find them either. Its attack ravaged the earth, killing all living creatures and crushing whatever else remained.

As the heavenly gods watched the flood waters pour forth upon the land and destroy everything that inhabited the earth, they too became frightened. They took refuge in their highest heaven, the heaven of Anu. There they crouched against the outer wall, trembling with fear like dogs. Nintu, the Mother Goddess, wept for the people who lived on the earth.

The goddess Ishtar cried out for the victims of the flood like a woman in labor. "All that used to exist upon the earth in days of old has now been turned to clay," she moaned, "and all because I added my voice to Enlil's in the assembly. How could I agree with the order to attack and destroy my people when I myself gave birth to them? Now the bodies of my people fill the sea like fish eggs!"

Humbled by the enormity of their deed, the heavenly gods wept with Ishtar. For seven days and seven nights the stormy south wind raged over the land, blowing the great flood across the face of the earth. Each day and each night, the windstorms tossed my giant ship wildly about upon the tumultuous sea of flood waters. On the eighth day, the flood-bearing south wind retreated, and the flood waters became calm. Radiant Shamash ventured forth once again. He spread his sunlight upon the heavens above and the earth below and revealed the devastation.

When my ship had rocked quietly for awhile, I thought that it would be safe to open a hatch and see what had happened. The world was completely still, and the surface of the sea was as level as a flat roof. All humanity except us had returned to clay. I scanned the expanse of the flood waters for a coastline, but without success.

As Shamash brought his rays of light and warmth inside my ship, I bowed my face to the ground before the powers of the universe. They had destroyed the world, but they had saved my ship. I knelt in submission and respect before Shamash, who nourishes human beings with his healing rays. In gratitude for our survival, I sacrificed an ox and a sheep to the heavenly gods. Then I sat and wept, letting my tears course freely down my face.

My ship floated upon the waters for twelve days. When I next opened the hatch and looked outside, far in the distance in each of the fourteen regions a mountain range had emerged from the surrounding waters. In time my ship came to rest, secure and stable, upon the slopes of Mount Nisir.

For the first seven days, Mount Nisir held my ship fast, allowing no motion. On the seventh day, I set free a dove and sent it forth. The dove could find no place to alight and rest, so it returned to the ship. Next I set free a swallow and sent it forth. The swallow could find no place to alight and rest, so it too returned to the ship. Then I set free a raven and sent it forth. The raven could see that the waters had receded, so it circled but did not return to my ship.

Then I set free all living things and offered a sacrifice to the heavenly gods. I set up fourteen cult-vessels on top of the mountain. I heaped cane, cedarwood, and myrtle upon their pot-stands, and I poured out a libation to the gods. They smelled the sweet aroma and gathered around me like flies. I prostrated myself before Anu and Enlil.

Then Ishtar arrived. She lifted up the necklace of great jewels that her father, Anu, had created to please her and said, "Heavenly gods, as surely as this jeweled necklace hangs upon my neck, I will never forget these days of the great flood. Let all of the gods except Enlil come to the offering. Enlil may not come, for without reason he brought forth the flood that destroyed my people."

When Enlil saw my ship, he became furious with the other gods. "Has some human being escaped?" he cried. "No one was supposed to survive the flood! Who permitted this?"

Ninurta, the warrior god, said to Enlil, "Do not be angry with us. Only Ea knows everything. Only he could have devised such a scheme!"

Ea then said to Enlil, "You are the ruler of the gods and are wise. How could you bring on such a flood without a reason? Hold the sinner responsible for his sin; punish the person who transgresses. But be lenient, so that he does not perish! Instead of causing the flood, it would have been better if you had caused a lion or a wolf to attack human beings and decrease their number! Instead of causing the flood, it would have been better if you had caused disease to attack human beings and decrease their number! Instead of causing the flood, it would have been better if you had caused famine to conquer the land. That would have weakened human beings and decreased their number!

"It was not I who revealed the secret of the great gods," Ea said craftily. "Utanapishtim, the most wise, had a dream in which he discovered how to survive your flood. So now, Enlil, think of what to do with him!"

I bowed my face to the earth in fear and submission before Enlil. He took my hand, and together we boarded my ship. Then Enlil took my wife aboard the ship and made her kneel at my side. He placed himself between us and touched our foreheads to bless us.

"Until now," Enlil said, "Utanapishtim and his wife have been human beings. From this time forward, they will live like the heavenly gods. I have brought down for them everlasting breath so that, like the gods, they may continue to live for days without end. Utanapishtim, the king of Shuruppak, has preserved the seeds of humanity and of plant and animal life. He and his wife will live far to the east, where the sun rises, at the mouth of the river in the mountainous land of Dilmun."

Utanapishtim concluded the story of his adventure. "That is how it came to pass that my wife and I became like the heavenly gods and will live for days without end. Enlil himself conferred everlasting life upon us. But Gilgamesh, king of strong-walled Uruk though you are, who will call the heavenly gods to assembly for your sake so that you can find the everlasting life you are seeking?"

Chapter 8

Utanapishtim challenges Gilgamesh to go without sleep for a week. When Gilgamesh fails the test, Utanapishtim gives him a magic plant and sends him on his way home. Gilgamesh loses the plant before he arrives in Uruk, but he returns home safely.

Utanapishtim, the Faraway, said to Gilgamesh, "If you wish to become like the heavenly gods and live for days without end, you must first possess the strength of a god. Even though you are mighty, I will show you that, like all human beings, you are weak. Starting with this night, I want you to remain upon your feet and stay awake for seven nights and six days."

Gilgamesh obediently squatted down and tried to stay awake. Despite his best intentions, sleep blew upon him like a soft mist and conquered him.

Utanapishtim said to his wife, "Look at this hero who wants everlasting life! Sleep fans him like a soft mist!"

Utanapishtim's wife advised her husband, "Touch Gilgamesh so that he will awaken and return safely to his strong-walled city. See to it that he will be able to return to his land the way he came, entering through the gate by which he left."

The Faraway responded, "In time, I will do as you advise. Meanwhile, Gilgamesh will try to deceive you by telling you he has not slept at all. We must devise proof of his slumber to show him how weak he really is. Each day, I want you to bake him a loaf of bread and place it by his head. And record how long he sleeps by placing a mark upon the wall behind him each day."

So each day that Gilgamesh slept, Utanapishtim's wife put a loaf of bread by his head and made a mark for that day upon the wall behind him. By the morning of the seventh day, Gilgamesh was still asleep. Six loaves of bread were lined up in a row by his head and there were six marks on the wall. The first loaf had dried out, the second had spoiled, the third had become soggy, the crust of the fourth had turned white, the fifth had a moldy cast, the sixth was still fresh in color, and the seventh was warm, having just been removed from the oven.

Utanapishtim touched Gilgamesh as his wife placed the seventh loaf of bread next to the others. Gilgamesh awoke and said, "I had hardly fallen asleep when you touched me and awakened me!"

Utanapishtim replied, "Gilgamesh, count the loaves of bread by your head so that you will realize how many days you have slept! Your first loaf is dried out, the second has spoiled, the third is soggy, the crust of the fourth has turned white, the fifth has a moldy cast, the sixth is still fresh in color, and I awakened you just as my wife put the seventh loaf, still warm from the oven, by your head."

Gilgamesh groaned in resignation and said, "What should I do now? Where will I go? Now that the robber Death is holding my limbs, I know that Death hides in my bedroom and I will never escape it! Wherever I place my feet, Death will be there with me! I will never become like the heavenly gods and live for days without end!"

Utanapishtim replied, "Let your heart not despair, Gilgamesh. It is true the heavenly gods have decreed that you, like all other human beings, cannot live for days without end. They have not granted you life everlasting. But Anu, Enlil, and Ea have granted you other gifts.

"The power to be unsurpassed in might they have granted you. The power to be skilled in wrestling they have granted you. The power to be skilled with the sword, the dagger, the bow, and the axe they have granted you. The power to be like a devastating flood in battle they have granted you. The power to lead attacks from which no one can escape they have granted you.

"The power to be unrivaled in heroism they have granted you. The power to seize and slaughter the Bull of Heaven they have granted you. The power to enter the Cedar Forest in the land of the living, to overthrow and kill Humbaba, and to fell the cedars they have granted you. The power to make the long, difficult, and dangerous journey to meet with me they have granted you.

"And as if extraordinary might and heroism were not sufficient gifts, the power to be supreme among human beings they have granted you. The power to rule your people as king and to be the greatest of leaders they have granted you. The power to bring light or darkness upon your people they have granted you. The power to free people or enslave them they have granted you. The power to teach your people and lead them to wisdom they have granted you.

"Therefore," Utanapishtim counseled, "cast away fear and sorrow. Rejoice in your heart that the heavenly gods love you and have smiled upon you!"

Utanapishtim then turned to his boatman and said, "Urshanabi, take Gilgamesh to the washing place that he may cleanse himself. Let him wash his long hair until it is as clean as snow. Let him remove his animal skins and let the deep sea carry them away, so that the beauty of his appearance may be seen. Let him replace the band around his head with a new one, and let him put on a new cloak to cover his nakedness. Then accompany him on his journey back to strong-walled Uruk."

Urshanabi took care of Gilgamesh as the Faraway had directed. When Gilgamesh was clean and newly clothed, the two of them climbed into Urshanabi's boat and prepared to sail away.

Utanapishtim's wife then said, "Gilgamesh made a long, difficult, and dangerous journey to meet with you. In appreciation of his effort, what gift will you give him to take back with him to his city?"

Utanapishtim asked Urshanabi to bring the boat close to the shore. Then he said, "Gilgamesh, because you have made a long, difficult, and dangerous journey in order to meet with me, I will send you back to strong-walled Uruk with a secret thing created by the heavenly gods. The plant that you see growing deep in the water there is like the rose. Its thorns will prick your hands when you try to pick it. However, if you can gather that plant, you will hold in your hands the gift of everlasting youth. This plant cannot make you live forever, but it will keep you young and strong all the days of your life."

Gilgamesh replied, "I can gather the plant if you will give me two heavy stones." He tied one stone to each of his feet and placed his dagger between his teeth. Using a pole to push the boat out into the deep water near the plant, he jumped overboard. The stones pulled his body down into the deep water where he could reach the plant. He picked it successfully even though it pricked his hands. Then he cut the heavy stones from his feet and let the water carry him up to the surface of the sea.

Gilgamesh climbed into the boat once again, stowed the plant safely, and set off with Urshanabi. They successfully crossed the waters of death; in three more days, they covered the distance that would have taken another craft a month and a half.

In time they saw the cottage of Siduri and knew that the first part of their journey was behind them. Being tired and hungry, they steered the boat toward an inviting shore and beached it.

To protect his plant, Gilgamesh removed it from the boat and carried it with him. He wandered over the land, enjoying the freedom of moving about on firm ground and stretching his legs. He followed a freshwater stream inland until it formed a pool. There he put the plant upon the ground along with his clothes and went for a refreshing swim.

A serpent in the water smelled the appealing fragrance of the plant. It glided out of the water, slithered up the bank, took hold of the plant with its mouth, and carried it back into the water. As it returned to the water it shed its skin, emerging younger and fresher looking.

By the time Gilgamesh noticed what had happened, it was too late to save the plant. He sat down and wept. Then he took the hand of Urshanabi and said, "For whom have my hands labored? For whom does the blood of my heart work? I have obtained nothing for myself. I have only helped the serpent! Now the tide will carry the plant back into the depths of the sea!"

After composing himself Gilgamesh continued, "Since it is impossible to retrieve the plant, I must become resigned to my loss. We will leave the boat on the shore as we had planned and continue our journey overland toward strong-walled Uruk."

When they had walked sixty miles, they stopped to eat. After another ninety miles, they prepared to spend the night. After many days and nights they saw the strong walls of Uruk in the distance. As they walked toward the city, Gilgamesh explained to Urshanabi, "Uruk is composed of four sections: the city, the orchards, borderland, and the precinct of the Temple of Anu and Ishtar."

As they entered the gates, Gilgamesh said, "Urshanabi, I want you to notice the strong walls of our city of Uruk. I built these walls on a foundation created in ancient times by the seven wise men, who brought great knowledge to our land. The top of our outer wall shines with the brightness of copper, but it is made of burnt brick. Now study the inner walls of our city. Examine the fine brickwork. These walls, too, surpass all others! No human being, not even a king, will ever be able to construct more impressive walls than I have built around our city of Uruk! Now approach the majestic Temple of Anu and Ishtar. No mortal, not even a king, will ever be able to build a structure as beautiful as the one I have created! Climb up and walk upon the walls of Uruk. Examine the fine brickwork. Admire the majestic Temple of Anu and Ishtar. Gaze upon one man's supreme achievement!"

Gilgamesh inscribed these travels and these thoughts upon stone tablets and placed these tablets on the strong walls of Uruk so that his people could gain wisdom and remember him.

❧ QUESTIONS FOR
Response, Discussion, and Analysis

1. Why is Enkidu created as a wild, uncivilized human being? What does he lose when he becomes civilized, and what does he gain? Is the change desirable? Explain.

2. What makes Gilgamesh a hero? What qualities does he possess, and what deeds does he accomplish? To what extent are the gods necessary in his life? Do they detract from his heroism? Why?

3. Does Gilgamesh's journey in search of immortality make him appear cowardly because he fears death, or strong because he attempts to change his fate? Defend your point of view.

4. How are Gilgamesh and Enkidu alike? How are they different?

5. The author emphasizes the thoughts of Gilgamesh and Enkidu as they travel to meet Humbaba, but he gives only a brief description of the actual fight. What does this emphasis reveal about the nature of courage?

6. What is the purpose of the various trials that Gilgamesh must pass in order to reach Utanapishtim?

7. What does Gilgamesh learn from Utanapishtim? What makes him finally accept his destiny?

8. How does the knowledge that Gilgamesh acquires from his journey and from Utanapishtim change his life? How does he intend to gain immortality?

9. What character traits best describe Gilgamesh? Support your choice with examples.

10. Gilgamesh made a dangerous journey in order to acquire knowledge. Could a person today have a similar experience? Explain. Would you make such a journey if you could? Why?

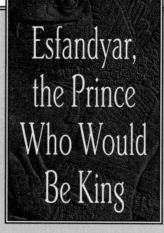

HISTORICAL BACKGROUND

Although Ferdowsi wrote the *Shahnameh* (*Book of Kings*) in about A.D. 1000, many aspects of the legends it contains are rooted in the ancient cultures of the Scythians, the Persians, and the Parthians. War is a major subject in the section of the *Shahnameh* that presents the history of Persia's legendary kings, and Ferdowsi's descriptions of implements of war and battle practices have a distinctly Scythian flavor.

Two groups of Scythians settled the area that in time became the Persian and later the Parthian empire. In about 1400 B.C., the first group settled the southwestern part of the Persian plateau and became the ancestors of the legendary kings of Persia. They called themselves Aryans ("Iranians" in Persian), meaning "the noble ones," and called their area "Iran," meaning "the land of the Aryans." Later, in the second century B.C., related Saka tribes moved southwest from Sakestan ("the land of the Sakas") to the area that became Seistan and Zabulestan on the eastern border of Persia, where they became the ancestors of Rostam and the other legendary Saka heroes in the *Shahnameh*.

Like their Scythian ancestors, the legendary kings and heroes in the *Shahnameh* are expert horsemen and archers. They view war as a way of life and hunting as a means of relaxing. Like their Scythian ancestors, they wear leather armor and carry a leather, metal-plated shield. They hang a case containing their bow and arrows from their waist at their left side; tied to their right thigh they wear a sheath containing a long knife or a short sword of bronze or iron. They carry both a battle-ax (used with the left hand) and a javelin (used with the right hand). In battle, they decapitate their enemies, and they are rewarded for their valor based on the number of heads they have taken. They make leather-bound drinking cups from the skulls of their most hated enemies, and if they are wealthy, they may line these skulls with gold.

Long before Ferdowsi was born, Persian history was a source of national pride and an appropriate subject for epic material. Approximately eight hundred years after the Scythians settled in Persia, Cyrus the Great (sixth century B.C.) had turned a country of people whose ancestors were nomads into an empire of almost two million square miles and about ten million people.

The Parthian kings considered themselves to be the legitimate successors to the great kings of the earlier Persian empire and to rule with the divine blessing of Ahuramazda, the chief god of Zoroastrianism, the religion of the Persians. Their empire, established in about 171 B.C., extended from the Caspian Sea on the north to the Persian Gulf on the south, and from the Euphrates on the west to India on the east, and therefore included Rostam's kingdom of Seistan and Zabulestan.

Because of their pride in their Persian heritage, the Parthian kings revived Persia's oral and written literature, which included the Rostam cycle of Saka legends. Undoubtedly, the Parthian aristocrats particularly enjoyed these ancient stories because they reflected their own interests and values. Like their Scythian ancestors and the legendary kings and heroes who have come down to us in the *Shahnameh,* the Parthians excelled as horsemen and archers and loved both war and hunting.

FERDOWSI AND THE ORAL TRADITION

Mansur ibn Ahmad, later known as Ferdowsi, was born into a family of landowners in about A.D. 935. His place of birth was the city of Tus, in the province of Khurasan, in what is now northeastern Iran. However, at that time the area extended into what are now Afghanistan and former Soviet republics.

Khurasan and the other eastern provinces of Persia could be called "the cradle of Persian civilization," since much of Persia's history had occurred in this area. Consequently, it was also here that the land-owning class had become responsible for preserving Persian oral and written literature as a way of maintaining the Persian values and traditions that had existed before the Arab Muslim conquest in the seventh century. Living during a time when the language, cultural traditions, and religion were different, these Muslims prided themselves on being the historians of their Persian heritage.

In time, a Persian cultural renaissance had occurred, with the result that, in Ferdowsi's day, the language spoken in the king's court was Persian rather than Arabic, and the court poetry was written in Persian. Consequently, Ferdowsi wrote a work that glorifies the mythological, legendary, and historical past of an old, non-Muslim empire, with its Zoroastrian religion and its vilification of the Turanians, or Tatars, as Persia's greatest enemy. The memorable human heroes within its pages revive cultural values and national issues that, for many people, had been long dead and forgotten.

Ferdowsi was a compiler and editor as well as an author and poet. He used a combination of written and oral sources. The age of Ferdowsi's oral sources—legends passed down from generation to generation for hundreds of years—is reflected by their preservation of Scythian implements of war and battle practices.

The *Shahnameh* covers a period of 3,600 years, from the creation of the world and the first Persian king (the first two-thirds of the book) to the Arab Muslim conquest of Persia by the Saracens in A.D. 636 (the last third). It provides a history of four dynasties and fifty Persian kings. The kings in the earliest dynasty are mythical; those in the second dynasty (beginning about 700 B.C.) are legendary; and those in the third and fourth dynasties (c. 150 B.C.–A.D. 632) are historical. Goshtasp is among the last of the legendary kings.

APPEAL AND VALUE

The *Shahnameh* contains a series of legends—including the legend of Esfandyar—that take their place among the greatest stories in world literature. These heroes, and the kings for whom they perform their deeds, are unforgettable characters who live forever in the reader's mind and heart. In the course of their adventures, they encounter the magic of demons, the power of monsters, and the skill of other valiant warriors. They experience the joys of friendship and the passions of love, jealousy, and hatred. They courageously encounter the challenges of danger, treachery, and death.

The *Shahnameh* bears approximately the same relation to Persian culture (prior to the 1979 Islamic Revolution) that the *Iliad* bears to ancient Greek culture and the *Ramayana* and the *Mahabharata* bear to ancient Indian culture. Like them, it aims to preserve and, in fact, to immortalize some aspect of its country's history. Like them, it defines, symbolizes, and perpetuates the values of its particular culture, thereby providing a sense of national and ethnic identity that enhances the self-esteem and dignity of its people.

Like the great epics from ancient Greece and India, the *Shahnameh* is a world treasure as well as a national jewel. The legends of Persia's heroes reach across time and space to touch the lives of those who live today just as they have touched the lives of countless others throughout Persia's long history.

Ferdowsi possessed the ability to create characters who are truly human and who possess a tragic nobility as they come to grips with their soul-rending conflicts. He composed all of his character's speeches and their letters, turning history into literature and skeletons into human beings who think and feel in ways that we can understand and appreciate.

Ferdowsi had an instinct for psychological high drama, and his genius illuminates both the bright and dark sides of human attitudes and behavior. He saw the potential for great good and great evil that exists in each human being. He saw the danger of excessive pride, the slippery slope that leads to rash and imprudent actions, and the inevitable retribution that follows. Moreover, he saw that basically good people can succumb to this personality pattern. Conversely, Ferdowsi saw that people who perform deeds that harm others are not necessarily evil people. They may refuse to consider the consequences of their actions, or they may be ruled by temporary passions, or they may simply behave differently in different situations.

Ferdowsi was fascinated by the human aspect of history—by the people who both shape the events and are shaped by them. In the legends that he recounts, he focuses on the personalities of kings and heroes, whose attitudes and behavior reveal their motivations, their goals, and their internal and external conflicts.

Rostam and Esfandyar are the greatest Persian heroes, and they are unforgettable individuals. In their speeches and actions, they advocate the universal principles of love, honor, loyalty, wisdom, justice, and freedom, along with such qualities as courage, strength, skill, and creative intelligence on the plain of battle. They are majestic figures because of their virtues and their valiant deeds.

However, they live on in the minds of those who come to know them because of the age-old conflicts between their obligation to themselves, given their own needs, desires, and values, and their obligations to their family and their society. The fact that each of these heroes must choose between important competing values—knowing that neither choice is satisfactory—heightens his stature while it creates his personal tragedy.

Tragedy abounds in the lives of the legendary kings and heroes of Persia. These human beings play out their lives on a dark stage, often like puppets. Given the frailties that are inherent in the human personality, the transitory nature of human life, and the inevitability of Fate that is integral to the Persian world-view, it cannot be otherwise. In such an environment, Rostam and Esfandyar strive to make their own lives worthwhile, recognizing that noble deeds are their only source of immortality. However, these heroes are not duplicates of some generic Persian hero. Each is unique in his personality and in his goals.

Rostam is one of the world's greatest traditional heroes. Like them, his fame resides in his many great deeds that make his society a better place in which to live. He is not only Persia's greatest hero, but he is the greatest hero of his time, and he takes pride in his greatness. Unlike Esfandyar, Rostam embraces heroism solely for its joy and its satisfaction. Having no greater ambition, Rostam is the friend of the just king and the enemy of all tyrants. Doing his best to serve Persia's kings and preserve Persia's autonomy has given him self-esteem, and he has earned the respect and admiration of these kings, his own family, and his peers.

Rostam's continued success in combat—whether against monsters, demons, or warriors—has earned him the epithets of "Rostam the Mighty" and "The Shield of Persia." His courage, strength, and skill have made him as great as his reputation. However, his pride makes him very human.

Because Rostam lives more than three hundred years, his life encompasses the reign of many kings, including that of Goshtasp. Rostam is an old man when his life becomes inextricably bound up with that of Esfandyar—the youth whom Ferdowsi introduces as Persia's greatest legendary hero. Certainly, Esfandyar is the most complex of these heroes. Because he is much younger than Rostam, Esfandyar's heroic life functions as a variation on Rostam's life, and many of his exploits mirror Rostam's early accomplishments. However, Esfandyar is a different type of hero. Unlike Rostam, he is a prophet of Zoroaster and his religion, and, unlike Rostam, the challenges in his life stem from his great ambition to become king of Persia.

However, Goshtasp—who is Esfandyar's father and the current king of Persia—is not ready to relinquish his power to his son. Consequently, Esfandyar's devotion to his religious principles eventually leads him to obey his father's command even when it is unjust, unnecessary, and ultimately self-destructive. The result is a tragedy that leads readers to question whether Esfandyar has enhanced his heroic image or whether he has tarnished it.

Taken together, Rostam and Esfandyar form a multifaceted portrait of the hero, both in ancient Persia and in any culture today. Like Rostam, people still choose to become heroes in order to help the society in which they live and to give meaning to their own lives through deeds that others will remember. Like Esfandyar, people still choose to become heroes in order to create an identity that others will recognize and value. Also, like Esfandyar, people still choose to become heroes in order to achieve another, greater goal, such as greater power.

Today, we can take these heroes into our hearts because we, too, know what it is to have to choose between our personal desires and our responsibilities to our families, friends, and society. Often, we too must choose between what others would like us to do, and even what we might wish to do, and our own moral and ethical values. We understand the temptation, we understand the torment of internal conflict, and, sometimes, we lose the battle against the external and internal forces that lead us to exercise bad judgment. In our own environment, we too must make our own lives worthwhile, and we too must recognize the importance of our good deeds in whatever type of immortality we hope to achieve.

THE PERSIAN HERO

The *Shahnameh* depicts a time in Persian legend and history when a strong Persian king means the difference between freedom and captivity. The King of Kings, or the Great King of Persia, demands total obeisance and obedience from his subjects. He is served by a large group of warriors who protect and increase his power. The greatest of these warriors are usually kings or chieftains in their own right, and they lead their own warriors into battle.

Because the Great King receives his right to rule directly from Ahuramazda (the supreme divinity in Zoroastrianism), each warrior's primary responsibility is to serve the Great King, and, by so doing, to serve Ahuramazda, as well. The warrior's responsibility to the Great King must take precedence over his responsibility to his own kingdom, to his family, and to himself. Moreover, the warrior is obligated to serve the Great King—whether the ruler is wise or foolish and just or cruel—with total and sacred loyalty.

Like his Scythian ancestors, the Persian warrior takes pride in his ability to ride a horse, to draw his bow, and to use his lariat. In war, he aims to behead his foe with one stroke of his sword. He enjoys the challenge of single combat, where he also uses such weapons as the war-club or ox-headed mace (a sign of kingship), the spear, and the dagger.

The Persian warrior's fate—like that of everyone else in his society—is written in the stars for the king's wise men to read, and what is written there comes to pass, no matter how he tries to avoid it. Since death comes to everyone sooner or later, the Persian hero aims to perform valiant deeds on the plain of battle in order to gain the immortality of lasting fame.

THE ROLE OF THE GODS

Goshtasp, a late legendary king in the *Shahnameh,* adopts the new religion of Zoroastrianism. In Zoroastrian belief, the human condition reflects the struggle between Ahuramazda (Urmazd) and Ahriman to control the universe. Ahuramazda is the god of wisdom, goodness, and light, and the constructive force in the universe, whereas Ahriman is the evil spirit, who represents deception, darkness, and the destructive force in the universe.

Ahriman is always busily using deception as a lure in his attempt to harm human beings and destroy the world of truth. Consequently, Zoroastrianism contributes an additional moral dimension to the *Shahnameh,* where a war on earth becomes a war, not only between Persia and Turan, but between good and evil, and where Ferdowsi reveals his characters' conflicts between the claims of their political and social selves and the demands of their moral selves.

The earliest existing manuscript of the *Shahnameh,* written in 1216 and only the first of two volumes, was recently discovered in Florence. The earliest complete manuscript, written in 1276–1277, is owned by the British Museum in London.

The following version of the Esfandyar legend is based upon James Atkinson's *The Shah Nameh of the Persian Poet Ferdowsi* (1832) and Helen Zimmern's *The Epic of Kings: Hero Tales of Ancient Persia* (1882).

 ℰ ∿

PRINCIPAL CHARACTERS

BAHMAN: the son of Esfandyar; the grand-son of Goshtasp; the king of Persia after Goshtasp
ESFANDYAR: a son of Goshtasp; a prophet of Zardosht and Urmazd
GOSHTASP: the father of Esfandyar; the grandfather of Bahman; the king of Persia
ROSTAM/TAHAMTAN ("giant-body"): the son of Dastan/Zal; Persia's greatest hero
ZAL/DASTAN: the father of Rostam; the king of Seistan and Zabul/Zabulestan

PRINCIPAL GODS, DEMONS, AND CREATURES

AHRIMAN ("Maker of Evil"): the Evil Spirit who represents deception and darkness and is the destructive force in the universe; the greatest Demon, who lives in the dark lands of the Demon peoples in the North; the great foe of Ahuramazda
AHURAMAZDA ("Wise Lord"): the supreme Zoroastrian divinity; the holy spirit who represents truth and light and is the constructive force in the universe; the god of wisdom, goodness, and light; the creator of the universe; the great foe of Ahriman
ARJASP: the demon-king of Turan, who is mortal, human in form, and a sorcerer
SIMURGHS: giant birds, known as "the bird of marvel"
URMAZD: the shortened name of Ahuramazda

ESFANDYAR, THE PRINCE WHO WOULD BE KING

Chapter 1

Esfandyar performs his first heroic deeds.

It came to pass that when Goshtasp took the throne of Persia, he became a mighty ruler to whom many kingdoms paid tribute. Similarly, Goshtasp was willing to pay tribute to King Arjasp of Turan until it came to pass that, early in his reign, the prophet Zardosht arrived in Persia with the goal of teaching about Urmazd, the God of Wisdom, Goodness, and Light. Once Goshtasp converted to the new religion, he announced that he would no longer pay tribute to Arjasp, who responded by declaring war on Persia.

Despite the fact that Arjasp's warriors were Demons, King Goshtasp called his son, Esfandyar, before him and announced, "My son, I am putting you in command of Persia's warriors! Conquer Arjasp, the Demon-king. And in return, I promise that I will give you my crown and my throne and make you king of Persia!"

Esfandyar was virtuous and valiant. His heart was as generous as rain-clouds which enrich the earth with their showers. However, his heart was also set on becoming the king of Persia.

As usual, war between Persia and Turan flared up like fire in a gale-wind. Just as autumn winds blow the leaves off the willow tree, so battle-axes battered both helmets and heads off the warriors. The battle-plain soon became a sea of blood, with waves of arrows, spears, and swords. Like ships, horses floated until they sank. At first, neither side could claim a victory. Finally, Esfandyar was victorious over the Demon-warriors, causing Arjasp to panic and flee from Persian soil, like a sheep from a ravenous wolf.

And so it came to pass that Esfandyar returned in triumph to King Goshtasp and declared, "Father, I have defeated Arjasp and his Demon-warriors! Now, give me your crown and your throne. And make me king of Persia as you have promised!"

To these words, Goshtasp responded, "My son, it is true that you are a valiant hero who has just won a great victory. However, one great victory does not entitle a prince to rule a kingdom! And your hunger for power does not become you! The king who would rule his people well must follow the teachings of Zardosht and pursue the path of truth through good thoughts, good words, and good deeds."

"Therefore, you must now go forth as a prophet of Zardosht and teach the peoples of the world to worship Urmazd and pursue the path of truth! Conquer other kingdoms in the names of Zardosht and Urmazd! Do this, and I promise that I will give you my crown and my throne and make you king of Persia!" declared Goshtasp.

Esfandyar agreed. And it came to pass that, while he was away on this mission, a jealous nobleman convinced King Goshtasp that Esfandyar intended to use his victories for his own glory, rather than for his father's, and that, in fact, Esfandyar intended to overthrow him. Goshtasp found this slander easy to believe since, when he was a young man, he had argued with his own father about receiving the crown and throne of Persia.

Once Esfandyar was victorious in his second task, he returned in triumph to King Goshtasp. "Father, not only have I defeated Arjasp and his Demon-warriors, but I have also conquered many kingdoms in the names of Zardosht and Urmazd," he declared. "Now, be true to your word! Give me your crown and your throne. And make me king of Persia as you have promised!"

Goshtasp responded to these words by saying nothing to Esfandyar. Instead, he turned to his nobles and commanded, "Counselors, tell me how a loving and righteous father and king should treat a son who has conquered many lands, but who has done this valiant deed in order to feed his own ambition. What should such a father and king do if he knows that his son plans to murder him so that he can rule in his father's place?"

To these words, the king's chief counselor replied, "King Goshtasp, such a prince would be guilty of treason! The king, at all cost, must defend his kingdom from such a prince, and, of course, he must protect his own life! Therefore, the king should kill the traitorous prince, despite the fact that he is his son! However, if the king cannot find the courage within his heart to commit such a dreadful deed, then, from this time forth until his son's days come to an end, he must keep his son in chains, imprisoned in the darkness of the dungeon that lies buried deep in the earth beneath his palace!"

"Your wise words will now become my deeds!" Goshtasp exclaimed. And turning to Esfandyar, he declared, "My son, because you are a traitor, you are hereby condemned to spend the rest of your days chained to the dungeon walls that lie hidden beneath this palace!"

It then came to pass that, when Arjasp the Demon-king learned that Esfandyar had been imprisoned, swift as an arrow from a warrior's bow, he gathered his Turanian warriors and invaded Persia. Once again, war between Persia and Turan flared up like fire in a gale-wind. Just as autumn winds blow the leaves off the willow tree, so battle-axes battered both helmets and heads off the warriors. The battle-plain soon became a sea of blood, with waves of arrows, spears, and swords. Like ships, horses floated until they sank.

King Goshtasp fled to Seistan, where he tried to command Rostam to be his shield against Arjasp and his Turanian warriors. Rostam the Mighty, whom men call Tahamtan, had been the Shield of Persia for many kings.

However, Rostam disliked Goshtasp. Therefore, the king's expectations roused Tahamtan to fury like a wolf, and he replied, "My father Dastan's kingdom of Zabulestan, as well as Kabulestan and the other kingdoms under his control, are independent of Persia and therefore not subject to your will, Goshtasp! You will just have to deal with Arjasp yourself!"

Meanwhile, Arjasp took advantage of the fact that Goshtasp was in Seistan. He entered the Persian capital with his Demon-warriors, killed the king's father, and captured Esfandyar's brother and his two sisters. The Demon-king also burned all of Urmazd's temples and many of the Persian palaces.

When Goshtasp returned home, his wise men looked into the heavens and read in the stars that only Esfandyar could deliver Persia from the Tatars. The king therefore called his son forth from the darkness of the dungeon that was his prison and freed him.

"Esfandyar, forgive me for doubting your loyalty!" Goshtasp exclaimed. "Only you possess the skill to be victorious against Arjasp. Therefore, once again, I am putting you in command of Persia's warriors. Lead them against the Demon-king, free Persia from Turan's tyranny, and rescue your brother and sisters! Do this, and I promise that I will give you my crown and my throne and make you king of Persia!"

Esfandyar agreed, and so it came to pass that, once again, he led Persia's warriors against Arjasp the Demon-king. This time, no dreams of glory made his heart sing. And no love for his father flooded his heart with fire! His heart burned to avenge Arjasp's capture of his brother!

Esfandyar was victorious against Arjasp. The great Persian hero caused the king of Turan and his Demon-warriors to panic and flee from the Persian warriors like sheep from a ravenous wolf. In the process, Esfandyar rescued his brother.

Chapter 2

Esfandyar performs "The Seven Stages."

And so it came to pass that Esfandyar returned in triumph to King Goshtasp and declared, "Father, first I defeated Arjasp and his Demon-warriors. Then, I conquered kingdoms in the names of Zardosht and Urmazd. Now, I have rescued my brother and freed Persia from Arjasp's tyranny. Therefore, be true to your word! Give me your crown and your throne, and make me king of Persia as you have promised!"

To these words, King Goshtasp responded, "My son, it is true that you are a valiant hero who has just won another great victory. However, great victories, alone, do not entitle a prince to rule a kingdom! And your hunger for power does not become you! Surely you have a rock for a heart! Otherwise, you would not set your heart on my crown and my throne when your sisters are imprisoned in Arjasp's Brass Fortress!"

"Therefore, my son, once again, I am putting you in command of Persia's warriors," Goshtasp announced. "Destroy Arjasp and his Demon-warriors and rescue your sisters from the Brass Fortress, and I promise that I will give you my crown and my throne and make you king of Persia!"

When Esfandyar agreed, King Goshtasp explained, "Now, two roads lead to the Brass Fortress, my son. Both are difficult and dangerous. The longer way is safer, but vengeance is successful only if it is as swift as an arrow sent forth from a warrior's bow. Therefore, I must advise you to take the shorter route, even though no one who has ever chosen this route has survived!"

"Your journey to the Brass Fortress will only take seven days, my son, but your path will be paved with peril," continued Goshtasp. "I hear that you will encounter seven successive challenges. If you kill all of the beasts and Demons that attack you, you will have survived only to have to cross the barren, fiery desert that lies between here and the Brass Fortress! Therefore, I will send one of my Demon-slaves to guide you. If anyone knows how to reach the Brass Fortress, surely he does!"

"I pray that Urmazd will bring you safely back to me," Goshtasp concluded. "But if it is written in the stars in the heavens that you are destined to be killed by the Demon-king, you can do nothing to change your fate. Sooner or later, Death's door swings wide for everyone who breathes the wind of life, and he who leaves behind him a trail of honor and glory is most blessed!"

"Do not fear for my life, Father!" Esfandyar exclaimed, undaunted. "Urmazd smiles upon the prophet of Zardosht and the warrior-son whose goal is to obey his king and father! If Arjasp the Demon-king dares to confront me, he will surely fall beneath my arm!"

So it came to pass that Esfandyar set forth upon this perilous journey accompanied by his brother, twelve thousand warriors, and the Demon-guide, whose job was to educate him as to the nature of each challenge so that he could prepare himself to meet it successfully. He took the short, dangerous route to the Brass Fortress.

THE FIRST STAGE

The Demon-guide had agreed to accompany Esfandyar to the Brass Fortress, but as soon as the prince chose the short route, he exclaimed, "Prince of Persia, we dare not go where no bird will dare to fly! We will surely die long before we reach our destination"

To these words, Esfandyar responded, "The brave warrior takes the shortest route! A man has only one life to live and one death to face! And what will come is written in the stars! So it is best to be virtuous and valiant!"

The Demon-guide told Esfandyar that his first challenge would be a pair of monstrous wolves, but to Esfandyar's surprise, the first day passed uneventfully. However, when the sun's bright shield had sunk from sight, it came to pass that, just as their guide had predicted, two great wolves charged forth from the forest. They were as large and strong as elephants, with long, spear-like fangs. As soon as they spied Esfandyar and his brother, they attacked them. However, quick as dust in the wind, each brother chose a wolf and sliced it in two with one mighty slash of his sword.

THE SECOND STAGE

The Demon-guide told Esfandyar that his next challenge would be a pair of ferocious lions, but to Esfandyar's surprise, the second day passed as uneventfully as the first. However, when the sun's bright shield had once again sunk from sight, it came to pass that, just as their guide had predicted, a pair of ferocious lions charged the prince as he rode at the head of his warriors. These beasts were so filled with rage that Esfandyar feared for his brother's life and chose to kill both lions himself.

Like fire in a gale-wind, Esfandyar first attacked the male, separating its head from its body with one mighty slash of his sword. However, when he turned to combat the female, she was so enraged over the death of her mate that she battled Esfandyar with a mad fury. It took all of the prince's skill to hold his own against her until, at long last, the moment came when he could slice her head from her body with another mighty slash of his sword.

THE THIRD STAGE

The Demon-guide told Esfandyar that his third challenge would be a great dragon, whose roar caused the mountains to shake in fear and whose poisonous foam felled all life that lay in its path. Therefore, Esfandyar built a horse-drawn, closed chariot which he covered with sharp spears and swords. As soon as it came to pass that the mountains echoed with the roar of a great avalanche, Esfandyar leaped into this chariot and drove the pair of horses off to meet the monster.

When the dragon smelled the scent of Esfandyar and his horses, it opened its mouth in delightful anticipation of a feast of flesh, bone, and blood.

The sight of the venom-spewing dragon turned the hearts of Esfandyar's warriors into water. However, the prince drove his horse-drawn chariot right into the dragon's gaping mouth, landing on its tongue.

Although the dragon expected to swallow horses, chariot, and driver in one great gulp, to its surprise, the chariot's projecting spears and swords tore its mouth to shreds, and it soon found that it was choking on its great feast. Consequently, quick as the flames of fire, the dragon spewed out this entire feast amidst its poisonous foam.

Esfandyar then leapt out of his chariot and, like fire in a gale-wind, plunged his sword into the dragon's brain. Before he fainted from the smell of the venom, he had cracked the dragon's head apart like a gigantic nut and had snuffed out its life.

THE FOURTH STAGE

The Demon-guide told Esfandyar that his fourth challenge would be a Demon-enchantress, who could transform herself into any shape. And, indeed, it came to pass that, when the sun next raised his shining shield, scattering the armies of night and brightening the earth with his brilliant light, a beautiful weeping princess appeared before Esfandyar and his companions with a tale of how she was the prisoner of a monstrous ghost. Esfandyar raised his lariat and lassoed her as soon as she came within range. She could not escape from his noose, even though she turned herself into a cat, a wolf, and, finally, an old man. Esfandyar rewarded her magic feats by chopping her into pieces with his sword.

No sooner had the enchantress lost her life then a flame-spitting Ghost-Demon materialized from the depths of a black cloud. Esfandyar rushed into the flames to do battle, fearless of the fire that was eating his armor and his clothing. Once again, quick as fire in a gale-wind, Esfandyar separated his antagonist's head from its body with one mighty slash of his sword.

THE FIFTH STAGE

The Demon-guide told Esfandyar that he would find his next challenge when they reached the high mountain pass that they had to traverse in order to reach the Brass Fortress. There, a giant simurgh—the bird known as the Bird of Marvel—was accustomed to swooping down and carrying off travelers as food for offspring that were the size of elephants. Esfandyar decided that he would cross the pass in his special chariot.

It took the Persian warriors an entire day to climb the mountain. They reached the pass just as the sun's bright shield was sinking from sight. To assure their safety, they set up camp in the darkness and ate their food cold.

It came to pass that, when the sun next raised his shining shield, scattering the armies of night and brightening the earth with his brilliant light, the simurgh looked down from her nest high upon the mountain cliff and spied Esfandyar's chariot. She swooped down upon it, intending to grab it in her talons and carry it off to her nest. However, the protruding weapons tore into her beak and her claws, weakening her.

Esfandyar then jumped forth from his chariot and, quick as dust in the wind, sliced the huge bird in two with one mighty slash of his sword. The simurgh's blood poured over Esfandyar's body, completely covering him from head to toe and making him invulnerable to any weapon. Being unaware of this disguised blessing, Esfandyar instinctively closed his eyes, and so it came to pass that the prince could only encounter injury if a weapon struck his eyes. When he had completed this task, and the giant bird lay dead at his feet, Esfandyar could not help but stare in wonder at the great size and majestic beauty of the Bird of Marvel.

THE SIXTH STAGE

The Demon-guide told Esfandyar that his next challenge would appear in the form of a fearful storm. However, when the sun next raised his shining shield, scattering the armies of night and brightening the earth with his brilliant light, Esfandyar and his warriors pushed ahead despite their guide's dire warnings. The Persian warriors were still making their way through the mountains when it came to pass that, just as their guide had predicted, the Demons descended upon them in the form of a terrible snowstorm that was accompanied by bitter cold and heavy winds. Fortunately, Urmazd answered their prayers by revealing a large cave that could shelter their entire group. There, they remained for three days, until, finally, the storm ceased.

THE SEVENTH STAGE

In a last attempt to prevent Esfandyar from reaching the Brass Fortress, the Demon-guide told Esfandyar that the final challenge of his journey would be to cross a waterless, fiery desert that was so scorched by the sun's shield that no lion or vulture, or even an ant or fly, would venture forth upon it. Esfandyar remained fearless. And when the sun next raised his shining shield, scattering the armies of night and brightening the earth with his brilliant light, he led his warriors forth on the last stage of their journey to the Brass Fortress. To their delight, they found that the storm had made the fabled desert fresh and green.

It then came to pass that Esfandyar told his guide that, upon reaching the Brass Fortress, he intended to kill Turan's greatest heroes and make slaves of their wives and children. The Demon-guide responded by cursing the Persian prince, and, quick as the flames of fire, Esfandyar beheaded him with one mighty slash of his sword.

Chapter 3

Esfandyar conquers the Brass Fortress.

As soon as the Persians reached the Brass Fortress, they could see that it was unconquerable. A massive brass wall surrounded the great city. And they could see that teams of four horsemen were riding side-by-side upon it. Esfandyar decided to win by cleverness what he knew that he could not win by combat.

Choosing two hundred sixty warriors and a hundred camels to accompany him, Esfandyar prepared to enter the city as merchants who had arrived with a caravan of luxurious merchandise to sell. Ten camels would carry embroidered clothes; ten camels would carry priceless jewels; and eighty camels each would carry a pair of chests. One hundred sixty Persian warriors would enter the Brass Fortress hidden in these chests, while one hundred additional warriors would enter the great Demon-city disguised as merchants, camel-drivers, and servants.

The plan was successful. Once the disguised merchants had been welcomed into the fortress with their wares, Esfandyar began to prepare a great feast for Arjasp and his Demon-chiefs. In the process, he discovered that his sisters were working in the kitchen of Arjasp's palace.

During the feast, Esfandyar saw to it that wine flowed like a spring mountain stream. The Demons drank heartily, and they soon fell into a heavy, drunken slumber. This was the moment for which all of the Persian warriors had been waiting. The merchant-warriors now opened their chests, releasing the warriors who were concealed within them. The Persians defeated the unsuspecting Demons, killing the warriors and making slaves of their wives and children.

After Esfandyar rescued his sisters, he fought Arjasp the Demon-king in single combat, finally gaining the advantage that enabled him to slice him in two with one mighty slash of his sword. Then, the Persian prince fought and killed Arjasp's sons so that they would not live to avenge their father's death.

Esfandyar and his warriors also went on to conquer the peoples of neighboring provinces, so that when he finally returned to Persia, in addition to having rescued his sisters, Esfandyar had expanded his father's empire and increased his treasure.

Meanwhile, back in Persia, it had come to pass that King Goshtasp listened to the wicked whisperings of Ahriman—the Evil One who is Urmazd's great enemy—and commanded his wise men to look into the heavens and read in the stars how his son, Esfandyar, would find Death. The wise men responded that the prince would find death in Seistan, from an arrow sent forth from the bow of Rostam the Mighty. Goshtasp decided that, as soon as Esfandyar returned to Persia, he would do his best to hasten his son's destiny.

It came to pass that, once Esfandyar was victorious in his tasks, he returned in triumph to King Goshtasp. "Father, in the past I defeated Arjasp and his Demon-warriors; I conquered many kingdoms in the names of Zardosht and Urmazd; I rescued my brother; and I freed Persia from Arjasp's tyranny," he declared. "Now, I have successfully completed the Seven Stages; I have rescued my sisters from the Brass Fortress; I have destroyed Arjasp and his Demon-warriors and brought you their treasures; and I have even won other wealthy provinces for your empire!

"Surely, having done all that you have asked of me, you will finally be true to your word! Please give me your crown and your throne, and make me king of Persia as you have promised!" Esfandyar exclaimed.

Chapter 4

Goshtasp plots Esfandyar's death.

To these words, King Goshtasp responded, "Esfandyar, it is because you are now the world's greatest hero and the shield of the Persian king that I have one more task for you. Rostam the Mighty, whom men call Tahamtan, has become too arrogant for Persia's good, and for his own good as well! He refused my command to be my shield against the king of Turan, denying that Dastan's kingdoms owe allegiance to the king of Persia."

"Therefore," Goshtasp declared, "I command you to bring the Champion of the World before me, chained hand and foot like a slave, so that he will recognize that both his life and his death are in my hands! Use force, use strategy, or use magic—I do not care which!—But subdue him! Do this, and I promise that I will give you my crown and my throne and make you king of Persia!"

"Do not ask this of me, Father!" Esfandyar exclaimed. "Tahamtan has been the glory of Persia for hundreds of years, and you have even been his guest and friend! Ask me to conquer any other ruler on the face of the earth, and, as swiftly as fire in a gale-wind, I will do it. But I will not do this! I will even give up the crown and throne of Persia, if I must!"

"Esfandyar, what you must do is obey your father—without question, and without comment!" the king replied. "And do not let me see you before you have brought Rostam to me!"

"Alas, Father!" Esfandyar exclaimed. "Obviously you do not want me to have your crown and throne, and so you have devised this task as a way to kill me! Every hero who has ever contested with Tahamtan has died, so my blood will be on your head! Yet, I am yours to command, and I will carry out your wishes."

So it came to pass that Esfandyar set forth with his son Bahman and the king's warriors. When they had traveled but a short distance, Esfandyar's camel lay down and refused to rise. Fearing an evil omen, the hero beheaded his camel and commanded the caravan to continue on to Seistan.

However, when Esfandyar arrived in Seistan, Rostam was away on a hunting trip in the mountains, so Esfandyar sent Bahman to find him and give him the king's message. Bahman traveled until he saw a group of Persians gathered around an old warrior who appeared to be as large as a small mountain. Knowing that this must be Tahamtan, and fearing for his father's life should any contest occur between them, Bahman climbed high above the hunting party, dislodged a huge boulder, and sent it crashing down upon the group below. Hearing the noise of thunder while standing beneath the sun's bright shield, Rostam looked up, spied the boulder, rose to his feet, and then kicked it far out upon the plain.

When Bahman arrived and delivered King Goshtasp's message, fury flooded Tahamtan's heart, but he lassoed his anger and courteously replied, "Noble Youth, tell your father that I look forward to meeting a hero who has brought glory to Persia. However, only Demons would demand that I subject myself to being a slave! And to try to force me will be like trying to confine a winter wind within a cage! I will forfeit my life before I bring such enduring shame upon my name!

"Instead," Rostam declared, "I invite your father to be my guest, and together we will return to King Goshtasp in friendship. When I talk with the king, his anger will disappear like the morning mist under the sun's bright blade."

Rostam returned to Seistan in order to welcome Esfandyar personally, but Esfandyar said to him, "I am not free to offer my hand in friendship, Tahamtan! And my task prevents me from eating your bread and salt, as much as I would like to do so! For if you will not come with me in chains, then we must fight each other in single combat, and if I have become your guest, then I cannot both keep my honor and fight against you."

"My heart floods with sorrow when I think that we two might have to fight each other," he explained, "but if I do not obey Goshtasp's commands, I have offended my father and king in this life, and Urmazd after my death. I would not act so as to bring dishonor upon myself in both worlds—even for you, Tahamtan!"

Esfandyar then did his best, through deed and word, to insult Rostam, thereby provoking combat between them. So it came to pass that sorrow also flooded Rostam's heart, for he knew that nothing he could say or do would change Esfandyar's mind.

"I will suffer no matter which choice I make!" Rostam exclaimed to his brother. "If I permit Esfandyar to lead me before King Goshtasp bound in chains, then I tarnish my glory by letting him imprison me, and no water can wash off such a stain upon my honor. Yet, if I kill this young hero in combat, I will also dishonor my name because I will have killed the king of Persia's son just because he insulted me."

So it came to pass that Tahamtan said to Esfandyar, "You give me no choice but to meet you in single combat tomorrow. But I fear that your father is bringing an evil fate upon you, for he is insisting that you combat a champion who has never yet lost a battle! Reconsider while you can, and agree to let me go in friendship with you to your father! Only a foolish youth would rush forth to meet my mighty mace, for there he meets Death as well!"

"My father is the king of Persia!" Esfandyar exclaimed. "Where is your respect, Tahamtan? Surely you do not expect to persuade me to disobey him! It is you who have much to consider before we prepare for combat. Are you now so old that your eyes shun the sight of the sun's bright blade? Are you now so tired that you long for the hard, cold bed of Death? Think well upon these questions, for if you face me in battle tomorrow, your eyes will look their last upon that blade, and the grave will become your lasting bed!"

When the sun's bright shield had sunk from sight, Esfandyar returned to his brother, who pleaded with him to avoid battle with Rostam. "Remember that Tahamtan is the champion of our people and the Shield of Persia!" he exclaimed.

However, Esfandyar responded, "Do not try to stop me! Tahamtan is a thorn, both in my ambition and in my faith. Unless I bring him to Father in chains, Father will not give me his crown and his throne, and I will never become the king of Persia. And Zardosht teaches that whoever disobeys his king is tortured upon his death. I bear Rostam no ill will, and I certainly have no wish to hurt him. But I dare not disobey Father's command!"

Chapter 5

Esfandyar and Rostam meet in single combat.

THE FIRST DAY

So it came to pass that when the sun next raised his shining shield, scattering the armies of night and brightening the earth with its brilliant light, Tahamtan called Esfandyar to combat. The two champions, one a youth and the other heavy with age, fought long and hard, first with their spears, until they were bent beyond use; next with their swords, until they were broken; and then with their war-clubs, until the maces had ripped their shields, pierced their armor, and dented their helmets. They wrestled, as each warrior tried to unseat the other from his horse, but just as mighty mountains withstand the blows of winter winds, so each warrior remained firmly planted on his horse.

Finally, with their throats choked with dust, their bodies dripping with sweat, their arms too worn to lift a weapon, and their horses exhausted, Tahamtan and Esfandyar stopped for a short respite. While they were resting, Bahman arrived with the news that two of his brothers had just been killed in battle against the warriors of Seistan.

"So, I see that old age destroys honor!" Esfandyar exclaimed, his heart flooding with fury and vengeance. "A plague on you, Rostam, and on your house of heroes for this treachery!"

Rostam's voice shook like leaves in an autumn wind as he responded, "I swear, by Urmazd and by all that I hold dear, that I know nothing about this! I will give you whoever is to blame, even if it is Dastan, my father!"

"No, villain!" Esfandyar exclaimed. "Only your own blood will avenge my sons' murder!"

And with these words, Esfandyar drew his bow and showered Tahamtan with sixty arrows, each of which left a great wound. Tahamtan was powerless against the assault, for his arrows fell from Esfandyar like water.

Esfandyar, seeing that his foe was seriously injured, smiled and exclaimed, "Surrender, Tahamtan, or I must kill you! Let me take you in chains to King Goshtasp!"

Noting with relief that the sun's bright shield was sinking from sight, Rostam announced, "Enough for today! It is time to rest!"

To these words, Esfandyar replied, "Is Rostam the Mighty, whom men call Tahamtan, now fleeing from battle? Where is the raging lion, the valiant chieftain of old? Where is your mighty arm? Has old age stolen your great name as well as your noble character?"

Tahamtan lassoed his anger at these words and replied, "Not at all! You will see for yourself when the sun's blade again brightens the earth!"

THE FIRST NIGHT

And with these words, the two warriors parted, the old man to recover his strength and seek help for his wounds, and the young man to marvel at Tahamtan's courage and strength.

Esfandyar returned to his brother and said, "Tahamtan must be made of iron or stone! For ordinary weapons cannot wound him! If it were not for my own charmed arrows, given to me as a prophet of Urmazd, I could never be victorious against him!"

However, it came to pass that Rostam, too, had access to charms. When White-haired Zal saw his son so sorely wounded, he said, "Let hope now push all fear and despair from your heart, my son! I still have the golden breast-feather which the Bird of Marvel gave me as its parting gift when it returned me to my father so long ago. It told me to burn it in time of need, so I will now toss it upon the flames."

He tossed it on the fire and waited, alternating between fear and hope. Quick as dust in the wind, a dark cloud wafted into the room, and Zal found himself looking into the eyes of the simurgh.

"Dastan, my son, what has happened that you need me?" it asked.

"My son Rostam is so wounded as to be close to death, as is his great war-horse," Zal replied, "and I can do nothing to heal either of them."

"My wings will heal them both," the Bird of Marvel replied.

So it came to pass that the simurgh first healed Rakhsh by drawing out the arrows with its golden beak and brushing its feathers over his gaping wounds. Then it healed Rostam by sucking the poison from his wounds and closing them.

"Wondrous nurse!" Rostam exclaimed. "Can you give me any magic power to use against Esfandyar?"

To these words, the Bird of Marvel replied, "Great son of Dastan, why have you chosen to fight against a hero who is the beloved of Zardosht? It would bring no shame upon your name if you were to bow before this son of King Goshtasp! Esfandyar has Urmazd's blessing! The further you stay from his invincible arm, the better! If you promise to try, once again, to get him to listen to you, I will give you what help I can, but I cannot save your life!"

"It is written in the stars that whoever succeeds in spilling Esfandyar's blood is doomed to a joyless life and an early death," the simurgh explained. "But, if you are prepared to take this fate upon yourself, bring a sharp dagger and come with me. I will teach you how to subdue your foe. And, if the stars reveal that now is his time to die, you will succeed."

"Surely, given who I am, the stars have decreed a painful death for me, no matter what I choose! Therefore, I will go with you," Rostam declared.

So it came to pass that the simurgh, as swiftly as clouds before a storm, took Rostam on a long journey to the shore of a great sea, next to which a garden grew. Brushing one of its feathers across Rostam's eyes, the simurgh took him to a tall tamarisk tree. "Choose a long, straight, flexible branch, the one best suited to become the shaft of an arrow, for Esfandyar's fate is bound to it. Remove the branch, harden it in fire, and feather it well with three feathers. Make the point into a forked arrow, and place two good arrowheads upon it. Then soak the point in grape juice," it commanded.

"Except for his eyes, Esfandyar's body cannot be injured by any weapon," the simurgh advised. "Therefore, if he continues to ignore your best efforts to make peace between you, prepare your bow, and aim the twin arrowheads at his eyes. If it is written in the stars that you are destined to kill Esfandyar at this time, your arrowheads will pierce his eyes, giving him a fatal wound."

"But having taught you this," the Bird of Marvel concluded, "I advise you to make peace with him so that you will avoid great sorrow in your own life!"

With these words, the simurgh, as swiftly as clouds before a storm, transported Rostam back to Zal's palace, where Rostam prepared the special arrow.

THE SECOND DAY

When the sun next raised his shining shield, scattering the armies of night and brightening the earth with its brilliant light, Tahamtan rode forth to battle. It came to pass that Esfandyar was so certain that he had killed Rostam the Mighty, that Tahamtan had to awaken him.

"Greetings, Old Champion!" the young hero exclaimed. "I see that Dastan is a master of magic! The wounds I gave you yesterday should have killed you and Rakhsh! You will wish for his magic today too, but by the time I have finished with you, it will be too late even for a Demon's tricks!"

To these words, Rostam replied, "Master of Archery! No arrow can hurt me! However, I have come, not to fight you, but, once again, to offer my friendship. Accept my hospitality, and I will accompany you to your father, freely and unchained, where I will make peace with him."

"It seems that you never tire of singing the same song!" Esfandyar exclaimed. "Nor do I! You must choose between the chains of bondage and Death! If I disobey the commands of my father, I give up both the crown and throne of Persia and the path to Urmazd. This I will never do! So, prepare for combat! But know that, before the sun's bright shield sinks from sight, I will kill you!"

So it came to pass that Tahamtan prepared his bow with the tamarisk arrow and then offered a silent prayer to Urmazd. "Oh, Creator of the World, you who move the hearts of mortals," he prayed. "See how I have tried my best to avoid this fight, and do not punish me for the blood I am about to spill!"

"You hesitate, I see!" Esfandyar exclaimed. "Is the old champion afraid to meet the young hero once again on the plain of battle?"

These words roused Tahamtan to fury like a wolf. As swiftly as clouds before a storm, he raised his bow, took aim, and released the fatal arrow. Quick as fire in a gale-wind, the arrow flew straight to its target, piercing Esfandyar's eyes.

Overcome with suffering, Esfandyar's world turned black before his eyes, causing him to drop his bow and fall from his horse upon the ground. Then, his mind cleared, and he called Tahamtan to his side.

As bloody tears from his heart fell upon the face of the young hero he had killed, Rostam said to him, "The bitter seeds you have sown have become a harvest of bitter fruit!"

"Oh, Rostam!" Esfandyar exclaimed. "Do not weep. For my father, not you, bears the blame for my death today! Father listened to Ahriman's wicked whisperings and sent me here to die. And Urmazd will curse him for it! But, surely this was written in the stars in the heavens, and what is written there is sure to come! You are only the arm of fate.

"In my heart, I never wanted to kill you!" Esfandyar declared. "I have loved you from the time I first heard your name and learned of your great deeds. My goal has always been to be just like you! But my father gave me no choice!

"Now, I want you to take Bahman, my son, and prepare him for the glory of Persia, just as you are preparing your own son Faramarz," Esfandyar concluded. "Teach him the arts of war and the banquet. Then, when Goshtasp dies, give him the crown and throne of Persia, and be his counselor. As for me, I curse my father's name and his Demon's heart! For I die the victim of his hatred!"

So it came to pass that Esfandyar died. His brother led the funeral procession out of Seistan and back to King Goshtasp. He walked next to Esfandyar's riderless horse, with its shorn mane and tail and the hero's armor hanging from its reversed saddle, and they were followed by the camel which carried Esfandyar's coffin.

Who among us can escape our fate? Who among us can use our wisdom, or our courage, or our strength, or our skill to this end? No one. What is written in the stars in the heavens is sure to come! So it was with Esfandyar. So it is with all who walk the earth!

❧ QUESTIONS FOR
Response, Discussion, and Analysis

1. Why does Ferdowsi (or his source) give Esfandyar the challenge of "The Seven Stages"?

2. Given the simurgh's advice, is Rostam supposed to go in chains to Goshtasp? Why or why not?

3. To what extent, if any, are the following responsible for Esfandyar's death? Who is most responsible? (a) Esfandyar; (b) Rostam; (c) Goshtasp; (d) the simurgh

4. Goshtasp and Esfandyar are Zoroastrian in their religious beliefs. Consequently, they should be committed to good thoughts, good words, and good deeds. To what extent, if any, do they remain true to these principles? Explain who is to blame for their relationship and how their problems could have been avoided.

5. Tragic heroes are good human beings whose greatest strength becomes their greatest weakness in that it leads them to act imprudently, without thinking of the consequences of their actions. Often, they belatedly realize how their own attitudes and actions brought their tragic fate upon themselves. What characteristics, if any, does Esfandyar possess that cause his tragic experiences with Goshtasp and Rostam? To what extent, if any, is Esfandyar a tragic hero?

6. What is the connection between Fate and prophecy in this legend? What does the prophecy about Esfandyar's death contribute to the legend? How does such a prophecy affect the legend's tone?

7. What does the simurgh contribute to this legend?

8. How does a person's view that every aspect of his or her life is predetermined affect how such a person might live life? What are the advantages and disadvantages of this world-view?

9. Repetition is characteristic of oral literature. How does Ferdowsi use this technique? What does it contribute to this legend?

Greece and Rome

The myths of Greece have earned universal fame and popularity. Recorded as early as approximately 775 B.C. (Homer's *Iliad*), and approximately 725 B.C. (Hesiod's *Theogony*), they reveal a universe that closely resembles our own. Their gods, their heroes, and their depiction of the human condition are consistent with our knowledge of human behavior.

The Greek gods are a large family, and each member of that family has a distinct personality. Love, hate, jealousy, and pride motivate their behavior just as those feelings motivate human behavior. The gods who first rule the universe are overthrown by Zeus. Zeus, along with his brothers, sisters, and children, then rules the world of human beings.

Zeus's sister, Demeter, and their daughter, Persephone, prefer the simple beauties of the earth to the majestic palaces of the gods on Mount Olympus. When Zeus's brother, Hades, abducts Persephone, we experience with Demeter the plight of every mother who has lost her beloved daughter. We also feel their bittersweet emotions when they are reunited: joy that they are together again and sorrow that their relationship will never be the same again.

Zeus expects human beings to conform to an unwritten code of respectable behavior. When King Lycaon and his nobility lose their respect for the gods and for other human beings, Zeus destroys almost the entire race with a flood. However, he promises to create another race in its place, and he keeps his word.

According to Hesiod, Zeus also created five races of human beings, each worse than the race that preceded it. People today speak of "the good old days" and wonder whether the human race will survive. Hesiod had the same concerns. It is interesting to compare his description of his generation with the prevailing attitudes of people today.

Heracles, whom the Romans called Hercules, is the most famous Greek hero. His accomplishments were so great that his name continues to be attached to any great task that humans face today. His courage, his strength, and his skill in the face of adversity provide a model of behavior for all of us.

Many other famous heroes walk through the pages of Homer's *Iliad*. Achilles and Agamemnon, among the Greeks, and Hector, among the Trojans, must choose between their own desires and the needs of their people. Their war is ancient, but their agony is modern. Once again, the courage with which they meet the challenges in their lives makes them impressive, yet very human, models of behavior for all of us.

The myth of *Jason and the Golden Fleece* was well known in ancient Greece. In Homer's *Odyssey,* from the eighth century B.C., the goddess Circe tells

Odysseus that the adventures of the Argonauts are known to all who walk the earth. However, we know the myth of Jason and the Argonauts primarily through Apollonius Rhodius's *Argonautica,* a Hellenistic epic from the third century B.C. Here, Apollonius depicts the youthful Jason and Medea who, in their maturity, will become the Jason and Medea made famous by Euripides. Apollonius's epic is a tale of youthful heroism and love. Jason is more human than traditional heroes, such as Heracles. Jason is successful because he is pragmatic and prudent. Being a man of words rather than a man of deeds, he is able to persuade others to use their courage, strength, and skill on his behalf. Medea's love for Jason in *The Argonautica* has given posterity one of the world's great love stories. Virgil so admired Apollonius's depiction of the maiden whose passion leads her to sacrifice family, home, and country for a heroic stranger that he adapted it for his own depiction of Dido in *The Aeneid.*

The myth of *Medea* has roots both in ancient Corinth, where Medea plays a prominent role in an eighth century B.C. epic about Corinth's heroic history, and in ancient Colchis (former Soviet Georgia). Medea is one of the greatest women in all of literature. Euripides' depiction of her in his *Medea,* a tragedy from the fifth century B.C., has continued to capture the human heart. When Jason leaves Medea for a younger woman, Medea loses whatever rights and privileges she had as Jason's wife. Her universal appeal resides in the depth of her outrage against injustice and the extent to which she is willing to rebel against it. Medea's many literary children continue to confront her issues in their own time and place. Jason's self-serving ambition is as destructive as Medea's passion for revenge. Therefore, it is interesting to evaluate Jason as a tragic hero, both from an Aristotelian and from a contemporary point of view.

Pyramus and Thisbe, Ovid's famous myth from ancient Rome (written at the start of the first century A.D.), involves thwarted adolescent love. The myth has inspired love stories that, in turn, have inspired related love stories. Best known are William Shakespeare's version of the myth in *A Midsummer Night's Dream* and *Romeo and Juliet.*

The Romans adopted the Greek gods and their myths. Virgil wrote his own myth, *The Aeneid,* to glorify Augustus Caesar and the founding of Rome. *The Aeneid* begins shortly after Homer's *Iliad* ends, and it describes the adventures of the Trojan hero Aeneas. Because Virgil patterned his epic upon Homer's two epics, it is interesting to compare the works of these two great authors, particularly their concept of the hero. Virgil's dramatic portrayal of the destruction of Troy is one of the most powerful descriptions in all of literature, and Aeneas' love, Queen Dido of Carthage, is one of the world's most noble heroines.

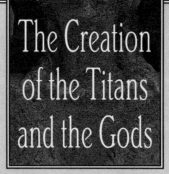

The Creation of the Titans and the Gods

Creation, according to the Greeks, moves from a mother-dominated society, in which the most important divinities are female, to a father-dominated society, in which the most important divinities are male. Just as the human family progresses through time from generation to generation, so the divine family, which was created in the image of the human family, moves from the rule of the parents, to the rule of the children, to the rule of the grandchildren.

Gaea, who is Mother Earth, is the first Great Goddess or Mother Goddess. The peoples who were living in Greece when the Bronze Age tribes invaded the land worshipped the Great Goddess because they were farmers, and the fertility of the earth was of prime importance to them. Their survival depended upon their ability to raise enough food to sustain them through the nonproductive months of the year, and upon their ability to have enough children to assure the continuity of their clan. These people drew a connection between a woman's ability to give birth to children and the earth's ability to "give birth" to all plants. Therefore, the earth spirit was feminine, and the principal divinities that the early Greeks worshipped were also feminine.

When Uranus becomes ruler of the world, his son, Cronus, dismembers him—just as priestesses of the Great Goddess or Mother Goddess in the female-oriented religion dismembered the sacred king. They used his blood, which they considered to be a prime source of fertility, to fertilize the soil so that it would produce an abundance of crops. Uranus' blood, too, produces "crops," in the form of monstrous offspring. In the matriarchal, or mother-dominated, society, a son owes a greater loyalty to his mother than to his father.

When Cronus becomes ruler of the world, the divine family is in transition from the mother-dominated society to the father-dominated society that will follow under the rule of Zeus. Rhea is a Great Goddess or Mother Goddess, just as Gaea, her mother, is. In the contest for power between husband and wife, Cronus is winning until Rhea solicits the help of her mother. Then the females win. Yet, Rhea uses her son, Zeus, to carry out her plan, and with her approval, he becomes the next principal ruler, even though he is male. He will rule with greater authority than either Uranus or Cronus did.

Cronus disposes of his infant children by eating them. Cannibalism is not unusual in history. Primitive people believed that they could acquire desirable characteristics—such as courage, strength, wisdom, and skill—by eating the important organs of another creature, often a fearsome enemy, who had possessed those characteristics. Consequently, early peoples might eat the meat of an animal they had killed, or they might drink the blood or eat the heart of the person who, until they killed him, had been a great enemy. In the matriarchal society, the priestesses would eat the flesh of the sacred king in order to acquire his fertility.

Hesiod tells this myth in the *Theogony*.

PRINCIPAL GODS (ROMAN NAMES ARE IN PARENTHESES)

THE FIRST GENERATION

GAEA: first Great Goddess or Mother Goddess in Greek mythology; Mother Earth, who nourishes all life

URANUS: son and husband of Gaea; ruler of the sky

THE SECOND GENERATION: CHILDREN OF GAEA AND URANUS

HUNDRED-HANDED GIANTS: triplets; best known: Briareus

CYCLOPES: triplets; one-eyed metalsmiths; servants of Zeus

TITANS: thirteen; race of immortals who, with their children, ruled the universe before the gods conquered them:

CRONUS (Saturn): youngest child; god of the sky after Uranus and ruler of the Titans; father of the first six Greek gods: Zeus, Poseidon, Hades, Hera, Demeter, and Hestia

RHEA (Cybele): sister and wife of Cronus; a Great Goddess or Mother Goddess like Gaea; mother of Zeus, Poseidon, Hades, Hera, Demeter, and Hestia

HELIOS: god of the sun before being replaced by Apollo in late Greek and Roman mythology

SELENE: goddess of the Moon before being replaced by Artemis in late Greek and Roman mythology

THEMIS: goddess of prophecy at Delphi before Apollo conquered her oracle

ATLAS: strongest Titan; condemned by Zeus eternally to hold up the sky

PROMETHEUS: most creative and intelligent Titan; created mortal man out of clay

EPIMETHEUS: brother of Prometheus; husband of Pandora (the first mortal woman)

THE THIRD GENERATION: THE GREEK GODS

Children of Cronus and Rhea

ZEUS (Jupiter, Jove): youngest, most intelligent, and most powerful child; lord of the sky after Cronus; ruler of the gods; maintains order in the world of mortals; protects strangers and guests

POSEIDON (Neptune): brother of Zeus; lord of the sea; causes earthquakes

HADES (Pluto): brother of Zeus; ruler of the Underworld; lord of the dead

HERA (Juno): sister and wife of Zeus; queen of Olympus; goddess of marriage and childbirth

DEMETER (Ceres): sister of Zeus; a Great Goddess or Mother Goddess like Rhea and Gaea; goddess of grain

HESTIA (Vesta): sister of Zeus; kindest and most loved of the gods; guardian of the home

Immortal Children of Zeus

APOLLO: twin of Artemis; god of prophecy, medicine, archery, and music; god of the sun in late Greek and Roman mythology

ARTEMIS (Diana): twin of Apollo; goddess of the hunt; goddess of the moon in late Greek and Roman mythology

ATHENA (Minerva): goddess of arts and crafts and defensive war; helper of heroes; goddess of wisdom in late Greek and Roman mythology

APHRODITE (Venus): goddess of beauty and sexual desire

PERSEPHONE (Proserpine): wife of Hades; queen of the Underworld

THE FATES: CLOTHO, LACHESIS, and ATROPOS: determine the length of each mortal's life

ARES (Mars): god of war

HEPHAESTUS (Vulcan): husband of Aphrodite; metalsmith of the gods, famous for his creativity and skill

HERMES (Mercury): Zeus' messenger; guides travelers and leads shades of the dead into the Underworld; helps merchants and thieves

THE CREATION OF THE TITANS AND THE GODS

Out of the original emptiness, which was called Chaos, emerged the first three immortal beings: Gaea (Mother Earth), Tartarus, who ruled the deepest, darkest region of the Underworld, and Eros (Love), whose great beauty inspired the creation of many of the deathless gods. Then Gaea, without any partner, gave birth to Uranus (Father Sky). She made him her equal, so that he would surround her on all sides and would provide a home for the immortal beings. Gaea also gave birth to Ourea (Mountains) and Pontus (Sea).

Gaea then married Uranus, and he ruled over all that came into being. The first immortal children of Gaea and Uranus were the three Hundred-Handed Giants. Each Giant had fifty heads and fifty arms extending from each shoulder.

Their next immortal children were the three Cyclopes. Each Cyclops had only one eye, set in the middle of his forehead. They were expert craftsmen, and they later built the palaces for the gods on Mount Olympus.

Uranus feared the terrible strength of these six children, and he hated them because they terrified him. So as each child was born, Uranus took him from his mother, bound him, and hurled him deep into Gaea's being, the earth. Each child fell for nine days and nine nights, finally landing in the region named after its ruler, Tartarus, on the tenth day. There Uranus kept the Hundred-Handed Giants and the Cyclopes, far from the surface of the earth and the light of the sun. His eyes now shone with pride and satisfaction, for he ruled without fear of any challenge to his authority, and he expected to rule forever.

Gaea was outraged by her husband's actions. She longed for her children, and she hated Uranus for what he had done to them. However, she buried her feelings deep in her heart and quietly waited for the time when she could take revenge.

The next immortal children born to Gaea and Uranus were the thirteen Titans. They and their children became the oldest generation of Greek gods. Helios was the god of the sun and drove it across the sky in his chariot. Selene was the goddess of the moon. Oceanus was the god of the river that surrounded the earth. Like her mother, Gaea, Themis was the goddess of prophecy at Delphi. Cronus married his sister Rhea, a goddess of the earth, and in time they became the parents of the Greek gods. Later, Atlas, by far the strongest of the Titans, held up the sky so that it would not fall upon the earth. Soon thereafter, Prometheus, the most intelligent and clever Titan, created mortal man out of clay and water. His brother, Epimetheus, married Pandora, the first mortal woman.

Gaea decided to use her Titan children as her means of revenge against Uranus. She took a large piece of flint and shaped it into a huge, sharp stone sickle. Then she approached her sons and said, "I want you to punish your father, for he is very cruel. He has imprisoned your brothers in the land of Tartarus against my wishes and against their will."

Almost all of Gaea's sons were so terrified of Uranus that they listened to her command in silence and refused to obey her. But Cronus, the youngest Titan, was very similar to his father in temperament, and he was much more courageous than his brothers. When he saw their reaction, he said, "If no one else will help you, Mother, I certainly will! If our father has been cruel to you and to our brothers, we should take revenge!"

When she heard Cronus's words, Gaea's heart overflowed with pride and satisfaction. It was gratifying to have one son who had the courage to help her. Now Uranus would learn what it was like to endure endless suffering!

So Gaea put the great flint sickle into Cronus's hands. She warned him to be careful with its sharp curved blade. Then she told him where to hide and what she wanted him to do. Later, when Helios had drawn the chariot of the sun across the sky and had retired for the night, Uranus joined his wife by the shore of the sea and lay down to sleep with her.

Selene shed the light of the moon upon the sleeping figure of Uranus. Cronus, from his place of hiding, raised the huge stone sickle and emasculated his father. Then he quickly threw the severed pieces into the sea and said, "Your reign is over, Father! Now I shall reign in your place. You may challenge me, but my power is clearly greater than yours. So, I advise you to submit to your fate."

Uranus, being immortal, could not die. However, he screamed in agony, for his immortality did not prevent him from feeling excruciating pain. Part of his anguish came from the realization that his power had suddenly ended.

From Uranus's blood, which flowed into the earth, Gaea brought forth the three black-clothed Furies. With eyes that dripped poisonous tears and breath that was too foul to bear, these immortal goddesses drove to insanity any child who killed one of his parents.

From the same blood, Gaea also brought forth another group of terrible beings, who were simply called the Giants. They looked fearsome, with their hairy heads and faces and their dragonlike feet. When they wore their shining armor and carried their long spears, they appeared to be invincible.

The severed pieces of Uranus's immortal body remained in the sea, where a white foam surrounded them. In time, Aphrodite, the goddess of beauty and sexual desire, was born from them, and she was often called the foam-born goddess.

Cronus became god of the sky, as his father had been before him. Like his father, he feared the Hundred-Handed Giants and the Cyclopes, so he ignored his promise to Gaea and kept his brothers bound and imprisoned in Tartarus.

Gaea, disappointed and angry, watched and waited for the next opportunity to free her children. Being a goddess of prophecy, she enjoyed informing Cronus that one day a son of his would overpower him just as he had overpowered his own father.

"I shall fool the Fates!" he exclaimed to himself, with a clever smile. "If I do not have any children, then I will be able to rule forever!"

However, it was not so easy to change his destiny. Cronus loved his wife, Rhea, and in time she gave birth to a lovely daughter, Hestia. When Rhea proudly presented their baby daughter to Cronus, the words of his fate screamed inside Cronus's head! His great fear of losing power brought a mad, distraught glint into his eyes. Without considering whether the baby was female or male, Cronus took the baby lovingly from his wife, opened his gigantic mouth, and swallowed the infant in one gulp. "Now," he thought with satisfaction, "I have cheated the Fates of their prophecy and my child of his throne!"

Four more children were born to Cronus and Rhea: Demeter, Hera, Hades, and Poseidon. Each time Cronus embraced the infant so lovingly that Rhea was certain he would accept this child. However, each time the glint of madness would steal into his eyes as the words of the prophecy roared in his ears, and each time he would open his gigantic mouth and swallow the infant in one gulp. Then, once again, Cronus would grin with satisfaction and think to himself, "I have cheated the Fates of their prophecy and my child of his throne!"

By this time, Rhea's heart was overflowing with grief. When she was about to give birth to her sixth child, she went to Gaea and said, "Mother, please help me! Cronus has robbed me of our children just as Uranus robbed you of the Hundred-Handed Giants and the Cyclopes. I cannot bear to let him steal this baby too! What can I do? Can we hide the infant from Cronus before he sees it? How can I trick him?"

Gaea replied, "My heart understands your pain, my daughter, and I think I can help you. I know that Cronus is destined to be overpowered by his son just as he overpowered his father before him. Surely the child about to be born to you is the son who is destined to take revenge upon Cronus for his treatment of his father, his brothers, and his own children.

"When your time to give birth arrives," Gaea counseled her daughter, "go to the island of Crete and take refuge in the deep, hidden cave high on the slopes of Mount Dicte. I shall see that nymphs nurse your infant son with goat's milk, and I will have them hang his cradle from a tree so that Cronus will not be able to find him on land, or sea, or in the air. Young boys, the Curetes, will march beneath his cradle, clanging their spears against their bronze shields to smother the sound of his cries.

"And as for how to trick Cronus," Gaea concluded, "he is so crazed with fear that an ordinary rock should be all you need to fool him!"

So it came about that Rhea gave birth to the infant, Zeus, in the cave of Mount Dicte, on Crete. She left her mother, Gaea, in charge of the baby and quickly returned home. She then found a rock about the size of her newborn infant and wrapped it in swaddling clothes as if it were an infant. Soon Cronus entered the room.

"How are you feeling?" he asked her sweetly. "Let me admire our latest child. Not every infant is born into such a royal family!"

Rhea forced herself to think of the fate of her other five children as she handed the well-wrapped rock over to her husband. As usual, Cronus took the bundle she gave him and lovingly embraced it. Then the words of the prophecy screamed in his head, and the look of madness shone forth from his eyes. Beside himself with fear of his destiny, Cronus opened his gigantic mouth and swallowed the rock in one gulp. "Now," he said to himself, smiling with the greatest satisfaction and relief, "once again, I have cheated the Fates of their prophecy and my child of his throne! I shall rule forever, after all!"

Years passed, and Zeus became a mature god. Cronus never realized that a son had escaped his eye and evaded his gigantic mouth. He ruled untroubled and unthreatened, never thinking that his destiny might be rapidly approaching.

One day when Cronus was thirsty, Rhea gave him a delicious drink. He was delighted and asked for more. A young stranger walked in and handed him the cup, and Cronus had swallowed the drink before it occurred to him that he had never seen the young man before.

"Who is he?" he wondered. "Why should he have brought me the drink? Why does my stomach feel so strange? Did I drink too much? Was the second drink different from the first drink? What if he has poisoned me?"

Suddenly, Cronus felt an excruciating pain in his stomach. He vomited up the rock, followed by Poseidon, Hades, Hera, Demeter, and Hestia, all of whom were fully grown by now.

Rhea then entered the room, with the young stranger, Zeus, by her side. "Your destiny is upon you, Cronus!" she exclaimed. "The Fates prophesied that a son would overpower you just as you overpowered your own father. That son, Zeus, now stands before you. You are reaping the fruits of the seeds you sowed when you swallowed our children and kept your brothers in chains in Tartarus! We will now see whether Zeus will rule with more intelligence and kindness than you did. Your mind has been as blind and your heart as hard as that rock you swallowed!"

"If this stranger, son of mine or not, thinks that he is going to take my kingdom from me, he is not as intelligent as you seem to think he is!" Cronus responded. "Anyone who wants to rule in my place will have to fight me, and all of the other Titans, too!"

So it came to pass that Zeus and his brothers and sisters, the first Greek gods, waged war against Cronus and the Titans who allied themselves with him. The gods and the Titans were so evenly matched in numbers and in strength that they fought for ten years without victory for either side.

Finally, Gaea, who had given Zeus the poisoned drink to give his father, helped Zeus once again. She told him about her lost children, the Hundred-Handed Giants and the Cyclopes, whom Uranus and Cronus had kept imprisoned beneath the ground at the borders of the earth, and how they were chained in grief and sorrow, far from the light of Helios and the companionship of the deathless gods. She prophesied that the gods would win their war if they brought the Hundred-Handed Giants and the Cyclopes up from Tartarus as their allies.

Zeus and his brothers went down to Tartarus to rescue Gaea's children and encourage their alliance. Once they had killed the guard, removed their uncles' bonds, and fed them, Zeus said, "Listen to these words from my heart. We have been fighting the Titans for ten years without success. If you will repay our kindness to you by fighting on our side, your great strength will make us victorious."

To these words one of the Hundred-Handed Giants replied, "We know that you are fighting to defend the deathless gods from the cruelty of Titan rulers. And we know what it is to be the victims of Titan power. Had you not freed us, we were doomed to face an eternity of darkness, bondage, and isolation. Uranus and his son Cronus do not understand suffering and know nothing of mercy. We know that you will rule the world with greater wisdom. Of course we will fight with you against the Titan tyrant!"

Then one of the Cyclopes said, "In return for our freedom, we present each of you with a special gift. To you, Zeus, we give the gift of thunder and lightning in the form of a thunderbolt, an invincible weapon against any enemy. We will make more of these for you when we set up on Mount Olympus.

"To you, Poseidon," he continued, "we give the trident. Not only is it a superior fishing spear, but you will find it a most effective device for shaking the earth and creating waves at sea. Until then, its three barbed prongs will make it a useful weapon against the Titans.

"And to you, Hades," he concluded, "we give the helmet of invisibility. In times to come, the hero Perseus will need your weapon to kill the monstrous Gorgon, Medusa. Until then, it will serve you well against Cronus and his Titan allies."

With high spirits, Zeus and his allies returned to the upper world and renewed the battle. The Hundred-Handed Giants broke cliffs off the mountains until they had a huge crag in each of their multitude of hands. Then they pelted the Titans with their stone weapons.

The Titans responded with arrows and spears. The combatants could not kill each other, for they were all immortal beings. However, they could injure and overpower one another. The battle caused an upheaval across the earth and sea. The mountains quaked, and even Tartarus felt the impact of the mighty rocks upon the earth high above him.

Then Zeus hurled his invincible lightning bolt, which engulfed in flames whatever it touched. The earth resounded with the roars of mighty thunder as the blazing woods and the scalding sea scorched the air. Finally, the Titans fled beneath the earth into Tartarus, where the Hundred-Handed Giants placed them in chains for eternity in that dark, dismal land. Zeus then commanded the Hundred-Handed Giants to guard the hated Titans forever. However, because of his size and his strength, Zeus forced the Titan Atlas hold up the sky upon his shoulders. The war was over.

When the three male gods drew lots for their kingdoms, Zeus drew the sky, Poseidon the sea, and Hades the Underworld. In addition to maintaining peace and order among all of the immortal beings in the world, Zeus taught human beings to be just in their treatment of one another. Those who did not respect the deathless gods and other mortals were severely punished. Poseidon could use his trident to cause earthquakes as well as storms at sea, but he also taught mortals how to tame horses to work for them and how to build ships. Hades taught mortals to have respect for the dead by conducting proper funeral ceremonies and following certain burial practices.

Zeus married his sister Hera, who became the goddess of marriage and childbirth as well as queen of Olympus. Hestia became the guardian of the home and taught mortals how to build houses. Demeter became the goddess of grain. She taught mortals how to save the kernels of wild corn, plant them where they wanted corn to grow, and harvest the mature plants.

Zeus became the father of many other gods: Athena, the goddess of arts and crafts and defensive war; Apollo, the god of prophecy, medicine, and archery; Artemis, the goddess of the hunt; Hermes, Zeus's messenger; Persephone, the queen of the Underworld; Ares, the god of war; and Hephaestus, the renowned metalsmith.

The rule of the Titans had ended. The rule of the gods had begun.

1. How is Gaea like a human mother?

2. Why is Zeus presented as being better than Uranus and Cronus?

3. The Mycenaean Greeks showed political sophistication by combining their patriarchal religion with the older matriarchal religion that they found in Greece. What examples show that they continued to respect female gods?

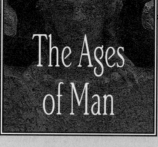

The Ages of Man

After Homer, the next important Greek poet was Hesiod, who lived toward the end of the eighth century B.C. Hesiod wrote a number of myths based upon myths that already existed. He shaped the following creation myth so that it would teach people how to lead satisfying lives in their own difficult times.

According to Hesiod, as human beings acquired more technology, their values deteriorated. Therefore, the first, golden race of mortals, which led the most simple life, was the most honorable and the happiest of all the races that Zeus created. They were a peaceful society of farmers, and they worshipped the Great Goddess or Mother Goddess (Mother Earth), who made them and their land fertile. In Greek history, this race conforms most closely to the peoples who inhabited Greece before about 2600 to 2000 B.C., when the Mycenaeans invaded the land.

The bronze race of mortals lived during the Mycenaean Age. This was a time of many wars, including the Trojan War, which is the setting of Homer's *Iliad*. The Mycenaeans were more aggressive and acquisitive than the peoples they encountered when they invaded Greece. They worshipped Zeus, and in their society, the male was more powerful than the female.

Hesiod's description in *The Works and Days* of the race of iron refers to the people living in his own time. We are still part of the race of iron. You may find it interesting to compare his vision of people in his time with your view of people today.

THE AGES OF MAN

Zeus, Lord of Mount Olympus, was the father of the Deathless Gods, as well as the father of human beings. The first generation of mortals to inhabit the grain-giving earth was known as the race of gold. These mortals were pure in heart and in deed. They respected both their fellow human beings and the deathless gods, and the immortals loved them in return. Because they treated one another justly, they needed neither written laws nor courts nor punishments. They lived carefree and easy lives, in freedom, safety, and peace. Since fear, grief, and hard labor never touched their lives, the passing years did not ravage their appearance or weaken their strength. Old age earned them respect and gratitude.

The weather treated the golden race kindly, providing the warmth, beauty, and sustenance of an eternal spring. Mortals did not have to work to house or to clothe themselves. Flowing nectar and milk formed their rivers, and the leaves of dwarf oak trees dripped honey. They feasted by gathering the wild grains and fruits that grew abundantly about them, and they shepherded their flocks of cattle and sheep in lush green pastures. They had the time and the desire to enjoy the wildflowers that radiantly blossomed in the sunshine and the stars that shone in the night sky.

The mortals of the race of gold had no wish to possess more than they already had. They were neither acquisitive nor aggressive. These people did not fashion boats in order to discover what lay beyond the borders of their own land. They did not threaten other human beings, and in return, no one threatened them. They had no need to build defensive walls around their towns nor to possess weapons. They had no armies, and they never heard the sound of a trumpet calling them to battle.

They died as peacefully as they had lived; death came in the form of a gentle sleep. After their bodies became part of the earth, their spirits roamed across the land, hidden by the mists. They protected the living from danger and taught them how to lead a just life.

When the first generation had passed away, Zeus created a second generation of mortals. They were the race of silver, and they were far less virtuous than the race of gold. Although their bodies matured with the passage of time, the silver race remained juvenile in spirit. For one hundred years each child stayed at home with his or her mother, isolated from the companionship and instruction of other human beings. During this time, these mortals devoted their lives solely to the pursuit of childish pleasures.

As a result, the lives of adults in the silver race were short and unhappy. They never learned to treat one another with kindness and consideration, and their selfish behavior created injustice and war. They did not respect the deathless gods and made no effort to please them.

Because the silver race honored neither gods nor mortals, Zeus became angry with them. The Father of Gods and Mortals changed the weather from eternal spring to a year of four seasons, which ranged from the icy cold of winter to the blistering heat of summer. Caves and sheltered forest areas no longer provided sufficient protection from the weather, so the silver race built the first houses.

Food was now less plentiful. The people began to yoke oxen in pairs and drive them across their fields, toiling each day during the growing season, first to plant seeds of corn and later to reap the mature ears. Zeus brought their life on the earth to an early end, and when their bodies became part of the earth, their spirits entered the Underworld.

Then Zeus, the Father of Gods and Mortals, created a third generation of mortals, which became known as the race of bronze because their weapons and tools were made of bronze. These mortals were far inferior to the silver race because they were so cruel. They loved Ares, the God of War, above all the other gods, and they lived by the sword. Their brute strength made them powerful, but their hearts were as unresponsive as the hardest rock.

Despite their strength and power, members of the bronze race died young. They brought black Death upon themselves through endless violence and war. When their bodies became part of the earth, their shades descended into the dark, dismal Underworld, and they left behind nothing of worth to give them a good name.

Next, Zeus created a fourth generation of mortals, which became known as the race of heroes. These human beings were more noble and virtuous than the members of the silver or the bronze race. Some of them died in the war against

Troy and in other wars, but Zeus placed those who survived upon the islands of the blessed at the ends of the earth. There, the heroes still live along the shore of Oceanus in a land that bears a harvest of honey-sweet fruit three times a year. Grief can no longer touch them; only the honor and glory they earned during their ordinary lifetimes survive. They are ruled by Cronus, whom Zeus freed from his bondage in Tartarus for this purpose.

The fifth generation of mortals that Zeus placed upon the grain-giving earth is our own, the race of iron. Now each day is filled with work and with grief, and each night many mortals die. The worst crimes in the history of humanity now occur throughout the world, and yet no mortal feels shame. Justice and faith have left the world; treason and fraud, violence and greed have replaced them.

The people of the iron race do not think of others' needs nor share the bounty of the earth. Instead, we have divided up the earth's surface into a multitude of private properties, and we keep as much as we can for ourselves. We feel that the earth has not provided enough wealth in the grains she gives, so we have built ships and sailed into the unknown in order to acquire more wealth.

We have torn into the grain-giving earth, searching for the riches she has hidden within her. We have found her secret treasure and have become powerful and wealthy from her deposits of iron and gold. The value of these metals has led to war, and mortal hands have become bloody as they greedily tried to grasp the golden treasures of victory.

If we do not change our ways, our behavior will destroy us. When the time comes that host and guest no longer act hospitably; when friend argues with friend and brothers are enemies; when children and their parents cannot agree with each other; when grown children forget what their parents have done for them and instead treat them with disrespect and dishonor, criticizing them and complaining bitterly because they have grown old and weak; when people who keep their word or are just or virtuous receive less respect than those who use their strength for violent and evil purposes; when those who are evil hurt those who are honorable, then Zeus will destroy our iron race, for we will have shown the Father of Gods and Mortals that we are unfit to inhabit the earth that sustains us.

❧ QUESTIONS FOR
Response, Discussion, and Analysis

1. What do you think led Hesiod to believe that the first of the four ages was the best?

2. Compare the Age of Iron to our own age. How does Hesiod's description apply to our own time?

3. Given the similarities between Hesiod's age and ours, what conclusions, if any, can you draw about human beings?

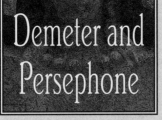

Demeter and Persephone

In ancient agricultural communities, productive soil was of primary importance, and the culture of the community was earth-oriented. Farmers observed that plants and animals were born, grew to maturity, and died, and that others like them were born the following spring. In the same way, people were born, grew to maturity, and died, but not before reproducing and thus continuing the cycle of human life. This cycle became the central focus of the matriarchal religion. Death was an accepted part of the life cycle because it was followed by rebirth or new life. The people worshipped the Great Goddess or Mother Goddess to ensure the fertility of their fields and themselves and, therefore, to ensure the survival of their community.

The Great Goddess functioned in three related forms. As Goddess of the Underworld, she controlled the three-stage cycle of life: first, the period of birth and childhood; then, the fertile period of maturity and reproduction; and last, the sterile period of old age, with its decline and death. As Goddess of the Earth, she controlled the three-stage cycle of the seasons: first, spring (the period of birth or rebirth and budding growth); then, summer (the fertile period of blossoming and harvest); and last, winter (the sterile period of decay, barrenness, and death or dormancy). As Goddess of the Sky, she was the great Moon Goddess, who appeared in her three-stage cycle of phases: first, as the new and waxing moon (the period of birth or rebirth and growth); then, as the full moon (the period of maturity); and last, as the waning moon (the period of decline and death or dormancy).

Before the Mycenaeans brought their patriarchal religion into ancient Greece and other parts of the Mediterranean region, the agricultural communities worshipped this Great Goddess or Mother Goddess. Different communities called her by different names, and the principal female divinities in Greek mythology were originally worshipped as the Great Goddess. For example, Aphrodite was worshipped on the island of Cyprus; Artemis in Attica, Asia Minor, and on Crete; Athena in Athens; Demeter in Eleusis (in Attica); Gaea in Delphi and throughout Greece; Hera in Argos; Persephone in Enna (in Sicily); and Rhea in Phrygia (in Asia Minor).

Wherever they settled, the Mycenaeans prudently incorporated into their own religion the Great Goddess that the particular matriarchal community was accustomed to worshipping. They made Zeus their principal divinity, and they transformed every local Great Goddess into an important member of his family. In the process, Gaea became Zeus's grandmother, while Rhea became his mother. Demeter became Zeus's sister, while Hera became both his sister and his wife. Athena, Artemis, Aphrodite, and Persephone became Zeus's daughters.

Then the Mycenaeans gave their gods and goddesses new roles. Zeus now became God of the Sky, and his brother Hades became God of the Underworld. There, Hades became God of the Dead—including the "dead" (dormant) earth, which revived each spring to burst forth with new plant life. Hades also became known as the God of Wealth because the earth contained copper and tin, from which the Mycenaeans made bronze. (Hades' other name, Pluto, is derived from *ploutos*, which means wealth.) Demeter now functioned only in the role of Goddess of the Earth, where, as Goddess of Grain, she taught mortals how to plant, raise, and harvest corn, wheat, and barley.

In contrast, Persephone (also known as Kore, which means "daughter") remained both Goddess of the Underworld and Goddess of the Earth. However, both in the Underworld, where she functioned as Hades' subservient wife, and on Earth, where she functioned as Demeter's loving daughter, Persephone lost her power as the life-giving Great Goddess. Although she still determined the seasons, her place of residence, rather than her life-giving power, controlled their cycle. Whenever Persephone lived on earth with her mother, it was Demeter who caused the seeds to sprout and the crops to grow; and whenever Persephone lived in the Underworld with her husband, once again, it was Demeter who caused the seeds to lay dormant within the earth.

The ancient tale of Demeter and Persephone is a fertility myth in that it explains the change of seasons and the annual rebirth of life-supporting nature. However, while the subject is generic, its treatment is truly remarkable. The author depicts the Great Goddess as a very human mother whose beloved daughter has been abducted. So great was his talent that his psychologically realistic narration of a mother's love and loss remains one of the most heart-rending and powerful depictions of motherhood—not only in all of mythology, but in later literature, as well. Therefore, it is not surprising that the hymn that relates this myth was thought to have been written by Homer until Hellenistic scholars (third centuries and later B.C.) attributed *The Homeric Hymns* to ancient but anonymous professional *rhapsodes* ("one who stitches songs together").

The second of *The Homeric Hymns*, "Hymn to Demeter" (seventh century B.C. or earlier), contains the most complete version of the following myth.

DEMETER AND PERSEPHONE

Demeter, the Great Goddess, bringer of seasons and giver of life-sustaining gifts, was the Olympian who most loved mortals and the earth that fed them, and they dearly loved her. She was delighted that farmers' wives set an extra place at the table in the hope that she would knock upon their door and join them for their evening meal. So she smiled when the gods teased her that she ate more meals in the humble homes of mortals than in the lofty palaces that Hephaestus had designed and the Cyclopes had built for the immortals on Mount Olympus. Demeter was kind, loving, and generous, but she was also the daughter of Cronus, feared ruler of the Titans, and the sister of Zeus, the Loud-Thunderer.

The joy of Demeter's eternal lifetime was her daughter, Persephone, whom she had borne to Zeus. Persephone loved sunshine, wildflowers, and laughter, and she had the gift of bringing what she loved into the lives of those who knew her. The wildflowers in Sicily were so beautiful that Persephone often roamed the fields there, carrying a large basket that she could fill with the beautiful blossoms. Bright-eyed Athena, the Goddess of Arts and Crafts, and Artemis, the Archer Goddess, usually accompanied her.

Aphrodite watched one day as Hades, the Lord of the Dead, drove his chariot around the island of Sicily. As usual, the King of Shadows was checking to see whether the unruly giant Typhon, who lay on his back under Mount Aetna vomiting fire and flaming ash, had created any cracks in the earth with his eruptions. Hades was quite relieved to find every piece of earth in its proper place, for he feared that if the earth opened above the Underworld and admitted the light of Helios's bright sun, his many subjects would tremble fearfully.

Calling her son, Eros, to her, golden Aphrodite said, "Few of the immortals have a high regard for our powers. Notice how Athena, Artemis, and Persephone all shun the idea of love. Zeus and his brother, the Lord of the Sea, have been subjected to our weapons, and it is time for us to rule the dark lord of the Underworld as well. Send one of your infallible arrows flying into Hades' heart, to make him fall madly in love with Persephone."

Eros's sure aim struck Hades and took him to Zeus for permission to marry Persephone. "Of course, I would be delighted to give you Persephone, dear brother," Zeus replied, "but our sister, Demeter, would never agree to such a marriage. She would not permit me to exchange Persephone's freedom to roam through flower-filled fields, shimmering under the light from Lord Helios's chariot, for the opportunity to be queen in your dark kingdom. Power does not mean that much to the Great Goddess or to Persephone.

"However," the lord of Olympus concluded, "since you are my brother and the ruler of a mighty kingdom, if you insist on having Persephone, that would be a great honor for her. Although I cannot force my daughter to marry you, I will secretly help you to seize her."

So it came to pass that one day, as Persephone was gathering flowers on one of the Sicilian meadows, she noticed in the distance an incredibly beautiful bloom that she had never seen before. Leaving her companions far behind, Persephone immediately ran over the fields toward this unusual flower. She had no way of knowing that her father secretly had commanded the earth to create this special flower to lure her to Hades.

As Persephone reached toward the fragrant flower to add it to her collection, the earth suddenly opened wide, and out came a golden chariot drawn by black horses and driven by the dark lord himself. Keeping his left hand on the reins, Hades seized Persephone with his right arm, placed her beside him in the chariot, and drove off at top speed before Persephone's companions realized that she had disappeared.

"Mother! Mother!" she screamed. "Help me! Father, help me!" But her mother was far away, and no one among the gods or mortals heard her screams. Only Helios, Lord of the Sun, observed the crime from his chariot as he traveled across the sky. By the time Artemis and Athena arrived at the meadow, the crevice had closed, the unusual flower had disappeared, and Persephone was gone. All that remained was the basket filled with flowers that the young goddess had dropped when she was snatched away.

Persephone continued to call for her mother as the chariot carried her through deep lakes and smoking pools. As long as she could see the grain-giving land, the swift-flowing sea, and Helios above her in his chariot, she hoped that someone would hear her cries. But when a sea nymph tried to stop Hades, he struck the earth, opened a crevice, and disappeared with Persephone into its dreary depths.

For some time after the earth had closed upon Persephone, the sound of her voice echoed from the mountain heights and issued forth from the depths of the sea. When the Great Goddess heard her daughter's cries, pain enclosed her heart in its mighty grip. From her lovely hair she tore its band, from her shoulders she loosened her dark cape, and freely she ran, like a wild bird, over land and sea, desperately searching everywhere for her lost child.

The deathless gods who knew where Persephone was remained silent. Mortals could not help the grieving and distraught mother. So that the darkness of night would not slow her search, the Great Goddess kindled two pine torches in the fiery crater of Mount Aetna. From that time on, neither Dawn nor the evening star found her at rest. But she searched the earth in vain.

At last, Demeter returned to Sicily, where Persephone had last been seen and her own fruitless search had begun. Not knowing who to blame, Demeter punished Sicily first. If no one could tell her what had happened to her daughter, she would withdraw her life-sustaining gifts. So she broke the plows, killed the oxen and the farmers who owned them, and commanded the earth to shrivel and mold the seeds it harbored. Soon the very land that had been famed for its fertility became barren. First, the country was plagued by drought. Then, blasting winds brought with them a deluge of rain. Corn that had not withered upon the stalk was devoured by greedy birds.

From Sicily, the Great Goddess wandered back across the earth, causing a year of drought and devastation for all of humankind. She so concealed the nourishing seeds within the earth that not one of them sprouted. Even when teams of oxen pulled curved plows over the fields so that the farmers following behind could plant white corn, golden-haired Demeter made all of their labor come to naught.

Then, still carrying her flaming torches, the Great Goddess approached the lord of the sun, who watched both gods and mortals. Placing herself in front of Helios's horse-drawn chariot, Demeter said, "I heard my daughter scream as though someone had seized her against her will, and yet I have been unable to learn what has happened to her. Since your chariot takes you high above the grain-giving land and the swift-flowing sea, did you see who took my child?"

To these words Lord Helios replied, "I will tell you the truth, Great Goddess, for I pity you in your sorrow. Zeus, the Cloud-Gatherer, gave Persephone to the Lord of the Dead to become his queen. You heard her cries as Hades carried her down to his gloomy kingdom. Yet the marriage is a good one, since the dark lord is your brother and rules a mighty kingdom. Try to put aside your anger and your grief."

Demeter's heart now overflowed with a deeper and more savage sorrow. Torn between fury and anguish, the Great Goddess determined to punish Zeus and the other Olympians by causing all mortals to die of starvation. Then the deathless gods would no longer be honored with sacrifices and gifts, and grim Hades would gain more shades to honor him.

Zeus, fearing that such might be her intent, sent wind-footed Iris to command Demeter to return to Mount Olympus. When the Great Goddess did not respond, Zeus commanded the other Olympian gods, one by one, to approach her and offer her greater honor and glorious gifts. However, Demeter refused all but the last of these messengers. To him she said, "Tell Zeus that I will set foot upon fragrant Olympus in order to talk with him, but I will not permit any seeds to sprout upon the earth until I have seen my beautiful child."

When the Great Goddess approached Zeus she said, "Father of Gods and Mortals, I come pleading to you on behalf of our daughter. Even if you do not care for me, surely you love Persephone! You know how she loves the light of the sun, the joyous sound of laughter, and the scent of flowers. How can you make her live in our brother's dark and dismal kingdom, ruling over the dead when she so loves life? And how could you permit her to marry someone who had to seize her against her will? Tell Hades that he must let her go!"

"Truly, Demeter," Zeus replied, "I share your love and your concern for our daughter. However, Hades seized Persephone because he loves her, and he is as great a god as I am. Only the drawing of lots gave the Underworld to him and Olympus to me. If our brother's love and power cannot make you put aside your anger and resentment, then I will let Persephone return to you—as long as she has eaten no food in Hades' dark kingdom. But if she has consumed the food of the dead she is condemned to remain in that dismal land, for so the Fates decree."

To these words the Great Goddess replied: "I will meet Persephone on the meadows she loves. Until then, the earth will remain lifeless and barren. Farewell."

As Demeter departed, Zeus sent his messenger Hermes, the Wayfinder, down to Hades' grim kingdom to persuade the dark lord with kind words to let Persephone return to her mother. Hermes found the Lord of the Underworld in his gloomy palace and said, "Hades, kind uncle and Lord of the Dead, my father has commanded me to bring Persephone up to her mother.

"The Great Goddess," Hermes continued, "has threatened to destroy all mortals by withholding their source of food, thus removing from the gods their source of honor and sacrificial offerings. She has hidden all seeds deep in the earth where they cannot sprout, and not one of the Olympians has been able to soften the rage and grief that fill her heart."

At these words, Hades smiled grimly, but to Persephone he kindly said, "Go now with Hermes to seek your dark-robed mother. But, in your heart, know that I too love you and want you here with me.

"Think of me with kindness," Hades continued, "for I will be a good husband to you. Remember that I am the brother of Zeus and my kingdom is also very great. While you are here, you will rule everything that lives and moves, and I will see that you receive the greatest honor among the deathless gods. I will punish for eternity anyone who wrongs you or who does not worship you with sacred rites and sacrifices."

When she heard her husband's words, Persephone's heart filled with joy. While the Wayfinder harnessed Hades' immortal horses to his golden chariot, the Lord of the Underworld gave Persephone a honey-sweet pomegranate seed to eat so that his beloved wife could not remain forever in the upper world. Persephone, unaware of the consequences, swallowed the seed.

When she had mounted the chariot, Hermes took the reins and the whip into his hands, and they quickly left the palace. Once the deathless horses reached the upper air, neither the swift-flowing sea nor grassy meadows nor the peaks of mountains were any obstacle to Hades' swift steeds.

Demeter waited for Persephone in a meadow that should have been ablaze with the colorful flowers of summer. Now, however, this ground, like the lands that in prior years had produced rich crops of corn and wheat, lay barren and idle. As soon as she saw Hades' golden chariot, the Great Goddess rushed to meet her daughter. Hermes had barely halted the horses before Persephone leaped down from the chariot and threw her arms around her mother's neck in a long, happy embrace.

As Demeter held her dear child in her arms, her heart filled with fear, and she suddenly asked Persephone, "My child, tell me truly, when you were in Lord Hades' dark kingdom, did you taste any food? If you ate nothing there, you can live here where the sun shines with your father and me. But if you had any kind of nourishment you must return to your husband, for the Fates have decreed that anyone who eats the food of the dead must remain in the dismal land of death!"

Persephone's eyes filled with tears, and she replied, "I will not attempt to deceive you, Mother. As Hermes was about to bring me to you, my husband gave me a honey-sweet pomegranate seed to eat. I swallowed it because I was hungry; I had no idea of the consequences."

Tears then flowed uncontrollably from Demeter's eyes, for it seemed that her visit with her dear child was doomed to be brief. Sorrow and despair threatened to push all the joy of their reunion from her heart. She felt she could not bear their eternal separation.

Suddenly, Demeter's spirits lifted with surprise and delight as she saw her own mother, Rhea, approaching them. With great love, the Mother of the Gods embraced her daughter and her granddaughter.

"Come, my child," said Rhea. "A mother must have the strength to bear pain as well as joy. Sorrow visits all of us. You must not let your grief destroy you.

"I have come from Mount Olympus," Rhea continued, "and I bring you a special message from your brother, Zeus. He wishes you to rejoin the Olympian family, where you will be highly honored among the deathless gods. He gives you his word that Persephone need spend only one-third of each year in Hades' dark and gloomy kingdom. When the time comes each year for the earth to bring forth the fragrant flowers of springtime, she will leave the kingdom of darkness and return to you. You will be together until all of the crops have been harvested and Helios, Lord of the Sun, has caused the days to become short and cool.

"So put aside your anger against Zeus, my child. Enjoy your lovely daughter for the seasons that you can be together, and make the earth once again yield the life-giving fruits that mortals need to sustain them."

Demeter heard her mother's words and smiled through her tears. She would have her daughter after all! These separations she could endure. Immediately, she caused the fertile land to blossom with leaves, flowers, and life-giving fruits. Then the goddesses joined the immortals on Mount Olympus.

Thus the pattern of the seasons became established. Each year, after the harvesting of the autumn crops, Persephone would return to her husband, the dark Lord of the Dead, for the winter months. Then, in her loneliness and sorrow, Demeter would allow the earth to lie leafless and idle.

As soon as Lord Helios once again warmed the earth with the sun, and the days became longer, the Great Goddess would see her beloved child joyously running toward her. Once again, in her great joy, Demeter would cause all flowers and seed-bearing plants to blossom upon the earth. Once again, she would bless the mortals she loved with her life-sustaining gifts.

Then people would often see a beautiful mother and daughter roaming together through sunny flowering meadows. Farmers' wives once again would set an extra place at their table for the evening meal, hoping that their beloved Demeter would join them to share the fruits of their labors.

❧ QUESTIONS FOR
Response, Discussion, and Analysis

1. What does this myth reflect about Zeus's personality and power?

2. The Greek gods are anthropomorphic, meaning they speak and act like human beings. What examples in this myth support this statement?

3. This myth celebrates the idea of the cyclical nature of life: birth, maturity, death, and rebirth. What role does Demeter perform? Hades? Persephone?

THE LABORS AND DEATH OF HERACLES

Heracles was the son of Zeus and a mortal woman. The lord of Olympus wanted to be certain that Heracles earned eternal fame, but he also wanted to please Hera, who hated his children by other women. Therefore, Zeus promised Hera that Heracles would have to perform for King Eurystheus of Tiryns whatever ten labors the king commanded. Only then would Zeus make Heracles immortal.

The name Heracles means "Hera's glory" (Hera + *cleos*). Heracles earned his name when he was eight months old, for Hera unintentionally caused him to win great fame. Wishing to kill him, she sent two huge snakes into his nursery. As the snakes approached his bed, Heracles gleefully extended his arms, grabbed a snake in each hand, and strangled both serpents.

Heracles continued to earn fame as he grew into manhood. He married a princess and became the father of three sons. Eurystheus, fearing that Heracles would become a threat to his power, commanded him to perform the labors. When Heracles refused to become Eurystheus's servant, Hera caused Heracles to become insane. In a fit of madness, he picked up his great bow and shot his only children, thinking that they were enemies.

Upon recovering his sanity, Heracles withdrew from all society, became purified of his crime, and sought the advice of the oracle of Delphi. The oracle informed Heracles that he must obey the will of the gods by performing whatever ten labors Eurystheus commanded, and that he would then become immortal. Heracles obeyed the oracle and placed himself in the service of the king.

Eurystheus first commanded Heracles to bring him the skin of the lion of Nemea. Heracles knew that the beast could not be hurt by stone or bronze, so he would have to devise some other way to kill it. When he came upon the lion, he learned that his arrows and his huge wooden club were also useless. The lion responded to Heracles' attack by retreating into a cave that had two exits. Heracles blocked one exit with a huge rock and entered the cave through the other opening. He wrestled with the beast until, finally, he was able to put one arm around the lion's neck, tighten his grip, and choke it to death. Heracles left the cave wearing the lion's skin as a fearsome trophy.

When Heracles returned to Tiryns dressed as the Nemean lion, Eurystheus was so frightened by the sight that he ordered Heracles to remain outside the city gates. Thereafter, Eurystheus communicated with Heracles by having one of his servants act as his messenger.

For his second labor, Eurystheus commanded Heracles to kill the Hydra of Lerna. This monster had nine snakelike heads upon its huge body, and the middle head was immortal. It lived in a swamp and scoured the nearby countryside in search of cattle to eat. First, Heracles forced the monster out of the swamp by shooting blazing arrows at it. Then he grabbed the Hydra and tried to smash its heads with his club. But wherever Heracles destroyed one head, two new heads replaced it. Seeing that such schemes would only multiply his problem, Heracles ordered his nephew and traveling companion, Iolas, to put a log into a fire and create a white-hot brand.

Then Heracles cut off the Hydra's mortal heads one by one. As he severed them, Iolas immediately seared and sealed the monster's raw flesh before a new set of heads could sprout. Heracles cut off the one immortal head and buried it under a huge rock by the side of the road. Finally, he sliced the Hydra's body into pieces and dipped his arrows into the monster's blood, for a wound infested with the Hydra's deadly poison was incurable. When Heracles returned to Tiryns, Eurystheus declared that this labor did not count because Iolas had helped perform it.

For his third labor, Eurystheus commanded Heracles to bring to Tiryns the swift deer with golden horns that was sacred to Artemis, Goddess of the Hunt. Heracles realized that if he wounded the deer, he would anger Artemis. So instead of shooting it, he pursued it for an entire year. Finally, the deer lay down, exhausted, and Heracles captured it. He enclosed it in a net, slung the net over his shoulders, and returned with it to Tiryns.

Heracles' fourth labor involved capturing the Erymanthian boar and carrying it, alive, back to Tiryns. This wild boar was extremely dangerous because of its sharp tusks, and it was incredibly fast in spite of its short legs. Heracles chased it up a mountainside into deep snow, where it could no longer run swiftly. When the beast was too exhausted to challenge Heracles with its tusks, the hero bound its feet and carried it back to Tiryns on his shoulders.

For his fifth labor, Eurystheus chose to humiliate Heracles by ordering him to clean the stables of King Augeas in one day. If the stables had ever been clean, no one remembered it, and many herds of cattle had left dung piled high. To preserve his dignity, Heracles did not mention Eurystheus's command. Instead, he approached the king and offered to clean the stables in a day in return for some cattle.

When Augeas agreed, Heracles changed the course of two nearby rivers so that they ran through the stables and washed away the dung. However, when the king learned that Heracles had been ordered to clean the stables, he would not pay him. Moreover, Eurystheus would not accept this labor because Heracles had performed it in return for a promise of payment.

For his sixth labor, Eurystheus commanded Heracles to chase the hordes of Stymphalian birds away from the lake of that name in Arcadia. The birds were robbing the farmers of the fruits of their orchards and were dangerous as well, for they would shoot their feathers like arrows. Athena helped Heracles by giving him a bronze rattle that made such a dreadful noise it frightened the birds away.

The seventh labor required Heracles to journey to Crete and capture the bull that Poseidon had sent to King Minos for a special sacrifice. When the king did not kill the beautiful bull as he had promised, the Lord of the Sea turned it into a ferocious beast. Heracles caught the bull, brought it back to Tiryns, and set it free.

For his eighth labor, Heracles had to capture the mares of King Diomedes, which ate human flesh. He found them chained to their bronze troughs, feeding upon the arms and legs of strangers. Heracles was so angered by the king's savage nature that he killed Diomedes and fed his body to his mares. Once the horses ate the flesh of the man who had trained them to enjoy eating people, Heracles could control them. He took them to Eurystheus, who set them free. The mares then climbed Mount Olympus, where wild animals killed them.

In the course of performing this labor, Heracles stopped to visit his good friend King Admetus, whose wife, Alcestis, had just died. Heracles wrestled with Death for her life and won the contest, thereby restoring Alcestis to her husband.

For his ninth labor, Eurystheus commanded Heracles to bring him the belt of the Amazon queen, Hippolyte, because his daughter wanted it. The Amazons were an aggressive tribe of female warriors, and Ares, God of War, had given Hippolyte a belt. When Heracles arrived, Hippolyte met him; once she knew why he needed it, she gave him her belt. Hera thought this was too easy, so the goddess disguised herself as an Amazon and shouted that Heracles was abducting their queen. When the warrior women attacked him, Heracles thought Hippolyte had betrayed him, so he killed her, took her belt, and returned to Tiryns.

For his tenth labor, Eurystheus commanded Heracles to bring him the beautiful red cattle of the monstrous giant Geryon, who had the form of three men joined together at the waist. Guarding the cattle was a two-headed dog named Orthus. When Orthus attacked him, Heracles clubbed the dog to death and began to herd the cattle. Geryon met Heracles by the river and tried to stop him. Heracles moved to the giant's side, raised his mighty bow, and killed Geryon by shooting one arrow through his triple body.

On his way back to Tiryns with Geryon's cattle, Heracles stopped along the Tiber River and lay down to rest. A monstrous, fire-belching giant named Cacus saw the beautiful cattle and stole the best oxen. Craftily, Cacus disguised the path to his cave by dragging the oxen backwards by their tails. When Heracles awoke, he noticed that some of his cattle were missing. He found the nearest cave, but the only animal tracks he saw led away from the cave rather than into it. However, as he moved off with his cattle they mooed, and to his surprise, Heracles heard a response from inside the cave.

Heracles then took his great club and headed for the cave. Cacus, seeing him approach, lowered a gigantic rock into the doorway, sealing himself and the stolen cattle within the cave. Three times Heracles climbed above and around the cave, trying to find a way to reach the giant. Finally, he set his weight against a large rock that was part of the roof of the cave and, with all of his might, pushed it upon its side. As the rock moved toward the earth, the murky interior of Cacus's den was revealed.

Gazing down upon the roaring, fire-spewing giant, Heracles saw pale, decaying heads of men nailed to the cave's walls and smelled the foul odor of blood. First he hurled huge rocks and tree trunks upon Cacus. Then, undaunted by the clouds of black smoke that issued forth from the depths below, he jumped into the cave, threw his arm around the giant's throat, and squeezed with all his strength. When he had permanently extinguished Cacus's fires, and the giant lay dead upon the floor, Heracles moved the stone from the doorway. He dragged the giant out by his feet, led forth the cattle, and went on his way.

Eight years had now passed since Heracles had begun his labors. For his eleventh labor, Eurystheus commanded Heracles to collect the golden apples of the Hesperides, daughters of the Titan Atlas, who held the sky upon his shoulders. Gaea had given the apple trees to Hera as a wedding gift, and they were guarded by a hundred-headed, immortal dragon who spoke in many different voices.

In order to locate the garden, Heracles had to consult Nereus, the old man of the sea. When Heracles found him along the shore and grabbed him, the sea god tried to frighten Heracles away by turning himself into a series of fearful sights. He became a raging fire, a roaring lion, a slithery snake, and a torrent of water, but through every change in appearance, Heracles held on to the figure beneath the apparition. In the end, Nereus gave up and gave Heracles the directions he needed.

On his way to the garden, Heracles passed through Libya, which was ruled by a giant son of Gaea named Antaeus. Antaeus was an unusually strong and skillful wrestler and challenged every stranger to a wrestling match. Antaeus inevitably won and put the loser to death. Then he hung the head of his latest victim next to his other trophies on the temple of Poseidon.

When Antaeus forced Heracles to wrestle with him, Heracles noticed that whenever any part of the giant's body touched the earth, he immediately became much stronger. Heracles realized that, in order to win this contest, he would have to prevent Antaeus' mother from renewing her son's strength. Therefore, Heracles hugged Antaeus and, using his deathly grip and all his might, he lifted the giant into the air and held him there, strangling, until he died. Then Heracles killed all the wild beasts in the country, enabling farmers to plant olive orchards and vineyards.

Heracles continued his journey, which took him to the Caucasus Mountains at the eastern end of the Euxine (Black) Sea in Scythia. There he found the Titan Prometheus nailed to the mountain and helpless as Zeus's eagle tore out his liver. Heracles raised his giant bow and killed the bird; then he freed Prometheus. In return, Prometheus advised Heracles that he should find Atlas and take the sky upon his own shoulders, sending Atlas for the golden apples instead of attempting to deal with the dragon and gather them himself.

Heracles followed Prometheus's advice. Atlas returned with the apples but announced that he was tired of holding the sky upon his shoulders and that he would take the apples to King Eurystheus himself. Heracles immediately agreed to take over Atlas's task, but craftily asked Atlas to hold the sky temporarily while he put a pad upon his head to make the weight more tolerable. Atlas helpfully put the apples upon the ground and accepted the sky. Heracles quickly picked up the apples and left the gigantic Titan with his awesome burden.

For his twelfth and final labor, Eurystheus commanded Heracles to enter the Underworld and return with Cerberus, the monstrous, three-headed dog that guarded the entrance to the dread kingdom of Hades. Heracles was accompanied by Hermes, the Wayfinder, who leads the shades of the dead down to the Underworld.

Heracles approached Hades and asked his permission to take Cerberus to King Eurystheus. The Lord of the Dead agreed on the condition that Heracles must capture the monstrous hound without using any weapon. Hades' command challenged Heracles because, in addition to its three heads, Cerberus's back was covered with snakes and the tail of a dragon. Heracles covered himself with his protective lion skin, embraced the three-headed monster, and never let go. He carried the hound up to Tiryns, showed the monster to Eurystheus, and then returned it to Hades.

Heracles continued to have numerous adventures after he had completed his labors. Many years later, Heracles' wife, jealous that he might be in love with another woman, sent her husband the gift of a tunic that had been soaked in the blood of the Hydra. An enemy of Heracles' had treacherously led her to believe that the tunic would cause Heracles to remain in love with her.

When Heracles put the tunic on, the heat of his body activated the poison, causing the tunic to stick to his skin and burn it. In agony, he immediately tore off the tunic, and with it his skin. Only death could relieve his misery, so he built a funeral pyre and lay down upon it. However, no one he asked was willing to put a torch to it and kill him. Finally, Philoctetes happened to pass by, and when he saw Heracles in such excruciating pain, he agreed to light the pyre. As a reward, Heracles gave Philoctetes his great bow and arrows, which the young man, in later years, took to Troy.

Just as the burning torch touched the wood of the funeral pyre, a bolt of lightning flashed in the clear sky and struck the pyre. A cloud immediately descended into the roaring mass of flames, enveloped Heracles, and carried him up to Mount Olympus. After the fire had consumed the entire pyre, not even Heracles' bones remained among the ashes. Zeus had kept his promise; Heracles had become immortal.

❧ QUESTIONS FOR
Response, Discussion, and Analysis

1. What heroic qualities does Heracles possess?

2. Heracles, like most heroes, must enter the Underworld. In your opinion, what is the reason for such a task?

3. Antaeus receives his great physical strength from Gaea, his mother. What strengths do you possess? From whom did you receive them?

4. What, if anything, would motivate you to perform a dangerous labor? Do you know of anyone who has done so? What do you think was that person's motive?

HISTORICAL BACKGROUND

The Iliad

The story of *The Iliad* occurs in about 1180 B.C., late in the Bronze Age. The action is located on the plain outside the great fortified city of Ilios (Troy), during the last year of the ten-year war between the allied Mycenaeans (the attackers) and the Trojans and their allies (the defenders).

In *The Iliad,* Homer's Greeks and Trojans speak the same language and appear to share other aspects of Hellenic culture, such as the same divinities. However, Ilios was located on the west coast of what is now Turkey—called Anatolia ("The East") by the Hellenes—across the Aegean Sea from Mycenaean Hellas. Therefore, in order to write a cohesive and comprehensible literary work about the Trojan War, Homer needed to Hellenize the Trojans or to transform the Hellenes into Anatolians. Since he lived relatively close to Troy, but in a Greek colony, Homer chose to Hellenize the Anatolian people of Ilios.

Throughout the ages, *The Iliad* was first considered to be historical, then legendary, and then mythical. However, when Heinrich Schliemann's excavations at Troy, in 1871, revealed the remains of many cities where Homer's Ilios could have stood, *The Iliad*'s historical basis became an intriguing question.

Unfortunately, the passage of more than three thousand years and the ravages of weather, war, and fire have destroyed the perishable remains of human life and culture. Moreover, victors, pirates, and new occupants have removed anything of value—from building materials to weapons and jewelry. Therefore, we can only evaluate archaeological remains, related scholarship, and literary references in order to learn about Mycenaean Greece, Anatolian Troy or Ilios, and Homer.

As early as about 2600 B.C., Indo-European-speaking tribes from the north invaded the area of northern Greece known as Macedonia. Between 1900 and 1600 B.C., the descendants of these peoples moved southward to inhabit the rest of Hellas. The golden age of their civilization occurred between 1450 B.C., when they conquered the island of Crete and adopted much of the technology and art of that advanced, non-Indo-European society, and about 1200 B.C., when their palace states began to be destroyed by civil wars and by sea raiders.

During this period, the Mediterranean and Aegean communities enjoyed a rich period of cultural exchange in that the Mycenaeans traded with the Hittites—whose empire in Anatolia and the Near East flourished from about 1800 until about 1200 B.C.—the people of Ugarit in Syria, and the Egyptians. (The Phoenicians became important after the Mycenaean Age.) Mycenaean religion, as well as art, literature, and technology, reveals the influence of other cultures. For example, the Mycenaeans adopted Athena and Hera from pre-Hellenic cultures; they combined their Zeus with the Minoan Zeus of Crete; and they adopted Apollo and Aphrodite from Anatolia and the Near East, respectively.

Our knowledge of the Bronze Age Mycenaean culture is based primarily on the ruins of a number of important sites in Greece. Fortunately, archaeologists have unearthed decorated objects, such as jewelry, pottery, and metal containers, and an assortment of war gear, such as shields, helmets, and weapons. In addition, archaeologists have found a large number of clay tablets that are inscribed with a language called Linear B, which they can read.

The Mycenaean civilization in full bloom far surpassed in complexity and wealth many of the Hellenic civilizations that followed it, including Homer's age. The Mycenaeans were an aggressive people who enjoyed fighting, hunting, and athletic contests. Except for the large peninsula known as the Peloponnese, their land was mountainous and their soil rocky and dry. Therefore, they took to the sea and became fearsome raiders of other communities.

In this way the Mycenaeans acquired extraordinary wealth. They lived and died with weapons by their sides. Fortunately for archaeologists, they buried their dead in tombs along with the war gear and wealth they had possessed in life. The Mycenaeans loved decorated objects. Whether of gold, bronze, or clay, their arts and crafts reflected their interest in war and in hunting ferocious wild animals.

The Mycenaean kings constructed palaces that were fortified strongholds. For example, the palace at Mycenae, built in 1350 B.C., had walls twenty-three feet thick. Each king's palace was the political, economic, and social center of his small kingdom. Connected with the palace were the numerous nobles, artisans, scribes, farmers, and common laborers needed to keep the complex organization operating. The king had to be a strong, able, and aggressive leader who could protect the people in his palace community and gain wealth for

its aristocratic members by sacking other communities.

Archaeological remains reveal very little about the religious practices of these people and nothing of their myths except the names of some of their gods. We can assume that the family was important because the dead are buried in family groups. We can assume that in an age of piracy and well-fortified palaces, hospitality was necessary for the traveler to survive, and yet people had to be very cautious about welcoming strangers.

As early as about 6000 B.C., a New Stone Age, or Neolithic, fortified community existed in southern Anatolia. It grew to become one of the earliest cities, with a population of 5,000 to 10,000 people who worshipped the Great Goddess or Mother Goddess. Between about 5500 and 3000 B.C., the descendants of these people migrated into other areas of Anatolia, including Troy. Known for its strategic location with regard to overland trade between Europe and Asia and marine trade between the Mediterranean palace states and northeastern Europe, as well as for its bronze work, Troy became the most famous Early Bronze Age (3000–2000 B.C.), Anatolian, fortified city.

Troy controlled the Hellespont strait (now called the Dardanelles), a narrow waterway that functioned as the gateway from the Aegean Sea to the Euxine Sea (now called the Black Sea). The Euxine Sea provided access to the communities along three major rivers: the Danube from Germany, the Don from Russia, and the Dnieper from the Ukraine. The Mycenaean Greeks and other ancient peoples valued items such as pure copper, tin, and gold that they could obtain in trade with those who inhabited the coastal lands of the

Euxine Sea and the lands of northeastern Europe.

However, the prevalence of unfavorable wind and current patterns in the Hellespont strait usually forced ships en route to the Euxine Sea to wait for long periods of time in Troy's harbor (now known as Besik Bay) until favorable conditions permitted them to continue their journey. For hundreds of years, Troy took advantage of this situation by collecting mooring fees for the privilege of using its harbor plus large tolls for the privilege of passing through the Hellespont.

Consequently, given its strategic location at the mouth of this major trade route, Troy—whether or not it is Homer's Ilios—was an extraordinarily powerful and wealthy Bronze Age city. Archaeological excavation reveals that Bronze Age Troy was actually the sixth of nine cities that existed on the same site and that it was destroyed twice. However, as yet, no conclusive proof exists that Troy VI is Homer's Ilios or that the Trojan War that Homer describes in *The Iliad* actually occurred.

During the centuries between the collapse of Rome and the birth of the modern age, most historians and other scholars viewed the entire narrative content of *The Iliad* as pure myth. However, in 1870, Heinrich Schliemann, a wealthy German merchant, decided to become an amateur archaeologist. He took his beloved copy of *The Iliad* in hand and let it lead him through the Homeric world for the next fourteen years. To everyone's amazement but his own, in 1873, Schliemann unearthed the ruins of Troy on an acropolis (a large hill) that, in modern times, is called Hissarlik ("Place of Fortresses").

Convinced that Homer's Ilios had to be one of the bottom layers of this nine-layer ruin, Schliemann dug until

he unearthed fabulous gold jewelry, silver knives, containers of gold, silver, and copper, and bronze weapons. Because he saw that the fortress that contained them had been destroyed by fire, he erroneously concluded that Troy II was Homer's Ilios, that the Trojan War had destroyed it, and that he had discovered the "Treasure of Priam." However, in 1995, new excavations revealed that Troy II was an impressive, late addition to Troy I, which burned c. 2480/20 B.C.—about 1300 years before the Trojan War and, therefore, too early to qualify as Homer's Ilios.

From 1932 to 1938, a team of scholars directed by archaeologist Carl Blegen (University of Cincinnati) discovered Troy VI (1700–1250/30 B.C.). This period is consistent with the period that Homer describes in *The Iliad,* and the remains of great towers and walls built with Bronze Age tools in about 1470 B.C. are consistent with the strongest Bronze Age city. However, Homer's description reveals Ilios to be a major trade center—a place where people from both western and eastern cultures would meet in order to transact business—whereas the Troy VI citadel occupies only five acres. Therefore, unless further excavation unearthed more extensive remains, Troy VI was clearly too small to be Homer's Ilios.

However, for the next fifty years—including World War II and the Cold War—Hissarlik was part of a military zone, and the partially excavated citadel remained undisturbed. Then, in 1988, the Turkish government invited German archaeologist Manfred Korfmann (University of Tubingen) to direct a new team of scholars in further archaeological excavation and analysis at Hissarlik. In 1996, the acropolis and its surrounding area officially became a national historic park.

Every summer since 1988, Korfmann and his team (specialists in the Bronze Age and earlier periods) have been working in conjunction with University of Cincinnati specialists in post-Bronze Age periods. Approximately one hundred scholars from Germany, the United States, Turkey, and ten other countries are involved—including anthropologists, archaeologists, architects, botanists, chemists, geographers, geologists, meteorologists, numismatists (currency specialists), philologists (literature and related language specialists), physicists, and zoologists. Computer specialists, filmmakers, photographers, restorers, scientific illustrators, and surveyors function as their support staff.

As the archaeologists have unearthed material remains, scholars have revised their ideas to conform with the latest discoveries. However, reputable reports may disagree about what has been excavated and its significance. Moreover, so much is still unknown that future discoveries may change what we currently "know" about the city that may be Homer's Ilios.

Current archaeological excavation has revealed that the great walls discovered by Blegen and his team enclosed only the citadel (fortress), rather than the city, of Troy VI. However, the citadel protected a lower residential city, at least nine times its size, that is located to the south of the acropolis. Whereas royalty and priests probably lived within the citadel, the Trojan people lived in the lower city.

Archaeologists have unearthed and mapped sixty-one significant structures from the period of Troy VI, including the remains of fifteen ancient fortifications (three of which are large forts located three miles south of the lower city). They have also discovered well-planned streets and many examples of Mycenaean pottery. Therefore, the size and complexity of this thirteenth century B.C., Bronze Age city reveals it to have been such a busy and prosperous community that it appears to be consistent with Homer's description of Ilios.

Recent archaeological excavations have also revealed a creative defense against the devastating war machine developed by the Hittites—a spoke-wheeled, lightweight chariot pulled by a team of swift horses. (Troy and the highlands of Anatolia were known for their horse-breeding.) Archers shot their enemies from these moving vehicles and then moved out of range before their enemies could retaliate.

In 1993, archaeologists discovered that, during the period of Troy VI, the lower city possessed an ingenious defense system against these chariots—an encircling trench, or moat, approximately twelve feet wide and twelve feet deep. Carved out of bedrock with hammers and chisels, the partially excavated moat now contains layers of debris, including a thick layer of Myceanean pottery shards at the bottom, as well as the remains of reeds and other aquatic plants.

However, in 1994, archaeologists unearthed part of a second huge trench, or moat, located one hundred yards beyond the first. Chariots could not cross these wide and deep expanses. Therefore, Troy's enemies—wearing armor and carrying weapons—would have been forced to climb down and then up the sloped sides of the trench, which would have made them vulnerable to attack.

Scholars believe that the Trojans also constructed a defensive wall or palisade behind the interior trench from which their archers defended the citadel and the lower city by attacking raiders with arrows. However, archaeologists have yet to find evidence of such a wall.

Approximately three hundred feet behind the interior trench, archaeologists have unearthed the stone foundation of a Troy II (after 2900–c. 2480/2420 B.C.) wooden palisade that was about ten feet thick and that probably consisted of a line of stakes in front of a platform. However, Troy II is probably much too early for the palisade to have remained in use.

Current excavations have also revealed that, between about 1250 and 1230 B.C., the palaces within the walled citadel of Troy VI were destroyed by earthquake, internal social upheaval, enemy attack, fire, or some combination of these. If enemy attack was responsible for this upheaval, the motive probably was economic—to obtain free access to the Euxine Sea or to obtain Troy's fabulous wealth. The enemy could have been the Mycenaean Greeks because their survival depended on trade—both the export of their pottery and crafts and the import of grain and other food. Therefore, any disruption in their foreign trade would have caused both economic deprivation and significant political dissatisfaction at home, and Troy controlled the access to the Euxine Sea.

Troy VI's first destruction initiated a century (c. 1250–1150 B.C.) marked by a tumultuous upheaval throughout the eastern Mediterranean. The great cities in Anatolia and the Near East began to fall like a house of cards. The Hittite empire, which extended south from the Euxine Sea to the plains of Syria, and east from the shores of the Aegean and the Mediterranean Seas to the Euphrates River, collapsed between 1225 and 1200 B.C., when Hattusha, its great fortified capital, was suddenly demolished. Meanwhile, the cosmopolitan Canaanite port of Ugarit (in Syria), a Hittite vassal state, was also sacked and burned in about 1200 B.C.

The dependence of the Mycenaean Greeks on foreign markets—and the devastating loss of many of these markets caused by the chaos of this period—may have led them to unite, in about 1190 B.C. (assuming a ten-year war), in order to lay siege to Homer's Ilios. Ancient Egyptian and Roman sources date the second destruction of Troy VI—Homer's Trojan War—at one year before the destruction of the Phoenician city of Sidon (c. 1179 B.C.). Radiocarbon dating and analysis of pottery shards, in 1995, also reveal that Troy was attacked, defeated, and completely destroyed by a devastating fire in 1180 B.C.

Scholars must depend on circumstantial evidence in order to determine the culture of Troy VI's inhabitants, and finding artifacts that contain written language would be most helpful. Unfortunately, if their assumptions are correct, archaeologists will not unearth a Troy VI library because later inhabitants probably destroyed it in order to build a great Temple of Athena.

However, Troy VI was such a cosmopolitan city that its educated citizens must have spoken and written several languages, including the various languages of their partners in trade, such as Colchis on the Euxine Sea; Mycenaean Greece on the Aegean Sea; and Ugarit on the Mediterranean Sea. Because pottery shards from Troy VI reveal that it had an active trade with Mycenaean Greece, Troy VI citizens probably wrote the Linear B hieroglyphic script and spoke the language used by the Mycenaeans from about 1450 to 1200 B.C. In addition, some among them must have known the

Akkadian language since bilingual poets were translating Akkadian literature into the Hurrian and Hittite languages from about 2000 to l000 B.C. Moreover, Akkadian was the language of diplomacy throughout Anatolia, Mesopotamia, and Egypt from about 1500 to 500 B.C.

Although evidence of the use of these languages in Troy VI has not been unearthed, in 1995, archaeologists discovered the first piece of writing in Troy VI—a bronze seal that contains a Luwian text written, as was the custom, in Hittite hieroglyphics. The Luwians entered Anatolia at approximately the same time (c. 3000–2000 B.C.) as the Hittites and spoke a closely related Indo-European language. Undoubtedly, all Troy VI citizens spoke, and some among them probably wrote, a local language. However, scholars cannot conclude from one bronze seal that this language was Luwian.

Nevertheless, in early Greek script, Ilios is written "Wilios," and evidence exists to support the idea that Wilios was a Luwian city that the Hittites called Wilusa. Recently discovered Hittite texts suggest that, like Wilios, Wilusa was also located in northwestern Anatolia. At different times, the Luwians were rivals, allies, or vassals of the more powerful Hittites. A Hittite treaty (c. 1280 B.C.) between King Muwatalli II and King Alaksandu of Wilusa, his vassal, lists three gods as witnesses for Wilusa: Appaliunas; the "Storm God of the Army;" and Dingir Kaskal Kur ("God of the Underground River," who is also associated with other sources of water and with wells).

The names of the king (Alaksandu) and the divinity (Appaliunas) closely resemble the names and functions of Paris and Apollo, respectively, in The Iliad. Paris, who is King Priam's second son, is also known as Alexandrus ("Defender of Men"), the name he earned while living as a shepherd on Mount Ida.

Apollo is the principal god of Homer's Ilios, and throughout the tenth year of the war, he functions as a local deity who is swift to protect Troy's heroes and punish the Hellenes. Although the Mycenaean Greeks adopted Apollo and revered him as the epitome of the "Hellenic spirit," originally, he was neither a Hellenic nor a pre-Hellenic divinity, but rather a god who was first worshipped in Anatolia. For thirty years, most scholars have viewed Apollo's origin as central Anatolian, and some scholars had already identified Apollo with the Hittite god Appaliunas.

With regard to the god of water mentioned in the treaty, archaeologists have unearthed artificial caves buried beneath the ruins of the Hittite capital of Hattusha. Because they were built next to a holy lake, they appear to relate to the worship of Dingir Kaskal Kur in Hattusha. Moreover, in 1997, archaeologists excavating Troy VI unearthed the same type of artificial well-cave, with three benches, that presumably relates to the worship of Dingir Kaskal Kur in Wilusa.

Further evidence indicates that the culture of Late Bronze Age Troy was probably Luwian-Hittite. First, the defensive trench and the gates to Troy VI resemble Hittite, rather than Mycenaean, architecture. In addition, most of the Troy VI pottery that has been unearthed is Gray Minyan Ware, rather than Mycenaean. Also, in 1995, archaeologists unearthed a small bronze figure of a warrior-god that resembles figures that have been found at Hittite and other near-eastern sites.

Moreover, 1996 research into the significance of the many *stelae* (inscribed or carved stone pillars or slabs used for commemorative purposes) that have been found at the gates of Troy VI reveals that they relate to the worship of Troy's principal god, who was probably Appaliunas. Similar Late Bronze Age stelae have been found to the east, in Luwian and Hittite Anatolia, but not in the regions that border on the Aegean and Mediterranean seas.

The extensive excavations and analyses that are scheduled for the remainder of the twentieth and the early twenty-first centuries may finally turn myth and legend into fact. However historians and Homeric scholars want archaeologists to discover more than Homer's Ilios. In order to determine whether Homer's account of the Trojan War is historically accurate, archaeologists must find some remains of the Hellenic camp that would have existed near the shore of Troy's harbor during the period of Troy VI.

HOMER AND TRADITION

Although ancient literature that was written on perishable materials has disappeared, in time the continued discovery and translation of clay tablets may reveal that the destruction of so many great cities between about 1250 and 1150 B.C. inspired the creation of ancient epics in Anatolia, Syria, and other parts of the near east that are, as yet, unknown. Fortunately, the war that destroyed Ilios inspired an active oral tradition in the Greek colonies located in or near Anatolia, so that we have *The Iliad* and *The Odyssey* from the eighth century B.C. as well as six later epics about the Trojan War that exist only in the form of ancient summaries.

One of the most important books in Western literature, *The Iliad* is also one of the two earliest examples of Hellenic literature, the other being its companion epic poem, *The Odyssey.* Most scholars attribute both works to Homer. However, we have no proof that Homer ever existed, and it appears that the ancient Greeks knew no more about him than we do. Today, many Homeric scholars think that Homer lived and worked in about 760 B.C. and later. It is possible that he composed *The Iliad* as a young man and that he was much older when he composed *The Odyssey.*

The linguistic aspects of *The Iliad* and *The Odyssey* place the epics no later than the eighth century B.C. and connect them with the language of Ionia, the central part of the east Aegean coast that includes the large islands of Samos and Chios. These conclusions are consistent with the fact that, in about 700 B.C., Arctinus of Miletus wrote *The Aethiopis* to be the sequel to *The Iliad,* thus placing *The Iliad* in the eighth century B.C. or earlier. They also support the traditional idea, dating from the period between about 650 and 525 B.C., that Homer was a blind Ionian poet from the island of Chios or the city of Smyrna (now called Izmir, in Turkey).

In Homer's time, the Greeks possessed an elaborate oral tradition that had developed during the dark age that followed the collapse of the great Mycenaean civilization. Successive generations of professionally trained poets, called *rhapsodes,* learned, taught, and performed a wealth of literary material orally. A rhapsode chanted his tales to the accompaniment of his lyre (a small, harplike instrument). If he was fortunate, he became attached to a particular king's household staff;

otherwise, he traveled from house to house, earning his food and lodging with his tales. The best rhapsodes were highly respected, for they provided one of the major forms of entertainment in their day. They combined radio, television, movies, albums, history books, and novels all in one human being.

Rhapsodes served a far more important purpose as well. In times of political instability and war, they kept alive the heroic past of Greece. By recounting the great deeds of mortal men, they provided their listeners with heroic models of behavior. In a culture that had no code of ethics or body of laws, their tales presented standards and goals for living one's daily life. Courage, strength, skill, intelligence, loyalty, respect for all forms of life, moral responsibility, and hospitality were prime values; glory and honor were principal goals.

At this time, it was still the custom for a poet to create narratives without attaching his name to them. As the opening lines of The Iliad reveal, Homer viewed himself as the anonymous voice of the Muse of Epic Poetry, a daughter of Mnemosyne, the goddess of memory. Homer was the last and greatest of these anonymous poets, eclipsing all who preceded him and casting his shadow upon all who followed him in the ancient world, including the next great epic poet, Virgil. Toward the turn of the eighth century B.C., the concept of anonymity was replaced by the concept of authorship, and the seventh-century epic poets, such as Hesiod, speak in their own voice.

We do not know whether Homer put The Iliad and The Odyssey into writing, or whether he dictated them to someone else, or whether other poets memorized and performed The Iliad and The Odyssey as Homer had created them until they were eventually written down. Many contemporary Homeric scholars think that one poet wrote both The Iliad and The Odyssey. All of the existing ancient copies of The Iliad agree in terms of dialect and plot details, thus reflecting the existence of one original version. The Iliad, which is longer and more complex in its structure, is organized as if it were going to be recited rather than read. However, a literate tradition can coexist with an oral tradition.

In 1595 B.C., the Hittites had destroyed Hammurabi's city of Babylon and with it his empire. However, they had adopted Babylonian Akkadian script and Babylonian/Sumerian literature and had introduced them to the coastal lands of Anatolia and the offshore islands in the Aegean and Mediterranean. Later, many of these areas had become Greek colonies. Meanwhile, by the thirteenth century B.C., Ugarit had a cuneiform alphabet, and by the twelfth century B.C., Phoenicia had one as well. Phoenician merchants, with their prized bowls of bronze and silver, also transported goods from other eastern cultures to western communities, and wherever such trade occurred, written language developed.

Therefore, by the mid-eighth century B.C., when Homer was creating The Iliad, communities from the Euphrates River in Mesopotamia on the east to Italy on the west had become literate. In Smyrna—and, therefore, possibly on the island of Chios, as well—people still spoke, understood, and wrote the Luwian language, and Akkadian cuneiform scripts (Babylonian/Hittite/Luwian) often coexisted with three related, alphabetic Semitic scripts—the Aramaic

(Syria/Palestine), the Phoenician, and the Greek.

Moreover, folded wooden or leather writing tablets, like the one Glaucus mentions when relating the tale of Bellerophon (*The Iliad*, Book VI) were used in Mesopotamia, Syria, and Palestine. In fact, a fourteenth century B.C. wooden writing tablet has been unearthed in Turkey. However, because leather and wood are perishable materials, with the exception of the Bible (which, being a sacred text, was treated with special care), the literature written on these materials has almost completely disappeared.

Homer is first mentioned in writing that scholars date at 660 B.C. By this time, *The Iliad* and *The Odyssey* were well known throughout Hellas and the Hellenic Aegean. The writer of one of *The Homeric Hymns* refers to himself as a blind poet, and when the ancient Greeks attributed these poems to Homer, they decided that he must therefore have been blind. Late in the sixth century B.C., Chios had a guild called the *Homeridai* ("the descendants of Homer") that trained rhapsodes. By this time, *The Iliad* and *The Odyssey* were considered an important part of a Hellene's education.

Until late in the fourth century B.C., students usually memorized *The Iliad* and *The Odyssey* by listening to others recite them. It is possible that an authoritative edition of *The Odyssey* existed in Athens in the sixth century B.C.; however, few copies of *The Iliad* have been found that were written prior to the mid-fifth century B.C.

In the fourth century B.C., books became more plentiful in Athens, and a larger segment of the Athenian public could read. Thus, it is not surprising that numerous fragments of both epics have survived from this period. In addition to being written on papyrus, which was scarce and expensive, the early copies were also written on rolls of leather or on wooden tablets. By this time, Athenian authors often quoted Homer in their writings.

Many contemporary Homeric scholars think that Homer created *The Iliad* and *The Odyssey* with the knowledge of other epics in mind. Homer's choice of subjects, the related knowledge that he obviously expected his audience to possess, and the existence of six other ancient Hellenic epics on the Trojan War all reveal that Homer and the other rhapsodes of ancient Hellas knew a larger body of myth on the subject of the Trojan War.

In *The Iliad*, for example, Homer chose one event from the last year of the ten-year Trojan War and developed it in depth. He assumed that his listeners would know the complete story of the war with Ilios, the stories of all the families of the major heroes in that war, and the stories of the Olympian gods that determine their ways of relating to one another.

In keeping with the oral tradition, Homer created *The Iliad* by taking traditional building blocks of material from the poets who preceded him and reshaping them to form the foundations of his artistic creation. These blocks included various myths about the gods and about the heroes of old (the fathers of the heroes of the Trojan War); myths about the war with Ilios and its various participants, from long before the start of the war until the last of the heroes had returned home; folk tales; set passages describing scenes of sacrifice, fighting, and funerals; and particular descriptive phrases, called *epithets,* that described people and nature. From these blocks of material, Homer created two dramatic tales that were new in the important sense that each had a focus that was uniquely his own. Although Homer was trained to work within a particular framework, like all rhapsodes, he was also free to manipulate much of the material so as to reflect his own artistic vision and to please a particular audience.

Homer believed that the Muse of Epic Poetry gave him the power to remember the heroes' exact words and to describe their actions as if he had personally observed them. Often Homer would repeat descriptions and speeches, sometimes exactly and other times with slight variations. Repetition not only made the storytelling process easier, but it reminded listeners about what the poet had been telling them, for these were always very complicated tales. Approximately one-third of the lines in The Iliad are repeated, often more than once.

Homer designed his tale in the form of a tree. The principal plot forms the trunk of the tree, and many other stories branch off from the trunk. Some of the auxiliary stories are included in order to instruct particular characters in the major plot; others are inserted artistically as comic relief or as parallel subordinate plots that reinforce the theme of the principal plot. Given the extensive connections among stories, Homer invariably begins his tale in the middle and moves in many directions simultaneously.

The Iliad and The Odyssey became incorporated into a group of six other Trojan War epics that had been written by various poets in the seventh and sixth centuries B.C., and this group of eight epics became known as the Epic Cycle. The later poets were so impressed by The Iliad and The Odyssey that they made no effort to deal with the subject of either epic.

Instead, each poet chose to supplement both epics by telling a part of the Trojan War narrative that Homer had chosen to omit.

By the sixth century A.D., all of these supplementary epics had disappeared. However, a writer by the name of Proclus had summarized them, and summaries of his work have survived to this day, along with 120 more or less scattered lines from the original epics. By studying this material, it is possible to discover details about the Trojan War that Homer does not include in The Iliad and The Odyssey, and it is also possible to see what Homer undoubtedly contributed to the traditional version of that narrative. For example, it is interesting to note that Patroclus's death and funeral in The Iliad are very similar to Achilles' death and funeral in The Aethiopis. Whether Arctinus copied Homer or both poets followed the earlier oral tradition is open to conjecture.

Consistent with Homer's treatment of Patroclus in The Iliad is his creative addition of a second shield for Achilles. In both The Aethiopis and The Little Iliad, Odysseus and Ajax (Telamon's son) compete for Achilles' shield. Consequently, it appears that, traditionally, Achilles only needed and possessed one shield.

Homer straddled two cultures—Hellenic and Anatolian. First, he lived in a Greek colony that was either on the coast of Anatolia (ancient Smyrna; modern Izmir) or on an offshore island (Chios). Therefore, he was much closer to Troy than to Hellas, and it is natural that he would have been very familiar with Anatolian literary materials and historical events.

The educated Hellenic Anatolians of Homer's time and place were a cosmopolitan people. Their location enabled them to be in touch with merchants who transacted business with the peoples of many diverse cultures who lived along the shores of the Mediterranean and the Euxine Seas. Therefore, many Hellenic Anatolians spoke and wrote more than one language, including Luwian, and they enjoyed an unusually rich literary heritage.

Being a Hellene, Homer had inherited a large body of Hellenic myth and legend. Living in Anatolia, he had inherited two additional literary traditions: the rich culture that the Hittites had preserved from Ancient Sumer and Mesopotamia and the rich culture that was indigenous to Anatolia.

Being a rhapsode, Homer performed other epics than his own. Particular details in *The Iliad* and *The Odyssey* reveal that he was familiar with the older epic literature from the Middle East, such as *Gilgamesh* from Sumer/Babylonia and *The Enuma elish* from Babylonia. (Both of these are included in *World Mythology*.) For example, Achilles and Gilgamesh can be shown to follow the same heroic pattern. Moreover, Homer apparently found the close friendship between the two heroes in *Gilgamesh* to be such an appealing idea that he increased Patroclus's importance in *The Iliad* in order to create a relationship between him and Achilles that parallels the relationship between Enkidu and Gilgamesh. Patroclus does not appear to have the same relationship to Achilles in the plot of *The Cypria*, which chronologically precedes the plot of *The Iliad* in the Epic Cycle.

Moreover, being a rhapsode, Homer's knowledge of other myths and legends—including those of Anatolia— enabled him to choose from a treasure chest of literary riches. Many Hellenic and Anatolian myths and legends may already have enriched each other by the time Homer became familiar with them; others Homer himself probably combined. For example, when Glaucus tells the tale of Bellerophon, a warrior who is a Lycian and a Trojan ally, he is relating heroic exploits that occurred in Lycia (located on the southern coast of Anatolia). However, at least in Homer's version, Bellerophon is a Hellene who is sent to Lycia, where he remains, because of someone else's connection with that Anatolian kingdom.

Like Homer's version of the Bellerophon tale, his other renditions of myth and legend are the earliest we have. Therefore, we can only evaluate them in connection with later Hellenic versions and similar material from other cultures. In the process, we can see how Homer may have taken details from a competing myth or legend and adapted them to enrich his own version of *The Iliad*. For example, Proclus's summary of *The Cypria* (written c. 660 B.C. by either Staninus of Cyprus or Hegesinus of Salamis) reveals that the Hellenes leave Aulis for Ilios but arrive, by mistake, at Teuthrania, in Mysia (located east of the large island of Lesbos, on the northwestern coast of Anatolia and therefore southeast of Ilios). Believing Teuthrania to be Ilios, they sack this Mysian city.

Meanwhile, the Mysian hero, Telephus—described in later versions as the king of Teuthrania—defends the city against the Hellenes. Depending on the version of this myth—and revealing ancient cultural exchange— Telephus is either born in Mysia, arrives there from Hellas as an infant, or appears there as an adult, where he discovers his mother.

Then, in a situation that resembles that of Philoctetes (See "The Death of

Paris," in the Epilogue to *The Iliad*, in *World Mythology*), Achilles wounds Telephus, and the Hellenes return to Hellas. Meanwhile, an oracle reveals to Telephus that Achilles alone can cure him of this wound and that he is destined to guide the Hellenes to Ilios. Therefore, Telephus finds Achilles in Hellas and, in return for Achilles' cure, agrees to lead the Hellenes to Ilios. As a result, the Hellenes gather at Aulis once again, and this time their voyage to Ilios is successful.

Proclus's summary of *The Little Iliad*, written c. 660 B.C. by Lesches of Mitylene (located on Lesbos), tells of the arrival of Philoctetes from the island of Lemnos, the healing of his wound, and his single combat with Paris in which he kills Paris with Heracles' bow. Lesches also continues the tale of Telephus, when, shortly before the construction of the wooden horse, Achilles' son arrives to help the Hellenes, Telephus's son arrives to help the Trojans, and, in the course of battle, the son of Achilles kills the son of Telephus.

Finally, it is also possible that Homer could have based parts of *The Iliad* on Luwian oral and written sources. Hittite tablets record several wars with Wilusa, and a passage from a sixteenth century B.C. Luwian cult song closely resembles a description in *The Iliad*.

APPEAL AND VALUE

The survival and fame of *The Iliad* and *The Odyssey* confirm that Homer was the supreme poet of ancient Greece. Because these epics are unusually long, they made great demands both on the rhapsode and on his audience. Performing *The Iliad* must have taken between six and ten three-hour sessions and, therefore, was a form of entertainment that would continue for a three- to four-day period. According to the great philosopher Plato (427–347 B.C.), Homer was the teacher of every Hellene. In fact, Homer profoundly influenced Hellenic civilization for a thousand years, for the people of ancient Greece knew and valued his words as people continue to know and value the Bible. Moreover, students of every generation have studied *The Iliad* and *The Odyssey*, for something in Homer appeals to every human being.

Without the existence of writing, it is amazing that information about any event could survive the gap of more than four hundred years between the Trojan War and the first written version of *The Iliad*. Yet archaeologists have confirmed a surprising number of Homer's details, such as the existence of most of the communities he mentions and his descriptions of war gear. Homer memorized lists of communities that no longer existed in his own day. He also retained the use of chariots as a means of transportation across battlefields, even though chariots no longer existed in Greece when he created *The Iliad*, and he did not know their real purpose. Homer's distance in time from the events he described resulted in some inaccuracies. For example, the Mycenaeans buried their dead; they did not cremate them. Homer also describes palaces that appear to have no historical basis at all.

However, Homer is not read primarily for his history. The universal appeal of Homer resides in his heroes. What survives of the other epics in the Epic Cycle reveals that Homer was a literary giant among poets. Unlike those who came after him, Homer was a born psychologist and was far more interested in creating heroes who thought and acted like real people in time of crisis than in repeating the multitude of factual details that traditionally described the events in the Trojan War.

Because of the individual he was and the fact that he lived in a community that was, in many ways, as close to Anatolian culture as to Hellenic culture, Homer reveals his sympathy for both the Greeks and the Trojans in the great war that provides the setting for his story. Because of his gift with characterization, we, too, sympathize with Achilles and Patroclus, who find themselves caught in circumstances beyond their control. Moreover, the plight of Hector, his parents (King Priam and Queen Hecuba of Ilios), his wife (Andromache), and their young son (Astyanax) gives them a lasting place in our hearts.

Homer's heroes in *The Iliad* are remarkable in that, unlike the earlier heroes of Hellenic myth and the traditional heroes of world myth, they do not achieve fame or immortality by killing evil human beings or monsters. Instead, they are simply good men who, due to circumstances beyond their control, find themselves called upon to fight and kill other good men in battle. Homer's heroes—Greeks and Trojans alike—fight with courage, strength, and skill, and they win honor, glory, and lasting fame. However, the price of victory is as great as the cost of defeat—overwhelming suffering and death.

Many details relating to the war in *The Iliad* no longer interest contemporary readers. However, Homer's characters remain vitally alive. As we watch them react to the problems in their lives, we realize that people have remained basically the same throughout the history of the humanity. Like those who lived at the turn of the twelfth century B.C., on whom the characters in the Trojan War are based, and like Homer and his eighth century B.C. contemporaries, we have the same needs, the same types of conflicts, and the same ultimate fate, which is death. Therefore, Homer's characters become so real to us that we identify with them, and, in the process, we gain insight into our own emotions and goals. This examination of our own attitudes and values may help us exert more control over the course of our own lives.

Human emotions and behavior obviously fascinated Homer, for the opening lines of *The Iliad* state that his focus will be the anger of Achilles and the devastation it caused all of the Greeks who were fighting in the war against Ilios. In keeping with his perspective, Homer's style is dramatic rather than narrative. He does not tell us what his characters are like; instead, he reveals their personalities by actively involving us in their moments of crisis. Homer enables us to listen to their private thoughts and public statements and to watch them interact with other characters. Often, two characters who are quite different in attitude and behavior react against one another.

This approach lets us see each major character from a variety of perspectives. Each hero becomes a vital, complex person who possesses a range of emotions and whose behavior varies as his emotions change. Because the issues he faces are complex and important, the decisions he must make are never obvious or easy. Given a particular hero's values and attitudes and the very human limitations of his personality, it is as difficult to categorize him as good or evil as it would be in real life. Homer almost always leaves the interpretation of his heroes' personalities and the evaluation of their behavior to the other characters and to us.

Homer's characters stand apart from the story of the Trojan War as a sculpture stands apart from its background. Homer gives us no idea of the timing of his story beyond its duration of a few days; neither the year nor the season interests him. He tells us that the Hellenic ships are swift, black, and "hollow," that men row them and that they have sails, but we still cannot picture them in our minds. We have even less of a feel for the appearance of Ilios and the wall that protects it. Homer is interested primarily in human beings, and anything else is included in the story only to the extent that it enhances his portrayal of the individual.

Homer's extended comparisons, known as *Homeric similes,* function in this way. In these comparisons Homer relates the appearance, emotions, or actions of one of his characters to something or someone in the natural world—a particular wild animal or bird, a forest fire, flood, or storm, or a farmer or artisan working. The scenes Homer describes in his similes provide additional emotional depth by showing, for example, how much fear, anger, grief, or happiness a particular character is feeling at that moment. In this way the Homeric simile increases the significance of human emotions and actions.

THE HOMERIC HERO

The principal characters in *The Iliad* are heroic aristocrats. Homer examines their attitudes and their behavior in crucial wartime situations. These aristocrats are no strangers to the demands of war. On the contrary, their families reared them to assume a major role in the warrior culture that dominated their age. In fact, many nobles were much happier fighting on the battlefield with their friends than living at home in peaceful isolation.

The Greek nobility in the Mycenaean age valued strength and skill, courage and determination, for these attributes enabled the person who possessed them to achieve glory and honor, both in his lifetime and after he died. The Mycenaean hero never forgot that death was his ultimate fate. Faced with a grim view of life after death, he chose to concentrate on the aspects of his existence he could control, notably the quality of his life and the manner in which he died.

The striving for excellence in particular areas of human behavior, called *aretē* by the ancient Greeks, is an integral part of the Homeric hero's life. Strength, skill, and determination are necessary and admirable attributes both on the athletic field and on the battlefield. Courage and moral responsibility are obviously components in the *aretē* of the warrior. *Aretē* in the form of intelligence, insight, or ingenuity is more common in the older hero. Years of experience in the warrior culture have made the older generation of heroes more expert in this area, and one of their major roles is to counsel the younger men.

The Homeric hero strives to be the best among his peers. His goal is to achieve the greatest glory in order to earn the highest honor from his peers, his commander, and his warrior society. He has the opportunity to exhibit the greatest *aretē*—and thus win the greatest glory—on the battlefield, for armed conflict presents the ultimate challenge to his abilities. How well the Homeric hero fights, how heroic his adversary is, and how well he faces death all combine to determine how well he will be remembered and honored, not only by his companions but by society and posterity. Given that suffering and death are an inevitable part of the human condition, honor, glory, and lasting fame compensate the Homeric hero for his mortality.

The Homeric hero judges his own *aretē* by what his warrior society thinks of him. Public approval is crucial to the Homeric hero's self-esteem. His commander confers a more tangible honor by rewarding him with wealth and prizes that represent in material terms the amount of honor he has earned. Such wealth includes gold and bronze, valuable objects and animals, land and the power to rule those who inhabit it, and female slaves captured when their cities were raided. The highest and most honored prize is called the prize of honor, and in *The Iliad* this prize is the most attractive, intelligent, and skilled female captive.

Moreover, once the Homeric hero achieves his goals of glory and honor, the poets will sing about his great accomplishments, conferring wide and lasting fame upon him. Such fame is the ultimate honor, for it is the only form of immortality that any mortal can acquire. Lasting fame places the Homeric hero lower than the gods but higher than ordinary men.

The greatest insult one can confer upon the Homeric hero is to withhold the honor he has earned. The hero then feels robbed of his proper status in society, and he feels the intolerable shame of public disgrace. The Homeric hero feels dishonored if he does not receive enough wealth or appropriately impressive prizes for his contributions in battle, or if he is judged the loser in a competition that he thinks he deserved to win.

Ultimately every Greek warrior must choose between dying as a hero and dying an obscure or disgraceful death. Despite his values, the choice of how to die is never easy, for the warrior loves life and believes that death will be an eternally dull existence. Moreover, his decision inevitably involves the welfare of his society, whether in the form of his companions on the battlefield or the people of the city he is defending. Sometimes he must choose between his loyalty and responsibility to the individuals he loves most and the loyalty and responsibility he owes to the larger community. The Homeric hero's decision to accept death in order to give significance and value to his life gives him a dignity, a nobility, and a grandeur that do not tarnish with the passage of time. When he is most vulnerable, most aware of his situation, and most alone, he is most noble.

The principal focus of *The Iliad* is on the consequences of a quarrel between Agamemnon, the commander of all the Greek forces, and Achilles, his greatest warrior. In a very human but very juvenile, arrogant, and callous act, Agamemnon publicly humiliates Achilles by taking away his prize of honor. Achilles retaliates by withdrawing from battle. His decision cripples the Greek forces and results in needless suffering and death among the Greeks, eventually including the death of his best friend, Patroclus. *The Iliad* demonstrates how the actions of these two great Greek heroes cause great harm to their community (the army) when each thinks only of himself. Homer's own attitudes toward war and its heroes are reflected in the values of Agamemnon, Achilles, Patroclus, and Hector.

The issues in *The Iliad* are not simple ones by any means. The removal of

Achilles' prize of honor is a blow to his reputation as well as to his pride. Moreover, Achilles knows that if he chooses to fight in the Trojan War, he will die an early death but will be remembered as a great hero; whereas if he refrains from fighting, he will lead a long but insignificant life and will not be remembered at all. He understandably vacillates between choosing life and choosing death.

Achilles personifies what is best and worst in human nature. As he moves from one crisis to another, he is at his best when he stands apart from his warrior society and questions the values by which he and they live. He is also at his best when he offers compassion and consolation that reveal his profound understanding of the human condition. However, at his worst, Achilles behaves like a selfish child and acts like a brutal beast. With striking psychological realism, Homer portrays the two sides of Achilles' nature as they exist in the human personality, like the two sides of one coin.

Achilles is considered to be the first tragic hero in literature, and his tragedy has many possible causes. He may be a tragic figure because he must sacrifice his life in order to achieve the lasting fame that confers immortality. He may be tragic because, given his values, he is not ultimately free to choose either life or death. His tragedy may also lie in the fact that his reason for reentering the war has nothing to do with his argument with Agamemnon, the principles for which he stood, or the Greek cause. Finally, it may be tragic that his view of his fellow warriors condemns him to be honored by those whose values he does not respect. Because Homer presents all these factors, he permits us to evaluate Achilles' situation for ourselves.

Homer changed the traditional Trojan War myth wherever necessary in order to create a psychologically cohesive narrative. For example, in The Aethiopis, Zeus permits Thetis to rescue Achilles from the funeral pyre and take him to White Island in the Euxine Sea, where he lives forever. The ability of a god to grant immortality to a favored mortal occasionally occurs in the earlier, traditional body of Greek myth, and, given Achilles' heroic stature, it is likely that he would have received this highest accolade. However, by permitting Achilles to die, Homer makes The Iliad more stimulating intellectually. It is interesting to consider how Homer's audience would have responded to The Iliad, since they would have known the story of Achilles' later rescue.

Homer's treatment of the Greek and Trojan heroes is unbiased. Although the Trojans are the enemy, in Homer's epic they are not villains. They are as human and heroic as the Greeks. The greatest of the Trojan warriors is Hector, whose sense of responsibility to his people stands in sharp contrast to his brother Paris's selfishness, and to Achilles' selfishness as well. Like Achilles, Hector knows that he will die fighting in the Trojan War. He too vacillates between choosing life and choosing death, even though an honorable death will bring the immortality of everlasting fame. His death at the hands of Achilles shows only that Achilles is the greater warrior. Hector's humane values and his ultimate courage reveal that he is the greater human being.

Yet, like Achilles, Hector is not perfect. At the base of his single-minded devotion to his people is the fact that above all else, above even his wife and child, he values his reputation. Therefore, in this respect, the motivating force behind Hector's behavior is similar to that behind Achilles' behavior. Hector's fear of disgrace, with its accompanying shame, causes needless death among the Trojans, including his own.

The ancient Greeks were fond of two precepts: "Know thyself" and "Nothing in excess." However, the Homeric hero, in striving for excellence, or *aretē*, was such an accomplished individual that it was easy for him to forget his human limitations and to think that he was even greater than he actually was. The ancient Greeks called such excessive pride and arrogance *hubris*. *Hubris* would lead the hero to think that he was greater than the heroes who were his peers and that he had the limitless power that he attributed to his gods.

As a result of this attitude, the hero inevitably would say or do something excessive, without thinking of the consequences. The ancient Greeks called such action *atē*, which means blind, rash behavior. *Atē* would inevitably lead to retribution, or *nemesis*. Sometimes the gods would punish the hero directly; sometimes other human beings would punish him. Either way, the Homeric hero brought his fate, which was often death, upon himself. The reader can follow the pattern of *aretē*, *hubris*, *atē*, and *nemesis* in the behavior of Agamemnon, Achilles, Patroclus, and Hector.

WOMEN IN THE ILIAD

The Iliad is dominated by men, since it is set during the Trojan War. However, the Homeric heroes clearly place a very high value upon women. The aristrocratic woman in Mycenaean society also possesses *aretē*, consisting of beauty, intelligence, loyalty, and excellence in handicraft work (usually weaving). Although the queen's place is in the home instead of on the battlefield, as mistress of the royal household she wields great power during her husband's frequent absences.

The Homeric hero's most honored prize is the female captive who possesses the greatest *aretē*. The heroes reveal, by both their actions and their words, that they cherish these women both as individuals and as symbols of honor. It is worth noting that the abduction of Helen caused the Trojan War, and that the anger of Achilles over the seizure of Briseis, the female captive who was his prize of honor, is the focus of *The Iliad*.

However, Homer also depicts this situation from the female point of view. Through Andromache, Homer eloquently expresses the plight of all aristocratic Mycenaean women who become war's victims. The woman who is so valued as to become a prize of honor is actually enslaved by the victorious nobleman who wins her. She is carried off to a new land, where she is relegated to a life of servitude and deprivation.

Female divinities play a major role in *The Iliad*. Athena, the goddess of defensive war, is the favorite child of Zeus, the ruler of all the Greek gods, because she is so intelligent and clever. She is also the favorite divinity of the Homeric hero, whom she inspires and guides. Since the ancient Greeks gave their gods the qualities they themselves possessed, the fact that Athena is a superlative being is another indication that they esteemed women highly.

THE ROLE OF THE GREEK GODS

Because *The Iliad* is the earliest written work from ancient Greece, it is the earliest presentation of the Greek gods. The Homeric gods are ageless and immortal, can possess great knowledge of the future, and are influenced by the pleas of one another and the prayers of mortals. They have not given any moral code to mortals, nor do they live by such a code themselves. In practice, they are simply a divine aristocratic family whose members possess the same variety of feelings and attitudes as mortals. Their behavior is often angry, jealous, deceitful, and, in some instances, amusingly juvenile. It is clear that the ancient Greeks did not require perfection, either in themselves or in their divinities.

The Homeric gods are not all-powerful. Unlike divine power in the earlier, traditional body of Greek myth, fate and death are even beyond the control of Zeus, who may talk as though he could control when a mortal dies, but never tries to do so. While mortals live, however, the gods may participate in their lives by giving advice (both good and bad), by supplying thoughts and ideas, strength and skill, courage and determination, and by causing weapons to hit or miss their mark. They may appear as their divine selves, or they may disguise themselves as any human being they choose, depending upon the purpose they have in mind.

The Homeric hero feels the presence or absence of his gods. He often attributes all of his success on the battlefield to them or blames them for his failures and bad luck. However, he always accepts the fact that the gods cannot prevent his death when it is his time (his fate) to die.

The relationship between the Homeric hero and his gods is complex. The Homeric gods clearly have their favorites among mortals and make an effort to help them. However, a mortal must earn divine esteem and goodwill by the way he treats both the gods and other mortals. The gods are particularly partial to heroes because they appreciate and enjoy heroic deeds. Their help enhances the heroic stature of those warriors who receive it.

Homer attributes to the gods powers that today we ascribe to science, human nature, human skill, luck, and fate. The Homeric gods do surprisingly few things that we can explain in no other way. Certainly only a god could whisk Paris off the battlefield and into his palace bedroom. Only a god could lure Hector into a direct confrontation with Achilles and then instantly disappear. However, a god need not be present to cause the strap of Paris's helmet to break, or to tell Achilles that it is better to hurl sharp words at Agamemnon than to stab him with his sword.

The Homeric gods do not change a mortal's personality or fate. Even though the gods may give advice or help, a mortal's actions in response to any given situation are determined by his or her own personality and ability. Consequently, a mortal's fate is created by the interaction between personality and situation. Because the Homeric gods are not all-powerful, mortals can be dignified, morally responsible, and important. The world of ancient Greece contains no puppets.

PROLOGUE TO THE ILIAD

THE BIRTH OF PARIS

Hecuba, the wife of King Priam of Troy, was about to give birth when she had a dreadful nightmare. She dreamed that instead of a baby, she gave birth to a flaming torch crawling with snakes. When she told her dream to the prophets, they told her that the baby must be killed, for if he lived he would cause the destruction of Troy.

As soon as he was born, Priam and Hecuba obediently gave the baby, whom they had named Paris, to two of their trusted servants and ordered them to kill him. The servants did not have the heart to kill Paris, so they left him exposed upon a mountainside, expecting that he would die of starvation or would be mauled by wild animals. Instead, Paris was found and raised by a shepherd couple. He grew to manhood as their son.

Many years later, this shepherd boy's favorite bull was chosen by King Priam's servants to be a prize in funeral games commemorating Paris's death. The young man went to the games and won all of the contests. Priam's daughter Cassandra, to whom Apollo had given the gift of prophecy, announced that this young man was, in fact, the son they thought had died. Then his parents welcomed Paris home.

THE JUDGMENT OF PARIS

While Paris was still living with the shepherd family, an event occurred that led to the eventual destruction of Troy. Zeus, Lord of Olympus, held a royal wedding celebration to honor the sea goddess Thetis and the great mortal hero Peleus. He invited all the gods except Eris, Goddess of Discord, for a wedding is no place for arguments. Highly insulted, Eris came anyway. When she was not permitted to enter, she threw a golden apple into the hall and announced that it was a gift for the most beautiful goddess.

Every goddess wanted the honor of receiving the apple, but finally all of them gave up except for Hera, Athena, and Aphrodite. They asked Zeus to decide which of them was most beautiful, but he refused to choose among his wife and two of his daughters. So he ordered Hermes, the Wayfinder, to take the golden apple and the three goddesses to Mount Ida and to have Paris, who was herding sheep there, judge among them. Each goddess thought Paris would choose her if she promised him a special gift.

Hera said, "If you give the apple to me, Paris, I will give you extraordinary wealth and will make you ruler over all mortals."

Athena said, "If you give the apple to me, Paris, I will make you the bravest and wisest of mortal men, victorious in war, and skillful in every craft."

Finally, Aphrodite said, "If you give the apple to me, Paris, I will give you Helen, the daughter of King Tyndareus and the most beautiful woman in the world, as your wife." (It did not matter to Aphrodite that Helen was already married to King Menelaus of Sparta.)

Paris liked Aphrodite's gift best of all, so he awarded the apple to her, and from that time on Hera and Athena hated all Trojans. Paris then sailed to Sparta, where he was the guest of Menelaus and Helen for nine days. When Menelaus left on a trip, Paris convinced Helen to return to Troy with him. She left her nine-year-old daughter at home, took all of her possessions, and sailed away on Paris's ship that night.

THE MARRIAGE OF HELEN

Helen's marriage to Menelaus had involved an unusual circumstance, which also contributed to the eventual destruction of Troy. Because of Helen's beauty, many of the greatest kings in Greece approached her father, King Tyndareus, for her hand. He was afraid to choose one of them for fear that the others would be furious enough to attack the chosen suitor and destroy the marriage. Odysseus, Ajax, Menelaus, and Patroclus were among the suitors.

Odysseus looked at his competitors and decided that Helen would never choose him, for he was not handsome. He approached her father and offered to help the king solve the problem of the suitors if, in return, King Tyndareus would help Odysseus win Penelope, who was the king's niece, for his wife. Odysseus suggested that before announcing his choice, the king should make all the suitors swear that they would punish anyone who tried to break up the marriage. Once the suitors had taken the oath, King Tyndareus chose Menelaus to be the husband of Helen and Odysseus to be the husband of Penelope.

PREPARATION FOR WAR: ODYSSEUS AND ACHILLES

When Menelaus returned to Sparta and heard that Paris had carried Helen away, he went to wide-ruling Agamemnon, his powerful brother, and asked him to raise an army to bring her back. He then sent heralds to many of the Greek kings, including Helen's former suitors, to remind them of the oath they had sworn. Many kings were delighted to have an occasion for heroism and adventure; Odysseus felt otherwise.

An oracle had warned Odysseus that if he went to Troy, he would return home, alone, twenty years later. So when Agamemnon and Menelaus came for him, he pretended to be insane by harnessing a horse and an ox, instead of two oxen, to his plow. Knowing that Odysseus was a man of many schemes, the two brothers tested him by taking his infant son, Telemachus, out of his cradle and putting the baby down in front of the plow. To avoid killing his son, Odysseus had to stop pretending to be insane. He made arrangements for organizing the soldiers who would go with him to Troy, and then he left with Agamemnon and Menelaus to find Achilles.

Achilles' mother, the sea goddess Thetis, could not accept the fact that Achilles was doomed to die since his father, Peleus, was mortal. (In order to be immortal, one must have both an immortal mother and an immortal father.) When Achilles was an infant, she tried to burn away his mortality by secretly placing him in a fire at night. However, Peleus suddenly awakened in the middle of the night, found his wife holding the baby in the flames, and commanded her to stop. Thetis was so infuriated that she abandoned her husband and returned to her home in the sea to live, leaving Achilles to be reared by his father.[1]

Thetis knew that Achilles would die if he fought in the Trojan War, so she hid him in the palace of a king who was a friend of hers. The king dressed fifteen-year-old Achilles as a girl, gave him a female name, and housed him with his daughters.

---

1 A Roman poet writing more than a thousand years after the Trojan War adds more detail to this story. He says that Thetis then took the infant Achilles down to the River Styx in the Underworld. There she held onto him by the heel of one foot and submerged the rest of him in the water. The river water protected from injury every part of his body it touched, so Achilles could be wounded only in the back of one heel—the Achilles tendon. Homer, however, does not indicate that he knew this story.

Agamemnon, Menelaus, and Odysseus heard that Achilles was in the palace, but the king would not admit it. He did agree to let them search the palace, but they could not find Achilles anywhere. Odysseus, a man of many schemes, then pretended to be a peddler. He returned to the palace with a tray of beautiful scarves and jewelry, plus a spear and a shield. When the daughters of the king and their handmaidens came into the forecourt of the palace to examine these beautiful articles, he had the servants sound an alarm and shout that the palace was under attack. Achilles immediately tore off his woman's clothing, grabbed the spear and the shield, and went looking for the attackers. Instead he found Odysseus, who told him of Helen's abduction. Achilles then promised the Greek kings that he would bring his soldiers to Troy.

DEPARTURE FOR TROY

The Greek kings, with all of their soldiers, gathered at Aulis and prepared to sail across the Aegean Sea to Troy. Time passed and the fleet remained beached, for the winds would not blow in the right direction. Finally, the prophet Calchas announced that favorable winds would blow only when Agamemnon appeased Artemis, the Goddess of the Hunt, by sacrificing his most beautiful daughter. Agamemnon had killed a deer that was sacred to Artemis and then bragged that he had killed a deer the Archer Goddess could not have hit. Therefore, he would have to soothe her rage.

Agamemnon sent Odysseus to his wife, Clytemnestra, with the false message that their daughter Iphigenia should come to Aulis in order to become the bride of Achilles. When lphigenia arrived, her father let Calchas place her upon an altar. As the prophet was about to kill her, Artemis secretly substituted a deer and carried Iphigenia off to become one of her priestesses. The winds shifted, and the Greeks set sail for Troy. But Clytemnestra never forgave her husband.

THE ILIAD

Chapter 1

Agamemnon insults the priest of Apollo, causing Apollo to punish the Greeks. In order to correct the situation, Agamemnon must give up his prize of honor. Achilles and Agamemnon argue, and as a result, Agamemnon takes Achilles' prize of honor. Achilles, in turn, retaliates by withdrawing from battle.

Sing, goddess, of the time when wide-ruling Agamemnon and godlike Achilles parted in anger. The wrath of Achilles brought numerous troubles upon the long-haired Greeks and sent down to Hades the shades of many brave warriors, while dogs and birds feasted upon their dead flesh.

Who set Agamemnon and Achilles against each other? Apollo, God of the Silver Bow, caused the argument when Agamemnon dishonored Apollo's priest. Agamemnon had been awarded the priest's daughter, Chryseis, as a prize of honor, but soon the priest arrived with a rich ransom. He spoke to Agamemnon, his brother Menelaus, and all the other Greeks. "May the Olympian gods permit you to destroy Troy, Priam's great city, and return safely to your homes if you will accept my ransom and free my daughter. Do this out of reverence for the son of Zeus, far-shooting Apollo."

All of the Greeks agreed to honor the priest of Apollo, except for Agamemnon, whose heart beat with resentment. The wide-ruling king warned the priest, "Do not let me find you by our hollow ships, old man, or even Apollo will not be able to protect you! I refuse to free your daughter. Instead, Chryseis will grow old in my house in Argos, far from you and her country. There she will weave on the loom and serve me. Go peacefully now, without arousing my anger."

Agamemnon's words put fear into the priest's heart. Silently he walked some distance along the shore of the salt sea. Then he prayed to Apollo, "Hear me, God of the Silver Bow! If I have ever pleased you, let your arrows repay the Greeks for my sorrow."

So he prayed, and Apollo heard him. Down from the peaks of Mount Olympus, the Far-Shooter came like night, with anger in his heart and his bow and arrows upon his shoulders. Each invisible arrow carried a deadly disease. First he shot the mules and dogs, and then he killed so many Greek warriors for nine days that funeral pyres were burning continuously everywhere.

On the tenth day the goddess Hera felt sorry for the Greeks and put into Achilles' heart the idea of calling the Greek leaders together in council. When everyone had assembled, godlike Achilles took the speaker's staff into his hands and said, "Agamemnon, son of Atreus, we are now being destroyed by plague as well as by war. Let us ask some priest or prophet to tell us why Apollo is so angry with us. Perhaps if we appease him with a sacrifice of lambs and goats he will end the plague."

When Achilles had finished speaking, the prophet Calchas, to whom Apollo had given knowledge of the past and the future, rose and took the speaker's staff. "Achilles, dear to Zeus," he began, "I will speak out if you will promise to defend me against the anger of the one who rules over all the Greeks."

To this Achilles replied, "Be brave, Calchas, and reveal what you know. I swear by Apollo, the dear son of Zeus whose gift you possess, that as long as I live and see, no man will harm you—not even if you fear Agamemnon himself, who states that he is by far the greatest of the Greeks."

Then Calchas revealed, "The Far-Shooter is punishing us because Agamemnon has dishonored his priest by not accepting his ransom and returning his daughter. Now Apollo will not remove the plague until we have returned Chryseis freely, without accepting any gifts in return."

Agamemnon rose angrily. With rage in his heart and fire in his eyes, he grabbed the speaker's staff and exclaimed, "You prophet of evil! You never reveal any good thing! Why must you blame me for Apollo's anger just because I want to keep Chryseis in my own house? I prefer her to my wife, Clytemnestra, and Chryseis is certainly Clytemnestra's equal in beauty, intelligence, and skill with handiwork.

"Yet even though I love her," Agamemnon continued, "if it is necessary, I will return Chryseis to her father. I prefer to see the Greeks safe rather than dead. Just give me another prize so that I am not the only noble Greek without this symbol of my rank and honor, for it is not appropriate for a person of my stature to have his prize of honor taken from him."

Achilles then took up the staff and answered him. "Great son of Atreus, most greedy of all men, how can the great-hearted Greeks give you a prize of honor? We have already distributed everything of value from the cities we have raided, and it is improper to take back what we have given. However, if you give up Chryseis, we will give you prizes worth three or four times her value when Zeus lets us sack well-defended Troy."

Agamemnon replied, "Brave you are, Achilles, but do not try to deceive me. Do you think that you can keep your own prize of honor while making me return mine? No! If the great-hearted Greeks give me another prize that pleases me, I will accept it. Otherwise, I will seize a prize of honor from you, or from Ajax, or from Odysseus, by force. However, I will deal with this later. Now let us return fair Chryseis and make suitable sacrifices to Apollo, the Archer God."

Then Achilles, his eyes glaring, exclaimed, "Oh, you shameless, cunning man! How is any Greek willing to obey you? I did not come here because the Trojans had injured me. They have never bothered my pigs or horses or my fields of grain, for great distance separates the rich soil of Phthia from Troy—shadowy mountains and the salt sea. Rather it was for you, shameless one, dog-face, for you and for your brother Menelaus that we came to wreak vengeance on the Trojans.

"Yet now," Achilles continued, "you threaten to take away my prize of honor, which I earned and which the Greeks gave to me. Whenever I sack a town, my prize is never as great as yours, even though I am the greatest Greek fighter. Even so, my small prize is my own. So now I will return to my homeland. I refuse to stay here, dishonored, in order to win greater wealth for you!"

To these words wide-ruling Agamemnon replied, "Run away if you wish! I will not ask you to stay. I have many others who honor me, even Zeus, Lord of Olympus. Of all the kings Zeus favors, I hate you most of all, for you are too fond of arguing and fighting. You are strong only because a god has given you that gift. So take your men and your black ships, and go home.

"I do not care about you or your anger," Agamemnon continued, "but know this. Because Apollo has taken my Chryseis from me, I will come to your hut and take your prize of honor, fair Briseis, from you. Then you will understand how much more powerful I am than you are, and in days to come, no other king will think that he can argue with me and treat me as his equal."

As Agamemnon said these words, Achilles debated within himself whether he should draw his sword and kill this arrogant son of Atreus, or whether it would be better to control his anger. While his hand was on his sword hilt, Hera sent Athena down to him, for Hera loved both Agamemnon and Achilles. Athena stood behind Achilles and pulled his golden hair, making herself visible to him alone.

Startled, Achilles turned and recognized the bright-eyed goddess. "Why are you here, daughter of Zeus?" he asked. "Have you come to watch how this insolent king will lose his life?"

To these words Athena replied, "Hera has sent me here to ask you to control your anger, for she loves both you and Agamemnon. If you will use words against Agamemnon instead of your sword, in days to come you will receive three times as many gifts."

"No matter how angry he is," Achilles replied, "a man must obey the two of you, for the gods will listen to those who obey them." So the son of Peleus leashed his fury, took up the speaker's staff, and attacked Agamemnon with strong words instead.

"You drunkard!" Achilles exclaimed. "You with the face of a dog but the heart of a deer! You have never been brave enough to arm yourself for battle with your countrymen or to take part in an ambush with the other Greek kings. You are as afraid of that as you are of dying! Instead, you much prefer to seize for yourself the prize of any Greek who disagrees with you. You must rule over mice, not men; otherwise you would not think that you could treat other people in this way."

Achilles then announced, "By the staff I am holding in my hands, I swear before you a mighty oath. When hundreds of Greeks fall to their deaths before man-slaying Hector and you cannot defend them, all the Greeks will long for Achilles' help. Then you will sorrow in your heart, knowing that by refusing to honor the best of the Greeks, you have caused their destruction."

Then sweet-speaking Nestor, the aged and wise king of Pylos, rose, took up the speaker's staff, and spoke. "Shame upon both of you!" he cried. "It is sad to see the Greeks divided like this. Surely Priam and his sons are delighted to have such strife between the two Greeks who are greatest in counsel and in fighting. Listen to me, for I am older than both of you, and long ago even better men than you paid attention to my words."

Nestor then advised, "You, Achilles, should not think that you can fight against a king. Although you are the mighty son of a goddess, Agamemnon is greater than you are, for he is king over more people. As for you, Agamemnon, powerful as you are, do not take Briseis, for the Greeks gave her to Achilles as his prize of honor. Control your anger, for Achilles is the Greeks' great defense in this war."

Then Agamemnon replied, "You are right, old sir, but this man thinks that he is the chief commander whom everyone should obey. The immortal gods made him a spearman, but did they also give him his insulting tongue?"

Achilles interrupted him. "Yes, for people would call me a coward and a mouse if I gave in to your demands. Order others if you will, but not me, for I will obey you no longer. I will not fight you for Briseis because you gave her to me. However, if you attempt to seize anything else that is mine, my spear will invite your dark blood!"

With these words, the two leaders rose and disbanded the assembly. Agamemnon sent Chryseis homeward, with Odysseus as captain. Then he commanded the Greeks to purify themselves in the salt sea and to sacrifice bulls and goats to Apollo.

Achilles returned to his huts, where he gave up Briseis to Agamemnon's two heralds. As they were about to leave, he announced, "Let the two of you be my witnesses before the immortal gods and mortal men and before that foolish king if the day comes that the Greeks need me to save them from destruction. For the wide-ruling son of Atreus does not have the sense to look ahead and see the consequences of his actions."

Chapter 2

Achilles' mother agrees to persuade Zeus to restore Achilles' honor by showing the Greeks that, unless he rejoins the war, the Trojans will defeat them. Zeus sends Agamemnon a false dream that tells the king to attack Troy now, for the attack will be successful. When the Greeks and Trojans meet on the battlefield, Menelaus and Paris fight one another but neither warrior is clearly victorious.

Then godlike Achilles sat down alone beside the shore of the loud-sounding sea and cried. Stretching out his hands, he prayed to his mother, silver-footed Thetis. "Seeing that my life will be so brief," he began, "surely Zeus, the Loud-Thunderer, should permit me to be honored. Yet wide-ruling Agamemnon has dishonored me by seizing Briseis, my prize of honor."

Thetis heard Achilles' prayer deep in the salty sea. Quickly she emerged like a mist, comforting her son as she listened to his tale of sorrow.

When he had finished, Achilles said, "As I was growing up in my father's house, I often heard you brag about how, of all the immortal gods, you alone saved Zeus of the storm-clouds when the other gods united against him and bound him up so intricately. You brought Briareus, one of the Hundred-Handed Giants, to rescue him, and in this way you earned his eternal affection and gratitude.

"So please help me now," Achilles pleaded. "Go to Zeus, Lord of Counsel, and ask him to help the Trojans for my sake, letting the Greeks die by their ships. Only through disaster will Agamemnon, that arrogant son of Atreus, discover how blind he was when he refused to honor the best of the Greeks."

Tearfully, Thetis replied, "Knowing how short your life will be, I wish that you could have been spared this grief. Instead, you bear sorrows that are too great for any one man. Do not attempt to leash your anger. Avoid all battle, and stay instead by your swift black ships. Meanwhile, I will go up to snow-covered Olympus and plan to convince Zeus to support us."

Achilles obeyed his mother's instructions. He no longer attended the council sessions where men win glory, and he remained idly by his ships, far from the battlefield. Yet he sorely missed the war cry and the fighting.

As she had promised, Thetis approached Zeus as he sat alone upon the highest peak of many-ridged Olympus. "Father Zeus," she prayed, "if ever I have helped you by word or deed, hear my plea. Bring honor to my son who is fated to die so young, for Agamemnon has dishonored him by taking his prize of honor. Please help the Trojans until the Greeks restore my son's honor and compensate him for their insult. Bow your head in agreement, or else deny my prayer and show me how little you honor me."

Zeus, the Cloud-Gatherer, replied, "You are making my life with Hera more difficult by asking this of me. She already complains that I have given the Trojans too much help in battle. Yet I will do as you wish."

While gods and mortals slept, Zeus considered how he could best bring honor to Achilles and kill many of the Greeks beside their black ships. He decided to send wide-ruling Agamemnon a misleading dream. Calling Dream to his side, he commanded, "Go, harmful Dream, and tell Agamemnon to rouse the long-haired Greeks to battle since now they can conquer the well-defended city of the Trojans. Hera has convinced all the gods to side with the Greeks."

So Zeus spoke, and Dream went to Agamemnon, appearing in the form of Nestor, king of sandy Pylos, whom of all the elder Greeks Agamemnon most honored. "Why are you asleep, Agamemnon?" Dream asked. "A leader in your position, in charge of the entire Greek army, should have too much on his mind to sleep the night away. Now listen carefully, for I bring you a message from Zeus, Lord of Olympus, who cares for you.

"Quickly rouse all the bronze-coated Greeks to arms because now is the time to take Priam's great city. Hera has won the support of all the deathless gods, and by the will of Zeus, Troy is doomed. Do not forget these words once you awaken." So Dream spoke to Agamemnon and departed.

Once wide awake, Agamemnon foolishly believed his dream to reflect reality. He put on his tunic, cloak, and sandals and hung his sword around his shoulders. He took his father's sceptre, fashioned by Hephaestus, in his hand and had his heralds call the Greeks to assembly.

When Agamemnon had explained to the council of elders the nature of his dream, wise Nestor spoke, "Friends, kings, and leaders of the Greeks," he began, "if any other Greek had had such a dream, we might think it false and therefore ignore it. However, since Agamemnon, who states that he is by far the greatest of the Greeks, has heard these words, let us prepare to attack."

Meanwhile, Zeus sent Iris, his wind-footed messenger, to the place where the Trojan forces had assembled. There she appeared in the form of the Trojan's principal watchman. "Old sir," Iris said to Priam, "I have been a part of many battles, but I have never seen such a large and impressive army marching across the plain to attack us. In numbers they are as great as the leaves in the woods or the sands along the salt sea!"

Then Iris turned to Hector of the shining helm. "Hector, godlike son of Priam, I place you in command of all the Trojans and our allies. Because those who have come to our aid speak many different languages, let each chieftain inform and lead his own countrymen out to battle." So Iris spoke, and Hector knew her true voice and obeyed her advice.

The horse-taming Trojans marched upon the field as noisily as cranes fly up into the sky toward the ocean when they flee from the heavy rains of winter. The bronze-coated Greeks silently approached them, each man with courage in his heart and eager for battle.

Just as the south wind spreads a mist over mountain peaks—a mist that the shepherd despises but the robber loves, for it hides the land and a man can see no farther than he can throw a stone—so the feet of these hundreds upon hundreds of marching men created a heavy cloud of dust over the armies as they moved quickly across the plain.

As the Greeks approached the Trojans, Paris became the Trojan champion. Carrying a bronze-tipped spear in each hand and upon his shoulders a panther skin, his curved bow, and his sword, he challenged the Greeks. "Come forth, any of you who think you are the best of the Greeks!" he announced. "I challenge you to fight me face to face to the death!"

Menelaus was pleased in his heart to see Paris emerge from the Trojan throng. Just as a hungry lion is delighted to come upon the carcass of a great horned stag or a wild goat, and he eats the tasty flesh even though he senses that young hunters with their pack of dogs are swiftly coming upon him, so Menelaus was delighted to see Paris, for the war-loving king of Sparta was anxious to take vengeance upon the Trojan prince who had taken fair Helen from her home and had carried her across the sea to Troy.

But when Paris saw Menelaus leap from his chariot in order to accept his challenge, Paris suddenly became terrified. As a man turns pale, trembles, and reels backward when he spies a snake on his mountain path, so did Paris shrink fearfully away from war-loving Menelaus and hide among the Trojan ranks.

When Hector observed this behavior, he criticized his brother with strong words. "Evil Paris! You are so handsome that women cannot resist you. It would have been far better for the Trojan people had you never been born or had you died unwed. As it is, your behavior is shameful. Your countrymen scorn you, and Greeks must be laughing indeed to see that the Trojan champion, for all his beauty, lacks courage and strength in his heart."

Hector then asked, "Are you the same man who crossed the salt sea to a strange land and returned with a beautiful woman, bringing sorrow upon your father, your city, and your countrymen and shame upon yourself? Do you really intend to evade Menelaus? You should learn what kind of man he is whose wife you took. You will find no help in your lyre or in the gifts Aphrodite has bestowed upon you, for Menelaus is a respected warrior who would send you, defeated, into the dust. The Trojan people must share your cowardice, or they would have stoned you to death long before this, for all the evils you have brought upon them."

To these words, Paris replied, "Hector, you are right to criticize me, but do not blame me for golden Aphrodite's gifts. Instead, command all the Greeks and

Trojans to stand aside while I fight Menelaus hand to hand for fair Helen and all her treasure. Then our people and their allies can return to their homes, and the Greeks can return to their lands in peace."

All the Greeks and Trojans were overjoyed to hear Hector's announcement, for the war rightfully was a conflict between Paris and Menelaus, and few were enthusiastic about continuing the fighting into this tenth year. The leaders of both forces united in prayer to Zeus and the other immortal gods, swearing to the terms of the agreement.

Wide-ruling Agamemnon raised his arms and prayed, "Father Zeus, observe our oaths. If Paris kills Menelaus, fair Helen and all her possessions will be his, and we will return to Greece empty-handed. But if fair-haired Menelaus kills Paris, then the Trojans must return Helen and her treasure along with suitable compensation for inciting us to war. Otherwise, I will remain on Trojan soil and continue to fight until I win what is rightfully mine."

When Paris and Menelaus had armed themselves, they entered the clearing between the seated Trojan and Greek forces, approaching each other with glaring looks and ready spears. Paris was the first to throw his far-shadowing spear, which bent its bronze point upon meeting Menelaus's round shield.

As Menelaus raised his spear, he prayed, "Zeus, Lord of Olympus, permit me to punish Paris for stealing my wife so that any guest hereafter will fear to commit an offense against his friendly host." His spear penetrated Paris's armor, but it did not draw blood, and when he smashed his sword upon Paris's helmet, the sword fell to the ground, broken into four pieces.

So war-loving Menelaus jumped upon Paris, grabbed the thick horse-hair crest of his helmet, pulled him around, and began to drag his body backward toward the seated Greeks. Paris would have strangled to death, bringing Menelaus endless glory, if Aphrodite had not observed Paris's plight and cut his helmet strap, permitting him to break loose from Menelaus's grasp. When Menelaus leaped after Paris with his bronze spear he could not find him, for Aphrodite had lifted him up, hidden him in a dense mist, and returned him to his bedroom in Priam's great city.

Agamemnon shouted, "Hear me, all you Trojans and your allies. Obviously Menelaus has won the duel, so return Helen and her treasure to her rightful husband, and compensate the Greeks for Paris's offense." So he spoke, and all the Greeks shouted in agreement.

However, Hera and Athena were still angry with Paris for choosing Aphrodite's beauty over their own. This meant that Zeus could keep his word to Thetis without offending them, and the immortals agreed that Athena should cause the battle to resume.

Athena chose the Trojan Pandarus and appeared to him in the form of a respected Trojan spearman. "Why don't you shoot Menelaus with one of your arrows?" she suggested. "Then you will win fame and honor in the eyes of all the Trojans, especially Paris. He surely will reward you most handsomely for killing Atreus's war-loving son!"

So bright-eyed Athena persuaded the foolish Pandarus to draw his bow upon the unsuspecting Menelaus. However, because Athena at heart was a friend to the king of Sparta, she directed Pandarus's arrow through Menelaus's belt, where it wounded but did not kill him.

Agamemnon was so outraged at the injury to his brother that no one could accuse him of reluctance or cowardice as the Trojans resumed the battle. Leaving his chariot, he went by foot through the ranks of the bronze-coated Greeks, eagerly cheering them on to battle and the winning of glory. "Father Zeus will not help those who do not keep their word," he cried, "so be of good strength and courage. Vultures will feed on Trojan flesh, and many Trojan wives and children will sail home with us once we have taken Priam's well-defended city."

Just as the waves of the salt sea pound the shore, one after the other, driven forward by the west wind, so did the Greeks return to the battle, group after group, in endless succession; and each chieftain commanded his respectful, silent men, gleaming in their armor.

The Trojans, on the other hand, were as noisy as herds of sheep impatiently waiting to be milked, for they included peoples from many lands who did not share a common language. Bronze clashed upon bronze until untold numbers of Greeks and Trojans remained upon the plain, intermingled, with their faces buried in the dust.

Chapter 3

Hector returns to Troy. He urges Paris to join the Trojan warriors and then he bids farewell to his wife and son.

Hector of the shining helm decided to leave the plain of battle and enter Priam's great city in order to ask the women of Troy to pray to the deathless gods for help. The bronze-coated Greeks were clashing against the horse-taming Trojans with a mighty uproar, and Hector was no longer confident of a Trojan victory. Louder than the waves of the sea as they crash upon the shore when they are driven from the ocean's depths by the harsh blowing of the north wind; louder than the roaring of a fire that rages among the trees of a forested mountainside; louder than the howling wind among the highest branches of the oak trees were the Greeks and Trojans as Hector left them.

When his mother spied him, she cried, "My dearest child, why have you left the dreadful battle to return home? Do you wish to offer prayers to Zeus, Lord of Olympus? Stay while I bring you honey-sweet wine for the prayer, and then relax and have some wine yourself." So Queen Hecuba spoke to her godlike son.

Man-slaying Hector replied, "Mother, do not bring me any honey-sweet wine unless you want to weaken me and make me forget my strength and my courage. I am so covered with the dirt and blood of battle that it is wiser for you and the other women to pray to Athena than for me to petition Zeus of the storm clouds. I am here to call Paris to battle if he will listen to me."

Hector found his brother at home in his bedroom aimlessly handling his shield and his bow while Helen sat among her servants and their handiwork. Again he addressed Paris with contempt. "Strange man! Your countrymen are dying in battle upon the wall and within the city, and here you sit! And yet you are the person responsible for the raising of the war cry around Troy. You yourself would be very angry with any coward you caught shrinking away from this hateful war. So arise and help defend your city before it is burned to the ground!"

"You are right, as usual, Hector," replied Paris. "Even Helen has been urging me to join the fighting. So either stay with us while I put on my armor or else go on your way. I will follow, and I will probably overtake you before you leave the city."

When Hector did not reply, Helen softly spoke to him. "I wish that on the day I was born, a great storm wind had carried me away to some lonely mountainside or to the shore of the loud-sounding sea, where the waves would have washed me away, for then this hateful war never would have occurred. Or, considering that the deathless gods determined these events, I wish that they had married me to a better man than Paris, one who could feel the anger and hatred of his family and his people. Paris will never change, so I fear that he will reap the bitter fruit of the seeds he has sown. But come and sit down, dear Hector, since Paris's foolishness and my shame have laid the heaviest burden upon your shoulders."

Hector replied, "Do not ask me to stay, Helen, even though you love me. I am most anxious to rejoin the Trojan forces, whom I know miss my help while I am within the city walls. Try to make Paris hurry so that he will be able to overtake me. Meanwhile, I will go home to see my dearest wife and baby, perhaps for the last time."

With these words, Hector went searching for his wife and child. They met near the Scaean Gates, the entrance to Priam's great city, for Andromache had been standing upon the wall of Troy, weeping as she searched the battlefield for him. Hector smiled silently as he gazed upon his infant son, but Andromache tearfully approached her husband, took his hand in hers, and pleaded with him.

"Oh, Hector," she cried, "your courage and your skill in battle will destroy you! You lack any pity for your baby son, who will become an orphan, or for the woman who will soon be your widow, for the bronze-coated Greeks will soon kill you.

"It would be better for me to die than to lose you," she continued, "for swift-footed Achilles has made me an orphan. He killed my kingly father in his armor and murdered my seven brothers as they were tending their sheep, and then Artemis killed my mother. So, dear Hector, you are my father, my mother, and my brother, as well as my husband. Have pity upon me, and remain here upon the wall of Troy."

Finally Andromache advised her husband, "Position the Trojans by the wild fig tree, for there the wall is most easily accessible. Three times already the greatest warriors among the Greeks have tried to enter there."

Hector responded, "Dearest wife, I too have thought of this, but our people would look upon me with shame if I were to shrink like a coward from battle. My own heart cannot tolerate such behavior. I was taught to be courageous always and to lead the Trojans into battle to win great glory for my father and myself.

"My heart and my soul tell me that the day will come when the Greeks will destroy our fair city and its people. Yet I do not grieve for anyone in my family as much as I do for you when some Greek steals your freedom and leads you across the salt sea against your will.

"There," Hector added, "as a slave in some Greek household, you will work at the loom as some mistress directs you, and you will carry water from the spring as part of your sad burden. And when he notices your tears, some stranger will say, 'Look. There goes the wife of man-slaying Hector, who was the greatest in war of all the Trojans in the days when man fought against man at Troy.' May I be dead and may the earth cover my body before the Greeks enslave you."

With these words, Hector stretched out his arms to his little son, but Astyanax, terrified by his father's shining bronze helmet with its wildly waving horsehair crest, tearfully withdrew from his embrace. Then Hector and Andromache laughed together, and Hector removed the helmet from his head and placed it upon the ground.

Taking his infant son in his arms, Hector kissed Astyanax and prayed. "Zeus and all you other immortal gods," he began, "permit my son to live and grow to be as I am: courageous and strong, and foremost among the Trojan people; and grant that he will become a great king of Troy. Then one day may someone say of him as returns from war, 'He is better far than his father!' and his mother will be glad in her heart."

Hector then placed Astyanax in his mother's arms, and she held him, smiling through her tears. This sight brought pity to Hector's heart, and he caressed Andromache as he said, "Dearest, please try not to be too unhappy. I will not die before my fate sends me down to Hades, and I share the same fate as every other mortal; neither the courageous nor the cowardly can escape it.

"So return home," her husband concluded, "and keep busy with your daily chores. War is the responsibility of the men of Troy and, therefore, mostly mine." Hector put his crested helmet upon his head and returned to his men.

Andromache walked home, frequently looking back tearfully. When she arrived, all the women of the household cried for Hector, even though he still lived, for in their hearts they knew that he would never return alive from this battle with the Greeks.

Paris did not dally long at home. Just as a well-fed horse breaks his rein and goes galloping across the field, anticipating a swim in the fast current of the river, and rejoices in his strength and splendor as he carries his head high and feels his mane waving upon his neck, so Paris in his sparkling armor moved through the streets of the city on his swift feet, laughing with the pure joy of being alive.

He met his brother as Hector was leaving the place where he had talked with Andromache. "Hector," Paris apologized, "I am sure that I delayed you and did not come as soon as you wished."

To these words Hector replied, "No one who is observant can criticize your skill in battle, Paris, for you are courageous and strong. But you are also irresponsible, and it makes me sad to hear the Trojans say truly that you are the cause of their troubles. However, let us go on our way. We will deal with this later if Zeus permits us to drive the Greeks from our land."

Chapter 4

Agamemnon's advisors counsel him to apologize to Achilles. He offers Achilles many gifts if he will rejoin the Greeks and keep Hector from burning their ships, but the warrior refuses.

The Trojans were fighting with skill, spirit, and success. With the allies they had summoned from many lands, they frustrated every attempt of the bronze-coated Greeks to subdue them.

Without Achilles to lead his countrymen, the Myrmidons, and without the gods to help them, the Greeks were not equal to Hector and the Trojan army. Just as farmers and their dogs force a lion out of the cattle pen so the wild beast cannot capture the fattest of the herd, and they remain on watch throughout the entire night and when the lion returns, skillful hands send arrows and dreadful flaming torches to frighten it away, until with the coming of rosy-fingered Dawn the lion finally retreats in anger, so the Trojans sent the Greeks back across the plain toward their hollow ships.

There Agamemnon, with sadness in his heart, commanded his heralds to call the Greek leaders to assembly. When everyone had arrived, the wide-ruling king rose and addressed them. As a waterfall pours down the face of a cliff into the dark stream below, so Agamemnon stood weeping before the gathering.

"My friends, leaders, and chieftains of the Greeks," he began. "Cruel Zeus, Lord of Olympus, has blinded me. Long ago he promised me, and he bowed his head to it, that I would not return home until I had destroyed well-defended Troy. Obviously he was deceiving me. So let each of us gather our countrymen into our hollow ships and return to our homeland, for we cannot hope to capture Troy. We need not feel ashamed to run from ruin, even in darkness, for it is better to escape and live than to be captured or killed."

Those assembled before him sat in complete silence. Finally, Odysseus rose. "Son of Atreus, do you mean these words you have just spoken? If so, it would be far better if you commanded some ordinary army. Do you really wish to leave Troy now, after we have fought here for nine years to destroy it? Remain quiet so that no other king will think to follow your poor example. You must have lost your senses to speak to us in this way in the midst of battle. Your advice would be the dearest wish of the Trojans."

Agamemnon replied, "Your words have touched my heart. I would not have the bronze-coated Greeks withdraw against their will. I welcome other opinions on this matter."

Nestor, the wise king of Pylos, rose. "Great son of Atreus, wide-ruling Agamemnon, I will begin and end with you, for Zeus has enabled you to rule all the men gathered here. It seems best to remind you of the day long ago when, against my advice and the consent of all gathered here, you took from godlike Achilles' hut his prize of honor, fair Briseis. By giving your pride free reign, you dishonored a mighty warrior whom the deathless gods honor. Consider how best to apologize, with what word to entreat him, and with what gifts to persuade him to rejoin us."

Agamemnon replied, "Old sir, you are right to remember my foolishness. I do not deny that I was blinded by my strong feelings. As a result, Zeus honors

Achilles, whom he loves in his heart, and is destroying us. To atone for my insult, I will give the son of Peleus an overwhelming number of impressive gifts.

"I will give swift-footed Achilles seven new tripods, untouched by fire; the weight of ten talents in gold; twenty shining cauldrons; and twelve strong, swift, prize-winning horses. I will also give him seven beautiful women who are skilled at handicraft, among them Briseis, whom I have never touched."

Agamemnon added, "Later, if the gods permit us to seize well-defended Troy, let Achilles pile gold and bronze into his hollow ships and choose for himself the twenty most beautiful Trojan women next to Helen. And if we return to the rich land of Argos, I will honor Achilles as I honor my son Orestes. Let him choose any one of my three daughters to be his wife, and he need offer none of the usual courting gifts. Finally, I will give him seven large cities near the salt sea on the border of sandy Pylos, cities that are rich in sheep and cattle, whose people will honor him as if he were a god.

"All this I will do for Achilles if he will put aside his anger. Only Hades, lord of the dead, is unrelenting, and he is, therefore, the god whom mortals hate most. The son of Peleus should agree to my proposal because I am older than he is, and I am a greater king."

So spoke Agamemnon, and everyone was pleased with his words. Nestor then said, "Great son of Atreus, no one could find fault with the gifts you are offering Achilles. So let us choose who will approach Achilles in your name. First let Phoenix, Achilles' tutor, lead the way, followed by Ajax and Odysseus."

The three men walked along the shore of the loud-sounding sea with prayers in their hearts that Poseidon, the Earthshaker, might help them persuade Achilles to their cause. When they arrived, Achilles greeted them warmly. "Welcome!" he cried. "Even in anger, you are my dearest friends! The bronze-coated Greeks must desperately need my help that they have finally sent you to me."

After Achilles had fed them, Odysseus discussed why they had come. He explained the successes of the Trojans under Hector's leadership, and he repeated the list of gifts that Agamemnon was offering Achilles if he would forget his anger and return to the war.

When he had finished recounting the gifts, Odysseus said, "But if you hate the son of Atreus and his gifts too much, then at least have pity for the rest of us! We will honor you as a god, for you will win great glory. Now you may easily kill Hector, for he thinks there is no one who can match him among the Greeks."

Achilles replied, "Odysseus, man of many wiles, I will say exactly what I think so that you will not think you can argue with me. I hate a man who thinks one thing but speaks another.

"Neither Agamemnon nor any other bronze-coated Greek will persuade me to rejoin the battle, for it seems that no one appreciates the warrior who fights without rest. He who remains at home receives the same gifts as he who fights his best; the coward is honored equally with the brave man; and death is the fate of both the man who is idle and the man who works hard. I have spent many a bloody day in battle and many a sleepless night in watch. I destroyed twelve Trojan cities from my ships and eleven more by land. I took much treasure from these cities and gave all of it to Agamemnon. He remained behind, beside his hollow ships, and from the treasures I gave him, he distributed a few and kept the rest. Some he gave to kings and chieftains, and they have been allowed to keep them. Only from me did he take a prize of honor."

Achilles went on to say, "Agamemnon has led all of us here to bring Menelaus's wife, fair Helen, back to Sparta. Are the two sons of Atreus the only mortal men who love their wives? Surely I love mine with all my heart, even if she is a captive I won with my spear.

"I know Agamemnon too well. He does not keep his word. He will not deceive me again, nor will he persuade me to come to his aid. Even his gifts are hateful to me; I would not accept them if they were as many as the sands of the salt sea and the dust of the earth, and I would not marry his daughter if she were as beautiful as Aphrodite and as skilled in handiwork as Athena.

"What are gifts compared to life!" Achilles concluded. "My goddess mother has told me that if I stay here and fight at Troy, I will never live to return home, although I will have gained eternal fame. On the other hand, if I return to my homeland, I will lose all fame but live a long life. I am choosing life, and I advise you to do the same. You will not conquer the great city of Priam, for the horse-taming Trojans are a courageous people, and Zeus is watching over them. So let the arrogant son of Atreus plan the best way to keep man-slaying Hector from burning the Greek ships. The wall and the ditch will not be sufficient to stop him, so courageous and confident is he now that I am not fighting. Return to Agamemnon with this message, but let Phoenix sleep here tonight so that he can sail home with me tomorrow if he chooses."

For a few minutes after Achilles had spoken, everyone remained silent, overwhelmed by what he had said and the strength of his feeling. Then Phoenix spoke through his tears. "If you are indeed determined to return home and will not help protect the Greek ships from Hector's fire, then I must return with you.

"I have loved you and reared you as I would my own son, Achilles. I ask you now to rule your pride, and let pity enter your heart. Even the deathless gods bend, and they are far greater than you are. If Agamemnon were not offering you gifts, I would not ask you to put aside your anger and help the Greeks in their need. But he is amply rewarding you, and he has sent the best warriors, your dearest friends, to plead with you. Do not look arrogantly upon their words or upon their visit here.

"Until now," Phoenix concluded, "no one could blame you for your anger, but the time has come for you to relent. It will be much harder to save the hollow ships once they are burning. So agree to help the Greeks while they are offering you gifts, and they will honor you as a god. If you enter the battle later, you will have given up the gifts, and you will have lost much honor even if you save the ships."

Achilles replied, "Phoenix, old sir, Father, I do not need the long-haired Greeks to honor me. Zeus, Lord of Olympus, has honored me, and his honor will be mine as long as I live. Do not annoy me by taking Agamemnon's part against me, or I will hate you as I hate him. Let the others return to the son of Atreus with my message. Meanwhile, spend the night with me, and in the morning we will discuss whether we should remain here or return home."

Ajax then said to Odysseus, "Let us be on our way, for we should quickly deliver Achilles' message, even if it is not a good one. The son of Peleus has no pity for his friends who have honored him above everyone else. A man accepts payment from the one who kills his brother or his son, and for a great price, the one who killed can continue to live in his own country.

"But you, Achilles, will not bend because of one woman, when we have offered you seven of the best women and many other gifts besides. Respect yourself and us, for we would like to be your dearest friends."

Achilles answered, "I would agree with you, Ajax, except that I am furious to think of how the arrogant son of Atreus has dishonored me among the Greeks as though I were some worthless stranger. So return with my message. I will not join the fighting until Hector brings fire to my own ships, and there I will stop him."

Ajax and Odysseus returned to Agamemnon. When Odysseus repeated Achilles' message, the hearts of the Greek leaders and chieftains were sad. They realized that the son of Peleus would fight only if and when his heart moved him to do so. Until then, the bronze-coated Greeks would have to rely upon their own courage and strength.

Chapter 5

Patroclus convinces Achilles to let him lead the Myrmidons into battle. Wearing Achilles' armor, Patroclus pushes the Trojans away from the Greek ships and back toward Troy. Finally, Hector kills him.

When Dawn, the rosy-fingered, shone forth upon gods and mortals, the war resumed. Just as reapers push into one another as they move through a rich farmer's field of wheat or barley, and many handfuls of grain quickly fall about them, so the bronze-coated Greeks and the horse-taming Trojans leaped upon each other and cut one another down, with no thought of retreat. Neither side gave in to the other, and they tore on like wolves.

Achilles stood at the stern of his black ship, watching the return of injured Greeks. Calling his closest friend to him, Achilles said, "Good Patroclus, dearest to my heart, I think the Greeks soon will be praying at my knees for me to help them, for they appear to be in great trouble. Go ask Nestor whom he has brought wounded from the field; I fear it is our doctor, and that, indeed, would be a cause of fear and grief."

When Patroclus questioned Nestor, the king of Pylos asked him, "Does Achilles suddenly pity the Greeks? Does he care that many of our greatest warriors are lying by their hollow ships sorely wounded by arrows or spears?"

Nestor then told Patroclus, "I remember that when Odysseus and I came to Phthia to ask Achilles to join wide-ruling Agamemnon and the other Greek leaders, your father told you to be your dear friend's adviser. Although Achilles is stronger than you are, you are older and, therefore, wiser than he is. Counsel him now. Perhaps he will take your words into his heart.

"And if, perhaps, some prophecy of his mother is restraining Achilles from fighting, let him place his armor upon you and permit you to lead the Myrmidons into battle. With godlike Achilles' armor upon you, the Trojans may think that you are indeed he, and they may retreat in fear."

Then Nestor concluded, "The Greeks need a chance to rest, for they are weary with fighting. Your countrymen are so well-rested that it will be easy for you to push the tired Trojans back from our huts and our ships across the plain toward Troy." So Nestor of sandy Pylos, in his wisdom, put fire into the heart of good Patroclus.

The Trojans, who had been fighting by the wall the Greeks had constructed to protect their huts and their ships, suddenly pushed forward. Just as a great wave upon the salt sea is forced by the fury of the strong wind into a mighty swell and rushes down upon the decks of a ship and engulfs it, so the Trojans, with a loud war cry, drove their chariots over the defensive wall to the sterns of the Greek ships. They fought the Greeks there face to face.

As a starving mountain lion courageously enters a well-built sheepfold to seize its prey, and although it sees that the shepherds are prepared to defend the sheep with their swift spears and their dogs, it is determined to capture a sheep or else die in the attempt, so did man-slaying Hector of the great war cry put courage into the hearts of the Trojans and lead them to set fire to the hollow ships of the Greeks.

By the time Patroclus reached Achilles, he was in tears. The son of Peleus pitied him and asked, "Patroclus, dearest of friends, why are you weeping like a little girl who runs by her mother's side and slows her down by pulling at her robe and tearfully crying up at her until her mother picks her up? Have you heard that your father or mine has died? Or are you grieving for the bronze-coated Greeks who are being killed beside their black ships because of their arrogance?"

Then did great-hearted Patroclus foolishly relate to Achilles the plight of the Greeks and his wish to lead the Myrmidons into battle in Achilles' place, for he did not realize that he was, in fact, pleading for his own death.

Patroclus's words weighed upon Achilles' heart, and he replied, "Dear Patroclus, it is not my mother's prophecy that keeps me from battle. I simply could not let a man who is my equal seize my prize of honor just because he is more powerful than I am. I did not intend to be angry forever, but I did say that I would not rejoin the Greeks until Hector threatened my own ships.

"However," Achilles relented, "put my shining armor upon your shoulders, if that is your wish, and lead the war-loving Myrmidons into battle yourself. Drive the Trojans from the hollow ships, for if they burn the ships, the Greeks will have no way to return home. Win enough glory that the Greeks will return Briseis to me along with many impressive gifts, but not so much glory that your success will lessen my own value and my own honor. Although you love the war cry, once you have cleared the Trojans from the ships and have sent them in retreat across the plain toward Troy, return to me."

When Patroclus, wearing the armor of Achilles, was ready to depart with the Myrmidons, Achilles prayed to Zeus. "Lord of Olympus, in the past you have heard my prayers. You have honored me, and you have brought destruction upon the Greeks. Now hear my prayer again. I am sending my dearest friend into war with my Myrmidons. Grant him success and glory, but when he has driven the Trojans from the hollow ships, let him return uninjured to me."

So Achilles, son of Peleus, prayed, and Zeus, Lord of Counsel, heard him. He permitted Patroclus to drive the Trojans from the swift black ships, but he did not permit him a safe return from battle.

With Patroclus in the lead, the war-loving Myrmidons marched into battle. Patroclus cried, "Myrmidons, friends of Achilles, courageously win honor for the son of Peleus, so that wide-ruling Agamemnon will realize how blind he was when he dishonored the best of the Greeks."

So Patroclus put strength and courage into the hearts of the Myrmidons as they joyfully prepared to attack the Trojans. Like wasps along the wayside that swarm angrily from their nests when young boys foolishly torment them for the fun of it, so the Myrmidons swarmed upon the Trojans with a great war cry.

When the Trojans saw Patroclus in Achilles' shining armor, fear entered each man's heart, for they thought that godlike Achilles himself would soon be upon them. They gave way before the Myrmidons and considered how best to escape total destruction.

Just as a winter rainstorm at its peak causes swift, swollen rivers to wash away whatever lines their banks, so Patroclus raged across the plain, causing many Trojans to fall beneath his sharp spear. If he had remembered to return to the ships, as Achilles had counseled him, he would have avoided his fate. However, blind in his heart, he forgot the words of his dearest friend and foolishly pressed on across the plain toward Troy.

Then the bronze-coated Greeks would indeed have captured high-gated Troy under the leadership of Patroclus, but Apollo came down from Mount Olympus to stand upon the well-built wall and help his favorites. Three times Patroclus climbed upon a corner of the high wall, and three times the Lord of the Silver Bow raised his immortal hands, pushed against Patroclus's shining shield, and threw him back.

When Patroclus, undaunted, made a fourth attempt to climb the wall, Apollo stopped him with a terrifying cry. Then he said, "Give up, Patroclus! It is not your fate to sack the great city of Priam with your spear; nor will swift-footed Achilles destroy this city, and he is a far better man than you are." Patroclus obeyed Apollo's command, having no intention of angering the Far-Shooter.

Meanwhile, Hector of the flashing helm was standing at the Scaean Gates and wondering whether it would be better to continue the fighting or to summon the Trojans inside the well-defended walls. Apollo assumed the form of Hector's uncle and said, "Godlike Hector, why are you not fighting? It is not honorable to stand about idly while others are winning glory for themselves and their fathers. If I were strong enough, I would punish you for your cowardice. Now drive your horses toward Patroclus and kill him; then Apollo, the Far-Shooter, will give you glory." So spoke Apollo, and Hector returned to the battle.

As long as the sun was high in the sky, the spears and arrows of Greeks and Trojans took an even toll. But when the sun revealed that the time had come to unyoke the oxen and stable them for the evening, then the bronze-coated Greeks took the lead.

Three times Patroclus, shouting the great war cry, killed nine men. As he raged on for the fourth time, far-shooting Apollo enveloped himself in a thick mist and came up behind Patroclus. Unseen, the Lord of the Silver Bow took his immortal hand and struck the warrior on the back with such a mighty force that his eyes whirled in his head. Then he knocked Patroclus's helmet to the ground, where it clattered as it rolled beneath the feet of the horses, and its horsehair crest became covered with blood and dust.

Still Apollo was not finished with Patroclus. The warrior's bronze-tipped, far-shadowing spear broke apart in his hands, his shield fell to the ground, and his armor loosened. Then his mind became blind, and as he was standing senseless, a Trojan came up behind him and speared him in the back. However, even this wound did not kill Patroclus.

Man-slaying Hector then approached and drove his spear clear through Patroclus's stomach. Just as a mountain lion overpowers a mighty boar when the two fight upon a mountaintop for the right to drink from a little spring, so did Hector, godlike son of Priam, end good Patroclus's life.

Standing over the fallen body of his enemy, Hector said, "Patroclus, you thought that you would sack Troy! You wanted to make slaves of our women and return with them to your homeland. You were a fool! Instead, vultures will feed upon your flesh. Even your dear friend, Achilles, with all his courage, strength, and skill, could not help you. He must have commanded you to kill me. He muddled your good sense!"

The dying Patroclus replied, "You can boast about my death only because Zeus and Apollo first subdued me. Otherwise, if twenty Hectors had attacked me, I would have killed them all with my spear. You were not first but third in my slaying.

"And remember this well," Patroclus concluded. "You yourself do not have long to live, for it is your fate to be killed by Achilles. Even now, your death is very close at hand." With these words Patroclus's shade left his body and went down to the kingdom of Hades.

Hector replied to the dead Patroclus, "Why do you prophesy my death? Maybe I will kill the son of Peleus!" He then removed Achilles' shining armor from Patroclus and took it for himself. He would have dragged off Patroclus's body as food for the dogs of Troy, but Ajax took his shield, which was like a wall, and defended the corpse.

The bronze-coated Greeks then fought the horse-taming Trojans for the body of Achilles' friend. All day long the battle raged. Just as a man gives the hide of a great bull, soaked in fat, to his people to stretch, and they arrange themselves in a circle, where they stand and pull it until the moisture evaporates, the fat penetrates the skin, and the hide is completely stretched out, so the Greeks on one side and the Trojans on the other pulled the body of Patroclus first this way and then that until, at long last, the Greeks were able to carry his corpse back to the hollow ships.

Chapter 6

As soon as Achilles hears that Hector has killed Patroclus, he is determined to kill Hector. He and Agamemnon formally settle their quarrel, and Achilles shows his skill on the battlefield. Hector flees from him, and Achilles chases Hector around the walls of Troy.

Meanwhile, back at his hut, Achilles was filled with foreboding. "Why are the Greeks being driven back again?" he asked himself. "My mother once told me that I would live to see the best of the Myrmidons felled by Trojan hands. Great-hearted Patroclus! My dearest friend! How foolish of him to ignore my words and fight against man-slaying Hector."

While he was thinking such thoughts, the son of Nestor arrived in tears and announced, "I am so sorry to bring you very sad news, Achilles. Hector has killed Patroclus and has taken his armor. Now our warriors are fighting the Trojans for his very body!"

These words enveloped Achilles in a black cloud of grief. With both hands he covered his head and clothing with black soil. Then he lay himself in the dirt and tore his hair.

As he moaned in grief, silver-footed Thetis appeared before him. "My child, why are you crying?" she asked. "Zeus, Lord of Counsel, has indeed granted your wish, and the bronze-coated Greeks are sorely in need of you."

Achilles replied, "Mother, even if the deathless gods have heard my prayer, what joy can I have when Patroclus, dearest of all to me, is dead? I no longer care to live unless I slay the godlike son of Priam who killed my friend!"

"You are then fated to die soon," Thetis replied, weeping, "for your own death will rapidly follow the death of Hector."

"Let me die, then," responded Achilles, "since I was not able to stand with Patroclus against Hector. I now realize at what great price I sat uselessly by my ships, enjoying anger far sweeter than honey against wide-ruling Agamemnon. Hector has killed good Patroclus and many other friends. May such anger, which upsets even the wisest, no longer afflict the deathless gods and mortal men!"

Achilles then announced, "I will go forth to slay Hector, who killed the man I loved. I will accept my fate whenever Zeus and the other immortals bring it upon me. Until then, may I win great fame and glory, and may every Trojan realize that the greatest of the Greeks no longer remains apart from battle. If you love me, Mother, do not attempt to prevent my return to battle."

"I will not try to dissuade you, my child," Thetis replied. "I ask only that you wait until Dawn has brought early light. Then I will return to you, bringing you new armor forged by Hephaestus himself. You will enter battle wearing shining armor that will bring glory to the immortal craftsman who fashioned it and to you."

When the Greeks finally had carried Patroclus's body back to the hollow ships, wise Polydamas advised Hector. "Godlike son of Priam, listen to my thoughtful counsel. I think that we should return to Troy. It was safe for us to remain by the Greek ships, far from our well-defended city, as long as Achilles was angry with wide-ruling Agamemnon. Now, however, I fear the wrath of the swift-footed son of Peleus. He will fight relentlessly to destroy our city and to capture our wives. If we remain here, many of us will become food for dogs and vultures, and we will weaken the defense of Troy. We can fight Achilles far better if we take a stand upon our walls."

To this advice, Hector of the flashing helm angrily replied, "Polydamas, your words do not please my heart. Are you not tired of being confined within walls? I will not permit any Trojan to listen to you! We will fight the bronze-coated Greeks at their hollow ships. If Achilles enters the battle, I will fight him face to face, and one of us will win great glory."

So Hector commanded the horse-taming Trojans. His countrymen foolishly supported him, for bright-eyed Athena robbed them of their good judgment. They praised man-slaying Hector for his poor counsel and refused to listen to wise Polydamas.

When rosy-fingered Dawn brought light to gods and mortals, Thetis appeared before Achilles as she had promised, with Hephaestus's shining armor. Following her advice, the son of Peleus then called the Greeks to assembly in order to end his argument with Agamemnon.

Once they had gathered together, Achilles rose and said, "Agamemnon, did we gain anything by fighting in this way over a woman? Would that Artemis the archer had slain her when I captured her! My mighty anger has caused the deaths of my dearest friend and many other Greeks and has brought great glory to Hector and the Trojans. Now it is time for us to put aside the past and unite once again against our enemy. Few will escape the fury of my spear!"

Agamemnon replied, "Often the long-haired Greeks have criticized me, even though I was not at fault. The evil goddess Ate blinded me and Zeus stole my judgment on the day that I seized your prize of honor. Therefore, I am willing to compensate you for the injury I have caused you. I offer you, once again, all of the gifts that Odysseus promised you in my name when he came to your hut."

Achilles answered, "Great son of Atreus, wide-ruling Agamemnon, whether you give the gifts, as is proper, or whether you withhold them is your decision. But let us put an end to this talk. Instead, we should quickly prepare for battle, for that is an unfinished task. Let everyone watch as I destroy the Trojans with my far-shadowing bronze spear!"

Soon the plain shone with shining bronze as the Greeks met the Trojans in battle. Achilles' desire for revenge combined with his courage, strength, and skill to ravage the Trojan army. Swift-footed Achilles pushed ever onward to win glory. As a wildly raging fire sweeps through the parched forests on a mountainside, and the wind scatters flames everywhere, so the godlike son of Peleus raged among the Trojans, causing the black earth to swim with Trojan blood.

Now that Patroclus was dead, Achilles could feel no pity. When one of the Trojan warriors begged for his life, Achilles explained, "Until Patroclus died, I enjoyed sparing Trojan lives. Many I captured alive and sold across the sea. But now no Trojan who comes into my hands will avoid death. Great-hearted Patroclus died, and he was a far better man than any of you. Even I, goddess- and hero-born, and as skillful as I am, will die in this war, either by some Trojan spear or by an arrow from a well-aimed bow."

Hector was standing near the Scaean Gates of Troy with his father when they saw Achilles approaching. "My dearest child," Priam pleaded, "do not go forth to meet Achilles alone lest he kill you, for he is a far better warrior than you are. Cruel man! I wish the immortals valued him as I do! I would let the dogs and vultures ravenously feed upon him as I left him, unburied, upon the dirt. Do not bring great glory to the swift-footed son of Peleus by offering him your life!"

As Hector of the shining helm watched Achilles come toward him, he thought to himself, "If I retreat within the walls of Troy now, Polydamas will remind me that I have caused our troubles. After I killed Patroclus, I ordered the Trojans to remain near the Greek ships. Thinking that we had nothing to fear, I was quick to criticize Polydamas's wise counsel. How blind I was to think that we could defeat the bronze-coated Greeks once godlike Achilles returned to the battlefield!

"Now Achilles has sent the shades of many fine Trojan warriors down to the kingdom of Hades, and I feel ashamed in front of the armored men and long-robed women of Troy. I fear they will say I brought destruction upon my people because I was too confident in my ability to fight Achilles. It would be far better to face Achilles man to man and either kill him or die with honor.

"On the other hand," Hector thought, "what if I lay down my shield and crested helmet, rest my far-shadowing spear against the wall, and go forth unarmed to meet Achilles, promising to return Helen and all the treasure that Paris took from Sparta? We could give the sons of Atreus half the treasure of Troy as well.

"But how can I even consider this? If I approach Achilles in a submissive way, he will neither respect me nor pity me but will kill me as I stand unarmed before him. No, the first approach is the better one: to fight it out and learn which of us will gain glory."

As Hector stood thinking, Achilles approached him. The godlike son of Peleus was a terrifying sight as his father's ash spear rode upon his right shoulder and his bronze armor blazed like the fiery sun. Fear grabbed Hector's heart, and he fled. Swift-footed Achilles immediately pursued him. As a falcon in the mountains, the swiftest of birds, swoops easily after a trembling dove and pursues it with shrill cries, so Achilles chased Hector.

Around the walls of Troy they ran, past where the Trojan people sat upon the wall, past the observation post, past the wild fig tree, along the wagon track, and by the two springs that feed the Scamander River, the one steaming hot and the other icy cold. As swiftly as Hector ran, a faster man ran after him, for they were not running a race to win a beast of sacrifice or a bull's hide as a prize. They were running to see who would win Hector's life!

Three times around the walls of Troy they ran, as all the deathless gods watched from Mount Olympus. Just as a hunting dog stirs a fawn from its den and chases it through woods and meadow, and though the fawn escapes for a while by hiding in thick underbrush, yet the dog tracks its scent and follows it until he finds it, so swift-footed Achilles pursued man-slaying Hector.

Whenever Hector tried to come close enough to the Scaean Gates for the Trojans upon the wall to shoot at Achilles, the son of Peleus would take an inside track and drive Hector back toward the plain. Apollo helped Hector for the last time by increasing his strength and hastening his feet so that swift-footed Achilles could not overtake him.

Meanwhile, Achilles signaled the Greeks that they should not try to kill Hector. The godlike son of Peleus wanted to win that glory for himself.

Chapter 7

Athena tricks Hector into fighting Achilles face to face. It is Hector's time to die, and Achilles kills him. Hector reminds Achilles that his own death will soon follow.

As the race around the well-built walls of Troy continued, the Lord of Olympus commented, "I pity Hector, whom I love, but Achilles is a good man too. Should we save Hector from death, or good as he is should we let Achilles kill him?"

Bright-eyed Athena replied, "Oh, Father, lord of the bright lightning and of the dark cloud, how can you suggest that we have a choice? Do you intend to change a mortal's fate that was set long ago? Save him if you wish, but know that all of us do not agree with you."

As Hector and Achilles were approaching the hot and cold springs for the fourth time, Zeus raised his golden scales and set the two fates of death upon them: on the one hand, that of swift-footed Achilles; on the other, that of man-slaying Hector. When he held the scales in the middle to see how they would balance, the scale bearing Hector's fate sank. Now Apollo would have to leave him, for a god may not help a mortal on the day he or she is fated to die.

Athena went down to Achilles and said, "Great Achilles, dear to Zeus, now we will kill Hector. He can no longer escape from us, no matter what Apollo may try to do to save him. Rest here while I persuade the son of Priam to fight you face to face."

When the goddess left Achilles, she appeared before Hector in the form and voice of his dearest brother, Deiphobus. "Dear brother," she cried, "let us stand here together and deal with Achilles as he deserves!"

Hector of the shining helm replied, "Deiphobus, you have always been the dearest of my brothers to me, but now I honor you in my heart even more because you have left the safety of the walls for my sake, while everyone else has remained within."

The bright-eyed goddess then said, "It is true that our father and mother and many friends pleaded with me to remain there, so terribly afraid are they of Achilles, but my heart was with you. So let us now attack the son of Peleus with all of our strength and skill, and learn if, in fact, he will kill both of us or whether your spear will put an end to him." In this deceptive fashion Athena tricked god-like Hector into confronting his fate.

Hector approached the son of Peleus and said, "I will no longer run from you, Achilles, but will fight you man to man until one of us has taken the life of the other. But first, let us call the deathless gods to witness this pledge: I will treat you fairly if Zeus, Lord of Olympus, gives me the strength to slay you. Once I have removed your splendid armor, I will return your dead body to your country-men, and I want you to promise to do the same."

Achilles angrily replied, "Do not talk to me of promises, Hector. Just as lions and men do not make pledges to one another, nor do wolves and lambs agree but rather continually plot evil against each other, so it is impossible for you and me to treat one another as friends and promise anything at all.

"Instead," Achilles continued, "summon all your courage, strength, and skill as a spearman, for you are about to die. You can no longer escape your fate, for by my spear Athena, bright-eyed daughter of Zeus, will take your life. Now you will finally pay for all the sorrow you brought me by slaying good Patroclus with your bronze-tipped spear."

With these words Achilles raised his own far-shadowing spear and hurled it at Hector. The son of Priam accurately judged its path, and moved so that the spear flew over his head and lodged in the earth behind him. Unseen by Hector, Athena removed the spear and returned it to Achilles.

As he prepared to hurl his swift spear, Hector announced, "You missed me, Achilles! You have also missed knowing my fate, sure as you were of it. You tried to frighten me into losing my courage and my strength and fleeing, but I will not give you the chance to drive your spear into my back. You will have to plunge it straight through my chest. Now, avoid my spear if you can!"

Hector's spear hit Achilles' shield as planned, but then it bounced off and fell to the ground out of Hector's reach. He called upon his brother for another spear, but Deiphobus was nowhere in sight.

Then in his heart Hector understood the truth. He thought, "The deathless gods have indeed brought me to my death! I thought that Deiphobus was by my side, but he is within the walls of Troy. Athena has deceived me! The Lord of Olympus and his far-shooting son must long have intended this, even though they have usually been quick to help me.

"My death now awaits me," Hector concluded. "I see no way to avoid it. At least I will die with honor, so that men in times to come will hear of my valor."

He drew his great sword from his side and rushed upon Achilles. As a mighty eagle soaring high into the sky spies a little lamb or rabbit far below and, swiftly changing its course, swoops down through the dark clouds to the meadow to seize its trembling prey, so Hector of the shining helm attacked the son of Peleus.

Achilles met Hector's attack with rage in his heart. In his right hand, his spear shone like the brightest evening star. He paused briefly while he studied his old bronze armor in order to find the best place to strike. He had given that shining armor to great-hearted Patroclus, but now it was protecting man-slaying Hector. Hector's only visible flesh was at his throat, where he would die most quickly. There Achilles plunged his bronze tipped spear.

As his foe lay dying in the dust, the son of Peleus cried joyfully, "Hector, slayer of men, while you were busy killing Patroclus, you were foolish to give so little thought to how I would repay you for your evil deed. Good Patroclus will receive a proper burial, but your body will be ravaged by dogs and birds!"

Hector replied with the last of his strength, "I plead with you, do not take me to your hollow ships to be consumed by dogs. Instead, accept the gifts of bronze and gold that my father and mother will give you for my body so that the Trojan people can bury me with honor."

Achilles furiously responded, "Do not implore me, you dog! So great is my anger at what you have done to me that if I could, I myself would tear apart your flesh and eat it raw. Therefore, no one can keep the dogs away from your head, not for ten or twenty times the proper ransom, not even if Priam were to pay me your weight in gold. Your mother will not be able to mourn before your body, for you will be completely devoured by dogs and birds far from Priam's great city."

The dying Hector then said, "I knew that I could not hope to persuade you. Your heart is truly made of iron! Be careful, though, for I may bring the wrath of the deathless gods upon you on the day when, in spite of your courage, your strength, and your skill, my brother Paris and far-shooting Apollo will kill you at the Scaean Gates."

With these words, death came upon him. Godlike Hector's shade left his lifeless body and went down to the kingdom of Hades.

Achilles spoke to the dead Hector. "Lie dead, Hector! As for me, I will accept my death whenever Zeus, Lord of Olympus, and the other deathless gods bring that fate upon me." Then the son of Peleus withdrew his bronze spear from Hector's neck and put it aside. He removed from Hector's body the bloody armor that had been his own.

The bronze-coated Greeks then approached the lifeless Trojan. As they stood admiring their greatest foe, they took their bronze spears and, one by one, each warrior drove his spear into godlike Hector's corpse.

Achilles announced, "Come, let us return to our hollow ships singing our song of victory, and let us take with us this warrior who has brought so much evil upon us. We have won great glory, for we have killed Hector of the shining helm, whom the horse-taming Trojans worshipped as though he were a god."

The son of Peleus then punctured the tendons of Hector's feet between the ankle and the heel, inserted a narrow strip of oxhide through each slit, and tied Hector's body to his chariot, leaving the hero's head to trail behind in the dust. After that, he put the shining armor into his chariot, climbed into it, and drove his horses forward at top speed, dragging Hector's body behind him.

Chapter 8

The Trojans mourn Hector's death and are angered that Achilles will not return his corpse. Finally the gods order Achilles to accept Priam's ransom and surrender Hector's body. After Priam returns to Troy, the Trojans conduct a royal funeral.

Hector's father and mother agonized over the death of their dearest son and his foul treatment at the hands of Achilles. Priam cried, "My friends, although you love me, let me leave the city by myself and go across the plain to the Greeks' hollow ships. There I will plead with this evil man for the body of our son. Perhaps he will be ashamed before his companions and will pity me in my old age, for he himself has a father like me."

Andromache, who heard the cries and wailing from the wall while she was at home weaving, reached the wall in time to see Achilles' horses swiftly dragging Hector's body off toward the Greeks' hollow ships. Darkness like night came over her eyes and she collapsed, tearing from her head the veil that golden Aphrodite had given her on the day she had married Hector.

When Andromache regained consciousness she cried, "Oh, Hector, you have left me in deep grief, myself a widow and our infant son helpless without you. Even if he survives this war, he is now doomed to a hard, sad life, for other men will seize his lands.

"Once a child becomes an orphan," she continued, "his friends leave him. With a bowed head and tears on his cheeks, he approaches his father's friends, tugging at their coats. The one who pities him will offer him a cup for a moment, enough to wet his lips but not enough to fill his mouth. And a child whose parents still live strikes him and pushes him away from the table, saying: 'Go away! No father of yours is eating with us!' So the needy child tearfully returns to his widowed mother. Poor Astyanax, who has known only the best of love and care!" So Andromache spoke, weeping, and all the Trojans wept with her.

That night, Achilles mourned for Patroclus until he finally fell asleep by the shore of the loud-sounding sea. Then the shade of his dearest friend appeared before him, looking and sounding exactly as he had when he was alive.

"You have forgotten me," Patroclus admonished Achilles. "Bury me quickly so that I may enter the kingdom of Hades! Until you do this, the shades will not let me cross the River Styx and join them. You, too, are fated to die beneath the well-defended walls of Priam's city. When that time comes, let our bones lie together in the golden urn with the double handles that your mother gave you."

Achilles replied, "I will do just as you wish, dearest friend, but come closer that we may clasp our arms about each other and grieve over our separation."

The son of Peleus reached toward Patroclus with his hands, but he could not touch him. Like a mist, the shade of his friend disappeared into the earth. Achilles proceeded to hold the funeral ceremonies and games in honor of Patroclus as he had promised.

Many days after the funeral, Achilles still kept the body of Hector, unburied, by his hollow ships. Whenever he felt the desire, he would attach Hector's body to his chariot, drag it around and around Patroclus's tomb, and then leave it lying face down in the dust. Since Apollo loved Hector even in death, he preserved Hector's corpse from decay and destruction.

The God of the Silver Bow finally prevailed upon his father, Zeus, to convince Hera and Athena that Achilles should not be permitted to have his way with Hector's body. This was not an easy task, for even Hector's death had not softened the hatred that Hera and Athena felt for the Trojans. The insult of Paris's choice of Aphrodite's beauty and gift over their own had not faded with time. Nevertheless, they finally permitted Thetis to counsel her son.

When Thetis entered Achilles' hut, he was sitting with his head upon his arms, still mourning for Patroclus. She sat down beside him, stroked his head, and said, "My child, how long will you continue this sorrow? Since your life will be so short, I would like to see you enjoy it. I have come as a messenger from Zeus, Lord of Olympus. All the deathless gods are angry because you have not returned Hector's body for proper burial. Accept the ransom for the dead and give him up."

While Thetis was persuading Achilles to return Hector's body, the Lord of Olympus sent wind-footed Iris down to advise King Priam to go alone to Achilles' hut with ample ransom. In order to calm his fears, Hermes, the Wayfinder, would be his guide.

Great-hearted Priam collected a wondrous array of gifts. As the eternally young god and the old king made their way together across the plain of Troy toward the hollow ships of the Greeks, Hermes reassured Priam that the immortals had protected Hector's body from both the ravages of time and Achilles' harsh treatment. Once they reached Achilles' hut, Hermes took leave of Priam and returned to Mount Olympus.

The old king entered the hut, took Achilles by the knees, and said, "Remember your father, godlike Achilles, who, like me, will soon become an old man. While you are alive, his heart is joyful. As for me, although I fathered fifty sons, you and war-loving Ares have killed the best of them. And for none do I mourn as I do for my son Hector, who guarded Troy and its people. I have come to you with numerous gifts as ransom for his body. Pity me, for I am forced to beg the man who killed my valiant sons."

Achilles wept in sympathy with Priam in his sorrow. Then the swift-footed son of Peleus asked, "How did you have the courage to come alone to the hollow ships and look into my eyes when I have killed so many of your brave sons? Surely your heart is made of iron!"

Achilles continued, "The deathless gods spin the threads of mortals' lives to bring them grief, while the gods themselves live free of pain. Zeus, Lord of the Thunderbolt, sits between two urns, one filled with blessings and the other containing evils. The one to whom Zeus gives only evil gifts is despised both by mortals and by the gods. That man wanders upon the earth searching for honor but finding none. However, the one to whom Zeus gives gifts from both urns at some times finds good and at other times evil in his life.

"So it is with you. In the past the deathless gods gave you great gifts: the blessings of land, wealth, and many fine sons. Now, with this hateful war, the gods have brought evil upon you. The bronze-coated Greeks have killed many of the sons you loved. However, you must endure the pain. A heart overflowing with sorrow will not help you, for grief will not return the dead to life. So come now and sit down. Together we will put an end to our tears."

Priam replied, "Do not ask me to sit down while my son Hector lies unburied and away from Troy. Instead, bring him to me immediately so that I can look upon him, and accept the great ransom I have brought you."

Achilles angrily replied, "Do not incite me to fury, old sir, or I may harm you even while you are a guest inside my hut and, in doing so, anger Zeus. I intend to give your son back to you, for Zeus, Lord of Counsel, sent my mother to advise me. I know in my heart that some god must have led you to my hut. No mortal, no matter how young and strong, would have had the courage to come into the camp of the bronze-coated Greeks, nor could he have done so without arousing the guards."

Then Priam became frightened and silent. Achilles, however, leaped forth like a lion, accepted the ransom, and prepared to return the body of Hector to his father. He also agreed to halt the war for eleven days so that the Trojans could prepare and hold a proper funeral for Hector. He shook the old king's hand to confirm his promise.

With Hermes to guide him once again, Priam returned to Troy with Hector's body. Andromache, Hecuba, and Helen led the women in wailing over the death of Hector, recounting his loss to them as husband, son, and dear friend.

The gathering of wood for the funeral pyre took nine days. On the tenth day, as rosy-fingered Dawn shone forth, the people of Troy assembled at the pyre. They laid godlike Hector's corpse upon it and set fire to his body. When Dawn next gave light to gods and mortals, they quenched the flames, gathered Hector's bones, and put them into a golden urn. They wrapped the urn in purple robes and placed it in a hollow grave. After they had covered the grave with large stones, they built a mound and set a watch upon it to protect it from the Greeks. The funeral concluded with a great feast in the palace of King Priam.

In this way the horse-taming Trojans held the funeral of godlike Hector of the shining helm.

EPILOGUE TO THE ILIAD

THE DEATH OF ACHILLES

With the help of Apollo, Paris killed Achilles at the Scaean Gates by shooting an arrow into his heel. A great battle for Achilles' corpse followed. While Odysseus fought off the Trojans, Ajax was able to pick up Achilles' body and, through a shower of Trojan arrows, carry it back to the Greek ships. The Greeks burned the body of Achilles and placed his bones with those of Patroclus as they both had wished. However, Thetis actually rescued Achilles from the funeral pyre and took him to White Island in the Euxine Sea, where he is immortal.

After the funeral games, the Greeks decided to award Achilles' armor to the warrior who had contributed the most to the Greek effort. Odysseus, the best strategist, and Ajax, the best fighter, competed for this prize. Odysseus, with the help of Athena, won the votes of the Greek leaders. Ajax was so humiliated by his defeat that he went insane. Thinking that the Greeks' cattle were the warriors who had voted against him, he killed them. When he realized what he had done, he was so ashamed that he killed himself.

THE DEATH OF PARIS

When the Greeks sailed for Troy, Philoctetes accompanied them carrying the bow that Heracles had given him before he died. At one of their island stops, Philoctetes was bitten by a snake. The wound smelled so terrible that the Greeks left him behind on the island. Ten years later, the prophet Calchas (or the Trojan seer Helenus), whom Odysseus captured, told the Greeks that they needed Heracles' bow in order to defeat the Trojans. So Odysseus and Diomedes returned to the island and brought Philoctetes and the bow to Troy. There his wound was healed and he shot Paris in single combat.

THE DEFEAT OF TROY

After the death of Paris, his brother Deiphobus married Helen. Odysseus brought Achilles' son, Neoptolemus, to Troy and gave him his father's armor. Athena taught Epeius to build a great wooden horse, whose body would accommodate the greatest of the Greek warriors. Meanwhile, Odysseus, in the disguise of a beggar, entered Troy. Helen recognized him and plotted with him to capture Troy. However, she later changed her mind and tried to expose the men who were hiding inside the horse.

The Greeks left the horse outside the walls of Troy and hid on a nearby island. The Trojans were suspicious of the horse, but when two serpents attacked the priest of Apollo, who had warned against accepting a Greek gift, they took it inside. Then, certain that the war had finally ended, they celebrated their great victory.

Later that night, while the Trojans slept soundly, the Greeks who were hiding inside the horse, including Odysseus, Menelaus, and Neoptolemus, disembarked and opened the Trojan gates to the Greek armies, who had secretly returned. The Greeks then looted and burned the great city.

Menelaus killed Deiphobus and recovered Helen. The women in Hector's family became enslaved, as he had known would be their fate if Troy lost the war. The greatest Greek warriors were entitled to special prizes of honor, which, now, were the greatest of the Trojan women. Agamemnon claimed Hector's sister Cassandra, who had received but spurned Apollo's love. Odysseus claimed Hecuba. Neoptolemus, who had killed Priam, chose Andromache. Hector's son Astyanax was grabbed from his nurse by either Neoptolemus or Odysseus and thrown to his death, either from a tower or from the Trojan wall.

❧ QUESTIONS FOR
Response, Discussion, and Analysis

1. *The Iliad* focuses on the behavior of warriors in time of crisis and examines what each person owes to him- or herself and to the community. What does each of the following characters owe to himself and to others: (a) Agamemnon? (b) Achilles? (c) Patroclus? (d) Hector? (e) Paris?

2. Achilles is acknowledged to be the greatest Greek warrior. Yet Homer focuses on Achilles' quarrel with Agamemnon and its effect upon the Greeks rather than on his heroic exploits. Why?

3. In *The Iliad*, why is a person's reputation worth more than wealth and power? Is this still true today? Explain.

4. Why does Homer choose an argument over a woman as the cause of a tragic quarrel between Agamemnon and Achilles? Does it matter what actually causes the quarrel? Explain.

5. When we evaluate a human being, we consider what kind of person he or she is as well as the deeds he or she accomplishes. What kind of person is Agamemnon? What tests of character confront him? To what extent does he pass those tests? What temptations does he find irresistible? Why? How does his behavior affect his heroic image?

6. Describe Agamemnon as Achilles sees him. Is Achilles' evaluation correct? Consider the following:
   a. What makes Agamemnon apologize to Achilles?
   b. Why does he give Achilles so many gifts?
   c. Why does he send others to kill Achilles instead of going himself?

7. Based on *The Iliad*, what kind of person is Achilles? What tests of character confront him? To what extent does he pass them? Which temptations does he resist, and which does he find irresistible? Why? How does his behavior affect his heroic image?

8. Why does Achilles refuse to fight for the Greeks when Agamemnon takes Briseis: love of Briseis? honor? pride? Defend your opinion.

9. When Achilles chooses to remain by the Greek ships but refuses to fight, what options does he have?
   a. Can he return home to Peleus? What will his father think of him?
   b. Should he permit Agamemnon to take Briseis? Without protesting? After protesting? What will be the result of each choice?
   c. Should he accept Agamemnon's gifts? If he does, will this change his relationship with Agamemnon? If so, in what way?
   d. Should he send Patroclus into battle? Why or why not?
   e. Can he keep Patroclus as well as himself out of battle? If he does, what will be the result?

10. Achilles criticizes the way in which his warrior society operates. Why? What are his objections? To what extent, if any, are they valid?

11. Achilles is considered to be the first tragic hero in Western literature. Evaluate the extent to which each of the following factors contributes to his tragedy:
    a. Achilles knows that he will gain lasting fame, but at the cost of an early death, if he continues to fight in the war against Troy.
    b. Achilles leaves the war in order to teach a lesson to Agamemnon and, to a lesser extent, the other Greek leaders. However, he must put that reason aside and reenter the war in order to avenge the death of Patroclus.
    c. Achilles leaves the war because he is denied Briseis, the tangible symbol of the honor that he needs and has earned from Agamemnon and the other Greek leaders. Yet he criticizes the obligations and the method of reward under which all Greek warriors fight, and his abdication is neither understood nor accepted by the other Greek warriors whom he would have honor him.

12. In *The Aethiopis,* by Arctinus of Miletus, Zeus permits Thetis to confer immortality upon Achilles when he dies. However, in *The Odyssey,* Homer rejects the traditional view of Achilles' immortality. How do you think Achilles' immortality would have affected audience resposne to *The Iliad* in Homer's time? How would it affect your own response?

13. To what extent, if any, are each of the following beings, both human and divine, responsible for Patroclus's death: (a) Nestor; (b) Achilles; (c) Patroclus; (d) Apollo; (e) the Trojan who first wounds Patroclus in the back; (f) Hector?

14. Why does Homer have Apollo weaken Patroclus before others kill him? How does this affect the image of Patroclus? Does it help the stature of a hero to have a god's help? Defend your opinion.

15. What kind of person is Hector? What tests of character confront him? To what extent does he pass them? Which temptations does he resist, and which does he find irresistible? Why? How does his behavior affect his heroic image?

16. Why does Homer demonstrate Hector's fear of Achilles? Is his purpose to enhance Achilles? to enhance Hector? Does the fact that Hector runs from Achilles make him appear to be a coward or more courageous once he fights Achilles? Defend your point of view.

17. How do you react to the fact that Athena tricks Hector into fighting Achilles? How would you have written this part of the myth?

18. Once Hector knows that Troy is doomed to lose the war, does he have any viable choice except to continue fighting? Does Hector have any option other than to fight Achilles? Explain.

19. After Achilles has killed Hector, he says, "We have won great glory. We have killed Hector." Who does he mean by "we"? Athena? Patroclus? The Greeks? Could he have any other reason for saying "we" instead of "I"?

20. Why does Homer make Achilles so barbaric in his treatment of Hector's corpse? Is this a comment on the nature of a warrior? Of a hero? Explain.

21. In *The Odyssey,* Achilles tells Odysseus that it is better to be a live servant than a dead hero. Do you think Achilles would have chosen to return to the Trojan War if he had known what awaited him after death? Why or why not?

22. What kind of a person is Paris? What tests of character confront him? To what extent does he pass them? What temptations does he find irresistible? Why? How does his behavior affect his heroic image?

23. *The Iliad* reflects the view that life is not fair. Give examples from the myth to support this statement. In your experience is life fair? Give examples to support your point of view.

24. *The Iliad* shows the tragic truth that a person's greatest strength is often his or her greatest weakness. Which characters in *The Iliad* illustrate this statement? Explain your choices. Do you know anyone who illustrates this statement?

25. Agamemnon, Achilles, Patroclus, and Hector all suffer the consequences of the behavior pattern in which *arete* (excellence) leads to *hubris* (excessive pride), which in turn leads to *ate* (rash or imprudent behavior) and finally results in *nemesis* (retribution). Explain these characteristics in terms of the attitudes and behavior of the four heroes. Do you know anyone whose behavior fits this pattern?

26. Does the personality of any of the major characters change in the course of *The Iliad?* Defend your opinion with examples.

27. Why did Homer choose to end *The Iliad* so abruptly? How would you have concluded it?

28. In *The Iliad,* Homer implies that each person must strive to live in such a way that his or her life enriches the lives of other people. Which characters achieve this goal? How? Do you think this is a good goal? Why or why not?

29. Based on the heroes in *The Iliad,* what qualities make a person heroic? What qualities make a person heroic today?

30. How are Achilles and Hector alike? How are they different? What motivates each of them? What would Hector have done if his commander had taken away his prize of honor? If you were a soldier, who would you prefer as your commander? Why? Who is the greater hero? Why?

31. How are Hector and Paris different? What motivates each of them?

32. How are Paris and Helen alike? How are they different?

33. Why does Homer portray only the leaders of the Greek and Trojan forces? Would the effect of the myth be different if the principal characters were ordinary men and women? Why?

34. What do the values and behavior of the following characters in *The Iliad* reveal about Homer's attitudes toward war? (a) Agamemnon; (b) Achilles; (c) Patroclus; (d) Hector; (e) Paris; (f) Andromache; (g) Helen.

35. Why do the Greek gods participate in the Trojan War? Are they a help or a hindrance? Defend your point of view.

36. Find examples to support the idea that the Greek gods represent forces we attribute to: (a) nature, (b) human thought, (c) human skill, and (d) luck. How many examples can you find of circumstances where only the action of a god explains the situation?

37. If, like Achilles, you could choose between a short life with eternal fame or a long life with no lasting recognition, which would you choose? Why?

38. Compare the values in *The Iliad* with the values that people hold today. To what extent are dignity, pride, honor, glory, fame, and revenge still important? How do people achieve them today?

39. What do Homer's similes reveal about the time in which he lived? What effect do they have on the story?

HISTORICAL BACKGROUND

Jason and the Golden Fleece

Jason and the Golden Fleece is one of the oldest and most famous myths in the western world. The ancient Greeks thought that the great kingdom of the sun existed far to the east, where Helios, their god of the sun, began his daily journey through the heavens. At least as early as the eighth century B.C., they viewed Colchis as that kingdom. Homer assumed that his audience knew the myth because, in Book XII of *The Odyssey,* Circe tells Odysseus, "No ship bearing mortal sea-farers has ever survived that passage, except for the *Argo*—known to all who walk the earth—on her way home from Aeetes; and even she would have crumbled against those great rocks if Hera, out of her great love for Jason, had not pushed her through."

The voyage of Jason probably takes place in the mid-thirteenth century B.C. and involves fifty-two Greek heroes aboard a ship called the *Argo*. Jason and his companions, called the Argonauts, sail from the kingdom of Iolcus to the eastern shore of the Euxine Sea and the Phasis river—a distance of fifteen-hundred sea miles—in order to find the kingdom of Colchis and fetch the Golden Fleece from King Aeetes. The Argonauts are the fathers of Homer's heroes, who set sail for Troy about twenty years later, and whom we know from *The Iliad* and *The Odyssey.*

The Argonauts' voyage takes them from Greece to the former Soviet Georgia, on the shore of the Black Sea—the end of the known world— and back again. It is a sea journey of three thousand miles, and from start to finish it is filled with adventures.

Scholars always want to prove whether a story of such antiquity is myth (fiction in a historical sense), legend (partly based on historic fact), or history. The earliest writers considered these tales part of the history of their culture. Later writers viewed them as the product of imaginative minds and, therefore, as myths. However, with the development of archaeology, scholars have found evidence that much of their content has some historical basis.

Some scholars think that the Golden Fleece was actually amber, a commodity so valued in ancient times that the Greek peoples decided to unite—for the first time in their history—in order to acquire it. Others have considered the Golden Fleece to be a symbol of fertility and agricultural prosperity. However, Tim Severin, a specialist on the history of exploration, carefully read *The Argonautica* and actually simulated the *Argo's* voyage. Early in the 1980s, he set forth on a twenty-oared ship that replicated Jason's fifty-oared open vessel, and he made the sea journey from Volos (ancient Iolcus) to the Republic of Georgia (ancient Colchis). The following information is part of what he discovered.

First, Greeks living in 1245 B.C. could have made such a voyage on such a ship. Archaeological evidence reveals that the ancient Greeks sailed as far as the Black (ancient Euxine) Sea in about 3300 B.C. in order to learn how to create bronze. Pottery shards excavated in Volos show a Greek vessel from between 1600 and 1500 B.C. The *Argo,* sailing about three hundred years later, is described as the largest ship of its time, being powered by fifty rowers plus a steersman and a stroke-master. Homer, in writing about the Trojan War of c. 1225 B.C., describes ships rowed by fifty men.

Second, Greeks were living in Iolcus in 1245 B.C. Archaeologists have discovered a Mycenaean town on a site that would have been a good seaport for Iolcus. Moreover, on the outskirts of Volos, they have unearthed the walls of a small Mycenaean manor house or palace, with a royal burial tomb. Apparently, it was occupied for no more than a century and then peacefully abandoned.

Although the story of Jason and the Golden Fleece contains elements of myth and folklore, Jason's quest may have a historical basis. People have lived on the eastern shore of the Black Sea and along the Rhioni (ancient Phasis) River for at least five thousand years. Archaeologists have excavated a late Bronze Age site, dating back to c. 1300–1200 B.C., near the Phasis and Aea, King Aeetes' capital city. The name *Aeetes* means "ruler of Aeae" and may refer to the entire kingdom of Colchis as well as to its capital.

Linguistic evidence reveals that the Mycenaean Greeks must have known about Colchis some time before 1000 B.C.—when the Colchian language changed—because their words for Colchian objects reflect the earlier Colchian language. For example, the ancient Greeks called Georgia's great river the Phasis, rather than the Rhioni. Moreover, the ancient Greek word for *sheepskin* is related to the ancient Colchian word for *fleece.*

Although archaeologists have not discovered any physical evidence that Mycenaeans, such as Jason and the Argonauts, reached Colchis, archaeological excavations in the Rhioni River valley and Tim Severin's conversations with the Svan people who live in the nearby mountains cast an interesting light on many aspects of Jason's experience in Colchis.

Archaeological excavations throughout the Rhioni River valley may explain why King Aeetes demands that Jason perform a test that involves plowing a field. Agriculture appears to have been a very important activity in ancient Colchis. Archaeologists have uncovered late Bronze Age stockaded settlements where kings were buried with farm implements.

Moreover, when Jason must yoke Aeetes' fire-breathing bulls if he hopes to win the Golden Fleece, these bulls may symbolize the real bulls—sacred to members of the bull cult—that lived in the sacred grove and near the sacred tree on which the Golden Fleece hung. Archaeologists have excavated a site on the coastal plain by the Rhioni, where Jason could have anchored the *Argo.* Called *Namcheduri,* the site contains the remains of a late Bronze Age wooden, stockaded building that was probably a temple, since it contains evidence of a bull cult. Within the building, archaeologists have found collections of bull totems fashioned from stone and clay.

Even the Golden Fleece was probably real because, in the Bronze Age, the ram was sacred to the people of Svanetia, who lived in the foothills of the Caucasus Mountains of Georgia and in the Rhioni River valley. The Svan culture is at least four thousand years old, and for thousands of years the Svan people created symbolic forms of the ram. Archaeologists have found a double spiral of ram's horns in a Svan grave from about 1500 B.C. The church in the village of Kala, near the Svan capital of Mestia, contains a small bronze ram that dates from the time of Jason's arrival in Colchis. A Svan folktale describes a secret cave in the Caucasus mountains where a golden ram, tied with a golden chain, guards a secret treasure.

Ancient Colchis was famous for its gold, and Svanetia was the principal source of that gold. Today, the Svan people live in the Caucasus Mountains, but their language, beliefs, and traditions are still rooted in the Bronze Age. As recently as the 1980s, Svan men told Tim Severin about having gathered gold in the following ancient way.

Each spring, when the glaciers and snowfields in the mountains would begin to melt, they would carry sheepskins, scrapers, and flat wooden boards up to the high valleys. They would find their favorite stream, where the water would contain gold that had been washed from veins in the rocks. Then, using new or last year's boards, they would nail their sheepskins, fleece-side up, to their boards, and they would place the boards, in a descending series, on the floor of the stream-bed, weighing them down with rocks so that the water would flow over them.

As the stream flowed down the mountain, the gold particles, being heavy, would drop to the bottom and become lodged in the wool of the sheepskins. When they were satisfied with the amount of gold that had collected in their sheepskins, they would remove them from the stream-bed and, using scrapers, water, and a wooden trough, they would clean the fleece and collect the gold particles that had lodged in the wool.

In a richly laden stream, the highest fleece would often be so filled with gold that it was truly a "golden fleece." The Greek geographer Strabo (64 B.C.–c. A.D. 25) wrote: "It is said that, in their country (Colchis), raging mountain streams carry pieces of gold, which the barbarians use perforated troughs and fleecy skins to collect, and this is the origin of the myth of the Golden Fleece."

Finally, evidence reveals that a serpent would have guarded a golden fleece because it was a cult object. Near Namcheduri, archaeologists at Kobuleti have found clay tablets that combine forked bull's horns with a zigzag groove that may symbolize a serpent guardian. Possibly the ancient Colchians kept snakes inside their temples to guard their sacred objects, just as, until recently, many Georgian families in the Rhioni River valley kept a protective snake within their homes. Since ancient pottery from the Rhioni River valley has been found in the Caucasus Mountains, it is possible that, in the Bronze Age, the mountain people may have given a golden fleece to the powerful king in the valley, either as a gift or as tribute. If the Colchians considered the fleece to be a cult object—which, in *The Argonautica*, they did—then they would have placed it in the wooden temple where they worshipped the bull, and the serpent guardian of the temple would have protected it.

Today, the legend of the Argonauts is well known in the Republic of Georgia. Medea and the Argonauts are folk heroes, and parents name their daughters Medea. Students study the voyage as a source of their history because it records the first contact between their ancestors and the ancient people of the Mediterranean.

RELIGIOUS BACKGROUND

Traces of an earlier matriarchal religion in ancient Greece are present in the myths connected with the myth of Jason and the Golden Fleece. When Argus tells Jason that Medea serves Hecate, the Night-wandering Goddess, he is describing Medea in a later and transformed human form. Yet Argus reveals Medea's earlier identity when he declares that she can manipulate all the herbs that grow on land and all that live in the sea, that she can call forth blazing fires and quiet rushing rivers, that she can make spring flowers bloom in summer and make grain ripen for harvesting in winter, and that she can make the chariot of the moon appear next to the chariot of the sun in the sky.

Argus's description of Medea's powers reveals her to be the Great Goddess or Mother Goddess of an earlier matriarchal religion. The Great Goddess functioned in three related forms. As Goddess of the Underworld, she controlled the three-stage cycle of life: first, the period of birth and childhood; then, the fertile period of maturity and reproduction; and last, the sterile period of old age, with its decline and death. As Goddess of the Earth, she controlled the three-stage cycle of the seasons: first, spring (the period of birth or rebirth and budding growth); then, summer (the fertile period of blossoming and harvest); and last, winter (the sterile period of decay, barrenness, and death or dormancy). As Goddess of the Sky, she was the great Moon Goddess, who appeared in her three-stage cycle of phases: first, as the new and waxing moon (the period of birth or rebirth and growth); then, as the full moon (the period of maturity); and last, as the waning moon (the period of decline and death or dormancy).

In a matriarchal community, the reigning priestess of the Great Goddess or Mother Goddess took a young male consort to be the community's sacred king for the new year. In order to earn this honor, young male contenders competed with other candidates in contests that took unusual courage, strength, and skill. Then, as part of his coronation ceremony, the winner performed additional tasks that took remarkable courage, strength, and skill. One task usually involved wrestling with a bull. The community thought that the bull brought rain because its fiery breath was like lightning, and its roar sounded like thunder. The new sacred king's goal was to grab hold of one of the bull's horns so that he would gain the bull's rain-making magic and increase his own powers of fertility. Another task often involved cleaning or plowing a hill or a field in one day. The tasks that King Aeetes (as an enthroned sacred king) demands of Jason (a contender for his throne) conform to this pattern.

The principal purpose of a sacred king was to ensure the human and agricultural fertility of his community. In order to assure this fertility, the priestesses ritually killed their enthroned king while he was still young and healthy and then put a young and healthy successor in his place. Once the sacred king was dead, the priestesses tore apart his body and either ate his raw flesh, or they stewed the pieces of his corpse in a soup and ate his flesh cooked. By doing this, they expected that his spirit—particularly, his powers of fertility—would pass into them. They would become pregnant, and nine months later, in the next lambing season, the spirit of the sacred king would be reborn in their infants. The priestesses sprinkled the farm animals and the earth with the sacred king's blood in order to fertilize them as well.

At first, the sacred king was ritually sacrificed in midsummer, on the last day of the thirteen-month lunar year. Later, he was permitted to experience a mock death each year while a boy surrogate was enthroned for one to three days and then ritually sacrificed in his place. In this way, the sacred king was able to reign for one hundred lunar months, or approximately eight years, before he was sacrificed.

The myth of Phrixus, told in the Prologue to *Jason and the Golden Fleece,* conforms to this pattern. Phrixus is a sacred king whose impending sacrifice will mark the end of his reign. His community intends to obey the oracle and sacrifice him because of crop failure and famine. They expect that his death will restore the fertility of their land. Of course, Phrixus would prefer to live, and he is fortunate that his attempt to escape is successful.

A ram's fleece was a symbol of the sacred king because he used it in his annual rain-making ceremony. In ancient Greece, in matriarchal times, Zeus was a storm god rather than a sky god, and the fleece was purplish black—the color of clouds before a thunderstorm—rather than gold. The fleece became gold when religion became more patriarchal, and Zeus became a sky god as well as a weather god. The myth of Phrixus reveals that rams were sacred to Zeus. Nephele, Phrixus's mother, prays to Zeus, who sends a ram to rescue Phrixus, and Phrixus flees to Colchis on its back. Later, communities accepted a ram as a substitute sacrifice for human beings. Apparently, in Classical Greece, an old man wearing a black sheepskin mask was still symbolically killed on the summit of Mount Pelion and then restored to life by companions who were dressed in white fleece.

The fact that Medea cuts up Jason, Pelias, and (in some versions) Aeson and then puts them into cauldrons of rebirth and rejuvenation also reflects earlier religious practices. The myths, legends, and folktales of other cultures—including those of Italy, Germany, Russia, Scandinavia, and the Celts in Ireland—involve similar magic cauldrons. Priestesses would cut up a living human being or animal, put the fragments of the corpse into a magic broth, and then recite proper incantations as a fire caused the soup to boil. The corpse would then revive and emerge rejuvenated. Because fire was thought to be an aspect of the sun, it was sacred in cultures where people worshipped a sun god. Therefore, the fire, as well as the broth, was necessary for the renewal of youth and the extension of life.

APOLLONIUS AND ALEXANDRIA

The oldest, most complete version of *Jason and the Golden Fleece* that we have, *The Argonautica,* was written by Apollonius Rhodius, a Hellenic (Greek) scholar-poet living in Alexandria, Egypt, in the third century B.C. during the Golden Age of Hellenistic poetry. These Hellenes had inherited the empire established by Alexander the Great in the prior century. Many were now living far from Hellas (Greece), in foreign lands. There, they were the most prosperous citizens. Their members formed the governing body of their community, and they viewed the native people with whom they lived as resident aliens. They shared their Hellenic language with these Egyptians,

Romans, or Jews, but they alone lived under Hellenic law. They surrounded themselves with Hellenic culture, but they shared it only with other Hellenes throughout the empire.

Alexandria was the intellectual and artistic center of the Hellenic world. The Alexandrian Museum gained fame as an institute for research in all fields, including science, philosophy, and literature. The great Alexandrian Library was the largest in the western world. It contained between 100,000 and 700,000 volumes (estimates vary), and it supported a large staff of important scholars and scribes.

To the Hellenes of Alexandria, Alexander the Great was more of a hero than Alexander's own hero, Heracles, because they were no longer a warrior culture. In time of war, foreign warriors (mercenaries) fought on their behalf. The goal of the Alexandrian Greeks was to avoid unnecessary wars—by declaring neutrality wherever possible and by settling disputes peacefully through arbitration.

The prevailing values in Alexandrian society emphasized intelligence and diplomacy rather than physical strength and skill, cooperation rather than individuality, and socialized, rational behavior that would enable citizens to relate peacefully with others. Many educated Hellenes found the old religion—with its focus on the Olympian gods of Homer and Hesiod and on the superhuman, mythic heroes of earlier centuries—to be irrelevant to their lives.

Little is actually known about Apollonius. Early in his adulthood, he was put in charge of the great Alexandrian Library, where he wrote scholarly works on Homer and Hesiod, as well as poetry. He was still a young man when he gave a public reading of his epic, *The Argonautica*. The

members of his audience knew the story of Jason and the Golden Fleece since they had learned other versions of it—along with the epics of Homer and the tragedies of the great fifth-century playwrights—as part of their cultural history. Moreover, they were familiar with Medea's homeland since trade between Alexandria and Colchis was frequent. Like Mycenae, Colchis was famous for being "rich in gold," and ancient gold objects from the far end of the Euxine Sea helped keep the tales of the Argonauts' voyage alive.

However, for some reason, Apollonius's audience strongly disliked his version of the ancient story, and Apollonius was so disturbed by their reaction that he retired to the island of Rhodes, where he may have remained for as long as twenty years. There, he revised his epic and gained fame as a fine teacher. In time, he returned to Alexandria with the finished product and offered his epic to the public once again, this time with great success.

APOLLONIUS AND THE LITERARY TRADITION

The myth of Jason and the Golden Fleece is as old as the myth of the Trojan War, and it, too, has roots in the oral tradition. The folktale motifs that it contains reveal both its age and its universality. For example, anyone with knowledge of fairy tales finds the plot of Jason, Medea, and the Golden Fleece familiar when it is related in its generic form, as follows: A powerful and jealous king (Pelias) forces a prince (Jason) to venture forth to the kingdom of a wicked king (Aeetes) in search of a valuable object. There, the wicked king gives the prince a series of impossible tasks, which the prince must perform if he is to win the object for which he has come. The wicked king's daughter (Medea) falls in love with the prince and secretly helps him perform these tasks. However, when the king discovers his daughter's behavior, he refuses to give the prince his prize. Once again, the princess helps the prince, this time by stealing the prize for him. The prince must now flee, and he takes the willing princess with him. The wicked king pursues them, but they escape by tossing items behind them that he will want to collect.

In other familiar tales, a youth (Jason) encounters a stranger in the form of an old man or woman, who, in myth, is usually a god or goddess in disguise (Hera). The stranger asks the youth for some form of help, which turns out to be a secret test of the youth's character. Previous youths have ignored the stranger, but this youth sympathetically offers assistance, thereby revealing the proper human values. Because the youth is kind, the stranger befriends the youth and helps the youth perform otherwise impossible tasks. In still other familiar tales, a father/king (Aeetes) imposes difficult tasks on any suitor (Jason) who wishes to marry his daughter (Medea), or a youth (Jason) must succeed in accomplishing difficult tasks, which are tests he must pass in order to claim his inheritance, or a jealous stepmother (Ino) contrives to kill her stepchildren (Phrixus and Helle), thereby causing the children to flee.

We cannot know much about Apollonius's sources because, according to one scholar, Apollonius probably had fifty times more Greek literature available to him than we do. For example, only seven of Aeschylus's, seven of Sophocles', and nineteen of Euripides' tragedies still survive. Most were

destroyed in 47 B.C. when Julius Caesar was in Alexandria and the Library was burned. Fortunately, Hellenic scribes had made copies of the most revered and popular works—including the epics by Homer and Hesiod, the lyric poetry of Pindar, and certain tragedies by Aeschylus, Sophocles, and Euripides. These were available throughout the Hellenic empire, and their multiple copies and broad distribution enabled them to survive to this day.

However, Aeschylus wrote eighty-three tragedies, including the lost *Athamas, Argo,* and *Phineus.* Sophocles wrote one hundred twenty-three tragedies, including the lost *Athamas* (I and II), *Phrixus, Phineus* (I and II), *Women of Colchis* (Jason's adventures in Colchis, including the murder of Medea's brother, Apsyrtus), *Root-Cutters* (about Medea's gathering of her special herbs), and *Scythians* (Jason and Medea's escape and a second version of Apsyrtus's murder). Moreover, Euripides wrote about seventy tragedies, including the lost *Phrixus* (I and II) and *The_Daughters of Pelias.* Fortunately, Euripides' *Medea* was so valued that multiple copies enabled it to survive the passage of centuries. Therefore, we know from the surviving plays and from the titles of lost plays that myths about Jason and Medea provided stimulating material for the great writers of ancient Greece. Further, we know that almost all of these were available to Apollonius.

Our earliest sources of *Jason and the Golden Fleece* are those of Hesiod (late eighth century B.C.) and Pindar (fifth century B.C.). Hesiod's version, in *The Theogony,* is brief and without detail. He states that, "having accomplished the terrifying tasks imposed on him by the wicked King Pelias, Jason, by the will of the gods, led Medea,

King Aeetes' daughter, forth from her father's house to his swift ship, and after much suffering, he returned to Iolcus with her and made her his wife. Medea submitted to Jason, shepherd of the people, and bore him a son."

Pindar is the earliest known writer to tell a brief but complete version in his Fourth Pythian Ode. Reflecting his interests and the time in which he lived, Pindar celebrates a male's athletic victory by emphasizing Jason's heroic feats rather than Medea's. Aphrodite teaches Jason how to win Medea away from her parents, and it is Jason who cleverly kills the serpent that guards the Golden Fleece.

In contrast, Apollonius is more interested in the psychological aspects of human behavior, particularly as these are revealed in the love story of Jason and Medea. Apollonius's choice of epic poetry enables him to relate the quest for the Golden Fleece in great detail, and he designs aspects of his characterizations and style to remind readers of Homer's *Iliad* and *Odyssey*.

By supplying the earlier part of the myth, Apollonius's *Argonautica* also reminds readers of Euripides' *Medea*, written two centuries earlier. Apollonius makes the attitudes and actions of his youthful Jason and Medea consistent with the attitudes and actions of their mature counterparts in Euripides' tragedy. However, he carefully avoids Euripides' subject by stopping his version with Jason's successful return to Iolcus.

APPEAL AND VALUE

At a time when short, original poems were popular and realism was fashionable, Apollonius chose to write a long, derivative poem about mythical heroes and their great deeds. However, given his talent as a poet, the nature of his subject, and his treatment of it, he deserved the success he finally achieved.

First, *The Argonautica* is one of the world's great stories. As told by Apollonius Rhodius, the love story of Jason and Medea is unique in ancient literature, being the first psychologically accurate description of falling in love and the first work of literature in which love plays the major role in the development of the plot. Its nature and quality have continued to influence later writers of romance, beginning with Virgil and Ovid, and the nature and quality of their stories, in turn, have continued to influence other writers. Therefore, Apollonius can be considered the father of romantic literature.

The Argonautica is also one of the world's great adventure stories, second only to the *Odyssey* of Homer. Few readers from Apollonius's time to ours can resist such a well-told tale. Yet the adventures of Jason's companions remain peripheral to Jason's myth in that Apollonius could have inserted other adventures of other heroes in their place.

Unlike Homer, Apollonius has neither the need nor the interest to explore the nature of the ideal warrior or king. Apollonius did not create *The Argonautica* to be an entertaining model for ideal human behavior but, rather, to be valued as a captivating work of literature. Like Homer and Euripides, Apollonius is interested in the human psyche and, specifically, in Jason and Medea's choices—although he leaves the consequences of their choices to Euripides, whose *Medea* cannot be surpassed. Apollonius's psychological insight, his skill with conversation, and his sense of humor are so effective that

The Argonautica captures the imagination and heart of the reader.

Second, in preserving ancient Greek myth as historical fact, Apollonius gave value to Greek culture and united Greek-speaking peoples at a time when they lived in many lands and so were happy to retain and confirm their identity. For all of us, through the centuries, who are not Greek, *The Argonautica* has continued to give value to ancient Greek culture and to confirm the common human bond that unites the people who lived in the past with those who live in the present.

Third, Apollonius was sensitive to the needs and interests of his audience, and these determined both his depiction of Jason and the nature of the *Argo*'s voyage. Homer was the Shakespeare of Apollonius's time and place, and the *Iliad* and the *Odyssey* were still the model for all epic poetry. His audience could recite much of Homer from memory. Therefore, Apollonius's readers appreciated the many parts of *The Argonautica* that either reflected or contrasted with Homer's epics. They appreciated Jason because mercenaries fought their wars, and they had little personal interest in Bronze Age values and the Homeric type of hero. They understood Jason's pragmatism and prudence—his willingness to delegate to others whatever they could do better than he—because they lived in a law-abiding society that valued cooperation more than individualism in daily life. The contrast between Jason's ability to persuade others to use their courage, strength, and skill on his behalf and the individual feats of Homeric heroes, such as Achilles, Hector, and Odysseus, captured reader interest. Moreover, Medea's heroic role offered a valued change from Homer's male-centered

world and the role of the female as helpless victim.

Fourth, Apollonius was sensitive to the psychological nature of human beings. The ancient Greeks believed that all human beings, through their attitudes and actions, are capable of bringing sorrow upon themselves. In Homer's *Odyssey* (Book I), Zeus tells the gods, "It is shameful how quickly mortals blame the gods for the evils that beset them! But they, not we, are to blame. Their own blind recklessness brings them pain and sorrow that we have not decreed."

In Greek mythology and literature—and in modern life—people bring sorrow upon themselves when their attitudes and actions form a particular pattern known to the ancient Greeks. First, a person must possess some type of excellence (*aretē*) or superior ability. A person may be unusually handsome, clever, or skilled. Unless that person is careful, excellence is followed by excessive pride (*hubris*) in oneself because of one's superior ability. Excessive pride, without words and deeds that express it, is harmless. However, it usually leads to rash behavior or blind recklessness (*atē*), because the person's superior ability leads her or him to feel entitled to overstep important natural boundaries. Finally, having said or done what one is not entitled to say or do, the person experiences some form of retribution (*nemesis*) because the gods—acting directly or through other human beings—do not tolerate such inappropriate behavior.

This behavior pattern is an important part of Jason and Medea's love and, therefore, Jason's quest for the Golden Fleece. Because we, too, are vulnerable to this pattern of behavior, seeing how characters in literature bring their suffering upon themselves engages our sympathy and our concern for ourselves, or, in Aristotle's terms, it arouses our pity and fear.

Finally, Apollonius was sensitive to the nature of the human condition. Despite the "modern" Hellenistic age, he knew that gains in human knowledge never change the fundamental nature of the human condition. Therefore, *The Argonautica* has captured the imagination of its audience from Apollonius's time until the present. Like the members of his audience, we still are vulnerable when we have to confront the forces of nature, the unknown, and the consequences of our actions. Therefore, our lives, like theirs, are still unpredictable and dangerous. We, too, can identify with the characters in *The Argonautica* and value both human magic and the superhuman marvels of the gods.

Apollonius published two versions of *The Argonautica,* but only the later version—probably because its popularity resulted in multiple copies—exists today.

The following version of Jason's quest for the Golden Fleece is adapted from Apollonius's *Argonautica* and focuses on Jason, Medea, and the acquisition of the fleece. Medea's rejuvenation of Jason is adapted from several literary works from ancient Greece (sixth century B.C. and later).

CHARACTERS

ACASTUS: the son of Pelias, king of Iolcus; an Argonaut; later, the king of Iolcus
AEETES: a son of Helios; the father of Medea, Chalciope, and Apsyrtus; the maternal grandfather of Argus; the king of Colchis, in Scythia
AESON: the half-brother of Pelias (They share the same mother); a first cousin of Phrixus (Their fathers are brothers); the legitimate king of Iolcus, in Thessaly
APSYRTUS: the son of Aeetes; the brother of Medea and Chalciope
ARGUS: the eldest son of Phrixus; a grandson of both Athamas and Aeetes; a nephew of Medea; a second cousin of Jason (Their paternal grandfathers are brothers)
CHALCIOPE: a daughter of Aeetes; a granddaughter of Helios; the sister of Medea; the wife of Phrixus; the mother of Argus and his three brothers
JASON: the son of Aeson; a second cousin of Argus; the husband of Medea and later, of Glauce; the leader of the Argonauts
MEDEA: a daughter of Aeetes; a granddaughter of Helios; the sister of Chalciope; an aunt of Argus; Jason's first wife; a priestess of Hecate; a sorceress
PELEUS: the king of Phthia, in Thessaly; an Argonaut
PELIAS: a son of Poseidon; the half-brother of Aeson (They share the same mother); the illegitimate king of Iolcus
PHINEUS: a Thracian king; a seer
PHRIXUS: the son of Athamas and Nephele; a first cousin of Aeson (Their fathers are brothers); the husband of Chalciope; the father of Argus and three other sons

THE GODS AND OTHER IMMORTAL BEINGS

APHRODITE: a daughter of Zeus; the goddess of sexual desire
APOLLO: the son of Zeus and Leto; the twin brother of Artemis; the god of prophecy, with his oracle at Delphi; the god of disease and medicine
ARES: a son of Zeus and Hera; the bloodthirsty god of war
ARTEMIS: the daughter of Zeus and Leto; the twin sister of Apollo; the goddess of wild animals; the goddess of the hunt; a goddess of childbirth; the patron goddess of Iolcus
ATHENA: a daughter of Zeus; the goddess of arts and crafts and defensive war; later, the goddess of wisdom; the patron goddess of heroes; the architect of the Argo
BOREAS: the god of the north wind; the north wind itself; the father of two winged sons who are Argonauts

CHEIRON: the immortal centaur

EOS: the goddess of dawn

EROS: the son of Aphrodite; the god of love

GAEA: the mother of all the gods and of all life; Mother Earth; the Mother Goddess

HADES: a brother of Zeus, Poseidon, and Hera; the ruler of the Underworld

HECATE: a goddess in Hades' kingdom

HELIOS: the father of Aeetes; the paternal grandfather of Chalciope, Medea, and Apsyrtus; the maternal great-grandfather of Argus; the god of the sun

HEPHAESTUS: the son of Zeus and Hera, or of Hera; the metalsmith of the Olympian gods

HERA: a sister of Zeus, Poseidon, and Hades; the wife of Zeus; the mother of Ares and Hephaestus; an aunt of Aphrodite, Apollo, Artemis, Athena, and Hermes; the queen of Olympus; the goddess of marriage

HERMES: a son of Zeus; Zeus's messenger; the patron god of travelers

IRIS: Hera's messenger

NYX: the mother of Thanatos; the goddess of night

POSEIDON: a brother of Zeus, Hades, and Hera; the ruler of the sea; the god of earthquakes

SELENE: the goddess of the moon

THANATOS: the son of Nyx; the god of death

ZEUS: a brother of Poseidon, Hades, and Hera; the father of Aphrodite, Apollo, Ares, Artemis, Athena, Hephaestus, and Hermes; the king of Olympus and ruler of all the gods; the god of justice, hospitality, and rain; the patron god of suppliants, fugitives, and strangers, with his oracle at Dodona

GEOGRAPHICAL LOCATIONS

AEA: the capital city of Colchis, located near the mouth of the Phasis River, in Scythia

BOEOTIA: the region in the central, eastern part of Hellas

COLCHIS, SCYTHIA: the region at the eastern end of the Euxine Sea and south of the Caucasus Mountains (now the Republic of Georgia)

CORINTH: the region of Hellas that includes part of the northeastern Peloponnesus and most of the isthmus that connects the Peloponnesus with Attica and Boeotia to the east

DELPHI: a city on Mount Parnassus, in Phocis, in Hellas; the site of the oracle of Apollo and, therefore, the principal religious center of the Hellenes

DODONA, EPEIRUS: a city in the region in Hellas that borders on the coast of the Adriatic Sea (now southern Albania); the site of an ancient oracle of Zeus

HELLESPONT: (Sea of Helle) the narrow sea channel, or strait, that connects the Aegean Sea with the Sea of Marmara

IOLCUS, THESSALY: a city in the region north of Boeotia, in the eastern part of Hellas (now Volos, in Magnesia)

LIBYA: the region bordering on the African coast of the Mediterranean Sea, between Egypt on the east and the Pillars of Heracles, which line the Strait of Gibraltar, on the west

MOUNT OLYMPUS: a high, snow-covered mountain near the Gulf of Salonika, in the region of Pieria, in northern Thessaly, in Hellas, where the gods of the Hellenes live

MOUNT PELION: a mountain near the city of Iolcus, in Thessaly

PHAEACIA: the island of Drepane; Homer's Scheria; thought to be located "at a far end of the sea" (now Corfu)

PROLOGUE TO JASON AND THE GOLDEN FLEECE

THE GOLDEN FLEECE

King Athamas of Boeotia married the immortal Nephele, and she bore him two children, whom he loved: a son named Phrixus and a daughter named Helle. Later, Athamas fell in love with Ino and made her his second queen. Ino bore Athamas two sons and was determined that they, rather than Nephele's children, should inherit the kingdom. In order to carry out this plan, she secretly ordered the farm-women of Boeotia to sow the new crop of wheat with roasted seeds, which she knew would never sprout.

When Athamas saw that his people would starve, he sent messengers to Delphi in order to ask the oracle of Far-shooting Apollo what he should do to restore the fertility of his land. However, Ino intercepted the messengers and told them they must return to Athamas with this message: "The children of the king's first queen have poisoned the soil of Boeotia. Sacrifice them to Far-seeing Zeus. And the soil will bloom with sweet, life-sustaining grain."

At first, Athamas refused to sacrifice Nephele's children. However, when the people of Boeotia learned that he refused to accept the advice of Apollo's oracle, they gathered before the palace and shouted, "Athamas, you may not save your children while our children die! Sacrifice Phrixus and Helle to Far-seeing Zeus. Or we will do it for you!"

While Athamas prepared for the sacrifice, Nephele prayed to Zeus to save her children. He heard her prayers and sent his son, Swift-footed Hermes, to her with a ram whose fleece was of shining gold. "Go forth to my father's altar. Cut your children loose. And order them to climb on the ram's back," commanded Hermes. "It will carry them to Colchis, in Scythia. And there I will meet them."

Before the ram reached Scythia, Helle fell into the sea, known thereafter as the Hellespont (Sea of Helle), where she drowned. However, the ram carried Phrixus safely to Colchis. There, Hermes told Phrixus to sacrifice the Golden Ram to Zeus and to take its Golden Fleece to King Aeetes. Aeetes accepted both Phrixus and the gift because Hermes had told him to obey the will of Zeus. Then Phrixus married Chalciope, the king's older daughter, and became the father of four sons.

Meanwhile, Aeetes nailed the wondrous fleece to a great oak tree in a grove that was dedicated to Ares. However, Shining Helios told Aeetes, who was his son, that members of his family would contrive deceitful schemes that would lead to treachery and destruction. Therefore, Aeetes placed a sleepless serpent by the fleece to guard it.

JASON AND THE GOLDEN FLEECE

Muse—divine daughter of Far-seeing Zeus, Father of Gods and Mortals—sing of the ways of the human heart. Sing of how the heart floods, like the storm-tossed salt sea, with waves of love, hatred, ambition, and revenge, enslaving the human mind with these passions and making all who walk the earth its victims. And sing of the Olympian gods—the deathless ones—who observe all who are mortal, judge them, and then respond in ways mortals do not expect. And through your song, reveal who is to blame for the troubles that plague all who walk the earth.

Muse—divine daughter of Far-seeing Zeus, Father of Gods and Mortals—sing of Jason's arrival in Iolcus. Sing of how King Pelias sends Jason forth to fetch the wondrous Golden Fleece. Sing of Phineus. Sing of Jason's arrival in Colchis. Sing of the tasks King Aeetes demands of Jason. Sing of Medea. And sing of the capture of the Golden Fleece.

Chapter 1

Jason claims the throne of Iolcus. Then King Pelias commands him to fetch the Golden Fleece, and the Argo departs for Colchis.

In Thessaly, Pelias—mad for power and without respect for law—took the royal scepter, the throne, and the kingdom of Iolcus from his half-brother, Aeson, who was the rightful king. In time it came to pass that Aeson's wedded lady gave birth to a son, whom they named Jason. Jason was the rightful heir to the throne. Thus, Aeson and his wedded lady feared that, swift as the wind, Pelias would push their son into the grasping hands of Thanatos. And there he would look his last upon light and life. So Aeson secretly gave little Jason to the centaur Cheiron to rear.

In time, it came to pass that, like Aeetes, Pelias lived in fear of the grasping hands of Thanatos. For the oracle of Far-shooting Apollo at Delphi caused the king's heart to flood with terror by declaring, "Pelias, beware of a man wearing a single sandal—whether he is a stranger or one of your own people—who comes to the bright land of Iolcus from a home on the mountain."

So the oracle had prophesied. And in time, it came to pass that Jason left Cheiron's cave high on Mount Pelion. And he set forth to find his real parents, for he intended to claim the royal scepter, the throne, and the kingdom in the name of his father. And as he strode down the mountain path, Jason looked like one of the deathless gods. Uncut curly locks framed his godlike face and danced upon his back as he walked. The clothing of a hunter graced his godlike form. A leopard skin lay draped across his shoulders. And in each hand he carried a great spear.

Now when Jason approached the towers of the royal city of Iolcus, he found that the river that flows past the city had become a roaring flood-tide with a treacherous current. For Shining Helios's golden rays had warmed the snow-covered meadows high on Mount Pelion. And the snow had fled, sending cascades of water down into the valley below.

But Jason knew that, if he wanted to find his parents, he would have to cross the churning waters as best he could. So he plunged into the icy river and began to push his way through the roaring winter flood-tide. And as he fought his way through the mighty current, he lost his left sandal in the swollen floodwaters. So it came to pass that Jason walked through the gates to the royal city—and arrived in the marketplace of Iolcus—wearing only his right sandal.

Now the marketplace was crowded with people. But everyone stood silent and still when the godlike stranger suddenly appeared among them. For just as a rippling brook sparkles like a jewel beneath the golden rays of Shining Helios's gold-yoked chariot, so Jason's beauty, strength, and vigor now shone forth from his youthful face and form.

Swift as the wind, Rumor flew to the royal palace. "A strange youth—surely as godlike as Far-shooting Apollo or Death-dealing Ares—has entered the marketplace of Iolcus!" she whispered into every ear. So it came to pass that King Pelias heard the news. Swift as the wind, he went forth to the marketplace. And there he did not have to look far to find the stranger. For just as a great oak tree towers over the surrounding pine trees in a forest, so Jason stood head and shoulders above the people.

And so it came to pass that Jason and King Pelias came face to face. Jason stood silent and still before the king. Plans of revenge now flooded his mind. And his heart overflowed with courage. Pelias, too, stood silent and still. For the sight of the godlike stranger flooded his eyes. And so, swift as the wind, his eyes flew straight as an arrow from the youth's face down to his feet. And seeing that the stranger was wearing only one sandal, the king's mind flooded with the prophecy of Far-shooting Apollo's oracle. And so his heart flooded with waves of fear and anguish.

But Pelias acted as if he had nothing to fear. "Welcome, Stranger!" he exclaimed. "What land do you call home? And whom do you call Father? Let your words fly as swift and straight as a well-aimed arrow. For my heart easily floods with rage."

So King Pelias spoke. And to his words, Jason replied, "My lord, my home and my father's name are best revealed within your palace."

"Then come with me, Stranger," replied Pelias.

There, Jason announced, "My lord, I call Cheiron—the deathless and renowned centaur—Father. For he is the only father I have ever known. And I call his cave on Mount Pelion my home. There, I have lived while twenty years have followed one upon the other as Gleaming Selene follows Shining Helios across the heavens. And there Cheiron has reared me. But I was born in Iolcus. And my true father is Aeson, a grandson of King Aeolus. And so I have come to the royal city of Iolcus in order to reclaim my birthright.

"Cheiron has told me about you, Uncle. And plans of revenge have flooded my mind. But that is an old path, Uncle. And now, we need to make a new one. And so open the doors of your mind to my words. For, like well-aimed arrows, they will fly forth straight and true. Being related by blood, surely we do not need to threaten each other with swords or spears in order to gain what, by birth, is rightfully ours. For your part, Uncle, you may keep my father's fields, his flocks of sheep, and his herds of oxen—though, by taking them, you increased the wealth that was already yours.

"But Uncle—in the name of Far-seeing Zeus, Lord of Justice—I ask you to return the royal scepter, the throne, and the kingdom that rightfully belongs to my father. Only a reckless man keeps power unlawfully. His eyes are blind to what will come to be, and so he walks in the dark. And he bears a burden that weighs heavily on his mind and his heart."

So Jason spoke. And to his words, Pelias replied, "Cheiron has taught you to speak with a honeyed tongue, Jason. And your words are as wise as they are sweet. For Time—who ravishes all Mother Gaea's children—has left his mark on me. And I am now like an autumn leaf—no longer fresh and green—but old and stiff and weak.

"You are like a spring fruit, with your ripeness still to come. And so I give you my sacred promise—with Far-seeing Zeus, Lord of Justice, as my witness—that I will soon give you the royal scepter, the throne, and the kingdom of Iolcus. And you will rule—not in your father's name—but in your own."

So Pelias spoke, but his honeyed words concealed the rage that flooded his heart.

It came to pass that the godlike youth became reunited with his parents. And soon thereafter, Pelias invited Jason to join him in his offerings to Lord Poseidon and to the other Olympian gods. But the king was so distraught that he foolishly neglected to make the offerings that would honor Golden-throned Hera. For his mind was still flooded with the prophecy of the Far-shooter's oracle. And his heart was still flooded with waves of fear and anguish at the presence in Iolcus of the single-shod young man. And so his mind could think of nothing but the best way to destroy Jason.

"Surely Jason must look his last upon light and life. For only in this way will I escape my fate. And yet, I cannot kill him. For Far-seeing Zeus protects strangers and guests. And Aeson's son is both. Surely I do not want Zeus's heart to flood with wrath toward me. Instead, Thanatos must embrace Jason far from the shores of Hellas at the hands of some other man or between the jaws of some wild beast."

So Pelias mused. And so it came to pass that he approached Jason at the sacrifice and said, "Jason, tell me what you would do under the following circumstances. Assume you are a great king. For you will rule this kingdom. And assume you learn from Far-shooting Apollo's oracle at Delphi that, in time, one of your subjects will push you into the grasping hands of Thanatos. And there you will look your last upon light and life. Then later, you discover the identity of the man you fear. Once you know who he is, what would you do?"

So the king spoke. And to his words, Jason replied, "Why, Uncle, I would summon the man I fear. And—if he appeared to have the courage, strength, and skill of a heroic young man—then I would command him to go forth on a great quest. I might send him to Aeetes' kingdom of Colchis, in Scythia. For it lies at the far, eastern shore of Oceanus—at the end of the world we know. And there I would command him to fetch the Golden Fleece that belongs to King Aeetes.

"Now Uncle, the man I fear—if he appeared to have the courage, strength, and skill of a heroic young man—would surely look upon my command as a great opportunity. For the wondrous Golden Fleece is the prize of all prizes! And the heart of King Aeetes and mercy are strangers. So the heart of the man I fear would flood with joy, for he would welcome the challenge and the adventure I would be offering him. And he would look upon this quest as the way to win the glory that brings lasting fame.

"And yet, Uncle, I would be pushing the man I fear into the grasping hands of Thanatos. For that dreadful god would embrace him! He might find him on the voyage to Colchis. Or in Aeetes' kingdom. Or on the return journey. But he would surely embrace him. And so the man I fear would look his last upon light and life."

So Jason spoke. And to his words, the king replied, "Jason, my heart floods with joy at your clever scheme! And so I now command you to go forth to Colchis. For you are the man to whom the Far-shooter's oracle referred. Fetch the Golden Fleece, Jason. And when you return to the towers of Iolcus, present it to me as a gift.

"Now I will build you a fifty-oared ship for the journey. And you, Jason, will invite the crew to man her. I expect that—by the time your companions have assembled and the well-benched ship is ready to sail—spring blossoms will have become summer flowers. But summer is a good time for sailing the salt sea, for it brings favorable winds, and you will need all the help you can get!"

So King Pelias spoke to Jason. Meanwhile, Golden-throned Hera had been looking down from Mount Olympus, watching and listening to Jason and Pelias, in order to see how she could contrive to punish the king. And when King Pelias pretended to ask Jason's advice, her heart had flooded with joy.

"Pelias's scheming mind will now prove to be his undoing!" she had silently exclaimed. "Already I can see him in the embrace of Thanatos. For swift as the wind, I will flood Jason's mind with the idea of fetching the Golden Fleece from King Aeetes. And Pelias will accept Jason's scheme."

So the White-armed Goddess had decided. And so it had come to be. And so now, she silently exclaimed, "How clever I was to make the most of Pelias's challenge to Jason, for now my plan to punish Pelias begins! And my heart floods with joy when I think of all that will come to pass!"

And it came to pass that, swift as the wind, the greatest heroes of Hellas accepted Jason's invitation to accompany him on his quest. For each hero longed for adventure and the opportunity to win the glory that would bring him lasting fame. And soon after they all had arrived, Jason's well-benched ship, the Argo, was ready to sail upon the salt sea. Jason went forth to join his companions with his heart flooded with the call of glory and lasting fame. And so it was with the other Argonauts. And as they took their places at the benches, every hero gleamed like the shining stars in Nyx's robe, and every heart flooded with joy.

And joy flooded the heart of King Pelias, as well. "Now Jason will surely look his last upon light and life," the king thought, "for Thanatos will surely embrace him. He may find him on the voyage to Colchis. Or in Aeetes' kingdom. Or on the return journey. But of this one thing, I am certain. Jason will never return to Hellas alive!"

So King Pelias mused. But he did not know his only son, Acastus, was planning to join the Argonauts. And when he discovered this, his heart flooded with grief. For he feared that Acastus as well as Jason would soon give up light and life.

When the shipbuilder, too, joined the Argo's crew, Jason's heart overflowed with joy. "This quest may not be the death of me after all!" he silently exclaimed, "for Pelias would never send his only son on a doomed voyage. And the shipbuilder has such pride in his craft, he, too, has chosen to accompany us."

Now everyone knew that, if Jason captured the Golden Fleece, then poets would sing of it for as long as mortals walk the earth to hear of it. And so as the Argonauts prepared to row out of the harbor of Iolcus, Pelias's subjects thronged the shore and cheered their voyage. And on Mount Olympus, the deathless gods, too, watched as the Argonauts stowed their gear and prepared to work their oars. For aboard the Argo were two sons of Far-seeing Zeus, four sons of Earth-shaking Poseidon, one son of Far-shooting Apollo, one son of Strong-armed Hephaestus, two sons of Swift-footed Hermes, and one son of Gold-helmeted Helios. And other Argonauts were favorites of the deathless gods.

Now when the Argonauts finished their final preparations, they raised the anchor of their well-benched ship. And Jason raised a golden goblet—a cup as bright as the golden rays of Shining Helios's gold-yoked chariot. "Far-seeing Zeus—Father of Gods and Mortals—and Earth-shaking Poseidon—Lord of the Sea—I call upon you. Smile on our great venture," he prayed. "Grant us favorable winds and friendly waves. Protect us as we sail upon strange waters and discover strange peoples. And bring us safely back to our homes in Hellas."

So Jason prayed. And the great deathless gods heard his prayer. For Zeus, the Loud-thunderer, responded. Swift as the wind, the ears of those aboard the Argo—and the ears of those standing by the shore of the salt sea—flooded with the rumble of the god's thunder. And their eyes flooded with the flash of the god's bright lightning-bolt. And yet, Shining Helios was still driving his gold-yoked chariot across the heavens. And so everyone now stood silent and still. And their hearts flooded with awe. For they knew they were witnessing the signs of the greatest of the Olympian gods.

And this most favorable of omens caused the heart of every Argonaut to flood with joy. One and all, they raised their voices in a mighty cheer, and the hearts of those by the shore of the salt sea flooded with joy, as well. And they, too, raised their voices in a mighty cheer. And so it came to pass that the well-benched Argo departed for King Aeetes' kingdom of Colchis—at the far, eastern shore of Oceanus and at the end of the known world.

Chapter 2

The Argonauts rescue the seer Phineus and the sons of Phrixus. At last, the Argo reaches Colchis. Jason and Medea meet in Aeetes' palace.

In time, it came to pass that the Argo entered the narrow passage that leads to the great eastern salt sea. In time, the Argonauts anchored her in a small harbor on the western shore. For their eyes flooded with the sight of a great hall. And they went ashore to find its lord.

And it came to pass that—at the sound of their feet and voices—a blind and decrepit man slowly rose to his feet and came forth from his hall to greet them.

With trembling arms and hands, he reached out for walls and objects that would guide his shaking legs. And as he walked, his withered knees and feet found it hard to support the weight of his lean form.

"Welcome, Jason! Welcome, heroes of Hellas!" exclaimed the blind and decrepit man. "And may you, Far-seeing Zeus, and you, Far-shooting Apollo, see that my heart floods with gratitude for your gift of these heroes."

So the blind man greeted his visitors. But Jason and the Argonauts only stood silent and still, for their eyes flooded with the sight of this wreck of a man who was now staggering toward them. He was gazing at them with eyes that could not see. His dry skin was thin and filthy. And having no flesh beneath it, it clung to his bones like a finely-woven, but very wrinkled robe.

At last, Jason replied, "We thank you for your welcome, my lord. And please forgive our silence. But your greeting has caused our hearts to flood with waves of pity and wonder. Why do we find you in this sad state? And how do you know who we are?"

So Jason spoke. And his decrepit host replied, "Heroes of Hellas, let your eyes flood with the sight of my ravaged face and form, for Far-seeing Zeus is the most fearsome foe of all who do not recognize and respect the privilege and power of the deathless gods.

"Heroes of Hellas, you must not walk in my foot-steps! And so open the doors of your mind to my words, for, like well-aimed arrows they will fly forth straight and true. My name is Phineus, and in time of old, I was king of the Thracians. And I was renowned—not for my wealth and power, great as they were, but for the godlike gift of prophecy that Far-shooting Apollo has given me.

"In time of old, my heart flooded with good will toward all who walk the earth. And so I did my best to help everyone who came to me in need. Time after time, I revealed everything about each needy person's fate. For I know all there is to know about what will come to be.

"And it came to pass that my greatest talent caused my suffering. For time after time, I revealed more than Far-seeing Zeus wants mortals to know about what is to come. And when Zeus looked into my heart, he saw presumption where I saw compassion. As I saw it, my heart overflowed with kindness. But the Lord of Olympus saw that my heart overflowed with pride.

"Heroes of Hellas, Far-seeing Zeus has shown me that good and evil often appear dressed in each other's robes. And so we mortals—all too often, the best among us!—can find it difficult to recognize which is which. Our eyes can look upon Shining Helios's golden rays and see them. And yet, we can look upon our thoughts and our deeds but not see them. Then we are blind. For we do not know ourselves. And so we act recklessly.

"Far-seeing Zeus has shown me that, though we are mortal, the deathless gods permit us to be godlike. But we must always remember we are only mortal. We may not think and act as if we are one of the deathless gods. And should we forget, sooner or later the gods will punish us. They themselves may punish us. Or they may use other mortals to punish us. But they will surely punish us.

"Now those among us who remain blind usually blame the deathless gods when a disastrous change of fortune befalls them. But those who learn to know themselves will surely discover that they themselves—through their own thoughts and deeds—caused their own suffering.

"Heroes of Hellas, open the doors of your mind to my words. For when you have won the glory of great deeds, and when your deeds have brought you lasting fame, they will protect you.

"Far-seeing Zeus has sorely punished me for my pride and my blindness. Because I looked but did not see, the Lord of Olympus decreed that I should look my last upon the light of Shining Helios's golden rays. But, alas, Zeus did not decree that I should give up the wind of life that blows through me! And so Thanatos has refused to embrace me. My face and form reveal how Time—who ravishes all Mother Gaea's children—has continued to leave his mark on me. And so I would welcome the embrace of Thanatos. But that dreadful god has turned his back on me.

"And whenever I must eat or drink, Zeus's hounds—the Harpies—descend on me. You may know them as the Snatchers. Swift as the wind, they fly down from the clouds like the Loud-thunderer's lightning-bolts. They snatch whatever I wish to eat or drink from my hands before I can put it into my mouth. And they cast the disgusting smell of decay over whatever food and drink remains. The stench is so strong, only a starving mortal would dare to come near it!

"Heroes of Hellas, the winged sons of Boreas stand here among you. And they alone possess the power, and the permission of the deathless gods, to save me from the Harpies. So, Jason, permit them to save me! And in return, I will reveal as much of what is to come as Far-seeing Zeus will permit. None of the deathless gods—not even the Lord of Olympus—can remove a god's gift once it has been given. And so the Far-shooter's gift of prophecy is still mine."

So Phineus spoke. The heart of every hero flooded with pity for their blind and decrepit host. And to his words, Jason replied, "Flood your heart with hope, my lord, for your words reveal that the gods have decided to rescue you. And we have arrived to carry out their will. So command your servant bring forth your food and drink, and the sons of Boreas will attack the Harpies as soon as they appear.

So Jason spoke to Phineus. And it came to pass that, swift as the wind, the sons of Boreas rose to meet the Harpies. And they would have killed Zeus's hounds, but Golden-winged Iris suddenly appeared and declared, "Sons of Boreas, Far-seeing Zeus will not permit you to destroy his hounds. But he promises they will never attack Phineus again."

And it came to pass Phineus kept his word. For he revealed whatever Far-seeing Zeus would permit of what was to befall the Argonauts. Then Jason said, "Phineus—respected lord of those who walk the earth—you have told us how, if the deathless gods smile on us, we will reach Colchis. Now tell us. How will we fare with King Aeetes? For I have heard that his heart and mercy are strangers. And tell us. Will our eyes ever again look upon our homes in Hellas? For my heart floods with fear that our return will have no familiar signs to mark the way."

So Jason questioned Phineus. And in response, the blind seer declared, "My friends, at the far shore of Oceanus you will come upon the Phasis River. And not far from where this great river joins the salt sea, you will see the towers of the royal city of Aea and the wondrous palace of King Aeetes. And you will see the sacred grove of Death-dealing Ares, where the wondrous Golden Fleece you seek hangs upon the branches of a leafy oak tree. The fleece is guarded—both day and night—by a deathless dragon whose watchful eyes never close in sweet sleep.

"Guides will help you reach Colchis and find King Aeetes. And one of the deathless gods will guide your return to Hellas. But the success of your quest, Jason, will depend on Foam-born Aphrodite. However, Far-seeing Zeus forbids me to reveal more about this."

So Phineus spoke. And it came to pass that the Argonauts soon continued on their way. They beached the Argo on the island of Ares the Death-dealer, as Phineus had directed. And help came to them from the angry waves of the salt sea, as Phineus had foretold. For there, Jason and his companions rescued four shipwrecked youths. They were Phrixus's sons, and Argus, the eldest, advised and guided Jason on the rest of their voyage.

Meanwhile, once again Golden-throned Hera had been looking down from Mount Olympus in order to see how her plans for Jason were progressing. And when she saw that the well-benched Argo would soon reach the kingdom of Colchis, her heart flooded with joy. "Now I can proceed with my plan for Pelias!" she silently exclaimed. "Foam-born Aphrodite must have her son, Eros—whose love-inspiring arrows flood even the hearts of the Olympian gods with fear—aim his bow at King Aeetes' maiden daughter. For Medea must fall in love with Jason. And then she will use her great skill with magic to help him acquire Aeetes' wondrous fleece."

So Golden-throned Hera decided. And so it would come to pass that Laughter-loving Aphrodite and Love-inspiring Eros would help Jason in his quest for the Golden Fleece, for the Foam-born Goddess spoke with her son. And swift as the wind, Eros put on the golden belt from which his quiver of love-inspiring arrows hung. Then he picked up his curved bow and sped down through the air to Aeetes' kingdom of Colchis. There, he waited by the Phasis River—and not far from the royal city of Aea—for the arrival of the Argo.

While Love-inspiring Eros was making his way toward Colchis, the Argonauts were rowing their well-benched ship into the swirling waters that formed the broad mouth of the Phasis. And as they rowed, Jason declared, "My friends, surely our safety lies in our secrecy. And so, Argus, guide our well-benched ship into a quiet cove. For there we will anchor her. And there I will offer honey and wine to the great Colchian gods of earth and sky—Mother Gaea and Gold-helmeted Helios. May they welcome us here, and may they help us with our quest!"

So Jason spoke. And so it came to pass. And then Jason announced, "Friends, I want you to remain here while the sons of Phrixus lead me forth to King Aeetes. I will greet the king with the honeyed words of friendship. It may come to pass that the heart of Aeetes will flood with the warmth of hospitality, and he will give me the wondrous Golden Fleece as a host-gift. Then we will not have to rise against him in battle and take it by force."

So Jason spoke. And in reply, Argus announced, "I speak for my brothers and myself when I declare that the strength of the sons of Phrixus will forever be at your service, Jason. For we owe our lives to you! But Jason, open the doors of your mind to my words, for, like well-aimed arrows, they will fly forth straight and true.

"The task King Pelias has laid upon you is a hopeless one! King Aeetes is the son of Shining Helios—the Gold-helmeted God who drives his gold-yoked chariot across the heavens and into the western waves of Oceanus. And he is our grandfather, so his ways are well-known to us. He commands warriors beyond number. Just his war cry floods every mortal heart with fear! For no one can defeat him in battle. His heart and mercy are strangers. And whoever opposes him becomes food for birds and dogs!

"Grandfather will never give you the Golden Fleece, Jason. Nor will you be able to steal it from him, for a great deathless dragon lies coiled around the tree from which the wondrous fleece hangs. It is a child of Mother Gaea, and so it is more than mortal. Its watchful eyes never close in sweet sleep, and its skin defies the strongest and sharpest of weapons, so no mortal possesses the skill to defeat it.

So Argus spoke. And his words caused the heart of every Argonaut to flood with fear. But then, as everyone sat silent and still, Peleus pushed fear from his heart and declared, "Argus, my friend, your words have caused courage to panic and flee from our hearts, but we possess the courage, strength, and skill to defeat King Aeetes and his warriors on the plain of battle. Many of us are sons of the deathless gods, and if Aeetes will not give us the wondrous fleece in friendship, then—strong as he is—he will not be able to stop us from taking it!"

So Peleus replied to Argus. And then Jason declared, "Surely Peleus speaks for all of us. But I will now speak for myself alone. I do not take your words lightly, Argus, but I have not come all this way in order to retreat now! The coward flees from danger. But he who meets life with courage greets danger as a welcome friend. And in this way, the brave man earns the respect and love of the deathless gods. My heart and fear are strangers! And so I will proceed with the task Pelias has given me, come what may!"

So Jason spoke to Argus. Meanwhile, once again, Golden-throned Hera had been looking down from Mount Olympus, watching and listening, in order to see how her plans for Jason were progressing. And now she silently exclaimed, "My eyes flood with the sight of Love-inspiring Eros. For he has arrived in Colchis! And now he rests near the Argo, so Jason will surely have to pass him as he walks toward the towers of Aea. My heart floods with joy when I think of all that will now come to pass!"

So White-armed Hera mused. And it came to pass that the goddess watched as Argus and his brothers led Jason forth to the royal city and the palace of King Aeetes. She watched as—unseen by mortal eyes—Love-inspiring Eros left his resting-place and began to walk at Jason's side. And she watched until Jason and the sons of Phrixus approached Aea's walls. Then, swift as the wind, she wrapped a cloak of thick, gray fog around the royal city, for she knew Jason could only meet Medea if he reached Aeetes' palace and entered its grounds in safety.

And it came to pass that, as the young men walked through the city, Argus declared, "Jason, once we enter Grandfather's palace, your eyes will flood with the sight of many marvels, for in a time now past, Shining Helios helped Hephaestus.

And so the Strong-armed god built this wondrous palace for my grandfather, and he gave him the marvelous gifts that will flood your eyes."

So Argus spoke. And indeed it came to pass that Jason's eyes flooded with the sight of marvels as soon as he stepped through the palace gates. First, he noticed a plow that had been fashioned from an unbreakable stone. It rested beside an enormous but empty field. Then he noticed a pair of huge bulls, grazing nearby, that pulled this great plow. Jason was astonished to see that these bulls had bronze feet. They also breathed fire from their bronze mouths, and so they were scorching the grass they were eating.

It came to pass that soon after Jason and his companions entered the home of the royal family, their eyes suddenly flooded with the sight of the beautiful maiden princess. Medea was a priestess of Night-wandering Hecate, the dreaded Underworld goddess from grim Hades' lifeless kingdom. And so she usually spent her days at the goddess's temple. But White-armed Hera had found reasons to keep her at home.

When Medea's eyes suddenly flooded with the sight of her nephews, swift as the wind, she cried out in surprise. For her mind flooded with questions about their return home. And at first, her eyes did not mark the presence of the godlike stranger among them. And swift as the wind, her cry brought her sister to her side. And when Chalciope's eyes suddenly flooded with the sight of her children, she too cried out in surprise. And her eyes did not mark the presence of the godlike stranger among them.

Meanwhile, swift as the wind, Eros drew forth his curved bow and aimed one of his love-inspiring arrows at Medea just as her eyes flooded with the sight of the godlike stranger.

And just as a poor woman heaps dry sticks around a small log in order to kindle a blazing fire—and as she watches, the burning log ignites the sticks and they suddenly erupt into a blazing sheet of flame—so Eros's arrow now caused Medea's heart to flood with flames of love and longing for the godlike stranger. Then, having completed his task, the son of Laughter-loving Aphrodite flew back to his home on Mount Olympus.

Chapter 3

King Aeetes plans to kill the strangers from Hellas. He demands that Jason perform tasks in order to win the Golden Fleece. Argus promises to help Jason. Medea has a strange dream.

And it came to pass that Aeetes held a great feast in honor of the return of his four grandsons. But only after everyone had feasted on the sumptuous fare did the king declare, "Argus, the time has come for you to answer two questions. First, why have you returned home? And who is the stranger whom you have brought with you?"

So Aeetes spoke. And his words caused Argus's mind to flood with thoughts of Jason's quest and the debt he owed him. So it came to pass that Argus answered the king with honeyed words. He explained how Jason had rescued them. He spoke of Jason's family. And he explained why Jason had come to Colchis.

"Give Jason your wondrous fleece, Grandfather," advised Argus, "and he will pay you well for it. For with courage, strength, and skill, Jason and his companions will fight the enemies who lie to the north of us. They are the greatest heroes of Hellas. Many are children of the deathless gods, and the gods look with delight on them all."

So Argus spoke, but his honeyed words only caused Aeetes' heart to flood with fury. And swift as the wind, Aeetes' eyes sent forth fiery golden rays—rays as blindingly bright as the gold-yoked chariot his father, Shining Helios, drives across the heavens each day.

"Argus, you must think I am soft of mind and weak of heart that you prey upon me with honeyed words," he declared "Jason has not come for my wondrous fleece. He wants my royal scepter, my throne, and my kingdom!"

So Aeetes spoke. And with these words, he turned toward Jason and exclaimed, "I wish I had not entertained you as my guest! For I would now cut out your tongue and chop off your hands so that you could not return and try to overthrow me! But you have become my guest, Jason. And so I will give you a choice. You may return to your companions and your ship, and then I will guarantee you safe passage from Aea and the kingdom of Colchis. Or you may try to earn the Golden Fleece for which Argus says you have come. But, before you choose, open the doors of your mind to my words, for, like well-aimed arrows, they will fly forth straight and true.

"To perform all the tasks I will demand of you, you will need courage, strength, and skill that equal my own. For when Blushing Eos makes the new day light, it is my custom to go forth to the Plain of Ares the Death-dealer and yoke my two bulls to my plow. Next I plow and sow the field. Then, at the proper time, I reap the harvest. But I am performing no simple set of tasks.

"As you entered the palace grounds, surely your eyes flooded with the sight of the huge fire-breathing bulls and the great, deep-cutting plow of unbreakable stone that Strong-armed Hephaestus gave my father, Shining Helios. When Blushing Eos makes the new day light, I force the yoke on these bulls, though fiery flames spurt forth from their mouths and burn me, and their bronze hooves kick me.

"Once I have plowed the field, I sow 'seeds' that are the terrible teeth of Death-dealing Ares' dragon. And once I have planted them, swift as the wind, they begin to grow into armed men. By the time Father has driven his chariot two-thirds of the way across the heavens, each tooth will have sprouted into a fearsome bronze-clad warrior. Now each of these warriors comes forth from Mother Gaea wielding a double-pointed spear, and they will push me into the grasping hands of Thanatos unless I kill them first.

"These bronze-clad warriors are Mother Gaea's children. But, fortunately for me, my own spear can force them to give up light and life. And so I slice off their heads, or their trunks, and I push them into the grasping hands of Thanatos before they push me. Every earthborn, bronze-clad warrior looks his last upon light and life, and by the time I have finished this harvest, Father has driven his gold-yoked chariot into the western waves of Oceanus.

"And so, Jason, if you choose to earn the Golden Fleece for which Argus says you have come, you will need to be well rested, both in mind and in body. For when Blushing Eos makes the second day light, you must go forth to the Plain of Death-dealing Ares, and there you must plow, plant, and reap the field just as I would do.

"Complete these tasks, Jason, and I will reward you with the wondrous Golden Fleece. And I will permit you to return with it to Hellas. For then you will have proved that you are my equal in courage, strength, and skill, though surely you will not be my equal in power! But if you do not agree to undertake these tasks, Jason, then you are a coward, and swift as the wind, you must leave my kingdom. No man of courage lets a coward have his way!"

So King Aeetes spoke in his great pride, and his words caused Jason's heart to flood with despair. "Argus was right. Both Pelias and Aeetes want to kill me!" he silently exclaimed. "But I must quiet my quaking heart, and I must be brave before this cruel king, for his heart and mercy are strangers. And in courage lies my only hope!"

So it came to pass that Jason responded, "King Aeetes, it is your right to make me win the Golden Fleece if I would have it. And so I accept your challenge. At the appointed time, I will go forth to the Plain of Death-dealing Ares. There I will plow, plant, and reap the field just as you would do. And I will prove I am your equal in courage, strength, and skill."

"As you have agreed, Jason, so it will be," declared Aeetes. "Return now to your companions and rest well, for, at the appointed time, we will meet again— on the Plain of Death-dealing Ares."

Jason and the sons of Phrixus returned to their well-benched ship. And there Jason gathered the Argonauts and announced, "My friends, my heart overflows with despair, for the heart of King Aeetes floods with rage toward us. And so he has commanded me to complete a series of tasks only a godlike mortal like himself can perform. And yet I have agreed to do all Aeetes demands of me, for I had nothing better to offer."

So Jason spoke to the Argonauts, and swift as the wind, Peleus responded, "Jason, let us determine for ourselves whether your heart has cause to overflow with despair. What are these tasks King Aeetes now commands you to perform?"

So Peleus questioned Jason. And so Jason described the tasks Aeetes was demanding of him. And his words caused every heart to flood with despair.

But then Peleus declared, "Jason, open the doors of your mind to my words, for, like well-aimed arrows, they will fly forth straight and true. Look into your mind and heart, and see if you are willing to perform all the godlike tasks that Aeetes now demands of you. For your heart must flood with courage. And your limbs must go forth with strength and skill. If you are willing, then you should honor your promise.

"But what if you cannot summon the courage you will need? What if you are uncertain of your strength and skill? Then Jason, I will go forth in your place. And I will perform all the tasks that King Aeetes now demands of you, for I have nothing to lose. If I am successful, I will win the glory of the great deed. And if I fail, Thanatos will embrace me. Why should my heart flood with fear? Heroes and cowards alike share the same fate. For that dreadful god will clasp all who walk the earth in his grasping hands. And so if I must look my last on light and life, let it be when I am performing great deeds. For I would choose a death that brings glory and lasting fame!"

So Peleus responded to Jason. And his words caused the hearts of other Argonauts to flood with courage as well.

But swift as the wind, Argus declared, "Peleus's heart overflows with courage, but even he lacks the strength and skill to yoke my grandfather's bulls and do battle with Mother Gaea's bronze-clad children. Believe me, my friends, when I tell you Jason is in dire straits! And surely now, Jason, you realize what a hopeless task King Pelias has given you! So open the doors of your mind to my words, for, like well-aimed arrows, they will fly forth straight and true.

"I have a plan, Jason. And, if you agree with it, you will be able to perform all the tasks my grandfather demands of you, for I have an aunt—my mother's younger sister, Medea. She is still a maiden, but she is wise far beyond her years. She serves Hecate, the Night-wandering Goddess, and the goddess has caused her to be gifted in the ways of charms and magic. And so if my mother can get Medea to help you, surely you will succeed!"

"For in Medea's skillful hands, all the herbs that grow on land and all that live in the salt sea become drugs and charms. She can call forth blazing fires. She can quiet rushing rivers. And in the heavens, she can make Silver-horned Selene drive her silver-yoked chariot next to the gold-yoked chariot of Gold-helmeted Helios. She can make spring flowers bloom in summer. She can make the grain grow ripe for harvesting in winter. And she can make the floor of heavily-wooded forests reflect Shining Helios's golden rays."

So Argus spoke. And in reply Jason declared, "Fear not, Argus. Whatever will ensure my success, I will do. I will even rely on a woman! And so kneel before your mother. Clasp her knees. Take her chin in your hand. And with honeyed words, plead on my behalf."

So Jason spoke to Argus. And in time, it came to pass that the eyes of all the Argonauts closed in sweet sleep.

But within the royal palace, sweet sleep fled from King Aeetes. For his mind flooded with thoughts of his grandsons and the stranger from Hellas. And he knew that, as soon as Blushing Eos made the new day light, he would call the warriors of Colchis to assembly, and he would flood their ears with his commands.

And sweet sleep fled from Medea as well. For she had been present at the great feast that had celebrated the return of her nephews. And so she had heard her father challenge the stranger from Hellas. And she had heard the stranger's response. She had stood silent and still, for the sight of this stranger had flooded her eyes, and the godlike beauty of his face and form had caused her heart to flood with waves of love and longing. Even after the stranger had left the great hall, she still could see how he looked as he sat and as he walked. And she still could hear his courageous words.

As the maiden sat on her bed, her mind flooded with waves of conflicting thoughts. "This stranger from Hellas towers over all other men!" she silently exclaimed. "Stranger though he is, my heart would have to be made of stone or bronze to resist him. What a pity Father's bulls will cut his life short! But I cannot reveal the love that floods my heart for this stranger, for he is my father's enemy, and to befriend him would be treason. Yet I must help the man I love, or Thanatos will soon embrace him. And there he will surely look his last upon light and life!"

So Medea mused, and the thought of the stranger's impending death caused her heart to flood with grief, and tears flowed freely from her eyes. And so the maiden now called on the Underworld goddess whom she served. "Oh hear me, Night-wandering Hecate. Smile on this stranger from Hellas. And help him!" she prayed. "Lead grim Hades—Lord of the Dead—to take no interest in him. Help this stranger return safely to his home in Hellas. And help me show him that, in me, he has a loyal friend in this land where he is an unwelcome guest."

So Medea prayed. And it came to pass that the maiden, weary from the overwhelming passion that flooded her heart, lay down and fell into a troubled sleep. And in her sleep, she dreamed the stranger had not come to recover the Golden Fleece. Instead, he had come to wed with her. And she dreamed he planned to take her, as his wedded lady, back to his home in Hellas.

Moreover, in her dream, Medea—and not the stranger—performed all the tasks her father demanded of him. She yoked the fire-breathing bulls, she sowed the terrible dragon's teeth, and she reaped the harvest of the fearsome earthborn warriors. Her skill in magic enabled her to perform these tasks easily. And so she saved the stranger's life.

But her father's heart flooded with rage, for the stranger from Hellas had not performed these tasks, and so her father refused to give up the Golden Fleece. His refusal caused the stranger's heart to flood with wrath, and so the stranger argued angrily with her father. At last, they agreed to have her choose between them. And swift as the wind, she chose the stranger from Hellas. Her decision caused the hearts of her parents to flood with waves of anguish and anger, and their cries awakened her.

"What a terrifying dream!" Medea silently exclaimed. "My heart quakes like a great oak tree in a storm wind! But I must offer this stranger my help—no matter what happens. And may the deathless gods see into my heart and forgive me, for that is the only way to stop the anguish that floods my own heart."

So Medea mused, and these thoughts caused tears to flow freely from her eyes. The eyes of King Aeetes had long since closed in sweet sleep, and now only Medea lay awake in the dark silence, for waves of terror and love flooded her heart, preventing sleep's arrival.

When Blushing Eos with her sparkling eyes made the new day light, King Aeetes gathered his armed men. And it came to pass that more than the storm-tossed waves of the salt sea, more than the grains of shining sand on its shores, and more than the autumn leaves on the floor of the oak forest were the Colchian warriors who now responded to their great king's call for revenge.

And when they had assembled in front of the royal palace, the great king of Colchis declared, "Warriors of Colchis, open the doors of your mind to my words, for, like well-aimed arrows, they will fly forth straight and true. The sons of Phrixus are traitors! They have joined these strangers from Hellas, for they want to steal my royal scepter, my throne, and my kingdom!

"My father, Shining Helios, warned me of this. He told me to beware of deceitful schemes. He said they would lead to treachery and destruction, and he warned me that those of my own blood would contrive them. Now surely I have no cause to fear my daughters or my son. It is only my grandsons—the sons of Phrixus—whom I cannot trust.

"And so, warriors of Colchis, I will treat my grandsons—as well as these strangers from Hellas who have corrupted them—as they deserve. One and all, they must give up light and life! My bulls will tear Jason's limbs from his trunk, and I will leave his lifeless flesh as food for birds and dogs. Then, as soon as Jason falls, you must go forth to the forests that clothe our wooded hill-sides, and there you must fell the trees and make fiery torches of them. Then you must find where these strangers have hidden their well-benched ship, and you must destroy her and all who would escape on her.

"For just as bees will always return to their hive, so the Argonauts—with the sons of Phrixus among them—will surely return to their ship. So keep close watch, for not one of them must escape your torches. One and all, they must look their last upon light and life!"

So Aeetes spoke to his armed men. Meanwhile, Argus kept his promise to Jason. As soon as Blushing Eos with her sparkling eyes made the new day light, he secretly went forth to speak with his mother. There, he knelt before her. He clasped her knees. He took her chin in his hand. And with honeyed words, he pleaded on Jason's behalf.

Chapter 4

Medea decides to help Jason win the Golden Fleece, and she prepares him for his tasks.

Argus's words sent Chalciope forth to her sister's room. And when she saw her, she exclaimed, "Medea, tears are flowing freely from your eyes! Why does your heart flood with grief?"

"Oh, Chalciope, I dreamed your sons became food for birds and dogs!" exclaimed Medea. "For I dreamed that Father killed them, along with the strangers who have come here from Hellas! When Blushing Eos makes the new day light, we often see our dreams flee, swift as the wind, like snow beneath Grandfather's golden rays. But I fear my dreams reveal events that will indeed come to pass, for your sons have shown Father they support the stranger from Hellas and his quest for the wondrous Fleece. And so they are traitors!"

So Medea spoke, and her words caused Chalciope's heart to flood with fear. And so Chalciope now knelt before Medea. She clasped her sister's knees. She took her sister's chin in her hand. And tears flowed freely from her eyes as she exclaimed, "Then I plead with you, Medea. You must save my sons, for you have powers that are greater than Father's."

So Chalciope spoke. And in reply, Medea declared, "You give me more power than I possess, Chalciope, but I hereby take the sacred oath of our people. And with the great, deathless gods of earth and sky as my witnesses, I promise I will do my best to save your sons, Chalciope."

So Medea spoke, and in reply, Chalciope declared, "For you to save my sons, Medea, you must find a way for the stranger from Hellas to accomplish all the tasks Father demands of him. And then, swift as the wind, you must help him take the Golden Fleece. For my sons plan to leave Colchis with the Argonauts, and they all must escape before Father forces them to give up light and life!

"In fact, Argus is here in the palace. He wants you to help the stranger from Hellas perform the tasks Father demands, and he is waiting for my reply. He says the stranger will gladly accept whatever help you can give him, for the stranger knows that, without your help, Thanatos will surely take the wind of life that blows through him. This is what brought me to your room, Medea, but your tears distracted me. Now what message should Argus give the stranger?"

So Chalciope spoke, and her words caused Medea's heart to flood with joy. "Chalciope, this stranger from Hellas has put the lives of your sons, as well as his own life, in danger. And may my eyes look their last upon light and life if I let anything come before you and your sons! So I will now prepare to go forth to Night-wandering Hecate's temple, and I will take powerful herbs that will act as charms against Father's bulls. Tell Argus to lead the stranger forth to meet me at the temple, and there I will give him the charms he will need."

So Medea spoke, and her words caused Chalciope's heart to flood with joy. Swift as the wind, she left Medea and gave Argus the welcome news.

And so it came to pass that, once again, Medea was alone in her room. And once again, her mind flooded with waves of conflicting thoughts. "What madness! I have vowed to help a stranger whom Father regards as his enemy!" she silently exclaimed. "Surely it is better to forget my oath and welcome the embrace of Thanatos, or to place myself at the mercy of the deathless gods. I should pray they punish me by making me live the life of a loyal daughter whose heart never floods with joy.

"I wish Artemis—the Archer-Goddess—had killed me with one of her golden arrows before my eyes had seen this godlike stranger, for love only floods the heart with anguish! I can choose to help the stranger from Hellas, or I can choose to die, or I can choose to suffer in silence. But the end will be the same—unbearable anguish! For if I do not help him, then he will surely die, and my heart will never know another love. And yet, if I do help him, how can I face Father, for how can I hide my treachery?

"I should save the godlike stranger. And then I should welcome the embrace of Thanatos, for I know which herbs to swallow. But even my death would not wash away my crime. Not only the Colchians but all who walk the earth would come to hear of it, for poets would sing of the maiden who dishonored her family and her people because of her love for a godlike stranger. And other poets would sing these songs even in times yet to come. No, I must give Thanatos the wind of life that blows through me, but I must do it now—before I do any harm!"

So Medea mused. And with these thoughts it came to pass that she found and opened the box in which she kept all her powerful herbs—those that cured ills as well as those that created them. And with tears flowing freely from her eyes, her sure hand chose those herbs that, swift as the wind, would invite Thanatos to embrace her and cause her to look her last upon light and life. But waves of a conflicting passion now flooded the maiden's heart. "Surely it is dreadful to choose an early death! For my heart floods with longing for life!" she silently exclaimed.

"What would it be like to give up light and life? My heart would never again flood with the joy of embracing someone I love! My ears would never again flood with the sound of a bird's sweet song! And my throat would never again be moistened by sweet water from sparkling streams! My eyes would never again flood with the sight of Grandfather's chariot! And my skin would never again flood with the comforting warmth of his golden rays! My eyes would never again flood with the sight of fields of flowers. And my nose would never again flood with the smell of their sweet fragrance!

"And so how can I face grim Hades' lifeless kingdom and all the shades of the dead who live there? How can I choose death when my heart floods with love of life? No, I cannot give Thanatos the wind of life that blows through me! And so I will keep the sacred oath I made before Chalciope and the deathless gods. I will meet with the stranger from Hellas. I will give him the herbs he needs. Yes, I will save the man I love! And the poets can sing of it!"

So Medea decided. And so it came to pass. For Golden-throned Hera had been looking down from Mount Olympus, watching Medea and listening to the maiden's thoughts, in order to see how her plans for Pelias were progressing. And Medea's plan to invite the embrace of Thanatos had caused the goddess's heart to flood with wrath. "I cannot permit Medea to give up the wind of life that blows through her!" the goddess had silently exclaimed. "For without Medea, my plans to avenge Pelias's insult to my honor cannot succeed. And so I must now flood the maiden's mind and heart with the love of light and life."

So the White-armed Goddess had decided. And so it came to pass that Medea now washed her tears from her cheeks and rubbed a sweet-smelling oil into her skin. Then she artfully arranged her golden hair and put on a lovely robe. She covered her head with a silver veil, and she chose just the herbs that would help the stranger from Hellas.

"The man who covers his body with these drugs will be invincible!" she silently exclaimed. "For one day his strength and skill will prevail against any flames from a blazing fire and any blow from a bronze weapon. He will be more than mortal, for these drugs will prolong his strength, and they will give him the power of renewed youth."

So Medea mused. And with these words, she tucked the powerful herbs into the folds of her waistband and left the palace. Then she drove her chariot to Night-wandering Hecate's temple. It came to pass that she arrived before Jason, and as she performed her tasks, her ears remained alert to every sound that might herald the arrival of the godlike stranger.

Meanwhile, Argus was leading Jason forth to the goddess's temple. However, as soon as they could see the structure in the distance, Argus declared, "Jason, you must now go forth alone to meet the Colchian maiden at the Night-wanderer's temple. Win her heart with honeyed words, and she will surely help you with your tasks."

So Argus advised Jason. And it came to pass that, at last, the sight of the stranger from Hellas flooded Medea's eyes. The maiden now stood silent and still as once again the beauty of his face and form caused her heart to flood with waves of love and longing, for White-armed Hera had made Jason even more godlike in his beauty.

Swift as the wind, Medea's cheeks flushed a fiery red, and her limbs felt too weak to move. Just as oak and pine trees in a mountain forest stand side by side but silent and still when no breeze stirs them, and yet, later, they will rustle constantly when a brisk wind blows upon them, so the maiden from Colchis and the stranger from Hellas now met face to face but stood silent and still. And yet, later, love would unleash a steady stream of words.

Jason saw Medea's confusion and declared, "I come to you alone, lovely maiden, so you need not fear me. You appear to be both gentle and kind. I know the deathless gods have given you the power to save me, and that you have promised to give me the charms I will need if I am to accomplish my tasks. And so I now kneel before you. I clasp your knees. I take your chin in my hand. And as I ask you to keep your word, I invoke both Far-seeing Zeus, who protects suppliants and guests, and Hecate, the Night-wandering Goddess from grim Hades' lifeless kingdom who is honored by this temple.

"Lovely maiden, you hold my life and my death in your hands. If your heart floods with the pleasure of power, you will choose to destroy me by withholding your help. But if your heart floods with the glory of the great deed, then you will choose to save my life by giving me whatever help you can. And your decision will confer life or death on my companions as well. Help me, lovely maiden! And in gratitude I will praise you to all who walk the earth! Everyone will know your name and your deed. My companions aboard the well-benched Argo will praise you as well, and their mothers and wives, in turn, will praise you, for you will have saved the lives of us all."

So Jason spoke to the Colchian maiden. Meanwhile, once again, Golden-throned Hera had been looking down from Mount Olympus, watching and listening, in order to see how her plans for Jason and Medea were progressing. And now she silently exclaimed, "How clever I was to put honeyed words into Jason's mind and heart, for they will tear Medea's heart away from her loving parents. And now her heart will overflow with waves of love and longing for Jason, for so it must be if I am to use Medea to avenge Pelias's insult to my honor."

So the White-armed Goddess mused. And so it came to pass that the stranger's honeyed words caused Medea's heart to overflow with waves of love and longing for him. The maiden took from her waist-band certain of the herbs that would save the stranger's life, and she handed these drugs to him. For she saw that the stranger from Hellas needed her, and she saw the love that passed from his eyes to hers. And—if he had only asked her—she would have handed him her soul as well.

"Stranger, open the doors of your mind to my words, for, like well-aimed arrows, they will fly forth straight and true," declared Medea. "When Nyx ascends her throne and covers Mother Gaea with her star-filled robe, you must go forth alone. First you must purify yourself by bathing in the lively stream that flows near this temple. And then you must honor the Night-wandering Goddess by pouring her an offering of honey. Only then, may you ask her to help you perform the tasks my father demands of you.

"Then you must return to your companions. But you must take care never to look back, for when the goddess hears your prayers, she will leave grim Hades' lifeless kingdom and come forth to accept your sacrifice. Remember, Stranger, dreadful sounds will flood your ears. And terrifying sights will flood your eyes, but you must not look back.

"Your ears will flood with the sound of fearsome hissing, for deadly serpents writhe in woven coils among the leafy oak twigs that form the goddess's crown. Your ears will flood with the sound of furious barking, for grim Hades' fearsome hounds always accompany the Night-wanderer when she walks upon Mother Gaea. And your ears will flood with the dreadful cries of the nymphs who live in marsh and stream, for when their eyes flood with the sight of the Night-wanderer, their hearts will flood with terror.

"The goddess's torches will chase Nyx from her throne, for the Night-wanderer's lamps gleam like Shining Helios's gold-yoked chariot. And so your eyes will flood with the sight of fields that, swift as the wind, now shine as brightly as when Shining Helios bathes them in his golden rays. Meanwhile, the goddess's feet will cause even Mother Gaea to quake with fear. And so—beneath your own feet—you will hear and feel her trembling.

"The dreadful sounds that flood your ears and the terrifying sights that flood your eyes will surely cause even your own heroic heart to flood with fear. But you must not look back! If you forget my warning, you will dishonor the goddess. You will ruin your sacrifice. And you will look your last upon light and life. You will not be safe until you have rejoined your companions.

"When Blushing Eos makes the new day light take this herb I now place in your hand, and soak it in water until it becomes soft. Then remove your clothing, and rub the softened herb into the skin of your entire body. Rub it on your shield and on your sword and spear, as well.

"You already possess the necessary courage and skill to perform the tasks that await you, Stranger. But if you do just as I say, then the flames of my father's fire-breathing bulls will not harm you. Nor will the double-pointed spears of the fearsome bronze-clad warriors—those children of Mother Gaea who will spring forth from the furrows where you have sown the terrible dragon's teeth—leave a mark upon you.

"Once you have sown the dragon's teeth, you must stand aside from the Plain of Death-dealing Ares. Rest from your labors in the shade of a great boulder that lies nearby. And in time it will come to pass that the field will shine with the gleaming, plumed helmets of the earthborn ones.

"Then you must surprise these warriors by suddenly tossing that great boulder among them. For just as starving dogs will tear into one another in order to grab hold of a piece of meat—fighting until they have given up light and life—so the fearsome bronze-clad warriors will now fight to their death in order to possess the boulder you have thrown among them. And now, swift as the wind, you must go forth to kill the earthborn ones while they are fighting each other! And if you do just as I say, Stranger, then you will win the wondrous Golden Fleece.

"Once the fleece is yours, I will lead you to it and enable you to take it, for despite your victory, Stranger, my father will never give it to you. And without my help, you will never be able to take it from him, for a great deathless dragon lies coiled around the tree from which the fleece hangs. It is a child of Mother Gaea, and so it is more than mortal. Its watchful eyes never close in sweet sleep. And its skin defies the strongest and sharpest of weapons. No mortal possesses the skill to defeat it. But I will subdue it for you.

"And then, Stranger, you must take the wondrous fleece. And, swift as the wind, you must flee, for your victory will cause my father's heart to flood with fury. He commands tribes of Colchians beyond number. Before Blushing Eos makes the new day light, his warriors will have made fiery torches of the trees that clothe our wooded hillsides. And they will carry their flaming weapons forth to your well-benched ship, for surely my father will have commanded them to destroy both your ship and all who have come here with you. Stranger, no one can defeat my father in battle! And he will not rest until you and all your companions have become food for birds and dogs!"

So Medea advised Jason. Her heart now flooded with grief as her mind flooded with the thought of his leaving her, and so tears flowed freely from her eyes as she declared, "Once you have returned safely to Hellas, Stranger, do not forget me! For I will not forget you! But if you forget me, then, swift as the wind, Rumor will fly across the sea to Colchis with the news. And you will find that I am your unexpected guest in Iolcus. Then I will remind you of how I helped you perform all the tasks my father demanded of you, and how I helped you capture the wondrous Golden Fleece."

So Medea spoke, and her tearful words caused Jason's heart to flood with love for the weeping maiden. And he replied, "Your heart floods with waves of fear and sorrow without cause, lovely maiden. And so your words are as empty as a lone cloud when Shining Helios bathes Mother Gaea in his golden rays. For if I live to return safely to Hellas, day and night, for as long as I live, I will remember you!"

So Jason spoke. And it came to pass that, as Medea stared into Jason's eyes, her own eyes shone with love for the godlike stranger. And as she continued to look at him, her eyes grew brighter and brighter until they sent forth fiery golden rays, rays as blindingly bright as the gold-yoked chariot her grandfather, Shining Helios, drives across the heavens each day. Beset by Medea's gaze, Jason saw nothing but that blindingly bright light. And then he saw nothing at all. His knees gave way, and his body collapsed gently upon Mother Gaea. And there he lay in a deep sleep.

Medea recited an incantation over the sleeping stranger that put him into an even deeper sleep—a deathlike state from which only she could awaken him. Then she brought forth a pile of firewood, a tripod, and a large bronze cauldron from Night-wandering Hecate's temple. These she arranged one upon the other. Last, she brought forth a sharp, wood-chopping blade. And this she put to one side.

Medea filled the great pot with water from the stream that flowed nearby. And she ignited the wood beneath the tripod. Next she removed handfuls of herbs that she had stored in the waistband of her robe, and she sprinkled these drugs into the water. Then she picked up a large, dead olive branch, and she began to stir the brew in the cauldron carefully and well.

At first it came to pass that, as the broth in the cauldron became hotter, the bare olive branch began to grow strong and green. Then, as the broth became even hotter, the branch sprouted a host of green leaves. And at last, as the broth began to boil vigorously, a wealth of firm, ripe olives grew upon the branch. Meanwhile, wherever the pot boiled over and the broth splattered upon the earth, Mother Gaea sent forth fresh green grass and fragrant flowers.

Medea now stopped stirring and returned to the stranger, who still lay silent and sleeping as if he were dead. She picked up her wood-chopping blade and chopped the stranger's body into pieces and dropped them into her boiling brew. "Stranger, for this one day, my herbs will give you the power of a god!" she exclaimed. "My broth will fill you with such strength, you will feel as if divine ichor, and not the blood of a mortal, flows within you. When you awaken, you will have the strength to yoke Father's great bulls, and you will be able to plow Death-dealing Ares' fearsome field."

So Medea spoke. And indeed, it came to pass that, swift as the wind, just as Medea's brew had restored the olive branch to life and youth, so the stranger's body now became restored and renewed as it cooked in the boiling broth. And so the maiden now lifted him from the broth and laid him, once again, upon Mother Gaea.

Then Medea returned to the cauldron. Now she added herbs that would render the broth powerless, and she put out the fire. She emptied the cauldron. She returned the great pot and its tripod to Night-wandering Hecate's temple, and she swept away the ashes. Last of all, she recited a second incantation over the sleeping stranger, and so Jason awoke from his deathlike sleep. And it came to pass that he remembered only the love he had seen shining forth from the maiden's eyes.

"Come with me to Hellas, lovely maiden," he declared. "And there the Hellenes will treat you with the honor and respect they give one of the deathless gods, for you will have saved the lives of their sons, their wedded lords, and their kinsmen. Come with me to Hellas, lovely maiden. For there I will make you my wedded lady. There I will keep you safely at my hearth. And there—for as long as the wind of life blows through me—I will let nothing destroy our love!

"For I will love you, Medea, as long as Shining Helios drives his gold-yoked chariot across the heavens and into the waves of the western sea. But if Shining Helios should tire of his journey—if instead, he closes his eyes in sweet sleep when Blushing Eos beckons him with her light—then still I will love you.

"And I will love you, Medea, as long as Nyx ascends her throne and covers Mother Gaea with her star-filled robe. But if the goddess should tire of her robe— if instead, she wraps herself in a robe of blushing red or leafy green or even a robe of gleaming silver or shining gold—then still I will love you.

"And I will love you, Medea, as long as Lord Poseidon causes the salt sea to send forth its waves upon Mother Gaea's shores. But if the heart of the Earthshaker should flood with anger—if instead, he causes the sea to disappear like a drop of water beneath Shining Helios's golden rays—then still I will love you.

"And I will love you, Medea, as long as Mother Gaea sends forth grains and fruits from the earth on which we mortals walk. But if the heart of Mother Gaea should flood with anger—if instead, she causes the earth to become as dead as grim Hades' lifeless kingdom—then still I will love you.

"So come with me to Hellas, lovely maiden. And there our days will follow, one after the other, like blossoms of shining gold upon a golden chain."

So Jason spoke. And his loving words flooded the maiden's heart with joy and her soul with longing. Medea now stood before the stranger, silent and still. She flooded her eyes with the godlike beauty of his face and form. And it came to pass that her soul flew into the stranger's keeping.

At last, Jason spoke again. "Lovely maiden, swift as the wind, we must now part. For we have tarried here too long already. Someone might pass by this sacred place. And we must not be seen here together.

"But first, open the doors of your mind to my words. For, like well-aimed arrows, they will fly forth straight and true. If it comes to pass that, with your help, I accomplish the tasks your father demands of me. And if, with your help, I claim the wondrous Golden Fleece, then your life will be in danger, and you will have to flee with me. Remember! You must take your little brother with you!"

"Surely the loss of my brother—my father's only son—will be more than Father can bear, Stranger!" exclaimed Medea. "And it floods my heart with terror to think of how he will respond to it!"

"Lovely maiden, if your little brother remains behind with your father, in time, he will have to avenge our theft of the wondrous fleece. But if we manage to escape with him, he will grow up with our love. Then he may choose to remain loyal to us. So do not let your heart rule your mind in this matter. Do just as I say, and we will fare well."

So Jason spoke. And with these words, he returned to his companions, and his heart flooded with joy. "Medea will help me! And so I will perform all the tasks Aeetes demands, and I will capture the wondrous Golden Fleece!"

So Jason mused. Meanwhile, his words about Apsyrtus flooded Medea's mind. "The godlike stranger's promise of lasting love floods my heart with love for him! But when my mind floods with thoughts of the deeds I have promised to perform, then my heart floods with horror! For by choosing to help the stranger from Hellas, I am forsaking my parents, my home, and my homeland. And so from this time forth, whatever this stranger wants, I will have to give him."

So Medea mused, and so it had to be, for so White-armed Hera had contrived. And with these words, the maiden returned to her father's palace.

Meanwhile, once again, Golden-throned Hera had been looking down from Mount Olympus, watching and listening, in order to see how her plans for Jason and Medea were progressing. And now she silently exclaimed, "My heart floods with joy! For with Medea's help, Jason will capture the Golden Fleece. He will return safely to Iolcus. And he will bring more than the wondrous fleece. He will bring Medea! And through Medea I will avenge Pelias's insult to my honor, for his fate must remind all who walk the earth that I will not tolerate anyone who dishonors me!"

Chapter 5

Because of Medea's help, Jason performs his tasks.

In time, Shining Helios drove his gold-yoked chariot into the western waves of Oceanus. Nyx ascended her throne, and she covered Mother Gaea with her star-filled robe. And so it came to pass that Jason set forth to perform the tasks Medea had given him. He felt that her love had renewed his youth, so he carefully performed the offering to Night-wandering Hecate. And then he returned to his companions. He did not look behind him. But all the sounds the maiden had told him he would hear now flooded his ears. And all the sights she had told him he could safely see now flooded his eyes.

And it came to pass that, when Blushing Eos with her sparkling eyes made the new day light, Jason applied the special herb Medea had given him. And as soon as he rubbed it into his skin, he felt like one of the deathless gods. Just as a war horse that longs for battle first raises its head and its ears and neighs—and then it prances about and paws at Mother Gaea with its hooves—so Jason now flexed his limbs and longed for his tasks to begin. And just as lightning flashes forth from summer stormclouds, so Jason leapt into the air with his ash spear in one hand and his bronze shield in the other.

Jason now went forth to the Plain of Ares the Death-dealer, for he was ready to perform all the tasks King Aeetes was demanding of him. When he reached the field, his eyes flooded with the sight of all the Argonauts as well as with the sight of King Aeetes, his warriors, Medea and the other members of the royal family, and a great crowd of Colchians who had already gathered nearby.

King Aeetes was surely the strongest of all who walk the earth, but on this day, Jason surpassed him, for now Jason was truly godlike! Surely Death-dealing Ares had entered his mortal body, and Far-shooting Apollo had entered his spirit. And all whose eyes flooded with the sight of the stranger from Hellas knew that the fearsome king of Colchis had met his equal.

So it came to pass that King Aeetes dropped the terrible dragon's teeth into Jason's bronze helmet. And the stranger from Hellas set forth to yoke the king's fire-breathing bulls. Just as a blacksmith places his bellows into his furnace and works it in order to raise a great fire, resting only after he has created a fiercely roaring flame, so Aeetes' bulls now thundered with rage and sent furious flames soaring forth from their mouths. Like blasts of storm-winds, their fiery breath lashed Jason's face and body as he labored to place the bronze yoke on their backs. And like bolts of lightning, their bronze hooves kicked him.

However, Medea's wisdom and skill came to Jason's aid, for her drug gave him the protection he needed in order to succeed with this task. And so, in time, it came to pass that Jason yoked Aeetes' fire-breathing bulls. Meanwhile Aeetes stood by and watched, and his heart flooded with waves of anguish and anger as he marveled at his adversary's might.

Then Jason drove Aeetes' fearsome bulls and his great, deep-cutting plow of unbreakable stone onto the Plain of Ares the Death-dealer. And there he began his next two tasks. First he plowed the field, forming deep furrows on Mother Gaea's surface. Meanwhile, Aeetes still stood by and watched, and once again his heart flooded with waves of anguish and anger as he marveled at his adversary's might.

Next Jason walked beside the furrows, and he tossed the terrible dragon's teeth into the beds that were far from him, for his heart would often flood with terror as he sowed these strange seeds. And then he would turn his head—now this way, and now that way—in order to be certain he was not in danger, for he feared the bronze-clad, earthborn ones would spring forth from their mother before he was prepared to fight them.

In this way, in time, it came to pass that Jason finished sowing the Plain of Death-dealing Ares. Shining Helios had now driven his gold-yoked chariot two-thirds of the way across the heavens, and Jason now left the field. He rested from his labors in the shade of the great boulder that lay nearby. And as Jason rested, he watched as—here and there, before his eyes—the earth he had so recently plowed suddenly began to move. First, spear-points on wooden shafts began to push up through the soil. Then gleaming helmets with waving plumes began to burst forth from the furrows where he had sown the dragon's teeth.

As Jason continued to watch, faces began to appear beneath the plumed helmets, followed by bronze-clad shoulders and chests and pairs of arms with hands that held oxhide shields as well as double-pointed spears. And at last pairs of bronze-clad legs with shod feet emerged from Mother Gaea.

Just as Shining Helios's golden rays warm the snow-fields winter storms have left high on a mountain-side, causing the snow to flee and sending cascades of water down into the valley below—and the stream that is lazily making its way through that valley suddenly begins to swell, and its waters increase until it becomes a roaring flood-tide with a treacherous current—so a host of fearsome, bronze-clad warriors now began to flood the furrows where Jason had so recently sown the terrible dragon's teeth.

Meanwhile, as Jason watched the growing army of earthborn warriors, Medea's advice flooded his mind. And so he relaxed by the side of the field until the gleaming helmets and shining armor of the bronze-clad ones covered the Plain of Death-dealing Ares, setting the field ablaze with golden rays that were as bright as those cast by Gold-helmeted Helios and his gold-yoked chariot. Then it came to pass that Medea's voice suddenly flooded his ears, rousing him from his rest. "Stranger!" urged the voice. "Lift the rock that now comforts you, and, swift as the wind, throw it among the warriors!"

And with these words, Jason noticed the immense size of this rock. All hope now fled from his heart. And just as a heavy spring rain flows freely from the roof of a house, so Jason's feeling of renewed youth now poured forth from his body. His heart now flooded with despair. His arms now hung weakly at his sides, and his feet now remained rooted to the earth as if they were planted in Mother Gaea. "Stranger!" urged Medea's voice, once again. "Do not let the size of the rock weaken your will! Four of the strongest youths, working together, could not lift it off Mother Gaea. But you will be able to do it!"

So Medea's voice resounded in Jason's ears. And in response Jason slowly rose to his feet and put his arms around the great rock. And it came to pass that his heart flooded with surprise. For he found that, despite the rock's immense size, he could move it. Swift as the wind, his heart flooded with joy. He lifted the rock off Mother Gaea, and he tossed it among the bronze-clad warriors. And then, swift as the wind, he crouched behind his shield, for he did not want any of the earthborn warriors to see who had thrown the rock into their midst. And there—behind his shield—his heart flooded with courage. Meanwhile, once again, Aeetes stood by and marveled at his adversary's might.

And what Medea had described to Jason indeed came to pass. Just as a pack of hungry wolves will break into a sheepfold—tearing into the frightened flock of sheep and fighting fiercely over the carcass of a lamb they have killed—so the fearsome earthborn ones now leapt upon the great boulder and fought to their death in order to possess it. And just as storm winds batter great oak trees—and cause them to fall lifelessly upon Mother Gaea—so the fearsome warriors now began to destroy each other.

Then it came to pass that, just as a fiery star shoots through the star-filled robe of Nyx and leaves a trail of bright light, so, swift as the wind, Jason now went forth to battle, unleashing his shining sword and leaving a trail of blood. And just as stalks of grain fall to the earth beneath a farmer's newly-sharpened sickle, so beneath Jason's sharp blade, the bronze-clad bodies now fell lifelessly upon Gaea, their mother.

By the time Shining Helios had driven his gold-yoked chariot across the heavens and into the western waves of Oceanus, the furrows Jason had plowed ran red with a flood of blood, and every earth-born warrior lay dead upon the field, having given up both light and life to the point of a sword—and to the grasping hands of Thanatos. Bloody corpses now littered the Plain of Death-dealing Ares like beached sea-monsters on the shore of the salt sea. Some lay with just their heads protruding from the earth. Others lay with their chests and arms exposed, but their legs still buried in Gaea, their mother. While still others lay stretched out upon the earth, fully formed, but sliced apart.

Nyx ascended her throne, and she covered Mother Gaea with her star-filled robe. And then it came to pass that King Aeetes and his family silently returned to their palace. The king's mind flooded with thoughts about the events on the Plain of Ares that had flooded his eyes. And so it came to pass that his heart now flooded first with despair, then with grief, and at last with rage.

"Jason has successfully completed all the tasks I demanded of him, and so the wondrous Golden Fleece should be his. But he could never have performed these tasks without the aid of powerful magic! Who dared to help him? A traitor must live in my own house! Now the sons of Phrixus, though I have doubted their loyalty, lack all knowledge of drugs and charms. And my daughter Chalciope, too, lacks such knowledge.

"And so only Medea could have committed this traitorous deed. My own daughter! Why did she choose to dishonor her father, her family, and her homeland? It is beyond belief! And yet my mind knows Jason has not honored the terms of our agreement, and my heart knows Medea is the traitor, for only Medea's drugs and charms could enable Jason to perform all the tasks I demanded of him. And so he has no right to the wondrous Golden Fleece!

"These thoughts flood my heart with rage! I will treat Medea and my grandsons—as well these strangers from Hellas who have corrupted them—as they deserve! I have already decreed death for every Argonaut, and for the sons of Phrixus, as well. Now I must also decree death for Medea, for one and all, they must now give up light and life. And I will leave their lifeless flesh as food for birds and dogs.

"My warriors must now rid Colchis of these enemies. They must go forth to the forests that clothe our wooded hillsides. And there they must fell the trees and make fiery torches of them. Then they must find where these strangers have hidden their well-benched ship. And they must destroy her and all who would escape on her. For just as bees will always return to their hive, so Jason and the Argonauts—with the sons of Phrixus, among them—will surely return to the Argo. And now Medea will surely flee there, as well. So my warriors must keep close watch, for no one must escape their torches. Thanatos must embrace them all!"

So King Aeetes mused. And with these thoughts, he went forth to speak with those who led the warriors of Colchis.

Chapter 6

With Medea's help, Jason captures the Golden Fleece. Then the Argonauts escape from Colchis with Medea, Apsyrtus, and the sons of Phrixus.

Meanwhile, Medea returned to her room in the royal palace. "Father surely knows what I have done!" the maiden silently exclaimed. "And how could I have done it? Was my heart so flooded with passion for the stranger from Hellas that my judgment abandoned me? Whatever the answer, it is too late for such thoughts. The question is what to do now?"

And just as a frolicsome fawn freezes with terror—as, deep within the woods, it suddenly hears the cries of deer-hounds—so Medea's heart now flooded with dread as she became certain that news of her treachery would spread like a forest fire throughout her father's kingdom. "Swift as the wind, the ears of one and all will flood with the news of what I have done!" she silently exclaimed. "First everyone in the palace will hear of it. Then everyone in Aea will hear of it. And then everyone in Colchis will hear of it.

"And so what should I do now? My room is spinning before my eyes! I cannot breathe! What is left for me but to swallow poisonous herbs and put an end to my agony? And yet I cannot face grim Hades' lifeless kingdom and all the shades of the dead who live there. I cannot choose death when my heart floods with love of life. No, I cannot give Thanatos the wind of life that blows through me! And so I must now flee from my father's palace, from Aea, and from Colchis. My heart may flood with passion, or it may flood with shame, but I must now forsake my parents, my home, and my homeland. And I must cast my lot with the stranger from Hellas!"

So Medea decided. And so it came to pass. For once again, Golden-throned Hera had been looking down from Mount Olympus, watching Medea and listening to the maiden's thoughts, in order to see how her plans for Pelias were progressing. And Medea's desire to invite the embrace of Thanatos had caused the goddess's heart, once again, to flood with wrath. "I cannot permit Medea to give up the wind of life that blows through her!" Hera had silently exclaimed. "For without Medea, my plans to avenge Pelias's insult to my honor cannot succeed. And so I must now, once again, flood the maiden's mind and heart with the love of light and life."

So the White-armed Goddess had decided. And so it came to pass that Medea now emptied her container of powerful drugs, and she stored them within the folds of her waistband. Meanwhile, tears flowed freely from her eyes. "How my heart floods with grief to leave everyone I love!" the maiden silently exclaimed.

"For I must now go forth with a stranger to a strange land. And stranger, how I wish the salt sea had swallowed you before you ever reached Colchis!"

So Medea mused. And with these words, the maiden stole into her little brother's room and gathered his sleeping form into her arms. And just as a female captive is forced to leave her wealthy home—and she must now depend on the warrior who has claimed her and his wedded lady's harsh hands—so Medea now left her home and her city and went forth to find Jason and the well-benched Argo. And as she fled from the royal palace and the towers of Aea, she hid her brother beneath her robe.

Upon reaching the Phasis River, the maiden spied her nephews as they celebrated Jason's victory with him on the opposite shore, and so she called to the sons of Phrixus. And led by Jason, they rowed forth to meet her. As soon as Jason stood before her, Medea knelt at his feet. She clasped his knees. And she reached up to take his chin in her hand, for her heart flooded with anguish.

"Jason, see how, as a suppliant, I now clasp your knees and take your chin in my hand. For you must save me from my father! And you must save yourself, my brothers, and all your companions, for Father is aware of our treachery! And we must escape before Blushing Eos makes the new day light! Now, swift as the wind, I will lead you to the Golden Fleece, and there I will put the great deathless dragon that guards it to sleep. You must take your own prize, for Father will never give you the wondrous fleece!

"In return, I ask but this of you, Jason. Before the deathless gods and all your companions, promise me that you will remember that I helped you perform all the tasks my father demanded of you. Promise me that you will remember that I helped you capture the Golden Fleece. For far from home, I will be a stranger in a strange land. I will have no family to protect and defend me. And so Jason, you alone will stand between me and all who will look upon me with contempt.

"And so Jason, promise me that, once we have reached Hellas, your mind will not flood with the thought that I am a traitor to my family and my homeland. Promise me that your heart will not flood with contempt for me and that you will not abandon me. Promise me that you will uphold my honor and that you will protect me from any danger."

So Medea spoke to Jason. And these words caused tears to flow freely from her eyes.

And it came to pass that Medea's words caused Jason's heart to flood with waves of gratitude and love. He raised the maiden to her feet and embraced her. "Medea, I give you my sacred promise—with Far-seeing Zeus, Lord of Escape and Protector of Strangers, and with White-armed Hera, Protector of the Wedding-bond, as my witnesses—that once we have reached my home in Hellas, I will make you my wedded lady. There I will keep you safely at my hearth. And there I will love you until Thanatos embraces me!"

So Jason gave Medea his sacred word. And his promise reassured Medea. And it came to pass that Jason now declared, "I hope that your little brother now lies hidden beneath your cloak, for we must keep watch over him."

"He sleeps cradled in my arm, Jason," replied Medea. "But what thoughts now flood your mind? For surely you are hiding something behind your words!"

"Lovely maiden, your brother's heart now floods with love for you. But I assure you it will not always be so. He is a great threat to us. He may remain at home, or he may go forth with us. But he is a threat to us, for—as I know all too well—a son must always avenge any wrongs against his father. Your brother is the prince of Colchis. And so the time will surely come when he must avenge the loss of the wondrous Golden Fleece. So we may be safe now, but we will only be truly safe once Thanatos has embraced him, for your brother must give up light and life!"

So Jason spoke. And in reply, Medea exclaimed, "Do my ears deceive me, Jason? Can it be that you want to kill my little brother? Is it not enough for you, Jason, that I helped you perform all the tasks my father demanded of you? And that I am about to help you capture the wondrous Golden Fleece? By helping you I have forsaken my family, my home, and my homeland! Do not ask more of me than this, Jason! To everyone in Colchis, I am a traitor. But I have acted so as to save lives. I have not destroyed them! Thanatos can wait until my brother is an old man, or until he becomes a valiant warrior. Surely we do not have invite that dreadful god's embrace!"

So Medea spoke. And to her words, Jason replied, "Then we will speak no more of this. For now is the time for other deeds. And words, too, are a threat to us now. Swift as the wind, we must capture the Golden Fleece and leave Colchis. Gleaming Selene's silvery beams can guide our way. Indeed, they must! For too soon, Blushing Eos will make the new day light. And then Aeetes will pursue us. So lead us toward the wondrous prize, lovely maiden!"

So Jason spoke. And so it came to pass that Medea directed the well-benched Argo toward the sacred grove of Ares the Death-dealer. Nyx still covered Mother Gaea with her star-filled robe. But in time a golden glow became visible in the distance, and the hearts of the Argonauts flooded with joy, for the wondrous Golden Fleece hung from the leafy branches of the great oak tree like a cloud that blushes beneath the sparkling eyes of Blushing Eos. And now it was only a short distance away.

The Argonauts rowed their well-benched ship into a small cove, and there they anchored her. Then they remained aboard while Medea and Jason went ashore to capture the fleece from the great deathless dragon that guarded it.

The sleepless serpent soon spied Medea and her companion. And it hissed at them with such fury that, throughout the royal city of Aea and the surrounding countryside, the hearts of newborn infants flooded with fright, causing their mothers to awaken in sudden terror at the sound of their screams and to rush to shelter them protectively in their arms. And just as countless swirling wreaths of smoke rise from the fire that smolders beside a sleeping shepherd—climbing one after the other to form a tall column—so the dragon's countless, scale-covered coils now slithered behind its menacing head, causing Mother Gaea to tremble as they scraped her.

Jason now stood silent and still, for the sight of the great deathless dragon flooded his eyes. And so, swift as the wind, his heart now flooded with terror. "Why this serpent is longer and broader than the well-benched Argo!" he silently exclaimed. "And the white foam that drips from its jaws will surely kill me! I dare not go any closer, for the fiery fumes that flood the air will choke me long before the serpent's tongue stings me! But for Medea I would give up my quest for this fleece. Swift as the wind, I would return to the Argo and sail back to Hellas!"

So Jason mused. And while his heart overflowed with fear, Medea's heart flooded with confidence. For the sight of the fearsome serpent flooded her eyes, as well. But Medea did not stand silent and still. Instead, swift as the wind, she sweetly began to sing a chant. In part of it, she asked Night-wandering Hecate to help her capture the wondrous fleece.

And so it came to pass that the great deathless dragon found itself fighting off an overpowering need to sleep. Under Medea's gaze, it relaxed its wreathed coils, but it raised its menacing head, for it expected to capture Medea and Jason between its fiery and venomous jaws. But Medea's heart remained flooded with confidence. She continued her chant. And while she sang, she cut a sprig of juniper. Then she dipped it into one of her drugs, and she shook the sprig over the serpent's eyes.

And it came to pass that, swift as the wind, the deathless dragon now fell into a deep sleep. Then Medea began to rub the juniper charm into its head. And as she rubbed, she told Jason how to remove the Golden Fleece from the great oak tree on which it hung.

And so it came to pass that Jason removed the wondrous fleece from the leafy branches of the great oak tree. And his heart flooded with joy as he gathered the heavy fleece in his arms. "What a prize I have won!" he silently exclaimed. "To gain this wondrous fleece, Pelias sent forth the greatest heroes of Hellas aboard the well-benched Argo. And Aeetes—surely the greatest of kings—had a great deathless dragon protect it. But now the Golden Fleece is mine!"

This thought caused Jason's mind and heart to overflow with pride. Remembering how Heracles liked to wear the hide of the Nemean lion across his shoulders as a trophy, Jason now placed the hide of the Golden Ram across his own shoulders. And he wore the Golden Fleece like a great cloak. And with Medea at his side, he now set forth for the well-benched Argo. Silver-horned Selene's silver-yoked chariot still sent forth silvery beams to guide them. And the shining fleece cast its own glow upon the path before them. And so he walked with bright eyes and a happy smile.

But now and again fearful thoughts would flood Jason's mind and cause his heart to flood with dismay. "A great prize like this brings with it the burden of great risk!" he silently exclaimed. "Now if one of Aeetes' warriors tries to take the wondrous fleece from me, swift as the wind, he will surely give up light and life! But what if one of the deathless gods appears and commands me to give up the fleece? What then?"

So Jason mused. And with these thoughts, he would gather the fleece between his arms and clutch it tightly to his chest, lest anyone should try to take it from him. So it came to pass that—now with his heart flooded with pride, and now with his heart flooded with fear—Jason made his way back to the well-benched Argo. He and Medea arrived just as Blushing Eos with her sparkling eyes was making the new day light. And swift as the wind, the Argonauts gathered around Jason. But they stood silent and still, for the sight of the wondrous Golden Fleece flooded their eyes.

"Friends, we may now return to our homes in Hellas," Jason announced. "For with Medea's help, I have performed all the tasks King Aeetes demanded of me. And with her help, I have captured the Golden Fleece. But we are taking more than Aeetes' wondrous fleece, for he has even greater treasures! His daughter—this beautiful and wise maiden—has agreed to return to Iolcus with me. There, I will make her my wedded lady. And Medea's little brother and the sons of Phrixus have also joined us.

"And so, my friends, you must now help me save Medea from her father and his warriors. But for Medea, Aeetes already would have stretched forth his hands against us. And already he would have pushed us into the grasping hands of Thanatos! And so, one and all, we must thank the great Colchian gods of earth and sky—Mother Gaea and Gold-helmeted Helios—for they welcomed us here. And they helped us with our quest! Aeetes discovered Medea's plans too late!

"But while we remain here, Aeetes' heart is overflowing with rage over the loss of his treasures. And as surely as Shining Helios follows Blushing Eos at the start of each new day, he will now gather his warriors and pursue us. Before the Argo enters the great salt sea, he will try to reclaim all that we have taken from him. And if he succeeds, he will surely kill the strangers from Hellas who captured them. So we must leave at once! For every delay brings Aeetes and his warriors closer. Swift as the wind, half of you must now take your places at the benches and begin to work the oars. The rest of you must now put on your armor, gather your shields and your weapons, and prepare for battle.

"And as we prepare to fight Aeetes and his warriors, we must flood our hearts with courage, we must flood our hands with strength and skill, and we must flood our minds with one thought: How we meet the Colchians in battle will determine whether we win—for ourselves, for our families, and for all of Hellas—the lasting fame of victory or the lasting shame of defeat."

So Jason spoke to his companions. And so, swift as the wind, the Argonauts left Colchis. Medea, little Apsyrtus, and the four sons of Phrixus were safely aboard the Argo. And together, they all set forth for Hellas.

    ◆ **QUESTIONS FOR**
    Response, Discussion, and Analysis

1. What do Jason's encounters with Pelias reveal about Pelias? Analyze Pelias's attitudes and behavior in terms of the behavior pattern of excellence (*aretē*), excessive pride (*hubris*), blind, reckless behavior (*atē*), and retribution (*nemesis*).

2. What do Jason's encounters with Pelias reveal about Jason? Consider how Jason introduces himself to Pelias. Consider also how Jason reacts to Pelias's theoretical problem.

3. Why does Jason suggest to Pelias the idea of fetching the Golden Fleece, when, later, he reveals that he was aware of the trap?

4. Analyze Phineus's attitudes and behavior in terms of the behavior pattern of *aretē, hubris, atē,* and *nemesis.*

5. Aphrodite's son, Eros, is Cupid. Whomever his arrow hits must fall in love with the next living person or thing she or he sees. Explain what Eros's arrows symbolize.

6. What does King Aeetes' palace reveal about him? Should Aeetes give Jason the Golden Fleece as a host-gift? Why or why not? Analyze Aeetes' attitudes and behavior in terms of the behavior pattern of *aretē, hubris, atē,* and *nemesis.*

7. Why does Jason accept the challenge of the tasks that Aeetes demands of him? Why, instead, does he not accept Aeetes' guarantee of safe passage from Aea? How does Jason's decision affect his character? His heroism?

8. Compare the approaches of Jason and Peleus to the following situations: (a) Preparing to deal with King Aeetes; (b) preparing to perform the tasks that Aeetes demands of Jason. Consider the extent to which Jason's attitude is typical of how he handles problems. Note his earlier attitude toward Pelias. Consider the extent to which Peleus's attitude is consistent. Contrast the attitudes of Jason and Peleus, and explain who appears to be more heroic.

9. To what extent, if any, does a hero choose to do whatever will ensure his or her success? What does Jason's attitude reveal about him? Analyze Jason's attitudes and behavior in terms of the behavior pattern of *aretē, hubris, atē,* and *nemesis.*

10. Compare and contrast Jason with Heracles and Odysseus/Ulysses, who are traditional heroes. Consider (a) their goals; (b) their quest; (c) their tasks; (d) their *aretē;* and (e) their values.

11. Explain why Medea decides to help Jason. Analyze Medea's attitudes and behavior in terms of the behavior pattern of *aretē, hubris, atē,* and *nemesis.*

12. Phineus tells the Argonauts that good and evil can appear in each other's clothing, To what extent, if any, do good and evil appear in deceptive form to Jason and Medea?

13. What is the significance of Medea's dream? What does it reveal about wishful thinking and reality? What does it predict about the future?

14. How does Medea manipulate Chalciope? What does Medea accomplish by doing this?

15. Situational irony is the difference between what a character expects will happen and what actually happens. What is ironic about the prophecy that Helios shares with Aeetes?

16. What does Medea's vacillation achieve? Why does Medea refuse to commit suicide?

17. How does Jason get Medea to help him?

18. What future possibilities does Medea's rejuvenation of Jason suggest?

19. Contrast Medea's thoughts with Jason's (a) following his declaration of love; and (b) once they have separated. What does this contrast reveal about each of them?

20. What later event do Jason's words about Apsyrtus suggest? Why does he not use the boy's name?

21. What do Hera's remarks about Medea's role in Jason's quest reveal about the goddess's character? What type of divinity does she appear to be?

22. The chapter in which Jason performs the challenges that Aeetes demands contains many similes. The long, extended comparisons are called *Homeric similes*. Find and analyze three Homeric and five shorter similes. Which are more effective? Why? What do all of these similes have in common?

23. Note the author's depiction of Jason as he performs his tasks. Using specific details, analyze whether his thoughts and behavior enhance his heroism or detract from it.

24. Evaluate Medea's reaction to her treachery. To what extent, if any, is it psychologically realistic?

25. Only after Medea flees from her family, does she call Jason by his name, instead of using the term *stranger*. What is the significance of this change?

26. What are Jason's priorities? What is the nature of his character? Consider (a) the changes in Jason's commitment; (b) Jason's concern about Apsyrtus; and (c) Jason's reaction to Medea's response to the problem of Apsyrtus.

27. Contrast the behavior of Jason and Medea with regard to the serpent. To what extent, if any, is Jason's behavior consistent with the nature of his character?

28. How is Medea's attitude toward Jason similar to Jason's attitude toward the Golden Fleece? What is ironic (the opposite of what one might expect) about Jason's attitude?

29. Why does Jason acknowledge Medea's help to the Argonauts when, in the privacy of his thoughts, he appears to forget it?

30. Explain the extent to which Jason and Medea are responsible for Jason's success in his quest for the Golden Fleece. Who is more responsible?

31. Note that Jason is introduced as being godlike in his appearance. What does his physical appearance contribute to his myth? What difference(s) would it have made if he had been short and homely?

32 Evaluate Jason as a human being and as a hero. To what extent, if any, does the nature of Jason's character affect the quality of his heroism? Give three examples to support your point of view.

33. According to a popular saying, "Nothing succeeds like success." Given Jason's success in acquiring the Golden Fleece, what does the nature of his success teach him? What does Jason fail to learn from it?

34. Analyze the significance of the Olympian gods in the lives of Jason and Medea. To what extent, if any, do they control the events in this myth? First, consider the role of Aphrodite and Eros in Medea's life. Second, consider Zeus's responses to (a) Jason's prayer and (b) Phineus's behavior. Third, consider Hera's role in response to (a) Jason's response to Pelias's "theoretical" problem; (b) Jason's solicitation of Medea's help; and (c) Medea's contemplation of suicide.

35. What do the Olympian gods contribute to the reader's response to the myth?

36. Long before Jason reaches Colchis, the seer Phineus tells the Argonauts as much as Zeus will permit about what they are destined to experience. What is the role of prophecy in Jason's quest?

37. Pelias, Phineus, Jason, and Medea all become victims of the behavior pattern that Phineus described to the Argonauts. Give examples of situations in real life where a person becomes the victim of the pattern of *aretē, hubris, atē,* and *nemesis.*

38. When the *Argo* departs from Iolcus, Heracles is one of the Argonauts. However, he leaves his companions before they reach Colchis. How would Heracles' presence in Colchis have changed Jason's myth?

HISTORICAL BACKGROUND

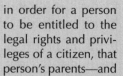

Medea is among the most enduring and famous women in mythology. Her story combines myth, legend, and history from three areas: former Soviet Georgia (ancient Colchis, in Scythia, which was Medea's home); Volos (ancient Iolcus, in Thessaly, which was Jason's home); and Corinth (the ancient home of Medea and Jason in Hellas).

In the eighth century B.C., the ancient Greeks considered Colchis to be the great kingdom of Helios, god of the sun. It lay far to the east, and, there, Helios began his daily journey through the heavens. The myth of the Argonauts has remained well-known in Georgia, where the people are direct descendants of the Colchians, Medea's people. The Georgians of today view the Argonauts as folk heroes, and parents name their daughters Medea. Jason's home, Iolcus, was a Mycenaean palace-state, and archaeologists have unearthed the remains of buildings from that ancient time. The introduction to *Jason and the Golden Fleece* provides additional information about both of these areas.

Homer assumed that his audience knew Medea's story because, in Book XII of *The Odyssey,* Circe tells Odysseus, "No ship bearing mortal seafarers has ever survived that passage, except for the *Argo*—known to all who walk the earth—on her way home from Aeetes [Medea's father]." However, Medea owes her enduring fame to Euripides, one of the great writers of tragic dramas in fifth century B.C.

Euripides was a man of fifty-four and living in Athens when, in c. 431 B.C., his *Medea* was first performed. According to Athenian law at that time, in order for a person to be entitled to the legal rights and privileges of a citizen, that person's parents—and the families of both parents, as well—must be citizens. Euripides set his *Medea* in Corinth, Medea's traditional Greek home, but he assumed that the political environment of Corinth was similar to that of Athens. It is possible that, despite the fact that Jason was a prince from Iolcus and entitled to the throne of that kingdom, if he had moved to Athens, he would only have qualified for Athenian citizenship if he married an aristocratic Athenian woman. A Colchian like Medea would have been a foreigner, and Jason's marriage to her would have had no legal validity. Athenian law would have viewed their children as illegitimate as well, and, therefore, their sons would not have been eligible for citizenship.

The characters in Euripides' plays reflect the time in which Euripides was writing. In Athens, even native-born women from aristocratic families had few rights and privileges, and a woman who was a resident alien had none. An Athenian woman lived in a man's world, with little status to call her own. She left her own family when she married, and from that time forth she had to depend on (and therefore please) her husband and his family. Medea's speech on the plight of women is the most famous feminist statement in ancient literature, and it reveals the nature of marriage in fifth-century, male-dominated Athens.

Moreover, once Jason marries Glauce, Medea is a resident alien, and she needs another male citizen to sponsor and protect her. Without that sponsorship, she has no valid place in the community. As an unprotected alien, her legal status is precarious. Moreover, she is vulnerable in that others do not have to honor and respect her. They are free to treat her with contempt without suffering consequences.

In addition, Jason's speech on the value of being Greek reflects the Athenian view of its intellectual and social superiority. Medea's attitude toward her friends and her enemies—reflecting total love and total hate, respectively—and her pursuit of revenge in the form of retributive justice reflect contemporary Athenian values that the great Athenian writers were examining in their plays.

Moreover, in Euripides' time, in order for society to function effectively, people were expected to keep their oral promises. The Athenians viewed oaths as sacred. The gods would honor and protect those who kept their sacred word and would punish those who betrayed their oaths.

RELIGIOUS BACKGROUND

Traces of an earlier matriarchal religion in ancient Greece are present in the myths about Medea.

When King Aeetes thinks that Argus must have told Jason that Medea serves Hecate, the Night-wandering Goddess, Aeetes is describing Medea in a later and transformed human form. Yet Aeetes reveals Medea's earlier identity when he declares that she can manipulate all the herbs that grow on land and all that live in the sea, that she can call forth blazing fires and quiet rushing rivers, that she can make spring flowers bloom in summer and make grain ripen for harvesting in winter, and that she can make the chariot of the moon appear next to the chariot of the sun in the sky.

Aeetes' description of Medea's powers reveals her to be the Great Goddess or Mother Goddess of an earlier matriarchal religion. The Great Goddess functioned in three related forms. As Goddess of the Underworld, she controlled the three-stage cycle of life: first, the period of birth and childhood; then, the fertile period of maturity and reproduction; and last, the sterile period of old age, with its decline and death. As Goddess of the Earth, she controlled the three-stage cycle of the seasons: first, spring (the period of birth or rebirth and budding growth); then, summer (the fertile period of blossoming and harvest); and last, winter (the sterile period of decay, barrenness, and death or dormancy). As Goddess of the Sky, she was the great Moon Goddess, who appeared in her three-stage cycle of phases: first, as the new and waxing moon (the period of birth or rebirth and growth); then, as the full moon (the period of maturity); and last, as the waning moon (the period of decline and death or dormancy).

The fact that Medea cuts up Jason, Pelias, and (in some versions) Aeson and then puts them into cauldrons of rebirth and rejuvenation reflects earlier religious practices. The myths, legends, and folktales of other cultures—including those of Italy, Germany, Russia, Scandinavia, and the Celts in Ireland—involve similar magic cauldrons. Priestesses would cut up a living human being or animal, put the fragments of the corpse into a magic broth, and then recite proper incantations as a fire caused the soup to boil. The corpse would then revive and emerge rejuvenated. Because fire was thought to be an aspect of the sun, it was sacred in cultures where people worshipped a sun god. Therefore, the fire, as well as the broth, were necessary for the renewal of youth and the extension of life.

Medea's banishment from Iolcus and Corinth (and eventually from Athens, as well) may reflect the Mycenaean conquest of the matriarchal cultures that already existed in Greece. Instead of prohibiting the earlier matriarchal religion in these communities, the Mycenaeans grafted their more patriarchal religion onto it. In the process, the Great Goddess lost her triple form and became less important. For example, in matriarchal religions, the serpent was the symbol of rejuvenation and immortality because it shed its skin, and the serpent-drawn chariot belonged to the great Moon Goddess. Therefore, Medea originally possessed a chariot drawn by winged dragons on which she traveled through the heavens in order to bring help and joy to mortals. However, later, when religion became more patriarchal, the serpent-drawn chariot was given to Helios, god of the life-giving sun. In the myth of Medea, Helios loans this chariot to Medea because she is (now) his granddaughter.

Earlier literary sources relate—and the text of Euripides' *Medea* alludes to—the murder of Medea's children by the people of Corinth and the Corinthians' subsequent need to atone for their crime. This type of murder and expiation suggests that human sacrifices were a religious ritual in Corinth's earlier matriarchal culture. However, when the Mycenaeans established their more patriarchal religion in Corinth, they dethroned Medea as the Great Goddess, and they prohibited human sacrifice, which they viewed as barbaric. The question of who murdered Medea's children now needed a new explanation, and who committed the foul deed (Medea, Jason, or the

Corinthians) became a sensitive issue for the Corinthians. At the end of his *Medea,* Euripides casts Medea in her earlier, divine form—a solution that pleased the Corinthians.

EURIPIDES AND THE LITERARY TRADITION

Our oldest sources of Medea's myth are those in Hesiod's *Theogony* (c. 700 B.C.) and Pindar's Pythian Ode IV (fifth century B.C.). Hesiod's version is brief and without detail. He states that, "having accomplished the terrifying tasks imposed on him by the wicked King Pelias, Jason, by the will of the gods, led Medea, King Aeetes' daughter, forth from her father's house to his swift ship, and after much suffering, he returned to Iolcus with her and made her his wife. Medea submitted to Jason, shepherd of the people, and bore him a son."

Euripides, the playwright who brought Medea lasting fame, lived between c. 485 and 406 B.C., in Athens. He first entered the annual dramatic competition in 455 B.C., where he depicted Medea as the murderer of Pelias in the lost *Daughters of Pelias*. His *Medea*, produced in 431 B.C., was as shocking in its own time as it is in ours because, as far as we know, Medea is the first woman in Greek myth and literature consciously, rather than in a fit of insanity, to murder her own children.

Many sources were available to Euripides that were lost, in 47 B.C., when Julius Caesar was in Alexandria, Egypt, and fire destroyed the great Alexandrian Library. However, copies of the most valued and popular material survived in other places, and these, plus fragments and scholar's summaries of lost works give us some idea of what Euripides—with his large library—must have known.

For example, in Eumelus's *Corinthiaca,* an epic about the heroic history of Corinth (written between 750 and 700 B.C.), the sun god, Helios, gives Corinth to his son Aeetes, but Aeetes moves to Colchis and leaves the rule of Corinth to a son of the god Hermes. When Hermes' son dies without an heir, the Corinthians send to Iolcus for Aeetes' daughter Medea (after the death of Pelias), and they enthrone her as their queen. Jason accompanies Medea, and through her he becomes king of Corinth. In time, Medea saves Corinth from a plague of famine. Then Zeus, father of gods and mortals, falls in love with Medea, but, fearful of the goddess Hera's vengeful wrath, Medea rejects Zeus's love. Hera gratefully rewards Medea by promising to make Medea's children immortal if Medea will bring them to her sanctuary. Therefore, Medea takes her children to the Temple of Hera Akraia (Hera of the Heights), where she leaves them at the goddess's altar or hides them beneath the floor of the temple. Either way, the children die, and the Corinthians honor them with a cult. However, when Jason discovers how Medea has been treating their children, he is outraged by her behavior, and he returns to Iolcus. Then Medea either leaves, or flees from, Corinth.

According to Didymus (a reputable first century B.C./A.D. Homeric scholar in Alexandria, Egypt), Creophylus of Samos relates a competing but related ancient legend in his epic *The Taking of Oechalia* (seventh century B.C.). In this version, Medea lives in Corinth, and she uses her knowledge of poisonous drugs to murder King Creon. Expecting retaliation, Medea prepares to flee. However, she decides that her sons are too young to follow her to Athens, so she leaves them as suppliants at the altar in the sanctuary of Hera Akraia. She assumes that Jason will also protect them. However, Creon's relatives and friends do not respect the goddess's sanctuary, and they murder the children at Hera's altar. Then they spread the rumor that Medea has murdered her children as well as Creon.

Based on different earlier sources, the scholar Parmeniscus (second/first century B.C.) relates still another competing but related ancient legend. In this version, the Corinthian women are displeased that their queen, Medea, is both foreign and skilled in the use of poisonous drugs. Therefore, they decide to kill her children (seven boys and seven girls). Medea's children hear of this plan, and they take refuge in the Temple of Hera Akraia. However, the Corinthians ignore the sanctity of the temple and brutally murder them at the goddess's altar. The Corinthians then experience a devastating plague, severe famine, and many infant deaths. When they ask the advice of a divine oracle, they learn that the goddess Hera and Medea's dead children have cursed them. Moreover, in order to calm their wrath, every year the Corinthians will have to choose seven boys and seven girls from among their aristocratic families and send them—with their heads shaved and their bodies clothed in black (symbols of mourning)—to the Temple of Hera Akraia, where they will live for one year. There, they will serve Hera in her sanctuary and offer sacrifices to Medea's dead children.

Parmeniscus also relates that the Corinthians paid Euripides five talents of silver if he would blame Medea, rather than their ancestors, for the death of Medea's children. Of course, this may not be true. However, the scholarship of Parmeniscus and Didymus reveals why the Corinthians had reason to be self-conscious. Moreover, in his *Medea*, Euripides reveals his knowledge of Corinth's legendary history. In the course of the play, Medea reveals her fear that the Corinthians will avenge Glauce's death by murdering her sons, since it was they who delivered Medea's gifts. Then, at the end of the play, Medea commands the Corinthians to establish the Akraia, an annual sacred festival with holy rites that will atone for the "impious" murder of her children.

Pausanias, the Greek geographer who published reliable historical information based on his travels throughout Greece c. A.D.160, relates a fourth competing but related ancient legend. According to his sources, the Corinthians stone Medea's children to death because they brought Medea's poisonous gifts to Creon's daughter, Glauce. The ghosts of Medea's children then take revenge upon the Corinthians by killing their infant children. Finally, a divine oracle commands the Corinthians to erect a monument to Terror (the figure of a frightening woman) and to establish the Akraia, the annual tradition of having their children cut their hair and wear the black clothes of mourning, and to offer sacrifices to Medea's dead children. According to Pausanias, the Akraia continued until the Romans sacked Corinth. Between 1930 and 1933, British archaeologists unearthed the Temple of Hera Akraia (dated at c. 800 B.C.) at the site called Perachora, not far from the modern city of Corinth.

APPEAL AND VALUE

Aristotle states in his *Poetics* that Euripides is "certainly the most tragic of the dramatists" because he is the best at enabling the members of his audience to identify with his characters and to feel pity (for the characters) and fear (for themselves). Certainly what made Euripides controversial during his lifetime is what has made him more appealing in the centuries after his death. Euripides' mind and heart lay with the outsider, which often made the subject of his plays politically incorrect, and he was interested in realistic psychological depiction of character rather than in the larger than life issues of the ideal and the heroic.

As discussed in the introduction to *Jason and the Golden Fleece,* the ancient Greeks believed that all human beings, through their attitudes and actions, are capable of bringing sorrow upon themselves. In traditional myth, characters are all larger than life; nevertheless, even they become victims of this behavior pattern. Under Euripides' pen, characters like Medea and Jason become real and ordinary human beings—like the men and women who walked the streets of Athens in his day and, in many ways, like us. His principal characters are often women rather than men, and he forces his audience to view life from the point of view of those who, like Medea, are powerless in their society. He accomplishes this by taking familiar characters from the ancient myths and placing them in their time of crisis so that he can explore their attitudes, values, and behavior under stress. It is a powerful theatrical experience for members of the audience (or readers) to see how characters who think and feel like ordinary people—in fact, like themselves—bring tragedy into their lives.

Noting that nothing human is new, the problems Euripides' characters face on stage reflect the injustice of prevailing contemporary Athenian attitudes and behavior. Consequently, at a time when the Athenians valued tragedy for its nobility of character, plot, and theme, Euripides' heroes (like Jason) behave unheroically, his women (like Medea) are society's victims, and the consequences are tragic. In this way, Euripides holds a mirror before the eyes of his masculine audience—an audience that reveled in its superiority and would have preferred to turn its eyes and ears away from Euripides' tragic drama.

The continued popularity of Euripides' *Medea* confirms Aristotle's judgment, for Medea has left an indelible mark upon the human heart from Euripides' day to our own. Throughout history, audiences have identified with the woman whose husband leaves her for a younger woman. Moreover, in many other societies, racial, religious, cultural, or social differences have placed groups of people outside the establishment, where, like Medea, they have been denied rights and privileges. Women—because of their gender—have either been second-class citizens or else have been treated like resident aliens.

Medea is unforgettable because of her courage, her skill, her conviction, and her moral strength. She scorns society's view of women, and by refusing to accept Jason's shoddy treatment, she reveals that women, too, have a sense of honor, a need for status, and causes for revenge. Euripides makes Medea speak like a woman of flesh and blood, and audiences identify with her thoughts and feelings. Her universal appeal resides in the depth of her outrage against injustice and the extent to which she is willing to rebel against it. In the twentieth century, she represents anyone who is an outsider, a feminist, a foreigner, or an outcast.

Jason is unforgettable because of his ambition, his pragmatism, his prudence, and his moral blindness. From the period of his heroism in the myth of *Jason and the Golden Fleece* to his maturity in the myth of Medea, Jason willingly delegates to others what they can do better than he. He is accustomed to persuading others to use their courage, strength, and skill on his behalf, and, therefore, he uses Medea—as he uses everyone—to further his own goals. However, with the murder of Medea's brother, Jason's self-serving ambition becomes destructive as well as callous, and his rejection of Medea leads to Medea's equally destructive passion for revenge. Therefore, it is interesting to evaluate Jason as a tragic hero, both from an Aristotelian and from a contemporary point of view.

Alexandrian scholars produced *The Collected Works of Euripides* in about 200 B.C., when ten of Euripides' eighty-eight plays (probably few of his tragedies) were already lost. This collection is the source of all the ancient papyrus fragments and all the medieval manuscripts.

The following version of the myth of Medea is an adaptation of Euripides' *Medea*, with the addition of selected passages from Seneca's *Medea* and descriptions of the death of Pelias from several literary works from ancient Greece (fifth century B.C. and later).

CHARACTERS

ACASTUS: the son of Pelias; an Argonaut; later, the king of Iolcus, in Thessaly

AEETES: a son of Helios; a brother of Circe; the father of Medea, Chalciope, and Apsyrtus; the king of Colchis, in Scythia

AEGEUS: the king of Athens

AEOLUS: the king of Aeolia; the lord of the wind

AESON: the half-brother of Pelias (They share the same mother); a first cousin of Phrixus (Their fathers are brothers); the legitimate king of Iolcus

ALCINOUS: the king of Phaeacia; the husband of Arete

APSYRTUS: the son of Aeetes; the brother of Medea and Chalciope

ARETE: the wife of Alcinous; the queen of Phaeacia

CREON: the king of Corinth; the father of Glauce

GLAUCE: the daughter of Creon; Jason's second wife

JASON: the son of Aeson; the husband of Medea and later, of Glauce; the leader of the Argonauts

MEDEA: a daughter of Aeetes; a granddaughter of Helios; a niece of Circe; the sister of Chalciope; Jason's first wife; a priestess of Hecate; a sorceress

PELIAS: the half-brother of Aeson (They share the same mother); the illegitimate king of Iolcus

PHINEUS: a Thracian king; a seer

PHRIXUS: a first cousin of Aeson; the husband of Chalciope; the father of four sons

THE GODS AND OTHER IMMORTAL BEINGS

APHRODITE: a daughter of Zeus; the goddess of sexual desire

APOLLO: the son of Zeus and Leto; the twin brother of Artemis; the god of prophecy, with his oracle at Delphi; the god of disease and medicine

ARES: a son of Zeus and Hera; the bloodthirsty god of war

ARTEMIS: the daughter of Zeus and Leto; the twin sister of Apollo; the goddess of wild animals and the hunt; a goddess of childbirth; the patron goddess of Iolcus

ATHENA: a daughter of Zeus; the goddess of arts and crafts and defensive war; later, the goddess of wisdom; the patron goddess of heroes; the architect of the Argo

BOREAS: the god of the north wind; the north wind itself; the father of two winged sons who are Argonauts

CIRCE: a daughter of Helios; a sister of Aeetes; an aunt of Chalciope, Medea, and Apsyrtus; a great sorceress

EOS: the goddess of dawn

EROS: the son of Aphrodite; the god of love

GAEA: the mother of all the gods and of all life; Mother Earth; the Mother Goddess

HADES: a brother of Zeus, Poseidon, and Hera; the ruler of the Underworld

HECATE: a goddess in Hades' kingdom

HELIOS: the father of Aeetes and Circe; the paternal grandfather of Chalciope, Medea, and Apsyrtus; the god of the sun

HERA: a sister of Zeus, Poseidon and Hades; the wife of Zeus; the mother of Ares and Hephaestus; an aunt of Aphrodite, Apollo, Artemis, Athena, and Hermes; the queen of Olympus; the goddess of marriage

HERMES: a son of Zeus; Zeus's messenger; the patron god of travelers

NYX: the mother of Thanatos; the goddess of night

SELENE: the goddess of the moon

THANATOS: the son of Nyx; the god of death

ZEUS: a brother of Poseidon, Hades, and Hera; the father of Aphrodite, Apollo, Ares, Artemis, Athena, Hephaestus, and Hermes; the king of Olympus and ruler of all the gods; the god of justice, hospitality, and rain; the patron god of suppliants, fugitives, and strangers, with his oracle at Dodona

GEOGRAPHICAL LOCATIONS

AEA: the capital city of Colchis, located near the mouth of the Phasis River, in Scythia

AEAEA: an island off the western coast of Italy, south of Rome, where Circe lives after leaving Colchis

AEOLIA: one of the Lipari islands (now Stromboli), located to the north of eastern Sicily at the sea approach to the Strait of Messina

BOEOTIA: the region in the central, eastern part of Hellas

COLCHIS, SCYTHIA: the region at the eastern end of the Euxine Sea and south of the Caucasus Mountains (now the Republic of Georgia)

CORINTH: the region of Hellas that includes part of the northeastern Peloponnesus and most of the isthmus that connects the Peloponnesus with Attica and Boeotia to the east

DELPHI: a city on Mount Parnassus, in Phocis, in Hellas; the site of the oracle of Apollo and, therefore, the principal religious center of the Hellenes

DODONA, EPEIRUS: a city in the region in Hellas that borders on the coast of the Adriatic Sea (now southern Albania); the site of an ancient oracle of Zeus

IOLCUS, THESSALY: a city in the region north of Boeotia, in the eastern part of Hellas (now Volos, in Magnesia)

LIBYA: the region bordering on the African coast of the Mediterranean Sea, between Egypt on the east and the Pillars of Heracles, which line the Strait of Gibraltar, on the west

MOUNT OLYMPUS: a high, snow-covered mountain near the Gulf of Salonika, in the region of Pieria, in northern Thessaly, in Hellas, where the gods of the Hellenes live

MOUNT PELION: a mountain near the city of Iolcus, in Thessaly

PHAEACIA: the island of Drepane; Homer's Scheria; thought to be located "at a far end of the sea" (now Corfu)

PROLOGUE TO MEDEA

JASON AND THE GOLDEN FLEECE

In Thessaly, Pelias unlawfully took the royal scepter, the throne, and the kingdom of Iolcus from his half-brother, Aeson. Then Aeson's wife gave birth to a son, whom they named Jason. Fearing that Pelias would kill Jason, Aeson had Jason reared in secrecy.

Years later, Jason returned to Iolcus and claimed the throne in the name of his father. Pelias then commanded Jason to go forth to Aeetes' kingdom of Colchis and fetch the wondrous Golden Fleece. Pelias expected that this dangerous quest would kill Jason, but Jason accepted the challenge in order to win lasting fame.

Pelias was so upset by Jason's return that he neglected to offer a sacrifice to Golden-throned Hera. The goddess's heart flooded with wrath, and she decided to use Jason and Aeetes' maiden daughter, Medea, to punish Pelias for having dishonored her.

Jason invited the greatest heroes of Hellas to accompany him on his quest, and they set forth. They rescued the seer Phineus, who gave them valuable advice about their journey. Then they rescued the sons of Aeetes' son-in-law, Phrixus. Long before, Phrixus had given the Golden Fleece to Aeetes and had then married Aeetes' older daughter, Chalciope.

When Jason arrived in Colchis, Aeetes demanded that he perform tasks in order to win the Golden Fleece. Hera asked Foam-born Aphrodite to have her son, Eros, shoot one of his love-inspiring arrows at Medea so that she would fall in love with Jason and help him. Hera's plan succeeded, and because of Medea's help, Jason captured the Golden Fleece. The Argonauts—together with Medea, her little brother, and the sons of Phrixus—then fled Colchis and the rage of Aeetes.

MEDEA

Muse, divine daughter of Far-seeing Zeus, Father of Gods and Mortals, sing of the ways of the human heart. Sing of how the heart floods, like the storm-tossed salt sea, with waves of love, hatred, ambition, and revenge, enslaving the human mind with these passions and making all who walk the earth its victims. And sing of the Olympian gods, the deathless ones, who observe all who are mortal, judge them, and then respond in ways mortals do not expect. And through your song, reveal who is to blame for the troubles that plague all who walk the earth.

Muse, divine daughter of Far-seeing Zeus, Father of Gods and Mortals, sing of how Medea accompanies Jason and the wondrous Golden Fleece back to Iolcus. Sing of the death of Medea's brother. Sing of how Golden-throned Hera avenges King Pelias's insult to her honor. Sing of Medea's life in Corinth. Sing of Jason's wedding with Glauce. And sing of Medea's revenge.

Chapter 1

Aeetes pursues the Argo. Jason would give up Medea. Instead, they kill Apsyrtus. The Argo's speaking beam reveals Far-seeing Zeus's anger. Jason and Medea marry on the island of Phaeacia. Then Zeus punishes the Argonauts.

King Aeetes now paced back and forth in front of his throne. And his mind flooded with thoughts. "Medea helped Jason perform all the godlike tasks I demanded of him. And now, my heart floods with fear!" he silently exclaimed. "For surely she will help him steal the wondrous Golden Fleece. And this deed may already have come to pass! I have searched the royal palace. And Medea has fled. No doubt, she has already fled from Aea, as well. And she had taken little Apsyrtus—my only son!—with her.

"Medea's mind and heart must have flooded with the fearful thought that, if Apsyrtus remained here, the day would come when he would avenge her treachery! Or else, Jason's mind and heart flooded with the fearful thought that Apsyrtus would avenge his deeds. And so, once again, he asked Medea to help him—this time, by stealing my son. And she did it! For Medea does whatever Jason asks! How my mind floods with the wonder of it.

"Long ago, my father, Shining Helios, warned me of this. He told me to beware of deceitful schemes. He said they would lead to treachery and destruction. And he warned me that those of my own blood would contrive them. And so, I have always feared that the sons of Phrixus would become mad for power. And that, without respect for law, they would contrive to take my royal scepter, my throne, and my kingdom.

"But I never thought to fear Medea's treachery! And so, her deeds have surprised me. But Medea is a maiden. And Jason must have set forth to corrupt her mind and her heart. For surely he knew that, without her help, he would never capture my Golden Fleece. He must have flooded her mind with honeyed words. And so, her young heart flooded with waves of love and longing for the handsome stranger from Hellas.

"And I was right to fear the sons of Phrixus. For they, as well as Jason, are surely to blame. They must have told Jason that Pelias had given him a hopeless task. For why else would he have sent Jason forth to fetch my Golden Fleece? And they must have told him that, without Medea's help, he would never capture it. For Hecate has smiled on Medea and made her gifted in the ways of magic. And in Medea's skillful hands, all the herbs that grow on land become drugs and charms.

"They must have told Jason that Medea can call forth blazing fires. That she can quiet rushing rivers. And that she can make Silver-horned Selene drive her silver-yoked chariot next to the gold-yoked chariot of Gold-helmeted Helios. They must have told him that Medea can make spring flowers bloom in summer. That she can make the grain grow ripe for harvesting in winter. And that she can make the floor of heavily-wooded forests reflect Father's golden rays. And they must have contrived for Jason to meet her.

"Yes, Medea's gifts have made her god-like. But in the ways of the heart, she is young and foolish! How could she be so blind as to forsake her family, her home, and her homeland for a handsome stranger? How does she think she will fare as a stranger in a strange land? Does she know the Hellenes look upon all strangers as barbarians? And she has chosen a man who apparently will do anything as long as he thinks he will profit from it. Does Medea really think she can hold onto light and life by casting her lot with him?"

So Aeetes mused. And his heart flooded first with surprise, then with grief, and at last, with rage. "Surely Medea knows the ways of my heart!" he silently exclaimed. "She knows that she has always flooded my heart with waves of pride and delight and love. And she knows that a father's heart longs to flood with pity for her! But she also knows that her treachery now floods my heart with rage. And she knows that my heart and mercy are strangers! And surely Medea knows the ways of my mind. She knows that I will come after her. And she knows that my watchful eyes will not close in sweet sleep until I find her!

"Dread that day, Medea! For I will find you! I will find you in the kingdom of Colchis. Or on the salt sea. Or in the land of Hellas. But I will surely find you! And then, I will avenge your treachery. You are my daughter. But I will push you into the grasping hands of Thanatos. And birds and dogs will feast on your lifeless flesh!"

So King Aeetes mused. And with these thoughts, he gathered his armed men. And it came to pass that more than the storm-tossed waves of the salt sea, more than the grains of shining sand on its shores, and more than the autumn leaves on the floor of the oak forest were the Colchian warriors who now responded to their great king's call for revenge.

And when they had assembled in front of the royal palace, the great king of Colchis declared, "Warriors of Colchis, open the doors of your mind to my words. For, like well-aimed arrows, they will fly forth straight and true. You have heard my command to rid Colchis of the well-benched Argo and all who would flee aboard her. Except for one among them, they must not escape your torches. They must look their last upon light and life! And birds and dogs must feast on their lifeless flesh!

"But one among them—my daughter Medea—you must return safely to me. Find her in Colchis. Find her on the salt sea. Or find her in Hellas. But find her! For I myself will avenge her treachery. Find her! Or Thanatos will clasp you in his grasping hands. And birds and dogs will feast on your own lifeless flesh."

So King Aeetes spoke. And it came to pass that he led his well-benched ships in pursuit of the Argo. He knew a direct route. And so, before long, he discovered her.

As soon as Jason spied the Colchian fleet, he approached Medea and declared, "Medea, you must contrive a way to save us! Or we are surely lost! Your father might be satisfied if I return you and your little brother to him. And perhaps that would be best for everyone! Certainly we cannot hope to escape. Nor can we hope to win a battle against him."

So Jason spoke. And his words caused Medea's heart to flood with waves of rage and terror. And so she replied, "Jason, where is your heart? Your gratitude? Your loyalty? Now that you have the wondrous Golden Fleece, will you really abandon me now, after all I have done for you?

"How quickly your success makes you forget your sweet promises to me! And how lightly you regard the sacred vows you made before the deathless gods—before Zeus, Lord of Escape and Protector of Strangers, and before Hera, Protector of the Wedding-bond! Your words, both sweet and sacred, melt like the spring snow beneath Grandfather's golden rays. Surely your heart is made of shifting grains of sand. For swift as the wind, you bow before every wave of the salt sea! And surely your courage is no stronger than a wisp of a tree. For swift as the wind, you rush to bend before every wind.

"Well, I am made of stronger metal! Your sweet promises and your sacred vows have burned their way into my heart. You swore before the deathless gods that, when we reached your home in Hellas, you would make me your wedded lady! You swore you would keep me safely at your hearth. And you swore you would love me until Thanatos embraces you! And though you are a Hellene, Jason, I took you to be a man of honor—a man who keeps his word! And so, I chose to help you. I was willing to forsake my family, my home, and my homeland. For my heart flooded with grief to think that my father would kill a godlike mortal. And I knew that I, alone, could save you.

"A man of honor would protect and defend me! But you long to sacrifice me for my good deeds! Now if love and honor have truly fled from your heart, Jason, then draw forth your sword, and slash my throat! And may the heart of Far-seeing Zeus—Protector of Strangers and Lord of Justice—and the heart of Lady Hera—Protector of the Wedding-bond—flood with wrath when they know your scheming mind and your cold heart. May the wondrous Golden Fleece vanish, like a drop of water, into the depths of the salt sea. And may the Furies, those fearsome avengers of unspeakable crimes, pursue you and prevent your return to Hellas!"

So Medea spoke to Jason. And so she prayed to the deathless gods. And her words caused Jason's heart to flood with fear. "You are wrong to think I have forgotten all that I owe you, Medea," he responded. "But, if your father and his warriors capture the Argo, then neither you, nor I, nor any Argonaut, will escape the grasping hands of Thanatos!"

At these words, Medea turned away from Jason and looked toward the Colchian fleet. And just as a young shepherd, while watching over his flock high in a mountain meadow, runs after a stray lamb, though it is heading toward the steep, rock-strewn edge, and as the boy reaches the edge, he stumbles on a rock and tumbles down the mountain-side, his heart flooding with terror, and his hands grasping wildly at every rock, hoping this one or that one will stop his fall as he tries desperately to escape from the grasping hands of Thanatos, so Medea's heart now flooded with terror as she recognized the truth in Jason's words. And her mind flooded with fear as she sought frantically for a way to survive.

"Foolish heart!" she silently exclaimed. "Why did you flood with pity for this stranger? Could you not see beneath his godlike face and form? And foolish mind! Why did you choose to help a stranger from Hellas? Why did you allow a foolish heart to rule you? What led you who are so wise to be so blind? For now my eyes see clearly, but too late! I have paid for Jason's life with my own. And what a poor trade I have made! For I have given true gold. And I have received its glittering fake! Jason does not have the heart of a good man. His heart is that of a scoundrel!

"Should I return to my father? His heart and mercy are strangers. And swift as the wind, he will push me into the grasping hands of Thanatos. But, if I must give up light and life, surely I should invite the embrace of that dreadful god. For my ways are far more gentle than my father's.

"And yet, I love light and life too much to join Hecate in grim Hades' lifeless kingdom. I want my heart to flood with the joy of embracing someone I love! I want my ears to flood with the sound of a bird's sweet song! And I want my throat to be moistened by sweet water from sparkling streams! I want my eyes to flood with the sight of Grandfather's chariot! And I want my skin to flood with the comforting warmth of his golden rays! I want my eyes to flood with the sight of fields of flowers. And I want my nose to flood with the smell of their sweet fragrance."

So Medea mused. And with these thoughts, it came to pass that that she now turned back to Jason and replied, "You are right, Jason. My father must not capture the Argo. For then, we would surely look our last upon light and life.

"And so, I will save us! And yet, my heart floods with horror and my mind quails in terror as these words come forth from my mouth! For we must push little Apsyrtus into the grasping hands of Thanatos! And may the deathless gods hide their eyes as I now give him the drugs that will make our unspeakable deed easier—for him, as well as for us."

So Medea spoke. And in reply, Jason declared, "Medea, I told you before we left Colchis that the time would come when you would have to face this dreadful deed. For as long as the wind of life blows through him, your brother will threaten our lives. The time would come when he must uphold his father's honor. Then he would have to avenge your treachery. And he would have to avenge my capture of the Golden Fleece. So give him the necessary drugs. And then, I will help you chop off his limbs. For we must prevent his shade from leaving grim Hades' lifeless kingdom and taking revenge on us. And let the deathless gods who rule the Underworld welcome him there!"

So Jason spoke. And to his words, Medea declared, "After we have chopped off my brother's limbs, we must remember to lick his blood and spit it out three times. For only in this way can we hope to atone for our dreadful deed. And then, we must toss the pieces of his corpse into the salt sea that flows behind the Argo. For this—and this alone—will save us! My father will stop his pursuit. For he will collect what remains of his son. And he will turn back in order to give the little corpse a proper burial. Meanwhile, we will escape. But let your tongue, like mine, remain forever silent about this unspeakable deed. For my heart and my mind recoil from what our hands must do!"

So Medea spoke to Jason. And it came to pass that the maiden gave her brother the powerful herbs that she had earlier considered taking herself. And just as a butcher picks up his blade, and he chops a slaughtered ox into pieces in order to provide food for gods and mortals, so Medea and Jason picked up sharp wood-chopping blades and began to chop away at little Apsyrtus's corpse. Meanwhile, the Argonauts turned away from Jason and Medea. They said nothing. And they did nothing. One and all, they remained silent and still.

And it came to pass that Medea's ears flooded with the sound of a great sigh that came forth from the mouth of her little brother's shade. And just as leafy boughs shiver and shake—now here, and now there—as a summer storm-wind buffets them, so the maiden now felt her body tremble. And her heart flooded with terror at the sound of Apsyrtus's sigh. However, with Jason's help, she continued to chop away at her brother's small form. Her mind and her heart recoiled from the sight and sound of her unspeakable deed. But, with Jason's help, she persisted until her little brother's corpse was in pieces.

And now, Medea's eyes flooded with the sight of her brother's blood-drenched hand. For it bounced up from the Argo's planks. And it smeared its gore on her robe. And just as when Loud-thundering Zeus sends forth a lightning-bolt that kindles a fire in an old forest, and the flames greedily fasten on the dry wood and suddenly burst into a wondrous blaze, so the maiden suddenly felt as if her heart was now blazing within her. "I am being roasted alive!" she silently exclaimed. "A great fire is raging within me. And its flames are hungrily feeding on my flesh. Thanatos is surely embracing me. And swift as the wind, I will now look my last upon light and life!"

But what Medea feared did not come to pass. The flames that raged within her subsided as she and Jason performed the ritual act of atonement. Then they tossed Apsyrtus's limbs into the salt sea that flowed behind the Argo. And indeed, it came to pass that King Aeetes gave up the chase in order to rescue the pieces of his son's corpse and then bury them. And he commanded the Colchian fleet to return to the royal city of Aea.

Meanwhile, the well-benched Argo continued safely on her way toward Hellas. And it now sped, swift as the wind, over the salt sea. Gray-eyed Athena had fashioned a plank from one of many oak trees that were Far-seeing Zeus's ancient oracle at Dodona. And she had placed it in the Argo's prow. These sacred trees revealed Zeus's prophecies by rustling their leaves. And it now came to pass that the goddess's plank spoke to the Argonauts in a commanding mortal voice.

"Hear me, Argonauts!" exclaimed the voice. "Open the doors of your mind to my words. For I speak the words of Far-seeing Zeus, Father of Gods and Mortals, and Lord of Justice. And just as Blushing Eos makes the new day light, so what I now tell you will surely come to pass. Every one of you will suffer for Medea and Jason's unspeakable deed. For you all stood by, silent and still, and so, gave them your support!

"And so, this well-benched ship will be battered by fierce storm-winds and carried by unfriendly currents. She will now take you far past the shores of Hellas. And at last, you will reach the land of the Etruscans. Nearby, Circe, the great sorceress, makes her home. And there, you must go. For Jason and Medea must petition the goddess to absolve them of their unspeakable deed. And only this daughter of Shining Helios can remove their blood-guilt.

"And in time, it will come to pass that you will find yourselves stranded in a barren and arid land. There, you will be compelled to work long and hard at tasks that will test the limits of your strength and your endurance. And you will think only of food, water, and rest from your hard labors."

So spoke the voice of Loud-thundering Zeus. And the sound of his voice flooded the heart of every Argonaut with waves of terror and despair. For no word spoken by Far-seeing Zeus can be changed.

And it came to pass that whatever Zeus foretold, indeed came to be. The Argo sailed past the shores of Hellas to the land of the Etruscans. And Circe performed the necessary cleansing rites that Far-seeing Zeus requires of those who have taken the life of another mortal without cause.

But then, the goddess declared, "I have performed the rites for which you came. But I am your father's sister, Medea. And my heart, like his, floods with blame toward you. First you took this stranger, whoever he is, into your heart. And so, you were disloyal to your father. And then, like a coward, you fled from your family, your home, and your homeland. And with this stranger, you committed an unspeakable deed. But since you are my niece, and you have come to me as a suppliant, I will not harm you or your friend."

So Circe spoke. And her words caused Medea's heart to overflow with waves of fear and anguish. Then the Argonauts resumed their voyage. And in time, it came to pass that they reached the island of Phaeacia. King Alcinous and Queen Arete gave the Argonauts a joyful welcome. But the arrival of a great fleet from Colchis interrupted them. And, swift as the wind, the Colchian commander sent his herald forth with a message for the Phaeacian king.

"King Alcinous, King Aeetes of Colchis gives you this choice," declared the herald. "Demand that the leader of the Argonauts release the princess of Colchis to the commander of the Colchian fleet. For King Aeetes waits impatiently for his daughter's return. Or prepare to engage the warriors of Colchis in battle, where you Phaeacians will surely look your last upon light and life!"

So the Colchian herald spoke to King Alcinous. And to his words, the Phaeacian king replied, "Tell your commander that I must give his words careful thought. And so, when Blushing Eos makes the new day light, I will announce my decision."

So King Alcinous declared. And, swift as the wind, it came to pass that Medea's ears flooded with the sound of the herald's words. And so, swift as the wind, the maiden went forth to seek audience with Queen Arete. There she kneeled before the queen, and with honeyed words, she spoke of how her heart had flooded with pity for the godlike stranger from Hellas. She spoke of how she had used her skills to help him, and she spoke of how she had cast her lot with the Argonauts.

Then Medea declared, "Oh, Queen Arete, I am still a maiden. As I kneel before you this day, I am as pure as I was in my father's house, but I am doomed to give up light and life unless the king's heart floods with pity for me! And so, I clasp your knees. And I take your chin in my hand as I ask this favor of you. Save me from my father's vengeance! Open your heart. And let it flood with pity for me. Send your sweet words forth to find their way into the king's heart. And may Far-seeing Zeus, Protector of Strangers and Fugitives, cast his smile on you, on your family, and on your fair city!.."

So Medea spoke. And just as a young widow works in the darkness, turning her spindle round and round about in order to twist her wool into yarn, while her little ones cry out for their father and tears flow freely from the widow's eyes as she bemoans her sorry fate, so Medea now wept as she thought of what would surely become of her.

And it came to pass that the queen pleaded with the king on Medea's behalf. And to her words, Alcinous replied, "My dear, let the doors of your mind now open to my words. For, like a well-aimed arrow, they will fly forth straight and true. No kingdom is safe when Aeetes chooses to go to war against it! For his heart and mercy are strangers. And yet, I would protect Medea. But to decide in her favor may displease Far-seeing Zeus, Lord of Justice. And so I will attempt to give a balanced judgment. If Medea has been living as Jason's wedded lady, then I will protect her wedding bond. If not, then Jason must return her to her father."

So Alcinous spoke. And with these words, he fell asleep. Swift as the wind, the queen then sent her messenger forth to Jason with the king's decision. And so it came to pass that the Argonauts found a sacred cave. There, they prepared Jason and Medea's wedding bed with the wondrous Golden Fleece. For they wanted White-armed Hera—Protector of the Wedding-bond—to honor their wedding. And they hoped the wondrous fleece would help their wedding live on in poets' songs for as long as mortals walk the earth to hear them. And so it came to pass that the stranger from Hellas wedded with the maiden from Colchis. And Lady Hera blessed their sacred union.

Meanwhile, once again, Golden-throned Hera had been looking down from Mount Olympus, watching and listening, in order to see how her plans for Jason and Medea were progressing. And now, she silently exclaimed, "How clever I was! For I put the idea of revealing Alcinous's decision into Arete's mind and heart. And Jason's wedding with Medea causes my heart to flood with joy! For now, Medea will surely return to Iolcus with Jason. And through Medea, I will avenge Pelias's insult to my honor. For his fate must remind all who walk the earth that I will not tolerate anyone who dishonors me."

So the White-armed Goddess mused. And it came to pass that, when Blushing Eos with her sparkling eyes made the new day light, King Alcinous, accompanied by his armed warriors, met with Jason and the Colchian commander.

And Alcinous formally declared the conditions he had privately stated to Arete. And Jason declared that Medea was his wedded lady.

When the Colchian warriors realized they would have to return to King Aeetes without Medea, their minds flooded with thoughts of their king's rage. And their hearts flooded with terror, for they knew that Aeetes' heart and mercy were strangers. And so, they remained on the island of Phaeacia, and they became King Alcinous's allies.

And now, it came to pass that Far-seeing Zeus called Glad-hearted Hermes, his swift-footed messenger, to him and said, "My son, even Lady Hera must admit that I have let her have her way with Jason, that Hellenic youth who apparently has captured her heart. But now, the Argo is leaving Phaeacia. And the time has come to punish Jason and Medea for their unspeakable deed. And I will punish the other Argonauts as well. For they stood by, silent and still, and so, gave them their support.

"And so, go forth to the palace of King Aeolus, Lord of the Wind. And command him to release only Boreas. For he must now lash the salt sea, causing foaming waves, like great snow-capped mountains, to pierce the heavens. And he must drive the well-benched Argo to the coast of Libya."

So Far-seeing Zeus commanded. And so it came to pass. There, the tide carried the Argo into a shallow gulf. And there, she sank into the soft sands that lay beneath the salt-water shallows. No wind ever blew here. No fresh water flowed here. And no living form survived here. And so it came to pass that, step by plodding step, the Argonauts carried the Argo across the scorching and lifeless wasteland.

Twelve times Nyx watched them as she ascended her throne and covered Mother Gaea with her star-filled robe. And twelve times Gleaming Selene watched them as she drove her silver-yoked chariot across the heavens. For they trudged on and on. Twelve times Blushing Eos watched them as, with her sparkling eyes, she made the new day light. For they trudged on and on. And twelve times Shining Helios watched them as he drove his gold-yoked chariot across the heavens and into the western waves of Oceanus. For when they did not lie beneath their cloaks with their eyes closed in troubled sleep, they trudged on and on.

But it came to pass that they found the salt sea and set sail once again. And at last, they saw the mountains of Hellas. Meanwhile, once again, Golden-throned Hera was looking down from Mount Olympus in order to see how her plans for Jason and Medea were progressing. And when she saw that the well-benched Argo was approaching the mainland of Hellas, her heart flooded with joy. "At last I will avenge Pelias's insult to my honor!" she silently exclaimed. "For his fate must remind all who walk the earth that I will not tolerate anyone who dishonors me!"

Chapter 2

At last, the Argo returns to Iolcus. There, Medea avenges Pelias's insult to Golden-throned Hera.

It came to pass, in Iolcus, that Silver-horned Selene, appeared four times in her new robe. But still the Argonauts had not returned. And so King Pelias now determined to kill Aeson. For despite Pelias's power, as long as the rightful king of Iolcus lived, Pelias's heart remained flooded with fear. He feared losing his kingdom. And he feared losing his life. However, Aeson gave up light and life by drinking the blood of a bull. And then, his lady cursed Pelias and gave up light and life by hanging herself.

Now the freshly fallen snow of a new winter was already covering the peak and the high meadows of Mount Pelion when the well-benched Argo approached the harbor of Iolcus. The Argonauts cloaked their arrival in secrecy so that Jason could learn what had occurred during his absence. And so it came to pass that he quietly called Medea aside and declared, "My dear one, open the doors of your mind to my words. For, like well-aimed arrows, they will fly forth straight and true. It is bad enough that Pelias took the kingdom of Iolcus from my father. And that he sent me forth to fetch the Golden Fleece with the hope that I would look my last upon light and life.

"But now, I have learned that Pelias has caused my parents to give up light and life. And so, I am the lawful king of Iolcus. Surely I must reclaim my father's throne! And I must avenge the deaths of my parents! The only question is how to kill Pelias. For I must kill him before he kills me. And you must help me decide what path is best."

So Jason spoke. And in reply, Medea declared, "If you wish, Jason, I will contrive to have Pelias see the last of light and life."

"Medea, even before the deed is done, your words cause my heart to flood with gratitude! What do you have in mind? And what weapons will you need? For whatever I have, is yours!"

So Jason responded. And to his words, Medea replied, "My plan will work best if I keep my own counsel, Jason. And, if I have been successful, you will learn of it. For my mind floods with a clever scheme, and I have the herbs I need."

So Medea spoke. And it came to pass that she fashioned a small, hollow statue of Artemis, the Archer-Goddess. And she placed certain powerful herbs within it. Then she transformed herself into a very old woman. And with the statue in her arms, she went forth into the royal city of Iolcus. "I am a priestess of Artemis, the Archer-Goddess, who protects Iolcus," she declared to everyone who crossed her path. "And I have come to tell you that the goddess will confer good fortune on King Pelias, his family, and all his subjects."

So Medea, in her disguise, spoke. And her words caused the hearts of the people of Iolcus to flood with gratitude toward the Archer-Goddess for her blessings. And so, swift as the wind, they went forth to Lady Artemis's temple. And there, they honored her with sacrifices. Meanwhile, Medea, still in her disguise, and still holding the statue in her arms, entered the royal palace. There, she asked to meet with King Pelias and his royal family. And since she appeared to be a priestess of the Archer-Goddess, the king honored her request. So it came to pass that Medea came into the presence of King Pelias and his daughters. But Pelias's son, Acastus, was still with the Argonauts.

"My lord, thank you for being so kind as to receive a priestess of the Archer-Goddess," declared Medea. "Lady Artemis has searched throughout Hellas. And she has found that you, my lord, of all the kings who walk the earth, are the most pious ruler. And so, the goddess has sent me to you. For she wants to confer her special blessings on you and your family.

"My lord, infirmity is a great liability, both in time of war and in time of peace, and certainly in one who is the leader of his people. Strength and vitality should course through your body as they did in days of old. But you have become an old man. Time, who ravishes all Mother Gaea's children, has left his mark on you. For your limbs, have become weak. And your legs now go forth slowly. And so, my lord, if you approve, my first deed will be to strip your old age from your body. And in its place, I will confer all the blessings of youth upon you."

So Medea, in her disguise, spoke. And her words caused the king's heart to flood with waves of pride and longing for his lost youth. And so it came to pass that Pelias replied, "Priestess, your presence honors the kingdom of Iolcus and the royal family. My heart floods with delight at your desire to bless me with the gift of renewed youth. And my mind floods with the thought that I should accept your wondrous gift.

"But Priestess, my mind floods with thoughts of caution, as well. And it urges me to request some proof of your power. For you are asking me to place my life in your hands. Now if you are truly the priestess of the Archer-Goddess, you have nothing to fear. And I have nothing to fear. For if the Archer-Goddess acts through you, as you declare she does, then you will restore the flower of my lost youth. And so, I ask you, Priestess: Are you willing to demonstrate your godlike skill? Will you show me exactly how you strip some living thing of its age? For my heart floods with the desire to see an example of renewed youth."

So King Pelias spoke to the woman who appeared to be the priestess of the Archer-Goddess. And in reply, Medea declared, "My lord, your words reveal that you are as wise as you are pious! Have your servants bring me a cauldron of fresh, warm water in which to bathe. And I will reappear before you stripped of my own white hair and wrinkled skin. And what I do for myself, I am prepared to do for you, as well."

So Medea, in her disguise, spoke. And swift as the wind, her words caused Pelias to command his servants to fetch the cauldron of water. And then, he commanded his daughters to watch Medea while she bathed. And it came to pass that Medea carefully chose certain of the powerful herbs that she had stored in the hollow statue of Artemis. And she sprinkled handfuls of these herbs into the warm water in the cauldron. And as she bathed, the white of her hair vanished like drops of water into the depths of the salt sea. And the wrinkles that lined her skin vanished, as well. And so Medea reentered the king's hall in the form of a beautiful maiden.

Now Pelias rose to his feet. And he stood silent and still. For his eyes flooded with the sight of the priestess's restored youth. And his heart now flooded with waves of amazement and delight. "Priestess, you have indeed restored you own lost youth! And so, surely you can restore my own lost youth, as well! But I will not yet entrust my life to you. For while my heart floods with hope, my mind still floods with doubt. And so, I need further proof of your godlike skill."

So King Pelias spoke to the woman who appeared to be the priestess of the Archer-Goddess. And in reply, Medea declared, "My lord, your words give me further proof that you are as wise as you are pious! And so, have your servants bring me the oldest ram from the royal flock. Have them bring me another cauldron of fresh water, a tripod, and firewood. And have them bring me a sharp, wood-chopping blade. Then before your eyes and the eyes of your lovely daughters, I will restore the ram's lost youth."

So Medea, in her disguise, spoke. And her words caused Pelias to command his servants to return with all that Medea now requested. And so it came to pass that the king's servants set the large bronze cauldron upon the tripod that had been placed over the pile of firewood. Medea ignited the wood beneath the tripod. Then she carefully chose certain of the powerful herbs that she had stored in the hollow statue of Artemis. And just as she had done before Jason went forth to perform the tasks that King Aeetes had demanded of him, she now sprinkled handfuls of these drugs into the water. Then she picked up a large, dead, olive branch. And she began to stir the brew in the cauldron carefully and well.

And it came to pass that, as the broth in the cauldron became hotter, the bare olive branch began to grow strong and green. Then, as the broth became even hotter, the branch sprouted a host of green leaves. And at last, as the broth began to boil vigorously, a wealth of firm, ripe olives grew upon the branch. Meanwhile, wherever the pot boiled over and the broth splattered upon the earth, Mother Gaea sent forth fresh green grass and fragrant flowers.

Medea now stopped stirring. She approached the aged ram and took it between her hands. Next she picked up the wood-chopping blade and slit the ram's throat. Then she chopped its corpse into pieces and dropped them into her boiling brew. And it came to pass that, just as it had done with Jason, swift as the wind, Medea's broth now restored the ram's youth.

Once again, Pelias rose to his feet. And his daughters rose to their feet, as well. And they all stood silent and still. For a frisky, young lamb now jumped out of the cauldron. The broth had restored its body. And new flesh now clothed its strong, young bones. The eyes of Pelias and his daughters flooded with the sight of the ram's restored youth. Their minds flooded with wonder. And their hearts flooded with awe. For they knew they were witnessing the work of the Archer-Goddess.

Then the king's heart flooded with joy. And he exclaimed, "Priestess, with this act, you have proved beyond a doubt that the goddess whom you serve has chosen to act through you! And so, I now command you to do to me what you have done to yourself and to the aged ram. Strip me of my old age. And renew in me the flower of my lost youth!"

So King Pelias spoke to the woman who appeared to be the priestess of the Archer-Goddess. And in reply, Medea declared, "My lord, your trust in the Archer-Goddess, and in my humble talent, flood my heart with joy! However, a king's children should have the honor of restoring their father's lost youth. Do you not agree?"

So Medea, in her disguise, spoke. And in response to her words, Pelias declared, "Once again, the priestess of the Archer-Goddess speaks words of wisdom. And so, my daughters, when Blushing Eos makes the new day light, I command you to listen well to our honored guest. And whatever this priestess of Lady Artemis tells you to do with me, I command you to do it."

So King Pelias spoke. And so it came to pass that, as soon as Blushing Eos made the new day light, Medea, in her disguise, gave the daughters of Pelias a drink that would put their father into a death-like sleep. And the princesses gave this drink to their father. But then, their hearts flooded with terror at the thought of the grisly deed that would follow. And so, despite Pelias's command, they balked like frightened horses. "Oh, Priestess, we clasp your knees. And we take your chin in our hands. For we beg you! Be the one who picks up the wood-chopping blade! And if it must be, then be the one who chops up Father! For he is more than a tree. And we will not make firewood of him!

"This deed will invite the embrace of Thanatos. And surely that dreadful god will take the wind of life that blows through him! Patricide is an unspeakable deed—a crime against Mother Gaea. And so, as surely as Blushing Eos makes the new day light, our deed will invoke the Furies, those fearsome avengers of unspeakable crimes. They will chase us until we go mad and fall into the grasping hands of Thanatos. And there, we will surely look our last upon light and life. So we beg you, Priestess. Take Father's fate from our hands!"

So Pelias's daughters spoke. And to their words, Medea replied, "Come, Princesses! You hold in your hands your father's youth, and not his death. And so, if you truly love him, you will use the wood-chopping blade to free him from the heavy burden of old age. Your wounds will be a blessing, and not an evil. For they will restore your father's strength and vigor. And surely these are necessary qualities in one who leads his people. So come, Princesses! The cauldron is on the tripod. The fire is blazing. And the broth is coming to a boil. If your father could speak, he would demand that, swift as the wind, you let your hearts flood with courage. And he would command that you obey his wishes!"

So Medea, in her disguise, spoke to Pelias's daughters. And with these words, the first princess picked up the wood-chopping blade. Meanwhile, her sisters prepared to take their turn. But the thought of their deed flooded their hearts with waves of dread and disgust. And so they did not permit their minds to flood with the thought of what their hands were about to do. Each sister took her turn in chopping up their father. But she closed her eyes lest they should flood with the sight of her unspeakable deed and so bear witness against her.

And so it came to pass that, since they were closed, the eyes of Pelias's daughters never flooded with the sight of Artemis's priestess. If she chose any of the powerful herbs that she had stored in the hollow statue of Artemis, their eyes never saw it. And if she sprinkled drugs of any kind into the boiling broth, their eyes never saw it.

But swift as the wind, the princesses blindly chopped their father's body into pieces. And swift as the wind, their hands tossed these pieces into the boiling broth. Then they opened their eyes. And they stood, silent and still, by the side of the cauldron. For their eyes now flooded with the sight of their father's chopped and stewing body. And they were watching and waiting for the Archer-Goddess to restore their father's body and the flower of his lost youth.

But it came to pass that, without the proper herbs, the king's body simply stewed in the boiling broth. Without the proper herbs, his body did not revive. And without the proper herbs, the broth did not restore his lost youth. Instead, the pieces that had been Pelias floated into the embrace of Thanatos. And there, without a whimper of protest, the great king gave that dreadful god the wind of life that blew through him.

Meanwhile, the eyes of the princesses remained flooded with the sight of their father's chopped and stewing body. And their hearts now flooded with waves of horror and rage. "The Archer-Goddess is not restoring Father's life and youth! And surely that woman is not her priestess! She is a fiend from grim Hades' kingdom!" they exclaimed. "And we must search the palace, and Aea, until we find her! For she has contrived to have us commit this unspeakable deed!"

So Pelias's daughters spoke. But it came to pass that they did not find Medea. For swift as the wind, she had taken advantage of their interest in their father. And she had stealthily and safely returned to Jason.

Meanwhile, once again, Golden-throned Hera had been looking down from Mount Olympus, watching and listening, in order to see how her plans for Pelias were progressing. And her mind flooded with many happy thoughts as she now rejoiced in her success. "My heart overflows with joy to see Pelias's stewing corpse!" she silently exclaimed. "For at last, he has reaped the fate I determined for him! And surely his fate will live on in song for as long as mortals walk the earth to hear of it. And so, it will be a lasting reminder that I will not tolerate anyone who dishonors me!

So White-armed Hera mused as she celebrated the death of King Pelias of Iolcus.

Chapter 3

Acastus banishes Jason and Medea from Iolcus, and they take refuge in Corinth. Years later, Jason weds with Glauce. King Creon banishes Medea and her children, and Medea learns of it.

It came to pass that Acastus buried the dismembered corpse of his father. And being his father's only son, he inherited the throne of Iolcus. Acastus knew he was obligated to avenge his father's murder. But waves of conflicting thoughts flooded his mind. And waves of conflicting passions flooded his heart. "I must avenge Father's murder by pushing Medea into the grasping hands of Thanatos. But the Colchian witch cannot have acted alone," he thought. "Father was no threat to Medea that she should have contrived to murder him. For they were strangers.

"Jason must have shared the deed with Medea. And so, he must share her punishment. But how can I push him into the grasping hands of Thanatos when he has been my leader and my companion. Just the sound of his name causes my heart to flood with waves of affection and loyalty as well as with anger. And so, surely it would be far better to banish Jason and his wedded witch than to kill them."

So Acastus mused. And with these thoughts, he called Jason and Medea before him. And he announced, "Jason, open the doors of your mind to my words. For, like well-aimed arrows, they will fly forth straight and true. You, as well as Medea, murdered my father. But Pelias killed your father. And we have been companions aboard the well-benched Argo. So my mind does not flood with the thought to kill you. And my heart does not flood with the hatred or wrath that would push my hands to do the deed.

"But I hereby banish you and Medea from the kingdom of Iolcus. From this time forth, until it comes to pass that you look your last upon light and life, I condemn you to live as strangers in a strange land. Or to wander from place to place. But I warn you. Never return to Iolcus. For as surely as Shining Helios follows Blushing Eos at the start of each new day, when my eyes next flood with the sight of you, I will kill you!"

So Acastus spoke to Jason. And so it came to pass that the leader of the Argonauts and his wedded lady left the towers of Iolcus and went forth to the kingdom of Corinth. There, King Creon welcomed them. For Jason was the greatest hero of Hellas. And there, it came to pass that ten years followed one upon the other as the silver-yoked chariot of Silver-horned Selene follows the gold-yoked chariot of Gold-helmeted Helios across the heavens.

And it came to pass that Jason and Medea lived happily together in Corinth. As Jason had promised, their days followed one after the other like blossoms of shining gold upon a golden chain. Medea bore Jason two sons. And Jason's heart flooded with pride. For just as the golden rays sent forth by Shining Helios shine forth more brightly than silvery beams sent forth by Gleaming Selene, so Medea's beauty now outshone the beauty of all the women of Hellas. And yet, Medea wore the crown of modesty upon her head.

However, it came to pass that Time, who ravishes all Mother Gaea's children, came to Medea and left his mark upon her. She had become a matron. And just as the leaves on the oak tree lose their brightness as they age, so Medea's beauty was now more subdued and mature. And when Jason's eyes flooded with the sight of Time's mark on Medea's face and form, they shouted a warning to his mind and heart. And so, Jason's mind flooded with the thought that a glaring stain now indelibly marred Medea's face and form. And from that time forth, whenever his eyes flooded with the sight of his wedded lady, or whenever his mind flooded with the thought of her, that glaring stain caused his heart to flood with disgust.

And so it came to pass that Jason's heart now flooded with desire for Glauce, the daughter of King Creon. And his mind flooded with thoughts about why she should now become his wedded lady. "This maiden should be mine!" he silently exclaimed. "For she is young and beautiful. And she is the daughter of a powerful king! Surely such a wedding will prove to be an advantage to me. For when Creon dies, I will become the king of Corinth!

"Glauce—and Creon, as well—will be happy to have me! For who among those who walk the earth is my equal? Surely I wear the crown of the greatest hero of Hellas! And so, poets will sing of my adventures for as long as mortals live to hear of them! For I led the Argonauts forth to fetch the wondrous Golden Fleece. And so, I have won great praise. And I have won the glory that brings lasting fame!"

So Jason mused. And so it came to pass that he wooed Creon's daughter. And when he saw that Glauce's eyes returned his love, he asked King Creon for permission to make her his wedded lady. And in response, the king declared, "Jason, open the doors of your mind to my words. For, like well-aimed arrows, they will fly forth straight and true. My heart floods with joy to have my daughter become your wedded lady. The deathless gods will surely smile on your wedding. For it will be good for you, good for me, and good for the people of Corinth. I have no son to inherit my royal scepter, my throne, and my kingdom. And so, Corinth could have no better future than to be ruled by the greatest hero of Hellas!"

So Creon spoke. And in response to his words, Jason asked, "My lord, does it not bother you that I live here in exile, banished from my own land?"

"No, Jason," replied Creon. "A lawful prince should have the opportunity to become king. And you cannot claim the royal scepter, the throne, and the kingdom of Iolcus. For they now belong to Acastus. And if you return to the towers of Iolcus, Acastus will push you into the grasping hands of Thanatos. For he holds you, as well as Medea, responsible for his father's murder. And he longs to avenge it. And yet, you are innocent of that dreadful deed. Medea claims she acted on your behalf. She claims her heart held no anger against Pelias. And she had nothing to gain from his death. But the scheme was hers. And she made Pelias's daughters hold the blade and spill their father's blood."

So Creon spoke. And to his words, Jason replied, "Medea will not come between Glauce and me! For it is Glauce I love! But my lord, does it not bother you that Medea is already my wedded lady?"

"No, Jason," responded Creon. "For Medea is not one of us. She is a barbarian from a barbaric people. And she is not your lawfully wedded lady! For no true Hellene regards the wedding of a Hellene with a stranger as proper or acceptable. And all strangers are barbarians. Clearly, as your quest for the Golden Fleece and your return to Hellas prove, your wedding with Medea was nothing more than a necessary convenience. Why, I have even heard you enjoyed its first fruits in a cave! My mind floods with laughter to think of it. For if there is a more appropriate place for a barbarian, I have yet to hear of it!

"But now, all that is past, Jason. You must choose one of your own kind—a Hellene—to be your wedded lady. But if you are to become my daughter's wedded lord, you must put aside the barbarian who presently calls herself your wedded lady. You must renounce Medea. And from this time forth, she must take care of herself."

So King Creon spoke. And in reply, Jason declared, "If that is your will, my lord, then certainly I will do it!"

And so it came to pass that Jason left Medea and wedded with Glauce. And then, swift as the wind, Creon took counsel with himself. For his mind flooded with disturbing thoughts that caused his heart to flood with fear. "Surely I must banish Medea and her sons from Corinth," he mused. "For deeds of wonder and terror drip from her name like honey from a stick! Poets will surely sing of them for as long as mortals walk the earth to hear of them. But we must not suffer from them!

"All wise men should be wary of a spurned woman! For rejection and disdain flood the female heart with wrath. And just as dry timber will burst into a mountain of flame when it is struck by a bolt of lightning, so Jason's wedding with my daughter will now surely cause Medea's fury to erupt into a mighty blaze. And her wrath will endanger the royal family and Corinth. Already I have heard that

Medea's heart floods with hatred for Jason and the royal house of Corinth. Tales of her ranting and raving flood my ears. And so, I will banish Medea and her sons from Corinth. Swift as the wind, I must send them on their way!"

So Creon mused. His decision caused his heart to flood with relief. And so he called for his messenger and commanded, "Tell the Colchian woman that, swift as the wind, she must prepare to leave Corinth. She must take her sons. And she may take whatever possessions she can push in a cart. But once Shining Helios begins his next journey across the heavens, she must be on her way. Be sure she understands that, if she overstays her welcome, I will push her into the grasping hands of Thanatos. And there, she will look her last upon light and life."

So King Creon commanded. And so it came to pass that he banished Medea and her children from Corinth. And his decree caused Medea's mind to flood with thoughts that caused her heart to flood first with anguish, then with despair, and at last with wrath. "Oh, how my mind, my heart, and my life overflow with woe!" Medea silently exclaimed. "For what I have most feared has now come to pass! Jason has forgotten his honeyed words. And he has broken his sacred promises. For he has betrayed me! And he has abandoned me in order to wed with Creon's daughter! His behavior shames him! And his shameful deed clothes me in dishonor as well!

"And now, I face banishment and exile! What can I do? What can any woman do when the man whom she has loved, the man to whom she has devoted her life, abandons her? Of every living thing, surely women are the least fortunate! First, a woman must offer some form of wealth if she hopes to get a wedded lord. And then, she must subject her mind and her body to his rule, whether or not she has chosen well. She has no real choice. For once she weds, a woman can only choose between breaking the sacred wedding bond and keeping her honor. And unlike her wedded lord, if a woman is displeased with her life, she cannot escape from her home and take refuge with a friend.

"Men are fond of saying that a woman has an easy life. She can remain safely at home in time of war. And so, men think she has no cause to complain. But men have no idea of what it is like to be a woman. And so, their words are as empty as a lone cloud when Grandfather bathes Mother Gaea in his golden rays! Surely I would rather fight three blood-filled battles than give birth to one child!

"Oh, how my mind, my heart, and my life overflow with woe! For I am a stranger here in Corinth. And now that Jason has betrayed and abandoned me, what man will protect me? The other women have parents or friends who will comfort and support them. But I have no one! And being clever does not help me. For my talents have only caused others to fear and hate me! Surely if parents are wise, they will make every effort to prevent their children from learning too much. For people only resent those who surpass them!

"Oh, Hecate—Night-wandering Goddess whom I serve—smile on me now as I plan to avenge Jason's betrayal. Flood my mind with thoughts of some scheme. Help me deceive, and through my deception destroy, Glauce and her father. And through that royal pair, help me destroy my hateful wedded lord. For my heart overflows with wrath toward Jason!"

So Medea mused.

Chapter 4

Jason offers to help Medea, and they argue.

Now it came to pass that Jason came forth to see Medea. And seeing him, Medea silently asked, "Why does the sight of that man's hateful face and form now flood my eyes? Why is he coming here? By now, his mouth must suffer from an excess of honeyed words. And so he feels compelled to share them. Then let him share them with Creon's daughter. She is welcome to them. And to him! For she cannot have one without the other!"

So Medea mused. And just as, high on a mountain pass each spring, the melting winter snow swells the stream that meanders through the meadow, and it rushes headlong over the rocky cliffs and down the steep mountain-side, where it overflows its banks, fells ancient trees, and dislodges great boulders as its strength increases, so Medea's heart now overflowed with rage. And a torrent of angry words burst forth from her lips before Jason could say a word. "Since you have come, open the doors of your mind to my words. For, like well-aimed arrows, they will fly forth straight and true," she declared.

"Is your heart so shameless, Jason, that you now dare to face your wedded lady? For you have betrayed me! You have abandoned me! You have left me to be a stranger in a strange land! And is your heart so hard, Jason, that you can forget our wedding vows, the sacred promises you, as well as I, made before Far-seeing Zeus, Lord of Justice, and before White-armed Hera, Protector of the Wedding-bond? Surely you are the most shameless and ungrateful of men! For you promised you would remember how I saved you from every danger. How it must amuse you that I controlled fire-breathing bulls and a deathless dragon. And yet, I have no power over you!

"And now, Creon has banished me from Corinth. But where can I go? After what I have done for you, who will take me in? Surely not my own people! Or yours! And so, Creon has condemned me to wander from place to place. I will always be a stranger. At house after house, I will beg for food and shelter. But the people will lock their doors against me. How could you let this happen to me, Jason? And what about our boys? Creon has expelled them, too. Has your heart forgotten them as easily as it has forgotten their mother?

"I wish I had never let the beauty of your eyes rob mine of their clear sight! For now I see—but too late—that I let my heart flood with love for a man who puts himself first in everything! I have sacrificed my life for a man who will do anything as long as he will profit from it! I should never have believed a stranger's sacred vows. For I did not know the man who was making them! Oh, Far-seeing Zeus, father of the deathless gods and those who walk the earth, why did you mark true gold so that we can tell it apart from its glittering fake? And yet, you put no mark on a mortal's face or form so that we can tell the heart of a good man from the heart of a scoundrel!"

So Medea spoke. And in reply, Jason declared, "Enough, Medea! Do not batter me with a storm of words. And like poorly-aimed arrows, they miss their mark. But open the doors of your mind to my words. For mine will fly forth straight and true. You are wrong to place such high value on your clever devices and kind deeds. Surely you know that you did not cause me to capture the Golden Fleece and return safely to Hellas. For Foam-born Aphrodite and Love-inspiring Eros, alone among gods and mortals, win that praise."

"Aphrodite? Eros? Surely my ears deceive me, Jason! And surely my mind floods with words you have not spoken!"

"No, Medea. On our way to Colchis, we rescued Phineus. Far-shooting Apollo gave him the gift of prophecy. And Phineus declared that the success of my quest would depend on Lady Aphrodite. And surely it was Eros's arrow that made you fall in love with me, Medea. For why would you turn against your own family and your own people in order to save the life of a stranger from Hellas? Admit it, Medea! If you were in control of your heart, you would never have been so foolish!

"And you have received far more from me than you have given, Medea. For I took you away from a barbarian people. And I brought you to live among the civilized people of Hellas. Your people—like all others!—use force to solve their problems. But we Hellenes solve our problems peacefully. We live under the rule of law. And we honor justice, not force. Because of me, you are so fortunate, Medea! For few barbarians ever receive the gift of living among us. And because of me, you are famous, Medea! For if it were not for the voyage of the Argo, no one would know of you! But now, poets will sing of your deeds for as long as mortals walk the earth to hear of them!

"And my new wedding proves that I am wise and prudent. Neither you, Medea—nor any other woman!—can see beyond love and sex in a wedding. But I did not wed with Creon's daughter for love. Nor to father more children. I wed with a princess in order to obtain the social position and the security to which my own royal blood entitles me!

"You unleash your serpent's tongue against me, Medea, as if I am the cause of your problems. But you are to blame! Where was your judgment? Can you never be silent? Can you never be still? Your ranting and raving against the royal family have brought your exile upon you! Did you think Creon would not hear of your threats? He is no fool, Medea! Like any man of honor, he must protect himself and his family! And so, you have made your fate far worse than it would have been. For I was not wedding with Creon's daughter for myself alone. You and your sons would also have profited from it. Surely it is a shame that women are necessary in order to have children. For it is women who bring trouble into the world!

"But you do not realize how fortunate you are, Medea! For Creon has only decreed exile for you. He could have decreed death! He even gives you this day to make your plans. In fact, that is why I have come, to offer my help. Your heart floods with hatred for me. But my heart overflows with good will toward you. And so, how can I help you?"

So Jason spoke. And to his words, Medea replied, "Jason, I wish your good deeds were as many as your words. For then, you would be godlike! And speaking the truth is not a disease, Jason! It should not cause your heart to panic and your feet to run from it! Why, it is easier to find a small flower beneath the dead branches of a tree that lies fallen in a forest than it is to uncover the truth in what you have said! For just as a swollen stream buries its shores beneath its waters, so your words conceal the shameful injustice of your behavior."

So Medea spoke. And to her words, Jason replied, "Enough of what is past, Medea. Instead, tell me how I can help you. I have come to offer you money. And I will give you introductions to my friends. For if you approach them, I want them to help you. Do not be foolish, Medea. Accept my offer. Then you will not be condemned to wander from place to place. You will not have to be a stranger. And you will not have to go from house to house, begging for food and shelter from people who will lock their doors against you.

"But before you respond, Medea, I want something from you in return. Something that is already mine. Give me my sons, Medea. For I am the father of your boys. And I love them with a father's love. Exile will surely be too harsh for them. With me, they will prosper. And here, they will comfort my heart as much as they would comfort yours in your exile. So give me my sons, Medea. For they mean more to me than my life! Before I would part with them, I would rob my eyes of their sight. I would chop off my own limbs. And I would even welcome the embrace of Thanatos. For without my sons, I would rush to give that dreadful god the wind of life that blows through me!"

So Jason spoke. And to his words, Medea replied, "Accept help from you, Jason? Never! And not in any form! Nor will I accept anything from your friends. For your base nature surely taints whatever you touch! And one can never trust a gift from an enemy! And I will not give up my sons, Jason. They mean more to me than they mean to you. For Creon's daughter is sure to give you others. And your new sons will replace mine in your heart. Creon has banished my sons. I will take them with me into exile. And there, no matter what fate brings, they will lighten my burden.

"And so, Jason, you can do nothing for me. But at least I have discovered something that is dearer to you than your own life! But I wish you valued me as much as you value the sons I have given you. For then, you would not have broken your wedding vows! Why is it, Jason, that your eyes can look upon Shining Helios's golden rays and see them? And yet, you look upon your own thoughts and deeds and do not see the shame of them? Either you no longer honor and respect the deathless gods. And so, you easily break your wedding vows—your sacred promises. Or else, you think that the Olympian gods have created new laws. And that those who walk the earth are now free to lead their lives as they choose!

"Whatever thoughts flood your mind, Jason, I now leave you to the deathless ones, to those who rule the earth on which we live, as well as the world above and the world below. Who you are will surely determine what will become of you. And in the end, the deathless gods will deal justly with you."

So Medea spoke. And in response to her words, Jason replied, "Call upon the deathless gods, if you will, Medea. But the judgment of the greatest Olympian gods, even that of Far-seeing Zeus, Father of Gods and Mortals, does not flood my heart with terror. For Father Zeus honors justice on earth as he does on Mount Olympus. And he has surely looked down from his palace and witnessed my generous offers to help you. And he has witnessed your foolish refusal to accept them. And so, I have nothing to fear."

So Jason spoke. And in reply, Medea asked, "Nothing to fear, Jason? Can you know so little about yourself? And can you know so little about the deathless gods? Listen. And learn what can happen to a man like you! For as we stand here face to face, I call upon Father Zeus, who honors and protects sacred promises and those who make them. And I call upon Mother Hera, Protector of the Wedding-bond.

"Father Zeus and Mother Hera, look down and see how I suffer. See how Jason has betrayed me. See how he has abandoned me after all I have done for him! And see how he has deserted me when I am a stranger in a strange land! Let my plight cause your hearts to flood with pity for me. And so, help me! Defend me! Protect me!

"Father Zeus and Mother Hera, may Jason reap the seeds he has sown. May I see Jason and his new lady ruined! And then, destroy Jason! For he has forgotten his sacred vows. And so, may he suffer a fate far worse than death. May he live to the end of his days always condemned to wander. And wherever he wanders, may he always be a stranger. May he find no friend to give him comfort. May no home become his refuge. May Hunger and Thanatos always follow, like dogs, at his heels. And may they be his only companions. May Time, who ravishes all Mother Gaea's children, wither his face and form. And only then, may Thanatos embrace him. And may Jason die alone, without honor, and without respect."

So Medea prayed. And then, she said, "Now leave my house, Jason. And return to your new bride. For I have nothing more to say to you. I have flooded your ears with my prayers to Father Zeus and Mother Hera. Now let your mind, if it will, flood with thoughts of those prayers."

But Jason only stood silent and still. And so Medea took him by the arm and silently ushered him out of the house that they had once shared. And then, Medea stood, silent and still. For her eyes remained flooded with the sight of Jason's retreating figure until, at last, he disappeared.

Chapter 5

King Aegeus arrives in Corinth and speaks with Medea. Then Medea sends Glauce beautiful gifts, and Glauce permits Jason to keep his sons.

And it came to pass that, while Medea was standing in front of her house, her eyes suddenly flooded with the sight of King Aegeus of Athens. Medea knew the aged king. And so, swift as the wind, she exclaimed, "Welcome to Corinth, Aegeus! What brings you to Creon's kingdom? I hope that all goes well with you!"

"Warm greetings to you, Medea!" Aegeus replied. "The sight of you floods my heart with joy! But I live with a heart that overflows with sorrow. For I am an old man. And I still have no child. I fear that the time will soon come when I will look my last on light and life. And then, no son will live after me. And no one of my blood will inherit my royal scepter, my throne, and my kingdom. And so, I am returning from Delphi. For I have asked the oracle of Far-shooting Apollo to advise me.

"But forgive me, Medea. I have spoken too long of my own problems. And I fear that all is not well with you. For my eyes flood with the sight of the tears that flow freely from your eyes. So tell me, my friend. What has happened to make your own heart flood with sorrow?"

So King Aegeus spoke. And in reply, Medea declared, "Oh, Aegeus! I fear that the source of my grief will make your heavy heart overflow with sorrow. For my wedded lord has abandoned me! He has left me in order to wed with Creon's daughter!"

"Abandoned you? Jason? Surely my ears deceive me, Medea!" exclaimed Aegeus. "And surely my mind floods with words you have not spoken! For I have always considered Jason to be an honorable man. And a man of honor remains loving and loyal toward his wedded lady. For such a man would not bring shame upon his own name. And so, swift as the wind, let your words now tumble forth like a river that is swollen with spring rain. And tell me exactly what has happened."

So King Aegeus spoke. And in reply, Medea declared, "Jason's eyes can look upon Shining Helios's golden rays and see them. And yet, he can look upon his own thoughts and deeds and not see the shame of them. For his eyes flood with the sight of a beautiful young princess and the great king who is her father."

"Ambition floods the eyes of many who walk the earth, Medea," responded Aegeus. "It blinds them, and so, they act recklessly. And then, the gods punish them for it. But tell me about Creon, Medea. He knows that you are Jason's wedded lady. And so, surely he did not want Jason to wed with his daughter!"

"He who is both a king and a father blessed their wedding, Aegeus!" exclaimed Medea. "Creon considers Jason to be the greatest Hellenic hero. And he could not resist such a fine wedded lord for his daughter. And now, Creon has banished me from Corinth."

"Surely Creon should know better!" exclaimed Aegeus. "For with age should come wisdom. Could Jason not soften his hard heart?"

"Jason has done nothing to temper Creon's decree. Instead, he has hardened his own heart against me," explained Medea. "He tells me that I have brought exile upon myself. And that I deserve my fate. And so, he has not only betrayed me. He has abandoned me. And a woman, if she is to survive, must have a man who will help and protect her."

So Medea spoke. And in reply, Aegeus declared, "Medea, these sorry deeds flood my heart with waves of terror and pity! Not so much for you—though you are now in a dreadful state. But for Jason and Creon, and even for Creon's daughter. For those who dishonored you are inviting the gods to judge them. And all who walk the earth should honor the deathless gods and respect their power! But what has been done cannot now be undone. And so, how can I help you, Medea? For your heart overflows with sorrow. And Far-seeing Zeus smiles on the man whose heart floods with pity for one who suffers."

So King Aegeus spoke. And in response, Medea fell to her knees before him and said, "I now clasp your knees as a suppliant, Aegeus. I take your beard in my hand. And before you, I hereby take the sacred oath of my people. And with the great, deathless gods of earth and sky as my witnesses—you, Mother Gaea, who are the mother of all that lives and all that has died and who are first among all who are more than mortal—and you, Shining Helios—dear grandfather!—whose gold-yoked chariot crosses the heavens each day so your golden rays will bring light to all who walk the earth—I give you my sacred word, Aegeus, that I am not to blame for Jason's behavior.

"And I give you my sacred word, Aegeus, with the great deathless gods of your people as my witnesses—Far-seeing Zeus, Lord of Justice, and White-armed Hera, Protector of the Wedding-bond—that I am not to blame for Jason's behavior. I have been a loving and loyal lady to my wedded lord. And I have given Jason two sons. And so, if your heart truly floods with pity for me, then rescue me, Aegeus! For I have no family, no home, and no homeland. Befriend me, Aegeus! Let your home, your palace in Athens, be my refuge. And in return, I promise you the children for whom you long. For I possess powerful herbs. And my chants will bring this to pass.

"And if you will help me, Aegeus, just as I have given you my sacred word, now give me yours. For your oath will protect us if my enemies come to Athens and ask you to banish me. And just as I have called the gods of your people to witness, I now ask you to call the gods of my people to witness."

So Medea spoke. And with these words, the king of Athens took her arms and raised her to her feet. And then, he said, "Dry your tears, Medea. And come to me in Athens. For before you and the great deathless gods of earth and sky, both those of the Colchians and those of the Hellenes, I give you my sacred word, Medea, that I will protect you from anyone who seeks to harm you! Come to me in Athens, Medea. And I give you my sacred word that my palace will be your home for as long as you wish. But I cannot help you leave Corinth, Medea. For here, I am Creon's guest. He is my friend. And so, he is also a friend of Athens."

So King Aegeus spoke to Medea. And to his words, Medea replied, "Aegeus, your words have caused my sorrow to melt away like spring snow beneath the golden rays of my grandfather's gold-yoked chariot! And in its place, gratitude now floods my heart. May you fare well on your journey! Before long, you will see me in Athens. There, I will take refuge with you. And there, I will return your kindness!"

So it came to pass that King Aegeus went on his way. And just as a wolf stands outside a sheep-fold, staring into the pen and looking for a way to spring on a sheep and carry it off, while the sheep are not yet aware of their coming terror, and nearby, the shepherds and their dogs doze peacefully, as yet unaware of the wolf's presence, so Medea's mind now flooded with thoughts about how she could avenge Jason's betrayal and abandonment.

And it came to pass that Medea prayed to the goddess whom she served. "Oh hear me, Night-wandering Hecate—Great Goddess from grim Hades' lifeless kingdom—as I now call upon you," she prayed. "Help me as I avenge Jason's betrayal and abandonment. For Creon's daughter must regret the day her eyes ever flooded with the sight of my wedded lord! And her father must regret that day, as well!

"Help me, Lady Hecate, as I contrive to bring Jason to his knees. And by this act, may I raise myself. I have no choice. If I let Jason abuse me, and yet I do nothing, my enemies will laugh at me. And their laughter will echo from the hills and roof-tops of Corinth. And wherever I walk upon Mother Gaea, I will hear it mock me.

"Help me, Lady Hecate, as I send Jason's sons forth to Glauce bearing wedding gifts—a beautiful, finely-woven robe in which to wrap her lovely form. And a beautiful wreath of shining gold to wear upon her lovely brow. Let my evil gifts arrive clothed in the innocence of beauty. And when Glauce unwraps them, swift as the wind, let her heart flood with waves of love and longing for them. And let her hands hunger to hold them and put them on.

"Surely Jason has told Glauce that he wants to keep his sons. And so, she will think I have sent her these gifts to make her heart flood with love for his children. And that will be the beauty of my deception! For with your help, Lady Hecate, I will have soaked my gifts in a poison that no mortal eye can see. Glauce's fingers will touch them without harm. But the poison will do its work when she wears them. May Glauce then forget her love for Jason. And instead, may she long for the embrace of Thanatos! May her screams fly through the walls of her palace. Swift as the wind, may they flood my ears. And like sweet music, may they soothe the wrath that floods my heart!"

So Medea prayed. And so she planned to avenge Jason's betrayal and abandonment. And just as the flames of a raging fire fly through a parched forest on the swift wings of the wind, leaving every tree charred and lifeless in their wake, so Medea now prepared to let her blazing fury rage through the royal palace of Corinth until Thanatos embraced Creon's daughter—and the king, as well.

"And I must not spare our sons!" Medea now silently exclaimed. "For surely, life without the love of family is worse than death! Jason has let selfishness and cruelty flood his heart. And to punish him, I must deprive him of everything he loves. Without Glauce, he will have no royal wealth, no princely power, and no other children. And then he will turn to our sons for comfort. Already, he has told me they are dearer to him than life! So now, he must lose them! For only when Jason is alone, with no source of comfort, will I have avenged his betrayal and abandonment.

"Oh, Hecate—Night-wandering Goddess whom I serve—may my unspeakable deed teach Jason, and anyone else who would dishonor me, that Far-seeing Zeus, Lord of Justice, still rules those who walk the earth! May it teach Jason that, like men, women possess courage, strength, and skill. And may it teach Jason that I am as fearsome a foe as I am a helpful friend."

So Medea prayed. And she now sent for Jason and their sons. And when they had gathered around her, she declared, "Jason, open the doors of your mind to my words. For, like well-aimed arrows, they will fly forth straight and true. Please forgive me for flooding your ears with foolish talk. When you took Glauce for your wedded lady, panic reared its frightened head. And swift as the wind, my common sense fled. But that is past now. And may the love we once shared help you to forget how my heart flooded with rage toward you. Your new wedding is surely in my own best interest. And Creon should permit you to rear our sons. This is your desire as well, Jason. And so, do your best to persuade him.

"I will send your new lady beautiful gifts—a finely-woven robe and a golden wreath. Grandfather—Shining Helios—gave them to my family long ago. And they are a wedding dowry fit for a goddess! So let our sons now carry these gifts forth to Glauce. And may her heart, in loving them, flood with love for our sons, as well."

So Medea spoke. And in response, Jason declared, "Medea, do not sacrifice gifts Shining Helios gave your family! For Glauce neither needs nor wants them, great as they are. Yet she will gladly honor my request to rear our sons. For her heart floods with love for me!"

So Jason spoke. And to his words, Medea replied, "Jason, great gifts influence even the deathless gods! And to all who walk the earth, a fine gift of gold is worth more than ten thousand words. So I gladly give Glauce these gifts. And if it would spare our sons a hateful exile, and if it would persuade you to rear them, I would gladly give up light and life! And so, Jason, let our sons now go forth, with their tutor, to the royal palace. But go forth with them. For our sons must put my gifts into Glauce's hands."

"Since your heart floods with generosity, Medea, I am happy to honor your wishes," replied Jason.

So it came to pass that Medea now called for the gifts that she had so carefully prepared and wrapped. She put them into her sons' hands. And then, they went forth to Creon's daughter. And their tutor and Jason went forth with them.

And just as Shining Helios's golden rays melt the winter snow that covers the mountain meadows—and the mountain streams become swollen rivers that tear down into the valley below and sweep away farms, villages, and even towns in their blind fury, so Medea's heart now overflowed with rage toward Jason as she sent Glauce these wedding gifts. For the wrath of a spurned lady is greater than a spear that soars forth in swift flight, greater than a raging storm, and greater than a blazing fire. For a love that changes to hate knows no limits and fears nothing, not even the embrace of Thanatos.

And it came to pass that the tutor soon returned with Medea's sons. "Lady, Princess Glauce has accepted your wedding gifts," he reported. "And they have flooded her heart with joy! For she will let your sons remain with their father."

So the boys' tutor spoke. Then Medea gathered her sons to her and exclaimed, "Let your hearts now flood with joy! For you have been spared the harsh life of exile. Instead, you are going to a new home. And there, you will live with your father and a new mother. And so, I now embrace you, my dear ones. And I now bid you farewell. For I must. I kiss your hands, your cheeks, and your lips for the last time. And tears flow freely from my eyes. For I love you! And without you, my heart will know only sorrow. But you will have happy lives in your new home. And that thought comforts me. And so, leave me now, children. And go inside. For I have much to do, and little time, before I leave Corinth."

So Medea spoke to her children. And obediently, they left her.

Chapter 6

Medea hears of the death of Glauce and Creon. Then she kills her children. Jason confronts Medea. Medea then reveals his future and departs.

And so it came to pass that Medea was alone once again. And now her mind flooded with waves of conflicting thoughts.

"Oh, heart! How you flood with a mother's love and anguish!" she silently exclaimed. "For just as Grandfather's golden rays melt the spring snow, and it swiftly streams away, so my sons' smiling faces have now melted the wrath that flooded you. And swift as the wind, it too has flowed away. I cannot kill my sons! Why should they suffer for their father's dishonorable deeds? Why should I deprive them of their growing up, their wedding, and their happy times? For they carry no blame upon their small shoulders!

"And surely this unspeakable deed would hurt me twice as much as it would hurt Jason! I would never be able to share my sons' thoughts, their deeds, and their happiness. And when it comes to pass that Time, who ravishes all Mother Gaea's children, makes me old and withered, my sons would not be there to care for me and to comfort me. And when Thanatos embraces me, they would not be there to wrap my body in its last cover and place it in Mother Gaea's arms. And so, I will take my sons with me into exile. It will be harsh on them. For they are very young. But they will still look on light and life. And no matter what fate brings, their presence will lighten my burden!

"Oh, heart! You may not flood with a mother's love and anguish! For I cannot let Jason abuse me! Or he will laugh at me! Everyone will laugh at me! And their laughter will echo from the hills and roof-tops of Corinth. And wherever I walk upon Mother Gaea, I will hear it mock me. And so, heart, you must flood once again with wrath! For Jason must suffer just as he has made me suffer!"

So Medea mused. And then, she silently asked, "Why do I torment myself like this? Why do I think of choices when I have no choice! The poisoned robe and wreath must now be feeding on Glauce's flesh. And surely Thanatos has already embraced her. And since my sons gave Glauce these gifts, surely the hearts of the people will flood with rage toward them. And if my sons must die, then I, the mother who gave them life, must be the one who kills them. But these are empty words. It is you, heart, and not the people of Corinth, who are to blame! For rage and not moderation rules you. And your rage compels me to commit this unspeakable deed.

"I am not a fool! I know that passion is moderation's great enemy. And I know that those who permit passion to rule in place of moderation cause their own suffering. But passion's heart floods with contempt for moderation. For it is strong, And moderation is weak. Just as spring snow melts beneath Grandfather's golden rays, so moderation melts beneath passion's gaze. And just as a stream that is swollen from heavy spring rains rushes down the mountain-side, and as it flows, it tears loose the great boulders and uproots the towering trees that would break its path, so the rage that floods you, heart, pushes aside every attempt of my mind and my love for my sons to restrain my hands.

"But a mother's heart floods with a mother's horror at what I am now about to do. My cheeks are pale from the tears that flow freely from my eyes. My arms hang motionless from my shoulders. And my legs quake with terror. For what mother can kill her children?"

So Medea mused. And with these thoughts, it came to pass that one of Jason's servants came rushing toward her.

"Escape while you can, lady!" he exclaimed. "For your gifts have destroyed the princess! And the king, too, has given up light and life! The sight flooded my eyes. And I could not tear them away, despite the horror of it!"

So the servant spoke. And to his words, Medea replied, "Welcome! I have been longing to hear news of my gifts. So swift as the wind, tell me everything!"

So Medea commanded Jason's servant. And in reply, he declared, "Lady, open the doors of your mind to my words. For, like well-aimed arrows, they will fly forth straight and true. I accompanied Jason and the children into Princess Glauce's private room. And when her eyes flooded with the sight of your sons, her heart flooded with waves of disgust and anger. And so, she turned away from them. But swift as the wind, my lord and master corrected her. 'Glauce, you must love my sons! For I love them,' he declared. 'So accept the wedding gifts they now bring you. And ask your father to let them remain with us. For they are innocent. And exile will be too harsh for them.'

"So Jason spoke to the princess. And so, she took your gifts from the boys' hands and unwrapped them. When her eyes flooded with the sight of their beauty, her heart flooded with delight. And swift as the wind, she agreed to accept your sons. Then Jason and the tutor took hold of the boys' hands. And they left the princess to enjoy her new gifts.

"Swift as the wind, she now put on the beautiful robe and wreath. She picked up a bright mirror. And, with her face wreathed in smiles, she carefully arranged her hair. And she admired her lovely reflection. Then her heart overflowed with joy. And so, she danced around the room.

Then, swift as the wind, her face grew as white as new-fallen snow. Foam began to stream forth like a river from her mouth. Her limbs began to shake like trees beneath the blows of a storm-wind. And her heart flooded with such agony that her screams surely flew through the walls of the palace. At last, she was no longer able to stand securely on her feet. And she fell into the nearest chair.

"At first, her servants stood silent and still. For sight of their lady's agony flooded their eyes. Then their hearts flooded with terror. And they fled from her room, screaming for the king and for help. Meanwhile, the princess's eyeballs rolled up into her head. For her wreath had become a crown of fiery flames. Her robe had fastened itself to her skin. And there, too, fiery flames were now feasting on her flesh.

"The poor princess now got up from her chair and began to run madly around the room. Just as when a shepherd finds a great swarm of bees living within a crevice of a rock, and he lights a torch and smokes them out of their hive, for he wants to collect their honey so it will sweeten his bread, and the bees fly round and round in confusion as they try to escape from their hive, darting this way and that through the smoke, so Princess Glauce now ran round and round her room, turning this way and that, as she tried to shake the blazing crown from her head. But she only fanned the fiery flames.

"Then King Creon ran into the room. And swift as the wind, he tripped over his daughter. For she lay on the floor at his feet. And when she flooded his eyes, his heart flooded with waves of love and pity and sorrow. He fell to his knees. He gathered her blazing form to him. And he embraced her. Her head was a mass of fire and blood. And her body was a mass of fiery, torn flesh and scorched, bloody bones. Yet a father's mind must have flooded with the hope that, if he smothered what remained of the flames, his daughter would look, once again, upon light and life. But her heart had long since overflowed with unbearable agony. And when Thanatos had embraced her, she had welcomed him.

"Oh, Lady! When that sight flooded my eyes, my heart overflowed with sorrow! For there lay the great king on the floor with what remained of his beautiful daughter. And all his power and all his wealth could not help him! And as the king embraced her, his heart overflowed with grief. Tears flowed freely from his eyes. And his voice groaned as he cried out, 'My poor child! Who among the deathless gods has so cruelly destroyed you? Has Thanatos already embraced you? Why did he not seek me? For, without you, I would gladly welcome him!'

"So King Creon spoke. And soon he tried to separate himself from his daughter. But her robe was now feasting on his flesh as well as on hers. He tried to pull himself away from the greedy cloth. But it would not release his flesh. And so he found himself locked in an embrace, not just with his daughter's corpse, but with Thanatos! By now, his own heart overflowed with unbearable agony. And so, he welcomed the embrace of Thanatos.

"And now, Lady, I have told you everything! For the sights still flood my mind. The sounds still flood my ears. And my heart overflows with waves of grief and horror!"

So Jason's servant spoke. And to his words, Medea replied, "You have been a fine witness. And my heart floods with gratitude for your loyalty. For you are Jason's servant. Now, leave me. For swift as the wind, the time comes when I must leave Corinth."

So Medea spoke. And with these words, once again, she was alone. And her mind flooded with thoughts. "Surely I am the most miserable of all who walk the earth!" she silently exclaimed. "For the time has come when I must act. And so, heart, become as hard and strong as a rock. Flood with hatred for Jason. And let that hatred leave no place for a mother's love. Mind, flood with the thought of a wedded lady's dishonor. And let that dishonor leave no place for a mother's thoughts. Hands, go forth to do what you must do. And eyes, restrain your tears!

"Oh, mind, heart, and eyes! For these moments only, forget my sons! For I have loved them with a mother's love. Later, for as long as I look upon light and life, you, mind, will flood with thoughts of this unspeakable deed. You, heart, will flood with waves of love and grief. And you, eyes, will mark my loss with tears that flow freely down my cheeks. But now, you must forget my sons!"

So Medea mused. And with these words, she gave her sons the powerful herbs that, long ago, she had given Apsyrtus. And then she killed them.

Then, swift as the wind, it came to pass that Jason appeared in front of Medea's house. His heart was flooded with waves of rage and grief. And when he saw servants standing outside, he asked, "Where is Medea? I have come for my sons! For the people of Corinth would make them suffer for their mother's unspeakable deeds. And I must protect them! But Medea will reap what she has sown!"

So Jason spoke. But the sight of Jason now flooded Medea's eyes. And before a servant could reply, she called out, "Jason, you will find no one within. Instead, cast your eyes upon the roof of the home you abandoned. For here we are! See how I have avenged your betrayal and your abandonment. Let the sight of your sons' corpses now flood your eyes, your mind, and your heart! And feel the loss that hurts more than death! My heart floods with joy that you have come, Jason!

For the fiery flames of my revenge lick happily upon your knowledge of it. And surely my victory is greater because you have learned of your defeat from my own tongue."

So Medea spoke. And in response, Jason exclaimed, "Oh, Medea! Surely serpents flood your monstrous heart! You have destroyed me! For you have taken all that I have loved from me! My heart floods with grief! And my mind floods with anguish as I think of all I have lost!

"Swift as the wind, may the gods of your people—Mother Gaea and Shining Helios—now destroy you, Medea! For as long as the wind of life courses through you, you curse whatever you touch! Surely most cursed is the day I brought you on board the Argo! I was foolish enough to believe a barbarian could change by becoming the wedded lady of a Hellenic hero. But our ways have washed off your back like ebb-tides off the shore of the salt sea. No Hellenic woman would ever murder her own children. I should have chosen to wed with one of them! But foolishly I chose you. And grievously, I have paid for it! Now let me bury my sons. And never again let my eyes flood with the sight of you!"

So Jason spoke. And to his words, Medea replied, "Call me what you will, Jason. But I have done what I had to do. I have caused your heart to overflow with agony. And I could only do this by taking all you loved from you.

"And now, I will not give you your sons, Jason. I, who gave birth to them, will bury them on the acropolis of Corinth, in the sanctuary of White-Armed Hera of the Heights. For there, none of my enemies will dare to desecrate their graves and violate their bodies. Tell the people of Corinth I command them to establish a sacred festival. For from this time forth, they must perform solemn rites that will atone for this impious murder."

So Medea spoke. And in response to her words, Jason prayed, "Father Zeus—Lord of Justice—look down from Mount Olympus. See how Medea has murdered her children. And see how she will not let me bury them. See that Medea is not a woman, but a monster! And so close your heart to her prayers. Close your ears to her curses. And punish her for her unspeakable deeds!

"Father Zeus—Lord of Justice—let your heart flood with pity for me. For I have lost my new wedded lady. And I have no children. Defend me against anyone who would seek to tarnish my name. For I am one of the greatest heroes of Hellas. I have won praise as a great leader. I have won the glory of the great deed. And I have acted as any Hellene would have acted in my place."

So Jason prayed. And to his prayer, Medea responded, "Jason, your winged words surely will reach the ears of Father Zeus, and Mother Hera, as well. But they know all I have done for you. And they know you have broken your wedding vows, your sacred promises. You have betrayed me. You have abandoned me! And so, you have dishonored me!

"Just as Shining Helios follows Blushing Eos at the start of each new day, you will now begin to reap the seeds that you have sown, Jason. You have let selfishness and cruelty flood your heart. And so, you have turned the hearts of the deathless gods against you. And from this time forth, until, at last, you give up light and life, they have condemned you to wander. And wherever you wander, you will be a stranger. You will find no friend to give you comfort. And no home to give you refuge. For all who walk the earth will now shun you. For no one who respects and fears the gods will dare to help a man whom the gods have condemned!

"Hunger and Thanatos will always follow, like dogs, at your heels. And they will be your only companions. And so, your heart will flood with waves of grief and despair. And you will walk with your head bowed toward those who live below the earth. For you will long for the embrace of Thanatos. But it is decreed that you will not soon give up the wind of life that blows through you. Your face and form will reveal how Time, who ravishes all Mother Gaea's children, will continue to leave his mark on you. But the dreadful god will turn his back on you.

"And the years will follow one upon the other as the silver-yoked chariot of Silver-horned Selene follows the gold-yoked chariot of Gold-helmeted Helius across the heavens. At last, aged and alone, without honor, and without respect, it will come to pass that you will seek refuge beneath the shadow of the well-benched Argo. And there, while your eyes are closed in sorrowful sleep, the prow of your old ship will fall on your head. And only then will you look your last upon light and life.

"But before that day comes, Jason, may you gain wisdom through suffering. May you learn that no mortal knows what the new day will bring. Some find themselves raised up. Others find themselves brought low. If they are wise, mortals will expect the unexpected. For no one who walks the earth can presume to know the will of the deathless gods. And it is they who rule the earth on which mortals live, as well as the world above and the world below."

So Medea spoke to Jason. And with these words, it suddenly came to pass that a great chariot, drawn by two winged and fire-breathing dragons, came down from the heavens and landed beside Medea on the roof. She took the corpses of her sons and seated herself in the chariot.

And then she announced, "Jason, our sons will ride with me in this chariot that Grandfather—Shining Helios—has sent down to me in order to protect me from my enemies. I will bury our sons. And then, I will go forth to Athens. For there, King Aegeus will welcome me and give me refuge."

So Medea spoke to Jason. And with these words, she picked up the reins and drove off into the heavens. And as she left, Jason called after her, "Corinth is well rid of you, Medea! Bury my sons! And find refuge in Athens, if you can. But as you fly through the heavens, discover what I now know. Those who walk the earth bear the heavy yoke of suffering. But the deathless gods are not to blame. For there are no gods!"

1. The depiction of a character's unspoken thoughts as if she or he is thinking them aloud is called *interior monologue*. What does Aeetes' interior monologue reveal about him? What reason(s) might he have for wanting to punish Medea himself? What function does his monologue serve at the opening of this myth?

2. What does Jason's reaction to the appearance of the Colchian fleet reveal about him?

3. What does Medea's monologue reveal about her? What does Medea say that reveals that she is suffering from the behavior pattern of excellence (*aretē*), excessive pride (*hubris*), blind recklessness (*atē*), and retribution (*nemesis*)? Explain how this pattern applies to her. What function does her monologue serve at this point in the myth?

4. What has Medea said that frightens Jason? To what extent, if any, should he be frightened?

5. Examine the function of Medea's interior monologue. What does the long, extended comparison (called a *Homeric simile*) that precedes it contribute to Medea's depiction? To what extent, if any, are her thoughts psychologically realistic?

6. Given what you know about Jason, explain whether he would have murdered Apsyrtus if Medea had opposed it. Why does Jason volunteer to help Medea with her terrible task?

7. Medea is capable of performing great magic feats. Why does this myth give Medea no choice but to kill her brother? For example, why, instead, does Medea not create a fog in which to hide the *Argo?*

8. What is the significance of Apsyrtus's sigh and blood-drenched hand?

9. Why do the Argonauts do nothing to stop the murder of Apsyrtus?

10. How does Alcinous solve the conflict between his obligation to Jason and his fear of the Colchians?

11. Why does Jason decide to marry Medea?

12. How do you evaluate Hera's claim to having influenced Arete's thoughts?

13. Evaluate whether Zeus, Lord of Justice, is, in fact, just when he punishes all the Argonauts for Jason and Medea's murder of Apsyrtus. Why does Medea not help the Argonauts when they arrive in Libya?

14. Why does Medea kill Pelias? What does her murder of Pelias reveal about Hera? about Medea's nature? about Jason's nature? What might you predict based on this knowledge?

15. Why would Hera have wanted Medea to be in charge of Pelias's death? Why does Medea arrange to have Pelias's daughters kill their father rather than choose to perform the deed herself?

16. What does Hera's response to Pelias's death reveal about her?

17. What do Zeus's punishment of the Argonauts and Hera's punishment of Pelias reveal about the nature of the universe in which Medea and Jason live? What might you predict based on this knowledge?

18. Why does Creon consider Jason to be the greatest hero of Hellas? Whose point of view does this value judgment represent? What does this evaluation reveal about heroes?

19. In what ways is Medea an ideal wife, even according to Hellenic values? Evaluate whether, if it had been possible, and if the situation had presented itself, Medea would have betrayed and abandoned Jason in order to improve her life.

20. Evaluate Jason's decision to leave Medea for Glauce. What does Jason's interior monologue reveal about his character? What does he say that reveals that he is suffering from the behavior pattern of *aretē, hubrise, atē,* and *nemesis?* Explain how this pattern applies to him. What function does his interior monologue serve at this point in the myth?

21. What does Creon's conversation with Jason reveal about Creon's character? What does Creon say that reveals that he is suffering from the behavior pattern of *aretē, hubris, atē,* and *nemesis?* Explain how this pattern applies to him. What function do Creon's statements serve at this point in the myth?

22. How do Creon's decisions about Medea lead to her banishment? What is the significance of this deed?

23. Medea's interior monologue, upon learning of her banishment, is the most famous passage in Euripides' *Medea* and the most feminist statement in ancient literature. How does Medea describe the position of women in Greek society? To what extent, if any, does it reflect the position of women in your society? In other societies today?

24. Analyze the components of Medea's rage. Explain why she hates Jason and why she might also hate herself. Why does she choose to destroy Jason by destroying Glauce and Creon? Why does she intend to use deception in order to do this?

25. When Medea confronts Jason, what do her accusations achieve?

26. Analyze Jason's response to Medea's accusations. What does it reveal about Jason and the society in which he lives? To what extent, if any, are his statements correct?

27. What is the significance of Jason's request for his sons?

28. Why does Medea refuse to accept Jason's help and leave quietly? To what extent, if any, is this an error of judgment on her part?

29. Medea tells Jason that who he is will determine what will become of him, and that, in the end, the Olympian gods will deal justly with him. Explain whether the audience or reader is supposed to accept Medea's statements as predicting what, in fact, is going to happen to Jason.

30. What does Jason's response to Medea's statements reveal about him? What aspect of his response would anger the Olympian gods? Why?

31. What is the significance of Medea's curse? To what extent, if any, might it predict Jason's future? Explain.

32. What does Aegeus contribute to this myth? What does he say that influences Medea's behavior? How does he influence the reader's reaction to Medea's situation?

33. Why must Medea's gifts be especially appealing? Why does she ask Jason to forgive her "foolish talk"? What do her gifts and comments reveal about Medea's insight into human nature?

34. Explain Medea's vacillation about murdering her children. To what extent, if any, does she really have a choice? How does this affect her characterization?

35. Why is it important that Medea knows herself, in contrast to Jason, who does not? To what extent, if any, is Medea a tragic figure?

36. What function does the servant's gruesome description of the deaths of Glauce and Creon perform in this myth?

37. What do Jason's response to Medea's murder of his sons and his prayer to Zeus reveal about Jason's character?

38. Note Medea's command that the Corinthians must establish a sacred festival in order to atone for this impious murder. What do Medea's command, her prophecy of Jason's future, and her definition of human wisdom reveal about her?

39. Why does Helios send his chariot down to Corinth to rescue Medea? What function does his chariot serve?

40. Although in one version of this myth, Medea unintentionally is responsible for the death of her children, Euripides is probably the first writer to have Medea murder them. What does the depiction of Medea gain from this change? In contrast, consider how the audience and reader would view Medea if she did not murder her children.

41. Why does Jason deny that the Olympian gods exist? To what extent, if any, does this myth confirm his point of view?

42. *Situational irony* (also called *dramatic* or, in a myth such as this, *tragic irony*) is the difference between what a character expects will happen and what actually happens. Because the audience or reader knows more about the character's situation than the character does, the character's words and deeds become significant examples of that character's faulty perception of the consequences of her or his behavior. Consider the reversals of fortune that occur in this myth. Explain whether they are examples of tragic irony.

43. Consider the extent to which each of the following is to blame for the troubles that plague Medea: (a) Jason; (b) Creon; (c) Glauce; (d) Medea; (e) Hera; (f) society. Based on your analysis, who is most responsible?

44. To what extent, if any, do the attitudes and behavior of Medea and Jason encourage readers to sympathize with them?

45. Medea both wins and loses in her contest with Jason over her integrity and her control over her own life. What does she win, and what does she lose? To what extent, if any, is Medea a hero? A villain?

46. According to Aristotle, tragic heroes must be better than ordinary people in that they are admirable, but they must not be preeminently virtuous and just. Throughout the plot, their attitudes and behavior must always be psychologically consistent. Through a great error in judgment (not vice or depravity), they blindly commit a rash act in that they do not anticipate the consequences. These consequences—a destructive or painful event—surprise this hero, cause the hero great suffering, and involve a reversal from happiness to undeserved misfortune. Therefore, members of the audience pity this tragic hero and fear that what has happened to the hero can happen to themselves. However, these heroes gain self-knowledge through suffering, and they discover the relationship between their earlier rash act and these devastating consequences. To what extent, if any, is Jason an Aristotelian tragic hero? Explain whether you view him as a tragic figure.

47. Evaluate the myth of Medea as a moral tale. Consider the attitudes and actions of both Medea and Jason. What do they reveal about human behavior? What do they reveal about how human beings should strive to behave?

48. What does the end of this myth reveal about the significance of the Olympian gods in the lives of Medea and Jason?

49. *Homeric similes* are long, extended comparisons. Find five examples of this type of simile. What does each contribute to the story? What type of comparisons does the author use? What do they, in themselves, reveal?

50. If you have read the preceding myth, *Jason and the Golden Fleece,* how do Medea and Jason, as maiden and hero, enrich the myth of Medea? To what extent, if any, do the attitudes and behavior of the younger Medea and Jason predict the attitudes and behavior of the older couple? What impact does this have on the myth of Medea?

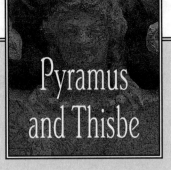

The myth of "Pyramus and Thisbe" appears in Ovid's most popular work, a treasury of myths and legends called *Metamorphoses*. The work has been called "the *Arabian Nights* of the Roman world," and it can also be compared with Boccaccio's *Decameron* and Chaucer's *Canterbury Tales*.

HISTORICAL BACKGROUND

Ovid (Publius Ovidius Naso) was born in the town of Sulmo (Sulmona), located seventy-five miles to the east of Rome, in 43 B.C., the year that Julius Caesar was assassinated. His family was wealthy, and Ovid studied in Rome in order to become prepared to hold public office. However, he found that he preferred to write poetry, and, therefore, he went to Athens, where he became familiar with Greek art. When he returned to Rome, Ovid joined a literary group that included the great Roman poet Horace.

In his early twenties, Ovid established his literary reputation with *Amores* (*Loves*), a collection of short, innovative love poems. In addition to *Metamorphoses,* Ovid wrote two other books that reflect his love of myths: *Heroides* (*Heroines*), which is a collection of fifteen letters from famous women of myth and legend to the lovers who had abandoned them; and *Ars amatoria* (*The Art of Love*), which is a handbook on love with examples from mythology.

Ovid was fifty-one years old and polishing the manuscript of *Metamorphoses* when, in A.D. 8, Augustus suddenly banished him from Rome. It has been suggested that the emperor found Ovid's *Ars amatoria* to be offensive at a time when he was trying to improve the moral values of Roman citizens. Augustus forced Ovid to live in the frontier community of Tomi, located on the shores of the Black Sea. (Later, when more Romans settled in the region, they renamed the town Constanta and the land Rumania.)

Ovid continued to write during his years in exile. Although he hoped to be pardoned or transferred to a more pleasant location, in A.D. 17, Ovid died in Tomi at the age of sixty.

LITERARY BACKGROUND

Ovid divided his *Metamorphoses* into three sections that move in chronological order from the time of Creation to the death of Julius Caesar. In Latin, the poetry of *Metamorphoses* has the rhythm of *The Iliad, The Odyssey,* and *The Aeneid.* Ovid's sources for this work include Homer, the ancient Greek dramatists, several Hellenistic collections of mythology, and a Latin collection, as well as myths and legends from Babylonia and countries to the East. Although many of the approximately two hundred fifty selections in *Metamorphoses* involve one of the many faces of love, and all involve some type of miraculous change or transformation, the myths and legends vary greatly from one another.

Fortunately, *Metamorphoses* was complete when Ovid went into exile. Although he burned the manuscript before he left Rome, the concluding verses of *Metamorphoses* reveal that he expected it to bring him lasting fame, and he knew that friends had made their own copies of it. When Augustus prohibited Rome's public libraries from possessing the work, Ovid's friends privately distributed copies of it. Within two years, the work was being imitated by poets and studied by children.

Metamorphoses was so popular that it continued to be copied after the collapse of the western Roman Empire. Chretien de Troyes (c.1140–c.1200), the first great French poet, translated parts of *Metamorphoses* into Old French, and he may be responsible for the fact that "Pyramus and Thisbe" is one of the earliest secular poems in French. The first printed edition of *Metamorphoses* was published in 1471. Shortly thereafter, in 1480, William Caxton translated and published it in England.

Dante (1265–1321), Boccaccio (1313–1375), Chaucer (c.1342–1400), Shakespeare (1564–1616), and Milton (1608–1674) relied upon Ovid's *Metamorphoses* for their knowledge of mythology. Boccaccio retells several selections from *Metamorphoses* in his own *Amorosa Visione*. Chaucer uses Ovid's versions of "Pyramus and Thisbe," among others, in *The Legend of Good Women*, and he admired the structure of Ovid's *Metamorphoses* enough to use a similar structure in his own *Canterbury Tales*.

From the Middle Ages into the nineteenth century, Ovid was considered to be the best Roman poet after Virgil and was one of the most popular ancient authors. Dante ranked Ovid with Homer and Horace. Shakespeare's favorite Roman author was Ovid, and he included a humorous version of "Pyramus and Thisbe" in *A Midsummer Night's Dream*. Moreover, although Ovid was not Shakespeare's source for *Romeo and Juliet*, "Pyramus and Thisbe" obviously influenced Shakespeare's sources, and Shakespeare's version is the finest version of this myth.

APPEAL AND VALUE

Ovid's versions of the myths and legends in *Metamorphoses* are known for their realistic detail and their author's knowledge of human nature. "Pyramus and Thisbe" is one of Ovid's most popular myths, and his version is the earliest version that exists. The myth has universal appeal in that it is about two devoted young lovers whose love for one another results in their death. Hostile parents, adventure, Fate, and youthful passion all play important roles.

Because Ovid tells his version of the myth swiftly, with simple characterization and a straightforward plot, many later writers chose to embellish the myth by making the personalities of the lovers and their situation more complex. Shakespeare's *Romeo and Juliet* is the most famous example in English. Other famous variants include versions of *Tristan and Isolde* from Celtic Wales, Norway, and Germany, and *Aucassin and Nicolette* from France.

The most famous English editions of *Metamorphoses* are those by Arthur Golding (1567), George Sandys (1626), and the composite translation edited by Samuel Garth (1717). The following version of "Pyramus and Thisbe" is based upon Sandys' version of Ovid's work. Chaucer's version of "The Legend of Thisbe" in *The Legend of Good Women*, Boccaccio's version in canto 20 of his *Amorosa Visione*, and both Golding's translation and Garth's edition of the myth were useful as well.

❧

PYRAMUS AND THISBE

Long, long ago, in the Assyrian city of Babylon—you may remember the city, for its arched brick walls gained everlasting fame as one of the seven wonders of the ancient world—there lived a youth by the name of Pyramus and a maiden by the name of Thisbe. Now Pyramus was more handsome than any other youth in the East, and as for Thisbe, those who saw her compared her beauty to that of the immortal Juno, Minerva, and Venus.

From the time of their birth, Pyramus and Thisbe had lived next door to one another. In fact, their houses shared one roof and had a common wall between them. Therefore, it was natural that the children had become good friends, and it came to pass that, as they grew, their childish affection for one another grew into an all-consuming love. One could not say that Pyramus had a greater love for Thisbe or that Thisbe had a greater love for Pyramus. In the hearts of both, their blood blazed with flames of equal passion.

The two lovers lived in happy anticipation of a long, shared life until they told their respective parents of their desire to become man and wife. Neither father looked with kind eyes upon their love. Instead, their paternal hearts flooded with rage, and they passionately opposed what their children so passionately desired. First, they tried to dissuade Pyramus and Thisbe from their intent. And when that failed, they prohibited them from seeing one another.

So it came to pass that Pyramus and Thisbe concealed their love from their parents. But, in the heart of both the youth and the maiden, the flames of love's fire only blazed brighter because of their need to keep it hidden. Having no one to help them, they communicated with silent signs—evident in a silent glance here or in a quiet nod there—that could be noticed by anyone who had the eyes to see them. However, their parents were blind to this, and they were satisfied that their children had obeyed their wishes.

Those who are old and wise often tell us that that love will find a way. And so it came to pass that, being equally desperate about their passion for one another, Pyramus and Thisbe discovered a slender crevice in the common wall of their homes, a crack that had remained undetected until they discovered it. Yet, this crevice had actually existed since their houses had been built, for the mortar that cemented the bricks in their common wall had shrunk as it had dried.

Therefore, you can imagine the lovers' surprise and their mutual delight when they realized that their whispers could travel from mouth to ear through the crevice. They had discovered a safe way to communicate with each other! And now it came to pass that, day after day, Pyramus and Thisbe stuck themselves to this crack in the wall like two snails, each greedily listening to the beloved voice of the other, happy even to hear the sound of the other's breathing.

Day after day, the two lovers shared their joys and sorrows and whispered their undying passion for one another. And, day after day, in the heart of both the youth and the maiden, the flames of love's fire blazed ever brighter. In fact, it came to pass that Pyramus and Thisbe's love became more desperate, because the crevice in the wall, which they now considered to be their enemy as well as their friend, brought them so near and yet continued to keep them very far from each another.

"Oh, Wall!" they would exclaim. "We do not mean to sound ungrateful for what you have given us, but surely you must be the most envious of structures! For you insist on separating those whom Love has joined! Please bend enough for us to embrace each other! And if the Fates will not permit you to do so much, at least allow us space for our lips to meet!"

The lovers' heartfelt whispers continued day after day. Night after night, they bid each other farewell by kissing the cold brick wall that separated them. Day and night, each yearned for the beloved, who stood waiting and yearning in return just beyond the crevice. However, day after day and night after night, the crevice did not widen and Pyramus and Thisbe's parents did not relent.

It came to pass that Saturn, whom the old ones often call Father Time, ushered in what appeared to be another ordinary day. Once again, Aurora, goddess of the Dawn, chased away the stars of Night. Once again, Phoebus Apollo followed Aurora, transporting the sun across the heavens in his chariot. And once again, Pyramus and Thisbe returned to their places by the crevice in the wall that separated them.

However, this was no ordinary day at all! For on this day, the two lovers decided that the time had come to put an end to their mutual suffering. As they conferred in whispers, Pyramus confided his plan.

"The only way that we can freely love each other," he announced, "will be if we leave our parents and friends and go off on our own! If you agree, and if you share my courage, I have a plan."

"I'm ready to go with you!" Thisbe replied in a whisper. "What do you suggest?"

"We can leave tonight," Pyramus explained, "as soon as everyone at home is asleep. We can slip by those on guard and steal into the countryside. However, it will be so dark in the fields beyond the walls that we might miss each other. Therefore, I think that we should meet at the tomb of Ninus." (Ninus was Assyria's first king, and both Pyramus and Thisbe were familiar with the location of his tomb.)

"This historic place will be ideal for us," Pyramus told Thisbe. "The great mulberry tree will reveal the tomb despite the darkness, for Luna will shine her silver beams upon its snowy berries, and they will glow like a thousand candles. The deep shadows beneath the tree's branches will shelter and protect us, and the cool spring nearby will be there to quench our thirst."

"We can wait there until Aurora chases away the stars of Night." Pyramus concluded, "Then, we can enter the woods and escape to some town where no one will know us. There, we will be able to live as we choose!"

Thisbe, as eager as Pyramus to join their lives, agreed with her lover's plan.

That day, Apollo must have known what the Fates had decreed for these lovers for he drove his chariot very slowly across the heavens, prolonging the sun's rays as if he hoped to delay Luna's journey through Night's domain and prevent the events that she would observe. However, the god finally became tired and drove his chariot toward his home beneath the waves in the sea.

Meanwhile, Thisbe stood watching Apollo's journey from her window, and her love for Pyramus flooded her heart with courage. As soon as everyone in her home had settled down for the night, she quietly unbarred the doors to her house and stole forth into the dark night. Lest she be recognized, she drew her hooded cloak over her face, and passing like a phantom through the shadows of the city, she made her way unseen to Babylon's great protective wall. There, she waited until the guards stopped to talk with each other, and then she quietly and quickly stole through the gates into freedom.

As Thisbe had hoped, Luna illuminated the mulberry tree's snowy berries with her silver moonbeams and made it easy for Thisbe to find the tomb of Ninus. The deep shadows beneath the tree's branches invited her to take refuge within their safe shelter, so Thisbe wrapped her cloak tightly around her body for warmth against Night's chill air, and then sat down to wait for Pyramus.

However, it was not Pyramus who came. Instead, a lioness ambled out of the woods, her jaws dripping with the blood of cattle that she had just slaughtered and eaten. Spying the spring, she rushed past the mulberry tree in order to quench her thirst with its refreshing waters.

Luna, ever the friend of maidens as well as wild animals, took pity on Thisbe and directed her moonbeams so that Thisbe noticed the lion just as the bloody beast was leaving the woods. At first, Thisbe froze with fright. But then, swift as the wind, she sought the safer refuge of a deep cave, located within the cliffs by the tomb, that beckoned to her from afar. The lioness so terrified Thisbe that she preferred the cave's dark and unknown recesses to the more welcoming but less reliable protection of the mulberry tree. Thisbe ran with such trembling abandon toward more certain safety that her cloak slipped from her shoulders to the ground as she ran past the spring. She missed it once she reached the cave, but it was too late to retrace her steps and retrieve it.

It came to pass that, once the savage lioness had drunk her fill from the stream and had begun to make her way back toward the woods, she noticed Thisbe's cloak upon the ground. Wondering what type of animal it might be, she approached the cloak and investigated it, tearing it apart with her still-bloody teeth. Then, when it no longer interested her, she discarded it and ambled off into the woods, heading in the direction from which she had so recently emerged.

Meanwhile, it had taken Pyramus much longer to make a safe escape from his home. As he approached the mulberry tree, Luna alerted him to the possible danger by shining her moonbeams upon the lioness's fresh tracks in the loose dirt. Surprised by the great silence that greeted him in place of Thisbe's welcome, Pyramus turned pale with fear and shuddered with apprehension.

"Thisbe should have called out to me by now," Pyramus thought to himself. He looked around for his beloved, and, instead, he spied her torn and bloody cloak upon the ground by the spring.

"A lion has killed my Thisbe, my love!" he exclaimed. "But now that you have been taken from me, Dear One, this one night will bring death to two lovers! You deserved to live long and happily," he sobbed, "and I am to blame for your death! For it was my idea that we meet at this dangerous place, and now I have arrived too late to save you!"

"So, Lion, come forth once more from your den beneath this cliff! Tear into my foul body with your fierce teeth! Feast upon my hated flesh! Chew my vile limbs! Eat my evil guts! I despise myself, and I deserve the worst from the Fates!"

Then, Pyramus paused and reconsidered. "No," he thought. "To wish for death is the coward's way to die. The brave take death into their own hands!"

So it came to pass that Pyramus carried Thisbe's cloak to the trunk of the mulberry tree, where he had expected to meet his beloved. There he stood in the shade cast by the tree's branches, kissing Thisbe's torn and bloody garment with his trembling lips and washing it with his tears.

"Now," he announced to the sorry cloak, "drink my blood as well as Thisbe's! Let our blood combine and dye your cloth an even deeper red! For I will die with my true love, and I will be her companion in Pluto's dark kingdom."

With these words, Pyramus drew forth his sword from the ivory scabbard that he wore at his waist and quickly plunged its blade deep into his side, giving himself a mortal wound. Then, while Death slowly drew forth his life from his body, Pyramus withdrew the bloody weapon and collapsed upon the ground. His warm blood gushed forth into the air like water from a broken lead pipe, traveling upward in an arc and spraying the mulberry's white berries a dark red. Meanwhile, the tree's roots drank his blood and sent it coursing up the trunk and across the branches to feed its fruit.

Then it came to pass that Thisbe, who had hidden too far from the mulberry tree to know about Pyramus's plight, gathered her courage and left the shelter of the cave. "Surely the beast has drunk its fill by now," she thought. And in an attempt to reassure herself, she added, "Besides, lions do not usually harm people!"

Thisbe hastened toward the mulberry tree, fearing that she had disappointed her lover by her absence. In her mind and in her heart, she could see that Pyramus was eagerly waiting for her, and she entertained herself by rehearsing the tale of terror and escape that she would tell him for his amusement.

Finally, Thisbe could see a mulberry tree in the darkness. She recognized its shape and location, but this tree had dark red berries! "This cannot be our mulberry tree!" she exclaimed to herself. "Luna shone her silver beams on white berries, not red ones!"

Thisbe lowered her gaze and then suddenly spied a prostrate form which lay trembling and gasping upon blood-stained earth by the tree's trunk. Startled by the sight, she gasped, stopped, and then recoiled, as if by this action she could reverse the passage of time as well. Her blood fled from her cheeks, and she trembled like the sea's surface beneath a gentle breeze. Thisbe's heart knew Pyramus before her mind recognized him.

Thisbe then ran to her lover, wailing, beating her breast, and tearing her hair with inconsolable grief. Kneeling at his side, she gently raised his limp body, embracing his still form and filling the bloody cavern of his mortal wound with her tears. She then raised his head and kissed his lips—which Death had already made cold—trying desperately to restore her beloved to life.

"My Love, who has been so cruel as to kill you?" she asked. "Oh, Pyramus! Look at me! Answer me! Your dear Thisbe is calling to you! Please speak to me! Do not leave me without a word! Oh, why have the Fates cheated us?" she sobbed.

Death had not yet taken Pyramus away, but he held the last of the youth's ebbing life in his hands. When Pyramus heard Thisbe's name, he did his best to open his eyes and look his last upon the maiden he loved. However, Death had made his eyes too heavy and too dim to do his bidding. They fluttered open for a brief moment and barely saw Thisbe before Death closed them forever and took Pyramus's shade down to Pluto's dark kingdom.

Thisbe then looked around and spied both her lover's empty scabbard and her own torn and bloody cloak upon the ground nearby.

"Now I understand it all!" she cried. "Dear Soul! You took your own life because of your love for me! Together we would have lived long and happily, but, now, I am the one who is to blame for your death! Well, Pyramus, my love is as strong as yours, and it will give my hand the courage and the strength to take my own life with as sure an aim!"

"For without you, life means nothing to me, and my only joy will be to follow you down to Pluto's dark kingdom," Thisbe declared. "In death as in life you will be my friend and my partner. Death alone was strong enough to take you from me, and yet, even Death will fail to separate us. The Fates will surely let him conquer me as well!"

Thisbe then added, "I have one last request, Cruel Parents—if only you were here to hear it! Please put aside your anger and your envy and bury us together in one tomb! Our constant love united our hearts while we lived, and now that love has brought us to our untimely end. And just as the Fates have eternally joined our shades in death, so I would have you join our earthly remains!"

"And I have one last request for you as well, Mulberry Tree," Thisbe concluded. "Soon, your branches will shade our two corpses. But once Pluto's dark kingdom has become our home, in lasting memory of our great love, always remember our death. Clothe your white berries in the bloody color of mourning forevermore! Let your roots continue to drink our blood, and let the dark red fruit upon your branches become a living and lasting memory of our double death!"

With these words, Thisbe found Pyramus's sword lying on the blood-stained earth by his arm. "Why, this weapon is still warm with my lover's blood!" she exclaimed. "May the Fates give all who truly love each other a better destiny than ours!"

Thisbe then raised the sword, pointed it at her heart, and threw herself upon it, giving herself the mortal wound she sought.

The gods looked down upon the lovers and gave Thisbe her last wishes. The four parents mourned their own loss and the tragedy of their children's love. After the funeral fires had consumed the corpses of their children, they tearfully mixed Pyramus and Thisbe's ashes together and placed them in a golden burial urn.

And it has come to pass that mulberries now become dark red as they ripen, eternally mourning Pyramus and Thisbe's tragic love.

1. What themes about the relationship between parents and their children can you find in this myth?

2. To what extent, if any, do the events of the plot reveal that the lovers' fathers may have been correct to prohibit their marriage?

3. Why do you think that Ovid blames the lovers' fathers more than he blames their mothers for their initial situation?

4. Tragedy has been defined as "the disaster which comes to those who represent and who symbolize those flaws and shortcomings which are universal in a lesser form." What universal flaws, if any, do Pyramus and Thisbe symbolize?

5. According to Aristotle, tragic heroes bring misfortune upon themselves through a great error of judgment. Apply this idea to Pyramus and Thisbe.

6. According to Aristotle, tragedy arouses pity and fear in the audience. To what extent, if any, do you pity Pyramus and Thisbe? Why or why not? To what extent, if any, does their myth create fear with regard to some aspect of your own life? Explain.

7. Consider the tragic aspects of this myth. To what extent, if any, does the tragedy reside in the nature of a character's personality? To what extent, if any, does tragedy reside in the characters' situation?

8. What is the role of Fate in this myth? To what extent, if any, is this myth simply a tale of bad luck?

9. To what extent, if any, does Ovid imply that Pyramus and Thisbe should have obeyed their parents?

10. Chaucer retells this myth very much as Ovid tells it, with one interesting exception. Chaucer omits the mulberry tree and the transformation of its berries from white to red. What, if anything, does the mulberry tree add to the myth?

11. In your opinion, which of the two lovers, Pyramus or Thisbe, is the greater character? Explain your choice.

12. In your opinion, what qualities have made this myth so popular with writers throughout the ages?

HISTORICAL BACKGROUND

The founding and destiny of Rome are the focus of *The Aeneid.*

The same peoples who invaded Greece from the north between approximately 2600 and 100 B.C. also invaded Italy. The first tribes who arrived brought copper and bronze into the area; much later, a second wave of invaders brought iron tools and weapons. In time, these two groups intermingled and inhabited all of the Italian peninsula.

These tribes settled in the lower valley of the Tiber River, called the plain of Latium, and the people became known as the Latins. Archaeologists have found that small Latin settlements existed on many of the seven hilltops there by 753 B.C., which, according to legend, is the year Romulus founded Rome. According to the chronology of *The Aeneid,* however, Aeneas founded Rome in 1176 B.C., eight years after the end of the Trojan War.

Archaeologists think that the small Latin villages united sometime between 800 and 700 B.C. By 700 B.C., the Latins had built a common area, called the Forum, for commercial purposes, including a cattle market. By 625 B.C., many huts had sprung up around the Forum. The Latins could not use much of the area at the base of the hills, because the waters of the Tiber often flooded it. The lowland remained swampy, malaria-infested, and largely uninhabited until the Etruscan peoples, with their advanced technological knowledge, invaded the area.

Between approximately 900 and 800 B.C., the Etruscan people left their homeland in Asia Minor to invade Italy. They brought with them the idea of the city-state. When they conquered the Latin villages in 607 B.C., they built sewers leading into the Tiber and drained the lowland areas at the base of the seven hills, making a city in that location possible. In about 575 B.C., the Etruscans leveled the existing primitive huts and constructed the large public Forum (the Forum Romanum) as the commercial and political center of a large new city, which they named Rumlua. Romulus (the legendary first ruler of Rome) and Roma (Latin) are both derived from the Etruscan Rumlua.

Meanwhile, in approximately 800 B.C., the Phoenicians established the city-state of Carthage on Numidian land, on the coast of North Africa to the southwest of Sicily. By 750 B.C., the Greeks had begun to establish colonies on the island of Sicily and on the Italian peninsula.

The Etruscans were an enterprising people who learned whatever they could from the cultures with whom they came into contact. They adapted many religious and artistic ideas and much of their technology from the Greek colonies—including the Greek gods and the phonetic alphabet. They also made a political alliance with Carthage in about 545 B.C., when Carthage was wealthy and powerful and controlled the western part of the Mediterranean Sea.

From 509 to 133 B.C., Rome developed into a major power. By 270 B.C., it had conquered the Italian peninsula, including the Etruscans and the Greek colonies. Then it conquered Carthage, Greece, and part of Asia. The three wars with Carthage (the Punic Wars) have remained famous because of the amount of blood spilled and because of the unusual strategic skills of two of the generals involved. After Hannibal, a Carthaginian general, led forty thousand men, nine thousand cavalry troops, and African elephants over the Alps from Spain into Italy, it took the Romans almost twenty years to find a general (Scipio) who could defeat him.

At home, the Romans established a more democratic form of government than their original monarchy, giving the common people many rights and displaying the laws of Rome on twelve tablets in the Forum. The Romans were also more democratic than many of their neighbors in the treatment of the countries they conquered. Unlike the Greeks and many other peoples of that time, the Romans did not kill or enslave most of their enemies. The defeated countries had to pay taxes to Rome and supply troops to defend all of the provinces, but they remained free to govern themselves in most respects. In return, Romans brought their roads and other technological advances, their legal system, and their language and culture to all of their provinces.

The wars of conquest left Rome with numerous social and economic problems at home, provoking civil wars between 133 and 30 B.C. In 59 B.C., Julius Caesar was elected Consul for a nine-year term; he then made himself ruler for life. His greatest achievement was to conquer Gaul (France), for this brought Roman culture into northern Europe. He was murdered in 44 B.C. by senators who felt that he had turned the Roman republic into a dictatorship.

Julius Caesar was followed by the joint rule of Mark Antony and Octavian. When Antony fell in love with Cleopatra, the queen of Egypt, and gave her Roman provinces as a gift, Octavian went to war against him. Octavian's forces won the famous sea battle of Actium, in 31 B.C., and conquered Alexandria, in Egypt, the following year. With the victory against Antony, one hundred years of civil wars came to an end.

Octavian inherited a dismal economic, social, and moral scene. Roman aristocrats were accustomed to being unpatriotic, selfish, and lazy. In addition, Rome was plagued by hordes of unemployed people from other levels of society—such as displaced farmers, dissatisfied war veterans, and slaves from foreign countries—who were accustomed to free bread, free entertainment, and little work. From this economic shambles, Octavian created a professional civil service (a core of trained workers that anyone of ability could join) and a permanent, professional army, which would remain on the borders of the empire and defend them.

The Roman Senate named Octavian "Augustus" (the revered), and the nature of his rule supports such a tribute. Augustus created the Golden Age of Rome. Under his leadership all Roman lands were governed as one large empire, and he instituted conditions under which the Roman world lived in peace for two hundred years, known as the Pax Romana. Augustus worked with the Roman Senate to rule Rome and the empire. He gave the Senate the power to make laws, and he consulted its members. However, he alone controlled the Roman army so that no one could overthrow him.

Under Augustus, the Romans built an elaborate system of roads throughout their empire and numerous cities. Self-government under Roman law brought a long period of prosperity and peace. This stable environment encouraged the various races and cultures of the many Roman provinces to intermingle freely. The Romans took whatever they valued from the various cultures, synthesized it, and spread this greater knowledge throughout the empire along with their public buildings, aqueducts, roads, and bridges.

Augustus also worked to revive the Roman values of a strong family dominated by the father; a respect for ancestral customs and current laws; a strong sense of justice, self-control, and piety; and loyalty both to family and country.

The Romans took their cultural heritage from the Greeks. They adopted the Greek pantheon of gods, giving most of them new Roman names. They also adopted Greek myths, architecture, sculpture, and literature. Greek tutors taught them the Greek language, and a Greek slave translated Homer into Latin between 250 and 200 B.C. The Roman poet Ovid (43 B.C.–17 A.D.) told many of the Greek myths with such skill that his stories provide the basis for most of the versions read today.

Virgil, who has for centuries been acknowledged as the greatest Roman poet, used *The Iliad* and *The Odyssey* as the basis for his great epic, *The Aeneid*, in which he glorifies Rome. Indeed, almost every significant event in *The Aeneid*—including the Trojan War, the dangerous adventures of Aeneas, the befriending of Aeneas by Dido, and the slaying of the Latin warrior Turnus—has a parallel in either *The Iliad* or *The Odyssey*.

VIRGIL AND THE AENEID

Publius Vergilius Maro (Virgil) was the son of a farmer in Mantua, but like many young men of his time, he was educated in the larger cities of Milan and Rome. Augustus recognized Virgil's great literary talent and became his patron.

Augustus had been adopted by his great-uncle, Julius Caesar; through him, Augustus traced his ancestors back to the Trojan hero Aeneas, and thus to Aeneas's divine mother, Venus. Romulus had been the legendary founder of Rome according to the Latin tradition. However, Aeneas had been considered the heroic founder of Rome within the Etruscan culture, and he was also part of the Greek historical and literary tradition. The Romans felt that the Greeks had traditionally been more civilized than the other Latin peoples, and they did not want to have arisen from barbaric ancestors. So they created close political and cultural bonds between themselves and the Greeks in whatever ways they could, including accepting Aeneas as the founder of their principal city.

The atmosphere of Rome at the time of Augustus and Virgil was optimistic and patriotic. The people felt that they were witnessing the dawn of a new age, one of peace and prosperity unprecedented in the history of the world. The fact that Rome had risen to become the major world power in such a relatively short time and from such ordinary beginnings encouraged their belief in a divine destiny for their nation. It was natural for Virgil to choose the myth of Aeneas's founding the city of Rome as the subject of an epic poem, to base the epic's content and structure upon *The Iliad* and *The Odyssey,* and to design it to glorify Augustus and his period in Roman history.

Unlike Homer, Virgil created his epic for a literate audience. The fact that he was writing for readers rather than listeners removed certain limitations and permitted a new set of standards. Virgil was not bound to an elaborate oral tradition that dictated his subject matter and many aspects of its treatment. For his audience, repetition was a liability. He could add much more detail to his plot and description, and he could afford to pay very careful attention to his choice of words and the structure of each line.

Virgil began writing *The Aeneid* in 29 B.C., two years after the battle of Actium, and he continued to work on it for the next ten years of his life. First he wrote the entire story in prose. Then he began the intense process of molding it into the style of an epic poem. Each day he created a few lines of poetry, concentrating on the structure of each line and the particular words that would best create the effect he wanted to achieve.

In 19 B.C., Virgil set out for Greece and Asia, where he intended to spend three years revising the entire poem. In Athens he met Augustus, who convinced the poet to return to Italy with him. In Megara, Virgil contracted a fever, which got steadily worse; he died of it at the age of fifty-one. As he was dying, Virgil requested that *The Aeneid* be burned, but Augustus ordered the work to be published in spite of Virgil's wishes.

APPEAL AND VALUE

The Aeneid has been valued throughout the ages, both for the nature of its story and for its style. Students and poets of many historical periods have considered it the single greatest work of literature in the world after the Bible. The great Italian poet Dante Alighieri (A.D. 1265–1321) idolized Virgil and immor-talized him in his own great epic, *The Divine Comedy.* Even Anglo-Saxon poets were influenced by his style. The Christians of the early Middle Ages were pariularly sympathetic to the virtue of Aeneas, to the higher purpose of his life, and to the conflict in the external world between the forces of good and evil, because these ideas were also present in Christianity. Most people agree that, like Homer and Shakespeare, some aspect of Virgil speaks to every generation.

The decisive event of *The Aeneid* occurs when Aeneas leaves Dido in order to found Rome. He leaves the woman he loves and sacrifices his personal desires to fulfill his destiny. His act causes a great personal tragedy, for Dido commits suicide. Although Aeneas mourns for her, his resolve to pursue his historical mission never weakens.

The central role that Aeneas's divinely sanctioned and prophesied destiny plays in *The Aeneid* is lacking in both *The Iliad* and *The Odyssey,* where human motivations predominate. For example, Odysseus leaves Calypso as Aeneas leaves Dido—but he does it simply because he wants to go home, rather than to fulfill his divinely sanctioned destiny.

THE VIRGILIAN HERO

The Virgilian hero theoretically has the power to create history by the choices he makes in life. Yet at the same time he is a pawn of the gods and, beyond them, of Fate, the mysterious power that directs and controls all events. Although some of the gods may know the hero's destiny and may be able to postpone it, even the most powerful among them cannot alter it. Prophets and deceased relatives may also know the hero's destiny, and they or the gods may reveal aspects of it to him. However, the hero's knowledge of his destiny is always limited by how much those who reveal it know and how much they choose to tell him.

The Virgilian hero must cope with beings who help him on his way, as well as with beings who deter him. Presumably, the hero is free to reject both their help and his own destiny. In reality, the nature of the hero's personality and the persuasive powers of those who reveal his destiny to him combine to make it unlikely that he will disobey their directions.

In *The Aeneid,* the Virgilian hero's destiny is good for the world in which he lives or for the world of the future. Therefore, the beings who help him are good, and those who deter him are evil. The Virgilian hero usually has one or more divine beings on his side, including his own patron god or goddess. These gods appear to him directly or in dreams and give him advice. The hero also receives advice from his deceased relatives.

In addition to beings who help him, the Virgilian hero also must cope with beings who hinder him. Various non-Virgilian heroes act as deterrents, or as forces of evil. They are being guided by their patron gods just as the Virgilian hero is being guided by his own patron divinity. The gods' intervention sometimes causes the plot of *The Aeneid* to resemble a highly competitive chess game, one in which each divinity directs his or her favorite pawns across the board. The gods may take time out from the chess game to try to manipulate one another, for like the various heroes, each immortal is either Virgilian or non-Virgilian in temperament and attitude. The gods may also influence the natural environment by sending good or bad weather to help or hinder their particular heroes.

The Virgilian hero and his divinities represent the forces of order, self-discipline, rational thinking, and constructive behavior. Opposed to them—in the world of human beings and nature, and in the world of the gods as well— are the forces of disorder, passion, irrational thinking, and violence. *The Aeneid* examines the interplay between passion and reason, war and humanity, the primitive and the civilized. Even when the Virgilian hero is destined to create order and civilization out of disorder and chaos, Virgil forces his readers to evaluate the worth of that hero's sacrifices and the nature of his victory.

PRINCIPAL CHARACTERS

THE TROJANS

AENEAS: son of the goddess Venus and Anchises; founder of what becomes the Roman people

ANCHISES: husband of Venus; father of Aeneas

ASCANIUS: son of Aeneas and his wife Creusa (daughter of Priam and Hecuba)

ACHATES: close friend of Aeneas

PRIAM: king of Troy; husband of Hecuba; father of Hector, Paris, Cassandra, Creusa, and Helenus

HECUBA: queen of Troy; wife of Priam; mother of Hector, Paris, Cassandra, Creusa, and Helenus

HECTOR: son of Priam and Hecuba; commander of the Trojan forces; greatest Trojan warrior

PARIS: son of Priam and Hecuba; abductor of Helen (wife of King Menelaus of Sparta)

HELENUS: son of Priam and Hecuba; prophet

LAOCOON: priest of Neptune in Troy

THE GREEKS

AGAMEMNON: older brother of Menelaus; king of Mycenae; commander of all Greek forces in the Trojan War

MENELAUS: younger brother of Agamemnon; king of Sparta; husband of Helen

HELEN: wife of Menelaus and queen of Sparta until abducted by Paris and taken to Troy

ULYSSES (Odysseus): master of strategies for the Greek forces

NEOPTOLEMUS: son of Achilles; great warrior in his own right

SINON: Greek spy who deceives the Trojans

THE ITALIANS

LATINUS: king of Latium; husband of Amata; father of Lavinia

AMATA: queen of Latium; wife of Latinus; mother of Lavinia

LAVINIA: daughter of Latinus and Amata; destined wife of Aeneas

TURNUS: king of the Rutulians; betrothed to Lavinia; greatest Italian warrior

EVANDER: king of Pallenteum; ally of Aeneas against the Latins

PALLAS: son of Evander; heroic young warrior

SIBYL: priestess of the oracle of Apollo in Italy

The Romans adopted the Greek gods and gave them Roman names. For a list of the gods, see page 83.

THE CARTHAGINIANS

DIDO: founder and queen of Carthage
ANNA: Dido's sister

THE AENEID

Chapter 1

Venting her hatred of the Trojans upon Aeneas and his group of Trojan refugees, Juno forces them to travel stormy seas on their way to Italy. Finally, they land near the city of Carthage, on the coast of North Africa, and meet Dido, its great queen.

I sing of arms and the man, Aeneas, who, after many years of wandering, came to Italy and the shores of Lavinium. Fate forced him to leave his homeland of Troy when the Greeks sacked Priam's great city. Then cruel Juno, with unrelenting hatred for all Trojans, forced him to endure stormy seas and war in Italy before he could build a city there and bring his gods into Latium, thus establishing the Latin race, the lords of Alba Longa, and high-walled Rome.

Goddess, tell me why the Queen of Olympus forced such a good man to endure so much suffering and danger. Was it not enough that the Trojans were defeated by the Greeks and pitiless Achilles? Yet Juno has kept them wandering for seven years, driven over all the seas and always far from Latium. Why does one of the immortal gods harbor so fierce an anger?

Above all other lands Juno loved the ancient city of Carthage. The city had been founded by its queen Dido and other settlers from Tyre (in Phoenicia) and was famed for its wealth and its skill in war. However, Juno knew that some day an aggressive people of Trojan descent, who ruled many other lands, was fated to conquer her fair city. Moreover, the Queen of Olympus had not forgotten Paris's judgment against her beauty, and even the Trojans' defeat at the hands of the Greeks had not satisfied her hatred.

"Why should I allow their fate to prevent me from punishing the Trojans before they reach Italy?" Juno thought. "If Minerva can sink Greek ships and drown their sailors because of the arrogance of one Greek leader, surely I—the queen of the gods, and the sister and wife of Jupiter—should be able to subdue this people."

With such thoughts enraging her heart, Juno came to Aeolia, homeland of storm clouds, where King Aeolus confines and soothes the struggling winds and the roaring gales deep in a dreary cave. "Aeolus," she greeted him, "a people whom I hate are sailing the Phoenician seas, bringing Troy's household gods into Italy. I want you to arouse your mighty winds and hurl them furiously upon these Trojans, sinking their ships and strewing their bodies upon the waves of the sea."

"I will do as you wish," replied Aeolus, "for you and Jupiter have made me lord of clouds and storms." He struck the side of the cave with his spear, commanding the winds to emerge and attack the Trojan ships with mighty waves and great gales.

As the Trojans watched, clouds suddenly turned day into night. The men cried out with dread as flashes of lightning illuminated the clouds and the rumbling of thunder surrounded them. Aeneas stretched his arms toward the heavens and cried, "Compared to us, three and four times blessed are those who were fated to die before their fathers' eyes upon the plain of Troy!"

His words were followed by a shrieking gust of wind that struck his sail full force and raised mountainous waves, causing the oars to snap and the ship to turn broadside to the waves. As water cascaded into the ship, the sailors were washed overboard. Some were carried high upon the crests, while others could glimpse the ground between the swells. The storm drove three ships upon concealed rocks; three others were forced upon a willow sandbar. One was completely swallowed by a swirling whirlpool of waters. The sea now wore the planking of ships and the bodies of men intermingled with its collection of weapons of war and Trojan treasure.

When Neptune became aware of this wild turbulence, he raised his head above the waves in order to learn more about the storm. He immediately recognized his sister Juno's anger behind the destruction of Aeneas's fleet, so he summoned the East Wind and the West Wind and said, "How dare you raise such a tempest without my command? Return quickly to your king and remind him that I, and not he, am the Lord of the Sea!"

Neptune calmed the sea and sent the clouds away, letting the sun shine forth once more. As when argument and strife tear apart a great country, and the common folk rage at one another until suddenly they see a man honored for his good character and worthy service, and they become silent and listen attentively while he soothes their passion with his words, so the sea sank into silent submission as the Lord of the Sea drove his chariot over the waters.

Aeneas and his remaining companions, weary from battling the sea, headed for the coast of Libya, which was the closest shore. Upon finding a good harbor, the seven remaining ships pulled into the sheltered waters. The Trojans disembarked, glad to feel firm ground beneath their feet.

Aeneas and his companion, Achates, set off to see what they could learn about their missing ships. From the edge of a nearby cliff they had a good view of the sea, but they could see no sign of the ships. They did see three huge stags, each leading a herd of deer, grazing along the shore. Aeneas took his bow from Achates and shot the three leading stags and four other large remaining deer, providing one deer for each of the ships. Then the two men descended the cliff, picked up the deer, and carried them back to the ships, where Aeneas divided them among his company.

As Jupiter looked down upon them, Venus approached him, her eyes brimming with tears. "Oh, Ruler of the Gods, what terrible crimes have Aeneas and the Trojans committed that they cannot reach Italy? You promised that from their lineage would be born the Romans, a people who would rule both land and sea. Is this how you reward my son's virtue?"

The Father of Gods and Mortals smiled and replied, "Have no fear, Daughter. I have not changed my mind, nor has the fate of your Trojans changed. You will see the city of Lavinium and the fame of great-souled Aeneas. Then his son, Ascanius, will move the capital to Alba Longa, where for three hundred years Hector's race will rule Italy. Finally, the priestess Ilia will bear twins to Mars, and one of them, Romulus, will found Rome.

"The Romans will rule with no divine limit upon either the extent of their lands or the duration of their power. The day will come when the Roman descendants of the Trojans will conquer Phthia, the city of Peleus and Achilles; Argos; and Agamemnon's famous Mycenae.

"Augustus Caesar will be born from this noble line of Trojans," Jupiter continued. "Only the oceans will limit his empire, and the stars alone will limit his glory. This renowned Caesar will close the temple of Janus, imprisoning within it savage Rage. Sitting on his death-dealing weapons, with his hands tied in one hundred bronze knots, this Fury, powerless, will shriek with ghastly, bloodstained lips. Then wars will cease, and an age of law will reign on earth. In spite of her present anger, Juno, too, will cherish the Roman people, who will rule the world. Fate has willed it so."

With these words Jupiter sent his messenger, Mercury, down to Carthage, so that Dido, ignorant of her fate, would welcome the Trojans. Because it was the will of Jupiter, the people of Carthage put aside their warlike thoughts, and their mighty queen became compassionate toward the Trojans.

With the light of morning, Aeneas concealed his ships within the shelter of a hollow rock and, with Achates, set forth to explore the strange country. Soon he saw his mother, Venus, disguised as a young huntress, come across his path.

"Tell me, young men," she began, "have you seen my sister hunting in this area?"

"I have neither heard nor seen your sister," Aeneas replied, "but who are you? You look and sound like a goddess. Please tell us, if you will, where we are. We were driven here by a storm at sea and have no idea who lives here."

"A people native to Tyre live here in the city they are building, called Carthage," Venus explained. "The powerful kingdom of Libya surrounds them. Dido, their queen, founded this city when she fled from her brother after he killed her husband. But who are you? Where are you from? And where are you going?"

"I am from ancient Troy, goddess, if the name means anything to you," Aeneas replied. "I am Aeneas the Good, and my fame is known on Mount Olympus. I am carrying with me my household gods that I saved from enemy hands, and I am heading for Italy, my new country. Of the twenty ships I started with, only seven remain, and these have been heavily damaged by wind and waves."

"Whoever you are," Venus said, "the immortal gods must favor you, or you would not have survived to reach this city. Just follow the path, and go to the queen's palace. Unless my parents only pretended to teach me the art of prophecy, you will find that the winds have driven your missing ships and the men who sailed upon them safely into Carthage."

Venus concealed Aeneas and Achates in a thick fog so that they could enter the city without being seen or questioned. Their path took them to the top of a hill from which they could survey the city below. Aeneas marveled at the impressive buildings and the paved roads. Everywhere workers were busy with more construction. As bees in early summer go about their tasks of making honey, some busy in the sunshine gathering nectar from fields of flowers and others storing the liquid in cells bursting with sweet honey, so the people of Tyre were hard at work building their new city.

Concealed in the fog, Aeneas and Achates entered the majestic temple dedicated to Juno. As soon as Queen Dido arrived and seated herself, their lost shipmates came forward to speak with her.

"Oh, Queen, whom Jupiter has permitted to found this new city," their spokesman began, "we unhappy Trojans ask you to spare our ships and our lives. We have not come to attack you or to rob your homes. We have been driven by storms from sea to sea and have lost our king, Aeneas, greatest of all men in virtue and in deeds of war. Allow us to beach our storm-shattered ships while we fashion new planks and oars. If we find our king and our comrades, we will sail to Italy and Latium. If not, we will return the way we came to those among our people who have settled near the straits of Sicily."

Dido replied, "Put all fear from your hearts, Trojans. We are aware of Aeneas's people, of Troy's brave soldiers and their deeds in the war against the Greeks. If you wish to return to Sicily, I will send you forth with an escort for your safety and with wealth to sustain you. If you prefer, you may remain in my city. I will not distinguish between Tyrian and Trojan. Meanwhile, beach your ships while I send scouts along the coast and through Libya. Aeneas may have been shipwrecked along the way."

The mist suddenly disappeared, revealing Achates and godlike Aeneas, whom Venus made radiant. "Here I stand before you," Aeneas said, "Aeneas of Troy, snatched from the Libyan waves. Neither words nor deeds can thank you, Dido, for offering to share your home and your city with us. If the immortal gods respect virtue and justice, may they reward you."

"What fate drives you through such dangers, Aeneas?" Dido asked as she led him inside the palace. "Unhappy fortune has driven me also through evil times, but at last I have found peace in this land."

While Dido sent a feast down to Aeneas's comrades in the harbor, Aeneas asked Achates to bring his small son, Ascanius, to the palace, along with gifts snatched from the flames of Troy.

At the same time, Venus decided that it would help protect Aeneas against Juno's schemes if Dido were passionately in love with him. So the goddess called her son Cupid to her side and said, "For just this one night, pretend to be Ascanius, and when Dido hugs you at the feast, breathe into her the hidden fire and poison of passion."

Everything went according to Venus's plan. As Dido listened to Aeneas and embraced Cupid, thinking him to be Aeneas's young son, her love for her dead husband faded, and a living passion for Aeneas invaded her sleeping heart. To prolong the evening, Dido continued to question Aeneas about Priam, Hector, and Achilles. Finally, she said, "Tell us, from the beginning, about the strategy the Greeks devised to capture Troy, about the suffering of your people, and about your wanderings over land and sea for these seven long summers."

Chapter 2

Aeneas tells Dido about the Trojan horse and the destruction of Troy.

The Tyrians sat in hushed silence, all eyes directed upon Aeneas as he began to speak.

Words cannot express, oh Queen, the grief you are asking me to remember: how the Greeks overthrew Troy's great and wealthy kingdom and the sickening sights I saw. Even a warrior like Achilles or stern Ulysses could not refrain from tears as he told such a tale! However, if you wish to hear about Troy's destruction, I will tell you, though my mind shudders to remember the events and recoils in pain from the details.

Being unable to conquer Troy through the skills of war in nine years of fighting, the Greek leaders decide to follow Minerva's instruction and build a horse of mountainous bulk from the wood of the fir tree. They pretend that it is a religious offering and let such a rumor spread throughout Troy. Meanwhile, deep inside the horse's cavernous belly, the devious Greeks secretly hide a group of armed warriors, chosen for their courage and skill.

We think that the Greek forces are sailing back to Mycenae, but, in fact, their ships are hidden upon the barren shore of Tenedos, an island near Troy. So we rejoice to be free of war at last. The Scaean Gates are opened to all, and the people venture forth to see where Achilles camped, where the Greek ships were beached, and where the battles were fought.

Many stare in wonder at Minerva's deadly gift. Some among us are certain that we should drag the horse within our walls, but others, who are wiser in counsel, advise us to hurl this strange Greek gift into the sea, or to heap flames beneath it to feed upon it, or, at least, to explore its hollow belly by piercing its wooden sides with our spears. Noisily the crowd argues, this way or that.

Then the priest of Neptune, Laocoon, comes running down from the fortress, calling to us from afar, "Oh wretched citizens, you must have lost your senses! Do you believe the Greeks have sailed homeward? Do you imagine that any Greek gifts are without guile? Do you not know Ulysses? Either Greek warriors are hiding within the wooden body of this beast, or this is a war device that can look beyond our walls and into our homes. Some evil surely lurks within its belly or will descend upon our city from above. Do not trust the horse, Trojans. No matter how it appears, I fear the Greeks, even when they bear gifts."

With these words the priest hurls his great spear with mighty force into the curved side of the horse. As the spear quivers in the wooden belly, the cavernous interior emits a hollow, groaning sound. If the gods had supported us and our judgment had been sound, Laocoon would have convinced us to destroy the Greek sanctuary with our bronze weapons. Then Priam's great city would still be standing. However, the priest's counsel falls upon deaf ears.

Meanwhile, the shouts of some Trojan shepherds draw our attention toward a young man they are dragging before Priam. With his hands tied behind his back, the prisoner is so obviously at our mercy that we do not question his honesty. It does not occur to us that he has courageously chosen to place himself where we would discover him and that he is prepared to deceive us with his lies or to die as our prisoner. Our youth immediately approach him from all sides and taunt him. But as soon as he speaks, he will teach all of you how treacherous the Greeks are.

The prisoner stands among us, unarmed and afraid. "Alas!" he cries. "What land or sea will take me? What fate will next befall me? The Greeks have cast me away, and the Trojans angrily clamor for my death."

With these words he arouses our sympathy. "Tell us who you are and where you are from," we reply, "and why you are here."

When he is no longer afraid, he says, "I will tell you the truth, oh King, come what may. I, the most unfortunate of men, am called Sinon, and I am of Greek birth. But I do not want to tell you a tale that does not interest you. If you hate all Greeks just because of their birth, then kill me now. Ulysses would be pleased, and Agamemnon would pay you to do it!"

Then, of course, we cannot wait to hear his story. Trembling, the prisoner begins his tale, speaking with guile and with false feeling.

"Often the Greeks wished to retreat, being weary of the tiresome war and longing for home. How I wish that they had done so! Many times a severe tempest at sea frightened them and kept them on Trojan soil. Then, when the wooden framework of this horse had already been built, storm clouds rumbled throughout the sky. The soldiers could not interpret the omen, so they asked the oracle of Apollo. The god responded, 'In order to reach the shores of Troy, oh Greeks, you had to appease the winds with the blood of a maiden's sacrifice. Now, in order to return to your homeland, you will have to please the winds with the blood of a warrior's sacrifice.'

"When the Greeks heard these words, their hearts froze and a cold shudder ran through them. Whom was Apollo choosing? Ulysses dragged the prophet Calchas forward and told him to discover Apollo's will. Calchas sat speechless in his tent for ten days, refusing to proclaim a warrior's death. Finally, the demands of the Greeks overcame his reluctance, and he announced my doom. Of course no one objected, for each was relieved that my fate was not his own.

"When the day I dreaded arrived, I ran from death. I broke my bonds and hid for the night in a marsh. I hoped that the Greeks would sail away without discovering me, and they did. Now I can never hope to see my homeland, my loving children, or my dear father. I am sorry that the Greeks may make my family atone for my crime by demanding the life of one of them in my place. But I ask you, by the gods above, to pity me, for I do not deserve such suffering."

We cannot resist the prisoner's plea. We not only pity him, we grant him life. Priam commands that his bonds be removed and then addresses him with kind words.

"Forget that the Greeks were your people," the king tells him. "From this time forth, you are one of us. Now explain to me truthfully: Why have the Greeks constructed this monstrous horse? Who designed it, and why? Is it a weapon of war? An offering to one of the gods?"

The young man raises his arms to the heavens and replies, "May I be free to put aside my loyalty to the Greeks and hate them for the suffering they have caused me. I am no longer bound by the laws of any country, so surely I can reveal their secret purpose. Only keep your promise, Trojans, and save me in return for the help I am giving you.

"From the beginning of the war, the Greeks could count on Minerva to help them. But this year the Greeks captured your prophet and forced him to tell them how they could win. The clever Trojan told them that they first would have to remove from Troy the statue of Minerva. So Ulysses, the contriver of crime, and the ungodly Diomedes secretly enlisted the help of Helen and stole the statue from its shrine, defiling it with their bloody hands. From that time on, Minerva ceased to favor the Greeks, and their strength was broken.

"As soon as they placed the statue in their camp, its eyes flashed with flames, salty sweat ran down its body, and three times the goddess herself leaped from the ground with her shield and quivering spear. Their prophet then told them that they would not be able to take Troy unless they first returned to Argos and found new, favorable omens there. So the Greeks are sailing for Mycenae, but they will return.

"Meanwhile, the Greeks have followed Calchas's counsel and have left this huge wooden horse here in order to atone for their insult to Minerva. The prophet commanded them to build it so large that you Trojans could not bring it through your gates and have it protect you. For if you move the horse into your great city, then you are fated to take the war across the sea to the cities of the Greeks and destroy them. On the other hand, if you harm this gift to Minerva, then Priam's country is doomed to utter destruction."

So well does Sinon tell this tale that we believe him. His guile and tears conquer us when ten years of Achilles could not! Then we see the most dreadful omen: Laocoon is sacrificing a mighty bull upon the altar of Neptune when, over the peaceful sea from Tenedos—I shudder to remember—we see two snakes with countless coils glide through the waters side by side and head for our shore. Their heads rise high above the wave, and the rest skims along the surface of the water behind them in endless coils, causing the sea to foam and roar. Their eyes blaze forth with blood and fire, and quivering tongues dart from their hissing mouths. We watch them as they cross the land and head directly for Laocoon. Then, terrified, we run from the site.

Upon reaching the altar, the two snakes coil themselves around the bodies of Laocoon's two young sons, enfolding them in a deadly embrace and sinking their fangs into the children's soft flesh. Then, as their father raises his weapons against them, the serpents entwine themselves around him, twice winding themselves around his waist, twice encircling their scaly bodies around his throat, and raising their heads high above his own.

Laocoon is covered with their poisonous black venom and gore. He strains his hands to tear their deadly coils from him, and he screams to heaven, as a wounded bull bellows as it shrugs off a poorly aimed axe and runs from the altar, but he is helpless. With the death of the priest, the serpents glide away to Minerva's shrine, where they take refuge under the goddess' feet and the curve of her shield.

This omen horrifies us. "Laocoon has been punished for his crime," some say. "He hurled his spear into the sacred body of the horse and angered Minerva."

"Pull the horse within the walls to Minerva's shrine," everyone cries. "We must atone for our priest's deed!"

So we make an opening in our walls, clearing the way into the city. Everyone takes part in the work. We place sliding rollers under the horse's feet, tie ropes around its neck, and then pull the monster up our walls. As it moves forward, boys and maidens sing hymns and happily handle the rope halter. So the horse glides dangerously into the very center of Priam's great city. Oh, Troy, famous in war!

Four times the horse halts near the gates to the city, and four times armor sounds within its cavernous belly. Yet, with ears that do not hear and eyes blinded by fright, we push it ever forward, until the ill-omened monster finally rests within our city walls. Even when Priam's daughter Cassandra reveals to us our coming doom, we do not believe her, for Apollo's angry gift to her was to be able to predict the future but not to be believed. And at the close of day, never aware that it is our last, we joyously decorate the shrines of the gods with colorful wreaths and begin an evening of celebration.

In time, night rises from the sea, wrapping in its mighty robe earth and sky and the scheming Greeks. While we sleep in comfort, unaware of our fate, the Greek ships leave the island of Tenedos and return to the familiar shores of Troy. Then, when Agamemnon's royal ship sends forth a flaming signal, Sinon quietly approaches the monstrous horse and opens its secret hatch.

Joyfully the Greek leaders, one by one, leave the monster's belly and slide down the lowered cable into the night air. Dreadful Ulysses, Menelaus, Neoptolemus, who is the son of Achilles, and Epeus, who designed this devious device, are among them. They kill our guards, open the gates to our city, and welcome back their thousands of companions. Then they attack while we sleep.

Chapter 3

Aeneas continues his story, describing to Dido the destruction of Troy.

While I am asleep the figure of Hector, weeping, appears before my eyes. His hair is coated with blood, his body is black with gory dust, and his swollen feet are still punctured with the thongs Achilles used to drag his body around the walls of our city. "Run, goddess-born!" he cries to me. "Save yourself from the flames! The Greeks hold our walls, and Troy is burning to the ground. You have done all you can for Priam and our country. If strength could have saved Troy, the Greeks would never have breached our walls. Troy now gives to you her holy things and her household gods. Take them with you as you search for the place you will establish a city." With these words he brings forth the cloth bands, the eternal fire, and the Great Goddess Vesta from their inner shrine.

As I force myself to awaken, I fear that I recognize the sounds of war in the distance—screams, cries, the clash of armor on every side. I climb up to the roof of my father's house and strain my ears to learn more, for land and trees stand between our house and the rest of Troy. As a lone shepherd high upon a rocky peak hears the far roar of a swollen mountain stream as it buries the crops and hurls down the forest, so I become aware of Troy's destruction. Now I understand the meaning of Sinon and the monstrous wooden horse. The Greeks' treacherous scheme has succeeded.

I rush inside and grab my weapons. I know that I will not have time to use them, but my heart blazes with rage and resentment. I long to gather a group of my comrades and fight the Greeks to the death, for that is the most honorable way to die.

At my door I find Panthus, priest of Apollo and father of Hector's friend, the wise Polydamas. He holds his grandchild with one hand and carries the sacred articles and the household gods in the other. "Troy's last hour is upon us!" he cries. "Troy is dead, the Trojan people are dead, and our great glory is dead. Jupiter has given everything to the Greeks, who now are lords in our burning city. Armed warriors issue forth from the monstrous horse, and Sinon, arrogant with victory, spreads flames wherever he goes. Thousands of Greek warriors are everywhere among us, guarding our wide-open gates and barring passage on our narrow streets."

I take the sacred objects from him and prepare to do my part for my country. I go out to the moonlit streets, and my companions gather around me. When I see that they, too, are eager for battle, I tell them, "Men, if your hearts lead you to be courageous in this hopeless cause, follow me. The fate of our people is clear. The gods who supported our kingdom have left us, and our city is in flames. Let us die fighting!"

Who can describe to you the chaos of that night? Who can describe its bloodshed? Whose tears can equal our troubles? Like ravenous wolves in a black fog, whose hunger drives them blindly forth and whose cubs wait back in their den with tongues that already taste the food they expect, so we go forth, sheltered by black night, into the heart of our city to meet certain death. We gaze upon the queen of cities, now fallen. We step among the piles of lifeless bodies that litter the streets. Not all the corpses are Trojan, however. We who have been conquered summon enough strength and courage to take many of our Greek victors on man's long, last journey. Most of my companions are killed. Pain is everywhere; panic is everywhere; and Death is everywhere!

The clash of weapons draws us to Priam's palace, where a terrible battle rages. Ladders cling to the walls; Greek warriors clutch them with one hand and in the other hand hold a shield against an attack of arrows. Meanwhile, Trojans are on the roof, tearing down the towers and ripping up the roof, using whatever objects they can find as weapons for their final self-defense. We make our way to the roof to help the defenders. Below, other Trojans guard the doorways to the interior of the palace.

From the roof we see Neoptolemus, Achilles' son, leading a group of warriors to Priam and Hecuba's private rooms. As a snake fed on poisonous plants casts off its old skin and emerges from its hole with the warm days of spring, shining with the splendor of youth, and flicks its three-forked tongue from its mouth, so Neoptolemus shines in his father's lustrous, bronze armor. Using his battle axe, he bursts through the doorway, tearing the bronze-plated doors from their hinges.

Neoptolemus forces his way into the confusion with the strength of his father. Neither bolts nor guards can stop him. A foaming river that bursts its banks and overflows, its violent motion tearing away all barriers as it rushes furiously over the fields, sweeping herds and pens away, is more calm than this son of Achilles.

I also see Hecuba, with her one hundred daughters, and Priam. The old king has put his long-abandoned armor upon his aged shoulders, grabbed his useless sword, and is preparing to meet his death among the invading Greeks. Hecuba and her women have tried to take refuge among the household shrines. They press together there, clutching the statues of the gods, like doves driven forth by a black tempest.

When Hecuba sees her husband in the armor of his youth, she asks him, "What madness moves you to put on your old armor? Where do you intend to go? Even if Hector were here, you could do nothing to save us. Come join me. Either this sacred altar will protect us, or we will die together."

Then one of Priam's sons comes running toward his parents. Through enemies and arrows he desperately tries to escape Neoptolemus's sword. Finally, Achilles' son spears him through the back, and the boy falls dead at the feet of his parents.

Being face to face with death does not silence the old king's fury or his tongue. "May the gods reward you as you deserve for making a father view the murder of his son!" he exclaims.

"Achilles, the warrior you falsely claim as your father, treated his enemy Priam more respectfully than this!" The old king hurls his spear at Neoptolemus, but his arm is so weak that the spear merely catches upon a bronze decoration on Achilles' great shield and hangs there harmlessly.

Neoptolemus replies, "I will send you to my father with a message. Tell him how poorly I fight and how shameful I am! Now die!" He pulls the trembling old king toward the altar. When Priam slips in the pool of his dead son's blood, Neoptolemus grabs Priam's hair in his left hand and with his right hand plunges his flashing sword into the old king's side.

So ends the life of one of the great kings of Asia. He was doomed to live long enough to see his sons murdered and his city in flames. His corpse now lies by the shore of the sea, a headless, nameless body.

As I gaze upon the dead king, in my mind I see my own father, my wife and son, and our plundered house. When the vision leaves me, I find that I am alone. The women have either leaped to the ground far below or have thrown themselves into the fire.

Suddenly, in the light of the fires, I notice Helen quietly hiding by the shrine of Vesta. The hateful woman is at a loss. She knows the Trojans despise her for causing the destruction of Troy. On the other hand, she fears the vengeance of the Greeks and the anger of Menelaus, whom she abandoned. My heart blazes with resentment as I gaze at the source of all our woes, and I want to make her pay for all of the death and destruction. For her sake, Troy has burned. For her sake, Trojan land is soaked with blood. For her sake, our good king has been murdered.

Without thinking, I say aloud, "How will Helen pay for her crime? Will she sail back to Sparta without injury, a queen returning in triumph from a major victory? Will she have the pleasure of returning to her father's house and living among her family? There is no honor in killing a woman, yet it will bring me great satisfaction to avenge the ashes of my family."

Suddenly, my mother appears before me in all of her divine radiance. "My son," she says, "it is not Helen or Paris who is to blame; the gods have destroyed Troy. Now return home and see if your father, your wife, and your child are still alive. If my love of your family had not prevented it, Greek swords would have drunk their blood, and flames would have consumed their bodies."

My first thought when I return home is to carry my aged father to the safety of the hills. But he steadfastly refuses my pleas. "You are young and strong enough to flee," he tells me. "I will take my own life and leave my possessions to the Greeks."

I look at my father aghast. "Do you expect me to flee and leave you here?" I ask him. "If the gods intend to burn our great city to the ground and you firmly intend to remain here, then Neoptolemus, who is already bathed in Priam's blood, who murders the son in front of his father by a sacred shrine, that Neoptolemus will bring death here.

"Is this why you brought me home, Mother? Did you save me from the sword and the fire so that I could watch the Greeks enter my house and murder my father, my wife, and my son? Never! I will die fighting the Greeks and avenging our people!"

I have put on my sword and have my shield upon my arm when my wife holds up our little son and pleads with me. "If you are leaving here to die," she says, "then take us with you, for you are abandoning us to the Greeks. Otherwise, use your armor to defend your own home."

And as my wife stands there weeping, a wondrous omen appears. Upon the head of our little son, Ascanius, flames that do not burn suddenly play upon his hair, illuminating his face with their ruddy glow. Frightened by the blaze, we quickly quench the holy fire with water.

But my father joyously raises his eyes and his arms to the heavens and prays, "Jupiter, Father of Gods and Men, if we deserve your favor, confirm this omen with some sign." He has hardly finished speaking when we hear a sudden crack of thunder and see a star shoot down from the heavens into the forest, leaving a trail of light in the evening sky. "Now I will go with you, my son," Anchises tells me, "wherever you lead us. Gods of my fathers!" he prays. "Save my house and my grandson. If you have sent this omen, then Troy must remain under your protection."

By this time, I can hear that the roaring flames are closer to us. "If we do not leave here quickly, we will be engulfed in a flood of fire," I tell my family. I then spread a lion's skin over my shoulders and neck, stoop down, and say, "Come, father, climb upon my shoulders, and hold onto my neck. Carry with you the sacred objects and Troy's household gods. It is not right for me to carry them until I have washed off the blood of battle in a bubbling stream. Whatever happens, you and I will endure it together. Little Ascanius, take my hand and try to keep up with me. Wife, follow us quickly!"

We pass through burning Troy, protected by the darkness. As we approach the gates, my father cries, "Run, my son! I see the bronze shields of the Greeks drawing near!"

Fearing for my father and my son, I head for the back streets and a more devious course, forgetting that my wife is behind us. So I lose her to Troy's shadows. I never know whether she stops, or whether she tries to follow and loses us. I do not even think to look back for her until we reach the mound sacred to Ceres, where we find our household servants.

Then, of course, I am frantic! I leave Anchises and Ascanius in a hidden spot and run back home, trying to retrace my steps. I do not see my wife, but towering flames are devouring our house. In a mad frenzy I rush among the city's ruins, calling her name again and again.

Suddenly the sad form of my wife appears before my eyes. As I stand speechless, the vision says, "Do not sorrow, dear husband. The lord of high Olympus will not permit me to join you on your journey. Years of wandering are your fate, followed by kingship, a royal wife, and satisfaction in the rich land that surrounds the Tiber River. I will never be a slave to some Greek woman, but will stay here with Cybele, the great mother of the gods. Love our child. Farewell."

I stand there, weeping, with so much I want to say to her. Three times I try to embrace her, but each time the vision escapes my grasp, drifting away like a light breeze. Finally, with the coming of dawn, I return to my family.

To my surprise a large number of Trojans have joined us and are prepared to follow me wherever I lead them. Since Greeks are guarding the city gates, we leave by back roads toward the mountains.

Chapter 4

Aeneas finishes his tale by telling Dido about his wanderings.

Once we have built our ships, we leave our homeland and set out to sea. We sail for days through tempests and for nights without a star to guide us. We are now far off our course. Finally, I see mountains and rising smoke ahead, so we sail in that direction.

Leaving our ships in a good harbor, we move quickly to spear some of the untended cattle and goats that we see scattered about us. As we sit down to a feast of fresh food, we call upon Jupiter and the other gods to share it with us.

Suddenly, we hear the noisy clanging of large wings. Looking up, we see huge winged creatures swooping down toward us from the mountains. The Harpies are upon us! These monstrous birds have the face of a woman—but thin and drawn with hunger—bronze feathers, clawed hands, and a dreadful scream. As they fly above our food, they snatch whatever they wish and spoil all the rest by dropping their foul-smelling filth upon it.

We then notice a deep, recessed area beneath an overhanging rock that is surrounded by bushes. Since it looks well-protected, we set up a fresh feast there. However, from some hidden home in the opposite direction, the noisy birds dive upon us once again, snatching and spoiling our food as before.

In hungry desperation, we hide our shields and keep our swords deep in the grass ready for their next assault. When the filthy birds arrive, we are waiting for them. But we have little success. Swords cannot wound their bodies and blows do not injure their wings. We chase them away, but they have fouled our food once again.

Then I notice that one Harpy has remained behind, perched on a high rock. "Are you bringing war upon us, Trojans? Would you drive innocent Harpies from their homeland? You have butchered our cattle and have fought us. Now plant these words in your heart. What Jupiter told Apollo and Apollo told me, I, the first-born of the Harpies, will reveal to you.

"You are bound for Italy, and her harbors will welcome you," the Harpy foretells. "However, because of your violence toward us, you will not build the walls of your fated city until you are so famished that you chew and swallow your tables!" With these shrill words, the bird-like monster flies off into the forest.

My companions become so frightened that their blood freezes. With prayers to the gods, we hastily leave this country. We sail past Ulysses' kingdom of Ithaca and curse the land that sustained him. Eventually, we reach the city where Priam's son, the prophet Helenus, now rules.

After we have been warmly welcomed, I ask Helenus about the Harpy's prophecy. "Oh, goddess-born," he replies, "do not fear the chewing of your tables, for the Fates will find a way to help you. Meanwhile, since Jupiter is in charge of your destiny, I will tell you how to travel safely over the seas.

"You are close to Italy," Helenus begins. "But you must sail past Circe's island and avoid the shores of Italy that are washed by the tide of our own sea, for evil Greeks dwell there. When you reach the coast of Sicily, sail to the left even though the route is a long one. By all means avoid the shore and the water on the right, for that marks a narrow channel between Sicily and Italy. The monster Scylla guards the right side of the strait, while greedy Charybdis guards the left.

"Three times each day, Charybdis swallows the sea and then hurls it into the heavens, lashing the heavens with water. Scylla lives in a deep cave. Above the waist she has a human form; below she is a monstrous sea-dragon, with dolphin's tails joined to her stomach, which is covered with wolves. With her mouths she pulls ships upon the rocks. It is far better to travel the long way around than to meet Scylla in her huge cave above the rocks.

"When you reach the shores of Italy," Helenus concludes, "find the town of Cumae, for a prophetess lives deep in a rocky cave there, chanting prophecies and writing them on leaves. She will tell you about the nations of Italy, future wars, and the proper way to perform or avoid every labor. In the end, she will grant you a good voyage. Finally, I advise you always to honor Juno first in your prayers, and try to win her favor with gifts."

Having received this prophecy from Helenus, we sail forth once again. In time, we can see Mount Aetna on Sicily. In the distance, we hear the roar of the waves upon rocks. We are certain that we have reached the channel of Scylla and Charybdis, so we head into the tossing sea to our left. The winds have stirred up the waves to lofty heights. First our ships seem to climb up to the heavens upon a mountain of water, and then they swiftly drop down to the depths of the sea.

Finally we enter a large, safe harbor and go ashore for the night. Nearby, Mount Aetna terrifies us with its thunder and hurls blazing rocks into the heavens. We hide in the forest and try to forget the monstrous noises that seem to surround us all night long.

The next morning, when Dawn has brushed the shade from the sky, a strange man comes out of the woods and stretches forth pleading hands to us. He seems starved for food. His face is as pale as death, his beard is unshaven, and from what remains of his tattered clothing, he appears to have once been a Greek warrior.

As soon as he notices our Trojan clothing and weapons, he becomes afraid. But his desperate need overcomes his fear, and he rushes toward us, asking us to take him away with us. Once my father assures him that he is safe with us, he tells us what has happened to him.

"I come from the country of Ithaca, and I was a comrade of the unfortunate Ulysses. I went to Troy with him and left with him, but he abandoned me here in the huge cave of the Cyclops Polyphemus.

"That den is as dark as it is vast," he continues, "and its floor and walls are littered with the remains of bloody feasts and gore. The giant who lives there strikes the sky with his head when he stands upright—may the gods remove this monster from the earth!—and one cannot safely speak with him, for he feeds on human flesh and blood. Before my eyes, he seized two of my companions in his monstrous hand, crushed their bodies upon the rocky wall of his cave, and ate them.

"Yet Ulysses would not let the Cyclops' bloodthirsty deeds remain unpunished. When Polyphemus had gorged himself upon his human feast, Ulysses offered him such great quantities of tasty wine that he sank to the floor of his cave in a drunken sleep. While pieces of flesh mixed with blood and wine dribbled from his mouth, we prayed to the gods and treated him with the same kind of courtesy he had shown our companions. Together, we raised a large, pointed pole and pierced the one great eye that lies beneath his savage brow.

"My companions managed to escape, but in their haste, they forgot that I was not with them. By the time I escaped from the cave, they had already sailed."

The Greek then counsels, "We should quickly board the ships and leave this terrible place, for one hundred other monstrous Cyclopes shepherd their flocks upon these mountains and live along these shores. I have been hiding from them in the forest for three full moons, in constant fear of the sound of their footsteps and their voices. I have lived on nuts, berries, and roots, all the time hoping to see a ship pass by. I prefer to die by your hands than to be eaten by one of the Cyclopes!"

The Greek has barely finished his tale when we see Polyphemus heading down to the shore from the mountaintop with his flocks. The blind monster is terrifying as he steadies himself with his staff; even without sight, he moves swiftly and surely down the familiar trail. When he reaches the sea, he walks into the waves and washes away the blood that constantly oozes from his eye socket, groaning and grinding his teeth with the pain. Then he strides through the open sea, whose water reaches only as high as his waist.

We make every effort to leave the harbor quickly and silently, but Polyphemus hears the sound of our oars. He turns toward the sound, and when he cannot see us to grab us, he gives a mighty roar. The other Cyclopes, hearing him, run down from the mountains and out of the woods. We watch them gather upon the shores of the harbor and glare at us, but we seem to be safely out of their reach.

In our terror, our first thought is to sail in any direction as long as we move quickly, but we remember Helenus's warnings about Scylla and Charybdis and avoid their channel.

My final trial before reaching Carthage is the death of my dear father. Neither the Harpy nor Helenus had mentioned that sorrow to me.

With these words Aeneas concluded the tale of his wanderings and was silent.

Chapter 5

Dido and Aeneas love each other, and for a time Aeneas forgets his obligation. Aeneas leaves Carthage and Dido commits suicide.

Dido was so in love with Aeneas that all she could think about were his appearance, his words, his deeds. When Dawn lighted the earth with the lamp of Apollo, the queen confided in her sister.

"Anna," she said, "my dreams frighten me. This Trojan stranger who is our guest is so noble and brave that I fear I might marry him in spite of my firm decision never to marry again. Aeneas has rekindled a flame within me, and I must confess that he is the first man to weaken my resolve since my dear husband died."

"Oh, dearest," Anna replied, "do you intend to live your entire life lonely and sad, without ever enjoying love and motherhood? Do you think that the buried shade of your husband would appreciate such a sacrifice?

"I think the Trojan ships have been directed here by Juno," she continued. "What a great city would result from your marriage to Aeneas! With Trojan weapons to help us, what glory we could win! I advise you to make pleasing sacrifices to the gods, give Aeneas the warmest welcome, and delay his departure as long as possible. It is to your advantage that his ships are shattered and winter passage upon the sea is stormy."

Her sister's words relieved Dido's guilt, put hope into her heart, and fanned the passions that burned within her. As a deer is struck with an arrow from the bow of a shepherd, who is hunting from such a distance that he does not know it has reached its target, and the deer is forced to run through woods and meadows with the deadly shaft clinging firmly to its side, so Dido wandered with Aeneas through the city of Carthage with Cupid's arrow burning within her.

She could not hear the sad story of Troy too many times, and even when she was not with Aeneas, in her mind she saw him and heard his voice. Meanwhile, with Dido's attention distracted, many activities in Carthage lay idle. Training for war and the building of defenses ceased, and partly constructed buildings remained unfinished.

One day Dido and Aeneas went hunting together. Stags crossed the open meadows and wild goats walked over the mountain ridges, both providing good challenges. When a sudden storm caused the streams to swell with swift-running currents, Aeneas and Dido took refuge in a cave. There they consummated their love, and fires flashed in the sky to mark the gods' approval. But the event ushered in grief and death. Dido honored the divine ceremony as a legal one, and Rumor told the story far and wide.

Rumor is the fastest of all evils, and she gains strength and energy as she travels. She is as fast on foot as she is in the air. Monstrous in appearance, she has as many observant eyes along her belly as she has feathers on her wings and back, and her ears and her mouths each equal her eyes in number. She may be afraid at first, but in the end she walks the earth with her head in the heavens. She never sleeps. At night she goes squawking through the darkness. By day she sits on top of buildings, shouting lies disguised as truths.

When Rumor entered Libya with tales of Dido's passion for Aeneas and her neglect of her kingdom, she infuriated King Iarbas, whom Dido had rejected. Iarbas complained to Jupiter. "Dido has built Carthage on valuable land that I removed from my own rule and allowed her to buy. Since she has refused to marry me, how can you permit her to take Aeneas as her lord and thereby give to him all the benefits that by right are mine? Do you possess the power we mortals have believed, or are our sacrifices in your temples useless?"

Jupiter heard his words and sent Mercury, his messenger, down to Aeneas. "Tell him," the lord of Olympus commanded, "that it was not for this that we chose his mother's son to rule over Italy, nor was it for this that we rescued him twice from death at the hands of the Greeks. Moreover, if he has no interest in acquiring such fame and glory for himself, he should not steal his son's future. He must set sail at once!"

When Aeneas saw Mercury facing him in the clear light of day, he was speechless with fright. Jupiter's message so terrified him that he wanted to leave Carthage immediately, but he was reluctant to tell Dido. After much thought, he decided that it would be best to prepare the ships for departure in secret. This would give him time to find the right words and the best occasion for breaking the unwelcome news.

Rumor, however, quickly informed Dido, and she immediately confronted Aeneas with a torrent of questions and pleas. "You hypocrite!" she began. "Did you expect to leave here secretly? Can neither our love nor our promise keep you here? Are you choosing to leave me, or do you wish to acquire more fame? Would you choose to return to Troy in stormy winter weather? Pity me and stay. Because of you, the tribes of Libya, the Nomad chieftains, and even my own Tyrians hate me. For you I have given up honor, fame, and the political security of my country. What is left for me except death? At least if I could bear your child, you would leave me with some meaning in my life."

As he listened to Dido's reproach, Aeneas kept Jupiter's command in his mind and struggled to bury his anguish deep in his heart. "I admit that you deserve the best from me," he began, "and I will cherish my memories of you as long as I live. I would not have left without telling you—but remember, I never married you.

"If the Fates had permitted me to design the course of my own life," he continued, "I would have remained in Troy and rebuilt it. But Apollo has told me that my love and my country are in Italy. You have chosen Carthage; I can choose Italy. In my dreams, my father warns me not to sacrifice the destiny of my son, and now Jupiter has sent his messenger to me in the light of day to command me to leave. So spare yourself, and spare me your anger. I am sailing for Italy because I am not free to choose what I do with my life. My destiny is to found a great country. I may not satisfy my personal wishes as other people do."

Dido angrily replied, "False one! You are no son of goddess and mortal, but of some rocky mountain! You have no pity. You cannot even spare a tear or a sigh for me! Why have faith in the gods, when they are unjust? I welcomed a ship-wrecked, homeless man and gave him love and part of my kingdom. I saved his ships and his companions. Now the gods tell him to leave. So, go to Italy! But if the gods are just, you will suffer for it! And when I am dead, my shade will torment you. I will make you pay for what you have done to me!" With this curse, Dido left Aeneas.

Good Aeneas longed to comfort her, for his heart overflowed with his great love for Dido. However, he followed Jupiter's command and returned to his ships, where the Trojans were already preparing to leave. As a black column of ants crawls over the plain, through the grass, and along a narrow path with its plunder, and some strain with their shoulders to shove the huge grains of corn while others push them from behind and lament the delay, so some of Aeneas's men set their ships afloat while others carried branches from the forest to make into oars, each busy with some necessary task.

Meanwhile, Dido was observing their activity from the palace. "Anna," she said to her sister, "do you see how happy the Trojans are to leave? I can muster the strength to bear this sorrow, for I could foresee it. But do me one favor. Aeneas is your friend; convince him to wait and depart with good winds. I will not plead with him to stay beyond that."

However, Aeneas refused Anna as he had refused Dido, for Fate had closed his ears to tearful pleas. As roaring winds descend from the heights of a mountain and try to uproot a mature oak tree, but the tree continues to cling to the rock, so Aeneas rejected pleas from every side. Although his heart was sad, he remained determined to leave.

Then Dido planned her death. Pretending to have a strategy for returning Aeneas to her or freeing herself of her love for him, she commanded her sister to prepare for the fatal occasion. "Construct a funeral pyre in the inner courtyard," she said, "and place upon it our bridal bed, Aeneas's weapons, and everything else that he has left here. I intend to destroy everything associated with that traitor as the priestess advises." As this was just what Dido had done when her husband had died, Anna obeyed her directions.

That night, when all the tired creatures on the earth were sleeping, Dido lay awake, tormented by choices. "What will I do?" she asked herself. "Should I find marriage among my old suitors, who will laugh at me, or among men I have thought beneath me? I could follow the Trojan ships, but who would accept me? Or should I gather my Tyrians about me and drive the Trojans from Carthage, forcing them to sail the stormy seas? No, I should die by the sword, for I have broken my vows to my dead husband! "

While Aeneas was asleep that night, Mercury appeared in his dream and said, "Goddess-born, how can you sleep when you are in such danger? Dido is considering all kinds of dangerous plans. Quickly leave these shores while favorable winds make your escape possible!"

Frightened by his dream, Aeneas forced himself awake and called, "Quickly, men, awake and set sail! A god from high Olympus has come down and ordered us to leave immediately! As we joyfully obey your command, oh Jupiter, please be with us and help us."

When early Dawn was spreading her rays upon the earth, Dido saw that Aeneas had departed. Filled with grief and dismay, she said to herself, "That vile stranger has made a fool of me! I should have grabbed him, torn him apart, and strewn his pieces upon the waves when I had the chance. I should have killed his men and even his son, and served Ascanius to his father as part of my welcoming feast.

"I summon you, Apollo, and Juno, and you avenging Furies," Dido continued. "Hear my prayer. If that traitor must reach Italy, then may he be faced with war, driven from his land, and torn from his son, and may he witness the death of his friends. Then, when he has agreed to an unfair peace, may he die early and lie unburied upon the shore.

"And this last prayer I make with my blood. May you Tyrians, my people, honor me by hating the race of Aeneas now and for all time to come. May a peace treaty never exist between our people and his. May the Trojans, their children, and their children's children be faced with war."

Then Dido turned to her husband's old nurse and said, "Dear Nurse, I am going to begin the ceremony. Ask my sister to come and bring with her the offerings."

Feverish with determination, Dido entered the inner courtyard, climbed upon the high pyre, and unsheathed Aeneas's sword. "Release me from my troubles!" she prayed. "I have built a great city, and now my queenly shade will pass beneath the earth. Happily do I enter the darkness. Let the hard-hearted Trojan witness these flames from sea and take with him the omen of my death." With these words, Dido fell upon the sword and died.

Screams and wailing tore from the palace. Rumor flew through Carthage, shocking the Tyrians with the dreadful news. Anna, hearing about her sister's death from Rumor's mouth, rushed back to the palace. Tearing at her face and beating her chest, Anna cried, "By taking your own life, you have also destroyed me, your city, its government, and its people!"

Aeneas was far out to sea when he saw funeral flames rising from within the walls of Carthage. He sensed, with great sadness, that Dido was dead.

Chapter 6

A storm forces Aeneas to return to the land where his father, Anchises, died. The shade of Anchises directs Aeneas to let many of his people settle there. Aeneas then consults the Sibyl, who leads him into the Underworld to talk with his father. There, Anchises reveals to Aeneas the future of Rome.

"The winds are against us," the helmsman advised Aeneas. "If we allow them to guide us, we can reach Sicily, where our people live. "

"Then let us direct our ships in that direction, for I long to revisit my father's ashes," Aeneas replied.

Once on land, Aeneas held athletic contests in memory of his father. While the men were participating in the games, Juno decided to delay further Aeneas's journey to Italy. She sent her messenger, Iris, down among the women, who after seven years of wandering wanted to establish a permanent settlement. Under Iris's leadership, the women set fire to the Trojan fleet.

Aeneas was dismayed at the sight. "Great Jupiter," he prayed, "if you have any regard for the Trojans, save our ships. Or, if I deserve your wrath, kill the few of us who are left with your mighty thunderbolt! " As he finished speaking, black clouds gathered overhead, bringing with them a raging thunderstorm that poured torrents of rain upon the burning ships and extinguished the flames. Thus the Trojans were able to save all but four of their ships.

That night, the shade of Aeneas's father appeared before him. "Dearest Son," he began, "Jupiter has sent me to tell you to leave the aged, the weak, and the fearful here, and take only the bravest Trojans with you to Italy, for there you will have to fight a strong people. But first seek the Sibyl in Italy, and let her lead you down to the kingdom of Pluto, where you will find me among the blessed in Elysium. There I will reveal to you the future of all your race. Farewell."

Aeneas immediately summoned his company and informed them of Jupiter's command. As soon as their ships were ready, they set off for the shores of the Sibyl and the oracle of Apollo in Italy. They found the Sibyl's cave concealed high in the mountains. The huge cavern where she was seated contained one hundred interior entrances, so that her words echoed from one to the other. As soon as they entered, the prophetess commanded, "It is time to ask the god! Pray, Aeneas!"

"Apollo," Aeneas began, "you have always been kind to the Trojans. You guided Paris's hand and arrow as he killed Achilles. Protect us when we reach our destined shores of Italy. Sibyl, I ask for no more than the destiny I have been given."

Through the one hundred openings in the cavern came this reply: "You will reach Lavinium, Trojans, but you will fight grim wars there and the Tiber will run red with blood. In Latium, you will fight a goddess-born hero like Achilles, and Juno will set herself against you, forcing you to seek help from many peoples in Italy. As with Helen, the cause of Trojan suffering will be a foreign bride and a foreign marriage. Yet face your destiny with steadfast courage. Your help, surprisingly, will come from a Greek city." Thus the Sibyl voiced her prophecies, hiding the truth in words of darkness.

Aeneas replied, "Thank you, Sibyl. Now, the shade of my father wants you to help me find him in the Underworld. He told me that the gate to Pluto's kingdom is not far from here."

"Goddess-born," the Sibyl responded, "it is easy to enter the gloomy Underworld, for the gates are always open. The difficult task is to leave the kingdom of death once you have entered it! Only a few sons of the gods favored by Jupiter have been able to do that.

"If you have such love for your father in your heart," the Sibyl counseled, "then you first must find within the forest a bough bearing golden leaves that is sacred to Proserpine, for Pluto's queen requires this gift. If you are destined to have this bough, you will be able to break it off, and it will follow you. Then, when you have made a sacrifice of black cattle, you will be able to enter the kingdom of the dead while you are still alive."

Aeneas entered the forest and wondered how he would ever discover the golden bough buried among so many branches. However, as soon as he wished to see it, twin doves—his mother's birds—landed on the grass in front of him. They led him to a tree within whose green leafy branches Aeneas could see the shimmer of gold. At his touch, the branch broke off in his hand. Once Aeneas possessed the golden bough, he returned to the Sibyl and sacrificed the black cattle.

With the first rays of dawn, tremors deep within the earth caused the ground beneath them to tremble, the forests to shake, and dogs to howl. "Run, run!" the Sibyl cried. "All of you who are not sacred must now leave! You, Aeneas, unsheath your sword, gather your courage, and follow me."

The Sibyl rushed deep into the cave, and Aeneas fearlessly followed her. At the entrance to Pluto's dark kingdom, he came upon the evils that afflict human beings—Cares, Distress, Diseases, Old Age, Grief, Fear, Famine, Discord, War, and Death.

There, too, he found many famous monsters: the half-human, half-horse beings called Centaurs, the Hydra of Lerna with its hissing heads of snakes, and the triple-bodied giant called Geryon, all of whom the great Hercules killed; the flame-breathing Chimera, whom Bellerophon killed; Medusa, the serpent-haired Gorgon with the face that turned mortals to stone, whom Perseus killed; the six-headed Scylla, who ate six of Ulysses' companions; the Hundred-Handed Giant Briareus, who saved Jupiter when the Olympian gods revolted against him; and the Harpies. Aeneas turned his sword upon them and would have killed them, but the Sibyl reminded him that these were only the monsters' shades.

From there Aeneas followed the Sibyl toward the River Acheron, where the aged Charon, grim ferryman of the shades of the dead, stood guard in his boat. The flames blazing forth from his bony eye sockets, his untended beard, and his filthy clothing knotted upon his shoulders terrified the shades as Charon tended the sails, poled his boat, and chose which beings could journey across the Acheron.

Aeneas watched as a crowd of shades rushed toward the arriving boat, clamoring to be taken aboard. As many as the autumn leaves that fall in the forest with the first frost, and as many as the birds that flock to warm lands when cold winds bring winter upon northern shores, the shades stood, arms outstretched, pleading with Charon to take them across to the opposite shore. The gloomy boatman carefully chose his passengers, taking some and pushing others away.

Aeneas asked the Sibyl, "Why do all of these shades crowd here at the river's edge? Why does Charon accept some but reject others?"

"Aeneas," the Sibyl replied, "You see before you the river on whose waters the Olympian gods swear their sacred oaths. Charon ferries across it the shades of those who have been properly buried so that they can enter the kingdom of Pluto. Those he denies have not received a proper burial. The unburied must wander upon this shore of the river for one hundred years before they can gain entrance into Pluto's dark kingdom."

As he walked toward the Acheron, Aeneas met the captains of the ships that had been swamped in the storm that had washed the rest of his company ashore near Carthage. He talked with the helmsman of his own ship, who had fallen overboard and had drowned in stormy seas.

Charon spied Aeneas and the Sibyl before they reached the shore. "Who are you," he asked, "who, living and bearing arms, approaches the land of Shadows, Sleep, and Night? Stop where you are, and tell me your purpose. I may not ferry the living across this river in my boat. I took Hercules, Theseus, and Pirithous across only because their fathers were gods. Hercules carried off Cerberus, Pluto's three-headed watchdog, and the other two tried to steal Pluto's queen."

The Sibyl replied, "Have no fear. We do not come to cause any harm. Cerberus may continue to frighten the bloodless shades with his endless barking, and Proserpine will remain here in safety. The goddess-born Trojan, Aeneas, famous for his virtue and his skill in war, must see the shade of his father. If you do not believe me, this golden bough surely will convince you."

Gazing with wonder upon the golden bough, Charon cleared his boat and made way for Aeneas and the Sibyl to climb aboard. The boat groaned under Aeneas's weight and water leaked through the cracks in its seams, but it carried Aeneas and the Sibyl safely across the Acheron.

Cerberus, crouching in his cave, howled with all three heads. Upon seeing the snakes entwining his necks rise with anger, the Sibyl tossed the dog a cake soaked with sweet honey and sleep-inducing drugs. Greedily, all three mouths swallowed the sweet food, and the monstrous dog immediately fell alseep. Aeneas left the banks of the Acheron and entered the kingdom of Pluto.

Among the first shades he passed were the victims of love, with Dido among them. Lovingly, Aeneas addressed her. "Poor Dido! I swear to you by all that is sacred that I did not want to leave you! The gods, who now force me to make this journey, drove me from Carthage. I never thought my departure would cause you to take your own life!"

Dido ignored Aeneas's tears and his soothing words. She kept her eyes fixed upon the ground and showed as little emotion as a rock. Finally, she turned away from Aeneas, whom she still regarded as her enemy, and ran back to her loving husband. Aeneas, dismayed by her unjust fate, wept with pity as she left him.

Continuing on their way, Aeneas and the Sibyl came upon the shades of war heroes. Aeneas's Trojan friends were happy to see him. But as soon as the Greek heroes saw Aeneas, with his sword glittering in the gloom, they trembled and fled.

Next they came to a fork in the path. "Your father and Elysium are to the right," the Sibyl said. "To the left, behind that triple wall and encircled by the flaming Phlegethon River, is the castle where great criminals are punished. Each of them has committed some monstrous offense. Even if I had one hundred mouths and a voice of iron, I could not relate to you all of their crimes and all of their punishments. Imprisoned there are those who killed a parent or who hated their relatives, those who refused to share their wealth, those who committed adultery, and those who engaged in civil war."

The Sibyl continued, "One king accepted bribes to change the laws and then sold his country to a tyrant for a payment of gold. One is condemned to shout: 'I warn you to be just and not to slight the gods.' Sisyphus continually rolls a huge boulder up a steep hill; Ixion hangs outstretched upon an endlessly revolving wheel of fire; Pirithous sits eternally upon the stone chair of forgetfulness, to which he is bound and attached. But come, let us find your father and achieve your purpose here. I see the arched gates where we are to place the golden bough."

Then Aeneas and the Sibyl entered the Happy Forest, a land of woods, meadows, and rivers on which a special sun and special stars shone. Some of the shades were wrestling, some were dancing, and others were singing. Here Aeneas saw Dardanus, the founder of Troy, as well as the greatest heroes who died defending their country, and the greatest priests, poets, and philosophers.

When Anchises saw Aeneas approaching, tears streamed down his cheeks. He stretched out both hands and cried, " At last you have come! Your love for your father has given you the courage to make this fearsome journey. What dangers have befallen you? I was afraid that Carthage would harm you."

"Your sad shade, father, often came to me and directed me along the right path. So I have come to find you in this kingdom. Let me clasp your hand and embrace you!" So Aeneas, weeping, spoke to Anchises. Three times he tried to embrace him, but three times his father's shade fled from his grasp like a light breeze. "Who are all of those people?" Aeneas then asked.

"They are spirits who are waiting for Fate to give them second bodies," Anchises replied. "When they have been here one thousand years, they drink from the River Lethe and forget their entire past. Then they return to the world above in a new body. I have long wanted to show them to you, for they are the future beings of your race. With this knowledge, you will be more pleased about your destiny in Italy.

"Come now and see what glory your Trojan line will achieve, what fame and honor your Italian children will bring our name," Anchises said. "There is Silvius of Alban, who will be the last child born to you and your Italian wife, Lavinia. He will be a king and a father of kings, and through him our race will rule in Alba Longa.

"Then Romulus, a child of Mars and Ilia, will join his grandfather, Numitor. You can see how Mars has marked his son with a twin-plumed helmet like his own, so his place upon the earth is even now assured. Under his rule, a single wall will enclose Rome's seven hills. His empire will encompass the earth, and Roman spirit will equal the gods' Olympus.

"Now look at your Roman race. Here are Julius Caesar and all his children, who also are destined to appear on the earth above. That is Augustus Caesar, son of a god, who will bring forth the Golden Age in Latium and extend the Roman Empire to lands that lie beyond the stars and beyond the paths of the sun. Not even Hercules traveled over so much of the earth, although he captured the Arcadian deer, brought peace to the woods of Eurymanthus, and killed the Hydra of Lerna.

"There is Numa, the second king of Rome, called to kingship from a poor land, who will give the city a code of law. And there are Mummius, who will be famous for the Greeks he slays and the conquest of Corinth, and Aemilius Paulus, who will destroy Argos and Agamemnon's Mycenae, thus punishing the Greeks for destroying Troy. There, too, are great Cato, Cossus, and the mighty Fabius Maximus, who will restore the Roman state.

"Finally, there are the two Marcelluses: the first will defeat the Carthaginians and the Gauls, and then the gifted young Marcellus will so reflect the nobility of his Latin ancestors in virtue, honor, and skill in war that the Fates, fearing his potential power, will not let him live long. Remember, Roman, that your great contribution will be to rule the nations in your empire in peace under law, to tame the proud through war, and to treat the conquered with mercy!"

When Anchises had kindled in Aeneas the love of future glory, he told him about the wars he would have to fight, about the Laurentine peoples and the city of Latinus, and how to avoid or face each trial.

Then Anchises took Aeneas and the Sibyl to the gates of Sleep, where he dismissed them. Aeneas quickly returned to his ships and rejoined his companions, and they continued on their way.

Chapter 7

Aeneas and his companions arrive in Italy. As prophesied, they must fight the Latin people, led by the warrior Turnus. Aeneas is helped by Pallas, whom Turnus slays. Finally, Jupiter forces Juno to put aside her anger. Aeneas and Turnus fight in single combat, and Aeneas kills Turnus when he sees him wearing Pallas's sword-belt.

With favorable winds, Aeneas and his companions set sail on a moonlit night. They passed Circe's island, where they heard the daughter of the Sun singing as she wove upon her loom. They also heard the roaring of her chained lions, the raging of her boars and bears in their cages, and the howls of her wolves. With magic herbs, the cruel goddess had transformed men into all of those monstrous beasts.

Neptune filled the Trojans' sails with strong winds to move them safely past this dreaded land.

As the rays of dawn painted the sea red, Aeneas saw a great forest with the Tiber River running through it to the sea. Colorful birds sang as they flew among the trees. Joyfully, Aeneas directed his ships into the wide mouth of the peaceful river; there they moored the ships and went ashore.

When the travelers set forth their food, Jupiter inspired them to use their grain cakes to keep the wild fruits they had gathered off the ground. After they had eaten the fruit, they ate the cakes. Young Ascanius laughed, "Look! We are eating our tables, too!"

Aeneas immediately remembered the prophecy of the Harpy and said, "Hail to the faithful gods of Troy! Here is our home; here is our country."

King Latinus welcomed the Trojans, for an oracle had pronounced that his daughter, Lavinia, would marry a stranger, and their children would beget a race that would establish a great empire. Juno, still unwilling for Aeneas to have his Latin destiny, directed a goddess from the Underworld to go forth among the people of Latium and create war.

First she inspired Amata, Lavinia's mother, to remind her husband of his pledge to marry Lavinia to the warrior Turnus. Then she appeared in Turnus's dreams and inspired him to defend Italy against Aeneas and the invading Trojans. Finally, she caused a fight between a group of Latins and some of the Trojans. Popular sentiment now opposed the Trojans.

Although King Latinus steadfastly tried to avoid war with Aeneas by refusing to open the twin doors of the Temple of Janus, which would have declared a state of war, Juno came down from Olympus and opened them herself. Turnus then raised the flag of war and marshaled his troops.

As Aeneas slept on the bank of the Tiber, worried about the coming war, the river god came to him and counseled, "Arise, Goddess-born. Your home is here, and your gods support you. Do not fear these threats of war. In thirty years, Ascanius will found the great city of Alba. Meanwhile, seek King Evander in Pallenteum. He perpetually wars with the Latins, and he will become your ally."

With two ships and a group of chosen men, Aeneas then rowed up the peaceful Tiber River to the city of Pallenteum, which would one day become the renowned Rome. As Aeneas arrived, the king, his son Pallas, and the city officials were offering sacrifices to the mighty Hercules and the gods in a grove near the city. When he heard the purpose of Aeneas's visit, King Evander welcomed him warmly, remembering Anchises and King Priam from his own youth. Then he explained to Aeneas the history of the rites honoring Hercules, who had killed the giant Cacus at the base of the cliff where they were presently sitting.

Evander told Aeneas that he would support him against the Latins, although his resources were few. He would send Pallas and four hundred men. Then Venus signaled Aeneas with thunder in the sunny sky that she would bring him armor fashioned by her husband, Vulcan, the famed metalsmith of the gods. Afterward, Aeneas and Pallas led their men to fight Turnus and the Latins.

Meanwhile, in Aeneas's absence, the Latins attacked the Trojans. Many on both sides died. After Ascanius killed Turnus's brother-in-law, Apollo said to him,

"Be satisfied, son of Aeneas, that Apollo grants you this glory. You have the courage and skill of the son of gods and the father of gods to be. Now refrain from further fighting." Eager as the boy was to continue, he obeyed the command of the great god.

The Trojan captains marshaled their men against Turnus, who stood alone against them. As a furious lion faces the spears of a band of hunters and reluctantly retreats, backing up because its courage and anger will not let it turn around yet unable to force its way through the armed hunters, so Turnus retreated toward the river, with rage blazing in his heart. Pressed upon by the Trojans, Turnus found his weapon was useless. Darts, stones, and finally a storm of spears attacked his helmet and his armor. With a leap, he jumped into the Tiber in full armor, and the water supported his body and carried him back to his men.

The fighting was in full force when Aeneas arrived with his allies. Pallas killed many Latins. Then Turnus decided to rescue the warrior Lausus and fight Pallas in single combat. Turnus left his chariot as a lion rushes down from the mountain to attack a bull it has spied upon the plain. Pallas, aware of how much mightier Turnus was than he, prayed to Hercules, "By my father's welcome, help me to strip the bloodstained armor from Turnus's dying body, and may Turnus's last sight be of his conqueror. "

When Hercules wept to hear this prayer, Jupiter soothed his son. "Each mortal has his or her fated day to die," the Father of the Gods counseled, "and none has a long life. The courageous man performs deeds that will give him lasting fame, for fame survives after death. Turnus, too, is fated to die when his time comes."

Pallas's spear grazed Turnus's shoulder. Then Turnus's spear tore through the center of Pallas's shield and pierced his heart. Standing over Pallas, Turnus cried, "Greeks, tell Evander that I grant him Pallas's corpse and a proper burial." He then stripped Pallas's heavy sword-belt as a trophy of victory, unaware of how soon he would regret that gesture.

Juno, afraid of Aeneas's vengeance, received Jupiter's permission to rescue Turnus and postpone his inevitable fate. From the mist, she fashioned a shade of Aeneas in his war gear. The phantom appeared at the front of the Trojan forces, provoking the enemy with its spear and its defiant cry. When Turnus attacked it, the spirit turned and fled, and Turnus pursued it, sword in hand.

The phantom took refuge on a moored ship. As soon as Turnus followed it on board, Juno broke the anchoring cable, causing the ship to float out with the ebbing tide. The phantom then became a black cloud and drifted into the sky, leaving Turnus helplessly being blown out to sea.

"Father Jupiter!" Turnus cried. "Why are you punishing me like this? I am ashamed to have left my companions to face their deaths without me. I wish that the earth would open and swallow me! Winds, pity me, and destroy this ship, or take me where no one will ever hear of my shame."

Upon receiving the corpse of Pallas, Evander sent Aeneas a message that it was now his duty to avenge Pallas's death by slaying Turnus. Meanwhile, the battle continued to rage. With Turnus absent from the Latin forces, the Trojans were victorious.

When Aeneas received envoys from the Latins asking for a truce in order to bury their dead, he said, "I favor peace for the living as well as for the dead. Fate brought me to your shores, and I never desired war. If Turnus was so set on war, it would have been far better for him to fight me in single combat than to cause the deaths of so many people."

By this time Turnus had returned, and the Latins had become divided. Some wished to continue the war, but others said, "Turnus, pity your countrymen and surrender. We have seen enough of death! If you are determined to win glory or a royal wife, then fight Aeneas in single combat. Why should we die, unburied and unwept upon the plains, for your own private gain and glory?"

Turnus replied, "Many of you speak well but fear the battlefield. If the Trojans call me to face Aeneas in single combat, I will confront him with courage even if he surpasses the great Achilles and wears armor fashioned by Vulcan!"

The argument was cut short by the arrival of messengers, who announced that the Trojans and their allies were marching from the Tiber across the plain to their city. "Citizens!" Turnus cried. "You sit here in the council praising peace while the enemy rushes to attack our walls!"

When Turnus realized that the Latins were defeated and that they lacked further spirit to fight, he became furious. As a lion becomes aroused to anger once it has been wounded in the breast, and it defiantly tosses its shaggy mane, roars with its bloodstained mouth, and snaps the implanted weapon, so Turnus blazed with rage. "Arrange for me to fight Aeneas in single combat," he told King Latinus. "Either I will remove our nation's shame or the Trojan will win Lavinia as his bride and be our conqueror."

The Latin people were dismayed by the prospect of the unequal contest, and even those who had longed for rest and safety wished for weapons and a way to avoid Turnus's unjust fate. Therefore, one among them broke the truce. As war resumed, Aeneas cried, "Curb your anger! Honor the truce! I will enforce the treaty. Peace will reign in Italy!" But Turnus ignored Aeneas's words and fought his way across the field, killing many. Aeneas, too, brought death to many, causing the field to turn red with blood.

Venus then inspired Aeneas to realize that he could conquer the city. Queen Amata, watching the course of the fighting from the roof, saw the Trojans advance without opposition, scale the walls of the city, and toss blazing torches into the houses. Frantically, she searched the plains for Turnus, but she could not find him. Thinking that he had been killed and blaming herself for her people's destruction, she hanged herself. Latinus, faced with the death of his wife and the conquest of his city, tore his clothes, covered his head with dirt, and walked the streets in stunned horror.

When Turnus heard about the disasters, he turned to gaze upon the burning city, and his heart filled with the conflicting emotions of shame, grief, and anger. "I am determined to fight Aeneas," he said. "I will bear the bitterness of death; no longer will I stand ashamed."

Turnus leaped from his chariot and rushed past his enemies' weapons to the city walls. As a great rock rushes headlong down the steep mountainside and bounces upon the ground, crushing trees, herds, and men, so among the scattered troops Turnus rushed to the city walls, where the earth was drenched with blood and the sound of clashing spears clamored in the air.

"Withdraw from battle!" he shouted. "Whatever my fate, it is better that I take upon myself the outcome of this war and decide it with my sword."

Hearing his words, Aeneas left the fighting to approach him. They attacked each other as two bulls charge into deadly conflict head to head, while their herders retreat in terror, the entire herd stands in quiet dread, and the heifers wonder who their next leader will be. As the bulls viciously gore each other with their horns, their necks and shoulders swimming in blood and the forest echoing their bellows, so Aeneas and Turnus clashed shield to shield, filling the air with a mighty clamor.

Jupiter, high above, picked up his balanced scales and placed the fate of each hero upon a scale to see whose life the battle would doom, for the loser's impending death would cause his scale to sink with the weight of his destiny. Turnus's sword blade broke off like brittle ice upon meeting Vulcan's armor. Regretting that he had hastily left his father's sword behind, Turnus ran from Aeneas. The Trojan, despite an arrow wound in his knee, pursued him.

As a hunting dog chases at the hooves of a stag that is confined by a stream, the stag running frantically this way and that while the dog clings close to those hooves, his greedy jaws ajar in anticipation of the tasty flesh, so Aeneas chased Turnus. Turnus called among his countrymen for another sword, but Aeneas threatened death to the one who supplied it.

Five times they ran full circle, and as many times they ran in reverse. They were racing not for a mere trophy but for Turnus's life! When another goddess restored a sword to Turnus, Venus helped Aeneas retrieve his spear from the tree in which it had lodged.

Then Jupiter said to his wife, "You know that Olympus claims Aeneas as the hero of Italy. We have come to the end, so stop grieving and do not contend against me. You have chased the Trojans over land and sea, started this evil war, brought death into a royal home, and caused the bride great grief. I forbid you to interfere further."

"Knowing your feelings," Juno replied, "I have remained aloof here with you, when I would have chosen to be fighting the Trojans myself on the battlefield. I now yield completely to your wishes. I ask only that when Aeneas and Lavinia marry, you permit the Latins to keep their ancient name and language. Preserve Latium, let Alban kings rule, call the race Roman, and let Troy's name die with its city."

Jupiter smiled and replied, "In the depths of your anger, you prove that you are my sister and Saturn's child. I hereby grant your wish. From Aeneas and Lavinia I will create a blended race of one people, one language, and one set of laws and rituals. They will surpass all mortals and gods in virtue and in your worship."

Aeneas pressed on against Turnus with his great spear. "Why delay further?" he asked. "Let us fight hand to hand with our weapons instead of foot to foot."

"Do not think that you are my mighty enemy, Aeneas," Turnus replied. "Jupiter and the other gods are my greater foe!" With these words, Turnus spied an ancient, massive boulder that twelve strong men could hardly have lifted upon their shoulders. This he quickly grasped and tried to hurl at Aeneas. But as he raised and threw the stone, his knees trembled, his blood froze, and the rock, falling short of its goal, failed to wound his target. The dread goddess, Fate, had denied Turnus success, and the hero trembled with fear at the approach of Aeneas's spear and certain death.

Seeing Turnus falter, Aeneas aimed his deadly spear and hurled it upon his enemy. The spear pierced Turnus's shield and armor and then passed through his thigh. The huge warrior sank to the ground upon his injured leg. "I do not beg for mercy," Turnus said. "But think of your father and give my body back to my family. You are the victor, and Lavinia is yours to wed. Do not press your hatred further."

Aeneas, awesome in his armor, relaxed his sword arm and felt compassion for his fallen foe until he saw upon Turnus's shoulders the sword-belt of young Pallas. Memory of the courageous boy revived Aeneas's great grief and overwhelming anger. "How can you expect to win my pity when you wear as a trophy the belt of my dear friend whom you mercilessly killed?" he roared. "It is Pallas who demands this payment of your blood and here strikes you dead!" Aeneas furiously buried his sword deep in Turnus's chest. Turnus's limbs grew limp and chill, and, with a moan, his life fled resentfully down to the shades below.

❧ QUESTIONS FOR
Response, Discussion, and Analysis

1. Aeneas's Trojan wife, Anchises, and Dido all die. What effect does this have upon Aeneas and the myth?

2. How does Aeneas change as the myth progresses? At what point does this change occur?

3. Compare Aeneas and Dido as leaders of their people. Who is more effective? Why?

4. Why does Aeneas leave Dido: fear of the gods? personal ambition? Defend your opinion.

5. Should Aeneas have left Dido? Why? What does this incident reveal about Aeneas? What would you have done? Why?

6. How does Dido's love for Aeneas affect her life? Give as many examples as you can.

7. Does Virgil want his readers to believe that Dido is evil because she tries to persuade Aeneas to stay with her in Carthage? Explain.

8. Why does Dido commit suicide? What other choices does she have? Explain the consequences of each choice.

9. Is Dido an appealing character? Would you choose to be like her? Why or why not?

10. Should Aeneas kill Turnus? Why? What does this incident reveal about Aeneas? Would you kill Turnus? Why?

11. Who is more appealing, Aeneas or Turnus? Why?

12. Why does Virgil have so many people prophesy Aeneas's great achievements?

13. What does Aeneas give up in order to found Rome? Is his achievement worth the sacrifice to him? Do you think Virgil wanted the reader to find it worth the sacrifice? Would you find it worth the sacrifice? Explain.

14. What kind of person is Aeneas? What tests of character confront him? To what extent does he pass them? Which temptations does he resist, and which does he find irresistible? Why? How does his behavior affect his heroic image?

The Far East
and the
Pacific Islands

The myths of the Far East and the Pacific Islands represent a number of different cultures and were recorded over a wide range of time. The earliest myths from India reflect the culture of the Indo-European peoples who invaded the country in about 1500 B.C. Later the Hindus adopted and adapted some of these myths, among them the creation myth and the myth of Rama.

Most of the Chinese myths were recorded during the Han dynasty (206 B.C.–A.D. 220). They are the earliest Chinese myths still in existence because in 213 B.C. the first emperor of China burned all books that were not about medicine, prophecy, or farming.

The Japanese crossed the Korea Strait into Japan during the early period of the Han dynasty. Much later, in the eighth century A.D., they recorded their myths. The epic *Kotan Utunnai* is a modern transcription of a myth of the aboriginal Ainu people, who were living in Japan when the Japanese arrived.

The Polynesian peoples migrated from Asia to Tahiti, and then from Tahiti to New Zealand, Hawaii, and other Pacific islands. The fate of Polynesian mythology was determined, island by island, by the interaction between a particular group of Polynesian people and particular Christian missionaries, many of whom arrived during the first quarter of the nineteenth century. Maori mythology shows little Western influence. However, many Hawaiian myths were changed or lost due to the missionaries' intervention in the native peoples' culture. The first collection of Polynesian (Maori) myths was published in the middle of the nineteenth century.

Both the Indian and the Chinese creation myths that follow begin with an egg, involve creating the universe from the body of a divinity, and explain the creation of human beings. However, the Indian myth, which is Hindu, involves regeneration and the cyclical nature of time. It sets forth four ages of man. The Maori creation myth emphasizes the development from nonbeing to thought to creation. In this myth, the creation of the natural world reflects human nature, and New Zealand is created by a trickster-hero.

The Japanese and Hawaiian fertility myths included here are traditional in that they relate how a god or demigod saves the world from a great threat.

Each hero myth has its own special appeal. The Hindu *Ramayana* is one of the world's great epics. Not only is it a superb adventure story, but its emphasis on responsibility and righteous behavior make us think about our own values. In the Chinese myth, a virtuous young woman risks her life for the welfare of her community. Chi Li must use creative intelligence as well as courage, strength, and skill to conquer her adversary. The Ainu *Kotan Utunnai* is unusual in that its ancient, pristine quality gives it a primeval power.

The Creation, Death, and Rebirth of the Universe

Just as the Hindu religion accommodates a number of different religious views, it accepts a number of different creation myths. Vishnu, who was associated with the sun, and Rudra, who was associated with storms, existed as divinities before the Hindus gave Vishnu major importance and cast Rudra as the destructive side of Vishnu. The following myth was probably written down sometime between A.D. 300 and 500, and it contains a number of elements that are distinctively Hindu.

First, the idea of reincarnation is a Hindu concept. The Hindu creation myth reveals Vishnu in three forms: as Brahma, the creator of life on earth; as Vishnu, the preserver of life on earth; and as Shiva-Rudra, the destroyer of life on earth. The myth also explains how Vishnu often descends to earth and becomes reincarnated as a human hero to protect gods and mortals against the forces of evil beings (demons).

The duty of each person to live according to his or her *dharma*—a definite pattern of righteous behavior required by that person's position in society—is also a Hindu concept. Vishnu establishes dharma as a way of preserving civilization. Without it society disintegrates, war results, and civilization destroys itself.

Finally, the unending cycle of time and life is a Hindu concept. Creation is always re-creation, part of a cycle that has no beginning and no end. The universe progresses from birth to maturity to death to rebirth, over and over again. The four stages of life on earth progress from the ideal golden age to the dark age and back to the golden age, over and over again.

Vishnu, in his three forms, directs the life cycle of the universe from creation to disintegration to dissolution to re-creation, over and over again.

Thus, in Hindu thought, a sense of unity and pattern remains at the foundation of all apparent differences. Vishnu creates, preserves, and destroys. His names change, and his roles change, but the great god remains the same. The golden age will inevitably disintegrate into the dark age, which in turn will inevitably lead back to the golden age.

Like the four ages of the Greeks, the Hindu ages reveal the moral disintegration of society and show how people bring suffering upon themselves through their selfish and unjust treatment of one another. In each case, the ages become progressively worse. The last age is always a time of cruelty, pain, grief, and unnecessary death, and it is always the age in which the reader is living.

THE CREATION, DEATH, AND REBIRTH OF THE UNIVERSE

The world is created, destroyed, and re-created in an eternally repetitive cycle. It continuously moves from one Maha Yuga (great age) to the next, with each lasting for 4,320,000 years. Each Maha Yuga consists of a series of four shorter yugas, or ages, each of which is morally worse and of shorter duration than the age that preceded it.

The beginning of each Maha Yuga is the Krita Yuga, the age of virtue and moral perfection—a bright, golden age on earth. The great god Vishnu, in his form of Brahma, the grandfather and creator of the world, is the presiding god, and dharma (ideal, righteous behavior or moral duty) walks steadily and securely upon all four feet. The Krita Yuga lasts for 1,728,000 years. During this period, human beings need no shelters, whether they live in the mountains or by the sea. Gift-giving trees provide them with an abundant supply of food, clothing, and decorative objects. Everyone is born good and lives a happy, contented, unselfish, and beautiful life. People are devoted to meditation, the highest virtue, and spend their lives being loyal to dharma. They work for the pleasure of it, rather than from necessity. Sorrow does not exist.

The second age in each Maha Yuga is the Treta Yuga. *Treta* means three and refers to the fact that dharma now walks less steadily, on three of its four feet. Virtue and moral perfection still exist, but they have declined by one-fourth. The duration of the age has similarly declined by one-fourth. Vishnu, lord of heavenly light and the preserver of life on earth, is the ruling god. People are now devoted to the pursuit of knowledge, which they consider the highest virtue.

In the Treta Yuga the gift-giving trees supply food and clothing to everyone in abundance until greedy people try to make them their private property. Then the special trees disappear, and life on earth becomes difficult for the first time. Heavy rainfall creates rivers, and the mixture of earth and water makes the soil fertile for the growth of many new kinds of trees. Although the new trees bear fruit and are useful to human beings, they are ordinary trees rather than gift-giving trees. Therefore, people must work hard to acquire food and clothing. Because of the rain and severe changes in the weather, they also need to construct houses for shelter.

In the Treta Yuga people are more passionate and greedy. They are no longer happy with what they have. Dissatisfaction, resentment, and anger replace satisfaction, peace, and contentment in their hearts. They covet their neighbors' possessions. The strong take land from the weak in order to possess more food and greater wealth. Many men take the wives of others.

The third age in each Maha Yuga is called the Dvapara Yuga. *Dva* means two, and eternal dharma now totters unsteadily on two of its four feet, creating a precarious and shifting balance between good and evil. Virtue and moral perfection still exist, but they have declined to one-half what they were in the Krita Yuga. Correspondingly, the duration of this age is half that of the Krita Yuga. Vishnu, the preserver of life on earth, is still the ruling god, and people devote themselves to sacrifice, which they consider the highest virtue.

In the Dvapara Yuga, disease, misfortune, suffering, and death are part of everyone's existence; people have become more passionate and greedy, and war is commonplace. Religious doctrines are developed in an attempt to guide human behavior toward dharma, but the gradual process of moral deterioration continues.

The fourth age in each Maha Yuga is the Kali Yuga. This is the dark age, as *kali* means quarrel and war. Dharma drags along on only one of its four feet, and virtue barely exists. This age is one-fourth the length of the golden Krita Yuga. The great god Vishnu is the ruling god, in his form of Shiva-Rudra, the destroyer of life on earth.

In the Kali Yuga people achieve noble rank in society based on the amount of money and property they own rather than their moral virtue. The quality of virtue is measured only in terms of material wealth. Sexual passion alone binds husband and wife together in marriage. People become successful in life through a succession of lies, and their only source of enjoyment is sex. They live with continuous fear of hunger, disease, and death.

In the Kali Yuga only the poor are honest, and the only remaining virtue is charity. To escape the oppression of greedy kings, a few people retreat to isolated mountain valleys. They clothe themselves with rough-hewn garments made from the leaves and bark of trees, and they live by gathering wild fruits and edible roots. Harsh weather and primitive living conditions make them prey to devastating illnesses. One who lives to the age of twenty-three is considered very old.

VISHNU AS SHIVA-RUDRA, DESTROYER OF LIFE ON EARTH

At the end of one thousand Maha Yugas, which is one day of the life of the world, the great god Vishnu will take on the form of Shiva-Rudra and will destroy all life on earth. He will usher in one night in the life of the world, a period lasting as long as the day. First he will enter the sun's rays and intensify them for one hundred years, causing great heat to evaporate all water on the face of the earth. All three worlds—heaven, earth, and the Underworld—will burn up from this intense heat. The great drought and scorching fire will create a wasteland. Famine will stalk the universe, and by the time the one-hundred-year period ends, no living creature will remain.

When the fires have consumed all life on the three worlds, Shiva-Rudra, the destructive form of Vishnu, will exhale dreadful storm clouds. Accompanied by terrifying thunder and lightning, these clouds will move across the face of the earth, blocking the sun and covering the world in darkness. Day and night, for one hundred years, a deluge of rain will pour forth until everything in the world has been buried beneath the deep waters of a devastating flood. Besides the desolate sea, only the great god Vishnu will continue to exist, for the fire and flood will have destroyed all of the other gods along with the rest of all life.

Just as the great flood begins to bury all life, a large golden egg will appear. This egg will contain the seeds of all forms of life that existed in the world before the flood. As the world drowns, the egg will float safely upon the waters of the boundless ocean.

When the ocean completely covers all three worlds, Vishnu will exhale a drying wind. For one hundred years this wind will blow across the world, scattering the storm clouds. For the remainder of the one thousand Maha Yugas, that night in the life of the world, Vishnu will sleep and the world will lie asleep also.

VISHNU AS BRAHMA, CREATOR OF LIFE ON EARTH

At the end of the long night of one thousand Maha Yugas, Vishnu will awaken. A marvelous lotus flower will emerge from his navel, and Vishnu will emerge from the lotus flower in his creative form of Brahma, creator of life on earth. The lotus will become the foundation of the three worlds. Once he has emerged from the blossom, Brahma will rest upon it. Realizing that the flood has killed all life, Brahma will break open the egg to begin the process of rebirth. Thus, as the god Brahma, Vishnu will usher in the next day in the life of the world, a new period of one thousand Maha Yugas.

The image of all three worlds, complete with gods, demons, and human beings, exists within Brahma. First Brahma the creator will bring forth water, fire, air, wind, sky, and earth, with mountains and trees upon the earth. Then he will create the forms of time, as a way of organizing the universe.

Soon thereafter, Brahma will concentrate upon creating gods, demons, and human beings. First he will bring forth the demons from his buttocks. He will then cast off his body, creating the darkness we call night, which belongs to the enemies of the gods. Taking a second body, Brahma will bring forth the gods from his face. He will cast off this body as well, creating the lightness we call day, which belongs to the gods. From successive bodies, Brahma's powers of concentration will bring forth human beings and Rakshasas, snakes and birds. Then Brahma will bring forth goats from his mouth, sheep from his chest, cows from his stomach, antelope, buffalo, camels, donkeys, elephants, and other animals from his arms and legs, horses from his feet, and plant life from the hair on his body.

Thus the great god Vishnu exists eternally in his three forms. First he is Brahma, the grandfather and creator of the world. Then he is Vishnu, the preserver of life on earth. As Vishnu, he protects human beings with dharma, a code of civilized behavior, and often defends them from their greatest enemies by descending to earth and being born as a human being in order to help them. Finally he is Shiva-Rudra, the destroyer of life on earth.

1. This myth describes life as a continuously repetitive cycle. What aspects of life support such a view?

2. In addition to the view of life as a continuously repeating cycle, alternative views of life include one in which life continues to improve and one in which life continues to get worse. Which of these three views of life do you find most realistic? Why? Which do you find most appealing? Why?

3. What are the advantages and disadvantages of living according to the principle of dharma? Does the concept of dharma support or oppose an effort to correct social injustice? Explain.

 The Ramayana

HISTORICAL BACKGROUND

The Ramayana reflects the traditions of two politically powerful peoples, represented by Rama's family and Sita's family, who lived in northern India between 1200 and 1000 B.C. They were the most cultured of many cultured peoples who lived in India at that time. Their kings were as famous for their great learning as for their military skills. Their religious leaders founded universities of such high academic excellence that students came from other countries to attend them.

Scholars believe that *The Ramayana* was composed sometime between 200 B.C. and A.D. 200, with the last chapter added later, possibly as late as A.D. 400. The poet Valmiki, to whom this epic poem is attributed, is almost as vague a figure as Homer. He was probably born a Brahman and probably had some close association with the kings of Ayodhya. He collected the myths, songs, and legends about Rama and shaped them into a connected poetic narrative using meter and style of his own invention. The epic itself states that Valmiki is a contemporary of Rama's and explains how Valmiki created *The Ramayana.*

Valmiki provides a window onto the ancient past. Through him we see the culture of the ancient Hindus. We see something of their political, social, and religious life, and we are introduced to their values. Valmiki viewed the period in which the poem is set as the Golden Age of India. Dasa-ratha is the ideal king of the ideal city. Rama is the ideal prince, and Sita is the ideal wife.

A direct relationship exists between *The Ramayana,* which is a moral epic, and the life and values of the ancient Hindus. Just as Rama spends fourteen years living as a hermit in the forest, so in ancient times every Hindu boy from a religious home left his parents when he was very young in order to live with his teacher. For a period of twelve, twenty-four, or even thirty-six years, the young man lived a hard, simple life. He wore a garment made of rough cloth, went from door to door begging for food, and served his teacher as a menial servant. Endurance and suffering were as important a part of his training as traditional learning, for devotion to duty was the foundation of a righteous and successful life.

An interesting aspect of *The Ramayana* is the close relationship between human beings and animals. The monkey Hanuman is a great hero without whose help Rama would not have succeeded. Their partnership reflects the respect that the creators of the Rama myths and legends felt for other living creatures.

APPEAL AND VALUE

Like *The Iliad, The Ramayana* tells of the rescue of an abducted queen. Like *The Odyssey,* it tells of the adventures of a hero in the course of a long journey. As Odysseus is blown from one land to another during his journey from Troy to Ithaca, so Rama travels from northern to southern India and finally to Ceylon.

Certainly one reason for the lasting appeal of *The Ramayana* is that it is a superb adventure story. Its focus is the battle between the forces of good and the forces of evil. Heroes combat villains, magic adds interest, and humane, intelligent animals lend a very special flavor.

The Ramayana has had a phenomenal impact on its culture. It has molded the values of Indian society by presenting a variety of models for heroic human behavior to countless generations of people. For many centuries *The Ramayana* was a required part of every Indian child's education, since it provided moral instruction as part of an adventure story. The characters in *The Ramayana* have long served as models of proper behavior among Hindus. The person who based his or her actions under stress on what Rama or Sita would do in that situation could be sure of doing the right thing.

The Ramayana is still a living tradition and, for many, it is part of a living religious faith. Indian children are raised with stories from the epic. *The Ramayana,* whole or in part, is celebrated and dramatized in religious festivals and is the subject of books and movies.

Despite the fact that Rama, Sita, Lakshmana, and Bharata are ideal figures, they are still very appealing human beings. The ordeals that Rama and Sita endure so virtuously are exaggerated versions of the trials that ordinary men and women must face. Each serves as a role model for his or her sex and teaches the satisfaction to be found in devotion to one's duty and righteous behavior.

Readers today can identify with Sita, Rama, and Rama's brothers. We all enjoy seeing people behave at their best under very difficult circumstances, for righteous behavior elevates the person and thus the human race. Like the ancient Hindus, we value love, friendship, loyalty, dedication, and perseverance. We too know how it feels to be jealous, envious, and greedy; we too experience grief and suffering. We are often called upon to act our best in difficult situations.

However, contemporary Western codes of behavior sometimes differ from those portrayed in *The Ramayana*. For example, some readers may find it incomprehensible that Rama renounces Sita because of her abduction by Ravana and that he drives her away for the same reason many years later.

The Ramayana centers on the love between husband and wife, with parental relationships and society's values operating as complicating factors. At the root of almost every incident are the affection and responsibility between two people: husband and wife, parent and child, two brothers, two friends, or, on a larger scale, the king and his subjects.

Because *The Ramayana* is a very personal story about people's emotions as they face their tasks and trials, its appeal is universal. Noble or peasant, ancient Indian or modern American, we all have the same basic needs and emotional responses.

THE HINDU HERO

According to ancient Hindu tradition, each person should be loyal to dharma, or righteous behavior. A prescribed code of behavior exists for each role in life—king, queen, father, mother, son, daughter, brother, sister, friend. Therefore, each person knows what he or she ought to do in each situation that occurs. Conflicts between loyalties present problems, as always. However, suffering and sorrow are part of the righteous life, and each person must endure whatever life brings.

In ancient Hindu society, a wife's obligation is to dedicate her life to her husband. Her love must be pure and faithful, her devotion complete. The extent to which she can meet the ideal standard despite all trials and temptations determines her self-worth and the worth society assigns to her. The greater the challenge, the greater the success. If she meets the standards of her society despite many difficult circumstances, she is a great heroine.

To the ancient Hindus, a woman should not think of herself or function as an independent human being. Thus, in terms of her own tradition, Sita is one of the greatest females in literature. She represents the highest ideal of female love, devotion, and faithfulness, and Hindu society has loved her throughout the ages.

The obligation of the husband is more complex. He functions in a male-dominated culture and therefore has more responsibilities to fulfill, in society as well as at home. He is expected to remain devoted to duty while enduring trials and deprivation. Lakshmana is a great hero because he is a loyal brother and friend and an exceptional warrior. Reflecting his primary loyalty, he does not take his wife with him when he goes into exile with Rama. Similarly, Bharata feels a greater obligation to Rama, his brother, than to his father, his mother, or himself.

As the king, Rama has a special obligation to society. Kingship involves putting his responsibilities to his subjects ahead of his personal life. Because he is the model for proper behavior among his subjects, Rama's personal behavior must be beyond criticism. Therefore, to his dismay and grief, he must honor the attitudes of his subjects and obey their wishes—even when they are wrong.

The Rakshasas are the enemy, but they are not evil within their own society. While they feel free to indulge in violence and deception with outsiders, among themselves they have the same values as Rama's people do. They show love and loyalty and are courageous and skillful in battle. Ravana is not a good king, because he puts his personal wishes before the needs of his subjects. Yet he is a great hero. His brother, Vibhishana, will be a good king.

THE ROLE OF THE GODS

The gods in *The Ramayana* are immortal and powerful, but they are not omnipotent. The Hindu gods can be conquered by a skillful enough adversary. Thus, Ravana is able to wield great power.

Like the Greek and Sumerian gods, the Hindu gods come down to earth and interact with heroes but do not determine their behavior. Human beings bring their misfortunes upon themselves. In *The Ramayana* it is Sita's attitude that makes her abduction possible.

The heroes of *The Ramayana* are free to choose between proper and improper behavior, between good and evil. Their human natures often lead them to react with emotion rather than with reason, and that always brings unnecessary suffering. The Rakshasas are to be feared because they are evil and devious, and they can transform themselves into creatures of rare beauty. As such, they conquer good people through deception and temptation. Evil often comes disguised as good, and its temptation is always difficult to resist, whether a Rakshasa is at the root of it or not.

The Ramayana expresses the Hindu idea that a person's behavior in one life determines what happens to him or her in the next life. Thus, Sita wonders what evil she committed in a previous life to reap such suffering and sorrow in this life. The scene in which Rama and his brothers renounce life on earth and ascend to heaven reflects Hindu beliefs about the death of the righteous.

PRINCIPAL CHARACTERS

DASA-RATHA: king of Kosala; father of Rama, Bharata, Lakshmana, and Satrughna
RAMA: one earthly form of Vishnu; eldest and favorite son of Dasa-ratha; brother of Bharata, Lakshmana, and Satrughna; husband of Sita
BHARATA: second earthly form of Vishnu; second son of Dasa-ratha; brother of Rama, Lakshmana, and Satrughna
LAKSHMANA: third earthly form of Vishnu; third son of Dasa-ratha; brother and companion of Rama; brother of Bharata and Satrughna
SATRUGHNA: fourth earthly form of Vishnu; youngest son of Dasa-ratha; brother and companion of Bharata; brother of Rama and Lakshmana
JANAKA: king of the Videhas; husband of Mother Earth; father of Sita

SITA: earthly form of Lakshmi, Vishnu's wife; daughter of Mother Earth and Janaka; wife of Rama
RAVANA: demon king of Lanka and the Rakshasas; enemy of both gods and mortals
MARICHA: Ravana's adviser; a Rakshasa demon
KUMBHA-KARNA: giant brother of Ravana; greatest Rakshasa warrior
VIBHISHANA: youngest and good brother of Ravana; king of Lanka and the Rakshasas after Ravana's death
SUGRIVA: monkey king who helps Rama fight Ravana
HANUMAN: son of the wind; great monkey hero who helps Rama
NARADA: great wise man who tells Valmiki the story of Rama's life
VALMIKI: hermit; poet who composes *The Ramayana;* teacher of Rama's twin sons

PRINCIPAL GODS

INDRA: king of the gods; god of rain
VISHNU: preserver of life on earth
BRAHMA: Vishnu in the form of creator of life on earth
SHIVA: Vishnu in the form of destroyer of life on earth
LAKSHMI: goddess of beauty and good fortune; wife of Vishnu
MOTHER EARTH: mother of Sita
YAMA: lord of the dead
AGNI: god of fire

THE RAMAYANA

Chapter 1

The god Vishnu, preserver of life on earth, descends to earth in order to kill Ravana, a monster who is an enemy of both gods and humans. Vishnu is reborn as the four sons of King Dasa-ratha: Rama, Bharata, Lakshmana, and Satrughna. Rama wins the hand of Sita, daughter of Mother Earth.

We sing of the way of Rama, the great hero. We sing of kings and queens, of humans and animals, of heroes and monsters who lived long ago. One wanted power and would do anything to acquire it. Others, when power was given to them, chose to reject it. We sing of love and loyalty and of courage and kindness in the face of jealousy, greed, and violence. We sing of trials and temptations and of sorrow and suffering, for these are part of devotion to duty and righteous behavior. Listen to our words and become wise, for this tale will reveal what is good, what is true, and what is beautiful.

In time of old a great king, Dasa-ratha, ruled his kingdom of Kosala from the capital city of Ayodhya. He had been born into the ancient Solar Race. As a human being and as a leader of his people, King Dasa-ratha outshone other men as the full moon outshines the stars. His city was known far and wide for the intelligence, righteousness, loyalty, generosity, self-restraint, piety, and happiness of its citizens. Dasa-ratha lacked only one thing: a son to rule the kingdom after his death.

The king had made many sacrifices, hoping that the gods would hear his fervent prayers and grant him a son. But all his prayers had been in vain. Finally he told his priests, "Sacrifice a horse to the gods above. Perhaps they will accept this greatest of all offerings and give me the son I long for."

So the priests set free for one year a magnificent horse, one that was lithe, graceful, and strong. When the horse returned, the wise men announced that King Dasa-ratha would become the father of four sons. These words fell sweetly upon the king's ears. His three wives beamed with delight, their faces shining like lotus flowers when they first open to the warmth of the sun's rays after many months of winter cold.

Meanwhile, the gods above were complaining to Brahma. "Ravana, the wicked Rakshasa king, is destroying us with his tyranny!" they exclaimed. "He wields unlimited power. You are to blame for our troubles, for you made Ravana immune to attack by either the gods or his own people. If you do not want this monster to control both heaven and earth, you had better devise some way to destroy him. Unless you act quickly, evil will triumph over good, and we will be ruined!"

Brahma, the grandfather and creator, replied, "It is true that Ravana asked me for protection from his own people and from every creature who lives above and below the earth, and that I gave him that gift. However, he very foolishly did not ask for protection from either humans or animals because he saw no threat from them. Therefore, by human and animal he will be killed. Just be patient, and you will see for yourselves!"

No sooner had Brahma spoken than the great god Vishnu, preserver of life on earth, joined the assembly. The gods honored and respected Vishnu as their great defense in time of need, so they pleaded with him for help. "Ravana, king of the Rakshasas, is terrorizing both heaven and earth!" they cried. "His evil ways know no end. Yet we are powerless to stop him. Only you can help us! Descend to the kingdom of Kosala and accept birth as King Dasa-ratha's four sons. As one man, you can destroy Ravana."

"This I will do," Vishnu replied. "My goddess-wife, Lakshmi, will accompany me and become my mortal wife on earth."

Vishnu changed himself into the form of a tiger and appeared to Dasa-ratha in the midst of the king's sacrificial fire. "King Dasa-ratha, tiger among men," Vishnu called from within the flames. "Brahma, the grandfather and creator, has sent me to you with this sacred rice and milk. Give it to your wives, and they will bear you sons."

So it came to pass that King Dasa-ratha's three wives gave birth to four sons, each of whom embodied Vishnu, preserver of life on earth. Rama was born first, Bharata second, then Lakshmana and Satrughna. The gods also created a band of monkeys whose courage, strength, and wisdom would help Vishnu destroy the wicked Ravana and the Rakshasas who supported him.

Rama and his three brothers became known for their virtue and their courage. Lakshmana was Rama's constant companion, while Satrughna always accompanied Bharata. In their sixteenth year, one of the great wise men said to King Dasa-ratha, "Most honored king, I request a gift from you."

"Ask whatever you wish, and it will be yours!" the king replied.

"Most honored king," the wise man replied, "I need your son Rama's help to fight Ravana and the Rakshasas. Without his aid, we cannot make our sacrifices. We have no hope of stopping the destructive acts of this monstrous creature and his demons!"

"Why do you ask for my Rama, when the gods can help you?" King Dasa-ratha asked.

"Unfortunately for all of us," the wise man exclaimed, "the gods are powerless against Ravana! He has already subdued all who live above and below the earth. Only the best of men can destroy him, and Rama is that man. Do not worry. Your son will be successful!"

So Rama and Lakshmana set out to accompany the wise man with their father's blessing. Indra, king of the gods, smiled upon the young men as they set out with their bows in one hand and their swords at their sides. He poured down upon them a shower of blossoms, a great rain of flowers from the heavens.

When Rama had easily destroyed the troublesome Rakshasas, the wise man said to him, "Now accompany me, lion among men, to the sacrifice to be held by King Janaka. This great king is married to Mother Earth, and he possesses a marvelous bow, which the god Shiva, destroyer of life on earth, gave to his ancestor long ago. None of the gods above, none of the Rakshasas, and none of the kings and princes of the earth has been able to string it. I would like you to try it!"

When the king had told Rama and Lakshmana the history of the bow, he announced, "Whoever can bend and string my mighty bow of war, long prized by kings of this land, will win my daughter Sita, child of Mother Earth. This child, the light of my life, arose from the soil one day as I plowed and blessed my field. Many men of fame have tried to conquer the bow and win my daughter, but in vain. Rama, I now offer that trial to you. If you succeed, Sita, the most fair and virtuous of women, will become your wife."

"Most honored king," Rama replied, "it is my pleasure to accept your invitation and to try my hands upon your mighty bow. To win your glorious daughter would be the greatest of honors!"

Word quickly spread far and wide that the great prince Rama had agreed to test himself against King Janaka's mighty bow. Kings, chiefs, famous warriors, noble suitors, and ordinary people from many nations gathered at Janaka's palace to witness the event.

Janaka's mighty bow was indeed great. It took the king's strongest lords and warriors, working together, to pull the weapon slowly forth on an eight-wheeled iron chariot.

Rama lifted the cover of the bow case and admired the awesome weapon of war. "With your permission," he said to the wise man, "I will place my hands upon this bow. Then I will lift and bend this greatest of weapons."

The wise man and King Janaka replied, "May it be so!"

Rama lifted the great bow from its case with ease and grace. He bent and strung it as if it were as supple as a leaf. Then he took the stance of the archer and drew the bow, but the strain was more than the wood could bear. It snapped in two with a clap like the roar of thunder. The earth quaked, and the hills resounded. So terrifying was this sudden sound that kings, and warriors—everyone except Rama, Lakshmana, Janaka, and the wise man—fell cowering to the ground.

King Janaka said to the wise man, "My old eyes have seen Rama perform this marvelous deed. It brings me special pleasure to know that my daughter—who has no equal—will wed the godlike son of King Dasa-ratha. I will be true to my promise, for Sita has been fairly won by a man whom no one can surpass in valor and in worth."

As Rama and Sita stood together to take the sacred marriage vows, King Janaka said, "Rama, this is my child, Sita, who is dearer than life to me. From this moment on she will be your faithful wife. She will share your virtue, your prosperity, and your sorrow. Cherish her in joy and in grief. No matter where life takes you, she will follow like your shadow, and she will be with you in death as in life." The king, tearful in his joy, sprinkled holy water upon the bridal couple.

Then King Janaka married Lakshmana to Sita's sister and Bharata and Satrughna to two other beautiful maidens. Indra, king of the gods, smiled as the four couples walked around the sacred fire celebrating their weddings. He poured down upon them a shower of blossoms, a great rain of flowers from the heavens.

So Rama married Sita, queen of beauty, who was as faithful and devoted as she was beautiful.

Chapter 2

King Dasa-ratha plans to give his kingdom to Rama, but Bharata's mother forces him to give it to her son instead. Rama is banished from Ayodhya for fourteen years. Sita and Lakshmana accompany him on his journey.

Of King Dasa-Ratha's four sons, Rama was the dearest to his father and to all the people of Ayodhya. He was the ideal male figure: loyal, devoted, even-tempered, trained in all the arts of peace and war, and kind to all. When the king sent his gentle second son, Bharata, to live with his grandfather for a year, Satrughna, the king's youngest son, accompanied him.

During their absence, Dasa-ratha thought, "I will give up my throne to Rama, for I am old and no longer possess the strength I had in my younger days. What is best for me is surely best for my subjects as well. I will end my days in ease, and since Rama is unmatched in virtue and valor, Ayodhya and the kingdom of Kosala will prosper under his rule."

The king then called the leaders of his country to council: chiefs, princes, and leaders of the army. His voice pealed like thunder as he announced, "I have cared for my people as a father cares for his children, without excessive pride and without anger. Now, in the evening of my life, I am very tired. Honoring royal obligations and carrying out the laws of our land require more strength and skill than I now possess. I hope that you will accept my son Rama in my place. Rama combines the courage of Indra, king of the gods, with the knowledge of sacred lore of a wise priest. Among those who walk the earth, he has no equal!"

The king's subjects applauded his announcement with such enthusiasm that the sky above and the ground below trembled with their joyous acclaim. "We would see Rama seated on your revered throne, for his heart is blessed with valor, his words and deeds show virtue, his love of truth and loyalty to dharma are unsurpassed. He is our father in time of peace and our protector in time of war. He towers above those who walk the earth as Indra towers above the gods in the heavens. He is as forgiving as Mother Earth."

So the city of Ayodhya prepared to celebrate Rama's coronation. Flags and banners proclaimed the event. Actors, dancers, and musicians entertained the gathered throngs of citizens from all parts of the kingdom.

Rama entered the assembly as beautiful as a full moon in the autumn sky. King Dasa-ratha seated him on his throne and counseled, "Rama, dearest and most honored of my sons, tomorrow you will be crowned king. You must be even more dedicated and virtuous than you already are. You must practice restraint in all things. You must be fair to everyone. You must maintain the military strength and the wealth of our nation. My heart is content knowing that I am leaving my subjects and my kingdom in your hands."

Rama returned to Sita and Lakshmana. To Sita he said, "We must prepare for our sacred fast." To Lakshmana he said, "Prepare to rule Mother Earth with me, for my good fortune is always yours as well. I value my life and my kingdom only because of you."

Not everyone, however, was happy with King Dasa-ratha's decision. Bharata's mother was watching the festivities with a mother's joy when her nursemaid placed deep and deadly thoughts in her heart.

"Why are you so happy when this is your time of greatest sorrow?" the nurse-maid asked. "Another queen's son has won the throne, not your son. Yet your son is the better of the two, being unmatched in merit and in fame. Because Rama fears Bharata's virtue and valor, he will spring upon his brother like a wolf and tear him to pieces! And Rama's mother and his wife will treat you and Bharata's wife as bond-slaves!"

Bharata's mother replied, "You speak wicked words, woman! Rama is as dear as Bharata to me. He loves his brothers as he loves himself, and he will protect them as a father protects his sons. King Dasa-ratha is obligated by ancient custom and the law of the land to leave his throne to the oldest and best of his sons, and that son is Rama. My Bharata will rule after Rama because he is younger."

"You must be blinded by madness, my fair queen!" the nursemaid responded. "Rama's son, not Bharata, will inherit the throne. Brothers do not divide their reign. In fact, once Rama is king, he will force your son to wander from land to land, alone and friendless. Bharata will be a man without a home and without a country!

"Trust your old nurse!" she continued. "I have lived long years, and I have seen many dark deeds performed in the most noble of palaces. Rama's allegiance is to Lakshmana, not to Bharata. Your son has already been ordered to leave the kingdom. You must save his life! Speak to your husband before it is too late. Otherwise, Rama will force Bharata to serve him and will hate Bharata if he refuses."

The nursemaid's words seeped into Bharata's mother's heart like a serpent's deadly poison, awakening her jealousy and her fears for her child. She entered the room reserved for mourning the death of loved ones, and there she lay upon the cold ground and wept. The old king found her lying there like a blossoming vine that has been uprooted. The sight of such sadness sorely distressed him, for he loved his young wife more than his own life.

"Why do you lie here in tears?" he asked. "Are you suffering from some sickness? Has someone insulted you? Speak, and your words will dissolve your anger as the sun's rays melt the winter snows. My great love for you gives you great power. I promise you that my court and I will obey your wishes, whatever they may be!"

The love-blinded king thus gave his sacred oath to the jealous queen. The sun, moon, and stars, the earth, and the household gods heard King Dasa-ratha's words. As he was an honorable man, his promise was unbreakable.

His wife began, "Years ago, when the Rakshasas sorely wounded you, I cared for you and saved your life. In gratitude, you granted me two rewards. I did not ask for them then, but I do now. If you will not honor them, I will die! First, let Bharata be crowned king in place of Rama. Second, make Rama live as a hermit in the wild forestlands for fourteen years. These are the rewards I now claim from you. I will be satisfied with nothing less!"

The aged king could not believe his ears. "This must be a monstrous dream!" he exclaimed. Then anger dried his tears, and he said to his young wife, "You are a traitor to me and to your family! What cause can you possibly have to hate a son who loves you as a mother? I feel as if I have been harboring a poisonous snake in my palace!

"Banish my wives, if you will," the old king continued. "Take my kingdom and my life from me, if you insist. But do not make me part with my son Rama! The world can continue to turn without the light of the sun. The harvests can survive without the moisture the rains bring. But I cannot survive without Rama! I am an old man, and I am weak. I do not have long to live. Be kind to me, dear wife! Ask for cities; ask for land; ask for treasure. But do not ask for Rama. Do not force me to break my sacred word to my son and to my people. That would be the greatest of crimes!"

The queen replied, "If you, who have always been known for your honesty and your virtue, break your sacred word to me, the world will know how poorly you rewarded the loyal, loving wife who saved your life. The world will know that you caused me to die of a broken heart. I demand kingship for Bharata and banishment for Rama. I will accept nothing less!"

On the following morning—the day of the coronation—Rama, accompanied as always by Lakshmana, approached his father. He found Bharata's mother sitting at the king's side. King Dasa-ratha was so sad of heart that he could speak nothing more than Rama's name. Rama asked, "Mother, what have I done to cause my father such distress? Why do tears glisten upon his cheeks? Is Bharata all right?"

Bharata's mother calmly replied, "The only pain grieving your father is that he cannot bring himself to tell you the bad news. Many years ago, he gave me his royal promise. Now, because of his great love for you, he would break it if he could. Yet you know that King Dasa-ratha cannot break his sacred word. If you are a true and righteous son, you will be loyal to dharma. Prove your virtue by holding your father to the vow that, in time long past, he made to me."

Rama exclaimed, "Tell me what I must do. I will obey my father even if he wishes me to drink poison and die!"

"If you would save your father's honor, act upon your words. Leave here immediately and live in the wild forestlands as a hermit for the next fourteen years. Wear your hair matted and clothe your body with the skins of animals and the bark of trees. My son, Bharata, will return to Ayodhya and rule your father's kingdom in your place."

Rama accepted these words with a calm heart. He was neither sad nor angry. "I hope that my journey will bring peace to your heart, Father," he replied. "Send for Bharata; I will leave as soon as I have seen Sita and my mother."

As the two brothers left the hall, the young and loyal Lakshmana gave vent to his rage. "Why should you let Bharata's mother destroy your life? Our father surely suffers the illness of old age to let her rule him in matters of state! Fight for your rightful title, and I will stand at your side!"

"No, Lakshmana," Rama replied. "I have no wish to rule our father's kingdom under these circumstances. Other men in our family have had difficult tasks placed before them. Surely this time in the forest is part of my destiny. I will live my life with honor, obeying my father as a good son is expected to do. That is the way of dharma."

Rama then told his mother and Sita, "Remain here in peace while I am in the wild forest. Mother, no matter how unhappy you are, your place is with my father. If you leave him to accompany me, he will die. Sita, I want you to watch over my mother. Love Bharata and Satrughna as your brothers, for they are dearer to me than my life."

The gentle and devoted Sita replied, "Just as your mother's place is with your father, so my place is with you! What is the moon without its light? A flower without its blossom? A lute without its strings? A chariot without its wheels? Without you I am nothing! Fine clothes, rich food, and palace comforts are nothing! Your banishment will be mine as well. The berries and roots that will sustain you, will nourish me. The beauty of the forest will bring joy to our eyes, and I will fear neither fierce wild animals nor the hard life of a hermit. As long as I am by your side, I will not count the years!"

"I too will accompany you!" Lakshmana exclaimed. "I am happy and content if I can be wherever you are. It will be my pleasure to find the forest paths and to gather food. How bad can exile be when we are together?"

So Rama, Lakshmana, and Sita went into exile. King Dasa-ratha angrily left Bharata's mother to herself and took comfort in Rama's mother. On the evening of the fifth day of Rama's journey, the old king's heart could no longer bear its burden of grief, and he died. Then sorrow flowed over the land, for without a king a kingdom is like a river without water, a meadow without grass, or a herd of cattle with no one to herd them. The people feared for their safety and their well-being, so the palace officials sent for Bharata.

Chapter 3

Bharata learns of his mother's treachery and tries to convince Rama to return, but Rama refuses. A wise man gives Rama weapons of the gods. Ravana's sister becomes infatuated with Rama, and when he rejects her, a Rakshasa army attacks him. Rama manages to kill the entire army.

On the seventh day Bharata, accompanied as always by Satrughna, arrived in the city of Ayodhya and immediately went to see his mother. He grieved to hear of his father's death. "Where is Rama?" he asked his mother. "To me Rama is father, brother, and friend. It brings me joy to serve him."

Bharata's mother told her son the truth about Rama's departure, for she expected him to be pleased with his good fortune. To her surprise and dismay, Bharata was furious.

"If it were not for Rama's love for you, I would renounce you as my mother!" he exclaimed. "In spite of your treacherous designs, I will not rule my father's kingdom! It is too great a task for me, and the kingdom is Rama's to rule. I will search the broad forestlands for Rama. And once I have found him, I will bring him home to rule as is his right.

"As for you," Bharata continued, "your fate will bring you misery both in this life and in your life to come. You deserve to be banished, or hanged, or burned for your dreadful deed!"

Bharata refused the throne when it was formally offered to him. Instead, he and Satrughna gathered together a huge host of nobles, cavalry, learned men, and traders and led them through the wild forestlands in search of Rama. In the course of the journey, they encountered a wise man who said to Bharata, "Each man's destiny takes him along strange and unforeseen paths. Do not blame your mother for Rama's banishment. His exile is destined to benefit both humans and gods alike. Be patient, and remain true to dharma."

Finally Bharata and his companions found Rama. Bharata wept when he found his brother living with Sita and Lakshmana in a leaf-thatched hut and dressed in clothing made of deerskin and bark. Yet in spite of his simple manner of living, with his mighty arms and lion-like shoulders, Rama seemed like Brahma, the grandfather and creator of the wide earth.

"Are you that Rama, prince among men, whose people placed him on the throne of Ayodyha to rule the kingdom of Kosala?" Bharata asked him. "You have exchanged your luxurious robes for forest leaves and animal skins, and you have left your palace for the solitary life of a hermit. The very sight of you fills my heart with sadness!"

Rama embraced Bharata and Satrughna and lovingly welcomed them into his simple home. Then he asked, "Bharata, why have you sought me in my forest dwelling? Tell me, did our father ask you to come? Is he well? Do our warriors guard our kingdom as they should? Do the king's counselors serve him as they should? Surely some serious matter has moved you to undertake this long and difficult journey into the wilderness to find me!"

Bharata tearfully replied, "Rama, our father is dead! He walks the paths of heaven now instead of earth. His death has brought my mother to her senses and made her ashamed of her treacherous deed. I have come to ask you to return with me to Ayodhya and rule the kingdom of Kosala as the eldest son of King Dasa-ratha should. It is your duty according to the ancient law of our land. Besides, I need you! You are not only my brother; you are my father and my teacher."

Rama replied, "Bharata, I cannot return with you to Ayodhya, no matter how you plead with me to do so. I cannot claim the throne of our kingdom, for I cannot disobey the command of my father and king. Even though he is dead, I cannot break the promise that I made to him.

"And, Bharata, have kindness in your heart for your mother. She is not to blame for my exile. As for you, you must rule our kingdom and protect our people during my years in these wild forestlands. That is the way of dharma. As a dutiful son, you also must obey our father's wishes."

Rama concluded, "You must remember to care for the ordinary people in our country. Think of the herders who tend their cattle and the farmers who work their land. Make certain our soldiers guard our borders. Guard our nation's great treasure. Give gifts of food and wealth to all who are worthy, not just to the nobles. Always rule with justice, defending those who are innocent, no matter who they happen to be."

Bharata replied, "Rama, in truth, I cannot rule your kingdom. Our people look to you, not me, as their leader."

"Nonsense!" Rama exclaimed. "You possess the virtue and the strength to rule an empire that is as great as the world. Surely, then, you can rule the kingdom of Kosala. Our father's trusted counselors will advise and guide you.

"As for me," Rama concluded, "I am as firm in my resolve as a great rock. Your pleas, no matter how eloquent, cannot move me. The pleas of your entire company cannot move me. The moon may lose its glow and the mountains may lose their snow, but I cannot forget my promise to our father."

"So be it, then," Bharata replied. "Give me your golden sandals. I will place them upon the throne of Ayodhya to rule in your absence. They will give me the courage and the will to keep our kingdom for you. As for me, I will spend the next fourteen years as a hermit, even though I live in the royal palace. I will dress and eat as you do. If you do not return at the end of that period, I intend to die in the flames of a funeral pyre."

"So be it," Rama replied. "Take my sandals, then, and return to Ayodhya with Satrughna and your companions. We will meet again in fourteen years. You have my respect, my love, and my friendship."

So the ever-true Bharata and the righteous Rama parted. At first Rama wandered from place to place in the pathless forest, accompanied by his faithful Sita and his loyal Lakshmana. He met many of the holy hermits who lived within its dark shelter. To many people, the endless forest seemed nothing more than a dark, gloomy, and fearsome wilderness. But within its trackless depths Rama and his companions, like the holy hermits, found purity and peace. Ripe, wild fruits hung from broad, bending trees. The fragrant lotus and the lily rested on quiet inland waters. Drops of sunlight glittered upon lush, green leaves that sheltered grazing deer. Both day and night, the air was alive with the songs of birds.

In the course of their wanderings, Rama and his family came upon a mighty wise man, one of the holy hermits who also made the wild forestlands his home. "Rama," he said, "you are a hero, but even in this forest you will need weapons of war. Here is Vishnu's bow. Take it with you, for it is truly a wondrous weapon that was shaped in the heavens. Here is Brahma's shining arrow. In the hands of a good bowman, it will never miss its target. Here is Indra's large quiver filled with sharp-tipped arrows. They will never fail you in battle. Finally, take this case of burnished gold. Within it rests a sword with a golden hilt that should belong to a valiant warrior and a king.

"The enemies of the gods," the hermit continued, "know and fear these great weapons. So make them your constant companions because you will need them often. Here in the peaceful forest you will meet Rakshasas, those evil hunters who haunt the forest ways at night. Only you can defend us from those who disturb our prayers and defile our holy shrines. Even here, a hero will find deeds of honor to perform."

"Thank you, respected sage," Rama replied. "You have blessed my exile with your kindness and your friendship."

Rama, Sita, and Lakshmana lived in the forest for ten years, defending the hermits against the attacks of the Rakshasas who hunted in the night. The young and valiant Lakshmana built a comfortable house of bamboo and leaves for them in an area where food was plentiful. Their clearing was surrounded by date palms and mango trees. Nearby, a river teemed with fish and the forest with deer. Both fragrant lotus flowers and ducks made their home upon a beautiful, small lake.

All was well until the sister of Ravana, king of the Rakshasas, came upon Rama's forest home, observed Rama, and fell in love with him. "Who are you," she asked Rama, "dressed like a hermit, yet armed with a mighty bow? Why do you live in a lonely house in this dark forest where the Rakshasas are accustomed to having their way?"

When Rama had explained the nature of his stay in the forest, he asked the maiden about herself. She replied, "Ravana, king of Lanka, is one of my brothers. I usually wander through this forest with my brothers, but my love for you has caused me to leave them to their own pursuits. My kingdom is broad and boundless, so you should feel honored that I have chosen you to be my husband and my lord. Put your human wife aside; she is not as worthy a companion for you as I am! Rakshasas feed on human flesh. With no effort at all, I can kill your wife and your brother. Compared to the Rakshasas, humans are weak, fragile, puny beings."

Rama repressed a smile, but he could not resist teasing the brash maiden. "You do not want a married man for your husband," he replied. "Instead, you should consider my brother, Lakshmana. You see no wife of his in this forest home of ours!"

When Ravana's sister approached Lakshmana, he smiled and rejected her advances. "You certainly would not be satisfied with me!" he exclaimed. "I am Rama's slave. Given your royal birth, you would not become the wife of a slave, would you?"

These words caused unrequited passion to unite with wounded pride, igniting a blazing rage in the maiden's heart. "You insult me, Rama, by not treating my feelings seriously," she announced. "That is very foolish of you! Apparently you have not felt the fury and wrath of an injured Rakshasa. No female will live as my rival!" Like a demon of destruction, she moved to attack Sita, who fell to the ground shuddering with terror.

Rama placed himself between his wife and the savage maiden. "I was wrong to treat any Rakshasa lightly," he said to Lakshmana. "My humor provoked this danger, and now we must deal with this shameless female as best we can."

Lakshmana wasted no time with words. The threats of the Rakshasa struck like lightning in his heart. He quickly raised his sword and sliced off the maiden's ears and nose before she could defend herself. Her cries of anguish tore through the forest as she fled to her brothers.

With only one glance at their sister's bloody face, they sent a group of fourteen Rakshasas to avenge her. Rama raised his mighty bow and killed them all with his arrows. With mounting fury, the maiden's brothers then assembled a force of 14,000 Rakshasas, each as cruel as he was courageous.

Rama ordered Lakshmana and Sita to take refuge in a well-concealed cave. He was determined to protect them and to fight the enemy alone, so he put on his armor and waited for the Rakshasas to arrive. Many of the gods in heaven came down to earth to watch the battle.

Like the waves of the ocean, the 14,000 Rakshasas attacked Rama. The gods fled at the sight of them. Rama, however, stood firm, without fear in his heart. Like stinging raindrops in a raging storm, his arrows fell upon the Rakshasa warriors. In return, the Rakshasas dislodged mature trees and mighty boulders and hurled them upon Rama. But even these missiles could not stop the defender of the earth. He killed all 14,000 demons, leaving alive only their leader, one of Ravana's brothers.

Rama and the Rakshasa leader then faced one another in a fight to the death. They fought long and hard, like a lion against an elephant. Finally Rama triumphed and the Rakshasa leader lay lifeless upon the bloody earth. The forest floor was strewn with the bodies of the enemy.

Indra, king of the gods, smiled upon Rama. He poured down upon him a shower of blossoms, a great rain of flowers from the heavens.

Chapter 4

Ravana is determined to capture Sita. His adviser, Maricha, devises the deception that makes it possible. After Sita is captured, Rama seeks the help of the monkeys to find her. When the monkey Hanuman learns where she is, Rama and the monkeys set out to kill Ravana and rescue Sita.

When Ravana heard of the death of his brother and the total destruction of his army, he became determined to destroy Rama by capturing Sita. His adviser, Maricha, objected to his plan. "If you provoke Rama, you will destroy your city of Lanka and every Rakshasa in your kingdom!"

"You speak of an empty threat," Ravana replied. "Rama is but a man, and all men are easy prey for a Rakshasa. You must either help me or forfeit your life. I have no use for cowards in my kingdom!"

So Maricha devised a plan to capture Sita by deceptive means. He transformed himself into a beautiful golden and silver deer, with antlers of sapphire and skin as soft as the petals of a flower. He wandered in the forest near Rama's house until Sita noticed him.

When the gentle Sita saw the beautiful creature, she was as enthralled as Maricha had hoped. "Please, Rama," Sita begged. "Follow that deer and capture it for me. I long to have it for my companion, or if you must kill it, I will cherish its shining hide as a golden and silver carpet. I have seen many graceful creatures roaming the forest ways, beautiful antelope and frolicsome monkeys, but never have I seen such a one as this deer! Its beauty illuminates the forest as the moon lights up the sky."

"Beware, Rama!" Lakshmana warned. "No real deer possesses such beauty. This creature must be a Rakshasa in disguise! Their ability to change their shape makes them a treacherous foe. Remember how quick they are to slaughter unwary victims." Thus he prevailed upon Sita to view the animal in its true light.

"On the contrary, Lakshmana," Rama replied, "if this creature is really a Rakshasa, then I feel obligated to kill it before it threatens us. Guard Sita in my absence. I will not be gone long, and I will bring Sita that star-studded deerskin."

Maricha led Rama on a long, tiresome chase through the deep forest. Finally he came within bowshot and killed the creature with an arrow. As Maricha lay dying, he resumed his own shape. Making one last attempt to help Ravana, he disguised his voice as Rama's and called out, "Lakshmana! Help me! I am dying, helpless, in this forest!"

Rama heard these words with a sense of terror and impending doom. He immediately set out for home, painfully aware of the long distance he had to travel.

"Lakshmana," Sita asked, "did you hear Rama's cry? You must go, right now, to help him. What a fool I was to send my dear lord after that deer! If bloodthirsty Rakshasas have found him, they will slaughter him as raging lions slaughter even a fearsome bull."

"It must be some clever Rakshasa trick," Lakshmana protested. "No one in heaven or earth or the netherworld can conquer Rama! Besides, I gave my word that I would guard you from all danger."

"You must be a wicked monster of a man!" Sita replied angrily. "You only pretend to be compassionate. Your heart is as callous as a stone! You cannot love Rama as much as you claim if you will not go to his aid when he needs you."

"All right, Sita. I will do as you wish, although I fear the outcome. A clever trick has clouded your mind. I do not deserve the dishonor you cast upon me. May the guardian spirits of the forest protect you in my absence, and may I soon see Rama by your side!"

Ravana, who was secretly watching nearby, bided his time. Changing himself into a holy hermit, he appeared before Sita with a staff in one hand and a beggar's bowl in the other. As leafy trees conceal a deep, dark cave, so Ravana's disguise artfully concealed his evil purpose. However, all of nature knew what Sita could not sense. Aware of Ravana's dark plans, the fragrant forest breeze ceased to blow, and the trees stood like silent sentinels. No sound of any kind could be heard.

Beneath his pious exterior, Ravana gazed upon Sita with illicit passion. Even in her simple clothing, Rama's queen illuminated her forest home as the moon's silver rays illuminate a starless sky. He spoke of her great beauty with flattering eloquence. Then he said, "Why do you live in this lonesome forest, where dangerous beasts wander and terrifying Rakshasas haunt the gloomy woodland? Your beauty deserves silken robes instead of leafy garments, a palace instead of the trackless forest, and thousands of servants instead of none.

"Choose a royal suitor," Ravana concluded, "a king and a mighty hero, who will treat you with the attention you deserve! I am not the pious hermit that I appear to be. I am Ravana, king of Lanka and the fearsome Rakshasas. My courage and skill have made me ruler of both the heavens and the wide earth. I have many lovely wives, but your beauty has so won my heart that I offer to share my glory and my empire with you alone!"

The faithful Sita angrily replied, "My husband is Rama, a lion among men! Why should the woman who has his love desire yours? In valor and virtue, in word and deed, Rama shines with the brightness of the full moon. You could sooner tear a tooth from the mouth of a hungry lion as it feeds upon a calf, touch the fang of a deadly serpent as it reaches for its victim, uproot a majestic mountain as it stands rooted in rock, than you could win the wife of the righteous and mighty Rama!"

Sita's words did not deter Ravana. Resuming his monstrous shape, he grabbed her hair in one hand and her body in the other. He carried his prisoner to his golden chariot and away through the sky to his distant kingdom.

"Rama! Rama!" Sita cried to the dark forest below. "Save me! Attack the evil Ravana who assaults your faithful wife! Lakshmana, save me from Ravana! Your warning was true, and my charge against you was false. Forgive me! Oh you towering mountains and wooded hills, tell Rama of my abduction."

While all of nature grieved for Sita, Brahma, in the heavens above, was delighted. "Now Ravana surely will die!" the grandfather and creator exclaimed.

Gentle Sita, scanning the land below for some sign of life, spied a group of monkeys sitting on a mountain peak. Secretly, she threw down to them her jewels and her golden veil in the hope that Rama would somehow find her tokens and learn of her fate.

When Rama returned to his house with Lakshmana, whom he had met along the way, his worst fears were realized. Tirelessly the two brothers searched the forests, the mountains, and the plains for Rama's beloved wife without success. In the course of their journey, they mortally wounded a Rakshasa who said, "You will find Sita if you enlist the aid of Sugriva, the great monkey king, and his band. They too can change their shapes, and they know where to locate every demon."

So Rama sought Sugriva, king of the monkeys. "Rama," the monkey king said, "We do not know where Ravana lives, but we do know that he has captured

Sita. We were sitting on a mountaintop when Ravana's chariot passed overhead, and Sita dropped these tokens down to us." Sugriva handed Rama Sita's golden veil and her jewels.

Once Rama held Sita's possessions in his hands, joy brightened his face as the light of the full moon illuminates the midnight sky. "Can you and your people help me find her, Sugriva?" he asked.

"We can certainly try!" the monkey king replied. "I will summon the monkeys from all over the earth. We will divide the earth into four quarters and send one-fourth of the monkeys searching in each direction. I place my greatest hope in the ability of Hanuman, son of the wind. He is strong enough to leap into the heavens and to reach every place on earth, and his courage and intelligence are as great as his strength."

Hanuman, who was standing next to Sugriva, grinned with delight at the praise. "If anyone can find Sita, I can!" he assured Rama. "As a child, I leaped nine thousand miles into the heavens because I hoped to pull down the sun as if it were a ripe fruit swinging on the branch of a tree. Brahma, the grandfather and creator, has made me invincible. Indra, king of the gods, has given me the power to choose my own death. Surely I am the one to perform this heroic deed!"

Hanuman's words caused hope to shine in Rama's eyes as the evening journey of the sun causes the stars to glow in the heavens. "I too feel certain that, if Sita is still alive, you will be able to find her," Rama said. "If your search is successful, Hanuman, show Sita this signet ring of mine. It will make her trust you, and it will remind her of my great love for her."

The monkey band divided into four groups and set out to search the earth for Sita. Hanuman's band was in charge of the southern quarter. They learned that Ravana lived in Lanka, an island that lay on the other side of an ocean 300 miles wide. The broad sea stopped all of the monkeys except Hanuman himself.

Using his extraordinary strength, Hanuman leaped over the great body of water. He glided gracefully across the heavens as a duck moves smoothly upon the water, landing safely and energetically upon the far shore. He rested until the evening journey of the sun brought darkness upon the land.

Then, in order to perform his secret mission, the monkey transformed himself into a cat. In this inconspicuous form, Hanuman entered the golden-walled city and prowled the streets until he learned that Ravana's palace was located on a mountaintop. Again, protective walls were no deterrent. However, no matter where he looked, Hanuman could find no sign of the gentle Sita. He finally returned to the wall of the city and sat down to consider what he should do.

"I hope the Rakshasas have not killed and eaten Sita!" the monkey king thought. "I cannot leave here until I know what has happened to her. If I return without any news, Rama will die of grief!"

Hanuman decided to search the wooded area that lay beyond the city wall. He sprang down from the wall like an arrow leaving a bow and set off among the trees with renewed hope in his heart.

He found Sita deep within the forest, guarded by a number of female Rakshasas. She looked pale, thin, and worried, but her beauty shone through her grief as moonlight shines through a covering layer of clouds. Hanuman hid among the leafy branches of a tree and waited in silence.

He watched Ravana approach Sita and offer her power, wealth, and comfort if she would accept him. He watched Rama's devoted wife hide her face from her captor and sob. He heard her exclaim to Ravana, "One of these days, Rama will arrive and kill you!" He heard Ravana reply, "My patience with you is fast coming to an end! If you have not given yourself to me by two months from this day, it is you who will be tortured and killed."

Once Ravana departed, Sita took refuge at the base of the tree in which Hanuman was hiding. He wished to attract her attention without frightening her or alerting her guards. So he softly spoke about Rama's life in Ayodhya and the major events that had followed, concluding with the search for Sita and his own discovery of her.

At first Sita feared that Hanuman was simply a Rakshasa in another disguise. But when he gave her Rama's signet ring, she plied him with questions. "Does Rama live in safety, and does Lakshmana still serve him faithfully? Does he miss me? Does he still love me? Is he planning to kill Ravana and the Rakshasas for this insult to my honor?"

"Be at ease, gentle Sita," Hanuman replied. "Rama remains as loyal and courageous as ever. He thinks of you day and night. Without you, he takes no pleasure in eating and finds no joy in the beauties of nature. His only goal is to destroy Ravana and rescue you."

Devoted Sita's face brightened as the sky glows once dark clouds move away and reveal a full moon. "Give Rama this jeweled token from my hair," she said, "and tell him to rescue me soon. It has been ten months since I last saw him, and each day of each month creeps to an end. Good luck, heroic monkey! In coming here, you have done what no human could have done, and you have brought the light of hope into my life again."

Rama too revived when he learned that Sita was still alive. "Hanuman, your heroic deed has made you as dear as a brother to me!" he exclaimed. "Tell me again how Sita looked and what she said to you. Your words are like water to a thirsty man, like food to a starving man. Speak to me of my gentle wife, who weeps in sorrow, surrounded by wicked Rakshasas. Then let us arm at once and prepare to cross the ocean. My heart longs to invade Ravana's kingdom and avenge my faithful Sita's honor!"

So it came to pass that Sugriva and Rama led the huge host of monkeys south to the great sea.

Chapter 5

Rama and the monkeys invade Lanka, Ravana's kingdom. After many difficult battles, they defeat the Rakshasas, and Rama kills Ravana. Rama makes Sita prove her purity in an ordeal by fire. Rama, Sita, and Lakshmana then return to Ayodhya, where Rama rules for 10,000 years.

Hanuman had burned a large part of the city of Lanka before returning across the sea. Therefore, Ravana gathered his leaders together to discuss retaliation. Most of them told Ravana what they thought he wanted to hear and advocated total war against Rama and the monkeys. However, two of Ravana's brothers were more thoughtful in their comments.

Kumbha-karna, the mightiest warrior of all the Rakshasas, awoke from his usual slumber and said, "Ravana, stealing Sita was a foolish thing to do, and it has brought needless strife to our land. However, I will continue to support you, for you are my brother and my king. I will slay Rama and tear his limbs apart! Then you can marry Sita."

Vibhishana, Ravana's youngest brother, was more critical. "Ravana, who can fight a war against Rama and win? Rama has a righteous cause behind him, and you are the offender. The warrior who fights with right on his side is doubly armed. Sita has brought evil omens into our land. The cows give no milk, serpents sleep in our kitchens, and wild beasts howl all night long. Like a falcon diving upon its victim, Rama and the monkeys will swoop upon our land with bow and with fire. If you value virtuous behavior and peace, you will save the lives of your people. I advise you to return Sita to Rama and cleanse yourself of your foul deed. Then we can avoid the war that would surely destroy us."

Ravana angrily replied, "Sita is mine, and she will remain mine no matter whom I must fight in order to keep her! I would have taken her by force long ago if Brahma, the grandfather and creator, had not warned me that I would die for such an action."

Ravana concluded, "Either you are jealous and want my kingdom and my queen for yourself, or else you are a traitor. If you were not my brother, I would kill you for what you have said. Because you are of my blood, I order you to leave the kingdom at once. Join Rama, since your heart is already with him!"

"I will leave you, Ravana," Vibhishana replied, "but I pity you, for you cannot see the wisdom of my words. You cannot see the danger and the destruction that will follow if you listen to those who misguide you with their self-serving, honeyed speech. You have lost the ability to save yourself!"

So it came to pass that Vibhishana flew across the sea and joined Rama and the monkeys as an important adviser. In return for his help, Rama promised him the kingship of Lanka once they had killed Ravana. The monkeys collected rocks and trees and placed them in the sea to create a bridge across the broad expanse. Ravana's enemies crossed the bridge, and the war began.

Battle raged both day and night, for the Rakshasas always were most aggressive at night. Rama was the greatest fighter on the field, but Ravana was second only to him in might, and each had a brother who was also a great warrior to support him. The forces were thus closely matched. Clouds of dust from charging elephants obscured friend and foe alike. Arrows fell like hissing serpents upon all warriors. The best on both sides were strong enough to hurl mountaintops upon their enemies. Streams of blood from hundreds of slain Rakshasas and monkeys flooded the earth like summer rains.

Ravana was so certain of victory that he let his great warrior-brother Kumbha-karna sleep through most of the war; he himself did not enter the battle until the monkeys had killed all of his strongest warriors. Ravana seemed invincible as he fought his way across the battlefield in his chariot. But Rama gained the advantage when that mighty son of Dasa-ratha climbed upon Hanuman's back and fought a fierce battle with Ravana. He demolished Ravana's chariot, broke the Rakshasa's crown in two, and severely wounded him with an arrow.

Then, instead of killing Ravana while the advantage was his, Rama said, "You are too weak to fight, so return to Lanka and rest. When you have recovered your strength, we two will fight again. Then I will show you how strong I really am!"

Ravana decided that the time had come to seek the aid of his great warrior-brother Kumbha-karna, who was fast asleep as usual. Kumbha-karna often slept for as long as ten months at a time and awoke only to gorge himself with food. So the Rakshasas first prepared for the huge creature a mountain of food: heaps of buffalo and deer meat, rice, and jars of blood.

Once they could feed him, they tried to awaken him. They shouted and beat their drums so loudly that the birds in the sky died of fright, but Kumbha-karna did not wake up. In unison, 10,000 Rakshasas yelled at him, beat 1,000 kettle-drums, and struck his body with huge log clubs, but Kumbha-karna still did not wake up. Then they bit his ears, poured pots full of water upon him, drove 1,000 elephants against him, and wounded him with spears and maces. At long last, Kumbha-karna woke up.

The monstrous Rakshasa ate the mountain of food and drank 2,000 flasks of wine. Then he put on his golden armor and marched upon the monkeys. They fled from this moving mountain in terror—with good reason, for whomever Kumbha-karna caught, he devoured.

Rama, Hanuman, and the monkeys gathered around him as clouds cling to a mountain peak. Although they hurled massive rocks and huge trees upon him, their weapons splintered against the giant Rakshasa's metal coat. Meanwhile, Kumbha-karna killed hundreds of monkeys with each thrust of his mighty spear, and he ate twenty or thirty monkeys at a time, the excess blood and fat dribbling from his mighty mouth.

Having wounded the best of the monkey leaders, he came face to face with Lakshmana. "You are the finest of warriors, Lakshmana," Kumbha-karna said. "You have shown great skill and have won great glory. I have no desire to fight you because I intend to pit my might and skill against the only human who is greater than you are, your brother. I will fight Rama to the death."

Kumbha-karna's fortune turned when he fought Rama, for Dasa-ratha's son sent deadly flaming arrows against him. Rama severed the giant's two arms with two of his arrows. He sliced away the giant's two legs by hurling two sharp-edged discs at him. Finally Rama aimed Indra's great arrow at the giant's neck. It pierced his armor and severed his head from his shoulders. His headless body crashed upon the bloody earth and tumbled into the sea, where it created such violent waves that it seemed as if a tempest were stirring them.

Lakshmana killed Ravana's son. Soon thereafter, he was severely wounded by a flaming arrow that he intercepted in order to save the life of Vibhishana, Ravana's brother who had become their ally. These two incidents brought Ravana and Rama against one another in their final battle.

From the heavens the gods were watching the great battle. When Ravana entered the battle in a new chariot drawn by fresh horses, Indra, king of the gods, announced, "We gods always help those who are righteous and brave. The time has now come to help Rama in his fight against Ravana. Rama already has my quiver filled with sharp-tipped arrows. I will now give him golden armor that was fashioned in the heavens and my own golden, horse-drawn chariot, driven by my own driver."

Now Rama's war gear was superior to Ravana's. Nevertheless, Ravana was such a great warrior that the battle raged long and furiously. Some of Ravana's arrows wore fiery, flame-spewing faces that turned into hissing poisonous snakes. Against these, Rama used Vishnu's bow, and arrows belonging to Vishnu's golden-winged bird, for these arrows turned into birds and consumed the snakes on Ravana's arrows. Still the battle raged. In terror, the brilliant sun turned pale, the winds ceased blowing, and the mountains and the sea shook. With Indra's mighty arrows, Rama sliced off Ravana's ten heads one by one, but each time he severed a head another grew in its place. Finally Rama lifted Brahma's shining arrow, which blazed like the fire of the sun and had wings like Indra's lightning bolt. It shattered Ravana's heart, killing him.

Indra smiled upon Rama. He poured down upon the bloody earth a shower of blossoms, a great rain of flowers from the heavens. The sun shone forth in its full brilliance. Gentle, cool breezes rustled the leaves on the trees, perfuming the air with their fragrance. Heavenly harps played celestial music, and Rama heard a heavenly voice exclaim, "Rama, champion of the righteous and doer of virtuous deeds, now you have completed your noble task. Peace reigns in the heavens and on the earth. We shower our blessings upon you!"

Rama unstrung his bow and joyfully put aside his weapons. When Vibhishana mourned Ravana's death, Rama said to him, "Ravana was one of the earth's great warriors and heroes. Even Indra, king of the gods, could not stand against him. Such heroes should not be mourned when they die in battle, for they have died with honor, and none of us can escape death."

After giving Ravana a hero's funeral, Rama sent Hanuman to Sita with news of the victory. She returned freshly bathed and dressed. At the sight of her husband, her face shone with the radiance of the full moon in the midnight sky.

Rama said, "Dear Sita, with the help of Hanuman, Sugriva, and Vibhishana, I have kept my promise to you and have performed the obligation of a man on whose honor a stain has been placed. I have cleansed my family and myself of dishonor by killing Ravana.

"However," Rama continued, "you bear the stain of a woman who has lived with a man other than her husband. Ravana gazed upon you and touched you. No man of honor can accept such behavior in his wife. Therefore, I must publicly renounce you. You may live with whomever you choose—Lakshmana or Bharata, Sugriva or Vibhishana—but you may not live with me!"

Sita trembled like a leaf in the wind and sobbed as she heard these words. Then she dried her tears and said, "If you doubted my faithful devotion to you, my purity of heart, why did you cross the broad ocean and risk your life for me? Have you forgotten that I am the daughter of Mother Earth and that I followed you into the wild forestlands with a woman's deep devotion? At no point in my life have I ever been unfaithful. If Ravana gazed upon me and touched me, you must realize that I had no power to stop him.

"However," she continued, "when the shadow of dishonor casts its shade upon an innocent woman's life, death by fire is the only way to restore the honor she deserves. So, Lakshmana, if you love me, build a funeral pyre for me and light it. I would rather die than live with a stain upon my name."

Rama showed no sign of weakness or anguish at these words. So Lakshmana, with an aching heart, did as Sita had asked him.

As she stood before the roaring flames, Sita announced, "If in thought and in deed I have been faithful and true, if in my lifelong devotion to dharma I have lived without a stain, may this fire defend my name!" Then, showing courage and faith and no sign of fear, the gentle Sita entered the flames and disappeared. All who watched her wept with grief and awe.

The gods descended from the heavens in their golden chariots and said to Rama, "Preserver of life on earth, how can you act like a common man and treat Sita in this way? Do you not remember that you are the first of all the gods, the grandfather and creator of all? As you were in the beginning, so will you be in the end."

Rama replied, "I believe that I am Rama, eldest son of Dasa-ratha. If I am wrong, then let the grandfather tell me who I am."

Brahma said, "Rama is an earthly form of the great god Vishnu, who lives forever. In your heavenly form, you are both creation and destruction, the savior of all gods and holy hermits, the conqueror of all enemies. You live in every creature and in every part of nature. Day comes when you open your eyes, and night comes when you close them. I am your heart. Sita is the earthly form of your heavenly wife, Lakshmi.

"Now that you have killed Ravana," Brahma concluded, "you can assume your divine form and return to heaven, for you have accomplished the task for which you adopted human form. Those who love you and who tell your story will be rewarded."

The flames parted and Agni, the god of fire, appeared with faithful Sita. The flames had not touched her. Her face, her hair, and her clothing were as fresh as the grass in the morning. Agni said to Rama, "Son of Dasa-ratha, reclaim your devoted wife. She resisted all the temptations Ravana put before her and has remained pure in both thought and deed."

Rama's eyes glowed with the radiance of the sun as he announced, "In all the years that I have known her, I have never doubted my Sita's virtue. Now the whole world knows what I know, for Agni has attested to her pure and shining name. I reclaim her with delight in my heart, now that my people know that the eldest son of Dasa-ratha puts the law of his country above his own personal desires." Rama then embraced his loving wife, who understood the reason for her trial and forgave him.

The gods then revealed the presence of King Dasa-ratha in their midst. "Rama," his father said, "not only have you helped the gods and the holy hermits, but you have saved my honor. Your exile is now at an end. Return as a victorious hero to Ayodhya, and rule there with your brothers. May you live a long life!"

King Dasa-ratha turned to Lakshmana and said, "My son, you are ever true to deeds of virtue. Continue to take care of Rama, and may you have a good life."

Finally the king turned to Sita and said, "Forgive Rama. It was for your own good that he spoke against you in public. You have earned glory that few women can ever achieve."

Then Indra, king of the gods, appeared before Rama and said: "Righteous Rama, lion among men, in return for what you have done for us, ask whatever you wish, and the gift will be yours!"

Rama replied, "Lord of heaven, please grant renewed life to all those who fought on my behalf against the Rakshasas, and provide them with food and fresh water wherever they may go."

"So be it," Indra replied.

When it was time for Hanuman to leave Rama, he said, "Rama, I ask you to grant me one special gift. As you may remember, Indra, king of the gods, gave me the power to choose my own death. I ask you to permit me to live on earth as long as people tell the tale of your glorious deeds."

"So be it, Hanuman," Rama replied, "and as a token of my gift to you, I also give you this jeweled chain from around my neck and place it, with love and respect and gratitude, around yours."

So Rama, Lakshmana, and Sita returned to Ayodhya after an absence of fourteen years. Bharata had remained true to his word. His face now glowed with the radiance of a great wise man, for he had been loyal to dharma. He had faithfully honored Rama's sandals as the token of Rama's kingship and had lived the life of a holy hermit within the palace walls.

Rama and Sita became the king and queen of Ayodhya and ruled their kingdom of Kosala for 10,000 years. During all of that time, neither terrible diseases nor untimely death visited their land. Yama, lord of the dead, let infants grow to maturity and husbands live to old age. Farmers rejoiced, for rains came reliably and winds were friendly. In gratitude Mother Earth provided bountiful harvests, fruitful trees, and rich pastureland. The people were loyal to dharma and loved their neighbors and their king. Those who lived in towns and cities worked at their customary tasks on the loom or the anvil without fearing liars and robbers. It was truly a time of happiness and peace for all.

Chapter 6

The people of Kosala again question Sita's virtue, and Rama banishes her. In exile she gives birth to Rama's twin sons. Valmiki teaches them *The Ramayana*. When Rama hears his story and meets his sons, he brings Sita back and asks that her purity be tested again. Instead, Sita returns to Mother Earth, her mother. After 1,000 years of additional rule, Rama and his brothers return to heaven as Vishnu.

When Rama had reigned for 10,000 years, Sita became pregnant and decided to visit the hermitage of the wise men along the holy Ganges River. The night before the start of her journey, Rama asked his friends and advisers, "What do my subjects say about my brothers, Sita, and me?"

One replied, "They speak admiringly of your alliance with the monkeys and your conquest of the Rakshasas and Ravana."

"Surely that cannot be all they speak of," Rama said. "Do they not say more?"

Another replied, "Since you press us, you should know that your subjects criticize you for taking Sita back after she had lived with Ravana in Lanka. They feel they must accept improper behavior from their own wives because their king has done so."

Rama's heart flooded with dismay. He dismissed his companions and sent for his brothers. Tearfully, he told them what he had just heard. "My heart knows that Sita is pure, and she has proven her purity by fire. Yet my subjects force me to renounce my devoted wife for a second time. A king cannot reign with disgrace upon his name.

"Therefore," Rama continued, "I want you, Lakshmana, to take Sita to Valmiki's hermitage along the Ganges River as if you are simply honoring her request. Then, however, you must leave her there."

When Lakshmana had brought Sita to Valmiki and had told her of Rama's position, she said, "In some past life I must have committed grave sins to be punished this way twice in spite of my purity! I would drown myself in the Ganges if I were not carrying within me Rama's child.

"Return to Rama with this message," Sita concluded. "Tell him that, as always, I will be loyal to dharma. I will continue to serve my husband with a woman's deep devotion no matter what the circumstances. I accept my exile but grieve over my false reputation."

Lakshmana gave Rama Sita's message. Then he said to his brother, "Do not grieve over what you have had to do. Each of us must accept whatever life brings. Wherever there is growth, there is decay. Wherever there is birth, there is death. Wherever there is prosperity, there is poverty. Wherever there are friendship and love, there is separation."

In time, Sita gave birth to twin sons, who grew up with their mother and the holy hermits in the forest. The hermit Valmiki taught them wisdom and the skill of recitation. Then he taught them to sing *The Ramayana*.

Valmiki knew the story of Rama because one day, years earlier, he had asked the great wise man Narada, "Is there any man alive who possesses perfect righteousness and courage?" Narada had replied, "Rama is such a man. I will tell you about him."

Soon after that, Brahma, grandfather and creator of the world, appeared before Valmiki. "I have watched how you live your life. Your thoughts and your deeds have shown me that you are a wise and compassionate man. Therefore, I have chosen you to fashion the story of Rama into beautiful verses that will reveal truth from beginning to end."

Brahma continued, "Be confident that you already possess the understanding of human nature and the gift of poetry. Whatever more you need to know about Rama's story I will see that you discover. Your *Ramayana* will be told from one generation to another as long as snow-covered mountains rise from Mother Earth and sparkling seas wash her shores." With these words, Brahma disappeared.

As Valmiki sat in deep thought, the people in Rama's life came alive in his mind and revealed their tale. The holy hermit shaped their words and deeds into verses. Thus he was able to teach *The Ramayana* to the sons of Rama and Sita.

After many lonely and joyless years had passed, Rama decided to hold the sacred sacrifice of the horse. During the year that the horse wandered in freedom, the king gave many gifts to the poor: clothing to the needy, food and drink to the hungry, shelters to the weak and aged, and gold and homes to orphans. He invited all of his subjects as well as the monkeys and Vibhishana, king of the Rakshasas, to the final ceremony.

When the time came, Valmiki arrived with Rama's sons. He instructed them to sing *The Ramayana* from beginning to end, reciting twenty of the 500 cantos each day from morning until night. "Do not speak of your own misfortunes," he advised them. "If Rama asks who your parents are, tell him that I am your teacher and your father here on earth."

The children captivated everyone who heard their song. The people whispered to one another how much like Rama they looked. As the days passed and the boys continued their performance, Rama realized that these were his own sons. He called Valmiki to him and said, "I long to have Sita at my side again, for I have never forgotten our love. Let her prove her purity before the assembled guests once more. Then she can again share my throne and my kingdom with me."

When Sita arrived in Ayodhya, Rama said, "Gentle, devoted, faithful Sita. Let the world once again know of your virtue. I have never questioned your purity. Forgive me for banishing you in order to please my subjects. It was a shameful deed and an error, but I knew no other way to stifle the voice of rumor."

Sita looked upon the assembled throng. She saw her husband and king, as bright as a star. She saw her sons performing as hermit-minstrels, as radiant as two moons. She saw kings from many lands and the gods from heaven. "How many times should I have to prove my purity?" she asked herself. "I am Rama's queen and the daughter of Mother Earth and a great king. Surely it is time to put this life behind me and leave the earth."

So Sita sadly announced, "If my thoughts and deeds have been pure from the day of my birth, and I have been loyal to dharma in my devotion and duty to my husband, I call upon you, Mother Earth, to receive your child. Put an end to the pain and shame of my life, and claim me as your own!"

Before the astonished eyes of the crowd, the earth opened, and a golden throne rose from its depths, supported by serpents from the netherworld as a rosebud is enfolded by leaves. Mother Earth stretched forth her loving arms to embrace her virtuous daughter and to place her upon her own throne. Then mother, daughter, and throne descended into the earth, which closed above them.

Rama watched the spectacle with grief and anger. Brahma, the grandfather and creator, then appeared before him and said, "Rama, do not grieve for Sita or for yourself. Sita is pure and innocent, and her reward is to join her mother. Remember that you are the great god Vishnu. You will be with Sita once again in heaven, where she is your wife, Lakshmi. The end of Valmiki's story will reveal your future to you."

Rama reigned for another thousand years without joy. He had his craftspeople fashion a golden statue of Sita, which he kept by his side. His kingdom prospered.

One day the figure of Time entered Rama's palace and said to him, "As Rama, you have reigned on earth for eleven thousand years. The grandfather has sent me to ask you: Do you wish to reign longer over mortals, or are you ready to reign once again over all of the gods?"

Rama replied, "I am ready to return to my place among the gods in heaven."

When Rama announced that he was going to leave the earth and return to heaven, his brothers left their thrones to their children and joined him. Sugriva, king of the monkeys, also joined him. "Wherever you go," he said, "I will follow!"

Rama permitted any monkey who chose to follow him to do so—except Hanuman. "Do you remember the gift you asked of me long ago?" he asked Hanuman. "You asked to live on earth for as long as people spoke of my great deeds. Therefore, you will live here forever. May you be happy!"

Vibhishana, king of the Rakshasas, prepared the departure rites. When Rama's brothers and their wives, his counselors and servants, all the people of Ayodhya, the Rakshasas, monkeys, bears, and birds had assembled, Brahma arrived on earth with 100,000 chariots. Indra, king of the gods, smiled upon the loyal host. He poured down upon them a shower of blossoms, a great rain of flowers from the heavens.

Brahma exclamed, "Hail, Vishnu, preserver of life on earth! Enter heaven in whatever form pleases you."

Rama and his brothers entered heaven in the form of Vishnu, and all of the gods rejoiced and bowed before him. Then Vishnu said, "Brahma, all of those who assembled wish to follow because they love me. In order to remain with me, they are renouncing their lives on earth. Therefore, give each his or her place in heaven."

So it came to pass that those who followed Rama assumed their godly forms, and now they live in heaven.

So ends *The Ramayana*, created by Valmiki and honored by Brahma, the grandfather and creator. Those who recite it will earn rich gifts of cows and gold. Those who hear it or read it will become cleansed of all sin. They will have a long and honored life. They will enjoy the blessing of children and grandchildren, both on earth and in heaven.

❧ QUESTIONS FOR
Response, Discussion, and Analysis

1. How does the nurse change Bharata's mother's attitude toward Rama? Are her fears realistic? Explain. Is Bharata's mother's attitude realistic? Defend your point of view.

2. How does Dasa-ratha put himself in a position from which he feels he cannot retreat? Could he have retreated? Should he have retreated? Defend your point of view.

3. Is Lakshmana's dharma less than Rama's because he encourages Rama to fight for his title as king? It not, why does he do it? Defend your point of view.

4. Is Rama right to obey his father when he knows that Dasa-ratha was forced to banish him? Is Rama right to continue to obey even after his father's death? Defend your point of view.

5. What is the nature of dharma that Lakshmana leaves his wife to accompany Rama, yet Rama takes Sita with him?

6. Is Bharata's treatment of his mother justified? Defend your point of view. What is the nature of dharma that Bharata treats her this way? Why did she not anticipate his response?

7. What is the nature of dharma that Bharata pleads with Rama to take the throne?

8. How much flexibility is possible within the concept of dharma? Since Rama, Bharata, and Lakshmana are all earthly forms of the god Vishnu, why do they exhibit extremely different points of view? Does Valmiki intend to show that a variety of responses is justifiable in any complicated situation? Does he intend to show that Rama is the greatest of the brothers by contrasting his attitudes and behavior with theirs? Defend your point of view.

9. A wise man gives Rama Vishnu's bow, Brahma's arrow, Indra's quiver of arrows, and a special sword. What is the purpose of such weapons in a myth? How do they enhance the hero's stature? How do they detract from his heroism?

10. Why does Rama tease Ravana's sister? What does this reveal about Rama?

11. When Sita makes Lakshmana leave her to search for Rama, how does Valmiki make her a sympathetic character in spite of the fact that she is criticizing the loyal, devoted Lakshmana?

12. What kinds of temptations does Ravana use upon Sita? What is so tempting about them?

13. Why are the monkeys such appealing allies? What does their role add to the myth?

14. How does Hanuman's ability to choose his own death affect the decisions he makes? How does this gift permit him to be more heroic? Less heroic?

15. Ravana's two brothers, Kumbha-karna and Vibhishana, disagree about supporting him. Which brother do you think is correct? Defend your point of view.

16. How does Valmiki's portrayal of Kumbha-karna and Vibhishana mold the reader's opinion of the Rakshasas? How does their characterization affect the myth as a whole?

17. Why is Vibhishana not considered a traitor?

18. How does Valmiki portray Kumbha-karna with humor? How does Valmiki portray Kumbha-karna with respect? What do these characterizations add to the myth?

19. Should Lakshmana have intercepted an arrow meant to kill Vibhishana? Why or why not? What does this reveal about Lakshmana's character?

20. Why does Rama give Ravana a hero's funeral? What does it reveal about Ravana? What does it reveal about Rama? What would you have done in Rama's place? Why?

21. Is Rama right to renounce Sita publicly the first time? Defend your point of view.

22. How does Sita feel about this renunciation? How would you feel as Sita?

23. Is Rama right to renounce Sita publicly the second time? What, if anything, has changed? Defend your point of view.

24. Why does Rama make Sita prove her virtue a second time while acknowledging that he was wrong to have banished her? Is he right to do this? Defend your point of view.

25. How does Sita feel about this denunciation? Is her revenge justified? Defend your point of view.

26. In Hindu society Rama and Sita are the ideal couple because Rama provides a model of proper behavior for a husband, and Sita a model of proper behavior for a wife. What do you think of Rama as a husband? Of Sita as a wife?

27. Compare the values presented in this myth with the values you consider most important in a marriage. Describe what you consider to be the ideal husband and the ideal wife.

28. Why is Rama such a great hero? What temptations does he resist? What tests of character does he pass? What tasks does he accomplish? Which seem more important, the tests or the tasks? How does his behavior affect his heroic image?

29. Why is Rama a greater hero than Bharata and Lakshmana? What does he do that they do not do?

The Creation of the Universe and Human Beings

Scholars believe that many of the Chinese myths that have come down to us are not as old and authentic as the myths from other ancient cultures. The problem began in 213 B.C., when the first emperor of China burned all books that were not about medicine, prophecy, or farming. Then, during the great Han dynasty (202 B.C.–A.D. 220), the emperors instituted the teachings of Confucius as the state religion and banned religions that involved nature worship. Many of the old myths that had been passed down orally were recorded anew during this period. However, Han scholars revised them to reflect their own attitudes and the political and religious climate of their time.

Fortunately, the Han scholars were also great collectors, and unlike earlier scholars, who were more aristocratic in their focus, Han scholars collected oral myths, legends, and folktales from the common people. Therefore, some myths that appear for the first time during the Han dynasty are actually from an earlier period.

The Chinese have three basic creation myths, involving Yin and Yang, Nu Kua, and P'an Ku. Yin and Yang, who are two gods, appear in the *Huai-nan Tzu* (*Master Huai-nan*), compiled early in the Han period (c. 139 B.C.) by Liu An, the king of Huai-nan (c. 170–122 B.C.). In these myths, Yin ("shaded") and Yang ("sunlit") arise out of chaos and represent complementary essences in the universe that, taken together, comprise the whole. Yin is the female principle in nature—heavy, dark, earthy, passive, submissive, and cool. Yang is the male principle—light, bright, celestial, active, aggressive, and warm. Just as male and female unite among humans, so the sun, a god representing the qualities of yang, marries the moon, a goddess representing the qualities of yin. Even earth (yin) and heaven (yang) represent complementary aspects of the whole.

In her earliest form, Nu Kua is a Great Goddess or Mother Goddess who functions as an independent divinity. In the *Feng su t'ung-yi* (*Explanations of Social Customs*), compiled later in the Han period by Ying Shao (c. A.D. 140–c. 206), Nu Kua creates human beings. The fact that, in this Nu Kua myth, the other forms of life have already emerged from P'an Ku's corpse reveals that the myth of P'an Ku already existed, at least in an oral form.

In Liu An's *Huai-nan Tzu*, Nu Kua appears as the Great Goddess or Mother Goddess, who is also Goddess of Fertility. In this myth, the second of China's four flood myths, Nu Kua repairs all the damage caused by Kung Kung, a primeval warrior-god. She puts an end to the great flood by building dams. She also restores the damaged universe by repairing the sky and its supporting columns. Moreover, like the Great Goddess in other matriarchal cultures, she rides in a dragon-drawn chariot. Kung Kung is the principal character in the first of China's flood myths. However, in the myth of Nu Kua that appears in the *Huai-nan Tzu*, his role in causing the flood forms the setting for Nu Kua's drama.

P'an Ku ("Coiled Antiquity"), a semidivine giant, is the principal character in the two most detailed of the existing Chinese creation myths. Both myths were originally compiled by Hsu Cheng, who lived in southwestern China in the period of the Three Kingdoms (third century A.D.). These male-dominated myths soon became the authoritative Chinese versions of creation. In Hsu Cheng's *San Wu li chi* (*Historical Records of the Three Sovereign Divinities and the Five Gods*), P'an Ku creates order out of chaos by separating the sky from the earth. Given Hsu Cheng's location, this myth may have reached China by way of Central Asia and then Tibet.

The second part of the P'an Ku myth appears in Hsu Cheng's *Wu yun li-nien chi* (*A Chronicle of the Five Cycles of Time*). Here, P'an Ku's death preserves and increases the order that he earlier established. His corpse provides additional structure by differentiating the surface of the earth into a variety of natural forms, such as mountains, oceans, and forests, and by differentiating the heavens as well. The resemblance of this myth to many Indo-European creation myths leads scholars to conclude that it is probably Indo-European in origin. Hsu Cheng may have collected it from Central Asian sources. However, it is also similar to the ancient Near Eastern (Akkadian/Babylonian) myth of Apsu and Tiamat.

THE CREATION OF THE UNIVERSE AND HUMAN BEINGS

YIN AND YANG AND THE CREATION OF THE UNIVERSE

In a time long past, before Heaven and earth came to be, there was only chaos. The universe was vast, obscure, and barren. For there was only a great, gaping expanse of desolate space—without light, without form, and without life. Images alone appeared and disappeared within the mist.

Then it came to pass that chaos gave birth to two gods. They wove the fabric that became the heavens. And they molded the substance that became the earth. So great were these gods that they were beyond understanding. They could move higher into the heavens and lower into the depths than anyone could imagine. And no one knew where they took their rest.

After the two gods had fashioned Heaven and earth, it came to pass that they became separate in form and in function. They divided into Yin and Yang. And Yang gathered into himself all that was bright and light. And, like a mist, Yang drifted upward into Heaven and became one with it. And Heaven became round. Then Yin gathered into herself all that was dark and heavy. And, like a thick, plodding mass, Yin sank downward into the earth and became one with it. And earth became square.

Yang's hot breath became intense and gave birth to fire. And his fiery breath became the sun. Yin's cold breath became intense and gave birth to water. And her watery breath became the moon. Stars spun off from the sun and the moon. And, being part of Yang, the sun, the moon, and the stars all settled in the sky, while, being part of Yin, rivers and seas, rainwater, silt, and dust all settled on the surface of the earth. The complex essence of Yang and Yin became the four seasons that dwell on earth in an endless cycle. And the essence of the four seasons became the ten thousand things in nature that populate the earth. Substances became hard or soft. And a multitude of living things came into being. The vapor that was dense and cloudy took the form of insects. And the vapor that was pure took the form of human beings.

NU KUA, CREATOR AND PRESERVER OF HUMAN LIFE

Nu Kua, the Great Goddess or Mother Goddess, created the first people. She herself was formed like a human being, except that instead of legs she had the tail of a dragon. Nu Kua glided over the earth. And as she traveled, she admired all of the beautiful forms that had emerged from P'an Ku's corpse. She loved the trees, the plants, and the flowers. But she was most interested in the fish and the animals. For these living creatures were more active.

Nu Kua decided that she wanted to watch the fish and the animals, and so she stopped gliding and studied them. And after studying them for a while, Nu Kua decided that creation was not yet complete, for animals and fish were not intelligent enough. She decided that she would now create creatures who would be superior to all other living things.

And so Nu Kua glided along the Yellow River, and she decided to use the yellow earth of this riverbed to form human beings. And so she sat down along the shore of the river. She then took handfuls of wet clay from the riverbed, and she formed them into little people. She made them look almost like her, but instead of dragon-tails, she gave each of them two legs to match their two arms.

As soon as her little people were prepared to walk, Nu Kua breathed life into them. Some she infused with Yang, the masculine, aggressive principle in nature. And these little people became men. Others she infused with Yin, the female, submissive principle in nature. And these little people became women.

Nu Kua worked quickly, but it was very hard work. And so, after a while, she became too tired to continue to fashion people one at a time. She decided that she would try to find a way to create her little people faster and more easily.

And so Nu Kua glided along the shore of the river. And it came to pass that she soon spied a twisted rope—the type of measure that builders would use in time to come. Nu Kua studied the rope, and she decided that it would help her make her little people faster and more easily.

And so Nu Kua picked up the twisted rope. She held onto one end, but she placed the rest of the rope on the wet clay of the riverbed. Then she rolled the rope around in the wet clay. And as she turned it, Nu Kua was delighted to see that, as she had hoped, the wet clay was sticking to it.

At last, the upper end of the rope was completely covered with wet clay. Nu Kua then lifted the rope off the riverbed, and she shook it over the shore. And Nu Kua was delighted to see that, as she had hoped, each drop of clay that fell off became a human being.

Nu Kua was pleased that she had created her little people faster and more easily. But her two methods did not create exactly the same type of human beings. The people whom Nu Kua had fashioned by hand from the rich yellow earth of the riverbed were high-born, wealthy, and intelligent. But the people who had fallen in drops from her rope were low-born, poor, common folk. Nevertheless, all of Nu Kua's children built homes and settled into villages and farms in order to provide for their daily needs.

In time it came to pass that Kung Kung, an age-old god, became so angry at another god that he attacked him. But Kung Kung did not look where he was going, and so he rammed his head into one of the mountains that supports the sky. The mountain came tumbling to the ground. And as it fell, it tore a great hole in the sky, and it caused the earth to crack open in many places.

Flames blazed forth from some of the crevasses, burning homes and crops. And these fires raged far and wide, for no one could smother them. Rivers overflowed their banks, and torrents of underground water gushed forth from other fissures. These surging waters flooded the land and created a vast sea where once there had been villages and farms, for no one could provide a drain.

Now everything was at the bottom of the sea. And the few animals and people who remained alive could find nothing to eat. And so it came to pass that starving animals became ferocious and feasted on whatever people they could find. Meanwhile, starving birds of prey swooped down from the heavens. They grabbed all who were old and weak in their talons, and then they carried them off to their nests. No one could stop them.

Nu Kua watched in horror as hundreds of her little people starved to death or drowned. She decided that she had to act quickly if she hoped to save any of the children she had created. And so, first, she set fire to the reeds that grew beside the river. She then stuffed their ashes into the burning cracks in the earth to smother the raging flames. Next Nu Kua piled up more of the reed ashes to form dikes. These dams forced the swift flood-waters to seep into the earth and to flow in controlled river channels. And so it came to pass that Nu Kua's children returned to their farms and villages, for they could resume their daily occupations.

Then Nu Kua glided over to the Yellow River and chose a number of stones in five different colors. She melted them in a forge and covered the hole in the heavens with them. Next she removed the four legs from a giant tortoise and used one at each corner of the earth as an additional pillar to support the sky. In this way, Nu Kua repaired the devastation that Kung Kung had so thoughtlessly created. But she knew of no way to raise the northeast corner of the earth on which the fifth pillar had fallen. And so, from that day to this, that land is lower than the rest of China, and rivers flow eastward across that land and into the sea.

Nu Kua continues to watch over her children. Her swift, winged dragons pull her thunder-chariot through the heavens and bring forth the rains that nourish all that grows upon the earth. And so the hearts of Nu Kua's children are filled with gratitude for all that the Mother Goddess has done for them and for all that she continues to do.

P'AN KU, CREATOR OF THE UNIVERSE

In the beginning an egg—like that of a chicken—contained the entire universe. Within the egg was one chaotic mass. Heaven and earth were identical. And all was always dark, for neither the sun nor the moon existed. From within this dark mass, P'an Ku, the first living being, was formed.

Then, finding himself alive in darkness, encased within an egg, and surrounded by chaos, P'an Ku decided to bring order into the universe. First he broke open the world egg. Yang, the lighter part, rose and became the heavens. And Yin, the heavier part, sank and became the earth.

P'an Ku tried to stand upon the earth. But the heavens pressed heavily upon his head. He realized that no life would ever be able to exist on earth if the heavens were not high in the sky. And so he sat down and thought about how to solve this problem.

That day, P'an Ku went through nine transformations. And it came to pass that P'an Ku became more godlike than Heaven and more wise than earth. He decided that the only way living objects and creatures would form and survive upon the earth would be if he held up the sky.

For the next eighteen thousand years, P'an Ku worked constantly to keep the heavens from crushing the surface of the earth. He ate only the mists that blew into his mouth, and he never slept. At first he could only rest on his knees with his elbows bent. And yet, summoning all of his great strength, he pushed his feet against the earth, and he pushed his hands upward against the sky. Each day he pushed the heavens ten feet higher, and he forced the earth to sink ten feet lower. And each day he became ten feet taller.

The time came when P'an Ku could rise to his feet. But his knees were still bent as he pushed his feet down against the earth, and his elbows were still bent as he pushed his hands upward against the sky. At last the time came when P'an Ku could stand at his full height. And then he pushed his feet down against the earth with straight legs, and he pushed his hands upward against the sky with his arms stretched out to their full length.

Day after day and night after night, month after month and year after year, P'an Ku stood upright, as firm as a rock column. He never stopped pushing the earth lower with his feet, and he never stopped pushing the heavens higher with his hands.

P'an Ku's pushing caused the earth and the sky to move ten feet each day. And so it came to pass that, little by little, the earth sank lower and lower beneath the sky. And it came to pass that, little by little, the sky rose higher and higher above the earth. And the lower the earth sank, and the higher the heavens rose, the taller P'an Ku became.

At last the earth rested far below the heavens. And the heavens rested high above the earth. And only then did P'an Ku realize that he was very, very tired. He looked up at the heavens above his hands, and then he looked far, far down to the earth beneath his feet. And P'an Ku felt certain that the distance between heaven and earth was so great that he could lie down and rest without fearing that the sky would collapse and crush the earth.

So P'an Ku lay down and fell asleep. And it came to pass that P'an Ku died in his sleep. But he had not done all that he could do, for living objects and creatures could now survive upon the earth, but as yet they had no form.

And so it came to pass that P'an Ku's corpse gave shape and substance to the universe. His head formed the mountain of the East, while his feet formed the mountain of the West. His right arm formed the mountain of the North, while his left arm formed the mountain of the South. And his torso formed the mountain of the Center. These five sacred mountains defined the four corners of the square earth and its center. Each stood firmly upon the earth like a giant stone column, and each did its part to hold up the heavens.

From the hair on P'an Ku's head, chin, and eyebrows came forth the planets and the stars. His left eye became the sun, while his right eye became the moon. His breath formed the clouds and the wind. His voice became lightning and thunder. And his perspiration and body-fluids became the rain and the dew.

P'an Ku's flesh formed the soil of the earth, while his blood and his semen became the oceans and rivers that encircle it. His veins and muscles gave shape to the earth's surface. His teeth and his bones formed rocks and minerals, while his bone marrow became jade and pearls. From the hair on his body came forth trees, plants, and flowers.

Then the wind that had come forth from P'an Ku's breath blew upon the mites that lived on his skin. And these mites became fish, animals, and the black-haired people.

❧ QUESTIONS FOR
Response, Discussion, and Analysis

1. In what significant way does the myth of Yin and Yang differ from the myth of Nu Kua?

2. How does the myth of Yin and Yang present the relationship between divinity and human beings?

3. What is the nature of Nu Kua? Why did the myth-makers have her create human beings using two different methods?

4. What is the nature of P'an Ku? If he were a human being, what kind of person would he be? What tasks would you give him to do? Why?

Chi Li Slays the Serpent

The story of Chi Li and the serpent has been told for hundreds of years in the form of ballads. However, the story probably originated in the mythology of an even older period. The first emperor of China, who created the Ch'in dynasty (221–207 B.C.)—the period from which this story dates—burned all books that were not about prophecy, medicine, or farming, as a way of giving China a new beginning. Consequently, most, if not all, previously recorded Chinese myths were destroyed. However, the scholarly class remained prestigious in the new China, and many myths from the old oral and written traditions reappeared in a new form and with a revised content that made them politically acceptable.

Historically, in many societies throughout the world, the serpent represented immortality because it shed its skin each year. Ancient peoples connected the serpent's ability to emerge renewed from its old skin to the regeneration and rebirth that they observed in nature. Therefore, throughout the world, cults arose that worshiped the snake as a form of divine spirit.

Serpents that control the sources of water and demand human sacrifices are common in world mythology. They are a form of water god and may be among the fertility gods to whom people offered human sacrifices in the hope of assuring a successful growing season for their crops.

The society's choice of young maidens for human sacrifice, instead of young men or old people, implies that their sacrifice was connected with the issue of fertility. Maidens were often designated for human sacrifice because of the connection between their own fertility and the fertility of the earth. As part of the sacred ceremony, their blood would be used to fertilize the fields.

Young maidens have been chosen for sacrifice because they were more expendable than males. Certainly, this is true in the Chinese society that is depicted in this later version of the story.

Chi Li is unusual in that she is a female hero; moreover, she is unusual among other heroines. Not only does she possess the typical hero's courage, strength, and skill, but her creative intelligence is equally responsible for saving her life. Chi Li is an independent thinker. She does her best to determine the course of her life and criticizes those who merely accept their fate.

The following version of this story appears in the *Sou shen chi* (*A Record of Researches into Spirits*), compiled by Kan Pao in about A.D. 317. Like other selections in this anthology, the original myth has been preserved in the form of a fictional narrative that resembles a folktale.

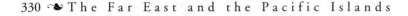

CHI LI SLAYS THE SERPENT

In a time long past, in the ancient kingdom of Yueh, a monstrous serpent had made its home in a cave that was located on a high pass between the towering peaks of the Yung Mountains. For nine years, on the appointed day in the eighth month of the year, the Yung serpent had demanded the flesh of a young maiden for its nourishment. For nine years, long before the appointed day, this serpent had communicated its demand to the people of Chiang Lo County through an oracle and through the dreams of men.

The people of Chiang Lo County lived in terror of the monstrous Yung serpent. No one had found another way to pacify it. And no one had been able to slay it. Local villagers had tried offering the serpent their best sheep and oxen, but its demands had continued until it received a human sacrifice.

The villagers had appealed to the officials of neighboring counties, and courageous magistrates and officers of the law had come to their aid. They, too, had tried to slay the Yung serpent. But its body spanned the distance of the tallest tree, and its girth was greater than the span of ten hands. Therefore, despite their skill and their number, the monstrous serpent had killed many magistrates and officers of the law, and the survivors had fled in panic down the mountainside.

Hearing of their defeat, other magistrates had sent word of the Yung serpent to the capital city of Yueh, and the king's chief minister had responded by sending the king's royal warriors under experienced commanders to slay the Yung serpent. However, once again, despite their skill and their number, the monstrous serpent had killed many of the king's warriors, and the survivors had fled in panic down the mountainside.

And so it came to pass that, with all of their resources exhausted, no choice remained for the people of Chiang Lo County but to appease the demands of the Yung serpent. Each year, the county officials tried to find a maiden whose sacrifice would not be a great loss to her community. Therefore, the magistrates would choose the maiden from among the daughters of criminals or from among female slaves.

Each year, on the appointed day of the eighth month of the year, county officials would bind the maiden and take her high into the Yung Mountains to the area where the serpent had made its home. There they would leave the maiden in a temple that they had built near the mouth of the serpent's cave. They would then retreat to a safe distance and watch while the monster glided forth from its den, swallowed the maiden, and withdrew once again into the recesses of its den.

It had now come to pass that the tenth year of this sacrifice had arrived, and the county magistrates were already considering who this year's sacrifice should be.

Meanwhile, in the village of Fukien, in Chiang Lo County, a man by the name of Tan Li and his wife had reared six daughters but had no son. Their youngest daughter, Chi, learned that the county magistrates were currently searching her village for a possible sacrifice, and she became determined to volunteer.

One day, when the family had gathered for the evening meal, Chi declared, "Father and Mother, I want you to know that I have decided to place myself in the hands of the county authorities and to volunteer to be sacrificed to the Yung serpent."

"We will never consent to that, Chi!" Tan Li exclaimed. "We may have been deprived of the joy and honor of having a son, but we love and value every one of our daughters, and we love and value you none the less because you are the youngest of the six!"

"I know that, Father, and I love you for it!" Chi responded. "Nevertheless, everyone knows that parents who have only daughters might just as well have no children at all. For what can a daughter do for her family? As long as I am alive, I only eat food that, if I were not here, would nourish the rest of you. And I surely will not be able to support you when you and Mother become too old to work. I can only sell myself to the county magistrates and give you the money from my sale.

"You know as well as I do, Father," Chi concluded, "that wealthier parents than you and Mother have killed their newborn daughters because, if they remained alive, they would be too much of a burden on their family. Everyone must die sooner or later. And since my life can do nothing for you, I would like my death to improve your lives in some way."

To these words, Tan Li replied, "Chi, all of your arguments fall upon deaf ears! You are our beloved daughter, and we will not sacrifice your life for anyone or anything! So do not let such thoughts invade your mind or let such feelings flood your heart. In this house they are unwelcome guests!"

However, it came to pass that Chi Li defied her parents' wishes. She secretly appeared before the county magistrates and volunteered to be that year's sacrifice to the Yung serpent. Having a volunteer made their job much easier, and the magistrates of Chiang Lo County readily accepted Chi Li's offer.

Chi Li then declared to the chief magistrate, "Your Honor, I have three requests to make of you. When the appointed day arrives, I would like you to provide me with a serpent-hound on a leash and a sharp-pointed, sheathed sword. And I would like you to give me the freedom to make use of them."

To these words, the chief magistrate replied, "Chi Li, neither the hound nor the sword will be able to save you from the Yung serpent, but I respect your courage, and I promise that they will indeed be yours and that we will give you the freedom to make use of them."

The months of the year came and went with the faces of the moon until, finally, the eighth month and the appointed day within that month arrived. As the chief magistrate had promised Chi Li, the county officials who took her to the serpent's den left her in the temple with a leashed serpent-hound, a sharp-pointed, sheathed sword, and the freedom to make use of them. In preparation for her ordeal, Chi Li had worn a belt and had brought with her a large bag of rice balls, which she had moistened and flavored with malt sugar.

As soon as the county officials had retreated, Chi Li took a deep breath and said to herself, "At last, the time has come! And who knows? The gods may look with favor upon those who do their best to help themselves. If they do, I pray that I will have their blessing as I try to slay this serpent!"

With these words, Chi Li strapped the sheathed sword to her belt, picked up her bag of rice balls, and then led the serpent-hound on its leash toward the mouth of the Yung serpent's cave. She kept the hound close to her side as she withdrew the rice balls from her bag and placed them at the mouth of the serpent's den.

As she had anticipated, the serpent smelled the malt sugar and quickly glided toward the mouth of its cave. As soon as she saw it, terror flooded Chi Li's heart, and she exclaimed to herself, "Why, the monster is even greater than I have heard! Its eyes shine like two large mirrors, and its huge mouth could hold a barrelful of rice!"

But then, quick as the wind, she declared, "Come now, Chi Li! The child of terror is certain death! So push fear from your heart, and force your mind to think only of the task at hand! Watch the serpent closely so that you will know when to proceed with the next step!"

It came to pass that the Yung serpent was so attracted to Chi Li's rice balls that it did not even notice Chi Li! And as soon as it opened its mouth to swallow the delicacy, Chi Li unleashed the serpent-hound. Then, quick as the wind, the hound leaped upon the monstrous serpent and dug its teeth into the serpent's throat. And quick as the wind, Chi Li ran behind the serpent and plunged her sword first into the back of the monster's head and then into its neck. Once she had made several deep thrusts with her weapon, Chi Li called off the serpent-hound, and they retreated into the safety of the temple. There, Chi Li prepared to do further battle with the Yung serpent if that proved to be necessary.

Thrashing wildly about from the pain of its wounds, and spurting cascades of blood, the Yung serpent blindly scattered the remaining rice balls and began to die. Before long, the monster lay stretched out lifeless upon the ground.

When Chi Li was certain that the serpent could no longer threaten her, she took her sword, the serpent-hound, and her rice-ball bag and entered the serpent's cave. There she found the skulls and bones of the serpent's nine sacrificial victims.

"But for the blessing of the gods, my skull and bones would be resting here among yours!" she exclaimed softly.

Then, one by one, Chi Li collected the skulls of the serpent's victims and put them into her bag. They would be proof of her victory, and then she could give them a proper burial.

"Poor girls!" she thought. "The monster conquered you because you were too timid to put up a fight! How pitiful!"

In silent awe, the county officials had witnessed Chi Li's battle with the serpent from a safe distance. And so it came to pass that Chi Li was triumphantly escorted down the mountainside by those who had brought her to the temple to die.

Faster than the speed of the wind, word of Chi Li's heroism traveled to the king of Yueh. Upon hearing the tale, the monarch announced to his ministers, "Such a maiden surely is a worthy wife for the king of Yueh. Tell my messengers that I wish them to go forth to the village of Fukien in Chiang Lo County and bring this maiden and her family to the royal palace!"

It came to pass that the king's messengers brought Tan Li, his wife, and his six daughters to the royal palace. Chi Li became queen of Yueh. Tan Li became the magistrate of Chiang Lo County. And Chi Li's mother and her five sisters became wealthy women.

The months continued to come and go with the faces of the moon. No other monster ever again dared to trouble the kingdom of Yueh. And poets continued to celebrate Chi Li's heroism in ballads that have been read from that day to this.

1. Why does Chi Li tell her parents that she wishes to volunteer to die and yet not mention that she hopes to attempt to kill the monster serpent?

2. If Chi Li's parents had known what Chi Li was going to attempt to do, to what extent, if any, would they have been more encouraging?

3. What heroic qualities does Chi Li possess? Find an example in the story that supports each quality.

4. The gods have faded far into the background of this tale. How might they have blessed Chi Li?

5. Why does Chi Li view the serpent's victims as timid and pitiful? What behavior would she have expected of them? To what extent, if any, is her attitude toward them realistic? To what extent is Chi Li the unusual person?

6. What does this story reveal about the Chinese society of its time?

Amaterasu

The Japanese were not the original occupants of the islands that now comprise Japan. Mongoloid peoples crossed the Korea Strait and invaded these islands during the second and first centuries B.C. and brought their Shinto religion with them. This religion included the worship of nature, ancestors, and heroes.

The Japanese did not record their religious beliefs for hundreds of years. By then, the influence of China on Japanese culture was widespread. The year A.D. 552 marks the beginning of the great Chinese influence on Japan in the areas of religion, literature, and art. However, it was not until the early eighth century that the Japanese recorded anything of their religion.

The *Kojiki (Records of Ancient Matters)*, written in A.D. 712, and the *Nihon Shoki (Chronicles of Japan from the Earliest Times to A.D. 697)*, written in 720, are the two major sources of Japanese mythology, including the myth of Amaterasu. They were written at a time when the Japanese accepted their traditional myths as fact. The authors of these books made an effort to minimize the Chinese and Indian influences on their earliest religious beliefs.

The Amaterasu myth is part of the Shinto religious tradition, which assumes that every aspect of nature contains a divine spirit. Amaterasu Omikami is the principal Japanese deity. She is the Great Goddess or Mother Goddess, who, in her role as sun goddess, is responsible for fertility. She is also the ruler of the gods and the universe. Moreover, she has the personality and skill to remain in power. In her multiple divine roles, Amaterasu reflects the important role of women in early Japanese life, where they were rulers, seers, and warriors.

The myth of Amaterasu reflects the Shinto interest in fertility and rituals associated with it. The myth explains the separation between the sun and the moon, the origin of food on earth, and the beginning of agriculture and the silkworm industry. As is the case with most cultures, the Japanese gods are anthropomorphic in that they are human in appearance, thought, speech, and deed.

In many other cultures, two different deities are responsible for the shining of the sun and for fertility. However, this myth reflects the logical connection that exists between the two. Without the sun, no plants would grow; and without plants, human beings would starve for lack of food. The gods would also starve, since they eat the same food that humans do, either directly or in the form of sacrifices offered to them. Thus, when Amaterasu locks herself in the cave, her action brings the ultimate catastrophe upon both gods and humans.

Presumably, as long as Amaterasu was treated with respect, the sun would continue to shine and human beings would prosper. This optimistic view of nature was supported by the abundance of plant life, wild animals, and fish in Japan at the time the myth was created.

AMATERASU

Amaterasu Omikami, goddess of the sun and of the universe, was reigning in heaven when she sent her brother and husband, the god of the moon, down to the reed plains to serve the goddess of food. As soon as the goddess saw him, she turned toward the land and spit boiled rice from her mouth. Next she turned toward the sea and spit all kinds of fish from her mouth. Finally, she turned toward the mountains and spit a variety of fur-coated animals from her mouth. She then prepared all of these as food and placed them upon one hundred tables for the moon god to eat.

When the moon god saw what she had done, he was furious. "How dare you feed me with food that you have spit from your mouth!" he exclaimed, "You have made the food filthy and disgusting!" He drew his sword and killed the goddess. Then he returned to Amaterasu and told her of his deed.

To his surprise, Amaterasu exclaimed, "You are an evil god! I can no longer stand the sight of your face. Take yourself from my presence, and see to it that we do not meet face to face again!" So the sun and the moon lived apart from one another, separated by day and by night.

Amaterasu sent her messenger, the cloud spirit, down to the goddess of food. He found that the goddess was indeed dead. However, he also found that the ox and the horse had issued forth from her head, grain had grown from her forehead, silkworms had come forth from her eyebrows, cereal had emerged from her eyes, rice had grown from her stomach, and wheat and beans had grown from her abdomen. The cloud spirit collected all of these and returned to Amaterasu with them.

The goddess of the sun was delighted with the variety of foods. "You have given me great cause for rejoicing!" she exclaimed to her messenger. "Human beings will be able to eat these foods and survive."

Amaterasu extracted the seeds from the various grains and beans and planted them in the dry fields. She took the rice seed and planted it in the water fields. She then appointed a heavenly village chief and let him supervise the sowing of these seeds. The first harvest that autumn was a pleasure to behold. Meanwhile, Amaterasu placed the silkworms in her mouth and collected silken thread from them. Thus, the sun goddess initiated the art of raising silkworms.

Not long thereafter, Izanagi and Izanami gave their son Susano-o-no-Mikoto the netherland to rule and banished him there. Before he took his place in the netherland, he decided to visit his shining sister. He was such a violent god that the mountains and hills groaned aloud and the sea frothed in tempestuous tumult as he made his way up to heaven.

When she saw him coming, Amaterasu thought, "Surely my wicked brother is coming to visit me with no good purpose in mind. He must want my kingdom, the plain of heaven. Yet our parents assigned a particular realm to each of us. Susano-o-no-Mikoto should be satisfied with the kingdom they have given him. I had better prepare for the worst!"

The goddess bound up her hair in knots and tied her skirts into trousers as if she were a male. She placed two quivers upon her back, one containing one thousand arrows and one containing five hundred. At her side she placed three long swords. In one hand, she carried her bow upright in shooting position, with an arrow ready on the bowstring; in her other hand, she firmly grasped one of her swords.

When the two gods came face to face, Amaterasu felt confident that her appearance would intimidate her brother. "Why have you come to me?" she calmly asked him.

"You look as if you are expecting trouble!" Susano-o-no-Mikoto replied. "Certainly you should have no fear of me. I have never had a black heart, although our parents dislike me and have condemned me to rule the netherland. I simply wanted to see you before I left the world of light. I do not intend to stay long."

Amaterasu, wishing to believe the best of her brother, put away her weapons. She welcomed him among the heavenly gods and hoped that his visit would be as brief as he had said.

But Susano-o-no-Mikoto stayed longer than he was wanted, and his behavior was very rude. He and Amaterasu each had three rice fields of their own. Whereas Amaterasu's fields thrived in spite of excessive rains or prolonged drought, Susano-o-no-Mikoto's rice fields were always barren. In times of drought, the soil was parched and cracked; in heavy rainfall, the soil washed away. Finally Susano-o-no-Mikoto became possessed by jealous anger. When the rice seeds were sown in the spring, he removed the divisions between the fields, filled up the channels, and destroyed the troughs and pipes. Amaterasu, wishing to believe the best of her brother, remained calm and tolerant.

In the autumn, when the grain was mature, Susano-o-no-Mikoto freed the heavenly colts and caused them to lie down in the middle of the rice fields. Again Amaterasu remained calm and tolerant.

Then Susano-o-no-Mikoto spoiled the harvest feast of first-fruits by defiling the purity of the palace with disgusting filth. Again Amaterasu remained calm and tolerant.

Finally, while Amaterasu sat weaving cloth for the clothing of the gods in her sacred weaving hall, her evil brother silently removed some roof tiles in order to create a hole in the ceiling. Then he threw a colt of heaven into the room. Amaterasu was so startled that she pricked herself with her shuttle.

This time the sun goddess could not forgive Susano-o-no-Mikoto. In great rage, she left the palace and entered the rock cave of heaven. She locked the door and remained there in isolation. Now that her brilliance no longer illuminated heaven and earth, day became as black as night. The universe was forced to exist in total, continuous darkness. Without the sun, plants could not grow. People everywhere stopped their activities, watching and waiting to see how long they would have to be in darkness.

All of the gods gathered along the banks of the Peaceful River of Heaven and discussed how to placate Amaterasu's wrath. They placed a statue of the sun goddess outside the rock cave and offered prayers to it. They also made many special offerings—including fine cloth, rich jewels, combs, and a mirror—which they hung upon a sakaki tree—and goddesses danced and chanted by the door.

Amaterasu heard the music and said to herself, "I hear both beautiful prayers of supplication addressed to me and the sounds of music and dance. Why are the gods so happy when my seclusion in this rock cave has brought constant darkness to the central land of fertile reed plains?" Her curiosity overcame her anger, and she opened the door a crack to look outside.

This was just what the gods had hoped Amaterasu would do. Rejoicing in the return of the sun's brilliant rays, they took Amaterasu by the hand, had her among them, and convinced her to rejoin them.

The gods punished Susano-o-no-Mikoto by demanding from him 1,000 tables of offerings. They also plucked out his hair and the nails on his fingers and toes. Finally they said to him, "Your behavior has been intolerably rude and improper. From this time forth, you are banished from heaven and from the central reed plains as well. Go forth with all speed to the netherland. We have had enough of your wicked ways!"

So Susano-o-no-Mikoto left heaven forever and began his journey to the netherland.

◆ QUESTIONS FOR
Response, Discussion, and Analysis

1. What role does Amaterasu have in fertility?

2. Why does Amaterasu permit Susano-o-no-Mikoto to visit her? When he misbehaves, why does she not banish him?

HISTORICAL BACKGROUND

Kotan Utunnai

The Ainu people, remaining members of a Stone Age Asiatic people, lived in Japan before the islands were invaded by the Mongoloid people, who became the Japanese. Because they lived in isolated river valleys and had an abundant food supply to feed their small population, the Ainu remained unaffected by civilization for hundreds of years. Their people had no system of writing, no political organization beyond the small village, no domesticated farm animals or system of agriculture, and no bronze or iron metalwork of their own.

Ainu life remained unchanged from ancient times until about 1670, when the people began to have much closer contact with the Japanese. About 200 years later the Japanese began a concerted effort to settle the island of Hokkaido, on which most of the Ainu were living. The Japanese cleared the land of forests and wild animals and set up permanent fishing nets. No longer able to continue in their traditional way of living, the Ainu men became migrant farm workers. In time, alcoholism and disease ravaged their society.

In the early twentieth century, 15,000 to 16,000 Ainu still were living on Hokkaido. Because their society placed great value upon oral recitation, it was easy to find an Ainu who had a superb command of his oral tradition. Most of the Ainu literature we have today was collected and recorded in the 1920s and 1930s. By the 1940s, Ainu adults spoke both Japanese and their native language, but Ainu children spoke only Japanese. By 1955, fewer than twenty Ainu in all of Hokkaido could speak their native language fluently. The plight of the Ainu had become a public issue by the 1970s, and an interest developed in trying to preserve the Ainu heritage.

The epic of *Kotan Utunnai* is particularly important among the literary works acquired from the Ainu. John Batchelor, an English missionary, recorded it between 1880 and 1888, at a time when the ancient Ainu traditions still were vital. *Kotan Utunnai* was first published, in both Ainu and English, in an 1890 volume of the *Transactions of the Asiatic Society of Japan.*

Aspects of this epic are so old that they were unfamiliar to those who recited it. The Ainu of the 1880s and later years did not know who the Repunkur (people of the sea) were. Many years later, archaeologists discovered that the term refers to the Okhotsk, a people who lived on the northern coast of Hokkaido. The Ainu, who were the Yaunkur (people of the land), defeated the Okhotsk (the Repunkur) in a series of wars between the tenth and the sixteenth centuries. *Kotan Utunnai,* like a number of other Ainu heroic epics, reflects these wars.

APPEAL AND VALUE

The epic of *Kotan Utunnai* is appealing because it is an unusual adventure story. The hero fights against strange adversaries. The blending of the divine with the human throughout the story provides surprise, magic, and mystery. The hero is a human being, but he possesses such godlike qualities that even those who are supposed to be gods are not certain that he is human. Similarly, the hero is not certain whether those who battle against him are divine or human.

The epic reminds us of how similar human beings are to one another, even when separated by hundreds of years and by very different cultures. We understand and identify with the heroic characters because they have the same need to prove their excellence and to acquire fame that the characters in other major epics have—and that we have.

As in other epics, the best of human beings on both sides in *Kotan Utunnai* are heroic figures. The major characters possess courage, affection, loyalty, and perseverance, whether they are friend or foe. For example, the hero's "older sister" is not really his sister at all—she is a member of one of the enemy communities. She rescues the hero when his parents die and then rears him. She fights side by side with him, and he repays her loyalty. The ruler of Shipish is as much a hero as the narrator is. He fights only because the hero insists upon fighting him. When the sister of the ruler of Shipish leaves her brother and joins the hero, the author provides her with credible motivation for her decision.

The epic of *Kotan Utunnai* is also appealing because of its simplicity. The characters live in a world that they do not question. They know their strengths and their limitations, and they accept themselves and their destiny. They accept death as an integral part of life, and they know that those who lead good lives will be reborn after death; those who do not, however, will remain dead.

The world of the gods is an ever present part of the world of these human beings. The spirits of the gods rumble, and human ears hear their presence. Each human being possesses divine qualities just as each god possesses human qualities. Thus, a sense of unity and order exists in the universe depicted in *Kotan Utunnai*.

These special qualities are transmitted by the epic's style. Like the other Ainu epics, *Kotan Utunnai* was recorded as it was sung, in the form of a first-person narrative. The first-person narrative is the most immediate kind of narration. The narrator is the hero of the epic, and he describes his own experiences as they unfold. We see what he sees as he sees it, and we hear what he hears as he hears it. We know only what the narrator knows. Because in a first-person narrative we as readers participate in the thoughts and actions of the hero, we become completely immersed in the narrator's world.

All the major characters of *Kotan Utunnai* are members of the nobility, just as they are in the major epics from every other culture. The subject matter reflects the values and concerns of its noble audience. Thus, the major subject is war, and the major values are courage, strength, and skill. The marriages of the hero and his brother to princesses of the enemy may have been used by the Yaunkur to justify and popularize their rule over the Repunkur.

One interesting feature of *Kotan Utunnai* is that the female characters possess great power and skill and are considered the equals of men. Aristocratic women fight side by side with their fathers, husbands, and brothers. The hero's mother dies in battle with her husband, and we are told that she has been a warrior all her life. The hero appreciates both his older sister and Shipish-un-mat because their courage, strength, and skill on the battlefield equal their great beauty.

KOTAN UTUNNAI

Chapter 1

The hero, who is the narrator, learns that the Repunkur killed his parents. Taking his father's war gear, he sets out to avenge their deaths. In Repunkur country, he finds his older brother a prisoner. With his sister's help, the hero frees his brother and kills his captors.

I was reared by my older sister in the land of the Repunkur. For many years, we lived in a little grass hut. I would often hear a rumbling sound throughout our land. My sister told me that this was the sound of gods fighting. When many gods were dying, the sound would go on and on without interruption.

When I grew older, I would often hear similar sounds made by the spirits of the Yaunkur upon the roof of our grass hut. I could not understand this, so I said, "Older Sister, you have reared me well. Now it is time to tell me how this has come to be."

As my sister looked at me, her eyes trembled with fear and shining tears coursed down her cheeks. She replied, "I intended to tell you the story when you were older. I shall tell you now, since you wish it, but I must warn you not to act rashly when you have heard it.

"Although I have reared you, you and I belong to different people," she began. "Mine are the Repunkur, people of the sea. Yours are the Yaunkur, people of the land. Long ago your father ruled the upper and lower regions of Shinutapka. He was a great warrior and hero. One day he decided to go across the sea on a trading expedition. He invited his second son, Kamui-otopush, and your mother to join him on his journey. Since you were just a baby, she strapped you to her back and took you along.

"When they sailed by the coast of the island of Karapto, the people invited them ashore. Although they were Repunkur, they offered a sign of peace and wine to drink. Day and night, the people of the island encouraged your family to drink that poison. Your father became drunk with the wine, and his mind became clouded. He announced that he and his family intended to buy the major treasure of the people of Karapto and take it away.

"Your father's announcement caused fighting to break out, which spread to neighboring lands, including my own. My country is a land of many great warriors, and in one of his battles against the Repunkur, your father was killed.

"I was there when he died," my sister continued. "I took your father's war helmet and his clothes from his dead body. To help your mother, I took you from her back and tied you securely to me with my baby-carrying cords. With my sword, I did my best to protect your mother's life, but she had been a warrior all her life, so she insisted on fighting. Like your father, she was killed in that battle.

"Seeing that both your mother and your father were dead and that you were far too young to help your brother or survive on your own, I carried you to this land where we have been living all these years. It is a safe and isolated place; neither gods nor humans ever visit it.

"Since the time of your parents' death," my sister concluded, "your older brother, Kamui-otopush, has been fighting all alone against the Repunkur to avenge them. I must tell you this, for you asked to hear the whole story. However, remember that it would be unwise for you to act rashly."

I listened to the words of my older sister with complete surprise. My heart overflowed with rage. Was she not my enemy? Her own people had killed my parents. It took a great effort to calm myself and refrain from killing her!

I did not feel like thanking her for saving my life, but I forced myself to be polite. "You have reared me well, Older Sister," I said. "Now I would like you to find my father's clothes and give them to me."

She immediately entered the hut, untied the cord of her treasure bag, and brought forth six magnificent robes, a belt with a metal buckle, a small metal helmet, and a wondrous sword. All of these she held out to me.

With great pride and pleasure I put on my father's robes, placed his belt around my waist, tied his helmet on my head, and thrust his sword beneath his belt. My father's heroic spirit infused my body through his war gear. I strode up and back in front of the fireplace, flexing my shoulders and stamping my feet. Soon I felt my body go up the smoke hole of our little hut. Then I found myself being pushed through the air by a strong wind.

The mighty breeze blew me into a country formed of majestic mountains. I landed on the shore of the sea, not far from the mountains. My older sister dropped down at my side with the roaring of the wind. We traveled over a series of metal spruce forests, which clinked and clanked as the wind struck their branches. Certainly only great gods would live in a land such as this!

Suddenly I smelled smoke. When I descended into the lower regions of the forest, I found its source—a great bonfire. Along one side of the fire sat six men wearing stone armor. Next to them sat six women. Across the fire from them sat six men wearing metal armor, and next to them sat six women.

At the far end of the fire, between the two groups of warriors, stood a very strange-looking being I had never seen before. I wondered whether he could possibly be human, for he looked more like a small mountain that had arms and legs sprouting from it. His face looked like a cliff sheared off by a landslide. His huge nose looked like an overhanging rock. Strapped to his side he wore a sword as large as the oar of a boat. I knew that he must be the evil human demon called Dangling Nose, a famous Repunkur warrior.

While I stood gazing upon this strange group, the earth beneath my feet moved this way and that, and the metal branches of the spruce trees clinked and clanked as they struck each other. When my eyes left the group by the fire and searched the trees, I saw the most surprising sight. A gravely wounded man was tied to the top of a large spruce tree. Now and then he would rearrange his bound limbs, and it was his movements that were causing the earth beneath my feet to move this way and that. Even though I had never seen him before, I knew that he must be Kamui-otopush, my older brother.

My older sister said, "Younger Brother, this man is too sorely wounded to accompany us to battle. His presence will only hurt us. Let me carry off his body while you fight these people alone."

As soon as my ears had heard her words, the six warriors in metal armor announced together, "We are the people of Metal River, six brothers and six sisters. We were hunting in the mountains today when we came upon Kamui-otopush. He was returning to his country, for he had finished fighting. He was moving slowly, for his many battles had sorely wounded him. We would have killed him then and there if we did not fear the anger of Shipish-un-kur, our mighty uncle and ruler. So we tied him to a large spruce tree."

They added, "Soon these six warriors of Stone River came by with their sisters, and they stopped here with us. And now you also have come along. Are you a god, or are you human? Together, let us take Kamui-otopush as a gift to Shipish-un-kur. He surely will praise us when he sees this trophy!"

The man standing at the head of the fire proclaimed, "The famous warrior Dangling Nose adds his deep voice in agreement."

While he was speaking, my older sister went to the top of the spruce tree and freed my older brother. The sound of his loosened ropes falling on the metal branches drew the eyes of all the demons in that direction.

I did my best to prevent them from seeing me in my human form. Like a light breeze I flew with my sword into their midst. Beginning on one side of the fire, I raised my father's wondrous sword and sliced into the flesh of three of the warriors in stone armor with a single stroke, slashing three of their women as well. Turning to the other side of the fire, I sliced into the flesh of three of the warriors in metal armor with a single stroke, slashing three of their women as well.

Swinging my sword back, I aimed to kill Dangling Nose. However, he flew over my blade like a light breeze and said, "I thought that Kamui-otopush was bound to the top of the spruce tree, but he has strength enough to kill our people. I doubt that we would be able to kill such a man in battle. Let us take him to the battle-chasm, for it will be easier to kill him there."

Meanwhile, our sword blades gleamed as he and I fought fiercely against one another. In the midst of our battle, my older sister dropped down at my side with the roaring of the wind. "I have taken the body of your older brother back to your country," she announced. "There I found your oldest brother, now the ruler of your land, and your oldest sister. It is fortunate that your parents left them behind when they set off on that trading expedition across the sea so many years ago.

Before I left, we restored Kamui-otopush to life, so do not let concern for him distract your fighting."

While my older sister was speaking, the remaining six women attacked her with their swords. Wicked women can be brave and strong fighters! My sister raised her sword, her blade shining against theirs. She was a match for them, but she would not be able to kill them easily.

As their battle carried the women toward the distant mountains, an attack by the six remaining warriors and Dangling Nose directed my attention back to the men. I raised my sword, my blade shining against theirs. I was a match for them, but I would not be able to kill them easily. I did my best to prevent them from seeing me in my human form. Like a light breeze, I flew with my sword over their blades.

As we fought, I noticed a river flowing from one group of mountains to the next. Between them, it descended into a deep ravine. When I saw many sharp sword-blades and spear-blades of stone rising from the poisonous water, I knew that this must be the battle-chasm Dangling Nose had mentioned.

The warriors banded together and forced me toward the chasm. Time and again they almost killed me, but I did my best to prevent them from seeing me in my human form. Like a light breeze, I flew with my sword over their blades.

Meanwhile, I chanted, "Hear me, gods of the chasm, gods of the deep ravine! I am one Yaunkur against many Repunkur. If I die here, my blood will give you little wine to drink. Take my side against these warriors, and you can gorge yourselves upon their blood!"

With these words, my heart flooded with renewed spirit and strength. With my father's wondrous sword, I drove the Repunkur toward the battle-chasm. The oldest of the warriors in stone armor was the first to fall to the bottom of the ravine and be sliced into chunks of human meat. His spirit left his body with a loud roar and rumbled as it flew off to the west.

Next, the largest of the warriors in metal armor fell to the bottom of the ravine and was sliced into chunks of human meat. His spirit left his body with a loud roar and rumbled as it flew off to the west.

In time I killed all but Dangling Nose. One by one, their spirits left their bodies with a loud roar and rumbled as they flew off to the west. Not one among the dead would be restored to life.

Dangling Nose and I then fought to the death. Time and again he almost killed me, but each time I returned his sword thrust with one of my own. Finally he said, "Great warriors fight in more than one way. I now challenge you to a contest of strength!"

He did not wait for my response but quickly rushed toward me. As we wrestled together, he enclosed me between his mighty hands and began to press the breath out of me. My heart fluttered with pain, but I made a quick twist and escaped from his hands as running water rushes through open fingers.

Finally I was able to hurl Dangling Nose down into the deep ravine. When his body hit bottom, the sharp blades of the stone swords and stone spears sliced him into chunks of human meat. His spirit left his body with a loud roar and rumbled as it flew off to the west. He would not be restored to life either.

Chapter 2

The hero travels to Shipish to fight the fearsome Repunkur ruler. The ruler's sister helps the hero. Together, they rescue the hero's older sister and kill her Repunkur enemies. Then they fight two storm demons. Victorious, they return to the hero's homeland, where they are reunited with the hero's older brother and older sister. The two Yaunkur men marry the two Repunkur women and live in peace.

In the quiet time that followed, I walked along the river and said to myself, "Who is this fearsome ruler who would have received my older brother as a trophy? If I were to return to my country without seeing Shipish-un-kur, my people would look upon me as a coward. He may kill me, but I must see how we two warriors compare with one another."

A light breeze carried me above the river as it flowed down to the sea. At its mouth I found the large village of Shipish surrounding a lone, majestic mountain. Its peak soared so far into the heavens that it was wrapped in clouds of mist. I followed the winding trail to the stockade at the top. Fearsome spirits rumbled their warnings from the top of the stockade, but I entered in spite of them.

Peering through the windows of the large house, I saw the fearsome ruler of this country. The sight of Shipish-un-kur filled my heart with awe, for he wore magnificent robes and carried wondrous swords. However, he was only a young man. Whiskers had just begun to grow upon his chin.

As he sat by the side of the glowing hearth, the most beautiful young woman I had ever seen sat next to him. Even my older sister was not this beautiful! I could tell from her face that she possessed the magical powers of a prophet, and their conversation soon proved my judgment correct.

"Shipish-un-mat, dear younger sister," I heard him say, "ever since you were a child, you could tell the future. Tell me, then, why do I have the feeling that danger is approaching?"

Shipish-un-mat tied her hair with the band of a prophet and picked up her magical wand. A prophecy immediately streamed forth from her mouth. "By the battle-chasm of our river," she began, "I can see that people have joined together to fight a Yaunkur. At times the blood and gore conceal my view of the scene. At other times, I see the tangle of their swords in battle. Then I see the broken swords of the Repunkur disappear into the west. Meanwhile, the sword of the Yaunkur is brightly shining in the east.

"Then," the prophetess continued, "I see the Yaunkur, in the form of a marvelous little bird with speckled feathers, flying downstream above our river. Fierce fighting suddenly breaks out in our land, completely destroying our villages. I see your sword entangled with the sword of the Yaunkur. At times the blood and gore conceal my view of the scene. At other times, I see the tangle of swords in battle. Then I see a terrible sight—your broken sword disappearing under blood and gore. Meanwhile, the sword of the Yaunkur is brightly shining in the east. Then the entire vision disappears."

"You have spoken dreadful, wicked words!" Shipish-un-kur exclaimed, with rage blazing forth in his eyes and in his voice. "The gods may be speaking through you, but their words infuriate me. I fight only against the gods; I keep peace with human beings. The evil Repunkur may have fought against the young Yaunkur all his life, but I will not fight him! Should he ever come here, I will greet him with kindness and peace in my heart."

I flew through the window and up to the rafters of their large house. I walked this way and that on the beams, stamping my feet so that the rafters creaked and the household gods rumbled with fright. Then I dropped down beside the young ruler with the roaring of the wind. I caught him by his hair and twisted his head this way and that.

As I tossed him about, I said, "Tell me, Shipish-un-kur, why was Kamui- oto-push taken prisoner and bound at the top of a spruce tree? I avenged him by fighting the Repunkur. They spoke of you as a fearsome ruler who would have received my older brother as a trophy. I knew that if I were to return to my country without seeing you, my people would look upon me as a coward. So I have come. If you greet me with kindness and peace in your heart, I cannot accept that. I must see how we two warriors compare with one another. Even if we kill each other, our hearts will be content. Show me your courage, strength, and skill."

With these words, I grabbed the great warrior's younger sister and carried her toward the smoke hole, while she screamed for help. Shipish-un-kur quickly drew his sword and prevented me from leaving through the smoke hole. I then dashed to the window, but again I could not get past his sword. The two of us flew from side to side beneath the ceiling like a pair of birds. Angry at her prophecy, the great warrior became determined to kill his sister.

I carried Shipish-un-mat before me as a shield, believing that her brother would spare us both because of his loyalty to her. I was wrong. Shipish-un-kur's repeated sword-thrusts finally turned Shipish-un-mat against him, and she became determined to kill him. As soon as I released her, she drew a dagger from her robes and began to attack him, gaining strength from the wrath in her heart.

Hearing the commotion, throngs of armed men rushed in and attacked us. My companion spirits joined the local spirits on top of the stockade, and they rumbled together like one great spirit. The gods sent a fearsome wind rushing into the house, fanning the flames in the hearth until they left their bounds and began to consume the house itself. We escaped just before the building collapsed.

When I saw armies of spearmen coming toward me, I chased them toward Shipish-un-mat. Somewhat to my surprise, she proved to be as courageous and as skilled as she was beautiful. She stood her ground and fought them off, slashing as if she were facing only a few warriors rather than hundreds of them. The flashing of her sword concealed all other swords. She cut down the warriors like blades of grass, and corpses soon covered the earth like a blanket.

Strong as we were, we could not have killed hundreds if a mass of clouds had not blown toward us as swiftly as an arrow in flight. While a mighty god rumbled a warning, my older brother dropped down beside me with the roaring of the wind. We saluted one another with our swords, and then Kamui-otopush began his attack.

Although I swung my father's wondrous sword against the warriors, my skill was small compared to that of Kamui-otopush. The flashing of his sword concealed all other swords. He cut down the warriors like blades of grass, and corpses soon covered the earth like a blanket.

Suddenly Shipish-un-mat screamed, "Valiant Yaunkur warrior, your older sister is fighting mighty demons in a far land. Unless we hurry to her aid, they may kill her, and you will never see her again! Kamui-otopush has the strength and skill to stand alone against all the warriors here. Let us quickly depart!"

Shipish-un-mat flew into the heavens. I sheathed my sword and quickly flew behind her. When we came to the land Shipish-un-mat had seen in her vision, we heard the loud rumbling crashes that told of many dying gods. Below us, battle-mists concealed the earth. Through the clamor we could hear the sad rumblings of my older sister's companion spirits.

The rumbling of my sister's spirits led me to her rescue. I saw with dismay that she was gravely wounded. She would swing her sword once or twice but then faint from the effort. When she regained consciousness, she would swing her sword again. I dropped down at her side with the roaring of the wind.

I unsheathed my father's wondrous sword and swung it against the warriors, but my skill was small compared to that of Shipish-un-mat. Once she began her attack, the flashing of her sword concealed all other swords. She cut down the warriors like blades of grass, and corpses soon covered the earth like a blanket.

Then my older sister collapsed to the ground while a host of spears fell upon her. I pulled her into my arms and held her body up toward the heavens. "Oh gods," I said, "you to whom my father prayed, my older sister reared me lovingly and well. Reward her for the care she gave me. Even though she is the child of my enemy, I pray you to restore her to life!"

The gods heard my words, and their hearts were kind. My sister's spirit left the body in my hands as a new, living spirit. It flew up with a loud roar and rumbled all along its eastward journey to our land, the land of the Yaunkur.

Shipish-un-mat and I continued the fight with renewed spirit. We did not stop until we had avenged my older sister by completely destroying those who had fought against her. When we had finished and all was quiet, Shipish-un-mat's eyes suddenly filled with tears. She said to me, "I can see that to the west of this land, the storm demon and his younger sister are preparing to attack us, man to man and woman to woman!"

Before long a mass of clouds rose in the west, bringing stormy weather upon us. I watched as two creatures walked toward us. First came a very strange-looking being whom I had never seen before. I wondered whether he could possibly be human, for he looked more like a small mountain that had arms and legs sprouting from it. His face looked like a cliff sheared off by a landslide. Strapped to his side he wore a sword as large as the oar of a boat. Behind him came a woman dressed in leather armor sewn from the skins of both land and sea animals. She walked toward Shipish-un-mat with a red knife poised in her hand. As Shipish-un-mat had foretold, the storm demon fiercely attacked me, and his younger sister fiercely attacked her.

I did my best to hold onto my life. I flew here and there like a light breeze, avoiding the storm demon's sword-thrusts. Then I discovered how his armor was tied together. Holding my father's wondrous sword like a spear, I stabbed the storm god through those ties. Good fortune smiled upon my blade, for the tip went right into his flesh, and he fell flat upon the earth. "He must be human after all!" I thought.

To my surprise, a handsome young boy jumped out from beneath the storm god's armor! He looked at me and said, "You amaze me, young Yaunkur! Even the greatest gods cannot destroy my armor, and yet you have succeeded. But great warriors should fight without armor. I must see how we compare with one another. Even if we kill each other, our hearts will be content, for everyone will speak of our fame. Now show me your courage, strength, and skill!"

He drew his sword and thrust it at me. Again I flew here and there like a light breeze, avoiding his sword-thrusts. Finally good fortune smiled upon my blade, for the tip of my father's wondrous sword slashed right into his flesh, and I heard his spirit leave his body and fly up with a loud roar.

Meanwhile, Shipish-un-mat and the storm demon's younger sister were also fighting fiercely. I discovered how the demon's armor was tied together. Holding my father's wondrous sword like a spear, I stabbed the goddess through those ties. Good fortune smiled upon my blade, for the tip went right into her flesh, and she fell flat upon the earth. "She must be human after all!" I thought.

To my surprise, a beautiful young woman jumped out from beneath the leather armor! She looked at me and said, "You amaze me, young Yaunkur! Even the greatest gods cannot destroy my armor, and yet you have succeeded. But do not let Shipish-un-mat hurt me!"

Shipish-un-mat angrily replied, "I must see how we compare with one another. Even if we kill each other, our hearts will be content, for everyone will speak of our fame. Now show me your courage, strength, and skill!"

Shipish-un-mat drew her sword and thrust it at the demon. Good fortune smiled upon her blade, for the tip of her sword slashed right into the goddess's flesh, and I heard her spirit leave her body and fly up with a loud roar. Her living spirit rumbled as it traveled to the east.

Shipish-un-mat said to me, "I know that after we left them, Kamui-otopush and my brother fought one another until your older brother killed mine. Because my brother was your enemy, perhaps you think of me as your enemy also. If you choose to kill me right now, my heart will be content. Or you may choose to pity me and take me to your country. Either way, it is time to stop fighting."

I chose to take Shipish-un-mat with me, for I knew that no other woman could ever compare with her. We traveled to my country, the land of the Yaunkur, which I had never seen. When we dropped down at the majestic house of my father, I called out to the herald, "Have my older brother and my sister who reared me arrived? If not, I will leave right now to fight the Repunkur."

The herald replied, "Kamui-otopush has finished fighting and has returned. The gods have restored your older sister to life, and she is here also."

It was as he said. My older sister had indeed been restored to life, and she was now more beautiful than ever. In gratitude for saving my life, my oldest brother gave my older sister to Kamui-otopush in marriage. In gratitude for saving my life, he gave Shipish-un-mat to me in marriage.

From that time until this, we have lived in peace.

❧ QUESTIONS FOR
Response, Discussion, and Analysis

1. Does the fact that the hero is the narrator make the epic more interesting? Defend your point of view. What is the disadvantage of a narrator who is one of the characters?

2. How is the narrator's youth unusual? How does this affect the epic?

3. What heroic tasks does the narrator perform? What trials, if any, does he experience? Explain.

4. What kind of person is Older Sister? What qualities does she possess? Support each adjective with an example.

5. When Older Sister tells the narrator not to act rashly, what does she fear he will do?

6. Many ancient cultures believed that a person gained the desirable qualities of another by eating the flesh or drinking the blood of that person. For example, the Greek warriors in The Iliad dip their weapons in Hector's blood to increase their power. How does the narrator in this myth gain the heroic qualities of his father? What might people in our society do if they wish to gain the qualities of a friend or relative?

7. How is Shipish-un-kur different from what the Repunkur warriors say about him? Is his attitude realistic? Defend your point of view.

8. What godlike or magical qualities does the narrator possess? What other characters share these qualities? Do they enhance or detract from the characters' heroism?

9. Why do the characters in this epic find it difficult to recognize who is divine and who is human? What test provides the answer?

10. When the narrator asks the gods to help him, he acts as if they possess human qualities. How does he gain their aid? What may his promise reveal about the practices of warriors in that culture?

11. What determines whether a dead person's spirit is restored to life? Why do the spirits of those who will remain dead fly to the west, while those who will be restored to life fly to the east?

12. Does Shipish-un-mat act properly when she turns against her brother and helps the narrator? What justification does she have? What would you have done? Why?

13. Why does Shipish-un-mat help the narrator? What options does she have, and what would be their consequences?

14. What good qualities does the narrator possess? Support your choice of adjective(s) with examples.

15. With whom do you sympathize most: the narrator? Shipish-un-kur? Shipish- un-mat? Why? With whom do you sympathize least? Why?

16. What qualities does the narrator value in Shipish-un-mat? Why does he marry the sister of his enemy? How is the reader prepared for a lack of prejudice? Does this add to or detract from the quality of the epic? Defend your point of view. Could you marry the sister or brother of your enemy? Why or why not?

The Creation Cycle

The ancestors of the Polynesian peoples originated in Asia. Conflict over land and available food probably led them to cross the Pacific and settle on Tahiti and other nearby islands. When conditions on Tahiti could no longer sustain their population, groups once again took to the sea in search of a new home.

One group of Polynesians traveled southwest and became the first inhabitants of New Zealand. They called their land *Aotearoa* (long white cloud) and themselves *Maori* (a person of this place). In their myths, they refer to their land of origin as *Hawaiki* (homeland). Although another group of Polynesians traveled east to the islands of Hawaii, whose name is derived from Hawaiki, scholars have concluded that the Polynesian land of origin was not the Hawaiian Islands.

Although the first Christian missionary, Samuel Marsden, arrived in New Zealand in 1814, Maori mythology shows little Christian influence. The earliest written collection of myths from the Maori oral tradition is Sir George Grey's *Polynesian Mythology and Ancient Traditional History,* published in 1855.

The Maori creation myth is unusual in its emphasis on the development from nonbeing to thought to the creation of the universe and human beings. The myth focuses on the relationship between nature and human beings. The behavior of Father Rangi and Mother Papa's six sons explains physical aspects of the environment while reflecting important characteristics of human nature.

Maui is the trickster-hero of Polynesia. Like many of the great heroes in mythology, he is a demigod, the son of a goddess and a mortal father. Maui can be compared with other trickster-heroes in mythology, such as Hermes, Loki, and Raven.

The cycle of myths that depicts Maui's exploits traveled with the Polynesian people to their new lands, including Tahiti and Little Tahiti, New Zealand, Samoa, and the Hawaiian Islands. The cycle includes Maui's mysterious birth, his theft (in another version, his capture) of fire, his taming of the sun, his fishing for New Zealand (in other versions, Tahiti and Little Tahiti or the Hawaiian Islands), and his quest for immortality (in another version, his introduction of death). These episodes may be very similar, or they may vary considerably from one island to another. Their broad distribution is an indication of their great age.

THE CREATION CYCLE

THE CREATION OF THE UNIVERSE AND THE GODS

In the beginning, there was nothing but an idea. The idea was remembered. It then became conscious. Finally, it became a wish to create. So it came to pass that out of nothing came the power to live and to grow, even in emptiness.

And it came to pass that out of this power to live and to grow came the deep, dark, long, and gloomy Night, a presence felt, but unseen, in the sightless, empty universe.

And it came to pass that out of this power that was the Night came life, in the form of the sky, far-reaching Father Rangi. Father Rangi lived with rosy dawn's pale light and created the moon. He lived with golden morn's warmer rays and created the sun. Then he tossed both the moon and the sun into the deep, dark, and gloomy Night so that they would light the universe and be its eyes. Now there were both Night and Day.

Father Rangi then lived with Mother Papa, the Earth. In love, he lay upon her, and they created land.

Father Rangi and Mother Papa produced many children, who lived in the darkness of the small space that existed between their parents. Mother Papa's body was covered with low plants, and the sea was as black as Father Rangi.

Father Rangi loved Mother Papa and clung to her. No light could come between them. Their first children became tired of living in everlasting darkness, and their six sons met together to discuss what they could do to improve their situation.

"We can kill Father Rangi and Mother Papa, or we can force them apart. For only then will we be able to escape this darkness. Which will it be?"

Tu, the fierce father and god of war-spirited human beings, finally exclaimed, "We must kill them!"

To these words, Tane, father and god of trees, birds, and insects, replied, "No, it would be better to push Father Rangi away from Mother Papa, to live like a stranger far above us. Meanwhile, we could let Mother Papa remain where she is under our feet, so that she can continue to nourish us with the foods that she grows for us."

Tane's words were so wise that even the warrior Tu was quick to agree with his brother's advice. But one brother, Tawhiri, father and god of all winds and storms, stood alone against the others. Now and forever, he separated himself from his brothers, fearing the loss of his own power and regretting his parents' separation. In defiance he held his breath and would do nothing. So it came to pass that five of Father Rangi and Mother Papa's six sons made an effort to try to separate their parents.

First came Rongo, father and god of the sweet potato and other edible cultivated plants. He lacked the necessary strength to separate Father Rangi and Mother Papa. Next came Tangaroa, father and god of all fish and sea reptiles. Tangaroa was stronger than Rongo, but no matter how hard he pushed, he could not separate Father Rangi and Mother Papa either. Third came Haumia, father and god of the fern root and other edible wild plants. However he, too, was unsuccessful. Then, confident in his own strength, Tu, the fierce father and god of war-spirited human beings, grabbed an axe-like tool and chopped away at the tendons that bound his parents together. The blood from these tendons created sacred red clay. However, Father Rangi and Mother Papa remained bound together.

Finally, Tane, father and god of forests, birds, and insects, took his turn. Just as a young tree pushes up from the earth, increasing in strength as it grows, so Tane slowly used his body to force his parents apart. First he tried to use his arms and his hands, but all their might could not move Father Rangi up and away from Mother Papa. Then, he decided to rest his head and shoulders against Mother Papa and to use his feet to push up against Father Rangi. Very, very slowly, Tane's continuous pressure stretched and then tore the tendons that bound his parents together. Despite their anguished cries, he pushed Mother Papa far under him and thrust Father Rangi far above him. So it came to pass that Tane freed all of Father Rangi and Mother Papa's other children from their dark world.

Tawhiri, father and god of winds and storms, had sympathized with his parents' love for each other and had considered their attachment to be appropriate. Living in darkness was also compatible with the nature of his power, whereas living in a lovely, bright world was not. Tawhiri greeted Tane's success with jealousy and anger. Tane had created exactly what Tawhiri dreaded—Day, with its power to push away the gloomy darkness of Night and light up and beautify the universe. The father and god of winds and storms feared that there would no longer be a place for him in this new world.

So it came to pass that Tawhiri hurried to join Father Rangi. The god of the sky and weather was pleased to have this son's companionship and help. Together, they worked to create many great winds and storms that flew north, south, east, and west, battering those on Mother Papa with their blows. Tawhiri sent winds that delivered fiery blows, winds that delivered freezing blows, winds that dumped rain, and winds that dumped sleet. Finally, Tawhiri came down to his mother's realm as a hurricane. He surprised Tane by tearing apart his forests and leaving his mighty trees to rot away, broken and useless upon the earth.

Having felled Tane's forests, Tawhiri then attacked Tangaroa's seas. Tangaroa loved to live along the seashore, but now he found himself battered by great tides, churning whirlpools, and mountainous waves. Terrified, he ran and hid in the deepest part of the ocean, where Tawhiri would not be able to find him.

Meanwhile, Tangaroa's two grandchildren, the father of fish and the father of reptiles, together with their own children, argued about whether they would be safer on land or in the sea. Shark tried to persuade Lizard and the other members of his family to seek refuge in the sea with the fish. "If you are captured on land," he warned, "you will have to endure death by fire before being eaten!"

"That may be," Lizard replied, "but all of you will be caught and eaten as well!"

And so it came to pass that the children of Tangaroa separated forever. Tangaroa became furious with Tane for sheltering Lizard and his children in the forests, and from that time to this, the god of the sea has been at war with his brother Tane. Tangaroa continues to nibble away at the forests that grow along the seashore, causing Tane's trees to fall prey to his waves. And Tangaroa enjoys chewing the wood from houses and trees that floods bring him. Meanwhile, Tane provides his brother Tu's children with the means to capture Tangaroa's sea-bound children by supplying human beings with wood for their canoes, fishing spears, and fish-hooks, and with flax and other plant fibers for their fishing nets. In response, Tangaroa attacks Tu's children with his waves and tides, capsizing their canoes and claiming their lives.

During the war between Tangaroa and Tane, revenge continued to occupy Tawhiri's thoughts and actions. After he was satisfied with his punishment of Tangaroa, he attacked Rongo and Haumia, the gods of planted and wild food. However, Mother Papa came to their rescue. Knowing that her other children needed the sweet potato and the fern root in order to survive, she hid Rongo and Haumia where Tawhiri could not find them.

Finally, Tawhiri attacked his last brother, Tu, the father and god of war- spirited human beings, and the one brother who originally had suggested that the gods kill Father Rangi and Mother Papa. However, Tu was ready for the assault. He placed his feet upon Mother Papa's chest, where they took their strength from their mother. Thus Tu survived Tawhiri's strongest storm-winds. Tu's victory caused Tawhiri to give up his battle.

Peace had little opportunity to reign on earth, however. Once Tu, the eternal warrior, had proved himself against Tawhiri, he became angry with his four other brothers. Not one of the gods of the earth and the sea had shown the courage and strength against Tawhiri that he had. Tane had been surprised by Tawhiri's attack and had made no effort to stop the father and god of winds and storms from destroying his forests. Tangaroa had avoided any confrontation with Tawhiri and, instead, had taken refuge in the depths of the sea. Rongo and Haumia had let Mother Papa protect them from Tawhiri by hiding them.

Tu was most angered by the fact that not one of his brothers had had the courage and the sense of loyalty to help him in his own fight against Tawhiri. The eternal warrior, therefore, set out to punish the four of them by taking control of their kingdoms.

The fierce father and god of war-spirited human beings decided to attack Tane's children first, before they became numerous enough to outnumber and overwhelm his own children. He fashioned leaves into nooses and hung them cleverly to trap Tane's birds. Once caught, he defiled them by cooking them, and then he ate them.

Next, Tu attacked Tangaroa's children. He wove the flax from Tane's plants into nets and dragged them through the sea to catch Tangaroa's fish. These, too, he defiled by cooking them, and then he ate them.

Finally, Tu attacked the children of Rongo and Haumia. He fashioned a digging stick from one of Tane's trees and wove a flaxen basket from one of Tane's plants. With these, he dug up and collected the sweet potato and the fern root. Once again, he defiled them by cooking them, and then he ate them.

So it has come to pass that, from the time that Tu conquered Tane, Tangaroa, Rongo, and Haumia, the warrior god and his human children have dominated and eaten the children of these gods of earth and sea. To this day, the human family continues to eat Tane's birds, Tangaroa's fish, Rongo's sweet potatoes, and Haumia's fern roots. Tu has never been able to gain power over Tawhiri, but, to this day, he continues to fight him, for Tawhiri's winds and storms remain a destructive force on both earth and sea.

THE CREATION OF HUMAN BEINGS

Before there was man, there was woman, and it was Tane who created the first woman. He molded her from the sacred red clay that had received the blood from the tendons that had bound Father Rangi and Mother Papa together. When he had finished, he blew the breath of life into her nostrils and called her Hine Ahu One, the Earth-Maiden.

Tane loved the woman he had made, and from their love, a daughter called Hine Titama, the Dawn-Maiden, was born. Tane loved Hine Titama as well, and from their love, children were born who became the first men and women.

All was well until Hine Titama asked Tane, "Who is my father?"

When she learned that Tane was her father as well as her husband, she exclaimed, "Because I am so ashamed, Tane, I must now leave you, and our children, and this world of light that I love! I will find my grandmother, Mother Papa, deep in the Underworld, and I will remain there with her from this time forth and forever. I will make a path as I walk, for I know that, in time, our children, their children, and all who come after them will know death and will follow me into the lower world."

In order to be certain that no one attempted to prevent her going, Hine Titama cast a spell of weakness upon Tane and a sleeping spell upon her children. Down, down, down, she traveled from the world of light into the eternal darkness of the lower world.

At the entrance to the Underworld, a guard confronted her. "Return to the upper world, Dawn-Maiden," he advised, "while you still can. Our spirit world is not for one like you! Here it is always black and grim. You would never choose to be here, for this is truly a joyless place!"

"I know that what you say is true," Hine Titama replied. "But it is here that I intend to live, and it is here that I will watch over my children who will be coming to me from the world above."

As Hine Titama turned from the guard to walk through the gates, her eyes fell upon Tane. Despite the deep gloom, she could see that he was tearfully following her.

"Poor Tane!" she cried. "Return to the upper world, and be a father to our children while they live in the world of light. Know that, in time, all of our children, and their children, and their children's children, from this time forth and forever, will follow this path that I have made.

"For death should come to all men and women," she explained, "and then, they should return to the dark world from which they came. That is why I intend to remain here. I want to be a mother to them when it is time for them to join me."

With these words, Hine Titama turned and walked into the Underworld, where she became known as the Night-Maiden and the goddess of Death. From that day to this, the sun begins its morning journey in the east and returns to its home in the west, while Tane follows it on its journey. And men, women, and children follow Hine Titama's path down into the Underworld when Death claims their spirits.

Meanwhile, despite their forced separation, Father Rangi and Mother Papa have continued to feel a great love for each other. In the beginning, Father Rangi cried so long and hard that his tears caused the sea to flood and swallow up most of the land and its people. Most of these people continue to live beneath the sea. Many of them have become so accustomed to living in their murky world that if the sun's rays ever were to touch them, they would die.

Some of Father Rangi and Mother Papa's sons began to fear that the upper world would entirely disappear into the sea unless they could find a way to stop Father Rangi's tears. They decided to ease their parents' grief by turning Mother Papa's face down upon the earth so that she and Father Rangi would not be able to see each other's tears. Their plan succeeded. The flood-waters that lay upon the upper world subsided, and from that time until this, Father Rangi's tears form the morning dew, while Mother Papa's tears form the morning mist.

Her sons turned Mother Papa's body while her infant son, young Ruaumoko, was drinking at her breast. At first Ruaumoko continued to cling to his mother. Then he fell into the Underworld. In time he grew up. Now whenever he walks around the Underworld, he creates earthquakes in the upper world. Some say that he has become Hine Titama's husband.

THE CREATION OF NEW ZEALAND

Maui, the son of the goddess Taranga and the mortal Makea, was a hero, a trickster, and an inventor. It was he who tamed the sun so that those who live on the earth would have an easier life. However, it was also he who, for a prank, stole fire from those who live on the earth, thereby making life more difficult. And, it was he who first thought of using a barbed spear-point to capture birds and a barbed fish-hook to catch fish.

Maui's success in acquiring food for his wives and children was much greater than the success that his brothers had using traditional fishing methods, and since he never revealed the secrets of his success, his brothers preferred to hunt and fish without him.

One day, Maui overheard his wife complaining that she needed more fish than Maui caught for her. "If you want more fish," he announced, "why don't you simply ask me! You forget my magic powers. If it's fish that you want, I'll catch a fish that is so large that it will spoil before you can finish eating it! And then, I'm sure you will complain about the food that you had to throw away!"

So it came to pass that Maui used a piece of his grandmother's jawbone to create a magic fish-hook. Once he had recited the proper chants over it, he was determined to accompany his brothers on their next fishing trip. He expected that they would set out in their canoe just as the sun set out on its morning journey.

He knew that his brothers would be watching out for him, even in one of his transformations, so he decided to hide beneath the planking in the canoe.

The canoe was safely out to sea before Maui decided to reveal his presence. Even then, his brothers were determined to take him home. So it came to pass that Maui resorted to magic. While his brothers were turning the canoe around, Maui so extended the distance between their canoe and land that they decided that it was more trouble to return Maui to shore than to keep him with them.

All was well until the brothers stopped at their usual fishing spot. Then, Maui suddenly spoke up and exclaimed, "Don't anchor here today! There's better fishing farther out!"

So the brothers resumed their paddling and continued toward their second fishing spot. By this time, they were very tired, but Maui was undaunted. "You don't want to anchor here, either!" he told them. "If you really want to catch a boatload of fish, let me take you to the place that I like best!"

Lured by the promise of fine fish, Maui's brothers agreed to paddle further out to sea. Finally, when they no longer could see the land they had left, Maui announced, "Here we are! Throw in the anchor and prepare your lines!"

Just as Maui had promised, fish continually bit their bait and were caught. Soon the canoe was weighted down with a huge load of fish, and the brothers prepared to return home.

"Wait a minute!" Maui cried. "You can't leave just yet! I have to try my own hook!"

"Your own hook!" his brothers exclaimed. "You don't own a hook, and if you mean to use one of our hooks, you can't have it!"

"Don't worry! I don't want one of your hooks," Maui replied. "I have my own right here."

Maui's brothers gaped in astonishment as he reached under his loincloth and pulled out a marvelous fish-hook. At one end of the sparkling, shell shank, a tuft of dog hair waved in the sea breeze. At the other end, Maui had fastened a hook that he had made from his grandmother's jawbone.

Maui found a fishing line in the bottom of the canoe, but his brothers refused to let him use their bait. Therefore, he gave himself a nosebleed and used his blood instead.

"All right now," he told them. "I am ready to fish. Do not say anything, no matter what I say or do! One word from you could make me lose my catch!"

He then threw out his line and recited this spell: "Blow kindly, winds, both you from the northeast and you from the southeast. I have come for my great land. Line, be strong and straight, and lead me to my catch!"

The line suddenly caught, and Maui pulled on it, causing the heavy canoe to tip and take in water. Maui's magic fish-hook had grabbed onto the house of Tangaroa's grandson.

"Let go, Maui!" his brothers screamed, as they frantically bailed out the seawater. They were sure that they would drown, but Maui refused to obey. He was busily using his fishing skill and his magic chants, and he impatiently replied, "What Maui has caught, he cannot set free! He is catching what he has come to catch!"

Meanwhile, Maui's brothers sat in silent terror in their quaking canoe, fearing the tumultuous waves that Maui's fishing had caused. Just when they could endure their fears no longer, they saw a group of thatched, pointed roofs, followed by the houses themselves, and, finally, the great piece of flat land on which the community stood, all slowly emerge from the waves. Maui's "fish" was no creature of the deep. It was a huge island filled with living people who were busily occupied with village life.

Maui tied his fishing line onto a paddle that lay securely in the canoe, and then he told his brothers, "I am going to the sacred place in this village so that I can perform the ritual offering to the gods. Until I have returned to you, you must not eat any food, and you must leave my fish just as it is. If you do not listen to me, you will anger Tangaroa and bring great trouble upon us!"

Despite Maui's warning, his brothers only waited until he was out of sight before they began to eat the sweet fruits of the land. The gods were quick to retaliate. Maui's fish began to thrash about, just as if it were an ordinary fish. Its movements caused the land to become mountainous and, therefore, difficult for human life. When the sun ended its day's journey, the fish finally became quiet. However, the surface of the land had permanently settled into the shape that it has had from that time until this.

Meanwhile, Maui and his brothers paddled back to their home on Hawaiki, where their father greeted them with a song of praise for Maui. "Maui Tikitiki, you are my pride and joy!" he exclaimed. "You have rescued our ancient land from its burial place at the bottom of the sea. This land disappeared long ago when Father Rangi, being angry over his separation from Mother Papa, helped Tawhiri take vengeance on his brothers by flooding the earth with his rain of tears.

"In times to come," Maui's father continued, "you will become the father of human beings like myself, and not gods like your mother. Some of your children and your children's children will continue to live here in our homeland of Hawaiki, but others will live on the islands that you have rescued from the sea. Therefore, your catching of your great fish will be as important an event to them as the separation of Father Rangi and Mother Papa!

"Your wonderful catch has made you a great hero!" Maui's father concluded. "And for this, you will have everlasting fame! From this time forth and forever, the Maori people will call their fish-shaped north island, 'The Fish of Maui,' their south island, 'Maui's Canoe,' and the cape at Heretaunga, 'Maui's Fish-Hook.'

"In fact," he laughed, "your deed is so great, Maui, that Hawaiki peoples of other lands will also claim that you rescued their islands from the bottom of the sea. And they will call their lands "The Fish of Maui" as well!"

Response, Discussion, and Analysis

1. In what ways are the Maori gods like human beings?

2. What appears to be the greatest natural enemy of the Maori? Cite evidence from the creation myth to support your point of view.

3. What view of humankind does the Maori creation myth have?

4. Does Maui's being a trickster-hero add to his heroic image in this myth or detract from it? Explain.

HISTORICAL BACKGROUND

Since the Hawaiians and the Maori of New Zealand share the same Polynesian origins, the introduction to the Maori creation myths includes a discussion of historical background that also applies to the following Hawaiian fertility myth.

Polynesian society in the Hawaiian Islands was divided into social classes that consisted of chiefs and royalty at the top, then priests, then the common people, and, finally, slaves at the bottom. Each ruling chief claimed a divine ancestor through whom he had inherited his land.

Because Hawaii is a fertile land and fish are plentiful, life for the Polynesians was easy, and leisure time existed for the development and enjoyment of oral tales. Bards sang or recited poetic stories. Some were part of the chief's court, while others traveled from one court to another. Both types of bard performed only for the aristocracy.

The Polynesians worshipped nature gods who are important in their legendary history. In the Polynesian myths, the gods are often depicted as chiefs who live in distant lands or in the heavens. Like the Hawaiian chiefs, who claimed divine ancestors, the heroes of Hawaiian myth are also related to the gods, either by birth or by adoption. Consequently, in Hawaiian mythology, divine power flows from the gods to their human relatives.

Captain James Cook, the British navigator and explorer, discovered the Hawaiian Islands in 1778, nine years after he had reached New Zealand. The first missionaries arrived in 1820, and they had a profound effect upon the native Hawaiians and their mythology. Under their direction, the Hawaiian chiefs discarded their native religion and adopted Christianity. The Polynesian creation myth disappeared from the culture and was replaced by one that is consistent with the account in the Bible.

During this period, the native oral language was given a written form, and by the 1860s, Hawaiian newspapers included Western literature. As a result, native Hawaiian literature became heavily influenced by foreign ideas.

Moreover, the first people who collected native Hawaiian literature chose to ignore the tales that collectors on other Polynesian islands had chosen to preserve. Consequently, the literature that survives from the Polynesian culture on Hawaii is later than the literature obtained from the Maori of New Zealand and from the native peoples of Tahiti and Samoa.

Two collections of Hawaiian mythology are particularly interesting. *The Legends and Myths of Hawaii,* by His Hawaiian Majesty King David Kalakaua, published in New York in 1888, presents a selected group of Hawaiian legends and folklore in a form designed to promote Hawaiian nationalism and cultural pride. The author rescues his subject from being viewed as mere children's tales by writing in a grandiose style and treating his Hawaiian material as if it were similar to the Bible, *The Iliad,* and the heroic myths and legends of medieval Europe.

The second collection is a series of books and articles written by William Drake Westervelt, an ordained minister who settled permanently in Hawaii in 1899 and became an authority on the customs and legends of the islands. His first book, *Legends of Ma-ui* (1910), tells the myth of Maui's capture of the sun and also includes Polynesian sources of the tale from such islands as Samoa and New Zealand.

APPEAL AND VALUE

The Hawaiian version of "The Taming of the Sun" is very similar to the Maori version of the same myth. Like "The Creation of New Zealand" (and its counterpart, "The Creation of Hawaii"), "The Taming of the Sun" is another of the demigod Maui's great deeds, and it provides an accurate depiction of this trickster-hero at work. Like the Hawaiian chiefs, Maui also has both divine and human relatives, being related to the gods through his mother, who is the patron goddess of kapa-beating (bark cloth-making) and other women's tasks.

A common theme in fertility myths involves a hero saving the world from a great threat. Sometimes the hero is a god, like Indra and Raven; sometimes, he is a demigod, like Ahaiyuta; and sometimes he is simply an ordinary mortal, like Bao Chu. Maui's deeds compare with those of other trickster-heroes in mythology, such as Hermes and Loki.

THE TAMING OF THE SUN

Life was easier for those on earth after Maui had raised and fastened the sky high above. However, life was still very difficult because the sun god now traveled quickly across the sky and made each day much too short.

In fact, it was impossible for trees and plants to produce enough food for the human family because it took them so long to grow. And it was impossible for men and women to finish any one task within the few hours of available light. Farmers did not have time to plant or to harvest a crop. Hunters did not have time to set their traps or to empty them. Fishermen did not have time to reach their fishing grounds or to return from them. And women did not have time both to prepare and to cook the day's food, or to make the bark cloth that they used. Even prayers to the gods were completed after the sun had returned to his home. For most of each day, the world was damp, dreary, and dark.

From the time that he could remember, Maui would watch his mother, Hina-of-the-Fire, as she tried to make the bark cloth, called kapa, during the brief time that the sun was traveling across the sky. It was a long and complex task at best.

First, Hina-of-the-Fire had to take branches from the mulberry trees and soak them in seawater until their bark was soft enough for her to remove it. Once she had removed the bark, she had to separate the inner layer from the outer layer, since she would only be able to use the inner bark to make kapa. She would stack the wet pieces of inner bark in bundles and lay them upon the kapa board where, beginning at one end of the board and moving to the other end, she would pound them with a four-sided wooden beater until the bark had become soft, thin sheets of pulp. Finally, she would paste these thin sheets together into large cloths that would make fine clothes to wear and mats on which to sleep.

Since the sun traveled so quickly across the sky, the process of collecting the bark took one month. The process of soaking it took a second month. The process of separating it took a third month. And the process of pounding it into thin sheets took six more months. In the early stages of this process, it was difficult to keep the bark wet. After the sheets had been pasted together, it was difficult for the kapa to dry. The entire process could take as long as a year, and making kapa was only one of a woman's daily tasks!

Maui watched his mother hard at work day after day, rushing to prepare her materials for one task, working faster at another task, sighing in despair as the sun entered his home before she had completed anything, and his heart ached for her. And the more Maui's heart ached for his mother, the more his heart filled with anger at the sun. So it came to pass that Maui turned his attention away from his mother and toward the sun. In order to observe the sun more carefully, he climbed the extinct volcano that can be found on the northwest side of the island. From there, he noticed that each morning as the sun began his journey, the sun would travel up and over the eastern side of the great mountain called Haleakala (the House of the Sun).

Then one day Maui asked his mother, "Why does the sun have to travel so quickly? Why doesn't he care about those who live on the earth? Is there a way to stop him from behaving so selfishly? I am going to tame him! What if I cut off his legs? That should keep him from running so fast!"

"The sun does what he has always done and what he will always do," his mother replied. "No ordinary person can confront him and live to tell about it. If you are going to try to change his behavior, you have set yourself a great task, and you will need to prepare yourself well. The sun is very large and powerful, and his rays are fiery hot. Once you come face to face with him, your courage will dry up in his heat as if you were no more than a dead plant!

"I think that you had better visit your grandmother and ask her to help you," Hina-of-the-Fire suggested. "She can give you good advice, and she has just the weapon that might bring you success.

"Your grandmother lives on the side of Mount Haleakala, not far from where the sun always begins his morning journey. You will know that you have found the place when you come upon a large wiliwili tree. Your grandmother prepares breakfast for the sun every morning, and he stops there to eat before he begins his journey.

"Your grandmother cooks bananas for the sun to eat," Hina-of-the-Fire explained. "You must be at the wiliwili tree as the sun makes the sky rosy-red with his first rays. A rooster stands watch by the tree, and he announces the sun's arrival by crowing three times. It is then that your grandmother will come out with a bunch of bananas and put them on the ground while she makes a fire in order to cook them for the sun to eat. You must take these bananas.

"Your grandmother will then come out with a second bunch of bananas and put them on the ground in order to cook them for the sun to eat. You must take these bananas as well."

Maui's mother concluded, "Your grandmother will then come out with a third bunch of bananas and put them on the ground in order to cook them for the sun to eat. She will notice that someone has taken the first two bunches of bananas and will begin searching for the thief. It is then that you must present yourself to her. You must tell her that you are Maui, and that you are the son of Hina-of-the-Fire."

So it came to pass that, while the sun was asleep, Maui set out to climb Mount Haleakala. Just as the sun made the sky rosy-red with his first rays, Maui saw the great wiliwili tree painted in black against the pale-colored sky. The rest happened just as his mother had told him it would. The rooster crowed three times. The old woman, who was his grandmother, appeared two times with a bunch of bananas that Maui took. When she discovered that these two bunches were missing, she cried, "Where are the sun's bananas?" and began to search for the thief.

Maui's grandmother was so old that she was almost totally blind. As she searched for the thief, she came close enough to Maui to smell the scent of a man. She then approached him, peered into his face with her clouded eyes, and asked, "Who are you? And what do you want with the sun's bananas?"

"I am Maui, the son of Hina-of-the-Fire," Maui replied, "and I have come for your help. I want to tame the sun! I need to find a way to stop him from behaving so selfishly. He travels much too quickly! He makes each day so short that even my mother cannot finish any of her tasks. It can take her a full year to make kapa! Those who are not gods must have an even more difficult time!"

Maui's grandmother listened carefully to his words. And as she listened, the things of the earth and sky praised Maui. In his honor, thunder roared and the rainbow bridge appeared. In his honor, pebbles chattered and ants sang. In his honor, dogs without fur walked the land. Surely, Maui was born to be a hero among men!

So it came to pass that Maui's grandmother decided to help him. "Listen carefully to my words, my grandson," she said, "and I will help you tame the sun. First, you must make sixteen ropes that you must twist from the strongest coconut fiber. Then, you must ask your sister, Hina-of-the-Sea, to give you enough of her hair to enable you to make a noose for the end of each of them.

"When these are ready," she concluded, "return to me, and I will tell you how to arrange the ropes so as to catch the sun. I will also give you a magic axe of stone so that you will have a great weapon to use against the sun."

Given the short days, it took many months for Maui to make the ropes and nooses, but finally he was ready to return to his grandmother's home. While the sun slept, she showed him how to set the nooses as traps and how to tie the ropes to the great wiliwili tree. Then Maui dug a hole for himself by the roots of the great tree and hid inside the hole so that the sun would not be able to see him when he began his morning journey.

When the sun made the sky rosy-red with his first rays, Maui was ready for him. Soon, the sun's first ray appeared over the top of Mount Haleakala and became caught in one of Maui's nooses. Then the sun's second ray appeared over the top of Mount Haleakala and became caught in one of Maui's nooses. One by one, the fourteen other rays of the sun came over the top of Mount Haleakala, and, one by one, each ray became caught in one of Maui's nooses. Finally, the sun, dressed in his bright crimson robe, stood on top of Mount Haleakala. He was ready to begin his morning journey, but he was unable to move even one of his rays.

At first, the sun violently thrashed this way and that, desperately trying to pull his rays out of the nooses and to retreat down the back of Mount Haleakala into the sea-home from which he had come. But he could not pull the ropes off the wiliwili tree, and the roots of that great tree held the tree fast.

"Who has trapped me in these snares? And what do you hope to gain by it?" the sun roared.

"I am Maui, the son of Hina-of-the-Fire," Maui replied, "and I have come for your help. You must stop behaving so selfishly. You travel much too quickly! You make each day so short that my mother cannot finish any of her tasks. It can take her a full year to make kapa! Those who are not gods must have an even more difficult time!"

"I do not care about your mother and her kapa!" the sun exclaimed. "And I certainly do not care about those who are not gods! The faster I travel each day, the longer I can sleep each night. This is what I have always done, and this is what I will always do! As for you, if you do not release me from these snares right now, you will not live to see your mother again!"

Maui immediately bent down, but he did not intend to release the sun's rays. Instead, he picked up his grandmother's magic axe and waved it threateningly at the sun.

The sun responded by turning his blazing face upon Maui. He seared Maui with his fiery breath, hoping to burn him quickly to ashes.

Maui retaliated by attacking the sun. Despite the intensity of the sun's heat, Maui mercilessly struck the sun, again and again, with the stone axe.

Finally, the sun screamed, "Stop it! I cannot stand the pain any longer! If you keep beating me like this, you are going to kill me! And if I die, you and everything that lives will die as well! As it is, I am going to hobble all the way home!"

"I will stop," Maui replied, "if you promise me that you will travel slowly across the sky each day."

"Do I have to travel slowly every day from this day forth and forever?" the sun wailed.

"No," Maui replied, relenting. "It will be good enough if you travel slowly for just half of the year. Your light and your heat will enable plants to grow faster and produce more fruit, and they will permit men and women to get their work done faster and more easily. Then, for the other half of the year, you can travel as fast as you wish."

The sun was quick to agree to this compromise. So it came to pass that Maui released the sun's sixteen rays from the nooses. However, as a daily reminder of their agreement, he left the ropes and nooses next to the great wiliwili tree on the side of Mount Haleakala, where the sun would be sure to see them as he climbed over the top of the mountain.

So it came to pass that, because of Maui's efforts, life became much easier for human beings. Each day during the long season that came to be known as summer, the sun traveled across the sky so slowly that the days were very long.

Now it was possible for trees and plants to produce enough food for the human family because they grew fast and well. And now it was possible for men and women to finish a difficult task within the long hours of available light. Farmers now had time to plant or to harvest a crop. Hunters now had time to set their traps or to empty them. Fishermen now had time to reach their fishing grounds or to return from them. And women now had time to prepare their food and to cook it, or to make the bark cloth that they used.

In honor of Maui's taming of the sun, the people celebrated and sang, "How good it is that the sun's journey is long and that he now gives us the light we need for our daily work!"

∾ QUESTIONS FOR
Response, Discussion, and Analysis

1. In what way does the setting of this myth reflect life in the Hawaiian Islands?

2. What does this myth reveal about Maui's nature? Do you like him? Explain.

3. What does magic contribute to this myth? Does it enhance or detract from the myth? Explain.

4. Does Maui's being a trickster-hero add to his heroic image in this myth or detract from it? Explain.

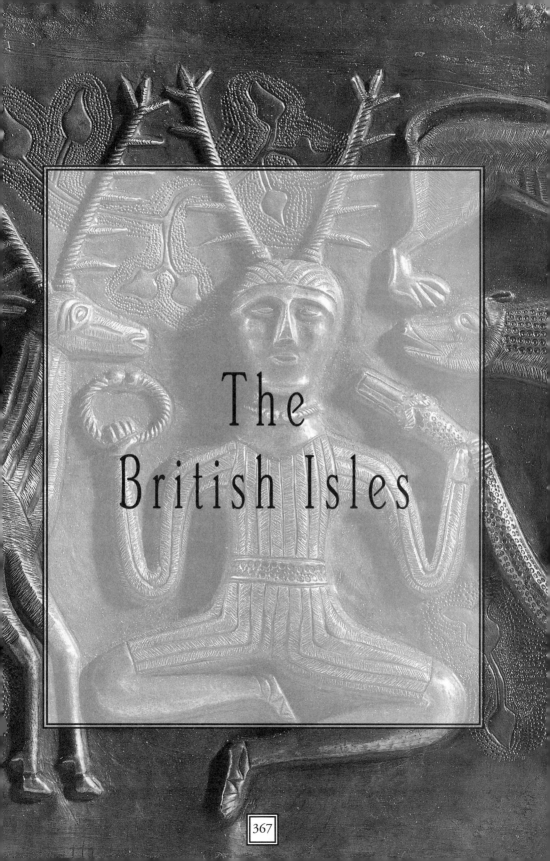

The British Isles

The British Isles were settled by various European cultures, and their myths reflect this diversity. The epic of *Beowulf,* which was written in the early eighth century A.D. by a Christian who loved the pagan tradition, reflects the Norse tradition transplanted to English soil. The Irish myths were recorded by monks between 1100 and 1600. Finally, the story of King Arthur shows a combination of Welsh, English, and French traditions ranging from the early twelfth century to the late fifteenth century.

The Irish myths connect mythology and history by describing the settling of Ireland by successive waves of Celtic peoples. The battles between the race called the Fomorians (local residents who represent the forces of darkness) and the Celts (invaders who represent the forces of light) reflect Ireland's harsh northern environment and its uncertain political future. The use of magic enlivens all these tales, including the creation and fertility myths.

Beowulf is the earliest surviving major work of Germanic literature, and it is a masterpiece. The anonymous writer has created a thematically unified work in which every detail relates to the piece as a whole. Moreover, the writer's ability to create psychologically complex characters is unique among the surviving works from Northern Europe. However, the epic can be appreciated on a less serious level as well. After all, Beowulf is a hero who resembles Superman, and he combats three memorable monsters. Readers of *Beowulf* understand why writers continue to create their own versions of this epic and why students will learn Anglo-Saxon in order to read this work in the original language.

The legend of King Arthur is equally amazing, but in a different way. The story assigns to King Arthur whatever is great in the Western heroic tradition. For example, his ancestors come from the burning city of Troy. His father and uncle are connected with Stonehenge. Merlin, part prophet and part magician, sprinkles his marvels throughout the early part of the tale. Moreover, Arthur's famous knights enliven the story with adventures of their own.

Like Beowulf, Arthur fights a monster. Like Alexander the Great, he is one of the world's great conquerors, becoming the head of the Roman Empire. Finally, from a French tradition comes the tragic love story of Arthur, Guinevere, and Lancelot, in which personal desires overcome the characters' responsibility to society and cause the destruction of a great kingdom. The story of King Arthur has something for every taste. Therefore, year after year, it continues to enchant readers and and to inspire writers.

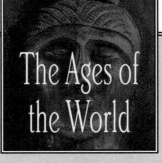

The Ages of the World

Scholars believe that the first people to settle the British Isles migrated there from northern Africa and Spain. They were the resident population when the Celts arrived from Northern Europe.

The druids were the religious leaders of the Celts. They were the priests, prophets, poets, magicians, scientists, and doctors of their tribes. Experts in human knowledge, the druids also could deal with the gods. They were so highly respected that they ranked next to kings and chieftains in importance. The druids performed particular rituals and sacrifices in the belief that they could persuade the gods who controlled all natural phenomena to grant their people fertility and prosperity.

The Celts worshipped the sun, which represented light, fertility, and life. Their four major holidays focused on the sun's relationship to the earth: the two solstices (summer, when the sun is closest to the earth, and winter, when it is farthest from the earth) and the two equinoxes (the beginning of spring and of autumn). The Celts may have used the prehistoric monument Stonehenge (which marks the sun's progress through the year) as a religious site.

For the Celts, life was fragile and nature was harsh. The powers of darkness brought to the northern countries an early, freezing winter, long months when crops could not grow, and the risk of early death from illness, starvation, or harsh weather. The Celtic year's-end festival on the night before Samain, now celebrated as Halloween, was truly a fearsome holiday because it marked the beginning of winter, when the sun's power would become increasingly weak and the forces of darkness would become increasingly strong. Survival was uncertain.

Halloween was a time of monsters and human sacrifice. As part of the religious festival, residents of villages and towns would appear dressed as the demons of darkness, disorder, destruction, disease, and death so that the other residents could chase them away. Celts would also construct figures representing these demons and burn them in the town square as part of the religious ceremony. They also sacrificed one-third of their healthy children to their gods every year, hoping to motivate the gods to provide the grains and grass that they and their animals needed to survive.

The Celtic myths were preserved by Christian monks in Ireland, Scotland, and Wales between A.D. 1100 and 1600. The Irish and Scottish monks recorded an older and more authentic Celtic tradition in the *Lebor Gahala Erenn* (*Irish Book of Conquests*) than the Welsh monks did in *The Mabinogion*. The latter collection of myths and tales has the setting and tone of medieval chivalry and often involves the adventures of King Arthur and his knights. Consequently, the Celtic creation and fertility myths are found in manuscripts from Ireland and Scotland rather than from Wales.

According to Irish tradition, ancient history and mythology are the same real event—the settling of Ireland by successive races of divine and human peoples. It was a time when gods walked the earth like human beings, using their supernatural powers to bring fertility, civilization, and peace to Ireland. (It is possible that because of their own Christian bias, the Irish and

Scottish monks made the Celtic gods act, and even die, as if they were human warriors.)

The Celtic gods live on Irish soil rather than in the heavens. The male gods are warriors who protect the tribe. The female gods are usually fertility goddesses, but may be warriors as well. When the chieftain marries a fertility goddess, he is increasing the protection and survival of the people.

Whatever race of gods rules Ireland, the force of darkness—in the shape of the Fomorians—opposes it and is often successful in battle. The Fomorians represent the gods worshipped by the native, Mediterranean peoples, while the Túatha Dé Danann (the peoples of the Mother Goddess Danu) represent the gods worshipped by the Celts.

PRINCIPAL CHARACTERS AND GODS

LADHRA: leader of the first race in Ireland
PARTHOLON: leader of the second race in Ireland

NEMED: leader of the third race in Ireland
FIR BOLG: fourth race in Ireland; first to survive on Irish soil
TÚATHA DÉ DANANN: fifth and greatest race in Ireland; they conquer the Fir Bolgs and the Fomorians
DANU: Mother Goddess or Great Goddess; Túatha Dé are her people
ERIU: Mother Goddess or Great Goddess; queen of the Túatha Dé
BADB CATHA: great Celtic war goddess
DAGDA: god of fertility; great skill in magic; one of the two greatest Túatha Dé warriors
LUG: god of the sun; one of the two greatest Túatha Dé warriors
NUADA: great king of the Túatha Dé
BRES: son of the king of the Fomorians and a Túatha Dé; replaces Nuada as king of the Túatha Dé
FOMORIANS: race of giants; enemy of all the Irish races
MILESIANS: sixth race in Ireland; conquerors of the Túatha Dé
AMERGIN: great druid and poet of the Milesians
DONN: oldest of the Milesians

THE AGES OF THE WORLD

In the beginning, Ireland existed, and it was the world. In the first age of the world, the first race inhabited Ireland. Ladhra, a great leader, had sixteen wives. He was the first person to die on Irish soil, and after his death Ireland was buried by a great flood. Ladhra's entire race perished by drowning. For the next 268 years, the land of Ireland remained uninhabited.

In the second age of the world, the second race invaded Ireland. This was the race of Partholon, the first of the Irish divine ancestors. The race consisted of forty-eight gods; half were males and half were females. For most of the second age, which lasted for 300 years, the Partholons ruled supreme upon the land. In time, their numbers grew from the original forty-eight to 5,000.

When the race of Partholon arrived, Ireland had no grass or trees, but three lakes and nine rivers already provided fresh water. Partholon created seven additional lakes and made the soil fertile. Then he created three more treeless, grassless plains, and his people began to till the soil. One Partholon merchant imported herds of cattle, which became the prize of farmers. Another merchant introduced gold. Agriculture became the principal activity, and the community flourished.

During Partholon's lifetime, the people built the first houses and guest houses, made the first cauldron, and brewed the first beer from large, wild ferns. They established the beginnings of legal and educational systems and devised formal religious practices involving prophecy and sacrifices.

Although this second age was a time of general prosperity, disagreements sometimes disturbed the peace. The first duel was fought, and adultery first occurred. While Partholon was away, his wife and his servant slept together. When Partholon learned of their crime, he demanded that they pay him a price of honor.

Partholon's wife replied that he was at fault rather than she, and it was she who deserved compensation. She argued that a wife was part of her husband's property, and a husband was responsible for protecting his property. In leaving, Partholon had not properly protected his wife. Therefore, she was entitled to the price of honor. The legal system supported Partholon's wife in the dispute, and the judgment against him became the first legal decision in Ireland.

The Fomorians, a native race of divine, monstrous sea-people who had inhabited the islands off the coast of Ireland for 200 years, envied the Partholons' abundant food supply and attacked. They fought with their one eye, their one hand, and their one foot, and they were adept in the use of magic. A mighty battle raged between the two races for seven days. Finally, the Partholons succeeded in driving the Fomorians off their land. But the victory was only temporary; the Fomorians returned to their islands, where they watched and waited for their chance to conquer the people who had civilized Ireland.

On the first of May, the great feast day of Beltine that marked the beginning of summer, the entire race of Partholon was destroyed by a strange plague. Ireland remained uninhabited for thirty years. Yet the contributions that the Partholons had made to Irish life remained to enrich the lives of races who came after them.

In the third age of the world, the divine race of Nemed (sacred) invaded Ireland. The Nemedians created four more lakes and cleared twelve more plains. They imported sheep, which so thrived upon Irish soil that soon they far outnumbered the cattle of the Partholons. Under Nemedian rule, agriculture became more widespread and the people more prosperous.

To protect themselves against the Fomorians, the Nemedians built two forts. Four times the race of Nemed fought against the Fomorians, and four times they emerged from battle victorious. Then a great disease killed Nemed and 2,000 of his people. The Fomorians took advantage of their vulnerability and attacked again. This time they easily conquered the Nemedians in battle, and then they enslaved them. Thereafter, every year on the first of November, the great feast day of Samain that marked the beginning of winter, the Nemedians had to give the Fomorians two-thirds of their children, two-thirds of their milk, and two-thirds of their corn.

The Nemedians could devise no way to avoid this devastating tribute. In desperation, they made one final attack upon the Fomorians in which 16,000 of the race of Nemed died. Those Nemedians who survived abandoned their homes and farms and left Ireland.

In the fourth age of the world, the race of Fir Bolg invaded Ireland on the first of August, the great feast day of Lugnasad that marked the beginning of autumn. Although the Fir Bolgs consisted of many different tribes, they functioned as one race and lived under one king who held complete power in Ireland. They were the first of the races to survive on Irish soil. Unlike their enemies, the Fomorians, they were not divine.

During the reign of the Fir Bolgs, Ireland became more than an agricultural society. The Fir Bolgs were warrior-aristocrats who introduced the iron spearhead. Their king was the first to establish justice in the land, and under his rule the soil became very fertile. The rains fell as gentle dew, and each year's harvest was a bountiful one. Nevertheless, in spite of their warlike skills, the Fir Bolgs were defeated by a new wave of invaders.

In the fifth age of the world, the divine race of Túatha Dé Danann (peoples of the Mother Goddess Danu) invaded Ireland on the first of May. When they landed, a dense cloud concealed their arrival from the Fir Bolgs. As a sign of their determination to remain on Irish soil, they immediately burned all of their boats; no matter what trials lay before them, they would either have to succeed or die.

Their religious leaders, the druids, blew fog and rain clouds over the entire island. These clouds unleashed a torrent of blood and fire upon the Fir Bolgs, causing them to hide in sheltered places for three days and three nights. The religious leaders of the Fir Bolgs cleared the air by performing their own magic spells. Finally, the two races declared a truce of 105 days in order to give each side time to prepare for war.

The Túatha Dé Danann were divided into two groups, gods and non-gods. The gods were the artisans, artists, and aristocratic warriors, for they possessed the power and talent of the race. The non-gods were farmers and common laborers of the fields.

The Túatha Dé were a very talented and learned race of gods. In the islands of northern Greece they had learned many arts and crafts, along with magic. Their wisdom, their magic, and their four talismans gave them divine power. The three greatest Túatha Dé were Dagda the Good, Lug of the Long Arms, and Nuada of the Silver Arm. Dagda earned his name because he was the god of fertility, and he possessed great skill in magic. Lug, the god of the sun, emitted a great brilliance during the day and reflected the glow of the sun from dusk until dawn. He and Dagda were the greatest of the Túatha Dé warriors. Nuada was the great king of the Túatha Dé.

The first treasure of the Túatha Dé was Dagda's bronze Cauldron of Plenty, which always fed each person the amount of food he or she deserved and yet satisfied the hunger of each person who ate from it. Their second treasure was the Stone of Destiny, which emitted a human cry whenever the lawful king of Ireland stepped upon it.

The third treasure of the Túatha Dé was the Spear of Nuada, which always hit its target and brought death to anyone it wounded. Their fourth and last treasure was the sword of Lug, which flashed and roared with fiery flames and brought certain victory to whoever wielded it. Lug's sword always longed for the taste of blood and searched for a way to appease its hunger. Lug kept its blade stored in a container of juice made from pulverized poppy leaves, for the narcotic put the sword safely to sleep until it was needed. Once Lug unleashed it, his sword would tear into the enemy and tirelessly slay warrior after warrior, feasting upon their warm blood.

By using their great skill in magic, the Túatha Dé won their first battle against the Fir Bolgs. Their warriors killed 1,100 of the enemy, and the few who survived the battle fled to the islands west of the Irish mainland. This became known as the first battle of Mag Tured.

In the course of the war, one of the Fir Bolgs cut off the arm of King Nuada. The Túatha Dé doctor and metalsmith worked together to create a silver arm for Nuada that could move with the life and vitality of the original arm. But even with his wondrous silver arm, Nuada was still considered to be maimed. Since the king had to be in perfect health, Nuada of the Silver Arm had to give up his throne.

The chieftains of the Túatha Dé Danann chose Bres the Beautiful to replace Nuada of the Silver Arm as king of Ireland. Bres was a son of the king of the Fomorians, but his mother was one of the Túatha Dé and he had been reared among them. The Túatha Dé chieftains hoped that their choice of Bres as king would ensure peace between the Fomorians and their race.

However, Bres was a very poor king. He was stingy when he should have been generous. He did not offer beer to his chieftains or grease their knives with fat. He refused to employ musicians, acrobats, clowns, and poets to entertain them, for he wished to keep his wealth for himself. He demanded heavy taxes in the form of jewels and food. He also treated the chieftains of the Túatha Dé as non-gods, forcing them to perform menial chores such as carrying firewood, digging ditches, and constructing forts and castles.

When Bres foolishly mistreated the Túatha Dé poet, who was the god of literature, he brought disaster upon himself and the Fomorians. Bres sheltered the poet in a barren, dark hut without the comfort of a bed or a fire and gave him only three dry biscuits for dinner. In retaliation, the poet used his magical power with words to curse the king. "May it become the fate of Bres to live as he has forced others to live: without food upon his plate, without cow's milk in his cup, and without the comforts of a house to protect him from the dismal night!"

The power of the poet was so great that when the chieftains of the Túatha Dé heard these words they forced Bres to give up the throne of Ireland. Bres asked his father, the king of the Fomorians, to attack the Túatha Dé. His father, hearing the true story, refused to help his son, but the other Fomorians gathered together a fearsome army and prepared for battle. The Túatha Dé also prepared for battle.

Meanwhile, Nuada's shoulder became infected where his silver arm was attached to it. When Nuada heard that the young son of the doctor who had designed his silver arm could perform even more wondrous medical feats than his father, he asked the son to cure his infection. The doctor asked Nuada what had been done with his real arm, and Nuada told him it had been buried. The doctor dug up the arm, placed it next to Nuada's shoulder, and recited the words, "Arm, join Nuada's shoulder, nerve to nerve and sinew to sinew."

After three days and three nights, Nuada's arm returned to life and connected itself to his shoulder once again. So it came to pass that Nuada of the Silver Arm was completely healed of his old injury and resumed his position as king of the Túatha Dé Danann.

The young doctor's father was so jealous of his son's medical skill that he raised his sword and struck his son on the head with it, just cutting the skin. The son easily healed his own surface wound. His father then raised his sword and struck his son on the head again, this time slicing through to the bone. Again, the son easily healed his wound. His father then raised his sword a third time and struck his son on the head, this time slicing through to the brain. Again, the son easily healed his wound. Finally, his father raised his sword a fourth time and struck his son on the head, this time slicing his brain in two. With this stroke, the older doctor killed his son.

Upon the young doctor's grave grew 365 stalks of grass. Each blade could cure an illness in one of the 365 nerves in a person's body. The young doctor's sister carefully collected the stalks and arranged them in proper order upon her cloak so that the Túatha Dé doctors could use them to heal their patients. She knew that with these stalks her brother had produced the cures for all illnesses. Her father, however, was so jealous of his son's contribution to medicine, even in death, that he overturned his daughter's cloak and hopelessly mixed up the stalks. Thereafter they were useless, for no one could determine which stalk could cure which illness.

Lug of the Long Arms arrived at court just after Nuada had returned to the throne. The porter greeted Lug politely but announced, "Although you look as royal as our king, Nuada, you will have to prove that you are master of a particular skill in order to be accepted among the nobility of the Túatha Dé Danann."

Lug replied, "Go before your king and tell him that I am a skilled and strong warrior, an excellent carpenter, a fine metalsmith, a gifted harpist, poet, and teller of tales, a knowledgeable doctor, and a talented magician. I challenge King Nuada to produce another of the Túatha Dé Danann who possesses as many skills as I do!"

When the porter repeated Lug's qualifications to the king, Nuada challenged Lug to a game of chess against the best player of the Túatha Dé. When Lug had won the game, he sat on the Seat of Wisdom and watched as the strongest of the Túatha Dé pushed a huge piece of flagstone across the floor of the palace. The stone was so heavy that it would have taken more than eighty teams of oxen to move it. After the stone had been moved, Lug picked it up, carried it outside, and placed it in its original location.

King Nuada then commanded Lug to play Dagda's harp for them. Lug played a melody that was so sad all the gods cried. Then he played a melody that was so cheerful they all laughed. Finally he played a melody that put all the gods to sleep until the following day.

Seeing that Lug was indeed as talented as he had claimed, Nuada gave him kingship for thirteen days so that he could direct the preparations for war against the Fomorians. Lug called upon each of the Túatha Dé gods to reveal his or her particular skills. The chief magician promised to remove the twelve mountains of Ireland and hurl them as missiles against the Fomorians.

The chief cupbearer promised to hide the waters from Ireland's twelve principal lakes and twelve principal rivers so that the Fomorians would find no water to drink. Yet these lakes and rivers would continue to supply fresh water for the Túatha Dé, even if the war lasted for seven years.

The chief metalsmith promised to create weapons that would not fail those who carried them into battle. His lances would always hit their targets and kill their victims. Moreover, he would continue to supply fresh weapons even if the war were to last for seven years.

The chief doctor promised that, as the battle raged, he would cure the wounded so quickly that they could return to battle the following day. He also advised the Túatha Dé to toss the corpses of their slain warriors into a particular well; his chants would cause the dead to emerge from the well restored to life.

The chief druid of the Túatha Dé promised to cause three streams of fiery rain to wash the faces of the Fomorians. Moreover, he promised to remove two-thirds of each Fomorian's strength and courage, while each of the Túatha Dé would receive renewed strength and courage with every breath. Consequently, even if the war lasted for seven years, the Túatha Dé would be able to wage war without tiring.

Finally, Dagda the Good promised that his great club, which could bring both death and the restoration of life, would crush the bones of the Fomorians as the feet of horses crush hailstones. This eight-pronged war club was so heavy that it would take eight strong men to carry it. In battle, Dagda would pull it behind him on a cart, then lift it and kill nine men with one motion.

The Túatha Dé were now prepared. Soon thereafter, the second battle of Mag Tured was fought upon Irish soil. In this fierce combat, both the Túatha Dé Danann and the Fomorians used every kind of magic they possessed. Although the wondrous magic of the Túatha Dé surpassed that of the Fomorians, the giants were so strong that the Túatha Dé could not win. Consequently, the battle between the gods and the giants raged on and on.

The chieftains of the Túatha Dé had decided that Lug of the Long Arms was so valuable they could not risk his death in battle. They had placed him under the guard of nine mighty warriors, but Lug became increasingly impatient with his captivity. Finally he escaped from the guards, climbed into his chariot, and entered the war. He drove among the Túatha Dé warriors shouting, "Be of good courage! It is far better to face death in battle than to live as a slave and pay taxes to a conqueror!"

The Fomorians saw the brightness of the sun shining forth from among the Túatha Dé warriors and exclaimed, "What dreadful fate is upon us? The sun rises today in the west instead of in the east! Surely that must be Lug of the Long Arms, god of the sun, who will help the Túatha Dé win the war!"

Seeing the fields red with the blood of fallen giants, the surviving Fomorians ran for their lives, with Lug and the other Túatha Dé in relentless pursuit. So many Fomorians died in the battle that it would be easier to count the trampled blades of grass under the feet of many galloping horses, the waves in a stormy sea, the sands upon a beach, the drops of dew upon a broad meadow in the spring, the hailstones in a sudden autumn storm, the flakes of snow in a raging winter blizzard, and the stars in the heavens on a clear night than to count the corpses of the Fomorians.

The decisive Túatha Dé victory put a permanent end to the Fomorian threat in Ireland. As the gods were celebrating their victory over the giants, their great war goddess, Badb Catha, stood before the assembled host and chanted, "We have chased the Fomorians from our land, but all is not well. I see the end of our age and the dawn of a new age.

"I see the race of human beings who will invade our land. They will not honor us, and they will not accept our ways. Under their rule, the summers will bear no flowers, the trees will bear no fruit, the cows will give no milk, and the seas will bear no fish. Women will have no pride, men will have no strength, old men will tell no truths, and rulers will not make just laws. Friends will steal from one another, warriors will betray one another, and all that is good and virtuous will perish from the world."

So it came to pass that in the sixth age of the world, the Children of Mil invaded Ireland on the first of May. They had to sail around the island three times before their 36 ships could set anchor, because the druids of the Túatha Dé Danann had shrouded the land in dense fog.

As soon as the Milesians stepped ashore, they were greeted by the Great Goddess Eriu, a queen of the Túatha Dé Danann. "I am the goddess Eriu," she said, "and this land bears my name. I welcome you to this island. You will find none better between the setting sun and the rising sun. It will belong to you and to those of your race who live after you as long as mortals walk the earth. May you honor me by calling this land the land of Eriu, or Ireland."

The great druid and poet of the Milesians, Amergin of the Fair Knee, responded, "We thank you, Great Goddess, for your welcome and your gift of this land. We are grateful that you honor us. In return, we promise to honor you and to keep your name upon this island forever!" But Donn, the oldest of the Children of Mil, interrupted. "Goddess, the poet Amergin does not know what his mouth speaks! His mind is clouded and his words make no sense. We owe no gratitude to you, for you have done nothing for us. Our own gods brought us to this land. It is they who will sustain us here, and it is they whom we will honor!"

Eriu replied, "Because you cannot accept us along with your own gods, your gods will sustain your race, but they will not sustain you! You will not live to enjoy this land, and no child of yours will either!"

Eriu's words proved to be true. Donn drowned very soon thereafter. The Milesians buried him on an island off the western coast of Ireland, which they called the House of Donn. Since that time, whenever one of the Children of Mil dies, his or her spirit goes to live in the House of Donn.

Then Amergin said, "Mother Goddess, I ask you to unite your forces with mine and bring prosperity to this land. Bring forth fertility from the mountain, the forest, and the sea. For I, too, have great power. I am the wind that blows upon the sea, the roaring of the surf, the powerful ox, the courageous wild boar, the predatory eagle, the rays of the sun, the most beautiful of plants, the imagination of all art, and the champion wielder of mighty weapons.

"Like one of the gods," Amergin continued, "I can change my shape. I can change the shape of the hills and the valleys. I know the age of the moon. I know where to find springs of fresh water. I can summon the fish from the sea. I see a great battle before us in which we will win victory. We will make our home upon this island, and here we will live in safety and peace."

Amergin and the other leaders of his race then confronted the chieftains of the Túatha Dé Danann and said, "We claim this land as our own. You may submit to our rule, or you may choose to fight us! Know, however, that we possess great power."

So it came to pass that the Túatha Dé Danann fought the Children of Mil. Some chronicles state that the Milesians killed the Great Goddess along with a large number of the Túatha Dé Danann, and that those who survived left Ireland. But the common people know the truth. The great gods of the past continue to live in Ireland and will remain there as long as mortals walk the earth. Their spirits dwell within the hills and beneath the earth.

➤ QUESTIONS FOR
Response, Discussion, and Analysis

1. Study the Irish ages. What pattern emerges? What is the significance of the sixth age?

2. Based on this myth, what values were important to the Irish Celts?

3. Like many of the other races that inhabited Ireland, the Túatha Dé Danann are gods with human traits. Give examples of their human and their divine characteristics.

4. Does the emphasis on magic enhance or detract from the appeal of this myth? Explain.

Dagda the Good

The Irish creation and fertility myths are so closely related that the introduction preceding "The Ages of the World" applies here as well. In the creation myth, several of the races that invade Ireland bring fertility to the land. The Partholons create additional lakes, introduce cattle, cultivate the soil, and turn the island into a successful agricultural society. The race of Nemed continues the work by creating more lakes and fertile plains and introducing sheep. The Túatha Dé Danann are described in the greatest detail; their fertility god is the subject of the myth that follows.

In Irish myth the force of light, fertility, and life must always be on guard against the force of darkness, sterility, and death. These two forces often fight against each other for control of Ireland. Sometimes the force of light— represented by the Partholons, Nemedians, and Túatha Dé Danann—wins, and sometimes the force of darkness—represented by the Fomorians—wins.

What is interesting in the Irish myths is that both forces appear able to assure fertility of the soil, although it is the force of light that civilizes the people. Consequently, the conflict in the Irish fertility myth is quite different from that in most other cultures' fertility myths. This myth does not follow the usual pattern of the insulted or deprived fertility god. Instead, two forces— each possessing powers of fertility—confront each other for control of the land.

DAGDA THE GOOD

In the fifth age of the world, the divine race of the Túatha Dé Danann possessed great powers of fertility, and Dagda the Good was one of its major gods. He cared for his people because he was the lord of all knowledge. He nourished them because he was the lord of abundance, and he protected them because he was the lord of life and death.

Dagda could perform great magic. His skill was evident both in the wondrous objects he possessed and in his own activities. He could control the weather and assure a bountiful harvest. He brought forth the seasons, each in its proper order, by playing his harp. He also owned a wondrous bronze Cauldron of Plenty, which fed each person the amount of food he or she deserved, yet satisfied the hunger of each. Dagda also owned a grove of fruit trees whose fruit was always ripe. And he had two wondrous pigs; at any time one was cooking in order to be eaten, and the other was living, waiting its turn to be cooked.

Dagda's eight-pronged war club was so heavy it would take eight strong men to carry it. With one end of the club he could kill nine people with a single blow; with the other end he could restore them to life. He took this club into battle against the Fomorians, the giant race of monsters who were the enemy of the Túatha Dé Danann.

Dagda was as fertile and vital as the forces in nature that he commanded. He loved to eat, and the Fomorians once challenged his enormous appetite. Pretending to be very hospitable, they said, "Welcome, Dagda. We know that you must be very hungry, so we are preparing your favorite meal for you: porridge."

Dagda watched with interest as the Fomorians poured into a great cauldron—a pot as large as the fists of five giants—eighty gallons of milk along with flour, fat, and bacon. To this they added whole carcasses of pigs, sheep, and goats. They cooked the mixture over a fire until it boiled and then lifted the pot from its tripod and poured the contents into a hole in the ground.

"Now, Dagda," they informed him, "we insist that you eat your porridge if you wish to remain alive and return to your own people. We certainly do not want you to tell the Túatha Dé Danann that the Fomorians are inhospitable and are sparing with the food they feed their guests. We would kill you before we let you tell such a false tale!"

Dagda was undaunted by this challenge. He picked up a spoon so large that two human beings could recline comfortably in its bowl. With it, he lifted out huge hunks of bacon and salted pork. "It certainly smells delicious!" he exclaimed. Then he proceeded to eat all of his porridge. Using his fingers, he even scraped up and ate the last drops from the bottom of the hole, including some gravel.

As he walked off to find a place to rest, the Fomorians laughed at the sight of him. Dagda's stomach was so bloated from his meal that he waddled. It was larger than the largest cauldron a large family would possess, and it puffed out in front of his body like a sail on a ship moving downwind.

But the last laugh was on the Fomorians. Dagda's purpose in visiting the enemy was to distract them from the coming war and to give his own people more time to prepare for battle. Like the Túatha Dé Danann, the Fomorians possessed great power over fertility. When their prince, Bres, was captured by the great warrior Lug of the Long Arms, Bres pleaded with Lug not to kill him.

"What price will you pay me for your life?" Lug asked him.

"I can promise that your cows will always give milk," Bres replied.

"That is not enough," Lug said, "unless you can make the cows live longer."

"I cannot do that," Bres replied. "But I can promise you that year after year the Túatha Dé will have a fine harvest of wheat."

"That is not enough," Lug responded. "We already have the four seasons. We have spring for plowing and planting, summer for growing, autumn for harvesting, and winter for eating our bread. However, if you can tell me exactly when to plow, when to plant, and when to harvest, I will give you your life."

"That I can do," said Bres. "Always perform each of these tasks on a Tuesday." Lug accepted Bres's advice and let him return to the Fomorians.

1. The myths of many cultures depict a deprived or insulted fertility god whose anger must be appeased, or a heroic god who restores fertility by combating a monster. What conditions might have caused the creators of this myth to depict a battle for control of Ireland where both forces possess great powers of fertility?

2. Why is it important that Dagda is as powerful a warrior as he is a god of fertility?

HISTORICAL BACKGROUND

Beowulf

The epic poem *Beowulf*, written in Old English, is the earliest existing Germanic epic and one of four surviving Anglo-Saxon manuscripts. Although *Beowulf* was written by an anonymous Englishman in Old English, the tale takes place in that part of Scandinavia from which Germanic tribes emigrated to England.

Beowulf comes from Geatland, the southeastern part of what is now Sweden. (The Swedes lived to the north of the Geats and were their great enemies.) Hrothgar, king of the Danes, lives near what is now Leire, on Zealand, Denmark's largest island.

The *Beowulf* epic contains three major tales about Beowulf and several minor tales that reflect a rich Germanic oral tradition of myths, legends, and folklore. The minor tales, deleted in the version of *Beowulf* that follows, are thematically consistent with the larger tale and are recited by bards in the mead-hall during the principal meal of the day. The tale of King Volsung and his twins, Sigmund and Signy, is the oldest form of *Sigurd the Volsung* (also in *World Mythology*) that exists. All of these tales reflect aspects of life in two cultures: first, the Germanic culture in which the plots are set, and second, the culture in which the Anglo-Saxon *Beowulf* poet lived.

The *Beowulf* epic reveals interesting aspects of the lives of the "North-men" who lived in northern Europe in both the Bronze and the Iron Age but prior to the Vikings. The Roman historian Tacitus's *Germania* (*On the Origin and Country of the Germans,* published in A.D. 98) is largely based on Pliny the Elder's twenty-book history *The German Wars* and discusses various Germanic tribes north of the Rhine and the Danube rivers.

The lives of warriors in the *Beowulf* epic reflect many of the historical observations in Tacitus's work. For example, based on the historian's statements, Hrothgar's Heorot functions as the typical mead-hall in the Bronze Age. It is the clan center, where warriors eat, drink, sleep, and transact all of their business, from political treaties to marriage contracts. Because it is the king's hall, its size and decoration reflect his wealth and power.

Like the *Beowulf* warriors, the Northmen were people of unusual courage, strength, and skill who prized their weapons. According to Tacitus (*Germania,* chapter 13), "They transact no business, public or private, without being armed. But it is a rule that no one shall carry arms until . . . he will be competent to use them. Then, in the presence of the Assembly, either one of the chiefs or the young man's father or some other relative presents him with a shield and a spear. . . . the first distinction publicly conferred upon a youth, who now . . . becomes a citizen. Particularly noble birth, or great services rendered by their fathers, can obtain the rank of 'chief' for boys still in their teens."

Later, when as adults they took their place as warriors in their society, like the *Beowulf* warriors, they received their weapons as gifts from their chieftain, both as rewards for their accomplishment in battle and as a symbol of their responsibility to defend him. Because skill in battle was so important, the quality of their weapons reflected their social status as well as their courage and skill.

Beowulf and his warriors wear helmets that are decorated with stern, gilded boars. The boars serve the spiritual purpose of protecting the helmet-wearer by keeping watch over his life and keeping Death at bay. Tacitus (chapter 45) describes a neighboring land where "they worship the Mother of the gods, and wear, as an emblem of this cult, the device of a wild boar, which stands them in stead of armor or human protection and gives the worshipper a sense of security even among his enemies."

Some clans made a practice of fighting at night and would blacken their bodies and their shields in order to terrify their foes. Others, like Beowulf's people, the "Sea-Geats" or "War-Geats," were sea-warriors who engaged in shore-raids as well as in commerce. Beowulf's lord, King Hygelac, may be the historic king who was killed on a raid, in about A.D. 520, when he went into the North Sea and then up the Rhine River. In the *Beowulf* epic, the Danes and the Geats cross the seas in "curved-necked" ships. Tacitus (chapter 44) describes their boats as having "a prow at each end so they are always facing the right way to put in to shore." Like the shields of the *Beowulf* warriors, the shields of the Northmen were fashioned from the wood of the linden tree.

After Grendel kills one of Beowulf's warriors, Hrothgar sends a compensatory payment, known as *wergild,* to his family in Geatland. According to Tacitus (chapter 21), "Even homicide can be atoned for by a fixed number of cattle or sheep, the compensation being received by the whole family. This is to the advantage of the community: for private feuds are particularly dangerous when there is such complete liberty."

In the third of the *Beowulf* plots, Beowulf must fight a dragon, and all but one of his attending warriors desert him. The deserters receive a calamitous punishment. However, Tacitus explains this when he says (chapter 14), "On the field of battle it is a disgrace to a chief to be surpassed in courage by his followers, and to the followers not to equal the courage of their chief. And to leave a battle alive after their chief has fallen means lifelong infamy and shame. To defend and protect him, and to let him get the credit for their own acts of heroism, are the most solemn obligations of their allegiance."

Moreover, the third of the *Beowulf* plots reflects aspects of the Bronze Age, as well as the Iron Age, in Scandinavia. The Bronze Age, which ended in about 500 B.C., is Scandinavia's greatest prehistoric period. At that time, the Northmen were skilled seamen, and the numerous northern waterways were their highways. Their work in bronze and in gold was superior to the work of any other European people of the period, and archaeologists have unearthed beautiful swords and daggers like those described in the *Beowulf* epic.

Beowulf's best sword-blade is unreliable. Its inability to "win glory" testifies to the strength of Beowulf's adversaries. However, it also reveals something about the nature of bronze, which is a combination of copper and tin. The proper proportion was critical because a sword-blade that contained too much tin would shatter, and one that contained too little tin would bend. Because of the importance of the bronze industry and bronze trade, a wealthy class emerged in which metalsmiths, such as the legendary Weland, were highly regarded and rewarded.

The dragon that Beowulf fights sits in a tomb, called a barrow, and guards a hoard of treasure. In the Bronze Age in Northern Europe, wealthy men and women, along with treasure and other valuable objects, were buried in massive mounds, known as barrow graves. These graves were usually located on a hill and constructed out of large stones, which were more plentiful than earth. These stones also protected the grave contents from animals and grave-robbers. Once the builders had constructed the barrow, they would strip away turf from a large surrounding area and place these earth-strips in layers on top of the stones. Some stone-barrows were so large that later peoples used them as stone quarries. Many of these mounds can still be found in Sweden and Denmark.

The Bronze Age, with the skills and objects that produced prehistoric Scandinavia's Golden Age, appears to be the great bygone age of the "giants" in the *Beowulf* tales. Weland, the far-famed giant smith, is credited with having forged the wondrous weapons of war. The great stone-barrows, with their arches and columns and their beautiful, handmade, golden treasures, are also the work of giants.

After his death, Beowulf's corpse is cremated, but his ashes, along with a hoard of treasures, are placed in a barrow that is built according to his directions. This actually reflects a time of cultural transition in Scandinavia, when, between 900 and 500 B.C., cremation gradually became popular and the interest in creating barrow-graves decreased.

According to Tacitus (chapter 27), "The bodies of famous men are burned with particular kinds of wood. When they have heaped up the pyre . . . only the dead man's arms, and sometimes his horse too, are cast into the flames. The tomb is a raised mound of turf. They disdain to show honor by laboriously rearing high monuments of stone. . . ."

The old woman's lament at the end of Beowulf's funeral is a poignant reminder of the period in which the tale is set, a time when a strong warrior-king makes the difference between the life and death of his people. Tacitus (chapter 27) explains why tradition may have given a woman, rather than a warrior, this lament when he says, "Weeping and wailing are soon abandoned; sorrow and mourning not so soon. A woman may decently express her grief; a man should nurse it in his heart."

Cremation, in which the corpse and particular possessions were burned on a funeral pyre, may reflect a change in religious ideas, from one in which the body as well as the spirit of the deceased entered a renewed existence in an afterlife to one in which the body was simply the fragile vessel in which the human spirit lived until death freed it and the flames of the funeral fire carried it up to heaven. Eventually, the change in burial practices had a substantial economic impact on Bronze Age culture because once the corpse and any accompanying possessions would be burned, people no longer were interested in purchasing expensive grave-objects.

The *Beowulf* warriors have a foot in both the Bronze and Iron Ages. Their mead-halls reflect the wealthy living of the Bronze Age Northmen, and their wooden shields, wood-shafted spears, and bronze-hilted swords are those of the Bronze Age warrior. However, they carry iron-tipped spears, and their best swords have iron or iron-edged blades. Beowulf also orders an iron shield for his fight with the dragon.

Iron replaced bronze because it produced a blade with a cutting edge that was stronger and sharper. The Northmen learned how to forge iron in about 500 B.C. Although they had been superior to the European Celts in bronze work, it was the Celts who taught them how to make and design iron work. Iron was accessible everywhere in Scandinavia, usually in the form of "bog-iron" found in the layers of peat in peat bogs.

The *Beowulf* epic also reveals interesting aspects of the lives of the Anglo-Saxons who lived in England at the time of the anonymous *Beowulf* poet. The Germanic tribes, including the Angles, the Saxons, and the Jutes, invaded England from about A.D. 450 to 600. By the time of the *Beowulf* poet, Anglo-Saxon society in England was neither primitive nor uncultured. Christianity had been introduced in about A.D. 600, and the Anglo-Saxon monasteries contained large libraries of ancient and contemporary works, both secular and religious. Virgil's *Aeneid* was well known, as was the large body of Germanic myths and legends.

Society was well organized, with a large number of wealthy aristocrats. The Sutton Hoo royal ship burial, dating from between 650 and 660, was discovered in Suffolk, England, in 1939. Its artifacts authenticate the details of court life described in *Beowulf*. Like the epic itself, these articles combine aspects of Anglo-Saxon culture with the contemporary Christian culture.

Although the *Beowulf* manuscript was written in about A.D. 1000, it was not discovered until the seventeenth century. Scholars do not know whether *Beowulf* is the sole surviving epic from a flourishing Anglo-Saxon literary period that produced other great epics or whether it was unique even in its own time. Moreover, they disagree as to whether this *Beowulf* is a copy of an earlier manuscript. Many scholars think that the epic was probably written sometime between the late seventh century and the early ninth century. If they are correct, the original manuscript was probably lost during the ninth-century Viking invasions of Anglia, in which the Danes destroyed the Anglo-Saxon monasteries and their great libraries. However, other scholars think that the poet's favorable attitude toward the Danes must place the epic's composition after the Viking invasions and at the start of the eleventh century, when this *Beowulf* manuscript was written.

The identity of the *Beowulf* poet is also uncertain. He apparently was a Christian who loved the pagan heroic tradition of his ancestors and blended the values of the pagan hero with the Christian values of his own country and time. Because he wrote in the Anglian dialect, he probably was either a monk in a monastery or a poet in an Anglo-Saxon court located north of the Thames River.

Anglo-Saxon literature, like that of Iceland, has a distinctive style. First, it is unusually alliterative. Each line divides into two parts, and the initial sounds of words in the first part are repeated in the second part. Moreover, nouns are paired and placed together, giving them heightened descriptive power. These word pairs, known as kennings, have come down to us in the form of compound words, such as *afterlife, bedroom, blood-stained, bygone, handmade, iron-tipped, seamen, sometimes, sword-blade,* and *waterway.* In fact, the preceding paragraphs of this introduction contain many of them.

Beowulf's people are known as the Sea-Geats, Storm-Geats, War-Geats, and Weather-Geats, whereas Hrothgar's people are known as the Bright-Danes, Ring-Danes, and Spear-Danes. These kennings are used interchangeably when referring to these people, not based on their meaning but based on their alliterative relationship to other words in the lines in which they occur.

The Anglo-Saxon language, know as Old English, is the earliest form of the English language. A few words are the same, such as *under, hand,* and *help(e).* More are recognizable, such as *mōdor* (*mother*); *gōd* (*good*); *waes* (*was*); *sunu* (*son*); *grund* (*ground*); *ond* (*and*); *waepna* (*weapon*); *sweord* (*sword*); and *cyning* (*king*). However, most words are unrecognizable, and therefore students must learn to read Anglo-Saxon as they learn a foreign language.

APPEAL AND VALUE

Beowulf interests contemporary readers for many reasons. First, it is an outstanding adventure story. Grendel, Grendel's mother, and the dragon are marvelous characters, and each fight is unique, action-packed, and exciting.

Second, Beowulf is a very appealing hero. He is the perfect warrior, combining extraordinary strength, skill, courage, and loyalty. Like Heracles, he devotes his life to making the world a safer place. He chooses to risk death in order to help other people, and he faces his inevitable death with heroism and dignity.

Third, the *Beowulf* poet is interested in the psychological aspects of human behavior. For example, the Danish hero's welcoming speech illustrates his jealousy of Beowulf. The behavior of Beowulf's warriors in the dragon fight reveals their cowardice. Beowulf's attitudes toward heroism reflect his maturity and experience, while King Hrothgar's attitudes toward life show the experiences of an aged nobleman.

Finally, the *Beowulf* poet exhibits a mature appreciation of the transitory nature of human life and achievement. In Beowulf, as in the major epics of other cultures, the hero must create a meaningful life in a world that is often dangerous and uncaring. He must accept the inevitability of death. He chooses to reject despair; instead, he takes pride in himself and in his accomplishments, and he values human relationships.

Like Beowulf and the other epic heroes, we too are faced with our own mortality. We too must create a meaningful life in a dangerous world. Like them, we must learn to reject despair and adopt a code of behavior that will permit us to take pride in ourselves, our accomplishments, and our relationships with other people. Beowulf kills monsters to protect his society from those life-threatening dangers. Today, it is just as necessary for us to fight against the monsters of famine, sickness, injustice, and war.

THE GERMANIC HERO

The aristocratic society of Beowulf's time involved groups of warriors clustered around particular princes or kings. War was the customary occupation of the Anglo-Saxon nobleman, and he slept with his armor by his side. Under the leadership of the king, warriors spent their time defending their own country from hostile invaders and raiding other countries for wealth. A king was obligated to provide his warriors with food, drink, weapons and armor, land, and jewels. In return, a warrior was obligated to fight to the death to defend his king. In such a society courage, skill in battle, and loyalty were the principal virtues.

The only acceptable justice was retributive justice, usually a death for a death. Wergild (man-price), the specific monetary value placed on the life of an individual, varied according to a person's social status. Retributive justice created an environment in which vengeance and feuds were common and self-perpetuating.

The pagan warriors of the northern lands believed in Wyrd, an unalterable fate. Both gods and humans were completely subject to Wyrd, which included their inevitable death. Without an afterlife, immortality could be achieved only through fame that lasted beyond one's death. In an environment where everyone had to face the difficulties of war, severe weather, food shortages, illness,

uncomfortable old age, and death, it made sense to take pleasure in whatever good things life offered. So eating, drinking, receiving gifts, and achieving fame and honor were highly valued.

PRINCIPAL CHARACTERS

BEOWULF: the great hero of the Geats; later, their king
BRECA: Beowulf's childhood friend and competitor
GRENDEL: a giant
HROTHGAR: the king of the Danes
HYGELAC: Beowulf's uncle; king of Geatland
UNFERTH: the greatest warrior of the Danes
WIGLAF: Beowulf's nephew; a young Geatish warrior

BEOWULF

Chapter 1

Hrothgar, king of the Ring-Danes, builds Heorot (Hall of the Hart), a great mead-hall. After the giant Grendel murders Hrothgar's warriors there, Heorot lies empty. Beowulf arrives from Geatland to fight Grendel.

Hear me! We have listened to many a tale about the Ring-Danes in days of old. We have heard about their mighty kings, for their deeds of daring and danger won them honor, glory, and wealth. They defeated fierce foes, and they ruled with such might that folk across the whale-road paid them tax and tribute. At home, they were gracious and generous gift-givers. And so, when war came, their war-comrades were loyal and served them well in battle. They were good kings! And the Lord of Life, Giver of Glory, showered them with fame.

When the time came for such a king to die, his soul made the journey to God, and it remained in peace there forever. That king's war-comrades honored him. Their hearts flooded with a surging sea-swell of love as they carried his corpse down to the sea-shore. And they brought his body aboard a ring-prowed sea-ready ship that was moored in the ice-cold sea-flood. They placed their dead king, their beloved ring-giver, against the mast. And they surrounded him with a treasure-trove—gold and jewels from far-off lands; gleaming ring-meshed battle-shirts; gold-glittering war-helmets; gold-rimmed shields; iron-tipped spears; and sharp-bladed battle-swords, blood-hardened and shining. All these went with their king on his last, lonely journey.

Then, when all was ready, they cast loose the anchor, and they launched the broad-beamed boat upon the deep waters of the whale-road to wander where it would. Long after the ring-prowed ship was out of sight, its golden banner waved high above the sea-waters. Bold-hearted war-comrades and wise counselors watched and waited with heavy hearts as the surging sea-swell carried that wealthy cargo into the deep waters of the pathless sea-road.

Hrothgar was one of these mighty kings who ruled the Spear-Danes. Holy God, Lord of Life, granted him wisdom, war-skill, and good fortune in battle. Warriors followed him, for he was fierce in war and generous with gifts. And so, soon he led a mighty band of warriors.

Hrothgar decided to build a high, horn-gabled mead-hall. It would be so splendid that folk in lands far and wide would speak of it. He wanted his high-born war-comrades to gather in his great hall to feast, drink, and receive treasure as their reward for bold hearts and battle-skill. And when it came to pass that the Hall of Heroes was finished, Hrothgar named it Heorot, the Hall of the Hart, for the hart (stag) was a fitting sign for a war-king.

And so, it came to pass that Hrothgar and his high-born war-comrades feasted in their horn-gabled mead-hall. And the treasure-giving war-king gener-ously gave his war-comrades all the treasure—gold rings and shining armbands—that God had granted him. But he did not give lives of men or land belonging to the Dane-folk, for these alone were not his to give.

Hrothgar and his high-born war-comrades heard the sounds of the harp, and they sang happy songs in Heorot, unaware that someone was watching them and waiting. For Grendel, a joyless giant of a man, ghastly and grim, lived somewhere in the lonely border-land. He dwelled at night deep in the darkness of that murky moor. And by day, shielded by its mist from the eyes of ordinary men, he haunted that marsh-land.

Grendel's hard heart was always flooded with a surging sea-swell of hatred, for he despised the Dane-folk. Descended from the race of Cain, Grendel bore the age-old curse, the mark of murder, of his death-dealing ancestor. Like Cain, Grendel had been banished from life among happy folk. He was condemned to live in a lonely lair, where only his mother and sea-monsters kept him company.

Day after day, Grendel heard the sounds of the harp and the happy songs of heroes, and he hated them. And it came to pass that, one day, he waited until the sun, that bright candle of the world, had glided over the land. And then, that shadow-walker, ghastly and grim, left his lonely lair in the marshy border-land. And shielded by the darkness and mist, he strode forth upon silent feet toward King Hrothgar's Hall of Heroes, that gold-gleaming treasure-house, for his hard heart longed to spy on the Spear-Danes.

He found it easy to enter, for no one feared that he would come. He stepped softly into the Hall of Heroes, and there he found a band of bold-hearted warriors. The mead had flooded their bodies, and so their sleep was heavy, and the mead had dulled their minds. So, for this short time, they were free of thoughts of sorrow and woe in the world about them.

At the sight of the Spear-Danes, a sea-swell of hatred surged forth in Grendel's hard heart. Grim and greedy, furious and fierce, that monster of a man grabbed thirty warriors. And he slew them while they slept, for he gave them gruesome death-wounds by biting into them with his blood-stained teeth. A great serpent's-skin bag hung from his shoulder, loathsome and large, and into it he tossed the blameless bodies of his victims. The good fortune was his. And so, gloating and gleeful over his plunder, he hurried home to his lonely lair with his frightful feast.

For the time being, Grendel left Heorot to the living. But he would come again.

Not until bright daylight once again shone forth over the land did King Hrothgar and the Dane-folk learn of this disaster. And when they entered Heorot, that bright hall of bold-hearted men, the blood-filled sight filled them with horror. The woeful sounds of weeping and wailing now replaced the happy songs that had come forth from the tower-tall, timbered mead-hall.

The Ring-Danes recognized Grendel's foot-prints, and they feared his power. But they did not think that he would return. And in this, they were wrong.

Once the sun, Heaven's jewel, had glided over the land, and the bright heavens again had darkened with the shadows of dusk, it came to pass that Grendel left his lonely lair in the marshy border-land. And shielded by the darkness and mist, that shadow-walker, ghastly and grim, strode forth upon silent feet toward King Hrothgar's Hall of Heroes, that gold-gleaming treasure-house. For his hard heart still flooded with a surging sea-swell of hatred, and now, it longed to murder more men.

And so, once again, the man-eating monster stole into Hrothgar's high, horn-gabled mead-hall. Now grim and greedy, furious and fierce, he grabbed thirty Bright-Danes in his frightful battle-grip, and he slew them while they slept. Again he mangled them with his blood-stained teeth. The great serpent's-skin bag still hung from his shoulder, and into it he tossed the blameless bodies of these victims. Then, gloating and gleeful over his plunder, he hurried home to his lonely lair with his frightful feast.

The hearts of the Dane-folk now flooded with a surging sea-swell of despair. And so, day after day, as soon as the bright heavens darkened with the shadows of dusk, they deserted Heorot, that bright hall of bold-hearted men. For night after night, the dark death-shadow of that frightful fiend left the misty marsh-land and stalked toward Heorot. And he haunted that tower-tall, timbered mead-hall.

Grendel's ravenous appetite for human flesh drove him to wage war against all the Dane-folk. The monster knew nothing of justice, and he desired no peace. King Hrothgar could not reward him, nor could he appease him. For the frightful fiend valued neither gold nor treasure. And so great was his power that he feared no form of retribution and no avenging death.

And so it came to pass that the Dane-folk gathered in their heathen temples. And there, they offered sacrifices to their idols and prayers to Satan, the Slayer of

Souls. They did not know that they were neglecting the Lord of Heaven. Nor did they know that their salvation would never come from Hell.

And so, for twelve long winters, Grendel haunted Heorot. Now, this frightful fiend, and not King Hrothgar, ruled the Ring-Danes. Grendel's ravaging raids flooded the hearts of even the most bold-hearted heroes with a surging sea-swell of terror, for they had neither the strength nor the battle-skill to kill him.

But the tale of Grendel's terror spread far and wide. Bards sang of his destructive deeds, of the Spear-Danes' hopeless struggle, and of their endless war. And so it came to pass that the Sea-Geats heard about Grendel's dreadful deeds. Beowulf was the strongest of the Geat-folk, bold of heart and strong in strife. And he decided to sail across the deep waters of the whale-road to help Hrothgar, the treasure-giving war-king of the Bright-Danes. And he chose fourteen bold-hearted war-comrades to accompany him.

A ring-prowed sea-worthy ship was suitably fitted for the journey. Then Beowulf and his bold-hearted war-comrades eagerly boarded it. They stowed their splendid battle-gear deep within the hold of their broad-beamed boat—gleaming ring-meshed battle-shirts; hard war-helmets, with battle-ready boars, gold-glittering and stern; sharp-bladed battle-swords, blood-hardened and shining; iron-tipped ash-wood spears; and gold-rimmed linden-wood shields.

The Storm-Geats set forth with a spirit of adventure, and a brisk wind sent their bent-necked ship speeding across the deep waters of the whale-road like a sea-bird, its curved prow like a foamy bill. And when bright day-light again shone forth over the land, the sun, Heaven's jewel, shone upon the lofty, sheer-cut sea-cliffs, the high hills, and the broad head-lands of the Bright-Danes.

The Sea-Geats soon beached their broad-beamed boat. Then they stepped ashore, their ring-meshed battle-coats clanking. And they thanked God for granting them safe paths for their sea-crossing.

By now, from the top of the sea-cliff, sheer-cut and lofty, the watchful warden upon horse-back had seen the group of strange battle-ready warriors, bearing shining shields and gleaming war-gear, step ashore. And so, holding his ash-wood spear ready in his hand, he galloped down to meet them.

"What men are you? And who are your fathers?" he challenged, "And why have you come to the land of the Bright-Danes wearing ring-meshed battle-shirts and carrying gleaming war-gear? One of you is the greatest warrior I have ever seen! And if his looks do not lie, he is matchless among noble men!"

So the coast-guard spoke. And in reply, Beowulf, the leader of the band, unlocked his own word-hoard. "We are Weather-Geats. King Hygelac is my blood-kin, my hearth-friend, and my war-comrade. My own father, Ecgtheow, was known in folk-lands far and wide, for he was bold of heart, strong in strife, and a leader of men. His blood-hardened sharp-bladed battle-sword sang a greedy war-song. And it doomed many a battle-skilled sword-man to death. Wyrd wove bright threads into his life before Death, that dreaded destiny, took his life at the end of many winters. And so, every man of wise mind remembers him well.

"We seek your treasure-giving lord, Hrothgar. For we have come to kill the frightful fiend whose deadly deeds terrify the Dane-folk."

So Beowulf spoke to the coast-guard. And to his words, the warden replied, "Then I will lead you forth to our king. Take your battle-weapons. And take your gleaming war-gear. But let my men watch your ring-prowed ship. They will protect it from any foe."

So it came to pass that the War-Geats walked toward the Hall of Heroes. And as they walked, the stern battle-ready boars glittering upon their hard war-helmets kept watch over their lives. At last, they saw Heorot, King Hrothgar's Hall of Heroes, famed beyond all others in folk-lands far and wide. There the warden left them to return to his sea-watch. But Beowulf and his band of war-comrades continued along the stone-cobbled street toward the Heorot, that bright hall of bold-hearted men. And as they walked, their gleaming war-gear sang a clattering, iron battle-song.

At last, they rested their broad, gold-rimmed linden-wood shields and their gray-tipped, ash-wood spears against the wall of the high, horn-gabled mead-hall. There, Hrothgar's herald came forth to greet them. And there, the herald questioned them as the coast-guard had.

And it came to pass that the herald returned to his white-haired king and said, "My lord, a warrior named Beowulf has sailed the deep waters of the whale-road to our land. He leads a band of Storm-Geats, and he wishes to speak with you. Grant him your ear, gracious Hrothgar, for his gleaming war-gear reveals him to be worthy of great respect."

So the herald spoke to his king. And to his words, Hrothgar replied, "I knew Beowulf when he was a child. His kin-folk and I are hearth-friends. I have heard from sea-faring folk that Beowulf has the strength of thirty men in his mighty battle-grip! I hope that holy God has sent him to help us fight Grendel! I will give him glorious gifts for his bold heart and his battle-skill. And so, welcome the Storm-Geats, and ask them to come before me."

So King Hrothgar commanded his herald. And so, Beowulf came to stand before the old, treasure-giving war-king. The youth stood straight and tall in his gleaming ring-meshed battle-shirt and his hard war-helmet, with its battle-ready boars, gold-glittering and stern.

"Hail to you, Hrothgar, mighty war-king of the Spear-Danes!" he exclaimed. "I am King Hygelac's blood-kin and war-comrade. In Geat-land, I have heard sea-faring folk speak of Grendel, that ghastly and grim man-eater. And they say Heorot, your gold-gleaming treasure-house, lies deserted and useless once the bright heavens darken with the shadows of dusk.

"From the days of my youth, I have won honor and glory by doing deeds of daring and danger. I have slain savage sea-monsters upon surging sea-swells in the dark of night. And now, I will wage war with Grendel, that joyless giant, frightful fiend though he is.

"I ask only one favor of you, my lord. Let your folk rest while my bold-hearted war-comrades and I cleanse your horn-gabled mead-hall of this monstrous man-eater. I have heard that Grendel has contempt for weapons of any kind. And so, I will fight without my sharp-bladed battle-sword and my broad linden-wood shield. My mighty battle-grip will be my only war-weapon. And I will grapple with that frightful fiend, hand to hand, until Death takes one of us.

"If Grendel wins the battle, he will leave you with no bodies to bury. For I have heard that he does not feast in your mead hall, and so, he leaves no bones behind. He will bear my blood-bathed head and body to the moor, and there, he will chew upon them at his leisure in his lonely lair. Just send my ring-meshed battle-shirt, this hand-linked and hand-joined age-old treasure, back to my king, for Weland, that far-famed master smith, made it with his own hands. Wyrd always weaves as it must."

So Beowulf spoke. And to his words, the treasure-giving king replied, "Beowulf, my friend, you alone can save us from this savage man-eater, for Grendel has weakened my bold-hearted war-comrades, and he has wasted my mead-hall. So, welcome! Join the Ring-Danes now in a joyful feast. And speak to my war-comrades of your purpose and plan."

Chapter 2

The Danish hero Unferth unjustly criticizes Beowulf. Beowulf meets Grendel in single combat and kills him.

After the feast, the warrior Unferth sat at the feet of King Hrothgar. Unferth was the foremost fighter of the Spear-Danes and had earned honor and glory among his own folk, but now, the hero's heart burned with shame and anger. For Beowulf, a bold-hearted sea-farer, had crossed the deep waters of the whale-road and had come uninvited to this land in order to kill Grendel, the ghastly and grim man-eater that Unferth himself was afraid to meet in battle. And so, Unferth now unlocked his hoard of angry words.

"Are you that Beowulf," he began, "who, foolishly boastful, risked your life by striving against Breca in a swimming-match upon the surging sea-swells of winter's swollen sea-waters? I heard that no man, loved or loathed, could turn you from your desire, despite the danger, and that you swam in the swollen sea-flood's frightful battle-grip for seven days and nights.

"But I also heard that Breca, being stronger than you are, surpassed you in swimming. And the early tide then carried him near his folk, his home, his town, and his treasure.

"And so, I warn you. If you decide to spend a night here, waiting for Grendel, I foresee a harder match and a worse destiny for you, though you are bold of heart and strong in strife."

So Unferth spoke to Hrothgar's guest. And, in reply, Beowulf unlocked his own word-hoard. "Unferth, my friend, your mind is muddled with mead. And it has twisted your tale about Breca and me," he declared.

"The truth is that no man has more strength in surging sea-swells than I have. Breca and I were still boys when we made that childish boast and decided to risk our lives in the deep waters of the whale-road. We swam forth into the swollen sea-swell bearing our sharp-bladed battle-swords in our hands to guard against the frightful battle-grip of fierce sea-fish. And we swam side by side for five days. But, at last, the surging sea-swells and the bitter, battle-fierce north-wind drove us apart.

"The rough waves roused the wrath of the fierce sea-fish. I was glad I was wearing my ring-meshed battle-shirt, hand-linked and hand-joined, for a savage sea-beast dragged me to the bottom. And there it held me fast in its frightful battle-grip. But my hand-woven war-coat protected my chest.

"The sharp point of my sword pierced the hard heart of that mighty monster. And I gladly buried my blood-thirsting battle-blade in its breast. Then, other savage sea-beasts, starving for warm food, pressed close about me, hungry and hopeful. Eagerly they clutched at the gleaming chains that guarded my chest, for they expected to seize me and feast upon my dead flesh. But I gladly gave each of them the sharp point of my sword. And so, my blood-thirsting battle-blade robbed them of their reward.

"And it came to pass that, when bright day-light next shone forth over the land, it found nine monsters belly-up on the beach. They were blood-smeared from the wounds made by my blood-hardened battle-blade. And they lay there, silent and still, death-doomed by my sword-strokes. Never again would they bother sea-farers crossing the deep waters of the whale-road!

"I have never heard of a harder fight at night. Or of a man in worse trouble in the surging swells of the sea-flood. But when the waves subsided, I could see the head-lands and the wind-swept walls of the Finns. And it came to pass that the swollen sea-flood swept me to their land. So Wyrd often spares a man who is not marked for death, that dreaded destiny, if he is bold-hearted.

"But I have heard of no daring deeds of yours, Unferth. No strife where you faced such terror with your own blood-hardened battle-blade. Your heart is not as bold as you would have me believe, for then Grendel, that ghastly and grim man-eater, would not rule here in this land. That frightful fiend slaughters and eats whomever he chooses whenever he chooses, sparing no one. For he has learned that he need not fear the anger of the Ring-Danes.

"But the spirit, strength, and skill of the Storm-Geats will now bid Grendel to battle. And when daylight once again shines forth over the land, the Dane-folk will be able to return to this mead-hall without fear!"

So Beowulf spoke. And hearing of Beowulf's great deeds, King Hrothgar, giver of treasure and shepherd of the Dane-folk, was confident that Beowulf would conquer Grendel. Then, as was her custom, Hrothgar's gentle-mannered queen, dressed in golden splendor, greeted their guests and offered them the mead-cup, that age-old treasure. And Hrothgar's Heorot echoed with the sounds of the harp and the happy songs of heroes.

But the time soon came when the sun, Heaven's jewel, had glided over the land. And now, the bright heavens had darkened with the shadows of dusk. And so, quick as the wind, the king and his gentle-mannered queen rose to seek their night's rest. And all the Ring-Danes rose with them and followed the royal couple out of the mead-hall, for they knew that Grendel, that shadow-walker, ghastly and grim, would soon leave his lonely lair in the marshy border-land. And shielded by the darkness and mist, he would stride forth upon silent feet toward their tower-tall, timbered mead-hall.

Hrothgar then said to Beowulf, "Never since my hands could carry a sword and shield have I trusted anyone other than Dane-folk to guard Heorot. Keep in your mind your great deeds. And let this frightful fiend know your battle-skill and your strength in strife. If you succeed, I will reward you with a treasure-trove."

To these words, Beowulf replied, "When I boarded my broad-beamed boat, I vowed that, in your great mead-hall, I would do deeds of daring and danger that befit my birth, or Grendel would mangle me with his frightful battle-grip. And so it will be. I will win honor and glory, or I will be beaten in battle. And then Death will take my life, for I will not run from my destiny. Wyrd always weaves as it must."

So Beowulf spoke. And so it came to pass that the Storm-Geats prepared to spend the night in Heorot, that bright hall of bold-hearted men, where the Bright-Danes feared to sleep. Trusting in his mighty strength, Beowulf removed his gleaming ring-meshed battle-shirt; his hard war-helmet, with its battle-ready boars, gold-glittering and stern; and his age-old, sharp-bladed battle-sword, blood-hardened and shining. And he gave his treasured war-gear to one of his war-comrades to guard until bright day-light would again shine forth over the land.

Then, before he lay down, Beowulf, bold-hearted in battle, declared, "I am as bold of heart and strong in strife as Grendel! I could easily slay him with my blood-thirsting battle-blade, for the monstrous man-eater is not skilled in the use of war-weapons. But since Grendel fights without battle-sword and shield, so will I. May God award good fortune to the one He chooses!"

Then Beowulf lay down, awake and alert, watching and waiting. He was anxious for the battle to start, for his heart flooded with a surging sea-swell of anger toward his foe, that monstrous man-eater.

But Beowulf's bold-hearted war-comrades, sea-weary from their journey across the deep waters of the whale-road, lay down to sleep. Every War-Geat knew that Grendel took savage joy in slaughtering the men he found in this high, horn-gabled hall. And so each warrior quietly thought of his home-land. In his heart, he feared that never again would he see his kin-folk, his home, or the town in which he had been reared.

But God had woven defeat for Grendel. And He gave the War-Geats the good fortune to conquer their foe through one man, the most bold of heart and most strong in strife. Mighty God rules mortals forever!

By now, the shadow-walker, ghastly and grim, had left his lonely lair in the marshy border-land. And shielded by the darkness and mist, he was striding forth upon silent feet toward the Hall of Heroes, that gold-gleaming treasure-house. For Grendel bore God's anger, and so his hard heart knew nothing of joy. It still flooded with a surging sea-swell of hatred. And now, it longed to murder more men.

And so, the frightful fiend angrily placed his hands upon the great door of the high, horn-gabled hall and pushed against it. And quick as the wind, the door gave way. Its fastenings had been forged in fire, but they could not hold beneath Grendel's savage strength.

Grendel now strode inside the mead-hall. The deeds that he determined to do were dreadful. And a blazing light burned in his eyes like a furious flame. His hard heart flooded with a surging sea-swell of laughter when he saw that, once again, warriors were sleeping in the high, horn-gabled mead-hall.

Grendel expected to slaughter each and every one of them and then retreat to his lonely lair, for the sight of such a full feast filled him with a raging hunger. But Wyrd had woven a different destiny for that man-eater. And after this night, Grendel would never again feed upon human flesh.

Silent and still, Beowulf watched as Grendel set about his beastly business. He watched as the monstrous man-eater suddenly seized one of his own sleeping war-comrades, tore the man's body to pieces, and then bit into his flesh and chewed through his bones. Silent and still, he watched as that frightful fiend drank down his war-comrade's blood and then devoured him piece by blood-smeared piece. Silent and still, he watched as the monster consumed the entire corpse of his comrade. But his heart flooded with a surging sea-swell of fury toward his foe.

Grendel then stepped toward the reclining figure of Beowulf, and he gripped the bold-hearted hero in his frightful iron-nailed hand. But Beowulf, battle-ready and strong as the storm-wind, angrily seized Grendel's arm in his own mighty battle-grip.

Grendel had never met a more frightful foe. And swift as a warrior's sword-stroke, his hard heart flooded with surging sea-swells of terror and panic. He wanted only to flee into the darkness. Using the dark night as his shield, he wanted only to return to his lonely lair in the misty marsh-land.

But Beowulf held the frightful fiend fast in his own mighty battle-grip. And the bold-hearted hero now sprang to his feet and clutched at Grendel's hand with all his strength. The man-eater turned and tried to pull away, but Beowulf hung onto his hand.

The high, horn-gabled mead-hall clanged and shook as the two foes raged against each other in a savage and unyielding death-doomed struggle, and its walls shattered. But the iron bands within and without kept the Hall of the Hart standing in spite of the frightful fight.

Far from the fight, the hearts of the Ring-Danes had flooded with a surging sea-swell of terror as they heard Grendel's howling screams of pain and his shrieks of defeat. And by now, Beowulf's bold-hearted war-comrades were trying to help him by using their blood-hardened sharp-bladed battle-swords, handed down by their fathers, to slash at Grendel from every side. But that frightful fiend had placed a spell upon every sharp-bladed war-weapon.

So it came to pass that the two foes fought fiercely on. Beowulf kept Grendel's hand clasped in his own mighty battle-grip. And Grendel kept trying to break free. Grendel's fingers snapped. And then a growing and gruesome death-wound slowly opened in his shoulder. At last, the sinews snapped apart, and the bones split at the joint. Beowulf had ripped Grendel's arm from the rest of his body. He had won the battle. And he had won great glory and lasting fame.

Grendel, beaten in battle, ran in dreadful pain back to his lonely lair in the misty marsh-land. He knew that his life was at an end. He dived, death-sick and death-doomed, into the depths of a loathsome lake. And there, Death, that dreaded destiny, took his heathen life, and Hell received him.

Beowulf, who had come from afar and who was bold of heart and strong in strife, had kept his word to Hrothgar, the treasure-giving war-king of the Spear-Danes. The hero had cleansed Heorot of deadly deeds, for he had conquered the frightful fiend. And so, his heart flooded with a surging sea-swell of joy. And as sign of his good fortune, Beowulf mounted Grendel's gruesome, blood-smeared shoulder, arm, and iron-nailed hand beneath the high, horn-gabled roof of the great mead-hall for all the Dane-folk to see.

It came to pass that, when bright day-light again shone forth over the land, King Hrothgar, giver of gold rings, and his gentle-mannered queen entered the Hall of the Hart. And they gazed with wonder at the terrifying token of Beowulf's bold heart and strength in strife. Unferth, too, came and looked. From this time forth, he would think less of his own heroic war-deeds, and he surely would not boast of them.

"I thank God for this sight!" Hrothgar exclaimed, gazing up at Grendel's gruesome arm. "Not long ago, while horn-gabled Heorot stood blood-smeared and gory, I feared that no one in the wide world could help us.

"But you were true to your word, Beowulf. And so, from this time forth, I will love you like a son. As long as I live, you will never want for wealth. I have given great treasure to weaker warriors for far less service. Your deeds here have given you great glory and fame that will live forever! May God continue to give you a good life!"

So Hrothgar spoke. And then, many bold-hearted warriors wandered within the Hall of Heroes. And seeing Grendel's great shoulder, arm, and iron-nailed hand, they marveled at the sight. Neither Spear-Dane nor Storm-Geat sorrowed at the thought of the maimed man-eating monster, defeated and dying, wending his way back to the misty marsh-land with a weary heart.

Heorot, that bright hall of bold-hearted men, was completely cleaned, repaired, and decorated for the great feast that would celebrate Beowulf's bold heart and battle-skill. That gold-gleaming treasure-house needed many repairs, for by the time the frightful fiend had fled, only the high, horn-gabled roof of the tower-tall, timbered mead-hall was whole. At last, gold-gleaming tapestries once again shone forth from the shattered walls.

By the time the sun, that bright candle of the world, had glided over the land, the food and drink were ready. And so, Beowulf and his war-comrades joined the Spear-Danes, and they joyfully returned to the Hall of the Hart for the celebration. Then, as was her custom, Hrothgar's gentle-mannered queen, dressed in golden splendor, greeted their guests and offered them the mead-cup, that age-old treasure. And Heorot, that bright hall of bold-hearted men, echoed with the sounds of the harp and the happy songs of heroes.

During the feast, Hrothgar's bard, who knew many an age-old saga, was already skillfully weaving a war-tale of Beowulf's bold heart and strength in strife. He compared Beowulf to Sigurd the Volsung, who had slain a frightful fire-serpent and won its hoard-heap of golden treasures.

After the feast, Hrothgar gave Beowulf a rich array of gifts—a great treasure-sword; an embroidered war-banner; eight golden-bridled horses; and an age-old jeweled saddle that had once been the war-seat of a high-king. The treasure-giving war-king also gave gifts to Beowulf's bold-hearted war-comrades. And remembering the War-Geat whom Grendel had killed, the king gave Beowulf *wergild* (a payment in gold) to give to that man's kin-folk.

And it came to pass that the feasting, drinking, telling of tales, and giving of gifts came to an end. And then, Hrothgar and his gentle-mannered queen rose to seek their night's rest, and all of the warriors rose with them. Beowulf, with his war-comrades, and most of the Spear-Danes followed the royal couple out of the mead-hall. They left Heorot to the warriors who would sleep there as they had often done in times past.

The Ring-Danes who remained behind in the high, horn-gabled mead-hall covered the floor with beds and pillows. And they pushed the mead-benches to the head of their beds. Before they lay down to sleep, they placed their hard war-helmets upon these benches. They set their shining linden-wood shields and their sharp-bladed swords, unsheathed, at their heads. And they placed their gleaming ring-meshed battle-shirts and their iron-tipped ash-wood spears at their sides. For it was their custom always to be ready for war.

The Spear-Danes were good warriors, but they were unaware of what Wyrd had woven for them.

Chapter 3

Grendel's mother invades Heorot and murders Hrothgar's best friend. Beowulf plans to kill the giant.

Deep within the misty marsh-land of the moor, and doomed to dwell in Grendel's dark and dreary den, lived the joyless giant's mighty mother. Ordinary men had loathed Grendel, but his mother had dearly loved him. And so, when Death, that dreaded destiny, took Grendel's heathen life, her mother's-heart flooded with surging sea-swells of sorrow and rage.

And it came to pass that, when the sun, Heaven's jewel, had glided over the land, and the bright heavens had darkened with the shadows of dusk, the mournful mother left her lonely lair in the marshy border-land. And shielded by the darkness and mist, this shadow-walker, ghastly and grim, strode forth upon silent feet toward the Hall of Heroes, that gold-gleaming treasure-house.

Her mother's-heart was intent on invading that bright hall of bold-hearted men, for there her son had met his dreadful destiny. There, he had received the war-wounds that had doomed him to death.

Grendel's mother found it easy to enter the tower-tall, timbered mead-hall, for no one feared that she would come. But she stepped softly into the Hall of Heroes. And there, she found a band of bold-hearted war-comrades. At the sight of the Spear-Danes, a sea-swell of hatred surged forth in her mother's-heart.

The mead from their feast had flooded the bodies and dulled the minds of the Bright-Danes, but they were not as yet asleep. And seeing Grendel's mighty mother step into their hall, the mind and heart of every warrior flooded with a surging sea-swell of terror.

But the Bright-Danes told themselves that they were bold of heart and strong in strife and that they could trust their blood-hardened sharp-bladed battle-swords and their shining linden-wood shields. And they comforted their minds with the fact that this giant, mighty as she appeared to be, could not harm them.

For she was a woman, and women were much weaker, more fearful, and far less fierce in fighting than any man.

And these thoughts spurred the Spear-Danes to take some action. And so, they grabbed their war-weapons and prepared attack the giant. But in their haste to harm the wondrous woman, they forgot to put on their hard war-helmets and their ring-meshed battle-shirts.

Despite their muddled minds, God wove good fortune for the Ring-Danes, for their movements signaled danger and daunted the mourning mother. Swift as a warrior's sword-stroke, her mind and heart flooded with a surging sea-swell of fear for her destiny. And in its wake, her war-fury abated. And all thought of avenging her son's death-wound fled. Now, she only longed to save her own life.

And so, that mighty mother seized only one warrior, the closest Dane. She held him in a grasp that was stronger than the storm-wind. And then she bit into his flesh with her frightful teeth, giving him a gruesome death-wound.

At last, clutching the man's corpse, she turned to run from the hall. But she spied Grendel's gruesome shoulder, arm, and iron-nailed hand beneath the high, horn-gabled roof. And so, she reached up and seized it, too. Then she departed, disappearing into the darkness.

The sound of the Spear-Danes' heart-rending cries suddenly awakened Hrothgar. Swift as a warrior's sword-stroke, the old treasure-giving war-king went forth to his high, horn-gabled hall. And there, he heard that a second frightful giant, a woman, had come uninvited into his mead-hall. And she had savagely killed his dearest friend. The news crushed the king's spirit, and his heart flooded with a surging sea-swell of sorrow. For the death-doomed Dane had been his beloved hearth-friend, his most trusted counselor, and his bold-hearted war-comrade, and he was a far-famed warrior.

And so, as soon as bright day-light again shone forth over the land, Hrothgar summoned Beowulf and his War-Geats to the Hall of Heroes. The treasure-giving war-king then unlocked his word-hoard. "Beowulf, my heart floods with grief and sorrow," he declared. "For, after we left Heorot, another joyless giant, a woman, invaded that bright hall of bold-hearted men," he declared. "And she gave a Dane, a man who was dear to me, a gruesome death-wound.

"Now, I have heard tales of her. Some told by country folk. Some told by counselors, hearth-friends, and war-comrades in my own hall. They would speak of two frightful folk, ghastly and grim shadow-walkers, who lurked in the lonely border-land. During the day, the mist shielded them. And at night, the darkness of the murky moor-land shrouded them.

"These joyless giants seemed drawn to the dwellings of happy Dane-folk. They would come near the out-skirts of farm-folk, and they would stand there, silent and still. Shielded as they were by the mist, it was hard to get a clear view of them.

"But the larger one seemed to be a giant of a woman. The other was younger and misshapen. But still, he was a giant of a man. The old folk had named him Grendel. And bold-hearted Dane-folk often peered into the murky mists for some sight of his father, but they never saw a third shadow-walker.

"Those who spoke of them said the joyless ones lived in the lonely marsh-land of the moor. A few fearless folk even dared to follow their trail.

Wyrd wove good fortune for them. And so, they lived to tell of it, and this is what they told.

"At first, the foot-path takes folk through the woods. But then, it travels across the moor-land, murky and wild, loathsome and lonely. It leads onto a high head-land. And there, peril awaits folk on all sides, for the path is rope-thin and rock-strewn. It twists and turns through the frightful marsh-land, with its treacherous mist and mud. It runs past rugged ravines, by wild wolf-slopes, and along sheer-cut and lofty wind-swept cliffs. It climbs high into the hills, and it crosses steep, rough-hewn rock-slopes. It touches many a water-serpent's cave and many a monster's lair.

"At last, the path comes to the place where a foaming mountain-stream flows down a steep rock-slope. It gathers strength and speed as it plunges over the rocks, becoming a terrifying torrent. And it rushes over the cliff-wall in a great water-fall.

"And below, at the base of the cliff, the flood-waters form a lonely lake, dark and dreary, that is surely haunted by evil spirits. There, the frightful flood-waters sink beneath the muddy marsh-land and disappear into unknown depths beneath the earth. But those who have seen that loathsome lake have seen sea-monsters frolicking there. And so, the flood-waters must flow beneath the head-land and empty into the surging sea-flood.

"There, wood-land fir and pine trees lean gloomily out from the rough-hewn rocks of the cliff, casting their dark and dismal shadows upon the flood-waters. The lake itself is a frightful sight, for once the bright heavens darken with the shadows of dusk, its flood-waters burn with furious flames. And when the storm-wind stirs up unwelcome weather, and day-light turns dark, its flood-waters bubble and boil, and a murky mist rises into the heavens.

"No one knows the depth of that dark, dreaded marsh-land, with its lonely lake of frightful flood-waters. Even the stalwart stag, that roaming heather-stepper who depends upon its horn-strength for safety, will stop at the edge of the cliff-wall, upon the brink of that marsh-land. When chased by deer-hounds, it gladly chooses to give its life to the hunter, for it knows better than to leap into that loathsome lake, with its frolicsome sea-monsters, in the hope of saving its life.

"And so, Beowulf, once again, only you can help us. For of all warriors, you are the most bold of heart and strong in strife, and you have become the shield and sword of the Dane-folk. That giant of a woman who invaded Heorot and killed my comrade must be Grendel's mighty mother, for surely there is no other. And she took small pleasure in her savage deed, for her goal was to avenge the death-wound the Bright-Danes had given her son. (She knows nothing of Weather-Geats.) And so, she took a life for a life. But that cannot be the end of it, for I must now take a life for a life, as well. I must avenge the death of my trusted counselor and beloved comrade.

"And so, Beowulf, I charge you with the greatest of challenges, and I hope you will dare to do it. Kill Grendel's mighty mother. Her wild, wind-swept, and lonely land is not far-off. Go there, and seek her in her dark and dreary den. For, ghastly and grim, she guards the depths that lie beneath the frightful flood-waters of that loathsome lake. Go there and slay her. Do this deed for me, and I will reward you with a trove of gracious gifts—age-old treasures and twisted gold."

So the old treasure-giving war-king spoke. And to his word-hoard, Beowulf replied, "You are a wise king, my lord. And so, put aside your sorrow. It is better to avenge the death of your friend than to mourn over-long for him. Wyrd always weaves as it must. And soon or late, Death, that dreaded destiny, takes the life of every man. So, the warrior who can, should win honor and glory before Death takes his life. Then, when his life comes to an end, his good name will live on after him.

"And so, my lord, quick as the wind, let us seek Grendel's foot-prints, for they are blood-stained. And surely his mighty mother has chosen to take the same path. If we leave soon, that path should be plain to see. For the sun, that bright candle of the world, is shining, and it has just begun to glide over the land.

"I promise you that no shelter will protect Grendel's mighty mother from my blood-hardened sharp-bladed battle-sword. For wherever that wondrous woman hides, I will find her. Even if she takes refuge in the heart of the earth, or in the high mountain wood-land, or at the bottom of the surging sea-flood, I will find her. And then, my blood-thirsting battle-sword will sing its greedy war-song. And strong as that mighty mother is, its savage stroke will give her a gruesome death-wound. Just be patient this day, my lord."

So Beowulf spoke. And Hrothgar thanked God that the hero from Geat-land was the shield and sword of the Spear-Danes. The old war-king then called for his horse, for he would join Beowulf and his bold-hearted war-comrades as they searched for Grendel's mighty mother. King Hrothgar rode in state, accompanied by a band of shield-bearers on foot.

And so it came to pass that Beowulf, King Hrothgar, and their bold-hearted war-comrades traveled through the woods and across the moor-land, murky and wild, loathsome and lonely. Danger greeted them on all sides of the high head-land. And the rope-thin foot-path was filled with peril. At last, the bold-hearted old war-king dismounted. And he and his band of war-comrades went forth to the edge of the cliff-wall.

Suddenly Hrothgar spied the severed, blood-bathed head of the man who had been his trusted counselor and beloved comrade. It was lying, like one of the rocks, at the edge of a steep rock-slope. Beowulf had advised them well, for Grendel's mighty mother had taken this path across the moor-land, bearing the body of the best of Hrothgar's men.

The king and the war-comrades stood silent and still at the sight. Then they approached the blood-bathed head. And every heart flooded with surging sea-swells of grief and sorrow to see the destiny of that far-famed warrior.

At the edge of the cliff-wall, they looked over the rough-hewn rocks to the muddy marsh-land that lay far below. It was seething with grisly gore. And the frightful flood-waters of its loathsome lake, lonely but for the sea-monsters that frolicked there, were surging and swirling, and bubbling and boiling with fire-hot blood.

In silence, the king and the two companies of war-comrades sat down and watched the scene below. Strange sea-serpents were swimming here and there. And savage sea-dragons, which grieve sea-farers upon the whale-road by attacking their ring-prowed ships, were resting upon the flat surfaces of rocks that protruded from the head-land slope. Then, the warriors blew a blaring battle-song upon their war-horns. The sudden sound startled the sea-serpents, and they all swam away.

Chapter 4

Beowulf descends to the underwater den of Grendel's mother, where he kills her. Then he returns to Geatland.

Beowulf put on his battle-garments. "I have no fear for my life," he declared. "My ring-meshed battle-shirt, hand-linked and hand-joined, will protect my body from any sea-serpent's battle-stroke or frightful battle-grip. And that clever smith covered the face of my age-old war-helmet with battle-ready boars so that no sword-blade can bite through it."

So Beowulf spoke. And it came to pass that Unferth, the foremost fighter of the Spear-Danes, now forgot the taunting words that mead had led him to speak. He knew that he lacked the bold heart and the battle-skill to do a warrior's duty and risk his life beneath the blood-filled waves. And so, he offered Beowulf his own blood-hardened sharp-bladed battle-sword.

"Beowulf, take Hrunting with you," he said. "It is one of the most valued of the age-old treasures, war-tested and true, for its battle-blade is iron-edged and blood-hardened, and its shining serpent-shapes are deadly. Many warriors who have wielded it have tread ways of terror. But Hrunting has never betrayed anyone who has clasped it in battle!"

"Thank you, my friend" replied Beowulf. "I will be glad to have such a trusted friend! And I will win glory with Hrunting, or I will be beaten in battle. And then Death will take my life, for I will not run from my destiny. Wyrd always weaves as it must. But you must take my own sharp-bladed battle-sword, for it, too, is a trusted. age-old war-weapon."

Beowulf was now battle-ready for whatever danger his daring journey would bring. And so, he said to Hrothgar, "Remember, my lord, should Death take my life, you must care for my war-comrades. Send the treasure you gave me to my king. I want him to know what a gracious ring-giver you are and how rewarded I was for my deeds while I lived."

So Beowulf spoke. And with these words, he climbed down the rough-hewn rocks to the bottom of the cliff-wall. There, he walked to the shore of the loath-some lake and plunged into its swirling and seething blood-filled waves. Beowulf sank deep and ever deeper beneath the lake-face. And the sun, that bright candle of the world, glided high into the heavens and shone forth over the land. Still, Beowulf sank ever deeper beneath the lake-face. And then, the sun began to glide toward its home. But still, Beowulf sank ever deeper beneath the lake-face. At last, beneath the flood-waters, he felt his feet touch the firm lake-floor.

Grendel's mighty mother had guarded the flood-waters' depths for fifty winters. And now, she spied Beowulf as he searched for her secluded sea-cave. At first, the warrior did not see her. But suddenly her frightful face swam before his eyes in the murky waters.

Swift as a warrior's sword-stroke, the giant seized him. And she held him in a grasp that was stronger than the storm-wind. And as she clutched him in her terrible claws, she tried to find his flesh. She wanted to bite into it with her frightful teeth and give him a gruesome death-wound. But she could not even scratch his skin, for her foul iron-nailed fingers could not tear through his ring-meshed battle-shirt.

And so that mighty mother carried Beowulf toward her lonely lair. And strong as he was, Beowulf could not wield his battle-weapons. So it came to pass that many strange sea-beasts pressed their treacherous tusks close to him. And they were able to break through his stout, ring-meshed war-shirt and scratch his skin.

Soon, Beowulf found himself in a sheltered sea-cave, deep beneath the flood-waters. It was a high-roofed hall where no water could enter. Bright fire-light flickered upon the walls. And against it, Grendel's mighty mother cast a shadow, ghastly and grim.

Safe within her lonely lair, the giant relaxed her grasp. And swift as a warrior's sword-stroke, Beowulf raised Hrunting, Unferth's sharp-bladed battle-sword. And he smashed that mighty mother upon her head with such strength that the blood-hardened blade sang its greedy war-song.

But that blood-thirsting war-weapon could not bite the flesh or break the life of that wondrous woman. Its iron-edged blood-hardened battle-blade betrayed Beowulf in his time of greatest need. In the past, Hrunting, that battle-friend of heroes, had bitten through many a hard war-helmet and ring-meshed battle-shirt. And so, it had given gruesome wounds that had doomed warriors to death. But now, Unferth's treasured war-sword won no glory.

Beowulf's heart flooded with a surging sea-swell of rage. He angrily threw Hrunting aside. And now, he put his trust in his own mighty battle-grip. For every man must rely upon his own strength in battle. And the warrior who wants to win glory and lasting fame must put aside all fear of death, that dreaded destiny.

So, Beowulf eagerly seized Grendel's mother by the shoulders. He was so bold-hearted and swollen with wrath that he could throw her to the ground. But swift as a warrior's sword-stroke, the mighty giant clasped him in her own frightful battle-grip. She pushed and pulled him, and Beowulf's spirits sank as he struggled to survive. He was the strongest of warriors, but Grendel's mother was stronger than the storm-wind. And so, at last, Beowulf staggered and fell to the floor of her high-roofed hall.

Grendel's mighty mother hurled herself upon her foe. And then she drew forth her broad, sharp-bladed dagger. And Beowulf, the foremost fighter of the War-Geats, would have met Death there in that sheltered sea-cave, deep beneath the flood-waters, but the stout mesh of his hand-linked battle-shirt saved him. The hand-joined chain-links withstood the thrust of that giant's dagger-point and blood-hardened blade. Those ring-links shielded his chest and sheltered his life.

And Holy God, wise Lord and Ruler of Heaven, granted Beowulf good fortune in battle. For Beowulf was bold of heart and strong in strife. And so, swift as a warrior's sword-stroke, Beowulf now pushed away the mighty giant and sprang to his feet.

Beowulf then spied a wondrous age-old battle-sword hanging upon the wall of the sea-cave. In a bygone age, it had been forged and fashioned by a giant smith for those of his race. And now, the mightiest of men could not bear this weapon into battle. But Beowulf's heart was flooded with surging sea-swells of rage and fury. And so, he seized that wondrous war-weapon, and he let it sing its greedy war-song.

But God had woven defeat for Grendel's mighty mother. And so, she had no good fortune in battle. And it came to pass that, in Beowulf's hand, the blood-thirsting battle-blade of the giant-sword slashed into her neck with such savage strength that it broke her bones and sliced through her body. And Grendel's mighty mother, beaten in battle, dropped to her death at Beowulf's feet.

Beowulf gazed at the blood-smeared battle-blade of the giant-sword. And he gloried in his great deed. Then, suddenly, the fire that had lighted the wall of the sheltered sea-cave blazed forth. And it filled the lonely lair with light as bright as the sun, Heaven's jewel.

And so it came to pass that Beowulf could search the cave-floor for Grendel. At last, he found the frightful fiend's lifeless, broken body. Beowulf then swung the wondrous giant-sword with such an angry blow that, once again, it sang its greedy war-song, and it separated Grendel's loathsome head from his lifeless body.

Above, the bright heavens would soon darken with the shadows of dusk. Eight hours had passed, and the ninth hour was upon them. But King Hrothgar and the two groups of war-comrades were still patiently keeping their long cliff-watch. Suddenly, the face of the frightful flood-waters began to swell and swirl with a new surge of blood-filled waves.

The Bright-Danes were sure that Grendel's mighty mother had slain Beowulf. Their hearts flooded with a surging sea-swell of sorrow. And they decided to leave the head-land and return to Heorot.

But the Sea-Geats sat there still, keeping their cliff-watch. They stared into the frightful blood-filled flood-waters of that loathsome lake. And their hearts flooded with a surging sea-swell of despair. They dared not hope to see their leader and lord. But they were as rooted to the edge of the cliff-wall as the trees that leaned gloomily out from the rough-hewn rocks.

Below, in the sheltered sea-cave, deep beneath the flood-waters, Beowulf was watching the boiling blood and gore of the frightful fiend and his mighty mother feast upon the giant-sword's battle-blade, for just as ice begins to melt when God, who rules the times and the seasons, breaks the frost-bonds and unwinds the flood-fetters, so the broad battle-blade now burned up.

Beowulf saw many treasures in that lonely lair, but he decided to take nothing but Grendel's gruesome head and the wondrous jeweled hilt of the giant-sword. And carrying one in each hand, he swam up to the lake-face. The frightful flood-waters now slept beneath the clouds, calm and still, but the boiling blood and gore from the cave below had risen. And so, the lake-face was still clothed in a gruesome color.

Beowulf swallowed the fresh air and feasted his eyes upon the golden glow of the cloud-filled sky. His heart flooded with a surging sea-swell of joy as he swam to shore and began to climb the rough-hewn rocks to the top of the cliff-wall. His war-comrades jumped to their feet and cheered. Then they went forth to join him, for they were joyful at the safe return of their leader and lord. And they delighted in his battle-skill and good-fortune.

When, at last, Beowulf and his war-band left the lonely lake, it took all the strength of four men to carry Grendel's gruesome head upon their spear-shafts. Again they crossed the moor-land, murky and wild, loathsome and lonely. And again danger greeted them on all sides of the high head-land, and the rope-thin foot-path was filled with peril. But they walked carefully and with good cheer. And at last, they made their way through the wood-land and back to Hrothgar's tower-tall, timbered mead-hall.

The bright heavens had long since darkened with the shadows of dusk. And at last, Beowulf and his war-comrades walked up the stone-cobbled street toward the Heorot, that bright hall of bold-hearted men. The king, with his gentle-mannered queen, and the high-born noble-men among the Ring-Danes were still in the high, horn-gabled mead-hall, where they had gathered for their evening meal. But Beowulf and his war-comrades did not hear the sounds of the harp and the happy songs of heroes. For the Ring-Danes were sure that Death, that dreaded destiny, had taken the life of the War-Geat who was their shield and spear, and every heart was now flooded with sorrow.

But suddenly, in the sad silence, the Spear-Danes heard the clattering, iron battle-song of Beowulf's war-band. And then, swift as a warrior's sword-stroke, Beowulf, boldest of heart and strongest in strife, strode into the Hall of Heroes. He walked toward the mead-benches dragging Grendel's gruesome head by its hair and bearing the hilt of the wondrous giant-sword. King Hrothgar and every Ring-Dane jumped to his feet and cheered. And then, they ran to join the hero. For they were joyful at his safe return, and they were eager to gaze in wonder at the tokens of his battle-skill and good fortune.

As soon as he would be heard, Beowulf unlocked his word-hoard. "My lord, my heart floods with joy, for I have brought you these tokens, gruesome and glorious, of my good fortune," he declared. "My struggle with Grendel's mighty mother was stern and savage, for she was stronger than the storm-wind.

"First, she tried to steal my life by clutching me in her terrible claws and chewing my flesh with her terrible teeth. Then she tried her blood-hardened sharp-pointed battle-knife. But the stout mesh of my hand-linked battle-shirt saved me from her foul iron-nailed fingers and her blood-thirsting battle-blade, for those hand-joined ring-links shielded my chest and sheltered my life.

Then that mighty mother tried to kill me by crushing my limbs. I barely escaped from her frightful battle-grip! And then Hrunting sang its greedy war-song. But its blood-thirsting battle-blade could not help me, for it could not bite the flesh or break the life of that wondrous woman. And so, that treasured war-sword, that best of battle-blades, won no glory.

"Then, Holy God, Ruler of Men, who often guides the friendless, shielded me. He showed me a wondrous, age-old battle-sword. Suddenly I saw it hanging upon the wall of that sheltered sea-cave, deep beneath the flood-waters. It had been forged and fashioned by a giant smith for those of his race, but it could still sing its greedy war-song.

"And so, I slew Grendel's mighty mother. And then I separated Grendel's loathsome head from his lifeless body. Their boiling blood and gore burned up that wondrous battle-blade. But I have brought you Grendel's gruesome head and the wondrous hilt of that giant-sword. For these tokens show that Death, that dreaded destiny, has taken God's foes, that frightful fiend and his mighty mother. And so, from this time forth, you and your war-comrades can sleep free from care in this high, horn-gabled hall."

So Beowulf spoke. And with these words, he placed the jeweled sword-hilt into the hand of the joyful, old war-king. The hilt depicted the age-old tale of the frightful flood. Those rushing waters had ravaged and ruined the giant race because they had lived lawlessly. Decorated with dragon-shapes, the age-old letters still told that terrifying tale.

The smiling, treasure-giving old king gazed at the wondrous gift in his hand. And then he looked up at Beowulf and unlocked his word-hoard, for the old war-king had wise words to share with the young warrior who stood before him. "My son, folk in lands near and far will know of your fame," he declared. "And so, maintain your war-might with a wise heart. Be a comfort to the Geat-folk and a help to your war-comrades.

"Like you, old King Heremod towered in strength above other men, but he became blood-thirsty. He let his heart flood with surging sea-swells of anger toward his own folk. And so, he killed his own comrades. Heremod lived for himself alone, and so he lived without joy. He suffered for his vengeful deeds. And he died as he had lived, alone.

"Mighty God rules all things. He permits a high-born noble-man to want to gain and keep power, land, and treasure. And so, such a man can satisfy his every wish. The shadows of sickness and old age do not bother him. Sorrow does not darken his spirits, and strife does not threaten his kingdom. All the world bends to his will.

"And so, that man does not realize that pride is growing within him. He decides that he does not possess enough power and wealth. And so, he greedily keeps his gold rings. If he is not careful, a poisoned war-shaft suddenly strikes him in the chest, for the blessings of God, the King of Glory, blind him to the future and his inevitable destiny. But, in the end, his body dies, as it must, and another king acquires all his possessions.

"You are now a far-famed warrior, Beowulf. For a while, you will be in the flower of your strength. But later, the sword-blade's bite or the spear-shaft's flight, the flood-waters' frightful grip or the flaming fire's grasp, sickness or sad old-age will rob you of your strength. Your bright eyes will dim and darken, and you will be beaten in battle or in soft sleep. And so, Death, that dreaded destiny, will take your life. For it must.

"But enough of an old man's advice. Go now. Taste the joy of the feast. And when bright day-light again shines forth over the land, I will give you many treasures."

So Hrothgar spoke. And when the sun, that bright candle of the world, again shone forth over the land, the Weather-Geats were eager return to their homeland. And they were ready to cross the deep waters of the whale-road. And so, Beowulf gave Hrunting, that age-old blood-hardened battle-sword, back to Unferth.

And then Beowulf said to Hrothgar, "My lord, we sea-faring folk from afar are ready to return to Geat-land. You have treated us well in every way. If ever I may do more to help you, I will be ready. If your neighbors attack you, I will come to your help with a thousand warriors. Hygelac, my lord and king, is young, but he will support me in word and in deed."

So Beowulf spoke. And to his words, Hrothgar replied, "Never have I heard one so young speak so wisely. If it comes to pass that the iron-tipped spear, the sharp-bladed battle-sword, or sickness kills your king, the Geat-folk could have no better king than you. And while I am king, the Spear-Danes and the War-Geats will live together in peace. We will share treasure and tokens of love."

Hrothgar then gave Beowulf twelve treasures. And tears fell from the white-haired king's eyes as he kissed the young warrior, for he loved him like a son. Beowulf was so dear to him that his heart hurt. He yearned to keep the young warrior in his own kingdom. And so, his heart flooded with surging sea-swells of grief and sorrow at their parting, for he knew that Death, that dreaded destiny, would take him before he could look upon Beowulf's face and form again. And he feared for the future of his kingdom, for the warrior who was the shield and spear of the Dane-folk was returning to Geat-land.

Beowulf, the gold-proud warrior, took his twelve treasures. And then he and his band of bold-hearted war-comrades walked down the stone-cobbled street toward the sea-coast. The battle-ready boars, gold-glittering and stern, upon their hard war-helmets had kept watch over their lives. And their clanking ring-meshed battle-coats had kept Death, that dreaded destiny, at bay.

The warden welcomed them at the sea-shore. There they placed Hrothgar's gift-hoard—the horses, the splendid battle-gear, and the treasure-trove—on board their ring-prowed broad-beamed boat. Beowulf then gave the ship's watch-man an age-old gold-hilted battle-sword, a treasure that would bring that warrior great respect among his comrades.

So it came to pass that Beowulf, that safe-guard of warriors, and his bold-hearted war-comrades set out once again upon the deep waters of the whale-road. And a brisk wind sent their bent-necked ship speeding across the sea-swell like a sea-bird, its curved prow like a foamy bill. The ship sailed forth to the lofty sheer-cut sea-cliffs of Geat-land.

There, the coast-guard was ready and eager to welcome the war-comrades home. King Hygelac had his mead-hall prepared for a great celebration. And there, Beowulf told the tale of his adventures to the warriors who had stayed behind in Geat-land. He then set Hrothgar's gift-hoard before his king, for these were royal gifts from one treasure-giving king to another.

King Hygelac then rewarded Beowulf for his deeds of daring and danger. He gave the far-famed warrior an age-old gold-hilted sword, Naegling, that was the best of treasures among the Weather-Geats, a prince's high-seat, a fine hall, and a large estate. And so, Beowulf was now the most highly honored of men.

Chapter 5

Beowulf has been king for fifty years when a dragon ravages his kingdom. The fire-serpent gives Beowulf a wound that dooms him to death.

It came to pass that blood-hardened, sharp-bladed battle-swords slew King Hygelac. And in time, Beowulf became king of Geat-land. He was a wise, treasure-giving war-king, and he ruled his realm well for fifty winters.

But, suddenly, in the fiftieth year of Beowulf's rule, trouble struck Geat-land. The sun, Heaven's jewel, had glided over the land, and the bright heavens had darkened with the shadows of dusk. And then it had come to pass that a frightful fire-serpent, shielded by the darkness, had soared into the night sky.

And this savage serpent had flown over Geat-land, swooping down over the villages and farms of the Geat-folk. And like a fiery forge, it had spewed forth a blazing torrent of furious flames. These flames had killed the folk of town and country, and they had burned the buildings of the Geat-folk down to smoldering coals and ashes. For the fire-serpent's hard heart had become flooded with a surging sea-swell of rage.

And it came to pass that the dreaded dragon crowned itself King of the Night, and its rule was a reign of terror. For night after night, its fiery breath spread furious flames over the land.

The dreaded dragon haunted lofty Eagle's-Cliff, part of a high heath-covered head-land that jutted out into the sea-flood. Above Eagle's-Cliff stood a steep stone-mound, built as a tower-tall barrow, in a by-gone age, to hold all that was left of a high-born noble-man and his wealth.

Beneath the stone-barrow, and down the side of lofty Eagle's-Cliff, lay a steep, secret foot-path. This path had been hidden so cleverly that men had not known of it for a thousand winters. And it led down the rough-hewn rock-cliff to a barrow-cave that lay hidden within the lower reaches of the cliff-side.

The barrow-cave opened onto a rock-shelf that rested safely above the sea-flood, for a steep lower cliff-wall protected it from the swollen and surging sea-swell and from sea-faring men. Still, the barrow-builders had cleverly hidden its entrance.

In a by-gone age, the barrow-hall had been a lofty earth-cave that rose high inside the sea-cliff. Giants had found this earth-cave, and they had cleverly fashioned it into a fine earth-hall. Inside the hall, they had put up great stone-arches, and they had supported them with stone-pillars. This stone-work held the earth-wall in place.

Many hundreds of winters ago, it had come to pass that a lone warrior was the last living member of his clan. Long before, Death, that dreaded destiny, had taken the lives of all his kin-folk, all his hearth-friends, and all his war-comrades. And so, he was the sole guardian of his clan's treasure-rings. He knew that all men are doomed to die, and he knew that he would soon sleep the lasting-sleep of his comrades and kin-folk. But before Death took his life, he wanted to preserve the precious wealth of his high-born clan.

And so, the warrior searched for a place to protect his treasure-trove. It came to pass that he found the hidden foot-path, and the path led him to the giant's earth-hall. As soon as he saw this hall, he said, "I will store my clan's treasure-trove in this well-built barrow-hall. It is below the stone-cliff and above the surging sea-waves. And so, it will be secret and safe."

So the warrior spoke. And with these words, he collected his clan's precious, age-old treasures. He carried them the down the secret foot-path, and he hid them within that earth-hall. And the treasure-trove made a high heap upon the earth-floor. For there were jewels and there were rings, for fingers and arms, of twisted gold. There were wondrous wall-hangings, woven with golden thread. There were jeweled and gold-plated cups, bowls, and platters. And there were gold-plated war-helmets, ring-meshed battle-coats, and gold-hilted, sharp-bladed battle-swords.

The lone warrior hid all of these treasures in the earth-hall. And then, once again, he spoke. But this time, he unlocked his hoard of words. "Earth, hold now this high-born clan-wealth, for its war-comrades can no longer keep it. It was within your rich body that good men first found the gleaming gold," he declared. "And so, now, I am returning your wealth to you.

"No one is left to shine the gold-plated bowl and the precious drinking-cup. And the hard, gold-plated war-helmet is tarnished now, for those whose job it was to shine it sleep the lasting-sleep.

"No one remains to wield the gleaming war-blade. The ring-meshed battle-shirt waits in vain to protect the warrior in battle. Both are decaying into dust. And the war-gear that survived such strife, that withstood the crash of shining battle-shields and the bite of blood-hardened sword-blades will crumble, too.

"No one lives to enjoy the mead-hall, to hear the harp-song, to ride a horse, or to see the hawk. For Death, that dreaded destiny, has destroyed all my kin-folk, all my hearth-friends, and all my bold-hearted war-comrades. Death has taken every-one in my clan, and my heart is flooded with sorrow."

So the lone warrior spoke. And with these words, he then protected his clan's treasure-trove by placing a curse upon it. "May destruction and death, that dreaded destiny, follow whoever disturbs this hoard-heap of treasures," he prayed. "And may my curse last until the Day of Doom!"

And it came to pass that, soon thereafter, Death clutched at that warrior's heart and took him, too. And for seven hundred winters, no one touched that hoard-heap of golden treasures.

But then the fire-serpent discovered the barrow-hall, and it made that lonely lair its own. It coiled contentedly upon the golden goods, and it became the hoard-guard of the age-old treasure-trove. It passed countless hours enjoying its possessions, and it kept a silent and secret watch over them. It knew every treasure by sight, and before and after every sleep, it counted each precious piece. In this way, three hundred winters passed peacefully for the serpent, for no one discovered the barrow and disturbed its life.

But it came to pass that, in the fiftieth winter of Beowulf's reign, a slave angered the high-born noble-man who was his master. And seeing that his master's heart had flooded with a surging sea-swell of rage, the slave's heart flooded with terror. And fearing a lashing, he fled.

Now that he had lost his home, he needed a secret hiding-place that would shelter him. He searched beneath the tower-tall stone-mound on lofty Eagle's-Cliff, and he stumbled upon the age-old steep, secret foot-path to the earth-hall that lay hidden in the lower reaches of the stone-cliff. He discovered its hidden entrance, and he took refuge within its stone walls.

The slave did not know that the earth-hall was a burial-barrow from a bygone age. And so, he was surprised to find a treasure-trove of jewels, woven gold-work, gold-plated objects, and age-old battle-gear. The hoard was heaped upon the ground, and a sleeping fire-serpent was protecting it.

When the slave saw the frightful fire-serpent, his heart flooded with surging sea-swells of terror and panic. Near the serpent's head, he noticed a glorious age-old goblet, jeweled and golden. He thought this shining treasure-cup would serve him well. And so, he stealthily crept up to the sleeping serpent, and he snatched the cup. Then quick as the wind, he sped away from the dreaded dragon's den. And Wyrd protected the slave, for it had not woven this to be his day of destiny.

And so it came to pass that the slave offered his master the treasure-cup. The slave hoped the goblet would purchase forgiveness and peace. And his master accepted the gift, for the age-old goblet was fine and rare.

When the frightful fire-serpent awoke, it counted each precious piece of its hoard-heap, and it discovered that its glorious golden goblet was missing. Its hard heart flooded with surging sea-swells of fear and rage. And so, it frantically slithered here and there within the barrow-hall, desperately searching for the treasure-cup. It looked high and low. It looked in every dark corner. It looked beneath every bright banner. But it could not find the cup anywhere within its high stone-hall.

At last, the frightful fire-serpent smelled the thief's foot-prints. And its hard heart flooded with a surging sea-swell of fury. Following the thief's scent, the serpent left its lonely lair. And it slithered, eagerly, along the rock-shelf, sniffing as it went. And as it sniffed, the serpent's thoughts turned from rage at the theft to the joy of revenge.

The frightful fire-serpent became determined to avenge the theft of its precious treasure-cup. It would punish all the Weather-Geats for one slave's crime. The winged dragon restlessly waited until the bright heavens had darkened with the shadows of dusk. Then it slithered out of its den. It spread its great wings, and it soared into the night sky.

The dreaded dragon then flew over Geat-land, swooping down over the villages and farms of the Geat-folk. And like a fiery forge, it spewed forth a blazing torrent of furious flames. These flames killed the folk of town and country and burned the buildings of the Geat-folk down to smoldering coals and ashes.

The blazing fires cast their golden glow high into the heavens, displaying the serpent's savage strength far and wide. And the heart of every Sea-Geat flooded with a surging sea-swell of horror at the fire-serpent's frightful fury and its dreadful deeds.

When it came to pass that the sun, Heaven's jewel, would soon shine forth over the land, the dreaded dragon flew back to its earth-barrow, for it loved its secret stone-hall and its hoard-heap of golden treasures. And it trusted that its frightful war-skill and the lonely location of its lair would secure its safety. But the fire-serpent deceived itself. It was destined to live no longer than the treasure-giving war-king of the Weather-Geats, for even as an old man, Beowulf was the shield and spear of the Geat-folk.

Beowulf, that best of kings, learned of the frightful fire-serpent's ravaging raids first-hand, for the savage serpent attacked his own glorious gift-hall. Quick as the wind, the tall timbered mead-hall was consumed in a bright blaze. And when Beowulf saw that the dragon's fiery breath had reduced his Hall of Heroes to smoldering coals and ashes, his heart flooded with surging sea-swells of grief and anger. He feared that he might have bitterly angered the Eternal Lord, Ruler of the World, by breaking some age-old law. And so Beowulf announced to his high-born noble-men that it was his duty to kill this frightful fire-fiend.

"Oh, my lord, do not come face to face in combat this greedy gold-guard!" they pleaded, "Let the savage fire-serpent lie safely in its lonely lair. Let it remain buried in its barrow-hall, that dark den, until the Day of Doom!"

So the best of the War-Geats spoke. But they could not dissuade their treasure-giving war-king from this heroic act. They could not make their lord, the shepherd of the Geat-folk and the shield and safeguard of warriors, accept their wise words. The Lord of Rings held to his high destiny, for he was a good king!

"I am no longer a youth, but I will always be the shield and spear of the Geat-folk!" Beowulf declared. "And so, I will now seek this savage serpent. But not with many war-comrades, for I have no fear of fighting. Nor do I fear the frightful fire-serpent's great strength and battle-skill.

"Many times I have been in great danger. But I have always been bold of heart and strong in strife, and I have always lived to tell the tale. I have slain many mighty sea-serpents. And I killed Grendel and Grendel's mighty mother. And so, I will now try to slay this frightful fire-serpent! But I will risk no life but my own."

So Beowulf spoke to his high-born noble-men. And then the old treasure-giving war-king of the Weather-Geats commanded his smiths to create a new battle-shield for him, one of gleaming iron. For his gold-rimmed linden-wood shield could not protect him from the blazing breath of this frightful fire-fiend.

Beowulf then chose eleven trusted war-comrades, the most bold of heart and strong in strife, to accompany him. The Lord of Rings had learned the cause of the savage fire-serpent's wrath. And so, he ordered the thief to lead them to its lair. Fear gripped the hearts of most of those men, for the fire-serpent was a frightful foe. And only the most bold-hearted heroes would dare to come near its earth-hall, for there, he would have to face the dreaded dragon's flaming fury.

Soon it came to pass that Beowulf and his band of trusted war-comrades arrived at the edge of lofty Eagle's-Cliff, the head-land cliff-wall high above the frightful fire-serpent's earth-hall. And there, Beowulf, the gold-friend of the Sea-Geats, sat down and said fare-well to his war-comrades. The old war-king had been bold of heart and strong in strife, but now his spirit was sad and restless within him. It was ready for Death, that dreaded destiny. For Wyrd would seek the treasure of his soul, and then Death would separate his spirit from his flesh.

And so, the Lord of Rings, that bold shield-bearer, unlocked his word-hoard. "I remember how in my youth I braved countless battles and times of peril," he declared. "And now, if the savage fire-serpent will leave its lonely lair and seek me, I will fight it. My hand and Naegling's blood-thirsting battle-blade will wage war for the treasure-trove!

"Now, if Wyrd, Ruler of All, will permit, my stout sword will sing its greedy war-song, and then I will win honor and glory, for this is a deed of daring and danger. And so, my bold heart and my battle-skill will force the greedy fire-serpent to give up its gold, or I will be beaten in battle. And then Death will take my life, for I will not run from my destiny. Wyrd always weaves as it must.

"If I could, I would bear no battle-sword or other war-weapon against this savage serpent. I would clasp the frightful fire-fiend with my mighty battle-grip as I once clasped Grendel. But now, I will have to face flaming fire and frightful fumes. And so, I will wear my ring-meshed battle-shirt, and I will use an iron shield. I am eager to fight! And so, I do not need to boast of my bold heart or my battle-skill.

"And now, comrades, sit here upon lofty Eagle's-Cliff. And permit me go down to the barrow-hall below and face the peril there. For this daring deed is not for you to do, though you are bold of heart and strong in strife. The task is mine alone."

So Beowulf spoke to his eleven trusted war-comrades. And so it came to pass that the old treasure-giving war-king, safe-guard of the Geat-folk, walked down the path that led to the treasure-guard's lonely lair. Beowulf carried his war-shield of gleaming iron beneath lofty Eagle's-Cliff, for he was battle-bold, and he was sure of his own strength and war-skill. No faint-hearted warrior would choose this fight!

The entrance to the earth-hall was not hidden now. For a sea-flood of flames was flowing forth from within the barrow. And the Lord of Rings knew that, if he tried to enter the hall and approach the hoard-heap of golden treasures, the fire-flood would burn him to death.

Beowulf's heart flooded with a surging sea-swell of hatred toward the savage fire-serpent. And so, he raised his voice in a battle-shout and angrily challenged the dreaded dragon to come forth to meet him in battle. His voice echoed off the stone walls in the barrow-hall like the clanking of gleaming war-gear.

Beowulf's war-cry caused the frightful fire-serpent's hard heart to flood with a surging sea-swell of rage. So now, its fiery breath burst forth from the barrow in a blazing torrent of furious flames. Even the rock beneath Beowulf's feet rumbled with their roar.

The hoard-guard then slithered forth from its lonely lair. And now, the sight of Beowulf caused its hard heart to flood with a surging sea-swell of joy, for it was eager to meet its foe in battle and flood that warrior's heart with terror.

The lord of the Geat-folk raised his gleaming iron shield, and from its sheath he drew forth Naegling, his age-old, blood-hardened battle-sword. Then he waited, bold-hearted in his war-gear, while the frightful fire-fiend sent forth a blazing torrent of furious flames, and it coiled for battle.

And as the dreaded dragon moved to meet its destiny, Beowulf approached his own destiny, for Wyrd would not grant the good, old, war-king good fortune in battle. Beowulf raised Naegling and struck the frightful fire-serpent with all of his strength. And Naegling sang its greedy war-song, but that age-old, blood-hardened war-weapon, that battle-friend of heroes, won no glory in this fight, for it could not bite through the fire-fiend's hard scales. And beaten in battle by the serpent's war-gear, Naegling's mighty blade became blunted.

Beowulf was now beset by evils. Naegling had lost its strength. And Beowulf's gleaming shield could not guard his body and save his life, for it was melting beneath the seething flames of the savage serpent's fiery breath. Beowulf knew that he would not be able to boast of his battle-skill and good fortune, for at last he faced Death, that dreaded destiny.

Beowulf knew that his long life, with its great glory and lasting fame, was no longer bright, but life at any age was worth living. Fame came second. And so, now that Death, that dreaded destiny, was waiting to take him, Beowulf was unwilling to leave the earth. The old war-king did not want to make that last journey to a far-off dwelling-place. Yet all men must meet their destiny when their days on earth come to an end.

It came to pass that Beowulf's battle-stroke only caused the dragon's hard heart to flood anew with a surging sea-swell of rage. And so, the savage serpent spewed forth a second blazing torrent of furious flames. And the old treasure-giving war-king, shield and spear of the Storm-Geats, found himself drowning in a frightful flood of fire.

The Storm-Geats who had accompanied Beowulf, his band of bold-hearted and trusted war-comrades, watched the savage fire-serpent beat their king in battle, and their hearts flooded with surging sea-swells of horror, terror, and panic. They should have been loyal to their lord and king. And so, they should have rushed to rescue him, but they thought only of saving their own lives. And so, swift as a warrior's sword-stroke, they rose from their places on lofty Eagle's-Cliff and fled into the forest.

Of Beowulf's eleven trusted war-comrades, only his nephew, young Wiglaf, was bold of heart and loyal. This would be the youth's first fight. He remembered all the honors his king had bestowed upon him, and he thought of the wealth and property of his kin-folk. "I cannot, with honor, repay my king's kindness by running away," he declared to himself. "To let my king die without help is a crime without pardon."

So Wiglaf spoke to himself. He knew that his war-comrades would hear his words if he spoke to them. And so, he unlocked his word-hoard, and he shouted, "Comrades! Remember how, in the mead-hall, we drank to our lord and king, who gave us our rings. We promised that, if he ever needed our help, we would repay him for our battle-shirts, our helmets, and our war-gear. Beowulf chose us to join him on this journey because of our bold hearts, our battle-skills, and our delight in deeds of glory.

"Our treasure-giving king, that most bold-hearted and battle-skilled warrior, has won honor and glory by doing deeds of daring and danger. And so, alone, he expected to fell this frightful fire-fiend. But now he needs our bold hearts and our battle-skills. And we must help him!

"God knows I would rather be enfolded in the fire-serpent's flaming fury than doomed to live like a faint-hearted warrior. And so, I will now go forth to help my lord and king!"

So Wiglaf spoke. And with these words, he gripped his linden-wood shield, drew forth his sharp-bladed battle-sword, and ran toward Beowulf. Wiglaf's shield might scorch and his sword might melt, but his spirit was of the strongest metal. Bold of heart and strong in strife, he would confront the savage fire-serpent's blazing breath and the stench of slaughter.

So it came to pass that Wiglaf fought his way through the fiery fumes to his lord and king. And then, he said, "Beloved Beowulf, remember how in your youth you swore to win honor and glory as long as life was yours? Now you must summon all your strength and save your life. And I will help you!"

So Wiglaf spoke. And at the sound of his words, the savage fire-serpent's hard heart flooded anew with surging sea-swells of rage, and it wrapped these war-comrades whom it loathed in its blazing breath. A frightful flood of flames scorched the linden-wood shield of the young warrior. And so, Wiglaf sought refuge behind Beowulf's iron shield.

Wiglaf's presence caused the old king's mind, once again, to flood with thoughts of glory. And once again, Beowulf's heart flooded with a surging sea-swell of hatred toward the savage fire-serpent. Swift as a warrior's sword-stroke and with youthful battle-might, Beowulf raised Naegling and rushed to meet his foe.

The mighty war-weapon sang its greedy war-song as it tore through the serpent's head-scales and into its soft flesh. Naegling's blood-thirsting battle-blade gave the serpent a sore battle-wound, but not one that doomed it to death. And then that blood-hardened battle-blade betrayed the old war-king in his time of greatest need, in this, his last battle. That treasured war-weapon, that battle-friend of heroes, won no glory, for its broad, blunted blade broke, beaten in battle by Beowulf's foe.

It was Beowulf's destiny that the mightiest man-made sword would never bring him good fortune in battle. His hand was too strong to wield that war-weapon. And so, his heart now flooded with a surging sea-swell of despair, and he withdrew from the wounded fire-serpent, knowing now that he would be beaten in battle.

Seeing its foe retreat, the savage fire-serpent attacked Beowulf for the third time. Again it spewed forth a blazing torrent of furious flames. But now, it rushed upon the old war-king, gripped him by the throat, and sank its fierce blood-thirsting fangs into his neck-flesh. And Beowulf's life-blood rushed forth from his blood-smeared body like a surging sea-swell.

Chapter 6

With Wiglaf's help, Beowulf kills the dragon. Beowulf dies, and Wiglaf becomes king. Wiglaf then punishes the disloyal warriors and prepares for Beowulf's funeral.

Wiglaf then showed his bold heart and his battle-skill. The blazing breath of the savage serpent was scorching his body, but the young warrior ignored its flaming fury and struck the dreaded dragon deep in its chest with his own blood-thirsting battle-blade. And at last, the fire-serpent's flames began to fail.

The death-sick war-king, shield and spear of the Geat-folk, fought off his destiny and reached for the battle-sharp dagger that he wore upon his ring-meshed battle-shirt. With one savage war-stroke, he slashed at the frightful fire-serpent and sliced it in two.

Destroying the dreaded dragon was Beowulf's last heroic deed, for his own death-wound began to burn and swell, and the fire-serpent's poison began to pulse in his chest. While he still had some strength, the old warrior dragged his body to the entrance of the earth-hall. There, he sat against the stone wall and gazed at the wondrous giant-work within the barrow.

Wiglaf, that worthy young warrior, found water, gathered it in his hands, and washed his king's blood-smeared body. Then he loosened Beowulf's hard battle-helmet.

Beowulf knew that his life was ending, and with it his joy. And so, he said to Wiglaf, "My son, the dreaded dragon now lies still and slain, sleeping from its sore war-wounds and taken from its treasure-trove. And so, quick as the wind, go and gaze upon the hoard-heap of golden treasures that lies within the barrow and bring forth some of that wondrous wealth, for I would see that golden treasure and enjoy the jewels before I die. My winning of it may make it easier for me to give up my life and leave the land I have ruled for so long!"

So Beowulf spoke. And Wiglaf was swift to do his lord's bidding. Within the age-old earth-hall, the young warrior saw a bright wondrous banner, woven with golden threads. It hung high over the boundless barrow-hoard, and its light shone upon all the treasures heaped high upon the floor. And so Wiglaf saw many glittering jewels, shining golden objects fashioned by an age-old giant smith, arm-rings that had been woven with shrewd skill, and wondrous wall-hangings.

The young warrior found drinking-goblets and dishes, and jars and bowls, all from a by-gone age, and all now unpolished and stripped of their decorations, for they had rested in that barrow for a thousand winters, with no one to clean them. He found swords that had shone in a by-gone age, but had now been eaten through with rust, and he found many an age-old rust-eaten war-helmet. Such a treasure-trove can make mortals overly proud, arrogant, and greedy, try as they will to hide that fact.

Swift as a warrior's sword-stroke, Wiglaf filled the inside of his ring-meshed battle-shirt with wine-cups and platters, and he took that golden banner, the brightest of beacons. He wanted his beloved lord to look upon this treasure before Death, that dreaded destiny, took his life.

When Wiglaf returned his lord's side, Beowulf was blood-bathed and at his life's end. And so, the young warrior sprinkled water upon him to revive him.

Beowulf admired the gold. And then the dying king unlocked his last word-hoard. "I give thanks to the Eternal Lord, the King of Glory, and the Ruler of All, for He has permitted me to see these treasures and to gain this gold for the Geat-folk before I die. And I have paid for this precious wealth with my life."

"Though my death-wound pains me, Wiglaf, I leave life with a happy heart. For I have ruled the Geat-folk long and well. For fifty winters, I have been their shield, and fear of my battle-spear has kept all other folk-kings from invading Geat-land. I have killed no kin-folk, and I have kept well what a king should keep.

"Let my battle-famed war-comrades burn my body upon lofty Whale's-Cliff and let them build me a barrow there. Make that broad mound rise tower-tall to remind the Geat-folk of me and call it Beowulf's Barrow. It will stand upon the high head-land. And so, it will serve as a sign for sea-farers, as well, for they must sail their broad-beamed boats across the deep waters of the whale-road when mists have made their way dark."

"Now, I would give my war-garments and my battle-sword to a son born of my blood, but Wyrd did not give me that heir. And so, Wiglaf, you must lead the Geat-folk and look to their needs, for you are the last of my blood-kin, and you have earned all that is mine. So take my gold-twisted collar-ring. Take my war-helmet, with its battle-ready boars. And take my ring-meshed battle-shirt, for it was hand-linked and hand-joined by Weland, that far-famed master smith. And use them wisely and well as you rule the Geat-folk.

"Young and old, Wyrd wove the destiny of all our kin-folk and brought it upon them. And now, I, too, must take that last, lonely journey. I must follow."

So Beowulf spoke to Wiglaf, and these were the old war-king's last words. His cold corpse remained behind, but his spirit went forth to receive the reward of the good, the loyal, and the just.

Wiglaf's heart flooded with surging sea-swells of grief and sorrow as he looked upon the body of his bold-hearted lord and king, but he gazed with pleasure at the corpse of the savage fire-serpent that had slain him. That dreaded dragon, lying uncoiled in its fifty foot-lengths, had fallen, death-sick, upon the rock-shelf near the earth-hall entrance. Its scales had been scorched by its own furious flames, and it had died of its death-wounds, beaten in battle by the iron-edged blood-thirsting battle-blades of bold-hearted war-comrades.

And so, the dreaded dragon-king ruled no longer. Never again would the frightful hoard-guard hover over its treasure-trove beneath lofty Eagle's-Cliff. Or haunt the high stone-barrow upon that headland height. Or spread its great wings and fly over Geat-land, swooping down over the villages and farms of the Geat-folk and spewing forth a blazing torrent of furious flames.

Then Wiglaf returned to Beowulf's side, and he sprinkled his lord and king with water, hoping without hope to awaken him. And it came to pass that the ten trusted war-comrades, those battle-shy and fear-beaten oath-breakers, now left the shelter of the woods and came down the footpath that led to the earth-hall. And they gathered around the body of their fallen treasure-giving king. Shame-faced, they still wore their gleaming battle-shirts and carried their shining shields.

Wiglaf looked at his war-comrades. Among men, they had been most honored, but now, they were most loathsome. And so, the new king unlocked his hoard of angry words. "You left your king when your battle-skill could have saved him! Faced with that battle, you threw away his gift of war-gear and fled!" he declared.

"And now, you will suffer for it. For you and all your kin-folk must give up your birth-rights and your land-rights. You must give up your homes. You must give up your gifts of war-garments and battle-weapons. You must give up all your wealth and treasure. And you must leave Geat-land, now and for-ever.

"Know that, quick as the wind, your disloyal deed will fly forth before you, to lands near and far. And there, all high-born noble-men, having heard of your battle-flight, will drive you from their shores. And so, you will learn that Death is a far better destiny for a warrior than the wretched life of dishonor and disgrace."

So King Wiglaf spoke. And then he sent word of the battle to the shield-bearing band of noble-men, for they were waiting behind lofty Eagle's-Cliff, at the fort, to hear of Beowulf's death or the dragon's. And the news caused their hearts to flood with surging sea-swells of grief, sorrow, and fear, for with the death of their beloved war-king, the Geat-folk had lost their shield and their spear. And war would surely follow. Swift as a warrior's sword-stroke, the Franks and the Frisians would reach their shores and wage war, and the Swedes would renew their age-old feuds with the War-Geats.

Wiglaf then commanded all folk-leaders and warriors, house-holders and land-holders from near and far, to bring wood to lofty Whale's-Cliff for Beowulf's great funeral pyre. The Geat-folk constructed a great pyre. Then, around it, Beowulf's war-comrades placed splendid war-gear—gleaming ring-meshed battle-shirts; hard war-helmets, with their battle-ready boars, gold-glittering and stern; gold-rimmed linden-wood shields; iron-tipped ash-wood spears; and sharp-bladed battle-swords, blood-hardened and shining.

At last, King Wiglaf stood before the gathering of Geat-folk and unlocked a hoard of wise words. "Let us now burn our honored king with a trove of the dragon's gleaming gold, for Beowulf, our beloved ring-giver and battle-shield, bought that treasure with his life-blood. And so, let him enjoy the wondrous wealth that he won," he declared.

"Such treasure gives no lasting gladness to anyone. Now that our beloved king has left the world of laughter and joy, let none of the Geat-folk wear these treasures, for the dragon's wondrous wealth has brought only disaster. It has caused the death of our beloved Beowulf, our bold-hearted war-king.

"Now, without Beowulf, our battle-shield and safe-guard to protect us, we will be forced to raise our ash-wood spears and face the terrors of war. For, swift as a warrior's sword-stroke, foes from lands near and far will now invade our home-land. The dark raven will cry with craving over the corpses of our battle-weary war-comrades, and the wolf will slash away at the slain."

So Wiglaf spoke. And it came to pass that the new king led a band of seven war-comrades, the most respected high-born noble-men, down the foot-path to the earth-hall. Together they entered the barrow, for they sought the dragon's hoard-heap of golden treasures, which now lay unguarded upon the floor. They loaded this treasure-trove onto a wagon that would take it to the funeral pyre. Then they pushed the slain fire-serpent over the steep wall of the lower sea-cliff, and they watched as the surging sea-swell claimed it.

Then they carried the body of their bold-hearted war-king up to the pyre upon lofty Whale's-Cliff, and their hearts flooded with surging sea-swells of grief and sorrow as they laid their beloved lord upon it. They kindled the death-fires at the base of the funeral pyre. And as the dark wood-smoke soared high above the raging flames, the sounds of woeful weeping and wailing mixed with the roar of the fire.

And an old Geatish woman, with her hair bound up, wove a sorrowful song. It was a lament for her lost lord, and for herself, and for all the women-folk of Geat-land. Again and again, she sang of the enemy raids that would come and the terror of the bloodshed and slaughter of their men-folk. She sang of the ravage and ruin of their home-land and the captivity and shame of their women-folk.

In time, the blaze consumed Beowulf's bones. And so, all that was left of the far-famed Lord of Rings was a pile of ashes.

Then Wiglaf announced, "Let us listen to our beloved Beowulf's wishes. Around these ashes let us build, for our Lord of Rings, a barrow that will be as great as his fame."

So Wiglaf spoke. And so it came to pass that, upon lofty Whale's-Cliff, the Geat-folk built a tower-tall burial mound, with worthy walls that sea-farers could see from afar. And this barrow became to the sea-farers the beacon that Beowulf, their bold-hearted war-king, had been to the Geat-folk.

Within the barrow, the War-Geats buried the part of the dragon's treasure-trove that they had not burned with Beowulf. Good men had first found that gleaming gold within earth's rich body. And now, the Geat-folk returned earth's wealth to her.

Then twelve war-comrades, the most bold of heart and strong in strife among the War-Geats, rode around the barrow, and they gave Beowulf the honor and praise that is proper when a leader dies. They spoke of their sorrow, and they told tales of their far-famed king's bold heart, battle-skill, and strength in strife. And they spoke of the honor and glory he had won by doing deeds of daring and danger.

And so, Beowulf's kin-folk, his hearth-friends, his war-comrades, and all of the Geat-folk grieved for their Lord of Rings, for Beowulf had been the greatest of all kings. He had been the most gracious, the most gentle, and the most kind of men. And he had been the most eager to win praise.

❧ QUESTIONS FOR
Response, Discussion, and Analysis

1. Why does *Beowulf* begin and end with a funeral? What does this reveal about one of the themes of the myth?

2. Does Beowulf live in a time of peace or war? Support your answer with details.

3. In the *Beowulf* epic, the swords of heroes have names (such as Naegling or Hrunting), but the slaves remain anonymous. What does this reveal about the values of these people? What other heroes possess famous swords?

4. What purpose does Unferth's drunken welcoming speech serve? Does it matter that Unferth is also a hero? Explain. Consider Beowulf's response. Which speech is more important? Why?

5. Why does the *Beowulf* poet not describe the appearance of Grendel and his mother? Should he have done so? Why or why not?

6. Why does Beowulf permit Grendel to kill one of his warriors? Is his decision wise? Is it heroic? Why or why not? What would you have done? Why?

7. Why does the *Beowulf* poet make Grendel's mother stronger and more difficult to kill than her son? What effect does this have on Beowulf's heroism and the myth?

8. Why does Beowulf kill monsters instead of men? Consider the heroic effect of each option.

9. If Hrothgar had not honored Beowulf for killing Grendel, would Beowulf have killed Grendel's mother? Why or why not? Should a hero perform a second great deed if he has not been honored for the first one? Why or why not?

10. The Beowulf poet presents segments from Beowulf's life in his youth and as an old man. How did he decide which incidents to include and what to omit?

11. Compare Beowulf as a young man and as an old man. How is he the same? How has he changed?

12. Beowulf's relationship to Hrothgar in the first part of the epic is similar to Wiglaf's relationship to Beowulf in the second part. Explain. How is Beowulf different from Wiglaf as a young man and different from Hrothgar as an old man?

13. Why does Beowulf ignore the advice of his nobles and insist on fighting the dragon: (a) desire for glory? (b) fame? (c) wealth? (d) need to prove his courage? (e) strength? (f) heroism? (g) desire or need to protect his people? Is his decision wise? Why or why not?

14. Why does the *Beowulf* poet make Beowulf's men desert him? Does this enhance or detract from Beowulf's heroic image? Defend your view.

15. Why do Beowulf's men desert him when they know their responsibilities to their king and the punishment for shirking those responsibilities? What would you have done? Why?

16. Why does Beowulf die in his fight against the dragon: (a) his age? (b) his fear of death? (c) his lack of self-confidence? (d) his poor weapons? (e) his poor judgment? Discuss the possible role of each in the outcome of the battle.

17. How does Beowulf's attitude toward death change as he ages? Why? Does his attitude affect his battle against each of the three monsters? If so, how? Does his fear enhance or detract from his heroic image?

18. What kind of person is Beowulf? What tests of character confront him? To what extent does he pass them? Which temptations does he resist, and which does he find irresistible? Why? How does his behavior affect his heroic image?

19. What is the Beowulf poet's attitude toward gold? Explain whether wealth is good or evil.

20. How does the *Beowulf* poet use light and darkness as symbols of good and evil? Find examples to support your point of view.

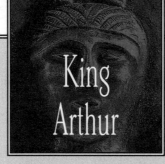

HISTORICAL BACKGROUND

Tales of King Arthur, the great legendary hero of Britain, have been popular for more than eight hundred years, but scholars have been unable to learn much about the real Arthur, since no contemporary accounts of his deeds exist. Some scholars think the real Arthur was probably a Welsh cavalry general named Artorius, who led twelve successful attacks against the invading Saxons between A.D. 500 and 517.

In 1985, however, Geoffrey Ashe, a prominent Arthur scholar, published evidence that challenges the traditional understanding of King Arthur's historical identity. Ashe bases his view upon the writings of Jordanes (sixth century), William (eleventh century), Geoffrey of Monmouth (twelfth century), and on a letter from a Roman aristocrat to a fifth-century British king called Riothamus (High King) who was then in Gaul (France). Ashe identifies Arthur with Riothamus, thereby placing the reign of King Arthur from A.D. 454 to 470 and including in it a British military campaign in Gaul in the late 460s. Geoffrey of Monmouth's description of Arthur's military exploits in Gaul have usually been regarded as fiction, but Riothamus actually led an army of 12,000 men into Gaul, where he fought courageously but unsuccessfully against the Goths in Burgundy. Moreover, like Arthur, he was betrayed by one of his associates, and he probably retreated by way of a French town that is still called Avallon.

Whatever his accomplishments, the real Arthur was such an appealing figure, both in his own day and in the years that followed, that an oral tradition of Welsh folklore became associated with his name. The earlier references to Arthur are found in Nennius' *Historia Brittonum* (c. 800) and William of Malmesbury's *Gesta Regum Anglorum* (c. 1125).

Arthur first appears in literature as Britain's major national hero in Geoffrey of Monmouth's *Historia Regum Britanniae* (*History of the Kings of Britain*), written in Latin in 1136. Arthur was already a popular subject in the oral tradition of Wales when Geoffrey recognized the need for a book about the history of Britain. He chose to make Arthur the major figure in his history, which covers the 1,900-year period from 1200 B.C. to A.D. 689.

Although Geoffrey cites sources for his material, scholars believe that he created fictitious sources in order to legitimize his use of folklore and his own imagination. His work must therefore be considered primarily literature rather than history.

To Geoffrey we owe the creation of Arthur as the great British king who conquered all of the British Isles and most of Europe as well. In Geoffrey's version Arthur would have conquered Rome also, had he not been called home to fight his nephew, who had taken over the kingdom in his absence. Geoffrey also introduces the world to Arthur's unusual birth and death; Guinevere, his beautiful, unfaithful wife; Merlin, the magician; and the concept of chivalry. Geoffrey was most interested in Arthur as a military leader, but he included just enough about Merlin, Guinevere, magic, and chivalry to inspire other writers to deal with them in greater depth.

Geoffrey's history is so well written that it was popular not only in his own day but with succeeding generations as well. The poet Wace freely translated Geoffrey's history into Norman-French verse in 1155. He concentrated on the Arthurian material, used additional sources, and added a more courtly flavor to the work. It is Wace who mentions the Round Table for the first time.

After the appearance of Wace's poem, Chretien de Troyes wrote five romances set in King Arthur's court. Being French, Chretien had little interest in Arthur as the national hero of Britain or as the conquering king. Instead, he wrote of the world of chivalry, where King Arthur reigns over a court of knights who are heroes and lovers. He introduced the idea of courtly love, in which the woman is superior to the man and the lover is completely obedient to the wishes of his lady. In his *Lancelot,* the love between Lancelot and Guinevere appears for the first time. Chretien was such a good storyteller that his romances were widely read and imitated.

King Arthur finally appeared in the English language when the poet Layamon freely translated Wace's poem into early Middle English in 1205. Layamon added more details to Wace's story and gave it a decidedly English flavor by emphasizing Arthur's courage and his love of adventure. Like Geoffrey of Monmouth, Layamon was patriotic, so he chose to ignore Chretien's romantic version of the Arthur story.

Still another version of the King Arthur story, *Morte Arthure,* appeared in English in the middle of the fourteenth century. Again the focus was nationalistic, with the proud warrior-king, Arthur, presented as a great hero in battle. The author had no interest in love, chivalry, or a court of knights. Sir Gawain is Arthur's principal knight, and Lancelot has only a minor role. This presentation resembles the French epic *Chanson de Roland* and the Anglo-Saxon epic *Beowulf.*

Many years later, in 1485, Sir Thomas Malory published what became the definitive story of King Arthur, *Le Morte D'Arthur.* He combined the English tradition of Geoffrey of Monmouth with the French tradition of Chretien de Troyes. In Malory's version Arthur becomes one of the world's greatest rulers, the equal of Alexander the Great. He does not return to England until he has been crowned emperor in Rome. Malory takes Mordred's treachery and Guinevere's infidelity from Geoffrey, but he combines it with the love affair of Guinevere and Lancelot. In addition, he broadens the picture of Arthur's court by presenting a number of tales about Arthur's principal knights. In this romantic version of English history, the collapse of the Round Table brings tragedy into a number of lives and marks the end of a Golden Age.

APPEAL AND VALUE

The story of King Arthur has appealed to writers and readers for hundreds of years because it is so complex and varied. Something in the story is likely to appeal to almost every taste. Unlike most of the major epics, the story has a broad focus and contains a large cast of important characters. Whether the reader is interested in adventure, magic, chivalry, courtly love, or a great and tragic love story, *Le Morte D'Arthur* is the book to read.

Readers who are familiar with the basic version of the King Arthur legend will find many modern versions of great interest, because the focus of each is different. Enjoyable nineteenth-century versions include Mark Twain's *A Connecticut Yankee in King Arthur's Court* and Alfred, Lord Tennyson's *Idylls of the King.* Writers in the twentieth century continue to be fascinated with the Arthurian legend. John Steinbeck, T. H. White, and Mary Stewart are among the writers who have carried on the tradition. Some versions simply retell the tale from the point of view of one of the major characters—such as King Arthur, Lancelot, Guinevere, Mordred, or Merlin. Some of the modern versions have been written with a historical focus, some with a comic focus, and some with a feminist focus.

The theme of the conflict between personal desires and responsibility to others is common to many ancient epics, yet it is as contemporary as the decisions we must make in our own lives. Readers today can still understand and sympathize with the conflicts Arthur, Lancelot, and Guinevere face.

loved. He was also expected to be courteous and gentle, particularly in the presence of ladies. In addition, he was expected to be courageous at all times, whether fighting for his lord in a battle, participating in a contest or tournament, or helping friends or ladies in distress. Finally, he was expected to be a man of honor, to live in such a way that the other members of the nobility held him in high esteem. The challenge was to balance these different values with a minimum of conflict.

It is important to understand that courtly love was often extramarital love. In the society that Chretien and Malory depicted in literature, and in the real world as well, marriages among the nobility were arranged by the young couple's family or by the ruling lord for political, social, or economic reasons. The participants' feelings were not considered, and divorce did not exist. Therefore, it was not unusual for a married person to find love outside the marriage relationship.

THE ARTHURIAN HERO

The principal characters in *Le Morte D'Arthur* are heroic aristocrats. In the age of chivalry, only a man born to the nobility could become a knight. As a young page he learned how to behave at court, and later, as a squire, he learned the necessary martial skills. By his teens, a young man was well on his way to knighthood.

When a man became a knight, he took an oath that obligated him to live according to certain values. He was expected to be loyal to the king, to his relatives and friends, and to the lady he

PRINCIPAL CHARACTERS

BRUTUS: great-grandson of Aeneas; leads Trojan exiles to Britain and establishes a kingdom

AURELIUS AMBROSIAS: son of King Constantine; older brother of Uther Pendragon; king of Britain; creates Stonehenge

UTHER PENDRAGON: son of King Constantine; younger brother of Aurelius Ambrosias; king of Britain; husband of Igraine; father of Arthur

IGRAINE: wife of the Duke of Cornwall; later, wife of Uther Pendragon and queen of Britain; mother of Arthur and Margawse

ARTHUR: son of Uther Pendragon and Igraine; husband of Guinevere; father of Mordred; king of Britain; established the knights of the Round Table

ECTOR: foster father of Arthur

KAY: son of Ector; foster brother of Arthur; knight of the Round Table

GUINEVERE: daughter of King Leodegrance; wife of Arthur; queen of Britain

MERLIN: great magician and prophet; adviser to three British kings: Ambrosias Aurelius, Uther Pendragon, and Arthur

LUCIUS HIBERIUS: mythological emperor of the Roman Empire until Arthur defeats and replaces him

MARGAWSE: daughter of Duke of Cornwall and Igraine; half-sister of Arthur; wife of King Lot of Orkney; mother of Mordred by Arthur; mother of Gawain, Agravain, Gaheris, and Gareth by Lot

MORDRED: son of Arthur and his half-sister Margawse; stepbrother of Gawain and Agravain; knight of the Round Table

GAWAIN: nephew of Arthur and one of his two favorite knights; son of Margawse and King Lot of Orkney; brother of Agravain, Gaheris, and Gareth; stepbrother of Mordred; second greatest knight of the Round Table

AGRAVAIN: son of Margawse and King Lot; brother of Gawain, Gaheris, and Gareth; stepbrother and friend of Mordred; knight of the Round Table

GAHERIS: son of Margawse and King Lot; brother of Gawain, Agravain, and Gareth; knight of the Round Table

GARETH: son of Margawse and King Lot; brother of Gawain, Agravain, and Gaheris; knight of the Round Table

LANCELOT: son of King Ban of Benwick; greatest knight of the Round Table; one of Arthur's two favorite knights; champion of Guinevere and her favorite knight

BORS: son of King Bors of Gaul; nephew of Lancelot; knight of the Round Table

PELLINOR: knight of the Round Table

BEDIVERE: knight of the Round Table; last knight to see Arthur alive

KING ARTHUR

Prologue

Brutus, great-grandson of Aeneas, leads a group of Trojan exiles to establish a second Troy on an island north of Gaul (France). He names the island Britain, after himself.

At the conclusion of the Trojan War, Aeneas fled from his flaming city with his father, his son Ascanius, and some of his people. His destiny led him by ship to Italy, where he established a new nation. After the death of Aeneas, Ascanius became king. He founded the town of Alba on the Tiber River, and became the father of Silvius. Silvius, in turn, became the father of Brutus. Seers prophesied that Brutus would cause the death of both of his parents, would therefore be banished from Italy, and would wander homeless through many lands, until finally he would settle in Britain, where he would become highly honored.

The prophecy proved correct. Brutus's mother died during his birth. When he was fifteen, he killed his father in a hunting accident, and his relatives banished him from Italian soil.

He first sought refuge in Greece, among people who were descendants of Priam, king of the Trojans. Brutus's courage and wisdom enabled him to free those Trojans from the tyranny of local Greek rule. He surprised the Greeks with a night attack, and the Trojans slaughtered the Greeks like wolves attacking slumbering sheep. Brutus married the daughter of the local king he had conquered and then sailed away with the Trojans for another land.

They came to an island that had been deserted for many years. Investigating an abandoned city, Brutus found a temple of Diana, goddess of the hunt, and offered sacrifices to her. "Oh mighty goddess, both terror and hope of the wild woodlands," he prayed, "tell me where we can safely settle and worship you throughout the years to come."

When he lay down to sleep that night, Diana appeared before him and said, "Brutus, far beyond the setting of the sun, past Gaul, you will find an island in the sea that was once inhabited by a race of giants. This land will suit you and your people for years to come. It will be a second Troy for all those who come after you. There from your blood a race of kings will be born, and the whole earth will kneel before them."

When he awoke, a fair wind was blowing. Brutus took this as another sign from the goddess, and he and his people immediately resumed their journey. They sailed up the coast of Africa, past the pillars of Hercules at the western end of the Mediterranean Sea. There they escaped from the sea monsters known as the Sirens, who almost sank their ships.

Brutus and his companions then came upon another group of Trojan exiles. The two groups decided to join together and share a common future. The Trojans, who were now formidable, fought their way through Gaul acquiring wealth. Finally they returned to the coast and set sail for the island Diana had revealed to Brutus in his dream.

When the Trojans landed, they found that the island was uninhabited except for a few giants, whom they killed. They saw that they would thrive here, for the soil was fertile, wild animals lived in the forests, and numerous fish swam in the many rivers. Under Brutus's direction, the Trojans divided up the land, built houses, and began to farm.

Brutus searched the island for the best location for a capital city. He decided to build it along the Thames River, and he called it Troia Nova (New Troy). He named the island after himself: It became Britain, and Brutus and his companions were called Britons. Brutus gave the city of Troia Nova to his people, and he also gave them a code of laws to help them live in peace with one another.

However, many years of civil wars and invasions followed Brutus's death, including the conquest of Britain by the Romans. After the Romans were called back to defend Rome in about A.D. 400, the Britons had to depend upon their own meager resources for defense against barbarians. Seeking more land, the Teutonic tribes had already moved into Gaul, leaving the Britons isolated on their island. Early in the fifth century the Saxons, along with the Angles and the Jutes, invaded and conquered Britain. King Constantine was the first king of Britain who was able to defeat them. His sons, Aurelius Ambrosias and Uther Pendragon, ruled Britain during the period when the Saxons were their principal adversaries.

Chapter 1

When Arthur is fifteen years old, a sword in a stone miraculously appears in the churchyard in London. Upon the stone is written: "Whoever pulls out this sword is the lawfully born king of Britain." Unaware of its meaning, Arthur pulls out the sword and learns that he will be king.

With the death of Uther Pendragon, the kingdom of Britain fell into a period of great danger, both from without and within. Every noble Briton who had the support of an army of loyal followers wished to become the next king. Meanwhile, other nations wished to invade Britain and establish settlements upon its rich soil. Unless a leader could emerge who was strong enough to unite the independent dukes and rally them to defend their land, Britain was certain to be consumed, bite by bite, by foreigners.

The great enchanter Merlin recognized this danger. He advised the Archbishop of Canterbury to summon all of the nobles to London at Christmastime, when the rightful king of Britain would be revealed to the world.

From all parts of the British Isles, nobles and their loyal supporters crowded into the city of London. They all attended the first mass. When they left the cathedral, they were amazed to see that a huge, square, marble stone had miraculously appeared in the churchyard. An iron anvil protruded from this stone, and plunged into the anvil was a beautiful, unsheathed sword. When the nobles excitedly gathered around the sword, they found written in gold letters: "Whoever pulls out this sword from this stone and anvil is the lawfully born king of all Britain."

Many proud knights immediately tried to remove the sword, but none could budge it, so securely lodged was it within the stone and anvil.

"The rightful king of Britain is apparently not with us," announced the archbishop, "but be assured that God will make him known to us at the proper time. Let us gather here on New Year's Day and let all the knights of the kingdom mount their horses and participate in a tournament to reveal their skill with the sword and the spear. Afterwards, whoever wishes may try to withdraw the sword from this stone and anvil."

The archbishop commanded that a tent be placed over the marble block containing the sword. He ordered ten of the most honorable knights to keep a constant watch over the sword, five throughout each day and five throughout each night.

On New Year's Day, Sir Ector, accompanied by his son, Sir Kay, and his foster son, Arthur, prepared to participate in the tournament. Kay had recently become a knight, and Arthur, being only fifteen years old, was his squire.

Arthur watched with admiration as Sir Kay fought courageously and skillfully in the tournament. Suddenly, however, a strong stroke by another knight shattered his sword. "Do me a favor, Arthur!" he cried. "Ride back to the tent and bring me another sword. Hurry, for I do not want to lose my place in the contests!"

Although Arthur searched everywhere in the tent, he could not find another sword. He said to himself, "I know—I will ride into the churchyard and take the sword that is lodged in that stone. Kay will just have to manage with that one!"

When he arrived, the churchyard was deserted, for even those who were supposed to be guarding the sword in the stone had gone off to participate in the tournament. Arthur dismounted, walked up to the stone, grasped the hilt of the sword in his right hand, and easily withdrew it from the anvil.

Thinking little of his accomplishment, Arthur returned to his brother, handed him the sword, and said, "I could not find a sword back at the tent. Use this one!" Sir Kay immediately recognized the sword as the one that had miraculously appeared in the churchyard. Since he was older and stronger than Arthur, he assumed that he could certainly do whatever his younger brother could do. He said to Arthur, "Tell no one that you found this sword, and I promise that you will become very rich! Now, let us ride over to Father.

"Father!" Kay exclaimed to Sir Ector. "Look! I have drawn this sword from the stone! Therefore, I must be the lawful king of Britain!"

Ector replied, "That may be, Kay, but be certain that your words are more than an empty boast. Let us return to the churchyard. If you are telling the truth, you are indeed the rightful king of this land. But first you will have to prove it by thrusting this sword back into the stone and drawing it free again. If you could do it once, then surely you can do it again. If you cannot, then you will shame yourself before every nobleman in London, for they too will demand proof of your right to kingship!"

Back at the churchyard Sir Kay replaced the sword, but no matter how hard he tried, he could not pull it out again. In the cathedral, Sir Ector commanded Kay, "Place your hand upon this holy Bible and swear that you will tell me truthfully how you came to possess this sword!"

"Sir, the truth is that Arthur brought it to me," Kay replied humbly.

"Yes," Ector responded, "that I can believe. Now, Arthur, how did you acquire this sword?"

Arthur explained, "During one of the contests, Kay's sword broke, so he asked me to get him another one from the tent. When I arrived, I could find no sword, no matter how carefully I searched. Fortunately, I remembered the sword in the stone. I knew how important it was for Kay to have a sword, so I rode over here and took it for him! It was easy—when I put my hand on the hilt and pulled, the sword simply slid from the anvil!"

"Were there no knights here as you did this?" Sir Ector inquired.

"No one was here. They must all have gone to the tournament."

"Arthur," Ector said. "Have you any idea what you have done? You are telling me that you are the rightful king of Britain!"

"Why do you say such a thing?" Arthur asked. "It does not make any sense, and it cannot be true!"

"Sir," Ector respectfully answered his foster son, "you are the rightful king of Britain because God has chosen you for this highest of honors. Only the rightful king of this land could have drawn this sword out of its stone. Now, let me watch you return the sword to its place in the anvil and then withdraw it once again."

"It is a simple task," said Arthur. He replaced the sword in the stone, drew it out, and returned it.

Sir Ector then tried to pull out the sword. But no matter how hard he tried, the sword would not budge. It stuck fast in its marble block.

"Now, you try it again!" Ector commanded Kay.

Sir Kay tried with all his might to pull out the sword, but he could not budge it either.

When Arthur easily withdrew the sword once again, Sir Ector and Sir Kay immediately knelt before him.

"Oh, no!" Arthur cried. "Dear Father and Brother, you have no reason to kneel before me. I am no king of Britain. I am your son!" he said to Ector. "And I am your brother!" he said to Kay.

"No, Arthur, I am not your father. In fact, I am not related to you at all. When you were just an infant, the great enchanter Merlin arrived at our home one night bearing you in his arms. He never told me whose child you were, but he commanded me to rear you as my own son, and so I have."

These words filled Arthur with great sadness. "You have suddenly made me feel all alone," he said to Sir Ector. "I feel as if I have lost my father, and my mother, and my brother! You are the only family I have ever known. You are the ones I love most in the world. I do not know how to be the king of Britain!"

"You have not lost us, Arthur. We will love you as we always have! Think instead about what it is that makes a good king. I am certain Merlin will reappear to advise you."

The next morning Sir Ector gave Arthur armor and weapons and conferred knighthood upon him. Then he sent him off to the tournament. All that day Arthur showed his courage and his skill in many contests, and he earned great honor and praise.

On the following day, Sir Ector went to the archbishop and said, "I know a young knight who is noble, valiant, and well skilled in the use of weapons. He will be king of Britain according to the law, for he can draw the sword forth from the stone in the churchyard."

The archbishop replied, "Bring him here, and I will summon all of the nobles."

When everyone had arrived, all of the nobles in turn tried to pull out the sword, but not one of them could budge it. When they watched Arthur easily accomplish what no mighty effort of theirs could do, they were ashamed and angry. "It is ridiculous that a mere boy should have the right to rule over all of us!" they exclaimed.

The archbishop decided to postpone the decision of kingship until the next holiday, and the knights continued to watch over the sword in the marble stone. At that time, more dukes and barons gathered, and all were given the chance to try to withdraw the sword. Again only Arthur could perform the deed, but the nobles still were not satisfied.

Easter arrived, and the archbishop repeated the contest. Once again only Arthur could remove the sword from the stone, but the nobles still were not satisfied. The archbishop agreed to postpone the decision one more time. The following holiday, everyone was again given the opportunity to pull upon the sword, but no one was able to budge it. Arthur then performed the task as easily as he had before.

This time when Arthur held the sword in his hand, both the common folk and the nobles knelt at his feet and exclaimed, "We will have Arthur as our king, for it is God's will that he rule us!" "And," many added, "we will kill anyone who tries to prevent Arthur's reign!"

Arthur then knelt before the archbishop. Holding one end of the sword in each hand, he raised his arms and offered the sword upon the altar. He took the oath of kingship, promising to be true to both the common people and the nobility and swearing to reign justly all the days of his life. Then he listened to the complaints of his subjects and restored property to those from whom it had unjustly been taken.

As the people left the cathedral, they passed the place where the stone had been and noticed that it was no longer there. It had disappeared as miraculously as it had appeared.

Shortly thereafter, Arthur held a great feast in the city of Caerleon, in Wales. The dukes of northern Britain, Scotland, Ireland, and Wales, accompanied by their attendant knights, were present, but they would accept no gifts of friendship from the new king. Instead they told Arthur's messengers, "We will accept no gifts from a beardless boy! We will give him appropriate gifts of our own choosing— our swords plunged into his heart! It is shameful to see such a noble land as this ruled by an ordinary boy!"

Arthur's barons advised their king that his life was truly in danger. He chose 500 soldiers and retreated to a strong, well-provisioned castle, to which the hostile nobles promptly laid siege. Arthur and his men had been imprisoned there for two weeks when Merlin arrived in Caerleon.

The nobles greeted Merlin warmly and asked him, "Why has that boy been made king of Britain?"

"Sirs," Merlin replied, "his blood is more noble that your own! Arthur is King Uther Pendragon's son, born in wedlock to Igraine, the Duke of Cornwall's wife."

"Then Arthur is a bastard!" they all exclaimed.

"Not so!" Merlin replied. "Arthur was conceived more than three hours after the Duke of Cornwall died, and King Uther married Igraine soon thereafter. This is ample proof that Arthur is not a bastard. Indeed, Arthur will long be king of Britain, and he will rule many other countries as well!"

Not all of the nobles took Merlin's words seriously. Some laughed derisively, and others called him a witch. However, they did agree to let Arthur come out and speak with them.

Merlin entered the castle and said to Arthur, "Many nobles have gathered outside and would speak with you. Appear before them without fear in your heart. Answer their questions as their chief and their king, for you are destined to overpower all of them, no matter what harm they hope to bring upon you. But let me tell you something about your parents and your country before you face them. Knowledge will fortify your heart."

Chapter 2

Merlin explains to Arthur the circumstances surrounding his birth. He tells Arthur about his uncle, Aurelius Ambrosius, and his father, Uther Pendragon, each of whom reigned as king of Britain.

"Arthur," Merlin began, "I will start with the tale of your birth."

In the days when Uther Pendragon was king of all Britain, he fought long and hard against the Saxon invaders. The Duke of Cornwall, an old man of great experience in warfare, had aided Uther in these wars. When the king held a great feast in London, he invited the Duke of Cornwall and his wife, Igraine.

Igraine's reputation had preceded her arrival. She was the most beautiful woman in Britain, and she was as good as she was beautiful. It was not surprising that King Uther fell in love with the duke's wife at the banquet. Ignoring his other guests, the king repeatedly sent his servants to her bearing plates of food and golden goblets of wine. Meanwhile, he kept smiling at her and engaging her in conversation. He could not keep his eyes from her, and he showed her as much as he dared of his love.

His attentions did not escape the notice of the Duke of Cornwall, who decided that he owed no allegiance to a king who would tempt his wife. Without a word the duke rose from the table, took Igraine by the hand, and left the hall. No one could convince the duke to return; even the king's orders did not persuade him, so precious to him was his wife.

The duke returned to Cornwall, where he confined his wife under guard in the castle of Tintagel. Uther became determined to make love to Igraine. Since the fortress was surrounded on all sides by the sea, except for a narrow, rocky pathway to its entrance, Uther asked my help to achieve his goal.

When I saw the depths of the king's passion and the intensity of his resolve, I said, "Sir, I will see to it that you have your wish, for it is destined that Igraine will bear you a son. This son will become the most marvelous king of Britain. He will live to the end of eternity, for people will remember his glory as long as the world exists. All who live in Britain will kneel at his feet. Bards will sing of his adventures, and poets will take inspiration from his deeds. The strongest and bravest will seek his company, for his spirit will live within them as well. Stone walls will crumble before his attack. Dukes and barons will retreat into submission. He and his knights will conquer many peoples in many lands, some far across the sea, and all will live in peace under his laws.

"However, for you to win Igraine, I will have to use magic. Even the strongest of men will never be able to storm the strong, high walls of Tintagel Castle. Enough food is stored within the fortress that a siege will be useless. Moreover, Igraine is so closely guarded that access to her is hopeless. And even if you were able to reach her, you could only despair, for there is no woman more loyal to her husband than Igraine is to the Duke of Cornwall.

"Therefore," I explained, "I will use my drugs to give you the appearance of the duke in every respect. Your face, your body, your speech, your deeds, your clothing, even your horse will duplicate those of Igraine's husband. I will change my appearance and that of your friend Ulfius to resemble the duke's closest companions. We will all be able to enter the castle without suspicion, for no one will doubt our identity." This was my advice to Uther, your father.

So it came to pass that Uther Pendragon dined with Igraine in Tintagel Castle and spent the night with her. Given his appearance and his conversation, Igraine never knew that her companion was not her husband. The real duke was killed in battle that day, and later that evening you were conceived.

When the duke's men arrived in the morning bearing the news of their lord's death, they found Uther with Igraine. Uther convinced them that he was the duke, and that he was indeed alive and well. He said he intended to leave immediately to summon additional troops, for Tintagel Castle was in danger of attack from King Uther Pendragon. Once the three of us were safely outside, we resumed our proper shapes.

Uther mourned the death of the duke while he rejoiced in Igraine's freedom. He returned to Tintagel, conquered the castle without bloodshed, and married Igraine. In time Igraine gave birth to you, and two years later Uther died. He and your mother loved each other dearly and were true to one another.

When Igraine was about to give birth to you, Uther asked her whose child she was carrying. "Tell me truthfully," the king said, "and I will love you all the more for it." Igraine explained that she had treated a stranger as if he were her husband because he appeared in all respects to be the Duke of Cornwall. Uther laughed and replied, "All that you say is indeed true, for it was I who came to you in the shape of the duke, and it is I who am the father of your child!" Igraine's heart filled with joy, for she was relieved and happy to know and to love the father of her child.

Shortly before you were born, I said to the king, "It is not safe for your child to live with you; as the heir to the throne of Britain, he will have many enemies. I know a lord who is loyal and good, Sir Ector by name. Let his wife nourish your baby as a foundling. Deliver him to me at the back gate before he is christened."

The elves themselves were present at your birth. They enchanted you with their strongest magic and presented you with special gifts. They gave you the courage and the strength to be the the best of all knights. They gave you the intelligence to become a mighty king, combined with the generosity that would bring you lasting devotion and fame. And finally they gave you the gift of a long life.

The king commanded your mother to wrap you in a golden blanket and have two of her ladies in waiting, accompanied by two knights, bring you out to me. I appeared in the guise of a poor man, so no one recognized me. I brought you to Sir Ector and had you christened by a holy man. And that is how you came to be reared in the home of Sir Ector.

Your father is buried beside his brother, Aurelius Ambrosius, inside the Giants' Ring at Stonehenge. I will tell you of how Aurelius and I came to build that ring. King Aurelius wished to construct a memorial structure that would honor the many noble leaders who had fallen to the Saxons and were buried near Salisbury. Because of my fame as a prophet and as a builder, the Archbishop of Canterbury suggested that he send for me.

I received a royal welcome! Aurelius came forth to meet me, accompanied by many knights. I told him, "If you want to erect a lasting and awesome monument upon the burial site of these patriots, then send for the Giants' Ring in Ireland. That structure is of stone, and there is not another like it throughout the wide world. The stones that form that mighty circle are so enormous and so heavy that no ordinary man, no matter how strong, will ever be able to move them."

Aurelius simply laughed in my face. "Merlin," he asked, "if those stones are beyond the ability of any man to move, then how do you expect my stonemasons to move them? And why would you ever want to move stones from Ireland to Britain? Can't we find large enough stones in our own land?"

"First of all," I replied, "it will take skill and talent, rather than strength, to move those stones, for they are not ordinary stones. Long ago, when the giants lived in Ireland, they brought those stones from Africa because they possessed certain religious and medicinal properties. Whenever a giant became ill, he or she would bathe at the foot of those stones and would become well. No other medicine was needed.

"Knowledge and skill are better than might," I concluded. "So assemble an army and I will accompany them to Ireland. You will honor the burial place with the memorial you wish, and you yourself will be buried there when your life comes to an end."

My explanation convinced Aurelius, so he sent your father and 15,000 knights with me to Ireland to transport those stones to Britain. The Irish met us with an army of their own. Their king could not believe the reason for our invasion. "It is no wonder that the Saxons could invade the island of Britain!" he exclaimed. "The Britons must indeed be fools if they believe that our stones are better than their own! Who in his right mind would cross the sea and invade a country for so poor a treasure? However, they will not remove one stone from the Giants' Ring! We will teach them how foolish it is to love stones, by causing their blood to flow upon Irish soil!"

We did meet the Irish in armed conflict, but they were a peaceful people and did not wear armor. Their fields welcomed their own blood rather than ours. More than 7,000 Irishmen fell there!

When our men had removed their armor and rested from the battle, I led them to the Giants' Ring. Your father and his knights were awestruck by it. "Only Giants could have arranged these stones and placed them upon one another!" they exclaimed.

"Knights," I said, "you are champions! See if you are strong enough to transport these stones to our ships!"

But 15,000 strong men, using sail ropes and pushing and pulling together, could not budge the stones. I said to them, "Withdraw from the circle, and watch me. I will prove to you that knowledge and skill are far more valuable than physical strength. Do not approach the stones again until I advise you to do so."

I entered the Giants' Ring and walked around the stones. Three times I walked around the ring, both within and without, silently speaking to the stones as I passed them. When I had finished, I said to the men, "Now, enter the ring and move the stones. The rocks will be as pebbles in your hands, and you can transport them to your ships with little effort!" And it was so.

Once we arrived back in Britain, Aurelius summoned clergy and Britons, both rich and poor, from all over the kingdom, to the burial-place near Salisbury. After the Archbishop of Canterbury rededicated the burial-place, I arranged the stones in their proper order so that they formed a circle as they had on Irish soil. The monument became known as Stonehenge.

Not long thereafter, the King was poisoned to death. That night your father, miles away from Aurelius, saw in the heavens a huge star of extraordinary brilliance. A single beam extended from the star, ending in a ball of fire that spread out in the shape of a dragon. Two rays of light shone from the dragon's mouth. One pointed in the direction of Gaul, and the other divided into seven smaller rays and pointed toward the Irish Sea. Three times this wondrous star appeared in the heavens!

Like everyone else, Uther was terrified by this strange sign, and he sent for me. "Merlin, dear friend, prove your wisdom and tell me what I have seen and what it means!"

At first I sat as in a dream. When I awoke and stopped trembling, I said, "Sorrow has befallen our land! Aurelius Ambrosius, the noblest of kings, is dead! Of all your noble family, Uther, you alone remain alive. You will become a good king, but first you must march against the Saxons. The star revealed your brother's death. The fiery dragon beneath it represented you, Uther. You will conquer the Saxon invaders and become king of all Britain.

"The ray of light that pointed toward Gaul represented the son that you will have (you, Arthur!). Your son will become a powerful king and will rule over all of the kingdoms that the beam shone upon. The ray of light that pointed toward the Irish Sea represented the stepdaughter you will have, who will be very dear to you. The seven bands within her ray represent her seven sons and grandsons who will be kings of Britain after your son has died." Thus I prophesied to your father the events of years to come.

After Uther had succeeded in killing many of the barbarous Saxon hordes, he held an elaborate funeral ceremony for Aurelius at Stonehenge. The great king was buried within the Giants' Ring that he had brought to Britain.

Your father was then crowned king of Britain. He was a good king. He upheld good laws and loved his subjects. He became known as Uther Pendragon (head war-leader) because the dragon he had seen with the star signified his kingship. When Uther and his men faced the last of the Saxon leaders, they set upon the Saxons in a surprise night attack and captured their two chieftains. With that victory your father, Uther Pendragon, finally put an end to Saxon terror in Britain.

"And that brings my story back to the point at which I began," Merlin concluded. "Now you know what you need to know in order to feel confident. You come from a family of honored kings, and you yourself will be an even greater king. Go forth and face the dukes of northern Britain, Scotland, Ireland, and Wales with courage in your heart. In time they will kneel before you and will fight at your side."

Chapter 3

Merlin foresees that Arthur's illegitimate son, Mordred, will kill Arthur. The Lady of the Lake gives Arthur her sword, Excalibur. Arthur marries Guinevere, even though Merlin foresees that she and Sir Lancelot will love each other more than they will love Arthur.

King Arthur was a born leader. Despite his youth, he possessed the qualities necessary in the best of knights: strength, courage, and skill. He also possessed the qualities necessary in the best of kings. He met arrogance with self-confidence and pride, yet treated the weak and poor with sympathy and understanding. He was a father to the young and a comfort to the old. He was strict with those who acted unwisely or unlawfully, yet he was generous and courteous to all. He used his wisdom, his strength, and his treasure to improve the lives of his people. His subjects loved him. His kingdom brought him fame from the early days of his reign, and he towered above the other kings of his time.

However, many powerful dukes and barons resisted King Arthur's effort to unify Britain. He had to conquer the outlying parts of his kingdom by force of arms. With Merlin to advise him, King Arthur spent the first years of his reign subduing the dukes of northern Britain, Scotland, Ireland, and Wales. He sailed to Iceland and added that island to his kingdom.

During this time, he met and loved Queen Margawse, the wife of King Lot of Orkney. Only later did Merlin reveal that she was Arthur's half-sister. "God is angry with you, for you have slept with your sister, and she has given birth to your son, who will destroy you and all of the knights of your kingdom. It is your destiny to die in battle against him as punishment for your foul deed."

Merlin advised King Arthur to save his life by collecting and secretly killing all the male children of noble blood who had been born on the day Margawse gave birth. Given the penalty of death for withholding such a child, many infants arrived at King Arthur's court. He put them all into a small boat and sent it out to sea. He expected that the infants would drown, or if by chance the boat remained afloat, that they would surely die of exposure or starvation.

The small boat crashed on the rocks by a castle and broke apart. Unknown to Merlin and Arthur, Arthur's son survived the catastrophe and was rescued by a good man, who named him Mordred and reared him to the age of fourteen. Then Mordred returned to the household of his mother and King Lot, where he trained with their four sons to become a knight. Arthur always believed that Mordred was one of his nephews.

When King Arthur's subjects learned of their children's deaths, they were outraged. Many blamed Merlin.

One day soon thereafter, Arthur was riding in the forest when he saw three peasants pursuing Merlin. Arthur forced the peasants to flee and said to Merlin, "You would have been killed if I had not happened to ride by and save you!"

"You are wrong," Merlin replied. "I could have saved myself. You are the one who is riding toward your death, for God is not your friend!"

The two friends came to an armed knight sitting in a chair by a fountain. "I challenge any knight who comes this way to a duel," the knight announced, "and so I challenge you!"

"So be it!" King Arthur replied.

The two men fought fiercely on horseback, breaking their spears to splinters upon one another's shields. When King Arthur reached for his sword, the knight said, "It is better if we continue to fight with spears. My squire will supply us with two good ones."

The two fought on with the new spears until they too shattered. Again King Arthur reached for his sword. "Let your sword rest," the knight said, "for you are the best spearman I have ever encountered. Let us do battle with spears once more for the love of knighthood! "

The squire brought two good spears, and the two men resumed their contest. This time, however, King Arthur's spear shattered while the knight's spear remained whole. The knight gave Arthur such a mighty blow upon his shield that he knocked both Arthur and his horse to the ground. Arthur drew forth his sword and said, "I will fight you on foot, Sir Knight, since I can no longer fight on horseback."

Thus began a new contest, sword to sword, with each knight on foot. They charged one another like two rams until the earth ran red with their blood. Finally the knight's sword sliced King Arthur's sword into two pieces, and the king was at the knight's mercy. But Arthur quickly leaped upon the knight, threw him to the ground, and removed his helmet.

The knight, realizing how vulnerable he now was, summoned all of his strength and overturned Arthur. He removed Arthur's helmet and raised his sword.

Before the knight could behead the king, Merlin cast a spell upon him, causing the knight to fall into a deep sleep. Merlin then picked up King Arthur and rode off with him on the knight's horse.

"What have you done, Merlin?" Arthur cried. "Have you killed that knight with your enchantments? He is one of the best knights I have ever fought!"

"I advise you not to worry about him, Arthur," Merlin replied, "for he is far healthier than you are! I have simply put him to sleep for a short time. He is indeed a great knight, and from this time forth he will serve you well, as will his two sons. His name is Sir Pellinor."

Merlin took King Arthur to a hermit skilled in the art of medicine, who healed the king. When they were leaving, Arthur said to Merlin, "I no longer have a sword."

"Do not be concerned," replied Merlin. "Not far from here you will find a suitable sword."

As they rode together, they came upon a lovely, wide lake. A woman's arm protruded from the middle of the water. It was clothed in a white embroidered silk fabric, and its hand held a beautiful sword. "There!" exclaimed Merlin. "Now you can see the sword I had in mind."

Then they noticed a lady in a boat upon the lake. "Who is that lady?" Arthur asked.

"She is the Lady of the Lake," Merlin replied. "She is coming to speak with you. Treat her well so that she will give you that sword."

When the lady arrived, King Arthur said to her, "Lady, what sword is being held above the water by that arm? I wish that it were mine, for I have no sword."

The lady replied, "King Arthur, that is my sword, Excalibur, but I will give it to you if you will give me a gift when I ask for it."

"I will give you whatever gift you wish," Arthur replied.

"Then take my boat and row out to the sword. Take both the sword and its sheath, and I will request a gift of you when I am ready to do so." Once Arthur took the sword and its sheath, the hand and arm withdrew beneath the water.

"Which do you prefer," Merlin asked, "the sword Excalibur or its scabbard?"

"I prefer Excalibur, of course!" Arthur replied.

"Then you are not wise," Merlin responded, "for the sheath is worth ten of the swords! As long as you wear the scabbard upon your body, no matter how wounded you are, you will not lose a drop of blood. So take care of that sheath, and always keep it with you!"

When King Arthur returned to Caerleon, his knights were amazed to hear of his adventure with Sir Pellinor. They were disturbed that he would risk his life in such a way, and yet they were glad to serve a king who would take the same risks they themselves did.

The time came when King Arthur said to Merlin, "My nobles want me to marry so that I will not leave the throne of Britain without an heir. Whom do you advise?"

"Whom do you love above all others?" Merlin asked.

"Guinevere, the daughter of Sir Leodegrance, who has in his possession the Round Table. She is the most beautiful lady alive!"

"If you did not love her as you do," Merlin replied, "I would find you another lady whose beauty and goodness would please you. But I can see that your mind is set on Guinevere, and I cannot hope to change it."

"You are right," Arthur responded. "But why would you want to change my mind?"

Merlin counseled: "As beautiful as she is, Guinevere will not be a good wife for you. In days to come, she and the great knight Sir Lancelot will love each other more than they will love you."

This prophecy did not deter King Arthur. He sent Merlin and a group of knights to Sir Leodegrance to request the hand of Guinevere in marriage.

Sir Leodegrance was delighted to have Guinevere marry the king of Britain. Since a dowry of land would be no gift for Arthur, Leodegrance decided to give him 100 knights and the Round Table, which Uther Pendragon had given him. "This is a most fitting gift for King Arthur," Sir Leodegrance said. "It will bring peace among all of his knights, since the table has neither a head nor a foot. Whenever the knights meet, their thrones, their services, and their relationship to one another will be equal."

King Arthur marrried Guinevere at Camelot in a solemn ceremony that was followed by a great feast. He appreciated the gift of the Round Table, which seated 150 knights. When the knights went to sit around the table, each found his name magically inscribed upon the throne that would be his.

Chapter 4

Lucius Hiberius, Emperor of Rome, demands tribute from Britain; King Arthur declares war upon Rome. Arthur fights and kills a giant in northern Gaul. He and his knights then defeat the Roman army, and King Arthur becomes the ruler of the Roman Empire.

King Arthur conquered Norway and Denmark. Then he conquered Gaul, which was a province of Rome. One day King Arthur was seated with his knights when twelve old men, their white hair encircled with gold bands, entered the hall two by two. Each man grasped the hand of his companion with one hand and held an olive branch in his other hand as he approached King Arthur's throne. They greeted the king and announced that they were ambassadors from Emperor Lucius Hiberius of Rome.

King Arthur read aloud to the assembled group from the parchment scroll they handed him. "From Lucius Hiberius, Emperor of Rome, to King Arthur, his enemy. Who are you that you can steal Roman land? Who are you to teach law to Rome, the father of justice? How dare you refuse to pay the tribute you owe to Rome?

"Why do you refuse to render unto Caesar that which is Caesar's?" the document continued. "Do you expect the lion to run from the calf? The wolf to fear the lamb? The leopard to quake before the hare? Such miracles do not occur in this world! Julius Caesar, our valiant ancestor, conquered Britain, and since that time, Britons have paid tribute to Rome."

King Arthur continued reading. "If you do not appear before the Roman Senate and pay what you owe, then I will come with a mighty army and take Gaul from you. I will burn all of Britain and crush your knights. Should you attempt to flee, I will pursue you and give you no rest until I have destroyed you. Even if you were to dig a hole in the earth and hide yourself there, you could not escape the might of Rome!"

The Roman emperor's words were greeted with such an angry uproar that King Arthur physically had to restrain his knights from harming the Roman ambassadors. Then he met with his private council in the Giant's Tower. King Arthur said, "Friends and companions, your skill has enabled me to acquire treasure and gold and to subject many neighboring kingdoms to British rule. A nation is entitled to keep whatever land it can conquer and defend. However, Rome is a mighty nation. We must decide what action is in our own best interest."

The council decided to go to war against Rome. King Arthur said to the ambassadors, "Tell your emperor that I intend to travel to Rome, but I will demand tribute, not pay it. I will bind and hang Lucius Hiberius. I will destroy your land and kill any knights who fight against me."

The Roman ambassadors returned to their homeland and reported King Arthur's decision. Emperor Lucius decided to fight King Arthur in the mountains of Gaul. Arthur and his noblemen also prepared for war.

On board the ship that was transporting him across the English Channel, King Arthur had a dream. He saw a dreadful bear flying through the air from the east. Its appearance was huge, hideous, and black as storm clouds. Lightning and thunder accompanied its flight, and the seacoasts trembled from its horrible roars. A fearsome dragon flew toward the bear from the west. The glare from the dragon's eyes illuminated the sea and the countryside. The bear fought valiantly, but it could not withstand the dragon's repeated attacks. The dragon's fiery breath burned the bear until its scorched body fell lifeless to the earth below.

When Arthur described his dream to his companions, they said, "The dragon symbolizes you. The bear represents a terrifying giant that you will have to fight. Just as the dragon overcomes the bear, so you will emerge victorious over the giant."

Arthur replied, "I disagree with your interpretation. To me, my dream represents my coming conflict with Emperor Lucius Hiberius. In time, God will reveal its true meaning."

Soon after the Britons arrived in northern Gaul, a knight came in search of King Arthur. "Lord king," he began, "for seven years a monstrous giant has been tormenting us. The fiend destroys the farmers' houses, tears up their crops, and devours their cattle, horses, sheep, goats, and pigs.

"We have even seen him seize and eat men alive! He carries off women and children to his den on Mont-Saint-Michel. So far he has eaten more than 500 people, including infants. On the cliff where he lurks, you will find more dead than you can count and more treasure than the Greeks found in Troy when they captured that ancient walled city.

"Now," the knight continued, "the fiend has captured the noble niece of the Duke of Brittany. He has been holding her on the crest of Mont-Saint-Michel for the past two weeks. By now she may even be dead. No one has been willing to risk death in order to save her. No one in this land, neither knight nor commoner, possesses the courage and strength to confront the giant. We no longer dare to attack him on land, for that means certain death. When we tried to attack him from the sea, he hurled huge boulders upon our ships and sank them, drowning those who were aboard. He roams wherever he wishes and does whatever he pleases.

"You must have noticed that our countryside lacks any sign of human life. To escape the giant's wrath, many people have hidden deep in the forests. Others are dying of starvation in their own secret hiding places. The fields have become a barren wasteland.

"We desperately need your help," the knight concluded. "The monstrous giant will destroy this entire land and all of its people unless you come to our aid!"

"Alas!" King Arthur replied. "Had I known about this giant, I would have offered him my life before I let him ravage this land. I will seek this fiend upon his crag. If it is treasure or land that he wants, I will appease his anger. If his hatred is implacable, I will fight him to the death! I doubt that he surpasses me in skill and strength!"

That evening Arthur took his foster brother, Sir Kay, aside and said, "At midnight tonight, without a word to anyone except our squires, I want you to come with me to find this giant. I intend to kill him myself—it is important for a king to set a fine example for his knights. I think my own strength and skill will be all that I need. However, if it looks as if I need help, come to my aid."

At midnight the two were riding toward Mont-Saint-Michel when they noticed a great fire blazing above the cliffs upon its crest. Reaching the inlet, they tethered their horses to a tree. They had to make the middle part of their journey in a small rowboat that was kept tied far up the beach, for whenever the tide was high, the hill rose straight out of the sea.

As they climbed toward the crest of the high cliffs, they heard the sound of a woman's cry echoing through the trees above them. King Arthur withdrew Excalibur from its sheath and bravely continued on his way. "I will walk on ahead of you, but follow me," he said to Sir Kay. "When we reach the crest of the hill, place yourself where you can observe what is happening. For your own safety, remain deep within the shadows. No matter what blows I may suffer, remain in hiding unless the giant pins me to the ground and has me at his mercy. It is not appropriate for anyone but me to fight the giant."

Upon the crest of the hill, King Arthur found the huge, blazing fire. Human bones lay scattered upon the ground, more or less picked clean of flesh. But there was no sign of the giant. Instead, the flames flickered upon the body of an old woman in torn clothing who was sitting by the side of a fresh grave mound. Her long hair fell over her face, and she was weeping and wailing with grief.

As King Arthur entered the lighted area with Excalibur ready in his hand, the woman stopped her wailing and turned in his direction. "Who are you, and what evil fate has brought you here?" she asked. "Are you an angel, or a knight? If heaven is your home, you may wander upon this mountain in safety. But if you are a knight and the earth is your home, then you are indeed an unfortunate man!

"I pity you, for you are about to be tortured to death by a giant, who will then tear your limbs to pieces. Even if you were made of the strongest metal, he would destroy you. Even if you had come with fifty knights as strong as you are, he would destroy you all! May his name be cursed!

"I have just buried the Duke of Brittany's niece," the woman continued, "and the giant will not hesitate to kill you as well! He attacked the best of all castles in Brittany. The gates fell to pieces in his hands. He pulled down the wall of the great hall. He tore the door to my lady's room into five pieces. He grabbed us and carried us into this wild, wooded area. My poor child was only fifteen years old. I was her nurse and had cared for her ever since the day of her birth. She died of terror in the monster's arms! I watched as the light of my life flickered and went out!

"Take my advice, fair lord, and flee while you can. To remain here is to seek your death. If the giant finds you, he will tear you to pieces and eat your flesh. Do not try to win him with words. He cannot be bought with lands, or with treaties, or even with chests of gold. He will rage where he chooses, regardless of the law, for he is his own master, and he answers to no one."

Then the woman's face filled with terror. King Arthur turned to follow her gaze and found himself staring at the monstrous giant.

The horrible appearance of the fiend was matched only by the terrible nature of his deeds. His face was darkly splotched like the skin of a frog. His eyebrows hung low over his eyes, which burned with fire. His ears were enormous, and his nose was hooked like a hawk's beak. His mouth was as flat as a flounder's, and his fat, loose, fleshy lips spread apart to display his swollen gums. His bristly black beard fell over his chest, concealing part of his fat body. He had the broad neck and shoulders of a bull. His arms and legs stretched out like the limbs of a mighty oak tree. From the top of his head to the tip of his shovel-shaped feet, he was thirty feet tall.

The giant wore a tunic made from human hair, fringed with the beards of men. He carried the corpses of twelve peasants tied together on his back. In his hand, he carried a club so mighty that the two strongest farmers in the land could not have lifted it off the ground.

The giant dropped the corpses by the fire and approached Arthur with broad strides. As Arthur fingered Excalibur, he saw that the giant's mouth was still smeared with the clotted blood and scraps of flesh from his last meal. Even his beard and his hair were strewn with gore.

Arthur said to him, "May great God in heaven, who rules the world, give you a short life and a shameful death! Surely you are the most foul fiend that was ever formed! Guard yourself, you dog, and prepare to die, for this day my hands will kill you!"

The giant responded by raising his fearsome club. He grinned like a ferocious boar, confident of its menacing tusks. Then he growled, and foam spilled from his gaping mouth.

King Arthur raised his shield and prayed to God that it would protect him against the fiend's mighty club. The giant's first blow fell upon Arthur's shield, making the cliffs clang like an anvil and shattering his source of protection. The shock of the impact almost knocked Arthur to the ground, but he quickly recovered.

The blow ignited King Arthur's rage, and he furiously struck the giant on the forehead with his sword. Blood gushed into the giant's eyes and down his cheeks, blinding him.

Just as an enraged boar, its flesh torn from the attacks of hunting hounds, turns and charges upon a hunter, so the giant, maddened with the pain of his wound, rushed with a roar upon King Arthur. Groping blindly with his hands, the giant grabbed the king by the shoulders and clasped him to his chest, trying to crush Arthur's ribs and burst his heart. King Arthur summoned all of his strength and twisted his body out from under the giant's grasp.

"Peace to you, my lord!" the giant exclaimed. "Who are you that fights so skillfully with me? Only Arthur, the most noble of all kings, could defeat me in combat!"

"I am that Arthur of whom you speak," the king replied. Then, quick as lightning, Arthur struck the giant repeatedly with his sword. Unable to see through the blood in his eyes, the giant never knew where the next blow would fall. Arthur's sword thrusts rained upon him relentlessly until one finally entered his ear and plunged into his skull.

The giant gave a dreadful roar and crashed to the ground like a mighty oak tree torn up by a furious storm wind. Arthur gazed upon his fallen prey and laughed with relief.

Sir Kay stepped into the firelight and said, "That was an impressive death blow! The fiend should have worn a helmet!"

"Take your sword, Kay, and slice off his head," Arthur commanded. "I want to take it back to our companions for everyone to admire. If we place our swords through his ears, we can carry the head between us all the way back to our tents. If you want any treasure, take whatever pleases you. I want nothing more than the fiend's tunic and his club."

The first glow of dawn was streaking the sky with shades of rose when King Arthur and Sir Kay entered their camp. Word had already traveled from tent to tent, so an enthusiastic group of knights greeted their return. They stared at the giant's huge, hideous head in awe, for its size and ugliness were beyond compare.

The Duke of Brittany built a chapel over his niece's grave on top of Mont-Saint-Michel, so that she would not be forgotten. By the time it was finished, the allies of King Arthur had arrived from Ireland and Scotland, and they all set forth to meet the Roman legions.

The two knights without equal in King Arthur's court were Sir Lancelot of the Lake and Sir Gawain, the king's nephew. Both showed their prowess in the war against Rome.

In the first battle, Sir Gawain received serious wounds but fought on. When the battle ended, Arthur's knights had killed more than 10,000 Roman soldiers, had taken many prisoners, and had sent the rest fleeing.

King Arthur put Sir Lancelot in command of the prisoners, who were to be taken to Paris. Emperor Lucius Hiberius sent 60,000 Roman soldiers to ambush Lancelot.

Lancelot's scouts warned him of the ambush. Even though the Romans outnumbered the Britons six to one, he met them in deadly combat. He was so strong and skillful that his soldiers won the battle, killing many Roman soldiers and forcing the rest to run from them as sheep run from a lion or a wolf.

But when he returned to the king, Arthur said, "Your courage nearly destroyed you, Lancelot! It is foolish to fight under circumstances where you are badly outnumbered."

Sir Lancelot replied, "No, it is not foolish, for once a person acts shamefully, he can never recover his honor."

The decisive battle followed. King Arthur met Emperor Lucius Hiberius in a long, mighty contest. Arthur received a serious wound, but ultimately he took Excalibur and sliced off the Roman emperor's head. That day, King Arthur and his men also killed sixty Roman senators and twenty kings of countries that were Roman allies.

"Bring these corpses before your Senate with this message," King Arthur commanded the three senators who remained alive. "Tell them this is the tribute they have demanded of me. Tell them also that if this is not sufficient, I will pay an additional tribute when I arrive in Rome. Make it clear to them that this is the only kind of tribute I will pay. Finally, tell them that they may never again demand a tribute or a tax of any kind from Britain."

Shortly after the funeral procession started, Arthur and his knights began their own march toward Rome. City after city in the provinces yielded to them. The cities of Italy—including Rome—also yielded. When the leading Roman officials asked for peace, Arthur agreed to hold his Round Table in Rome that Christmas and to be crowned Emperor of Rome at that time.

Thus it came to pass that King Arthur ruled all the lands of the Roman Empire. After he was crowned, Arthur rewarded his knights and servants generously with land. Each knight now longed to return home to his wife.

King Arthur himself had no desire to acquire more power. "We have achieved great glory and honor," he announced. "It is not wise to tempt God."

So Arthur and his army returned to Britain and received a royal welcome throughout the kingdom.

Chapter 5

Sir Lancelot has many adventures and performs many heroic deeds. He then returns to the Round Table and resumes his love affair with Queen Guinevere. He defends her against a charge of treason. In tournaments, he fights in disguise on the side against the king.

After King Arthur and his knights returned to Britain, Sir Lancelot became the leading knight of the Round Table. Not only had he performed outstanding feats upon the field of battle in Gaul, but at home he surpassed all other knights in tournament skills and in noble deeds. Queen Guinevere loved him above all other men, and he loved her above all other women.

Sir Lancelot loved to earn glory, honor, and praise. He soon tired of the routine of tournaments and other such contests of skill with arms. He decided to increase his honor by seeking adventures in which he could excel in other, equally noble ways.

One noble way in which Lancelot proved himself was in his loyalty to Queen Guinevere. After falling asleep under a tree, he awoke to find himself imprisoned by four queens. They said to him, "We know Queen Guinevere is the only lady you love, but she is lost to you forever. You must choose one of us or die in this prison."

Lancelot replied, "You have given me a difficult choice, but I will die rather than choose one of you. If I were free, I would prove to you that Queen Guinevere is true to her lord, King Arthur."

Sir Lancelot also proved himself by defending ladies in distress. Not long after his adventure with the four queens, he came upon a maiden in the forest who complained of a knight who assaulted any woman who passed his way.

"Are you telling me that a knight is a thief and a rapist?" Lancelot asked. "He brings shame upon the order of knighthood! He has broken his sacred oath, and he should die for it. Ride ahead of me, slowly, through the forest. If that knight bothers you, I will come to your rescue."

When the knight appeared and forced the maiden from her horse, Sir Lancelot challenged him to a duel and killed him. "Now, lady," he said, "what other service can I perform for you?"

"Nothing at this time, sir," the maiden replied. "But you need a wife. You are the most courteous of knights to all ladies, yet you love none of them. I have heard that Queen Guinevere has placed an enchantment upon you so that you will never love anyone but her."

"Fair lady," replied Lancelot, "I have no interest in marriage, for then I would have to remain with my wife and give up the tournaments, battles, and adventures that I love. To love a woman and not marry her would be even worse! God punishes such immoral behavior. Such knights are unfortunate in their contests and wars."

Sir Lancelot then left the maiden. After riding through the forest for two days, he found himself at the castle of Tintagel, where King Arthur had been born. Two giants approached him, each armed with a huge club.

Lancelot immediately raised his shield, fended off the blow of the first giant's club, and sliced off his head with his sword. Seeing this, the other giant ran for his life. Lancelot caught him and sliced through his body from the shoulder to the stomach.

Sir Lancelot then returned to the castle. When he entered the great hall, sixty ladies came and knelt before him in thanks.

"Most of us have been imprisoned here for seven years," they told him, "earning our food by embroidering silk. Who are you that you were able to deliver us from these giants? Many knights have tried, but their courage brought them only death. We thought that only Sir Lancelot of the Lake could save us, for these giants feared him alone."

"Fair ladies," Lancelot replied, "I am the very knight you hoped to see!" Then he left them to their freedom and went on his way.

Sir Lancelot had many more adventures. Word of his triumphs reached King Arthur and Queen Guinevere in various ways. Sir Lancelot asked some of the people he helped to go to Arthur's court and relate their stories to the queen and the knights assembled there. He also sent knights he had defeated to Queen Guinevere to become her prisoners. Other tales of Lancelot's heroic deeds were told by those of King Arthur's knights who met him in the course of their own adventures.

By the time Sir Lancelot returned to the Round Table, he had already earned the greatest name of any knight in the world and was honored by both the common folk and the nobility.

Lancelot's love affair with Guinevere resumed on his return. Their relationship was common knowledge at court. Lancelot was embarrassed by the gossip and began to spend his time helping the numerous maidens and ladies who asked for his assistance.

Queen Guinevere finally called Sir Lancelot to her and said, "Lancelot, your love for me must be dying, for you no longer seem to enjoy my company. Instead, you spend your time helping other women with their problems."

Lancelot replied, "Since I was last a part of the Round Table, I have given up all the pleasures of this world except my love for you. I might have chosen to become a holy man if I did not love you as I do. You are my earthly joy, and I love you too much to give you up for anyone—even Arthur, my lord and king.

"However, our continued boldness will bring great slander and shame upon us, and I do not want to see you dishonored. Surely you are aware, Guinevere, that many knights already speak openly of our love. I fear them more for your sake than mine, since if I must I can return to my own country across the sea. But you must remain here and face whatever is said about you.

"Therefore," Lancelot concluded, "I am making an effort to help various ladies so that the members of the court will think that I love attending all women, and not just you."

Queen Guinevere said, "I see from your words that you are a false knight. You love other women and have only scorn for me! Therefore, I will no longer love you. Leave this court and never return, for I never want to see you again!"

To prove that she loved other knights as much as she loved Sir Lancelot, Queen Guinevere gave a dinner for them. One of the knights ate a poisoned apple and immediately died. Because Queen Guinevere had prepared the feast, she was blamed for his death. Another knight came before King Arthur and the knights of the Round Table and accused the queen of treason, which was punishable by death.

King Arthur said, "Fair lords, my heart is heavily troubled. I must be the judge in this matter, so I cannot also defend my wife. I ask that one of you come to her aid so that she will not be burned for a crime she did not commit."

"Forgive me, my gracious lord," said the knight, "but not one of the twenty-four knights who attended the dinner is willing to defend the queen's innocence in this matter."

Arthur replied, "Be armed and ready for a contest in fifteen days. When that day comes, if no knight has come forward to defend the queen, then that will indicate her guilt, and she will be burned."

King Arthur then went to Queen Guinevere and asked, "Where is Sir Lancelot? He would defend you!"

"His relatives tell me that he has left Britain," she responded.

The king advised, "Ask his nephew, Sir Bors, to fight for you for Lancelot's sake!"

But Bors was unwilling to honor Queen Guinevere's request. "Madam," he replied, "how can I defend you when I attended that dinner? If I take your part, the other knights will suspect that I poisoned the apple!

"Sir Lancelot would have defended you even if you were guilty, but you drove him out of Britain although he worshipped you! How can you ask me to defend you when you have treated my uncle in such a cruel manner?"

King Arthur found Queen Guinevere pleading with Lancelot's nephew. "Gentle knight," he said, "have mercy upon the queen, for I am certain that she is innocent. Defend her for the love of Sir Lancelot!"

"My lord," replied Bors, "you are asking me to incur the wrath of my fellow knights. Nevertheless, I will defend the queen for Lancelot's sake and your sake, unless a better knight is willing to be her champion."

When Guinevere banished Lancelot from court, he went to stay with a hermit in the countryside. He received the news of Guinevere's distress with great joy, for now he had an opportunity to win back her favor.

The day of the contest arrived. The two knights were prepared to begin, when suddenly another knight, riding a white horse and bearing a shield with a strange coat of arms, galloped out of the woods and talked with Sir Lancelot's nephew. Sir Bors then announced that this stranger would defend the queen in his place. The strange knight defended Guinevere against her accuser and proved her innocent of treason.

After the contest King Arthur asked the strange knight to remove his helmet and reveal his identity. It was, of course, Sir Lancelot. Queen Guinevere rejoiced at his return and regretted her harsh treatment of him.

Arthur and the knights of the Round Table then prepared to participate in a great tournament at Camelot. The king asked Queen Guinevere to accompany him, but she said she was too ill to ride. Sir Lancelot also refused to attend the tournament because his wounds from his combat in defense of Guinevere had not yet healed. The coincidence provided those who loved scandal with much to discuss, and King Arthur left for Camelot with sadness and anger in his heart.

After the king departed, Queen Guinevere said to Sir Lancelot, "You were wrong to stay behind! Our enemies will accuse us of remaining here to make love!"

Lancelot decided to attend the tournament in disguise and fight on the side against the king. Guinevere could not convince him to appear in a more honest manner. But King Arthur recognized Lancelot when they lodged in the same town en route to Camelot and was pleased to see him.

All was not well, however. Since Lancelot never wore the token of any woman, he agreed to wear one as part of his disguise. During the course of the tournament, he was seriously wounded by his own nephew, Sir Bors. In time, Sir Gawain discovered Sir Lancelot's identity. Queen Guinevere was furious that her knight had worn the token of another woman, when he had always refused to wear her own token.

As a result, when the next great tournament was announced, Guinevere said to Lancelot, "I understand why you wore a maiden's token at the last tournament. However, from now on, I want you to wear my golden token upon your helmet as a sign of your love for me. And make certain that your relatives are well informed of your disguise so they do not injure you."

Sir Lancelot agreed, and at the next tournament he again rode against the knights of the Round Table, wearing Queen Guinevere's token. His relatives, who were also in disguise, fought on his side. Sir Gawain recognized them, and he counseled King Arthur that it would be better to let Sir Lancelot and his relatives win the day rather than to contest heavily against their own knights.

Chapter 6

Two of King Arthur's nephews reveal to him the love affair between Sir Lancelot and Guinevere. The queen is condemned to die, but Lancelot rescues her and takes her to his castle.

Sir Agravain and Sir Mordred, brothers of Sir Gawain, had long concealed their hatred of Queen Guinevere and Sir Lancelot. Finally Agravain's emotion conquered his good judgment, and he announced in a voice that many knights could hear, "What false men we are! I am amazed that we are all not ashamed to see how Sir Lancelot openly loves Queen Guinevere. Yet, day after day, we endure this shame and permit King Arthur to suffer this embarrassment without making any effort to punish the offenders! How long are we going to conceal Lancelot's treason? It is time to tell the king!"

Sir Gawain replied, "Do not speak of such matters within my hearing, for I will have nothing to do with that subject!"

"I will!" exclaimed Sir Mordred.

"You would do us all a service to leave the matter alone, my brother," Gawain replied, "and tend to your own affairs, for I know what will come of your mischief."

"Come of it what may," Sir Agravain answered, "I intend to disclose the affair to King Arthur."

"Not with my approval," said Sir Gawain. "If you proceed with this, you will cause a war between Lancelot and us. And as you well know, many dukes and barons will side with Lancelot. As for me, I will never take a stand against Sir Lancelot. He is my friend!"

"Do as you wish," replied Agravain. "I will keep silent no longer!"

"Your action will destroy the noble fellowship of the Round Table and bring ruin upon us!" Gawain exclaimed. "I urge you both to reconsider!"

But Agravain and Mordred could not be dissuaded. They told King Arthur of the relationship between Sir Lancelot and Queen Guinevere. "We will prove that Lancelot is a traitor to you," they concluded.

"You will need to prove it," Arthur replied, "for Sir Lancelot is the mightiest of knights, and he will kill the knight who insults his honor."

King Arthur had long been aware of the love between his wife and Lancelot. He had pretended ignorance because Lancelot had helped both him and the queen on many occasions, and King Arthur loved him. If their relationship became public, Arthur knew that, as king, he would have to consider his honor and his position and would be compelled to take action.

Yet Agravain was determined to make a public issue of the matter, so Arthur reluctantly consented to his plan. King Arthur would go hunting and send back word to Queen Guinevere that he would be away for the night. If Sir Agravain, Sir Mordred, and twelve knights found Sir Lancelot with the queen in his absence, they would bring Lancelot before him.

Lancelot was indeed with Guinevere when Agravain and his party of knights knocked on the queen's door. They called, "Sir Lancelot of the Lake, you are a traitor knight! Come out of the queen's bedroom! We intend to bring you before King Arthur."

"Alas!" Queen Guinevere cried. "Our love has destroyed us! Since you do not have armor and weapons, surely these men will kill you, and I will be burned!"

Lancelot put his arms around Guinevere and said, "Most noble queen, you have always been my lady, and I have at all times been your true knight. I have never failed you since King Arthur first made me a knight. Pray for my soul if I am killed here. My relatives will rescue you from the fire. Take comfort in that and return with them to my lands, for there you will live like a queen."

"No, Lancelot," Guinevere replied. "I will not choose to live once you are dead!" "Know that I will do my best to stay alive," Lancelot said, "although I am more concerned for you than for myself. Nevertheless, I would rather have my armor upon me right now than be lord of all Christendom! I would choose to die performing deeds that bring fame rather than to die a shameful death!"

With that, Sir Lancelot opened Queen Guinevere's door just wide enough for one knight to enter the room. Lancelot killed him, took his armor and weapons, and attacked those who had chosen to destroy him. Only Sir Mordred escaped.

Lancelot then said to Guinevere, "Because I have killed these knights, King Arthur will always be my enemy. I must leave Britain. Come with me! I will save you from the dangers that await you."

Guinevere replied, "No, Lancelot. I will not do more harm to the kingdom by fleeing. But if I am condemned to burn, please rescue me!"

"Have no doubt of that!" Sir Lancelot exclaimed. He kissed Queen Guinevere, and they exchanged rings.

Sir Lancelot returned to his lodgings, where he gathered his family and the knights who were loyal to him. "You all know," he explained, "that ever since I came to Britain, I have been loyal to my lord, King Arthur, and to my lady, Queen Guinevere. Tonight the queen sent for me to speak with her. King Arthur commanded Sir Agravain, Sir Mordred, and twelve knights to betray me while I was in her room.

"Now that I have killed these knights," he continued, "war is certain to follow. The king, in his anger and malice, will order the queen to be burned. I will fight for her and declare that she has been true to her lord."

Meanwhile, Sir Mordred returned to King Arthur and his knights with the terrible tale of his encounter with Sir Lancelot.

Arthur exclaimed, "The fellowship of the Round Table is broken forever, for many a noble knight will side with Sir Lancelot! Alas, that I wear this crown upon my head! Now I must lose the fairest fellowship of noble knights that a king has ever had!

"It must break with Sir Lancelot in order to keep my honor," King Arthur continued. "And the queen must suffer the penalty of death, for under the law, she is guilty of treason. She is responsible for the deaths of thirteen knights of the Round Table. Therefore, I command that she be put into the fire and burned!"

Sir Gawain said, "My lord, I counsel you not to judge the queen too hastily. Even though Sir Lancelot was found in her room, he may have been there for no evil purpose. You know that the queen owes more to Lancelot than to any other knight, for he has often saved her life and has fought for her when the entire court refused to do so. Perhaps she sent for him with good reason.

"Maybe," Gawain continued, "the queen asked Lancelot to come secretly to her room in order to avoid slander. Many times we choose what we think is the best course of action, only to learn that it is the worst! I say to you that Queen Guinevere is both good and true to you. As for Sir Lancelot, he will defend the queen's honor against any knight living, and he will take the crime and the shame upon himself in order to save her."

"I have no doubt that he will!" Arthur replied. "Sir Lancelot trusts so in his courage and his skill with arms that he fears nothing, neither man nor law. But this time I will not permit him to fight for the queen. She will suffer the consequences of her actions, for we all are subject to the law. And, if I can, I will bring a shameful death upon Lancelot."

Then Arthur asked Gawain, "Why are you defending Lancelot? He has killed two of your sons, and last night he killed one of your brothers and severely wounded another."

"They brought their deaths upon themselves!" Gawain answered. "I warned them of the perils of their action, but they refused to heed my counsel."

"Dear Nephew," the king commanded Sir Gawain, "put on your best armor, and with your brothers, Sir Gareth and Sir Gaheris, bring my queen to the fire. There she will receive her judgment and her death."

"No, my most noble lord," said Gawain. "That I will never do. My heart will not permit me to witness the shameful death of such a noble lady! And let no one ever say that I supported you in judging the queen guilty and condemning her to death!"

"Then," replied King Arthur, "permit your brothers to be there."

Gawain replied, "They feel as I do! However, they are too young to reject your command."

"Indeed, you may command us and we will obey you," Gareth and Gaheris said, "even though we are much opposed to the deed. But we will wear no armor and will carry no weapons."

Thus it came to pass that Queen Guinevere was led from the castle of Carlisle in a simple smock to face her death. Most of the lords and ladies wept with sympathy, and few would bear arms to support her execution.

Just as Guinevere reached the fire, a group of knights led by Sir Lancelot galloped forth to save her. Everyone who fought against the invading knights was killed, for Sir Lancelot had no equal on the field of combat.

A sword thrust intended to pierce some knight's armor struck the unprotected heads of Gaheris and Gareth, who were unarmed and unprepared for battle. It was Lancelot who cut them down, though he did not even see them in the heat of battle.

Once Sir Lancelot had killed or scattered anyone who would deter him, he placed a robe upon Queen Guinevere, sat her behind him on his horse, and rode off with her to the castle of Joyous Gard. There he kept her as a noble knight keeps a lady.

Sir Gawain had remained in his room, where he learned of Guinevere's rescue. He exclaimed, "I knew that Sir Lancelot would save the queen or die in the attempt! He would not have been a man of honor otherwise, since she was being burned because of his deed. I would have done the same thing myself in his place." Then Gawain was told of his brothers' deaths. He could not believe that Lancelot had killed them. "Gareth loved Lancelot better than he loved any of his brothers or the king!" he exclaimed. "If Lancelot had wished it, Gareth would have stood with him against all of us!"

Sir Gawain was overwhelmed with grief and anger. "How did Sir Lancelot slay my brothers?" he asked King Arthur. "Neither bore arms against him!"

"I can only tell you what I have been told," Arthur replied. "They were standing among a great group of armed knights, and he did not see them there. He did not know that he killed them. However, let us plan how to avenge their deaths."

"My king, my lord, and my uncle," Sir Gawain replied, "I now make you a promise that I will hold as sacred as my knighthood. From this day forth, no man on earth will convince me to make peace with Sir Lancelot of the Lake! I will not rest until I have met him in battle and one of us has killed the other! If necessary, I will seek Sir Lancelot throughout seven kings' kingdoms, but I will find him and avenge the deaths of my brothers!"

Thus the war between King Arthur and Sir Lancelot began.

Chapter 7

The siege of Lancelot's castle in Britain is unsuccessful. He returns Guinevere to King Arthur, but Sir Gawain compels Arthur to follow Lancelot across the sea in order to continue the war. Mordred seizes the throne, and Arthur returns to fight him. Sir Gawain is mortally wounded. Before he dies, he asks Lancelot to come to Arthur's aid in the war against Mordred.

Sir Lancelot and his knights prepared the castle Joyous Gard for a siege, and soon King Arthur and Sir Gawain arrived with a huge army. Although great fighting occurred, Lancelot and his best knights remained within the castle for almost four months and would not take part in the battle.

Finally Sir Lancelot spoke with King Arthur and Sir Gawain over the castle wall. "You win no honor here with this siege, since I refuse to do battle with you. I will never fight the noble king who made me a knight!"

Arthur replied, "Spare me your honeyed words! I am your mortal enemy until I die! You have killed my good knights and relatives. You have slept with my queen for many years. And now, like a traitor, you have taken her from me by force!"

"Most noble lord and king," said Lancelot, "say whatever you wish to me, but I will not fight against you. I am sorry that I killed your knights, but I did so only to save my own life. And as for Queen Guinevere, of all the knights under heaven, only you or Gawain could charge me with being a traitor and yet live! I will defend the queen's honor against any other knight alive, for she is as true to you as any lady living is to her lord.

"It is true that the queen has treated me kindly and has cherished me more than any other knight, but then I have deserved her favor. In your anger, more than once you would have had her burned, and I have saved her from the judgment and the flames. Then you loved me, and thanked me, and were loyal to me."

Lancelot continued, "I would have lost my honor if I had let the queen burn for my deeds. I have always taken her part in quarrels with others. How then could I leave her undefended when this quarrel concerned me? So, my good and gracious lord, take your queen and honor her, for she is both true and good!"

"You are a false knight!" Sir Gawain exclaimed. "I will never think shameful thoughts of the queen. But what cause did you have to kill my brothers? They were not even armed!"

"I know that you will not accept my excuse," Sir Lancelot replied, "but by the faith I owe to the high order of knighthood, I did not mean to kill them!"

"You lie, cowardly knight!" cried Gawain. "I will fight you as long as I live, until one of us kills the other!"

"From the moment I learned of their deaths," said Lancelot, "I knew that I would never again have your friendship and that you would cause my noble lord, King Arthur, ever to be my mortal enemy. If it were not for your abiding anger, I believe that I would again be in my king's good graces."

Sir Lancelot was indeed correct. The noble King Arthur would have welcomed his queen and made his peace with that valiant knight if Sir Gawain had permitted it. But Gawain's anger was implacable, and he led many of Arthur's knights to call Lancelot a false, cowardly knight.

To preserve his honor, Sir Lancelot was forced to leave the castle and fight for his good name. He pleaded with King Arthur and Sir Gawain to leave the field, but Gawain said that they had come to fight. Lancelot instructed his knights to fight everyone except those two.

Lancelot himself rescued Arthur from the sword of Sir Bors. "As dearly as I love you," Lancelot said to his nephew, "I will kill you before I see the noble king who made me knight either shamed or killed!"

As Lancelot put Arthur back on his horse, tears flowed from the king's eyes, for he knew that Sir Lancelot was more noble than any other man. "Alas, that this war ever began!" he moaned.

Finally news of the war reached the Pope in Rome. He sent King Arthur a papal order commanding him to accept his queen and make peace with Sir Lancelot. Gawain agreed that Guinevere should return to Arthur, but he would not permit the king to make peace with Lancelot.

Sir Lancelot rode with Queen Guinevere to King Arthur's castle in Carlisle. An escort of 100 knights, each clothed in green velvet and carrying an olive branch as a token of peace, accompanied Lancelot and the queen, who were dressed in white and gold. When they arrived at Carlisle Castle, Lancelot and Guinevere knelt before Arthur in the presence of Gawain and many great lords.

"My most honored king," Lancelot said, "It was never my thought to withhold your queen from you. My only desire was to save her from danger. I am a thousandfold happier bringing her here than I was taking her away."

He continued, "If any knight, except for you, my lord, dares to say that Queen Guinevere is other than true to you, I, Sir Lancelot of the Lake, will defend her good name. You have listened to liars, and they have caused this argument between us. Without the might of God on my side, unarmed and surprised as I was, I could never have killed thirteen armed knights who were determined to kill me. Remember how well I have always served you, and favor me with your goodwill."

"The king may make his peace with you if he chooses," said Gawain, "but I will never forgive you for killing my brothers! If you were not here under the Pope's command, I would fight you right now to prove that you have been false to both my uncle and me. Know that I will prove it once you have left Britain, wherever I find you! You must leave this land within two weeks."

Lancelot then said to Guinevere, so that everyone could hear him, "Madam, I must now depart from you and this noble fellowship forever. However, if any false tongues slander you, send me word and I will defend you." He kissed the queen and said, "Now let us see who will dare to speak against the queen and say that she is not true to my lord, Arthur."

With these words, Sir Lancelot handed Queen Guinevere to King Arthur and left the court. Neither king nor duke nor earl nor knight nor maiden nor lady could hold back a flood of tears. Only Sir Gawain remained unmoved, for his hatred of Lancelot was implacable.

King Arthur's heart ached with sorrow for his country. He knew that from this time forth, his kingdom would be torn with debate and strife. The fellowship of the Round Table had brought responsible leadership to Britain. Without that fellowship to sustain them, duke would fight duke, baron would fight baron, and knight would fight knight.

Sir Lancelot returned to his lands across the sea. King Arthur and Sir Gawain prepared to follow him with a huge army. Arthur decided to leave Britain in the care of his nephew, Sir Mordred. Mordred had virtues, but loyalty was not among them. He schemed to reign in King Arthur's place and marry Queen Guinevere, whom he loved.

Arthur was unaware of Mordred's evil plans. He left Mordred in control of all he possessed—his queen, his land, and his people. Then he left to fight Sir Lancelot, for he would remain loyal to Sir Gawain, and Gawain's heart was set on vengeance.

For six months Gawain fought Lancelot's knights, but Lancelot refused to appear and contest with him. Many knights were slaughtered on both sides. Finally Gawain appeared before the castle gates and shouted, "Where are you, Lancelot, you false traitor? Why do you hide within the walls of your castle like a coward?"

Then Sir Lancelot realized that he would have to fight the knight who had once been his dear friend. His own sense of honor could not let Sir Gawain publicly shame him. They agreed to do battle and told their knights that no man should come near to help until one of them died or yielded to the other.

Gawain possessed a gift that a holy man had given him: Every day of the year, from nine o'clock in the morning until noon, his might increased to three times its normal strength. Only King Arthur knew of this gift, and he always set the contests to resolve quarrels at that time of day.

Sir Lancelot was amazed to see Sir Gawain's strength gradually double and then triple. He fought more and more carefully, preserving his own strength. As noon passed and Gawain's strength began to diminish, Lancelot gave his helmet such a blow that it knocked him off his horse. Gawain lay defenseless on the ground, but Lancelot walked off and left him there.

"Turn around, traitor," Sir Gawain called after him, "and slay me! If you leave me as I am, when I am well I will fight you once again!"

Sir Lancelot replied, "You know very well, Gawain, that I will never strike a knight who is down!"

For the next three weeks, Gawain lay sick in his tent. When he felt well enough to resume the battle, he approached the castle and taunted Lancelot until he had to come out and fight. Again the contest between the two knights began at nine o'clock in the morning, and Lancelot carefully bided his time until after noon. Again Lancelot struck Gawain upon the helmet, reopening his wound, and again he walked away from the sorely injured knight.

As soon as Sir Gawain had recovered enough to speak, he called to Sir Lancelot. "Traitor knight, you know that I am still alive! Come and kill me, or I will live to do battle with you again! I will not give up until one of us lies dead!"

"I will do no more than I have done," Lancelot replied. "As long as you can stand on your feet, I will fight you. But I will not shame myself by striking a wounded man who cannot stand!"

This time Gawain lay sick in his tent for a month. He was preparing to resume the contest when King Arthur received news that Sir Mordred had formally been crowned king of Britain and that he intended to marry Queen Guinevere.

Fake letters claiming that Lancelot had killed Arthur had convinced the House of Lords of the need to crown a successor. Since Guinevere found the idea of marrying Mordred both shameful and distasteful, she told him she was going to London to prepare her trousseau. Then she stocked the Tower of London with food and knights and took refuge within it.

Try as he might, Sir Mordred could not win Queen Guinevere, who publicly announced that she would die rather than marry him. Then he received word that King Arthur had withdrawn the siege from Sir Lancelot and was returning home with his army.

Quickly Mordred wrote to barons throughout Britain asking for their support. Most of them sided with him, forgetting what a good king Arthur had been. They foolishly believed that King Arthur's reign had caused strife and war. With Sir Mordred, they thought that they would be able to live in joy and in peace.

The two armies met at Dover, and even the water ran red with blood. King Arthur was such a courageous leader that his knights followed him ashore with great spirit in their hearts. After a deadly battle, Sir Mordred and his forces retreated. Arthur returned to find Sir Gawain dying in one of the boats.

"Now all my earthly joy has left me!" the king cried. "I loved you and Lancelot above all other knights, and now I have lost you both!"

"Dear uncle, my lord and king," Gawain said, "I am dying because of my own rash judgment! Lancelot's wound is killing me. If he were still at your side this unhappy war would never have begun! When I set you against him, I caused the destruction of your kingdom. I beg you, give me paper, pen, and ink that I may write to Lancelot in my own hand."

Gawain wrote to Lancelot of Mordred's treachery, Guinevere's seclusion, Arthur's need for help, and his own impending death. He publicly cleared Sir Lancelot of blame and asked him to return to Britain to help Arthur and to visit Gawain's own tomb.

When his letter was finished, Sir Gawain told King Arthur to send for Sir Lancelot and to cherish him above all other knights. Gawain was given the last rites, and then he died.

Chapter 8

Arthur kills Mordred, but Mordred fatally wounds Arthur, as Merlin had predicted. Excalibur returns to the Lady of the Lake, and four queens take Arthur away with them. Guinevere and Lancelot recognize the destruction that their love has caused; she becomes a nun, and he a priest. Guinevere dies, and Lancelot dies shortly thereafter.

King Arthur had a dream in which he was sitting on a chair that was attached to a wheel. He was wearing his crown and a robe of rich, gold cloth, and all his knights were bowing before him. Far below him he could see deep, black water in which dragons, serpents, and wild beasts were fighting. The sight was terrible to behold! Suddenly his chair turned upside down, and he fell into the deep, black water. All of the monsters immediately swam toward him and began to attack him. Arthur cried out in his sleep.

Then in his sleep he saw Sir Gawain approach him. "My lord and uncle," Gawain said, "If you fight Mordred tomorrow, you and most of your knights will be killed. I advise you to offer Mordred a great reward if he will agree to postpone tomorrow's battle for one month. By that time Sir Lancelot will have arrived with his noble knights. They will kill Sir Mordred and those who support him." With these words, Sir Gawain disappeared.

Arthur revealed his second dream to his knights and sent two of them to Sir Mordred to bargain for the month's delay. Mordred had gathered 100,000 men and was prepared for battle. But he agreed to the postponement in return for the regions of Cornwall and Kent during King Arthur's lifetime and all of Britain after his death.

Arthur and Mordred each chose fourteen knights and met between the two armies to sign the treaty. The two leaders had so little trust in one another that each directed his men to watch for any drawn sword. At the first sign of an exposed blade, the knights were to kill every enemy in sight.

During the signing, a poisonous snake slithered out from a heath bush and stung one of the knights on the foot. The knight instinctively drew his sword to slay the snake. Seeing his drawn sword, both armies immediately clashed in warfare.

King Arthur sadly rode into battle, encouraging his knights and fighting his best. "Would that great God in heaven had destined me to die for all of you!" he exclaimed. "I would rather save your lives than rule all that Alexander possessed while he lived upon this earth!"

By dusk, 200,000 men had fallen upon the earth, their bodies as cold as the ground they lay upon. When the king looked about him, only one of his knights, Sir Bedivere, remained alive. "Alas, that I have seen this saddest of days!" Arthur exclaimed.

Then Arthur noticed Mordred standing among a great heap of dead men. The king said to his knight, "Give me my spear, for I see the traitor who caused all this woe! I will repay him for his treachery and treason!"

"My lord," Bedivere replied, "remember your dream and let him be. If you leave Mordred alone, your day of destiny will pass."

"Come death or come life," King Arthur replied, "I will kill him now." He took his spear in both hands and ran toward Mordred, shouting, "False knight and traitor! Dark death now comes upon you, and no man on earth will rescue you!"

Mordred ran toward Arthur with his sword drawn. The king struck Mordred beneath his shield with a mortal blow, but Mordred summoned his last strength and struck King Arthur on the side of the head, piercing through his helmet to his brain. Then Mordred's body crumpled to the earth.

King Arthur cried, "Ah, Lancelot, I sorely missed your help this day! The rich blood of my Round Table soaks this muddy earth. My loyal knights, who by the might of their hands made me master of the earth, have been struck down by treachery. This day's bloody deeds have drowned all my joy. I weep for the glory, the honor, and the fellowship that are no more. Even I have received my death blow."

Arthur then said to his knight, "Take my sword, Excalibur, to the lake that is nearby and throw it into the water. Then return and tell me what you saw there."

Sir Bedivere went off as King Arthur had directed, but when he saw that the hilt of the sword was covered with precious stones, he thought, "Nothing good can come from throwing such a valuable sword into the lake! Why waste all this wealth?" So he hid Excalibur under a tree.

When he returned and said that he had tossed the sword into the lake, Arthur asked, "What did you see?"

"Only the deep waters, the dark waves, and the wind," Bedivere replied.

"Then you have not done what I asked you to do. Return to the lake, and throw the sword into it!"

Bedivere went back to the lake, but again could not bear the thought of tossing away an object of such great value. He left Excalibur under the tree.

When he said that he had tossed the sword into the lake, Arthur asked, "What did you see?"

"Nothing but the water lapping upon the shore and the dark waves," Bedivere replied.

"Now you have twice betrayed me!" King Arthur exclaimed. "Go quickly and do as I have asked you, for your delay is endangering my life. Already I feel cold. If you disobey my command this time, I will kill you with my own hands!"

When Sir Bedivere approached the lake for the third time, he took Excalibur and threw it as far out into the water as he could. To his amazement, an arm rose out of the water and caught the sword in its hand. Three times the arm waved the gleaming sword aloft in the air; then, sword in hand, the arm withdrew into the water.

When the knight returned with this tale, King Arthur said, "Help me reach the lake, for I fear that I have stayed here too long."

So Bedivere carried the king to the edge of the lake. A rich ship, containing the Lady of the Lake and three fair queens, was waiting where the waves met the shore. The four women wore black hoods of mourning, and they wept and wailed as Bedivere brought Arthur aboard.

Bedivere watched as the queens rowed the ship out into the lake. "Farewell," King Arthur called. "I am going to Avalon, where I will be healed of my wound. Someday I will return to my kingdom and live among the Britons with great joy."

The last sounds the knight heard were the mournful sobbing and wailing of the queens on board the ship.

Sir Bedivere spent the night walking through the forest. The next morning he came upon a chapel near Glastonbury, where he saw a holy hermit praying beside a newly dug grave.

When he asked for whom the hermit was praying, the holy man replied, "Last night, at midnight, a number of ladies came here bearing a corpse, and they asked me to bury it. They gave me 100 candles and 100 gold coins."

"Alas!" exclaimed Bedivere. "That was my lord, King Arthur, whom you buried in this chapel. We have lost the best king who ever ruled Britain!"

When Queen Guinevere learned of the deaths of King Arthur, Sir Mordred, and their armies, she entered a convent and became a nun. She spent her days fasting, praying, and performing deeds for the poor. People marveled at how virtuous she had become.

By the time Sir Lancelot arrived in Britain to fight on the side of the king, Arthur and Mordred were both dead, and Queen Guinevere was in the convent at Almesbury. Lancelot visited the tomb of Sir Gawain, and then he set out to find Guinevere.

When he came to the convent, Guinevere said to the other nuns, "This man and I caused this terrible war and the deaths of the most noble knights in the world. Our love for each other caused my most noble lord, King Arthur, to be killed by Sir Mordred. "

Then Guinevere said to Lancelot, "I am determined to heal my soul of its sins. In the name of all the love we two shared, I ask you never to look upon my face again. Leave me now. Return to your kingdom across the sea, and work to keep war from destroying it. Take a wife, and live with her in joy and contentment. As much as I love you, I may not see you, for our love for each other has destroyed the flower of kings and knights. Pray for me, that I may be able to atone for my past life."

Lancelot replied, "My lady, you and you alone have been my earthly joy. If you were willing, I would now take you back to my kingdom to be my wife. But I will never marry anyone else. I have promised always to be true to you. I will turn away from the world as you have done, and I will always pray especially for you. I ask you to kiss me for the last time."

"No," Guinevere replied. "That I will not do."

Thus Sir Lancelot and Queen Guinevere parted. Even the hardest heart would have wept to see such pain in the noble knight and his noble lady.

Lancelot became a priest at the chapel where King Arthur was buried. There he served God by praying and fasting. One night a vision came to him and said, "Come to the convent at Almesbury, where you will find Queen Guinevere dead. Bury her beside her husband, the noble King Arthur."

Lancelot journeyed to the convent, where he found that Guinevere had died a few minutes earlier. He buried her next to her lord, the king. As Guinevere's body was lowered into the earth, Sir Lancelot wept. The holy hermit, feeling that it was inappropriate for a priest to lament the loss of his beloved lady, criticized his behavior.

Lancelot replied, "I trust that I do not displease God with the nature of my sorrow, for it is not sinful. When I saw King Arthur and Queen Guinevere lying together in their final earthly resting place, my heart overflowed with sorrow. I remembered her great beauty, and the nobility that she and her king both possessed. I remembered their kindness and my unkindness. I remembered how my pride and my fault destroyed both the king and his queen, who were without equal."

Thereafter, Lancelot took so little nourishment that he wasted away. Day and night he lay by the tomb of King Arthur and Queen Guinevere and prayed, and no one could comfort him. Finally, he died.

The body of Sir Lancelot was carried to his castle at Joyous Gard for burial. His brother gazed at his corpse and said, "Ah, Lancelot! You were the most courteous man who ever carried a shield. You were the kindest man who ever struck with a sword. You were the most courageous man who ever fought with the spear. You were the most loyal friend and truest lover who ever rode a horse. Truly, you were the greatest of all knights!"

So ends the story of King Arthur and his noble knights of the Round Table. Many people believe that King Arthur is still alive in Avalon and that, when Britain is in great peril, he will return and rescue his country.

◆ QUESTIONS FOR
Response, Discussion, and Analysis

1. Why did the creators of this myth begin the history of Britain by having Brutus, the great-grandson of Aeneas and the nephew of King Priam, build a second Troy where London now exists?

2. Stonehenge was already sacred to the Celts when the Romans arrived in England. Why did the myth-makers relate Arthur to kings who are supposedly buried at Stonehenge?

3. When the Greek hero Theseus is old enough to claim the throne of his father, the king of Athens, he pulls his father's sword from beneath a huge rock. Sigurd's father, Sigmund, pulls Odin's sword from a tree. Arthur becomes king of Britain because he pulls a sword from a stone. What are the advantages of such proofs of kingship? What is the significance of these similarities?

4. Many writers have been so fascinated by Merlin that they have given him a major role in their own versions of this myth. What makes Merlin so appealing?

5. Why did the authors of this myth not give Merlin perfect powers of prophecy? For example, why does he not warn Arthur about making love to Queen Margawse? Why does his plan to kill Mordred fail? How do Merlin's flaws affect his image?

6. What does the fact that Arthur's sword has a name reveal about the period in which this myth is set?

7. What tasks does Arthur perform that make him a great hero? What does each task contribute to his heroic image?

8. Why does Merlin prophesy about Guinevere? Why does Arthur not use the knowledge this prophecy reveals? To what extent, if any, is he wise to ignore it?

9. How do you think Guinevere feels about marrying Arthur? Does she love him, or is it a political marriage? Support your opinions with details from the myth. Would you agree to a political marriage? Why?

10. Why is Lancelot reputed to be the greatest knight in Arthur's court? Does his reputation give him more credit than he deserves? Explain.

11. Why is it important that Lancelot is a good person as well as a good knight? How does his character contribute to his crime? How does his crime affect his heroic image? In what way is he a tragic hero?

12. In what ways is Arthur the ideal king?

13. Are Agravain and Mordred wise to confront Arthur with Guinevere's infidelity? Why?

14. Arthur ignores the love affair between Guinevere and Lancelot until Agravain and Mordred make a public issue of it. Does Arthur's behavior reflect weakness or strength? Defend your point of view. What would you have done? Why?

15. Why does Guinevere refuse to flee with Lancelot? What does her attitude reveal about her character? What would you have done? Why?

16. In early versions of this myth, Gawain rather than Lancelot is Arthur's greatest knight. How is Gawain's reputation still great, even in this late version? Relate examples from the myth.

17. Does Mordred have any reason to lead a revolt against Arthur? Is he a good person with honorable and justifiable motives? An evil person with jealous or vindictive motives? An innocent victim of circumstances beyond his control? Defend your point of view.

18. Lancelot and Guinevere are among the great lovers in literature. What aspects of their love affair are tragic?

19. As people mature, they can change. Sometimes they become better human beings: self-confident, sensitive, thoughtful, and kind. Sometimes their experiences make them weak, or callous and cruel. Explain how and why the following characters change in the course of this myth: (a) Arthur; (b) Lancelot; (c) Guinevere; (d) Gawain; (e) Mordred.

20. Explain why you like or dislike (a) Lancelot; (b) Guinevere; (c) Arthur.

21. When a snake causes the truce between Arthur and Mordred to be broken, does this enhance or detract from the myth? Is such a chance event realistic? Explain. Have any historical events occurred because of an unpredictable, unintended circumstance?

22. Why does the myth end with the question of Arthur's mysterious death? Does it add to or take away from the myth? Explain. What do you think happened to Arthur at the end of the myth? Why?

Northern Europe

The myths of Northern Europe reflect a universe in which the physical environment often threatens human survival. Consequently, Norse (Germanic) myths are populated with evil giants and monsters that heroes—both divine and mortal—challenge in combat.

The myths were recorded primarily in Iceland during the thirteenth century A.D. It is not surprising that these myths depict a depressed and burdened society. The people faced long, cold winters, short growing seasons that often yielded a less-than-abundant harvest, and a lack of sophisticated medical knowledge. In Norse myths, it is impossible to escape Fate. According to these tales, everything in the Northern peoples' existence is predetermined, so they must accept their destiny without question or rebellion. The Norse gods have human personalities, and they interact with one another and with the giants in many delightful myths, such as "The Theft of Thor's Hammer." However, unlike the gods of the Greeks and the Sumerians, Norse gods involve themselves with human beings only on rare occasions.

The Norse gods share the same unalterable fate that mortals do. When Ragnarok, the last great battle, occurs, famous human warriors will fight alongside the gods against the giants. Nevertheless, the gods will be defeated by the giants. Odin, ruler of the gods, knows their destiny is defeat, but he can do nothing to change it.

The Norse creation myth introduces the major concept of the conflict between the forces of good and the forces of evil. The myth describes the destiny of the universe from its creation to the destruction and inevitable death of the gods and mortals.

The fertility myth of Balder is a central part of the creation myth. Like other Norse myths, it has been lifted from its earlier, agricultural culture and has been transplanted into the more aggressive Viking age, with an increased emphasis on death.

The myth of Sigurd provides the basis for the story of Siegfried in Richard Wagner's famous cycle of operas, *The Ring of the Nibelungen*. Like *The Odyssey*, the myth of Sigurd is one of the world's great adventure stories. The idea of a curse on a gold ring that destroys whoever possesses it is the root of many a modern tales, including J. R. R. Tolkien's *The Lord of the Rings*. In this myth, Sigurd's great love, Brunhild, is the original Sleeping Beauty. As in the other major Norse myths, unalterable Fate dominates *Sigurd the Volsung*. The saga's characters shine brilliantly against the blackness of their fate, but they are doomed, and they know it.

HISTORICAL BACKGROUND

The acceptance of Christianity in Iceland in A.D. 1000 formally brought pagan beliefs to an end in that country. However, many of the monks enjoyed the old poems and stories enough to record them.

During the next few centuries, many people thought that the gods Odin and Thor really existed as evil spirits who tempted human beings with evil thoughts and deeds. In response to such ideas, in about 1220 Snorri Sturluson wrote *Gylfaginning* (*The Deluding of Gylfi*). It tells the story of the creation of the world and other myths from the Norse, or Germanic, tradition.

NORSE RELIGION

The Norse gods reflect the nature and values of the people who worshipped them. Not only do the Norse gods speak and act like human beings, but they too are subject to the Norns (the Fate Maidens) and face the inescapable destiny of death. Like human beings, the Norse gods know and accept their fate and are determined to face it with courage and dignity. Like many of the human beings who worship them, they choose to die in battle. They kill the evil giants to make the world a better place for future generations.

Except for Odin, who occasionally helps a great hero such as Sigurd, the Norse gods do not protect human beings from the dangers of living.

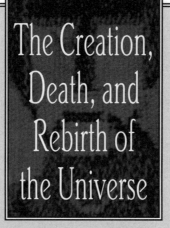

The Creation, Death, and Rebirth of the Universe

They usually keep to themselves, and their adventures involve the giants rather than humans. Similarly, the tales of human heroes do not usually include the gods.

The hierarchy of the Norse gods reflects the class divisions of Norse society. The Norse kings, as members of the warrior aristocracy, claimed Odin as their patriarch. Odin is both the god of war and the god of poetry. He brings both victory and defeat to warriors, and he inspires the court poets who create epics and songs about heroes and their battles. A fierce god, Odin demands human sacrifice from those who worship him.

Thor is the son of Odin and Frigg. Second to Odin among the Norse gods, he was worshipped by the peasant farmers, who needed his strength and dependability. Thor's hammer, Mjollnir, causes thunder and lightning, and is therefore related to the rain that helps produce abundant crops. Thor also uses his hammer to protect both Asgard, the home of the gods, and Midgard (Middle Earth), the home of mortals, from the evil giants.

Frey is the third most important Norse god. He is the son of Njord, god of plenty from the sea, and he is a fertility god like his father. Frey determines when the sun will shine and when the rain will fall. People prayed to him, his father, and his sister, Freya, for bountiful harvests and children. Like Odin, Frey demands human sacrifice from his worshippers.

Frigg and Freya are the most important Norse goddesses. Both are Great

Goddesses or Mother Goddesses and are worshipped for their powers to bring fertility to the land and to people.

APPEAL AND VALUE

Its broad cast of characters and great adventure make the Norse creation myth appealing. We recognize the giants, dwarves, and elves from our fairy tale heritage, which has Norse, or Germanic, roots. The concepts of gods who die and a world that is destroyed and reborn are fascinating. Readers of J. R. R. Tolkien will recognize that many names in *The Lord of the Rings* trilogy derive from Norse mythology, as do the names in C. S. Lewis's *Chronicles of Narnia* series.

PRINCIPAL GODS

ODIN (also, Woden, meaning "wild" or "filled with fury"): ancient Indo-European god of wind; son of Bor and Bestla; oldest and greatest of the gods; father and ruler of the gods; father of mortals, giving life and soul; god of war
FRIGG: originally, a Great Goddess or Mother Goddess; wife of Odin; mother of the gods; most important goddess; knows everyone's fate but does not reveal it

THOR: son of Odin and Frigg; second greatest god; strongest of all gods and mortals; god of thunder
BALDER: son of Odin and Frigg; most gentle and best loved of the gods
HODER: son of Odin and Frigg; blind brother of Balder
HERMOD: courageous son of Odin and Frigg
BRAGI: son of Odin and Frigg; husband of Idun; god of wisdom and poetry
IDUN: wife of Bragi; keeps the golden apples of eternal youth
NJORD (meaning "enclosing ships" or "the sea"): god of fertility; ruler of the winds and the sea
FREY: son of Njord; god of fertility of the earth and of mortals; ruler of the sun and rain; third most important god
FREYA: originally, a Great Goddess or Mother Goddess; daughter of Njord; gives advice about love; second most important goddess
HEIMDALL: ancient Indo-European god of fire, similar to Agni, the Hindu god of fire; watchman of the gods
HOENIR: ancient Indo-European god; son of Bor and Bestla; brother of Odin; along with Odin, father of mortals, giving intelligence and emotion; after Ragnarok, ruler of the surviving gods
LOKI: son of two Frost Giants, but considered a god; evil mischief-maker
HEL: monstrous daughter of Loki; ruler of the dead in Niflheim

THE CREATION, DEATH, AND REBIRTH OF THE UNIVERSE

In the days when King Gylfi ruled the land that is now known as Sweden, he transformed himself into an old man called Gangleri and visited the great gods in their hall in Asgard, in order to learn about the nature of the universe. Because Gylfi came in disguise, the gods did not reveal their true selves to him. They called themselves High One, Just-as-High, and Third.

"I am searching for the wisdom of the gods," Gangleri announced. "Is any one among you knowledgeable?"

"Ask of us whatever you will," High One replied, "and you will leave here wiser than when you arrived."

Gangleri asked, "Tell me, if you can, how did all things begin?"

High One explained, "In the beginning, nothing existed but Ginnungagap, which was an open void. In that ancient time, neither the heaven above nor the earth below, neither sand, nor grass, nor the cool, tossing waves of the sea had been fashioned."

Just-as-High added, "The first world to come into existence was Muspelheim (destroyers' home). It is a hot, bright, flaming world in the southern part of Ginnungagap and it sends forth sparks and glowing embers. It is guarded by the giant Surt, who possesses a flaming sword."

Third said, "The second world to come into existence was Niflheim (fog home), in the northern part of Ginnungagap. In the middle of Niflheim is a spring called Hvergelmir (bubbling cauldron), from which eleven fast and fearsome rivers arose and flowed far from their source. The foamy venom from their waves hardened and turned into ice. As it cooled, a drizzling mist arose from the venom and fell upon the firm ice, forming a second layer of heavy ice over the first. All this ice makes Niflheim cold, foggy, and harsh."

Gangleri asked, "Did anyone exist before human beings? Tell me about the giants and the gods."

High One replied, "The Frost Giants lived during the time of endless winters before the earth was formed. Where the soft, warm air from Muspelheim met the ice from Niflheim, the ice thawed. Life first grew from the drops of melted foam venom and developed into the first being, a Frost Giant named Ymir. The venom from which he was created made him wild, fierce, and evil. Then from the thawed ice a cow, Audhumla (nourisher), arose, and Ymir fed upon the four rivers of milk she produced."

Just-as-High added, "While Ymir slept, he sweated. From the moisture in the armpit under his left arm, a man and a woman emerged. Ymir became the father of all the families of Frost Giants. Like their father, they were evil creatures."

Gangleri said, "That is certainly a strange tale! How then did the gods first come to exist?"

High One explained, "Audhumla constantly licked a salty block of ice. By the evening of the first day, a head of hair had appeared. By the second day, the male's entire head had become visible. By the end of the third day, the whole male, called Buri, had emerged from the block of ice. Buri was tall, handsome, and strong, and he became the grandfather of the gods. He had a son called Bor, who married Bestla, the daughter of one of the giants. Bor and Bestla had three sons who became the first Norse gods: Odin, who was the oldest, then Vili, and finally Ve."

"Were the gods and giants friends or enemies?" asked Gangleri.

High One replied, "Odin, Vili, and Ve killed Ymir. So much blood poured from his wounds that, except for Bergelmir and his wife, all of the other Frost Giants drowned in the flood of Ymir's blood. Bergelmir escaped with his wife by quickly climbing into a boat he had made from a hollowed-out tree trunk. Thus, they became the parents of the next race of giants, who were also Frost Giants and evil creatures."

Gangleri asked, "How was the earth fashioned?"

High One replied, "The three gods took the corpse of Ymir, carried it into the middle of Ginnungagap, and made the world from it. From his flesh, they molded the earth. From the blood that poured from his wounds, they made the salt sea and laid it around the earth. From his mighty bones they fashioned the mountains, and from his smaller bones, jaws, and teeth they formed rocks and pebbles. From his hair they created the forests."

Just-as-High added, "They gave the lands along the shores of the salt sea, Jotunheim (giants' home), to the giants and their families. However, they wanted to protect the folk who would live in the inland part of the earth, called Midgard (Middle Earth), from the evil giants. So they used Ymir's eyebrows to build a barrier that separated the two groups of beings."

Third said, "From Ymir's skull, they made the sky and set it in the form of an arch over the earth, with a dwarf holding up each of its four corners. Then they tossed Ymir's brains into the air to create storm clouds."

Gangleri said, "I did not know that dwarfs existed before human beings. How did they come to be?"

High One replied, "Originally, the dwarfs came to life as maggots in Ymir's flesh. The gods gave them the appearance of people and also gave them human understanding. The dwarfs still live in dark places in the earth and in rocky caves in the land called Nidavellir."

Just-as-High added, "The gods fashioned the burning embers and the sparks that blew out of Muspelheim into stars and placed them in fixed locations in the midst of Ginnungagap to give light to heaven above and the earth below."

Third said, "They arranged for the sun and the moon to travel through the sky every day in order to create day and night and the seasons. The sun travels quickly because a wolf is chasing her. When this world comes to an end, at the time of Ragnarok (doom of the gods), he will catch her. Another wolf runs in front of the sun, chasing the moon. In the end, at Ragnarok, the moon too will be caught."

Gangleri asked, "How did human beings come to inhabit Midgard?"

High One replied, "When the three gods were walking along the shore of the salt sea, they found two trees, an ash and an elm. They created the first man, Ask, from the ash tree and the first woman, Embla, from the elm tree, and clothed them to give them dignity. Odin gave them blood and the breath of life. Vili gave them understanding and power of movement. Ve gave them shape and the ability to see, hear, and speak. Ask and Embla became the parents of the race of human beings, like yourself, who live in Midgard."

"What can you tell me about Yggdrasill? Is it not some kind of tree?" Gangleri asked.

High One replied, "The branches of this great ash tree spread throughout the whole world and extend over heaven. Three great roots support the World Ash Tree: one among the Aesir (the gods) in Asgard, a second among the Frost Giants, and the third over icy Niflheim."

Just-as-High added, "The root in Asgard is nourished by the sacred spring of Urd. There live the three Fate Maidens, called Norns. Their names are Urd (Past), Verdandi (Present), and Skuld (Future). They establish the laws that determine the lives of all human beings and seal their fate."

Third said, "There are other Norns as well. Some are the daughters of the elves; others are the daughters of the dwarfs. Those who come from good beings shape good lives—long, wealthy, and famous. Evil Norns confer short, poor, unfortunate lives."

High One added, "The root among the Frost Giants is nourished by the spring of Mimir, which is the source of wisdom and understanding. Like Mimir, who owns the spring, anyone who drinks that water will become wise. However, it is not a simple task. Odin, the All-Father, wished to have just a single drink; he had to sacrifice one of his two eyes before he could take it."

Just-as-High said, "The root over Niflheim is nourished by the spring of Hvergelmir, the source of the world's great rivers."

Gangleri then asked, "What did the gods do after they created human beings?"

High One replied, "Odin, Vili, and Ve built a stronghold for themselves in the middle of the world, called Asgard, where they and their families would live. There Odin sits on his high seat and surveys the entire world, seeing what everyone is doing and understanding everything. Two ravens, Hugin (thought) and Munin (memory), sit upon his shoulders. Each day, Odin sends them out at dawn to fly over the world. When they return, they tell him all that they have seen and heard."

"What is the most interesting palace in Asgard?" Gangleri asked.

High One replied, "That is surely Odin's golden-bright Valhalla (hall of the slain). It is roofed with spear shafts and golden shields. Valkyries (choosers of the slain), the valiant daughters of Odin, ride down to Midgard to award victory to certain warriors and to choose those who are destined to die. They bring the dead warriors up to Valhalla to fight on the side of the gods against the giants when Ragnarok arrives."

Just-as-High added, "Every day the dead warriors entertain themselves by fighting one another, eating an endless supply of boar meat, and drinking endless cups of mead."

Third said, "There are 640 doors built into Valhalla, and when Ragnarok arrives 960 warriors will leave to fight the fearsome wolf Fenrir."

Gangleri asked, "How can one travel between Asgard and earth?"

High One replied, "The gods built the Bifrost (quivering roadway) Bridge, which human beings see as the rainbow."

"In your opinion, what gods should human beings believe in?" asked Gangleri.

High One replied, "There are twelve gods and twelve powerful goddesses. Odin is the oldest and greatest of the gods. He is called the All-Father because he is the father of both gods and humans. He is also called many other names, such as High One and Father of the Slain, since he is worshipped by many different clans in Midgard and has had many adventures."

Just-as-High added, "Thor is the son of Odin and his wife, the earth goddess Frigg. Thor is the strongest god. He drives a chariot drawn by two goats. He owns three precious possessions: his hammer, Mjollnir; his mighty belt, which doubles his strength; and his iron gloves, which he wears when he wields Mjollnir."

Third added, "Another son of Odin's is Balder. He is as beautiful as he is good, and he is the best loved of the gods. He is the most wise and the most kind. Whatever he says can never be changed."

Gangleri asked, "Which other gods are most important?"

High One replied, "Njord is also very important. He was originally from Vanaheim, the home of the Vanir gods, who make the land and sea fertile. He is very important to sailors and fishermen because he controls the wind and the sea. He is wealthy and makes those who worship him prosperous also."

Just-as-High added, "Njord has two important children, Frey (lord) and Freya (lady). Frey is third in importance, after Thor and Odin. Frey decides when the sun will shine and when the rain will pour. Therefore, he is responsible for the fertility of the earth. Human beings pray to him for peace and prosperity, and for their own fertility as well as that of their fields."

Third said, "Freya is as important a goddess as Frigg. People ask her for help in matters of love."

High One added, "Of course, there are many other important gods and goddesses. Idun keeps the golden apples that the gods eat in order to remain young. Bragi, her husband, is known for his wisdom and skill in poetry."

Third said, "Heimdall is the watchman of the gods. He can hear the wool growing on the backs of sheep and the grass growing in Midgard. He can see farther than three hundred miles, even at night."

Gangleri asked, "Is Loki a god?"

High One replied, "Loki is the son of a giant, so evil flows in his blood. He is considered a god, but he is a mischief-maker. He is very clever, but he also lies and cheats. Some call him the Father of Lies and the Disgrace of Gods and Men. He often gets the gods into trouble—or out of it. He is the father of three monstrous children: the wolf Fenrir, Hel (goddess of the dead), and the World Serpent. He will be the enemy of the gods when Ragnarok comes upon us."

Just-as-High added, "Hel is a grim creature. Hunger and Famine are her companions. People who die from old age or disease live with her behind high walls in the land of Niflheim."

Gangleri asked, "What can you tell me about Ragnarok? Is there any way to escape it?"

High One replied, "The death of Balder will be the first indication that Ragnarok is approaching. Loki will be instrumental in causing both Balder's death and his confinement with Hel. As punishment, the gods will imprison Loki in a cave until Ragnarok arrives."

Just-as-High added, "Next, for three winters bloody wars will be waged throughout the world. Brother will strike brother with sword and axe, and both will die. Incest and adultery will become common. No mortal will show another mercy. Evil will run wild upon the earth, destroying relationships among family, friends, and clans. Finally the world will lie in ruins."

Third added, "Then three terrible winters, each lasting for an entire year with no summer between them, will bring biting winds, severe frost, and endless snow."

High One continued, "The wolf Hati will finally catch and swallow the sun, and the wolf Skoll will finally catch and swallow the moon. The giant Surt will tear apart the heavens with his scorching flames, causing the blazing stars, bursting with fire, to fall upon the earth. The earth will shake so forcefully that the trees of the forests will become uprooted and the mountains will collapse. This tremendous tumult will release Loki, Fenrir, and the monstrous dragon called the World Serpent, which lies deep in the salt sea that surrounds Midgard. The serpent will thrash about, poisoning the sea and the sky with its spurting venom and causing tidal waves to wash upon Midgard."

Just-as-High added, "Flames will flare forth from Fenrir's eyes and nostrils as he moves toward the plain of Vigrid with his mouth gaping in readiness. There he will meet the gathering of Frost Giants, the World Serpent, and all other creatures of evil. Heimdall will alert the gods to Ragnarok."

Third said, "Odin will fight against Fenrir; Thor will pit himself against the World Serpent; and Frey will battle Surt. The wolf will swallow Odin whole, but Odin's son Vidar, the fiercest of warriors, will tear Fenrir's jaws apart and kill him. Thor will slay the serpent, but its poison will kill him. Heimdall and Loki will kill each other, and Surt will slay Frey. Thus the high ones will be destroyed."

High One concluded, "With the fire from his flaming sword, Surt will set the entire earth ablaze. People will flee their homesteads in fear. With death as their destiny, the doomed and trembling human race will walk the road to join Hel. Finally, the charred and devastated earth will sink into the sea."

Gangleri exclaimed, "How horrible! What will happen after the whole world has been burned, and the gods and human beings are dead?"

High One replied, "The earth will rise out of the sea once again, fresh and green. The eagle will again fly down from mountain crags to capture fish. The daughter of the sun will travel the old paths of her mother and will brighten heaven and earth with her light. Fields will produce grain where seeds were never sown."

Just-as-High added, "After Surt's flames have destroyed the homes of the gods, Odin's sons Vidar and Vali will live where Asgard once was. Odin's grandsons Modi and Magni will join them and will claim Mjollnir, their father's hammer. Finally, Balder will return from the land of Hel and join the group. Together the gods will remember the knowledge of the high ones, the World Serpent, Fenrir, and Ragnarok. But evil will have left the world."

Third said, "Meanwhile, when the endless winter kills most human beings, one man, Lif (life), and one woman, Lifthrasir (desiring life), will seek safety by hiding among the branches of the great ash tree Yggdrasill. There they will survive by eating and drinking the morning dew. They will escape Surt's flames, and when the earth has revived they will become the parents of the next race of human beings."

High One then announced, "This ends our tale. We have answered all of your questions. Do what you will with all that we have told you."

Suddenly, Gangleri found himself in the midst of a tremendous uproar. When he came to his senses he found that he was alone upon a plain, and Asgard and the hall he had been visiting were nowhere in sight. He assumed his customary shape as King Gylfi and returned to his kingdom. There he told his people what he had learned. And from that day until this, these tales have been passed from one human being to another.

❧ QUESTIONS FOR
Response, Discussion, and Analysis

1. In what way(s) does the setting of this myth reflect life in Northern Europe?

2. How are the Norse gods like human beings?

3. What purpose does the idea of Ragnarok serve? What are some aspects or qualities of Ragnarok that have existed in the communities of Northern Europe?

HISTORICAL BACKGROUND

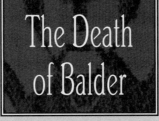

The Death of Balder

"The Death of Balder" and the Norse creation myth are so closely related that the introduction preceding the creation myth applies to this myth as well. The major source of the myth is Icelandic. Snorri Sturluson tells the story in his *Gylfaginning* (*The Deluding of Gylfi*).

Balder is one of a number of fertility gods in various mythologies who are killed, go down to the Underworld, and then come back to life. The pattern of life, death, and resurrection reflects the annual, cyclical pattern in nature of birth (spring), maturity (summer), death (autumn and winter), and rebirth (the following spring).

The myth of Balder begins during the period when the Norse gods are alive and well and life moves in an established pattern. However, as Odin knows, Balder's death is the event that initiates the destruction of that world. It ushers in a period in which the world order cracks apart and the gods and giants destroy each other in the last great battle of Ragnarok. Finally, the whole world is destroyed, first by fire and then by flood. Balder reappears only when the earth emerges from the flood—fresh, fertile, and ready to support a new race of gods and a new race of human beings.

This myth differs somewhat from the simple scheme of life, death, and rebirth in many other fertility myths. Balder's death is more final than that of the typical fertility god. His funeral is given major prominence, as if he were Beowulf, or any one of the other great Norse kings. The gods are unable to rescue him from the Underworld. In

some respects, Balder appears to be a fertility god in name only. His attitudes and actions do not affect the weather, and he does not teach human beings how to plant particular crops. Yet his murder does lead to the disintegration and destruction of society and the entire world.

The emphasis upon the finality of Balder's death may reflect the fact that this is a fairly recent myth that indicates a shift in the interests of the Norse peoples. During the fifth century A.D., Norse society had become less centered on peaceful agricultural pursuits, which depend upon the cyclical aspects of nature. Instead of farming, the Norse were beginning to turn their attention to accumulating wealth by the sword.

That Balder is resurrected at all testifies to the power of the original fertility myth and to the great appeal of the idea of rebirth and regeneration. Balder is the only major Norse god who returns from the dead to live in the new age. However, in his resurrection Balder reappears as one of a minor cast of divine characters whose function is, at best, undefined. Nonetheless, his influence remains long after his earthly death.

APPEAL AND VALUE

The myth of Balder has enduring appeal for many reasons. First, it reflects two universal desires of human beings: to be immortal and to bring back from the dead those loved ones who have died.

Furthermore, the myth of Balder reflects a parent's love for a child and a parent's anguish over a child's death. In striking contrast to this great love is an equally great hatred, spawned from jealous anger. Our sympathies are with the good child, his loving parents and friends, and his very vulnerable brother.

However, this myth is also fascinating because of the evil god Loki, who is determined to destroy the virtuous Balder. We are drawn to Loki's clever, evil mind, following him as he searches first for a way to destroy the victor, then for the weakest being to use as his unknowing accomplice, and finally for a way to prevent his own destruction. Although Loki achieves a great victory, we are glad that the fruits of his victory are not sweet and that evil does not triumph in the end.

THE DEATH OF BALDER

Balder was the son of Odin and Frigg. He was the favorite of everyone among the gods because he was so good. He was the best of the gods, the wisest, kindest, and most gentle of them all. Purity and virtue surrounded him. He was as handsome as he was good, and he shone with a special radiance.

One day Balder the Good approached the assembled gods and said, "Last night I had a dreadful dream! I dreamed I was in Niflheim, the land of the dead, and Hel herself embraced me. She led me through her palace. The rooms were all of gold and the halls were decorated with jewels. My dream terrifies me, for it shows that I shall die very soon!"

The gods were horrified at the thought that their beloved Balder would die. They decided to search the world for whatever could possibly endanger Balder's life and to remove any threat. They were certain they would be able to prevent his death. Frigg, Balder's mother, volunteered to take this great task upon herself.

She traveled from one end of the world to the other. She approached every plant and every animal, every bird and every serpent, every metal and every stone, every illness and every poison, every drop of water, every speck of earth, and every spark of fire. She made each in turn swear a sacred oath that it would do nothing to harm Balder. They were happy to do as Frigg asked, for they too loved Balder.

Once the gods knew that Balder was safe, they enjoyed testing his invulnerability. Some would throw darts at him, some would throw stones, and others would strike him with metal weapons. Balder's eyes would sparkle, and he would grin and announce, "Try again! I did not even feel that!"

Loki watched Balder's invulnerability and hated him for it. He disguised himself as an old woman and visited Frigg. "I have stopped by to talk to you woman to woman," Loki said in a disguised voice. "I hear that you are the queen of the gods, so surely you have great power here. Are you aware that the gods have gathered in assembly to throw things at one who stands among them? I must admit that he seems to enjoy it. But he is such a beautiful god, it would be sad if someone killed him! Maybe you should walk down there and see for yourself. You might want to do something about their foolish sport!"

Frigg replied, "How kind of you to come to me. You must be speaking about Balder. However, there is no reason for you to be concerned because nothing will ever hurt him. I have made everything take a sacred oath not to harm him, so he is quite safe."

"Have you really demanded an oath from everything in the world?" Loki asked.

"Oh, yes!" Frigg replied. "After all, Balder is my son! I have received an oath from everything: every plant and every animal, every bird and every serpent, every metal and every stone, every illness and every poison, every drop of water, every speck of earth, and every spark of fire. Nothing will hurt Balder. I assure you that he really is quite safe!"

"You certainly seem very sure of yourself," Loki said. "If it were my son, I would fear that I had overlooked something. But you must know that you have missed nothing."

"Well, I did miss one thing," Frigg replied, "but that was intentional. A little mistletoe bush grows west of Valhalla. I did not demand that it take a sacred oath because it seemed too young to harm anyone!"

"I am certain you were right about that," Loki replied, and then he left Frigg and casually strolled back in the direction of the assembled gods. As soon as he was out of sight, he resumed his own shape and quickly walked toward the west. He passed the hall of Valhalla and kept walking.

Sure enough, he found the little mistletoe bush exactly where Frigg had said it was. He pulled the plant up by the roots and took it to the palace where the gods had assembled. As he walked, he pulled off the berries, the leaves, and the small twigs. He sharpened the end of the stalk to a point and then tucked the twig into his belt. "No one will notice it," he said to himself. "In fact, I shall see to it that they hardly notice me!"

When Loki reentered the assembly, the game with Balder was still in full swing. The hall resounded with happy laughter as the gods hurled every kind of object at the beautiful god, all with no effect whatsoever. Loki looked around and noticed that Hoder, Balder's blind brother, was standing apart from the other gods. Hoder looked rather forlorn because he had no way to participate in this game. Loki said, "Hoder, why are you the only god who is not throwing things at Balder?"

"Because I cannot see where he is," Hoder replied. "And besides, I have nothing to throw."

"I can take care of that!" Loki exclaimed. "You should be able to honor your brother as the other gods do. My arm will direct your arm to where Balder is standing, and you can throw at him the twig I will give you."

Hoder took the twig of mistletoe that Loki gave him, and letting Loki guide his arm, he threw the twig at his brother. The twig went right through Balder's heart, and he fell to the ground dead.

The gods stared in silent shock at their dead friend. Tears streamed down their cheeks, reflecting the grief that overflowed their hearts. They could not speak. They were so stunned that they did not even try to lift Balder. Some of the gods turned in the direction from which the missile had come. When they saw

Loki walking quickly toward the door, they immediately knew who was to blame for the foul deed. However, they knew they would have to be patient. They were assembled in a sacred place and could not take vengeance upon Loki immediately.

Odin was the most upset of all the gods. Not only had he lost his dear son, but he alone knew that the death of Balder was the first in a series of events that would end in the destruction of their race.

Frigg was the first to speak. "Whoever among you would win my everlasting gratitude and affection will do what I now ask of you. Ride down to Niflheim and see if you can find my son in the kingdom of the dead. If you are successful, approach Hel and see if she will let him return to Asgard. Since she is Loki's daughter, it might be best to offer her a wergild payment in return for Balder's life."

"I am happy to do this for my brother's sake!" Hermod the Bold exclaimed. He took Odin's horse, Sleipnir, and galloped away.

Meanwhile, the gods carried Balder's body down to the sea. They placed it upon a funeral pyre on board his ship and then put his personal treasures next to his body. They even killed his harnessed horse and placed it on the pyre.

All of the gods were present to pay their last respects to the best of the gods. Thor directed the preparations. Odin arrived with Frigg, his Valkyries, and his two ravens, Hugin and Munin. Frey arrived in his boar-driven chariot. Freya arrived in her cat-driven chariot. Heimdall arrived on his horse. Even the Cliff Giants and the Frost Giants came to honor Balder the Good. Each god and guest boarded the funeral ship and added a treasured token of his or her own to the assembled pile of wealth. Finally, Odin added his own great treasure, his wondrous gold arm-ring that created eight more gold rings of equal weight every ninth night.

Balder's wife was so beset with grief that her heart burst and she died of sorrow. The gods placed her body next to that of her husband on the pyre. When the flames of the funeral fire roared toward the heavens, they set the ship afloat upon the sea for the waves to carry as they chose.

Meanwhile, Hermod rode for nine days and nine nights through such dark valleys that he could see nothing in front of him, nothing to the side of him, and nothing behind him. Finally, he reached the last river that divided the land of the living from the land of the dead. Stretching across it was a covered bridge with a roof that gleamed with gold even in the darkness.

As he approached the bridge, the maiden who guarded it asked him, "Who are you, and who is your father? Yesterday five troops of dead men rode across this bridge with less noise than you are making. You must be alive! Why then are you riding this road into Hel?"

Hermod the Bold replied, "I am Hermod, son of Odin the All-Father, and indeed I am very much alive! I must ride this road into Niflheim, for I must search the kingdom of the dead for my beloved brother, Balder the Good. Have you seen him cross your bridge?"

"Yes, Balder has crossed my bridge," the maiden replied. "Follow the road that goes continuously downhill and to the north, for that is the way to Niflheim. However, I warn you that the kingdom of the dead is surrounded by a very high wall. You will have to devise a way to get through its gates."

Hermod thanked her and rode on until he came to the gates of Hel's kingdom. These gates were high and locked to anyone who still had the wind of life within his body. Hermod dug his spurs into Sleipnir and said, "Take me over the gates!"

Sleipnir jumped so high that Hermod could see the gates far below as they cleared them. He rode up to Hel's palace, dismounted, and entered. The hall was crowded with the ghosts of the dead: male and female, old and young, rich and poor, virtuous and evil. Only the great heroes were spared eternal existence in the land of the dead. They were the fortunate ones, for Odin's Valkyries had chosen them when they died in battle and had brought them to the golden-bright Valhalla, where every day they prepared to fight on the side of the gods at Ragnarok in the last great battle.

Hermod walked through the hall, ignoring the hordes of ghosts. Balder was sitting on the high seat, as testimony to the great god that he was, and Hermod had eyes only for his brother.

Hermod spent the night with Balder, and in the morning he said to Hel, "My name is Hermod, and I am the son of Odin and Frigg. I have come from the home of the gods to ask if you will let me take my brother, Balder, back to Asgard. The hearts of all the gods are filled with grief at his death, so great is their love for him. Frigg promises you a fitting wergild in exchange for Balder's life."

Hel replied, "I shall release Balder only if you can meet one condition. You must prove to me that he is so loved that everyone and everything in the world, both alive and dead, will weep for him. If one thing objects to his return or refuses to weep for him, then Balder must remain with me in my kingdom."

"I am certain your condition will be met," Hermod replied. "My mother took an oath from everything in the world to protect Balder's life. Every plant and every animal, every bird and every serpent, every metal and every stone, every illness and every poison, every drop of water, every speck of earth, and every spark of fire promised to value his life. Surely they will weep for him!"

"For your sake, I hope you are right!" Hel exclaimed. "However, no matter how certain you are, I must have proof."

Balder then led Hermod out of the palace. As Hermod prepared to mount Sleipnir, Balder said to him, "Thank you for making this long, fearsome journey on my behalf. The gods call you Hermod the Bold with good reason. Only Father and the great Thor have as much courage as you! Do this favor for me. Return our father's wondrous golden arm-ring to him as a token of my love for him."

"This I shall do, Balder," Hermod replied. "Meanwhile, be of good courage! The gods are determined to free you from this dismal kingdom. I am certain that you will see the world of sunlight once again."

Hermod returned to Asgard and related his tale to the assembled company. The gods immediately sent messengers throughout the entire world requesting that every creature and form in nature, both alive and dead, weep for Balder to achieve his release from Hel. Everything they asked agreed, for Balder the Good was beloved by all that existed. Just as all things weep when they have been covered with frost and then are suddenly exposed to the hot rays of the sun, so every plant and every animal wept, every bird and every serpent wept, every metal and every stone wept, every illness and every poison wept, every drop of water, every speck of earth, and every spark of fire wept.

The messengers were returning to Asgard very pleased with the success of their journey when they came upon a giantess sitting in a dark cave. They greeted her and said, "Every other creature and form in nature, both alive and dead, is weeping for Balder in order to release him from the kingdom of the dead. Please add your tears to theirs, for Hel has demanded that no one must refuse to weep if Balder is to return to Asgard."

To their surprise the giantess replied, "No one will ever see tears flow from my eyes and course down my cheeks. Balder means nothing to me, whether he is alive or dead. If Hel has him in her kingdom, let her keep him there!"

No matter how the messengers pleaded with her, the giantess would not change her mind. They sadly returned to the assembled gods without having met the condition that Hel had set for Balder's release.

When the gods heard their story, tears streamed down their cheeks, reflecting the grief that overflowed their hearts. They knew who was to blame for this foul deed also. The giantess who refused to weep for Balder was none other than Loki in one of his many disguises. With grim determination they silently marched forth from Asgard to take vengeance upon him.

Loki, knowing that he had not fooled them, ran for his life. He hid high upon a mountainside above the sea, where he built a small, inconspicuous house with one door facing in each of the four directions. He hoped to see the gods coming soon enough to assure himself a quick escape. He tried to remain calm and unworried. He tried to take his eyes off the valley below. He tried not to jump at sudden sounds in the night. While he waited for the gods to discover him, Loki often changed himself into the form of a salmon and hid among the waters of a nearby waterfall, where he caught smaller fish for dinner.

At night he would sit in his house by the fire and amuse himself by trying to imagine what device the gods would use in their attempt to capture him. As his mind played with possibilities, he took linen threads and twisted them this way and that until he had created a mesh net. "This would certainly be a fine way to catch a fish!" he exclaimed. Then he shuddered and tossed the net into the heart of the fire as if it already had caught him.

Meanwhile, the gods continued their pursuit. Odin had sat upon his high seat from which he could see everything in the world, and he had watched Loki build his house upon the mountainside. Steadily and surely the gods approached Loki's hideaway. Their rage was implacable. They would capture this devious creature who often seemed to be one of them but whom they never could trust.

When they were near enough for Loki to hear them, he ran out of the back door, transformed himself into a salmon, and jumped into the waterfall.

The first of the gods to enter Loki's house was the wisest of them all. He looked carefully around the room, taking note of every detail as he searched for a clue to Loki's whereabouts. Finally, he spied the white ashes in Loki's fireplace and instantly recognized the pattern of a net. "Loki has taken the form of a fish!" he exclaimed. "Search the mountain stream by the waterfall, and I am sure you will find him there! I shall quickly make you a net like the one that Loki himself designed, and you can catch him with it."

Early the next morning the gods were at the waterfall with this clever device. Together they threw it into the water. Thor grabbed one side of the net and leaped across the mountain stream to the far side of the waterfall. All of the other gods stood on the near side. Together, they dragged the net through the waterfall and downstream toward the sea.

Loki fled deep beneath the cascade of water and hid himself in a crevice between two stones. The gods missed him the first time, but the second time they saw where he was hiding. They put weights into the net so that no fish could swim beneath it. Then they slowly moved the net from the waterfall downstream toward the sea. To avoid being caught, Loki was forced to swim downstream ahead of the moving net.

Finally, Loki saw that he had a difficult choice. He would either have to swim out to sea, which surely would kill him, or jump over the net and swim back upstream to the waterfall. Thor anticipated Loki's decision and waded into the rushing stream. When Loki jumped, Thor was ready to catch him. Salmon are slippery, however. No matter how Thor clutched at the body of the fish, it slid through his fingers. Finally, Thor dug his nails into the salmon's tail. Loki had lost the battle.

The gods took Loki up to a deep, dark cave in the mountain. They took three huge rocks and drilled a hole in each one. Next they captured Loki's two sons. They transformed Fenrir into a wolf, which proceeded to devour his brother. The gods then bound Loki to the three rocks using his dead son's intestines, which hardened into cords of iron. Then they hung a poisonous snake over Loki's head so that it would continuously drip venom on Loki's face. Satisfied with their vengeance, the gods returned to Asgard.

Fenrir found his mother and led her to Loki's side. She could not free her husband, but she tried to make his captivity more bearable by holding a bowl above his face to catch the snake's venom. When the bowl became full and she had to empty it, the venom would sear Loki's skin and he would writhe in excruciating pain, causing the whole earth to shake.

Loki remained imprisoned in this manner until Ragnarok, the time of the last great battle between the gods and the giants. When a violent earthquake caused even the great mountains to crumble, Loki's fetters snapped and he was free once more. He went down to Niflheim and brought his daughter and the fiends of Hel up from the kingdom of the dead to the battlefield. He and his monstrous children fought on the side of the giants. In the end he and Heimdall, the watchman of the gods, killed each other.

The entire world came to an end with Ragnarok. Gods and giants killed each other. Raging flames destroyed anything the earthquakes had left untouched. The earth became a wasteland, and in time a great flood covered it.

At the dawn of the new age, the earth rose forth from the sea, fresh, fertile, and green. Balder left the kingdom of the dead and joined the young gods who had survived the great destruction. The world as they had known it had disappeared, but they hoped to preside over a better world.

1. According to this myth, Loki killed Balder because he hated his invulnerability. Is this sufficient reason to kill him? What other reasons does Loki probably have for hating Balder? Would any of these be a better reason to kill him?

2. Does Hel expect that Balder will be freed on her terms? Why or why not? If not, what does that fact reveal about the Norse gods and their world?

3. This is one of the most famous Norse myths. Why do you think this is so? What do you like best about the myth?

The Theft of Thor's Hammer

The first written record of "The Theft of Thor's Hammer" is in the *Elder Edda,* where it is called "The Lay of Thrym." Dating from about A.D. 900, it is one of the oldest Norse poems. As a work of literature, it is the best of the short Norse myths.

"The Theft of Thor's Hammer" is a wonderfully appealing myth because of its great humor. The idea that Thor, the "superman" of Norse myth, should have to pretend to be a female must have brought smiles to listeners and readers throughout the centuries. Loki's role is also amusing. It is a pleasure to meet Loki, whose mischief is all too often evil, as a good-hearted conspirator, similar to Hermes among the Greek gods. Freya is a beautiful fertility goddess, and her sexual appeal is apparent in other Norse myths also.

THE THEFT OF THOR'S HAMMER

One morning when Thor the Hammer-Hurler awoke, he could not find Mjollnir, his hammer. His heart flooded with a violent rage. He angrily shook his red hair and tore his fingers through his beard as he looked first in one place and then in another, without success.

Finally, in desperation, he found Loki and said, "Someone has stolen my hammer. The gods in Asgard have not seen him. No one in Midgard has seen him. Whoever the culprit is, he is a crafty one!"

Loki replied, "Come with me to Freya's palace, Thor, and we will see what we can do about it."

Upon finding Freya, Loki said, "Will you lend me your falcon-feathered cloak so I can fly to Jotunheim to search for Thor's sacred hammer? Surely it is there somewhere, for no one but a giant would have taken it!"

"Of course, Loki," Freya replied. "I would give you my cloak even if it were made of pure silver or gold. Take it, and may it bring you what you are looking for!"

The falcon feathers whistled in the wind as Loki flew to Jotunheim. He found the Frost Giant Thrym sitting in the Hall of Giants, twisting strands of gold into collars for the hounds in his pen and combing the manes of the horses that he loved.

Hearing someone enter, Thrym looked up from his work and said, "Hello there, Loki! How are the gods? How are the elves? Why have you come to Jotunheim?"

Loki replied, "The gods and the elves are beset with grave trouble! Have you stolen and hidden the hammer of thunder?"

"Why, yes, indeed I have!" Thrym confessed. "I buried it eight miles deep in the earth. I shall not give it to any god until Freya agrees to be my bride!"

The feathers of Freya's falcon-coat whistled in the wind as Loki flew back to Asgard. Thor was waiting when he landed.

"I hope you have returned with a message and are not up to some mischief!" the Hammer-Hurler exclaimed. "Stay right where you are and tell me what news you bring."

"I do bring news and not mischief," Loki replied. "The giant Thrym has stolen your hammer and hidden it. He will not return it until we bring Freya to become his bride."

"Then let us see Freya immediately!" Thor replied.

Loki said to the goddess, "Place a bridal veil upon your head, Freya, for you must come with me to Jotunheim."

"What do you mean, Loki?" Freya asked angrily. Her palace quivered and quaked with her rage, and her Brising necklace, that glorious dwarf-crafted ring of twisted gold, split into pieces and fell to the floor. "The gods would think me a disloyal wife to Odr if I went to Jotunheim to marry another, and I certainly would never marry a Frost Giant!"

Thor, realizing the justice of Freya's attitude, asked Odin to call the gods and goddesses together in order to consider their next step. The hammer of thunder was a mighty weapon; its theft was no minor matter.

Heimdall, the wisest of the gods, devised the solution. "Thor himself is the answer to the problem!" Heimdall exclaimed. "We must dress him as Thrym's bride. We can repair Freya's Brising necklace and place it upon his neck. We can pin large brooches upon his chest, hide his legs behind a long dress, hang a bunch of women's keys at his waist, put a neat cap upon his red hair, and hide his face behind a bridal veil."

"Seeing me dressed as a bride will give all of you a mighty laugh!" Thor replied. "I am not certain it will accomplish anything else."

Loki replied, "Hold your tongue, Thunderer! We must capture your hammer if we are to defend Asgard against the giants. They would be all too glad to occupy our palaces."

So it came to pass that the gods placed Freya's necklace around Thor's neck, pinned brooches upon his chest, hid his legs behind a long dress, hung a bunch of keys at his waist, covered his hair with a neat cap, and arranged a bridal veil over his face.

When the disguise was complete, Loki announced, "I shall accompany you on your journey, Thor. I shall disguise myself as your handmaid, and together we will go to Jotunheim and make fools of the giants."

Thor drove his goats from their pasture and harnessed them to his chariot. The mountains echoed with the roar of thunder, and fires from mighty lightning bolts scorched the earth as Thor's chariot sped through the sky.

Meanwhile, in Jotunheim, Thrym eagerly prepared to receive his new wife. "Arise, Frost Giants, and place straw upon my benches. The gods may arrive at any time with my bride! I am happy that I have beautiful, gold-horned cattle grazing in my fields. I am happy that I possess a great treasure of gold and many gems.

I am happy that I have much to delight my eyes. I lack only Freya for my heart's content!"

Evening arrived, and with it Thrym's beloved. The giants set a feast of food and ale before the bride. She quickly consumed all the sweet dainties that had been reserved for the women, plus a whole ox and eight large salmon. She drank more than three horns of mead.

Thrym could not take his eyes off his beloved, and he could not help but wonder at what he saw. "Has any other bride ever had such a great appetite?" he asked. "Has any other bride ever taken such big mouthfuls of food or drunk as much mead?"

Loki, the handmaid, craftily replied, "Freya has so longed for her wedding day that she has not eaten for eight long days!"

Thrym, overcome with love for his bride, lifted her veil and leaned forward to kiss her. One look at her face sent him leaping backward the full length of his hall. "How fierce my beloved's eyes are!" the giant exclaimed. "Dangerous fires blaze forth beneath her brows!"

Loki craftily replied, "Freya has so longed for her wedding day that she has not slept for eight long nights!"

The unfortunate sister of the unfortunate giant then dared to command the bride, "Give me your golden rings! In return, I will give you my favor, my good-will, and my blessing!"

Then Thrym said, "Bring forth Thor's mighty hammer in order to bless the bride. Lay Mjollnir upon her lap, and wish us joy as we join hands and make our marriage vows."

Thor's heart leapt with joy when his mighty hammer was placed in his lap. Quickly he grabbed Mjollnir and smashed Thrym to the ground. Then, one by one, Thor killed all the Frost Giant's kin. The sister who had dared to demand bridal gifts received a deathly blow on her head instead of gold rings on her fingers. And Thor recovered his hammer of thunder.

✒ QUESTIONS FOR
Response, Discussion, and Analysis

1. What kind of human being would Thor be? Do you like him? Why or why not?

2. What does the element of humor reveal about the nature of the people who created this myth?

3. What role does humor play in other myths that you have read?

HISTORICAL BACKGROUND

Many scholars consider the Teutonic epic of *Sigurd the Volsung* to be *The Iliad* of the northern countries.

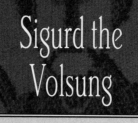

The story is found in Scandinavian, British, and German literature. The earliest existing version appears in the epic of *Beowulf* (written in about A.D. 1000), where a minstrel sings the tale as entertainment for the nobility. Clearly, the story was already famous at that time. *The Volsunga Saga,* written in 1300 by an anonymous author, is the definitive Norse version because it is the most detailed, cohesive, and complete version of the story.

The saga of *Sigurd* reflects the unstable political conditions in northern Europe between A.D. 400 and 600, before the arrival of Christianity in that part of the world. The wars between neighboring kingdoms produced many local heroes and villains, and their daring deeds became the subjects of popular songs and poems.

APPEAL AND VALUE

For hundreds of years the story of *Sigurd* disappeared from view, because its stark drama and pre-Christian values did not appeal to people living during those centuries. In the nineteenth century, *Sigurd* again became popular when writers recognized the saga's many attractions.

First, *Sigurd* is an outstanding adventure story. It contains magic, a monster, cursed treasure, passionate love, violent hatred, jealousy, treachery, danger, and death. Within its pages are both an early version of the Sleeping Beauty tale and a major source for the tale of the cursed ring that J. R. R. Tolkien used in *The Lord of the Rings* trilogy and Richard Wagner used in his cycle of four operas, *The Ring of the Nibelung.*

Second, Sigurd is an ideal hero. His wisdom is as great as his courage. He chooses to lead an honorable life by putting the needs of others above his own personal desires.

Third, the story contains numerous complex characters who are loyal to their families and friends until circumstances lead them to act treacherously. They are intelligent but they act foolishly, with tragic consequences. They cannot profit from prophecies because their human frailties doom them. No one in the saga is completely predictable or completely trustworthy, and this creates an atmosphere of suspense, excitement, and danger.

The reader can easily identify with the problems and emotions of the characters in *Sigurd*. They struggle to find happiness and to lead meaningful lives in a world that is uncaring, brutal, and treacherous. Death is inevitable, and the Norse gods offer no comfort. The characters cannot control their fates. They can try only to control their values, attitudes, and behavior. Their struggle to create meaning in their lives is viewed on a bare stage under harsh lighting. Life is a tragic experience, and the best the characters can hope for is to live with dignity.

The story of *Sigurd* strikes a sympathetic chord today because we too must create a meaningful life in a world that is often uncaring and dangerous. Ultimately, we must accept the inevitability of death. We must not give

The image in the background reads: **Sigurd the Volsung**

in to despair but must concentrate on the aspects of our lives that we can control. Like the characters in *Sigurd,* we cannot determine when we will die, but we can try to determine how we live.

THE NORSE HERO

In the Norse world, events are controlled by an unalterable fate. Both gods and humans know that their inevitable destiny is death. Since immortality exists only in the memory of the living, achieving honor and fame is the hero's principal goal.

The Norse hero creates his own meaning by living in such a way that others honor him. His greatness is measured by the quality of his life and his courage and dignity in facing death. Honor is earned primarily on the battlefield, where the hero attains glory according to whom he kills and the amount of treasure he acquires. The heroic goal is fame after death, the only immortality that a mortal can achieve. The hero aims to accomplish feats worth remembering—the type of great and glorious deeds that inspire poets and singers.

In the Norse world, a person's first loyalty is to his or her king. Family comes second, and friends third. No one else seems to exist. Gold is the greatest treasure. The noble person shares it generously, but the temptation to hoard treasure and let it corrupt one's personal values is very strong. Only the best human beings can withstand the temptation.

Retribution dominates Norse society. Justice is a private affair between one person and another or between one family and another. Even in the case of accidental death or murder, an individual takes full responsibility for his or her actions. The killer may choose to offer *wergild* (man-price), which is a designated payment as restitution for the death, but the recipient is free to reject the offer. As often as not, blood vengeance is the rule. The character accepts his or her punishment—death—without flinching, and the family feud continues to demand one life after another.

The fittest survive for a time, but raw courage and strength are not enough. Although the man or woman who is generous and loyal is less likely to have to stand alone against the human and natural world, in the Norse world no one is safe.

PRINCIPAL CHARACTERS*

SIGMUND: son of Volsung; king of Hunland; father of Sigurd
SIGURD: son of Sigmund; performs heroic deeds
HREIDMAR: father of Regin, Fafnir, and Otter; skilled in magic
FAFNIR: son of Hreidmar; brother of Regin and Otter; takes the form of a dragon
REGIN: son of Hreidmar; brother of Fafnir and Otter; tutors Sigurd
OTTER: son of Hreidmar; brother of Fafnir and Regin; often takes the form of an otter
ANDVARI: dwarf; possesses a magic ring and a hoard of gold
BRUNHILD: disobedient Valkyrie; rescued by Sigurd; wife of Gunnar
ATLI: brother of Brunhild; husband of Gudrun after Sigurd's death
GIUKI: king of a land south of the Rhine; husband of Grimhild; father of Gunnar, Hogni, Guttorm, and Gudrun
GRIMHILD: wife of Giuki; mother of Gunnar, Hogni, Guttorm, and Gudrun; skilled in magic

SIGURD THE VOLSUNG

Chapter 1

Sigmund, son of Volsung, pulls the god Odin's sword from the trunk of a tree. On the day that Sigmund is fated to die, Odin smashes the sword. Sigmund tells his wife to save the pieces for their son and then dies.

Listen to this tale from the heart of the north country, a land of snow-capped mountains, icy hills, and cold, gray seas. Hear of Sigurd, hero bright as the sun, and of Brunhild and Gudrun, who loved him. Hear of the treachery and woe that form the dark side of love and joy. Hear of men and women, heroes and villains, love and hate, life and death. Listen!

In days of old, Volsung, the great-grandson of Odin and the king of Hunland, was the greatest of all warriors—the strongest, most skilled, and most daring of all. He built his royal house around a huge oak tree, so the trunk of the tree grew through the center of the great hall and its many branches overshadowed the roof of the building.

The most noble of King Volsung's many children were his youngest, the twins Sigmund and Signy. King Volsung gave his daughter Signy in marriage to the king of Gothland. The Volsung family and their guests gathered in the great hall to enjoy the wedding feast. Suddenly a strange, old, long-bearded man walked, unannounced, into the room. He was barefoot and huge, and something about him seemed to speak of another, ancient time. He wore a blue cloak and a broad-brimmed hat that overshadowed his forehead, and he had only one eye. In his hand he held a shimmering long-bladed sword.

With broad steps, the old man strode up to the great trunk of the oak tree and plunged his sword deep into the wood, so that only the hilt of the sword was visible. While the family and their guests stood in amazed silence, the stranger announced, "Whoever draws this sword from this oak will have the sword as my gift to him, and will find that he never had a better friend in time of need." The old man then turned and left the hall. Everyone present realized that the visitor had been Odin, the All-Father.

Immediately, all of the noblemen rushed toward the sword in the tree. But it would not budge, no matter how hard they tugged. Finally, Sigmund put his hand upon the hilt and withdrew the sword as easily as if it lay loosely in the wood.

Sigmund announced, "I am destined to own this sword, for I have withdrawn it from its place in the tree. I will never give it up, even if a mighty king offers to pay me all the gold that he possesses!"

In time, Sigmund became the noble king of Hunland. So great were his courage and cunning, his skill in warfare, and the treasure he had won with his sword that his name was known throughout the northern lands.

After ruling wisely for many years, one day Sigmund was forced to fight an invading army. In spite of his age, he fought with great strength and skill. The battle raged furiously; the sky became gray with the passage of arrows and spears. Sigmund was covered with the blood of his enemies, yet he himself remained unwounded.

Suddenly, into the midst of the battle came an old, long-bearded man. He wore a blue cloak and a broad-brimmed hat that overshadowed his forehead, and he had only one eye. In his hand he carried a hooked spear. The old man approached King Sigmund and said, "Sigmund the Volsung, your time has come!" With that, he attacked the king.

Sigmund confidently struck the hooked spear with his own marvelous sword. But to his amazement the impact broke his sword into pieces, as if it were an ordinary weapon.

From that moment, Sigmund's success left him. No matter how well he fought, his enemies remained strong, while his men fell to their deaths all around him. Finally Sigmund received his death wound.

That night, the queen came out of hiding and searched among the corpses that littered the battlefield for her husband's body. She found Sigmund still alive.

While she comforted him, he said, "Odin, the All-Father, has brought an end to my days as a warrior. I am dying. Care for our son who is now within you and who is destined to be the most noble and famous of all the Volsungs. Preserve the pieces of my broken sword for him. They can be recast and will make a great sword called Gram, with which our son will accomplish deeds that will make his name live as long as there are bards on earth to tell the tale. Now let me rest here until Death claims me."

The queen sat with her husband throughout the night, and he died with the coming of dawn. The early morning light revealed many ships sailing toward them.

The young king of Denmark landed with his men and took Sigmund's queen and treasure back to his country. He promised the captive queen, "I will make you my wife, and you will live with honor in this kingdom. You will continue to be regarded as the best of women, and your son will be born into a royal home."

Chapter 2

Odin helps Sigurd choose his horse, Grani. His tutor, Regin, tells Sigurd about the dwarf Andvari's hoard of gold and the curse that Andvari placed upon it.

Sigurd, the son of Sigmund, was extraordinary from the time of his birth. He was raised in the royal house of Denmark, where he was loved and honored. All who met him marveled at his size, his strength, his courage, his skill, his intelligence, and his good heart. No one in the north lands could match Sigurd's gifts.

Sigurd's tutor was a gifted man by the name of Regin, who had earned fame as a metalsmith. Regin taught Sigurd to speak many languages, understand the ancient letters called runes, use weapons, and master all the other skills a prince was expected to know.

One day Regin said to Sigurd, "I am amazed to see that you are treated like a servant of the Danish king!"

"You are wrong!" Sigurd replied. "I can do whatever I want, and if I ever wish for anything, the king gives me what I desire with a cheerful heart."

"Then," Regin counseled, "I suggest that you ask him to give you a horse."

Sigurd went to the king and said, "I think that I am old enough now to have my own horse. I would like to train it myself."

The king replied, "Choose whatever horse you wish, Sigurd, and whatever else you desire as well."

Sigurd immediately left the great hall and set out to find the royal horses. He was walking through the forest when he came upon an old, long-bearded man whom he had never seen before. The man was wearing a blue cloak and a broad-brimmed hat that overshadowed his forehead, and he had only one eye.

"Where are you going, Sigurd, son of Sigmund the Volsung?" the old man asked him.

"Sir, I am going to find the royal horses," Sigurd replied, "for I intend to choose the best one for myself. You appear to be a very wise man. Would you like to come along and advise me?" he asked.

"That is just what I had in mind," the old man replied. "Let us drive the horses into the fast-flowing river. That should test their courage and strength!"

So the old man and the youth found the royal horses and drove them into the fast-flowing waters. Horse after horse shied away from the turbulent water. Some were so skittish that they would not enter the water at all. Others reared up on their hind legs in fright, turned around, and quickly regained dry land. Only one horse forged across the river. He was beautiful to see: gray in color, unusually large and strong in build, and yet quite young.

"The gray horse is the one I would choose!" Sigurd exclaimed. "I do not remember seeing him among these horses before today, or surely I would have remembered him. What do you think of my choice?"

"You have chosen wisely and well, Sigurd the Volsung!" the old man replied. "That gray horse is related to my horse, Sleipnir. Feed him well, and care for him. He will repay you by being the best of all horses!" And with these words, the old man vanished.

Then Sigurd realized that it was Odin, the All-Father, who had helped him. He called his horse Grani and trained him well.

Regin was still not satisfied. One day he said to Sigurd, "I marvel that you are satisfied to play here upon the royal grounds as if you were a peasant lad. Out in the world you would find treasure for the taking, and you would earn fame and honor by winning it. You are old enough and skilled enough. You have within you the blood of the mighty Volsungs. But tell me, do you have the courage needed for adventure?"

"Of course I do!" the youth replied. "What treasure do you have in mind? Where is it? And why is it available for the taking?"

Regin replied, "I have in mind the treasure that is guarded by the dragon Fafnir, whose den is on the Gnita Heath. He sits upon more gold than you will ever find in one place, and even the most greedy king would be satisfied with such a treasure!"

"Are you trying to help me or kill me?" Sigurd asked. "Young as I am, even I have heard of that treasure and that dragon! The monster is unusually large and evil. He continues to guard that treasure because there is no man alive who has the courage to fight him! How do you expect me to succeed where all others have failed?"

"Clearly you are no Volsung!" Regin replied. "Your father would never let children's tales fill his heart with terror! He had courage in his heart, not mush. Among those whose deeds have earned them lasting fame and honor, Sigmund the Volsung stood tallest. How ashamed he would be to think that his son was afraid of an ordinary dragon!"

"I am still so young that I am certain that I lack my father's strength and skill," Sigurd replied. "But I do not deserve to have you call me a coward! Why are you treating me like this? You must have some reason hiding behind your taunting words!"

"I certainly do!" said Regin. "I have a tale that I have been waiting many a year to tell you. You have come of age, and I have trained you well. You are ready. Listen to my tale, for it is the story of my life."

My father, Hreidmar, was a man of great strength and great wealth, and he taught us his skill in the arts of magic. He had three sons: Fafnir, Otter, and me. Fafnir was most similar to our father, both in physical strength and in greed. He possessed one extraordinary gift. He could change his shape to please himself.

Otter was completely different from Fafnir. He was simple, gentle, and kind. He loved to fish, and he was quite skilled at that pursuit. Like Fafnir, he could change his shape. He particularly enjoyed becoming an otter. In that form he would spend each day, from dawn to dusk, by the side of the river near the base of a waterfall.

Otter loved to plunge into the water to catch a fish, swim back to shore, and place it on the river bank. By the time the sun was setting, he would have stacked a sizable pile of fish. He would gather the fish he had caught into a net and bring them to our father. Otter would eat alone and then go to sleep. Nothing on dry land interested him, so he spent most of his time in the appearance of an otter, and he lived from one day's fishing to the next.

I was different from my brothers. I excelled in a more ordinary way. I loved to work with metals, and I became quite skilled at creating objects in silver and gold, and in working with iron as well.

Behind the waterfall near Otter's favorite fishing place lived a dwarf named Andvari. The waterfall itself was called Andvari's Force. Like Otter, Andvari could change his shape, and he too loved to fish. The dwarf fished in the form of a pike, and he ate the smaller fish that came over the waterfall. So many fish swam over the waterfall that there were always more than enough for both Otter and Andvari.

One day the gods Odin, Loki, and Hoenir were wandering upon the earth disguised as ordinary mortals. They enjoyed leaving Asgard, the home of the gods, to visit the homes of country folk. So it happened that the three gods came upon Andvari's Force. The sun was low in the sky, and it was time for supper. Otter had caught a salmon and was lazily lounging upon the bank of the river, about to eat it.

Loki spied both the otter and the salmon and said, "I think that I can kill that otter with the toss of one stone, and then we will have both otter and salmon to eat! That surely will satisfy our hunger!" He picked up a large stone, tossed it, and killed Otter. The gods then collected the otter and the salmon and walked toward our father's house.

"May we spend the night with you?" Odin asked my father when he opened the door. "We have brought enough food for all of us!"

Hreidmar courteously invited the visitors inside. However, when he noticed the otter hanging from Loki's hand, he became enraged. "What kind of guests are you?" he roared. "You have killed my son! I will return your kindness in equal measure!"

With these words, my father secretly signaled to Fafnir and me. We quickly grabbed our visitors and placed chains around them.

"Now prepare to die!" Hreidmar exclaimed. "You will pay with your lives for the crime you have committed!"

"You are being unduly harsh, sir!" Odin complained. "Your son's death was an accident! My companion killed what appeared to be an ordinary otter. How could we know that your son had transformed himself into an animal? If you agree to free us, we will pay you as much wergild as you demand. Will you accept treasure instead of our deaths?"

"All right, then," Hreidmar replied. "As payment for slaying my son Otter, I demand that you pay me the value I have set upon his life. Fill the interior of his otter skin with gold, then stand the skin upon its tail and cover the entire exterior with gold. Not one hair on the skin must be visible. If you refuse, I will kill the three of you as you killed my son!"

Hreidmar concluded, "You may discuss among the three of you who will collect the gold, for I intend to keep the other two here as my prisoners until you make this payment."

Odin and Hoenir looked at Loki in dismay. Then Odin said to Loki, "I think it is best that you locate the wergild for us, for you are far more clever than we are and you know where to look for it. As I look upon our host, I can tell that he is a man who will keep his word."

Once we had freed Loki, he went down to the bottom of the sea and borrowed a large net from the sea goddess Ran. He returned with it to Andvari's Force. He swiftly cast his net over the waters with such skill that it enclosed the pike before the fish became aware of the danger and could swim out of reach. Loki then drew the thrashing pike from the water and placed it, still confined in Ran's net, upon the bank next to him.

"Pike," Loki began, "if fish you truly are, how is it that you survive in the waterfall without being crushed, and yet you do not have the good sense to be aware that nets are no friends of yours? Who are you?"

"People call me Andvari," the pike craftily replied, "and in my true form I am a dwarf. The Norns, who determine the destiny of every mortal being, have changed me into the pike you see. They have forced me to spend all the days of my life swimming in rivers. I do not enjoy it, but I have no choice!"

"So you are Andvari!" Loki replied. "You need say no more! Nets are not the only enemies you have! If you intend ever to leave Ran's net alive, you must promise to give me all of the gold that you guard behind Andvari's Force in that cave of yours. Do not try to deny it, for I will kill you before I believe any other tales you create in order to deceive me!"

Loki convinced Andvari to resume his dwarf shape and bring him the gold that the gods needed in order to free themselves from my father's wrath and make amends for the death of my brother. Andvari soon returned to Loki in his true shape, lugging an enormous bag of gold.

Loki opened the bag and grinned with delight. Then he spied a beautiful gold ring upon Andvari's finger. "I'll take that, too!" he exclaimed.

"Let me keep just this one ring!" Andvari pleaded. "It is of little use to you. However, because I am a dwarf, I can use it to create more gold."

"No," Loki replied, "I intend to take every piece of gold you have, including that ring!"

When Andvari made no effort to remove the ring, Loki grabbed the dwarf from behind and pulled it from his finger. Satisfied that he had acquired every ounce of treasure, Loki then released the dwarf.

Andvari ran to the rocks by the waterfall and shouted, "From this time forth, that gold ring and all of the treasure that accompanies it will be the bane of every being who possesses it! Death and destruction will follow the gold as surely as night follows day, and no one who owns it will remain untouched by its curse. Only when the ring and the gold have returned to the deep waters will the bane end."

Loki ignored the dwarf's curse. He put the beautiful ring on his own finger and walked toward Hreidmar's house, dragging the bag of gold behind him.

Odin admired Andvari's beautiful ring, so Loki gave it to him. Then Loki took the otter skin and stuffed it with gold coins until the skin looked as if it might burst. When not another coin would fit into it, he stood the otter skin upon its tail and began to pile the gold around it. As Hreidmar had anticipated, in order for the fur to be covered it had to be completely buried in gold.

Loki was forced to use every gold coin in Andvari's bag to fulfill the terms of Hreidmar's wergild. Finally, Loki had emptied the bag and had arranged the coins so that even Hreidmar would be satisfied.

Hreidmar examined the pile with great care. "Ah!" he exclaimed. "I see an exposed hair—right there!"

Loki immediately moved a coin to cover the hair, but as soon as he did so, other coins moved also, uncovering more fur. Carefully, Loki set about rearranging them again so that they would completely cover the otter skin. When he had finished, he sat back with a smile of relief upon his face.

Hreidmar examined the pile again with great care. "Ah!" he exclaimed, with a sharp gleam in his eyes. "I see an exposed whisker—right there! If you do not have enough gold to cover that hair, I will be forced to take your three lives as payment for the life of my son Otter!"

Odin had so far made no attempt to add Andvari's beautiful gold ring to the pile. But when it became clear that the gold pieces were not sufficient, he said to Loki, "Take this ring and place it over the exposed whisker. Then we will have fulfilled the wergild agreement."

Hreidmar was satisfied, so he allowed the three gods to leave his house. Loki turned in the doorway to face Hreidmar and the two of us. Now that he felt safe, he exclaimed, "You have the wergild that you demanded of us, and a wealth of treasure it is! But I must warn you that every last piece of that gold carries with it the curse of the dwarf Andvari. The gold ring and all the treasure that accompanies it will be the bane of every being who possesses it! Death and destruction will follow the gold as surely as night follows day, and no one who owns it will remain untouched by its curse. Only when the ring and the gold have returned to the deep waters will the bane end."

As soon as our visitors had left, our father walked over to the otter skin and placed the beautiful ring on his own finger. Then he shook every last piece of gold out of the otter skin and locked it all away in a heavy wooden chest. He hung the key around his neck and said nothing more about it.

"Do you intend to keep the wergild all for yourself, Father?" I asked. "I think we should divide the treasure among the three of us!"

"You do not deserve a single coin!" Hreidmar replied. "Otter was my son, and the wergild is mine alone. I will not discuss the matter further!"

Fafnir was furious. Once we were alone, he exclaimed, "Regin, you and I each deserve one-third of that wergild! After all, Otter was our brother! Will you help me steal the key and remove our share of the treasure from the chest?"

"I am afraid that we may have to kill Father in order to get his key!" I objected. "You know how lightly he sleeps. The sound of grass growing is enough to awaken him! I am not certain I have what it takes to murder my father! I will have to think about it."

As it happened, I did not have long to consider the matter. When I awakened the next morning, the house was strangely quiet and my brother's bed was empty. I found our father stabbed to death in his bed. The key that had hung around his neck was gone. The ring that he had placed on his finger was gone. All of the wergild that he had put into the chest was gone.

I found my brother outside. "Fafnir, you certainly are brave to have had the nerve to kill Father!" I exclaimed. "Now we only need to divide the wergild between the two of us. That is even better!"

"I will never divide Andvari's treasure hoard with you, Regin!" Fafnir replied. "You were too cowardly to kill our father. Why do you think you deserve any of the gold? The risk was all mine, so the treasure is all mine! If you want it, you will have to fight me for it. I doubt if you have the courage to do that, either! I am much stronger than you are, you know. If you know what is good for you, you will leave here before I kill you as I killed Father!"

Fafnir entered the house and immediately returned wearing our father's helmet upon his head. We called it the Helmet of Terror because it caused the heart of anyone who gazed upon it to flood with great fear.

I took one look at Fafnir in that helmet and, seeing his sword in his hand, I fled. I sought employment with the king of Denmark. My fame as a metalsmith had preceded me, so he welcomed me.

In time, I learned that my brother had taken refuge in a cave on Gnita Heath and had turned himself into a fearsome dragon to protect the wergild he had stolen. He spent every day and night in his lair, with his body draped over Andvari's treasure hoard.

Chapter 3

Sigurd's uncle reveals his fate to him. Regin recasts Sigmund's sword, Gram, for Sigurd. With it, Sigurd kills Fafnir and then Regin. After taking Andvari's treasure hoard, Sigurd sets out to rescue Brunhild, the sleeping Valkyrie.

"Not long thereafter," Regin explained, "the king brought your mother to Denmark. I had bright hopes for my future, for I knew that the child she was carrying within her was a Volsung. I knew it was just a matter of time until I could avenge the death of my father and reclaim the treasure that is lawfully mine.

"I saw to it that your training would be in my hands. I have carefully reared you to reach this day. You have the courage, the strength, and the skill to kill Fafnir. All you need is the desire to help me. May I count on your help?"

Sigurd replied, "My heart is filled with sorrow to hear of your father's and your brother's greed. Surely, Andvari's curse is the bane of your family. Nevertheless, if you wish me to slay the mighty dragon who is your brother, I will do so. Fashion a sword for me that is equal to such a task. If any smith possesses such skill, surely it is you."

"That I will indeed do for you, Sigurd," said Regin. "You can put your complete trust in both my intent and my skill. For with that sword, Sigurd the Volsung will become known among all who walk the earth as Sigurd, Fafnir's Bane!"

Sigurd then decided to visit his mother's brother, who understood the lore of the dread Norns and could reveal the destinies of mortal folk. At first his uncle sat in silence. Then he said, "My nephew, it fills my heart with grief to speak of what those who rule men's fate have woven for you, for you are very dear to me.

"The fabric upon the loom of your life is a rich tapestry indeed, with intricate designs woven throughout in silver and gold thread. Truly, your life shines with the brilliance of the noonday sun! The patterns reveal that you will earn everlasting fame by slaying the fearsome Fafnir. You will also kill Regin, the tutor whom you trust, and win the treasure hoard.

"However," Sigurd's uncle added, "Andvari's treasure carries with it the curse of death and destruction to those who possess any part of it. This curse will destroy your love for Brunhild, the Valkyrie. Brunhild's vengeance will set your dearest friends against you, and you will be treacherously slain. You will leave behind a loving widow, who will avenge your death.

"Although you will die young, death is the common lot of all mortal folk," he concluded. "Always remember that it is the deeds you do while the wind of life blows within you that will bring you glory, honor, and lasting fame. You will be the most valiant of heroes: kind, courageous, fair, and skillful. A more noble man will never live beneath the sun!"

As he had promised, Regin fashioned a special sword for Sigurd. When Sigurd took the sword in his hand and struck the anvil with its blade, the blade broke into pieces. "You will have to make a better sword than this, Regin!" Sigurd exclaimed.

So the smith constructed a second sword for Sigurd. Once again, when Sigurd took the sword in his hand and struck the anvil with its blade, the blade broke into pieces. "Can you fashion no better sword than this, Regin?" Sigurd asked. "Or does treachery lurk in your heart as it did in the heart of your father and Fafnir? Do you intend Fafnir to kill me after I have killed him?"

Sigurd then approached his mother and said, "I have heard that my father asked you to save the pieces of his sword for me. If that is true, I wish to have them cast into a new sword. I intend to earn fame for myself by doing great deeds in the world!"

Sigurd's mother replied, "It is indeed true. As he lay dying, your father said to me, 'Carefully keep the pieces of my broken sword for our male child who is about to be born. They can be recast into a great sword called Gram. With it, our son will accomplish the deeds that will make his name live as long as there are bards on earth to tell the tale!'"

Regin was angry that Sigurd would not let him pursue his own craft in his own way. However, the master smith obeyed Sigurd's instructions and recast Sigmund the Volsung's sword. As Regin withdrew the finished blade from the fiery forge, blue flames burned all along its edges. "Here," he said to Sigurd. "Try this! If you are not satisfied I can do nothing more for you, even with all my talent."

Eagerly Sigurd grasped the sword that had been his father's. Raising it aloft, he swiftly brought it down on the anvil, as he had the other two swords. This time, however, the blade remained in one piece. In fact, it sliced straight through the anvil, dividing it in two down to its base.

"I think this sword will do," Sigurd said, "but I must put Gram to a more difficult test. Come with me."

Sigurd went down to the river, where he took a piece of wool and tossed it upstream. As it floated by him, he struck the wool with his sword, slicing it apart as he had split the anvil. "You have indeed served me well, Regin!" Sigurd exclaimed. "Gram will surely defend me against Fafnir!"

Sigurd and Regin set forth to find the mighty dragon. On the Gnita Heath they found the path that Fafnir traveled each day when he left his cave to quench his thirst. The path ended abruptly at the edge of a cliff, and they found themselves staring down at water splashing 180 feet below them.

"If your brother lies upon this path and drinks the water we see below us, then he has transformed himself into the largest dragon that has ever lived upon the earth!" Sigurd exclaimed.

"Fafnir's size should be of little matter to you, Sigurd!" Regin replied. "All you need to do is dig a hole where this path is. Make it deep enough for you to sit in it. Then, when Fafnir comes down the path toward the water, take your sword and thrust it up into his chest until it pierces his heart. What an easy way to earn glory, honor, and lasting fame! Fafnir's fiery breath will not scorch you with its venom. His spiked tail will not lacerate you. His scaly body will not foil Gram's search for blood. Intent on quenching his thirst, Fafnir will have no thought of the peril that awaits him as he glides forth on his vulnerable belly."

"That is all well and good," Sigurd replied. "But what if I should drown in the flood of Fafnir's blood?"

"You are hopeless, Sigurd!" Regin exclaimed. "No matter how well I advise you, your heart still overflows with fear! When your father died, he took the last of the Volsung courage with him! You will never be half the hero Sigmund was, for your heart is soft and weak! If you can find a better way to kill Fafnir, do it. I will be satisfied as long as you slay him!" With these words, Regin cloaked his own terror and rode off, leaving Sigurd alone upon the heath.

Sigurd set about digging the pit as Regin had advised. While he was working, he suddenly felt as if someone were studying him. He looked up to find standing above him an old, long-bearded man. He wore a blue cloak and a broad-brimmed hat that overshadowed his forehead, and he had only one eye.

"Sigurd, son of Volsung, why are you digging such a pit?" the old man asked. "Whoever gave you that treacherous counsel intends to destroy you! You are digging your own grave, for the flood of dragon's blood will drown you in this hole. It would be far better to dig many pits leading off from this one. Then, while you sit here and let Gram pierce the dragon's heart, Fafnir's blood will drain off into the other pits." The old man abruptly vanished, and Sigurd realized that it was Odin, the All-Father, who had counseled him.

When the tremendous dragon next slithered down the path toward the water, Sigurd was prepared with a network of pits and his trusted sword, Gram. Yet the young hero was unprepared for the terror that faced him. The weight of the monster caused the earth to rumble and shake as he moved along the path. The rhythmic explosions of his fiery venom caused the cliffs to echo with a progressively louder thunder as he approached Sigurd.

But Sigurd courageously remained hidden in his pit. Soon the body of the monster covered the pit like a slab, extinguishing all light. Sigurd plunged Gram up to the hilt into the dragon's vulnerable, exposed chest. Although he quickly withdrew his sword, the blood from Fafnir's gaping wound enveloped him. Fortunately, the side passages drained off the excess blood so that Sigurd did not drown as Regin had hoped.

Fafnir bellowed like an enraged bull as excruciating pain engulfed him. Frantically, he lashed out with his head and his tail, hoping to destroy his invisible enemy. Finally, as he lay dying, his eyes spied Sigurd, who was watching him from a safe distance.

"Who are you that you dared to match your sword against my might?" he asked Sigurd. "Surely my brother, Regin, must have challenged you to perform this deed. For I have terrified all who live in northern lands with my monstrous form and my poisonous breath, and folk for miles around live in dread of arousing my anger. I am comforted by the thought that he who led you to kill me also plans to kill you!"

"I am Sigurd, son of Sigmund the Volsung," Sigurd replied. "My courageous heart, my strength, and my sharp sword enabled me to bring your death upon you, and if Regin has cause to fear them, let him beware!"

"Little good your heart and your sword will be to you, Sigurd, son of Sigmund the Volsung, if you take my treasure," Fafnir replied. "The gold has been cursed by the dwarf Andvari. My beautiful gold ring and all the treasure in my cave are destined to be the bane of every being who possesses them! Death and destruction follow the gold as surely as night follows day, and no one who owns it will remain untouched by its curse. Only when the ring and the gold have returned to the deep waters will the bane end. So beware, lest my bane become yours as well!"

Sigurd replied, "I would fear Andvari's curse and leave your treasure if, by leaving it, I could avoid my death. However, each of us is fated to die sooner or later, so to live in fear of death serves no purpose. It is far better to perform courageous deeds and win treasure, glory, honor, and fame. If, like you, each of us can keep our treasure until the day of our death, we are indeed fortunate!"

When it was apparent that Fafnir was dead, Regin approached Sigurd. "Hail to you, Sigurd, son of Sigmund the Volsung and Fafnir's Bane!" he cried. "You have shown the greatest courage to face Fafnir and kill him. The fame this deed has brought you will endure as long as bards live upon the earth to sing of it!"

"The deed will surely bring you no fame," Sigurd replied, "for you left me alone to fight this mightiest of dragons!"

"Do not forget that I am the one who forged your sharp-edged sword!" Regin exclaimed. "Without it you would not have dared to attack Fafnir, because he surely would have destroyed you!"

"You are wrong, Regin," Sigurd replied. "What deed can a man perform, even with the greatest weapon, if he lacks the heart to do it? A brave man will win because he fights valiantly even if his sword is dull-bladed."

As Sigurd began to cut the dragon's heart out of his body, Regin said, "I have one small request to ask of you, Sigurd. Roast Fafnir's heart upon the fire, and let me eat it. I would like that token of my brother."

Sigurd obediently took the heart to the fire and roasted it upon a wooden spit. When he burned his finger on the bloody juices dripping from it, he put that finger into his mouth. To his amazement, as soon as the heart's blood entered his mouth, Sigurd could understand the language of the birds who sat watching him.

"There sits Sigurd," said one of the birds, "almost completely covered in Fafnir's blood. He cannot see that a linden leaf has stuck to his back between his shoulder blades and is pressed there by the dragon's caked blood."

"Sigurd does not realize that the dragon's blood possesses such protective powers that from this time forth, wherever Fafnir's blood has touched him no weapon of any kind will be able to harm him," added a second bird.

"If Sigurd could understand our words, he would protect his one vulnerable spot," said another bird. "For he can be wounded only where the linden leaf has prevented Fafnir's hot blood from touching his skin."

A fourth bird announced, "Sigurd foolishly is roasting Fafnir's shining heart for Regin. Sigurd should eat that heart himself, for then he, not Regin, would become the wisest of all men!"

"Regin is thinking about the best way to betray Sigurd," the second bird said. "He longs to avenge Fafnir's death. He will try to trick Sigurd with crooked words. Sigurd is foolish to trust him!"

"Sigurd should slice Regin's head from his neck. Then he would have all of Fafnir's treasure for himself!" added the third bird.

"Before Regin beats Sigurd to the deed!" the fourth bird exclaimed. "As the saying goes: 'Where wolf's ears are seen, wolf's teeth are close at hand!' If Sigurd is wise, he will take care of himself. He will ride to Fafnir's den, collect Andvari's hoard, then ride to Hindfell, where Brunhild sleeps. That is the road to wisdom!"

"Sigurd certainly has nothing to lose!" exclaimed the first bird. "He has killed one brother already. That is reason enough for the remaining brother to kill him."

"The birds are right!" Sigurd thought to himself. "Certainly, Regin will soon become my bane. If he shares Fafnir's destiny now, I will not have to fear him."

Sigurd approached the unsuspecting Regin, quickly drew Gram from its sheath, and sliced off Regin's head. He drank both Regin's and Fafnir's blood. Then he ate most of Fafnir's heart and saved the rest.

The birds chattered in a chorus: "Place Andvari's ring on your finger, Sigurd. You have little to fear. Then ride to Hindfell, where the Valkyrie Brunhild sleeps. High is the shield-hall that stands upon Hindfell, gleaming with gold within a ring of flames. The most beautiful of all maidens lies surrounded by gold, while red flame-shadows dance upon her. Long has the shield-maiden of Odin slept, put to sleep by the All-Father for disobedience in battle. She had pity in her heart and let the wrong warrior live, despite the dread Norns' decree. The sleep-thorn protects her until you come to win her! Place Andvari's ring on your finger, Sigurd. You have little to fear."

Once again, Sigurd obeyed the counsel of the birds. He mounted Grani and rode to Fafnir's den. There he found treasure beyond dreaming. He found Andvari's ring in a special place and slid it on his finger. He placed Hreidmar's Helmet of Terror on his head. Then he put the remaining treasure into two great chests and loaded them upon Grani's back. He planned to walk beside Grani to spare the horse his additional weight, but Grani refused to move. So Sigurd climbed onto his back. As soon as Grani felt the familiar weight of his master, he took off at a gallop as if he were carrying nothing but the wind.

Chapter 4

Sigurd awakens Brunhild and falls in love with her.

As Sigurd rode in search of Brunhild, his fame spread across the northern lands with the speed of the winter wind. Sigurd towered above other men in strength. He carried himself with such confidence that his extraordinary skill in handling the sword, casting the spear, bending the bow, and shooting an arrow were evident to all who gazed upon him. He carried a shield of blazing gold with the image of a red and brown dragon upon it. His suit of armor and his weapons were all of gold, and a similar dragon image decorated his helmet, his saddle, and his armor. Clearly, this was the man who had slain the fearsome dragon Fafnir.

Moreover, Sigurd possessed wisdom beyond that of ordinary humans. Since he could understand the language of birds, few events took him by surprise. He spoke with such eloquence and conviction that he could persuade anyone to his point of view.

He took great pleasure in pursuing challenging adventures, yet he also loved to help the common folk. He was known to take wealth from his enemies and give it to his friends. He was as courteous as he was strong. His courage never failed him, and he was afraid of nothing.

Sigurd rode far to the south, into the land of the Franks. Suddenly he saw before him a great light shining forth from the top of a hill. As he drew nearer, he could see that the source of the glow was a huge fire, whose flames soared toward the heavens. Within the ring of fire was a castle hung round about with shields. A banner floated above the topmost roof.

Knowing no fear, Sigurd rode Grani through the blazing ring of flame. The shield-hall was completely deserted except for a lone figure encased in a golden helmet and golden armor. The person appeared to be dead.

Sigurd removed the helmet. To his amazement, he discovered a maiden beneath the war gear. Her face blushed with the vigor of life, and Sigurd decided to awaken her. He moved her gently, but she remained fast asleep. He then noticed a thorn stuck into the back of her hand, and he removed it.

The maiden's eyes opened. She looked appraisingly at Sigurd, undaunted by the Helmet of Terror on his head. The man who stood before her was fair of face and awesome in stature. His eyes were so piercing that few were comfortable meeting his gaze. A great head of golden red hair tumbled down in heavy locks, and a thick, short beard surrounded his strongly chisled, high-boned face. His shoulders were as broad as the shoulders of two men. He was so tall that he could wear his sword Gram, which was seven sword-lengths long, upon his waist.

"Who are you," she asked, "who have awakened me from my long sleep? You must be Sigurd, son of Sigmund the Volsung, because you are wearing Hreidmar's Helmet of Terror upon your head, and you are holding Fafnir's Bane in your hand!"

"I am indeed!" Sigurd replied in surprise. "I have heard that you are the daughter of a mighty king and that you are as wise as you are beautiful."

Brunhild replied, "At Odin's command, I have slept for time without measure, helpless to awaken from the prick of his sleep-thorn. I was a Valkyrie, one of the warrior-maidens of Odin who are destined to live forever. I would descend upon the battlefield, bring death to the warrior of Odin's choice, and return with the dead hero to Valhalla in Asgard. There the hero would join other heroes to wait for Ragnarok, when they will help the gods fight the Frost Giants in the great battle that will bring this world to an end.

"In my last battle," Brunhild continued, "two great kings fought against one another. Since the old king was the greatest of warriors, Odin had commanded me to give the victory to him. I, however, decided to strike him down and let the younger king live instead. Odin's fury was implacable.

"'Because you have disobeyed my orders,' he told me, 'never again will I permit you to be a Valkyrie. Instead, you must marry a mortal and live for an ordinary span of years.'

"'If I must marry,' I replied, 'I promise you that I will marry only a man who never lets fear enter his heart!'

"'I will agree to that,' Odin replied. 'In your shield-hall on Hindfell, I will prick you with the sleep-thorn, and you will fall into a long, deep sleep. A ring of flames will rage around the walls of your castle to protect you.'

"He added, 'You will sleep undisturbed until the great hero Sigurd, son of Sigmund the Volsung, rescues you. Only he among mortals has the great courage you desire. He will ride through your blazing fire on his horse, Grani, who is kin to my own Steipnir. He will be carrying Andvari's hoard, for Sigurd, alone of all the men who walk the earth, will have had the heart to slay the fearsome dragon Fafnir and his brother Regin, the master smith.'

"And what Odin revealed to me has, indeed, come to pass," Brunhild concluded. "I have slept until this moment when you awakened me!"

"What knowledge can you teach me?" Sigurd asked. "You have a wisdom that belongs to the gods!"

"Let us drink together," said Brunhild, "and into your ale I will mix knowledge about life. I will give you knowledge of war to cut upon your sword, knowledge of the sea to cut upon the stern of your ship, knowledge of healing for the wounds of war, and knowledge of helping the simple, good folk.

"I advise you to speak carefully, and always keep your word. Be kind to your family and friends, even when they injure you, so as to win lasting praise. Beware of the presence of evil around you, and remove yourself from it lest it harm you. Be alert to the schemes of your friends so that you will know if one of your wife's relatives hates you and plans to take vengeance upon you. No matter how young he is, never trust the close relative of one you have killed, for even the wolf cub is a wolf.

"May you prosper with this knowledge until the gods bring an end to your days," Brunhild concluded. "May my wisdom bring you success and fame. And may you remember in the future what we have talked about here."

Sigurd embraced and kissed Brunhild. "You are the most beautiful maiden who has ever lived, and surely you are the wisest of all women!" he exclaimed. "I swear that I will have you as my own wife, for I hold you very dear to my heart."

"Then Sigurd, son of Sigmund the Volsung, I choose you above all other mortals!" Brunhild exclaimed. "You will be mine as I will be yours!"

As a token of his love, Sigurd gave to Brunhild Andvari's gold ring. "I will hold your love in my heart for as long as I live," he promised.

Brunhild looked at the ring that Sigurd had placed on her finger and replied, "We are not destined to live together, Sigurd. I am a shield-maiden. I wear a helmet as kings do in time of war, and I fight in battle. While I am enjoying the battlefield, you will marry Gudrun, the daughter of King Giuki."

"You cannot believe that I will be tempted by some king's daughter!" Sigurd exclaimed. "You alone have my heart, and I swear by the gods that I will have you as my wife or have no wife at all!"

Thus Sigurd and Brunhild pledged to love one another faithfully, and then Sigurd went on his way.

Chapter 5

Sigurd forgets Brunhild and marries Gudrun. Then he helps Gunnar win Brunhild as his bride. Gudrun reveals the truth to Brunhild.

After a journey of many days, Sigurd came to the palace of King Giuki, who ruled a kingdom south of the Rhine River. In addition to their beautiful daughter, Gudrun, King Giuki and his fierce-hearted wife, Queen Grimhild, had three sons: Gunnar, Hogni, and young Guttorm. All of their children were extraordinary in both goodness and skill, and the two older sons had earned fame through deeds of war.

When one of the nobles saw Sigurd in their town, he immediately went before King Giuki and said, "I have seen a man, who in form is like a god, riding into our town. Not only does he far surpass any man I have ever seen, but he is wearing gold armor, carrying golden weapons, and riding a horse that is far greater than any other animal of its kind."

King Guiki left the palace to welcome Sigurd and invite him to stay with them. Before long, the King treated Sigurd like his own son, Gunnar and Hogni treated him like the best of brothers, and Queen Grimhild decided that he would be the perfect husband for Gudrun. In addition to being impressed with his great wealth, King Guiki's family loved Sigurd because he was such a good human being. He was kind, loving, loyal, and generous.

Sigurd often spoke of his love for Brunhild. So Grimhild decided that the only way to win Sigurd for her daughter was to make him forget Brunhild. She accomplished this by giving Sigurd a drugged drink. As he drank it, she said, "Consider us to be your family, Sigurd. Giuki, Gunnar, Hogni, and I will now swear that we are father, brothers, and mother to you." The potion caused Sigurd to forget Brunhild entirely.

Sigurd had spent five seasons with the family when Queen Grimhild said to her husband, "Sigurd has the greatest of all hearts. Moreover, he is trustworthy and helpful. His strength makes our kingdom more powerful. Therefore, give him our daughter in marriage with wealth to spare and the right to rule what he chooses. Then he should be content to live with us forever."

Giuki replied, "Usually a king does not have to offer his daughter in marriage. Suitors apply to him for her hand. Yet I would rather offer her to Sigurd than accept the suit of any other noble."

So it came to pass that Sigurd was offered both power and the beautiful and good Princess Gudrun. He accepted with great pleasure. The older members of the family again swore oaths of brotherhood, and the royal wedding was a time of special joy for all.

With King Giuki's sons, Sigurd pursued the arts of war, returning home victorious and bearing great treasure in addition to glory, honor, and fame. He gave the part of Fafnir's heart that he had saved to Gudrun to eat, and she became even more wise and kind.

Now that her daughter was happily settled in marriage, Queen Grimhild turned her thoughts to her son Gunnar. "Surely Brunhild is the best choice for you," she told him. "I suggest that you set out to win her, and take Sigurd with you." Gunnar knew of Brunhild's beauty and fame, so he immediately agreed.

In high spirits, Gunnar, Hogni, and Sigurd approached Brunhild's father. When Gunnar asked for her hand in marriage, her father replied, "Brunhild will wed only the man whom she freely chooses. In order to win her, you must go to her castle high on Hindfell and ride through the wall of roaring flames around her golden shield-hall."

When the brothers arrived at the castle, Gunnar could not make his horse ride into the flames. No matter how he spurred and struck him, the horse would rear in terror and withdraw. So, Gunnar said to Sigurd, "My horse will never carry me through the fire. Will you lend me Grani?"

Sigurd did so willingly, but Grani would not take one step with Gunnar on his back. "Grani will carry no one but you!" Gunnar exclaimed. "Let us practice the art of shape-changing that my mother has taught us. Make yourself look just like me, and in my name ride Grani through the flames and win Brunhild for me. Meanwhile, I will remain here, looking just like you."

Having no memory of Brunhild and their love, Sigurd agreed to the adventure. He assumed Gunnar's shape, climbed upon Grani, took his sword in his hand, and spurred Grani into the heart of the raging flames. As Grani passed through the fire, the flames roared with an even greater fury and stretched their fiery fingers to the heavens above them, while the earth shook beneath the horse's feet. Nonetheless, Grani carried Sigurd safely through the blaze.

When Sigurd dismounted and entered Brunhild's palace, the warrior-maiden was sitting in the great hall with a helmet upon her head, armor encasing her body, and a sword in her hand. She looked at him and asked, "Who are you?"

"I am Gunnar, son of Giuki," Sigurd replied, "and I have come to claim you as my wife. For I have spoken with your father and have ridden through the flames that surround your hall."

"Do not speak to me of marriage, Gunnar," Brunhild replied, "unless you are the best of all men who walk upon the earth. You will have to combat all who would be suitors of mine, and I am reluctant to give up the life of a warrior, which I so enjoy."

"That may well be so," Sigurd as Gunnar replied, "but you swore a sacred oath that you would marry the man who rode through the ring of flames around your hall, and I have done so."

Brunhild then accepted the man she thought was Gunnar, and they exchanged rings as a sign of their love. Brunhild gave Andvari's ring to Sigurd, and Sigurd gave her a ring of Gunnar's to wear in its place.

Sigurd spent the next three nights with Brunhild. Since he was wooing her for Gunnar, Sigurd neither kissed Brunhild nor embraced her. Although they shared the same bed, each night Sigurd placed his sword between them. He told Brunhild that he could marry in no other way, and she did not question him.

Upon leaving Brunhild's castle, Sigurd had to spur Grani through the wall of flames once again. Then he and Gunnar exchanged shapes and rode to tell Brunhild's family of the news.

Later Brunhild visited her brother-in-law and said, "A king who claimed to be named Gunnar rode through the flames that surround my hall on Hindfell. I have promised to wed the man who possesses Andvari's hoard and who will ride Grani through the ring of flames that surround my shield-hall. But I know that only Sigurd could do this, for only he, of all the men who walk the earth, has the courage in his heart to have slain the fearsome dragon Fafnir."

Brunhild continued, "It is Sigurd whom I love, and Sigurd whom I pledged to marry. Now, what do I do about Gunnar? Rather than marry him, I would far prefer to remain chief over one-third of your army and to spend my time defending your kingdom."

Brunhild's brother-in-law replied, "You must marry Gunnar, for you cannot prove that he did not ride through those flames. Besides, Sigurd has married Gudrun, Gunnar's sister. What is past is dead; you cannot revive it. Only the present and the future are important. If you wish to keep my friendship and avoid my anger, you will forget Sigurd and marry Gunnar!"

So it came to pass that a second great wedding feast was held in the hall of King Giuki, to honor the marriage of Brunhild and Gunnar. The new couple appeared to be very happy. As the celebration ended, Sigurd's memory returned to him. Although he remembered the promises he had made to Brunhild, he never revealed by look, word, or deed that he had ever seen her before. He loved Gudrun and Gunnar, and above all he wanted peace among the members of his adopted family.

All was well until one day when Brunhild and Gudrun went to the Rhine River to bathe. Brunhild immediately walked into the river upstream of Gudrun. "I deserve the fresh water for rinsing my hair because my father is greater than yours, and my husband is more valiant than yours," she said. "Gunnar is known for his many famous deeds, not the least of which was riding through the wall of flames around my castle in order to win my love. Your husband's deeds are certainly no match for that!"

Gudrun waded upstream past Brunhild and angrily replied, "I suggest that you remain silent instead of criticizing my husband. In fact, it is my right to wash my hair upstream of you. You are foolish to demean your first love; all who have tongues to speak acclaim Sigurd as the most courageous man the world has ever known. It was Sigurd who killed Fafnir and Regin. Those valiant deeds gave him the right to Andvari's hoard of treasure."

Brunhild replied, "Well, it was Gunnar, not Sigurd, who rode through the raging fire that surrounds my shield-hall, and that took far more courage than the slaying of Fafnir!"

Gudrun laughed and said, "Brunhild, do you really think it was my brother who rode through those flames? Only Sigurd could have done that! He wooed you in Gunnar's name and shape, because Gunnar could not do it himself! You gave Andvari's ring to the man who shared your bed, and he gave it to me. If you do not believe me, just look at my hand, for I am wearing the ring that my husband originally gave to you!"

Brunhild recognized the ring immediately and became as pale as a corpse. She returned to the palace in silence and remained silent all evening.

Gudrun later asked Sigurd, "Why is Brunhild so silent? Is she not happy being famous, wealthy, and married to the man of her choice? I think I will ask her about it tomorrow!"

"Do no such thing, Gudrun," Sigurd replied, "for you will be very sorry if you do."

But Gudrun could not let the matter rest. The next day she said, "What is the matter, Brunhild? Did our conversation yesterday bother you, or is something else the matter?"

"You must have a cruel heart to return to that subject," Brunhild replied. "Do not pry into matters that are not good for you to know."

"What can you have against me?" Gudrun asked. "I have done nothing to hurt you!"

"I will not forgive you for having Sigurd, when he belonged to me! Gunnar may be wealthy and strong, but Sigurd killed the fearsome dragon Fafnir, and that is a greater deed than all of Gunnar's deeds. And Sigurd, not Gunnar, rode through the ring of flames that surround my shield-hall."

Brunhild added, "Your mother is to blame for this entire matter! Sigurd forgot me because she gave him a drugged drink."

"That is a lie!" Gudrun exclaimed angrily.

"Enjoy your husband, Gudrun, knowing that he would not be yours but for the craft of your mother! I wish you only trouble!"

That night as Gunnar lay asleep, Brunhild left the palace. Over the snow-capped mountains and the ice fields she wandered, letting evil thoughts inflame her heart. "Sigurd lies in bed embracing Gudrun, his queen, while I must live without his love and without his treasure," she said to herself. "My only joy will be in revenge!"

Chapter 6

Brunhild persuades Gunnar to slay Sigurd. He arranges for Guttorm to perform the deed. Gudrun becomes an unwitting accomplice to the treachery.

When Brunhild returned to the palace, she retired to her room and lay there as if she were close to death. Gunnar was concerned about her health and pressed her to tell him what was wrong. At first Brunhild remained silent. Finally she asked, "Gunnar, what did you do with that ring I gave you? I promised to wed the man who possessed Fafnir's hoard and who rode the horse Grani through my flaming ring of fire. That man could only have been Sigurd, for he alone, of all the men who walk the earth, has the courage in his heart to have slain the fearsome dragon Fafnir.

"You, Gunnar," she added, "have performed no great deeds in your life. What mighty treasure have you won? You may be a king, but you are not a noble leader. You have the courage of a dead man! I promised to marry the most noble man alive, and when I married you I broke that oath. Because Sigurd is not mine, I will cause your death. And I will reward Grimhild's treachery with the most evil of gifts, for never has a woman lived who is more vile than your mother!"

Gunnar quietly replied, "You are an evil woman who speaks with a poisoned tongue. You are criticizing a woman who is far superior to you. She has not spent her life killing folk, but has earned the praise of all."

"I have never performed evil deeds in secret, as your mother has," Brunhild replied. "However, my heart overflows with the wish to kill you! Never again will you find me in your hall happy to be your wife. Never again will you see me playing chess or plying my gold embroidery, drinking among friends, speaking kind words, or giving you good advice. My heart is filled with sorrow that Sigurd is not mine, and never again will there be love in my heart for you!"

Brunhild left her bed, tore her needlework to shreds, and opened her doors and windows so her sorrowful wailing would be heard far and wide. For seven days and seven nights she remained alone in her room, refusing food and drink and all offers of companionship. One by one Gunnar, Hogni, and the servants tried to reach her heart, but Brunhild's sorrow and anger were implacable.

Finally Sigurd said to Gudrun, "I fear that evil winds are blowing upon us. As Brunhild remains aloof in her room, in her heart she is plotting dreadful deeds against me!"

"Then please go talk with her!" Gudrun replied, weeping. "Offer her gold. Surely treasure will calm her grief and soothe her anger!"

Sigurd went to Brunhild's room, threw off her bed coverings, and exclaimed, "Awaken, Brunhild! You have slept long enough! The sun is shining, so let happy thoughts push grief from your heart."

"How dare you come before me!" Brunhild replied. "Of all who live upon the earth, I hate you the most, for you have been the most unjust to me."

"What evil spirit possesses you that you blame me for treating you cruelly? I have never had an unkind thought about you. You freely chose the husband that you have!"

"No, Sigurd!" said Brunhild. "I did not choose to wed Gunnar. He did not ride through my ring of flames; you did! I thought I recognized your eyes when I saw Gunnar standing before me in my hall. The Norns blinded me to what was good and what was evil, and so I accepted Gunnar in spite of my doubts. My heart has never loved him, although I have done my best to hide my true feelings. It was you who killed the fearsome dragon Fafnir and rode through the blazing fire for my sake, not Gunnar!"

"Brunhild, it is true that I am not your husband; yet you are wed to a famous man. Gunnar is the noblest of men! He has killed great kings. And he loves you with all his heart. You cannot buy such love with a hoard of treasure. How is it that you cannot love him? Why are you so angry?"

"My heart sorrows that a sword is not yet smeared with your blood!" she replied.

"I fear you do not have long to wait," Sigurd said. "We two are destined to enjoy only a few more days upon the earth."

"It is all the same to me," said Brunhild. "Since you betrayed me, I do not care whether I live or die!"

"I urge you to live, and to love both Gunnar and me!" Sigurd exclaimed. "I will give you all my treasure if you will but live!"

"You do not understand the feelings in my heart," Brunhild replied. "You, not Gunnar, are the best of all men, and you are the only man I have ever loved!"

"I loved you better than I loved myself," Sigurd replied, "and I love you still. However, I became the victim of Queen Grimhild's treachery and lost you. It was not until after Gunnar married you that my memory of you returned, and then my love for you returned as well. My heart sorrowed that you were not my wife, but I made the best of it. After all, I lived in a royal household with a loving wife, and we were all together."

"I have no pity for you, Sigurd! Your tale of love for me and sorrow over our plight comes too late to warm my heart. I swore an oath that I would marry the man who rode though my ring of flames; if I cannot keep that sacred oath, I choose to die!"

"I cannot stand the thought of your death!" Sigurd exclaimed. "If it comes to that, I will leave Gudrun and marry you!"

"No, Sigurd, it is too late. I will not have you or any other man! Without you, power and wealth mean nothing to me, life means nothing to me, and I choose to die."

With no more words to be said, Sigurd left Brunhild. His heart was so heavy with grief that it swelled with the pain and burst the iron rings on his chain-mail shirt. He did not tell Gunnar of Brunhild's anger or of his own grief.

When Gunnar next saw Brunhild, she said to him, "Sigurd betrayed both you and me by sleeping with me when, in your shape, he rode through the ring of fire to win me for you. For this offense Sigurd must die, for he committed it. Or you must die, for you permitted it. Or I will die, for the shame of it. Unless you agree to slay Sigurd, I will cause you to lose your wealth, your land, and your life. I will then return to my family and spend the rest of my days overcome with sorrow."

As Brunhild expected, Gunnar could not see beyond the tale she chose to tell him. All day long he sat with a heavy heart, pondering what he should do. His heart was torn between his love for Sigurd and the oath of friendship they had sworn and his love for his wife and the loyalty he owed her. Finally, he realized that he could not live with the shame of his wife's leaving him. "Brunhild is the best of all women," he thought. "She means more to me than anything on earth, and I would die before I would risk losing her love and her wealth."

Gunnar called his brother Hogni to him and said, "Evil times have come upon us. We must slay Sigurd, for he has been disloyal to us. Then we will divide his rule and his treasure between us."

Hogni replied, "Would you betray Sigurd because you want the treasure that he took from Fafnir? Or are you considering this treachery because you want Brunhild's wealth? We are honor-bound not to break our oaths of friendship with Sigurd. I know that Brunhild has persuaded you to do this, but I urge you to reconsider. If you slay Sigurd, you will bring dishonor and shame upon us all!"

"I am determined to do this deed," Gunnar said. "Let us arrange to have our brother Guttorm slay Sigurd, for he is too young to have sworn the oaths with Sigurd that we two swore, and he will believe whatever we choose to tell him."

"No good will come of this evil deed!" Hogni exclaimed. "Sigurd is an honorable man. If we betray his trust, our foul deed will fall heavily upon our own heads."

"Choose between us, Hogni," Gunnar replied. "Either we slay Sigurd or I will take my own life!"

Thus Hogni agreed to the treachery. The two brothers called Guttorm before them and offered him great power and wealth if he would slay Sigurd. They used some of the knowledge of witchcraft that their mother possessed. They chopped into paste the flesh of a certain worm together with the meat of a wolf and secretly added it to the wine they gave Guttorm to drink. The drug made Guttorm eager to do whatever they asked of him without thinking about it.

The brothers planned a boar and bear hunt as the occasion on which Guttorm would slay Sigurd. When Gudrun heard that Sigurd was accompanying her brothers on a hunting expedition, her heart filled with foreboding and fear. Knowing the depth of Brunhild's rage, Gudrun feared that Sigurd would be the target of her malice.

"Who can help me protect Sigurd from whatever evil scheme Brunhild devises?" she wondered. "I can no longer trust Gunnar. He will perform whatever deeds his wife asks of him. Hogni, of course, will support Gunnar, for they have always been inseparable. But Guttorm may be able to help me. He is not particularly close to Gunnar and Hogni. Yes, I think I can rely upon him!"

So it came to pass that Gudrun summoned her youngest brother, Guttorm, and said to him, "I fear that Brunhild may have planned some evil to befall Sigurd during the course of your hunting adventure. Sigurd has always been loyal to our family, and I do not want him to suffer for my foolish argument with Brunhild. I have already apologized for my quick tongue."

"I have always been very fond of Sigurd," Guttorm replied. "What would you like me to do, Gudrun?"

"I am afraid of some form of treachery that will appear to be a hunting accident," Gudrun replied. "I would like you to remain at Sigurd's side and guard him for me.

"Therefore," she continued, "I will confide in you a secret that Sigurd has shared with me alone. When he slew the dragon Fafnir, he became covered with that monster's blood. From that time forth, wherever the blood had touched my husband no weapon could harm him. However, as the blood from Fafnir's gaping wound enveloped Sigurd, the wind blew leaves off a nearby linden tree. One of those leaves stuck between his shoulder blades and warded off the bath of hot dragon's blood. I fear that, in some form of treachery, Sigurd will be shot in his one vulnerable spot and killed."

"If you will sew a design on Sigurd's jacket to mark the place where the leaf lodged, I promise to keep my eyes upon that spot," Guttorm replied.

"Oh, thank you!" said Gudrun. "I will add a leaf of red silk to the design of Sigurd's embroidered hunting jacket. It will stand apart from the rest because of its color, and yet it will blend in with the larger design so that only you and I will know its special meaning."

Gudrun's fears continued to torment her. By the morning of the hunting expedition, she was frantic with worry. "Oh, Sigurd," she cried, "last night I dreamed that as two boars chased you over the meadow, blood from your wound painted the flowers a deep red. Please do not join the hunt. I fear that someone will try to kill you!"

"Nonsense, dear Gudrun," Sigurd replied. "I am going with your kinsmen, and you know how well we love one another. I know of no one who hates me, nor anything I have done to cause such hatred. Be at ease. I will be back with you in a few days."

"Oh, Sigurd," Gudrun wept, "you are being foolish! Last night I dreamed that two mountains fell upon you and buried you, and I could never see you again. Please do not join the hunt. I know in my heart that someone will try to kill you!"

"Nonsense, dearest wife. You have no cause to fear. Be at ease. I will be back with you before you have had time to miss me!" And with these words, Sigurd embraced Gudrun tenderly and departed.

With an air of ease and good cheer, the hunting party headed toward the forest. Once they were deep within the woods, they stopped to discuss the best hunting strategy. "Let us divide into two groups to double the chance of success," Sigurd suggested.

"A fine idea," Gunnar replied. "Given your skill, let Hogni come with me while Guttorm accompanies you. Then we will be more evenly matched."

Sigurd and Guttorm hunted easily and well. Together they killed a number of elk and deer. Then they cornered a great wild boar, whose malicious tusks and sharp eyes challenged even the best of hunters. When the animal furiously charged toward Grani, Sigurd slew it with his sword.

They had just spied a bear when a horn blast echoed through the trees, signaling that the time had come to get together for supper. "We have done so well, Guttorm," Sigurd announced, "that I think it is time to have some fun. I intend to capture that bear and bring it back with us alive. That will surprise your brothers, and we will all have a good laugh."

Sigurd took Grani as far as he could. When the forest became too dense, he dismounted and chased the bear on foot. Sigurd was so quick and quiet on his feet that he caught the bear and tied it up without even needing to wound it first. He did not even get a scratch in the process. He dragged the bear back to Grani, tied it to his saddle, and set off with Guttorm to rejoin the other members of their party.

When they came upon a stream, Sigurd realized that he was very thirsty. He had not stopped for food or drink the entire day. Because the live bear was attached to his saddle, he tethered Grani to a sturdy tree. He then placed his hunting weapons near his horse, walked over to the stream, and bent down to take a drink.

Guttorm followed Sigurd's lead, walking behind him to the stream, his sword unsheathed in his hand. As Sigurd splashed the fresh water into his mouth, Guttorm suddenly plunged his sword through the red silk leaf embroidered on Sigurd's hunting jacket. The weapon sank deep into Sigurd's back and came out through his chest.

Blood gushed from Sigurd's back and chest. The stream waters ran red, and the ground was drenched with blood. Furiously, like an enraged, wounded boar, Sigurd turned to kill his murderer—but his weapons lay by the tree, and he was too weak to reach them. Thus, the greatest of heroes fell with his death wound among the wildflowers while Guttorm looked on from a safe distance. The boy gazed at Sigurd with growing horror, as the effects of the drugged drink wore off and his judgment returned.

"Guttorm," Sigurd whispered, "hear my last words and remember them well. Dear boy, you are only the arm of Brunhild's treachery. My uncle told me of my fate long ago, and Brunhild warned me, but I was blind to their words. Few among us can recognize our own destiny, and those who attempt to fight their fate are condemned to lose."

Sigurd added, "I swear to you that I have never harmed Gunnar in any way. I have never been more than a brother to his wife, even though she loved me above all other men. I have always honored our oaths to one another. Return to your kin with these words, for you have killed an honorable man this day."

Sigurd sank back upon the blood-drenched flowers. Death quickly stole upon him, for he had no weapon and no strength to keep it at bay.

Guttorm rode off to fetch Gunnar and Hogni. When they returned, they found Grani standing with his head bent low over Sigurd's body. They placed Sigurd upon his golden shield and prepared to return home. Gunnar said, "Hogni, when we return to the palace, describe how Sigurd went off hunting alone and must have been surprised by robbers as he drank from the stream. Then no one will suspect that we are to blame for this foul deed."

Chapter 7

Guttorm confesses his treachery. Brunhild reveals the future to Gunnar and then commits suicide. Gudrun mourns Sigurd's death. The corpses of Brunhild and Sigurd are burned together.

When her brothers returned to the castle bearing Sigurd's corpse, Gudrun was overcome with grief and anger. "Your tale of robbers may be true," she said, "but let me see you stand before Sigurd's corpse and proclaim your innocence. If you are guilty, his wound will condemn you by gushing forth fresh blood.

"When next you ride off to war," she added, "in vain will you wish that Sigurd were by your side to help you! He was your strength, and without him you will no longer prosper. Now look upon the corpse of your brother and swear that you had no part in his death!"

Guttorm replied, "Enough of false words! As Sigurd bent forward to drink from the stream, his back was toward me, and I struck him through the leaf you had embroidered upon his hunting jacket. I was doing my brothers' deed, dear sister, but Sigurd blamed Brunhild. Sigurd's dying words proclaimed his innocence. He swore that he was never false in any way to you, Gunnar, and that he was never more than a brother to Brunhild."

"Alas that you, my dear brothers, have brought this sorrow upon me!" Gudrun cried. "For breaking your oaths of love and friendship, may your kingdom become a wasteland! May Sigurd's gold drag you to your deaths! It was an evil day when Sigurd rode upon Grani to join you in the courtship of Brunhild. That woman is surely the most hated of all folk! She has destroyed a brave man and has brought nothing but sorrow to his wife!"

Hogni exclaimed, "Our destiny is unrolling before our eyes! Nothing good will come of this foul deed while we are yet alive!"

By now Gunnar had great misgivings about the murder he had instigated. When he heard Brunhild's mad laughter he said, "You laugh like one whose heart is made of stone! You must be evil to the core of your being. How would you feel if you killed your brother, Atli, and then had to look upon his corpse?"

"Atli will not die before my eyes!" Brunhild responded. "He will outlive both you and Hogni and will be a greater king! As for me, I will take my own life!"

"Choose life, not death!" Gunnar pleaded. "I offer you all of my wealth!"

When his wife would not listen, Gunnar asked Hogni to convince her. But Hogni said, "Let Brunhild die as she has determined. She has brought nothing but evil upon us!"

On the day that the corpse of Sigurd would be given to the fire, Brunhild collected the treasure she possessed and called everyone before her. She picked up her sword, plunged it into her side beneath her armpit, and lay back, calmly waiting for death to claim her. "Come," she said. "Let all who wish some treasure come forth and take my gold!"

Then she said to Gunnar, "While I still have the wind of life within me, I will tell you of your terrible future. You will ride into the arms of an enemy, and evil times will befall you and all your kin. For you broke your oath to Sigurd when you killed him, and you rewarded his loyalty with evil. Even when Sigurd won me for you, he was loyal to you. For the three nights he slept in my bed, he placed between us his sharp-edged sword, Gram, as a token of his honor.

"You will force Gudrun to marry my brother, Atli, against her will, and she will give him Andvari's ring. Atli will kill you to acquire Andvari's hoard, but in order to prevent the treasure from falling into his greedy hands, you will have buried it at the bottom of the Rhine River. Gudrun will avenge your deaths by murdering Atli and his sons. When she casts herself into the sea, Andvari's ring, like the rest of his treasure, will return to deep waters. Thus, Death will take you and your kin, and with the return of Andvari's hoard to the deep waters, the dwarf's curse will end."

Brunhild concluded, "Carry my corpse to Sigurd's funeral pyre. Place rich tapestries and golden shields around the pyre. Then place me next to Sigurd, with his sword between us as it was when he slept with me in my shield hall. We will burn as husband and wife and leave this earth together." With these words, Brunhild died.

Meanwhile, Gudrun sat dry-eyed and silent before Sigurd's covered body. Many queens came before her and spoke of their own loneliness when faced with the death of a loved one. They hoped that the warmth of friendship and the sharing of burdens would make it easier for her to accept the common lot of all human folk.

Finally Gudrun's sister pulled back the funeral shroud and said, "Look upon your husband, Gudrun, and kiss him, for I know of no love as true as yours among all who walk the earth. Sigurd was your greatest joy!"

Then Gudrun's heart melted, and her grief flowed from her eyes in a torrent of tears. "My Sigurd," she cried, "towered above all men as a stag stands above all beasts. He shone as gold in the presence of silver. He was the brightest jewel worn on a band, the most precious stone worn by a prince."

Gudrun continued, "As long as Sigurd was alive, I was held in highest regard by all noble warriors. Now that he is dead, I am no more than a lone willow leaf lost among a multitude of others on the tree. Like the leaves stripped from a twig, my joys have been cut off, and with no further nourishment they will wither and die. I miss my husband's sweet words, his love, and his friendship."

When the mighty pyre had been kindled, Gunnar did as Brunhild had wished. The corpse of Sigurd was placed upon it, along with the corpse of Brunhild, and Gram was placed between them. As the flames roared aloft, raising their rosy fingers to the heavens, they consumed wood and flesh alike. Thus, Brunhild burned by the side of Sigurd. She had joined in death the man she was destined never to have in life. As for Sigurd, his fame will last as long as folk live upon the earth.

∽● QUESTIONS FOR
Response, Discussion, and Analysis

1. What tasks does Sigurd perform to achieve the status of hero?

2. Why is Sigurd more heroic than Gunnar? Would Gunnar have been as heroic if he had accomplished Sigurd's deeds?

3. Early in the epic, Sigurd's uncle reveals his fate to him and to the reader. Does this reduce the impact of the story? Why?

4. Why does Sigurd take Fafnir's treasure hoard even though he knows it is cursed? Is it a mistake to take it? Explain.

5. Do the people who created this myth consider gold to be evil? Does this mean they think it is unwise to try to acquire wealth? Explain.

6. In what way are both Sigurd and Brunhild tricked? How do their different responses reveal the particular personality and character of each?

7. What kind of person is Sigurd? What tests of character confront him? To what extent does he pass them? Which temptations does he resist, and which does he find irresistible? Why? How does the role of magic in this epic affect his characterization? How does his behavior affect his heroic image?

8. Is Sigurd a perfect hero? If not, does his lack of perfection add to or detract from his heroic image? Explain.

9. Should any hero be perfect? Why or why not?

10. The myth of Sigurd the Volsung is filled with treachery and death. Which characters commit harmful deeds? Does each have a justifiable motive? Is any character completely evil? What effect do characters who commit evil deeds for good reasons have on the epic? How would the effect be different if they were completely evil?

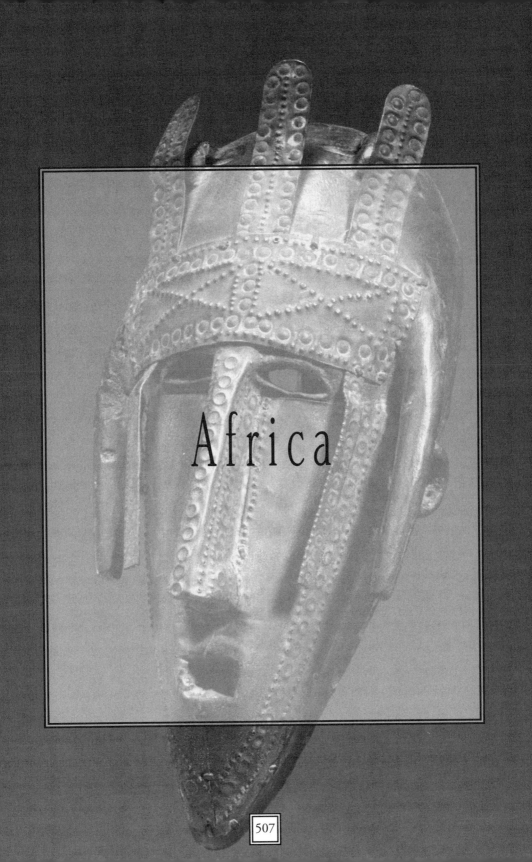

Africa

No one "African" culture exists. Instead, many different cultural groups live side by side on the same continent. Many of these cultures have existed for hundreds and even thousands of years.

The first creation myth in this section comes from the Yoruba people. The Yoruba gods make this myth appealing because they are caring and intelligent beings. It is also interesting to recognize that this myth shares similarities with the many other myths about people who suffer the damage and losses of a great flood.

The myth "Origin of Life and Fire" appears in similar versions among both the Boshongo and the Bakuba peoples of Zaire. The myth is particularly appealing because the creator-god leads his people to appreciate the wonder and beauty of the universe.

The fertility myth belongs to the Fon people of Benin (formerly Dahomey). It describes a family argument that results in an extensive drought. The myth is similar to two universal kinds of fertility myths: one in which a god saves the world from devastation, and one in which a god is insulted and must be appeased for fertility to be restored.

Gassire's Lute, the Fasa (Soninke) epic from Ghana, is a fascinating study of the conflict between an individual's personal desires and his or her responsibility to society. Gassire wants what almost every hero wants—everlasting fame. He is as courageous, determined, and skillful as the greatest of heroes. What is unique about this epic is that Gassire must choose between fame and his responsibility to his community.

Bakaridjan Kone, an epic of the Bambara people of Segu (now part of Mali), describes the journey of a hero from the time of his youth through the years of his maturity. Like the traditional hero, Bakaridjan has an unusual youth and performs heroic deeds that enrich his society. What is unique is that he must also cope with the loss of fame. His behavior raises the issue of whether a hero should question the nature of heroism and the appeal of its rewards.

The Creation of the Universe and Ife

The Yoruba people represent a major African culture that has roots extending back as far as 300 B.C., when a technologically and artistically advanced people lived just north of the Niger River. Today, more than ten million Yoruba people live in the southwest corner of Nigeria, from the Benin border north to the Niger River.

Like the ancient Greeks, the ancient Yoruba identified with the city-state in which they lived rather than with their larger culture. One Yoruba city-state was as likely to fight against another Yoruba city-state as against a neighboring culture.

Historically, Ife was the principal Yoruba city and was considered sacred. Religious ideas developed there and spread to other Yoruba city-states. The Yoruba religious system of prophecy even spread to other cultures in western Africa.

The mythology of the Yoruba people contains hundreds of gods, from major gods—the subjects of the following creation myth—to minor gods who protect local villages and regions. The Yoruba gods are human in form, thought, and way of life. They relate to one another as members of a large, human family, and they experience love, jealousy, anger, and sympathy. They enjoy human beings and like to spend time with them on earth. It is not surprising, therefore, that the Yoruba gods are sensitive to human problems and receptive to human prayers.

The Yoruba creation myth shares many characteristics with the creation myths of other cultures. For example, the creation of land is similar to the Japanese myth, the creation of human beings is similar to the Chinese myth, and the occurrence of a great flood is similar to the myths of the Greeks, the Sumerians and Babylonians, and the Scandinavians. The gods in the Yoruba myth are likable because they exhibit many of the best characteristics of the human personality, most notably creative intelligence and the ability to care about others.

The Yoruba creation myth is recorded in *The Treasury of African Folklore* (1975), edited by Harold Courlander, a noted scholar of the Yoruba. Courlander relates other Yoruba myths in *Tales of Yoruba Gods and Heroes* (1973).

PRINCIPAL GODS

OLORUN: ruler of the sky; creator of the sun; most powerful and wisest god
ORUNMILA: oldest son of Olorun; god of prophecy; advisor to Obatala
OBATALA: favorite of Olorun; creator of land and human beings
OLOKUN: ruler of the sea
ESHU: messenger god

THE CREATION OF THE UNIVERSE AND IFE

In the beginning the universe consisted only of the sky above and the water and wild marshland below. Olorun, the god who possessed the most power and the greatest knowledge, ruled the sky, while the goddess Olokun ruled the endless waters and wild marshes. Olokun was content with her kingdom, even though it contained neither vegetation nor animals nor human beings.

However, the young god Obatala was not satisfied. As he looked down from the sky, he said to himself, "The world below needs something of interest! Everything is water-soaked, and not one living thing enlivens the area! I must talk with Olorun and see what can be done to improve the situation."

Obatala said to Olorun, "Poor Olokun rules nothing but marshland, mist, and water! What she needs in her kingdom are mountains and valleys, forests and fields. All kinds of creatures and plants could live on that solid land."

Olorun replied, "Of course, solid land would be far better than this endless expanse of water. But who can create it? And how?"

"With your permission," Obatala replied, "I will create solid land."

"It is always my pleasure to give you whatever you wish, Obatala," Olorun replied. "You know that I love you as my son!"

So Obatala went to the house of Orunmila, the oldest son of Olorun, who had the gift of prophecy. Orunmila understood the secrets of existence, including fate and the future.

Obatala said to Orunmila, "Your father has given me permission to create solid land where now nothing exists except endless water and wild marshland. With your superior knowledge, you can teach me how to begin my project. I want to populate the earth with living beings who will be able to raise crops and build villages."

Orunmila replied, "First, Obatala, you must acquire a chain of gold long enough to reach from the sky above to the waters below. Then you must fill a snail's shell with sand. Finally, you must place that shell, a white hen, a black cat, and a palm nut in a bag and carry them with you as you climb down the chain to the wild marshland. That is how I advise you to begin your project."

"Thank you, Orunmila," Obatala replied. "I will find the goldsmith and begin at once."

The goldsmith said, "I will make you a chain of the length you need if you will bring me the gold I need to fashion it. I do not think you will find enough gold in the sky. But ask each of the gods for whatever gold he or she possesses, and you may succeed. I wish you well!"

Obatala approached the gods one by one. To each god he said, "I plan to create solid land where now there is nothing but water and wild marshland. Then I will create all sorts of plants and creatures to live on that land. Before I can begin, I need the goldsmith to make me a chain that will stretch from the sky above to the waters below. Will you contribute whatever gold you possess?"

The gods were sympathetic to Obatala's cause. They gave him their gold: necklaces, bracelets, rings, and even gold dust.

The goldsmith examined the gold Obatala had collected and said, "Can you not find more gold? This will not be enough!"

"It is the best I can do," Obatala replied. "I have asked every god in the sky, and each has given me whatever he or she owned. Make as long a chain as you can, with a hook at one end."

When the chain was ready, Orunmila accompanied Obatala while he hooked one end of the chain to the edge of the sky and lowered the rest of it toward the waters far below. Orunmila gave Obatala the sand-filled snail's shell, the white hen, the black cat, and the palm nut. One by one, Obatala put them into a bag, which he slung over his shoulder. Then he said farewell to Orunmila and began to climb down the golden chain.

Obatala climbed lower and lower and lower. When he was only halfway down, he saw that he was leaving the world of light and entering the world of twilight.

Again he climbed lower and lower and lower. As he reached the end of the chain, he could feel the mist rising cool and wet upon him and hear the splashing of the waves as they crashed upon the sea. But he could see that he was still far above the ocean.

`I cannot jump from here," he thought. "The distance is so great that I will drown!"

Then, from the sky far above, Orunmila called out, "Obatala! Use the sand in your snail shell!"

Obatala reached into the bag at his side, withdrew the snail's shell, and poured the sand on the waters below him.

No sooner had he finished when Orunmila called out, "Obatala! Free the white hen!" Obatala reached into the bag at his side, withdrew the white hen, and dropped it on the waters where he had poured the sand.

The hen fluttered down, landed upon the sandy waters, and immediately began to scatter the sand by scratching at it. Wherever the sand fell, it formed dry land. The larger piles of sand became hills, while the smaller piles became valleys.

Obatala let go of the golden chain and jumped to the earth. He named the place where he landed Ife. He walked with pleasure upon the solid land that he had created. The earth now extended farther in all directions than his eyes could see. It was still completely devoid of life, but it was a beginning.

Obatala dug a hole in the dry land and buried his palm nut in the soil. Immediately, a palm tree emerged and grew to its full height. The mature tree dropped its nuts upon the land, and they also quickly grew to maturity. Obatala built himself a house of bark and thatched the roof with palm leaves. He then settled down in Ife with his black cat for company.

Olorun wished to know how Obatala was progressing with his plan, so he sent his servant, the chameleon, down the golden chain to find out.

When the lizard arrived, Obatala said to him, "Tell Olorun, ruler of the sky, that I am pleased with the land I have created and the vegetation I have planted. But it is always twilight here. I miss the brightness of the sky!"

When the chameleon gave Obatala's message to Olorun, the ruler of the sky smiled and said, "For you, Obatala, I will create the sun!" Once Olorun tossed the sun into the sky, it shed light and warmth upon Ife as it moved across the sky on its daily journey.

Days passed. Months passed. Obatala continued to live on the earth that he had created with only his black cat for company. Then one day he said to himself, "I love my cat, but its companionship does not satisfy me. I would be happier if creatures more like myself could live in Ife with me. Let me see what I can do."

Obatala began to dig in the soil. He found that the particles held together in his hand, for the substance he dug up was clay. He laughed as he shaped little figures just like himself. One by one he finished them and set them aside to dry. Obatala worked on and on so enthusiastically that he was not aware of how tired and thirsty he was.

Finally his fatigue overcame him. "What I need is some wine to drink!" he thought. Obatala placed his last clay figure upon the ground and went off to make palm wine from the juice of the palm tree. Obatala drank bowl after bowl of the fermented palm juice, for he was very thirsty. He did not realize it, but the wine made him drunk.

Obatala returned to his task of making clay figures, but his fingers were clumsy now. The figures he created were no longer perfect. Some had arms that were too short, some had legs of uneven length, and some had backs that were curved. Obatala was too drunk to notice the difference. He continued to fashion one figure after another. In time, he was satisifed with the number of clay figures that he had created.

Obatala then called out to the ruler of the sky, "Hear me, Olorun, you who are like a father to me. I have created figures out of clay, but only you can breathe life into them and make them into living people. I ask you to do this for me so that I can have human companions in Ife."

So it came to pass that Olorun breathed life into the figures Obatala had created, and they became active, thinking human beings. When they noticed Obatala's house, they fashioned houses for themselves and placed them nearby. Thus they created the first Yoruba village in Ife where there had been only a solitary house.

When the effects of the palm wine wore off, Obatala realized that the creatures he had fashioned while he was drunk were imperfect. With a sad heart he announced, "I promise that I will never drink palm wine again! Moreover, I will devote myself to protecting all the people who have suffered from my drunkenness." And Obatala became the protector of all those who are born deformed.

The people prospered, and the Yoruba village of Ife grew into a city. Iron did not yet exist, so Obatala gave his people a copper knife and a wooden hoe to use as tools. The Yoruba cleared the land and began to raise grain and yams.

Obatala eventually tired of ruling his city of Ife, so he climbed up the golden chain and returned to his home in the sky. Thereafter, he divided his time between his home in the sky and his home in the Yoruba city.

The gods never tired of hearing Obatala describe the city that he had created on earth. Many of them were so fascinated with what they heard about Ife that they decided to leave their sky homes and live among the human beings on earth. As they prepared to leave, the ruler of the sky counseled them. "Remember,"

Olorun said, "that you will have obligations to the humans among whom you live in Ife. You must listen to their prayers and protect them. I will give each of you a specific task to fulfill while you are living there."

Not every god, however, was pleased with Obatala's success on Ife. Obatala had not consulted the goddess Olokun, ruler of the sea, when he had created solid earth and a Yoruba city in her kingdom. As the ruler of the sea watched one of the great sky gods usurp her power and rule a large part of her kingdom, she became angrier and angrier. Finally she conceived a plan that would avenge Obatala's insult to her honor.

Olokun waited until Obatala had returned to his home in the sky. Then she summoned the great waves of her vast ocean and sent them surging across the land that Obatala had created. One after another, the waves flooded the earth until water once again flowed as far as the eye could see, and only marshland existed amidst the waves of the ocean. Whole groves of palm trees became uprooted and floated away. Yams rotted and washed like dead fish upon the surface of the sea. People drowned in their fields, in their groves, and in their homes.

Those who still remained alive fled into the hills and cried out to Obatala for help, but he could not hear them over the roaring of the waves so far below him. So they sought the god Eshu, who was living among them. They knew that he could carry messages to Obatala and to Olorun. "Please return to the kingdom of the sky," they pleaded, "and tell the great gods of the disastrous flood that is destroying us!"

Eshu replied, "You must send a sacrifice along with your message if you want one of the great sky gods to listen to you."

The people sacrificed a goat to Obatala and said, "We send this goat as food for Obatala."

"That is not enough," Eshu replied. "I too deserve a gift for the service I am performing for you."

When the people had sacrificed accordingly, Eshu climbed the golden chain and told Obatala about how Olokun had flooded Ife and the rest of the earth.

Obatala did not know how to deal with Olokun, so he asked Orunmila for advice. Orunmila replied, "You rest here in the sky while I go down to Ife. I can make the waters withdraw and the land come forth once again."

So it came to pass that Orunmila climbed down the golden chain to the waters that covered Ife and the earth. Using his special knowledge, he caused the power of the waves to wane and the waters to retreat. Once the waves had subsided, he dried up the marshland and put an end to Olokun's attempt to recover the area that she had lost to Obatala.

The people who had survived greeted Orunmila as their hero and pleaded with him to stay and protect them. Orunmila had no desire to remain in Ife, but he agreed to stay long enough to teach the gods and humans who lived there how to tell the future so that they could begin to control the forces they could not see. When he had done so, Orunmila returned to his home in the sky, but, like Obatala, he often climbed down the golden chain to see how life was progressing in Ife.

The ruler of the sea made one final attempt to remain the equal of the ruler of the sky. Olokun was an excellent weaver of cloth, and she possessed equal skill in dyeing the fabrics she had woven. So the ruler of the sea sent a message to Olorun, ruler of the sky, challenging him to a weaving contest.

Olorun said to himself, "Olokun is a far better weaver than I am. However, I cannot give her the satisfaction of knowing that she is superior to me in anything. If I do, she will exert her powers in other ways as well, and that will disrupt the order that now exists throughout the universe. Somehow I must appear to accept her challenge and yet avoid participating in her contest. Now, how can I do this?"

Olorun thought and thought. Suddenly his eyes sparkled. With a smile, he summoned his messenger, the chameleon, to his side. "Go before Olokun, ruler of the sea," he ordered, "with this message: `The ruler of the sky greets the ruler of the sea. He asks you to display to his messenger samples of the cloth that you have woven. Let the chameleon judge your skill. If your cloth is as beautiful as you say it is, then the ruler of the sky will compete with you in the contest you have suggested.'"

The chameleon climbed down the golden chain and gave the goddess Olorun's message.

Olokun was happy to obey Olorun's request. She put on a bright green skirt, and to her amazement the chameleon turned a beautiful shade of bright green. She next put on a bright orange skirt, and to her amazement the chameleon turned a beautiful shade of bright orange. She then put on a bright red skirt, and to her amazement the chameleon turned a beautiful shade of bright red. One by one, the goddess Olokun put on skirts of various bright colors, and each time the chameleon turned into the particular color that she was wearing. Finally Olokun gave up.

The goddess said to herself, "If someone as ordinary as Olorun's messenger can duplicate the bright colors of my finest fabrics, how can I hope to compete against the greatest of the gods?"

She said to the chameleon, "Tell your master that the ruler of the sea sends her greetings to the ruler of the sky. Tell him that I acknowledge his superiority in weaving and in all other pursuits as well. Olorun is indeed the greatest of the gods!"

So it came to pass that peace returned between the ruler of the sky and the ruler of the sea, and that peace restored order in the universe.

❧ QUESTIONS FOR
Response, Discussion, and Analysis

1. Why do the Yoruba gods create human beings? What does this reveal about the nature of the gods?

2. What does the desire to explain the existence of deformed people reveal about the values of the Yoruba? Would you like to live in a society that has such values? Why or why not? Does our society share these values? Defend your point of view.

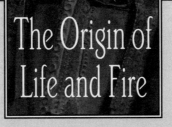

The following creation myth appears in similar versions among both the Boshongo and the Bakuba peoples of Zaire. Both groups speak a Central Bantu language and live in the western part of central Africa, immediately to the south of the tropical rain forest and centered on the Congo River and its tributaries. These may be the oldest of the Bantu-speaking peoples; their oral tradition records at least one hundred twenty rulers since their community originated in the fifth century.

At the time these myths were collected, both the Boshongo and the Bakuba people had an economy that depended on fishing and hunting as well as on the cultivation of crops. Trade was also an important activity. Traders used iron as money.

Scholars differ in their interpretation of certain elements in this myth. In both versions, the creator is a white god, and white can symbolize either death and the supernatural world or purity. Similarly, the stomach can symbolize either the house of the dead or the womb. If death is the controlling image, then Bumba enables life to emerge from death. If birth is the controlling image, then Bumba symbolizes great fertility. A particularly appealing aspect of this myth is the creator-god, who not only functions as a culture hero, but also leads his people to appreciate the wonder and beauty of the universe.

The following version is adapted from that of Maria Leach in *The Beginning: Creation Myths Around the World*.

THE ORIGIN OF LIFE AND FIRE

At first, only water existed, unseen in the darkness. Bumba alone was alive. The universe was barren and without life. However, Bumba, the white creator, lived.

Then it came to pass that Bumba felt terrible stomach pains. His pains grew and grew until, finally, he vomited up the sun. Now the sun's rays brightened the world each day. And the heat from the sun's rays caused much of the water to float into the sky and become clouds.

Then it came to pass that so much water floated into the sky that the hills rejoiced. They now climbed out of the waters and dried themselves off. Then it came to pass that so much water floated into the sky that the reefs and sand-banks rejoiced. They now climbed out of the waters and dried themselves off. And so it came to pass that now, when Bumba looked down upon the earth, he could see black reefs, black sand-banks, and the black edges of the world.

Then it came to pass that once again Bumba felt terrible stomach pains. His pains grew and grew until, finally, he vomited up the moon and the stars. Now the moon's rays and the stars' lights brightened the world each night.

Then it came to pass that again Bumba felt terrible stomach pains. His pains grew and grew until, finally, he vomited up the first living creatures. He vomited up Koy Bumba, the leopard. He vomited up Pongo Bumba, the crested eagle. He vomited up Ganda Bumba, the crocodile. And he vomited up Yo, the little fish.

Still Bumba was not finished. He vomited up old Kono Bumba, the tortoise. He vomited up Tsetse, the lightning—who was as beautiful and quick as Koy Bumba, the leopard, and as deadly as she was beautiful and quick! He vomited up Nyanyi Bumba, the white heron. He vomited up one beetle. And he vomited up Budi, the goat.

Then once again Bumba felt terrible stomach pains. His pains grew and grew until, finally, he vomited up the first human beings. He vomited up many men and women. But only one man, Loko Yima, was white like Bumba.

Bumba had now finished his part in the creation of the universe. However, it came to pass that many of the creatures that Bumba had produced now continued his work. Five of the nine living creatures that Bumba had produced now fashioned creatures who resembled themselves.

Nyanyi Bumba, the white heron, created all the birds that fly through the air, except for the kite. Ganda Bumba, the crocodile, created the iguana and all the serpents that crawl forth on the earth or swim in the waters. Budi, the goat, created every horned animal that walks the earth. Yo, the little fish, created all the fish that swim in the streams and rivers and in the lakes and seas. And the beetle created all the insects that fly through the air, crawl on the earth, and swim in the waters.

It then came to pass that Ganda Bumba's iguana proceeded to fashion all the animals that walk the earth—except for those with horns. And Ganda Bumba's serpents proceeded to fashion grasshoppers.

The creatures that Bumba had created had now finished their part in the creation of the universe. However, it came to pass that Bumba had three sons. And it was they who then finished their father's work.

Bumba's eldest son fashioned the white ants, but then he died from the strain of his creative effort. The ants were joyful to be alive, and, seeing that the lifeless body of their creator was lying desolate and exposed upon the barren sands, they decided to honor and protect him with a burial. Therefore, the white ants dug deep into the depths of the earth until they found black soil. They then carried this soil to the earth's surface, where they used it to bury the lifeless body of their creator and to cover most of the barren sands.

Bumba's middle son created a wonderful plant that scattered its seeds throughout the earth, and from these seeds grew all of the trees, shrubs, and grasses, with their flowers, fruits, nuts, and seeds.

Bumba's youngest son also wanted to be a creator, but he failed at everything he tried, with one exception. He finally succeeded in making the bird known as the kite.

The creation of the universe was now complete. And the beasts of the forests and fields, the birds of the air, the fish in the waters, and the men and women who walk the earth all respected one another. Tsetse, the lightning—alone of all that had been created—caused trouble.

It came to pass that Tsetse started many fires on the earth. And so Bumba told her that she would have to live in the sky. However, even from the sky, Tsetse can reach out and strike the earth. And from time to time, that is just what she does. So all who live upon the earth fear the fires that she causes.

Yes, Tsetse is a troublemaker because she starts fires where no one wants them. And yet, once Tsetse began to live in the sky, Bumba's human beings had to live without fire's gifts. They had to eat their food raw, and they could not make good tools.

And it came to pass that Bumba felt sorry for the men and women whom he had created. And so, he taught his people how to find the fire that lives in every tree, and how—by making and using the fire-drill—to take this fire home with them. Then Bumba walked the earth and visited each village. And in each village, he assembled his people and declared, "Men and women, rejoice! Look at the sky above. See the sun that brightens each day. See the moon and stars that brighten each night. See these wonders! And let joy flood your hearts that they are yours!

"Look at the land that lies at your feet. See the grasses that come forth from the soil. See their gifts of flowers and life-sustaining fruits, nuts, and grains. See these wonders! And let joy flood your hearts that they are yours!

"Look at the waters that flow past your feet. See their gift of refreshing and life-sustaining drink. See this wonder! And let joy flood your hearts that it is yours!

"Look at the birds of the air. See their grace and beauty, and hear their cheerful songs. See this wonder! And rejoice that it is yours!

"For I—Bumba—your creator and first ancestor, have created all the wonders that please the eye and the ear. I have created all the wonders that please the nose and the tongue. I have created all the wonders that please the hand and the foot. And as if that were not enough, I have created all men and women and all the animals that live in forest, field, and stream to live in peace with one another.

"And so, men and women, rejoice!"

❧ QUESTIONS FOR
Response, Discussion, and Analysis

1. How does this creation myth reflect the people to whom it belongs?

2. What is the nature of Bumba and the universe that he creates?

3. How does this myth view human beings and their purpose?

4. When Bumba visits each village and speaks of the wonders that he has created, what does this reveal?

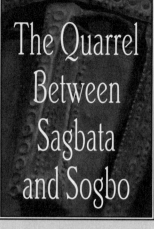

The Quarrel Between Sagbata and Sogbo

The following myth belongs to the Fon, the people of Benin (formerly Dahomey), a culture known since the early 1600s for their skill in battle. In the 1700s the Fon established a female army, which became a fixed part of their society.

The traditional enemies of the Fon were their neighbors, the Yoruba. Frequent battles resulted in extensive cultural contact. Consequently, the two cultures developed very similar religions, sharing the same complex system of prophecy and gods who had the same personalities, roles, and sometimes even the same names.

Like many other peoples, the Fon believed that the forces of nature were controlled by individual gods. In their location, the sun was a reliable force in daily life. Rain was less reliable, yet necessary if the Fon were to have enough to eat. The following myth explains why a particular drought occurred and why it will not happen again.

This myth combines two themes that are common in fertility myths. As in the myths of the Greeks, the Hittites, and the Japanese, a god is insulted and must be appeased for fertility to be restored. As in the myths of the Indians, the Chinese, and the Zuni, a god saves the world from a great threat.

The myths of the Fon people were collected by Melville and Frances Herskovits and published under the title *Dahomean Narrative* in 1958.

THE QUARREL BETWEEN SAGBATA AND SOGBO

When the Great Goddess Mawu had created the universe, she stepped aside and told her two sons, Sagbata and Sogbo, to rule the world together. However, Sagbata and Sogbo could not work well together. Each brother was always making decisions that annoyed the other.

Finally they had a great argument and Sagbata, the older of the two, said, "Sogbo, I cannot put up with you any longer! I am your older brother, and yet you do not think I am wise and you do not respect my decisions. Therefore, I am going to collect everything that is mine, and I am going to go down to the earth to live! I warn you that I am taking all of our mother's wealth with me. It is my rightful inheritance since I am the older son."

"Go then, if that is your wish," Sogbo replied. "I shall not miss you!

When Mawu heard of her sons' quarrel, she called them before her. "I disapprove of your quarrel, and I will not support one of you against the other," she announced. "You two must fit together like a closed calabash (a round gourd), and together you must rule the universe that exists within that calabash."

Mawu continued, "You, Sagbata, being my older son, should be as the lower part of the calabash and rule the lower part of the universe, which is the earth. To you will belong all my wealth. You, Sogbo, being my younger son, should be as the upper part of the calabash and rule the upper part of the universe. Sogbo, you too will possess great power, for you will rule with the thunder and fire of the lightning bolt. Now go, both of you, and rule your kingdoms in peace!"

Sagbata collected his possessions, including everything that belonged to his mother. As he put the treasures into a large bag, he thought, "If I put water into my bag, it will soak every treasure and then leak out. If I put fire into my bag, it will burn everything. Therefore, I have no choice but to leave water and fire behind."

Sagbata then finished packing and went down to live on the earth. The journey was so long and difficult that he realized he would never be able to return to his home in the sky.

Meanwhile, Sogbo remained near his mother in the sky. In time he won her great affection and her complete confidence. Once he had Mawu's support, it was easy to win the confidence of the other sky gods as well.

Sogbo then said to himself, "Now I have achieved just what I wanted, unlimited power. I can do whatever I choose, and no god can stop me! I will prove to my brother that I even have power over his kingdom. I will see to it that from now on, no rain will ever fall upon the earth! I will enjoy watching what my brother tries to do about that!" He laughed at the thought of it, rejoicing in his power.

When rains stopped nourishing the earth with their life-giving moisture, the people came to Sagbata and cried, "Now that you live among us and are our king, the rain no longer falls upon our land and our villages. Our food has withered and died. We too are withering and dying!"

"Do not worry," Sagbata replied calmly. "It will rain in a few days!"

But it did not rain in a few days. A year passed, and it did not rain. A second year passed, and it did not rain. A third year passed, and still it did not rain.

Then two sky-beings came down to earth in order to tell the people of the earth about destiny. They had brought with them seeds of prophecy. When someone needed the answer to an important question, the sky-beings would toss their seeds upon the ground and read the answer in the pattern formed by the fallen seeds.

Sagbata sent for the two sky-beings because he wanted to learn why it did not rain. When they came before him, he could tell that they spoke the truth. He watched as they tossed and studied the pattern of their seeds of prophecy.

Finally the sky-beings said to Sagbata, "It is clear from the arrangement of these seeds that you and your younger brother have argued because both of you want the same thing. It is also clear that if you are to live peacefully with your brother, you will have to meet his demands."

"I do not see how that will be possible," Sagbata replied. "The sky is too far above the earth, and I have never had the strength to climb back up there. Before I left the sky, my mother permitted me to take all of her wealth with me, since that was my right as her older son. I took everything but water and fire, leaving them behind only because I had no way to carry them. As soon as I arrived on earth, I realized that water is necessary here, but I have not been able to find a way to get it. Do you have a suggestion?"

"Yes, we do," the sky-beings replied. "We advise you to summon Sogbo's messenger, the bird Wututu, and tell him to fly up to your brother with an important message. Tell Wututu to tell Sogbo that you are offering him part of all of the riches on the earth in return for water. The bird will find a way to Sogbo's heart. He always does!"

Sagbata summoned Wututu and sent him to Sogbo. "Tell my brother," he said, "that I will let him rule my part of the universe as well as his own. From now on he, not I, will protect fathers, mothers, and their children. From now on he, not I, will rule over the villages and the countryside."

Sogbo directed Wututu, "Return to my brother with this message. Tell him that when he took all of our mother's wealth, which was his rightful inheritance, he was unwise to leave water and fire behind. Water and fire are so powerful that whoever controls them controls the universe. Therefore, I control Sagbata and all of his wealth whether he wishes it or not. However, tell him that I accept his offer and I will send nourishing rains down upon the earth!"

Wututu was halfway between the sky and the earth when suddenly a flash of lightning illuminated the universe, and the world resounded with the rumble of thunder. Streams of water began to pour forth from the sky. It rained and it rained. By the time Wututu arrived, Sagbata knew that his brother had accepted his terms, and he was delighted. He told his people that Wututu was a sacred bird and should never be killed.

From that day until this, Sagbata and Sogbo have remained friends, and nourishing thunderstorms visit the earth year after year. Rain falls on the grass, causing it to put forth new blades. Rain falls on the people, causing them to become fertile. Rain showers glory upon Sogbo, god of the thunderstorm!

☙ QUESTIONS FOR
Response, Discussion, and Analysis

1. In what ways are the gods Sagbata and Sogbo like human beings? Give examples from the myth.

2. What does this myth reveal about the daily life of the Fon? Consider the role of prophecy and the concept of inheritance.

HISTORICAL BACKGROUND

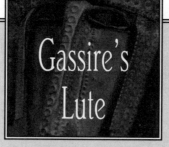

The African people called the Soninke have a history that is over two thousand years old. Their ancestors were an aristocratic nation called the Fasa, who moved inland from the seacoast in about the third century B.C. They settled in the fertile land of Faraka, an area that is bordered by the Sahara Desert on the north, the Senegal River on the west, the Sudan on the south, and the Nile River on the east.

The Fasa were an aristocratic people who fought on horseback with spears and swords for pleasure, as well as for military gain. Their goal was to achieve honor by displaying courage and skill in combat. They would fight in single combat only against those who were their social equals.

Wagadu was the legendary city of the Fasa. The four other cities mentioned in *Gassire's Lute* also have ancient roots. Dierra may have been located near Mursuk, where the ruins of Djerma are located; Agada may refer to Agadez, which is located north of the Hausa states in the central Sudan; Ganna and Silla may have been located on the upper Niger River.

The Soninke created the first empire in West Africa—Ancient Ghana—in the fourth or fifth century A.D. At its peak, their empire extended into the Sahara Desert and controlled all the land and peoples between the Senegal River and the upper Niger River. Trade in gold was the basis of its power. Mined in the south, gold was valued by the Berber Muslims of Morocco and Algeria in the north.

Wagadu became the cosmopolitan capital of Ghana. It was a city known for its artisans, traders, and Muslim teachers of the Koran. Agricultural produce, cloth, and the products of leatherworkers, blacksmiths, and goldsmiths, as well as items from many other nations, could be found in its great markets. Many languages, such as Mande, Hausa, and Arabic, were commonly heard on its streets.

Berber attacks that were designed to gain control of important trade routes, combined with politically motivated revolts by peoples who were subjects of the empire, led to Ghana's decline and fall during the twelfth to mid-thirteenth centuries.

Today the Soninke are a small group, mostly Muslim. They live in the desert oases of Tichit and Walatu, areas watered by the Niger River and its tributary, the Bani, in what is now Mali.

Gassire's Lute is an important part of the existing fragment of the Soninke epic *Dausi*, which was created as a group of songs between A.D. 300 and 1100. The influence of Islam on Soninke culture, combined with a long emphasis upon peaceful, agricultural pursuits, has contributed to the loss of much of the original Soninke epic. The epic reflects the Soninke heroic period of 500 B.C.

Gassire's Lute was recorded in the 1920s by a German anthropologist, Leo Frobenius. His study of Stone Age rock drawings led him to search for a common, prehistoric, European- African culture. His African expeditions, in turn, led him to investigate the mythology behind the pictures. He recorded numerous African folktales, legends, and myths, including *Gassire's Lute*, and published them as part of a series entitled *African Folktales and Folk Poetry.* In 1938 *Gassire's Lute* was published by Frobenius and Douglas C. Fox in a collection called *African Genesis.*

APPEAL AND VALUE

Like many other epics, *Gassire's Lute* focuses on the conflict between what an individual hero wants for himself and what is best for his family and the society in which he lives. Like many other heroes, what Gassire wants most of all is everlasting fame. Once he learns how to acquire such immortality, he pursues his goal with great courage, skill, and determination.

In most myths, the hero's great deeds help his or her people and win the hero the immortality that comes from fame. This myth is unique, however, because Gassire's heroic deeds will harm his family and his community. He knows this, but his desire for immortality is so great that he does not care about the consequences. It is interesting to consider how heroes from other cultures would have acted if they had been forced to choose between actions that would make them famous and immortal and actions that would help their family and their community.

GASSIRE'S LUTE

Four times beautiful Wagadu has existed. And four times Wagadu has disappeared from sight: the first time because her children were vain, the second because they were deceptive, the third because they were greedy, and the fourth because they were quarrelsome. Four times Wagadu has changed her name: first to Dierra, next to Agada, then to Ganna, and finally to Silla. Four times Wagadu has changed the direction she faces: first to the north, next to the west, then to the east, and finally to the south.

Wagadu receives the strength to endure from the four directions, which is why she has had four gates to her city: first to the north, next to the west, then to the east, and finally to the south. She has endured when her children have built her of earth, of wood, or of stone, or when she has existed only as a vision in the imaginations and desires of her children.

Wagadu actually is the strength that exists in the hearts of her children. She is visible in times of war, when the air resounds with the clash and clamor of battle as sword meets sword or shield. She is invisible when the errors in the hearts of her children tire her and make her fall asleep. Wagadu has fallen asleep four times: the first time because her children were vain, the second because they were deceptive, the third because they were greedy, and the fourth because they were quarrelsome.

If her children ever find Wagadu a fifth time, the vision of her beauty will shine so radiantly within their minds that they will never again lose her. Then, even if her children suffer from vanity, deception, greed, and dissension, these will never be able to harm her.

Hoooh! Dierra, Agada, Ganna, Silla! Hoooh! Fasa!

Each time the errors in the hearts of her children have caused Wagadu to disappear, she has reappeared possessing an even greater beauty. Her children's vanity created the great songs of heroes that bards sang in the second Wagadu and have continued to sing for countless generations, songs that all peoples of the Sudan still value today. Her children's deception brought forth showers of gold and pearls in the third Wagadu. Her children's greed created the need for writing in the fourth Wagadu, writing that the Burdama still use today.

Her children's quarrels will produce a fifth Wagadu that will continue as long as it rains in the south and rocks jut forth from the Sahara Desert. Then every man will carry a vision of Wagadu within his heart, and every woman will carry a vision of Wagadu within her womb.

Hoooh! Dierra, Agada, Ganna, Silla! Hoooh! Fasa!

Her children's vanity led Wagadu to disappear for the first time. Then she was called Dierra, and she faced north. The last king of Dierra was Nganamba Fasa. The Fasa were strong warriors and great heroes, but they were growing old. Every day of every month they had to fight their enemies. Day after day, month after month, without ceasing, they had to fight their enemies. Yet the Fasa remained strong. Each man was a hero in his own right, and each woman was proud of the heroic strength of each man.

King Nganamba was old enough to have a son, Gassire, who was the father of eight grown sons. Even these sons were the fathers of sons, making King Nganamba a great-grandfather among men. It was at the end of King Nganamba's rule that Wagadu disappeared for the first time. Would this have happened if Nganamba had died, and Gassire had ruled in his place?

Hoooh! Dierra, Agada, Ganna, Silla! Hoooh! Fasa!

Yet Gassire never had the opportunity to rule in his father's place. Gassire longed for his father's death and his own kingship. He listened for some sign of weakness in his father, and he searched for a sign of impending death as a lover searches the sky at dusk for the evening star, the first sign of night. Day after day and month after month passed, and still Nganamba did not die.

Each day Gassire raised his sword and shield and rode into battle against the Burdama, fighting like the great hero that he was. Each night, when evening shrouded the land in shadow, Gassire rode into Dierra and took his place in the circle among the men of the city and his eight grown sons. His ears listened to the praises the other heroes sang of his great deeds upon the battlefield, but his heart was jealous of his father's power.

Deep within, night after night and month after month, Gassire wept with longing for his father's death and his own kingship. He longed to carry his father's sword and shield, but they belonged to the king alone. His anger grew into wrath, his wrath grew into rage, and he could no longer sleep at night. So late one night Gassire quietly arose, dressed, left his house, and visited the oldest wise man in the city.

"Can you tell me when I shall become king of the Fasa?" Gassire asked.

"Ah, Gassire," the old wise man replied, "your father, King Nganamba, will die—but you will not inherit his shield and sword. That is for others, not for you.

You will carry a lute, and your lute will cause the disappearance of Wagadu! Ah, Gassire!"

Gassire said, "You lie, old man! It is clear that you are not wise at all. As long as her heroes can defend her, we shall not lose Wagadu! "

"Although you do not believe me, Gassire," the old wise man answered, "your path is not that of the warrior and hero. You will find the partridges in the fields, and when they speak to you, you will understand them. They will reveal your path and the path of Wagadu."

Hoooh! Dierra, Agada, Ganna, Silla! Hoooh! Fasa!

The next morning Gassire set out to prove that his path was indeed that of the warrior and hero. He said to the other Fasa heroes, "Today there is no need for you to fight the Burdama. I shall take them upon my spear and my sword without your help."

So it came to pass that Gassire fought against the Burdama, one against many. As a farmer's sickle cuts down the wheat in the field, so Gassire's sword cut down the Burdama.

The Burdama felt terror enter their hearts. "We are fighting more than a hero, and more than a Fasa!" they cried. "Against such a being, we have no strength and no skill." So each Burdama tossed away his two spears, turned his horse in retreat, and fled in fear.

As the Fasa heroes entered the field to gather the spears of their enemies, they sang, "Gassire has always performed the greatest deeds of any Fasa. He has always been the greatest of our heroes. Yet by winning so many swords, as one against many, Gassire has outdone himself today! Wagadu smiles with pride."

That night, when evening shrouded the land in shadow and the men gathered into their circle, Gassire wandered into the fields. He heard a partridge that was resting beneath a bush sing, "Hear the song of my deeds!" And then the partridge sang of its battle against a snake. "In time, all who live will die, will be buried, and will decay," the partridge sang. "Like all creatures, I too will die, will be buried, and will decay. But the song of my battles will live! Bards will sing my battle song again and again, long after heroes and kings have died and decayed. Wagadu will disappear, but my battle song will live on and on. Hoooh, that my deeds will become such a song! Hoooh, that I will sing such battle songs!"

Hoooh! Dierra, Agada, Ganna, Silla! Hoooh! Fasa!

Gassire returned to the old wise man. "I heard a partridge in the field brag that the songs of its deeds will live long after Wagadu has disappeared. Do humans also know great battle songs? And do these battle songs live long after heroes and kings have died and decayed?"

"Yes, they do, Gassire," the old wise man replied. "Your path is to be a singer of great battle songs rather than a great king of the Fasa. Ah, Gassire! Long ago the Fasa lived by the sea. They were great heroes then, too. They fought against men who played the lute and sang great battle songs. And those men were heroes also. Often they caused terror to enter the hearts of the Fasa. You too will play battle songs on the lute, but Wagadu will disappear because of it."

"Then let Wagadu disappear!" Gassire exclaimed.

Hoooh! Dierra, Agada, Ganna, Silla! Hoooh! Fasa!

The next morning Gassire visited the Fasa smith and said, "Master Smith, I want you to make a lute for me."

The smith replied, "Make a lute I will, but it will not sing!"

Gassire responded, "Master Smith, just make the lute. I will make it sing!"

When the smith had finished the lute, Gassire immediately tried to play it, but he found that it would not sing.

"Master Smith, what good is this lute to me? I cannot make it sing," Gassire complained. "Tell me what I should do."

The smith answered, "Gassire, until it develops a heart, a lute is only a piece of wood. If you wish to make it sing, you must help it develop a heart. When you next go into battle, carry your lute upon your back. Let it feel the thrust of your sword, and let it absorb the blood of your wounds. Right now, your lute is still part of the tree from which it was made. It must become a part of you, your sons, and your people. It must share your pain as well as your fame. It must absorb the lifeblood of your sons. Then the feelings of your heart will enter the lute and develop its heart. Your sons will die and decay, but they will continue to live in your lute. However, I must warn you. You will play battle songs on the lute, but Wagadu will disappear because of it."

"Then let Wagadu disappear!" Gassire exclaimed.

Hoooh! Dierra, Agada, Ganna, Silla! Hoooh! Fasa!

The next morning Gassire called his eight sons together and said, "Today, when we fight the Burdama, our sword thrusts will live forever in my lute. May we fight with such courage, strength, and skill that our deeds will create a battle song that surpasses the battle songs of all other heroes! You, my eldest son, will lead the charge with me today."

So it came to pass that Gassire hung his lute upon his shoulder and rode into battle with his eldest son at his side. They fought against the Burdama as more than heroes and more than Fasa. Together they fought against eight Burdama. As a farmer's sickle cuts down the wheat in the field, so Gassire's sword and the sword of his eldest son cut down four of the Burdama heroes.

Then a Burdama thrust his sword into the heart of Gassire's eldest son. He fell from his horse, his lifeblood pouring from him. Gassire sadly dismounted, lifted the corpse of his son upon his back, and returned to the other heroes and the city of Dierra. As he rode, the blood of his eldest son poured over the lute and was absorbed into the wood.

Hoooh! Dierra, Agada, Ganna, Silla! Hoooh! Fasa!

Gassire's eldest son was buried, and the city was solemn with mourning. That night Gassire tried to play his lute, but no matter how hard he tried, it would not sing. He called his seven sons together and said, "Tomorrow we again ride into battle against the Burdama."

Each of the next six days passed as the first day had passed. Each day, in the order of their birth, a different one of Gassire's sons joined his father in leading the charge against the Burdama.

Each day, one of the enemy thrust his sword into the heart of that son and he fell from his horse, his lifeblood pouring from him. Each day, Gassire sadly dismounted, lifted the corpse of his son upon his back, and returned to the other heroes and the city of Dierra. Each day, as he rode, the blood of his son poured over the lute and was absorbed into the wood.

By the end of the seventh day of fighting, the men of Dierra were angry, the women were weeping with fear and grief, and everyone was mourning the dead. That night, when evening shrouded the land in shadow and the heroes had gathered into their circle, they said, "Gassire, enough is enough! You are fighting out of anger, and without good reason. Gather your servants and your cattle, take those who would join you, and leave our city. Let the rest of us live here in peace. We too want fame, but we choose life over fame when the cost of fame is death."

The old wise man exclaimed, "Ah, Gassire! Today, for the first time, Wagadu will disappear."

Hoooh! Dierra, Agada, Ganna, Silla! Hoooh! Fasa!

So Gassire gathered his wives, his youngest son, his friends, and his servants and rode off into the Sahara Desert. Only a few of the Fasa heroes accompanied Gassire on his journey.

Gassire and his companions rode far into the lonely wilderness. They rode day and night, sleeping only when they could ride no farther.

One night Gassire sat awake and alone by the fire. The world around him was lonely and silent, for everyone else was asleep: his youngest son, the heroes, the women, and the servants. Gassire had just dozed off himself when a sudden sound awakened him. Next to him, as though he were singing himself, Gassire heard a voice singing. It was his lute, and it was singing his great battle song.

When the lute finished singing his great battle song for the first time, back in Dierra, King Nganamba died, and Wagadu disappeared for the first time. When the lute finished singing his great battle song for the second time, Gassire's anger disappeared and he wept. He wept with grief and with joy: grief over the death of his seven sons and the disappearance of Wagadu, and joy over the great battle song that would bring everlasting fame to him and his sons.

Hoooh! Dierra, Agada, Ganna, Silla! Hoooh! Fasa!

Four times beautiful Wagadu has existed. And four times Wagadu has disappeared from sight: the first time because her children were vain, the second because they were deceptive, the third because they were greedy, and the fourth because they were quarrelsome. Her children's quarrels will produce a fifth Wagadu that will continue as long as it rains in the south and rocks jut forth from the Sahara Desert. Then every man will carry a vision of Wagadu within his heart, and every woman will carry a vision of Wagadu within her womb.

Hoooh! Dierra, Agada, Ganna, Silla! Hoooh! Fasa!

1. Why is it important that Gassire is portrayed as a great hero?

2. Why does Gassire choose to play battle songs even if they make Wagadu disappear? Does he make the right decision? Defend your point of view. If you were given such a choice, what would you do? Why?

3. How and why does Gassire sacrifice the lives of his children to the lute? Why does the lute finally sing?

4. How do the citizens of Wagadu feel about Gassire's decision? Are they wise to make him leave? What happens after he leaves? What alternative do the citizens reject, and what consequences would have followed? How would you have voted? Why?

5. The myth says that Wagadu disappeared because of vanity. Explain the meaning of this statement.

6. What kind of person is Gassire? What tests of character confront him? To what extent does he pass them? Which temptations does he resist, and which does he find irresistible? Why? How does his behavior affect his heroic image?

7. Why has this epic been constructed in such a way that Gassire needs to shed blood in order to make the lute sing, and then, the lute sings very late?

HISTORICAL BACKGROUND

Bakaridjan Kone

Bakaridjan Kone depicts the life of Bambara nobility in the late eighteenth century, at the height of the Segu empire, in West Africa. The name "Bambara" is actually a Muslim term that means "unbeliever." The kingdom of Segu was founded by the Bambara early in the seventeenth century, a time when their neighbors—the Malinke, the Soninke, and the Fula (Fulani)—had adopted the Muslim religion. For the next two hundred years, as the kingdom of Segu became an empire that included city-states and lands of the Soninke and the Fula, the Bambara steadfastly refused to give up their religion. The empire of Segu reached its zenith under King Da Monzon, the ruler in the following epic. However, shortly thereafter (early in the nineteenth century), a Fula chieftain conquered Segu and brought Islam to the Bambara.

Located in the Western Sudan, in the area of the Upper Niger River (also called the Joliba River), the empire of Segu followed three earlier empires in that area—those of Ancient Ghana (dating from the fourth or fifth century A.D.), Mali, and Songhay. For centuries—from the origin of Ancient Ghana to the end of Segu—the Western Sudan was a battleground of wars fought in order to gain economic and political power.

Every male in Bambara society inherited a particular social status, which remained with him throughout his life and which he passed on to his children. At the top of the social ladder were the Bambara nobles, who were Segu's warriors. They were followed, in descending order, by the djeli or bard-historians, and then by the craftsmen and artisans, such as the blacksmiths (who were at the top of this social level) and the leatherworkers. Other social groups included magicians, farmers, and herdsmen. The lowest social group consisted of slaves.

The political and economic environment of the Bambara had a great effect on their values and their way of life. Theirs was a warrior society, and the hero was most valued by his king and among his peers. Consequently, Bambara warriors often attacked other communities, not because their own community was in danger, but simply for the excitement and the opportunity for heroism that such armed conflict afforded. A warrior's value in Bambara society depended on his courage, skill, and magical powers.

Moreover, the warrior's behavior was governed by a specific code. He would never fight a warrior who was afraid of him, nor would he fight a man of lower social status. It was the custom for the winner of a combat to behead the loser, and the severed head would become a trophy of the victory.

The Bambara djeli or bard-historian, who stood just beneath the warrior on the social ladder, not only inherited his profession, but he often inherited the family to whom he was attached. A djeli father taught his craft to his son, including the history of the family whom his grandfather and his father had served. A king's djeli served his master in many roles, such as those of counselor, spokesman, mediator in disputes, and ambassador. The djeli's power as the historian of his people ensured that he would get whatever he asked in return for his services. Typical gifts were cowrie shells, slaves, cattle, and land.

The Bambara blacksmith, who came next on the social ladder, worked in iron, wood, gold, and silver. He made iron farm implements and weapons of war, such as the gun, the spear, and the short sword. He carved wooden religious objects, such as fetishes and masks. He fashioned decorative pieces of jewelry. However, his great prestige as a craftsman came from the fact that he possessed great spiritual power and that this power entered the weapons that he fashioned.

Slaves, who stood at the bottom of the social ladder, were the personal property of their owners, and their well-being depended upon how their master treated them. They received no protection and had no rights since they were not citizens of the state. Many slaves were freeborn Soninke, Malinke, or Fula, whose capture in war had enslaved them. However, once a person became a slave, the condition and social status were both permanent and hereditary.

Magic was a potent factor in Bambara society. Certain Bambara were trained to predict future events based upon the toss of kola nuts. Morikes, who were Muslim (and Soninke or Fula rather than Bambara), predicted future events based upon their reading of the Koran as well as upon their toss of kola nuts. Therefore, they were thought to possess greater skill than the Bambara practitioners. However, both types of practitioners could use magic as a weapon and as a

protection, and Bambara warriors and kings called upon both of them.

In understanding *Bakaridjan Kone,* it is also important to know that the jinn is a type of supernatural spirit that appears in Muslim demonology. It exercises supernatural power and assumes various forms, often human, as it inhabits the earth.

Bakaridjan Kone depicts a world that has been confirmed from an objective point of view. The British Explorer Mungo Park visited Segu City as a tourist in 1795 when Da Monzon was king and, therefore, when the events in the following epic might have occurred. Fortunately for posterity, he kept detailed journals of what he saw.

According to Park, the empire's capital city actually consisted of four towns, two on the north bank of the Niger and two on the south bank, which housed a population of approximately thirty thousand people. The towns were protected by high mud walls and contained square, flat-roofed, often whitewashed clay houses. Some of these buildings were two stories high. Farms and pastureland for herds of cattle, sheep, and goats lay outside the city walls.

The towns' narrow streets were broad enough to support the crowds of people who used them. Farm produce, cloth, leatherwork, iron tools and weapons, gold and silver decorative objects, and wood religious objects were plentiful. Slaves transported horses and passengers across the Niger, from one set of towns to the other, in long wooden canoes. Each canoe was made from two tree trunks that had been hollowed out and then fastened end-to-end. A one-way trip cost ten cowrie shells, and the fare enriched the king's treasury.

An important appeal of the epic of *Bakaridjan Kone* is the interesting nature of Bakaridjan Kone himself, the extent to which he both resembles and differs from other epic heroes, and the nature of the life that he leads. Like many other traditional heroes, he has an unusual childhood, he distinguishes himself in competition with his peers, and he performs heroic deeds that enrich the society in which he lives. However, unlike most traditional heroes, Bakaridjan must also cope with the loss of fame. His behavior raises the issue of whether a hero

Bakaridjan Kone is also appealing because of the light that it casts on Bambara society at the end of the eighteenth century. Both the Bambara hero's code of behavior and his society's attitude toward its heroes invite comparison with the heroes of other times and places.

The source for the following version of this epic is Harold Courlander's *The Heart of the Ngoni: Heroes of the African Kingdom of Segu.*

BAKARIDJAN KONE

PART 1: THE RISE OF A HERO

Prologue

Heroes are born, not made. Some men can only be slaves. Other men can only be farmers. Still other men can only work in leather. Those who are fortunate must transfer their spiritual power into their craft and become blacksmiths. Others, who are more fortunate, must use their skill with words and become the bard-historians or djeli of their people. Still others, who are even more fortunate, must be nobles and become the warriors of their people. And a few nobles, who are the most fortunate of all, must become the heroes of their people.

The heroes who achieve lasting fame, who display such courage, skill, and honor that the king's djeli sings of their accomplishments, have weathered storm and strife, for fate is as fickle as the moon. Now it smiles upon the hero; now it frowns upon him. However, heroes, like all mortals, can only accept their fate. What will be, will surely come! So it is. So it has always been. So it will always be.

Chapter 1

Bakaridjan comes to Segu City and takes his place in the court of King Da Monzon.

In the region of Segu City one could find a small village called Diosoro Nko. In that village there lived a farmer who had been born a noble. This farmer did not value his wives, his work, or his life in the village. Thinking that the grass that grew within the compound of the court of great Da Monzon, king of Segu, was gold and would make him rich, this man left the members of his family to fend for themselves and went to Segu City.

When he arrived at the compound of the king, the farmer joined a group of men who made it their business to listen to the king's business every day and to praise his every word. To his sorrow, the farmer learned that gold did not sprout up from the ground like blades of grass, nor did it rain down from above. However, he and his fellow observers received leftovers from the king's meal and a few cowrie shells for their daily presence.

While this farmer was so occupied, he learned that one of his two wives had given birth to their child, a male infant. The man felt that he was too busy at court to attend his son's naming ceremony, but he told the king's djeli, who was also the king's spokesman, about the birth of his male infant. He hoped that the words of his tongue would reach the ears of the king and that great Da Monzon would present him with a handsome gift in honor of this special event.

King Da Monzon, however, had much wisdom between his ears. He did not respect those who lived only to praise his every word. And if such a man were a freeborn noble, why that was all the worse for him. Moreover, Da Monzon was blessed with a kingdom, wealth, and wives. His wives had given him twelve male children, so that he knew that one of them would inherit his kingdom and perpetuate his lineage. It was just a matter of which son it would be. And so, Da Monzon had no need for his group of praisers. And he had no interest in another man's son.

And so it came to pass that the king of Segu ignored the father of this newborn son. However, out of respect for the farmer's family, he sent one of his messengers to the infant's mother in the village of Diosoro Nko.

The man appeared before the woman and announced, "I have come from King Da Monzon with some cowries to help you plan a naming ceremony and with the king's request that you give your son the name Bakaridjan Kone."

When the mother heard these words, she replied, "Tell the great king of Segu that I will do as he wishes."

It then came to pass that years came and went like the sun and the moon. The king's sons were growing older in Segu City, and Bakaridjan was growing older in Diosoro Nko.

Meanwhile, heroes would come into Segu City in order to test their valor in contests with other heroes and in order to earn their place in the songs of the king's djeli. And since Da Monzon was growing older, when he saw these heroes, he now began to worry about the future of his kingdom.

And so it came to pass that great Da Monzon called his favorite morike to him and said, "You have earned great fame as a teacher of the Koran and as one who also knows the ways of magic. The hairs on my head now turn from black to gray. And I begin to think of the time when I must leave my kingdom to one of my sons. I worry that somewhere a hero exists who is greater than my sons, and that the brightness of his star will put an end to the light of their stars in Segu. So consult your Koran and toss your kola nuts. And then tell me what they reveal about the future. Your advice will earn you a bag of gold!"

When the morike had done as the king commanded, he returned to him and said, "Great Da Monzon, the only threat to you and your kingdom is a boy of Segu. Both the Koran and my kola nuts reveal that his star will be so bright that it will put an end to the light of your sons' stars in Segu. I do not know this boy's name. Nor do I know where he lives. But, if you will test every boy in Segu, you will surely find him!"

When the king heard these words, he exclaimed, "For a skilled morike, you certainly have not been able to learn much! Just what do you suggest as a test?"

"Great king of Segu, have every boy in your kingdom help you as you mount your horse," the morike replied. "Have him place his hand upon your stirrup to hold it steady. Meanwhile, lightly rest the point of your spear upon the boy's foot. Then, as you mount your horse, steady yourself by leaning heavily upon your spear. Your weight will force the spear-point into the boy's foot. And you will be hard-pressed to find a boy who will tolerate such pain without sound or deed. However, the boy who neither winces nor cries out is destined to become so great that he is surely the one whom you must fear!"

And so it came to pass that the king tested every boy in Segu City in this fashion. To his surprise, not one of his own sons could pass the test. And not one of the other boys in Segu City fared any better. One by one, each boy screamed in pain and ran away.

Da Monzon called his counselors before him and complained, "What am I to do about my morike? He has suggested a test that no boy can pass! Obviously, he has lost his powers!"

"Great king, do not be so quick to judge," replied a counselor who also had much wisdom between his ears. "You have tried the boys in Segu City, but many more boys live in the villages of Segu. One of them is Bakaridjan Kone, a boy whom you yourself named. Surely, you must test these boys, as well!"

And so it came to pass that even these boys came before King Da Monzon in Segu City. One by one, they were asked to help the king to mount his horse. One by one, they felt the king's spear-point puncture their foot. And one by one, they screamed in pain and ran away.

When all the boys had failed the test, the king of Segu commanded, "Tell me, slave, which of those boys was Bakaridjan Kone, that boy whom I myself named when he was born? As I recall, he is from the village where these boys live."

"Great king of Segu, that boy has yet to come to take the test," replied the king's slave. "When I went to the village of Diosoro Nko and visited the house of his mother, the only boy I saw there was an insolent ragamuffin who spoke to me as if he were the chief of his village. He answered every question of mine with an impertinent question of his own, so that I learned nothing at all about Bakaridjan Kone's whereabouts. However, the insolent boy did say that he would give Bakaridjan your message and that Bakaridjan Kone would indeed come!

"I can tell you nothing about Bakaridjan Kone," the king's slave declared. "But the words that came from the mouth of this ragamuffin earned him a good whack on his empty stomach. And for that, I was lucky to return to you with my life! He is a strange one, all right!

"I know that a king's ears are not interested in hearing a slave's words. But I advise you to let that ragamuffin take your test, for he surely is a child for even a king to fear! And if someone else will bring him here, I will point him out to you. However, I will face the point of your spear and certain death before I will deal with him again!"

It came to pass that while the slave was speaking these words, Bakaridjan Kone arrived in Segu City and entered the king's compound. "Great Da Monzon!" the slave exclaimed. "That's the very ragamuffin I have just been telling you about!"

King Da Monzon cast his sharp eyes upon the emaciated, dirty, and tattered young figure. "Boy, who are you?" the king asked. "And what do you want here in the compound of the king of Segu? If you are looking for food, one of my slaves will find something for you to eat."

"Great Whoever You Are, my name is Bakaridjan Kone," the boy replied. "And I have not come to beg for food or for anything else! I have come because Da Monzon, the great king of Segu, has summoned me to his compound. I would have come sooner, but the king did not think highly enough of me to send someone of rank. I am a freeborn Bambara. And I will not deal with any slave who acts as if he is superior to me!"

"Boy, learn your place!" Da Monzon replied. "One who is as poorly fed and clothed as you are must earn another's respect! It will not be handed to him in a gourd like food."

"Great Whoever You Are, who do you think you are that you dare to speak to me in this way? Your tongue has the authority of a king. And yet a great king has wisdom between his ears to match his power. He does not need to prove how great he is by cutting down one of his people like a blade of grass!" Bakaridjan declared. "As for me, I am a freeborn Bambara. And my ears do not have to listen to your words!" And with these words, quick as the wind, he turned to leave the compound.

"Bakaridjan Kone, come back!" commanded Da Monzon. "I am Da Monzon, king of Segu! It is I who named you! It is I who commanded that you come before me! And it is I who now ask you to help me mount my horse!"

"Great Da Monzon, if that is what you ask of me, then I will do it, for you are the great king of Segu. And this freeborn Bambara chooses to obey his king!" Bakaridjan replied.

And so it came to pass that Bakaridjan placed his hand upon Da Monzon's stirrup to hold it steady. And Da Monzon lightly rested the point of his spear upon Bakaridjan's foot. Then, as the king mounted his horse, he steadied himself by leaning heavily upon his spear. And his weight forced the spear-point into Bakaridjan's foot.

However, Bakaridjan did not even blink as the king's spear-point punctured his foot. He did not wince. He did not cry out. He did not move his hand from the stirrup.

And the words of his favorite morike thundered like the beat of a drum in the king's ears, proclaiming, "The boy who neither winces nor cries out is destined to become so great that he is surely the one whom you must fear!"

Da Monzon's heart flooded with terror. But then he said to himself, "When terror floods the heart, reason flees the head! A good king must have much wisdom between his ears! Surely I have nothing to fear from this insolent ragamuffin! Just look at him! He is ill-fed, ill-clothed, and untaught! I will try him again. And surely, this time, I will make him scream in agony!"

And so it came to pass that Da Monzon found a reason to dismount, leaning heavily upon his spear as he did so. Then he remounted his horse, again leaning heavily upon his spear. Then he dismounted once again, leaning heavily upon his spear. Now he was satisfied. Bakaridjan's foot had become a bloody pathway for his spear. And his weapon now lodged in the earth and held the boy's foot prisoner.

Still, Bakaridjan did not even blink as the king's spear-point ground a greater hole in his foot. He did not wince. He did not cry out. He did not move his hand from the stirrup.

And, once again, the words of his favorite morike thundered like the beat of a drum in the king's ears, proclaiming, "The boy who neither winces nor cries out is destined to become so great that he is surely the one whom you must fear!"

Da Monzon's heart flooded anew with terror. And, this time, reason fled his head. "Here is the hero I have dreaded!" he declared to himself. "This ragamuffin of a boy! Somehow, I will have to get rid of him!"

This is what the king thought to himself. However, to Bakaridjan the king exclaimed, "Oh, my poor boy! I have accidentally wounded you! I am so sorry! One of my slaves will clean and bandage your wound! And I will reward you for your valor! From now on, you will live in the king's compound, as one of my sons!"

Bakaridjan heard the king's words. And he replied, "Great Da Monzon, my tongue has not complained about my wound! Nor has my hand left the stirrup of your horse. You are my king. And I will obey all of your commands without question!"

And with these words, Bakaridjan walked unflinchingly on his wounded foot as he led the king's horse back toward the king's stable.

And the king's counselors, his djeli, his praisers, his servants, and all who were there to witness this event stood in silence and in awe. For they knew that one who was destined to become the greatest of Segu's heroes had entered their lives and was passing before them.

And so it came to pass that Bakaridjan Kone did not return to his mother and the village of Diosoro Nko. He remained in Da Monzon's compound, where he would spend each day sitting behind the king on a hide mat.

Da Monzon called his djeli to him—he who was the bard-historian of the Segu. And the king said to him, "Tell me, what should I do about this ragamuffin of a boy who does nothing but spend his days sitting behind me on his hide mat?"

The djeli heard his king's words. And he replied, "Great Da Monzon, let the boy do as he chooses. You cannot judge a seedling by the weak branch from which it falls! My songs tell of how Bakaridjan Kone comes from a great and noble tree. They tell of the heroes in his family and the great deeds they performed. The brilliance of this boy's star will be brighter than the light cast by the stars of your own sons! He will become the shield of Segu! He will become the right arm of Segu's great king!

The words of the djeli's tongue brought no joy to Da Monzon's heart. Instead, once again, the words of his favorite morike thundered like the beat of a drum in the king's ears, proclaiming, "The boy who neither winces nor cries out is destined to become so great that he is surely the one whom you must fear!"

Chapter 2

Bakaridjan deals with Da Monzon's sons.

And so it came to pass that Da Monzon called his twelve sons before him and declared, "See this boy who sits behind me each day on that hide. He chooses to be here, rather than outside playing games with all of you because he thinks that he is better than you are! His mind is flooded with thoughts of the heroes in his family and the great deeds that they have performed.

"He has heard the king's djeli declare that the brilliance of his star will be brighter than the light cast by your own stars!" Da Monzon exclaimed. "He has heard the king's djeli declare that he—Bakaridjan Kone—and not you will become the shield of Segu! He has heard the king's djeli declare that he—Bakaridjan Kone—and not you will become the right arm of Segu's great king. And that king is Da Monzon—your father, not his!

"The morike's Koran and his kola nuts say that this indeed will come to pass. And they do not tell false tales! My heart floods with grief because of it!" the king concluded.

The king's oldest son was quick to respond. "Then, push such grief from your heart, Father!" Da Toma exclaimed. "As long as your twelve sons are alive and well, the morike's Koran and his kola nuts will have another tale to tell! Like a cooking fire, Bakaridjan Kone's life may shine with the brilliance of the sun. But we will stamp it out before it can cause any harm!"

Poor Bakaridjan! Tears came to his eyes. And the thought of the heroes who were his ancestors did not console him. "What is my destiny?" he asked himself. "Why is it that I have been taken from my mother and my village and brought to live in this city, where the king has set his sons against me? I have done nothing to deserve this fate!"

Then courage flooded Bakaridjan's heart. And he thought to himself, "But I must deal with it! And I will remember the words of Da Toma, the king's oldest son!"

And it came to pass that, when the sun next made the day light, Bakaridjan accompanied the king's sons when they went off with sickles to cut grass for the king's horses. After they had completed their task, Da Toma challenged Bakaridjan to fight to the death. When Bakaridjan refused because of his injured foot, Da Toma ordered his brothers to bind Bakaridjan's arms and legs and beat him to death. Lakare, the youngest of the king's sons, objected to such dishonorable behavior. But the power of the oldest prince prevailed, and they obeyed.

The princes, believing Bakaridjan to be dead, gave him a grave of leaves and left him in the fields. However, the sorely wounded boy regained consciousness, managed to pick up his bundle of grass, and then returned with it to the king's compound.

When Da Monzon asked about Bakaridjan's wounds, the boy replied, "Great king of Segu, do not concern yourself! I neglected to keep my eyes on the path. And so, I tripped and fell upon a thorn-bush. But I have brought you your grain, for I would not return to the king's compound empty-handed."

In his heart, Da Monzon knew that his sons were reaping the seeds of jealousy that he had planted. And so his tongue remained silent.

And it came to pass that, when the sun made the second day light, Bakaridjan once again joined the king's sons in gathering grass. Once again, after they had completed their task, Da Toma challenged Bakaridjan to fight to the death. When Bakaridjan once again refused because of his injured foot, Da Toma ordered his brothers to bind Bakaridjan's arms and legs and beat him to death. Once again, Lakare, the youngest of the king's sons objected to such dishonorable behavior. But the power of the oldest prince prevailed, and they obeyed.

Once again, the princes, believing Bakaridjan to be dead, gave him a grave of leaves and left him in the fields. However, the sorely wounded boy regained consciousness, managed to pick up his bundle of grass, and then returned with it to the king's compound.

Once again, when the king asked Bakaridjan about his wounds, the boy replied, "Great Da Monzon, do not concern yourself! I neglected to keep my eyes on the path. And so, I tripped and fell upon spikes of sharp blades of grass. But I have brought you your grain, for I would not return to the king's compound empty-handed."

Once again, in his heart, Da Monzon knew that his sons were reaping the seeds of jealousy that he had planted. And so his tongue remained silent.

And it came to pass that, when the sun made the third day light, Bakaridjan once again joined the king's sons in gathering grass. Once again, after they had completed their task, Da Toma challenged Bakaridjan to fight to the death. When Bakaridjan once again refused because of his injured foot, Da Toma ordered his brothers to bind Bakaridjan's arms and legs and beat him to death. Once again, Lakare, the youngest of the king's sons, objected to such dishonorable behavior. But the power of the oldest prince prevailed, and they obeyed.

Once again, the princes, believing Bakaridjan to be dead, gave him a grave of leaves and left him in the fields. However, the sorely wounded boy regained consciousness, managed to pick up his bundle of grass, and then returned with it to the king's compound.

Once again, when the king asked Bakaridjan about his wounds, the boy replied, "Great Da Monzon, do not concern yourself! I neglected to keep my eyes on the path. And so, I tripped and fell upon the roots of a great tree. But I have brought you your grain, for I would not return to the king's compound empty-handed."

Once again, in his heart, Da Monzon knew that his sons were reaping the seeds of jealousy that he had planted. And so his tongue remained silent.

And so it came to pass that, when the sun made the fourth day light, Bakaridjan left the king's sons to their grass-gathering. And, instead, he walked the streets of the city until he found the shop of a skilled blacksmith. He waited there all day, helping the smith with small tasks as he pursued his work.

At last, the smith said to Bakaridjan, "Is there anything that I can do for you, my boy? You have watched me with patience and respect while the sun has made most of its journey, and you have helped me of your own free will. So tell me, have you come to learn about the trade of a blacksmith? Or do you want me to make something for you?"

Bakaridjan heard the blacksmith's words. And he replied, "Good Smith, if you would, I would like you to make me a knife that will be as long as my arm."

This the blacksmith did. And having given it to Bakaridjan, he would accept no payment for it. Instead, he declared, "I give this to you, my boy, as freely and as respectfully as you gave your help to me! You are a most unusual person!"

"Thank you, Good Smith!" Bakaridjan responded. "I will remember the generous deed of Segu's skilled blacksmith!"

Bakaridjan fashioned a scabbard for his long knife. And then returned to the king's compound, where, as always, he slept on his hide mat.

When the sun made the fifth day light, Bakaridjan once again accompanied the king's sons when they went off to gather grass. After they had completed their task, Da Toma said, "Bakaridjan, I would challenge you to fight to the death once again. But I know that you will refuse because of your injured foot. And so, prepare, once again, to be bound hand and foot and beaten! This time, know that we will surely take your life!"

"Not so, Da Toma!" Bakaridjan exclaimed. "Three times I have put up with your shameful behavior. And I have had enough of it! I do not know about my own destiny. But I do know that a hero's blood does not flow through your body! You have heard the songs that the king's djeli sings! What song praises the man who leads a group against a single adversary? What song praises the man who fights one who is not his enemy?"

"So let us now lay our weapons aside and fight hand to hand in single combat," Bakaridjan declared. "And let us agree that he who wins this combat will take the other's life."

"Agreed!" Da Toma exclaimed. "And, Bakaridjan, know that, this time, you will indeed give up your life!"

And so it came to pass that the two boys fought hand to hand, each trying to wrestle the other to the ground and to be victorious in their conflict. Da Toma was larger than Bakaridjan, yet he could not overpower him. And as the fight continued, Da Toma became more and more fatigued. "Come, help me, my brothers!" he called. "Let us put an end to this intruder's life, once and for all!"

"That is not the honorable way," Lakare responded. "And so we cannot help you in your battle. But know this. If Bakaridjan conquers you, each of us is willing to fight him as well. And like you, we will all fight him honorably, hand to hand in single combat."

And so it came to pass that the time came when Da Toma could no longer defend himself against Bakaridjan. And he fell to the ground beneath the weight of his adversary. In this way, Da Toma gave up his life. For, quick as the wind, Bakaridjan slew him with his mighty blade and then smeared himself with his enemy's blood.

"As Lakare has declared, so it will be," Bakaridjan announced. "Who among you is now ready to avenge Da Toma's death?"

As the king's eleven sons gazed upon Bakaridjan's blood-smeared body, terror flooded their hearts. Their ears heard Bakaridjan's words, but their tongues remained silent. Suddenly, they all turned and fled in panic with their lives, each taking refuge in his mother's house in the king's compound in Segu City.

Da Monzon saw that his sons were dashing into the compound overcome with terror, and he learned that Da Toma had given up his life to Bakaridjan Kone. The king immediately sent his armed guards into the bush with orders to find Bakaridjan, take his life, and leave his body there as food for eagles and dogs. However, when the guards encountered Bakaridjan, their hearts, too, flooded with terror. They thought that he must surely be protected by a jinn's magic. And so, they turned and fled in panic with their lives, each taking refuge in the king's compound.

And so it came to pass that Bakaridjan returned to the king's compound and entered the king's private rooms. There he found Da Monzon's great gun, which had the power to bring death upon four men with each shot. Then, gun in hand, he went out and faced Da Monzon, his sons, his djeli, his counselors, his armed guards, and his servants.

Speaking for the king, Da Monzon's djeli asked Bakaridjan, "Oldest Brother, what trouble has come between you and your younger brothers that the oldest of the king's sons is not here, while you appear before us gun in hand? I call you 'Oldest Brother' because you have earned our respect. Now, we would hear what you have to say."

Bakaridjan heard the djeli's words. And he replied, "Do not ask me, noble djeli! It is a matter for the king's true sons to tell you."

"Then let the king's true sons speak," the djeli responded.

Da Monzon's eleven sons heard the djeli's words. And one after the other, ten of the boys replied, "Do not ask me, noble djeli! My eyes did not see what happened. And so my tongue can only remain silent."

At last, it was Lakare's turn to speak. "Noble djeli, we were all there. And we have all seen what happened," he declared. "Father, the problem began when you told us that the brilliance of Bakaridjan Kone's star was destined to be brighter than the light cast by our own stars—when you declared that Bakaridjan Kone was destined to become the greatest hero in Segu!

"Da Toma heard your words, and he declared that Bakaridjan would give up his life before that ever came to pass. You heard Da Toma's words, but your tongue remained silent. And because you did not speak against Da Toma, we all knew that you would permit our oldest brother to carry out his threat," Lakare explained.

"Three times, we went forth together to gather grain," Lakare continued. "Three times, Da Toma challenged Bakaridjan to fight him. But three times, Bakaridjan refused. Three times, Da Toma ordered us to bind and beat Bakaridjan to the death. And three times, we left him beaten and buried in a grave of leaves.

"Three times, Bakaridjan returned to your court with his load of grain. And three times, you yourself saw his battered body," Lakare continued. "Yet, three times, your tongue remained silent. And because you did not speak against Da Toma, we all knew that you would permit him to carry out his threat.

"Today," Lakare continued, "we went forth together to gather grain once again. But this time, when Da Toma ordered us to bind and beat Bakaridjan, Bakaridjan refused to permit it. Instead, he challenged Da Toma to single combat, hand to hand, to the death.

"Da Toma accepted that challenge. And when he knew that he would lose the fight, he asked us to come to his aid," Lakare explained. "But that would not have been honorable. And so, we refused to do it.

"Bakaridjan won that combat. And he took Da Toma's life with his mighty blade. He then challenged us to avenge Da Toma's death and meet him in single combat, hand to hand, to the death. But terror flooded our hearts! Quick as the wind, we fled from him and took refuge in the safety of the compound!" Lakare concluded.

Da Monzon, his djeli, his counselors, his armed guards, and his servants all listened with silent tongues to Lakare's words. Then, the king's counselors said to him, "Great king, surely you cannot blame Bakaridjan for the death of your oldest son. Da Toma himself is to blame. And you yourself are to blame for permitting him to act as he did."

The king heard the words of his counselors. And he replied, "Your words hit their mark."

Then the king turned to Bakaridjan and declared, "You are in no way to blame for what has occurred, Bakaridjan,. From this time forth, you will have no need for my gun or your own blade among the members of the king's family and the people of Segu. You have proved by your actions that you are a man of honor, even though you are but a boy!"

Da Monzon's tongue spoke these words. But his heart was flooded with fear. "Bakaridjan Kone must not remain in Segu City!" he said to himself. "I cannot trust him! I will send him back to his village, where he can do no harm!"

Chapter 3

Bakaridjan responds to the Fula attack on Segu.

And so it came to pass that Bakaridjan Kone returned to the village of Diosoro Nko on a small horse that Da Monzon gave him. He had left as a boy. Now he returned as a boy, but he had become a hero. Fathers now wanted their sons to go to Diosoro Nko in order to spend time with Bakaridjan. These boys formed a club and made Bakaridjan their chief. And their club grew to include four hundred members. Together the boys hunted. Together the boys played war games. And together the boys grew to manhood.

When their manhood rite was close at hand, an army of Fula warriors from Massina staged a surprise raid against the capital city of Segu. They stole large herds of cows, goats, and sheep. Da Monzon commanded all who were skilled in the use of weapons to assemble in Segu City and set forth as an army to retrieve the animals and punish the Fula.

It came to pass that a thousand men on horseback and five thousand men on foot responded to the great king of Segu's call to arms. Bearing guns, spears, and knives, they were quick to leave Segu City and go forth to find the enemy. The four hundred members of Bakaridjan's club were part of this army.

But Bakaridjan was not leading the members of his club into battle. He was still at home in his village, sleeping. When his mother awakened him and called him to his task, he exclaimed, "Mother, we are too poor to own any cows, goats, or sheep. And so, the Fula warriors have done nothing to harm us! I will go to Segu City and present myself to King Da Monzon when I am ready!"

So it came to pass that Bakaridjan Kone reported to the great king of Segu long after the king's army had departed. Da Monzon greeted Bakaridjan by saying, "Bakaridjan, your manhood rite is close at hand. And yet when Segu has gone to war, you have not see fit to lead the members of your club into battle! What kind of behavior is that for a chief? Your tongue speaks words of courage. But your actions do not hit their mark!"

Bakaridjan heard the king's words. "Give me a large horse, so that I can look the Fula warriors in the eye, and I will show you that my actions obey my words!" he exclaimed.

To these words, Da Monzon replied, "I am sorry, Bakaridjan, but every horse has been given to the army!"

"Then I will ride your own special horse—the great white one, with the silver bit and bridle!" Bakaridjan declared. "Have no fear for his safety. He is carrying a great warrior into battle. And he will return to you carrying an even greater warrior!"

Before leaving, Bakaridjan stealthily entered the king's private rooms. There he found and took the king's two special weapons—the spear that could take the lives of two men with one throw and the gun that could take the lives of four men with one shot. Then, quick as the wind, he galloped out of Segu City, taking the route that Segu's army had taken before him.

Bakaridjan rode and rode toward Massina. But he could see no sign of an army. At last, he saw that the horizon was obscured by a dark cloud of dust. However, as he watched, the dark cloud appeared to be moving toward him! And it came to pass that Segu's army was returning home!

Bakaridjan's heart flooded with dismay. "The war has been fought and won before I could take part in it!" he exclaimed to himself. "How can this be? I have not delayed that long!"

As soon as the returning warriors had come close enough for Bakaridjan's eyes to meet theirs, he exclaimed, "I salute you! You have been victorious sooner than I expected! But where are Segu's herds? Are those who follow you driving them?"

The returning warriors heard Bakaridjan's words. "Your questions have hit their mark!" they exclaimed. "We are returning to Segu, but in defeat. As great as our warriors are, the Fula warriors are greater. We could not overcome them in battle. And we could not recover our herds!"

"Well, if warriors such as you cannot conquer the Fula, then no one can be successful against them!" Bakaridjan declared. "I will return with you, but first I need to relieve myself. So continue on your way, and I will catch up to you."

It came to pass that, once he was out of sight, Bakaridjan rode, quick as the wind, toward Massina. Meanwhile, Segu's army returned to the capital city and told the king of their defeat.

"And what of Bakaridjan Kone?" Da Monzon asked. "Did he ever find you?"

"He did," the warriors replied. "But by then, we had lost the battle and were returning to Segu. He left us to relieve himself, and we never saw him again!"

"So much for what the morike reads in the Koran and in kola nuts!" the king exclaimed. "If that boy is destined to become Segu's greatest hero, his path is most strange! The brilliance of even a small star will be brighter than the light that his star casts!"

Meanwhile, Bakaridjan rode on and on toward Massina. But he could see no sign of the Fula warriors. At last, he saw what could be a camp outlined against the setting sun. He quietly rode toward it, pausing only when he reached the outskirts of the camp. There, he waited long into the darkness of the night, until the campfires had become ashes and the warriors had gone to sleep. They had earned their rest! For, without pausing, they had come to Segu, stolen the herds, returned toward Massina, fought valiantly against the army of Segu, and continued on toward their home.

When all appeared to be safely still, Bakaridjan went into action. First, quick as the wind, he stole the warriors' horses. Once they were safely hidden, he crept into the Fula camp, fired two shots from Da Monzon's gun, and ran among the sleeping forms shouting, "To arms! To arms! The Bambara are upon us! To arms! To arms!"

Startled out of their sleep, the Fula warriors grabbed their guns and spears and wildly attacked any form that moved in the surrounding blackness. The ground soon became muddy with blood, but it was all Fula blood. Those who ran for their horses knew that the Bambara had stolen them. Before long, it became clear to the Fula chief that all was lost! "To Massina!" he cried. "Join me and flee to Massina!"

And so it came to pass that a small band of Fula returned to Massina. When the sun made the next day light, they saw that only forty of their army of four hundred warriors had survived the Bambara attack.

Meanwhile, Bakaridjan made his way back to Segu City, driving the horses of the Fula, and, of course, all of the Segu herds of cattle, goats, and sheep. The returning hero received a festive welcome. King Da Monzon accepted his spear and his gun with good humor. He called Bakaridjan "my son." And he gave him his own special horse—the great white one, with the silver bit and bridle—as a gift. The king's djeli created a song in Bakaridjan's honor that declared, "Bakaridjan Kone is Segu's mighty hero. Our great king, Da Monzon, is still our moon. But Bakaridjan Kone is our brightest star!"

It soon came to pass that Bakaridjan and the members of his club were initiated into manhood. And they took their place among the adult men of their kingdom. Bakaridjan Kone was a leader among leaders. He led Segu's army for Da Monzon. He conquered other peoples and brought them under Da Monzon's authority and power. Some djeli say that he added more than twenty kingdoms to Segu's empire, but others say that he added more than thirty. Because of

Bakaridjan's courage, strength, and skill, Da Monzon now ruled a large empire and collected tribute from many peoples. He built a treasure-house to hold all of his gold and cowries.

The great king of Segu rewarded Bakaridjan for his deeds. His mouth smiled with good humor that his eyes did not reflect, for Da Monzon's heart was flooded with fear. "I may be the moon of my people," he said to himself. "But how will I shine once the light cast by Segu's brightest star casts its shadow over my own light?"

And so it came to pass that Da Monzon called his favorite morike to him and said, "You have earned great fame as a teacher of the Koran and as one who also knows the ways of magic. My heart floods with fear that the light cast by Segu's brightest star will cast its shadow over my own light! And so, I wish to bring an early end to the life of Bakaridjan Kone. Consult your Koran and toss your kola nuts. And then tell me how I can accomplish this. Your advice will earn you a bag of gold!"

When the morike had done as the king commanded, he returned to him and said, "Great Da Monzon, no matter where I looked in the Koran and how I tossed the kola nuts, the answer was the same! You cannot take the life of Bakaridjan Kone! He is a true hero! He is pure of heart, pure of mind, and pure of soul!

"Bakaridjan has earned boundless praise," the morike added. "Yet he continues to respect all who attempt to lead good lives—whether young or old, rich or poor, strong or weak. He has become a man of wealth, yet he shares it with everyone. From his hands his friends receive gold, the poor receive cowries, and slaves receive land and cattle.

"Bakaridjan is strong," the morike continued. "Yet he takes the time to help those who are weak. He will carry a bundle of wood for one who is lame. And he will give food to a grandmother who has no children to care for her.

"Bakaridjan is the greatest of warriors, yet he will not fight a man whose status is less than his own. And he will not fight any warrior who is afraid of him. He fights to win, yet he shows compassion for those whom he has defeated in battle.

"Bakaridjan's virtue protects him more than any magic charm that he may wear," the morike concluded. "He radiates such power that he disarms every weapon. No spear-point or bullet can penetrate his skin. His code of honor is his life. And he owes his life to his code of honor! He has no wish to rule a kingdom, either yours or that of any other king, for he already possesses all that he wants. You may wish to take his life, but such a deed would bring dishonor upon your name."

Da Monzon heard his favorite morike's words. "Your words may hit their mark," the great king of Segu replied. "But the hairs on my head are now gray. And surely the time will soon come when I must leave my kingdom to one of my sons. Yet I do not have a son whose star shines with the brilliance of Bakaridjan's star! With such a hero in Segu as Bakaridjan Kone, how can any one of my sons hope to rule in my place?"

Da Monzon's favorite morike heard the king's words. And he replied, "Great king of Segu, push such fears from your heart! Bakaridjan Kone does not have designs upon your kingdom! He will honor the authority of any of your sons just as he respects your own authority as king of Segu. As long as he can be the shield of Segu and perform deeds that your djeli will transform into song, peace and contentment will flood his heart.

"And so, great king of Segu, let love flood your own heart! You are most fortunate to have a hero in Segu whose star shines with such brilliance!" the morike concluded.

Chapter 4

Bakaridjan confronts a water-jinn who has invaded Segu. Then the water-jinn challenges Bakaridjan to fight him. Bakaridjan receives valuable advice.

In time it came to pass that Segu had to bow to a powerful water-jinn named Bilissi. Water-jinns possessed a human form, but they neither looked like humans nor had human limitations. They had triangular heads, white arms and lower legs, and dark heads, torsos, and thighs. They were unusually strong, and they possessed magical powers. Neither spears nor guns could wound them.

The water-jinns lived in a world beneath the water that the human eye cannot see. In many ways, their kingdom resembled Da Monzon's kingdom. It too was ruled by a king. It too contained counselors, blacksmiths, leatherworkers, and slaves. And it too valued those who possessed a code of honor.

But Bilissi did not possess a code of honor. In fact, his behavior was so callous and cruel that he offended everyone he met in his own kingdom—nobles, craftsmen, and slaves alike.

At last, it came to pass that the king of the water-jinns met with his counselors. And they decided that it would be best to banish Bilissi. With the kingdom of the jinns now closed to him, Bilissi had nowhere to go but to a human kingdom. So he said farewell to his home beneath the water and set forth to make a new home for himself among human beings.

Bilissi wandered about on land until he entered Segu City in the kingdom of Segu. There, he built another house and settled into his new life. But he continued to be callous and cruel to one and all—nobles, craftsmen, and slaves alike.

The people of Segu knew that they were powerless against such an adversary. Because Bilissi was more than human, they called him Little God. And he had his way in everything. No one dared to stop Bilissi, for Bakaridjan was not in Segu at this time.

Now every week in Segu City a special cow was sacrificed in honor of Segu's greatest heroes. Its meat was the reward for all who had taken the lead in battle and had fought with courage, strength, and skill. No one else, even heroes of lesser standing, was entitled to participate in this rite.

But Bilissi announced that he was entitled to eat a portion of meat from the Cow of Heroes. And he proceeded to do so. "After all," he declared, "I am a greater hero than any of you! So treat me with the greatest respect! Stand aside and let me pass whenever you meet me. And set aside my portion from the Cow of Heroes, whether or not I appear in order to claim it."

Once again, no one dared to stop Bilissi. For Bakaridjan was not in Segu at this time. But in time it came to pass that Bakaridjan returned to Segu City. And when he saw that Bilissi had bent the city to his will, he said to Da Monzon, "Great king of Segu, this creature whom you call Little God is nothing but a petty tyrant! Surely, you have made an effort to stop him!"

"Bakaridjan, my son, what do you expect me to have done?" the king replied. "Little God is a water-jinn. And they possess magical powers. They are unusually strong, and neither spears nor guns can wound them. And so, the people of Segu are helpless!"

"You may be helpless, Father. But I am not!" Bakaridjan exclaimed. "This creature whom you call Little God may be more than human, but he is not a god. He must feed and water his body if he is to continue to live. And so, he shares the fate of every living thing. Now if you will not confront him, I will!"

"Open your eyes, my son, lest they lead your tongue to speak foolish words!" Da Monzon responded. "The people of Segu need your life more than they need Bilissi's death! To confront the petty tyrant is folly, not courage. And the seeds of folly bear deadly fruit! So forget your code of honor for once! Swallow your pride. And let the nasty creature have his way!"

"No, Father!" Bakaridjan exclaimed. "We must accept death and not fear it, for it is part of life. All things that live give up their lives sooner or later. Even the mountains crumble into rocks! Even the rocks crumble into sand! Even the sand gets washed away by the sea! And even the sea dries up! Death gives meaning to life by making how we choose to live important! And I will always choose to live with honor!

"And so," Bakaridjan concluded, "I will confront this water-jinn by taking his portion of the Cow of Heroes. And what will be, will come!"

So it came to pass that Bilissi arrived to take his portion of the Cow of Heroes only to find that, this week, his special portion did not exist.

"I want the portion that is always set aside for me!" Bilissi demanded. "Where is it?"

"I ate it!" Bakaridjan replied calmly.

"You ate it?" Bilissi replied. "Who are you? And what gave you that right?"

"I am called Bakaridjan Kone. I am a hero of Segu. And that gives me the right to eat your portion of the Cow of Heroes!" Bakaridjan replied. "When the Fula came and stole Segu's flocks and herds, I rescued them. Since I have become the shield of the king, the people of Segu no longer fear their neighbors. For their neighbors fear to attack them. Moreover, I have brought many kingdoms under Da Monzon's protection. And in return for that protection, they fill Da Monzon's treasure-house with bags of gold and cowries.

"Now, tell me, Bilissi, what have you done for the people of Segu except to act like a petty tyrant?" Bakaridjan asked.

"I do not have to listen to the words that your tongue speaks," Bilissi replied.

"Your words hit their mark," Bakaridjan replied. "You can walk away and return to your house. But since you are not choosing to do that, let us talk about a word that your tongue speaks too easily, the word 'hero.'

"The word hero is easy for the tongue to say, but to be a hero is a demanding task," Bakaridjan declared. "A man who would be a hero in deed must respect all who live—the old as well as the young, the poor as well as the rich, the weak as well as the strong. He must be pure of heart, pure of mind, and pure of soul.

"A man who would be a hero must be generous with his wealth and with his time, giving to whomever is in need," Bakaridjan continued. "From his hands, his friends must receive gold, the poor must receive cowries, and the slaves must receive land and cattle. He must take the time to carry a bundle of wood for one who is lame and give food to a grandmother who has no children to care for her. In battle, he must fight to win. But then he must show compassion for those whom he has defeated.

"Now, I ask you, Bilissi," Bakaridjan continued, "in what way have you ever behaved like a hero?"

The water-jinn's ears heard the words of the great hero, but his tongue remained silent.

"From what I hear, you are worse than an unruly child!" Bakaridjan continued. "And if you are indeed as great as you proclaim, then why are you here, living among ordinary human beings? If your own people valued you, they would never want to be without your protection!

"And so, as long as I am in Segu, you will know your place, and you will not overstep. The people of Segu have no reason to make way for you to walk. And the meat from the Cow of Heroes is not for you to eat!" he concluded.

So Bakaridjan spoke. And to his words, Bilissi replied, "Bakaridjan Kone, my ears have heard enough of your words! If this is how you choose to act, then you must defend your actions with your life! Tonight, the full face of the moon turns night into day. Let this face come and go. We will meet in combat when the full face of the moon shines forth once again."

"I am prepared to do that!" Bakaridjan responded.

"You know that neither spear nor gun can wound me!" Bilissi declared. "No iron object can penetrate my body."

"My ears have heard that this is so," replied Bakaridjan.

"Then, if I may ask, just how do you intend to defend yourself?" Bilissi asked.

"It is enough for you to know that I will be able to defend myself," Bakaridjan responded.

And so it came to pass that Bakaridjan sought the advice of a morike who was renowned as a master of magic. First the morike consulted his Koran. Then he consulted his kola nuts. At last, he communicated directly with the king of the water-jinns.

The king of the water-jinns apologized for his part in causing Segu's trouble. And he promised that he would quickly consult his older brother and return with help for Bakaridjan. He was as good as his word.

And so it came to pass that the morike told Bakaridjan how to win his battle with Bilissi. "Bakaridjan, I am giving you four charms—two that are red, one that is white, and one that is black," he began. "Now listen carefully to what you must do with them. First, you must buy a white ram and a black ram. Name the white ram 'Bakaridjan' and the black ram 'Bilissi.' Then you must hang the white charm around the neck of the white ram and the black charm around the neck of the black ram. Set the two rams against each other in battle. And observe which of the two rams is the victor. Your destiny will be the same as theirs.

"On the day of your battle with Bilissi," the morike continued, "wear one of the red charms in your hat. And put the other red charm into your pocket. Then keep your eyes on Bilissi's magical weapon, for your life will depend upon it! The jinn's weapon appears to be an ordinary rope that is used to prevent a horse from straying. But, in fact, it is deadly! Whatever living thing it touches instantly gives up its life! So do whatever you need to do in order to avoid Bilissi's rope. And if that means that you must retreat, then retreat!"

Bakaridjan accepted the four charms and replied, "Morike, my ears have heard your words. And I thank you for your help! I will remember the deed of the renowned master of magic!"

Chapter 5

Bakaridjan and the water-jinn fight to the death. Bakaridjan wins, but the water-jinn seriously injures Bakaridjan.

And so it came to pass that Bakaridjan bought a white ram and a black ram. He named the white ram "Bakaridjan" and the black ram "Bilissi." Then he hung the white charm around the neck of the white ram and the black charm around the neck of the black ram. At last, he set the two rams against each other in battle, so that he could observe which of the two rams would be the victor.

Their fight was long and arduous. Each ram was determined to overcome the other. The sun was completing its journey and heading toward its home when the white ram suddenly ran away from its opponent. The black ram instantly gave chase. Bakaridjan jumped on his special horse—the great white one, with the silver bit and bridle—and galloped after them.

The white ram ran on and on. The black ram ran on and on after it. And Bakaridjan galloped on and on after both of them.

In time, it came to pass that a dry well lay in their path. The white ram saw it, judged its width, and, without breaking pace, easily jumped over it. The black ram chased blindly after the white ram. And when the time came for it to jump, it misjudged the distance and fell into the well. With its body broken, quick as the wind, the black ram gave up its life.

In time, it came to pass that the full face of the moon shone forth once again. Bakaridjan and Bilissi met on horseback outside Segu City. The people of Segu cheered when they saw their greatest hero mounted upon his special horse—the great white one, with the silver bit and bridle. They stood upon the walls of their city and, where possible, upon rooftops, for they were locked inside their city's walls behind its barred gates. This would be a fight to the death. And Segu City would offer no refuge for the faint of heart, whether it was the unwelcome water-jinn or their own hero, Bakaridjan Kone.

"Well, Younger Brother, I see that you value heroism more than you value your life!" Bilissi exclaimed to Bakaridjan. "You are so foolish that I will give you the first move. Try your best. For your first move will be your last!"

Bakaridjan took aim with Da Monzon's gun that could take the lives of four men with one shot. He fired three times. And three times the bullets fell harmlessly from Bilissi's chest like loose leaves from a windswept bush.

"Younger Brother, you truly have no wisdom between your ears!" Bilissi exclaimed, laughing. "I remember telling you that neither spear nor gun can wound me, because no iron object can penetrate my body. You replied that my words were not strangers to your ears. And yet, here you are, wasting your one and only opportunity to conquer me by using an iron weapon! I will never understand you humans!"

Then all traces of humor fled from Bilissi's face. "Now, Bakaridjan Kone, I will lasso you!" the water-jinn exclaimed. "Say farewell to your people, to your city, and to the light of the sun, for you will see them no more!"

And with these words, Bilissi galloped toward Bakaridjan, swinging his rope as he approached. In order to avoid certain death, Bakaridjan suddenly turned and, quick as the wind, rode away from the jinn. Bilissi instantly gave chase. Bakaridjan galloped on and on. And Bilissi galloped on and on after him. Their chase was long and arduous since each rider was determined to be the victor.

The sun was completing its journey and heading toward its home when Bakaridjan saw that a dry well lay in their path. He judged its width, and, without breaking pace, he easily led his special horse—the great white one, with the silver bit and bridle—to jump over it.

The jinn thought only of capturing Bakaridjan Kone. And when the time came for his own horse to jump, he misjudged the distance. Together, he and his horse fell into the well. With its body broken, quick as the wind, the jinn's horse gave up its life. As for Bilissi, his body was broken beyond repair, but he did not give up his life.

When Bakaridjan returned to the well, Bilissi looked up at him and said, "Well, Older Brother, you are the victor! And I am content to have given my life to the greatest of heroes! The wind of life still blows through my body. But it is but a faint breeze that will soon depart. You have earned the right to take my head as a trophy. But even after I have given up my life, you can only use wood to do it. You see, it is wood—and not iron—that is the secret of my power!"

And so it came to pass that Bakaridjan rode toward the nearest tree, cut off one of its limbs, and fashioned it into a sharp-bladed knife. Returning to the well, with one stroke of his knife, Bakaridjan stabbed Bilissi through the chest. And, quick as the wind, he took Bilissi's life. With a second stroke of his knife, he sliced Bilissi's head from his body. But the jinn's head was so heavy that even Bakaridjan could not lift it from the well. And so it came to pass that Bakaridjan had to return to Segu City without any trophy to prove that he had, in fact, taken Bilissi's life.

Meanwhile, the people of Segu City were still locked inside the city's walls behind its barred gates. They had watched the fight from the top of the walls and, where possible, from rooftops. They had watched Bakaridjan Kone flee from Bilissi. And they were certain in their hearts that once the two adversaries were out of sight, Little God had vanquished their great hero. And so it came to pass that, when Bakaridjan returned to the walls of the capital city, the people of Segu City were certain in their hearts that the dust-covered figure on the great dust-covered horse was Little God and not their great hero. And so they refused to open the city's gates.

"King Da Monzon! Great king of Segu! Father!" Bakaridjan called. "Give me four of your mightiest warriors, and I will lead them to the well where Bilissi lies dead and decapitated. With their help, I can lift the water-jinn's head and bring it back to Segu City for all to see!"

Now, Bakaridjan had a son by the name of Simbalan who was not quite old enough to be initiated into manhood. When Simbalan saw the dust-covered figure upon the great dust-covered horse and heard his voice he went before Da Monzon and declared, "Great king of Segu, my father, Bakaridjan Kone, stands outside Segu City! Open the gates and let him enter! He is Segu's great hero! Surely Segu should treat him like one!"

Da Monzon's ears heard Simbalan's words, and he replied, "Simbalan Kone, it may be that you know your father well enough to recognize him. Or it may be that the magic that water-jinns possess has enabled Bilissi to transform himself into a figure who simply resembles your father. A good king protects his people. He must have much wisdom between his ears. And he must remember to think before he acts. And so, instead of rushing to open the gates to Segu City, I will first confer with my counselors."

So it came to pass that the king held this conference and then addressed his warriors. "Your ears have heard the words of a great warrior who stands outside the city's walls," Da Monzon declared. "Whoever he is, the dust-covered figure upon the great dust-covered horse wants the best among you to follow him into the bush to a certain well. There it is possible that you will see the corpse of Little God. If that is the case, then you may retrieve his head. Or else it is possible that there you will lose your lives!

"Since we have no way of knowing whether the dust-covered figure is Segu's greatest warrior or whether it is Segu's greatest villain, those of you who volunteer will have to be as courageous as you are strong!" Da Monzon exclaimed. "The people of Segu and its king ask four of you to take that risk! Bakaridjan Kone's son, Simbalan, will accompany you."

And so it came to pass that, before the people of Segu would open the gates to their city, Bakaridjan had to lead Da Monzon's four warriors, as well as his son, Simbalan, back to the well in order to recover Bilissi's head and bring it to the capital. That is how certain the people of Segu were in their hearts that it was Bakaridjan Kone who had given up his life.

But once the people of Segu saw the head of Little God, they rejoiced, for the tyranny of the water-jinn had come to an end. And Bakaridjan Kone had proved to be the greatest of Segu's many heroes. So Da Monzon's djeli sang, and so it was.

But it came to pass that Bilissi's magical powers were so great that, as he gave up his life to Bakaridjan, the water-jinn inflicted a dreadful disease upon the victor. Shortly after his return to Segu City, Bakaridjan suddenly became dizzy and weak. And his right side became paralyzed. He could not stand. He could not sit. He could only lie upon his mat and wait for death to claim him.

Da Monzon heard the news, and his heart flooded with joy. "At last, someone has been able to conquer Segu's greatest hero!" he exclaimed to himself. "Now that most brilliant of stars will no longer shine! My sons will be able to shine with the brightness of the moon. And no star's light will be brighter than their own! What most delights me is that I did not have to lift a finger to do it!"

But it came to pass that the king's joy was short-lived. For Simbalan Kone came before Da Monzon and demanded that he find a way to cure his father.

"Great king of Segu, I come before you as the son of Bakaridjan Kone, Segu's greatest hero. And as a freeborn noble in my own right. All the people of Segu know that your heart holds no love for my father, despite all that he has done for you and your kingdom. They know that your heart now rejoices in his illness," Simbalan declared.

"Great Da Monzon, you are a wealthy and powerful king," he continued. "You own the walled city of Segu and the land that surrounds it. You own large flocks and herds. You own a treasure-house that is filled with gold and cowries. But you owe your great prosperity to my father!

"And now you must repay that debt by restoring my father's good health. You have access to those who best practice the mystical sciences, both those who know the Koran and those who are of our own people, the Bambara. Call upon their skills. And give them forty days in which to succeed.

"I have not yet taken the rite of manhood," he concluded. "But know this, great king. If my father has not recovered his former health by the time that forty days have come and gone, I will take your life! You are the king of Segu. But I am a freeborn Bambara. And I am king of myself."

Da Monzon heard Simbalan's words. And his heart flooded with terror. "The young Bakaridjan Kone has been reborn in his son!" he exclaimed. "May Simbalan Kone grow to be to my sons what his father has been to me! If not, they will surely have more cause to fear him than I have had to fear his father!"

And it came to pass that Da Monzon summoned eighty of the wisest practitioners of the mystical sciences, forty of whom were morikes who knew the Koran, and forty of whom were Bambara.

"The water-jinn, Bilissi, has cast his magic upon Bakaridjan Kone and has paralyzed him," the king explained. "Segu's greatest hero now can neither stand nor sit. He can only lie upon his mat and wait for death to claim him."

"Now Bakaridjan's son, Simbalan, has threatened to take my life if his father is not well by the end of forty days. And so, I declare to all of you," Da Monzon concluded, "that you have forty days in which to find a way to destroy Bilissi's magic and restore Bakaridjan Kone to health. If you succeed, each of you will receive a bag of gold. If you fail, you will give me your lives before I am forced to give up mine to Simbalan Kone!"

"Put fear from your heart, great king of Segu," the morikes replied. "With our knowledge of the Koran and with our kola nuts, we will cure Bakaridjan Kone!"

"Put fear from your heart, great king of Segu," the Bambara replied. "With our knowledge of herbs, we will cure Bakaridjan Kone!"

And it came to pass that the eighty men with their magic arts were able to restore Bakaridjan's health before forty days had come and gone with the sun. Now everything was just as it had been before the water-jinn's magic had felled Segu's greatest hero.

PART 2: THE PRICE OF HEROISM

Chapter 1

Bakaridjan must compete with two other heroes for Aminata's love.

It came to pass that Segu's three greatest heroes all fell in love with the same Fula woman. Bakaridjan Kone was one of these heroes. The other two were Madiniko and Bamana Diase. As for the woman, she was young, she was beautiful, and her name was Aminata.

Aminata enjoyed the companionship of all three men and refused to choose among them. But the people of Segu were intrigued by the competition. And so, Da Monzon asked his djeli to think of a way for one of the three heroes to prove that he was the greatest of the three.

The king's djeli decided that an appropriate test of their heroism would be for each of the three to be challenged to return to Segu City with Dosoke Zan's gun. Now Dosoke Zan was a famous hunter who lived near the capital city. And he had won every battle that he had ever fought. No hero dared to challenge him, for everyone believed that the source of his unusual strength was a gift from the chief of the jinns. And so, he was invincible.

So it came to pass that the king's djeli announced the contest to Aminata's three suitors at a time when they were visiting with her together, as was their custom. To each hero, the djeli explained, "The people of Segu and their king consider it beneath the stature of a hero for him to be afraid to ask for a woman's hand in marriage for fear that he will lose to one of her other suitors.

"Now the three of you are not sheep that you should blindly follow each other as you do!" the djeli exclaimed. "Where is your courage? Where is your sense of honor?

"And so, the time has come for each of you to prove yourself to Aminata, to the people of Segu, and to Da Monzon, our great king," the djeli concluded. "Whoever succeeds in returning to Segu with Dosoke Zan's gun will be Segu's greatest hero!"

"And because of that hero's courage, strength, and skill, I will choose him above the others for my husband!" Aminata declared.

So it came to pass that each of the three heroes assured the king's djeli that he would return to Segu City with Dosoke Zan's gun before fourteen days had come and gone with the sun. But, in his own mind, not one of the three was at all certain that his hands could do what his words had promised. And so, each hero consulted his favorite morike.

Now it came to pass that Bakaridjan Kone's morike declared, "Bakaridjan, you will never be able to take Dosoke Zan's life—or even conquer him—because the chief of the jinns protects Dosoke Zan from every type of weapon. Now I have no power over the chief of the jinns. But I think I can protect you from harm. Just take these three white kola nuts and give them as charity to a young light-skinned boy."

And it came to pass that Madiniko's morike declared, "Madiniko, you will never be able to take Dosoke Zan's life—or even conquer him—because the chief of the jinns protects Dosoke Zan from every type of weapon. Now I have no power over the chief of the jinns. But I think I can protect you from harm. Just take these three red kola nuts and give them as charity to a young dark-skinned boy."

But it came to pass that Bamana Diase's morike declared, "Bamana Diase, you may be the hero who is able to take Dosoke Zan's life if you choose! The chief of the jinns protects Dosoke Zan from every type of weapon. And I have no power over this chief. But I know that you possess powers that are greater than those of Dosoke Zan. Dosoke Zan will know only whatever the chief of the jinns tells him. But you will have the power to know whatever the chief of the jinns has told Dosoke Zan!

"Meanwhile, take some goat's meat, cook it, and give it as charity to a young black-skinned boy. Be sure that you see the youth eat the meat!" the morike concluded.

That is what the heroes learned from their morikes. What the heroes did not learn is that the jinns have the power to know everything that happens in the world of humans. And so it came to pass that their chief heard about the contest and about the preparations as well.

The chief of the jinns then appeared before Dosoke Zan. He told him about the contest. And then he commanded, "When the sun next makes the day light, you must arrive at the gate to Segu City. Before you enter, take this powder that I am now giving you and rub some of it all over your skin. The powder will transform you into a young light-skinned boy. Then you must walk by Bakaridjan Kone's house. When Bakaridjan sees you, he will give you three white kola nuts as charity.

"Once you have collected Bakaridjan's nuts, you must find a secret place. And you must rub more of this powder all over your skin. This time it will transform you into a young dark-skinned boy. Then you must walk by Madiniko's house. When Madiniko sees you, he will give you three red kola nuts as charity.

"Once you have collected Madiniko's nuts, you must find another secret place. And once again you must rub this powder all over your skin. This time it will transform you into a young black-skinned boy. Then you must walk by Bamana Diase's house. When Bamana sees you, he will give you a portion of cooked goat's meat as charity. You must eat Bamana's meat while he watches you. And then you must return home," he concluded.

So the chief of the jinns spoke. And to these words, Dosoke Zan replied, "My ears have heard your words. And so, my hands and feet will do as you advise."

So it came to pass that when the sun next made the day light, Dosoke Zan entered Segu City. Dosoke Zan appeared in disguise before each of the three heroes. And each hero recited the prayer for the giving of charity. And he followed the directions that his morike had given him.

When Dosoke Zan had returned home, the chief of the jinns once again appeared before him. And now he declared, "Dosoke Zan, your three adversaries were given magic protective powers by their morikes. But you followed my advice. And so, you now possess all of those powers.

"But you can do more to protect yourself in the coming series of conflicts. You must learn whether any of your three adversaries possesses the ability to conquer you. And so, when the sun next makes the day light, you must go into the bush with three eggs. You must find a termite hill, and you must lay the eggs beside it. Then you must return on the following day and examine the eggs. If the three eggshells have remained intact, you will know that you will be successful against your three adversaries. But if even one shell is damaged in any way, to encounter these three heroes will be to invite certain death!"

So the chief of the jinns spoke. And to these words, Dosoke Zan replied, "My ears have heard your words. And so, my hands and feet will do as you advise."

So it came to pass that when the sun next made the day light, Dosoke Zan went into the bush and deposited his three eggs. On the following day, he returned to the site and discovered that the shell of one of the eggs had cracked.

"Now this has become a question of honor!" Dosoke Zan thought to himself. "If the chief of the jinns is correct—and he knows everything—I am destined to give my life to one of Segu's three greatest heroes. But I do not know in whose hands my life rests. If I refuse to fight all three men, I will save my life, but everyone will call me a coward. Life without honor is worse than death! And so, I will meet each of Segu's great heroes in combat. I will depend upon my courage, strength, and skill. And what will be, will come!"

Chapter 2

Bakaridjan and the two other heroes come forth to fight Dosoke Zan, but with surprising results.

And so it came to pass that fourteen days came and went with the sun. Then Bakaridjan Kone, Madiniko, and Bamana Diase rode forth together to confront Dosoke Zan in battle. Together, they arrived at Dosoke Zan's house. And together, they waited nearby. As always, Bakaridjan was mounted upon his special horse—the great white one, with the silver bit and bridle.

Dosoke Zan spied them hiding at the edge of the bush. And so, he called out, "You three cannot be the greatest heroes of Segu of whom the king's djeli sings! Those heroes would come forth and challenge me to fight, if that is why they had come! Now come forth and state your purpose. Or return to Segu City and leave me in peace!"

The three heroes conferred. And Bakaridjan agreed to be the first to confront their adversary. As he rode toward Dosoke Zan's gate, he saw that the hunter had already mounted and armed himself. In his hand he held his spear. Strapped to his chest was his short, sheathed sword. And slung over his shoulder was his gun.

"Dosoke Zan!" Bakaridjan cried. "You have earned fame as a man of courage, strength, skill, and honor! Now, come forth and defend yourself, for it is my goal to conquer you and bring your gun to Da Monzon's djeli!"

"That may be your goal now, Bakaridjan Kone!" replied Dosoke Zan. "But before you take action, listen to what I am about to say, for you may choose to withdraw your challenge and return in safety to Segu City."

"Dosoke Zan, my ears will hear your words. And then my hands will do as my heart tells them," replied Bakaridjan. "But tell me, how do you know who I am?"

"I know you are Bakaridjan Kone, for I am the young light-skinned boy to whom you gave those three white kola nuts! They were your only source of magical protection. And now they are in my power. And so, fight me if you will. But know that, if you do, you will surely give up your life!"

So Dosoke Zan spoke. And for the first time in his life, Bakaridjan Kone's heart flooded with terror. "Now this has become a question of honor!" he thought to himself. "It appears that I am destined to give my life to Dosoke Zan—unless I refuse to fight him! If I turn my back on him, I will keep my life, but I will tarnish my honor. The people of Segu will call me a coward. They will forget all my heroic deeds! And they will taunt and ridicule me whenever I show my face!

"I have never turned my back on a fight. But I have never faced an adversary such as this! Even Bilissi, the water-jinn, was no Dosoke Zan! And so, my courage has fled with the wind! And without it, I cannot depend on my strength and skill.

"Certain death leaves me no choice but to retreat! I have always said that life without honor is worse than death! But I am not yet ready to give up my life! And who knows what will come to pass? What will be, will come!" he concluded.

So Bakaridjan thought. But aloud he said, "Dosoke Zan, I am not so foolish as to fight a battle that I am destined to lose! And so, I will return in peace to Segu City!" And with these words, he turned his horse—the great white one, with the silver bit and bridle—and returned to the capital.

Madiniko was the next hero to approach Dosoke Zan. "My ears have heard the words that you have spoken to Bakaridjan Kone," he declared. "Do you then know who I am? And why I am here?"

"That I do," responded Dosoke Zan. "I know you are Madiniko, for I am the young dark-skinned boy to whom you gave those three red kola nuts! They were your only source of magical protection. And now they are in my power. And so, fight me if you will. But know that, if you do, you will surely give up your life!"

So Dosoke Zan spoke. And so, Madiniko thought to himself, "No wonder Bakaridjan Kone is leaving without a fight! And many in Segu view him as our kingdom's greatest hero! If a greater man than I will not face certain death, who am I to rush to my fate? And I will not be the only coward! What will be, will come to pass! And whatever it is, I can live with it!"

So Madiniko thought. But aloud he said, "Dosoke Zan, like Bakaridjan Kone I am not so foolish as to fight a battle that I am destined to lose! And so, I too will return in peace to Segu City!" And with these words, Madiniko turned his horse and returned to the capital.

At last, it was Bamana Diase's turn to approach Dosoke Zan. "My ears have heard the words that you have spoken to Bakaridjan Kone and to Madiniko," he declared. "So you must know who I am. And why I am here!"

"That I do," responded Dosoke Zan. "I know you are Bamana Diase, for I am the young black-skinned boy to whom you gave the portion of goat's meat! It was your only source of magical protection. And now it is in my power. And so, fight me if you will. But know that, if you do, you will surely give up your life!"

So Dosoke Zan spoke. And to his words Bamana Diase replied, "Your words have missed their mark, Dosoke Zan! Today you are in my power! And so, if you choose to fight me, it is you—and not I—who will surely give up your life!"

"My ears hear your brave words, Bamana Diase," responded Dosoke Zan. "But tell me, how is it that you are not daunted by my magical power? Two heroes—and they are certainly as great as you are!—have decided that it is better to be a live coward than a dead hero! Do you not agree with them?"

"If I knew only what they know, Dosoke Zan, I might well agree with them. But today I do not have to choose to be a live coward, for I am not destined to become a dead hero!" replied Bamana Diase.

"And so, the question is not whether I agree with Bakaridjan Kone and Madiniko. Do you agree with them, Dosoke Zan? For I too possess hidden knowledge!" Bamana Diase declared. "And my own magical powers are greater than yours, for you know whatever the chief of the jinns told you. But I know it too! I know what he told you to do with the three eggs. And I know what he advised you to do if you found even one damaged eggshell.

"My spirit had the power to crack one of those eggs. And it has the power to take your life! So give me your gun. Or prepare to give me your life!" he concluded.

So Bamana Diase spoke. And to his words Dosoke Zan replied, "Bamana Diase, like you I am a freeborn Bambara and a great hero! And so, I will not earn the name of a coward because I fear a cracked eggshell! Your omens and mine may mean nothing! And only our combat may determine our fate! I have lived with courage and with honor. And I am prepared to die as I have lived! And so, I now give you one last chance to reconsider. You may still choose to return in peace to Segu City."

So Dosoke Zan spoke. And to his words Bamana Diase replied, "I believe in my own power, Dosoke Zan, even if you doubt your own! And so, you may shoot me three times. You will see that the power of your first two bullets will throw me from my horse, but they will not injure me. Your third bullet will never leave your gun! And then you will give up your life!"

So Bamana Diase spoke. And it came to pass that his words hit their mark, for the first two bullets from Dosoke Zan's gun knocked Bamana Diase from his horse, but they fell harmlessly from his chest like loose leaves from a windswept bush. Then Dosoke Zan's third bullet became locked in his gun.

Bamana Diase now rode forth. And, quick as the wind, he knocked Dosoke Zan to the ground. He dismounted and bound Dosoke Zan, who was too weak to resist, with a strong rope. And then he took both Dosoke Zan and his gun to Da Monzon's djeli in Segu City. So it came to pass that Bamana Diase became Segu's greatest hero. And the king's djeli created new songs in his honor.

As for Dosoke Zan, the king's djeli respected both his nobility and his past heroism. And so, he freed him and permitted him to return to his home. But Dosoke Zan's defeat indelibly tarnished his fame as a hero.

As for Bakaridjan, his fate proved to be worse than death. The sight of him provoked the children of Segu City to taunt him. And the mention of his name provoked mocking laughter among the people of the capital. So it came to pass that Bakaridjan Kone—the man who had long been Segu's greatest hero—took refuge within his own house. There he remained out of sight. And the people of Segu City found it easy to forget him.

As for Madiniko, he was no longer important enough to the people of Segu City to become the object of their scorn.

Chapter 3

Bakaridjan attempts to restore his reputation. However, his plans do not succeed.

It came to pass that Da Monzon's djeli had compassion for Bakaridjan. He remembered all that Bakaridjan had done for Segu, and he decided to do his part to restore the hero's self-confidence and to restore the hero's reputation in the kingdom.

First, the king's djeli appeared at Bakaridjan's house and sang songs of praise. Then, when he had finished, he asked the hero for the gift of a cow. Bakaridjan consented. But the king's djeli had much wisdom between his ears, and he did not accept the cow that the hero offered him.

"Why, Bakaridjan Kone, this cow is much too skinny to offer Da Monzon's djeli!" the djeli exclaimed. "You know that, as a Bambara noble, you are obligated to give the king's djeli the gift of his choice, and I want a cow from the city of Samaniana! They have the best cattle. And I will accept no less than the best from you!"

"Noble djeli, your wish will be the father of my deed," Bakaridjan replied. "I will go forth to Samaniana. And I will capture every cow in their herds! When I have returned to Segu City, anyone who wishes to possess a cow from Samaniana will be able to have one!"

The king's djeli smiled. And he replied, "That is just as it should be, Bakaridjan Kone!"

But it came to pass that a man of Segu overheard the conversation between Bakaridjan and Da Monzon's djeli, and he decided that he could profit from it. And so, quick as the wind, he left Segu City and went forth to the capital city of Samaniana, a journey of four days from Da Monzon's capital. There he entered King Bassi's compound and revealed Bakaridjan's plan. The king found the information to be worth a modest reward. And, quite pleased with himself, the man returned to Segu City.

Shortly thereafter, Bakaridjan went forth to the capital city of Samaniana. He rode his special horse—the great white one, with the silver bit and bridle. He was accompanied by his personal slave, by his son, Simbalan, and by twenty-nine Bambara warriors. However, when he arrived, he could find neither farmers, nor herders, nor one head of cattle in the fields that surrounded the city. It appeared that the city had been deserted, or Samaniana's famous cattle, as well as its people, were now locked inside the city's walls behind its barred gates. And so, Bakaridjan and his men camped outside the city while they pondered how to enter it.

It came to pass that a young hero of Samaniana saw Bakaridjan Kone and his small band of Bambara warriors sitting outside the city's barred gates. And so, he went to King Bassi and declared, "Great king of Samaniana, you are wealthy and powerful! You own the walled city of Samaniana and the land that surrounds it. You own large flocks and herds. You own a treasure-house that is filled with gold and cowries. You own crops and wine.

"And so, why are you hiding from Bakaridjan Kone? You know he camps outside our city's gates. For he rides that great white horse—the one with the silver bit and bridle! And so, why do you not send forth your army and confront him in battle? Do you wish to make him a greater hero than he already is? Surely he rejoices to see these signs of your fear. And the people of Segu will mock you when they hear of it!

"You are the master of Samaniana. But I am a freeborn young man. I am the master of my own life, and I am free to use my own weapons. And so, if you are not willing to act, I myself will go forth and challenge Bakaridjan Kone!" he concluded.

So the young hero spoke. And to his words King Bassi replied, "Young man, your words miss their mark! A good king protects his people. He must have much wisdom between his ears. And he must remember to think before he acts.

"Bakaridjan Kone is the chief of Segu's army," the king explained. "He conquers other peoples and brings them under Da Monzon's authority and power. Some djeli say that he has added more than twenty kingdoms to Segu's empire. Others say that he has added more than thirty. The king who has wisdom between his ears knows that to fight Bakaridjan Kone is to lose his authority and power. And most likely to lose one's life as well!

"As king of Samaniana, I cannot sacrifice the lives and the freedom of my people unless I have no choice! Within our walls, we have ample food and water for our people and for our herds. If we do not antagonize him, Bakaridjan Kone will find that he has nothing to gain by continuing to sit outside our gates. And he will return to Segu City in peace.

"And so, I have commanded that all of our people, as well as our herds, must take refuge inside the city's walls. Our gates will remain barred. And no one may enter or leave!"

"But, young man, if you have developed a dislike for the light of the sun— and if you are in such a hurry to take leave of your life—I will not stop you! Since you are not a slave, you are free to go forth to your death if you choose. And your fate will teach the people of Samaniana a good lesson!"

So King Bassi spoke. And so it came to pass that, despite the king's warnings, the young man went forth to his death.

Thereafter, no one else left the city. And it came to pass that forty days came and went with the sun. Meanwhile, the people and cattle of Samaniana remained locked inside the city's walls behind its barred gates. And Bakaridjan, his personal slave, Simbalan, and twenty-nine Bambara warriors waited outside.

At last, as King Bassi had anticipated, Bakaridjan saw no choice. He mounted his special horse—the great white one, with the silver bit and bridle— and he returned to Segu City.

This failure was so humiliating that he and his companions entered the capital long after the sun had gone to its home. And once Bakaridjan entered his house, he remained hidden within it.

Simbalan Kone was ready to go forth to make a heroic name for himself, but Bakaridjan convinced him that he needed his help at home. He gave Simbalan the task of guarding the entrance to their house throughout each night so that, even then, no one could reveal that Bakaridjan Kone had, in fact, returned to Segu City. The ruse was successful. For no one, including Da Monzon's djeli, knew that Bakaridjan had returned to the capital without Samaniana's cattle.

In time, it came to pass that Bakaridjan's personal slave came to his master and said, "Master, I have a suggestion. Permit me to travel to Samaniana and tell King Bassi that you have died. If I can convince him of this, then he will surely open the gates to his city and let his herds of cattle return to their old grazing grounds, and then you can capture the cattle as you choose."

"My friend, you are my personal slave because you have much wisdom between your ears!" Bakaridjan exclaimed. "While you do your part, I will be waiting for Samaniana's warriors to appear. And when they do, I will do battle with them. Then their cattle will be mine. And Da Monzon's djeli will once again sing songs about my heroic deeds! My name will no longer be a flame that the wind has blown out! Once again, it will blaze like a raging fire!"

And so it came to pass that Bakaridjan's personal slave quickly left Segu City and went forth to the capital city of Samaniana, a journey of four days from Da Monzon's capital. Because he was only a slave, he was permitted to enter the city. And he even gained entrance to King Bassi's compound.

The king of Samaniana was happy to engage the slave in conversation about Segu City and Da Monzon. And it came to pass that Bakaridjan's slave found the opportunity to ask King Bassi, "Why is it, great king, that the fields surrounding Samaniana are deserted? Why is it that Samaniana's people—and even the cattle for which you are famous—are locked inside the city's walls behind its barred gates? I feared that some affliction had descended upon Samaniana that had caused everyone either to flee or to die!"

"Slave, your words both hit and miss their mark. That could have been Samaniana's fate," King Bassi replied. "However, by protecting ourselves in this way from Bakaridjan Kone, we possess our lives and our freedom!"

"If I may be permitted to say so, great king of Samaniana, you may possess your lives and your freedom just as well if you open the gates to your city and let your farmers till their fields and your herders tend to their herds. For Bakaridjan Kone is dead!"

"Dead!" King Bassi exclaimed.

"Yes, he is dead!" Bakaridjan's slave repeated. "An army of Fula warriors from Massina staged a surprise raid against Segu and stole large herds of cows, goats, and sheep. Da Monzon commanded all who were skilled in the use of weapons to form an army and go forth to retrieve our animals and punish those who had stolen them. Bakaridjan Kone went forth with the rest, but he failed to return."

King Bassi found this information to be worth a modest reward. And Bakaridjan's personal slave returned to Segu City quite pleased with himself.

Chapter 4

Bakaridjan captures Samaniana's cattle.

And so it came to pass that, once again, Bakaridjan went forth to the capital city of Samaniana. Once again, he rode his special horse—the great white one, with the silver bit and bridle. Once again, he was accompanied by his personal slave, by his son, Simbalan, and by twenty-nine Bambara warriors. And once again, when he arrived, he could find neither farmers, nor herders, nor one head of cattle in the fields that surrounded the city.

It still appeared that either the city had been deserted, or that Samaniana's famous cattle, as well as its people, were now locked inside its walls behind its barred gates. And so, Bakaridjan and his men once again camped outside the city. But this time they chose a secluded place where those who watched from the walls of the city would not be able to see them.

Meanwhile, King Bassi thought about what the slave from Segu City had told him. "A good king protects his people," he reminded himself. "He must have much wisdom between his ears. And he must remember to think before he acts. Many a fire's coals that have appeared to be cold have suddenly sprung into flames when they have found something to burn."

So the king thought. It came to pass that enough time had passed without incident that King Bassi began to think that it was foolish to continue to keep his kingdom protected from a disaster that might never occur. And so, he commanded that the gates to the city should be opened, and he permitted a brave Fula slave, one of freeborn descent, to take Samaniana's cattle forth from the city.

The Fula slave had not gone far from the city when he encountered Bakaridjan. The hero was mounted on his special horse—the great white one, with the silver bit and bridle—and he was armed for battle. In his hand he held his spear. Across his chest he had strapped his short, sheathed sword. And over his shoulder he had slung his gun.

"Slave, how is it that you, alone, are in charge of Samaniana's famous cattle?" Bakaridjan asked. "How can you hope to defend them against one such as I, who would take them from you? Call forth the king's warriors so that they can defend their property!"

"Who are you, stranger, that your tongue feels free to belittle me?" the slave responded. "I am a Fula of freeborn ancestry! And I possess courage, strength, skill, and honor even if I am a slave! The king has made me responsible for these herds, and I intend to defend them with my gun and my life!"

"I am Bakaridjan Kone, from the kingdom of Segu, and I cannot permit you to defend these cattle, for I am a freeborn Bambara. And despite your honorable ancestry, you are but a slave! The people of Segu know that to combat a slave is beneath the dignity of a freeborn noble. They will say that I have stolen Samaniana's cattle unless I fight honorably for them. And so, slave, summon King Bassi's warriors!"

"Your tongue still belittles me, stranger!" the slave exclaimed. "Your great white horse looks like Bakaridjan Kone's famous steed—with its silver bit and bridle. But everyone in Samaniana knows that Bakaridjan Kone is dead!

"But even if you were Bakaridjan Kone, my answer would be the same," the slave declared. "I am a slave, yet I possess courage, strength, skill, and honor! The king has made me responsible for these herds, and I will defend them with my gun and my life! And so, if you want the cattle, you will have to fight me for them!"

"Then so it will be," Bakaridjan responded. "But because I am Bakaridjan Kone, I am an honorable nobleman! And so, I will give you the first three shots!"

So it came to pass that the slave fired his gun at Bakaridjan, but his bullets fell harmlessly from Bakaridjan's chest like loose leaves from a windswept bush. And so, the slave then rushed headlong toward Bakaridjan. And he beat him with his gun.

"I thank you for your gift, slave!" Bakaridjan exclaimed. "Surely you know that a slave may not strike one who is a noble. And so, I may now take your life and still keep my honor!"

And with these words, Bakaridjan drew forth his short sword from its sheath on his chest. But, quick as the wind, the sound of a gunshot cut the air above his shoulder, and the slave crumpled to the ground, giving up his life then and there.

Bakaridjan spun around in fury, and he found himself face to face with Simbalan. "You have tarnished my honor by taking the life of an unarmed slave! And for this, Simbalan, I would take the life of any other man! But you are my son! The contest was mine, not yours! And I would have beaten the slave with my sword as he had beaten me with his gun. That is the path of honor. And you are old enough to know it!

"My son, you are too intent on becoming a hero! Just as clouds rush to conceal the sun before a rainstorm, your ambition rushes to conceal your judgment. A man who lacks judgment will never be a man of honor. And a man who puts aside his code of honor will never be a hero," Bakaridjan declared.

"Thank you, Father," Simbalan replied. "My ears have heard your words, and they have hit their mark!" Simbalan replied.

It came to pass that the sound of the gunshot aroused King Bassi's warriors. And so, they galloped forth from the city to protect Samaniana's cattle. However, as they approached the body of the dead slave, their chief recognized Bakaridjan Kone by his great white horse—the one with the silver bit and bridle. And, quick as the wind, the hero of Segu was charging toward them with his armed Bambara warriors.

"Retreat! Retreat! Before all is lost!" the Samaniana chief cried, quickly turning his horse back toward the walls of his city. "He has returned from the dead! Bakaridjan Kone himself rides against us! Flee with your lives! To Samaniana!"

The Samaniana warriors turned and galloped in panic toward the protection of their city's walls. Bakaridjan and his warriors galloped after them, taking the lives of so many of Samiana's warriors that the rest surrendered.

And so it came to pass that Bakaridjan returned to Segu City with the cattle of Samaniana, as well as a herd of horses and a band of new slaves. Once again, he received a hero's welcome from the people and a hero's acclaim from the king's djeli.

When the sun next made the day light, Bakaridjan summoned Da Monzon's djeli and announced, "Noble Djeli, you will remember that, in return for a song of praise, I gave you the gift of a cow. But you replied, 'Why, Bakaridjan Kone, this cow is much too skinny to offer the king's djeli! You know that as a Bambara noble, you are obligated to give a djeli the gift of his choice, and I want a cow from the city of Samaniana! They have the best cattle. And I will accept no less than the best from you!'

"And, Noble Djeli, you will also remember that to your words I replied, 'Your wish is the father of my deed! I will go forth to Samaniana, and I will capture every cow in their herds! And when I have returned to Segu City, anyone who wishes to possess a cow from Samaniana will be able to have one!'

"The task was no easy one," Bakaridjan explained. "It took many days of planning and patience, as well as courage, strength, and skill. King Bassi of Samaniana lived in fear of Bakaridjan Kone. And so, when I arrived, I could find neither farmers, nor herders, nor one head of cattle in the fields that surrounded the city. It appeared that the city had been deserted, or that Samaniana's famous cattle, as well as its people, were locked inside its walls behind its barred gates.

"At last I managed to lead the king to believe that it was safe to open the gates to his city and let his cattle return to their customary pastures. It was only then that I could do battle with the king's warriors. And with my band of Bambara warriors, I cut them from their horses as a sickle cuts grass from its roots!

"And so, you must choose your Samaniana cow before I let the people of Segu have their pick. As for me, I will keep only the Samaniana slaves whom I captured."

So Bakaridjan spoke. And so it came to pass that the king's djeli received the gift of his choice from Bakaridjan Kone. And, in return, he sang new songs of praise about the man who once again was Segu's greatest hero.

Chapter 5

Da Monzon attempts to murder Bakaridjan.

Years came and went like the sun and the moon. And it came to pass that Bakaridjan Kone continued to be a true hero! As always, he was pure of heart, pure of mind, and pure of soul.

Bakaridjan continued to earn boundless praise, yet he continued to respect all who attempted to lead good lives, whether young or old, rich or poor, strong or weak. He had become a man of great wealth, yet he continued to share it with everyone. From his hands, his friends received gold, the poor received cowries, and slaves received land and cattle.

Bakaridjan continued to be strong, yet he still would take the time to help those who were weak. He still would carry a bundle of wood for one who was lame. And he still would give food to a grandmother who had no children to care for her.

Bakaridjan continued to be the greatest of warriors, yet he still would not fight a man whose status was less than his own. And he still would not fight any warrior who was afraid of him. As always, he would fight to win, yet he still would show compassion for those whom he had defeated in battle.

Bakaridjan Kone was the shield of Segu! He was the right arm of Da Monzon, Segu's king! As always, his code of honor was his life. And he owed his life to his code of honor! And as always, he had no wish to rule a kingdom, either Segu or any other, for he already possessed all that he wanted.

Da Monzon, as always, rewarded Bakaridjan for his deeds. Yet the king's heart still remained flooded with fear. "I may be the moon of my people," he would say to himself. "But how will I shine once the light of Segu's brightest star casts its shadow over my own light?"

And so it came to pass that Da Monzon watched and waited for any opportunity to prove that Bakaridjan Kone was a real threat to him. He alerted his counselors and his servants to mark the words of Bakaridjan's tongue and the actions of Bakaridjan's hands and to be quick to report the least indiscretion.

And, in time, it came to pass that Bakaridjan was feasting with Segu's other heroes when they had a boasting contest. Bakaridjan listened to his companions in silence, but at last he decided to boast as well.

"I am so strong," he declared, "that if I were to stamp one foot, so much earth would give way that the entire kingdom of Segu would be swallowed up! But the people would have nothing to fear, for I could pull out all of Segu with one finger! But if I were to fall into that hole, all the people of Segu, working together, could not pull me out!"

Now it came to pass that Bakaridjan's words flew into Da Monzon's ears. And so the king called for his counselors. And he announced, "At last, I have Bakaridjan Kone just where I want him! He has stamped his foot and fallen into his own great hole! And all the people of Segu, working together, will not be able to pull him out!"

"No one—not even Bakaridjan Kone—is stronger than the great king of Segu! And so I, Da Monzon, accuse Bakaridjan Kone of speaking words of treason. And I hereby condemn him to death!

"But my condemnation must remain a royal secret between your king and yourselves," Da Monzon declared. "For Segu's greatest hero is too popular with the people, and I will not suffer a public outcry to save him. He is also too strong to condemn without risk to my own life. And so Bakaridjan Kone will give his life to my armed guards. But they will take his life in an ambush.

"I will invite him to a feast in my private room," Da Monzon explained. "And as you know, in order to enter this room, Bakaridjan will have to pass through six adjoining public rooms. Once he has reached my private room, I will have my guards conceal themselves in each of these six rooms. Every guard will be prepared to shoot Bakaridjan as soon as he reappears. And even a hero as strong as Bakaridjan Kone cannot survive six consecutive ambushes!

"Now my plan must remain a secret between you and your king. And so before I dismiss you, I must warn you that, if Bakaridjan becomes aware of this plot, all of you will be personally responsible. I will accuse you of treason. And my guards will take your lives!"

So Da Monzon spoke. And so it came to pass that he invited Bakaridjan to a private feast in his private room. He established a casual dress code. And so no one carried a weapon.

It also came to pass that Da Monzon's words remained locked in the ears of his counselors, and their tongues never slipped a word of what they had heard to anyone. But Da Monzon himself was not as careful. He was so proud of his plan that he could not resist confiding it to his favorite wife. And she could not resist confiding it to her personal slave.

Now, the years had come and gone like the sun and the moon. And it had come to pass that Simbalan Kone had become his father's son in courage, strength, skill, and honor. And so no one who knew Simbalan would have been surprised to learn that he had always treated the personal slave of Da Monzon's favorite wife with respect, kindness, and generosity. So it came to pass that this old woman now took the opportunity to repay Simbalan by telling him about Da Monzon's plan to ambush his father.

Now as these years had come and gone, Simbalan Kone had also become a man who had much wisdom between his ears. And so he decided that he would not tell his father what his ears had heard from the old slave woman. He decided that he would handle the matter himself.

In time, it came to pass that the dinner in Da Monzon's private room took place. Bakaridjan passed through the six adjoining public rooms that led to the king's private room. Then forty of the king's armed guards entered each of the six rooms. And each guard secreted himself in preparation for Bakaridjan's later departure.

The king feasted Segu's greatest hero well. And he plied him with drink. Then he withdrew his gun from a hidden place and pointed it at his guest. "Bakaridjan Kone, it has come to my ears that you declared, 'I am so strong that if I were to stamp one foot, so much earth would give way that the entire kingdom of Segu would be swallowed up! But the people would have nothing to fear, for I could pull out all of Segu with one finger! But if I were to fall into that hole, all the people of Segu, working together, could not pull me out!'

"Now, if you spoke these words, then you are a man who does not appreciate what his king has done for him! For I took you into my house and reared you as my son. I gave you my own special horse—the great white one, with the silver bit and bridle. I made you chief of my army and enabled you to win victory in battle. I have rewarded you with gold, land, and cattle. And my djeli has transformed your victories into songs of praise.

"Now, if you spoke these words, then you are a man who does not know his place, for surely you know that these are words of treason! And so I will give you a choice. You can admit that these are your words, or you can disown them. Now if you live with a code of honor, you will choose to admit that the words are yours. You will repeat them to me. And I will take your life from you, here and now, with this gun."

So Da Monzon spoke. And Bakaridjan's ears heard his king's words, but not knowing what to say, his tongue could only remain silent.

"I see that you cannot admit that the words are yours!" Da Monzon exclaimed. "And so let my ears hear you say, 'I, Bakaridjan Kone, disown the words of my tongue. And so I surrender my noble heritage. And since I no longer live with a code of honor, I am no longer a hero of Segu. And so let my name and my exploits be stricken from the mouth of the king's djeli.'"

So Da Monzon spoke. And Bakaridjan's ears heard his king's words, but not knowing what to say, once again his tongue could only remain silent.

At this moment, Simbalan Kone suddenly appeared in the king's private room. The old slave woman had done more than inform him of Da Monzon's plan. She had revealed to him the secret entrance to the king's private room.

Pointing his own gun at Da Monzon, who was still pointing his gun at Bakaridjan, Simbalan commanded, "Put down your gun, Da Monzon before I shoot the hand that holds it! Your behavior shames a great king!

"All the people of Segu know—as they have always known, Da Monzon—that your heart holds no love for my father," Simbalan declared. "But this has been true since he was a child. And in all the years that have come and gone, my father has never given you cause to fear him!

"When terror floods the heart, reason flees the head!" Simbalan continued. "A good king must have much wisdom between his ears! He must always remember that, above all, he protects his people! And before he acts, he must think of his people, not of himself!

"What did you do, Da Monzon, when the water-jinn terrorized Segu City?" Simbalan asked. "Because of Bakaridjan Kone, you—not Bilissi—are ruling here! Without Bakaridjan Kone, you might still be king of Segu, for Segu has other heroes to defend it against attack. But because of Bakaridjan Kone, you now rule an empire! In return for your protection, you now receive tribute from the kings of many other cities and lands! In fact, because of Bakaridjan Kone, you now own a treasure-house that is filled to the roof with all of your gold and cowries!

"So repeat the words of your boast, Father!" Simbalan commanded. "You are Segu's greatest hero! That is the way it is. And that is the way it will always be! And Da Monzon has no right to claim that it is treason for you say so!"

Bakaridjan heard Simbalan's words. And he exclaimed, "Thank you for defending me to the king, my son. A father who has such a son is most fortunate!

"But it was not necessary, Simbalan. My code of honor is my life. And that code does not permit words or deeds of treachery or treason! Apparently, my king still has not learned this about me. And so where I am concerned, I think that his heart will always be flooded with fear and not love.

"For me, life without honor is worse than death! And so I will risk death—if that is to be my fate!—in order to repeat the words of my boast so that Da Monzon's own ears will hear them from my own tongue. I am so strong that if I were to stamp one foot, so much earth would give way that the entire kingdom of Segu would be swallowed up! But the people would have nothing to fear, for I could pull out all of Segu with one finger! But if I were to fall into that hole, all the people of Segu, working together, could not pull me out!"

So Bakaridjan spoke. And to his words Da Monzon replied, "Well then, it is settled. It is good to know that Bakaridjan Kone is a man who will face death rather than dishonor his name. And because you could not know the reason for this test of your father's honor, Simbalan Kone, my ears will forget the disrespect that your own tongue has shown me.

"So put away your gun, Simbalan." Da Monzon commanded. "And I will put away mine. Whatever use we might have had for them has passed. And the time for sleep has come.

"And one more thing, Simbalan!" Da Monzon exclaimed. "You entered my private room through my private entrance. And so please leave with your father in the customary way! Go through the six adjoining public rooms to the public entrance, and there you will find the gate to the main street."

To these words, Simbalan replied, "I will put away my gun, great king, as soon as my father and I are safely out of your compound. And now I ask you to lead us through the rooms that you wish us to use and to see us safely to the gate as any loyal host and friend does, out of common courtesy!"

"It will be my pleasure!" Da Monzon replied, his mouth smiling with a good humor that his eyes did not reflect.

So it came to pass that Bakaridjan and Simbalan Kone safely made their way back through the six adjoining public rooms that led to Da Monzon's private room. As the king entered each room, he exclaimed, "Guards, at ease! The attack that your king expected has not come. And so let the king of Segu and his guests pass through in peace."

And so it came to pass that Bakaridjan and Simbalan Kone safely made their way through the gate that led from the king's compound into the main street of Segu City.

Epilogue

Bakaridjan Kone lived to perform many other heroic deeds for Da Monzon, his king. Years came and went like the sun and the moon. And Bakaridjan Kone continued to be a true hero! As always, he was pure of heart, pure of mind, and pure of soul.

Bakaridjan continued to earn boundless praise, yet he continued to respect all who attempted to lead good lives, whether young or old, rich or poor, strong or weak. He had become a man of great wealth, yet he continued to share it with everyone. From his hands, his friends received gold, the poor received cowries, and slaves received land and cattle.

Bakaridjan continued to be strong, yet he still would take the time to help those who were weak. He still would carry a bundle of wood for one who was lame. And he still would give food to a grandmother who had no children to care for her.

Bakaridjan continued to be the greatest of warriors, yet he still would not fight a man whose status was less than his own. And he still would not fight any warrior who was afraid of him. As always, he would fight to win, yet he still would show compassion for those whom he had defeated in battle.

Bakaridjan Kone was the shield of Segu! He was the right arm of Da Monzon, Segu's king! As always, his code of honor was his life. And he owed his life to his code of honor! And as always, he had no wish to rule a kingdom, either Segu or any other, for he already possessed all that he wanted.

Da Monzon, as always, rewarded Bakaridjan for his deeds. Yet the king's heart still remained flooded with fear. "I may be the moon of my people," he would say to himself. "But how will I shine once the light of Segu's brightest star casts its shadow over my own light?

"Long ago, my own ears heard my morike say, 'Bakaridjan Kone does not have designs upon your kingdom! He will honor the authority of any of your sons just as he respects your own authority as king of Segu. As long as he can be the shield of Segu and perform deeds that your djeli will transform into song, peace and contentment will flood his heart.'

"Long ago, my own ears heard my morike say that I would not be able to harm Bakaridjan Kone because of his great virtue. Time has proved that these words hit their mark.

"Now it is too late for me to try to plot against Bakaridjan Kone, for a second bright star rises over Segu—Bakaridjan's son, Simbalan Kone. To harm one hair on the father's head will be to meet certain death at the hands of the son!

"I must remember that when terror floods the heart, reason flees the head! I must remember that a good king must have much wisdom between his ears! My head knows that it would be far wiser for me to please Simbalan so that he may become to my sons what his father is to me. The question is, will my heart permit me to do this?" Da Monzon asked himself.

The tale of Bakaridjan Kone and his king, Da Monzon of Segu, ends with this question.

❧ QUESTIONS FOR
Response, Discussion, and Analysis

1. The heroes in myth and legend often have an unusual birth and child-hood. In addition, they must often pass tests that mark them as heroes. How are Bakaridjan's birth and childhood unusual? What tests does Bakaridjan pass? What do these factors contribute to his heroic stature?

2. Heroes in myth and legend perform tasks that benefit their society. What tasks does Bakaridjan perform? How does each benefit his society?

3. What does the rivalry among the three heroes contribute to the epic? What does it reveal about Bambara society at this time? Consider the public's attitude toward women, toward its heroes, and toward magic. What does it reveal about Bakaridjan?

4. What types of magic exist in this epic? What does each contribute?

5. What does the djeli's request of Bakaridjan reveal about the hero in Bambara society at this time?

6. What does the characterization of Da Monzon contribute to the epic? How do you think his question at the end of the epic will be answered?

7. Based upon the two kings in the epic, describe the ideal king. How close do Da Monzon and Bassi come to this ideal?

8. What does the characterization of Simbalan Kone contribute to the epic? How would you describe the relationship between Simbalan and

his father? Give examples to support your point of view. Why does Simbalan decide to keep his knowledge of Da Monzon's plot a secret from his father?

9. What does the epic reveal about the role of women in Bambara society at this time? Consider Aminata, Da Monzon's wife, and her favorite slave.

10. Based upon the role of slaves in this epic, evaluate the position of slaves among the aristocratic Bambara in Segu at the time of this story. Consider who they are, how they are regarded, and what they contribute to their society.

11. What personality traits characterize Bakaridjan? Support each with an example from the epic.

12. Bakaridjan is both the master and the victim of his fame. How does he become its master? How does he become its victim? In what ways does Bakaridjan act like a hero? In what ways is his behavior unheroic? Why?

13. Who is your favorite hero in the epic? Consider Bakaridjan, Simbalan, and Dosoke Zan, and give reasons to support your point of view.

The Americas

The New World has always been populated by many different cultural groups.

The Native American peoples represented in this book include those who were living in Central and South America when the Spanish invaded and conquered them in the 1500s, those who were living in North America when the French and the English invaded and conquered them from the 1500s to the 1800s, and those who remain living cultures today.

The American creation myths fall into two patterns: some describe the creation of the universe and human beings, and others describe the origin of the particular peoples to whom the myths belong. Like the creation myths of many other cultures, those of the Maya, the Aztecs, and the Aymara/Tiahuanaco, who preceded the Incas, describe the creation of the world. In unusually poetic language, the Mayan myth describes the great efforts of their creators to fashion a race of human beings who please them. It is interesting to follow the process and see what kind of people these gods desire and why.

The first part of the Aztec creation myth describes a series of worlds, inviting comparison with the Greek and Indian ages of man. It emphasizes the idea of blood sacrifice, a practice that permeated the Aztec culture. The final section of the myth is remarkable because it reveals the Aztecs' great love of the arts. A beautiful poem, rendered in prose in this chapter, describes the creation of music.

The creation myth of the ancient Tiahuanaco culture (the ancestors of the Aymaras in the Bolivian highlands) presents a god who is both creator and benefactor. An interesting description of the creation of human beings is followed by a journey in which Viracocha and his companions teach people how to lead civilized lives, with an emphasis on the humane treatment of other human beings.

In contrast, the creation myths of the Navajo and the Iroquois focus on the origin of their particular peoples. The Navajo myth describes how their people moved upward through four worlds into our fifth world, developing from insects into human beings in the course of this journey. Two aspects of the Navajo myth give it a distinctive flavor: the use of the sacred number four and the close relationship depicted between human beings and the animal kingdom.

The Iroquois creation myth envisions the earth as having been created by a female divinity. Good and evil are divided between twin brothers, who represent two sides of one personality. Unlike the myth of Quetzalcoatl, in the Iroquois myth the good brother destroys his evil brother. The Inuit myth explains the creation of sea animals in a manner that reflects the harsh environment in which the Inuit peoples have always lived.

The fertility myths from the Americas fall into three patterns: those in which a god or a supernatural figure teaches the people how to raise crops and thus achieve a higher standard of living; those in which a god or a godlike hero protects the fertility of the earth from some threat; and those in which an angered and vengeful god must be appeased in order for fertility to be restored. The Inca myth follows the first pattern. It also reveals the arrogance and prejudice of a conqueror toward the conquered peoples, whom the Incas describe as living like wild animals.

The Haida/Tsimshian/Tlingit myth follows the second pattern in that it tells the story of a god (Raven) who protects the earth. In the process it reveals much about the culture of its people. In contrast, the Micmac myth reveals the need of this Algonquian people for control over the natural environment. Finally, the Inuit myth follows the third pattern in that it focuses on a god (Sedna) whose anger must be placated by mortals.

The Yekuhana myth, from Venezuela, is both a creation and a fertility myth since Wanadi is both the creator and the culture-hero of his people. It describes the creation of the universe and human beings, including the origin of the Yekuhana people. Like the Ainu epic from Japan and the Micmac myth, it has an ancient, pristine quality that gives it a primeval power. Like the Ainu epic, it describes a world in which reality may not be what it appears to be. Like the Micmac myth, it depicts the magical world of the shaman, who protects and enriches the lives of his people.

The four hero myths resemble the traditional heroic pattern in that a hero performs a great task or tasks for the benefit of society. The Haida/Tsimshian/Tlingit and the Micmac myths are both hero and fertility myths because of the double focus of their subject. The Crow myth involves twins who perform a number of heroic feats, while always behaving like the children they are.

The Aztec myth "Quetzalcoatl" is one of the most fascinating of all hero stories, and it is truly remarkable given when it was written. In the Aztec creation myth, Quetzalcoatl and Tezcatlipoca are depicted as divine creators and benefactors, but here Quetzalcoatl is a traditional hero, a godlike mortal, and Tezcatlipoca is his enemy. With a focus that is completely modern, the myth describes how Quetzalcoatl is conquered by his alter ego or double.

The Creation

HISTORICAL BACKGROUND

The following creation myth comes from the Tiahuanaco culture, an important highland civilization that flourished in the region of Lake Titicaca before the Incas invaded. Since the 1960s, archaeologists have been investigating sites in the area of the famous ruins of Tiahuanaco. Monumental stone figures, located near the southern shore of Lake Titicaca in the Andean highlands of Bolivia, were built in approximately A.D. 500, and testify to the importance of the Tiahuanaco culture.

Archaeologists have discovered that the city Tiahuanaco began as a rural village in about 1000 B.C. and that it was occupied for over two thousand years, becoming important enough to influence the culture of the Andean peoples from about A.D. 500 to 1200. By 1200, Tiahuanaco had become the capital of the great Tiahuanaco empire, which may have included much of Chile and Peru, as well as the Andean highlands of Bolivia and Argentina. The reason for the empire's collapse remains a mystery, but the area it encompassed did not become unified again until the Incas conquered it sometime during the late fourteenth and early fifteenth centuries.

Scholars are mystified by the fact that the Spaniards could learn nothing about the culture from the Aymaras who were living in the area. The local population had no idea who the people were that had constructed the huge structures. One theory is that the Incas shifted populations from one area to another, so tribes could have been living in areas that were relatively new to them. Another theory is that the residents of the area, the Aymaras of that time, refused to communicate with the Spaniards about their ancestors.

Lake Titicaca, which extends from Peru to Bolivia, plays a major role in the mythology of both the Inca of Peru and the Aymara of Bolivia. When the Incas extended their rule to the Bolivian shores of Lake Titicaca, they adopted and transformed the myths of the native Aymara people and the Tiahuanaco culture to reflect their own nationalistic point of view. The Incas' political values also led them to establish their Quechua language as the official language of their empire, even though Aymara was the most widespread native language at that time. Although the Inca emperors demanded that the Aymara people accept their authority and their religion, they did not require the Aymaras to give up their own, older religion. Thus, the two religions coexisted.

Today, more than five million people continue to speak the Quechua language. However, the Aymara language also is a living language. Many of the Aymara people continue to live in the Andean highlands of Bolivia, where most of them are still involved in herding and agriculture.

APPEAL AND VALUE

Inca mythology and sun worship are directly related to the religion of the Tiahuanaco culture, since the Incas built their myths upon those of older civilizations. For example, the Incas adopted Con Ticci Viracocha (creator emerging with thunder) as their own creator-god.

The creator who is also a benefactor of the human race is common in American cultures, such as the Aztec and the Haida/Tsimshian/Tlingit. Other cultures also have a divine creator who teaches moral values and punishes those who ignore them. Like many other creators, Viracocha uses a flood to destroy a race of human beings who have acted immorally.

The role played by stone in this creation myth reflects the abundance of rock and the presence of ancient, rock-shaped figures in the area. The religious practice of worshiping natural phenomena is reflected in the birth of human beings from caves, rivers, mountains, and rocks.

The following myth was recorded in the early 1550s by Juan de Betanzos, the official interpreter for the Spanish governor of Peru. He took it from a Peruvian narrative song. Such songs were a customary way for Inca historians to preserve their nation's history.

THE CREATION

In the beginning, Lord Con Ticci Viracocha, prince and creator of all things, emerged from the void and created the earth and the heavens. Next he created animals and a race of gigantic human beings who lived upon the earth in the darkness of an eternal night, for he had not yet created any form of light. When the behavior of this race angered Viracocha, he emerged again, this time from Lake Titicaca, and he punished these first human beings by turning them into stone. Then he created a great flood. Soon even the peaks of the highest mountains were under water.

When Viracocha was satisfied that the flood had destroyed all forms of life, he caused the flood waters to subside until the face of the earth was revealed once again. So great was his creative power that he then created day by causing the sun to emerge from the island of Titicaca and rise into the heavens. In the same way, he created the moon and the stars, setting each brilliant light upon its proper path. With a wave of his hand and a command from his mouth, some hills and mountains sank to become valleys, while some valleys rose to become hills and mountains. With another wave and command, streams and rivers of fresh water sprang from the rocky cliffs, cascaded down the mountainsides, and flowed through the valleys.

Viracocha then turned his attention to creating new animals and a new race of human beings. First he created birds to fly in the air and fill the silence with song. He gave each type of bird a different melody to sing, sending some to live deep in the forested valleys and others to live in the high plains and mountains. Then he created the animals that walk the earth on four legs and the creatures that crawl on their stomachs. These too he divided between the lowlands and the highlands.

Once he had created all the animals, Viracocha was ready to create human beings. He decided to model them in stone, so he fashioned and painted stone men, stone women, and stone children.

He created some of the women in the condition of pregnancy. He created others in the process of caring for their young children, who were in cradles just as they would be once he brought them to life. He painted long hair on some figures and short hair on others. On each figure he painted the kind of clothing that that person would continue to wear. In this way Viracocha gave each human being the appearance that he or she would have in life. Then he fashioned a stone community in Tiahuanaco as a home for some of these stone people.

Finally Viracocha divided his stone figures into groups. He gave each group the food it would grow, the language it would speak, and the songs it would sing. Then he commanded all of the stone figures to sink beneath the earth and remain there until he or one of his helpers summoned them.

Viracocha explained their duties to the companions who had emerged with him from Lake Titicaca. "I want some of you to walk to the north, some to the south, and the rest toward the early morning sun. Divide among you the regions that I intend to populate with human beings. When you arrive in your region, go to the fountains, or the caves, or the rivers, or the high mountain plateaus. Summon from these places the groups of stone figures that I have assigned to your region."

So it came to pass that each of Viracocha's companions became a helper in the process of creation, and the land was populated with many groups of people. As each "viracocha" called forth his group of stone figures, Viracocha shouted, "Con Ticci Viracocha, who created the universe, commands his human beings to emerge from the stone figures he has created and occupy this empty land! Live in your area, and increase in number."

Viracocha himself walked the Royal Road across the Andes Mountains toward what would become the city of Cuzco. As he traveled, he called forth group after group of human beings and taught each group how to live on the land. He told them the name of each tree, each plant, each fruit, and each flower. He showed them which were good sources of food, which could heal sickness and injuries, and which would bring certain death. He also taught the people to treat one another with kindness and respect so they could live with one another in peace. Meanwhile, Viracocha's helpers were teaching the same knowledge to the groups of human beings who had emerged in their regions.

Viracocha continued this process until one group of people emerged armed with rocks. They did not recognize Viracocha, and they attacked him. Viracocha punished them by causing fire to fall from the heavens. The people immediately threw their stones to the ground and fell at Viracocha's feet in surrender. Viracocha extinguished the flames with three blows from his staff and explained that he was their creator.

These people constructed a great stone figure of Viracocha. They established a place of worship where Viracocha had brought down the fire and set the statue within it. Their descendants continue to present offerings of gold and silver in that sacred place.

Finally Viracocha reached the site of Cuzco, which he named. He created a ruler for the area and then returned to the seacoast. His companions rejoined him, and they set forth over the ocean toward the setting sun. Those who saw them last watched in fascination as Viracocha and his companions walked upon the waves as if the sea were solid land. The people called their creator Viracocha, which means "foam of the sea," in honor of this event.

Viracocha and his companions were never seen again.

❧ QUESTIONS FOR
Response, Discussion, and Analysis

1. Why does Viracocha cause his stone people to sink beneath the earth before they reappear? What difference does it make?

2. Why does Viracocha disappear the way he does? Is this better than vanishing into the air? Defend your opinion.

The Children of the Sun

Civilized peoples had lived in Peru for almost 4,000 years when, in the thirteenth century A.D., the Incas settled in the Cuzco Valley, high in the Andes Mountains. In the beginning, the Incas were simply one small group living among many others. Nothing distinguished them from their neighbors. Manco Capac became their first ruler, and at first other peoples willingly came under Inca rule.

By the early 1400s, the Incas had become more aggressive and had established themselves as conquerors. They had pushed outward from the Cuzco Valley and now dominated all of the land west to the coast of Peru, north to Quito, Ecuador, and southeast to Lake Titicaca.

By 1438, the Incas had created a great empire, which extended south from southern Colombia through Ecuador and Peru into southern Chile, and west across the highlands of Bolivia into the northwestern part of Argentina. The Inca emperor Pachacuti, who reigned from 1438 to 1471, transformed Viracocha from the god of the Aymara people to one of the great gods of the Inca. After Pachacuti dreamed that Viracocha helped him win a major military victory, the emperor had a solid gold statue of Viracocha created that was as large as a ten-year-old child. He then placed the golden image of the god in a great temple that he had had constructed and dedicated to Viracocha in Cuzco.

The Inca empire, the largest empire in the New World until the Spanish arrived, contained six million people. The empire thrived for the next 100 years, but fell to the Spaniard Francisco Pizarro and his conquistadores in 1532. Today, Quechua—the language of the Inca—remains the language of approximately five million people. Called the Quechua, these people live in Peru, Ecuador, and the highland regions of the Andes in Bolivia, Argentina, and Chile.

In many ways the Incas resembled the Romans. They conquered many civilized peoples and ruled them successfully by tolerating their cultural ways. As long as their subjects paid their taxes and worshipped the Inca gods, particularly the sun, they could live and worship in whatever other ways they chose. The Incas were skilled administrators, builders, and technicians. Their system of roads was one of the best in the world. They successfully farmed the mountainous regions of their empire by creating an elaborate system of terraces and a network of irrigation canals. Large surpluses of food supported the nonagricultural members of their society, including the nobles, priests, warriors, craftspeople, and artists.

Since they had no written language, the Incas were completely dependent on their oral tradition to record their past and preserve their fame for the future. A group of professional historians and performers was responsible for preserving and reciting Incan "history," a blend of fact, myth, legend, and self-serving propaganda. All of the Inca myths are part of this "history" and exhibit a double bias, both Incan and Christian. The Incas first adapted the myths of other peoples in order to glorify their own accomplishments.

When the Spaniards, under Francisco Pizarro, conquered the

Incas, they learned the Inca language and began to convert the Incas to Christianity. They sent reports back to Spain describing in great detail the characteristics of the people they had conquered, including their pagan beliefs. These reports reflected the Spaniards' own Christian attitudes, values, and beliefs.

The few writers who were Inca were new converts to Christianity. Their writings also reveal the influence of Christian doctrine, for it was all too easy in an oral tradition for new ideas to blend with the older ones.

The following myth was recorded by Inca Garcilaso de la Vega (1539–1616?) in Volume 1 of his masterpiece, *The Royal Commentaries of the Inca,* published in Spain in 1609. The author was born in Cuzco, Peru, the son of a Spanish conquistador and an Inca princess. Because he was illegitimate, he was given the name of Gomez Suarez de Figueroa instead of receiving his father's name. Garcilaso converted to Catholicism, and, in 1558, after his father's death, he moved to Spain in order to complete his education and attempt (unsuccessfully) to gain title to his father's estate. He took his lengthy notes on the Inca peoples along with him.

In 1590, Garcilaso was living in Cordoba under his father's name, to which he had added *Inca* in honor of his mother's people. His first book was published in that year. His third and last book, the second volume of his masterpiece, was published in 1617, close to the time of his death.

Garcilaso has long been regarded as one of the finest writers of Spain's Golden Age. Today, he is also valued as the first great South American author and the father of Spanish-American literature.

APPEAL AND VALUE

"The Children of the Sun" involves a supernatural being who leads humans to a more civilized life. It illustrates how the Incas took this common mythical theme and shaped it to suit their own purposes.

The Incas' goal was to glorify their heritage and their people. Therefore, they criticized the people who preceded them by describing them as living like wild animals. The myth shows the Incas improving the lives of the local inhabitants, changing them from a people who lived as migrant hunters and food gatherers, with no surplus of food and no leisure time, to a people who settled down as farmers and reaped the benefits of division of labor. (In reality, the local populations were as civilized as the Incas were.) The Incas who rescue and teach these "uncivilized" peoples are the children of the Sun, who is the kindly benefactor of all living creatures. Viracocha, the divine creator, is not mentioned in the myth.

The rod of gold indicates an awareness of the scarcity of good farmland in the Andean highlands and explains how Cuzco, the capital city of the Incas, came to be built. The end of the myth paves the way for creation of the Inca Empire.

THE CHILDREN OF THE SUN

In times of old, our land was one of shrubs and small trees and tall mountains. The people were unmannered and untaught. They lived as wild animals live, without clothes made from woven cloth, without houses, and without cultivated food. They lived apart from other human beings in small family groups, finding lodging as nature provided it, within mountain caves and in hollow places beneath the great rocks. They covered their bodies with animal skins, leaves, and the bark of trees, or they wore no clothes at all. They gathered whatever food they could find to eat, such as grass, wild berries, and the roots of plants, and sometimes they ate human flesh.

Father Sun looked down from the heavens and pitied these humans who lived like wild creatures. He decided to send one of his sons, Manco Capac, and one of his daughters, Mama Ocllo Huaco, down to earth at Lake Titicaca to teach them how to improve their lives.

When his children were ready to leave, the Sun said to them, "I devote myself to the well-being of the universe. Each day, I travel across the sky so that I can look down upon the earth and see what I can do for the human beings who live there. My heat provides them with the comfort of warmth. My light provides them with the knowledge that comes from sight. It is through my efforts that fields and forests provide food for them, for I bring sunshine and rain, each in its proper season.

"Yet all this, good as it is, is not enough. The people live like wild animals. They know nothing of living in houses, wearing clothing, or raising food. They have no villages, they use no tools or utensils, and they have no laws.

"Therefore," Father Sun continued, "I am making you the rulers of all the races in the region of Lake Titicaca; I want you to rule those peoples as a father rules his children. Treat them as I have treated you, with tenderness and affection, with devotion and justice. Teach them as I have taught you, for the races of human beings are my children also. I am their provider and their protector, and it is time they stopped living like animals.

"Take this golden rod with you," the Sun concluded. "It is only two fingers thick and shorter than the arm of a man, yet it will tell you how good the soil is for cultivating crops. As you travel, whenever you stop to eat or to sleep, see if you can bury it in the land. When you come to the place where the rod sinks into the earth with one thrust, establish my sacred city, Cuzco, city of the sun. Soft soil as deep as this golden rod will be fertile soil."

So Manco Capac and Mama Ocllo Huaco went down to Lake Titicaca and set out on foot to examine the land. Wherever they stopped they tried to bury the golden rod, but they could not do it. The soil was too rocky.

Finally they descended into a valley. The land was wild and without people, but the plant growth was lush and green. They climbed to the crest of a hill (the hill where Ayar Cachi and Ayar Ucho had turned to stone) and pressed the golden rod into the soil. To their great pleasure, it sank into the earth and disappeared.

Manco Capac smiled at Mama Ocllo Huaco and said, "Our father, the Sun, intends us to rule this valley. Here we will build his sacred city, Cuzco. Let us now go separate ways, you to the south and I to the north. Let us gather together the peoples we find and bring them into this fertile valley. Here we will instruct them in the ways of human beings, and we will care for them as our father has commanded us."

Manco Capac and Mama Ocllo Huaco set out for the mountain plateaus to collect the peoples of the land. The men and women they found in the barren regions were impressed with their clothing and pierced ears, their regal bearing, and their message. "Let us teach you how to lead a better life," the children of the Sun announced. "Let us teach you how to build houses, make clothes, and raise cattle and crops. Right now you live like wild animals. Let us teach you how to live like human beings. Our father, the Sun, has taught us and has sent us here to teach you."

The peoples of the land placed their confidence in these children of the Sun and followed as they led the way toward a new and better way of living. When many people had gathered together, Manco Capac and Mama Occlo Huaco divided the group into those who would be responsible for gathering food and those who would learn how to build houses. Their new life had begun.

Manco Capac taught the males which foods were nourishing so their diet would include both grains and vegetables, how to choose the best seeds, and how to plant and cultivate each kind of plant. In the process, he taught them how to make the tools and equipment necessary for farming and how to channel water from the streams in the valley for irrigation. He even taught them how to make shoes. Meanwhile, Mama Ocllo Huaco taught the women how to weave wool and cotton into cloth and how to sew that cloth into clothing.

So it came to pass that the Incas became an educated people. In honor of their great provider and protector, the Sun, the people built a temple on the crest of the hill where Manco Capac and Mama Ocllo Huaco had plunged the golden rod into the earth and from which they had set out to gather the Inca people together and teach them. Their prosperity drew other peoples to join them and learn their ways. Manco Capac finally taught the men how to make weapons—such as bows and arrows, clubs, and lances—so that they could defend themselves and extend their kingdom. The Incas were on their way to becoming a great people.

❧ QUESTIONS FOR
Response, Discussion, and Analysis

1. What reason is there to believe that this myth accurately describes the people mentioned at the beginning? What reason is there to believe that it is intentionally inaccurate?

2. Why does the Sun care about people? What other choices existed for the creators of this myth?

3. Why does the Sun claim responsibility for the fertility of the soil? To what extent, if any, do his reasons make sense? Explain.

4. What two purposes does this myth serve?

Wanadi, the Creator

The Yekuhana live in Venezuela, on the northern bank of the Upper Orinoco River. *Yekuhana* literally means "wood/log-water-people" and refers to their water-log or dug-out canoes. The Spanish conquistadors gave them the name of Makiritare when they found them in 1759. Therefore, they are known by that name, as well.

The Yekuhana consider themselves the "true people," who descended from Wanadi's first human beings. They speak the original language, and anyone who lives with them and learns their language becomes one of them. Their oral literature reveals that shamans, animals, and evil beings are all able to change their form. Therefore, what identifies a true Yekuhana is language. They view those who do not speak their language and who are not familiar with the *Watunna,* which is the collection of their religious doctrines and the record of their ancestral people and events, to be animals. Moreover, being nonhuman, they are enemies of the true people and the Yekuhana are entitled to hunt them.

The Yekuhana live in a region that is both mountainous and forested, and its great waterfalls prevent easy access. This environment protected them from Spanish conquest, and their region remains largely unexplored to this day. Agriculture, their principal activity, is based on a sophisticated slash-and-burn method that requires systematic movement from one place to another within a given area in order to permit the land to recover its fertility. They have no domesticated animals.

Being a forest people, the Yekuhana also have neither stone nor metal. However, they have adapted trees and plants to build frame houses, weave baskets and bark cloth, and create dug-out canoes. They also use clay soil along their riverbanks to make pottery.

As is evident in the myth of Wanadi, the tribe provides the individuals within it with their identity, and in these societies, the shaman is as important as the chief. The shaman perpetuates the tribe's religious history by controlling the religious practices that reinforce its traditions. He is the tribal doctor, and he functions as the intermediary between the people and their divinities, who, like Wanadi, are usually mythological culture heroes.

In another version of the following myth, the primal creative force is Father Sun, who drops three eggs on Earth. When the first two eggs break open, Wanadi and his brothers come forth. They represent all that is good in the universe, and, as culture heroes, they teach the ancestors of the Yekuhana people how to live well.

Because the third egg has become damaged by its fall, Wanadi rejects it and tosses it into the forest. This causes the third egg to break open, and Cajushawa comes forth, his heart filled with hostility. Cajushawa and his people, the *odosha* ("demons"), then multiply and live on earth. The human eye cannot see them, but they are responsible for all that is evil in life.

Wanadi and his brothers spend generations of time on earth, always trying to improve life. They introduce the cultivation of crops as well as social organization and religious practices. Meanwhile, they are always fighting against Cajushawa and his *odosha*. At last, they leave the earth to the Yekuhana and to Cajushawa. Thereafter, it is the responsibility of the Yekuhana to defend themselves against Cajushawa and his people.

The divinities in the *Watunna* are the Sky People, ancestors or "the old ones." Their ways provide the model for the behavior of their people. They reflect the law of the tribe, the tradition that itself is called *Watunna* and has been handed down from generation to generation in their oral tradition. The rituals in which the *Watunna* is recited include singing and dancing as well as the eating of cassava bread and the drinking of a special liquid. The people adorn themselves with jewelry and make bamboo flutes. They paint themselves with designs that reflect their myths. In the ceremony, a Master of Song will chant the myths that are the law of the tribe. The tribal elders know the traditions and have made contact with the spirits of their ancestors. In their society, they are respected and privileged.

The *Watunna* recited in ceremony is sacred doctrine, to be repeated exactly so that contact with the spirit world can continue. It is secret, and knowledge of it is limited to the initiated men of the tribe; thus, it is part of the initiation ceremony for the young men of the tribe. The end of the ceremony reflects the end of their initiation, and it closes with the initiates removing their costumes— feathered crowns, palm skirts, and sacred objects—and tossing them into the fire. In this way they take their leave of the spirits and prepare to return to their ordinary lives. Their final task is to stamp on the coals of the fire with their bare feet. They believe that they cannot be burned because they have acquired a new and magical power.

In addition to the sacred *Watunna,* a secular form exists. This form is as popular as the sacred form is secret. Everyone, including women and children, is free to retell the great tales in any imaginative form. Consequently, the popular versions are many, varied, and depend on knowledge, memory, and personal interpretation. However, these forms, too, unite the members of the tribe by reinforcing their common bond of a common cultural history. Therefore, the *Watunna* and its heroes of old remain alive and in daily use in a variety of forms. A tale from the *Watunna* can inform and enrich any daily activity, whether fishing, hunting, or basket-making.

The myth of Wanadi is appealing because it conveys the vulnerability of human beings in an environment that is far more powerful than they are. As we read it, we can sense the flickering shadows of the forest, and the fear that it conceals enemies. We can imagine a world in which nothing may be what it appears to be, either good or evil, and we can understand the importance of the shaman, with his magical ability to protect his people. We can sympathize with the Yekuhana people because we realize that we are vulnerable in our own environment, as well, because much that can happen to us, such as illness, storms, and war, is beyond our control. Moreover, we can understand the continuous and unending battle between good and evil that is externalized in the myth but that occurs within every human being in the form of endless temptations that, if we gave into them, would harm others or ourselves. Finally, we share the hope of the Yekuhana people that, by resisting these temptations, we will be able to make our homes, our communities, our country, and, therefore, the world, a better place to live.

The following version of Wanadi's myth has been adapted from Marc de Civrieux's *Watunna: An Orinoco Creation Cycle.*

WANADI, THE CREATOR

In the beginning, there was only Sky, the first place, and light, the first shining body. Clouds did not exist. Winds did not exist. And darkness did not exist. There was only light. And so, it was always day.

The first sun set creation in motion. He possessed some *wiriki,* the small quartz crystals that are the power stones of the shaman. And so, he blew on these *wiriki.* And Wanadi, the Creator, came into being. Wanadi lives in Sky. From there he sends forth his light like a sun that never sets. We who live on Earth cannot see him, and we cannot know him. But Wanadi is good, and he is the master of good.

Wanadi, the Creator, then blew on some *wiriki.* And the Sky People came into being. They built many houses and villages, all filled with Wanadi's light. Sky was a good place to live, for there were no demons. And so, there was neither sickness nor death, neither evil nor war. There was only life. No animals existed, but there was always plenty of food. And so, no one needed to work. The Sky People were wise and good, and they were always happy.

With Wanadi's light, the Sky People could see everything on Earth. But in the beginning, Earth was part of Sky. Sky and Earth were not separated, and Sky had no door. Earth, too, had only light, for Earth and Sky were one. And so, daylight was everywhere.

Wanadi I

In the beginning, no one lived on Earth. And so, it came to pass that Sky Wanadi, the Creator, said, "I want Earth to have good people and houses like the good people and houses in Sky." And so, Sky Wanadi blew on some *wiriki.* And Wanadi I, "Wanadi the Wise," came into being. And Sky Wanadi sent forth his first copy of himself, his first spirit double, down to Earth to be Master of Earth.

And so it came to pass that Wanadi the Wise came down to Earth. As soon as he was born, he cut his navel-cord and buried it. He did not know that Earth's worms would crawl into his navel-cord and begin to eat it.

But the worms did eat it. And so, the navel-cord rotted. As it rotted, it gave birth to Odosha. Odosha was ugly, for he was hair-covered, like an animal. Odosha was evil, for he became the master of all evil on Earth. But he lived with his own people, who were also demons, in dark caves in another land.

But Wanadi the Wise had not left Sky empty-handed. He had taken his tobacco. He had taken his gourd rattle, the maraca, so he could perform his magic. And he had taken some *wiriki* crystals to put into his maraca. And so it came to pass that Wanadi sat down to think. He sat silent and still, with his head in his hands and his elbows on his knees. And he thought. And he dreamed. And while he thought and dreamed, he smoked his tobacco. And he sang to the accompaniment of his maraca.

And so it came to pass that the first Earth People came into being. They came forth as Wanadi the Wise quietly blew out the tobacco smoke and dreamed of them. He created them as he dreamed them. And Wanadi the Wise gave these people the gifts of strength and knowledge, for he was the first and greatest of the shamans.

Now Odosha's hard heart flooded with waves of jealousy, resentment, and hatred whenever he thought about Wanadi the Wise. For Odosha knew that Wanadi was Master of Earth, and Odosha wanted to be Earth's master. And so, he spent day after day and night after night on Earth trying to become Master of Earth.

Odosha was clever. He whispered wicked thoughts into the ears of the first Earth People, and he misled them. A man was fishing, and he had caught lots of fish. And so, Odosha whispered to the Earth People, "If you kill that fisherman, you will have lots of fish." The Earth People listened to Odosha's wicked whisperings, and they killed the fisherman. And so, Odosha's hard heart flooded with joy at his success. But Wanadi turned the first Earth People into animals to punish them.

And yet, Odosha's power over the first Earth People was so great that Wanadi the Wise decided that he could not be Master of Earth. And so, he left the first Earth People, in their animal forms, with Odosha, and he went back to Sky to live.

Since the birth of Odosha, we never bury the navel-cord of our infants, for we do not want another Odosha to come forth and kill one of our infants.

Wanadi II

After Wanadi the Wise returned to Sky, it came to pass that Sky Wanadi, the Creator, thought, "The only people who live on earth are animals, and they are not good. I want good people to live on Earth." And with these words, Sky Wanadi blew on some *wiriki*. And Wanadi II came into being. Sky Wanadi sent forth a second copy of himself, his second spirit double, down to Earth. And so it came to pass that Wanadi II took the place of Wanadi the Wise on Earth.

When Wanadi II arrived, he thought, "New Earth People will be born again soon. But unless I do something about it, Odosha will cause them to become sick, and they will die. And so, I must show Odosha that I have the power to make Earth People live again, for Death is not real. It is only one of Odosha's tricks. And so, I must find a way to reveal my power to Odosha."

So it came to pass that Wanadi II sat down to think. He sat silent and still, with his head in his hands and his elbows on his knees. And he thought. And he dreamed. And while he thought and dreamed, he smoked his tobacco. And he sang to the accompaniment of his maraca. And he dreamed that his mother was born.

And so it came to pass that his mother came forth as Wanadi II quietly blew out the tobacco smoke and dreamed of her. And he created her as he dreamed her, in the form of a large, fully-grown woman.

As soon as his mother stood up, Wanadi thought, "Now I must make you die." So he sat silent and still, with his head in his hands and his elbows on his knees. And he thought. And he dreamed. And while he thought and dreamed, he smoked his tobacco. And he sang to the accompaniment of his maraca. And he dreamed that his mother died. And so it came to pass that Wanadi killed his mother as he quietly blew out the tobacco smoke and dreamed of her death. And he killed her as he dreamed of killing her.

Then Wanadi II repeated this process. When he thought and dreamed of his mother's life, she was born again. And when he thought and dreamed of her death, she died.

And so it came to pass that Wanadi II's mother became the symbol of his wisdom and his power. He had proved that Death was not real. It was just a trick.

The Huehanna

Now Wanadi II had brought the *Huehanna* with him from Sky. The *Huehanna* was a very large, hollow egg, and it had a thick, heavy shell that was as hard as a rock. Wanadi had brought it in order to create new Earth People, for the *Huehanna* contained many unborn people. Whoever stood beside it could hear their words, their songs, and their laughter, for all the unborn people were happily singing and dancing inside the *Huehanna*.

Now Wanadi II wanted the *Huehanna* to break open so that his people could emerge and settle Earth. "But I cannot open it now," he thought. "For my Earth People are good, and as long as Odosha wanders on Earth, he will kill my people. As soon as they come forth, he will cause them to become sick. And then they will die, for Odosha does not want good people. But if Odosha kills my Earth People, I will restore them to life, for I have the power and the wisdom to do it."

So Wanadi II thought. And so it came to pass that he killed his mother again. Then he thought, "My mother is dead now, but I will soon restore her to life. And when my Earth People come forth from the *Huehanna* and Odosha kills them, I will restore them to life, just as I have restored my mother."

So Wanadi II thought. And with these words, he called the orange-winged parrot to him. And Wanadi said, "Help me bury my mother here in the ground. Soon I will restore her to life, for she is the symbol of my power. And Odosha must learn of my power, for I am Master of Earth and Master of Life. And so, my people cannot die.

"Now I am going hunting, but I will be back soon. Guard my mother's grave while I am gone, for my mother will return to life here. When she comes forth from her grave and once again she is alive, then the *Huehanna* will break apart. For her return to life will tell my Earth People that it is time for them to come forth to settle Earth.

"Now when you see my mother's body begin to move, you must call me right away. You must screech, shriek, and scream so that I will hear you. And then I will come. But until I return, do not let Odosha near my mother's grave."

So Wanadi II spoke to the orange-winged parrot who served him. And with these words, he then called to his nephew, "Iarakaru, watch over the *Huehanna* while I am away!"

And so it came to pass that Wanadi II left to go hunting. But he forgot to put his *chakara,* his medicine bag, across his shoulder. And so, he left it behind. It contained his magic herbs and plants, his tobacco, and his power stones, the *wiriki,* and it contained the darkness of night. Whenever Wanadi became tired, he would just open his *chakara,* stick his head inside, and go to sleep. As soon as he woke up, he would close the *chakara.* And so, the darkness of night was always confined inside it.

Wanadi II went hunting. It came to pass that Odosha learned that his great enemy had left his mother's grave and the *Huehanna* guarded by others. And Odosha thought, "Wanadi II thinks everything belongs to him. And so, he thinks Earth belongs to him. He thinks the *Huehanna* will break open. And then his own Earth People will come forth to settle Earth.

"Wanadi II is too sure of his power! He thinks he will determine all that will come to be. He thinks he will make that woman in the ground live again. He thinks light will always keep Earth bright. How wrong he is! He even left two guards by the *Huehanna* to warn him when that woman begins to move.

"Wanadi II has power. But Earth is mine, not his. And I, too, have power. I have power over Wanadi's nephew. And I have power over the dead. So that woman will not come forth alive from the ground. She will not return to life. And then, the *Huehanna* will not break apart. And Wanadi's unborn Earth People will not come forth to settle Earth."

So Odosha thought. And so it came to pass that he went forth to find the *Huehanna,* for he knew that there he would find Wanadi's nephew. And when Odosha found Iarakaru, he hid from him. But he whispered to Iarakaru as if Iarakaru were hearing his words in a dream. "Open Wanadi's *chakara!* And then, Iarakaru, you will learn his secret!" he whispered.

So Odosha spoke. And Iarakaru thought he heard Odosha's words in his dream. Wanadi's nephew remembered that Wanadi II had said, "Iarakaru, never play with my *chakara,* for it contains my power. And if you open it, the darkness of night will escape and cover Earth."

So Wanadi II had commanded. But Iarakaru was very curious. "What is really hiding inside Wanadi's *chakara?*" he asked himself. "If it really is darkness, I want to see it. I want to smoke Wanadi's tobacco. And I want to have Wanadi's power."

So Iarakaru thought. And so it came to pass that he opened the *chakara.* And swift as a dart sent forth from a hunter's blowgun, darkness flew out and covered Earth. Night now hid Sky from Earth. And so, Earth no longer had light.

Odosha's heart now flooded with joy. "The night is mine!" he exclaimed. "And now, Earth is mine, as well. For Wanadi's people cannot live in darkness, and so they cannot live on Earth. But to my people, night is day. And so, they can now come forth and settle Earth, for I am Master of Earth."

And so it came to pass that, hidden within the darkness, Odosha created a hairy dwarf. And he said to the dwarf, "Darkness covers Earth, but night is day to you. So watch over this grave, and tell me when the woman begins to come forth."

And so, the dwarf watched the woman's grave. And at last he said to Odosha, "She is coming forth."

So the dwarf spoke. And when Odosha heard the dwarf's words, swift as a dart sent forth from a hunter's blowgun, Odosha urinated into a gourd, for he knew that his urine would destroy the woman in the grave. Then he gave the gourd to a small lizard. And he commanded, "Take this gourd to the woman's grave, and throw my urine on her body."

The orange-winged parrot was still watching the grave, as well. Suddenly— even in the darkness—the parrot saw the ground began to move. First, a hand came forth from the grave. And then an arm came forth. Swift as a rapids over-turns a canoe, the parrot began to screech, shriek, and scream for Wanadi II. Wanadi II was far-off, but he heard the parrot. And he came running, for he wanted to see what his new mother looked like. And he wanted to see if the *Huehanna* had broken apart.

Now the ground above the grave opened, and the woman, Wanadi's mother, began to come forth. But swift as a dart sent forth from a hunter's blowgun, the little lizard threw Odosha's urine on her body. So it came to pass that Odosha's urine covered the woman, and its flaming poison scorched her body, roasted her flesh, and ate into her bones. "I have done what Odosha commanded!" exclaimed the little lizard, and it returned to Odosha.

And the lizard accompanied Odosha as he went forth to break open the *Huehanna*. "I will smash the *Huehanna* to pieces!" exclaimed Odosha. "And then I will kill all the unborn Earth People who are waiting to come forth to settle Earth."

So Odosha spoke. But when he and his lizard began to beat the *Huehanna* with their clubs, they could not crack its thick shell, for it was as hard as a rock. And so, they were forced to leave the *Huehanna* just as it was.

Meanwhile, the darkness that Iarakaru had freed now blinded him. He could not see Sky. He could not see Earth. He could see nothing at all. And so, his heart flooded with terror. And swift as a dart sent forth from a hunter's blowgun, he started running in the dark. He did not know where he was running, but he ran.

Meanwhile, the parrot kept screaming, shrieking, and screaming for Wanadi II. And Wanadi II was running toward the *Huehanna* and his mother's grave. But as he ran darkness suddenly covered Earth. "Iarakaru disobeyed me. He must have opened the *chakara*!" he exclaimed. But he continued to run through the night that covered him.

At last, Wanadi II arrived at his mother's grave. And through the darkness, he saw that all that remained of her corpse was ashes and scorched bones. His parrot was silent. And his *chakara* was open.

"What can I do now?" Wanadi II asked himself. "My mother's corpse has no flesh. Her bones are useless, and so she cannot return to life. Earth is dark, and my Earth People cannot live in darkness. They would only die here. And so, Odosha has had his way. Earth is no longer mine. It now belongs to him. But what has happened to the *Huehanna*?

And so it came to pass that Wanadi II now went forth to find the *Huehanna*. And when he arrived, he saw that his nephew had fled, but the stonelike egg was still where he had left it. And so, Wanadi II picked it up. He heard the voices inside, and his heart flooded with joy, for his unborn Earth People were still inside the *Huehanna*. But now their hearts were flooded with fear, and so they were shrieking and screaming. But the *Huehanna* was still unopened.

"My Earth People are still unborn. And so, they have not died. But they will have to wait now, for this is no time for them to come forth to settle Earth," thought Wanadi II. "But it is still the beginning, and my people can come forth in time still to come. Until then, I must protect them from Odosha. And so, I will hide them."

So Wanadi II spoke. And so he took the *Huehanna* to the mountain called Mount Waruma. And there, he hid the *Huehanna* with all the unborn Earth People inside it.

As for Iarakaru, he had fled from the *chakara* like a white monkey, not like a man. And now Wanadi II punished his nephew for opening his *chakara* and letting the darkness escape. For Wanadi II turned Iarakaru into a white monkey. And so it came to pass that Iarakaru became the grandfather of the white monkey, and he gave all white monkeys his form, his speech, and his name.

Odosha's power on Earth was so great that Wanadi II decided that he could not be Master of Earth. And so, Wanadi II left Earth to Odosha. Like Wanadi the Wise, Wanadi II left the first Earth People, in their animal forms, with Odosha, and he went back to Sky to live. He put his mother's skull and bones into a palm basket and took them with him. And he threw her bones into Lake Akuena, the lake of life-everlasting, in the center of Sky, for its deep blue waters have the power to restore the dead to life. And so it came to pass that Wanadi's mother again returned to life. But she lives in Sky with Wanadi.

Wanadi III

After Wanadi II returned to Sky, it came to pass that Sky Wanadi, the Creator, thought, "The only people who live on Earth are still animals, and they still are not good. And so, I still want good people to live on Earth." And with these words, he blew on some *wiriki*. And Wanadi III, "House Wanadi," came forth. And Sky Wanadi sent forth his third copy of himself, his third spirit double, down to Earth. And so it came to pass that House Wanadi took the place of Wanadi II on Earth.

When House Wanadi arrived, Earth was still covered with darkness. Because of Odosha, light from Sky did not come down any more. And because of Odosha, all Earth People now suffered from hunger, sickness, and war, and they all were condemned to die.

Wanadi the Wise had transformed the old people into animals. And, like animals, they still lived in hiding, for their hearts were flooded with fear. They could not see, so they could not move about in the darkness. And so, they had no water, and they had no food. Hungry and wretched, they lived with Odosha. And Odosha made them sick and killed them.

Now Sky Wanadi, the Creator, sent House Wanadi down to Earth to make his people, for they would be good people. And so House Wanadi said, "I will make a sun, a moon, and stars for Earth. They will belong to Earth, and they will shine in the darkness. And so, once again, Earth will have light."

So House Wanadi spoke. And with these words, he made the sun to shine during the day, and he made the moon and the stars to shine at night. They were like people. And they lit up a new Sky for Earth People to see.

Now Wanadi the Wise had given the old Earth People the bodies of animals, but they could take human form when they wanted. And now, the hearts of the old ones flooded with joy. And one by one, they left their caves and looked at the new sun, for it was a new day. And they knew that, once again, Wanadi was with them.

And the old Earth People gathered around House Wanadi and complained, "You must do something about Odosha. Because of him, we are hungry. We are wretched. We are sick. And we die. Because of Odosha, we have no water. And we have no cassava bread to eat, for we have no yucca plants. Because of Odosha, we have no clothes, no hammocks, and no houses. We have no bows and no arrows. Because of Odosha, our hearts are always flooded with fear. And so, we are like animals."

So the old Earth People spoke to House Wanadi. And then it came to pass that House Wanadi saw Iarakaru, the monkey. Even he was now as thin as a rope. And Wanadi said to his nephew, "Iarakaru, you have caused all this suffering, for you opened my *chakara*. And so, as punishment, you, your children, your grand-children, and all the children who come after them will always be thin, for you opened the *chakara* and caused all this suffering on Earth."

And then House Wanadi thought, "I will now make Earth as it was in the beginning. And so, it will be good again."

So House Wanadi spoke. And with these words, he returned to Sky in order to look for food. And he searched until he found the house of Yucca Mistress, the good food-keeper who lived there. And when he asked Yucca Mistress for food, she sent her spirit messenger down to Earth with armfuls of cassava for the old ones. And so the Earth People could eat again.

But Odosha came upon the old ones. And when he saw that, once again, the Earth People were eating, his hard heart flooded with fury. "Wanadi has returned!" he exclaimed. "Once again, he intends to be Master of Earth. But, once again, I will spoil his plans."

And so it came to pass that Odosha dressed up like House Wanadi. He walked among the old Earth People, and he whispered wicked thoughts into their ears. The people listened to him, and they behaved in evil ways. They did not work together, for every person thought only of himself. They refused to have any chiefs, so there was no order, and there was no justice.

Now when it came to pass that House Wanadi saw how the old ones were behaving, he punished them once again. He made them sick. Yucca Mistress sent them no more food, and many of these Earth People died.

Then House Wanadi thought, "The old Earth People are not good people, for they only listen to Odosha's wicked whisperings. They do not want to be my people. And so, I must make new people, and my new people will not be like ani-mals. They will be real people."

And so House Wanadi took the form of the red-headed woodpecker. And by pecking on the wood, he built a house on Mount Wana. It was the first house. He made it for himself, to be his home on Earth. But he also made it to be a sign for the people, for House Wanadi wanted to show Earth People how to make their houses like those of the Sky People and not like the houses of ani-mals. And Wanadi made so many houses for the people that he made villages on Earth.

And it came to pass that Odosha came and saw House Wanadi's house on Mount Wana, and he like it. And so, Odosha built a house just like Wanadi's house, and he built it right in front of Wanadi's house.

Odosha's house caused House Wanadi's heart to flood with waves of fury and fear. "Once again, Odosha is trying to spoil everything! And so, I must work fast!" he exclaimed.

And so it came to pass that House Wanadi sat down to think by his house on Mount Wana. He sat silent and still, with his head in his hands and his elbows on his knees. And he thought. And he dreamed. And while he thought and dreamed, he smoked his tobacco. And he sang to the accompaniment of his maraca.

And so it came to pass that the second group of Wanadi's Earth People, the first human beings, came into being. And they came forth as House Wanadi quietly blew out the tobacco smoke and dreamed of them. And he created them as he dreamed them. And so, next to him on Mount Wana, Wanadi set down twelve men, and he gave these twelve men the gifts of strength and knowledge. But now he also gave his people wisdom.

House Wanadi remained seated after he had created his twelve men. And once again, he sat silent and still, with his head in his hands and his elbows on his knees. And he thought and he dreamed. And while he thought and dreamed, he smoked his tobacco. And he sang to the accompaniment of his maraca. "I am dreaming that my new Earth People have plenty of food," he said.

And then House Wanadi looked up, but no food came. And he saw that Odosha was sitting right in front of him. And Odosha was dreaming too, for he did not want House Wanadi to bring forth food. And so Odosha was dreaming evil dreams.

"I am dreaming that my new Earth People have cassava," said House Wanadi, dreaming.

"But I began to dream my dream first," replied Odosha. "And I am dreaming that all Earth People are hungry."

"I am dreaming that I killed five deer for my new Earth People," Wanadi said, dreaming.

"But I began to dream my dream first," replied Odosha. "And I am dreaming that there is nothing for Earth People to eat. And so, many of them are dying."

"I am dreaming my yucca plant is everywhere, and that there are nine kinds of bitter yucca and a sweet yucca, as well. I am dreaming that my plant is large and bushy and that I am cutting it down. I am dreaming that it makes a great harvest, for my new Earth People will use it to make all their food. And its bitter roots will give them cassava and manioc," said Wanadi, dreaming.

"But I began to dream my dream first," replied Odosha. "And I am dreaming that there are many sick people. And that they are all going to die."

So Wanadi and Odosha spoke. And at last Wanadi's heart flooded with rage. He looked down at his twelve men, and he said, "Because of Odosha's evil dreams, I cannot do anything for you here. And so we will leave my house on Mount Wana, and we will move somewhere else. We will find some place where Odosha cannot bother us."

So House Wanadi spoke to his twelve men. And so it came to pass that, together, they left Wanadi's house on Mount Wana. And they went forth to Wade's cave, at the foot of the tallest mountain, for Wade was House Wanadi's friend and his teacher, and he was good. He was one of the great ancestors, and he was one of the greatest shamans.

"We are running away from Odosha," announced House Wanadi. "And so we have come to live with you."

"You may stay with me," replied Wade.

And so it came to pass that House Wanadi and his twelve men lived with Wade in his cave. Wade was the grandfather of all the sloths, and he would take his sloth form whenever he wanted.

House Wanadi built Wade a house, and there he left his twelve people. And there Wanadi's people, the first human beings, fashioned their first garden. They cut down the forest and burned what remained. The men cleared the land, and they planted and cared for their crops. And so it came to pass that they had yucca, mostly bitter but also sweet. And they also planted some bananas, chili peppers, gourd, squash, sugar cane, and tobacco.

And one day it came to pass that House Wanadi said to Wade and his twelve men, "I am leaving you now in order to go hunting, but I will not be gone long."

And with these words House Wanadi took his poisoned darts and his blowgun, which he had fashioned from a long, straight bamboo stalk, and he went forth to hunt birds. And as he was walking through the forest, he saw a jaguar. Swift as a rapids overturns a canoe, Wanadi ran ahead of the jaguar. But the jaguar saw Wanadi, and it ran after him, for it wanted to eat him. But suddenly, Wanadi turned upon the jaguar. He quickly placed a dart inside his blowgun, and he shot the jaguar.

And it came to pass that the jaguar did not die, For it was a spirit jaguar. And so Wanadi could not kill it. But the jaguar fled.

So it came to pass that Wanadi continue on his way. And as he walked, he dreamed that he was killing birds. And every time he dreamed that he killed a bird, he really killed one. And so he brought many birds back to Wade's house for his twelve men to eat. And the hearts of Wanadi's people flooded with joy as they ate these birds.

Now, while they were eating, Wanadi said to Wade, "While I was walking in the forest, a jaguar jumped out. It wanted to eat me, but I shot it with my blowgun. My dart should have killed it, but it could not, for it was a spirit jaguar. And then the jaguar fled."

So House Wanadi spoke. And to his words, Wade replied, "Are you sure that the jaguar was not Odosha in disguise? He is a trickster, you know. And so, the next time you leave us, you had better take some form of disguise, as well. Then you will be safe.

So Wade spoke. And so it came to pass that, when Wanadi went forth into the forest again, he went in the disguise of a dirty old hunter. And this time, House Wanadi came face to face with the real Odosha.

Odosha stared at the hunter, but he did not know that this hunter was really Wanadi. And so, he asked him, "Have you seen House Wanadi?"

"Who is House Wanadi?" replied the hunter.

"He used to live on Mount Wana," said Odosha. "But he suddenly left, and I am trying to find him."

"I do not know House Wanadi," replied the hunter.

And so it came to pass that House Wanadi tricked Odosha. Wanadi then began to walk home. And as he walked, he dreamed that he was killing birds. And every time he dreamed that he killed a bird, he really killed one. And so he brought many birds back to Wade's house for his twelve men to eat. And the hearts of Wanadi's people flooded with joy as they ate these birds.

Now, while they were eating, Wanadi said to Wade, "While I was walking in the forest, I met Odosha. He asked me about House Wanadi, for he did not know me in my hunter's disguise. I told him that I had never heard of House Wanadi. And so, he left. He is still looking for me, but he is far away now.

So Wanadi spoke. And to his words, Wade replied, "That is very good. But now you know that you cannot go into the forest as House Wanadi."

And so it came to pass that House Wanadi disguised himself as a dirty old hunter once again. And in this form, he walked all over Earth. And at times, he would sit silent and still, with his head in his hands and his elbows on his knees. And he would think. And he would dream. And while he thought and dreamed, he would smoke his tobacco. And he would sing to the accompaniment of his maraca. And now, he dreamed of new houses and new people.

And it came to pass that new houses and new people came into being. And they came forth as House Wanadi quietly blew out the tobacco smoke and dreamed of them. And he created them as he dreamed them.

As for Odosha, he went away. He was still looking for House Wanadi. And for a long time, he did not return, for Odosha still did not know who the dirty old hunter was.

One day it came to pass that Odosha came looking for House Wanadi at Wade's house. "Have you seen House Wanadi?" he asked.

"Who is House Wanadi?" replied Wanadi's men. "We have never heard of him."

So Wanadi's men spoke. And so it came to pass that Odosha left Wade's house and continued his search, but he did not know where to look. And so he never found House Wanadi.

Now, while House Wanadi was walking all over Earth, he thought, "The old Earth People know only how to live like monkeys, for they only gather wild fruits. And so, the Food Master must teach my people what they need to know in order to survive and prosper."

So House Wanadi thought. And with these words, he returned to Sky in order to find Food Master. And when he asked Food Master to teach his Earth People how to raise food, Food Master sent his spirit messenger down to Earth. And his spirit messenger appeared to the people in the form of the chief of the birds. He brought Earth the first rain. And the rain made the soil soft and fertile. And so, tree-filled forests came forth from the soil and smaller plants bloomed. Then Food Master's spirit messenger showed Wanadi's people how to live like brothers. He showed them how to cut down trees, and he showed them how to plant seeds.

And so it came to pass that the chief of the birds taught all of House Wanadi's people what they needed to know in order to survive and prosper. When it had completed this task, it spread its wings and soared back to Sky and Food Master, but it left its bird-form and color behind on Earth for the birds that would follow.

And in time it came to pass that the old Earth People died. Wade left Earth, but he left his form, his speech, and his name on Earth for the sloths that came after him. And he went up to Sky to live as one of the Sky People. And the spirits of all the other animals and the birds returned to their masters, the Sky People, as well.

And so, House Wanadi thought, "The time is coming when I, too, will leave Earth and return to Sky. And I will move the twelve men whom I created—those men who, from the beginning, have lived with Wade—to my new house on Mount Kushamakari. But then there will be no one to care for Wade's garden. The plants will become wild, and the land will become what it used to be.

"And so, before I leave Earth, I must make two human beings, a man and his mate. I must build them a house. And I must give them the gifts of strength, knowledge, and enough wisdom to survive and prosper, for they will remain on Earth and take care of the food that grows here.

And so, once again, House Wanadi sat silent and still, with his head in his hands and his elbows on his knees. And he thought. And he dreamed. And while he thought and dreamed, he smoked his tobacco. And he sang to the accompaniment of his maraca. And now he dreamed of the first grandfather and grandmother of our people. He dreamed of finding clay. He dreamed of beating the clay. And he dreamed of shaping it into two figures that looked like clay dolls. Then he dreamed of drying them in a fire in order to make them hard. And he dreamed of their house.

And so it came to pass that first grandfather and first grandmother, the grandfather and grandmother of our people, the Yekuhana, came into being. And they came forth as House Wanadi quietly blew out the tobacco smoke and dreamed of them. And he created them as he dreamed them. And they took the gifts that Wanadi gave them, and they went to live in their house. First grandfather cleared away the trees and bushes so that first grandmother could plant the seeds, and they took care of Wade's garden. They taught their children how to make their own gardens and how to take care of them.

And it came to pass that the time came when House Wanadi would leave Earth and return to Sky. So he called our grandfathers together in order to say farewell. For three days, he feasted and drank, and he danced and sang with them. Then he announced, "I am going back to Sky, for Odosha has made himself Master of Earth. And so, there is sickness, every kind of evil, and death.

"But the time will come when Odosha will die. Then evil will disappear, and Earth as you know it will come to an end. The sun, the moon, and the stars will fall out of the sky, and darkness will disappear. For the sky that you see is not the real sky, and so it is not good.

"A new Earth, a good Earth, will take the place of Odosha's Earth. And Earth and Sky will be what they were in the beginning. Earth will be part of Sky, and it will be good, for Sky is good. And all Earth People will see the light that always shines forth from Sky Wanadi, the Creator.

"And it will come to pass that Wanadi, the Creator, once again will blow on some *wiriki*. And Wanadi IV, "Wanadi of the New Earth," will come into being.

Sky Wanadi will send forth a fourth copy of himself, his fourth spirit double, down to Earth. And so Wanadi of the New Earth will take my place on Earth and be Master of Earth.

"And Wanadi of the New Earth will go forth to find the *Huehanna* inside Mount Waruma. For within its stonelike shell, unborn people are waiting for Wanadi's spirit to release them so that they can settle Earth.

"But before that time comes, each of you will die. But your death will not be real, for Wanadi, the Creator's, spirit messengers will be tricking Odosha. Know that your real food and your real house is waiting for you in Sky. And Sky Wanadi, the Creator, will be waiting there for you, too.

"The body that your spirit has lived in here on this Earth will die, but your body is only a copy of your real body. Your spirit came down from Sky in your real body. And when you die, your spirit will return to Sky in your real body.

"And in your real body, your spirit will climb a ladder to your Sky house. And when your spirit reaches Sky, the Scissors Master will know whether your spirit has been good, or whether it has been in Odosha's power. And if your spirit has been good, the Scissors Master will permit it to enter Sky in your real body.

"But if your spirit has been in Odosha's power, the Scissors Master will slice your real body into pieces. They will fall back down to Earth. And here, they will remain with Odosha, and they will die with him when this Earth comes to an end.

"In Sky, you will find many houses and villages, all filled with Sky Wanadi's light. Sky is a good place to live, for there are no demons. And so, there is neither sickness nor death, neither evil nor war. There is only life. There is always plenty of food. And so, no one needs to work. All the people who live there are wise and good, and they are always happy.

"Now, until you die, you will live with Odosha. But you have my signs. And so you will know how to live. Let the old ones among you sing about Sky Wanadi, the Creator, and his spirit messengers. Let them sing about the ancient ways. Listen to the songs of the old ones. Repeat them. Remember them. Obey them. Teach them to your children. And have your children teach these songs to their children. In this way, the Yekuhana will always know about Sky Wanadi, the Creator, and his spirit messengers. And the ancient ways will teach your people how to work so that you will always have food."

So House Wanadi spoke to our grandfathers. And then he spoke separately with the twelve men whom he had created, those men who, from the beginning, had lived with Wade.

House Wanadi said to them, "I cannot take you all to Sky with me when I leave. And so, you must stay here on Earth for now. I have moved my house to Mount Kushamakari, that tall, flat-topped mountain called 'House of Kuchi,' the mountain that holds up Sky. For its beauty floods my heart with joy. I will now take you there to live, for you will not die like all the other Earth People.

"My new cave-house will be a safe house for you, for it is hidden deep within the mountains. Great rapids guard the path to it, and many anacondas lie hidden beneath them. They like to overturn the canoes that would pass over them. And those who, at last, find my cave-house must deal with the great bat that is always on guard.

"Only good people live in my house—the blowgun master, the grandfather of the tapir, and many other powerful people. And Sky's light always shines there.

"Odosha has no power to enter. Nor can his people enter, for they are evil. The anacondas will eat them if they try.

"But good people will come. The shamans of the Yekuhana will come. They will give up meat and women. And they will sing as they come.

"And so, wait in the cave-house that I have made for you, for Wanadi of the New Earth will return to Earth. He will look for Odosha's skull and for the *Huehanna*. And he will come for you."

So House Wanadi spoke to his twelve men. And then he led them forth to their new cave-house. And there, they are waiting for this world, Odosha's world, to come to its end.

We do not see the house of House Wanadi's twelve men. We can only see Mount Kushamakari. But our shamans can see it, for they are the great medicine men who have the power to protect and cure us. They have the power to control our supply of food. They have the power to rescue our body's double when Odosha captures it while we sleep.

Our shamans can see the cave-house of House Wanadi's twelve men. They can go up to the door of the cave, and they can speak with House Wanadi's twelve men through that door. They can tell them about us. They can ask them for food, good health, wisdom, and power. But they cannot enter their cave-house, and they cannot see them.

And so it came to pass that House Wanadi led his twelve men to their new cave-house. And then he returned. He put on a feathered headdress, and he began to sing. Then Odosha arrived. Like Wanadi, he wore a feathered headdress. Wanadi was still singing when the sun rose. And Odosha's hard heart flooded with joy as he watched Wanadi sing and dance.

And then, it came to pass that House Wanadi went away. He was still singing and dancing as he went toward the river. And Odosha was still singing and dancing, as well. But Odosha was watching House Wanadi as he left, for Odosha was ready to kill him.

Now, House Wanadi knew the ways of Odosha's mind and heart, and that is why he was moving toward the river. And so, swift as a dart sent forth from a hunter's blowgun, he suddenly jumped into a dug-out canoe and paddled away.

Odosha now stopped singing and dancing, and he ran after House Wanadi. He jumped into his own dug-out canoe. And swift as a rapids overturns a canoe, Odosha paddled after Wanadi. "I must catch House Wanadi before he returns to Sky!" he exclaimed. "For in Sky, he will always be safe."

It came to pass that House Wanadi placed fifteen piles of cooked food in the river, like rocks, but Odosha did not stop to eat. He left the meat in the river, and it turned into rocks, and rapids formed around the rocks.

Odosha then sent spirit animals forth to eat House Wanadi. He sent a dog, but the dog turned into a jaguar. And swift as a rapids overturns a canoe, House Wanadi killed the jaguar with his blowgun. Then Wanadi ground the jaguar's bones into a powder, and he blew on it. And mosquitoes and gnats came forth from that dust.

And then it came to pass that House Wanadi made his last people, butterflies. And he said to them, "Odosha is following me. And so, I am going to pretend to die. When Odosha asks you where I am, you must tell him that I went back to Sky. Tell him that I cut my stomach out. And that, swift as a dart sent forth from a hunter's blowgun, my body's double soared high above Earth."

And it came to pass that the butterflies obeyed House Wanadi. When Odosha heard how House Wanadi had died, he, too, cut open his own stomach. And he, too, pulled it out. That is what Odosha did, but his body's double did not soar high above Earth. And Odosha did not go to Sky. And so, he put his stomach back in its place, and he waited to recover.

As for the butterflies, they flew off to Colombia and became Colombians. They are good, and they are wealthy, for they helped Wanadi escape from Odosha.

And it came to pass that Wanadi took a new body. And then, he sat down to think. He sat silent and still, with his head in his hands and his elbows on his knees. And he thought. And he dreamed. And while he thought and dreamed, he smoked his tobacco. And he sang to the accompaniment of his maraca. And he dreamed of clear water.

And so it came to pass that the clear water came forth as Wanadi quietly blew out the tobacco smoke and dreamed it. And he created it as he dreamed it. And on that clear water, Wanadi left Earth, dreaming as he went. And he returned to Sky. And there he lives still, in peace.

As for Odosha, as always, he began to search for House Wanadi as soon as he was well enough. Odosha put on bird wings, and he flew through the clouds. He flew beneath the sun and the moon. He flew everywhere. But he was only flying through Earth's sky.

Odosha did not know that Sky, the real one, was higher, and he could not get there. And so, in the end, Odosha was tricked, for he did not find House Wanadi. But he is still looking for him.

And as for the *Huehanna,* it is still inside Mount Waruma. It has been waiting there, peacefully, since the world began. And it will stay there until this Earth comes to its end. The good people are still inside it, unborn. They are waiting for Odosha to die, for then this Earth will come to its end.

Odosha is Master of Earth, our Earth. But the time will come when Odosha will die. And then evil will disappear, and Earth as we know it will come to an end.

And a new Earth, a good Earth, will take the place of Odosha's Earth. Wanadi of the New Earth will come down from Sky. He will go to Mount Waruma. And he will tell the people inside the *Huehanna* that the time has come for their house to break open. And then, the good, wise people, who could not be born in the beginning, will at last come forth from the *Huehanna.* The light from Sky will shine on Earth again. And everything will be as good as it was in the beginning.

QUESTIONS FOR
Response, Discussion, and Analysis

1. What does the existence of both Wanadi and Odosha reveal about the Yekuhana's view of the universe?

2. How does Odosha exert power over Wanadi?

3. Why do Wanadi and Odosha never succeed in conquering each other?

4. What hope does this myth provide for the Yekuhana people?

5. Why does Wanadi always remain in Sky and send his spirit doubles down to Earth to help human beings?

6. What does the ability of people and animals to change their form at will reveal about the nature of the Yekuhana's view of the universe?

The Creation

HISTORICAL BACKGROUND

The Maya were one of the major cultures in the New World. Located in what are now Guatemala and the Yucatan Peninsula, they were farmers of a soil so rich that it was easy for them to acquire a surplus of food. Corn was their major and honored crop. Their surplus enabled them to devote as much as half their time to other pursuits, and they became well-known for their knowledge of astronomy, their construction of major pyramid-shaped temples and limestone palaces, and their works of art. The Maya were expert mathematicians, and they also possessed a written hieroglyphic language that they used in writing books.

The Spaniards conquered the Maya in A.D. 1524 and burned their principal city, including all of their books, to ashes. Spanish missionaries converted the Mayan population to Roman Catholicism and taught many of the Maya to write their own language in the Latin, phonetic alphabet. They encouraged the Maya to record their traditions and history in the Western form of writing. Today, more than 300,000 people continue to speak the Maya language.

The Mayan creation myth is part of an ancient epic known as *The Popol Vuh*, which is the greatest surviving Mayan document. It was written anonymously in the Mayan language using the Latin alphabet between 1554 and 1558. Scholars believe this document is either a translation of a manuscript in the ancient Mayan hieroglyphic language or a collection of stories and songs recorded directly from the Mayan oral tradition.

In about 1700, a Catholic missionary translated *The Popol Vuh* into Spanish. He spoke the Mayan language fluently, and he persuaded the Maya to show him this manuscript of their ancient history. There is no record that any other Spaniard ever saw the Mayan document.

The Spanish manuscript disappeared for 150 years. In the 1850s, it was discovered in the library of the University of San Carlos in Guatemala City; it was first published in Vienna in 1857.

APPEAL AND VALUE

The Popol Vuh is an ancient document of striking literary beauty. It reveals more than the talent of the anonymous recorder. It reflects the thoughts and values of this ancient people and the ability of their language to express them.

The part of the epic that tells the Mayan creation myth shows a Christian influence. The language and some of the ideas are similar to the opening chapters of the Old Testament. This is not surprising, given the fact that Spanish missionaries were already teaching the Maya about Christianity when the anonymous author recorded *The Popol Vuh*.

It is interesting to compare the type of human beings the Maya gods wished to create and the relationship between these gods and their people with those of other creation myths.

THE CREATION

In the beginning, only the sky above and the sea below existed in the eternal darkness, and they were calm and silent, for nothing existed that could move or make noise. The surface of the earth had yet to rise forth from the waters. Grass and trees, stones, caves and ravines, birds and fish, crabs, animals, and human beings had yet to be created. Nothing could roar or rumble; nothing could sing or squeak; nothing could run or shake, for there was nothing but the vacant sky above and the tranquil sea below.

Hidden in the water under green and blue feathers were the Creators. These great thinkers talked quietly together in the water, alone in the universe, alone in the darkness of the eternal night. Together they decided what would be. Together they decided when the earth would rise from the waters, when the first human beings and all other forms of life would be born, what these living things would eat in order to survive, and when dawn would first flood the world with pale light.

"Let creation begin!" the Creators exclaimed. "Let the void be filled! Let the sea recede, revealing the surface of the earth! Earth, arise! Let it be done!"

And so they created it. The Creators made it. Out of the mist, out of a cloud of dust, mountains and valleys rose from the sea, and pine and cypress trees took root in the rich soil. Fresh water ran in streams down the mountainsides and between the hills.

And the Creators were satisfied. "We have thought about it and planned it," they said, "and what we have created is perfect!"

Then the Creators asked, "Do we want only silence beneath the trees we have created? Let us create wild animals, birds, and snakes. Let it be done!"

And so they created them. The Creators made them.

"You, deer, will walk on four feet through the thicket and the pasture. You will multiply in the forest, where you will sleep in the cool shade of the ravines and in the fields along the banks of rivers. You, birds, will live in the branches of the trees and in the vines. There you will build your nests, and there you will multiply." This the deer and the birds were told, and this they did.

And the Creators were satisfied. "We have thought about it and planned it," they said, "and what we have created is perfect!"

Then the Creators asked for more from the living creatures they had created. "Speak, call, cry, as each of you can. Call us by name, praise us, and love us."

But all this the birds and animals could not do. They could scream, hiss, and cackle, but they could not call their creators by name.

The Creators were disappointed with the living creatures that they had made. They said to them, "We will not take from you that which we have given you. However, because you cannot praise us and love us, we will make other beings who will. These new creatures will be superior to you and will rule you. It is your destiny that they will tear apart and eat your flesh. Let it be done!"

And so they created them. The Creators made them. They decided to fashion an obedient and respectful creature who would praise and love them. First they tried to model him out of muddy earth, but the material was too soft. He was limp and weak. He could speak, but no mind gave meaning to the words he spoke.

"Creatures fashioned from mud will never be able to live and multiply!" the Creators exclaimed. So they destroyed this creature.

Next the Creators tried to carve their new creature out of wood. "This material seems to be just right! It is firm and strong," they said. "These creatures look and speak like human beings. Let us make many more of them. Let it be done!"

The wooden creatures lived and multiplied, but no mind gave meaning to the words they spoke, and no soul existed within them. Their faces lacked all spirit, their hands and feet all strength. Their flesh was yellow and dry, without a bloody moisture pulsing beneath the surface to nourish it. They wandered aimlessly on all four limbs and did not think of their creators.

"Creatures fashioned from wood are not good enough to be able to live and multiply!" the Creators exclaimed. So they determined to destroy these wooden creatures.

The Creators caused a great flood of sap to form in the sky and fall to earth, striking the heads of the wooden creatures and felling them like trees. Then an eagle descended upon them and tore out their eyes. A bat descended upon them and cut off their heads. A jaguar leaped upon them and broke and mangled their bones. The face of the earth became covered in darkness, and a black rain fell without ceasing.

Once they were powerless, these wooden creatures were beset by enemies. Animals, both large and small, attacked them. Sticks and stones, plates and pots attacked them. Dogs they had starved and taunted now tore into their faces with their teeth. Stones they had used for grinding now ground them. Pots and griddles they had burned upon the cooking fire now burned their faces.

Desperately fighting for their lives, the wooden creatures tried to climb to the roofs of their houses, but the houses collapsed and tossed them back to the ground. They tried to climb the trunks of trees and find safety in their branches, but the trees shook them off and threw them to the ground. They tried to enter caves, but the caves closed and refused to shelter them.

All but a few of the wooden creatures were destroyed. The others survived with mangled faces and jaws, and their descendants became known as monkeys.

The Creators then took counsel together in the darkness of the night. The sun, the moon, and the stars had yet to appear in the sky above them. "Let us try again to create creatures who will praise us and love us. Let it be done! Let noble creatures live on the surface of the earth. Let us search for the substance we can use to fashion them."

Four animals—the mountain cat, the coyote, the crow, and a small parrot—came before the Creators and told them of yellow ears and white ears of corn that grew abundantly nearby. The Creators took the road the animals showed them. They found the corn, ground it up, and fashioned their noble creatures from this food. "Let it be done!" they exclaimed.

And so they created them. The Creators made them.

So it came to pass that the four First Fathers were created. The Creators fashioned their bodies from cornmeal dough. They made corn drinks from ground yellow and white corn and fed them to their new creatures to give them muscles and flesh, and with these strength.

And the Creators were satisfied. "We have thought about it and planned it," they said, "and what we have created is perfect!"

These four First Fathers looked and talked like human beings. They were attractive, intelligent, and wise. They could see far into the distance. Mountains and valleys, forests and meadows, oceans and lakes, the earth beneath their feet, and the sky above their heads all revealed their natures to them.

When the four First Fathers saw all there was to see in the world, they appreciated what they saw, and they thanked their creators. "We thank you for having created and formed us," they said. "We thank you for giving us the ability to see, hear, speak, think, and walk. We can see what is large and what is small, what is near and what is far. We know everything, and we thank you!"

The Creators were no longer pleased. "Have we created creatures who are better than we intended? Are they too perfect?" they asked each other. "Have we made them so knowledgeable and wise that they will be gods like ourselves? Should we limit their sight so that they will see less and know less? Let it be done!"

So the Creators spoke, and they changed the beings they had created. They blew fog into their eyes so they could see only that which was close to them. In this way, the Creators destroyed the original knowledge and wisdom that the four First Fathers had possessed.

After the Creators had created and formed our grandfathers in this way, they said, "Now let us carefully create and form wives for the First Fathers. Let their wives come to them while they are asleep and be there to bring them joy when they awaken. Let it be done!"

And so they created them. The Creators made them.

And the Creators were satisfied. "We have thought about it and planned it," they said, "and what we have created is perfect!"

So it came to pass that the Creators made many more human beings like the First Fathers and the First Mothers. They lived and multiplied in darkness, for the Creators had not yet created light of any kind, neither sun, nor moon, nor stars. These human beings lived together in the east in great numbers, both light-skinned and dark-skinned, rich and poor, speaking different languages.

They made no images of their gods, yet they remembered their creators and were loving and obedient. They raised their faces to the sky and prayed, "Oh, Creators! Stay with us and listen to us! Let there be light! Let there be dawn! Let there be day! Let dawn flood the world with pale light, and let the sun follow. As long as the sun shines from the sky, brightening each day, grant us daughters and sons to continue our race. Give us good, useful, happy lives, and give us peace!"

With these words the people begged the sun to rise and to light with its golden rays the steps of those whom the Creators had made.

"So let it be!" the Creators said. "Let there be light! In the dawn of the universe, let the light of early morning shine upon all that we have created! For we have thought about it and planned it, and what we have created is perfect!"

And so they created it. The Creators made it. The sun rose from the waters and cast its golden rays upon the surface of the earth. And the animals and the people were joyful because of it. Large and small animals rose to their feet in the cool shade of ravines and along the banks of rivers and turned to face the rising sun. The jaguar and the puma roared, and the snake hissed. The birds stretched their wings and broke into song. The people danced around their priests, who were burning incense and making sacrifices. For the Creators had illuminated the earth with light, and it was perfect.

❧ QUESTIONS FOR
Response, Discussion, and Analysis

1. Why do the Creators create more than one race of human beings? Why could they not create the kind they wanted the first time? What does this reveal about the Mayan gods and about human beings?

2. Why do the Creators destroy the race of wooden people and change the race of cornmeal people? What do these actions reveal about the nature of the Mayan gods?

The Creation Cycle

Archaeological studies of the Mexican plateau reveal that human beings have been living in that region since 6000 B.C. From A.D. 900 to 1200, the Toltec people dominated the northern part of Central America, and their capital city of Tula was located just north of what is now Mexico City. The Toltecs captured the Maya who lived in the Yucatan Peninsula. Like the Maya, the Toltecs possessed a rich heritage of myths and legends. Their spoken language, Nahuatl, also had a rich cultural tradition. Toltec power was destroyed from within by civil war, which left Tula in ruins in 1200 and left the area without a dominant power for more than a century.

According to Aztec tradition, the Azteca (people of Aztlan) obeyed the command of their god and left Aztlan (located far north of the Colorado River) sometime in the twelfth century. They wandered from place to place until, in 1325, they finally settled the area that has become Mexico City. The Aztecs held the Toltecs in high regard both politically and culturally. The first Aztec ruler, who came to power in 1376, claimed to be a descendant of Quetzalcoatl, the founder of the Toltec people. Thereafter, Toltec culture became an integral part of Aztec culture.

The Aztecs adopted the Toltec language and their myths and legends, blending them with their own and recording them. Under Aztec rule, architecture, the arts, and literature flourished. Their largest cities were much larger than any Spanish city of that time, and they contained elaborate palaces, temples, and waterways. The Aztecs took pride in creating works of metal and of feathers, in carving wood and huge sculptures of stone, and in forming mosaics of gems. They had a great interest in history, in the form of myths and legends, and in poetry. Today, more than a million people continue to speak Nahuatl, the Aztec language.

When the Spaniards invaded Central America and conquered the Aztecs in 1519, Hernan Cortes was helped both by neighboring peoples and by the Aztec emperor himself. The bloody practices of the Aztecs had created many enemies, who mistakenly thought the invaders would be better. The Aztec emperor welcomed Cortes because he believed that the Spaniard was Quetzalcoatl, returning as their tradition said he had promised.

The Spaniards burned most of the literature of the pagan peoples whom they conquered. As with the Maya, whom they conquered five years later, they burned entire libraries because they feared the pagan materials were harmful to Christians.

The Spaniards preserved certain aspects of the Aztec culture by learning the language and recording the literature in Spanish. Their point of view is clear from the nature of their accounts. They were both fascinated and repelled by the non-Christian myths and legends.

In the process of converting the more educated Aztecs to Christianity, the Spanish friars taught them to write their own language in the Roman alphabet and to record their myths and legends in this more Westernized version of the Nahuatl language. The

Aztecs often blended newly acquired Christian concepts and literary style into their own, older oral tradition. These transcriptions, made by both Spaniards and Aztecs in the 1500s, reflect the Spanish influence and so are not entirely authentic.

"The Five Worlds and Their Suns" and "The Creation of Human Beings" were recorded in the sixteenth-century Nahuatl manuscript, the *Chimalpopoca Codex: Annals of Cuauhtitlan and Legend of the Suns.* "The Creation of the Earth" was recorded in a sixteenth-century French manuscript, *The History of Mexico.* The myths that relate how Quetzalcoatl is tricked and driven from the Toltec capital by Tezcatlipoca appear in two major, primary sources: the *Chimalpopoca Codex* and the *Florentine Codex: General History of the Things of New Spain,* a collection of Nahuatl texts made in the sixteenth century by the Spanish priest Fray Bernardino de Sahagun.

APPEAL AND VALUE

Like the Greeks, the Irish, and certain other cultures from the Americas, the Aztecs describe the creation of a succession of worlds, with their world being the current one. Like many other cultures, the Aztecs also describe a great flood.

The Aztecs did not create their myths; instead, they adopted existing Toltec myths to conform to their own beliefs. They identified the major Toltec god, Quetzalcoatl, with Huitzilopochtli, who was the Aztec god of the sun and of war. Aztec/Toltec myths are unusual in that both gods and human beings are required to make sacrifices in order to preserve the life of the universe and the lives of people. In "The Five Worlds and

Their Suns," human beings who live in the first four worlds are unwilling to do this, so the gods punish them.

The need to sacrifice human beings to the sun was an important religious concept among the Aztecs. The Aztecs knew that the fiery rays of a motionless sun would destroy the earth, and they lived in fear that the sun would halt in the midst of its daily journey. They believed that the heart and blood, divine or human, would quench the hot sun's thirst and renew its strength so it could continue its journey. The Aztecs were known to go to war to obtain these human sacrifices, evoking hatred from neighboring cultures.

The fifth world acquires light because two gods are willing to sacrifice their lives for the sun. According to another myth, Quetzalcoatl later makes the same sacrifice that Nanautzin does in this myth.

As part of their religious tradition, each year the Aztecs chose a boy to live like a god for the coming year and then, on the anniversary of his selection, to die in order to revitalize the sun. During that year, this boy was honored as the earthly form of the god Tezcatlipoca. He was dressed in fine clothing, given eight servants to accompany him constantly, and trained in music and religious practices.

Twenty days before his day of sacrifice, the boy put on the clothes he would wear at his death and married four virgins, to whom the Aztecs gave the names of goddesses. The five days preceding his death were filled with feasting and dancing.

On the day of his sacrifice, the boy was transported in a canopy-covered canoe to the temple. As he climbed the temple steps, he played and broke a succession of flutes. When he reached the top, waiting priests bound him to an altar, cut out his heart, and offered it to the sun. Then a new boy was chosen to perform this role for the following year.

The remaining myths in the Creation Cycle explain other aspects of Aztec life. "The Creation of the Earth" explains why the earth also needs to feast upon human blood. In "The Creation of Human Beings," Quetzalcoatl injures himself to provide the blood that will bring life to a new race of people. "The Creation of Music" reveals the importance of music in the Aztec/Toltec culture. The language is unusually beautiful because the source of the myth is a poem.

THE CREATION CYCLE

The Five Worlds and Their Suns

Five worlds were created, each with its own sun, each following upon the death of the preceding one. The first world was illuminated by the sun of earth. The people of this first world acted improperly, so the gods punished them by causing jaguars to feast upon their flesh. No one survived, and their sun died along with them.

The second world was illuminated by the sun of air. Its people acted without wisdom, so hurricane winds descended upon the earth, and the people were punished by being turned into apes. Their sun died when they became animals.

The third world was illuminated by the sun of the rain of fire. Its people acted without respect and reverence for the gods, refusing to sacrifice to them, so they were punished by earthquakes, volcanic eruptions of fiery ash, and other forms of flaming death. Their sun burned along with them.

The fourth world was illuminated by the sun of water. The great god Quetzalcoatl created a race of human beings from ash. The people were very greedy, so they were punished by a great flood. Their sun drowned when most of the people were transformed into fish.

The Supreme Being tried to save one human couple from the deluge. His voice came to them and said, "Find a mighty tree, make a hole in the trunk large enough to hide in, and take refuge there until the flood waters recede. You will survive if you master your greed and eat only one corncob each."

The husband and wife eagerly obeyed the instructions of the Supreme Being. They found a great tree, took refuge in it, and survived the flood.

When the waters had receded, they looked upon a strange world. Fish lay twitching on the ground where animals once had roamed. "Why should we gnaw on a corncob when fish are so plentiful?" they asked one another.

They proceeded to break off dry twigs from their tree, make a fire, and roast one of the fish. The gods smelled the savory smoke and became enraged at the greed and disobedience of this couple. They descended upon them in wrath and cut off part of their heads, giving them brains the size of animals'. Then they transformed them into dogs.

Before the gods created the fifth world, our own world, they gathered together in the darkness to choose who would illuminate it by creating the fifth sun, the sun of four movements. This sun would combine within it the earlier four elements of earth, air, fire, and water. One wealthy god, lavishly dressed in shining feathers of the hummingbird and in jewels of turquoise and gold, volunteered—thinking more about the praise he would receive than about what the deed would entail.

"One will not be enough for this great deed," the gods said. "We need a second volunteer." Each god remained silent. Finally the gods asked, "Will you help us, Nanautzin?"

Nanautzin looked up in surprise. Never before had he been worthy of their attention. He knew that the other gods despised him because he was misshapen, ugly, covered with disgusting-looking sores, and dressed in plain clothing made from woven reeds.

"If you will help us bring forth a fifth world, we will truly value you!" they said.

"If you wish it, I will do it," Nanautzin replied.

The two gods spent the next four days purifying themselves for the sacrifice. Then they approached the blazing fire upon the stone altar with their best gifts. The customary offerings were hay, dead branches, cactus needles, and bloody thorns. However, the wealthy god made a mighty show as he offered nuggets of gold, rich feathers, and gems. Nanautzin's offering seemed scanty as he placed in the fire three bundles of three green reeds, hay, the scabs from his sores, and thorns covered with his own blood.

All of the gods then built a towering pyramid of stone, made a bonfire on top of it, and let it burn for four nights while they too purified themselves. Finally they said to the wealthy god, "We are ready. Now perform the deed that you said you would do. Light up the world."

"How do you expect me to do this?" the wealthy god asked.

"You must leap into the center of the flames!" the gods replied.

The wealthy god's heart filled with terror, but he was ashamed to go back on his word. Four times he gingerly approached the flaming bonfire, and four times he retreated in the face of the terrifying flames and the great heat. "I know I volunteered, but I just cannot do this," he admitted in shame.

"Then, Nanautzin, it is your turn to perform this great deed," the gods said.

So Nanautzin forced courage into his heart and jumped into the flames. As the fire burned away his life, his blazing clothing lighted up the sky and gave life to the sun. The wealthy, cowardly god felt that he had no choice but to follow Nanautzin's brave example, so he too gathered the courage to sacrifice his life and he cast himself into the flames. But because Nanautzin had courageously led the way, from that time forth it was he who was honored among the gods. Many even say that Nanautzin was a form of the great god Quetzalcoatl.

The Creation of the Earth

Quetzalcoatl, the light one, and Tezcatlipoca, the dark one, looked down from the sky and saw only water below. A monstrous goddess floated upon the water, eating whatever she could find with her many mouths, for every joint in her body contained eyes sharp enough to spot any source of food and mouths that bit like wild animals.

"We must find some way to stop that goddess from devouring whatever we create," the two gods said to one another.

So it came to pass that the two great gods transformed themselves into two huge serpents. One of them quickly grabbed the goddess by her arms, while the other quickly grabbed her by the feet. Then, before she could resist, they pulled until she broke apart in the middle. Her head and shoulders became the earth, while the lower part of her body rose into the sky and became the heavens.

The other gods were angry at what Quetzalcoatl and Tezcatlipoca had done to the goddess. They came down to earth and decided to give her gifts that would compensate for her mutilation. They decreed that whatever human beings needed for survival, she would provide. They created trees, tall grass, and flowers from her hair, fine grasses and tiny flowers from her skin, small caves, fountains, and wells from her eyes, large caves and rivers from her mouth, hills and valleys from her nose, and mountains from her shoulders.

The goddess is often unhappy. Sometimes in the night, people can hear her crying. Then they know that she is filled with a ravenous thirst for human blood. Whenever this thirst comes upon her, the goddess will not provide the fruits of the soil and will not stop crying until the blood from human hearts has quenched her thirst. She who provides sustenance for human lives demands human lives in return for her own sustenance. So it has always been; so it will ever be.

The Creation of Human Beings

In the fifth world, our own world, the great god Quetzalcoatl prepared to create a new race of human beings. First he decided that his creations must have nourishing food to eat. He set forth across the face of the earth, stopping to examine every plant and animal to see if that particular food would be best for his people.

When the ants showed him the grains of corn they ate, Quetzalcoatl decided that this was the food for which he had been searching. But he knew the ants would never give him their corn. He would have to steal it from them.

So Quetzalcoatl transformed himself into a black ant. Along with the other black ants, he laboriously transported the corn from the field to a place of storage, grain by precious grain. But Quetzalcoatl only pretended to store the corn for the ant community. He was really building an enormous pile of grains for the people he was about to create. Finally he collected enough corn in his secret hoard to enable him to teach his people to plant it and produce a crop for themselves. He resumed his normal shape, put the corn into a huge bag, and returned to the heavens with it.

Quetzalcoatl was now ready to turn his attention to the second part of his plan, the creation of our present race of human beings. Each day he flew across the heavens from east to west, following the path of the sun. Each night he traveled through the Underworld from west to east, emerging at dawn. During one of his night journeys through the Underworld, Quetzalcoatl decided to find the Lord of the Dead Land and take the first step toward creating the new race of human beings.

"I would like you to give me the bones of my father that are buried in this land," he said to the Lord of the Dead Land.

"Why should I do you this favor, Quetzalcoatl?" the Lord of the Dead Land asked. "Whatever is buried belongs to me. What do you intend to do with these bones?"

Quetzalcoatl replied, "These bones are very dear to me, since they are all that remains of my father. The gods want another race of human beings to live upon the earth, and I intend to create them from my father's bones."

"Here they are, then," the Lord of the Dead Land replied. "The bones will be yours once you perform the deed I require of you. Take this conch shell in one hand and carry the bones in your other hand. Blow into the shell, making a great sound, as you walk four times around that circle of jade."

Quetzalcoatl took the bones and the conch shell from the Lord of the Dead Land and began to walk around the jade circle. When he tried to blow into the shell, it made no sound, for something was blocking its interior.

Quetzalcoatl called on the worms and the bees who lived in the Underworld to help him. First the worms entered the shell and pushed through the substance that was blocking it. Then the bees entered the twisting passages and cleared out any material that the worms had left behind.

Once Quetzalcoatl had successfully blown on the conch shell as he walked around the circle of jade, the Lord of the Dead Land had said he could take the bones. However, the lord secretly told his servants to examine Quetzalcoatl before he left and make certain that the god left the bones behind.

When the servants commanded Quetzalcoatl to leave the bones behind, the great god did not know how to evade the order. He called on his nahual, his animal double, for advice.

"Pretend to leave the bones, Quetzalcoatl," his nahual replied. "Then, once the servants have returned to their master, pack up the bones and take them with you."

So Quetzalcoatl pretended to obey the order to leave the bones, but he carefully wrapped them up and returned to the upper world.

The Lord of the Dead Land was not deceived by Quetzalcoatl's actions. He said to his servants, "Quetzalcoatl has disobeyed my orders and has taken the bones with him. Dig a pit that will trap him and cause him to drop the bones."

The servants of the Lord of the Dead Land dug a pit in the earth and concealed it well with leafy branches and dirt. As they had planned, Quetzalcoatl tripped and fell into the trap. Birds threatened him so menacingly that the great god fainted from terror, dropping his precious package. The birds then pecked apart the wrappings and the bones within them.

When Quetzalcoatl awakened, he wept with grief at his plight. "Oh, my nahual," he cried. "What should I do now?"

"Do not despair," his nahual replied. "Make the best of it, and continue your journey."

Quetzalcoatl gathered up the bones that the birds had pecked into tiny pieces, wrapped them as best he could, and returned with them as he had intended.

The goddess Woman Snake ground the bits of his father's bones into bone meal and placed the meal in a jade bowl. Then Quetzalcoatl pierced his body and moistened the meal with his own blood. From this mixture he molded the new race of human beings, both male and female.

The Creation of Music

One day Tezcatlipoca, god of the heavens, came down to earth and wandered from place to place, observing all the beauties of nature. As he walked, he said to himself, "Earth Monster has brought forth mountains and valleys, rivers and streams, forests and meadows. In the light of Sun's rays, her flowers sparkle like brilliant jewels among her blades of grass. Clearly, there is much on Earth to please the hearts of human beings. Yet creation is not complete. Something is missing. Animals roar and people talk, but I hear no music! My heart is heavy with sadness, for music delights the soul as nothing else can."

So Tezcatlipoca summoned Quetzalcoatl, in his form as Wind. "Wind, hear my voice and come to me!" he called to each of the four corners of the world.

Wind groaned complainingly and reluctantly gathered himself together from where he lay scattered over Earth's surface. He rose higher than the tallest tree and the mightiest mountain, and in the form of a great black bird, he came forth to meet the god of the heavens.

Tezcatlipoca heard the waves rise in tumult from the ocean depths and crash with a roar upon the sandy shore. He heard the branches of the trees creak and moan as their leaves tossed and touched. He smiled. Quetzalcoatl had heard his voice, and he was coming.

Quetzalcoatl arrived quickly. As usual, his tempestuous disposition gave him an angry look even when he was quiet. He rested at Tezcatlipoca's feet without complaint.

"Quetzalcoatl," Tezcatlipoca began, "I find that ripe fruits, colorful flowers, and the brightness of Sun's rays make the whole earth beautiful. Yet, in spite of such beauty, Earth is sick with sadness! Not one beautiful sound fills the silence. Not one animal, bird, or human being can sing! Even you know only how to whine and howl, or moan and groan!

"Life must contain music! Music must accompany the awakening dawn. It must inspire the dreaming man. It must comfort the waiting mother. One must be able to hear it in the wings of the bird overhead and in the waters of the nearby brook.

"You must travel high above to the roof of the universe, find the house of Sun, Father of All Life, and ask him to give you musicians to live on Earth and add their beauty to the world. Surely Sun can do this, for he houses many musicians and a flaming choir whose brilliance sheds light upon the earth. Choose the best among both and return to Earth with them.

"When you reach the shore of the ocean," Tezcatlipoca concluded, "You will find my three servants, Water Monster, Water Woman, and Cane and Conch. Command them to unite their bodies and create a bridge on which you can travel up to Sun."

Quetzalcoatl agreed. As he traveled across the face of Earth, he heard what Tezcatlipoca had described, either sad silence or harsh, raucous chatter. When he reached the seashore he found Tezcatlipoca's three servants, who created the bridge for him. Even with the bridge, it took all of his mighty breath to bring him to the house of Sun.

Sun's musicians strode about the halls in colors appropriate to the music they played. Those who played cradle songs and melodies for children wore gleaming white. Those who played songs accompanying the epics of love or war wore brilliant red. Those who wandered with their music as minstrels among the clouds wore bright blue, and those who sat in the golden rays of Sun playing their flutes wore radiant yellow. Quetzalcoatl could not find a musician dressed in a dark, sad color, for there were no sad songs.

As soon as the Father of All Life saw Quetzalcoatl, he exclaimed, "Musicians! I see Wind, that turbulent pest who annoys Earth, approaching our peaceful kingdom. Be silent! I want to hear no singing! I want to hear no playing of instruments! Whoever makes a sound when Wind speaks will have to return to Earth with him, and you will find no music there."

Wind climbed the stairways to the halls of Sun. As soon as he saw the musicians, he raised his deep voice and shouted, "Musicians! Singers! Come with me!"

Not one musician or singer replied to his call.

Wind shouted again, more harshly, "Come, musicians! Come, singers! The Supreme Lord of the Universe summons you to join him!"

Again, not one musician or singer replied to his call. They remained in frozen silence in obedience to the wishes of flaming Sun, like a colorful array of dancers suspended in the midst of their dance.

Then Tezcatlipoca, God of the Heavens, expressed his rage. From the four corners of the sky, flocks of black storm clouds rumbled ominously toward the house of Sun, lashed forward by the whip of their lord's lightning bolts. Mighty roars of thunder poured from the great god's throat, engulfing the house of Sun in torrential sound.

The storm clouds swallowed Sun, Father of All Life, who drowned like a flaming beast. Shivering with terror, the musicians and singers flew into the lap of Wind, who lifted them gently—so as not to crush their music—and happily carried them down to Earth, who was waiting far below.

Meanwhile, Earth scanned the heavens with her dark eyes, watching for the first appearance of Wind. Her face shone with a special radiance and she smiled with delight upon seeing that Quetzalcoatl's quest had been successful. All life welcomed the wanderers. Trees lifted their leafy branches, birds fluttered their wings, people and animals raised their voices, and flowers and fruits lifted their faces in greeting.

Sun's musicians and singers landed happily upon Earth and wandered off in small groups. One could not travel to the most distant corners of the world without meeting singers and musicians all along the way. Even Wind was now happy. No longer did he sadly sigh, moan, and groan as he had in former days. He now sang along with the rest of all life, refreshing the trees of the forest, the meadows, and the ocean waters with his gentle breezes.

So it came to pass that Tezcatlipoca and Quetzalcoatl helped one another to create music upon Earth. Music accompanied the awakening dawn. It inspired the dreaming man. It comforted the waiting mother. One could hear it in the wings of the bird overhead and in the waters of the nearby brook. From that time forth, every living thing could create its own kind of music.

❧ QUESTIONS FOR
Response, Discussion, and Analysis

1. What is the reason for having a succession of worlds?

2. Why is it an ugly, sore-infested god who makes the supreme sacrifice? Why is it important that his sacrifice is accepted and he is honored?

3. What is the reason for sacrificing human beings to assure fertility? Can you think of another way to appease Earth?

4. What aspects of Toltec/Aztec life do these four creation myths explain?

5. Based on these creation myths, what human qualities does Quetzalcoatl possess? Give an example of each quality.

HISTORICAL BACKGROUND

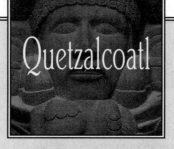

The myth of Quetzalcoatl and the Aztec creation myths are closely related, and the historical background preceding the creation myths applies here as well.

Scholars believe that the hero Quetzalcoatl is a combination of fact and myth. They may argue about whether Quetzalcoatl was one man or many, whether he was native to the Americas or a foreigner, whether he lived in one century or another. However, they all agree that his myth left a powerful, lasting impression on the major cultures of Central America.

An analysis of Quetzalcoatl's name reveals that he was a part of both the Toltec and the Mayan cultures. The quetzal is a rare, green-feathered bird found in the land of the Maya, particularly in Guatemala. *Co* is the Maya word for serpent, and *atl* is the Nahuatl word for water. *Coatl* is the Nahuatl word for snake. Consequently, Quetzalcoatl was a mythic being who combined earth (in the form of the snake), water, and air (in the form of a bird). He was identified with the wind, with the planet Venus, and, as a creator, with the sun. As the plumed serpent-god, he dominates the ancient monuments of Central America.

On the historical level, Quetzalcoatl was probably Topiltzin (Our Prince), the great leader of the Toltecs, a tenth-century-A.D. Nahuatl-speaking culture. Topiltzin had become a high priest of Quetzalcoatl, the great god of the Toltecs. He knew that other priests and kings had adopted Quetzalcoatl's name as the symbol of their own virtue. Consequently, once Topiltzin became king of the Toltecs, he changed his name to Quetzalcoatl. In 950, Topiltzin-Quetzalcoatl moved the capital of the Toltec nation to Tula, located fifty miles north of what is now Mexico City. There, he gave his people laws and ethical principles by which to live and taught them how to improve their standard of living. However, the historic Quetzalcoatl would not have had to teach his people to raise corn as food, because the peoples who inhabited Central America thousands of years before the Toltecs arrived already knew how to cultivate corn.

APPEAL AND VALUE

On the symbolic level, the myth of Quetzalcoatl may represent the conflict between those who supported Topiltzin in his desire to establish the benign, civilized Quetzalcoatl as the principal god of Tula and those who preferred to establish Quetzalcoatl's rival, the fierce warrior-god Tezcatlipoca, who exacted human hearts that were still beating and human blood that was freshly warm as part of his worship. Given the distinction between the two gods, the conflict had a political as well as a religious dimension, and the warlike Toltecs won.

The myth of Quetzalcoatl may also symbolize the conquest of the Toltec empire by the Aztecs. Tezcatlipoca was the god of the principal Aztec tribe, the Mexica. In the following myth, he destroys the Toltec people of Tula and succeeds in driving their ruler, Topiltzin-Quetzalcoatl, from power.

Two versions of the Quetzalcoatl myth exist. In one version, after

Quetzalcoatl becomes drunk and has sexual relations with his sister, he builds a funeral pyre and jumps into it just as Nanautzin does in the creation myth. In the version that follows, Tezcatlipoca successfully tempts both Quetzalcoatl and his people, first causing the king to become drunk and commit his immoral act, and then causing his people to bring their destruction upon themselves.

Tezcatlipoca is an unusually interesting figure. In the series of creation myths, he is a creator-god and a gift-giving god along with Quetzalcoatl. However, in the Quetzalcoatl myth, Tezcatlipoca is more than Quetzalcoatl's enemy. He is the dark side of Quetzalcoatl himself—his alter ego or double.

According to the Aztec tradition, Tezcatlipoca is invisible and intangible, which is most appropriate because his temptations represent all the evils that test the moral fiber of human beings. Whatever gifts he and Quetzalcoatl have given to human beings—food, wine, music, pride in self and country—Tezcatlipoca supplies in irresistible excess, and the gifts destroy the creatures they were designed to help. Even Quetzalcoatl himself, who personifies moral and ethical virtue, is unable to recognize his own weakness and his own potential for evil, thereby making it possible for Tezcatlipoca to destroy him. Everyone Tezcatlipoca destroys is ruled by emotion rather than by reason.

QUETZALCOATL

Quetzalcoatl was a large man. He often wore a conical cap made from the skin of the jaguar and a cloak made from the feathers of the quetzal bird. He wore a chain of seashells around his neck and a chain of rattles around his ankles. His voice was so strong that it could be heard for thirty miles. While he was alive, every cob of corn was as strong as a human being, pumpkins were as tall as human beings, and corn grew in many colors.

Quetzalcoatl was the son of Sun and the goddess Coatlicue. Coatlicue would sweep the heavens twice each day: once to usher in the night and the arrival of her children, the stars, and once to usher in the day and the arrival of her husband, Sun.

One day at twilight, after Sun had left the sky and Coatlicue's hundreds of children had yet to appear, a lone, multicolored feather floated down from the heavens. It was so lovely that Coatlicue picked it up and placed it in the neckline of her dress.

Later that night, when she had finished sweeping, Coatlicue sat down on the surface of the earth and rested. She reached for her feather, but she could not find it. She called to it, but it did not answer. In tears over her loss, she was heartbroken until she realized that she was pregnant.

When the stars heard that their mother was pregnant, they were determined to kill the father of the fetus. When they found that Sun was the father, they were not surprised. He was their father too, and they hated him. They were always attempting to kill him. As yet, they could not kill him for more than one night. In spite of their best efforts, every dawn he climbed into the eastern sky as usual.

It was not long before Quetzalcoatl was born, and in an even shorter time he grew to be the size of a nine-year-old. Soon thereafter, the stars killed Sun and buried his body in sand. Vultures saw the event as they flew through the sky. They quickly found Quetzalcoatl and told him of the murder. Quetzalcoatl sought the help of an eagle, a coyote, a wolf, and hundreds of moles, and together they followed the vultures to the burial site. The animals helped Quetzalcoatl dig up his father's body. Once again, the stars had been successful only temporarily.

When he had grown to be a man, Quetzalcoatl arrived as a stranger in the Toltec city of Tula. He taught the people how to raise corn and cotton, weave cloth, work with gold, jade, feathers, wood, and stone, and write, paint, and dance. Quetzalcoatl became famous for his moral principles. He had a great respect for all forms of life. He did not believe in killing flowers by picking them, or killing any of the animals of the forest. He became the ruler of the Toltec people, and even evil magicians could not tempt him to perform human sacrifices.

A powerful man, even when he is good, is never without enemies. Tezcatlipoca, who had worked with Quetzalcoatl to create the earth and to bring music to human beings, now wished to destroy his rival's power.

Tezcatlipoca was a formidable enemy. The Dark One had originally emerged from a cloud and descended to earth by means of a twisted spider's web. He was capable of performing deeds of virtue as well as deeds of evil. So great was his intelligence that he could create whatever his mind imagined. He could see into the depths of trees and rocks and into the minds and hearts of human beings. He had given human beings the gift of intelligence, and he was known to reward people who were good and to punish with disease those who were evil.

Once Tezcatlipoca set his mind to conquering Quetzalcoatl, he was clever enough to succeed where all others had failed. First, in the course of playing a game with Quetzalcoatl, Tezcatlipoca transformed himself into a jaguar and chased Quetzalcoatl from one community to another for the cruel enjoyment of it.

Next Tezcatlipoca held a mirror up to the ruler's face. "Oh," Quetzalcoatl groaned. "My skin is wrinkled like that of an ancient creature. My eyes look sunken like valleys in my face, and my eyelids are all puffed up. I am truly hideous to behold! I cannot walk the face of the earth if this is the way I look. I am so ugly that my people will be tempted to destroy me. I must leave the world of human beings!"

"Nonsense," Tezcatlipoca replied. "I can make you look handsome. Then you will be proud of yourself!"

Tezcatlipoca dressed Quetzalcoatl in splendid clothes. He covered his body with a robe made of feathers from the quetzal bird, he colored his face with red and yellow dye, and he placed a turquoise mask over his eyes. Finally he added a wig and a feathered beard. When his decoration was complete, he again held a mirror up to Quetzalcoatl's face. This time Quetzalcoatl was delighted. He looked so young and handsome that he gave up the idea of living a secluded life.

However, Tezcatlipoca had planted the seeds of fear in Quetzalcoatl's mind. His vision in the mirror had convinced him that he was an old man, and he began to have a great fear of death. Tezcatlipoca encourages this fear by offering Quetzalcoatl an intoxicating beverage. "Drink this, my friend," he said. "It will bring joy to your heart, peace to your mind, and youth to your body. It will chase away all thoughts of death as the rays of Sun scatter dark clouds."

"I have no interest in your drink, no matter what properties you say it possesses," Quetzalcoatl replied.

"Oh, come now!" Tezcatlipoca said. "You act like a man who is afraid of his own shadow! Dip the tip of your finger into the bowl and taste the wine. Surely you can have no fear of just a lick! How foolish you are being!"

Once Quetzalcoatl tasted the wine, he could not resist it. He drank bowl after bowl, until he had consumed five containers of wine and was very drunk. Quetzalcoatl's sister and his servants followed his lead, and soon they too had become very drunk. In this state, Quetzalcoatl no longer thought about living an honorable life. He forgot his religious practices and did whatever his senses enjoyed, without caring about the consequences.

When the effects of the wine eventually wore off, Quetzalcoatl realized that, among other immoral deeds, he had had sexual relations with his sister. He felt terribly ashamed. "Knowing what I have learned about myself, how can I walk among the Toltecs as a proud man?" he asked himself. "My people are weak. They need a strong man to lead them, a man they can admire and follow. However, if I leave them, they will only follow Tezcatlipoca. Surely they are better off if I remain their king."

So Quetzalcoatl remained king of the Toltecs. Tezcatlipoca also remained among them. "I have done all I need to do to destroy Quetzalcoatl," he said to himself. "Now it is time to destroy his people! I shall begin by making them sing themselves to death!"

Tezcatlipoca came before the Toltecs as a great entertainer, leading them in song after song. The people cheered as they sang along with him. They sang as the sun sank in the western sky. They sang as the stars appeared in the heavens. They sang throughout the night. The music Tezcatlipoca created pulsed within their hearts, faster and faster, stronger and stronger. One by one, their hearts cracked from the strain, and many collapsed and died.

Tezcatlipoca next transformed himself into a warrior and called the remaining Toltec men to join him in battle against a great enemy. Once they had assembled, he assumed his natural form and killed many more Toltecs.

Tezcatlipoca then transformed himself into a puppeteer. He appeared in the marketplace with a puppet of Quetzalcoatl and entertained the Toltecs by making the figure dance in the palm of his hand. The people gathered eagerly about him, captivated by his performance.

When he was satisfied with the size of his audience, Tezcatlipoca said, "Why are you watching us, you fools! Are we not trying to make you dance as, not long ago, we made you sing? Surely we deserve to be stoned to death! Who among you is sensible enough to throw the first stone?"

Tezcatlipoca goaded the Toltecs into stoning him. His body fell to earth as if rocks had killed him, and dreadful fumes began to issue from the fallen figure. Whoever smelled the fumes died. The wind blew the fumes throughout the city.

Finally Tezcatlipoca gave the Toltecs the courage to approach the figure and attempt to get rid of it. But the corpse turned out to be so heavy that it could not be budged.

In the meantime, the food the Toltecs raised began to have such a bitter taste that it was inedible. Before long the people began to starve to death. When they were desperate for food, Tezcatlipoca appeared in the marketplace in the guise of an old woman. He built a bonfire and began to roast kernels of corn.

The Toltec people could not resist the tantalizing aroma. It had been so long since they had eaten a tasty morsel that word spread like a summer storm, and they quickly gathered from all parts of the city, hoping to satisfy their hunger. When the last person had arrived, Tezcatlipoca assumed his natural form and killed them all.

So it came to pass that Tezcatlipoca destroyed Quetzalcoatl's people and forced their king to leave the city of Tula. Quetzalcoatl hid his wealth and his treasures deep within the mountains and canyons. He burned his rich palaces, turned cacao trees into desert brush, and ordered the birds to leave the area. Then he went on his way, traveling in a southeastern direction toward the sea.

At one point in his journey, Quetzalcoatl stopped, looked at his image in a mirror, and saw that he was as old as he had feared. In anger, he threw stones at a huge tree that was standing nearby; those stones have remained embedded in the trunk to this day.

At another point, Quetzalcoatl sat down to rest on a large rock. While he was sitting there, he wept tears the size and weight of hailstones. His body and his tears have left their impression upon that rock to this day.

Finally Quetzalcoatl came upon a group of demons who said, "Quetzalcoatl, stop and turn back! Where do you think you are going?"

"Sun has called me, and that is where I am going!" Quetzalcoatl replied.

"You may proceed, but only if you will agree to our conditions," the demons said. "You must toss away all your jewels and all your wealth. You must leave every skill that you possess with us: your ability to write, to cut gems and jade, to cast gold, to create objects from feathers, and to carve objects from wood and stone."

"If that is what I must do," Quetzalcoatl replied, "then I will do it. For I must go where Sun calls me."

Before he reached the end of his journey, Quetzalcoatl planted fiber-producing plants, built a ball court, built a house in the land of the dead, and proved that, even as an old man, he was strong enough to push a rock with his little finger that no other man could move at all.

Finally Quetzalcoatl reached the shore of the eastern sea. He wept with joy as he put on his feathered cloak and his turquoise mask. He climbed on a raft woven of snakes and set off toward Sun, who was beginning his morning journey across the heavens.

Some observers heard Quetzalcoatl exclaim, "Someday I will return to my people and my land!"

Others watched Quetzalcoatl's body burn up from the heat of Sun's rays. They say that his ashes became transformed into a colorful array of birds. The birds rose high into the air and carried his heart into the heavens, where it became the morning star that we call Venus.

1. Like many heroes, Quetzalcoatl has a remarkable birth. What is unusual about it, and how does it affect his heroic image?

2. What are the tasks Quetzalcoatl performs, and how do these accomplishments affect his heroic image?

3. Do you agree that a powerful person, even when he or she is good, is never without enemies? Defend your point of view.

4. Based on this myth, how are Quetzalcoatl and Tezcatlipoca alike? How are they different?

5. Like many heroes, Quetzalcoatl must confront tests of character in the form of temptations. What kinds of test does he face? What temptations does he find irresistible? Why?

6. What strength in Tezcatlipoca and what corresponding weakness in Quetzalcoatl make it possible for Tezcatlipoca to conquer Quetzalcoatl?

7. Why is Tezcatlipoca certain that he has destroyed Quetzalcoatl? In what way has he actually destroyed him?

8. How does Quetzalcoatl's behavior affect his heroic image? Do you think he is still a hero? Explain.

9. Why does Tezcatlipoca decide to destroy Quetzalcoatl's people? What qualities does Tezcatlipoca possess that enable him to destroy Quetzalcoatl's people? What qualities do the people possess that enable Tezcatlipoca to succeed?

10. How does Tezcatlipoca turn a person's good qualities into self-destructive qualities? Give examples.

11. What is ironic about the ways Tezcatlipoca chooses to destroy Quetzalcoatl's people?

12. Why did the creators of this myth have Tezcatlipoca destroy Quetzalcoatl and his people?

13. Why does Quetzalcoatl bury his wealth, turn sources of food into desert brush, and send away the birds before he leaves?

14. The Aztec emperor welcomed Cortes and his men because he believed that Cortes was Quetzalcoatl. Why would he welcome Quetzalcoatl back to Mexico?

15. Who is the greater being, Quetzalcoatl or Tezcatlipoca? Defend your choice.

HISTORICAL BACKGROUND

Sometime between A.D. 1000 and 1500, the people who became known as the Navajo left the northern woodlands, bringing with them the bow and arrow. They were accustomed to hunting and fishing, but they settled among the agriculturally oriented Pueblo peoples in northern New Mexico and northeastern Arizona.

The Navajo adapted the ideas of the peoples they met. When the Pueblo people fled from the Spanish invaders in the late 1500s, they took refuge among their Navajo neighbors. They introduced the Navajo to farming and weaving, and to their heritage of myths and religious ceremonies. With these new skills, the Navajo became known for their poetic, elaborate myths, their striking sandpaintings, and their beautiful blankets.

After the first Spanish colonists brought sheep, goats, and horses into New Mexico in 1598, the Navajo became a nation of shepherds. They also began to use Spanish silver and United States coins to fashion beautiful jewelry.

The Navajo nation, the largest group of Native Americans in the United States, presently comprises between 110,000 and 150,000 people. Most Navajos live on or near the Navajo reservation, a 24,000-square-mile area in northeastern Arizona, northwestern New Mexico, and southeastern Utah. This reservation is the largest in the United States and is comparable in size to West Virginia.

The Navajos are organized into matrilineal clans and, both on and off the reservation, often live in groups of extended families that are related through the women in the family. Women have social, political, economic, and religious importance in their society.

Agriculture is the basis of the Navajo economy. It includes the dry-farming of corn, beans, and squash and the herding of sheep. In addition, many Navajo men continue to be known for their beautiful work in silver jewelry, while Navajo women are recognized for their beautifully designed and woven wool rugs.

APPEAL AND VALUE

Every nation of people has an explanation of how it came into existence. In the Navajo creation myth, the Navajo progress from world to world and become more civilized as they move upward. Like other peoples, the first Navajo are created from a plentiful local material—in this case, two ears of corn. Like other peoples, the Navajo are the victims of a great flood—but the Navajo survive.

Four is a sacred number throughout the creation myth. There are four seasons, four directions, and four winds. The Navajo tradition also speaks of four sacred mountains (one in each of the four directions), four sacred colors (black, white, yellow, and blue), four sacred plants (corn, squash, beans, and tobacco), and a progression upward through four worlds. Moreover, four important human beings are created in the image of the gods (First Man, First Woman, First Boy, and First Girl).

One of the interesting aspects of this myth is the close relationship among insects, animals, and human beings. A distinctive feature of Native American mythology is the idea that all living creatures deserve respect, since they are all creations of the same Supreme Being.

The primary source for the following myth is Washington Matthews' *Navajo Legends,* published in 1897. Matthews continues to be respected for his pioneering research in Navajo religious ceremonies and texts during the last twenty years of the nineteenth century. He maintained the integrity of the material he transcribed by presenting it as it was believed and practiced and by preserving the inherent interrelationships that exist among the text, the songs, the prayers, and the sandpaintings.

THE EMERGENCE

In the beginning was the First World, or Black World. It consisted of a small area of solid land surrounded by burning resin, which provided the only available light. Most of the inhabitants were wingless insects and crawling creatures accustomed to living in holes in the ground, among them red ants, yellow beetles, black beetles, and white locusts. One day the insects gathered together and said, "This place is too small, too dark, and too unpleasant! We must find a new world that will be larger and lighter."

"How can we do that?" asked the ants. "You can see that we are surrounded by fire!"

Dragonfly replied, "We will all make wings for ourselves and fly toward the roof of our world."

The dragonflies, bees, flies, locusts, and ants tied wings to their bodies and flew upward. Locust noticed a crack in the roof through which a blue light came, and he led the insects through that crack into the next world.

The Second World, or Blue World, was larger and lighter than the First World. Each group of insects went off among the grasses and bushes to find a home. They had not gone far before four great birds, White Crane, Blue Heron, Yellow Loon, and Black Loon, flew from the four corners of the world and swooped down upon them. "This is our land!" the birds exclaimed. "You may not remain here! Besides, you will starve here for lack of food. We have to fly far away to the sea in order to find food, and your wings will never carry you that far."

"Have no concern for us," the insects replied. "We have no interest in your food. Here we have leaves, seeds, pollen, and honey. That is more than enough!"

"Then you may stay," the birds replied, "but see to it that you stay far away from us!"

So the insects remained in the Blue World. As time passed, they increased in number until there was not enough food to feed them all. In search of more food, they set out to find where the great birds lived. When the birds spied the swarms of insects flying toward them like great clouds of dust, they summoned all of their own kind to fight the invaders. Led by White Crane, Blue Heron, Yellow Loon, and Black Loon, the birds won the battle.

Locust gathered the surviving insects and announced, "We must move to another world. Follow me!"

With many birds flying in close pursuit, the insects followed Locust to the roof of the Blue World, where Blue Wind led them into the Third World, or Yellow World. This world was larger and brighter than the Blue World, and it was populated with animals and human beings. Together, these became known as First People.

Here there was food for all. Grass and bushes grew along springs and rivers, and the mountains that stood to the north, south, east, and west were covered with trees. All living creatures spoke the same language, and they all had the teeth, claws, feet, and wings of insects.

Human beings, however, wore their wings as part of their furry or feathered coats, which they could remove. They lived in caves, and they ate only food they could gather and eat raw, such as nuts, seeds, roots, and berries.

One autumn four gods—White Body, Blue Body, Yellow Body, and Black Body—appeared before First People for four days in succession. Each day they silently made signs and then departed. On the fourth day Black Body remained behind and said to First People, "The gods want to create people who look like them. Many of you have bodies like the gods, but you have the teeth, claws, and feet of insects and animals. Be clean and ready when we return to you in twelve days."

On the morning of the twelfth day, Black Body and Blue Body returned with two sacred buckskins. White Body returned carrying two perfect ears of corn, a white ear and a yellow ear. They placed the ears of corn on one of the buckskins, with the head of the buckskin facing west and the tips of the corn facing east. They placed an eagle's feather under each ear of corn, one from the white eagle under the white ear and one from the yellow eagle under the yellow ear. Then they covered both ears of corn with the second buckskin.

The White Wind entered from the east and the Yellow Wind from the west, and they blew on the ears of corn that lay between the two buckskins. When the gods lifted the upper buckskin, First People saw that the white ear of corn had become First Man and the yellow ear of corn had become First Woman. The winds had blown life into them just as they blow life into each of us.

For many years First People lived together peacefully in the Yellow World. Eventually, though, they increased in number until there was not enough food to feed them all. Those who were strong and fleet found food; those who were clever and stronger stole it. First People sent messengers to the four corners of the Yellow World to call all the people to assembly in order to choose one who would rule them all.

From the west came the Mountain People, who suggested that Mountain Lion should lead First People because he was both strong and wise. From the east came the Plains and Mesa Peoples, who suggested that Wolf should lead First People because he was both strong and clever. From the south came the Valley People, who suggested that Bluebird should lead First People because he was both wise and kind. From the north came the Forest People, who suggested that Hummingbird should lead First People because he was both swift and just.

When no group would accept the animal that another group suggested, Owl announced, "Let Lion return to his home in the west, Wolf to his home in the east, Bluebird to his home in the south, and Hummingbird to his home in the north. Let each of them bring back something that will help us. When we see what they can do for us, we can choose our leader."

Everyone agreed, and the four animals set forth. When eight days and nights had come and gone, Wolf returned. He was dressed all in white, from the cloud on his head and the robe on his body to the stalk of white corn and the white gourd rain-rattle in his hands. "Far to the east," he said, "I found these gifts for you: springtime rain, the light of morning, and young corn."

Wolf had hardly finished speaking when Bluebird arrived. He was dressed all in blue, from the cloud on his head and the robe on his body to the stalk of blue corn and the blue turquoise rattle in his hands. "Far to the south," he said, "I found these gifts for you: summer rain, blue sky, and soft corn."

Then, from the west, Lion arrived. He was dressed all in yellow, from the cloud on his head and the robe on his body to the stalk of yellow corn and the jasper rattle in his hands. "Far to the west," he said, "I found these gifts for you: autumn rain, evening light, and ripe corn."

Finally Hummingbird arrived from the north. He was dressed in the bright colors of the northern lights, from the cloud on his head and the robe on his body to the stalk of multicolored corn and the abalone-shell bowl of colored beans in his hands. "Far to the north," he said, "I found these gifts for you: northern lights for winter nights, dried corn and beans for winter food, and an abalone storage bowl that will always be full."

First People realized that they needed the gifts of all four leaders. They decided to be ruled by a council of wise people rather than by a single chief. From that day until this, in order to remind the Navajo people of the gifts they brought them, Wolf wears a silvery white coat, Bluebird a blue-feathered coat, Lion a coat of yellow fur, and Hummingbird a coat of many colors.

But solving the question of leadership did not solve the problem of food. First People did not know the proper way to plant the seeds they had, and they did not think to pray and bless the seeds before they planted them. Consequently, it was not long before First People knew that the time had come when they must move to another world or starve. They all flew up to the roof of the Yellow World, but they could find no cracks in it. They flew around and around, becoming more and more tired, but still they could see no way to enter the Fourth World.

Suddenly four voices called to them from the next world—one from the east, one from the south, one from the west, and one from the north. Four faces, each wearing a blue mask, were looking down from the four edges of the roof. First People divided into four groups, and each flew toward a different face. Those who became the first Navajo flew to the east and let First Woman direct them into the next world. The Bird People flew to the south and let First Girl direct them toward the warm part of the next world, where they spent each winter thereafter. The Animal People flew to the west and let First Man direct them toward the mountainous part of the next world, where they made their homes among the trees. The Insect People flew to the north and let First Boy direct them toward the cold part of the next world, where they immediately burrowed into the ground and waited for warmer weather.

To the surprise of First People, the Fourth World, or Black-and-White World, was already populated with other human beings. Their neighbors were the Hopi, Zuni, Acoma, and other Indians who lived in pueblos. They also met Comanche, Apache, and Ute nearby. First Man and First Woman taught their people how to live in the Fourth World, where the days were white and the nights were black. They added corn and beans to their diet of roots, seeds, nuts, and berries. "Learn from your neighbors who live in pueblos how to cultivate beans and corn," they advised.

First Man and First Woman had hardly finished talking when two dust columns blew upon them, one from the south and one from the north. The two columns met with a crash, deposited two bundles upon the land, rose into the air, and disappeared.

"Oh, dear!" First Man exclaimed. "The North Wind has given us Coyote, who thinks only of being lazy and playing tricks!"

"Do not worry!" First Woman responded. "The South Wind has brought us Badger, who has the industry and determination that Coyote lacks!"

One day Coyote went to the Pueblo People and challenged Water Monster to a game of chance. Since Coyote cheated, he won everything Water Monster had, even his fur coat. When Coyote returned home, he noticed Water Monster's two babies sleeping inside the pocket of their father's fur coat. "Oh, well! I will keep these along with the coat," he said. "And I will be very careful not to say one word about them."

When Water Monster found that Coyote had taken his babies along with his coat, his heart filled with rage. "I will destroy the land in the Fourth World and all the people who live on it!" he cried. He dived to the bottom of the sea and opened up all the dams that confined the waters beneath the earth. As these waters poured into the ocean, the sea rose and began to cover the dry land. As more and more water filled the ocean bed, more and more water washed upon the land in angry black waves. Higher and higher the waves stretched, until they formed a wall of water as tall as the highest mountains.

Turkey, who was a pet of First Man and First Woman, was the first to discover the invading flood. When people heard his story, they prepared to leave their homes and head for the high mountains to the west. The people were sad to leave their rich crops, but they had no choice.

Most of the Navajo, the Hopi, the Zuni, the Acoma, the Apache, the Ute, and the Plains Indians gathered a supply of food and necessary items and headed for the mountains. At the head of the procession was Coyote, who had Water Monster's children, along with many other possessions, in a great bag. By the time the last people reached the mountaintop, the land below them had completely disappeared under a great flood. Those who remained behind turned into water people, such as fish and seals.

Once the people had gathered on the mountain peak, one wise man from each of the thirty-two clans of the Navajo stood in a circle, and each of them planted a bamboo seed. For four days and nights the medicine men prayed for a quick, strong growth of bamboo. When the dawn of the fifth day arrived, the bamboo plants had joined together to form one huge, high, hollow, stalk-like tree. The people carved a door in the eastern side of the tree, and one by one went inside, using ladders they and Spider had made to climb higher and higher.

Turkey was the very last to reach the mountaintop. He had stopped to gather some of each kind of seed, which he buried in his feathers. White, blue, yellow, red, and multicolored corn, black and white beans, squash, melon, pumpkin, tobacco, and sunflower seeds were among them. As Turkey waddled up the trail, the black waters were angrily rushing upon him. Their foam brushed the tip of his tail as First Boy grabbed his head and pulled him inside the bamboo tree, and the marks of that foam remain on Turkey's tail feathers to this day.

Inside the tree, the people remained safe and dry. They showed First Woman the treasures they had brought from their homes in the Fourth World. Together they had collected everything they would need to begin life anew once the flood waters had receded. Only Turkey had remembered to bring the seeds of all the foods they ate, although these were the most important of all. The people honored Turkey for his good sense, and they honor him still.

As the black waters continued to swirl angrily around the great bamboo tree, rising higher and higher, the people climbed higher and higher inside the reed. Locust was the first to leave the bamboo stalk. He made a hole in the sky and won the island he found in the Fifth World for the peoples of the Fourth World. One by one the small animals entered the upper world, each using the treasures he or she had brought to make that world a better place. Badger, with a little help from Coyote, enlarged the tunnel so the creatures who were larger in size could also climb into the upper world.

So it came to pass that the last of the peoples of the Fourth World traveled up the tunnel into the Fifth World. The large animals were followed by the Hopi, the Zuni, and the other Pueblo people. The Apaches and the Plains Indians followed them. Finally the thirty-two Navajo clans emerged from the tunnel. First Woman was the last to leave. She brought Spider's ladder and the sacred eagle feathers. "From this time forth," she announced to her people, "we women will wear eagle feathers on our sacred headdresses, and we shall do the weaving for our people."

Even in the new land, the flood was still a threat. The angry waters continued to rise, and a lake began to form at the top of the tunnel. "Water Monster must be angry with us for some reason. Only he could create a flood as great as this!" First Woman exclaimed. "We had better find out what is wrong, or we shall all drown!"

"I am certain Coyote is to blame for our problem," First Man said. "Everywhere he goes, he wears a fur coat that is not even his. Let us search his possessions."

First Woman and First Man discovered Water Monster's babies in the fur coat Coyote had won."Look here!" First Woman exclaimed. "Coyote has Water Monster's two babies. No wonder Water Monster is punishing us with a great flood! We must return his children to him at once!"

First Man and First Woman placed Water Monster's coat, with his babies in the pocket, into a boat and sent the boat out into the lake. When the boat came near a large blue bubble floating in the middle of the lake, the bubble suddenly burst and the boat, coat, and babies disappeared. Water Monster never troubled the people again.

QUESTIONS FOR
Response, Discussion, and Analysis

1. What advantage exists in depicting living creatures becoming more complex and civilized as they move from one world to another?

2. How does this myth show a close relationship between human beings and animals? What does this reveal about the Navajo culture?

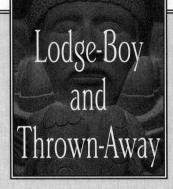

Lodge-Boy and Thrown-Away

The Native Americans known as the Crow are related to the Sioux. They traveled northwest into the Plains states sometime between A.D. 1200 and 1600. Originally they lived in small villages and farmed the land. The buffalo was not a major source of food at that time because it was so large and fast. However, after 1598, when the first Spanish colonists brought horses to New Mexico, the Crow way of life changed. The Spaniards traded their horses in exchange for peace with the Plains peoples, and a man on horseback could kill a buffalo. Native Americans measured wealth by their supply of food, and the buffalo made those who lived on the Northern Plains among the wealthiest native peoples in North America. Today, many of the Crow continue to live in southern Montana and to speak their native language.

tasks to make their community safer. Like all other heroes, they possess courage and skill. They also use their creative intelligence to compensate for their small size. They fit the heroic pattern of an unusual birth. What is most unusual and appealing about this myth is the fact that the heroes are young boys. Like ordinary boys their age, they cannot resist attempting anything their father tells them not to do.

The nature of these heroes and their adventures has probably contributed to the popularity of this myth, which exists in various but similar versions among the Native Americans who inhabited the Northern Plains. Stephen Chapman Simms included the following version in *Traditions of the Crows,* which was published in 1903.

APPEAL AND VALUE

Lodge-Boy and Thrown-Away are traditional heroes in that they perform many

LODGE-BOY AND THROWN-AWAY

One day while her husband was away on a hunt, a pregnant woman was murdered. The murderer cut open the victim, removed twin sons, and disposed of them separately. The murderer threw one behind the curtain in the tepee and the other into the spring.

The husband of the murdered woman returned home. As he sat eating dinner alone, his son Lodge-Boy, who had grown into a young boy, came out from behind the curtain and joined him. Thereafter, each day the father went out hunting, and each evening he returned to have dinner with his son.

One night Lodge-Boy said, "Father, I would like you to make me two bows and two sets of arrows."

His father made them and then hid to see how his son used the weapons. When he found Lodge-Boy playing with another boy of the same age, the father said, "Have your friend come and live with us!"

Lodge-Boy replied, "I will try to do that if you will make me a rawhide set of clothing. My friend lives in the spring and has the sharp teeth of an otter. Catching him will be difficult!"

The first day Lodge-Boy wore the rawhide suit, he enticed his brother, Thrown-Away, out of the spring by suggesting a game with the bows and arrows. In the course of an argument over the score, Lodge-Boy captured Thrown-Away and held him until their father arrived. Thrown-Away tried to bite Lodge-Boy, and the water in the spring flooded the land to aid him, but Lodge-Boy and their father were too strong. They carried Thrown-Away to the crest of a nearby hill, burned incense under his nose, and turned him into a human being. From that time on, both sons lived in the tepee with their father.

One day the boys decided to go to their mother's burial place and revive her. When they said, "Mother, your hide chest and your stone pot are both falling!" she sat up. When they said, "Mother, your bone crusher is falling!" she began to fix her hair. Then she exclaimed, "I have been sleeping a long time!" She stood up and returned home with her sons.

Another day the father said to his sons, "You may play wherever you wish, but do not go near the old woman who lives at the bend in the river. Whenever she sees a living creature, she tips her pot of boiling liquid in its direction. The creature is then pulled into her pot and boiled for her dinner."

The boys immediately went to the bend in the river, found the old woman asleep by her boiling pot, tilted the pot toward her, and watched as she was pulled into her own pot and boiled to death. They brought the pot home as a gift for their mother.

One day the father said to his sons, "You may play wherever you wish, but do not go over the hill."

The boys immediately went over the hill, where they found a huge serpent that resembled an alligator. The serpent opened its enormous mouth and swallowed the boys, and they found many other people inside. Some were dying, and some were already dead. The boys killed the serpent by cutting out its heart. Then they sliced open a passageway between its ribs, helped those who were still alive to escape, took a piece of the serpent's heart for their father, and returned home.

Another day the father said to his sons, "You may play wherever you wish, but do not go near the three trees that stand in the form of a triangle. They bend their branches to the ground and kill whatever comes beneath them!"

The boys immediately found the three trees. They ran toward them as if seeking the shade beneath their branches, but then they stopped short. The trees, expecting two victims, sent their branches crashing to the ground. The boys jumped on the bent branches and broke them so that they could never again rise and kill anyone.

One day the father said to his sons, "You may play wherever you wish, but do not go near the man who lives on top of the cliff with deep water at its base. He pushes anyone who comes near him over the cliff to become a meal for his father, who lives in the deep water!"

The boys immediately headed for the clifftop. As the man rushed toward them, the boys suddenly fell to the ground. The man could not stop running in time and fell off the cliff to become a meal for his father.

Another day the father said to his sons, "You may play wherever you wish, but do not go near the man who wears fiery moccasins. Whenever he wants anything, he walks upon it and burns it!"

The boys found the man and waited until he was asleep. They quietly stole his moccasins, and each boy put on one of them. Then they jumped on him, burned him to ashes, and carried the moccasins home.

One day as the brothers were walking, they felt themselves being lifted up and transported to the high peak of a mountain that rose out of a large lake. There they found themselves face to face with Thunder-Bird, who said, "I need your help. A great otter who lives in the lake below us eats all the young I produce. Please kill it for me!"

The boys prepared to kill the otter. First they made many arrows. Then they went down to the shore, built a fire, and heated many rocks. When the otter approached they shot their arrows into its open mouth, but the animal kept coming. They waited until it was within close range and then threw their hot rocks into its open mouth, killing it. Thunder-Bird thanked them and transported them back to their tepee, where they continued to live happily for many more years.

❧ **QUESTIONS FOR**
Response, Discussion, and Analysis

1. In what ways are the twins both courageous and skillful? Give examples.

2. How do the twins' accomplishments help their community?

3. Why did the creators of this myth make the heroes children? What are the advantages and limitations of having very young heroes? Do heroic children add to or detract from the appeal of a myth? Defend your point of view.

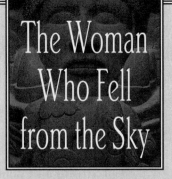

The Woman Who Fell from the Sky

The five Iroquois-speaking nations were, from east to west, the Mohawk (on the Atlantic coast), the Oneida, the Onondaga, the Cayuga (in central New York), and the Seneca (in the Lake Erie area). The Iroquois earned lasting fame by creating a great political organization, called the League of the Iroquois or the Confederacy of the Five Nations, in 1452. In its time, the League was more democratic than any other form of government, and it existed for more than 300 years. In fact, the League was such an impressive political structure that it influenced the formulation of the United States Constitution.

The fathers of the Iroquois League were Hiawatha, an Onondaga chief, and Deganawida, a Huron, each of whom had been adopted by the Mohawk nation. Organizing the League took political talent. The Onondaga joined on the condition that they would chair the council. Deganawida persuaded the fifth nation, the Seneca, to join by telling them to watch the sun when their corn became knee-high. They joined when, following his advice, they witnessed a total solar eclipse. The League enlarged to six nations in 1722, when the Tuscarora, an Iroquois nation that was then living in North Carolina, was admitted.

The Iroquois League was designed to facilitate equality, peace, and prosperity among its member nations. It was only concerned with the issue of war. The members decided that war could not occur without a unanimous vote, and that all the member nations would fight together on the same side. This agreement was a particularly great accomplishment, since the major way to achieve honor, fame, and glory was through war.

The League was run by fifty sachems or clan leaders, who had been nominated by women of noble rank in their nation and had been approved by their own nation's council. Each nation had proportional representation in the council. A second group of representatives—leaders who were called Pine Trees—could speak but not vote.

The Iroquois lived in stockaded villages that were organized according to matrilineal lines. All property was inherited through the mother. The women owned the houses in which they lived, taking their husbands in to live with them as visitors. The male head of the family was the brother of the oldest sister. Sisters and daughters lived in the same longhouse, which was large enough to house eight to ten families.

The women also owned the land and farmed their family's fields. They grew corn, squash, and beans. The Iroquois called the three crops the Three Sisters, believing that the crops were guarded by three spirit sisters.

In 1614, the Dutch navigated the Hudson River and built Fort Orange where Albany, New York, is located. The Iroquois traded beaver furs for Dutch guns and became wealthy and powerful. However, by the mid-1600s, they had exhausted the local beaver supply. In order to acquire the furs they needed to continue their trade, the Iroquois moved west and, in 1648, conquered the Huron, who also spoke the Iroquois language.

The Revolutionary War destroyed the Iroquois League by dividing the nations. The Mohawk, Seneca, Cayuga, and Onondaga peoples supported the British, while the Oneida and Tuscarora peoples supported the Americans. Consequently, in January 1777, the League's great council fire was extinguished in a formal ceremony.

In the years after the war, many of the Iroquois were given the land near Brantford, Ontario, that is known as the Six Nations Reserve. Today, more than 7,000 Iroquois live in that area. In the United States, most of the Oneida moved to Wisconsin in 1832, and most of the Seneca moved to Oklahoma.

The Iroquois council fire was rekindled in the l960s. As of 1971, the six nations were located on six reservations and had formed a modern republic. Many Iroquois continue to live within the Iroquois tradition, adhering to the values of their people and participating in longhouse ceremonies under the leadership of one of their chiefs.

The Huron, who call themselves the Wendat, were originally a confederation of four nations, numbering between 45,000 and 60,000 people when the Europeans first encountered them. The Huron lived in Ontario in large villages of from 4,000 to 6,000 people until the Iroquois destroyed most of them in 1648. The Huron took the side of the British in the Revolutionary War. Since 1867, many of them have lived in Oklahoma.

APPEAL AND VALUE

The special relationship between a divine grandparent and grandchild and the adventures of twin brothers are both common themes in mythology. When one twin is good and the other is evil, the twins can be viewed as representing the capability of any one human being to be both kind and cruel.

The Iroquois creation myth is remarkably similar from one Iroquois-speaking nation to another. One of the oldest versions was recorded by David Cusick, a Tuscarora Iroquois historian, whose *Sketches of Ancient History of the Six Nations* was first published in 1827. The oldest Huron version was related in 1874 by a seventy-five-year-old Huron sub-chief who had heard it as a child from those who had been alive in the mid-eighteenth century. It appears as part of Horatio Hale's "Huron Folklore," published in 1888. J. N. B. Hewitt, an important mythographer of Tuscarora descent, specialized in the Iroquois creation myth and collected detailed Mohawk, Seneca, and Onondaga versions for the Bureau of American Ethnology.

THE WOMAN WHO
FELL FROM THE SKY

When time was young, there were two worlds, the upper world and the lower world. Divine Sky People lived in the upper world. Great Water covered the earth in the lower world, and there the only living beings were the animals who knew how to swim. Great Darkness covered everything between Great Water and the upper world.

In the upper world, the Sky People had a great chief, who had a lovely daughter named Atahensic. It came to pass that the goddess Atahensic became very ill with a strange disease. The medicine man tried one remedy after another, but nothing would make her well.

A great corn tree stood near the chief's lodge and provided the Sky People with their principal food. It came to pass that a Sky Person dreamed that the goddess would be cured if the chief placed her on the ground by this tree and then dug up the great tree by its roots.

To the chief, the welfare of his daughter was more important than the welfare of his nation. Consequently, as soon as the chief heard the Sky Person's dream, he decided to follow its prescription without delay. He placed Atahensic beside the great corn tree and directed other Sky People to dig the earth away from its roots. The great tree soon toppled to the ground with a thunderous crash.

Alarmed by the terrifying sound, another Sky Person—a young man—ran toward the great corn tree and was horrified to see that it had been uprooted. It was clear that the chief had committed an outrageous act! The young man turned to his chief and unleashed his fury. "You have no right to destroy this tree!" he exclaimed. "Without its fruit, we will all die of starvation! Even the life of a chief's daughter is not that important!"

The removal of the corn tree's roots had left a large hole in the ground. The young man was so enraged that, before the chief could stop him, he kicked Atahensic into that hole.

Down, down, down the goddess fell, through the hole that formed a tunnel from the world above into the dark world below.

Loon was the first to see the glow that marked the fall of the goddess, and he decided to rescue her. He called out to the other water animals, "Look! Sky Woman is falling into our world! She needs our help, or she will drown!"

Loon caught Atahensic on his wings and then slowly descended with her to the Great Water on which he lived. Meanwhile, many of the animals wished to do their part to save Sky Woman's life, so they gathered together and made a raft of their bodies on which she could rest.

Sky Woman landed safely, and the animal raft was able to support her. However, the animals could not live forever in the form of a raft, and Sky Woman could not live forever upon their backs. The animals needed to rest, and the goddess needed to move about. So it came to pass that the water animals who were forming the raft said, "We must come up with a better plan to care for Sky Woman! We are all tired out! Do any of you have a good idea?"

Great Turtle was the first to volunteer. "Place her upon my back," he directed. "Mine is larger and stronger than all of yours put together!"

Once they had done this, Muskrat said, "That is all well and good, for now! But Sky Woman will surely die unless we can create a bed of earth upon which she can live. It will have to be large enough for her to be able to walk happily during the day and to sleep comfortably at night."

"I agree," Great Turtle said. "Those of you who think that you can do it should dive down to the bottom of Great Water, bite off a piece of the earth that you find there, and carry it back up here in your mouth."

It came to pass that Muskrat was the first to muster the courage necessary to make the deep dive. He was followed by Beaver, and then by Otter.

Beaver was the first to return alive. He was very tired and very short of breath, but when Great Turtle looked inside his mouth, he could find no earth. Otter returned quite a while after Beaver. He was more tired and more short of breath, but when Great Turtle looked inside his mouth, he could find no earth.

By this time, all of the water animals had become very worried about Muskrat, who had not yet returned from the deep. While they were discussing what to do, Muskrat's body suddenly reappeared on the surface of the water. He was dead. However, Muskrat had been as skillful as he was courageous, for clutched in his claws and lodged inside his mouth was earth from the bottom of the sea.

Great Turtle gave the earth to Sky Woman, who spread it carefully around the edges of Great Turtle's shell. The more earth she spread, the larger grew Great Turtle's shell and the more earth there was to spread. In fact, the earth continued to grow broader and deeper until it formed an enormous expanse of dry land, called Great Island. And from that day to this, Great Island has rested upon Great Turtle's shell.

It came to pass that on Great Island the goddess Atahensic recovered from her strange disease, just as the dreamer had dreamed she would. Sky Woman now built herself an earth lodge and, despite the eternal darkness, she lived happily with the water animals for neighbors. In time, she gave birth to a baby girl, who became known as Earth Woman.

It came to pass that one day, as Earth Woman was digging the wild potatoes that grew in the dirt of Great Island, she inadvertently forgot to face the west and, instead, faced the east. Not long after that, Earth Woman found that she had become pregnant. West Wind had blown into her body and had made her pregnant.

Just as her birth pangs were beginning, Earth Woman heard the twin sons within her body angrily arguing about when and how to be born. Evil Twin, who was bold and selfish, was determined to emerge first, from his mother's armpit. Good Twin, who was gentle and unselfish, was content to emerge second, in the usual way. So it came to pass that, while Good Twin was being born, Evil Twin impatiently burst forth from their mother's side, thereby causing her death.

Sky Woman buried Earth Woman on Great Island and reared her twin grandchildren by herself. Good Twin was her favorite. She had no love for Evil Twin, whom she blamed for the death of her daughter. Every day, she would sit by Earth Woman's grave and weep over her.

It came to pass that, in time, Good Twin became tired of living in eternal darkness. He told his brother, "I want to create a great light that will illuminate our world."

"Do not be absurd!" Evil Twin replied. "Our world is good enough as it is! Leave it alone!"

Despite his brother's opinion, Good Twin was determined to live in a bright world. Therefore, from his dead mother's face, he fashioned a brilliant sphere, which he tossed high into Great Darkness to shine upon Great Island each day. From the back of his mother's head, Good Twin then fashioned a smaller sphere and many tiny spheres, which he also tossed high into Great Darkness to shine upon Great Island each night. So it came to pass that Great Island and Great Water enjoyed Sun, Moon, and Stars, and with them, Day and Night.

It then came to pass that, nourished both by Sky Woman's tears and by Sun, the Three Sisters began to push through the earth that covered Earth Woman's body—the squash vine from what remained of Earth Woman's head, corn plants from her chest, and bean plants from her arms and legs. Good Twin loved these plants, and so he asked Thunder to provide the rain that they would need in order to flourish.

In their own time, the twin boys grew to become young men. They continued to have different personalities and different opinions. However, they agreed that the time had come to prepare Great Island for the Eagwehoewe people, who would soon live on it. They planned to start out together, to spend the day apart from each other, and to meet at their lodge, as usual, that night. When they separated, Evil Twin would walk toward the west, while Good Twin would walk toward the east. And, as they walked, each would create such things as lakes, forests, plants, and animals. Then, during the next two days, each brother would take the other to see what he had created.

So it came to pass that as Good Twin walked toward the east, he would reach down to the earth at his feet, pick up a handful of dirt, and toss it. Sometimes he tossed it in front of him; other times he tossed it behind him. Sometimes he tossed it to the right of him; other times he tossed it to the left of him. Sometimes he tossed it on the ground; other times he tossed it into the air. However, no matter where Good Twin tossed his handful of dirt, living plants or animals came into being. Meanwhile, wherever Good Twin had placed his feet, maple trees began to grow.

Still determined to be the first in everything, Evil Twin, whose Iroquois name means "like flint," was the first to show off his creations. Unlike Good Twin, he possessed an evil imagination and enjoyed creating mischief. Consequently, he had created a range of mountains on his part of Great Island. It was difficult to walk there because of all the rocks underfoot and the many treacherous ledges.

As they traveled, Good Twin was annoyed by the company of Mosquito, who was as large as Turkey. Finally, Good Twin told him to run away. Mosquito then ran toward a young tree, stuck his sharp, pointed nose into the slender trunk, and caused the tree to fall to the ground.

"You cannot do that, Mosquito!" Good Twin exclaimed. "The Eagwehoewe people are soon going to live on Great Island, and if this is what you do to a tree,

I can see what you will do to them! They are much weaker than a tree, and they will surely die from the thrust of your nose!"

With these words, Good Twin grabbed Mosquito and rubbed him between his hands until he had become very small. Then he opened his hands and blew Mosquito away. From that day to this, Mosquito has remained just as Good Twin changed him.

In the course of their walk, Evil Twin also showed Good Twin the fierce animals that he had made: Bear, Wolf, and Panther, as well as Fox, Porcupine, Raccoon, and Snake. These animals were all much larger than they are today.

Good Twin looked at these huge predators and exclaimed, "What have you done, Brother? The Eagwehoewe people are soon going to live on Great Island, and these fierce animals will surely kill them!"

Good Twin did not have the power to undo what his brother had created, but he was able to make each animal smaller, so that the Eagwehoewe people could hunt and trap them for their skin and their meat. It was then that Good Twin spied Partridge, whom he had created, but who was now on Evil Twin's land.

"What are you doing here, Partridge?" Good Twin asked him.

"Toad came onto our land and drank up all the water," Partridge replied. "I have heard that if there is any water left, I will only find it here in the land of Flint!"

"Where is Toad?" Good Twin asked his brother.

"I was just about to show him to you," Evil Twin replied. "Of all the animals that I have created, I love him the best! I have fashioned him to be so thirsty that he will drink every drop of fresh water on Great Island."

When Good Twin found Toad, he took one look at his bulging body and shot an arrow into his neck. Suddenly all of Great Island's fresh waters poured forth in a great waterfall that ran off in different directions as the first rivers.

Good Twin was quick to divide each river down the middle so that half the water flowed in one direction and half flowed in the other. "I want one side of every river always to flow downstream," he explained to his brother. "Then the Eagwehoewe people will not have to work at paddling their canoes. Instead, they can float with the current!"

"I cannot let you do this!" Evil Twin exclaimed. "The Eagwehoewe people will have to work for whatever they get!" And, with these words, Evil Twin changed all of his brother's rivers so that their waters flowed in only one direction. Moreover, he was not satisfied until he had placed waterfalls, whirlpools, and rapids in many places on each of them. From that day to this, the rivers have remained just as Evil Twin changed them.

Evil Twin was very angry that Good Twin had changed the animals, reptiles, and insects that he had created, but he did not say anything aloud. However, to himself he said, "Just wait until tomorrow, Brother, when you show me what you have created! You have seen what I have done to your rivers. Tomorrow, you will see what I will do to everything else that you have made to please the Eagwehoewe people!"

The following day, the twins walked toward the east so that Good Twin could show Evil Twin the fine animals and the beautiful trees that he had created.

Evil Twin was annoyed to see that the animals his brother had created—Buffalo, Elk, Deer, Dog, Rabbit, Squirrel, and Bird—would be useful to the Eagwehoewe people. They were so fat that they would be easy to catch and good to eat.

Later, Evil Twin returned to the area. Despite their cumbersome size, he quietly gathered together all of the animals that Good Twin had created and herded them toward a great cave. Using Good Twin's food as bait, he then imprisoned them inside the cave, blocking the entrance with a huge boulder. He smiled with satisfaction as he imagined how they would all die of starvation.

However, Bird had followed Evil Twin and watched him from above. Bird then flew to Good Twin and told him what Evil Twin had done. Good Twin followed Bird as he flew through the trees in the forest until, in time, Bird led him to discover the huge boulder that blocked the entrance to the cave. Good Twin gathered all his strength and pushed aside the boulder, permitting his animals to regain their freedom.

Evil Twin also noticed that his brother had created sycamore trees that produced sweet fruits and sugar-maple trees whose syrup dripped from the branches.

Of course, Evil Twin was not at all happy with what Good Twin had done. "Brother, I see that you and I can never agree on anything!" he exclaimed. "If I let you have your way, the Eagwehoewe people will have too happy a time! However, as you are beginning to see, I do not intend to let you have your way!"

So it came to pass that Evil Twin later went about from animal to animal, shaking each one until it became smaller and thinner. From that day to this, these animals have remained just as Evil Twin changed them.

Evil Twin then turned his attention to the sycamore tree and caused its fruit to become small and of no use. He changed the sugar-maple tree's syrup to a sweet water. And from that day to this, these trees have remained just as Evil Twin changed them.

It came to pass that one night not long thereafter, Earth Woman appeared to Good Twin in a dream. "Beware of your evil brother, my son!" she exclaimed. "He will try to kill you by any means. So, meet his treachery with your own!" And with these words, she disappeared.

The next morning, Evil Twin said to his brother, "It is clear that we will never be able to get along! I am furious with you for changing my creations, and you are furious with me for changing yours. So I suggest that we fight each other for the control of Great Island. Do you agree?"

"I agree to the idea of a contest, and I agree to the prize," Good Twin replied, "but I would like to avoid violence. We should just have a race."

"I agree to that," Evil Twin replied, "but I insist that the victor will then have the right to do whatever he wishes to the loser! And you may as well know that if I win—and, of course, I will win—I will take the wind of life from you!

"So tell me," Evil Twin concluded, "what is it that can hurt you? If you will confide in me, I will confide in you!"

"I fear the wild rose," Good Twin revealed.

"And I fear Buck's horns," Evil Twin confessed.

So it came to pass that once the twins had chosen their racing path, Evil Twin collected large quantities of the wild rose bush from their grandmother, the goddess Atahensic, who had created it. He placed its branches on the trees that grew along Good Twin's side of the path, and he scattered its flowers on the path itself. Meanwhile, Good Twin wandered through the forest collecting many of Buck's horns, which he then scattered upon Evil Twin's side of the path.

Just as the sun began its morning journey, the twins began their race. Evil Twin, who was always determined to be the first in everything, was so certain that he could outrun his brother that he permitted Good Twin to start first.

Evil Twin chased Good Twin all that day, tearing up mountains and trees like a great whirlwind as he raced after him. However, whenever Good Twin became tired, he would snatch some of the wild rose and eat it, thereby recovering his energy. Evil Twin found no such respite from his own fatigue because Buck's horns were constant thorns in his feet. Therefore, Evil Twin could not catch up to his brother that day. And no matter how Evil Twin pleaded, Good Twin would not stop and permit him to rest.

The sun began its journey on the second day while Evil Twin continued to chase Good Twin, tearing up mountains and trees like a great whirlwind as he raced after him. However, whenever Good Twin became tired, he would snatch some of the wild rose and eat it, thereby recovering his energy. Evil Twin found no such respite from his own fatigue because Buck's horns were constant thorns in his feet. Therefore, Evil Twin could not catch up to his brother that day. And no matter how Evil Twin pleaded, Good Twin would not stop and permit him to rest.

The sun was ending its journey on the second day when Good Twin became the first to reach the finish line. By this time, Evil Twin felt defeated by exhaustion as well as by the constant thrust of Buck's horns. He pleaded with Good Twin to let him stop where he was and rest, but Good Twin had the right of the victor to insist that his brother finish the race. At last, Evil Twin dragged himself to the end of the path and collapsed at Good Twin's feet.

"Do not kill me, Brother!" he pleaded.

"But, according to our agreement, that is exactly what I must do!" Good Twin exclaimed. "The idea of the contest was yours. The idea of the prize was yours. And, despite my objections, the idea of violence was yours. As the winner, I must treat you as you would have treated me if you had won!" And with these words, Good Twin picked up a branch of Buck's horns and beat his brother until the last wind of life had escaped from his body.

That night, the soul of Evil Twin came to Good Twin and said, "I would like to join you in our lodge."

"That I cannot permit you to do," Good Twin replied.

"Then, I bid you farewell, for you will never see me again!" Evil Twin exclaimed. "I will travel far to the northwest, to the Land of the Great Silence, and there I will wait for all among the Eagwehoewe people who die to join me. Know that, from this time forth and forever, it is I who will have power over the soul once the last wind of life leaves the body. The souls of the dead will leave Great Island and will live in my land forever." And with these words, Evil Twin left on his journey and became Evil Spirit.

Good Twin repaired the damage to the mountains and the trees that their chase had caused. Then he created the Eagwehoewe people, who would inhabit

Great Island. From the dirt at his feet, he formed a male and a female figure that resembled himself and his mother. He then bent down and breathed the wind of life into their nostrils, making their souls come alive. Then Good Twin disappeared from Great Island.

First Man and First Woman loved each other, and from their union the first six pairs of the Eagwehoewe people came forth from the heart of Great Island. They all spoke the Iroquois language, and they became the ancestors of all the Eagwehoewe people.

The first pair traveled toward where the sun begins its morning journey, and they settled beside a great river. They became the parents of the Mohawk people and the keepers of the eastern door. For two and a half days, the second pair traveled toward where the sun ends its journey, and they settled beside an enormous boulder. They became the parents of the Oneida, the "upright-stone people." The third pair continued to travel toward where the sun ends its journey, and they settled on Mount Onondaga. They became the parents of the Onondaga people and the keepers of the central council fire.

The fourth pair continued to travel toward where the sun ends its journey, and they settled by a long lake from which a mountain rises like a great pipe. They became the parents of the Cayuga, the "long-pipe people." The fifth pair continued to travel toward where the sun ends its journey, and they settled along the western border of the land of the Eagwehoewe people. They became the parents of the Seneca, the "great-hill people," and the keepers of the western door. The last pair traveled toward where the sun begins its morning journey and settled on the shore of Great Water. They became the parents of the Tuscarora people.

In the beginning, the first five families resolved that from that time forth and forever, despite differences in language and in location, they, their children, and their children's children would always understand each other and would remain united. It was they who established the great Iroquois nation. In time, the sixth family joined the Iroquois League.

So it came to pass that the Eagwehoewe people inhabited Great Island just as Good Twin had known they would. And their Confederacy of the Six Nations has brought everlasting fame to their nation.

**❧ QUESTIONS FOR
Response, Discussion, and Analysis**

1. Why is it that the female divinities create the earth and plant life, while the male divinities create animal life?

2. Why is there an Evil Twin as well as a Good Twin? Why are Good and Evil twins?

3. What is the significance of the fact that Good Twin kills Evil Twin? To what extent, if any, does Evil Twin's death reveal something important about the Iroquois view of life? Explain.

HISTORICAL BACKGROUND

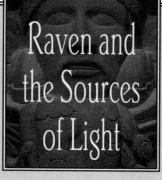

Raven and the Sources of Light

The Native American peoples known as the Haida, the Tsimshian, and the Tlingit settled along the Pacific Northwest Coast of Canada and the United States; the Haida in the Queen Charlotte Islands; the Tsimshian east of the Haida, along the coast of British Columbia; and the Tlingit from the southern part of the Alaska Panhandle north to Prince William Sound, near Anchorage, Alaska. They have traditionally been among the wealthiest of all Native American peoples because they have had the most abundant food supply. This, combined with the relatively moderate climate brought by the Japanese Current, gave them the time to develop a rich cultural heritage.

These peoples are known for their striking arts and crafts, their mythological dramas, performed in masks and costumes, and their potlatch feasts, in which the host would give an incredible array of valuable gifts to his or her guests (and would receive them in turn as a guest at another potlatch). The Haida, Tsimshian, and Tlingit peoples began to carve the totem poles that have made them famous some time between 1774 and 1779, when many American and European ships sailed up the Pacific Coast, bringing them their first iron tools and great wealth from the trade in sea-otter pelts.

APPEAL AND VALUE

The Haida, Tsimshian, and Tlingit peoples lived among animals of the forest, sea, and sky, and these animals provided them with both food and spiritual nourishment. The raven, the eagle, the crane, the whale, the salmon, and the bear are all familiar faces on their masks, totem poles, and carved wooden chests. In these cultures, animals are benefactors.

The role of Raven in this myth is that of animal hero and helper of human beings. In his study of the peoples of the Pacific Northwest, the anthropologist Franz Boas found forty-five principal myths about Raven. In Haida and Tlingit mythology, Raven is the bird called the raven. However, in Tsimshian mythology, Raven is the bird form of a supernatural being who often changes his shape. Raven is called Nankilslas (He Whose Voice Is Obeyed) in Haida mythology, Txamsem (Giant) in Tsimshian mythology, and Yetl (Raven) in Tlingit mythology. Moreover, depending on the particular myth, Raven may be a creator, a fertility-hero, or a trickster-hero.

The following myth combines Haida, Tsimshian, and Tlingit versions of the same myth. Although Raven is a creator, he is not a creator figure here. He brings light to the universe by taking what has already been created and placing it where it can benefit human beings. The Pacific Northwest is known for its heavy rainfall, so it is not surprising that the local Native American peoples have a myth about placing the sun in the heavens.

The major Raven myths are found in John Reed Swanton's *Haida Texts and Myths* (1905) and *Tlingit Myths and Texts* (1909), and in Franz Boas's *Tsimshian Mythology* (1916).

RAVEN AND THE
SOURCES OF LIGHT

Long ago when the world was young, the earth and all living creatures were shrouded in the darkness of an eternal night, for neither the sun nor the moon shone in the sky. It was said that a great chief who lived at the headwaters of the Nass River was keeping all this light for himself. But no one was certain, for the light was so carefully hidden that no one had ever actually seen it. The chief knew that his people were suffering, but he was a selfish man and did not care.

Raven was sad for his people, for he knew that without the sun the earth would not bring forth the food the Haida needed to survive. And without the moon his people could not see to catch fish at night. Raven decided to rescue the light. He knew that the way from the Queen Charlotte Islands to the source of the Nass River was very long, so he collected a group of pebbles. As he flew, whenever he became tired he dropped a pebble into the sea. And it formed an island where Raven could alight on solid land and rest for a while.

When Raven arrived at the chief's village, he said to himself, "I must find a way to live in the chief's house and capture the light." Raven thought and thought. At last he exclaimed, "I know just the way! I will change myself into something very small and wait in the stream to be caught."

So Raven transformed himself into a seed and floated on the surface of the nearby stream. When the chief's daughter came to draw water, Raven was ready. No matter how she tried to drink some of the water, the seed was always in her way. At last she tired of trying to remove it, and she drank it along with the water.

The woman became pregnant, and in time she gave birth to a son, who was Raven in disguise. The chief loved his grandson, and whatever the child wanted, his grandfather gave him.

As the boy crawled, he noticed many bags hanging on the walls of the lodge. One by one he pointed to them, and one by one his grandfather gave them to him. At last his grandfather gave him the bag that was filled with stars. The child rolled the bag around on the floor of the lodge, then suddenly let go of it. The bag immediately rose to the ceiling, drifted through the smoke hole, and flew up into the heavens. There it burst open, spilling the stars into the sky.

As the days passed, the boy still wanted to play with toys. He pointed to this bag and that box, stored here and there in his grandfather's lodge. His grandfather gave him whatever he chose.

At last the child cried, "Mae! Mae!" His grandfather took down a bag containing the moon and gave it to his grandson as a toy. The boy chuckled with delight as he rolled it around and around upon the floor of the lodge. Suddenly he let go of that bag just as he had let go of the bag of stars. The bag immediately rose to the ceiling, drifted through the smoke hole, and flew up into the heavens. There it burst open, spilling the moon into the sky.

The boy continued to play with bag after bag and box after box until one day he pointed to the last box left in the lodge. His grandfather took him upon his lap and said, "When I open this box, I am giving you the last and dearest of my possessions, the sun. Please take care of it!"

Then the chief closed the smoke hole and picked up the large wooden box he had kept hidden among other boxes in the shadows of one corner of the lodge. Inside the large box a second wooden box nestled in the wrappings of a spider's web, and inside that box, a third wooden box nestled. The chief opened box after box until he came to the eighth and smallest of the wooden boxes. As soon as the chief removed the sun from this box, his lodging was flooded with a brilliant light.

The child laughed with delight as his grandfather gave him the fiery ball to play with. He rolled the sun around the floor of the lodging until he tired of the game and pushed it aside. His grandfather then replaced the sun in its box and replaced the box inside the other seven boxes.

Day after day Raven and his grandfather repeated this process. Raven would point to the sun's box, play with it until he tired of it, and then watch as his grandfather put the fiery ball away into its series of boxes.

At last the day came when the chief was not as careful as usual. He forgot to close the smoke hole, and he no longer watched Raven play with the fiery ball. The child resumed his Raven shape, grasped the ball of light in his claws, and flew up through the smoke hole into the sky, traveling in the direction of the river.

When he spied people fishing in the dark, he alighted on a tree and said to them, "If you will give me some fish, I will give you some light."

At first they did not believe him. They knew that the light was well hidden and that Raven was often a lazy trickster. However, when Raven raised his wing and showed enough light for them to fish with ease, they gave him part of their catch. Day after day they repeated this procedure until Raven tired of eating fish.

At last Raven lifted his wing, grabbed the sun with both claws and tossed it high into the sky. "Now my people will have light both day and night!" he exclaimed. And from that day until this, the sun, moon, and stars have remained in the sky.

❧ QUESTIONS FOR
Response, Discussion, and Analysis

1. What does this myth reveal about the daily life of the people who created it?

2. What does this myth reveal about the personality of Raven? Would you enjoy having him as a friend? Explain.

3. What do the personality and the role of Raven reveal about the values and culture of the Haida, Tlingit, and Tsimshian peoples?

HISTORICAL BACKGROUND

Sedna

Ten thousand years ago, the ancestors of the Arctic peoples crossed the land bridge from Siberia to Alaska that today is known as the Bering Strait. Calling themselves the Inuit (the human beings), they remained in Alaska for about five thousand years and then began to move east across the Arctic, finally establishing themselves across a twelve-thousand-mile area that extends from eastern Siberia to lands east of Greenland. It was the neighboring Abnaki people who first called the Inuit by the name of Eskimo, an Algonquian term that means "eater of raw meat."

Although the Inuit have lived in Alaska for thousands of years, the Thule culture that identifies them is only about one thousand years old. It includes the use of dogsleds and boats made of animal skins. The Thule culture offered such great advantages over the previous way of life that, in less than four hundred years, it spread to all the Inuit communities from Alaska to Greenland.

The Inuit, now numbering about one hundred thousand, continue to live along the coasts of harsh lands, where the waterways are solid ice for all but the two summer months of each year. Those who live in small, isolated communities continue to live a traditional Inuit life as a society of hunters, and their life continues to focus on the annual cycle of procuring food. They hunt land animals, such as the caribou, and sea animals, such as the seal, and continue to rely upon these animals for food, clothing, and materials for their tents. However, today, supply boats bring modern food, clothing, building materials, rifles, outboard motors, and videotapes to large and small Inuit communities in the Canadian Arctic and Greenland. Many Inuit families use motor boats and snowmobiles, although dogsleds continue to be of major inportance in Greenland because of its mountainous terrain.

Some Inuit peoples no longer live in the traditional manner. In Alaska, members of the Inuit community have taken leading roles in the state's economic and political organizations. In Greenland, good Inuit students may choose to pursue higher education in Denmark. Many Inuit work in the radar warning stations and air bases that span the Arctic from Alaska to Greenland.

APPEAL AND VALUE

The myth of Sedna (She Down There) has been found among Inuit peoples across the Arctic. It is part of the oral tradition of a hunting people and thus reveals values that are important in the traditional Inuit culture. The Sedna myth reveals Inuit attitudes toward the relationship between men and women and reflects the harsh world in which the Inuit live. It also reflects the Inuit peoples' intense focus on the need to acquire food, the importance of land and sea animals to this hardy people, and their preoccupation with the need for balance and harmony as they interact with the natural world.

Sedna is one of the most powerful deities in mythology. She is the sole focus of Inuit myth and religious ritual and the supreme ruler of the Inuit supernatural world. She functions as the divine intermediary between the Inuit people and the animals (Sedna's children) that the Inuit need in order to survive.

Because she has been mistreated, Sedna is a hostile goddess, and she needs to be ritually appeased in order for the society to thrive. Sedna punishes her people by withholding their food supply whenever she feels that she has been insulted. Consequently, the Sedna myth reflects the Inuit need for taboos and, equally important, it sets forth rituals designed to appease Sedna and restore order whenever those taboos have been violated. These taboos and rituals enabled the traditional Inuit society to operate in an orderly and productive manner.

The Sedna myth also reveals the importance of the shaman, or medicine man, in Inuit society. In the eastern Arctic regions, the shaman must go into a trance that permits him, symbolically, to visit the goddess in her home beneath the sea in order to convince her to release her children—the animals on which the Inuit depend for food—for the well-being of the Inuit community. This ritual reflects the confidence of the Inuit people in their shaman's ability to increase their food supply when land and sea animals are scarce.

Today, some Inuit peoples continue to perform their traditional winter dances in which masked dancers enact their society's major myths. One such dance involves a woman named Ooyalu (the flinty-hearted, or the contrary woman), who rejects the many men who attempt to court her and is punished by being carried off by a monster.

Inuit myths were recorded by Franz Boas in the late 1800s and early 1900s, and by Knud Rasmussen in the early 1920s. The most famous version of the Sedna myth was originally told to Franz Boas in 1884–1885 by the Oqomiut and the Akudnirmiut people of southern Baffin Island, in Canada, shortly before Anglican missionaries converted those communities to Christianity. Franz Boas recorded this material in *The Central Eskimo*, published in 1888.

SEDNA

Long ago, an Inuit man lived alone with his daughter, Sedna, in a skin-covered tent on the shore of their lonely land. Sedna grew to be a beautiful maiden whom many young men wished to marry. However, no matter who approached her father and asked for her hand, he was not appealing to Sedna, so she refused to marry him.

Meanwhile, in another land across the water, a proud seabird—a stormy petrel or a fulmar—looked upon the female birds in his community with disdain and decided, instead, to choose a human wife from among the Inuit people. He flew over one Inuit household after another until he found the woman of his choice. Then he set about preparing for his conquest. He fashioned a striking sealskin parka to adorn his human form, and he built a swift kayak for his long journey.

Once the warm winds of spring caused the ice to break up, the bird-man kayaked to Sedna's homeland. He wore his magnificent parka because he was going to woo the most beautiful Inuit maiden to become his wife.

As he expected, the bird-man found Sedna by the shore of the sea, busily working at her tasks. Without beaching his kayak, he attracted Sedna's interest by calling to her from the water. Then, once her eyes rested upon him, he sang, "Come with me, my dear, to the land of my people, the land of the birds. There you will live in a beautiful skin tent, and you will sleep on the softest bearskin mat. My people will bring you whatever you wish. With the feathers they bring you, you can make your clothes. With the oil they bring you, you can light your lamp, and with the meat they bring you, you can cook your food. For my part, I will make you a necklace of ivory as a token of my love. Marry me, and put an end to cold, put an end to darkness, and put an end to hunger!"

Sedna was immediately impressed by such a handsome man. She loved the stranger's beautifully dark and intelligent eyes. She admired his magnificent seal-skin parka. And she longed for the luxury that he promised her in his song. At last, a suitor had come whom she could not resist.

Sedna ran to the tent, collected her few belongings in a sealskin bag, and announced to her father that she was leaving to marry the man of her choice. She did not care that the stranger was a bird-man, and no argument of her father's could convince her not to go. So Sedna returned to the stranger in the kayak, who had now beached his craft on the shore, climbed into the bow of his boat, and went off with him.

So it came to pass that Sedna became the wife of the well-dressed, promising stranger. The sea journey was difficult and tiring. When the couple finally reached the land of the seabird people, Sedna found that the bird-man's song had been nothing but a ruse to win her. Instead of having a tent made from beautiful skins, she had to live in a tent fashioned from smelly fish-skins that made so poor a cover that every blast of wind and flake of snow found its way inside. Instead of sleeping on a mat of the softest bearskin, she spent sleepless nights on the hard hide of the walrus. And instead of having tasty meat to eat, she had to eat whatever raw fish the seabirds brought her.

Sedna did not care that her husband loved her. She spent her long days and longer nights remembering all the suitors whom she had rejected with her proud heart. She would sing longingly to her father, saying, "Oh, Father! If you only knew how miserable I am, you would put your kayak into the water, paddle to this dreadful land, and rescue me from this terrible people! My tent does not shelter me; my bed does not comfort me; and my food does not nourish me! Oh, how I want to go home to my own people!"

In this way it came to pass that, once again, it was spring. Once the warm winds caused the ice to break up, Sedna's father paddled off in the direction that he had seen the stranger take his daughter, for he wanted to visit Sedna in her husband's homeland. He arrived to find that the bird-man was away fishing and that Sedna was home alone.

When Sedna's father saw how she was living, and when he heard Sedna's tales of her life among the arctic seabirds, his heart filled with rage. As soon as her husband returned, Sedna's father killed the deceitful bird-man who had enticed his daughter to come to this dreadful place. Then he took Sedna away with him in his kayak and paddled as quickly as he could toward their homeland.

It soon came to pass that the other seabirds returned to find that their friend had been murdered and that his wife had disappeared. Crying mournfully over their friend's death, they set out to sea in order to find and punish Sedna.

The seabirds did not have to fly far over the sea before they spied Sedna and her father in their kayak. Quick as the wind, they swooped down upon the water, stirring up a terrible windstorm as they violently flapped their wings. Their bodies darkened the sky, and the winds caused the waters of the sea to rise above the kayak in mountainous waves. The small boat was doomed to swamp and sink in such a sea!

Sedna's father knew that he was about to die unless he could think of a way to save himself. "This is no fault of mine!" he exclaimed to himself. "If Sedna had accepted a husband from one of our own people, this never would have happened! If I get rid of her, the seabirds may take pity on me and call off the storm-winds that are threatening my life!"

Sedna's father then grabbed his daughter and threw her overboard into the icy waters of the sea. "Take her, seabirds, if you really want her!" he shouted. "And let me return safely home!"

Having no wish to die an early death, Sedna swam to the surface and grabbed onto the edge of the kayak with her freezing fingers. Despite the tumult of the waves, she desperately hung on for her life!

Sedna's father, crazed by his own fears, took his sharp fishing knife and cut off Sedna's fingers from her nails down to the first joint. As her fingertips fell into the waves, her nails became whalebone, and her flesh became whales. They quickly swam away, very much at home in the tumultuous sea.

Sedna still had no wish to die an early death. So she once again grabbed onto the edge of the kayak, this time with what was left of her freezing fingers. Despite the tumult of the waves, she desperately hung on for her life!

Sedna's father, now more determined, took his sharp fishing knife and cut off Sedna's fingers from her first joint to the middle joint. As her bones and flesh fell into the waves, these pieces of her fingers became ringed seals. Like the whales, they quickly swam away, very much at home in the tumultuous sea.

Sedna still had no wish to die an early death. So she grabbed onto the edge of the kayak with what was left of her freezing fingers. Despite the tumult of the waves, she desperately hung on for her life!

Sedna's father, now even more determined, took his sharp fishing knife and, with two blows, first cut off the last of Sedna's fingers and then cut off her thumbs. As her bones and flesh fell into the waves, these pieces of her fingers became bearded ground-seals, while her thumbs became walruses. Like the whales and the ringed seals, the walruses quickly swam out to sea. However, the bearded seals swam in search of the nearest shore on which to make their home.

Watching the scene from above, the arctic seabirds flew away once Sedna's father had chopped off the last of her fingers and her thumbs. They knew that Sedna could no longer hang onto the kayak and so they were satisfied that she would drown. Their departure caused the winds to subside and calm waters to return.

Sedna's father then helped his daughter climb back into the kayak, and he paddled her back to their home. All the way home Sedna's heart pounded with rage against her father, and she thought and thought of how best to punish him for what he had done to her.

As soon as they arrived, they were greeted by her huskies. "That's the way!" Sedna exclaimed to herself. That night, when her father was asleep, she called her dogs into their tent and encouraged them to feed upon her father's hands and feet.

Her father awakened in agony and hurled a curse upon himself, his daughter, and her dogs. To his surprise, the earth began to rumble with a low roar. And as it rumbled, it began to shake. At first it shook so that one might hardly feel it. But then it shook more and more violently. Suddenly, the earth gave way beneath their home, engulfing daughter, father, dogs, and tent. Down, down, down they fell into the land of Adlivun, the Underworld. There, Sedna became its ruler and the supreme power in the universe.

From that day to this, Sedna lives at the bottom of the sea, where she rules over the living and the dead. Her hair remains in two fat braids, just as she wore it in her earlier life. However, she no longer has the fingers that are necessary in order to comb it. And so the animals that she created respond to her commands by giving themselves to those who are good and by hiding from everyone else.

Sedna insists that the Inuit people cook sea animals and land animals separately. To disobey this taboo angers her, and whenever Sedna becomes angry, her braided hair becomes tangled. She then withholds her animals from the Inuit hunters and creates the storms that swamp their kayaks and claim their lives.

Whenever this happens, the Inuit people must perform special, solemn ceremonies to win back Sedna's affection. Their shaman must make a spirit pilgrimage to her home beneath the sea, where he combs the tangles from her braided hair and pleads with her to forgive his people for breaking her taboos and to provide them with meat once again. Sedna is so happy to have the shaman's help that she generously rewards him and his people. Then, once again, the Inuit hunters find the animals that they desperately need in order to have food, clothing, and shelter in their harsh world.

❧ QUESTIONS FOR
Response, Discussion, and Analysis

1. What type of woman is Sedna? Choose two adjectives, and give an example from the myth to support each one.

2. To what extent, if any, is Sedna's father justified in killing the bird-man?

3. To what extent, if any, is Sedna's father justified in killing Sedna?

4. To what extent, if any, are the arctic seabirds justified in punishing Sedna for her husband's death?

5. What does a culture that has Sedna as its principal divinity reveal about itself?

HISTORICAL BACKGROUND

Caught by a Hair-String

The Micmacs were an Algonquian people who, for two thousand years, lived in the forested areas of Canada's maritime provinces, particularly in Nova Scotia and Prince Edward Island.

The name *Micmac* was given to these people by the French fur traders in the sixteenth century. The Micmacs called the French *nikmaq* (my kin-friends), and the French came to call the Micmacs by the same name. However, the Micmacs actually called themselves *Lnu'k* (the People).

Like the other Algonquian peoples, the Micmacs were involved in the fur trade with the French. The European demand for beaver pelts caused many wars between the Algonquian and the Iroquois peoples, who competed to trade their furs for European guns and metal implements. In time, the Micmacs were decimated by wars and disease. Finally, the surviving remnant ethnically disappeared through inter-marriage with the non-native communities.

The Micmacs lived in villages or camps, each composed of approximately one hundred families. Their society was patrilineal, with inheritance occurring from father to son. Their homes were long structures with rounded tops that were covered with birchbark. In small groups, the men hunted deer, elk, and beaver, which was the principal focus of the fur trade. They also used birchbark canoes to fish the waters of lakes, rivers, and streams.

Like the other Algonquian peoples, the Micmacs were known for their *wampumpeag,* or *wampum*—long strands or belts of strung beads made of seashell or bone. Long before the arrival of the French, men used wampum as money, as a memory device, and as a guarantee of an agreement. Women used strings of wampum as hair-ties, necklaces, bracelets, and belts, and as decoration for their head-coverings and their buckskin shirts. Strings of wampum played a role in marriages, where it was the custom for the groom's family to present the bride's family with wampum.

APPEAL AND VALUE

Like the other Algonquian peoples, the Micmacs viewed life as filled with dangers, and they felt the need to protect themselves against strangers, the animals that were their prey, and their enemies in war. Their myths reveal that they treated strangers with a blend of respect, caution, and self-assertion.

The Micmac both respected and feared the wildlife that they needed for their food, clothing, shelter, and trade. Possessing neither claws, wings, nor fins, the Micmac felt they were dependent upon the goodwill of their prey. Micmac society attributed supernatural qualities to the creatures of land, sea, and air, believing that they once had possessed human form and that they still had the power to adopt it if they chose to do so. Consequently, the Micmacs lived in a world that was infused with spirits, and they valued spiritual power in matters of marriage, hunting, and war.

The bones of animals had religious importance in Micmac society. The

Micmac believed that, after a creature's death, its spirit watched the hunter to be certain that he treated its bones with proper respect. The bones of water creatures had to be tossed back into the water, whereas the skulls of land creatures had to be hung up to the accompaniment of prayers and other rituals.

Some among the Micmac people developed the ability to surpass others in their perceptions and their talents. Such power usually came to a person who was already different from everyone else in some way and, therefore, already socially isolated from the group. This person acquired power privately, at some time when he or she was alone. This often occurred, either literally or symbolically, when the person was deep in the forest, through an encounter with a supernatural being who possessed the power and could confer it upon others.

However, Micmac myths reveal how society exacted a toll from those who gained such power. The unusually successful husband, hunter, or warrior separated himself from his more ordinary neighbors, and they retaliated by treating him with a hostility that reflected their jealousy, resentment, hatred, and fear. In extreme situations, the villagers ostracized and even banished from their community those who had spiritual power.

The medicine man held an important position in the Micmac world. Part of a medicine man's training involved a ritualistic form of death, which symbolized his leaving his old life behind and entering a new life in which he now possessed greater perception and comprehension.

Like the myths of all peoples, Micmac myths both preserve a particular way of viewing the world and enhance our own perception of the world in which we live. This is particularly true when the mythographer has the ability to communicate the spiritual nature of one people to those of a different culture. Silas T. Rand's *Legends of the Micmacs,* published in 1894, is an early source of Micmac mythology.

CAUGHT BY A HAIR-STRING

Deep in the woods, on the outer edge of a large camp of the People, lived an old man and his wife. They had two daughters who were very beautiful but were so shy that they hid from anyone who wished to see them. One suitor after another wished to marry them, but neither daughter would consider any of these young men.

Now the chief of the People had a son who wished to marry one of these daughters. So, as was the custom, the chief accompanied his son to the wigwam of the old couple one evening when the sun had gone to its rest. They had a fine time together, eating, playing games, and telling stories. Meanwhile, the maidens hid behind a screen in the wigwam so that they could listen to the chief and his son without being seen by them.

When it came time to leave, the chief announced, "My son is a fine hunter. He will be a fine husband. He wishes to marry one of your daughters, and it is time that he had sons of his own."

To these words, the maidens' father replied, "Thank you. I will have some word for you when the sun begins its morning journey."

After the chief and his son had gone, the father asked his daughters how they felt about this opportunity. The older daughter replied for both of them, "We do not choose to marry, even the son of the chief."

When the sun began its morning journey, the father kept his word and passed his daughters' words onto the chief, who repeated them to his son. Those words put great sadness into his son's heart.

Meanwhile, another young man lived among the People. He was very lazy and unattractive-looking, and he liked to joke about serious matters. The People wondered what maiden would ever want him for a husband!

When this young man heard that the beautiful maidens had rejected even the son of the chief, he laughed and bragged to his friends, "Those young women may have rejected everyone else, but they would not reject me!"

His friends could not resist such a challenge. "Is that so!" they exclaimed. "As soon as the sun has gone to its rest, let us go together to the wigwam of these young women. We should be clever and plan to arrive while the family is eating. We will surprise the maidens and get a good look at them before they have a chance to hide! Then we will see what comes of our visit!"

So it came to pass that the group of young men, the lazy and unattractive-looking fellow among them, appeared at the wigwam. They were in time to surprise the old couples' beautiful, shy daughters, and they were invited inside for a visit.

The young men spent the evening with the old couple and their daughters who, having been discovered, did not retreat from view. They had a fine time together, eating, playing games, and telling stories. The wigwam was filled with the joyous sounds of youthful laughter. Then, when it came time to leave, the young men all returned to their wigwams.

Not once during the evening had the lazy and unattractive-looking young man mentioned the idea of marriage, and, of course, none of his friends had mentioned it either. Before they went their separate ways, his friends laughingly said to him, "You have shown that you are one for big words and small deeds! We all had a fine visit, but it did not get you a wife for all that!"

Many moons came and went. One day, the lazy and unattractive-looking young man was hunting deep in the woods when he came upon a very old woman. She was sitting upon the trunk of a large tree, and she was so old that her weathered face was as wrinkled as a dried apple. She had pulled and twisted her gray hair into a bun at the back of her neck, and she had fastened it with many long and beautifully designed beaded hair-strings. These hair-strings hung over her rounded shoulders and draped over her clothing like a beaded robe that, in her seated position, reached down to touch her moccasins.

Upon seeing the lazy and unattractive-looking young man, the old woman looked up at him, her youthful eyes shining between strands of her hair-strings. "Where are you going, my grandson?" she asked.

"Oh, I am just walking through the woods," he replied. "But what about you, Grandmother? What brings you to this solitary part of the woods, so far from your wigwam?"

"Oh, I have not come as far as all that!" the old woman exclaimed. "I hear, my grandchild, that you would like to marry one of the two beautiful but shy daughters of the old ones who live on the outer edge of your camp."

"That is not correct," the lazy and unattractive-looking young man replied. "I was just bragging about that to my friends in order to give them a good laugh."

"You must tell me the truth in your heart, my grandson," the old woman replied, "because, if you wish it, I am able to help you win the love of one of those daughters and become her husband. Would you like that?"

"Oh, yes, Grandmother!" the lazy and unattractive-looking young man replied. "Just tell me what to do, and I will do whatever you advise."

"Then take this beaded hair-string that I am giving you," the old woman responded, "and put it into your medicine pouch. Do not tell anyone about my gift or our meeting. Just keep my hair-string with you until you happen to see the young woman whom you would choose to marry. Then approach her and, without making her aware of what you are doing, lay my hair-string upon her back." And with these words, the old woman disappeared.

So it came to pass that the lazy and unattractive-looking young man gathered his friends together and suggested to them, "As soon as the sun has gone to its rest, let us once again go together to the wigwam of the two beautiful, shy young women, and let us see what comes of our visit! Once again, we should be clever and plan to arrive while the family is eating. And, once again, we should surprise the maidens so that we get to spend the evening with them before they have a chance to hide!"

They readily agreed. So it came to pass that, once again, the group of young men, with the lazy and unattractive-looking fellow among them, appeared at the wigwam. They were in time to surprise the old couples' beautiful, shy daughters, and they were invited inside for a visit.

The young men spent the evening with the old couple and their beautiful daughters who, once again, having been discovered, did not retreat from view. They had a fine time together, eating, playing games, and telling stories. The wigwam was filled with the joyous sounds of youthful laughter. Then, when it came time to leave, the young men all returned to their wigwams.

Not once during the evening had the lazy and unattractive-looking young man mentioned the idea of marriage, and, of course, none of his friends had mentioned it either. Before they went their separate ways, his friends laughingly said to him, "Once again, you have shown that you are one for big words and small deeds! We all had a fine visit, but it did not get you a wife for all that!"

However, during one of the games, the lazy and unattractive-looking young man had found an opportunity to approach the younger sister. Without making her or anyone else aware of what he was doing, he had placed the old grandmother's beaded hair-string upon the back of the maiden of his choice.

When the sun began its morning journey, the lazy and unattractive-looking young man decided to take another walk deep into the woods. This time, he was not hunting animals, and he was not hunting beaded hair-strings. He was hunting the maiden whom he would marry!

The lazy and unattractive-looking young man was not surprised when he suddenly came upon the younger of the two beautiful, shy sisters walking all alone in the woods. The power of the hair-string had brought her to where the two of them would be able to speak to one another without the companionship of relatives or friends.

"What are you doing here in the woods?" the shy younger sister asked the lazy and unattractive-looking young man.

"That is an easy question," he replied. "I always hunt in these woods. But I have never found one such as you so far from our camp! Tell me, why is it that I have found you here alone? Have you lost your way?"

To his words, the shy younger sister only replied, "No, I have not lost my way."

"Then, if you are willing to have me accompany you, I will take you home to your mother and father," the lazy and unattractive-looking young man responded. "And if you are willing, I will tell them that I found you lost deep in the woods."

To his words, the shy younger sister replied, "I will accompany you, and you may tell my mother and father that you found me lost deep in the woods."

When the lazy and unattractive-looking young man brought the old couple's younger daughter back to them and told them how he had found her, her father said to him, "If you wish to marry my younger daughter, she is yours!"

The lazy and unattractive-looking young man was delighted, and the marriage was celebrated by a feast that all the People attended. Not long after that, a day came when the young husband found that his wife was wearing the beaded hair-string.

Taking his wife's beautiful face in his hands, he looked lovingly upon her and asked, "Where did you get this handsome hair-string?"

"Oh, one night I found it where I sleep," she replied.

The young husband thought of the old grandmother, her power, and his good fortune, and he smiled.

Once the lazy and unattractive-looking young man had acquired his beautiful wife, his thoughts turned to the chief's son, who had not been as fortunate as he in his attempt to win one of the two shy sisters. He liked the thought that, through marriage, they might become brothers, and he decided to see what he could do about it.

So it came to pass that the lazy and unattractive-looking husband went to visit the chief's son and said to him, "Now that I have married one of the two beautiful, shy maidens, the sister of my wife must be very lonely. Surely, now she would like to share her nights with one who would be as dear to her as her sister."

"I think that your words speak the truth," the chief's son replied. "I know, because I am also alone."

"You may not have noticed, but my wife now wears a very beautiful beaded hair-string that someone found in the woods. It seems to me that her sister might also like to be able to wear a beautiful beaded hair-string like that," the lazy and unattractive-looking husband suggested.

"Let me know when you plan to go hunting again in the woods, and I may go with you," the chief's son replied.

So it came to pass that when the sun began its morning journey, it looked down upon two young men who were walking deep into the woods. They were hunting, but they were not hunting animals. They were hunting beaded hair-strings!

Suddenly, the two young men came upon a very old woman. She was sitting upon the trunk of a large tree, and she was so old that her weathered face was as wrinkled as a dried apple. She had pulled and twisted her gray hair into a bun at the back of her neck, and she had fastened it with many long and beautifully designed beaded hair-strings. These hair-strings hung over her rounded shoulders and draped over her clothing like a beaded robe that, in her seated position, reached down to touch her moccasins.

Upon seeing the chief's son, the old woman looked up at him, her youthful eyes shining between strands of her hair-strings. "Where are you going, my grandson?" she asked.

"Oh, I am just walking through the woods," he replied. "But what about you, Grandmother? What brings you to this solitary part of the woods, so far from your wigwam?"

"Oh, I have not come as far as all that!" the old woman exclaimed. "I hear, my grandchild, that you would like to marry the elder of the two beautiful but shy daughters of the old ones who live on the outer edge of your camp."

"Well, yes, Grandmother!" the chief's son replied. "I have thought about that maiden now and then."

"Then this is what I would have you do," the old woman responded. "Take this beaded hair-string that I am giving you, and put it into your medicine pouch. Your brother will tell you what to do with it. Do not tell anyone about my gift or about our meeting. Just have many sons!" And with these words, the old woman disappeared.

So it came to pass that the chief and his son appeared at the wigwam once again. This time, they were in time to surprise the old couples' beautiful, shy elder daughter, and they were invited inside for a visit.

The chief and his son spent the evening with the old couple and their beautiful daughter who, having been discovered, did not retreat from view. They had a fine time together, eating, playing games, and telling stories. And during one of the games, the chief's son found an opportunity to approach the elder daughter. Without making her or anyone else aware of what he was doing, he placed the old grandmother's beaded hair-string upon her back.

When the sun began its morning journey, the chief's son decided to take another walk deep into the woods. This time, he was not hunting animals, and he was not hunting beaded hair-strings. He was hunting the maiden whom he would marry!

The chief's son was not surprised when he suddenly came upon the elder of the two beautiful, shy sisters walking all alone in the woods. The power of the hair-string had brought her to where the two of them would be able to speak to one another without the companionship of relatives or friends.

"What are you doing here in the woods?" the shy elder sister asked the chief's son.

"That is an easy question," he replied. "I always hunt in these woods. But I have never found one such as you so far from our camp! Tell me, why is it that I have found you here alone? Have you lost your way?"

To his words, the shy elder sister only replied, "No, I have not lost my way."

"Then, if you are willing to have me accompany you, I will take you home to your mother and father," he responded. "And if you are willing, I will tell them that I found you lost deep in the woods."

To his words, the shy elder sister replied, "I will accompany you, and you may tell my mother and father that you found me lost deep in the woods."

When the chief's son brought the old couple's elder daughter back to them and told them how he had found her, her father said to him, "If you wish to marry my elder daughter, she is yours!"

The chief's son was delighted, and the marriage was celebrated by a great feast that all the People attended. It pleased the new husband to see that his wife was wearing the beautiful beaded hair-string on this special occasion.

So it came to pass that the lazy and unattractive-looking husband and the chief's son became brothers. Like brothers, they always hunted together, and like brothers, they always talked together.

One day, the chief's son said to his brother, "If a person wanted to learn how to become a fast runner, it would be possible, although not many know how to teach this skill."

"That would, indeed, be a useful thing to know!" exclaimed the lazy and unattractive-looking husband. "Such a person could find more animals, and he could escape from his enemies. A person who knows how to teach this can find someone who wants to learn it!"

"Then," the chief's son advised his brother, "you must capture feathers from the birds in the woods, and you must save them for a day when the wind loves to whistle. On that day, free the feathers so that you and the wind can chase them. Let the wind chase you as you chase the feathers, and you will find that the power will grow in you and enable you to run faster than the feathers, faster than the wind, and, of course, faster than any other man. And once you can do this, you will always be able to do it!"

So it came to pass that the lazy and unattractive-looking husband became the fastest of runners.

Another day, the chief's son said to his brother, "If a person wanted to learn how to escape from a great danger, it would be possible, although not many know how to teach this skill."

"That would, indeed, be a useful thing to know!" exclaimed the lazy and unattractive-looking husband. "Such a person might find an animal that he cannot kill, or he might find an animal that can run even faster than he can. Then he would have to have the skill to save his life. A person who knows how to teach this can find someone who wants to learn it!"

"First," the chief's son advised his brother, "you must find some very old clothes, and wear them over your own. Then you must find someone and make him angry enough to grab you. As soon as he grabs you, you must pull yourself out of the old clothes, and run from him. You will find that the power will grow in you and enable you to do this. This man, like any man or animal, will believe that you are still inside the old clothes, and long after you have escaped to a safe distance, he will remain behind with those clothes, attacking and killing what he believes to be you. In this way, you can escape from any animal and, of course, from any man. And once you can do this, you will always be able to do it!"

So it came to pass that the lazy and unattractive-looking husband became the fastest at escaping danger.

Another time, the two young men were paddling a canoe down the river when the chief's son said to his brother, "If a person wanted to learn to see where all the moose in the woods are hiding, it would be possible, although not many know how to teach this skill."

"That would, indeed, be a useful thing to know!" exclaimed the lazy and unattractive-looking husband. "Such a person would become the greatest hunter and would provide the People with much more meat to eat and fur to wear. A person who knows how to teach this can find someone who wants to learn it!"

"First," the chief's son advised his brother, "you must catch some moose hair from the moose in the woods, roll it into a ball between your forefinger and your thumb, and then save it for a day when the wind loves to whistle. Then, on that day, you must free the fur ball so that the wind can chase it. You will find that the power will grow in you and enable you to see all the moose that are hiding in the woods. And once you can do this, you will always be able to do it!"

To these words, the lazy and unattractive-looking husband replied, "And a person who learns how to do this can decide to catch the hair from the other animals in the woods, roll their hair into fur balls between his forefinger and his thumb, and when the wind loves to whistle, free those fur balls so that the wind can chase them. Then such a person might be able to see all the other animals that are hiding in the woods along with the moose!"

"You may be right about this," the chief's son replied.

So it came to pass that the lazy and unattractive-looking husband became the greatest hunter. He could see all the animals that lived in the woods, no matter where they were hiding, and he could call them to him.

Another day the two young men were standing on the rocks along the river and spearing salmon, when the lazy and unattractive-looking husband said to the chief's son, "Fish do not have hair, but they have bones."

"You are right about this," the chief's son replied. "If a person wanted to learn how to see where all the fish in the river are hiding, it would be possible, although not many know how to teach this skill."

"That would, indeed, be a useful thing to know!" exclaimed the lazy and unattractive-looking husband. "Such a person would become the greatest fisherman and would provide the People with much more food to eat. A person who knows how to teach this can find someone who wants to learn it!"

"First," the chief's son advised his brother, "you must catch a fish and ask if you may have its bones. Next, you must take those bones, pound them into a powder, and save the powder for a day when the wind loves to whistle. On that day, you must free the powder so that the wind can chase it. You will find that the power will grow in you and enable you to see all the fish that are hiding in the river. And once you can do this, you will always be able to do it!"

So it came to pass that the lazy and unattractive-looking husband became a great fisherman. He could see all the fish in the river, no matter where they were hiding, and he could call them to him.

Many moons came and went. One day the two young men were talking together when the lazy and unattractive-looking husband said to the chief's son, "Now I dream dreams about whales and their songs."

To these words, the chief's son replied, "Whales do not die unless a person kills them."

So it came to pass that the lazy and unattractive-looking husband went alone to catch some whalebone by the side of the sea. When he found it, he burned it until he could crush it into a fine powder. He then saved the powder for a day when the wind loved to whistle on its way out to sea.

When that day came, the lazy and unattractive-looking husband walked out upon a rocky outcropping and freed a handful of the powder so that the wind could chase it. He found that the power grew in him and enabled him to see all the whales that were swimming far out in the sea. He freed a second handful of the powder, and as the wind chased the powder out to sea, he called the whales to him, and they came closer. He freed a third handful of the powder, and as the wind chased the powder out to sea, he called the whales to him, and they came even closer.

Three more times the lazy and unattractive-looking husband freed a handful of the powder. Three times, as the wind chased the powder out to sea, he called the whales to him, and with each handful the whales came even closer. The lazy and unattractive-looking husband freed a seventh handful of the powder, and as the wind chased the powder out to sea, he called a huge whale to him. To his surprise, the whale that he had called to him was Whale Person.

"Why have you have called me to you?" Whale Person asked the lazy and unattractive-looking husband.

"I have dreamed about you and about the power that you could give me, if you would be willing to do it," the lazy and unattractive-looking husband replied.

"I will give you the power that you wish to have," Whale Person replied. "When I open my mouth, reach under my tongue and take the medicine that you find there."

Whale Person then opened his mouth. The lazy and unattractive-looking husband reached into his mouth, found the medicine under his tongue, and removed it.

Once the lazy and unattractive-looking husband held the power medicine in his hand, Whale Person exclaimed, "Now you have the power to be invincible! My medicine will protect you against disease. My medicine will also protect you against the attacks of men and wild animals. My medicine will give you the power to do whatever you wish!"

And with these words, Whale Person dived deep into the sea and disappeared.

So it came to pass that the People in the large camp deep in the woods lived in peace and prosperity. Enemies did not attack them. The animals of the woods and the fish in the rivers permitted themselves to be caught and eaten. Fathers had sons, and, still, there was more than enough for all.

Many, many moons came and went. At last the chief was so old that he was not well enough to lead the People. The chief's son came to his brother and asked, "Are you able to return my father's youth and health to him?"

"A person should not tamper with nature," the lazy and unattractive-looking husband replied. "What will come at the end of a person's life should be permitted to come!"

So it came to pass that the chief finally died, leaving the leadership of the People to his son. The chief's son then came to his brother and said, "A chief should be a person who possesses great powers. The husband of my wife's sister is such a man. Maybe he, and not the chief's son, should be the new chief of the People!"

To these words, the lazy and unattractive-looking husband replied, "The new chief will be the son of the old chief! He is a person who also possesses great powers. And his brother will always stand beside him and help him!"

∾ QUESTIONS FOR
Response, Discussion, and Analysis

1. Why is the hero of this myth always described as a lazy and unattractive-looking young man?

2. What is significant about the relationship between the chief's son and the hero?

3. What is the role of the forest in the myth?

4. What is necessary for one to be able to acquire power in Micmac society?

5. What does the need for such power reveal about the Micmac people?

6. What would a person who hears this myth learn from it?

7. What type of power, if any, is available today? How does a person acquire it?

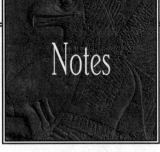

Notes

For each selection, the following Notes will provide you with the titles and publishers of the original sources (in fine translations), my primary sources, and selected supplementary sources for relevant background information, critical study, and further reading pleasure.

You will find additional information about original sources in the introduction to each myth. The Selected Bibliography provides a detailed listing of all sources mentioned in the Notes.

I have retold each myth in this book from scholarly English translations of the original material. In almost all instances, I have been able to work with at least two different sources. Most of the creation, fertility, and shorter hero myths are complete. However, most of the epics have been abridged because they were too long to include in this book.

In abridging the epics, my goal has been to retell the principal stories in a way that would preserve the characterization and language of the originals. Consequently, the major characters speak and behave as they do in unabridged editions. Secondary characters and subplots have been eliminated, and since one-third or more of an oral epic usually consists of repeated material, I have often included only one complete passage and then omitted or shortened repetitive passages. Any additions and omissions are explained in the relevant Notes.

THE MIDDLE EAST

Interest in the lands depicted in the Bible has always been strong. Therefore, the archaeological history of the Near East is a book in itself. However, the following highlights enhance our appreciation of the Middle East selections in *World Mythology* by providing a chronological framework for their discovery and their translation. The introduction to each selection contains further information that is particularly relevant to that literary work.

Carsten Niebuhr, in the 1760s, sketched the ruins of Nineveh, and, in 1778, he published the Persian inscriptions from Persepolis, which he had accurately copied by hand, that led to the translation of cuneiform.

However, understanding cuneiform was largely guesswork until, in the 1830s and 1840s, H. C. Rawlinson's military service in Persia enabled him to copy and translate it as a hobby. Rawlinson's source was a series of rock inscriptions, placed on five columns, and containing 414 lines of text. Because the inscriptions were located three hundred feet above the ground, Rawlinson constructed a scaffold, and at times he was lowered on a rope from the top of the rock in order to copy them accurately. His work was published in 1850–1851.

Meanwhile, in 1845, Austen Henry Layard began to excavate Nineveh and discovered the great library of King Ashurbanipal with its thousands of tablets and fragments. The first major excavation of Lagash, a Sumerian city, began in 1877 and unearthed thousands of clay tablets and fragments. Those at Nippur followed in 1889–1900 and unearthed thirty thousand more tablets and fragments, dating from 2500 B.C. to about 300 B.C., with publication of some of this material beginning in 1893.

In the second half of the twentieth century, and particularly in recent years, archaeologists have been able to find more material evidence from the ancient cultures of the Near East and Anatolia, and computer technology has enabled scholars to publish safely the contents of fragile clay tablets and fragments that are located in museums throughout the Near East, Europe, and the United States. More literature has come to light, and missing pieces have been restored to material published as recently as 1969. Besides technology, scholars have needed a time of peace and the cooperation of foreign governments to permit their work. Consequently, scholars know more about this corner of the ancient world than they have ever known, but their knowledge is far from complete.

The Enuma elish

Originally written in poetic form on clay tablets, primary sources of the Enuma elish provide linear translations of this material. My principal sources are "The Creation Epic," in a linear translation by Speiser, and "The Creation Epic—Additions to Tablets V–VII," in a linear translation by Grayson. Both are included in Pritchard's *Ancient Near Eastern Texts Relating to the Old Testament* (Princeton Univ. Press). Myths from Mesopotamia, linear translations by Dalley (Oxford Univ. Press) published after I had written *World Mythology*, appears to be another excellent primary source for the *Enuma elish*. Gaster's *The Oldest Stories in the World* (Beacon) contains an excellent modern version of this epic.

Osiris, Isis, and Horus

The most complete version of this myth is found in Volume I of *Osiris and the Egyptian Resurrection,* by Budge. My principal sources are both by Budge: *Egyptian Religion* (Bell/Crown reprint) and *Osiris and the Egyptian Resurrection* (Dover reprint). Two interesting discussions of this myth can be found in Breasted's *The Dawn of Conscience* (Scribner's) and in Frankfort's *Kingship and the Gods* (University of Chicago Press).

The myth of Osiris, Isis, and Horus was so well known in ancient Egypt that it is depicted on the walls of every major ancient religious structure in Egypt. Consequently, it is possible to understand and appreciate much of the visual art of ancient Egypt with only this myth in mind.

It is interesting to note that Osiris swallows Horus's eternal eye for the same reason that the Greek warriors stab Hector's corpse with their spears—to gain power through a magical transference. Other peoples have eaten the hearts or drunk the blood of enemies they have killed, thereby expecting to acquire the qualities that made those enemies great.

Telepinu

Originally written on clay tablets, the most complete version of this myth appears in Pritchard's *Ancient Near Eastern Texts Relating to the Old Testament* (Princeton University

Press). The myth appears as "The Telepinus Myth" in a linear translation by Goetze, and it is my principal source. Gaster relates an excellent prose version in *The Oldest Stories in the World* (Beacon).

The Hittites were an ancient people who built an empire in Asia Minor that included northern Mesopotamia and parts of Syria. It existed from about 2000 to 1200 B.C., so that the Hittites were contemporaries of the Mycenaean Greeks.

Many versions of the Telepinu myth exist. The particular god who vanishes differs from one version to another, and specific details about the same god differ as well. These variations support the idea that the myth was secondary to the ritual to which it belonged and that it was recited whenever the ritual was necessary.

Gilgamesh

Originally written in poetic form on clay tablets, primary sources of the *Gilgamesh* epic provide linear translations of this material. My principal sources are included in Pritchard's *Ancient Near Eastern Texts Relating to the Old Testament* (Princeton University Press). The Sumerian versions of the epic appear as "Gilgamesh and the Land of the Living" and "The Deluge," both in linear translations by Kramer. The Babylonian versions appear as "The Epic of Gilgamesh" and "Atrahasis" (the Babylonian Utanapishtim), both in linear translations by Speiser, and as "The Epic of Gilgamesh—Notes and Additions" and "Atrahasis—Additional Texts," both in linear translations by Grayson.

I have taken additional material from the following translations of Gilgamesh tablets: Gardner and Maier (Random House); Kovacs (Stanford University Press); Jacobsen, in his *Treasures of Darkness* (Yale University Press); and Kramer, in his *History Begins at Sumer* (University of Pennsylvania Press).

Myths from Mesopotamia, linear translations by Dalley (Oxford University Press) published after I had written *World Mythology,* appears to be another excellent primary source for the Gilgamesh epic. Excellent modern versions of this epic include the poetic versions by Ferry (Farrar Straus) and Mason (New American Library), and the prose versions by Gaster, in his *Oldest Stories in the World* (Beacon); Sandars (Penguin); and Silverberg, in his *Gilgamesh the King* (Arbor House).

Excellent supplementary sources for the study of *Gilgamesh* include: Heidel's *The Gilgamesh Epic and Old Testament Parallels* (University of Chicago Press); Kramer's *History Begins at Sumer* (University of Pennsylvania Press) and *The Sumerians* (University of Chicago Press); Oppenheim's *Letters from Mesopotamia* (University of Chicago Press); and Tigay's *The Evolution of the Gilgamesh Epic* (University of Pennsylvania Press).

In my version of the epic, I have combined Sumerian, Akkadian, and Babylonian material. The Akkadian version of the *Gilgamesh* epic takes its title from its opening words, "He who saw everything"—an appropriate epithet for Gilgamesh. I have added the gods' reasons for the flood from the Old Babylonian and Assyrian texts of the Atrahasis. Atrahasis means "exceedingly wise"—an appropriate name for Utanapishtim.

On the other hand, due to the limitation of space, I have found it necessary to shorten this epic. Fortunately, the style is so repetitive that, in most respects, it has been easy to preserve the impact of the original. However, I have had to shorten Gilgamesh's poignant, repetitive reply in which he responds to those who question him by justifying his emaciated, ragged appearance and his search for Utanapishtim. I have handled this problem by elaborating on the reply each time Gilgamesh responds, culminating with his final reply in which he provides his complete statement.

Esfandyar

The principal English sources of the legend of Esfandyar, originally found in Ferdowsi's *Shahnameh* (*The Book of Kings*), are: Atkinson's version in prose and verse, *The Shah Nameh of the Persian Poet Firdausi* (Routledge, 1832); Zimmern's prose version, *The Epic of Kings: Hero Tales of Ancient Persia, Retold from Firdusi's Shah-Nameh* (Macmillan reprint of the original 1882 text), which is based upon Mohl's French version; Levy's modern prose version, *The Epic of the Kings: Shah-Nama, the National Epic of Persia* (Arkana/Viking Penguin); and Picard's modern prose version, *Tales of Ancient Persia: Retold from the Shah-Nama of Firdausi* (Oxford University Press).

Ferdowsi wrote the *Shahnameh* in rhymed couplets. My prose version of the Esfandyar myth/legend is based primarily upon Atkinson and Zimmern, supported by Levy's modern, scholarly rendition and by two old, charming editions written for adolescents, Renninger's *The Story of Rustem & Other Persian Hero Tales from Firdusi* (Scribner's, 1909) and Wilmot-Buxton's *Stories of Persian Heroes* (Crowell, 1908). I chose the content of Zimmern and Levy in preference to Atkinson's content if theirs appeared to be more accurate. However, wherever Atkinson included material that I could not find in Zimmern or Levy, I relied upon Atkinson.

Esfandar's exploits are part of the Rostam cycle, since Rostam is first Esfandyar's heroic model and then the object of Esfandyar's greatest task. Before Ferdowsi chose to feature Rostam's adventures in his version of the *Shahnameh,* Rostam was a favorite hero among the Persians. In fact, tales about Rostam also existed in oral traditions with which Ferdowsi was not familiar. For example, Central Asian stories about Rostam exist in the Middle Persian language which have not appeared in any epic poetry. The legends of Rostam and the Persian kings reflect aspects of the earlier Scythian inhabitants of Persia, particularly their style of warfare and their treatment of their enemies.

Stylistically, I have made two changes in the Esfandyar myth/legend. First, I have repeated particular descriptions word for word throughout the story in a manner that is consistent with the oral epic tradition throughout the world. Such repeated patterns made it easier for the bard to remember his material and also unified the epic. Second, I have taken Ferdowsi's similes and metaphors and reworked them so that they read like a shortened form of Homer's similes.

I have also chosen to use "Persia," the English name for Iran until 1935, when the Shah of Iran announced that his country should be called "Iran." The use of Persia is consistent with the age of the epic and its translation into English.

Esfandyar is like the ancient Greek heroes, Heracles and Theseus, in that he takes a dangerous journey in which he kills a succession of monsters and evil beings.

The best secondary sources in English appear to be: Atkinson's notes; Levy's introduction; and Hanaway Jr.'s "The Iranian Epics," in Oinas' *Heroic Epic and Saga* (Indiana University Press, 1978), which is superb.

GREECE AND ROME

The following ideas enhance our appreciation of the selections in *World Mythology*. The introduction to each selection contains further information that is particularly relevant to that literary work.

Substantial evidence exists to support viewing Greek mythology, as well as many other aspects of Greek culture, in a Mediterranean context. First and foremost is Greece's location. The Mediterranean Sea was an international highway, across which language, ideas, and material goods traveled. Older, sophisticated cultures existed in the Near East and in Anatolia. When ancient tablets containing many of their myths and epics exist today, and when it is obvious that similarities exist between those myths and epics and the myths and epics of ancient Greece, it is reasonable to assume that the religious and literary influence traveled from the older cultures to the younger one.

This possibility seems so obvious just from looking at a map that it is difficult to understand why, at least for the last hundred years, this has been an unusual point of view. However, archaeology began as a hobby that was truly a labor of love for many of the people who made the greatest discoveries.

Since Heinrich Schliemann, in the 1870s, took his beloved copy of *The Iliad* and discovered many of the ancient Mycenaean palace centers and Anatolian Troy, archaeology has become a science rather than a treasure hunt. Thousands of clay tablets containing literature from the ancient Near East have been translated, and with their discovery and translation, the similarities between the literature of the ancient Middle East and the literature of ancient Greece have become apparent.

Moreover, in the second half of the twentieth century, and especially in recent years, archaeologists have been able to find more material evidence from the ancient cultures of the Near East and particularly from Anatolia. In addition, computer technology has enabled scholars to publish safely the contents of fragile clay tablets and fragments that are located in museums throughout the Near East, Europe, and the United States. Consequently, more literature has come to light, and missing pieces have been restored to material published as recently as 1969.

In recent years, thousands of Hittite tablets have been discovered in Anatolia, and, as a result, the Hittites have become a real rather than a fabled people. These discoveries, combined with the resumption of excavation at Troy, are leading many scholars to understand that Homer's Troy was a Hittite and not a Mycenaean city.

Besides technology, scholars have needed a time of peace and the cooperation of foreign governments to permit their work. Consequently, scholars know more about this corner of the ancient world than they have ever known, but their knowledge is far from complete.

For example, in following Jason's voyage to fetch the Golden Fleece, Tim Severin, who is a specialist in the history of exploration, sailed to Colchis, which is located in former Soviet Georgia. There he discovered excavated Bronze Age sites in the Rhioni River valley, and he was able to speak with people who live in the foothills of the Caucasus Mountains and who had prospected for gold in a way that sheds an interesting light on the true nature of Jason's Golden Fleece. However, this information was inaccessible to Westerners during the years of the Cold War, and much of the information is still not available to the public at large.

The following authors will be discussed frequently in this section of the Notes:

Aeschylus (525–456 B.C.): the earliest of the three great Athenian tragedians and the father of Greek tragedy. He wrote about eighty to ninety plays, seven of which survive.

Agias (or Hegias) of Troezen (writing after 700 B.C.): the author of the post-Homeric epic *Nostoi* (*Homecomings* or *Returns*), which describes the return of every great Hellenic hero except for Odysseus and ends where Homer's *Odyssey* begins. Proclus's summary and few fragments survive.

Apollodorus (working c. 140 B.C.): the Athenian author to whom the *Library*, probably written in the first or second century A.D., is attributed.

Apollonius Rhodius (c. 295–215 B.C.) the Hellenistic Greek scholar and poet, of Alexandria and Rhodes, who wrote *The Argonautica*, an epic about Jason and the Golden Fleece.

Arctinus of Miletus (writing after 700 B.C.): the author of two post-Homeric epics, *The Aethiopis* and *The Iliupersis*. *The Aethiopis* is the sequel to Homer's *Iliad* and describes Achilles' deeds and his death. Proclus's summary survives. *The Iliupersis* (*The Sack of Ilium*) is a sequel to *The Little Iliad* (see Lesches and Mitylene, below) and describes the fall of Troy. Proclus's summary and few fragments survive.

Callimachus (c. 307–c. 240 B.C.): an important Hellenistic Greek scholar and poet, whose work influenced later Roman poets, such as Ovid.

Diodorus Siculus (of Sicily) (c. 80–20 B.C.): the Greek historian who attempted to demythologize Greek myth in his *Library of History*.

Euripides (c. 485–406 B.C.): one of the three great Athenian tragedians; known for presenting people as they are, both physically and psychologically. Aristotle described him as "the most tragic of the poets," because he was the best at arousing pity and fear. Euripides wrote ninety-two plays, nineteen of which survive.

Hecataeus of Miletus (working in about 500 B.C.): one of the earliest authors of Greek prose history. In his *Histories* or *Genealogies*, he traces families back to the gods or heroes from whom they claim to have descended. Few fragments survive.

Hegesinus of Salamis (c. 660 B.C.): one of the two authors (see Stasinus, below) to whom the post-Homeric epic *The Cypria* (*Cyprian Lays*) is attributed. *The Cypria* functions as the prologue to Homer's *Iliad* in that it describes the events of the Trojan War up to the time when *The Iliad* begins. Proclus's summary and fragments survive.

Herodotus (c. 490–c. 425 B.C.): the author of the *Histories of the Persian Wars* and known as the father of history. Herodotus's style is lively, and his digressions about Egypt, Scythia, and Persia—given his interest in anthropology, archaeology, and ethnography—are as interesting as his principal subject.

Hesiod (writing in about 700 B.C.): the second earliest Greek epic poet and author of *The Theogony* and *Works and Days*.

Homer (writing in the eighth century B.C.): the earliest and greatest Greek epic poet; author of *The Iliad* and *The Odyssey*, and the author to whom the ancient Greeks attributed *The Homeric Hymns*, now believed to have been written from the eighth to the sixth centuries B.C.

Hyginus (64 B.C.–A.D. 17): a great scholar and friend of Ovid, to whom the *Fabulae*, probably compiled from Greek sources in the second century A.D., is attributed.

Lesches of Pyrrha (c. 660 B.C.): one of the two authors (see Mitylene) to whom the post-Homeric epic *The Little Iliad* is attributed. It is the sequel to *The Aethiopis* of Arctinus of Miletus (see above) in that it describes the events after Achilles' death. Proclus's summary and fragments survive.

Lycophron (born about 320 B.C.): a Hellenistic Greek poet, in Alexandria, and the author of *The Alexandra,* a dramatic monologue about the prophecies of Hector's sister Cassandra about the fall of Troy.

Mitylene of Lesbos (about 660 B.C.): one of the two authors (see Lesches) to whom *The Little Iliad* is attributed.

Ovid (43 B.C.–A.D. 17): the great Roman poet who is known particularly for his *Metamorphoses,* a collection of the Greek myths that involve transformations. Ovid's lively style has made his versions the most popular source for those who retell the Greek myths.

Pausanias (writing in about A.D. 160): the author of *Description of Greece* (*Guide to Greece*), in ten books, which reflects his own travels and presents historical information that is usually accurate.

Pherecydes (born in 584 B.C., in Syros, or a century later, in Leros): the author of history, in ten volumes, based on myth and legend. Fragments survive.

Pindar(os) (518–after 446 B.C.): the Greek lyric poet who wrote odes in honor of victors at the four great pan-Hellenic games: the Olympian; the Pythian; the Nemean; and the Isthmian. Pindar often used the heroes of myth and legend to reinforce his praise.

Seneca, the Younger (c. 4 B.C.–A.D. 65): the Roman author, whose philosophy as a Stoic infused his work. In addition to his essays, including many on the subject of ethics, Seneca wrote nine tragedies. He adapted four of them, including *Medea,* from the tragedies of Euripides.

Simonides (556–468 B.C.): a poet highly esteemed in ancient Greece for his lyric poetry, his elegies mourning the dead, and his epigrams.

Sophocles (c. 496–406/5 B.C.): the second of the three great Athenian tragedians and known for presenting people in a lifelike manner, but more noble than they are in reality. He wrote 123 plays, seven of which survive.

Stasinus of Cyprus (c. 660 B.C.): one of the two authors (see Hegesinus, above) to whom *The Cypria* is attributed.

Stesichorus (writing in 600 B.C.): a great Greek poet, in Sicily, who wrote very long narrative or choral lyric poems, later collected in twenty-six books by Alexandrian scholars. Stesichorus took his subjects from Homer and the Epic Cycle. Some scholars think that his version of the *Iliupersis* (*Sack of Troy*) may be the earliest source for Aeneas's journey to Italy. The following Notes on *The Iliad* contain an interesting story about him. Only fragments survive, most from papyrus found in the twentieth century.

Virgil (70–19 B.C.): a famous Roman poet, known then, as now, as the epic poet who, in *The Aeneid,* celebrated the greatness of Rome. Dante considered Virgil to be Italy's greatest poet.

The Creation of the Titans and the Gods

The Greek poet Hesiod (late eighth century B.C.) tells this myth, in poetic form, in the *Theogony.* My principal sources are two prose versions: *Hesiod, The Homeric Hymns, and Homerica,* translated by Evelyn-White; and Apollodorus's *The Library,* translated by Frazer (both Harvard University Press). Other excellent translations include versions in verse by Athanassakis (Johns Hopkins University Press) and by Lattimore (University of Michigan Press), and a translation in prose by West (Oxford University Press).

The Ages of Man

The Greek poet Hesiod (late eighth century B.C.) tells this myth, in verse, in his *Works and Days*. My principal source is *Hesiod, The Homeric Hymns, and Homerica*, translated in prose by Evelyn-White (Loeb Classical Library, Harvard University Press). Other excellent translations of Hesiod include versions in verse by Athanassakis (Johns Hopkins University Press) and by Lattimore (University of Michigan Press), and a translation in prose by West (Oxford University Press).

A helpful resource is Volume 1 of Bonnefoy's *Mythologies* (University of Chicago Press), which contains an elaborate analysis of the Greek gods.

Demeter and Persephone

The most complete version of this myth appears, in verse, in *The Homeric Hymns*. My principal sources are two prose versions: *Hesiod, The Homeric Hymns, and Homerica*, translated by Evelyn-White; and Apollodorus's *Library*, translated by Frazer (both Harvard University Press). Other excellent translations of *The Homeric Hymns* include verse versions by Athanassakis (John Hopkins University Press), by Boer (Spring Publications), and by Hine (Atheneum).

In his *Greek Myths and Mesopotamia: Parallels and Influence in the Homeric Hymns and Hesiod* (Routledge), Penglase discusses relationships between the Mesopotamian myths of Inanna and Dumuzi/Damu and the myth of Demeter.

Because she is a Great Goddess or Mother Goddess, Demeter drives a chariot drawn by winged serpents, and she teaches mortals how to cultivate grain. The limitations of space have made it necessary for me to limit my version of Demeter's myth to those aspects that best compare with other fertility myths. Therefore, I have omitted Demeter's relationship with Metaneira's infant son as well as Ovid's superb additions, in his *Metamorphoses*. First, Demeter is mistreated by an arrogant youth and turns him into a lizard (Book V, 450–563). Then, both Ovid (V. 643–661) and Hyginus, in his *Fabulae* (Triptolemus, CXLVII), relate how Demeter later gives Triptolemus seed-corn, a wooden plow, and her serpent-drawn chariot so that he can travel throughout the earth and teach mortals how to cultivate grain.

The Labors and Death of Heracles

The most complete versions of Heracles' labors appear in Apollodorus's *Library* and in Diodorus Siculus's *Library of History*. My principal sources are Apollodorus's *Library*, translated by Frazer, and Diodorus Siculus's *Library of History* (Volume II), translated by Oldfather (both Harvard University Press). *Gods and Heroes of the Greeks* by Simpson (University of Massachusetts Press) is another excellent translation.

Due to the limitation of space, I have found it necessary to omit the birth and youth of Heracles, the myth of Alcestis, Heracles' marriages, and the battle between the gods and the giants. The version contained in this book focuses on those aspects of the myth that best compare with other myths of the traditional hero.

Heracles was the great ancestral hero of Argos. He had such stature in ancient Greece that, when Athens was competing with Argos in the sixth century B.C., political and economic supremacy were not considered sufficient. The Athenians felt that they needed a hero from their past who could compete successfully with Heracles. They chose Theseus, who was Heracles' cousin, "found" Theseus's bones on an obscure island, and brought them back to Athens for a proper heroic burial. They also collected a variety of myths, including a series of exploits which imitate those of Heracles, and combined them into one elaborate myth, thus raising Theseus's stature to meet that of Heracles.

Helpful resources are Volume I of Bonnefoy's *Mythologies* (University of Chicago Press), which contains a detailed analysis of Heracles as the quintessential Greek hero, and the two books on mythology by Robert Graves, *The Greek Myths* (George Braziller) and *The White Goddess* (Farrar, Straus and Giroux).

Walter Burkert, in "Heracles and the Master of Animals," in his *Structure and History in Greek Mythology and Ritual* (University of California Press), discusses Heracles as an ancient hero with Sumerian and Babylonian roots. Cylinder seals of Sumer and Mesopotamia (dating at c. 2500 B.C.) depict a hero who conquers a series of monsters that are similar to those Heracles must fight in his labors.

The principal myth of Heracles is a variation of the Sumerian/Babylonian myth of Gilgamesh, which traveled to Greece by way of Phoenicia. Iolas is the counterpart of Enkidu. Heracles' wife is the counterpart of the goddess Ishtar. Both Heracles and Gilgamesh have a divine parent, kill a lion and wear its skin, seize a divine bull by the horns and overcome it, use clothing for a sail, experience what life is like in the Underworld, and possess the plant that confers invulnerability. According to Apollodorus (*Library* Book I, 6.1–2), when the Olympian gods must fight the giants, an oracle reveals that only a mortal can kill the giants. Mother Earth creates this plant to protect the giants, who are her children. However, under cover of darkness, Zeus quickly collects it, summons Heracles, and with Heracles' help, the gods win the battle.

According to Graves, the earliest legends associate Heracles with Libya and the Atlas Mountains in the Near East. This Heracles was a rainmaker. He would rattle his oak club in a hollow oak tree or rattle pebbles inside a gourd or stones in a wooden chest, or he would stir a pool of water with an oak branch in order to attract lightning. He was also the leader in hunting and in war and was accompanied by twelve comrades who were archers. However, other Heracles figures were farmers. They usually specialized in the cultivation of barley and were depicted with grain emerging from their shoulders.

In addition to the Heracles of Greek myth, as many as forty-four other legendary people are Heracles figures. They include: Orion the Cretan hunter; Polyphemus the Cyclops whom Odysseus blinds; Samson; Bran, Cuchulain, and the Dagda from Celtic Ireland; the Roman Romulus; both Cronus; both Zeus and Hermes; and Aeneas's father, Anchises.

Graves views Heracles as a sacred king who was adopted by pre-Hellenic Greece. Heracles, whose name means "the glory of Hera," would have defended the worship of Hera against the worship of the patriarchal gods of the invading Mycenaeans. Being a sacred king in Argos, Heracles would have been sacrificed at the end of his reign to Hera, the Argive Great Goddess or Mother Goddess. However, once the sacred king gained the power to extend his reign, a young surrogate would have reigned briefly before being ritually sacrificed, and then the sacred king would have returned and begun a new reign. In Greek myths, the children who die accidentally or who, like Heracles' children, are killed because someone, like Heracles, has gone mad and shot them are surrogates for the sacred king.

The pre-Hellenic Heracles would have fought a bull, a lion, and a boar or a scorpion; and then he would have dived into a lake and won a water-monster's (serpent's) gold. Heracles' twelve labors, numbered below, connect with pre-Hellenic matriarchal religion in the following ways. Killing a lion (#1) was a sacred king's marriage task. The heads of the hydra (#2), if fifty in number, symbolize the society of moon priestesses, who kept the land watered in a matriarchal society; if nine in number, they symbolize the Great Goddess or Mother Goddess in her role as Moon Goddess. Heracles' beheading of the hydra may record the historical conquest of the priestesses' sanctuary at Lerna and the suppression of their fertility rites. Killing the hydra was the task of a candidate for sacred king, and it symbolized the conquest of a serpent and the prize of its gold.

The capture of Artemis's deer (#3) connects with the pursuit of wisdom under a wild apple tree in Celtic mythology. The boar (#4) was sacred in a matriarchal society because its curved tusks were like the crescent moon, and it had a role in the midwinter coronation of the new sacred king. Cleaning Augeas's stables (#5) is a version of the clearing the land of stones and trees in Celtic mythology. Heracles' routing of the Stymphalian birds (#6) may record the historical conquest of a society of moon priestesses in Arcadia. Here, Heracles is acting as a doctor since rattles were used in ancient times to fend off fever demons.

Wrestling with a bull (#7) was a sacred king's coronation task. The bull was thought to bring forth rain because of his roar, and it was thought that the capture of its horn would enable the sacred king to fertilize the land in the name of the Moon Goddess by causing rainfall. The capture of Diomedes' mares (#8) reflects the practice of bridling a wild horse, and it was part of a sacred king's coronation rite in parts of ancient Greece. This labor also symbolizes the end of the matriarchal custom, where wild women wearing horse masks would chase and eat the sacred king at the end of his reign.

The capture of Hippolyte's belt (#9) symbolizes the conquest of a matriarchal society in the region of the Euxine (Black) Sea. Given the age of the Heracles myth, the ninth labor suggests that the people of ancient Greece were trading with communities in the Black Sea as early as 1500 B.C. The capture of Geryon's cattle (#10) represents the Hellenic patriarchal custom of having a husband pay the bride-price with cattle from a cattle-raid.

Heracles' need to acquire the golden apples of the Hesperides (#11) and his descent into the Underworld in order to capture Cerberus, the three-headed dog (#12), are reversed by some writers. Both are related to the journey of the deceased to the Celtic Paradise. There, Atlas ("long-suffering one") and Heracles would have held the sun-disk, rather than the sky, upon their shoulders. The capture of Cerberus is a reversal of a matriarchal practice.

In pre-Hellenic matriarchal religion, the three Hesperides ("Daughters of the Evening") would have been the Great Goddess in her three forms, and Cerberus, the three-headed dog, would have symbolized the Great Goddess.

As Goddess of the Underworld, the Great Goddess would have given the sacred king (Heracles) golden apples at the end of his reign and then carried him off to the land of eternity—called the Hesperides, the Islands of the Blessed, the White Island, or the Elysian Fields—where his spirit would have lived forever. However, in the myth of Heracles, the hero escapes from Hades' kingdom because he is immortal, or because his society has become patriarchal, and therefore, the sacred king is no longer compelled to give his life to the Moon Goddess.

Heracles' agonizing death reflects the agonizing death of a sacred king in midsummer. His blood would have been caught in a container and then sprinkled on the tribe in order to make them strong and fertile.

Philoctetes, who lights the funeral pyre's fire, was the sacred king's successor, and he would reign for the second half of that year. Then, in midwinter, he would be ritually sacrificed the Great Goddess by means of a snake-bite. Statuettes and inscriptions reveal that for hundreds of years after real sacred kings were burned, effigies of sacred kings were burned on Mount Oeta, where Heracles died.

The Iliad

Originally written in verse, my principal source for *The Iliad* is a prose translation by Murray (Harvard University Press). Excellent verse translations include those by Fagles (Viking), Fitzgerald (Anchor/Doubleday), Lattimore (University of Chicago Press), and Lombardo (Hackett).

The Selected Bibliography lists a number of books that are particularly worthwhile as supplementary sources for the study of *The Iliad*. Works whose titles may not immediately identify them as relating to *The Iliad* include: Burkert's *The Orientalizing Revolution: Near Eastern Influence on Greek Culture in the Early Archaic Age* (Harvard University Press); Chadwick's *The Mycenaean World* (Cambridge University Press); Jackson's *The Hero and the King: An Epic Theme* (Columbia University Press); and Vermeule's *Greece in the Bronze Age* (University of Chicago Press).

Information on the current excavations at Troy came from the following sources: "How Historic Is Homer?" *Archaeological Odyssey*. Premier Issue, 1998. Articles include: Brandau's "Can Archaeology Discover Homer's Troy?"; Griffin's "Reading Homer after 2800 Years"; McCarter's "Who Invented the Alphabet? A Different View"; Powell's "Who invented the Alphabet: The Semites or the Greeks?"; and Thomas's "Searching for the Historical Homer."

As the Introduction to *The Iliad* mentions, continuing summer excavations at Troy produce new discoveries and different conclusions. Therefore, information is quickly out of date. Readers who want the latest information about ancient Troy may contact Friends of Troy, Prof. Getzel M. Cohen, Institute for Mediterranean Studies, Cincinnati, Ohio. Friends of Troy publishes annual reports, "Recent Discoveries at Troy," and produces video lectures by C. Brian Rose on this subject.

Due to the limitation of space, I have selected conversations and incidents from the twenty-four books of *The Iliad* with the goal of telling the story simply and directly, while still preserving Homer's characterization of the principals, including their speeches. I have attempted to preserve key elements of Homer's style, occasionally moving suitable Homeric similes from one place in the text to another, in order to keep as much Homeric language as possible.

In order to reduce confusion over a multitude of names, I have omitted epithets that refer to a male character by stating his parent, such as "Son of Atreus" or "Leto's son." Instead, I have substituted other, less confusing epithets that also occur frequently in the original.

Because of space, I have had to omit the many anthropomorphic conversations among the gods on Mount Olympus. Moreover, I have found it necessary to omit Diomedes, whom many scholars view as the perfect Homeric hero, as well as Sarpedon and Aeneas. Consequently, I have omitted Homer's often quoted simile that equates the generations of mortals with the growth cycle of leaves (Book VI). In one instance (in Chapter 4), the omission of Diomedes required combining two scenes from the original. Early in Book IX and again in Book XIV, Agamemnon advises the Hellenic leaders to leave Ilios and return home. Diomedes responds in Book IX; Odysseus responds in Book XIV. Given my need to omit Diomedes, I have substituted Odysseus's reply.

The *Iliad* and *The Odyssey*, along with a later group of six epics (written after *The Iliad*, during the first half of the seventh century B.C., and now lost), became known as the (Trojan) *Epic Cycle*. Fragments of the six lost epics and Proclus's summaries of them have been published in *Hesiod, The Homeric Hymns, and Homerica* (Harvard University Press). *The Cypria, The Aethiopis, The Little Iliad,* and *Nostoi (Homecomings)* are discussed below, in relation to *The Iliad. The Little Iliad* (again) and the *Iliupersis* (*The Sack of Ilium*) are discussed in my notes to *The Aeneid. The Telegony* begins where Homer's *Odyssey* ends and concludes that myth.

The Cypria begins with Zeus's wish for the Trojan War. It then describes the apple of discord, the abduction of Helen, the gathering of the Hellenic armies, the sacrifice of Iphigeneia, the wound of Philoctetes and his desertion by the Hellenes, and the first nine years of the Trojan War. It concludes with the events in the tenth year that precede the argument between Agamemnon and Achilles.

The Aethiopis describes Achilles' deeds following Hector's funeral, his death from Paris's arrow, his rescue by Thetis, and his immortality. It concludes with the contest between Ajax and Odysseus for Achilles' armor.

The Little Iliad describes the events that follow the death of Achilles: the contest between Ajax and Odysseus for Achilles' armor; Ajax's madness and suicide following his defeat; and Odysseus' capture of Helenus, the Trojan seer. Helenus reveals the four conditions that the Hellenes must meet in order to conquer Ilios.

First, they must bring the bones of Pelops to Ilios. (Pelops, a towering figure in Greek myth, is the ancestor of Heracles, Theseus, Eurystheus, Agamemnon, Menelaus, and Aegisthus.)

Second, the Hellenes must use Heracles' bow and arrows against the Trojans. (Diomedes and Odysseus persuade Philoctetes, whom the Hellenes had abandoned on their way to Ilios more than nine years earlier, to rejoin them because he possesses Heracles' bow. His wound is cured, and, in a duel, he kills Paris.)

Third, Achilles' son Neoptolemus must fight with the Hellenes. (Odysseus brings him to Ilios.)

Fourth, the Hellenes must steal the Palladium from its guarded temple on the fortified acropolis of Ilios. (See my notes to *The Aeneid* for the Palladium's significance and its theft.)

The Little Iliad concludes with Athena's instructing Epeius to build the wooden horse and its acceptance by the Trojans. However, the epic originally may have concluded with the sack of Ilios. (See my notes to *The Aeneid*.)

Nostoi (Homecomings) describes the return of the great Hellenic heroes, with the notable exception of Odysseus. It includes Diomedes, Nestor, Neoptolemus, Agamemnon (including his murder by Clytemnestra and Aegisthus and Orestes' retribution), and Menelaus (last of all, except for Odysseus).

The Iliad and its related myths contain pre-Hellenic matriarchal roots that reflect the culture the Mycenaeans found in Greece. Here, as elsewhere, matriarchal communities worshipped the Great Goddess or the Mother Goddess (and her incarnations) in three forms, each of which performed different roles.

According to Robert Graves, the famous myth of the Judgment of Paris is a reversal of the matriarchal ceremony that marked the end of a sacred king's reign. The three Olympian goddesses were once the earlier Great Goddess (or incarnations of her) in her three forms: Athena, the maiden; Aphrodite, the mature and fertile woman; and Hera, the old, infertile woman.

At the end of Paris's reign as sacred king, Aphrodite, in her role as the incarnated Goddess of the Underworld, would have given him the golden apple of immortality. Then Paris would have been ritually sacrificed, and Aphrodite (now as the Great Goddess) would have carried him off to the land of eternity. However, when it is Paris who awards the golden apple to Aphrodite, and the apple has become the apple of discord, a later and competing religion is reversing an earlier religious tradition in order to reflect its own attitudes and values.

In contrast to Paris's relationship to Aphrodite, his relationship to Helen is firmly rooted in the pre-Hellenic matriarchal society. Helen would have been an incarnation of the Great Goddess, and Paris, in the role of sacred king, would have reigned as her consort for the prescribed period. Then, at the end of his reign, Helen would have given him the golden apple of immortality, and he would have been ritually sacrificed to the Great Goddess.

In the patriarchal culture of Trojan War, Helen is still immortal since she is the daughter of Zeus and the goddess Nemesis. (A fragment of *The Cypria* relates Zeus's love of Nemesis, and the myth of Leda and the Swan relates how Zeus gave Nemesis's egg to Leda, and how Leda and her husband, King Tyndareus of Sparta, reared Helen and Polydeuces along with their own children, Clytemnestra and Castor.) However, given the values and practices in a patriarchy, Helen should now be Paris's consort—a reversal of her status in a matriarchy.

Yet, even in Troy's patriarchal society, Prince Paris remains, in effect, the consort of Queen Helen. First, Aphrodite, who is the goddess of sexual desire, causes Helen to fall in love with Paris's form and face. Therefore, Helen chooses Paris as her new mate, and she permits him to abduct her and carry her off to Troy.

Second, in Troy, Paris reigns as the consort of the abducted Queen Helen until Troy falls. Technically, Helen is the consort of Paris. However, the members of the Trojan royal family and the elders of Troy respect and even revere Helen, whereas they have little respect, if any, for Paris. Moreover, Helen's rule of Troy as the incarnation of Great Goddess is confirmed by the fact that the Trojans never force Paris to return her to her lawful husband. They are besieged for ten years, during which they endure deprivation and death, and yet they never volunteer to end their crisis by giving Helen up. They view Helen as the jewel in the crown of their city, and yet, surely others among the Trojans, besides Hector, know that they are therefore bringing destruction and death upon themselves.

Third, at last, Philoctetes kills Paris with Heracles' bow and arrows, a manner of death that was customarily used for the ritual sacrifice of a sacred king. Queen Helen then returns to Sparta with another consort, who, in this patriarchal culture, is her original husband, King Menelaus.

Both Plato, in his *Phaedrus* (44), and Pausanias, in his *Description of Greece* (Book III, 19, 13), relate the tale of Stesichorus, who, in about 600 B.C., wrote two long poems about Helen. In the first poem, he presented the Homeric version, in which Helen goes to Ilios and is the cause of the Trojan War. Then he recited it in public, and he went blind. Helen then sent word to Stesichorus from the White Island (one of the Islands of the Blessed), where she was living, for eternity, with Achilles, Patroclus, and Ajax (also Iphigeneia and Medea) that she had cursed him with blindness because he had been unjust to her.

Therefore, Stesichorus wrote a poem of recantation in which he declared that he had used Homer's version in his first poem. However, in reality, Helen had never gone to Ilios. Hera and Athena had created a phantom in her image, and the entire Trojan War had been fought over that phantom. Stesichorus then recited his new version in public, and he regained his eyesight.

Years later, in 412 B.C., Euripides wrote *Helen,* his tragedy about Helen of Troy. However, whether or not he knew the story of Stesichorus, Euripides' play involves the phantom Helen, the real Helen, and Menelaus, who must discover who is real. The play ends happily, but the underlying idea is tragic—that the Trojan War was fought over a phantom.

According to Graves, judging from the manner in which they die, the heroes in *The Iliad* were sacred kings in an earlier matriarchal society. After his death, Menelaus, like a sacred king, spends eternity—in the Hesperides, the White Island, the Islands of the Blessed, or the Elysian Fields—with Helen.

Achilles' birth and death are also consistent with that of a pre-Hellenic sacred king. According to some writers (including Apollonius), and reflecting an early tradition, shortly after Achilles' birth, his father, Peleus, stops his goddess-mother, Thetis, from burning Achilles in the flames of their hearth because he senses that his wife must have killed their earlier infants in this manner. However, Thetis is outraged because she is certain that she would have made Achilles immortal.

This scene has pre-Hellenic, matriarchal roots. There, Thetis would be the incarnation of the Great Goddess, whose consort would be Peleus, the sacred king. Once the sacred king gained the power to extend his reign, a young surrogate would reign briefly as sacred king before being ritually sacrificed to the Great Goddess, and then the sacred king would return and begin a new reign.

The infant Achilles would have been one of those surrogates, and like all of Thetis's other "infants," he would have been ritually sacrificed to the Great Goddess. Then Thetis (as the Great Goddess) would have made him immortal by carrying them off to the land of eternity, and Peleus would have begun another reign as the sacred king.

Achilles' brief, far-famed life ends in the way that the sacred king of the waxing year would often have been killed at the summer solstice—with a fatal wound in his heel.
According to *The Aethiopis* summary, Thetis "bewails her son, whom she afterwards catches away from the pyre and transports to the White Island." Apollonius (Book IV, 811–15 of *The Argonautica*) also describes Achilles' immortality. Hera tells Thetis, "When he comes to the Elysian Fields, your son, Achilles, is destined to become the husband of Aeetes daughter Medea" (my phrasing).

The Introduction to *The Iliad* refers to the myth of Telephus and his roles in the Teuthranian and Trojan wars in Anatolia. Telephus is first mentioned in Proclus's summary of *The Cypria,* which relates how the Hellenes set sail for Ilios but arrive at Teuthrania. Thinking that Teuthrania is Ilios, they proceed to sack it.

Telephus, who is the king of Teuthrania, defends his city against the invaders and is wounded by Achilles. An oracle tells Telephus to go to Argos and guide the Hellenes to Ilios. *The Cypria* then continues with the second Anatolian invasion, this time involving the sacrifice of Iphigeneia and the Greeks' arrival at Ilios.

The double invasion of Anatolia by the same Hellenes, who return to Aulis between their two raids, opens the question of whether evidence exists of a Greek invasion of Teuthrania and whether a Hittite epic on that subject will be unearthed.

Telephus is discussed five times by Apollodorus, ten times by Pausanias (from Hecataeus and other sources), three times by Hyginus (including the wound and the oracle, from Sophocles' *Mysoi* [*The Mysians*]), as well as by Callimachus and Diodorus (from Sophocles and/or Euripides).

Unfortunately, most Telephus sources are lost. In Hesiod's lost *Ehoiai,* Telephus is born in Mysia. Aeschylus wrote at least two plays about Telephus: *Mysoi* (few fragments survive) and *Telephus* (few fragments survive), about his exploits in Anatolia and his journey to Argos to be healed.

Sophocles wrote at least five plays about Telephus. His "Telepheia" may consist of *Aleadai* (*The Sons of Aleus*) (fragments survive), a source for a fourth century B.C. summary of the Telephus myth; *Mysoi* (few fragments survive)*; Telephus* (lost); and *Eurypylus* (fragments survive), about Telephus's son, who participates in the Trojan War. However, Sophocles also wrote *Syllogus Achaean* (*The Assembly of the Achaeans*), produced in 438 B.C. (a fine fragment survives), about the second preparation for a Trojan invasion that will be directed by Telephus, and this play may be third in a trilogy that includes *Aleadai* and *Mysoi.*

The Telephus myth is also the subject of Euripides' *Telephus* (a fine Prologue fragment survives). Like Sophocles' *Syllogos Achaean,* Euripides' *Telephus* was produced in 438 B.C., and like Aeschylus's *Telephus,* it is set in Argos, where Telephus appeals to the Hellenes to heal his wound. Euripides also wrote *Auge,* about the plight of Telephus's mother.

The Telephus myth (based on Hecataeus's *Histories* and Euripides' *Telephus*) is also depicted on the second century B.C. frieze from the Great Altar at the Pergamon, which was discovered in 1878, excavated between 1878 and 1886, and then removed to Berlin, where it remains.

Jason and the Golden Fleece

My principal sources for *Jason and the Golden Fleece* are Apollonius's *Argonautica,* translated by Coleridge (Athens: Aspiote-Elka Graphic Arts) and by Seaton (Harvard University Press); and Pindar's "Pythian Ode IV," translated by Sandys (Harvard University Press). For Apollonius, I also used translations by Hunter (Oxford University Press) and by Green (University of California Press). Peter Green's edition contains a superb 160-page, line-by-line commentary, plus an elaborate glossary. For Pindar, I also used Nisetich's *Pindar's Victory Songs* (Johns Hopkins University Press).

Apollonius's work ends with the return of the Argonauts to Hellas. Therefore, the first part of the following myth, *Medea,* continues Apollonius's epic to its conclusion.

Tim Severin's *The Jason Voyage: The Quest for the Golden Fleece* (Simon and Schuster) provides historical background that is otherwise very difficult, if not impossible, to find. Colchis was located in what is now the former Soviet Republic of Georgia. As the *Jason* introduction explains, Severin's book introduces the reader to the Colchian part of the Jason myth, to the excavation of late Bronze Age sites in the Rhioni River valley, and to the old Svan method of gold-collecting, which involved using fleeces to trap the gold particles.

The quotation from Homer's *Odyssey* in the introduction is my own version. Before the Argonauts depart, Apollonius has Jason pray to Apollo, not Zeus. Given Zeus's more prominent role in Jason's expedition, I made the change.

According to Robert Graves, Pelias's neglect of Hera and her consequent anger may reflect a conflict between the people of Iolcus, who worshipped Hera as the Great Goddess, and the rulers of Iolcus, who worshipped Poseidon.

The voyage to fetch the Golden Fleece, like the later voyage to Troy, was so important that every Hellenic community sends an Argonaut to accompany Jason, and every hero has his important place in the epic. Different sources provide different names, and they can include as many as a hundred men aboard Jason's fifty-oared ship.

According to Apollonius, the Argonauts included: the musician Orpheus; Admetus, King of Pherae and husband of Alcestis; Telamon of Salamis, father of Ajax; Peleus of Phthia, father of Achilles; Heracles, son of Zeus; the twins Castor and Polydeuces, son of Zeus, of Sparta, brothers of Clytemnestra and Helen respectively; Meleager of Calydon; Zetes and Calais, the winged sons of Boreas, the North Wind; Acastus, the son of King Pelias of Iolcus; Argus, the shipbuilder (not Medea's nephew by the same name); and Jason, the son of Aeson, the legal heir to Iolcus.

Like most other epics, I had to shorten *The Argonautica*. Fortunately, because much of the plot involves the adventures of Jason's companions, I was able to limit my focus to Jason and Medea without compromising their story.

However, many interesting adventures could not be included. With the exception of Phineus, I had to omit the Argonauts' adventures en route to Colchis as well as most of the adventures on his return journey. These include: the island of Lemnos, inhabited only by women under the rule of Queen Hipsipyle; Heracles' departure to look for his companion (Zeus declares that Heracles must finish his labors rather than going to Colchis); Hera's help with the Clashing Rocks; the arrival of Phrixus's four sons on Ares' island; the help of Thetis and her sea goddesses with the Wandering Rocks; Triton; and Talus.

Apollonius had the ability to paint extraordinary word-pictures, and, unfortunately, I had to omit all of these as well. Examples include: the centaur Cheiron, holding the infant Achilles in his arms as the toddler waves good-bye to Peleus, his father; and Hera, pushing away one of the Clashing Rocks with one hand while she pushes the *Argo* through the narrow passage with her other hand.

Equally fine are: Thetis and her sisters, standing upon the Wandering Rocks, unseen in the smoke by the Argonauts, and tossing the *Argo* from one pair of hands to another like a great ball; Poseidon's horse, emerging from the sea and galloping off across the desert; Triton, half-god, half-dolphin, guiding the *Argo* out to sea; and Talus, the bronze giant, walking around the island of Crete and protecting it from strangers.

My additions are few. However, I created Jason's declaration of love to Medea. I thought this was appropriate because it is consistent with the pragmatic nature of Jason's personality and circumstances where his primary desire is to win Medea's help.

With regard to the sacrifice of Phrixus, according to Sir James Frazer (Apollodorus, Book IX.1), in the royal line of Athamas, the oldest son was vulnerable to human sacrifice, either to prevent or to cure crop failure. In later times the religious community accepted a ram as a substitute for the human victim.

Jason's loss of one shoe reflects the custom of Aetolian warriors to wear a shoe on their left foot only, which was the side on which they carried their shield. According to Sir James Frazer, this was related to the dangers of the soul and was a taboo designed to safeguard it.

Cadmus, Ino's father, killed Ares' dragon before he founded Themes. Athena then removed the dragon's teeth. She gave half to Cadmus and told him to plant them. She gave the other half to Aeetes of Colchis. According to Pherecydes, when Cadmus saw warriors sprouting out of the soil, he threw stones among them. The earthborn warriors thought that some among themselves had thrown the stones, and so they fought each other. The survivors became the first Thebans, in Boeotia. In versions related by Ovid and by Hyginus, the earthborn warriors fight each other without external provocation.

In Greek myth, taking a person or a god by the chin (or beard) and the knees is the customary pose of supplication. The theory behind the custom may be that physical contact makes it more difficult for the person or god whose help is needed to refuse to give it.

Pherecydes, Simonides, and Lycophron all say that Medea renews Jason's youth by cutting him into pieces and boiling them in a magic cauldron before he performs his labors in Colchis. Therefore, although I have followed Apollonius's version of Jason's myth, I have added this to my version.

Several different versions of the taking of the Golden Fleece exist. In a late seventh century (close to 600) B.C. account, the serpent swallows Jason, and Medea forces it to disgorge him. In Pherecydes, and in Pindar's "Pythian Ode IV" (462 B.C.), Jason kills the serpent. In *The Argonautica,* Medea puts the immortal serpent to sleep by waving a drugged juniper sprig over its eyes. Juniper was believed to offer protection against snakes.

Apollonius published two versions of *The Argonautica,* but only the later version—probably because its popularity resulted in multiple copies—exists today. The earliest and best existing text was copied in the tenth or early eleventh century A.D., and it is stored in the Laurentian Library in Florence, Italy. The principal edition based on that manuscript was later published in Florence in 1496. The earliest translation into English was made in 1780, but it is poor. A fine French translation was made in 1892.

Roman writers so admired Greek literature that they based much of their own writing upon it. Apollonius's Medea became the literary mother of Virgil's Dido in *The Aeneid* (Book IV), and, both in her own right and through Dido, Medea has had a lasting influence on writers from Virgil's day to our own.

Ovid included aspects of the myths of Jason and Medea in his *Metamorphoses* (Book VII). Here, Medea is a self-confident, accomplished, benevolent witch. She has no doubts about Jason; she is not afraid to leave her country; and Hera has no influence on her behavior. In Ovid's *Heroides,* "Medea to Jason" (XII) is based on Euripides' *Medea* and on *The Argonautica* (Books III and IV).

Thereafter, writers such as Corneille, Calderón de la Barca, Lope de Vega, and William Morris (*The Life and Death of Jason*) have worked with Jason and the Golden Fleece.

Medea

My principal sources for the myth of Medea are Apollonius's *Argonautica,* translated by Coleridge (Athens: Aspiote-Elka Graphic Arts) and by Seaton (Harvard University Press). I also used translations by Hunter (Oxford University Press) and by Green (University of California Press). Peter Green's edition contains a superb 160-page, line-by-line commentary, plus an elaborate glossary.

Once Apollonius's version comes to an end (when the *Argo* reaches Iolcus), my principal sources are Euripides' *Medea,* translated by Coleridge (Random House), by Kovacs (Harvard University Press), and by Morwood (Oxford University Press). Morwood's notes provide a superb line-by-line commentary. In addition, I consulted translations by Hadas (Bantam) and Warner (University of Chicago Press). A new translation by Wilner (University of Pennsylvania Press) has been well reviewed.

I have tried to enrich the myth of Medea by incorporating certain passages from Seneca's *Medea.* My principal source is Miller's translation (*Tragedies* I, Harvard University Press, and *The Complete Roman Drama,* Volume 2, Random House). I have also consulted translations by Ahl (Cornell University Press) and Slavitt (Johns Hopkins University Press).

The following eight passages in the myth of *Medea* include ideas from Seneca's *Medea:* (1) Medea on her wish for Jason's future (from lines 19–27); (2) Creon on the attitude of Acastus (from lines 251–270); (3) Medea on what Jason owes her and on her sacrifice (from lines 450–489); (4) Jason on his love for his sons (from lines 544–550), but note that I have reversed the request, from Medea to Jason, in order to be consistent with Euripides, my major source; (5) the Homeric simile when Medea gives Glauce's gifts to her sons and the simile about a spurned woman's wrath (from Chorus, lines 579–594); (6) Medea on her abilities, expressed by Aeetes in my version of *Medea,* and by Argus in my version of *Jason* (from lines 752–769); (7) Medea on her anguish after Glauce has received her gifts (from lines 924–953); and (8) Jason on the absence of gods (from lines 1026–1027).

Moreover, I have added the death of Pelias from Ovid's *Metamorphoses* and Diodorus Siculus's *Library of History.* My principal sources of Ovid are translated by Dryden, Pope, Addison, and Congreve (Heritage), by Sandys (University of Nebraska Press), and by Miller (Harvard University Press). I also consulted translations by Humphries (Indiana University Press), Innes (Penguin), and Mandelbaum (Harcourt Brace). Diodorus is translated by Oldfather (Vol. II, Harvard University Press).

Clauss and Johnston's book of essays on Medea (*Medea,* Princeton University Press) is a superb secondary source.

The quotation from Homer's *Odyssey* in the introduction is my own version. I have adapted both the content and the style of Euripides' *Medea* to conform with my version of *Jason and the Golden Fleece,* which precedes it. Medea and Jason speak as they do in Euripides. However, I have rephrased their words and arranged the placement of their speeches so that I could omit Creon and the Chorus.

The myth of *Medea* involves events where several alternative versions exist. The paragraphs that immediately follow discuss each of these events, the possible versions, and my choice.

Different versions of the prophecy that Aeetes receives from Helios, his father, include Herodotus, who says that Aeetes will be destroyed by one of his blood; Diodorus, who says that Aeetes will be destroyed by strangers take the Golden Fleece; and Hyginus, who says that Aeetes will keep his Kingdom as long as the Golden Fleece remains with him. I chose Apollonius (Book III, 594–600), who says that Aeetes will be the victim of treachery and disaster since he is not destroyed and he does not lose his kingdom.

Apollonius is the first ancient author to make Medea's brother an adult. In *The Argonautica,* Medea flees without Apsyrtus, and he leads his father's fleet in pursuit of her. When Apsyrtus finds the *Argo,* Medea treacherously lures him to meet with her on an island in the Danube, where Jason is waiting to ambush him. Jason kills Apsyrtus, and then he and Medea cut off Apsyrtus's hands and feet so that he cannot return from the Underworld. Finally, they secretly bury Apsyrtus on that island. Hyginus follows Apollonius in most respects.

In contrast, I have chosen Pherecydes' version, in which Jason tells Medea to take her little brother, Apsyrtus, from his bed and bring him with her when she flees from her father's house. Later, in order to delay Aeetes' pursuit, Jason and Medea kill Apsyrtus, cut up his corpse, and toss his fragments overboard into the Phasis River. Sophocles, in *The Scythians,* follows Pherecydes' version. However they throw the pieces of his corpse into the sea, and the murder takes place off the coast of Scythia. Apollodorus adopts Pherecydes' and Sophocles' version.

However, in *The Colchian Women,* Sophocles adopts still another version, where Apsyrtus is murdered in his father's palace. Euripides, in his *Medea* (1334), adopts the same version. Jason reminds Medea that she killed Apsyrtus at the hearth (the holiest place).

In Ovid's "Hypsipyle to Jason," in *Heroides* (Book VI, 129–130), Medea is said to be able to tear her brother apart and throw the parts over the fields. In "Medea to Jason" (Book XII, 113–116), Medea speaks of tearing Apsyrtus apart and tossing his parts into the sea.

According to some writers, the *Argo*'s speaking beam is in the center of the keel. Others place it in the *Argo*'s prow. I placed it in the prow.

Two sources reveal that Jason and Medea live happily with Pelias after Jason returns with the Golden Fleece. The summary of the *Nostoi* says, "Medea made Aeson a sweet young boy and stripped old age from him by her cunning skill, when she made a brew of many herbs in her golden cauldrons." In Pindar's "Pythian Ode IV," Pelias permits Jason to rule Iolcus after he returns with the Golden Fleece.

The earliest source in which Medea causes Pelias's death is a series of black-figured Attic vases (c. 530 B.C.), which depict Medea standing beside a cauldron as a ram jumps out. Here, Medea's power is not longer benign, and I used Apollodorus's brief version, in his *Library* (Book I, ix.27) as a guide. Ovid's *Metamorphoses* (Book VII, 296–350) and Diodorus Siculus's *Library of History* (Book IV, 51:1–52:3) supplied most of the details. However, I also added details from Medea's rejuvenation of Aeson in Ovid's *Metamorphoses* (Book VII, 179–293), but not the rejuvenation itself since Medea drains Aeson's body of old blood and replaces it with new blood by means of a magic brew.

Artemis is the appropriate goddess to be connected with the death of Pelias because she was the one Olympian who accepted, and who may have demanded, human sacrifice. Consequently, many Greek myths concern mortals who "forget" to honor her when they are honoring the other gods.

Many scholars have difficulty understanding the role of Aegeus in Euripides' *Medea*. According to Timothy Gantz, in his *Early Greek Myth: A Guide to Literary and Artistic Sources*, Aristotle thought that Euripides based his *Medea* on a similar drama by Neophron of Sicyon. Neophron wrote more than one hundred plays, but *Medea* is the only surviving title. A fragment of several lines from Neophron's *Medea* reveal that Aegeus comes to Athens in order to ask Medea to explain the oracle's advice. Since this makes more sense than having Aegeus pass through Corinth on his way to Troezen so that he can ask King Pittheus about the oracle's advice, some scholars wonder whether, in fact, Neophron based his *Medea* on Euripides' *Medea* and improved the part that involves Aegeus. Because Aegeus has an important role in Euripides' *Medea* regardless of the reason for his appearance, I have chosen to retain Euripides' version.

Euripides reveals that Apollo's oracle told Aegeus, "Do not loosen the wineskin's hanging neck until you return to the home of your father (Athens)" (phrasing mine). Medea offers no explanation. In the myth of Theseus, Pittheus also offers no explanation, but he understands that the oracle is telling Aegeus not to have sexual intercourse until he returns to Athens. Pittheus would love to unite his royal family with the Athenian royal family, and so he cleverly arranges for Aegeus to sleep with Pittheus's daughter. This is how the great Athenian hero Theseus is born. Years later, when Medea is still living with Aegeus in Athens and has borne him a son of her own, she tries to poison Theseus when he comes to claim his birthright from his father.

According to Robert Graves, Medea's expulsion from Corinth and her need to flee Athens reflects the Mycenaean rejection and suppression of the worship of the Great Goddess or Mother Goddess in ancient Corinth and Athens.

In Greek myth, taking a person or a god by the chin (or beard) and the knees is the customary pose of supplication. The theory behind the custom may be that physical contact makes it more difficult for the person or god whose help is needed to refuse to give it.

Medea mourns the loss of proper burial rites because, without them, her shade (her deceased form) will not be permitted to enter the Underworld. Parents expected their children to outlive them and to perform this function when they died.

The introduction to the myth of *Medea* contains ancient versions of Medea's behavior with regard to Creon, Glauce, and her own children. Diodorus relates that Medea disguises herself, enters Creon's palace at night, and sets a fire that no one can extinguish. Jason escapes, but Creon and his daughter burn to death.

What is most interesting is that Euripides, in his *Medea* (1378–1383), has Medea choose to murder her own children, yet he also chooses to have her establish a solemn festival and sacred rites in Corinth in order to atone for the impious murder of her children. Therefore, Euripides walks both sides of the line; he removes the murder of Medea's children from the Corinthians (who actually killed them), but he does not remove the consequences the Corinthians must suffer for their deed.

The ancient Greeks practiced a retributive type of justice. Medea avenges Jason's treatment of her and their children with a form of retribution. However, it is far more than "an eye for an eye."

Diodorus Siculus, in his *Library of History* (Book IV), discusses Medea in Corinth. Apollodorus adopts the versions of Apollonius and Euripides.

Among Roman writers, Ovid included aspects of Medea's myth in three works: a (lost) tragedy, *Medea;* a myth in his *Metamorphoses;* and a letter from Medea to Jason (Book XII) in his *Heroides.* Ovid depicts a more self-confident Medea in his *Metamorphoses,* a young woman who is not afraid to leave her country. Seneca depicts Jason more sympathetically in his *Medea.*

From A.D. 250, ten tragedies, among them *Medea,* were copied extensively and studied. Therefore, many medieval manuscripts of these plays are available. In contrast, the other nine existing plays all appear in one manuscript, which is located in the Laurentian Library, in Florence, Italy.

Euripides' *Medea* has continued to be imitated or adapted. Well-known authors include Pierre Corneille, Jean Anouilh, Calderón de la Barca, Miguel de Unamuno, Robinson Jeffers, and Brendan Kennelly. Marc-Antoine Charpentier, Luigi Cherubini, and Peter Sellars have written operas, Martha Graham has created a ballet, and Jules Dassin and Pier Paolo Pasilini have created films.

In the twentieth century, Medea has come to represent anyone who is an outsider, a feminist, a foreigner, or an outcast. For example, Medea's monologue on the problems of being a woman was recited at meetings of those who worked toward giving women the right to vote in the United States. Moreover, in a modern literature, Medea plays the following roles: an African Medea racially persecuted in Corinth; a black princess whose son loves a Corinthian princess; and a bohemian French woman in French society.

Medea also takes the following forms: a Malaysian woman in Salem, Massachusetts, in 1800; an African woman during the Portuguese colonization of Africa in the early 1800s; a Peruvian woman during the Spanish conquest of Peru; a Brazilian woman in a Brazilian shanty town; a French woman married to a German; an exiled Indochinese princess; a Spanish woman exiled during the Spanish Civil War; and a Greek woman caught in the partisan struggle in the Greek Balkans during World War II.

Pyramus and Thisbe

Ovid relates this myth, in verse, in his *Metamorphoses* (Book IV), and no earlier version currently exists. My principal source is Sandys' 1626 translation of *Metamorphoses* (University of Nebraska Press). I also considered the following five translations: Golding's, in 1567, (Harrison's William *Shakespeare: The Complete Works,* Harcourt Brace); the composite, edited by Garth, in 1717 (Heritage Press); Miller's (Harvard University Press); Chaucer's, in *The Legend of Good Women* (Houghton Mifflin); and Boccaccio's, in *Amorosa Visione* (University Press of New England).

Boccaccio (1313–1375) retells an abbreviated form of this myth in Canto XX of his *Amorosa Visione.*

Chaucer (1342–1400) retells this myth in Chapter 2, "The Legend of Thisbe" of *The Legend of Good Women.* He acknowledges that Ovid is the original author and gives a remarkably faithful rendition of Ovid's version, with one interesting exception. He omits the transformation of the mulberries and simply uses the tree in its generic sense within the story.

Shakespeare used Golding's version "Pyramus and Thisbe" as the basis for his own version of the myth in *A Midsummer Night's Dream.* Consequently, in his *William Shakespeare: The Complete Works,* Harrison reprints Golding's translation (except for the final section) in his introduction to the play.

Fine modern translations of Ovid's *Metamorphoses* include those by Humphries, in verse, (Indiana University Press); by Innes, in prose, (Penguin); and by Mandelbaum, in verse (Harcourt Brace).

The tale of Romeo and Juliet is a more embellished version of "Pyramus and Thisbe," and, even in Shakespeare's time, it was compared with Ovid's famous myth of tragic love. "Romeo and Juliet" first appeared in England, in 1562, when Arthur Brooke translated an Italian version of the tale. Thereafter, Brooke's poem, called "The Tragicall Historye of Romeus and Juliet," became so popular that Shakespeare may well have been familiar with different versions of it before he dramatized it as *Romeo and Juliet.*

Although I have retold Ovid's tale in prose, I have tried to preserve its charm.

The Aeneid

Originally written in verse, my principal source for *The Aeneid* is a prose translation by Fairclough (Harvard University Press). Excellent verse translations include those by Fitzgerald (Random House) and by Mandelbaum (University of California Press).

Excellent supplementary sources for the study of *The Aeneid* include: Beye's *The Iliad, the Odyssey and the Epic Tradition* (Peter Smith); Di Cesare's *The Altar and the City* (Columbia University Press); Galinsky's *Aeneas, Sicily and Rome* (Princeton University Press); Jackson's *The Hero and the King: An Epic Theme* (Columbia University Press); and Lawler's "The Aeneid," in Seidel and Mendelson's *Homer to Brecht* (Yale University Press).

Due to the limitation of space, I have selected conversations and incidents from among the twelve books of *The Aeneid* with the goal of telling the story simply and directly, while still preserving Virgil's characterization of the principals, including their speeches. I have attempted to preserve key elements of Virgil's style. In order to keep as much figurative language as possible, I have moved suitable Homeric similes from one place in Virgil's text to another.

The Aeneid can be divided into two parts: the first includes Aeneas's wanderings and is reminiscent of *The Odyssey;* the second involves the conquest of the Latin people in Italy and is reminiscent of *The Iliad.* From the first part, I have retold the sack of Troy, Aeneas's adventures en route to Italy, and the love affair between Dido and Aeneas—all in great detail. From the second part, I have retold in detail the fight between Turnus and Aeneas that concludes the epic. However, I have condensed the narrative that connects these two sections, and I have omitted many sections that glorify Rome.

As is mentioned in my notes on Heracles and King Arthur, among Western nations in ancient and medieval times, a great city-state or nation was expected to have a great heritage. Homer's Ilios was held in such esteem that writers who wished to authenticate their nation's heritage chose their founding fathers from among the heroes of the Trojan War. Consequently, Virgil chose Aeneas to become the founder of Rome.

Although Virgil's account of the wooden horse is famous, he did not create the myth. Two of the lost, post-Homeric epics that dealt with the Trojan War also related this event. The summary of *The Little Iliad* includes a description of how the Trojans take the wooden horse into the city, but it concludes without proceeding further with the fall of Troy. It is possible that it may originally have concluded with the sack of Troy, but Proclus chose not summarize it in *The Little Iliad* because he had already summarized a similar version in the *Iliupersis*. Some scholars think that Stesichorus's *Iliupersis* was also a source.

Pausanius, in his *Description of Greece,* describes the wooden horse as a device for breaking down the wall of Troy. According to Robert Graves, it would have been a wheeled wooden tower that was covered with wet horse-hides in order to protect it from the Trojan's flaming darts. It was located on the west side of the city, the weakest part of Troy's defense, "near the fig-tree."

This hollow wooden horse is obviously similar to the hollow wooden cow that was covered with cowhide, set on wheels concealed within its hooves, and was used in Crete as part of the sacred marriage between the sacred king (wearing a bull mask) and the Moon-Priestess. Therefore, Graves thinks that the wooden horse may have been used in a similar ceremony in matriarchal Troy, where the horse was a sacred animal.

The summary of *The Iliupersis* (*The Sack of Ilium*) describes the wooden horse, the death of Laocoon and his son, the role of Sinon, the return of the Hellenes from Tenedos, the death of Priam, and the reunion of Menelaus and Helen. It concludes with the murder of Astyanax, the enslavement of the leading Trojan women (prizes of victory for the leading Hellenic warriors), the burning of Troy, and Athena's plans to punish the returning Hellenic leaders for their theft of her Palladium.

The Palladium was an object of critical importance in the myth of the Trojan War. According to Apollodorus, it was a small wooden statue of the girl Pallas, which Athena created in memory of her dear friend. One day, as the girls were practicing their war skills, they had had an argument. When Zeus saw that Pallas was about to strike Athena, he became worried about his daughter's welfare. He distracted Pallas, thereby causing Athena, in the heat of their practice, inadvertently to give her friend a mortal wound.

In the *Iliupersis,* Zeus gives the Palladium to Dardanus, his favorite mortal son and the earliest ancestor of the Trojan people. From that time forth, the Palladium is so highly honored in Troy that the Trojans protect it by hiding the real statue and keeping an excellent copy of it on public view in the temple that had been built to honor it.

In *The Little Iliad,* when Odysseus captures Helenus, the Trojan seer tells him that the Hellenes will not conquer Ilios as long as the Palladium remains within the city's walls. Consequently, one night Odysseus and Diomedes secretly enter Ilios, kill those who guard the statue, steal the Palladium, and take it to their ships. In the *Iliupersis,* the Hellenes steal the copy of the Palladium. However, they still conquer Ilios.

Athena's attitude toward the Hellenes changes between the end of *The Iliad* and the beginning of *The Odyssey*. Her apparent indifference to the plight of Odysseus as he attempts to return to Ithaca may reflect her anger over his theft of the Palladium. Her attitude is consistent with her plans, as related in the *Iliupersis,* to destroy the Hellenic leaders as they return home.

The Palladium was such a treasure that accounts differ as to its fate. The Argives claim that Diomedes took the Palladium home with him to Argos. The Athenians claim that they raided the Argive ship that was transporting it, and, consequently, that they acquired the Palladium before it reached Argos. However, Virgil takes the Trojan point of view, and, in *The Aeneid,* Aeneas carries the Palladium out of Troy and takes it with him to Italy.

THE FAR EAST AND THE PACIFIC ISLANDS

The Creation, Death, and Rebirth of the Universe (India)

This myth is found in the Great Puranas, "stories of ancient times," which were written down between A.D. 300 and 1000 and became accepted throughout India. According to Indian tradition, Vyasa, the Hindu sage and seer, is the author of the Puranas in that he edited and compiled the material from earlier sources. "The Four Ages," "The Origin of Brahma from the Lotus in Vishnu's Navel," and "The Origin of the World from Brahma" are related in the Kurma; "The Kali Age" and "The Destruction of the World" are related in the Vishnu; and "The Cosmic Egg" is related in the *Vamana Saromahatmya.*

My only primary source of this group of myths is *Classical Hindu Mythology,* translated and edited by Dimmitt and Van Buitenen (Temple Univ. Press). Supplementary sources for further study of Hindu myth are Ions' *Indian Mythology* (Bedrick); *Hindu Myths* (Penguin); and Zimmer's *Myths and Symbols in Indian Art and Civilization* (Princeton Univ. Press).

The Ramayana

Although the epic poem called *The Ramayana* was composed sometime between 200 B.C. and A.D. 200 by the poet Valmiki, the story of "The Ramayana" is included, also in a Hindu edition, in the Great Purana called the *Garuda.* The Great Puranas, "stories of ancient times," were written down between A.D. 300 and 1000 and became accepted throughout India. According to Indian tradition, Vyasa, the Hindu sage and seer, is the author of the Puranas, in that he edited and compiled the material from earlier sources such as the Rig Veda.

My principal sources for *The Ramayana* are *Myths of the Hindus and Buddhists,* by Coomaraswamy and Nivedita (Dover reprint); *Classical Hindu Mythology,* translated and edited by Dimmitt and Van Buitenen (Temple Univ. Press); and *The Ramayana & The Mahabharata,* a poetic version by Dutt (Everyman's). Other excellent prose translations are those by Buck (Univ. of California Press) and Narayan (Penguin). *The Forest Book of the Ramayana of Kampan,* translated in verse by Hart and Heifetz (Univ. of California Press) is a twelfth-century Tamil (South Indian) version of *The Ramayana.* (See my notes on the creation myths of India for supplementary sources for further study of *The Ramayana.*)

I have followed the principal plot of *The Ramayana,* focusing on Rama's marriage to Sita, his banishment, Sita's abduction, the monkeys' search for Sita, Rama's conquest of Ravana, and Rama's two tests of Sita's virtue. I have chosen conversations and incidents with the goal of telling the story simply and directly, while still preserving Valmiki's portrayal of the principal characters. I also have attempted to preserve the beautiful figurative language of the original. Due to the limitation of space, I have found it necessary to omit the stories of such great characters as Sugriva and his brother Vali, and the heroic deeds of Hanuman.

The Creation of the Universe and Human Beings (China)

The myth about Yin and Yang appears Han Taoist work *Huai-nan-tzu* (*Master Huai-nan*), compiled early in the Han period (c. 139 B.C.) by Liu An, the king of Huai-nan (c. 170–122 B.C.). The material is found in Chapter 3, "The System of the Heavens," and Chapter 7, "Divine Gods."

The myth in which Nu kua controls the flood and repairs the damage to the universe also appears in the Han Taoist work *Huai-nan-tzu* (*Master Huai-nan*).

The myth in which Nu kua creates human beings appears in the *Feng su t'ung-yi* (*Explanations of Social Customs*), compiled later in the Han period by Ying Shao (c. 140–c. 206 A.D.). However, references to P'an Ku's corpse indicate that the myth of P'an Ku already existed, at least in an oral tradition.

The first part of the P'an Ku creation myth, in which P'an Ku creates order out of chaos by separating the sky from the earth, appears in Hsu Cheng's *San wu li chi* (*Historical Records of the Three Sovereign Divinities and the Five Gods*), written during the third century A.D., when Hsu Cheng was living and writing in southwestern China in the period of the Three Kingdoms. He may have collected this part of the myth from Central Asian and Tibetan sources. Now, this material exists only in fragments, which have been preserved in later texts.

The second part of the P'an Ku creation myth, in which P'an Ku's corpse provides the natural forms that exist in the sky and on the earth, appears in Hsu Cheng's *Wu yun li-nien chi* (*A Chronicle of the Five Cycles of Time*). Hsu Cheng may have collected this part of the myth from Central Asian sources. However it also resembles the ancient Near Eastern (Akkadian/Babylonian) myth of Apsu and Tiamat. This material also exists only in fragments, which have been preserved in later texts.

My principal sources for these myths are Birrell's *Chinese Mythology: An Introduction* (Johns Hopkins University Press), which is the most authoritative and informative text on Chinese mythology; Christie's *Chinese Mythology* (Newnes/Hamlyn); Bodde's essay "Myths of Ancient China" in Kramer's *Mythologies of the Ancient World* (Anchor/Doubleday); Mackenzie's *Myths of China and Japan* (Gresham); Walls and Walls' *Classical Chinese Myths* (Joint); and Werner's *Ancient Tales and Folklore of China* (Bracken reprint of *Myths and Legends of China*). The myth of P'an Ku also appears in Sanders' *Dragons, Gods, & Spirits from Chinese Mythology* (Schocken), which is an excellent collection of Chinese myths.

Chi Li Slays the Serpent

My version of this story is based upon Roberts' "Li Chi and the Serpent," in *Chinese Fairy Tales and Fantasies* (Pantheon, 1979).

Roberts' source is Kan Pao's version in his *Sou shen chi* (*A Record of Researches into Spirits*), an early fourth century A.D. collection of mythological, legendary, and fictional tales that Kan compiled in about A.D. 317. Many of these tales may date from the Ch'in Dynasty, founded by the first emperor of China, Ch'in Shih Huang Ti, who ruled from 221 to 210 B.C.

I have made the following changes in this tale. First, in the interest of clarity within the story, I have called the protagonist Chi Li (the American form of her name) instead of Li Chi (the Chinese form).

Second, I have assumed that victims were usually bound, and that those who delivered these human sacrifices remained to be certain that the sacrifice occurred. However, they also could have been drugged. Roberts omits the issue.

Finally, I have added Chi Li's statement that the gods favor those who try to help themselves. It is consistent with what was probably the religious nature of the original sacrifice, and her attitude toward what the gods value is consistent with her own behavior and her remarkable success.

Amaterasu

This myth is related in *Nihongi: Chronicles of Japan from the Earliest Times to A.D. 697*, translated by Aston (Tuttle), which, being the best, is my only primary source. (The title of this work is also transliterated as *Nihon Shoki*.) The myth of Amaterasu also appears in Davis's *Myths and Legends of Japan* (Graham Brash) and in Piggott's *Japanese Mythology* (Bedrick).

Kotan Utunnai (Ainu)

Batchelor's transcription of *Kotan Utunnai* was first published, in both Ainu and English, in the *Transactions of the Asiatic Society of Japan* in 1890. My only primary source, which is excellent, is Philippi's poetic translation in *Songs of Gods, Songs of Humans* (Princeton University Press).

In my prose version, I have retained the first-person narrative perspective because the narrator's limited omniscience recreates his magical world. In the course of the epic, the narrator has seven heroic adventures. Although I have followed the principal plot, I have found it necessary to omit three adventures due to the limitation of space: those involving the Pestilence Deities, the man and woman of Hopuni-santa, and the birdlike monsters.

I have omitted proper names that are infrequently used, such as those of the narrator (Poiyaunpe) and the woman whom he calls "Older Sister" (Chiwashpet-un-mat). "Dangling Nose" is a translation of that famous warrior's real name, Etu-rachichi, and, given his function in the story, I have preferred to use the more colorful translation. "Kotan Utunnai" refers to an isolated location in the land of the Repunkur (people of the sea).

The Creation Cycle (Polynesian/Maori)

Grey relates this myth in the chapter "The Children of Heaven and Earth," in his *Polynesian Mythology and Ancient Traditional History* (Auckland). My primary sources are Alpers's *Maori Myths and Tribal Legends* (Longman Paul), and Sproul's *Primal Myths* (HarperCollins), which is also the best contemporary version.

The Taming of the Sun

Westervelt relates this myth in his *Legends of Ma-ui* (1910). My primary sources are Colum's *Legends of Hawaii* (Yale University Press) and a collection of Westervelt's work, *Myths and Legends of Hawaii* (Mutual). Beckwith's *Hawaiian Mythology* (University of Hawaii Press) is an excellent source of supplementary information. *The Legends of and Myths of Hawaii,* by His Hawaiian Majesty Kalakaua (Mutual reprint), is stylistically fascinating.

THE BRITISH ISLES

The Ages of the World

My principal sources are Sjoestedt's *Gods and Heroes of the Celts* and Squire's *Celtic Myth and Legend.* The most complete versions of this myth appear in the following sources: Sjoestedt's *Gods and Heroes of the Celts* (Turtle Island); Squire's *Celtic Myth and Legend* (Newcastle reprint of *The Mythology of the British Islands*); and the recently reissued *Celtic Myths and Legends* by Rolleston (Dover reprint of *Myths & Legends of the Celtic Race*).

Excellent supplementary sources for further study of this cycle of Celtic mythology include: Chadwick's *The Celts* (Penguin); MacCulloch's *Celtic Mythology* (Dorset); and Rutherford's *Celtic Mythology* (Sterling).

Robert Graves, in *The White Goddess,* states that the Túatha Dé Danaan, the People of the Goddess Danu, are a confederation of tribes that are the descendants of the Greek Danaans. They left Greece, traveled through Spain, and invaded Ireland in 2028 and 1718 B.C., where they appear as the tribes of Partholon and Nemed, the second and third races, respectively. Given their Greek origin, it is not surprising that several Bronze Age Greek legends are similar to those of the Túatha Dé.

The Book of Invasions, which states that the Túatha Dé arrived in Ireland in the mid-fifteenth century (c. 1450) B.C., also states that Syrian invaders were the cause of their exodus from Greece. In this account, from Spain they traveled north to Denmark (the kingdom of the Danaans), and they acquired the name of their goddess Danu from their experience in Denmark. From Denmark, they crossed the sea to North Britain in 1472 B.C., and then they entered Ireland.

The Túatha Dé were a matriarchal society in which the mother named her son and gave him his weapons. Their sacred king was a type of sun king. When he died, he was buried beneath a barrow that was built like a fortress above and had the king's tomb beneath it.

Celtic myths were preserved by Christian monks in Ireland, Scotland, and Wales between A.D. 1100 and 1600. The Irish and Scottish monks preserved an older and more authentic Celtic tradition in the *Lebor Gabala Gahala* (*Irish Book of Conquests*) than the Welsh preserved in the *Mabinogion*. Nevertheless, the *Irish Book of Conquests* reflects its authors' discomfort as well as their interest in the pagan culture they were preserving.

Dagda the Good

The most complete versions of this myth appear in Squire's *Celtic Myth and Legend* (Newcastle reprint of *The Mythology of the British Islands*), which is my principal source, and also in the recently reissued *Celtic Myths and Legends* by Rolleston (Dover reprint of *Myths & Legends of the Celtic Race*). (See my notes on the Celtic "Ages of the World" for excellent supplementary sources for further study of this cycle of Celtic myths.)

Beowulf

Originally written in Old English (Anglo-Saxon) verse, my principal sources for *Beowulf* are the following translations: Chickering's, with the Anglo-Saxon on facing pages (Anchor/Doubleday); Child's, in prose (Houghton Mifflin); Kennedy's (Oxford University Press); Lehmann's (University of Texas Press); and Pearson's (Indiana University Press). Other excellent translations include: Alfred's, in prose, and with a superb introduction, in *Medieval Epics* (Random House); Donaldson's, for the Norton Critical Edition; Greenfield's (Southern Illinois University Press); Osborn's (University of California Press); and Raffel's (University of Massachusetts Press).

The Selected Bibliography lists excellent supplementary sources for further study of *Beowulf*. Works whose titles may not immediately identify them as relating to *Beowulf* include: Bruce-Mitford's *Aspects of Anglo-Saxon Archaeology* (Harper's Magazine/Harper); Jackson's *The Hero and the King* and *The Literature of the Middle Ages* (Columbia University Press); Owen's *Rites and Religions of the Anglo-Saxons* (Dorset); and Renoir's essay "Beowulf: A Contextual Introduction to Its Contents and Techniques" in Oinas's *Heroic Epic and Saga* (Indiana University Press). In addition, Tacitus's essay *Germania* (Penguin), based largely on Pliny the Elder's twenty book history *German Wars* (now lost), and *The Northmen* (Time-Life) are particularly interesting when read in connection with the *Beowulf* epic.

The new *Beowulf* introduction examines this myth in terms of two cultures: the Scandinavian culture from which it comes and the English Anglo-Saxon culture of its author. It is remarkable that the ten leading *Beowulf* translations consider only the culture of the *Beowulf* poet. Yet the myth itself is set in southern Sweden and in Denmark. Many aspects of Anglo-Saxon culture are present both in England and in Scandinavia. However, it is exciting to read Tacitus's *Germania,* written in A.D. 98, and find the prototypes of King Hrothgar, Beowulf, and the other warriors as well as an explanation of many of the values that are evident in the *Beowulf* epic. Archaeological excavations in Scandinavia have confirmed the existence of such barrows, weapons, and buried treasures in the Bronze Age, and Time-Life has produced a fine illustrated book, *The Northmen,* on this subject.

For this edition of *World Mythology,* I have retold *Beowulf* anew. I gained editorial support in restoring the key elements of Old English poetic style, particularly its use of kennings (the hyphenated word-pairs, such as whale-road and battle-blade), because these, along with alliteration, give Old English its distinctive quality. However, my version is not literal. First, my text is in prose, whereas the original is in poetry. Moreover, each Old English line is divided in half, with sounds from the first half repeated in the second half. I dispensed with the division and concentrated on the effect that alliteration achieves.

Then, I wanted readers to have a clearer mental picture of Grendel and his mother, the locations of Grendel's mother's den and the dragon's lair, and the timing of the battle in the underwater cave. I recognize that no one may ever have intended the giants or their locations to appear to be real. However, it may be just as possible that the original listeners lived in a world and in a location where these issues were part of their environment and did not have to be spelled out. In my opinion, giving them a reality enhances a reader's appreciation of Beowulf's bravery and his accomplishments.

In order to achieve this, I studied ten translations of the text, with interesting results. First, it is clear that Grendel and his mother are giants and not Godzilla-type monsters. They are primordial human beings. Grendel is cannibalistic, but his mother attacks Heorot in order to avenge Grendel's death. Therefore, I used the term *monster* where it seemed appropriate, and I dispensed with the word *demon*. Although *demon* reflect the poet's Christian attitude toward these pagan beings, often the poet used *demon, fiend,* and *monster* for their alliterative properties. By being more careful in their use, I have made these creatures more human, but they are just as terrifying.

It is easier to locate the underwater cave of Grendel's mother than to locate the dragon's lair. Her cave is beneath a lake, but its connection to the sea makes it possible for sea-monsters to inhabit it. In contrast, the timing is a difficult issue. It is agreed that it takes Beowulf either most of the day or all of the day to sink to the bottom of the lake. It is also clear that the Danes wait for Beowulf until the ninth hour arrives. However, translators do not agree as to whether it is the ninth hour of the day or the ninth hour of Beowulf's descent. Moreover, they do not agree as to the hour at which the new day starts. One translator defines the ninth hour as noon, while to another it is three o'clock in the afternoon. The others permit the reader who cares to deal with the ambiguity.

The Anglo-Saxon text is inconsistent and internally conflicting with regard to the dragon's barrow. Literally, the cave may be at the foot of a great cliff and on the shore where waves wash the sand. However, all translators agree that, after the dragon is killed, it is pushed off a steep cliff. No one transports the dragon anywhere, and therefore placing the cave "between the cliff and the seashore" cannot be correct.

Moreover, no thoughtful warrior would ever have chosen a sea-level cave for the safe storage of his treasure-hoard. A shore-level location would have been too vulnerable to stormy waves and the beaching of those curved-necked ships with their treasure-hungry warriors. Therefore, I created a cliff, a shelf that contains the cave, and then a lower cliff against which the surf crashes.

With the above exceptions, I have retained all of my earlier changes. The dragon section is still arranged more chronologically than it is in the manuscript in order to keep the action moving forward.

Due to the limitation of space, I have still selected conversations and incidents from *Beowulf* with the goal of telling the story simply and directly, while still preserving the author's treatment of the principal characters, including their speeches.

I have still found it necessary to omit the tales chanted by bards in the mead-hall. These mini-tales echo the major themes of the Beowulf epic, and one is the earliest existing version of *Sigurd the Volsung*.

King Arthur

The definitive version of the King Arthur epic is Malory's *Le Morte d'Arthur,* which combines various sources of Arthurian material. However, I constructed my version of King Arthur from sources that predate Malory. My primary sources are Geoffrey of Monmouth's *Historia Regum Britanniae* [History of the Kings of Britain, written in Latin in 1136 (Thorpe translation, Folio Society)]; Wace's *Roman de Brut,* written in Norman French verse in 1155 (Mason translation, Everyman's Library); Chreten de Troyes' *Lancelot or Le Chevalier de la Charrette* (*The Knight of the Cart*), probably written in French in the late 1170s, and part of the Guiot manuscript copied in the mid-thirteenth century

(Comfort translation, Everyman's); Layamon's *Brut,* written in early Middle English in 1205 (Mason translation, Everyman's); *From Camelot to Joyous Guard: The Old French La Mort le Roi Artu,* composed in approximately 1230 (Carman translation, University Press of Kansas); *Morte Arthure,* written in Middle English alliterative poetry in the mid-fourteenth century (Northwestern University Press); and Caxton's 1485 edition of Malory's *Le Morte D'Arthur* (University of California Press reprint).

Other excellent versions of these works include: Barber's *The Arthurian Legends* (Littlefield Adams); Barron and Weinberg's *Layamon's Arthur* (University of Texas Press); Brengle's *Arthur King of Britain* (Prentice-Hall); Gardner's poetic version of *The Alliterative Morte Arthure* (Southern Illinois University Press); Kibler's translation of Chretien de Troyes' *Arthurian Romances* (Penguin); Lumiansky's edition of *Malory's Le Morte D'Arthur* (Scribner's); Malory's *Le Mort D'Arthur* (Penguin); and Staines' *The Complete Romances of Chretien de Troyes* (Indiana University Press).

Excellent supplementary sources for further study of King Arthur include: Alcock's *Arthur's Britain* (Penguin); Benson's *Malory's Morte D'Arthur* (Harvard University Press); Jackson's *The Literature of the Middle Ages* (Columbia University Press); Morris's *The Age of Arthur* (Scribner's); and Ross and McLaughlin's *The Portable Medieval Reader* (Viking).

In my version, I have combined two principal plots: Arthur's heroic feats as a warrior-king (the English versions); and the relationship between Arthur, Guinevere, and Lancelot (the French version). However, due to the limitation of space, I have found it necessary to omit the many adventures of the knights of the Round Table that are irrelevant to the principal plot of the love triangle.

As is mentioned in my notes on Heracles and *The Aeneid,* among Western nations in ancient and medieval times, a great city-state or nation was expected to have a great pedigree. Homer's Troy was so highly regarded that writers who wished to authenticate or confirm their nation's heritage chose their founding fathers from among the heroes of the Trojan War. Consequently, in A.D. 1136, Geoffrey of Monmouth, in his *Historia Regum Britanniae,* chose the great-grandson of Aeneas to lead Trojan exiles to England, where they established New Troy (London) and the kingdom of Britain.

NORTHERN EUROPE

The Creation, Death, and Rebirth of the Universe

Snorri Sturluson (1178–1241), the Icelandic historian and poet, tells the most complete version of this myth in the part of his *Prose Edda* called *Gylfaginning* (*The Deluding of Gylfi*), written in about A.D. 1220. My principal sources are Taylor and Auden's translation of selections from the *Elder Edda* (Random House) and Young's translation of the *Prose Edda* (University of California Press). Other excellent poetic translations of this material include Hollander's *The Poetic Edda* (University of Texas Press) and Terry's *Poems of the Elder Edda* (University of Pennsylvania Press). *The Norse Myths,* retold by Crossley-Holland (Pantheon), contains a fine prose version of this material.

Excellent supplementary sources for the study of Norse myth include Branston's *Gods of the North* (Thomas and Hudson), Dumezil's *Gods of the Ancient Northmen* (University of California Press), and Volume 1 of Bonnefoy's *Mythologies* (University of Chicago Press).

Most scholars think that no unified Germanic religion or mythic tradition existed. Great discrepancies exist within the Icelandic versions of the Norse myths, reflecting contradictory sources for the same subject. The existing Norse myths show similarities to myths from Iran, from other Mediterranean areas, and from the Far East, suggesting the possibility that a group of ancient myths was common to all of these peoples.

Sturluson begins *The Deluding of Gylfi* with a description of the Allfather that does not completely match the description of Odin, who is called the All-Father. Apparently, in an earlier Norse creation myth, a god called Allfather wielded complete power over the universe. Odin, who appears later in Norse mythology, possesses many of the same characteristics as the earlier Allfather, but he has no power over the Norns (the Norse Fates). From Sturluson's tale and earlier material, it is also clear that the Aesir and the Vanir are two distinct groups of gods who fight against one another. As a result, some of the Vanir are adopted by the Aesir.

Situations such as these usually reflect a conflict between two religions. Both the Norse and the Greek myths reveal that the dominant religion adopted part of the religion that it supplanted. Another consideration is the fact that, under Christianity, the oral recitation of pagan literature was suppressed, and most of the written manuscripts were destroyed. Only the people of Iceland were permitted to enjoy pagan literature during the three hundred years that followed A.D. 1000. However, they read pagan literature that had been rewritten for a Christian audience, and, consequently, their versions of the Norse myths are more like fairy tales than like the powerful myths of any other culture. It is unfortunate that the Icelandic versions are the only Norse myths that have survived.

It is clear that the Norse creation myth reflects the geographical features of the land in which it was rewritten. Even today, Iceland is a land of fire and ice. It is composed of volcanic rock and contains an active volcano, geysers, glaciers, and waterfalls.

The Death of Balder

Snorri Sturluson (1178–1241), the Icelandic historian and poet, tells the most complete version of this myth in the part of his *Prose Edda* called *Gylfaginning* (*The Deluding of Gylfi*), written in about A.D. 1220. My principal source is Young's translation of the *Prose Edda* (University of California Press).

The Theft of Thor's Hammer

The poem "Thrymskvitha" ("The Lay of Thrym"), in the "Codex Regius" of the *Elder Edda* provides the most complete version of this myth. My primary source is Taylor and Auden's translation of selections from the *Elder Edda* (Random House). Other excellent poetic translations of this material include Hollander's *The Poetic Edda* (University of Texas Press) and Terry's *Poems of the Elder Edda* (University of Pennsylvania Press). *The Norse Myths,* retold by Crossley- Holland (Pantheon), contains a fine prose version of this material.

Sigurd the Volsung

Sigurd the Volsung has an interesting literary history. The story of Sigurd was well known in Norway between A.D. 600 and 1000. Part of it is related to the defeat of the Burgundians, an eastern Germanic people, whom the Huns defeated in 437. The neighboring Franks observed the event and transformed it into what became a heroic epic.

Four principal versions of the Sigurd epic exist, all based on Norse mythology. The earliest Icelandic version, the *Elder Edda,* was written down in about A.D. 1200 and combines poems from the oral tradition with prose transitions. In about 1241, Snorri Sturluson wrote the second Icelandic version, called the *Younger Edda* or the *Prose Edda,* which he based on the *Elder Edda.* He created passages of narrative to connect the famous poetic dialogues and scenes from the older version. Finally, the *Volsunga Saga* was written in about 1300 by an anonymous poet, and it became the most complete and definitive Icelandic version of the Sigurd epic.

Equally famous and complete is the *Nibelungenlied,* the Germanic version of the *Sigurd* epic, written in heroic poetry in about 1200 by an anonymous author who also used Norse sources. In this version, Sigurd is called Siegfried, and the story occurs in a medieval setting among nobles who emphasize knightly behavior and the chivalric code. The poet omitted major incidents in the basic story, however, so that without prior knowledge of the myth, certain aspects of the *Nibelungenlied* do not make sense.

After a lapse in interest that lasted for hundreds of years, writers once again turned to the epic of *Sigurd* in the 1800s. In 1857, the Norwegian dramatist Henrik Ibsen adapted material from the *Volsunga Saga* for *The Vikings at Helgeland,* and he continued to borrow ideas and themes from this epic for his later plays as well. In 1860, Richard Wagner wrote his *Ring of the Nibelungen* cycle of operas. Although he called his hero Siegfried, he drew most of his material from the *Elder Edda* and the *Volsunga Saga,* rather than from the *Nibelungenlied.* English poet William Morris translated the *Volsunga Saga* into English and also created his epic, *Sigurd* (1877), from this material.

My version of the *Sigurd* epic follows the Icelandic *Volsunga Saga,* although I have added a few details from the *Prose Edda.* I have taken the idea of Fafnir's protective blood, the linden leaf, and the manner of Sigurd's death from the *Nibelungenlied,* because this type of magic is consistent with the magic found in the *Volsunga Saga.* My principal sources are the *Volsunga Saga,* translated by Morris (Collier), and *The Saga of the Volsungs* by Schlauch (AMS reprint).

Three other editions of the Icelandic version that are of special interest are Anderson's *The Saga of the Volsungs,* which also includes his translation of related material from the *Prose Edda* and other sources (University of Delaware Press); Byock's prose version of *The Saga of the Volsungs,* taken from a 1400 manuscript that includes copies of much older texts (University of California Press); and Smith-Dampier's translation of a version from the Faroe Islands, called *Sigurd the Dragon-Slayer* (Kraus reprint).

Three fine versions of the *Nibelungenlied* exist: two prose versions, translated by Hatto (Viking-Penguin) and by Mustard (Random House), and a poetic version by Ryder (Wayne State University Press).

Volume 1 of Bonnefoy's *Mythologies* (University of Chicago Press) contains an analysis of Norse myth that is particularly worthwhile. Other excellent supplementary source for the study of *Sigurd the Volsung* are Jackson's *The Hero and the King* and *The Literature of the Middle Ages* (Columbia University Press).

Due to the limitation of space, I have confined my focus to Sigurd. Consequently, I have omitted both the first part of the story, which deals with Sigurd's father (Sigmund), and the last part of the story, which deals with Gudrun's revenge.

In one of the original versions of the epic, Brunhild is two different women: the Valkyrie and the princess. To make the combined woman a more consistent figure, I have omitted the scene in which Brunhild is living with her sister and brother-in-law and is working at handicraft. I have moved the ring gift that occurs in the handicraft scene to the scene in which Brunhild and Sigurd first pledge their love (in Chapter 5).

AFRICA

The Creation of the Universe and Ife

Courlander tells this myth in *A Treasury of African Folklore* (Crown), which, being the best, is my only primary source. Other interesting works on this subject are Courlander's *Tales of Yoruba Gods and Heroes* (Crown) and his novel, *The Master of the Forge* (Crown), which is based on Yoruba mythology.

The Origin of Life and Fire

Leach relates this Boshongo myth, which she calls "From Bumba," in *The Beginning: Creation Myths Around the World* (Funk & Wagnalls). She translated and adapted her version from Torday and Joyce's: "Les Boshongo" (Annales du Musee de Congo Belge. *Ethnographie Anthropologie,* Series 4. Brussels, 1910).

Eliade's "An African Cosmogony," in his *Gods, Goddesses, and Myths of Creation* (Harper Row), and Sproul's "Bumba Vomits the World," from her *Primal Myths* (HarperCollins), are reprints of Leach's version. Leeming's "Bumba's Creation," in *The World of Myth* (Oxford University Press), is a reprint of Eliade.

Cavendish, in "Central and Southern Africa: Myths of Origins," in his *Mythology: An Illustrated Encyclopedia* (London: Orbis), briefly summarizes the Bakuba version of the myth.

I have added a few details from the Bakuba to this Boshongo version. I have also added detail to the conclusion, where Bumba tells his people to appreciate the wonders that he has created. Whereas the content is almost all from Leach, the style is my own.

The Quarrel Between Sagbata and Sogbo

Courlander includes this myth in *A Treasury of African Folklore* (Crown), which is my only primary source. Courlander's source is Herskovits and Herskovits' collection of Dahomean or Fon myths, *Dahomean Narrative* (Northwestern University Press). Other excellent sources of African mythology are Parrinder's *African Mythology* (Hamlyn) and Radin's *African Folktales* (Schocken).

Gassire's Lute

Frobenius and Fox relate Gassire's Lute in *African Genesis* (Stackpole), which, in its reprint (Turtle Island), is one of my primary sources. My other sources of this epic, all of which include the Frobenius and Fox version, are Abrahams' *African Folktales* (Pantheon); Courlander's *Treasury of African Folklore* (Crown); and Rothenberg's revised and expanded edition of *Technicians of the Sacred* (University of California Press). *The Heart of the Ngoni,* by Courlander with Ousmane Sako (Crown), is an excellent collection of other West African epics.

Apparently, *Gassire's Lute* is an important part of the existing fragment of the Soninke epic Dausi. I have related *Gassire's Lute* in its entirety.

Bakaridjan Kone

Courlander relates this epic in *The Heart of the Ngoni: Heroes of the African Kingdom of Segu* (Crown). With the help of Ousmane Sako, he has provided the first English translation of this material.

Courlander quotes a late-eighteenth-century description of the capital of Segu, which can be found Mungo Park's journals, published in *Travels in Africa,* edited by Ronald Miller (London: Dent). Park visited Segu during the reign of Da Monson ("Mansong"), in 1795, and he returned to Segu again in 1805.

It is possible to find *The Journal of a Mission to the Interior of Africa, in 1805. Together with Other Documents, Official and Private, Relating to the Same Mission . . . An Account of the Life of Mr. Park* (London: John Murray, 1815). Mungo Park has been described as the "second great African explorer of British origin, after Bruce." He was the first European to reach the Niger River in "modern" times. Park's 1805 expedition appears to have been doomed from the start. With forty-four Europeans, he chose the wrong season for his second trip on the Niger, and, one at a time, forty members of his group died. The last five, including Park himself, drowned in the Niger as they tried to escape from "a party of natives." Apparently Park had his guide deliver his journal and letters "to Gambia" immediately before he and his four companions set out to explore the unknown part of the Niger where they all died, and the 1815 publication is based on these materials.

According to Park's journals, Sego was the capital of Bambara and consisted of four distinct towns: Sego Koro and Sego Boo, on the north bank of the Niger River, and Sego Soo Korro and Sego See Korro, on the south bank of the river. Da Monson lived in Sego See Korro. Moorish mosques had been built in each of the four towns, and Moors as well as the Bambara lived there.

With minor exceptions, I have followed the plot as Courlander has told it, even though details are not always consistent. However, in Courlander's version, it appears that the morike is not aware that Bamana Diase possesses supernatural powers that are superior to his own, and, therefore, Bamana Diase's knowledge about Dosoke Dan surprises the reader. Consequently, I have given the morike greater knowledge in order to prepare the reader for what eventually occurs.

The style of the version in the text is mine. I have given the characters additional thoughts and conversations, but these are consistent with Courlander's version.

THE AMERICAS

The Creation (Aymara/Tiahuanaco)

Juan de Betanzos, the official interpreter for the Spanish governor of Peru, took this myth from a Peruvian narrative song, the customary way the Inca historians preserved their nation's history. Juan de Betanzos relates this myth in his *Suma y Narracion de los Incas.* My source is Osborne's English translation of de Betanzos's version of the myth in *South American Mythology* (Newnes/Hamlyn). In the same volume, Osborne also includes English translations of two other, related Aymara/Tiahuanaco myths. The first is told by Pedro de Cieza de Leon in *Crónica del Perú,* Part II (Hakluyt Society, #68. London, 1883), which is his sequel to *The Travels of Pedro de Cieza de Leon.* Cieza de Leon was a Spanish chronicler who wrote fifteen years after the Spanish conquest of the Incas. The second related myth is told by Cristóbal de Molina of Cuzco in *The Fables and Rites of the Yncas,* translated and edited by Clements R. Markham in *Rites and Laws of the Yncas* (Hakluyt Society. London, 1873.).

Another excellent source, published two years after the first edition of *World Mythology,* is Bierhorst's *The Mythology of South America* (Morrow).

Viracocha is discussed in Volume 2 of Bonnefoy's *Mythologies* (University of Chicago Press).

The Children of the Sun

Inca Garcilaso de la Vega relates this myth in Volume 1 of *Commentarios Reales de los Incas* (*The Royal Commentaries of the Inca*), published in Spain in 1609. My primary source is Garcilaso de la Vega's *The Incas,* translated by Jolas (Avon). Osborne quotes Garcilaso's rendition in *South American Mythology* (Newnes/Hamlyn).

Bierhorst tells this myth and examines its relationship to other myths from this part of the world in *The Mythology of South America* (Morrow). Valdelomar relates creative versions of this and other Inca myths in *Our Children of the Sun* (Southern Illinois University Press).

Wanadi the Creator

The version of *Wanadi* in the text is taken from Marc de Civrieux's *Watunna: An Orinoco Creation Cycle,* edited and translated by Guss (North Point Press). The original version, which is different, is entitled *Watunna: Mitologia Makiritare* (Monte Avila Editores C.A., Caracas, 1970).

The word *Watunna* comes from the verb "to tell." And the first tellers were the Yekuhana/Makiritare of the Upper Orinoco in Venezuela. In order to write his version, Marc de Civrieux spent more than twenty years returning to the villages of the Yekuhana/Makiritare and listening to hundreds of fragments and episodes. He had many informants, and he eventually wove their tales into the work from which my version is taken.

Marc de Civrieux's version is long (about 175 pages), with repetitive, nonchronological, and occasionally conflicting details. In order to present a selection that reads as if it is complete in itself, I have selected particular chapters, rearranged the material chronologically, chosen among conflicting details, and incorporated information supplied in Guss's notes. Except for the description of the shaman's posture, which appears to be standard, the style is my own.

The version of Wanadi in the introduction to the selection is taken from Roe's "The Model" (pp. 220–221) in his *The Cosmic Zygote: Cosmology in the Amazon Basin* (Rutgers University Press). Roe's source is Nelly Arvelo-Jimenez's *Political Relations in a Tribal Society: A Study of the Ye'cuana Indians of Venezuela* (Ph.D. dissertation, Anthropology Department, Cornell University, 1971, p. 178).

The Creation (Maya)

The source of this myth is *The Popol Vuh of the Quiche Maya,* written by an anonymous author. It was translated into alphabetic script during the mid-1500s by Mayan scribes. My primary source is Goetz and Morley's *Popol Vuh* (University of Oklahoma Press).

An excellent version, published after I had first written *World Mythology*, is Tedlock's *Popol Vuh* (Simon and Schuster). Sproul's *Primal Myths* (HarperCollins) contains selections from the opening sections of my primary source, the Goetz and Morley translation.

Bierhorst compares this myth with the *Legend of the Suns* in *The Mythology of Mexico and Central America* (Morrow). Moreover, he enables readers to compare the *Popol Vuh* with other creation myths from this part of the world.

The Creation Cycle (Toltec/Aztec)

The Five Worlds and Their Suns can be found in the sixteenth-century Nahuatl manuscript, the *Chimalpopoca Codex: Annals of Cuauhtitlan and Legend of the Suns*, first recorded in alphabetic script by Aztec scribes in the mid-1500s. The first English edition of this manuscript became available late in 1992, translated by Bierhorst under the title *History and Mythology of the Aztecs* (University of Arizona Press). Bierhorst's edition includes the first translation, in any language, of the complete *Legend of the Suns*. My principal sources are Bierhorst's *Four Masterworks of American Indian Literature* (University of Arizona Press) and Nicholson's *Mexican and Central American Mythology* (Newnes/Hamlyn). Bierhorst compares this myth with the *Popul Vuh* in *The Mythology of Mexican and Central America* (Morrow). Moreover, he enables readers to compare the *Legend of the Suns* with other sun myths from this part of the world.

"The Creation of the Earth" can be found in a sixteenth-century French manuscript, *Histoyre du Mechique (The History of Mexico)*, published in a French journal in 1905. Andre Thevet, the translator, took his material from a collection (now lost) compiled by Spanish missionaries in 1543. My primary sources are Bierhorst's version in *The Red Swan* (Farrar Straus; University of New Mexico Press) and Nicholson's version in *Mexican and Central American Mythology* (Newnes/Hamlyn).

"The Creation of Human Beings" can be found in the *Chimalpopoca Codex*. According to Bierhorst, Quetzalcoatl's descent into the Underworld and his use of the bones exists in two other (unspecified) sixteenth-century versions as well. My primary sources for this myth are Bierhorst's *Four Masterworks of American Indian Literature* and Nicholson's *Mexican and Central American Mythology*.

According to Nicholson, "The Creation of Music" is a poem that can be found in one of the sixteenth-century Nahuatl manuscripts. It appears in Bierhorst's book *The Hungry Woman* (Morrow), and also in Nicholson's *Mexican and Central American Mythology*, which is my principal source.

Quetzalcoatl

The myths that relate how Quetzalcoatl is tricked and driven from the Toltec capital by Tezcatlipoca appear in two original sources: the *Chimalpopoca Codex: Annals of Cuauhtitlan* and *Legend of the Suns*, a 16th-century Nahuatl manuscript, first recorded in alphabetic script by Aztec scribes in the mid-1500s; and also the Nahuatl texts collected and recorded by the sixteenth-century Spanish priest, Fray Bernardino de Sahagun, under the title *Florentine Codex: General History of the Things of New Spain*. My primary sources are Bierhorst's *Four Masterworks of American Indian Literature* (University of Arizona Press) and Nicholson's *Mexican and Central American Mythology* (Newnes/Hamlyn).

Sahagun's *Florentine Codex* is available in an edition by Anderson and Dibble (University of Utah Press). Sahagun translated the Nahuatl texts known as the *Florentine Codex* in order to study the Nahuatl language, rather than to perpetuate Aztec beliefs. In practice, Christian priests and missionaries learned the Nahuatl language in order to preach about Christianity in the language of their audience. (See my notes on "The Creation Cycle" for information about the first English translation of the *Codex Chimalpopoca*.)

The Emergence

Matthews' 1897 transcription of the creation myth in his *Navaho Legends* (American Folk-Lore Society) is the classic source of this material. Another version is Klah's *Navajo Creation Myth*, recorded by Wheelwright (Museum of Navaho Ceremonial Art). My primary sources are the versions found in Gilpin's *The Enduring Navaho* (University of Texas Press) and Newcomb's *Navaho Folk Tales* (Museum of Navaho Ceremonial Art). The most complete version of this myth since Matthews' is Zolbrod's *Dine bahane: The Navajo Creation Story* (University of New Mexico Press). Burland relates a version of "The Emergence" in *North American Indian Mythology* (Newnes/Hamlyn). Erdoes and Ortiz' *American Indian Myths and Legends* (Pantheon) includes an extensive selection of other Native American creation myths.

Lodge-Boy and Thrown-Away

Simms relates this myth in his 1903 *Traditions of the Crows* (Field Museum Anthropological Series). My primary source is Thompson's classic version, in his *Tales of the North American Indians* (Indiana University Press). Thompson's source is Simms. *Tales of the North American Indians,* originally published in 1929, continues to be reprinted. Moreover, Thompson's versions of the myths, because they are based on primary sources, continue to be reprinted in anthologies compiled by other editors, such as Feldmann's *The Storytelling Stone* (Dell).

Coffin's *Tales of the North American Indians* (American Folklore Society) contains a Wichita version of this myth, entitled "Afterbirth and Lodge Boy." Bierhorst, in *The Mythology of North America* (Morrow), discussed the many variations of the "Lodge-Boy and Thrown-Away" myth. Excellent collections of other Native American myths from the Plains and Rockies include: Clark's *Indian Legends from the Northern Rockies* (University of Oklahoma Press); Grinnell's *By Cheyenne Campfires* (University of Nebraska Press); Marriott and Rachlin's *American Indian Mythology* and *Plains Indian Mythology* (Crowell); and Walker's *Lakota Myth* (University of Nebraska Press).

The Woman Who Fell from the Sky

Cusick, a Tuscarora Iroquois historian, relates this myth in the 1827 *Sketches of Ancient History of the Six Nations.* The oldest Huron version of this myth was related in 1874 by a seventy-five-year-old Huron subchief, and appears in Hale's 1888 "Huron Folk-Lore" (Journal of American Folklore). Hewitt, who was of Tuscarora descent, specialized in the Iroquois creation myth and collected detailed Mohawk, Seneca, and Onondaga versions that appear in his *Introduction to Seneca Fiction, Legends, and Myths 1910–1911* (Bureau of American Ethnology). He also worked with Curtin to write *Seneca Myths and Fictions* (Bureau of American Ethnology), and this is the source of the famous Seneca version of the Iroquois creation myth. Later, Curtin wrote *Seneca Indian Myths* (Dutton).

Each of my three principal sources uses one of the above original sources in relating the Iroquois creation myth. Clark relates Hale's Huron version in her *Indian Legends of Canada* (McClelland & Stewart). Emerson quotes extensively from Cusick's Tuscarora version in her 1884 *Indian Myths or Legends, Traditions and Symbols of the Aborigines of America* (Ross & Haines reprint). Thompson relates Curtin and Hewitt's classic Seneca version in his *Tales of the North American Indians* (Indiana University Press). See my notes on "Lodge-Boy and Thrown-Away" for information about Thompson's versions of the North American Indian myths.

Bierhorst presents a detailed discussion of this myth in *The Mythology of North America* (Morrow). A Huron version of this myth is discussed in Volume 2 of Bonnefoy's *Mythologies* (University of Chicago Press). Feldmann reprints Thompson's Seneca version of this myth in *The Storytelling Stone* (Dell).

The many versions of this myth are very similar in most respects. However, the twins have different names in different versions. In English translation, Cusick calls them "Good Mind" and "Bad Mind." Curtin and Hewitt call them "Little Sprout" and "Flint." Huron versions call them "Good Man" or "Good Brother" and "Like Flint" or "Evil Brother." Moreover, in some versions, Sky Woman does not have a daughter, and she herself gives birth to the twins. In some versions, the twins use bags of corn and beans as weapons in their final battle.

Raven and the Sources of Light

The major Raven myths were all originally published by the Bureau of American Ethnology and are found in Swanton's *Haida Texts and Myths* (1905) and *Tlingit Myths and Texts* (1909), and in Boas' *Tsimshian Mythology* and *Tsimshian Texts,* both published in 1916 and the best-known sources. These are my primary sources, as well.

Burland relates "Raven and the Moon," a Haida version, in *North American Indian Mythology* (Newnes/Hamlyn). Clark relates "How Raven Helped the Ancient People," a version from Puget Sound, in her *Indian Legends of the Pacific Northwest* (University of California Press). Coffin relates "Theft of Light," a Tahltan version, in his *Indian Tales of North America* (American Folklore Society). Coffin's version is fascinating in that it combines elements of the Tlingit and Tsimshian versions, while begin quite different in many of its details. Erdoes and Ortiz relate "The Theft of Light" (Tsimshian, from Boas/Thompson) in their *American Indian Myths and Legends* (Pantheon). Feldmann relates three raven myths (Boas/Thompson's Tsimshian, Clark's Puget Sound, and Swanton's Tlingit) in *The Storytelling Stone* (Dell). Goodchild's *Raven Tales* (Chicago Review Press) is an excellent source. Wherry relates a raven myth in his *Indian Masks and Myths of the West* (Bonanza/Crown).

The many versions of this myth are very similar in most respects. However, interesting variations exist, and in creating my own version, I have chosen elements and descriptive details from Haida, Tlingit, and Tsimshian versions.

In the major Haida version, the girl swallows Raven in the form of a conifer needle, which is floating in her water-dipper. Raven steals the moon, which is kept in a set of nested boxes, and returns with it under his wing.

In the major Tlingit version, the girl swallows Raven in the form of a small piece of dirt. Raven steals the stars, the moon, and daylight, which are contained in tied, separate, round bundles or bags. He threatens to let the daylight out of a box, and does.

In the major Tsimshian version, Giant removes his Raven-skin and transforms himself into a cedar leaf, which the chief's daughter swallows as it floats in her water-dipper. Giant steals Daylight, which is kept in a box, and, donning his Raven-skin, he escapes. Daylight emerges when Giant is taunted into breaking that box.

Sedna

The most famous version of this myth was originally told to Boas in 1884–1885 by the Oqomiut and the Akudnirmiut people of southern Baffin Island. Boas recorded this material in *The Central Eskimo 1884–1885* (Bureau of American Ethnology). My principal source is Thompson's classic version, related in his *Tales of the North American Indians* (Indiana University Press). Thompson's source is Boas. My second source is Caswell's *Shadows from the Singing House* (Tuttle).

Bierhorst reprints Thompson's versions in *The Red Swan* (Farrar Straus; University of New Mexico Press). Feldmann does also in *The Storytelling Stone* (Dell). Haviland reprints Caswell's version in *The Faber Book of North American Legends* (Faber and Faber). A version of this myth is discussed in Volume 2 of Bonnefoy's *Mythologies* (University of Chicago Press). Norman's *Northern Tales* (Pantheon) is an excellent collection of Inuit myths. However, it does not include the myth of "Sedna."

Caught by a Hair-String

Rand relates this myth in his 1894 *Legends of the Micmacs* (Longmans), but he does not reveal his source. My primary source is the version beautifully told by Whitehead in her *Stories from the Six Worlds* (Nimbus). Macfarlan's *American Indian Legends* (Heritage) contains another version of this myth.

Clark's *Indian Legends from the Northern Rockies* (University of Oklahoma Press) and *Indian Legends of Canada* (McClelland & Stewart), and Leland's *Algonquin Legends* (Dover reprint of *The Algonquin Legends of New England, or, Myths and Folk Lore of the Micmac, Passamaquoddy, and Penobscot Tribes*) are excellent collections of Canadian Native American myths. However, neither collection includes "Caught by a Hair-String."

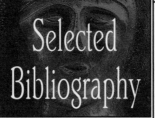

Selected Bibliography

The Middle East

Atkinson, James, trans. *The Shah Nameh of the Persian Poet Firdausi.* New York: Routledge, N.D.

"Atrahasis." (The Flood.) Trans. E. A. Speiser. *Ancient Near Eastern Texts Relating to the Old Testament.* Ed. James B. Pritchard. Third ed. with supplement. Princeton, NJ: Princeton UP, 1974.

"Atrahasis—Additional Texts." Trans. A. K. Grayson. *Ancient Near Eastern Texts Relating to the Old Testament.* Ed. James B. Pritchard. Third. Ed. with Supplement. Princeton, NJ: Princeton UP, 1974.

Beyerlin, Walter. *Near Eastern Religious Texts Relating to the Old Testament.* Philadelphia: Westminster, 1978.

Bonnefoy, Yves, ed. *Mythologies.* Vol. 1. Trans. Wendy Doniger. Chicago: U of Chicago P, 1991.

Breasted, James Henry. *The Dawn of Conscience.* New York: Scribner's, 1961.

Budge, E. A. Wallis. *Egyptian Religion.* New York: Bell/Crown, 1959.

---. *Osiris and the Egyptian Resurrection.* Vol. 1. New York: Dover, 1973.

Burkert, Walter. *The Orientalizing Revolution: Near Eastern Influence on Greek Culture in the Early Archaic Age.* Trans. Margaret E. Pinder and Walter Burkert. Cambridge, MA: Harvard UP, 1992.

---. *Structure and History in Greek Mythology and Ritual.* Berkeley: U of California P, 1979.

"The Creation Epic." Trans. E. A. Speiser. *Ancient Near Eastern Texts Relating to the Old Testament.* Ed. James B. Pritchard. Third ed. with supplement. Princeton, NJ: Princeton UP, 1974.

"The Creation Epic—Additions to Tablets V–VII." Trans. E. A. Speiser. *Ancient Near Eastern Texts Relating to the Old Testament.* Ed. James B. Pritchard. Third ed. with supplement. Princeton, NJ: Princeton UP, 1974.

Dalley, Stephanie. *Myths from Mesopotamia.* New York: Oxford UP, 1990.

"The Deluge." Trans. Samuel Noah Kramer. *Ancient Near Eastern Texts Relating to the Old Testament.* Ed. James B. Pritchard. Third ed. with supplement. Princeton, NJ: Princeton UP, 1974.

Durant, Will. *Our Oriental Heritage.* New York: MFJ Books, 1963.

"The Epic of Gilgamesh: Notes and Additions." Trans. A. K. Grayson. *Ancient Near Eastern Texts Relating to the Old Testament.* Ed. James B. Pritchard. Third ed. with supplement. Princeton, NJ: Princeton UP, 1974.

The Epic of Gilgamesh. Trans. Maureen Gallery Kovacs. Stanford, CA: Stanford UP, 1989.

The Epic of Gilgamesh. Trans. N. K. Sandars. New York: Viking Penguin, 1973.

"The Epic of Gilgamesh." Trans. E. A. Speiser. *Ancient Near Eastern Texts Relating to the Old Testament.* Ed.

James B. Pritchard. Third ed. with supplement. Princeton, NJ: Princeton UP, 1974.

Frankfort, Henri. *Kingship and the Gods: A Study of Ancient Near Eastern Religion as the Integration of Society and Nature.* Chicago: U of Chicago P, 1978.

Gaster, Theodore H. *The Oldest Stories in the World.* Boston: Beacon Press, 1952.

Gilgamesh: A New Rendering in English Verse. Trans. David Ferry. New York: Farrar, Straus, 1992.

Gilgamesh. Trans. John Gardner and John Maier. New York: Knopf, 1984.

"Gilgamesh and the Land of the Living." Trans. Samual Noah Kramer. *Ancient Near Eastern Texts Relating to the Old Testament.* Ed. James B. Pritchard. Third ed. with supplement. Princeton, NJ: Princeton UP, 1974.

Gilgamesh: A Verse Narrative. Trans. Herbert Mason. New York: New American Library, 1972.

Gilgamesh the King: An Epic Tale. Trans. Robert Silverberg. New York: Arbor House, 1984.

Goodrich, Norma Lorre. *Priestesses.* New York: Franklin Watts, 1989.

Hanaway, William L., Jr. "The Iranian Epics." Felix J. Oinas, ed. *Heroic Epic and Saga: An Introduction to the World's Great Folk Epics.* Bloomington: Indiana UP, 1978.

Heidel, Alexander. *Babylonian Genesis.* 2nd ed. Chicago: U of Chicago P, 1966.

---. *The Gilgamesh Epic and Old Testament Parallels.* Chicago: U of Chicago P, 1963.

Jacobsen, Thorkild. *The Treasures of Darkness: A History of Mesopotamian Religion.* New Haven, CT: Yale UP, 1976.

King, L. W. *Babylonian Religion and Mythology.* London: Kegan, Paul, 1899.

Kramer, Samuel Noah. *History Begins at Sumer.* Philadelphia: U of Pennsylvania P, 1981.

---. *Mythologies of the Ancient World.* New York: Doubleday/Anchor, 1961.

---. *The Sumerians: Their History, Culture, and Character.* Chicago: U of Chicago P, 1963.

Levy, Reuben, trans. *The Epic of the Kings: Shah-Nama, the National Epic of Persia, by Abol-Qasem Ferdowsi.* Rev. by Amin Banani. New York: Arkana/Viking Penguin, 1990.

Mackenzie, Donald A. *Myths of Babylonia and Assyria.* London: Gresham, N.D.

McCall, Henrietta. *Mesopotamian Myths.* Austin: British Museum and U of Texas P, 1990.

Montet, Pierre. *Everyday Life in Egypt.* Philadelphia: U of Pennsylvania P, 1981.

Myths from Mesopotamia. Trans. Stephanie Dalley. New York: Oxford UP, 1991.

Oppenheim, A. Leo. *Ancient Mesopotamia: Portrait of a Dead Civilization.* Chicago: U of Chicago P, 1972.

---. *Letters from Mesopotamia.* Chicago: U of Chicago P, 1967.

Penglase, Charles. *Greek Myths and Mesopotamia: Parallels and Influence in the Homeric Hymns and Hesiod.* New York: Routledge, 1994.

Picard, Barbara Leonie. "Isfendiar." *Tales of Ancient Persia: Retold from the Shah-Nama of Firdausi.* New York: Oxford UP, 1993.

Pritchard, James B. *The Ancient Near East.* Vol. 1. Princeton, NJ: Princeton UP, 1973.

Puhvel, Jaan. *Comparative Mythology.* Baltimore, MD: Johns Hopkins UP, 1987.

Renninger, Elizabeth D. *The Story of Rustem and Other Persian Hero Tales from Firdusi.* New York: Scribner's, 1909.

"The Telepinu Myth." Trans. Albrecht Goetze. *Ancient Near Eastern Texts Relating to the Old Testament.* Ed. James B. Pritchard. Third ed. with supplement. Princeton, NJ: Princeton UP, 1974.

Tigay, Jeffrey H. *The Evolution of the Gilgamesh Epic*. Philadelphia: U of Pennsylvania P, 1982.

Time-Life Books, eds. *Mesopotamia: The Mighty Kings*. Alexandria, VA: Time-Life, 1995.

Warner, Arthur G. and Edmond Warner. *The Shahnama of Abol-Qasem Ferdowsi* (9 vols.). London: Kegan, Paul, 1905–1925.

Wilmot-Buxton, E. M. *Stories of Persian Heroes*. New York: Crowell, 1908.

Zimmern, Helen. *The Epic of Kings: Hero Tales of Ancient Persia. Retold from Firdusi's Shah-Nameh*. New York: Macmillan, 1926.

Greece and Rome

Agias (or Hegias). "Nostoi." *Hesiod, The Homeric Hymns, and Homerica*. Trans. Hugh G. Evelyn-White. Loeb Classical Library. Cambridge, MA: Harvard UP, 1977.

Anonymous. *Phrixus*. Trans. D. L. Page. *Select Papyri III: Literary Papyri and Poetry*. Loeb Classical Library. Cambridge, MA: Harvard UP, 1970.

Apollodorus. *The Library and Epitome*. 2 vols. Trans. Sir James George Frazer. Loeb Classical Library. Cambridge, MA: Harvard UP, 1976; 1970.

---. *The Library: Gods and Heroes of the Greeks*. Trans. Michael Simpson. Amherst: U of Massachusetts P, 1976.

Apollonius Rhodius. *The Argonautica*. Trans. Edward P. Coleridge. Athens: Aspioti-Elka, 1957.

---. *Argonautica*. Trans. R. C. Seaton. Loeb Classical Library. Cambridge, MA: Harvard UP, 1967.

---. *The Argonautika*. Trans. Peter Green. Berkeley: U of California P, 1997.

---. *Jason and the Golden Fleece. (The Argonautica.)* Trans. Richard Hunter.

New York: Oxford UP, 1995.

Arctinus. "The Aethiopis." *Hesiod, The Homeric Hymns, and Homerica*. Trans. Hugh G. Evelyn-White. Loeb Classical Library. Cambridge, MA: Harvard UP, 1977.

---. "The Eliupersis." *Hesiod, The Homeric Hymns, and Homerica*. Trans. Hugh G. Evelyn-White. Loeb Classical Library. Cambridge, MA: Harvard UP, 1977.

Arnott, Peter D. "Later Tragedy: Euripides and the *Medea*." *An Introduction to the Greek Theater*. Bloomington: Indiana UP, 1967.

Bespaloff, Rachel. *On the Iliad*. Trans. Mary McCarthy. Princeton, NJ: Princeton UP, 1970.

Beye, Charles Rowan. *The Iliad, The Odyssey, and the Epic Tradition*. Gloucester, MA: Peter Smith, 1966.

---. "A New Athens." "The Variety of Tragic Experience." *Ancient Greek Literature and Society*. Garden City, New York: Anchor/Doubleday, 1975.

Boccaccio, Giovanni. *Amorosa Visione*. Canto XX. Bilingual Ed. Trans. Robert Hollander, Timothy Hampton, and Margherita Frankel. Hanover, NH: UP of New England, 1986.

Boedeker, Deborah. "Becoming Medea: Assimilation in Euripides." *Medea: Essays on Medea in Myth, Literature, Philosophy, and Art*. Ed. James J. Clauss and Sarah Iles Johnston. Princeton, NJ: Princeton UP, 1997.

Bonnefoy, Yves, ed. *Mythologies*. Vol. 1. Trans. Wendy Doniger. Chicago: U of Chicago P, 1991.

Bremmer, Jan N. "Why Did Medea Kill Her Brother Apsyrtus?" *Medea: Essays on Medea in Myth, Literature, Philosophy, and Art*. Ed. James J. Clauss and Sarah Iles Johnston. Princeton, NJ: Princeton UP, 1997.

Burkert, Walter. *Greek Religion*. Trans. John Raffan. Cambridge, MA: Harvard UP, 1985.

---. *The Orientalizing Revolution: Near Eastern Influence on Greek Culture in the Early Archaic Age.* Trans. Margaret E. Pinder and Walter Burkert. Cambridge, MA: Harvard UP, 1992.

---. *Structure and History in Greek Mythology and Ritual.* Berkeley: U of California P, 1979.

Burn, Andrew Robert. *The World of Hesiod: A Study of the Greek Middle Ages.* New York: Benjamin Blom, 1966.

Carpenter, Rhys. *Folktale, Fiction, and Saga in the Homeric Epics.* Berkeley: U of California P, 1946.

Chadwick, John. *The Mycenean World.* London: Cambridge UP, 1976.

Chaucer, Geoffrey. "The Legend of Thisbe." *The Legend of Good Women: The Poetical Works of Chaucer.* Boston: Houghton Mifflin, 1933.

Clauss, James J. *The Best of the Argonauts: The Redefinition of the Epic Hero in Book One of Apollonius's Argonautica.* Berkeley: U of California P, 1993.

---. "Conquest of the Mephistopheian Nausicaa: Medea's Role in Apollonius's Redefinition of the Epic Hero." *Medea: Essays on Medea in Myth, Literature, Philosophy, and Art.* Ed. James J. Clauss and Sarah Iles Johnston. Princeton, NJ: Princeton UP, 1997.

Crotty, Kevin. *Song and Action: The Victory Odes of Pindar.* Baltimore, MD: Johns Hopkins UP, 1982.

Di Cesare, Mario A. *The Altar and the City.* New York: Columbia UP, 1974.

Diodorus Siculus. *Library of History.* Vol. II. Trans. C. H. Oldfather. Loeb Classical Library. Cambridge, MA: Harvard UP, 1967.

Dodds, E. R. *The Greeks and the Irrational.* Berkeley: U of California P, 1951.

Dover, K. J., ed. *Ancient Greek Literature: Greek Literature 300–50 B.C.* New York: Oxford UP, 1980.

Dreyfus, Renee and Ellen Schraudolph, eds. *Pergamon: The Telephos Frieze from the Great Altar.* San Francisco: Fine Arts Museums, 1996.

Edwards, Mark W. *Homer: Poet of the Iliad.* Baltimore, MD: Johns Hopkins UP, 1987.

---, ed. *The Iliad: A Commentary.* Volume V. New York: Cambridge UP, 1991.

Euripides. *Medea.* Trans. Edward P. Coleridge. *The Complete Greek Drama.* Vol. 1. New York: Random House, 1938.

---. *Medea.* Trans. Edward P. Coleridge. *Seven Famous Greek Plays.* New York: Random House, 1950.

---. *Medea.* Trans. Moses Hadas. *Euripides: Ten Plays.* New York: Bantam, 1977.

---. *Medea.* Trans. Moses Hadas and J. McLean. *Greek Drama.* New York: Bantam, 1965.

---. *Medea.* Trans. David Kovacs. Loeb Classical Library. Cambridge: Harvard UP, 1994.

---. *Medea, Hipolytus, Electra, Helen.* Trans. James Morwood. New York: Oxford UP, 1997.

---. *Medea.* Trans. Rex Warner. *The Complete Greek Tragedies.* Vol. III. Chicago: U of Chicago P, 1959.

---. *Medea.* Trans. Eleanor Wilner. *Euripides 1.* Philadelphia: U of Pennsylvania P, 1998.

---. *Telephus.* (Prologue fragment.) Trans. D. L. Page. *Select Papyri III: Literary Papyri.* Loeb Classical Library. Cambridge, MA: Harvard UP, 1970.

Favre, Yves-Alain. "The Golden Fleece." Ed. Pierre Brunel. *Companion to Literary Myths, Heroes, and Archetypes.* Trans. Wendy Allatson, Judith Hayward, and Trista Selous. New York: Routledge, 1996.

Frazer, Sir James George. "The Renewal of Youth." Appendix VI. Apollodorus. *The Library.* Vol. II. Loeb Classical Library. Cambridge, MA: Harvard UP, 1970.

Galinsky, G. Karl. *Aeneas, Sicily and Rome.* Princeton, NJ: Princeton UP, 1969.

---. *Ovid's Metamorphoses: An Introduction to the Basic Aspects.* Berkeley: U of California P, 1975.

Gantz, Timothy. *Early Greek Myth: A Guide to Literary and Artistic Sources.* Baltimore, MD: Johns Hopkins UP, 1993.

Goodrich, Norma Lorre. *Priestesses.* New York: Franklin Watts, 1989.

Graf, Fritz. "Medea, the Enchantress from Afar." *Medea: Essays on Medea in Myth, Literature, Philosophy, and Art.* Ed. James J. Clauss and Sarah Iles Johnston. Princeton, NJ: Princeton UP, 1997.

Graves, Robert. *The Greek Myths.* New York: George Braziller, 1955.

---. *The White Goddess.* Amended and Enlarged Edition. New York: Farrar, Straus, 1976.

Hadas, Moses. "Alexandrian Literature and Learning." "Drama." *A History of Greek Literature.* New York: Columbia UP, 1965.

---. "Euripides." *Introduction to Classical Drama.* New York: Bantam, 1966.

Hainsworth, Bryan. *The Iliad: A Commentary.* Vol. III. New York: Cambridge UP, 1993.

Hendricks, Rhoda A. *Classical Gods and Heroes: Myths as Told by Ancient Authors.* New York: William Morrow, 1974.

Hesiod. *Theogony, Works and Days, Shield.* Trans. Apostolos N. Athanassakis. Baltimore, MD: Johns Hopkins UP, 1983.

---. *Theogony and Works and Days.* Trans. M. L. West. New York: Oxford UP, 1988.

---. "Works and Days." "Theogony." *Hesiod, The Homeric Hymns, and Homerica.* Trans. Hugh G. Evelyn-White. Loeb Classical Library. Cambridge, MA: Harvard UP, 1977.

---. *The Works and Days. Theogony. The Shield of Herakles.* Trans. Richmond Lattimore. Ann Arbor: U of Michigan P, 1991.

Homer. *The Iliad.* Trans. Robert Fagles. New York: Viking, 1990.

---. *The Iliad.* Trans. Robert Fitzgerald. Garden City, NY: Anchor Press/Doubleday, 1974.

---. *The Iliad.* Trans. Richmond Lattimore. Chicago: U of Chicago P, 1969.

---. *The Iliad.* Trans. Stanley Lombardo. Indianapolis: Hackett, 1997.

---. *The Iliad.* Trans. A. T. Murray. 2 vols. Loeb Classical Library. Cambridge, MA: Harvard UP, 1978; 1976.

The Homeric Hymns. Trans. Apostolos Athanassokis. Baltimore, MD: Johns Hopkins UP, 1976.

The Homeric Hymns. Trans. Charles Boer. Irving, TX: Spring Publications/U of Dallas, 1979.

"The Homeric Hymns." *Hesiod, The Homeric Hymns, and Homerica.* Trans. Hugh G. Evelyn-White. Loeb Classical Library. Cambridge, MA: Harvard UP, 1977.

The Homeric Hymn to Demeter. Trans. and ed. Helen P. Foley (with commentary and interpretive essays). Princeton, NJ: Princeton UP, 1994.

The Homeric Hymns and The Battle of The Frogs and the Mice. Trans. Daryl Hine. New York: Atheneum, 1972.

Hyginus. *Fabulae and Poetica Astronomica.* Trans. Mary Grant. Lawrence: U of Kansas P, 1960.

Jackson, W. T. H. *Hero and King.* New York: Cambridge UP, 1986.

Janko, Richard, ed. *The Iliad: A Commentary.* Vol. IV. New York: Columbia UP, 1986.

Johnston, Sarah Iles. "Corinthian Medea and the Cult of Hera Akraia." *Medea: Essays on Medea in Myth, Literature, Philosophy, and Art.* Ed. James J.

Clauss and Sarah Iles Johnston.
Princeton, NJ: Princeton UP, 1997.

Kerenyi, Carl. *The Heroes of the Greeks.*
New York: Grove, 1960.

Kerr, Walter. *Tragedy and Comedy.* New
York: Simon and Schuster, 1967.

Kingsley, Charles. *The Heroes.* Chicago:
Childrens' Press, 1968.

---. *The Heroes: Greek Fairy Tales.* New
York: Schocken, 1970.

Kirk, G. S. *The Iliad: A Commentary.*
Vols. I and II. New York: Cambridge
UP, 1985; 1990.

Kitto, H. D. F. "The Euripidean
Tragedy." *Greek Tragedy.* New York:
Doubleday/Anchor, 1954.

---. *The Greeks.* New York: Viking
Penguin, 1951.

Knox, Bernard M. W. "The *Medea* of
Euripides." *Oxford Readings in Greek
Tragedy.* New York: Oxford UP, 1983.

---. "The *Medea* of Euripides." *Word and
Action: Essays on the Ancient Theater.*
Baltimore, MD: Johns Hopkins UP,
1979.

Kott, Jan. *The Eating of the Gods: An
Interpretation of Greek Tragedy.* Trans.
Boleslaw Taborski and Edward J.
Czerwinski. New York: Random
House, 1973.

Krevans, Nita. "Medea as Foundation-
Heroine." *Medea: Essays on Medea in
Myth, Literature, Philosophy, and Art.* Ed.
James J. Clauss and Sarah Iles Johnston.
Princeton, NJ: Princeton UP, 1997.

Lamberton, Robert and John J. Keaney,
eds. *Homer's Ancient Readers.*
Princeton, NJ: Princeton UP, 1992.

Lattimore, Richmond. *The Poetry of Greek
Tragedy.* Baltimore, MD: Johns
Hopkins UP, 1969.

---. *Story Patterns in Greek Tragedy.* Ann
Arbor: U of Michigan P, 1969.

Lawler, Traugott. "*The Aeneid.*" *Homer to
Brecht.* Eds. Michael Seidel and
Edward Mendelson. New Haven, CT:
Yale UP, 1977.

Lesches. "The *Little Iliad.*" *Hesiod, The
Homeric Hymns, and Homerica.* Trans.
Hugh G. Evelyn-White. Loeb
Classical Library. Cambridge, MA:
Harvard UP, 1977.

Lycophron. *Alexandra.* Trans. A. W. Mair.
Loeb Classical Library. Cambridge,
MA: Harvard UP, 1977.

Mandel, Oscar. *Philoctetes and the Fall of
Troy.* Lincoln: U of Nebraska P, 1981.

Mimoso-Ruiz, Duarte. "Medea." Ed.
Pierre Brunel. *Companion to Literary
Myths, Heroes, and Archetypes.* Trans.
Wendy Allatson, Judith Hayward, and
Trista Selous. New York: Routledge,
1996.

Morford, Mark P. O. and Robert J.
Lenardon. "The Argonauts." "Local
Legends: Corinth." *Classical Mythology.*
New York: David McKay, 1977.

Nussbaum, Martha C. "Serpents in the
Soul: A Reading of Seneca's Medea."
*Medea: Essays on Medea in Myth,
Literature, Philosophy, and Art.* Ed.
James J. Clauss and Sarah Iles
Johnston. Princeton, NJ: Princeton
UP, 1997.

Ovid. "Medea to Jason." *Heroides.* Trans.
Daryl Hine. New Haven: Yale UP,
1991.

---. "Medea to Jason." *Heroides.* Trans.
Harold Isbell. New York: Penguin,
1990.

---. "Medea to Jason." *Heroides and
Amores.* Trans. Grant Showerman.
Loeb Classical Library. Cambridge,
MA: Harvard UP, 1977.

---. *Metamorphoses.* Trans. John Dryden,
Alexander Pope, Joseph Addison,
William Congreve, and others. New
York: Heritage, 1961. Reprint of
London: N.P., 1717.

---. *Metamorphoses.* Trans. Arthur Golding.
Reprint of London: N.P., 1567.

---. *Metamorphoses.* Trans. Rolfe
Humphries. Bloomington: Indiana
UP, 1967.

---. *Metamorphoses.* Trans. Mary M. Innes. New York: Penguin, 1977.

---. *Metamorphoses.* Trans. Allen Mandelbaum. New York: Harcourt Brace, 1993.

---. *Metamorphoses.* Trans. Frank Justus Miller. Loeb Classical Library. Cambridge, MA: Harvard UP, 1984.

---. *Metamorphoses: Englished, Mythologized, and Represented in Figures.* Trans. George Sandys. Lincoln: U of Nebraska P, 1970. Reprint of 1632 edition.

Padel, Ruth. *In and Out of the Mind: Greek Images of the Tragic Self.* Princeton, NJ: Princeton UP, 1992.

Pausanias. *Guide to Greece.* 2 Vol. Trans. Peter Levi. New York: Penguin, 1979.

Penglase, Charles. *Greek Myths and Mesopotamia: Parallels and Influence in the Homeric Hymns and Hesiod.* New York: Routledge, 1994.

Pindar. *Odes.* Trans. Sir John Sandys. Loeb Classical Library. Cambridge, MA: Harvard UP, 1978.

---. "Pythian Ode IV." Trans. Barbara Hughes Fowler. *Archaic Greek Poetry.* Madison: U Wisconsin P, 1992.

---. *Victory Songs.* Trans. Frank J. Nisetich. Baltimore, MD: Johns Hopkins UP, 1980.

Redfield, James M. *Nature and Culture in the Iliad: The Tragedy of Hector.* Chicago: U of Chicago P, 1978.

Richardson, Nicholas. *The Iliad: A Commentary.* Vol. VI. New York: Cambridge UP, 1993.

Rose, H. J. "Euripides and the Minor Tragedians." "Hellenistic Poetry." *A Handbook of Greek Literature.* New York: E. P. Dutton, 1960.

---. "The Cycles of Saga." *A Handbook of Greek Mythology.* New York: E. P. Dutton, 1959.

Schein, Seth L. *The Mortal Hero: An Introduction to Homer's Iliad.* Berkeley: U of California P, 1984.

Schibli, Hermann S. *Pherekydes of Syros.* New York: Oxford UP, 1990.

Schlesinger, Eilhard. "On Euripides' *Medea.*" *Oxford Readings in Greek Tragedy.* New York: Oxford UP, 1983.

Seneca. *Medea.* Trans. Frederick Ahl. Ithaca, NY: Cornell UP, 1986.

---. *Medea.* Trans. Frank Justus Miller. *The Complete Roman Drama.* Vol. 2. New York: Random House, 1942.

---. *Medea. Seneca VIII. Tragedies I.* Trans. Frank Justus Miller. Loeb Classical Library. Cambridge, MA: Harvard UP, 1979.

---. *Medea.* Trans. David R. Slavitt. *The Tragedies.* Vol. 1. Baltimore, MD: Johns Hopkins UP, 1992.

Severin, Tim. *The Jason Voyage: The Quest for the Golden Fleece.* New York: Simon and Schuster, 1985.

Seymour, Miranda. *Medea.* New York: St. Martin's Press, 1982. (a novel)

Sophocles. "Athamas," "Aleadae," "Mysians," and "Eurypylus." Trans. Hugh Lloyd-Jones. *Sophocles: Fragments.* Loeb Classical Library. Cambridge, MA: Harvard UP, 1996.

Stasinus (or Hegesinus). "The Cypria." *Hesiod, The Homeric Hymns, and Homerica.* Trans. Hugh G. Evelyn-White. Loeb Classical Library. Cambridge, MA: Harvard UP, 1977.

Steiner, George and Robert Fagles. *Homer: A Collection of Critical Essays.* Englewood Cliffs, NJ: Prentice-Hall, 1962.

Vermeule, Emily. *Greece in the Bronze Age.* Chicago: U of Chicago P, 1972.

Versényi, Laszlo. *Man's Measure.* Albany: State U of New York P, 1974.

Vickers, Brian. *Towards Greek Tragedy: Drama, Myth, Society.* New York: Longman, 1973.

Virgil. *The Aeneid.* Trans. H. R. Fairclough. 2 vols. Loeb Classical Library. Cambridge, MA: Harvard UP, 1978.

---. *The Aeneid.* Trans. Robert Fitzgerald. New York: Random House, 1983.

---. *The Aeneid.* Trans. Allen Mandelbaum. Berkeley: U of California P, 1971.

---. *The Aeneid.* Trans. David West. New York: Viking Penguin, 1973.

Vivante, Paolo. *Homer.* New Haven, CT: Yale UP, 1985.

Willcock, Malcolm M. *A Companion to the Iliad.* (Based on Lattimore's trans.) Chicago: U of Chicago P, 1976.

Wolf, Christa. *Cassandra: A Novel and Four Essays.* Trans. Jan Van Heurck. New York: Farrar, Straus, Giroux, 1984.

The Far East and the Pacific Islands

Alpers, Antony. *Maori Myths and Tribal Legends.* Auckland, NZ: Longman Paul, 1982.

Beckwith, Martha. *Hawaiian Mythology.* Honolulu: U of Hawaii P, 1977.

Birrell, Anne. *Chinese Mythology: An Introduction.* Baltimore. MD: Johns Hopkins UP, 1993.

Blackburn, Stuart H., Peter J. Claus, Joyce B. Flueckiger, and Susan S. Wadley. *Oral Epics in India.* Berkeley: U of California P, 1989.

Bodde, Derk. "Myths of Ancient China." *Mythologies of the Ancient World.* Ed. Samuel Noah Kramer. New York: Anchor/Doubleday, 1961.

Bonnefoy, Yves, ed. *Mythologies.* Vol. 2. Trans. Wendy Doniger. Chicago:U of Chicago P, 1991.

Christie, Anthony. *Chinese Mythology.* Felthan, England: Newnes Books, 1983.

Classical Chinese Myths. Ed. and Trans. Jan Walls and Yvonne Walls. Hong Kong: Joint, 1984.

Classical Hindu Mythology: A Reader in the Sanskrit Puranas. Ed. and Trans.

Cornelia Dimmitt and J. A. B. Van Buitenen. Philadelphia: Temple UP, 1978.

Colum, Padraic. *Legends of Hawaii.* New Haven, CT: Yale UP, 1987.

Coomaraswamy, Ananda K. and the Sister Nivedita. *Myths of the Hindus and Buddhists.* New York: Dover, 1967.

Durant, Will. *Our Oriental Heritage.* New York: MFJ Books, 1963.

Gray, J. E. B. *Indian Tales and Legends.* New York: Oxford UP, 1989.

Grey, Sir George. *Polynesian Mythology and Ancient Traditional History.* Auckland, NZ: H. Brett, 1885.

Hindu Myths. Trans. Wendy Doniger O'Flaherty. New York: Viking Penguin, 1975.

Ions, Veronica. *Indian Mythology.* New York: Peter Bedrick, 1984.

Jaffrey, Madhur. *Seasons of Splendour: Tales, Myths, and Legends of India.* New York: Atheneum, 1985.

Kalakaua, King David. *The Legends and Myths of Hawaii.* Honolulu: Mutual, 1990.

Kotan Utunnai. Trans. John Batchelor. *Transactions of the Asiatic Society of Japan* 18, Part 1. April 1890.

Mackenzie, Donald A. *India: Myths and Legends.* London: Bracken, 1985.

---. *Myths of China and Japan.* London: Gresham, N.D.

Narayan, R. K. *Gods, Demons, and Others.* New York: Bantam, 1986.

Nihongi: Chronicles of Japan from the Earliest Times to A.D. 697. Trans. W. G. Aston. Rutland: Tuttle, 1980.

Piggott, Juliet. *Japanese Mythology.* New York: Peter Bedrick, 1983.

The Ramayana. Ed. and Trans. William Buck. Berkeley: U of California P, 1976.

The Ramayana and the Mahabharata. Ed. and Trans. Romesh Dutt. New York: Dutton, 1972.

The Ramayana of Kampan, The Forest Book of. Trans. George L. Hart and

Hank Heifetz. Berkeley: U of California P, 1988.

The Ramayana: A Shortened Modern Prose Version (Suggested by the Tamil Version of Kamban). Ed. and Trans. R. K. Narayan. New York: Viking Penguin, 1987.

Roberts, Moss, Ed. and Trans. "Li Chi Slays the Serpent" *Chinese Fairy Tales and Fantasies.* New York: Pantheon, 1979.

Sanders, Tao Tao Liu. *Dragons, Gods, and Spirits from Chinese Mythology.* New York: Schocken Books, 1983.

Songs of Gods, Songs of Humans: The Epic Tradition of the Ainu. Trans. Donald L. Philippi. Princeton, NJ: Princeton UP, 1979.

Werner, Edward T. C. *Ancient Tales and Folklore of China.* London: Bracken, 1986.

Westervelt, William Drake. *Legends of Maui: A Demi-god of Polynesia, and His Mother Hina.* Honolulu: N.P., 1910.

---. *Myths and Legends of Hawaii.* Ed. A. Grove Day. Honolulu: Mutual, 1987.

Yuan Ke. *An Introduction to Chinese Mythology.* Trans. Kim Echlin and Nie Zhixiong. New York: Penguin, 1993.

Zimmer, Heinrich. *Myths and Symbols in Indian Art and Civilization.* Ed. Joseph Campbell. Princeton, NJ: Princeton UP, 1992.

The British Isles

Alcock, Leslie. *Arthur's Britain: History and Archaeology: A.D. 367–634.* New York: Viking Penguin, 1977.

(Alliterative) Morte Arthure. Ed. John Finlayson. Evanston, IL: Northwestern UP, 1971.

The Alliterative Morte Arthure, The Owl and The Nightingale, and Five Other Middle English Poems. Trans. John Gardner. Carbondale: Southern Illinois UP, 1979.

Ashe, Geoffrey and Debrett's Peerage. *The Discovery of King Arthur.* New York: Henry Holt, 1987.

---. *King Arthur: The Dream of the Golden Age.* New York: Thames Hudson, 1990.

---, ed. *The Quest for Arthur's Britain.* Chicago: Academy Chicago, 1988.

Barber, Richard, ed. *Arthurian Legends: An Illustrated Anthology.* Totowa, NJ: Littlefield Adams, 1979.

Benson, Larry D. *Malory's Morte D'Arthur.* Cambridge, MA: Harvard UP, 1976.

Beowulf. Trans. William Alfred. *Medieval Epics.* New York: Random House, 1963.

Beowulf: A Dual-Language Edition. Trans. Howell D. Chickering, Jr. New York: Anchor/Doubleday, 1977.

Beowulf and the Finnesburh Fragment. Trans. Clarence Griffin Child. Boston: Houghton Mifflin, 1904.

Beowulf. Trans. E. Talbot Donaldson. Critical Edition. New York: W. W. Norton, 1975.

Beowulf. Trans. Stanley B. Greenfield. Carbondale: Southern Illinois UP, 1982.

Beowulf: The Oldest English Epic. Trans. Charles W. Kennedy. New York: Oxford UP, 1977.

Beowulf. Trans. Ruth P. M. Lehmann. Austin: U of Texas P, 1988.

Beowulf. Trans. Marijane Osborn. Berkeley: U of California P, 1983.

Beowulf. Trans. Lucien Dean Pearson. Bloomington: Indiana UP, 1965.

Beowulf. Trans. Burton Raffel. Amherst: U of Massachusetts P, 1971.

Brengle, Richard L., ed. *Arthur King of Britain: History, Chronicle, Romance and Criticism.* Englewood Cliffs, NJ: Prentice-Hall, 1964.

Bruce-Mitford, Rupert. *Aspects of Anglo-Saxon Archaeology: Sutton Hoo and Other Discoveries.* New York: Harper's Magazine/Harper, 1974.

Chadwick, Nora. *The Celts.* New York: Viking Penguin, 1971.

Chrétien de Troyes. *Arthurian Romances.* Trans. W. W. Comfort. New York: Dutton, 1975.

---. *Arthurian Romances.* Trans. William W. Kibler. New York: Viking Penguin, 1991.

---. *The Complete Romances.* Trans. David Staines. Bloomington: Indiana UP, 1993.

From Camelot to Joyous Guard: The Old French La Morte le Roi Artu. Trans. J. Neale Carman. Lawrence: UP of Kansas, 1974.

Froncek, Thomas. *The Northmen.* New York: Time-Life Books, 1974.

Geoffrey of Monmouth. *The History of the Kings of Britain.* Trans. Lewis Thorpe. London: The Folio Society, 1969.

Irving, Edward B., Jr. *Introduction to Beowulf.* Englewood Cliffs, NJ: Prentice-Hall, 1969.

---. *A Reading of* Beowulf. New Haven, CT: Yale UP, 1969.

Jackson, W. T. H. *Hero and King.* New York: Columbia UP, 1986.

---. *The Literature of the Middle Ages.* New York: Columbia UP, 1962.

Kiernan, Kevin S. Beowulf *and the* Beowulf *Manuscript.* New Brunswick, NJ: Rutgers UP, 1981.

Layamon's Arthur: The Arthurian Section of Layamon's Brut. Trans. W. R. J. Barron and S. C. Weinberg. Austin: U of Texas P, 1989.

MacCulloch, J. A. *Celtic Mythology.* New York: Dorset, 1992.

Malory, Sir Thomas. *Le Morte d'Arthur.* Berkeley: U of California P, 1983.

---. *Le Morte d'Arthur.* New York: Viking Penguin, 1983.

---. *Le Morte d'Arthur.* Ed. R. M. Lumiansky. New York: Scribner's, 1982.

Morris, John. *The Age of Arthur: A History of the British Isles from 350 to 650.* New York: Scribner's, 1973.

Nicholson, Lewis E., ed. *An Anthology of Beowulf Criticism.* South Bend, IN: U of Notre Dame P, 1963.

Ogilvy, J. D. A. and Donald C. Baker. *Reading* Beowulf: *An Introduction to the Poem, Its Background, and Its Style.* Norman: U of Oklahoma P, 1983.

Owen, Gale R. *Rites and Religions of the Anglo-Saxons.* New York: Dorset, 1985.

Renoir, Alain. "*Beowulf:* A Contextual Introduction to Its Contents and Techniques." *Heroic Epic and Saga: An Introduction to the World's Great Folk Epics.* Ed. Felix J. Oinas. Bloomington: Indiana UP, 1978.

Rolleston, Thomas William. *Celtic Myths and Legends.* New York: Dover, 1990.

Ross, James Bruce and Mary Martin McLaughlin, eds. *The Portable Medieval Reader.* New York: Viking, 1977.

Rutherford, Ward. *Celtic Mythology: The Nature and Influence of Celtic Myth—from Druidism to Arthurian Legend.* New York: Sterling, 1988.

Sjoestedt, Marie-Louise. *Gods and Heroes of the Celts.* Trans. Myles Dillon. Berkeley, CA: Turtle Island Foundation, 1982.

Squire, Charles. *Celtic Myth and Legend.* Hollywood, CA: Newcastle Publishing, 1975.

Tacitus. *The Agricola and The Germania.* Trans. H. Mattingly and S. A. Handford. New York: Penguin, 1970.

Wace and Layamon. *Arthurian Chronicles.* Trans. Eugene Mason. New York: Dutton, 1976.

Northern Europe

Branston, Brian. *Gods of the North.* New York: Thames and Hudson, 1980.

Crossley-Holland, Kevin. *The Norse Myths.* New York: Pantheon, 1981.

Dumezil, Georges. *Gods of the Ancient Northmen.* Berkeley: U of California P, 1974.

The Elder Edda: *A Selection.* Trans. Paul B. Taylor and W. H. Auden. New York: Random House, 1969.

Jackson, W. T. H. *Hero and King.* New York: Columbia UP, 1986.

---. *The Literature of the Middle Ages.* New York: Columbia UP, 1962.

The Nibelungenlied. Trans. Arthur Thomas Hatto. New York: Viking Penguin, 1975.

The Nibelungenlied. Trans. Helen M. Mustard. New York: Random House, 1963.

Poems of the Elder Edda. Trans. Patricia Terry. Rev. ed. Philadelphia: U of Pennsylvania P, 1990.

The Poetic Edda. Vol. 1: Heroic Poems. Trans. Ursula Dronke. New York: Oxford UP, 1969.

The Poetic Edda. Trans. Lee M. Hollander. Rev. ed. Austin: U of Texas P, 1987.

The Saga of the Volsungs. *Together with Excerpts from the* Nornageststhattr *and Three Chapters from the* Prose Edda. Trans. George K. Anderson. Newark: U of Delaware P, 1982.

The Saga of the Volsungs: The Norse Epic of Sigurd the Dragon Slayer. Trans. Jesse L. Byock. Berkeley: U of California P, 1990.

The Saga of the Volsungs; The Saga of Ragnar Lodbrok Together with The Lay of Kraka. Trans. Margaret Schlauch. New York: AMS, 1978.

Sigurd the Dragon-Slayer: A Faroëse Ballad-Cycle. Trans. E. M. Smith-Dampier. New York: Kraus, 1969.

The Song of the Nibelungs. Trans. Frank G. Ryder. Detroit, MI: Wayne State UP, 1969.

Sturluson, Snorri. *The* Prose Edda: *Tales from Norse Mythology.* Trans. Jean I. Young. Berkeley: U of California P, 1973.

Volsunga Saga: The Story of the Volsungs and Niblungs. Trans. William Morris. New York: Collier, 1971.

Africa

Abrahams, Roger D. *African Folktales.* New York: Pantheon Books, 1983.

Biebuyck, Daniel. "The African Heroic Epic." *Heroic Epic and Saga: An Introduction to the World's Great Folk Epics.* Ed. Felix J. Oinas. Bloomington: Indiana UP, 1978.

Cavendish, Richard, ed. "Central and Southern Africa: Myths of Origins." *Mythology: An Illustrated Encyclopedia.* London: Orbis, 1980.

---, ed. *Legends of the World.* London: Orbis, 1982.

---, ed. *Mythology: An Illustrated Encyclopedia.* London: Orbis, 1980.

Courlander, Harold. *A Master of the Forge.* New York: Crown, 1983.

---. *Tales of the Yoruba Gods and Heroes.* New York: Crown, N.D.

---. *A Treasury of African Folklore.* New York: Crown, 1977.

Courlander, Harold and Ousmane Sako. *The Epic of Bakaridjan Kone, a Hero of Segu. The Heart of the Ngoni: Heroes of the African Kingdom of Segu.* New York: Crown, 1982.

---. *The Heart of the Ngoni: Heroes of the African Kingdom of Segu.* New York: Crown, 1982.

De Civrieux, Marc. *Watunna: An Orinoco Creation Cycle.* Ed. and Trans. David M. Guss. San Francisco: North Point, 1980.

Eliade, Mircea. "An African Cosmogony." *Gods, Goddesses, and Myths of Creation: From Primitives to Zen.* (Part I) New York: Harper Row, 1974.

Frobenius, Leo, and Douglas C. Fox. *African Genesis.* Berkeley, CA: Turtle Island Foundation, 1983.

---. "Gassire's Lute." *Technicians of the Sacred: A Range of Poetries from Africa, America, Asia, Europe, and Oceania.* Ed. Jerome Rothenberg. Rev. ed. Berkeley: U of California P, 1985.

Herskovits, Melville and Frances Herskovitz. *Dahomean Narrative.* Evanston, IL: Northwestern UP, 1958.

Leach, Maria. "From Bumba." *The Beginning: Creation Myths Around the World.* New York: Funk & Wagnalls, 1956.

Leeming, David Adams. "Bumba's Creation." *The World of Myth.* New York: Oxford Univ. Press, 1980.

Murdock, George Peter. *Africa: Its Peoples and Their Culture History.* New York: McGraw-Hill, 1959.

Okpewho, Isidore. *The Epic in Africa: Toward a Poetics of the Oral Performance.* New York: Columbia UP, 1979.

Park, Mungo. "Journals." *Travels in Africa.* Ed. Ronald Miller. London: J. M. Dent, 1954 and 1969.

Parrinder, Geoffrey. *African Mythology.* New York: Bedrick, 1991.

Radin, Paul, ed. *African Folktales.* New York: Schocken, 1983.

Radin, Paul, with Elinore Marvel and James Johnson Sweeney. *African Folktales & Sculpture.* Bollingen Series XXXII. Rev. Ed. New York: Pantheon, 1966.

Rothenberg, Jerome, ed. *Technicians of the Sacred: A Range of Poetries from Africa, America, Asia, Europe, and Oceania.* Rev. ed. Berkeley: U of California P, 1985.

Soyinka, Wole. *Myth, Literature and the African World.* New York: Cambridge UP, 1979.

Sproul, Barbara C. "Bumba Vomits the World." *Primal Myths: Creation Myths Around the World.* New York: HarperCollins, 1991.

The Americas

Anaya, Rudolfo A. *Lord of the Dawn: The Legend of Quetzalcoatl.* Albuquerque: U of New Mexico P, 1987.

Betanzos, Juan de. *Suma y Narración de los Incas.* Cited in Harold Osborne. *South American Mythology.* London: Hamlyn, 1968.

Bierhorst, John. Cantares Mexicanos: *Songs of the Aztecs.* Palo Alto, CA: Stanford UP, 1985.

---. *Four Masterworks of American Indian Literature.* Tucson: U of Arizona P, 1984.

---. *History and Mythology of the Aztecs: The Codex Chimalpopoca (Annals of the Cuauhtitlan and Legend of the Suns).* Tucson: U of Arizona P, 1992.

---. *The Hungry Woman: Myths and Legends of the Aztecs.* New York: Morrow, 1992.

---. *The Mythology of Mexico and Central America.* New York: Morrow, 1984.

---. *The Mythology of North America.* New York: Morrow, 1986.

---. *The Mythology of South America.* New York: Morrow, 1988.

---. *Myths and Tales of the American Indians.* Albuquerque: U of New Mexico P, 1992.

Boaz, Franz. "The Central Eskimo." *Sixth Annual Report of the Bureau of American Ethnology, 1884–1885.* Washington, DC: GPO, 1888.

---. "Tsimshian Mythology." *Thirty-First Annual Report of the Bureau of American Ethnology, 1909–1910.* Washington, DC: GPO, 1916.

---. "Tsimshian Texts." *Bureau of American Ethnology Bulletin 27.* Washington, DC: GPO, 1916.

Brundage, Burr Cartwright. *The Fifth Sun: Aztec Gods, Aztec World.* Austin: U of Texas P, 1979.

Burland, Cottie. *North American Indian Mythology.* Rev. ed. New York: Bedrick, 1985.

---, Irene Nicholson, and Harold Osborne. *Mythology of the Americas.* London: Hamlyn, 1970.

Caswell, Helen. *Shadows from the Singing House: Eskimo Folk Tales.* Tokyo: Tuttle, 1973.

Cieza de Léon, Pedro de. "Second Part of the Chronicle of Peru." Cited in Harold Osborne. *South American Mythology.* London: Hamlyn, 1968.

---. "The Travels of Pedro de Cieza de León, Contained in the First Part of His Chronicle of Peru, A.D. 1532–1550." Cited in Harold Osborne. *South American Mythology.* London: Hamlyn, 1968.

Clark, Ella Elizabeth. *Indian Legends from the Northern Rockies.* Norman: U of Oklahoma P, 1988.

---. *Indian Legends of Canada.* Toronto: McClelland & Steward, 1991.

---. *Indian Legends of the Pacific Northwest.* Berkeley: U of California P, 1953.

Coffin, Tristram. *Indian Tales of North America.* Philadelphia: American Folklore Society, 1961.

Cristóbal de Molina of Cuzco. *The Fables and Rites of the Yncas.* Trans. Clements R. Markham. Rites and Laws of the Yncas. London: Hakluyt Society, 1873.

Curtin, Jeremiah. *Seneca Indian Myths.* New York: Dutton, 1923.

---, and J. N. B. Hewitt. "Seneca Myths and Fictions." *Thirty-Second Annual Report of the Bureau of American Ethnology.* Washington, DC: GPO, 1918.

Cusick, David. *Sketches of Ancient History of the Six Nations: A Tale of the Foundation of the Great Island, Now North America, The Two Infants Born, and the Creation of the Universe.* New York: Lewiston, 1827. Cited in Ellen Russell Emerson. *Indian Myths or Legends: Traditions and Symbols of the Aborigines of America.* Minneapolis, MN: Ross Haines, 1965.

De Civrieux, Marc. *Watunna: An Orinoco Creation Cycle.* Trans. David M. Guss. San Francisco: North Point, 1980.

Edmonds, Margot and Ella Elizabeth Clark. *Voices of the Winds: Native American Legends.* New York: Facts on File, 1989.

Emerson, Ellen Russell. *Indian Myths or Legends: Traditions and Symbols of the Aborigines of America.* Minneapolis, MN: Ross Haines, 1965.

Erdoes, Richard, and Alfonzo Ortiz, eds. *American Indian Myths and Legends.* New York: Pantheon, 1985.

Garcilaso, Inca de la Vega. *The Incas. (Royal Commentaries of the Incas, 1609.)* Ed. Alain Gheerbrant. Trans. Maria Jolas. New York: Avon, 1964.

---. *Royal Commentaries of the Incas.* Cited in Emir Rodriguez Monegal. *The Borzoi Anthology of Latin American Literature: From the Time of Colum Rodriguez Monegal.* New York: Knopf, 1983.

---. *Royal Commentaries of the Incas.* Cited in Harold Osborne. *South American Mythology.* London: Hamlyn, 1968.

Gilpin, Laura. *The Enduring Navaho.* Austin: U of Texas P, 1987.

Goodchild, Peter, ed. *The Raven Tales: Traditional Stories of Native Peoples.* Chicago: Chicago Review, 1991.

Grinnell, George Bird. *By Cheyenne Campfires.* Lincoln: U of Nebraska P, 1971.

Hale, Horatio. "Huron Folk-Lore." *Journal of American Folklore* 1. Boston: American Folk-Lore Society/Houghton Mifflin, 1888.

Haviland, Virginia, ed. *The Faber Book of North American Legends.* Boston: Faber & Faber, 1979.

Hewitt, J. N. B. "Introduction to Seneca Fiction, Legends, and Myths." *Thirty-Fifth Annual Report of the Bureau of American Ethnology, 1910–1911.* Washington, DC: GPO, 1918.

"Histoyre du Mechique." ("History of Mexico.") Trans. Andre Thevet. *Journal of the Society of Americanistes.* Paris: 1905.

Josephy, Alvin M., Jr. *The Indian Heritage of America*. Boston: Houghton Mifflin, 1991.

Klah, Hasteen. *Navajo Creation Myth: The Story of Emergence*. New York: AMS, 1976.

Leland, Charles G. *Algonquin Legends*. New York: Dover, 1992. Reprint of *The Algonquin Legends of New England; or, Myths and Folk Lore of the Micmac, Passmaquoddy, and Penobscot Tribes*. Boston: Houghton Mifflin, 1884.

Levy, Jerrold E. *In the Beginning: The Navajo Genesis*. Berkeley: Univ. of California Press, 1998.

Macfarlan, Allan A., ed. *American Indian Legends*. New York: Crowell, 1968.

Matthews, Washington. "Navajo Legends." *Memoirs of the American Folk-Lore Society*. Vol. V. Boston: American Folk-Lore Society/Houghton Mifflin, 1897.

Monegal, Emir Rodriguez, ed. *The Borzoi Anthology of Latin American Literature: From the Time of Columbus to the Twentieth Century*. New York: Knopf, 1983.

Newcomb, Franc Johnson. *Navaho Folk Tales*. Albuquerque: U of New Mexico P, 1991.

Nicholson, Irene. *Mexican and Central American Mythology*. New York: Bedrick, 1983.

Norman, Howard, ed. *Northern Tales: Traditional Stories of Eskimo and Indian Peoples*. New York: Pantheon, 1990.

Osborne, Harold. *South American Mythology*. New York: Bedrick, 1986.

Popul Vuh: The Definitive Edition of the Mayan Book of the Dawn of Life and the Glories of Gods and Kings. Trans. Dennis Tedlock. New York: Simon & Schuster, 1985.

Popul Vuh: The Sacred Book of the Ancient Quiché Maya. Trans. Delia Goetz and Sylvanus G. Morley. Norman: U of Oklahoma P, 1950.

Popul Vuh: The Sacred Book of the Ancient Quiché Maya. Trans. Adrian Recinos. Norman: U of Oklahoma P, 1950.

Rachlan, Carol K. and Alice Marriott. *Plains Indian Mythology*. New York: NAL-Dutton, 1977.

Rand, Silas T. *Legends of the Micmacs*. New York: Longmans, Green, 1984.

Rivière, Peter. *Marriage Among the Trio: A Principle of Social Organization*. Oxford: Clarendon, 1969.

Roe, Peter G. *The Cosmic Zygote: Cosmology in the Amazon Basin*. New Brunswick, NJ: Rutgers UP, 1982.

Sahagun, Bernardino de, *Florentine Codex: General History of Things of New Spain*. Eds. Arthur J. O. Anderson and Charles E. Dibble. Santa Fe, NM: School of American Research/U of Utah P, 1950–1982.

Simms, Stephen Chapman. "Traditions of the Crows." *Field Museum Anthropological Series*. Vol. 2. Chicago: 1903.

Swanton, John Reed. "Haida Texts and Myths." *Bureau of American Ethnology Bulletin* 29. Washington, DC: GPO, 1905.

---. "Tlingit Myths and Texts." *Bureau of American Ethnology Bulletin* 39. Washington, DC: GPO, 1909.

Thompson, Stith. *Tales of the North American Indians*. Bloomington: Indiana UP, 1966.

Underhill, Ruth M. *Red Man's America*. Chicago: U of Chicago P, 1971.

Valdelomar, Abraham. *Our Children of the Sun: A Suite of Eight Inca Legends*. Carbondale: Southern Illinois UP, 1968.

Walker, James R. *Lakota Myth*. Ed. Elaine A. Jahner. Lincoln: U of Nebraska P, 1983.

Wherry, Joseph H. *Indian Masks and Myths of the West*. New York: Bonanza/Crown, 1969.

Whitehead, Ruth Holmes. *Stories from the Six Worlds: Micmac Legends.* Halifax, Nova Scotia: Nimbus, 1988.

Zolbrod, Paul G. Dine Bahane: *The Navajo Creation Story.* Albuquerque: U of New Mexico P, 1988.

General Mythology

Bachofen, J. J. *Myth, Religion and Mother Right.* Princeton, NJ: Princeton UP, 1967.

Bierlein, J. F. *Parallel Myths.* Ballantine/Random House, 1994.

Bonnefoy, Yves. *Mythologies.* 2. Vols. Ed. Wendy Doniger. Chicago: U of Chicago P, 1991.

Brunel, Pierre, ed. *Companion to Literary Myths, Heroes, and Archetypes.* Trans. Wendy Allatson, Judith Hayward, and Trista Selous. New York: Routledge, 1996.

Burrows, David, Frederick Lapides, and John Shawcross. *Myths and Motifs in Literature.* New York: Free Press, 1973.

Butterworth, E. A. S. *Some Traces of the Pre-Olympian World in Greek Literature and Myth.* Berlin: Walter de Gruyter, 1966.

Campbell, Joseph. *The Masks of God.* 4 vols. New York: Viking Penguin, 1991.

---, with Bill Moyers. *The Power of Myth.* New York: Doubleday, 1988.

---. *Transformations of Myth Through Time.* New York: Harper and Row, 1990.

Cavendish, Richard, ed. *Legends of the World.* London: Orbis, 1982.

---, ed. *Mythology: An Illustrated Encyclopedia.* London: Orbis, 1980.

Cotterell, Arthur, ed. *The Encyclopedia of Ancient Civilizations.* New York: Mayflower, 1980.

Doty, William G. *Mythography: The Study of Myths and Rituals.* Tuscaloosa: Univ. of Alabama Press, 1991.

Downing, Christine. *The Goddess: Mythological Images of the Feminine.* New York: Crossroads, 1984.

Dundes, Alan, ed. *The Flood Myth.* Berkeley: U of California P, 1988.

---. *Sacred Narrative: Readings in the Theory of Myth.* Berkeley: U of California P, 1984.

Eliade, Mircea. *Gods, Goddesses, and Myths of Creation: From Primitives to Zen.* Part I. New York: Harper and Row, 1974.

---. *Myths, Rites, Symbols.* 2 vols. Ed. Wendell C. Beane and William G. Dotz. New York: Harper, 1976.

Feder, Lillian. *Ancient Myth in Modern Poetry.* Princeton, NJ: Princeton UP, 1971.

Frazer, Sir James George. *The Golden Bough: The Roots of Religion and Folklore.* New York: Avenel/Crown, 1981.

Freud, Sigmund. *Totem and Taboo.* Trans. James Strachey. New York: Routledge, 1950.

Frye, Northrop. *Anatomy of Criticism.* New York: Atheneum, 1968.

Gaster, Theodor, ed. *The New Golden Bough: A New Abridgment of the Classic Work by Sir James George Frazer.* New York: Phillips, 1972.

Gimbutas, Marija. *Goddesses and Gods of Old Europe: 7000–3500 B.C.: Myths, Legends, and Cult Images.* Rev. ed. Berkeley: U of California P, 1982.

---. *Language of the Goddess.* San Francisco: Harper, 1991.

Graves, Robert. *The White Goddess.* Rev. ed. Magnolia, MA: Peter Smith, 1983.

Harrison, Jane Ellen. *Prolegomena to the Study of Greek Religion.* Princeton, NJ: Princeton UP, 1976.

---. *Themis: A Study of the Social Origins of the Greek Religion.* Rev. ed. Gloucester, MA: Peter Smith, 1974.

Higher, Gilbert. *The Classical Tradition: Greek and Roman Influences on Western*

Literature. New York: Oxford UP, 1949.

Jung, Carl G. *The Archetypes and the Collective Unconscious.* Princeton, NJ: Princeton UP, 1969.

---. *The Essential Jung.* Ed. Anthony Storr. Princeton: Princeton UP, 1983.

Kane, Sean. *Wisdom of Mythtellers.* New York: Broadview, 1994.

Kirk, G. S. *Myth: Its Meaning and Function in Ancient and Other Cultures.* Berkeley: U of California P, 1970.

Leach, Maria, ed. *Funk & Wagnalls Standard Dictionary of Folklore, Mythology and Legend.* New York: Harper, 1984.

Leeming, David Adams and Jake Page. *God: Myths of the Male Divine.* New York: Oxford UP, 1996.

---. *Goddess: Myths of the Female Divine.* New York: Oxford UP, 1994.

---. *The World of Myth.* New York: Oxford UP, 1990.

Lévi-Strauss, Claude. *Introduction to a Science of Mythology.* 2 vols. Trans. John Weightman and Doreen Weightman. Chicago: U of Chicago P, 1983.

---. *Myths and Meaning.* New York: Schocken, 1987.

---. *Mythologiques.* Vols. 3 and 4. Trans. John Weightman and Doreen Weightman. Chicago: U of Chicago P, 1990.

---. *Structural Anthropology.* Vol. 1. Trans. Claire Jacobson and Brooke Grundfest Schoepf. New York: Basic Books, 1974.

Middleton, John, ed. *Myth and Cosmos: Readings in Mythology and Symbolism.* Austin: U of Texas P, 1976.

Miller, James E., Jr., ed. *Myth and Method.* Lincoln: U of Nebraska P, 1960.

Murray, Henry A. ed. *Myth and Myth-Making.* Boston: Beacon, 1968.

Neumann, Erich. *The Great Mother: An Analysis of the Archetype.* Princeton, NJ: Princeton UP, 1964.

O'Flaherty, Wendy Doniger. *Other Peoples' Myths: The Cave of Echoes.* New York: Macmillan, 1988.

Olson, Alan M., ed. *Myth, Symbol and Reality.* South Bend, IN: U of Notre Dame P, 1980.

Porter, Thomas E. *Myth and Modern American Drama.* Detroit, MI: Wayne State UP, 1969.

Puhvel, Jaan. *Comparative Mythology.* Baltimore, MD: Johns Hopkins UP, 1989.

Radin, Paul. *Primitive Man as Philosopher.* Rev. ed. New York: Dover, 1957.

---. *Primitive Religion: Its Nature and Origin.* New York: Dover Publications, 1937.

Raglan, FitzRoy. *The Hero: A Study in Tradition, Myth, and Drama.* New York: NAL, 1979.

Rank, Otto, FitzRoy Raglan, and Alan Dundes. *In Quest of the Hero.* Princeton, NJ: Princeton UP, 1990.

Rothenberg, Jerome, ed. *Technicians of the Sacred: A Range of Poetries from Africa, America, Asia, Europe, and Oceania.* Rev. ed. Berkeley: U of California P, 1985.

Sebeok, Thomas. *Myth: A Symposium.* Bloomington, IN: Indiana UP, 1972.

Segnec, Jean. *The Survival of the Pagan Gods: The Mythological Tradition and Its Place in Renaissance Humanism and Art.* Princeton, NJ: Princeton UP, 1972.

Slate, Bernice, ed. *Myth and Symbol: Critical Approaches and Applications.* Lincoln: U of Nebraska P, 1963.

Slochower, Harry. *Mythopoesis: Mythic Patterns in Literary Classics.* Detroit, MI: Wayne State UP, 1970.

Sproul, Barbara C. *Primal Myths: Creation Myths Around the World.* San Francisco: Harper, 1979.

Stone, Merlin. *When God Was a Woman*.
New York: Harcourt, 1976.

Vickery, John B. *Myths and Texts:
Strategies of Incorporation and
Displacement*. Baton Rouge: Lousiana
State UP, 1983.

---, ed. *Myth and Literature: Contemporary
Theory and Practice*. Lincoln: U of
Nebraska P, 1969.

Weigle, Marta. *Spiders and Spinsters:
Women and Mythology*. Albuquerque:
U of New Mexico P, 1992.

Willis, Roy. *World Mythology*. New York:
Holt, 1993.

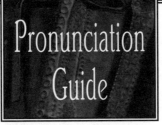

Pronunciation Guide

This index provides easy-to-pronounce English approximations of the original languages of the myths. The transcriptions are meant to serve as a guide to English-speaking readers. The following chart shows International Phonetic Alphabet (IPA) and American English values for the symbols used in this index.

[a, A] = IPA [æ]
cat

[ah, AH] = IPA [ɑ]
top

[ai, AI] = IPA [ɑɪ]
pie

[au, AU] = IPA [ɑʊ]
cow

[b, B] = IPA [b]
boy

[ch, CH] = IPA [tʃ]
church

[d, D] = IPA [d]
did

[dh, DH] = IPA [ð]
these

[e, E] = IPA [ɛ]
let

[ee, EE] = IPA [i]
feed

[ei, EI] = IPA [eɪ]
pay

[f, F] = IPA [f]
far

[g, G] = IPA [g]
get

[h, H] = IPA [h]
hoot

[I, I] = IPA [ɪ]
lit

[j, J] = IPA [dʒ]
judge

[k, K] = IPA [k]
kid

[l, L] = IPA [l]
lean

[m, M] = IPA [m]
my

[n, N] = IPA [n]
new

[ng, NG] = IPA [ŋ]
ring

[o, O] = IPA [ɔ]
law

[oi, OI] = IPA [ɔɪ]
coy

[oo, OO] = IPA [u]
moon

[ow, OW] = IPA [ow]
coat

[p, P] = IPA [p]
pink

[r, R] = IPA [r]
red

[s, S] = IPA [s]
suit

[sh, SH] = IPA [ʃ]
ship

[t, T] = IPA [t]
tight

[th, TH] = IPA [θ]
think

[u, U] = IPA [ʊ]
put

[uh, UH] = IPA [ə]
putt

[v, V] = IPA [v]
very

[w, W] = IPA [w]
what

[y, Y] = IPA [j]
you

[z, Z] = IPA [z]
zip

[zh, ZH] = IPA [ʒ]
garage

Index of Characters

Father Sky. *See* Uranus
Father Sun, 576–577, 578
Fenrir (FEN rir), 463, 464, 465, 473
Fir Bolg, 370, 372–373
First Boy, 619, 620
First Fathers, 597–598
First Girl, 618
First Man
    Iroquois, 633
    Navajo, 617–621
First Mothers, 598
First People, 617–621
First Woman
    Iroquois, 633
    Navajo, 617–621
Fomorians, 370, 371, 375–376, 378, 379
Food Master, 589
Forest People, 618
Freya (FREI uh), 459–460, 464, 470,
    475–477
Frey (frei), 459, 460, 464, 465, 470
Frigg (frig), 459–460, 464, 468–470
Frost Giants, 461–462, 463, 465, 470,
    475–477
Furies (FYOOR eez), 85
Future, 463

Gaea (JEE uh), 93, 168
    in "The Creation of the Titans and the
       Gods," 84–88
    in *Jason and the Golden Fleece*, 178
    in *Medea*, 210
Gaheris (guh HEIR is), 421, 445
Gangleri (gahn GLER ee) (Gylfi),
    461–466
Gareth (GAR eth), 421, 445
Gassire (gah SEE rei), 523–526
Gawain (guh WEIN), 421, 438, 442,
    443–449, 450
Geb (geb), 16
Geryon (GEIR ee uhn), 102–103
Giant(s)
    Antaeus, 103–104
    Cacus, 103
    Cliff, 470
    in "The Creation of the Titans and the
       Gods," 85

Frost, 461–462, 463, 465, 470,
    475–477
Geryon, 102–103
Hundred-Handed, 84–88, 131
and King Arthur, 435–438
Loki as, 472
slain by Lancelot, 440
Surt, 461, 465, 466
Gilgamesh (GIL guh mesh), 26–27,
    28–56, 116
Giuki (gee OO kee), 479, 494–496
Glauce (GLAU kei), 168, 210, 226,
    234–235, 238
Goddess of Arts and Crafts. *See* Athena
Goddess of Death. *See* Hine Titama
Goddess of Discord. *See* Eris
Goddess of Memory. *See* Mnemosyne
Goddess of the Earth. *See* Medea; Tiamat
Goddess of the Hunt. *See* Artemis
Goddess of the Sky. *See* Medea; Tiamat
Goddess of the Underworld. *See* Medea;
    Tiamat
Goddess of War. *See* Athena
God of the Dead. *See* Hades
God of the Heavens. *See* Tezcatlipoca
God of the Silver Bow. *See* Apollo
God of the Underworld. *See* Hades
God of War. *See* Ares
Good Twin, 628–633
Goshtasp (gahsh TAHSP), 61, 62, 63–66,
    70–71, 75–76
Gram (grahm), 481, 488, 491, 492, 503.
    See also Sigurd
Grani (GRAH nee), 483, 491, 492, 493,
    501, 502. *See also* Sigurd
Great Goddess, 90, 93, 107. *See also*
    Mother Goddess; specific names
    Amaterasu Omikami as, 335
    Demeter as, 93–99
    Eriu as, 376
    Frigg and Freya as, 459–460
    Ishtar as, 27
    Isis as, 14
    Mawu as, 518
    Medea as, 162, 205
    Nu Kua as, 324, 326
    Tiamat as, 4–5

birth of, 431
stealing the throne, 448, 449–451
Mother Earth, 299, 300
Mother Goddess, 11. *See also* Great
Goddess
Danu as, 372
Nintu as, 23, 28, 51
Mother Papa, 352–353, 354, 355, 356,
358
Mountain People, 617
Mummu (MOO moo), 5, 6
Munin (MOO nin), 463, 470
Muses (MYOOZ uhz), 171, 213

Naegling (NEI gling), 405, 409,
410–411, 412. *See also* Beowulf
Nanautzin (na nuh OOT zin), 603
Narada (nuh RAH duh), 299, 319
Nemean lion (ne MEE uhn . . .), 101
Nemed (NEM uhd), 370, 371–372, 378
Nemesis (NEM uh sis), 124
Neoptolemus (ne uhp TOL uh muhs),
154–155, 260, 269
Nephele (NEF uh lee), 168, 170
Nephthys (NEF thees), 16, 19
Neptune (NEP toon), 261. *See also*
Poseidon
Nereus (nir EE uhs), 103
Nestor (NES tr), 124
in Agamemnon's dream, 132
as Greeks' advisor, 130, 138–139
and Patroclus's death, 141–142
Nganamba Fasa (nah-gah-NAHM-bah
FAH-sah), 523, 526
Night, 352
Night-Maiden. *See* Hine Titama
Ninsun (NIN suhn), 27, 28, 32, 37
Nintu (NIN too), 5, 23, 28, 29, 51
Ninurta (ni NR tuh), 29, 52
Njord (nyord), 460, 464
Norns (nornz) (Fate Maidens), 459, 463,
485, 487. *See also* Fates; Wyrd
Nuada (NOO uh thuh), 370, 372–374
Nu Kua (noo KWAH), 324–325,
326–328
Nut (noot), 15, 16
Nyx (nix), 168, 210

Obatala (ow bah TAH lah), 509, 510–513
Oceanus (ow SHEE uh nuhs), 84, 92
Octavian. *See* Augustus Caesar
Odin (OW dn), 459
in Balder's death, 468, 470
in "The Creation of the Universe,"
460, 462, 463, 465
in *Sigurd the Volsung,* 480–481,
482–486, 489, 493
Odosha (ow DAH shuh), 580–593
Odr (OW dr), 476
Odysseus (ow DIS ee uhs), 124, 129,
141. *See also* Ulysses
and Agamemnon's apology to Achilles,
138–139
claiming Hecuba, 155
competing for Achilles' shield, 115
fighting for Achilles' body, 154
and marriage of Helen, 126
preparing for war, 126–127
Olokun (OW lo koon), 509, 510,
513–514
Olorun (OW lo roon), 509, 510–514
Ooyalu (oo YAH loo), 638
Orestes (uh RES teez), 124, 139
Orthus (OWR thuhs), 102–103
Orunmila (owr oon MEE lah), 509, 510,
511, 513
Osiris (ow SAI ris), 12–15, 16–18, 20
Otter (OT r), 479, 483–486
Ourea (YOO ree uh), 84

Pallas (PAL uhs), 260, 283, 284, 287
Pandarus (PAN duh ruhs), 124
Pandora (pan DOWR uh), 84
P'an Ku (pan KOO), 325, 326, 328–329
Panthus (PAN thoos), 268
Paris (PAR uhs), 111, 124, 147, 259
and Achilles' death, 150, 154
battle with Menelaus, 133–134
birth of, 124–125
combat with Philoctetes, 117
death of, 154
gods' influence on, 123
and Hector, 133–137
judgment of, 125, 151, 261
selfishness of, 121